CONTENTS

Production Manager: John Loubser
Cartographic Manager: Christine Flemington
Research Manager: Judy Graham (research@mapstudio.co.za)
Senior Cartographers: Braam Smit & Martin Endemann.
Cartographers: Charleen Mathys, Ryno Swart, Randall Watson & Willem van der Vyver
Research: Judy Graham, Derek Nel, Anthony Davids.
Graphic Design & Index: Martin Endemann.

0860 10 50 50
www.mapstudio.co.za

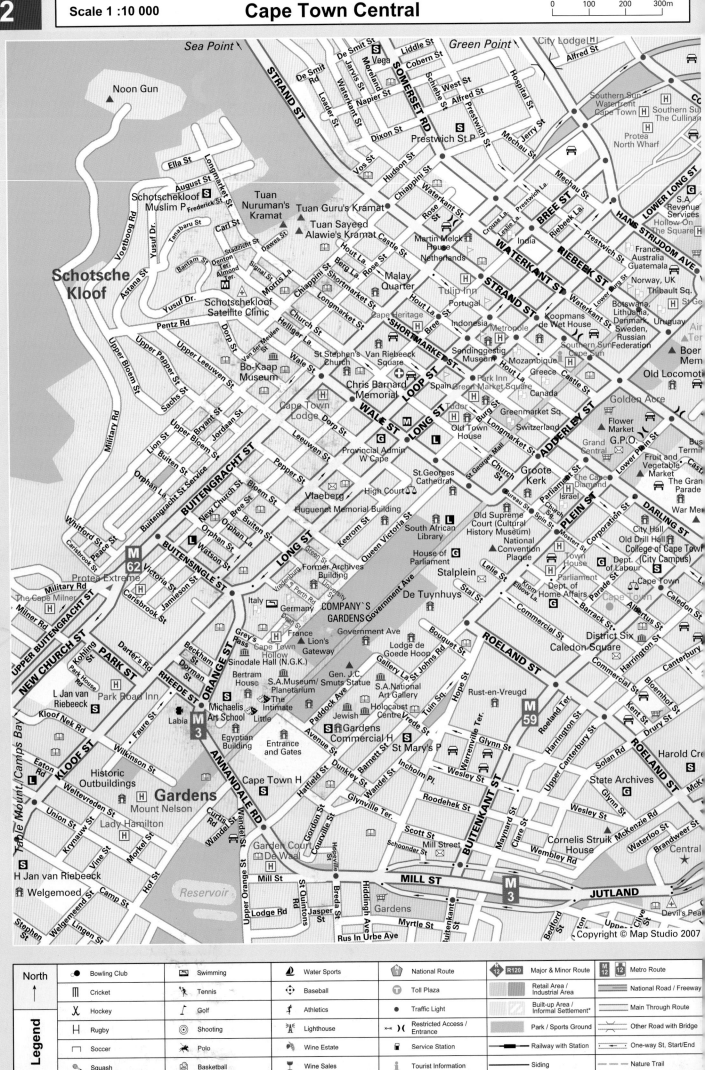

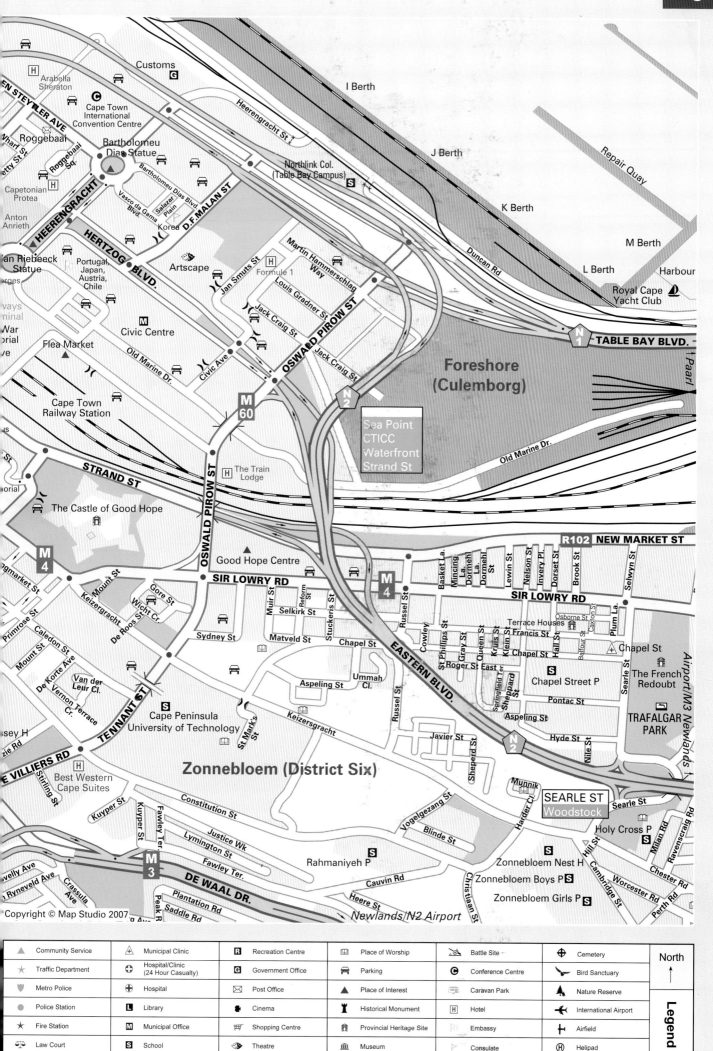

▲	Community Service	Ⓐ	Municipal Clinic	Ⓡ	Recreation Centre	📖	Place of Worship	⚓	Battle Site	⊕	Cemetery
★	Traffic Department	⊕	Hospital/Clinic (24 Hour Casualty)	Ⓖ	Government Office	🚗	Parking	Ⓒ	Conference Centre	⤙	Bird Sanctuary
▼	Metro Police	⊕	Hospital	✉	Post Office	▲	Place of Interest	🚐	Caravan Park	🌲	Nature Reserve
●	Police Station	Ⓛ	Library	✴	Cinema	🏛	Historical Monument	Ⓗ	Hotel	✈	International Airport
★	Fire Station	Ⓜ	Municipal Office	🛒	Shopping Centre	🏛	Provincial Heritage Site	‖	Embassy	✝	Airfield
⚖	Law Court	Ⓢ	School	🐟	Theatre	🏛	Museum	▷	Consulate	Ⓗ	Helipad

North
↑

Legend

ATLANTIC OCEAN

CITY OF CAPE TOWN METRO

False Bay

Copyright © Map Studio 2007

North ↑		Freeway / National Road	N2	National Route Marker	6	Page Number
Legend	⋯⋯	Through Route with Pass	R66 R102	Major and Minor Route Markers	**Newlands**	Suburb
	✈	International Airport	M6	Metro Route Marker	**DRAKENSTEIN**	Municipality

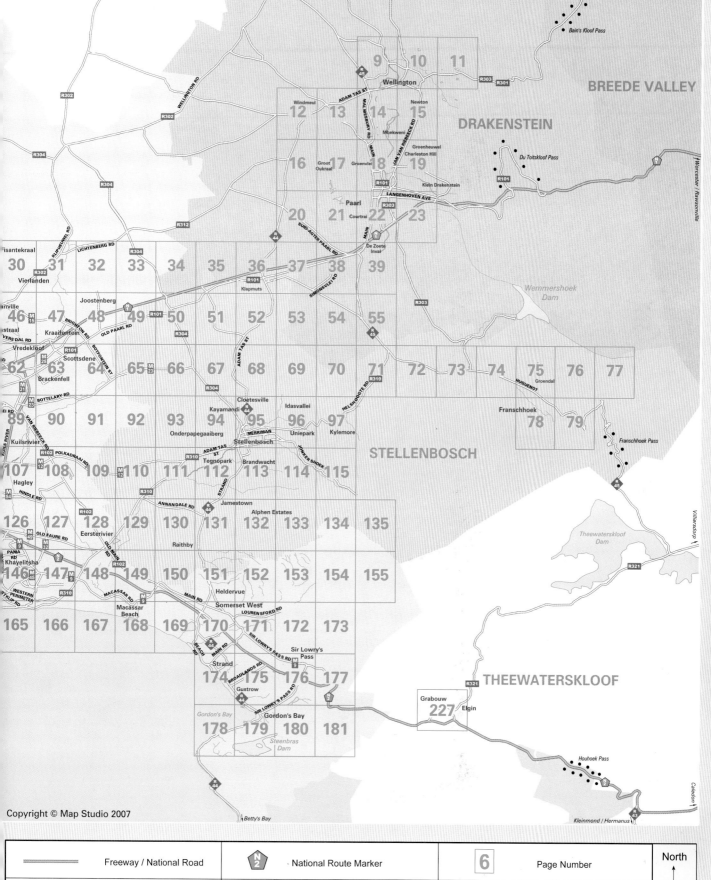

Freeway / National Road	N2 National Route Marker	6 Page Number	North ↑
Through Route with Pass	R66 R102 Major and Minor Route Markers	Newlands Suburb	
✈ International Airport	M6 Metro Route Marker	DRAKENSTEIN Municipality	Legend

					North
——— Freeway / National Road		National Route Marker			↑
——— Through Route	R66 R102	Major and Minor Route Markers	Newlands	Suburb	Legend
✈ International Airport	M6	Metro Route Marker	DRAKENSTEIN	Municipality	

Grid Reference System

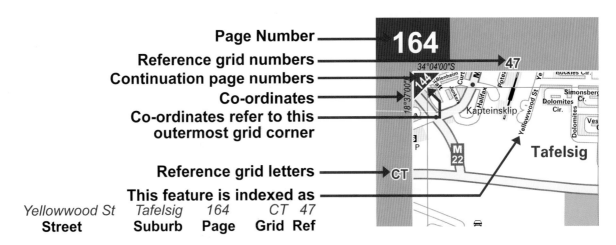

Page Number ——————————— **164**

Reference grid numbers —————— 47

Continuation page numbers ————

Co-ordinates ————————

Co-ordinates refer to this —————
outermost grid corner

Reference grid letters —————— CT

This feature is indexed as ————

Yellowwood St	*Tafelsig*	*164*	*CT 47*
Street	**Suburb**	**Page**	**Grid Ref**

Try This ▶ Look up the required Street, Suburb or Feature in the index at the back of the book, and note the grid reference. Turn to the appropriate page and identify the grid block.
Example: Yellowwood St   Tafelsig   164   CT 47
In the order of: Street Name, Suburb, Page No., Grid Letter, Grid number

The Key Plans

On pages 4-7, 196 & 214 the Key Plans gives an overall view of the areas covered by this guide. The numbered blue outlines represent the map pages of the book and are used to determine which page covers a particular area. Maps are arranged in double page spreads, with overlaps on three sides, to enable detail to be followed easily from map to map. All maps, except those indicated are arranged with North at the top.

Large Scale Maps

Large scale maps of Cape Town Central appear on pages 2 & 3.
Perspective maps of Airports and V&A Waterfront on page 308, 309 and 310.

Index Pages

The Index starting on page 230, features Street, Suburb and Wine Estate Indexes.

Co-ordinates

For your easy reference we have placed the co-ordinates on the outside corners of each page at the intersection of the blue grid lines. The grid lines on all maps that have a scale of 1 : 20 000 are at an interval of ½' (half a minute i.e. 30 seconds). This makes it easy to work out co-ordinates for the interval grid lines and for point features within the grid squares. On Map Studio street level mapping, the distance on the face of the earth covered by 30 seconds is approx. 0,9 km East-West and approx. 0,9 km North-South.

Datum

The datum used on this street guide is WGS 84 (World Geodetic System).

A reference panel on each map page

Symbols found on map
ie - there is a Cemetery
at that particular location

▲ Community Service	⚠ Municipal Clinic	R Recreation Centre	🏛 Place of Worship	⚔ Battle Site	✛ Cemetery	**North** ↑
★ Traffic Department	✚ Hospital/Clinic (24 Hour Casualty)	G Government Office	🚗 Parking	C Conference Centre	✈ Bird Sanctuary	
▼ Metro Police	✚ Hospital	✉ Post Office	▲ Place of Interest	🚐 Caravan Park	▲ Nature Reserve	
● Police Station	L Library	Cinema	𝕀 Historical Monument	H Hotel	✈ International Airport	**Legend**
★ Fire Station	M Municipal Office	Shopping Centre	🏛 Provincial Heritage Site	Embassy	Airfield	
⚖ Law Court	S School	Theatre	🏛 Museum	▷ Consulate	Ⓗ Helipad	

18°59'00"E

AO

10

AP

Berg

Bosmans

AQ

Lady Loch Bridge

LADY LOCH RD

R
45

AR

10

Katryntjiesdrif

Berg

Dis

AS

R
4

CHAMPAGNE ST

Wellington
Industrial
Park

S.P.C.A.

R
44

Elba

Oudepont

Oude

Rhebok
St

Warehorn
St

18°59'00"E

15

33°39'00"S

14

Copyright © Map Studio 2007

▲	Community Service	Ⓐ	Municipal Clinic	Ⓡ	Recreation Centre	🏛	Place of Worship	🗡	Battle Site
★	Traffic Department	⊕	Hospital/Clinic (24 Hour Casualty)	Ⓖ	Government Office	🚗	Parking	Ⓒ	Conference Centre
▼	Metro Police	⊕	Hospital	✉	Post Office	▲	Place of Interest	🚐	Caravan Park
●	Police Station	Ⓛ	Library	✴	Cinema	♜	Historical Monument	Ⓗ	Hotel
★	Fire Station	Ⓜ	Municipal Office	🛒	Shopping Centre	🏛	Provincial Heritage Site	🏳	Embassy
⚖	Law Court	Ⓢ	School	🎭	Theatre	🏛	Museum	▷	Consulate

⊕	Cemetery
🦅	Bird Sanctuary
⛰	Nature Reserve
✈	International Airport
✟	Airfield
Ⓗ	Helipad

North
↑

Legend

33°36'30"S
18°59'00"E

91   92   93   94

Tulbagh

AO

Jacaranda

9

Verailles 197

AP

1 Uit Kerk St (AR 93)

195m ▲

Malan de Versailles

Anglo-Boer Block House

AQ

Hexberg

Krom

D.G.B.

LADY LOCH RD

Onderwyskollege
Boland Sports Field

South African
Dried Fruit Co-op

Savingnac
de Versailles

Cape
Wine Cellars

Bosmans

Eshkol

Ferguson
Hall

Railway

Solomens

Kleinbosch
Wines

Wellington Resort

Huguenot Seminary

Wellington
Katryntjiesdrif
Wamakersvallei

Stasie

Wellington

Goosen St

Rossiter St

L Hugo Rust

Murray Jubilee Hall
& Samuel House

Huguenot
Museum

R303

CHURCH ST

MAIN ST

Wellington
CHC

Commissioner St

JOUBERT
PARK

Boland
Onderwyskollege

Huguenot Col.

AR

1st St
3rd St
4th St
2nd St

Fabriek

St Crispin Rd
Oxford St
Cillie St
Highfield St

Regent St

Wingfield St

MacCrone St

Schwartz St

Murray St

Joubert St

Jan van Riebeeck St

Keerom

Pentz St

College St

East St

Bain St

CHURCH ST

Malan St

Krom

Maynard Feenstra St

Marseilles St

Richer

Le Roux St
Albertyn St
Lombard St

L Pauw
Gedenk

Municipal
Clinic

Pentz St

Hope St

Melting

Malherbe St

Pins St

Short St

Rose St

Wellington

Granny's House

Palm Ave

Berg St

Doris Dr.

9

Carstens St
Pentz

Kweek St

Pentz St
Lilian St
Samson St

Jardine St

Abrahams St

Hoek St

Schoongezicht

West St

Park St

Kloof St

Zyster St

Kronberg St

Voor St

Dahlia St

MAIN ST

Breedt St

Wellington
VICTORIA
PARK

Memorial
Arch

First Govt
School

Minnie St

Bo Burg St

Jordan St

Fontein St

Eike Ave
Tecoma

Magnolia Ave

Doris Dr.

Wellington

Sylvester St

Loop St

Merriel St

Langham St

Upper Park St

Denne St

End St

Pine St

High St

Spin St

N.G.K.

L

1st Ave

Willem Basson St

Boland
Stadium

L Hugenote

AS

The James
Sedgwick
Distillery (Distell)

R44

Versailles St

Powell St

Minnaar St

Mintoor St

Hospital St

Desmore St

Wellington P

South St

Hospital St

R303

Gross St

4th Ave
5th Ave

2nd Ave

De Villiers St

1st Ave

3rd Ave

Dwars St

Kriel St

Blouvlei St

Charon St

Jasmyn St

H Hugenote H

Stephanie St

S

Gen Hertzog Dr.

Doris Dr.

New Cross

Grenach St

Wellington

L St Albans

Voor St

John
Gertse St

Levin St

Simonsberg Punt

CHAMPAGNE ST

H Bergrivier

Liebenberg St

Carmen St

Gardenia St

Alexander St

Forel St

Freesia St

Erika St

Dfea St

15

Copyright © Map Studio 2007

33°39'00"S
18°59'00"E

Copyright © Map Studio 2007

Legend									
North ↑	◑ Bowling Club	⊟ Swimming	♨ Water Sports	🛡 National Route	R120 Major & Minor Route	Metro Route
	Ⅲ Cricket	🎾 Tennis	⬦ Baseball	Toll Plaza		Retail Area / Industrial Area	National Road / Freeway
	✗ Hockey	⛳ Golf	🏃 Athletics	● Traffic Light		Built-up Area / Informal Settlement*	Main Through Route
	H Rugby	◎ Shooting	🅰 Lighthouse	Restricted Access / Entrance		Park / Sports Ground	Other Road with Bridge
	⊡ Soccer	🐎 Polo	🍷 Wine Estate	Service Station		Railway with Station	One-way St, Start/End
	◌ Squash	🏀 Basketball	🍸 Wine Sales	ℹ Tourist Information		Siding	Nature Trail

* Roads in these areas sometimes untarred

▲ Community Service	Ⓐ Municipal Clinic	Ⓡ Recreation Centre	Place of Worship	Battle Site	⊕ Cemetery	**North** ↑
★ Traffic Department	Hospital/Clinic (24 Hour Casualty)	Ⓖ Government Office	🚗 Parking	Ⓒ Conference Centre	Bird Sanctuary	
🛡 Metro Police	Hospital	✉ Post Office	▲ Place of Interest	Caravan Park	Nature Reserve	
● Police Station	Ⓛ Library	Cinema	Ⓨ Historical Monument	Ⓗ Hotel	✈ International Airport	**Legend**
★ Fire Station	Ⓜ Municipal Office	Shopping Centre	Provincial Heritage Site	Embassy	⊢ Airfield	
⚖ Law Court	Ⓢ School	Theatre	🏛 Museum	▷ Consulate	Ⓗ Helipad	

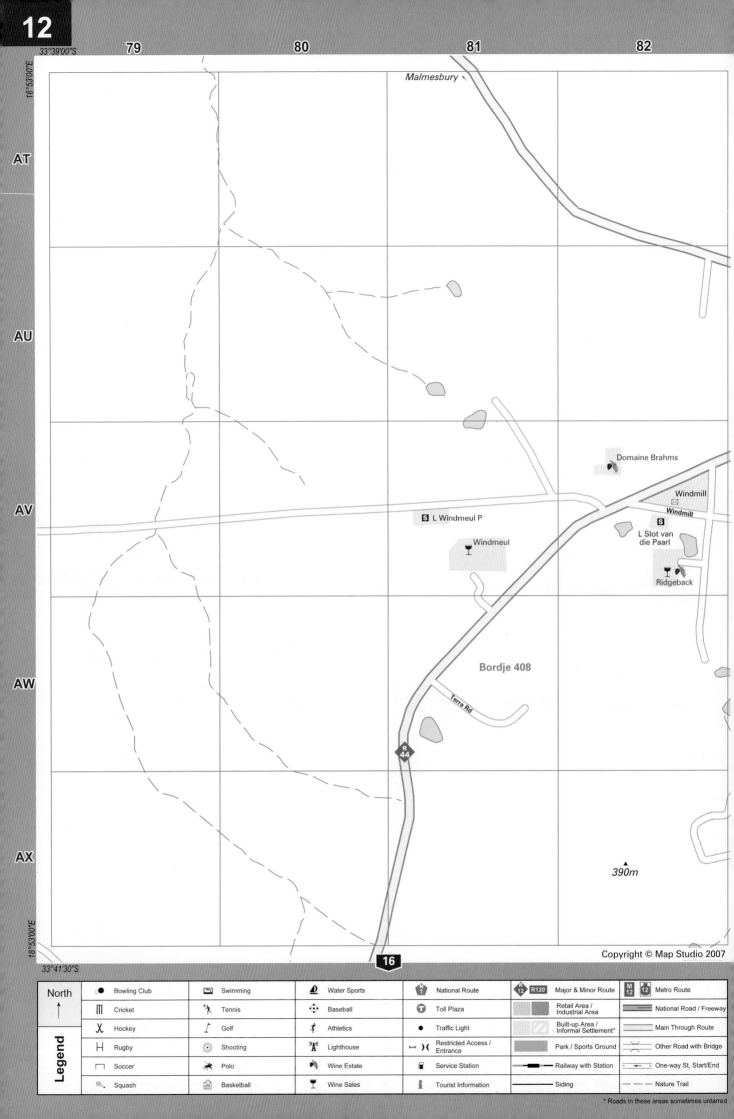

33°39'00"S

18°53'00"E

AT

AU

AV

AW

AX

18°53'00"E

33°41'30"S

79   80   81   82

Malmesbury

Domaine Brahms

Windmill

Windmill

S L Windmeul P

S

L Slot van
die Paarl

Windmeul

Ridgeback

Bordje 408

Terra Rd

R44

390m

16

Copyright © Map Studio 2007

North											
	Bowling Club		Swimming		Water Sports		National Route	R120	Major & Minor Route		Metro Route
	Cricket		Tennis		Baseball		Toll Plaza		Retail Area / Industrial Area		National Road / Freeway
	Hockey		Golf		Athletics		Traffic Light		Built-up Area / Informal Settlement*		Main Through Route
Legend	Rugby		Shooting		Lighthouse		Restricted Access / Entrance		Park / Sports Ground		Other Road with Bridge
	Soccer		Polo		Wine Estate		Service Station		Railway with Station		One-way St, Start/End
	Squash		Basketball		Wine Sales		Tourist Information		Siding		Nature Trail

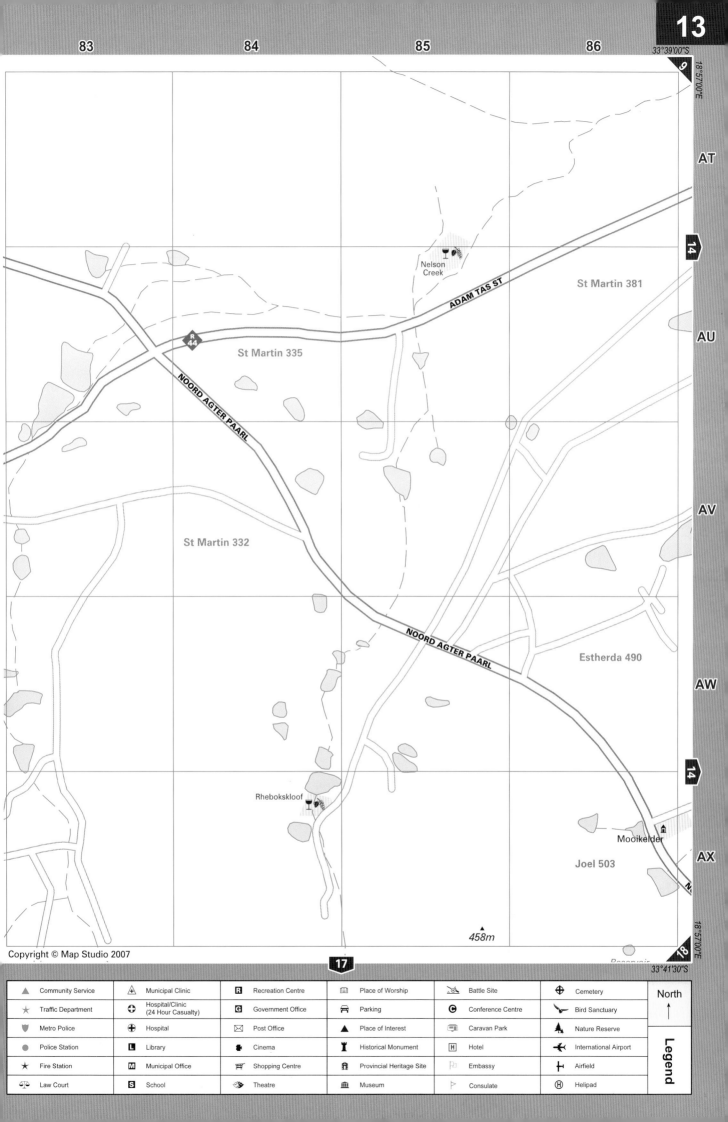

33°39'00"S
18°57'00"E

83　84　85　86

9

AT

14

Nelson
Creek

ADAM TAS ST

St Martin 381

R
44

St Martin 335

AU

NOORD AGTER PAARL

AV

St Martin 332

NOORD AGTER PAARL

Estherda 490

AW

14

Rhebokskloof

Mooikelder

AX

Joel 503

458m

18°57'00"E

18

33°41'30"S

17

									North
▲ Community Service	Ⓐ Municipal Clinic	Ⓡ Recreation Centre	📖 Place of Worship	⚔ Battle Site	⊕ Cemetery	↑
★ Traffic Department	⊕ Hospital/Clinic (24 Hour Casualty)	Ⓖ Government Office	🚗 Parking	Ⓒ Conference Centre	Bird Sanctuary	
🛡 Metro Police	✚ Hospital	✉ Post Office	▲ Place of Interest	Caravan Park	🌲 Nature Reserve	Legend
● Police Station	Ⓛ Library	Cinema	♜ Historical Monument	Ⓗ Hotel	✈ International Airport	
★ Fire Station	Ⓜ Municipal Office	Shopping Centre	🏛 Provincial Heritage Site	Embassy	⊢ Airfield	
⚖ Law Court	Ⓢ School	Theatre	🏛 Museum	▷ Consulate	Ⓗ Helipad	

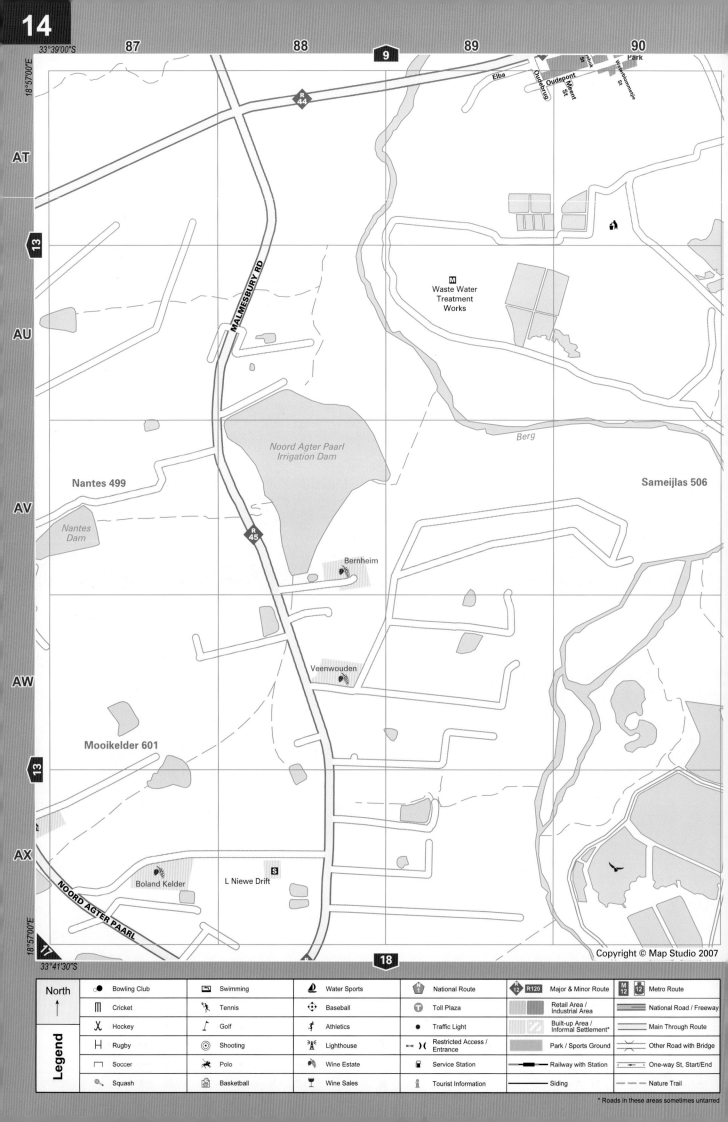

AT

13

AU

MALMESBURY RD

Elba
Meent St
Oudebrug
Oudepont
Park

Waspklommetjie St

Waspklommetjie

M
Waste Water
Treatment
Works

AV

Nantes 499

Berg

Noord Agter Paarl
Irrigation Dam

Sameijlas 506

Nantes
Dam

R
45

Bernheim

AW

Veenwouden

Mooikelder 601

13

AX

17

Boland Kelder

L Niewe Drift

S

NOORD AGTER PAARL

18°57'00"E
33°41'30"S

18

Copyright © Map Studio 2007

North ↑	● Bowling Club	🏊 Swimming	⛵ Water Sports	National Route	R12 R120 Major & Minor Route	M 12 12 Metro Route
	Ⅲ Cricket	Tennis	Baseball	Toll Plaza	Retail Area / Industrial Area	National Road / Freeway
	X Hockey	Golf	Athletics	Traffic Light	Built-up Area / Informal Settlement*	Main Through Route
Legend	H Rugby	Shooting	Lighthouse	Restricted Access / Entrance	Park / Sports Ground	Other Road with Bridge
	Soccer	Polo	Wine Estate	Service Station	Railway with Station	One-way St, Start/End
	Squash	Basketball	Wine Sales	Tourist Information	Siding	Nature Trail

* Roads in these areas sometimes untarred

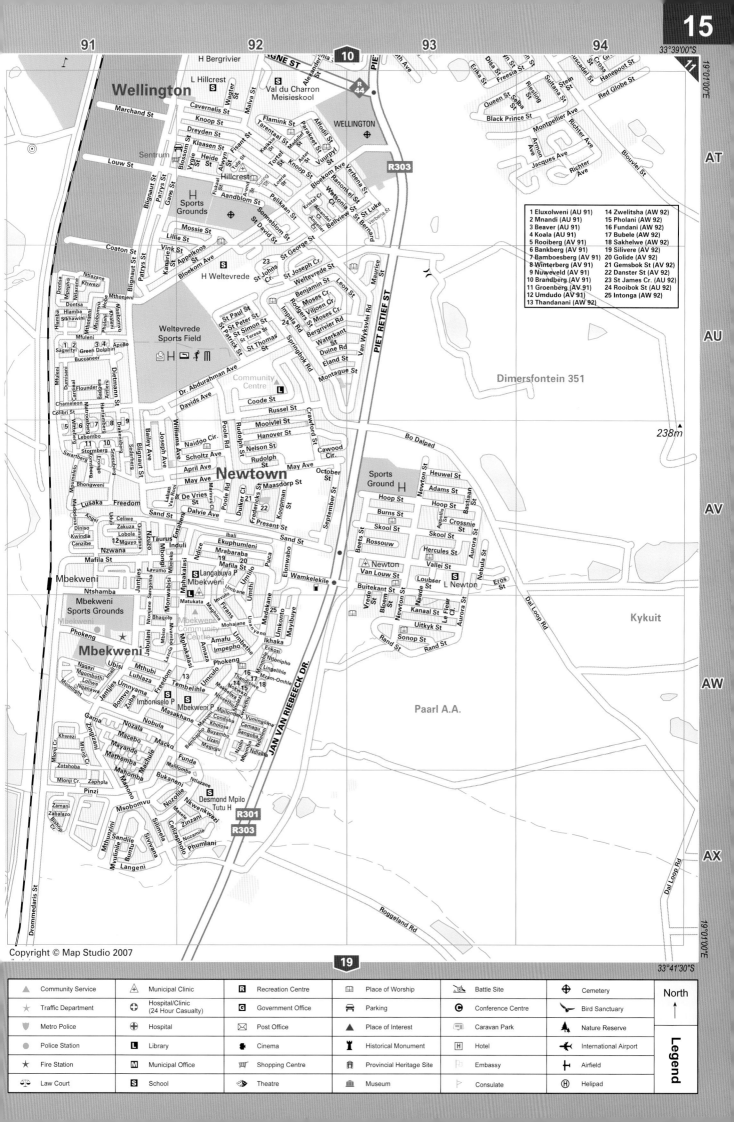

Wellington

L Hillcrest
Val du Charron
Meisieskool

WELLINGTON

R44

R303

Sentrum

Hillcrest

H Sports Grounds

H Weltevrede

Weltevrede Sports Field

Community Centre

Newtown

Sports Ground H

Dimersfontein 351

238m

Kykuit

Mbekweni

Mbekweni Sports Grounds

Mbekweni Community Centre

Paarl A.A.

Desmond Mpilo Tutu H

R301
R303

Newton
L Newton

1 Eluxolweni (AU 91)	14 Zwelitsha (AW 92)
2 Mnandi (AU 91)	15 Pholani (AW 92)
3 Beaver (AU 91)	16 Fundani (AW 92)
4 Koala (AU 91)	17 Bubele (AW 92)
5 Rooiberg (AV 91)	18 Sakhelwe (AW 92)
6 Bankberg (AV 91)	19 Silivere (AV 92)
7 Bamboesberg (AV 91)	20 Golide (AV 92)
8 Winterberg (AV 91)	21 Gemsbok St (AV 92)
9 Nuweveld (AV 91)	22 Danster St (AV 92)
10 Brandberg (AV 91)	23 St James Cr. (AU 92)
11 Groenberg (AV 91)	24 Rooibok St (AU 92)
12 Umdudo (AV 91)	25 Intonga (AW 92)
13 Thandanani (AW 92)	

10

19

AT

AU

AV

AW

AX

33°41'30"S

19°01'00"E

North ↑

Legend

▲	Community Service	⚠	Municipal Clinic	ℝ	Recreation Centre	🕮	Place of Worship	⚔	Battle Site	✠	Cemetery
★	Traffic Department	✚	Hospital/Clinic (24 Hour Casualty)	ℂ	Government Office	🚗	Parking	☯	Conference Centre	✈	Bird Sanctuary
▽	Metro Police	✚	Hospital	✉	Post Office	▲	Place of Interest	🚐	Caravan Park	🌲	Nature Reserve
●	Police Station	L	Library	🎬	Cinema	♟	Historical Monument	H	Hotel	✈	International Airport
★	Fire Station	M	Municipal Office	🏛	Shopping Centre	⌂	Provincial Heritage Site	📰	Embassy	✛	Airfield
⚖	Law Court	S	School	◈	Theatre	🏛	Museum	▷	Consulate	Ⓗ	Helipad

33°41'30"S

18°53'00"E

79   80   81   82

12

AY

R 44

AZ

Durbanville

R312

BA

Kanonkop
715m

BB

Groot-Waboom
729m

BC

R 44

18°53'00"E

33°44'00"S

20

Legend									
North	● Bowling Club	Swimming	⛵ Water Sports	National Route	R 12 R120 Major & Minor Route	M 12 12 Metro Route
↑	Ⅲ Cricket	Tennis	✛ Baseball	Ⓣ Toll Plaza	Retail Area / Industrial Area	National Road / Freeway
	X Hockey	Golf	Athletics	● Traffic Light	Built-up Area / Informal Settlement*	Main Through Route
	H Rugby	◎ Shooting	Lighthouse	⋈)(Restricted Access / Entrance	Park / Sports Ground	Other Road with Bridge
	Soccer	Polo	Wine Estate	Service Station	Railway with Station	One-way St, Start/End
	Squash	Basketball	Wine Sales	ℹ Tourist Information	Siding	Nature Trail

* Roads in these areas sometimes untarred

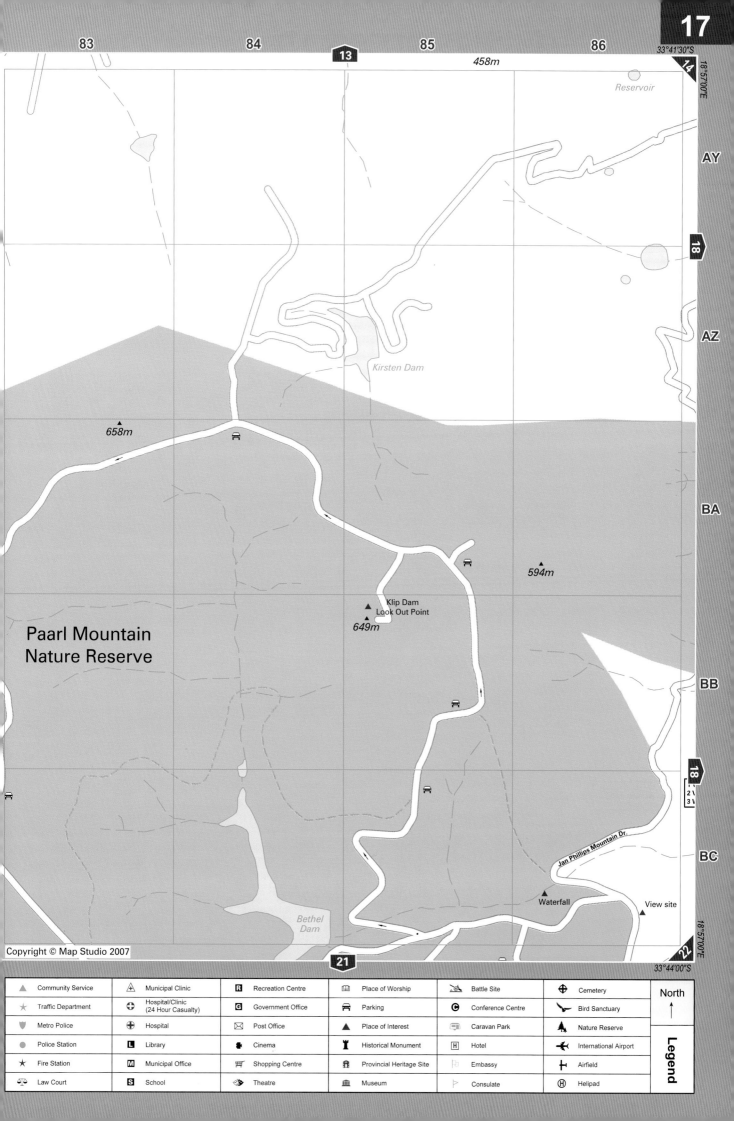

33°41'30"S

83   84   13   458m   85   86   33°41'30"S

AY

Reservoir

18

AZ

Kirsten Dam

BA

658m

Klip Dam
Look Out Point

594m

649m

Paarl Mountain
Nature Reserve

BB

18
2 V
3 V

BC

Jan Phillips Mountain Dr.

Waterfall   View site

Bethel
Dam

21

33°44'00"S

18°57'00"E

18°57'00"E

▲ Community Service	Ⓐ Municipal Clinic	Ⓡ Recreation Centre	📖 Place of Worship	⚔ Battle Site	✠ Cemetery	**North**
★ Traffic Department	Ⓗ Hospital/Clinic (24 Hour Casualty)	Ⓖ Government Office	🚗 Parking	▲ Place of Interest	Ⓒ Conference Centre	🐦 Bird Sanctuary	↑
♥ Metro Police	Ⓗ Hospital	✉ Post Office	▲ Place of Interest	🎥 Cinema	🚐 Caravan Park	🌲 Nature Reserve
● Police Station	Ⓛ Library	🛒 Shopping Centre	♜ Historical Monument	Ⓗ Hotel	✈ International Airport	**Legend**
★ Fire Station	Ⓜ Municipal Office	🛒 Shopping Centre	🏛 Provincial Heritage Site	🏦 Embassy	✚ Airfield
⚖ Law Court	Ⓢ School	👁 Theatre	🏛 Museum	⚑ Consulate	Ⓗ Helipad

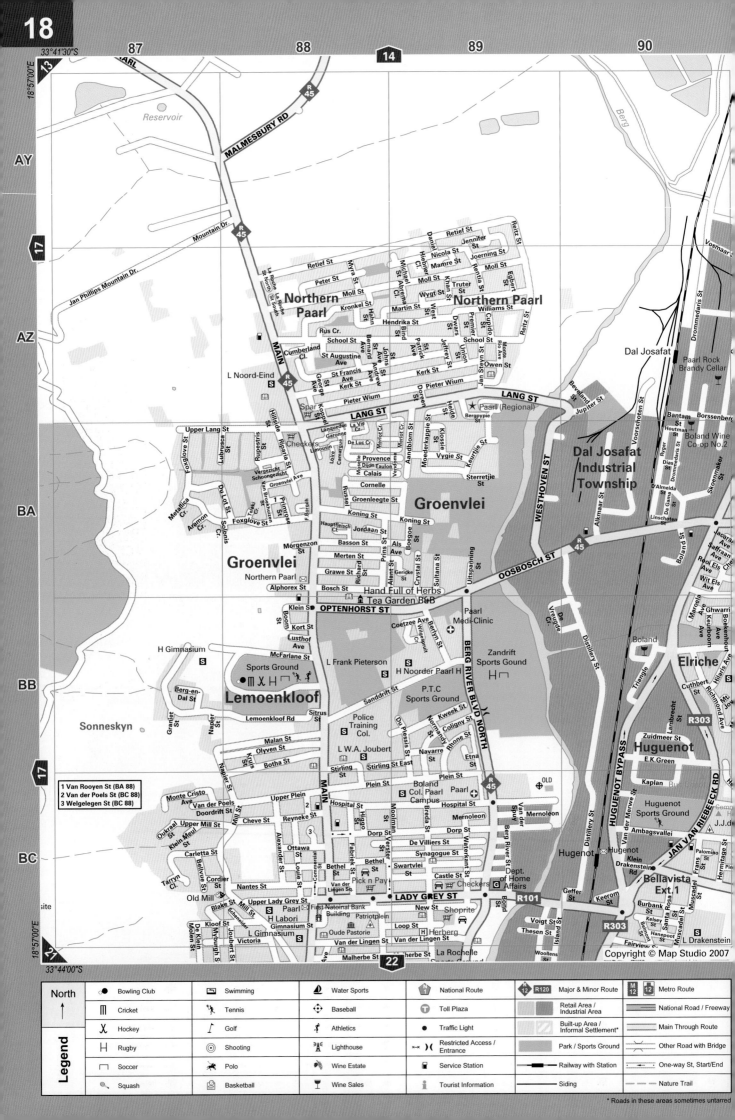

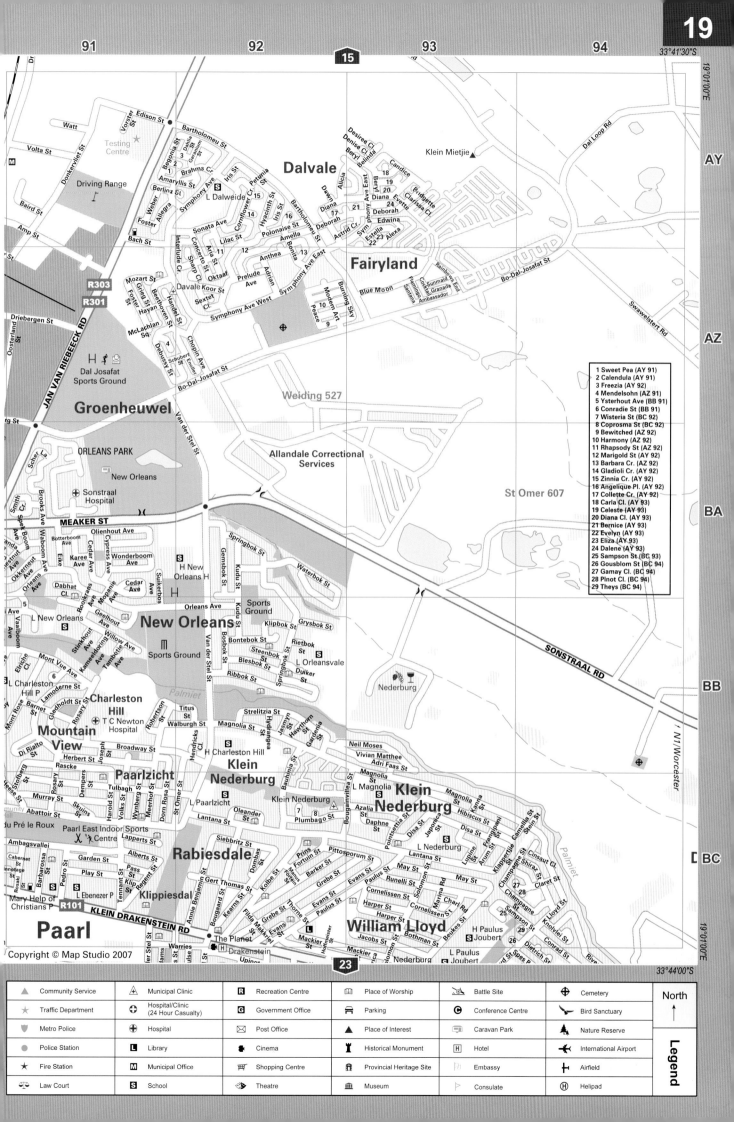

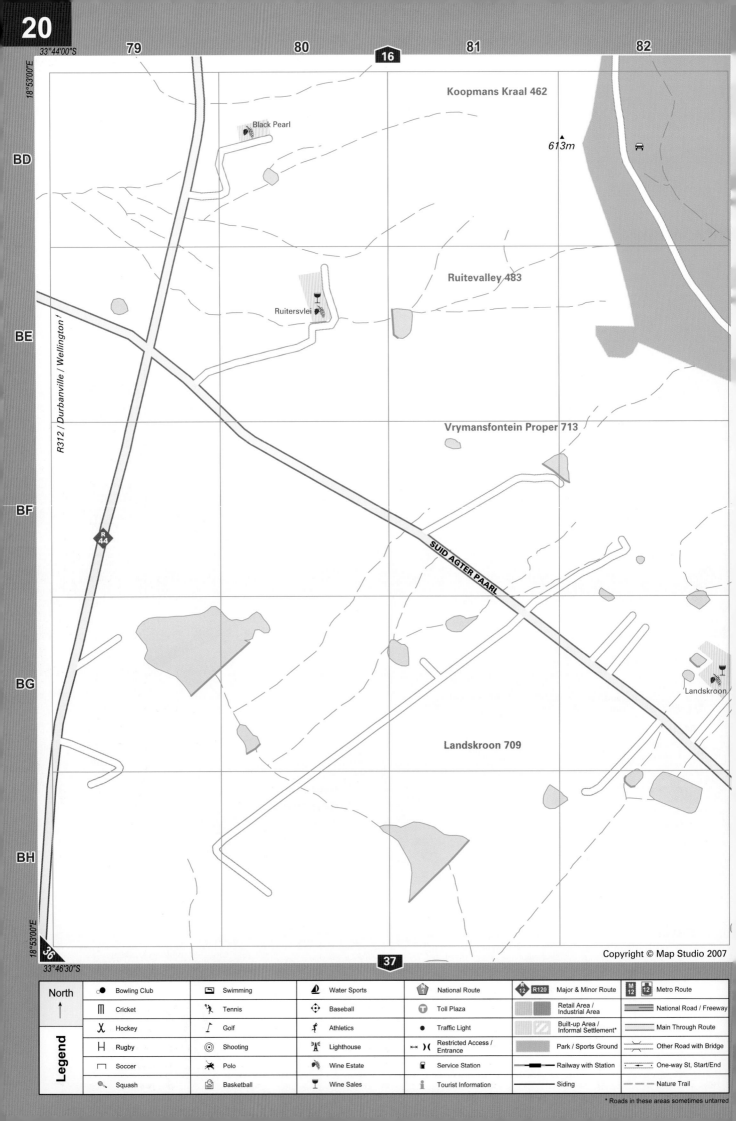

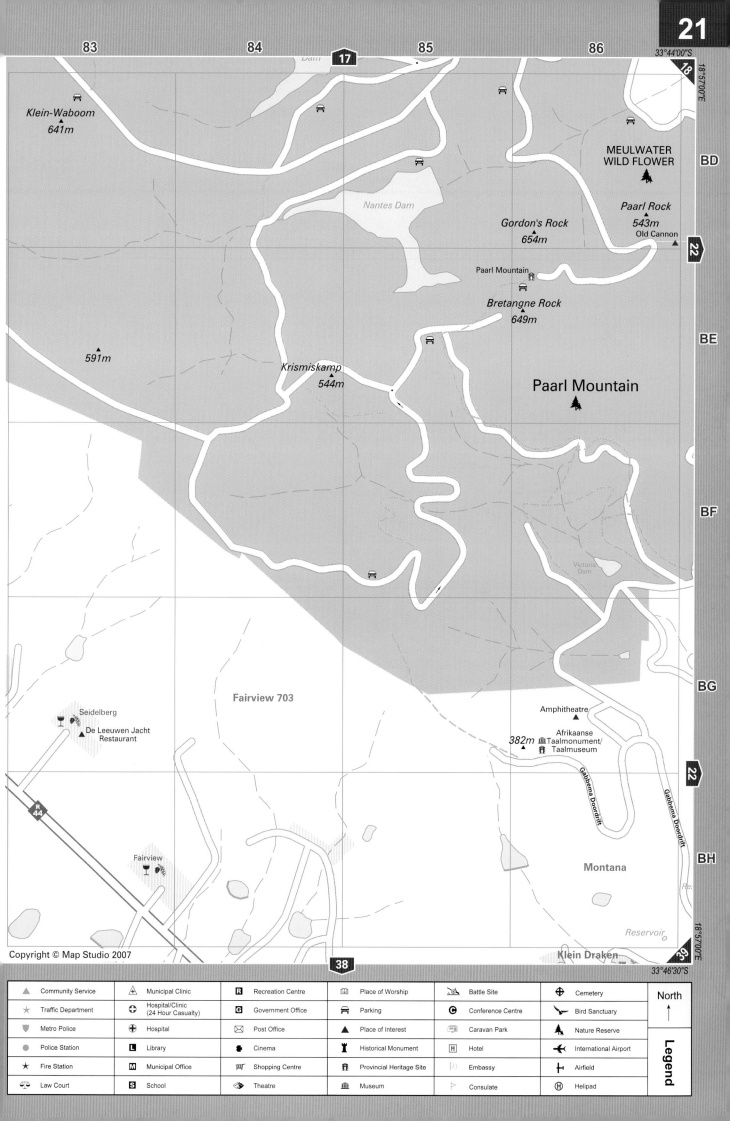

83　84　17　85　86

33°44'00"S
18°57'00"E

Klein-Waboom
▲
641m

18

**MEULWATER
WILD FLOWER**
♠

BD

Nantes Dam

Gordon's Rock
▲
654m

Paarl Rock
543m
Old Cannon
▲

22

Paarl Mountain 🏛
🚗

Bretangne Rock
▲
649m

BE

591m
▲

Krismiskamp
▲
544m

Paarl Mountain
♠

BF

Victoria Dam

Fairview 703

BG

Amphitheatre
▲

Seidelberg
🍷🍇
De Leeuwen Jacht ▲
Restaurant

382m
▲
Afrikaanse
🏛 Taalmonument/
🏛 Taalmuseum

R44

22

Fairview
🍷🍇

Montana

Reservoir

18°57'00"E
33°46'30"S

Klein Draken

38

▲ Community Service	🅰 Municipal Clinic	🆁 Recreation Centre	🏛 Place of Worship	⚔ Battle Site	⊕ Cemetery	**North** ↑
★ Traffic Department	⊕ Hospital/Clinic (24 Hour Casualty)	🅶 Government Office	🚗 Parking	🅒 Conference Centre	🦅 Bird Sanctuary	
🛡 Metro Police	⊕ Hospital	✉ Post Office	▲ Place of Interest	🚐 Caravan Park	♠ Nature Reserve	**Legend**
● Police Station	🅻 Library	🎬 Cinema	🏛 Historical Monument	Ⓗ Hotel	✈ International Airport	
★ Fire Station	🅼 Municipal Office	🛒 Shopping Centre	🏛 Provincial Heritage Site	Embassy	✛ Airfield	
⚖ Law Court	🆂 School	🎭 Theatre	🏛 Museum	▷ Consulate	Ⓗ Helipad	

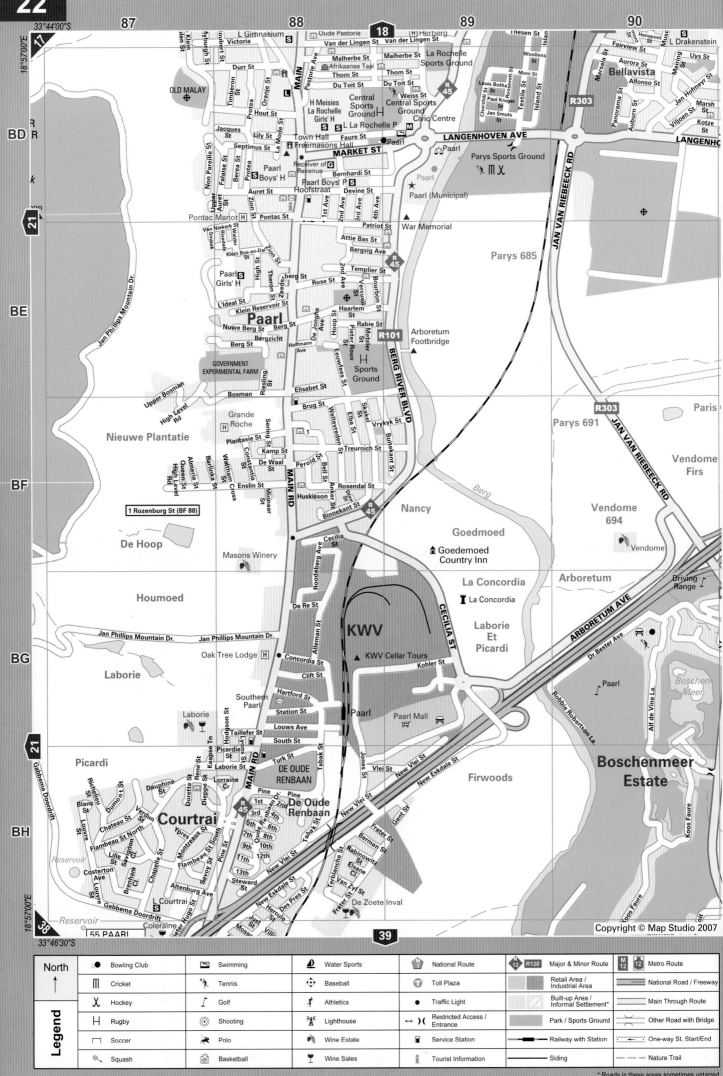

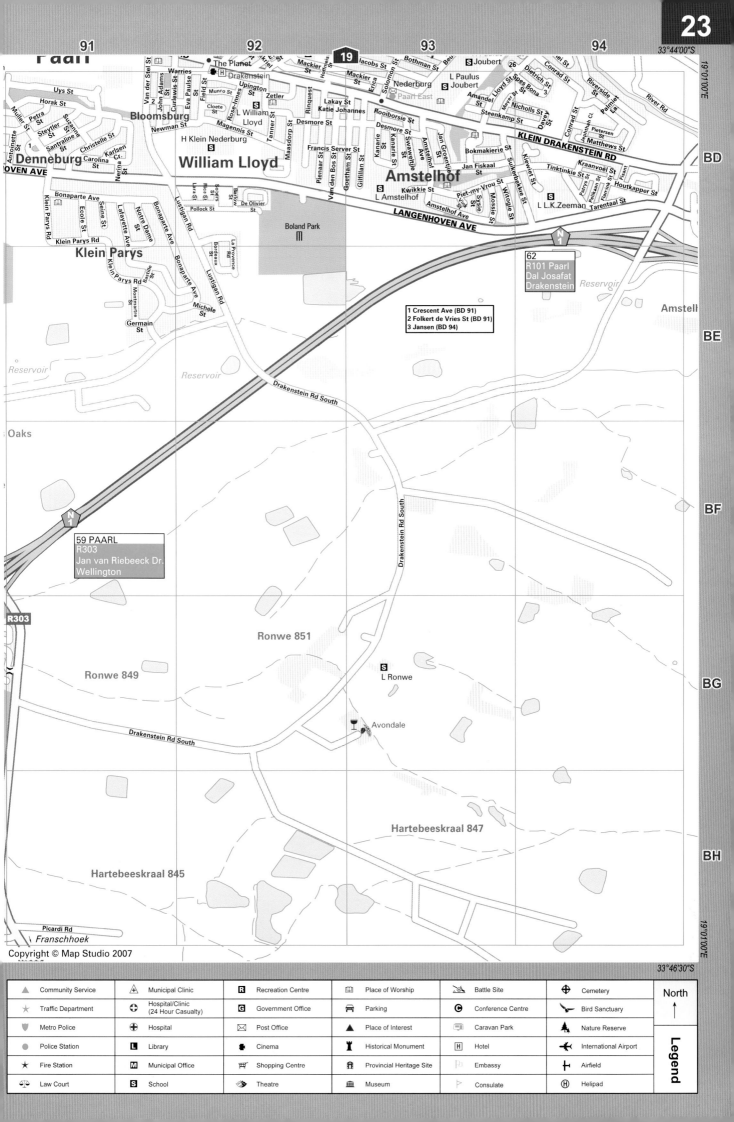

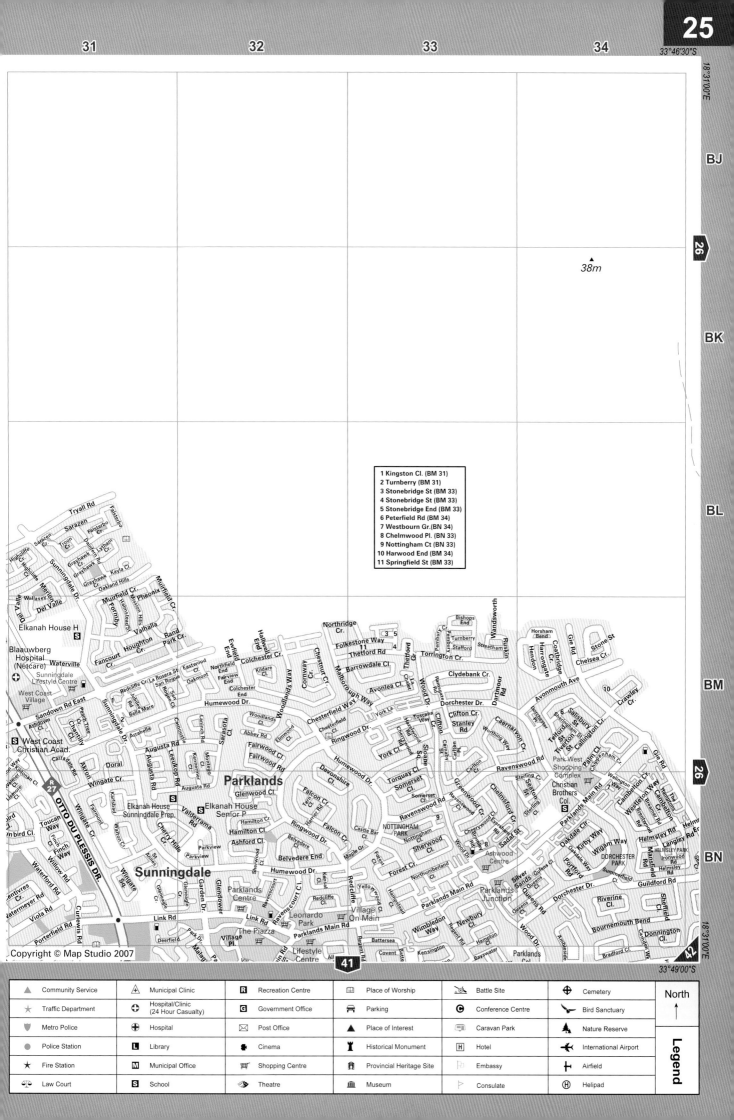

33°46'30"S

31 32 33 34

18°31'00"E

BJ

26

BK

38m

BL

1 Kingston Cl. (BM 31)
2 Turnberry (BM 31)
3 Stonebridge St (BM 33)
4 Stonebridge St (BM 33)
5 Stonebridge End (BM 33)
6 Peterfield Rd (BM 34)
7 Westbourn Gr.(BN 34)
8 Chelmwood Pl. (BN 33)
9 Nottingham Ct (BN 33)
10 Harwood End (BM 34)
11 Springfield St (BM 33)

BM

26

BN

18°31'00"E

33°49'00"S

▲ Community Service	Ⓐ Municipal Clinic	Ⓡ Recreation Centre	Place of Worship	Battle Site	⊕ Cemetery
★ Traffic Department	✚ Hospital/Clinic (24 Hour Casualty)	Ⓖ Government Office	Parking	Ⓒ Conference Centre	Bird Sanctuary
Metro Police	✚ Hospital	✉ Post Office	▲ Place of Interest	Caravan Park	Nature Reserve
● Police Station	Ⓛ Library	Cinema	Historical Monument	Ⓗ Hotel	International Airport
★ Fire Station	Ⓜ Municipal Office	Shopping Centre	Provincial Heritage Site	Embassy	Airfield
⚖ Law Court	Ⓢ School	Theatre	Museum	▷ Consulate	Ⓗ Helipad

North
↑

Legend

33°46'30"S
18°31'00"E

BJ

25

BK

BL

BM

25

BN

18°31'00"E
33°49'00"S

(Spoorlyn Kamp)

(Rooidakkies)

Malmesbury

Visserhok Uitspan 153

Visserhok Uitspan 152

Diep

(Doornbach)

Blan 215

1 Gousblom St (BN 37)
2 Geranium St (BN 37)

30 Nkunkwana (BO 37)

42

N7

M48

M5

POTSDAM RD

Old Farm Rd

Dunker Rd

Dunoon

Waxberry St

Tulip St

Loerie St

Amander St

Daisy

Dahlia St

Fig

Durmont

Siyabonga

Bujelan St

Yomelela Ave

Landelani

Jonga

Bulbinella Cl

Aloe St

Helmsley

Rd End

Fisherman's Wk

Earlswood Rd

Fernwood Rd

Copyright © Map Studio 2007

* Roads in these areas sometimes untarred

North		Legend		
Bowling Club	Swimming	Water Sports	National Route	R120 Major & Minor Route
Cricket	Tennis	Baseball	Toll Plaza	Retail Area / Industrial Area
Hockey	Golf	Athletics	Traffic Light	Built-up Area / Informal Settlement*
Rugby	Shooting	Lighthouse	Restricted Access / Entrance	Park / Sports Ground
Soccer	Polo	Wine Estate	Service Station	Railway with Station
Squash	Basketball	Wine Sales	Tourist Information	Siding

Metro Route
National Road / Freeway
Main Through Route
Other Road with Bridge
One-way St, Start/End
Nature Trail

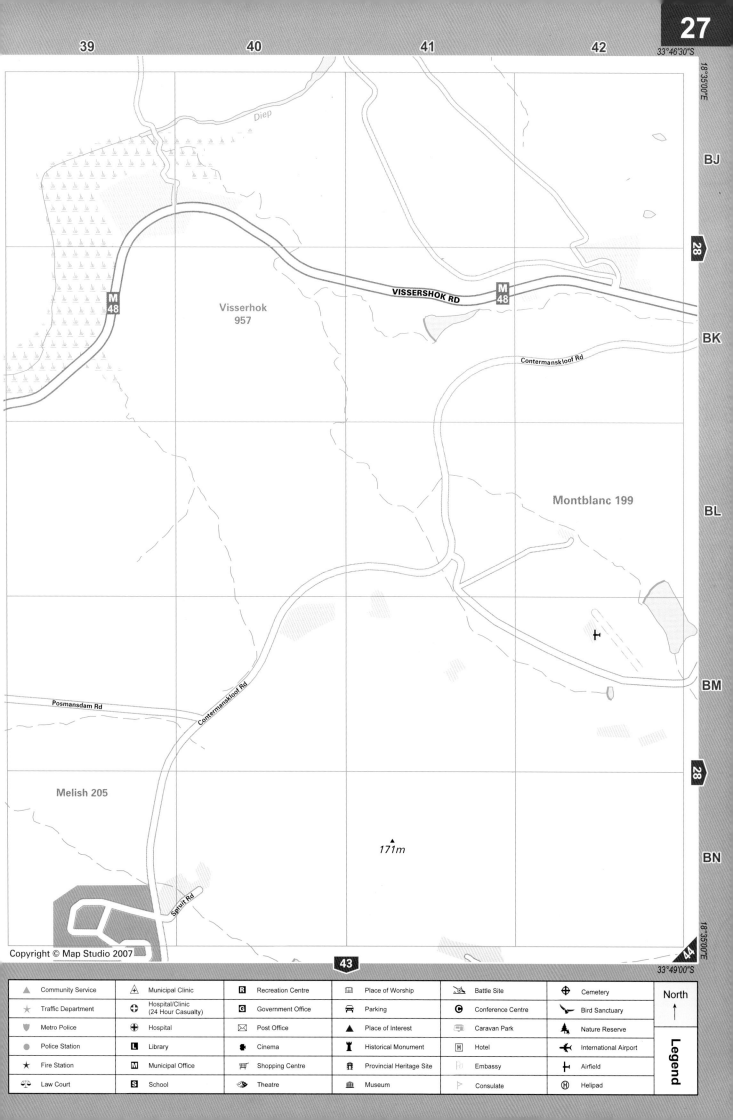

33°46'30"S

39 40 41 42

18°35'00"E

BJ

28

BK

Diep

VISSERSHOK RD

M48 M48

Visserhok
957

Contermanskloof Rd

BL

Montblanc 199

BM

Posmansdam Rd

Contermanskloof Rd

28

Melish 205

BN

_171m_

Spruit Rd

43

18°35'00"E

33°49'00"S

▲ Community Service	Ⓐ Municipal Clinic	Ⓡ Recreation Centre	Place of Worship	Battle Site	⊕ Cemetery	**North** ↑	
★ Traffic Department	⊕ Hospital/Clinic (24 Hour Casualty)	Ⓖ Government Office	Parking	Ⓒ Conference Centre	Bird Sanctuary		
Metro Police	⊕ Hospital	⊠ Post Office	▲ Place of Interest	Caravan Park	Nature Reserve		
● Police Station	Ⓛ Library	⚫ Cinema	Historical Monument	Ⓗ Hotel	International Airport	**Legend**	
★ Fire Station	Ⓜ Municipal Office	Shopping Centre	Provincial Heritage Site	Embassy	⊢ Airfield		
Law Court	Ⓢ School	Theatre	🏛 Museum	▷ Consulate	Ⓗ Helipad		

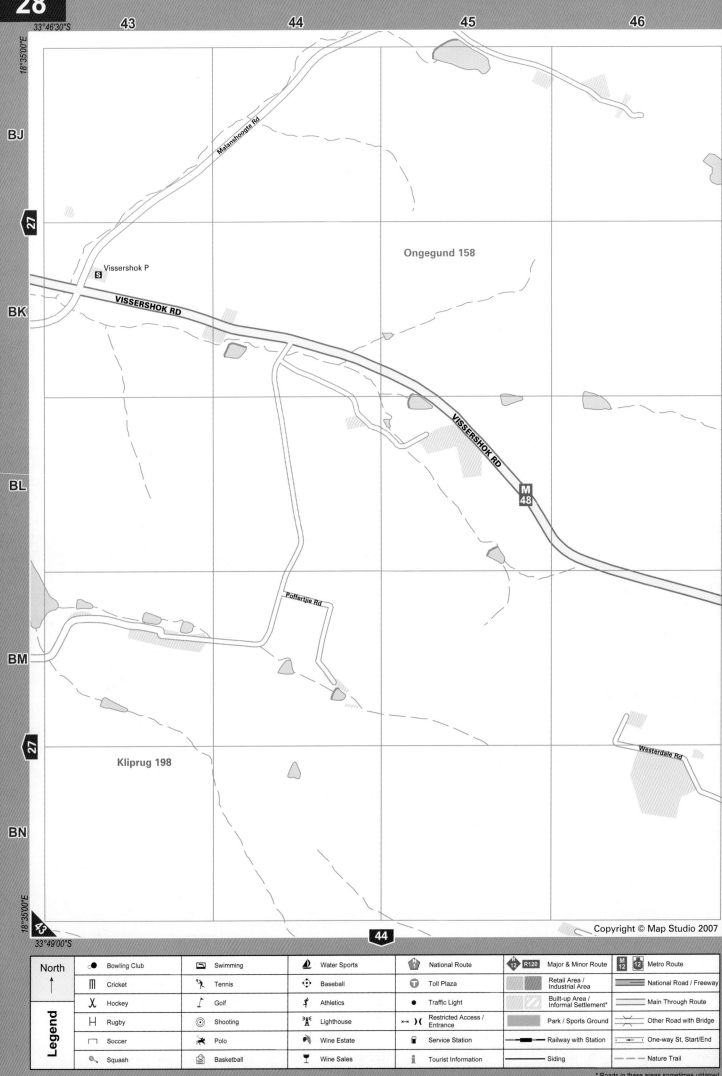

33°46'30"S
18°35'00"E

43   44   45   46

BJ

27

Malanshoogte Rd

Vissershok P
S

VISSERSHOK RD

BK

Ongegund 158

VISSERSHOK RD

BL

M
48

Poffertjie Rd

BM

27

Westerdale Rd

Kliprug 198

BN

18°35'00"E
33°49'00"S

44

Copyright © Map Studio 2007

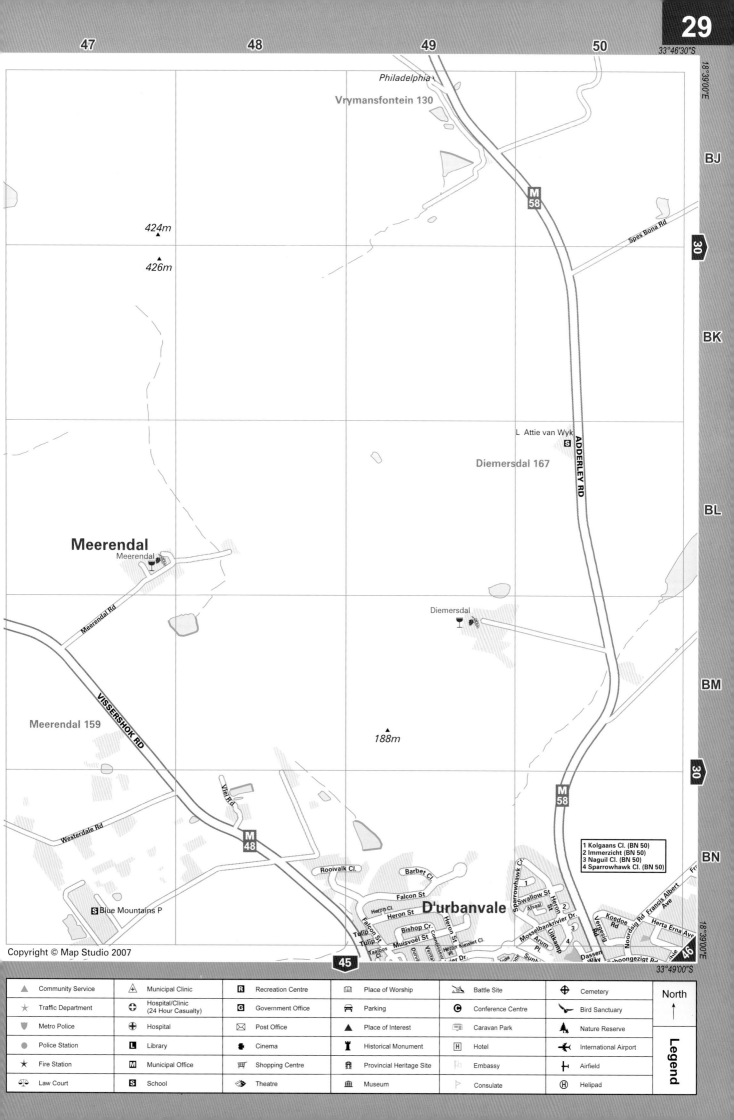

33°46'30"S
18°39'00"E

47   48   49   50

BJ

BK

BL

BM

BN

Philadelphia

Vrymansfontein 130

M 58

Spes Bona Rd

30

424m

426m

L Attie van Wyk
S

Diemersdal 167

ADDERLEY RD

Meerendal

Meerendal

Diemersdal

Meerendal Rd

VISSERSHOK RD

Meerendal 159

188m

30

M 58

Vlei Rd

M 48

Westerdale Rd

1 Kolgaans Cl. (BN 50)
2 Immerzicht (BN 50)
3 Naguil Cl. (BN 50)
4 Sparrowhawk Cl. (BN 50)

Rooivalk Cl.

Barbet Cl.

Falcon St

S Blue Mountains P

Heron Cl.

Heron St

D'urbanvale

Falcon St

Bishop Cr.

Tulip St

Muisvoel St

Sparrowhawk Cr.

Swallow St

Afsaal

Heron St

Pl.

Mosselbankrivier Dr.

Uitkamp

Koedoe
Rd

Vergesig

Noordsig Rd

Francis Albert
Ave

Herta Erna Ave

46

Dassen
Way

Schoongezigt Rd

45

33°49'00"S
18°39'00"E

Copyright © Map Studio 2007

▲ Community Service	Ⓐ Municipal Clinic	Ⓡ Recreation Centre	Place of Worship	Battle Site	⊕ Cemetery
★ Traffic Department	⊕ Hospital/Clinic (24 Hour Casualty)	Ⓖ Government Office	🚗 Parking	Ⓒ Conference Centre	Bird Sanctuary
Metro Police	⊕ Hospital	✉ Post Office	▲ Place of Interest	Caravan Park	Nature Reserve
● Police Station	Ⓛ Library	Cinema	Ⓨ Historical Monument	Ⓗ Hotel	International Airport
★ Fire Station	Ⓜ Municipal Office	Shopping Centre	Provincial Heritage Site	Embassy	Airfield
⚖ Law Court	Ⓢ School	Theatre	Museum	Consulate	Ⓗ Helipad

North ↑

Legend

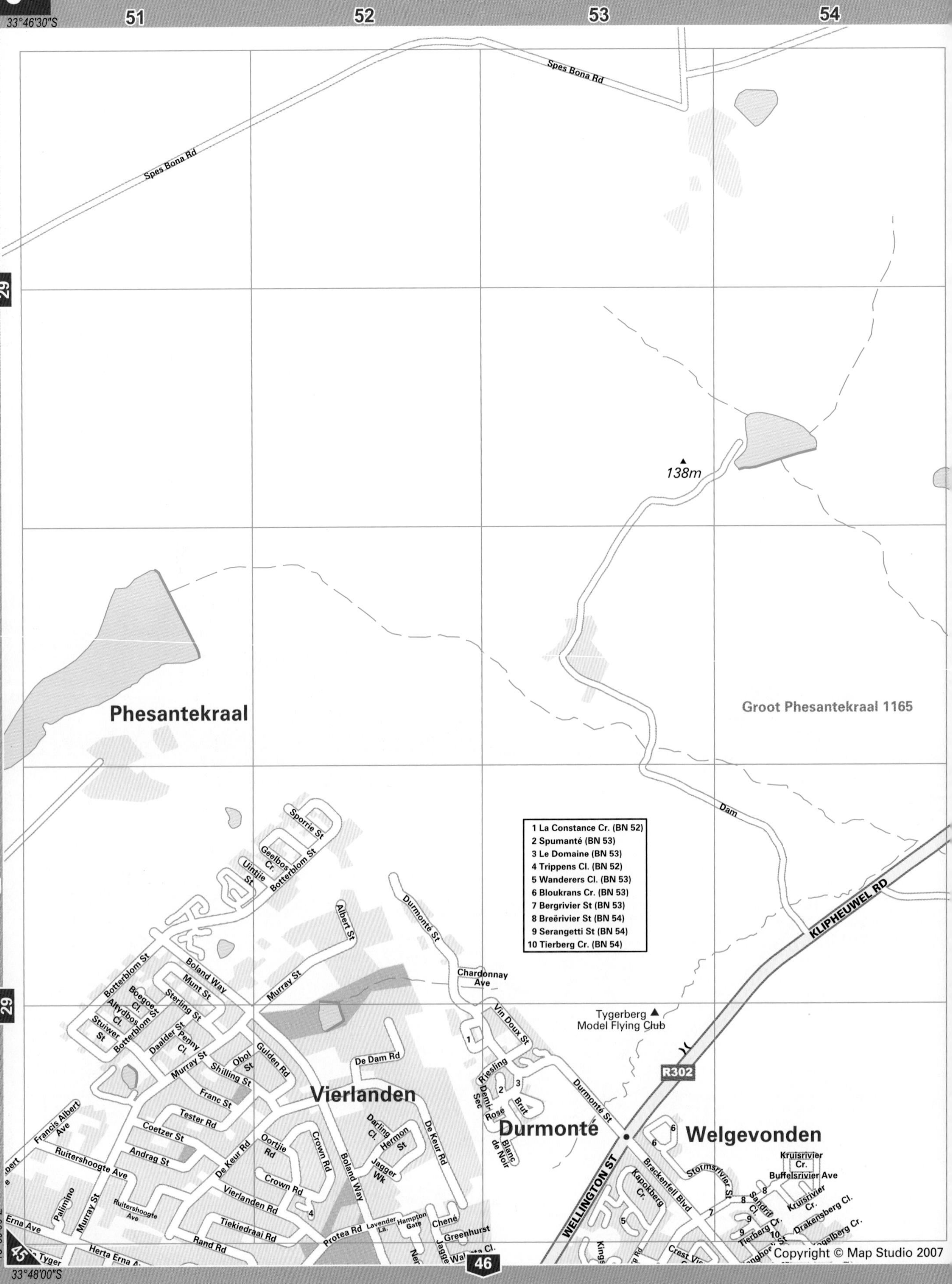

51   52   53   54

18°39'00"E

BJ

29

BK

138m

BL

Phesantekraal

Groot Phesantekraal 1165

Dam

BM

Spes Bona Rd

1	La Constance Cr. (BN 52)
2	Spumanté (BN 53)
3	Le Domaine (BN 53)
4	Trippens Cl. (BN 52)
5	Wanderers Cl. (BN 53)
6	Bloukrans Cr. (BN 53)
7	Bergrivier St (BN 53)
8	Breërivier St (BN 54)
9	Serangetti St (BN 54)
10	Tierberg Cr. (BN 54)

KLIPHEUWEL RD

Chardonnay Ave

Tygerberg ▲
Model Flying Club

29

Vierlanden

R302

Durmonté   **Welgevonden**

BN

WELLINGTON ST

Kruisrivier Cr.
Buffelsrivier Ave

18°39'00"E

45

33°48'00"S

Copyright © Map Studio 2007

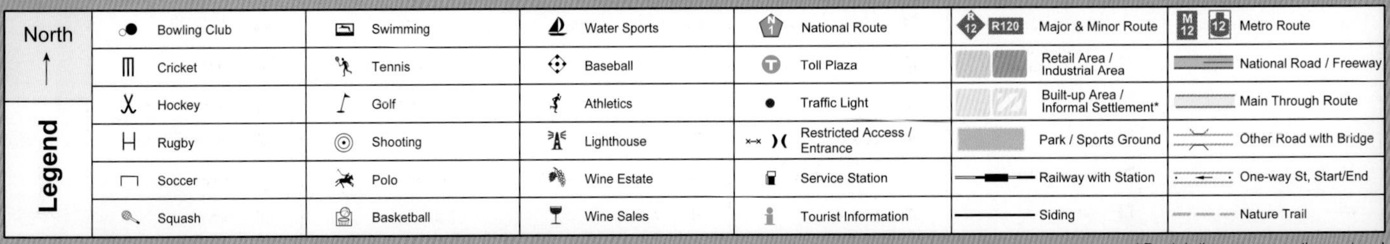

Legend

North ↑	●	Bowling Club	🏊	Swimming	⛵	Water Sports	National Route		R120	Major & Minor Route	12	Metro Route
	Ⅲ	Cricket	🎾	Tennis	✦	Baseball	Toll Plaza			Retail Area / Industrial Area		National Road / Freeway
	X	Hockey	Golf		Athletics		Traffic Light			Built-up Area / Informal Settlement*		Main Through Route
Legend	H	Rugby	◉	Shooting	Lighthouse		Restricted Access / Entrance			Park / Sports Ground		Other Road with Bridge
	□	Soccer	Polo		Wine Estate		Service Station			Railway with Station		One-way St, Start/End
	Squash		Basketball		Wine Sales		Tourist Information			Siding		Nature Trail

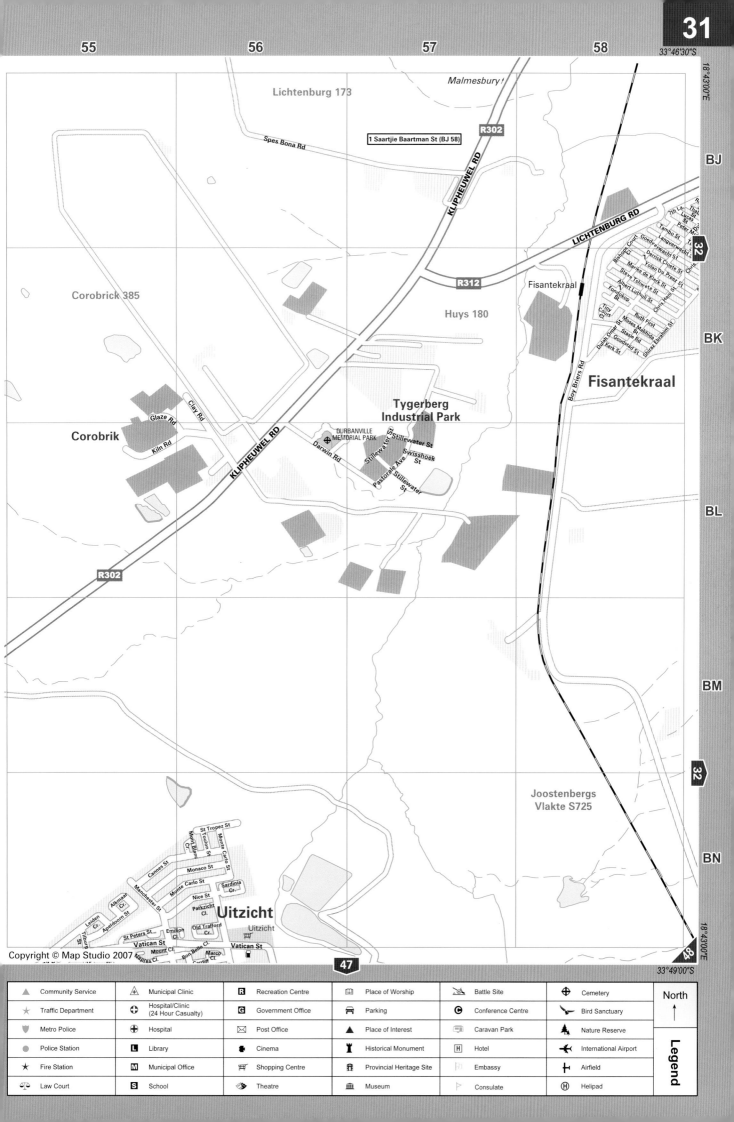

55   56   57   58

18°43'00"E

BJ

Malmesbury

Lichtenburg 173

Spes Bona Rd

1 Saartjie Baartman St (BJ 58)

R302

KLIPHEUWEL RD

LICHTENBURG RD

R312

32

Fisantekraal

Corobrick 385

Huys 180

BK

7th La
Lucas St
Peter Mo

Tambo St
Langverwacht S
Goedverwacht St
Bishops Court Cl
Derrick Cloete St
Yolan Du Preez St
Marike de Klerk St
Chris Hani
Steve Tshwete St
Albert Luthuli St
Fondokop St
Tiny Court
Ruth First
Moses Mabhida
Dulah Omar St   Stasie Rd
Goudsrid St
Shiraz Ebrahim St
Duli Kerk St

Boy Briers Rd

Fisantekraal

Tygerberg
Industrial Park

Corobrik

Clay Rd

Glaze Rd

Kiln Rd

KLIPHEUWEL RD

DURBANVILLE
MEMORIAL PARK

Darwin Rd

Stillewater St
Stillewater St
Stillewater St
Swisshoek St
Pastorale Ave
Stillewater St

BL

R302

BM

32

Joostenbergs
Vlakte S725

St Tropez St
Mont Blanc Cr
Toulon St
Monte Carlo St
Cannes St
Monaco St
Manchester St
Monte Carlo St
Sardinia Cr
Nice St
Patkzicht Cl
Leiden Cr
Alkmaar Cr
Apeldoorn St
Emilion Cr
Old Trafford Cr
St Peters St
Tilburg
Mount Cl
Vatican St
Bon Bello St
Marco Cl
Montes Cl
Cardiff

BN

Uitzicht

Uitzicht

Vatican St

18°43'00"E

48

33°49'00"S

47

▲	Community Service	⚕	Municipal Clinic	R	Recreation Centre	🕍	Place of Worship	⚔	Battle Site	⊕ Cemetery
★	Traffic Department	✚	Hospital/Clinic (24 Hour Casualty)	G	Government Office	🚗	Parking	©	Conference Centre	✈ Bird Sanctuary
⛊	Metro Police	✚	Hospital	✉	Post Office	▲	Place of Interest	🚐	Caravan Park	♠ Nature Reserve
●	Police Station	L	Library	✦	Cinema	🛡	Historical Monument	H	Hotel	✈ International Airport
★	Fire Station	M	Municipal Office	🛒	Shopping Centre	🏛	Provincial Heritage Site		Embassy	✚ Airfield
⚖	Law Court	S	School	👁	Theatre	🏛	Museum	⚐	Consulate	Ⓗ Helipad

North
↑

Legend

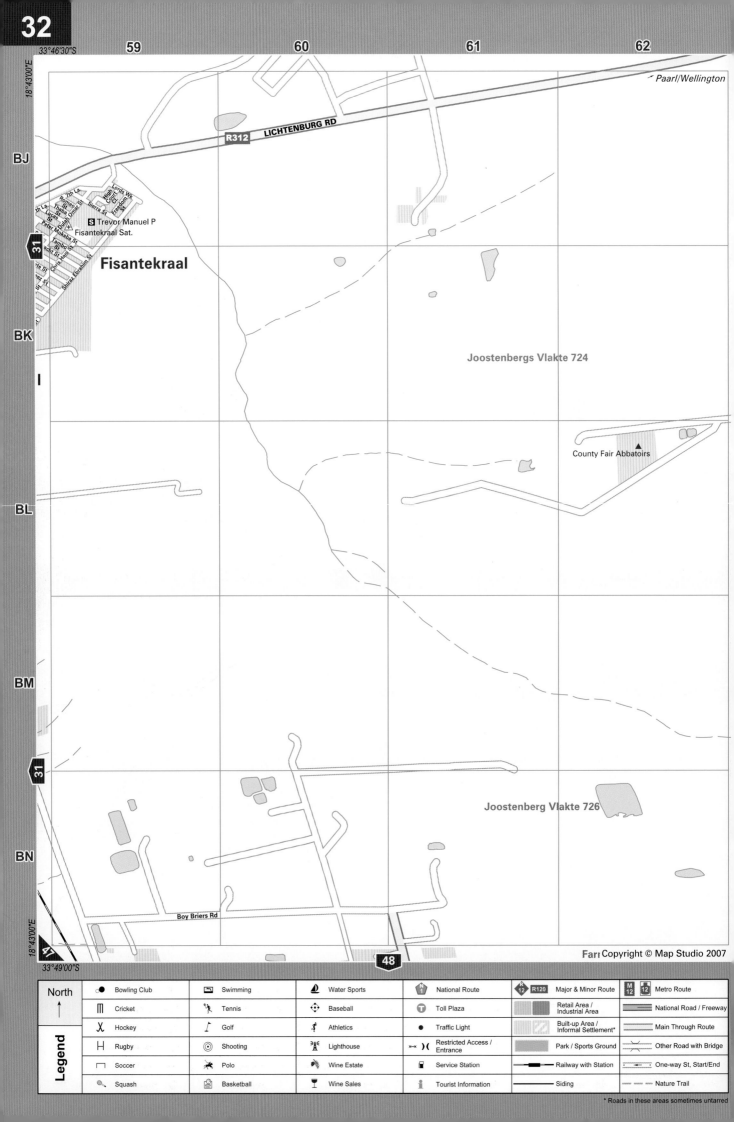

33°46'30"S
18°43'00"E

59   60   61   62

Paarl/Wellington

R312 LICHTENBURG RD

BJ

7th La.   Lords Wk.
Romeo st St   High   Freedom St
Thaba st   Court   St
Lucas   Dulah   Sierra St
Peter M   Ct
Tambo St
Chris Hani
Shiraz Ebrahim St

31

S Trevor Manuel P
Fisantekraal Sat.

Fisantekraal

BK

I

Joostenbergs Vlakte 724

BL

County Fair Abbatoirs

BM

31

Joostenberg Vlakte 726

BN

Boy Briers Rd

18°43'00"E
33°49'00"S

47

48

Farr Copyright © Map Studio 2007

North ↑											
	Bowling Club		Swimming		Water Sports		National Route	R120	Major & Minor Route	M12 12	Metro Route
	Cricket		Tennis		Baseball	T	Toll Plaza		Retail Area / Industrial Area		National Road / Freeway
	Hockey		Golf		Athletics	•	Traffic Light		Built-up Area / Informal Settlement*		Main Through Route
Legend	Rugby		Shooting		Lighthouse	)(	Restricted Access / Entrance		Park / Sports Ground		Other Road with Bridge
	Soccer		Polo		Wine Estate		Service Station		Railway with Station		One-way St, Start/End
	Squash		Basketball		Wine Sales	i	Tourist Information		Siding		Nature Trail

* Roads in these areas sometimes untarred

33°46'30"S

18°47'00"E

63 64 65 66

BJ

BK

BL

BM

BN

34

Paarl/Malmesbury

R304

Hercules Pillar Rd

34

50

18°47'00"E

33°49'00"S

49

North

Legend

Community Service	Municipal Clinic	Recreation Centre	Place of Worship	Battle Site	Cemetery
Traffic Department	Hospital/Clinic (24 Hour Casualty)	Government Office	Parking	Conference Centre	Bird Sanctuary
Metro Police	Hospital	Post Office	Place of Interest	Caravan Park	Nature Reserve
Police Station	Library	Cinema	Historical Monument	Hotel	International Airport
Fire Station	Municipal Office	Shopping Centre	Provincial Heritage Site	Embassy	Airfield
Law Court	School	Theatre	Museum	Consulate	Helipad

33°46'30"S

67   68   69   70

18°47'00"E

BJ

33

▲ Joostenberg
290m

Hercules Pillar Rd

BK

Joostenberg Brick ▲

Hercules Pillar Rd

Rd

BL

BM

33

R304

L Joostenberg P
S

Mӱn Burg

BN

Joostenberg

N
1

18°47'00"E

49

33°49'00"S

50

Copyright © Map Studio 2007

▲ The Pink Geranium Nursery

North ↑							
Legend	● Bowling Club	⊟ Swimming	⛵ Water Sports	🛡 National Route	R120 Major & Minor Route	M 12 / 12 Metro Route	
	Ⅲ Cricket	Tennis	⊕ Baseball	Ⓣ Toll Plaza	Retail Area / Industrial Area	National Road / Freeway	
	X Hockey	Golf	Athletics	● Traffic Light	Built-up Area / Informal Settlement*	Main Through Route	
	H Rugby	◉ Shooting	Lighthouse	⋈)(Restricted Access / Entrance	Park / Sports Ground	Other Road with Bridge	
	⊓ Soccer	Polo	Wine Estate	Service Station	Railway with Station	One-way St, Start/End	
	Squash	Basketball	♆ Wine Sales	Tourist Information	Siding	Nature Trail	

*Roads in these areas sometimes untarred

Zand Dam 479

Eenzaamheid Rd

Protea Rd

Protea Rd

N 1

R101

De Meye   Muldersvlei

51

Copyright © Map Studio 2007

▲ Community Service	Ⓐ Municipal Clinic	Ⓡ Recreation Centre	📖 Place of Worship	Battle Site	⊕ Cemetery
★ Traffic Department	⊕ Hospital/Clinic (24 Hour Casualty)	Ⓖ Government Office	🚗 Parking	Ⓒ Conference Centre	Bird Sanctuary
▽ Metro Police	⊕ Hospital	✉ Post Office	▲ Place of Interest	Caravan Park	♣ Nature Reserve
● Police Station	Ⓛ Library	✦ Cinema	Historical Monument	Ⓗ Hotel	✈ International Airport
★ Fire Station	Ⓜ Municipal Office	Shopping Centre	🏛 Provincial Heritage Site	Embassy	⊢ Airfield
⚖ Law Court	Ⓢ School	Theatre	🏛 Museum	▷ Consulate	Ⓗ Helipad

North ↑

Legend

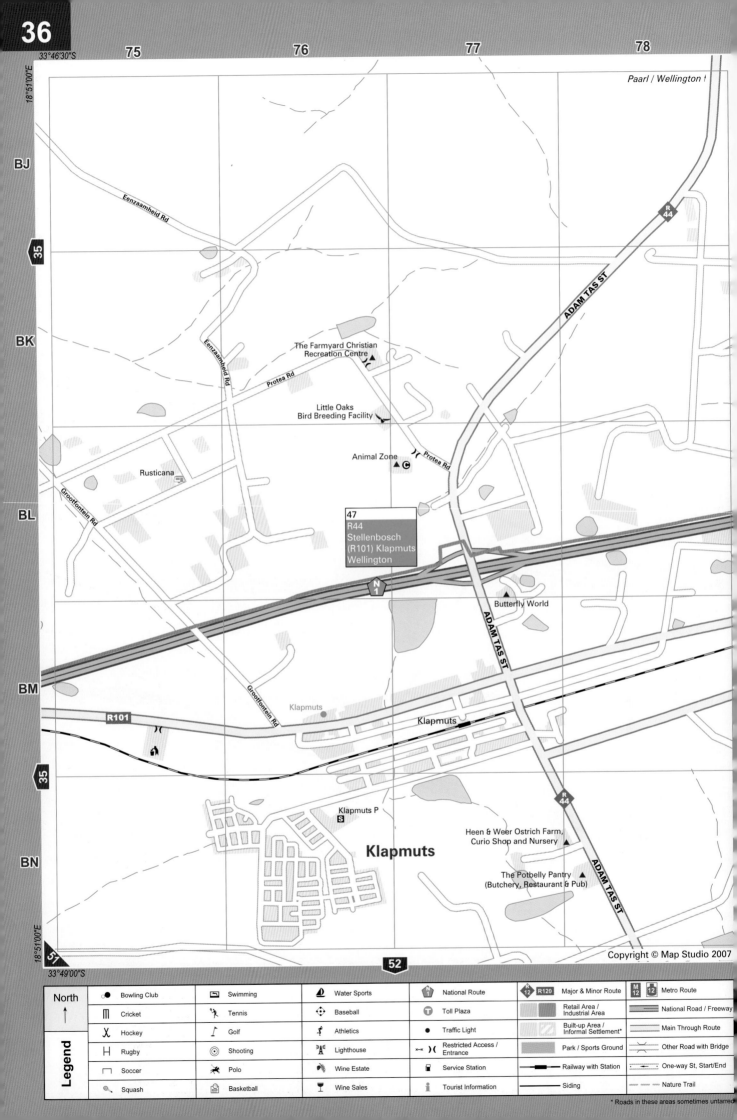

Paarl / Wellington

The Farmyard Christian Recreation Centre

Protea Rd

Little Oaks Bird Breeding Facility

Animal Zone

Rusticana

47
R44
Stellenbosch
(R101) Klapmuts
Wellington

Butterfly World

Klapmuts

Klapmuts

Klapmuts P

Heen & Weer Ostrich Farm, Curio Shop and Nursery

Klapmuts

The Potbelly Pantry
(Butchery, Restaurant & Pub)

North		Bowling Club		Swimming		Water Sports		National Route		Major & Minor Route		Metro Route
		Cricket		Tennis		Baseball		Toll Plaza		Retail Area / Industrial Area		National Road / Freeway
		Hockey		Golf		Athletics		Traffic Light		Built-up Area / Informal Settlement*		Main Through Route
Legend		Rugby		Shooting		Lighthouse		Restricted Access / Entrance		Park / Sports Ground		Other Road with Bridge
		Soccer		Polo		Wine Estate		Service Station		Railway with Station		One-way St, Start/End
		Squash		Basketball		Wine Sales		Tourist Information		Siding		Nature Trail

* Roads in these areas sometimes untarred

79 80 81 82

20

21

18°55'00"E

BJ

Bloemkoolfontein
Annex 701

38

BK

N1

BL

R101

Welgeleë

▲ Drakenstein
Lion Park

Welgemeend

BM

38

Anura
▲
Forest Hill
Cheeses

Glen Carlou

Hess Art
Collection

SIMONSVLEI RD

BN

18°55'00"E

54

53

33°49'00"S

▲	Community Service	Ⓐ	Municipal Clinic	Ⓡ	Recreation Centre		Place of Worship		Battle Site	⊕	Cemetery
★	Traffic Department	✚	Hospital/Clinic (24 Hour Casualty)	Ⓖ	Government Office	🚗	Parking	Ⓒ	Conference Centre	✈	Bird Sanctuary
	Metro Police	✚	Hospital	✉	Post Office	▲	Place of Interest		Caravan Park	♣	Nature Reserve
●	Police Station	Ⓛ	Library		Cinema	♛	Historical Monument	Ⓗ	Hotel	✈	International Airport
★	Fire Station	Ⓜ	Municipal Office		Shopping Centre	🏛	Provincial Heritage Site		Embassy	+	Airfield
⚖	Law Court	Ⓢ	School		Theatre	🏛	Museum	▷	Consulate	Ⓗ	Helipad

North
↑

Legend

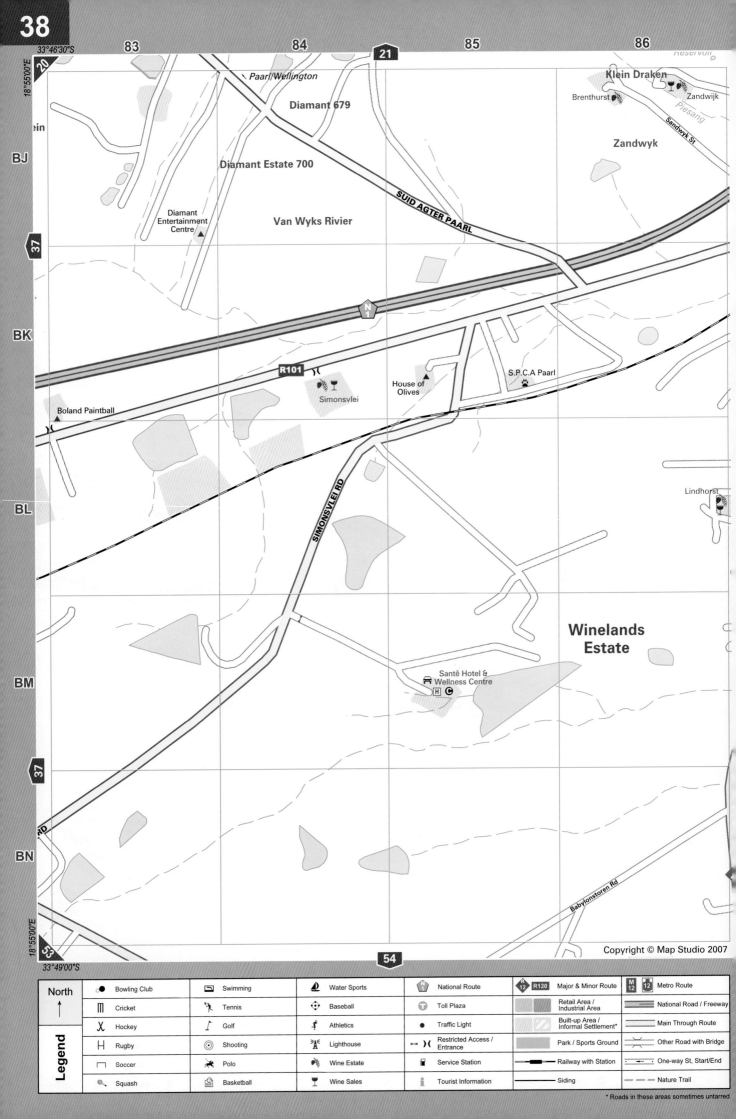

83　84　21　85　86

Paarl/Wellington

Diamant 679

Klein Draken

Brenthurst　Zandwijk

BJ

Diamant Estate 700

Zandwyk

Diamant Entertainment Centre

Van Wyks Rivier

SUID AGTER PAARL

37

N1

BK

R101

Simonsvlei

House of Olives

S.P.C.A Paarl

Boland Paintball

BL

Lindhorst

SIMONSVLEI RD

Winelands Estate

BM

Santê Hotel & Wellness Centre

H C

37

BN

Babylonstoren Rd

Legend

North ↑							
● Bowling Club	Swimming	Water Sports	National Route	12 R120 Major & Minor Route	M 12 12 Metro Route		
Ⅲ Cricket	Tennis	Baseball	Toll Plaza	Retail Area / Industrial Area	National Road / Freeway		
X Hockey	Golf	Athletics	Traffic Light	Built-up Area / Informal Settlement*	Main Through Route		
H Rugby	Shooting	Lighthouse	Restricted Access / Entrance	Park / Sports Ground	Other Road with Bridge		
Soccer	Polo	Wine Estate	Service Station	Railway with Station	One-way St, Start/End		
Squash	Basketball	Wine Sales	Tourist Information	Siding	Nature Trail		

* Roads in these areas sometimes untarred

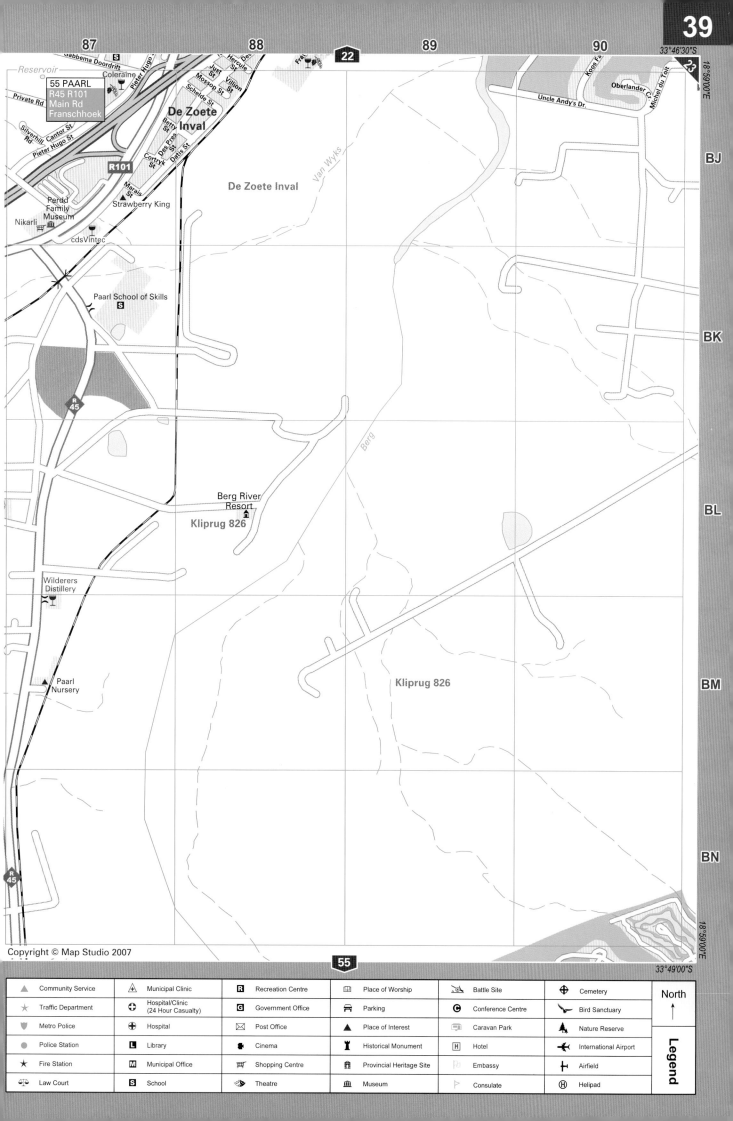

Reservoir

55 PAARL
R45 R101
Main Rd
Franschhoek

Private Rd

Gabbema Doordrift
Coleraine
Pieter Hugo
Silverhill Rd
Cantor St
Pieter Hugo Rd
R101

Just St
Hercule Des
Villion St
Mossop St
Schelde St
Betty St
Des Pres St
Datis St
Cortryk St

Marais St

De Zoete Inval

Perdd Family Museum
Nikarli
Strawberry King
cdsVintec

De Zoete Inval

Van Wyks

Uncle Andy's Dr.
Koos Fa
Oberlander
Michel du Toit

Paarl School of Skills
S

R45

Berg

Berg River Resort
Kliprug 826

Kliprug 826

Wilderers Distillery

Paarl Nursery

R45

R45

▲	Community Service	Ⓐ	Municipal Clinic	R	Recreation Centre		Place of Worship		Battle Site	✛	Cemetery
★	Traffic Department	✚	Hospital/Clinic (24 Hour Casualty)	G	Government Office	🚗	Parking	C	Conference Centre	✈	Bird Sanctuary
▼	Metro Police	✚	Hospital	✉	Post Office	▲	Place of Interest		Caravan Park	🌲	Nature Reserve
●	Police Station	L	Library		Cinema	♛	Historical Monument	H	Hotel	✈	International Airport
★	Fire Station	M	Municipal Office		Shopping Centre	🏛	Provincial Heritage Site		Embassy	⊣⊢	Airfield
⚖	Law Court	S	School		Theatre	🏛	Museum	▷	Consulate	Ⓗ	Helipad

North
↑

Legend

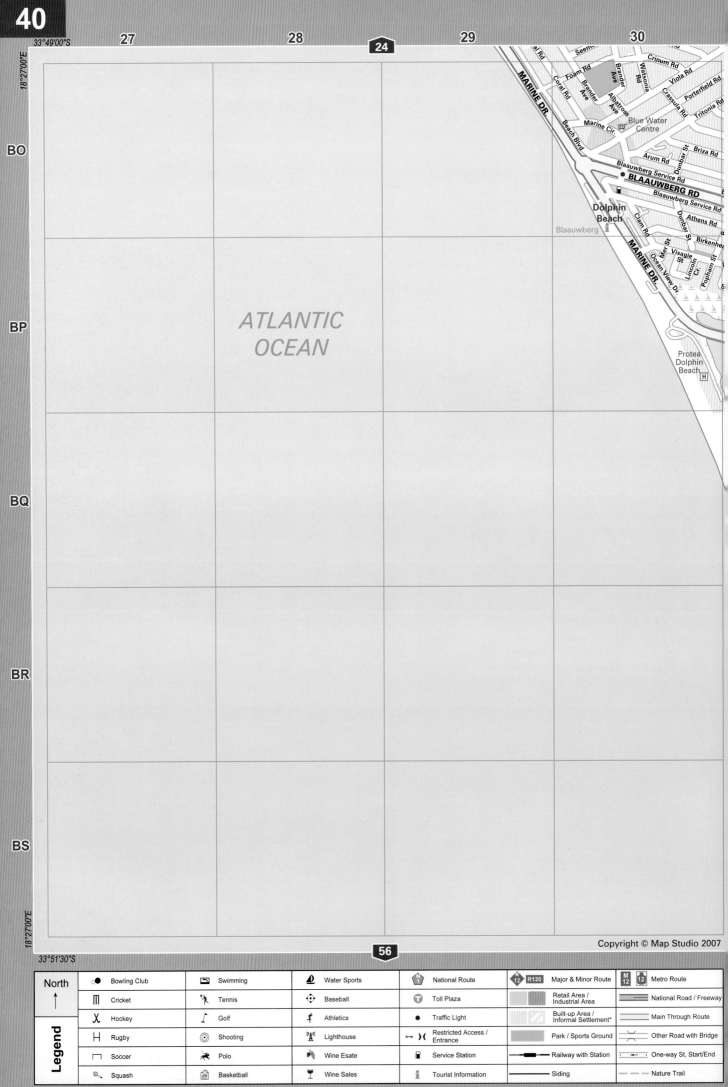

33°49'00"S
18°27'00"E

27   28   24   29   30

BO

BP

BQ

BR

BS

ATLANTIC
OCEAN

18°27'00"E
33°51'30"S

56

Copyright © Map Studio 2007

North		Bowling Club		Swimming		Water Sports		National Route		Major & Minor Route		Metro Route
↑		Cricket		Tennis		Baseball		Toll Plaza		Retail Area / Industrial Area		National Road / Freeway
Legend		Hockey		Golf		Athletics		Traffic Light		Built-up Area / Informal Settlement*		Main Through Route
		Rugby		Shooting		Lighthouse		Restricted Access / Entrance		Park / Sports Ground		Other Road with Bridge
		Soccer		Polo		Wine Esate		Service Station		Railway with Station		One-way St, Start/End
		Squash		Basketball		Wine Sales		Tourist Information		Siding		Nature Trail

* Roads in these areas sometimes untarred

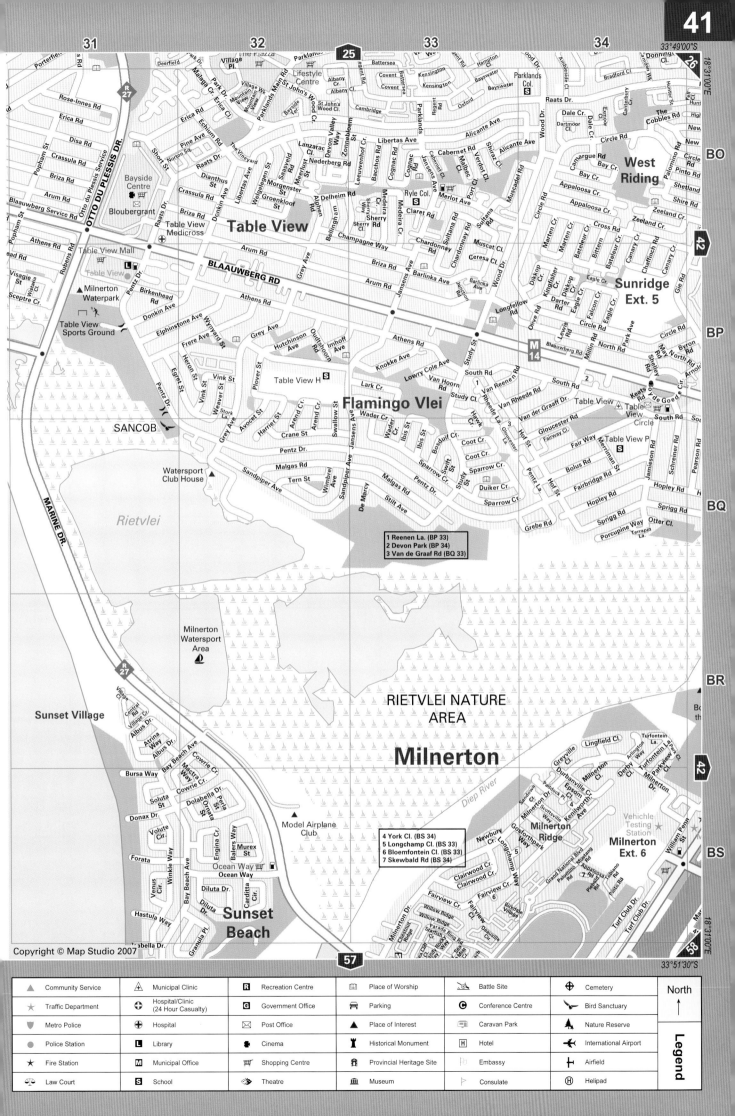

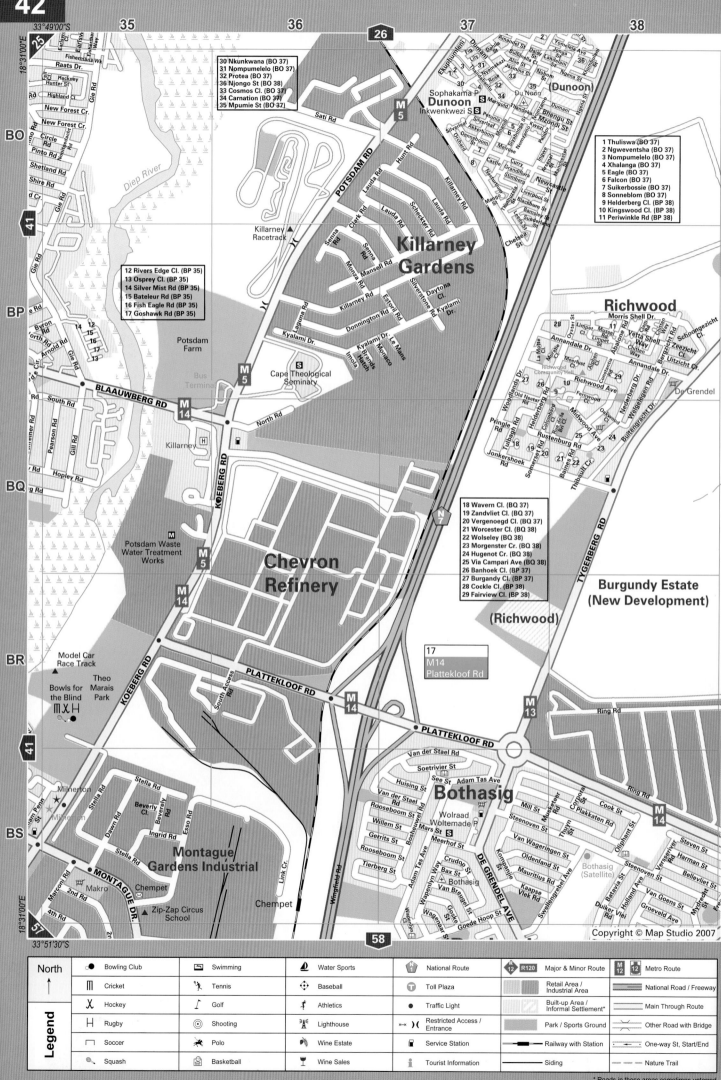

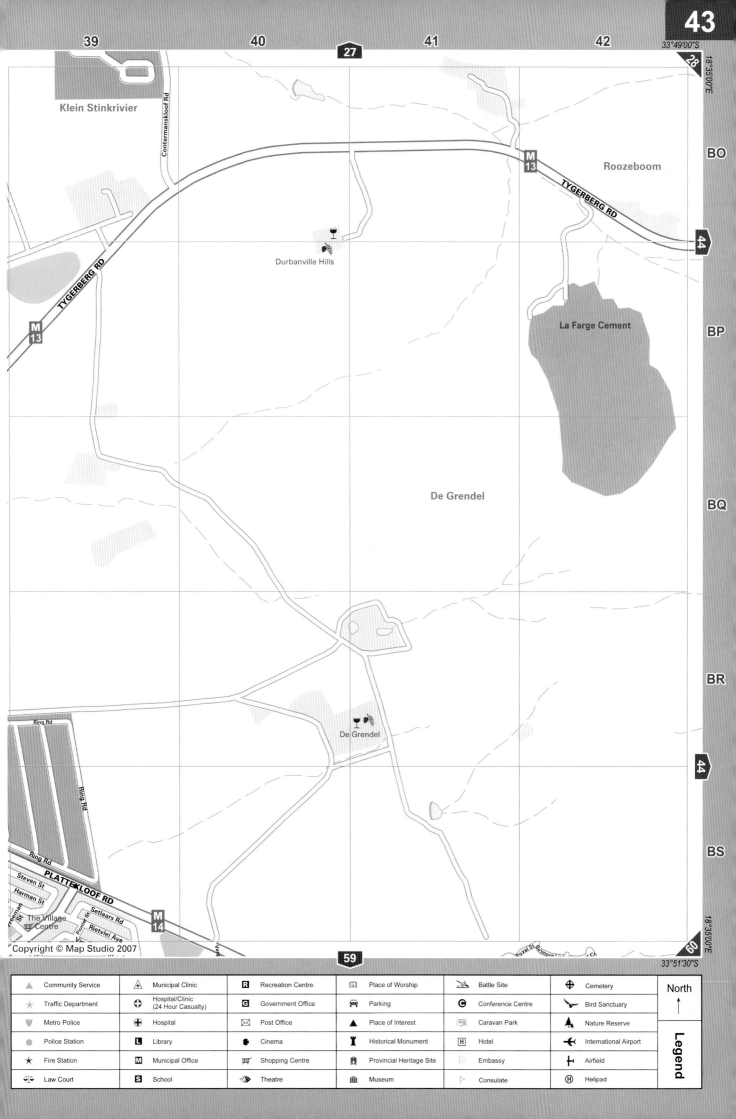

33°49'30"S

18°35'00"E

39 40 27 41 42 28

BO

Klein Stinkrivier

Contermanskloof Rd

Roozeboom

M 13

TYGERBERG RD

44

Durbanville Hills

TYGERBERG RD

M 13

La Farge Cement

BP

BQ

De Grendel

BR

Ring Rd

44

Ring Rd

De Grendel

Ring Rd

BS

Steven St

PLATTEKLOOF RD

Harman St

M 14

Setlaars Rd

The Village Centre

Rietvlei Ave

Pionier St

Royal St Belmont

Copyright © Map Studio 2007

59 60

33°51'30"S

18°35'00"E

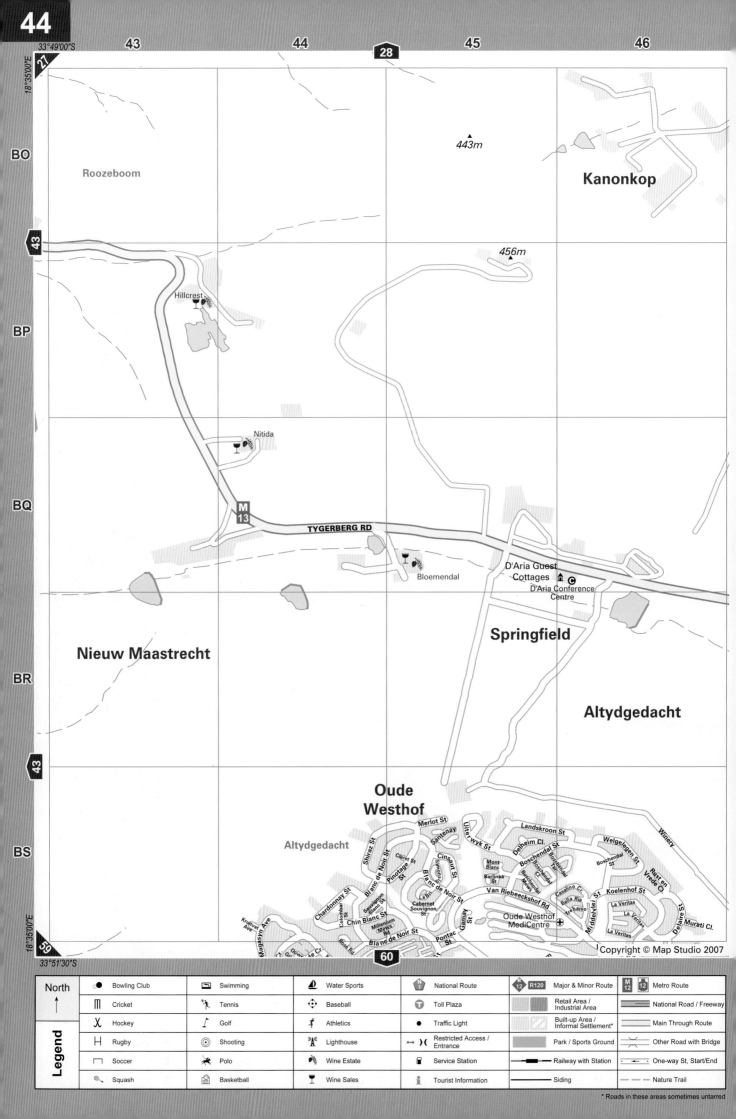

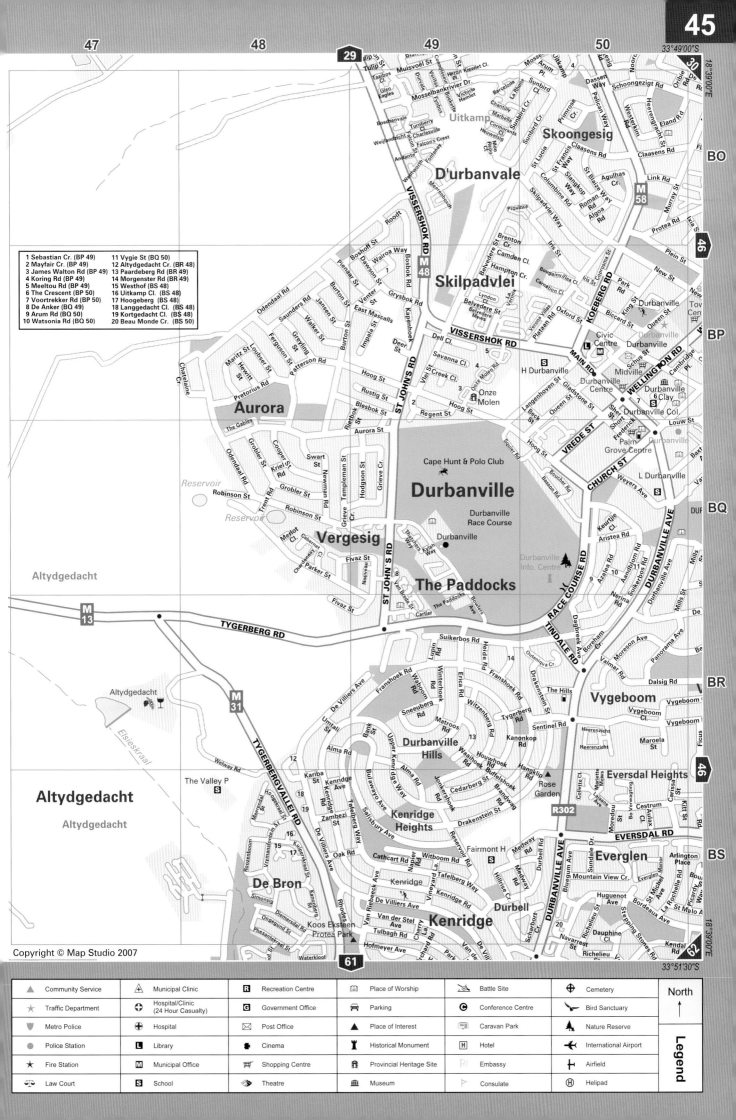

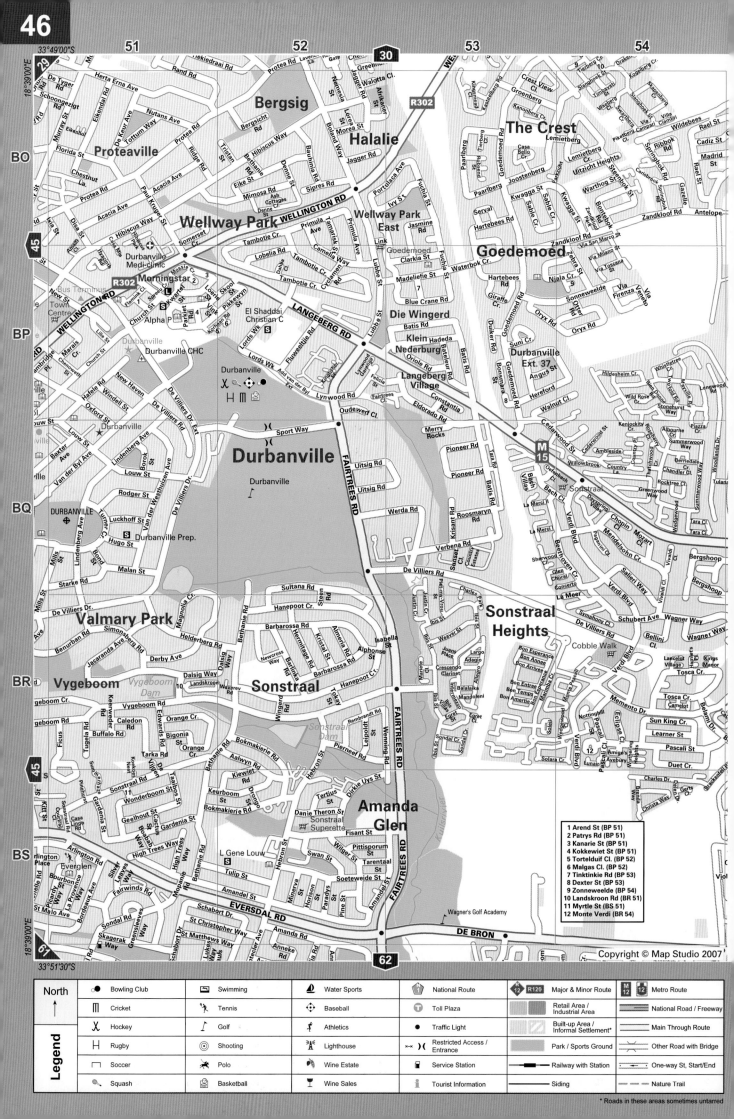

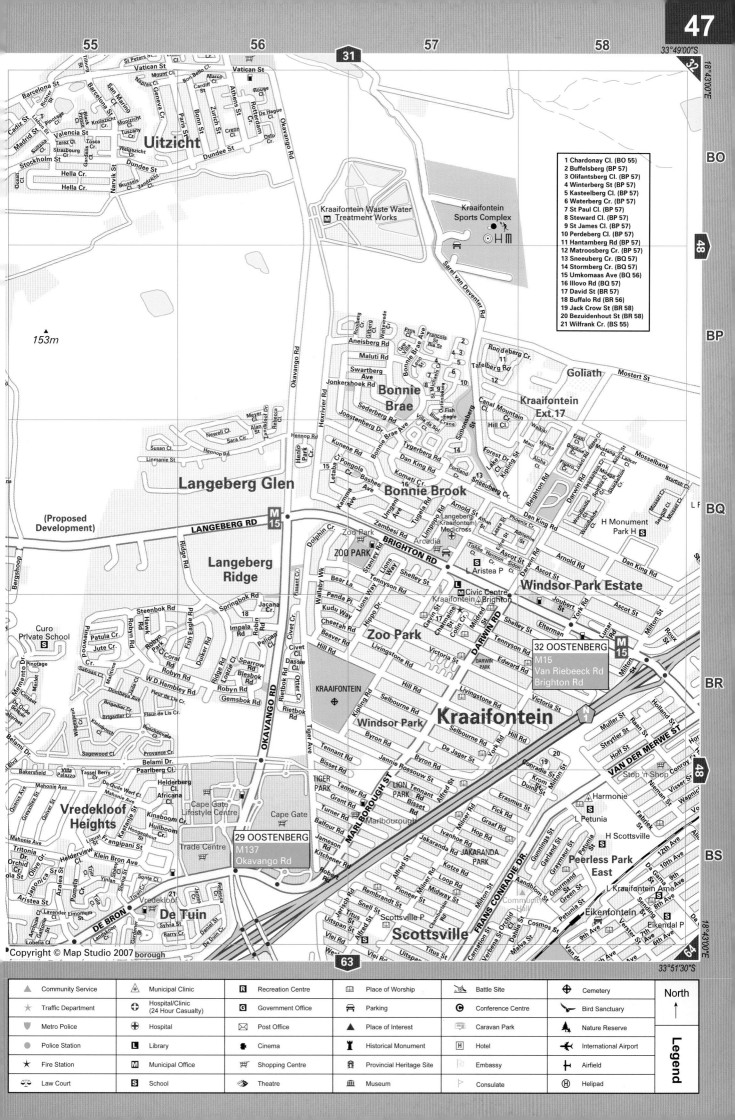

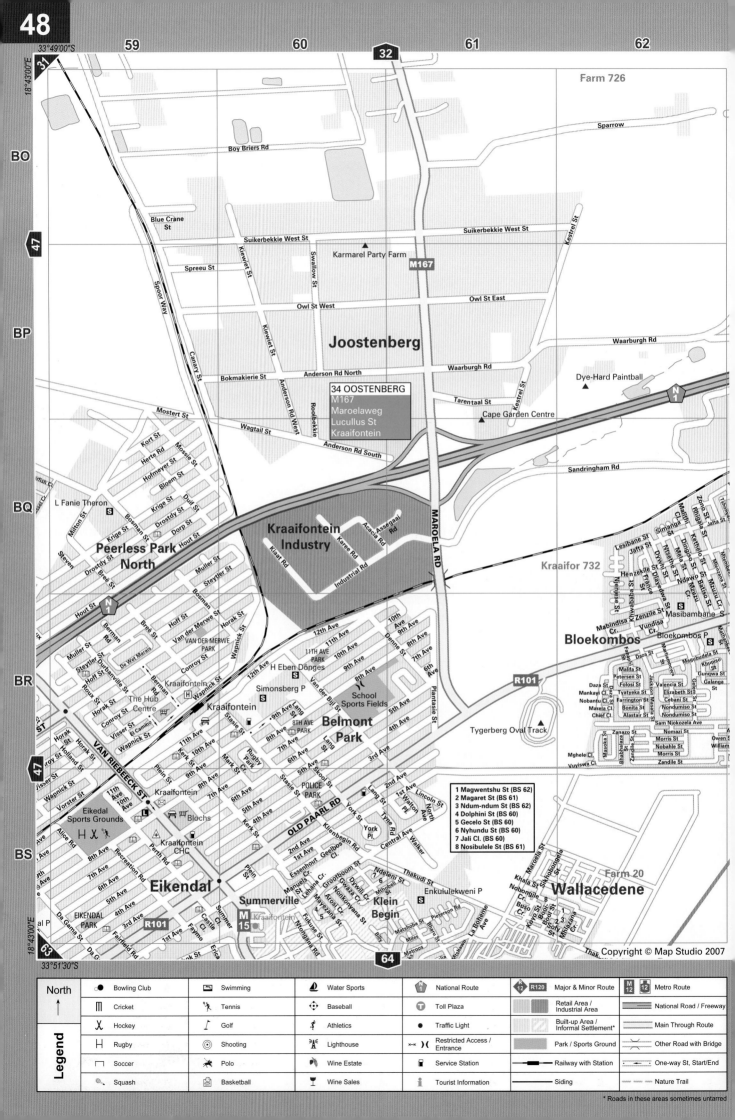

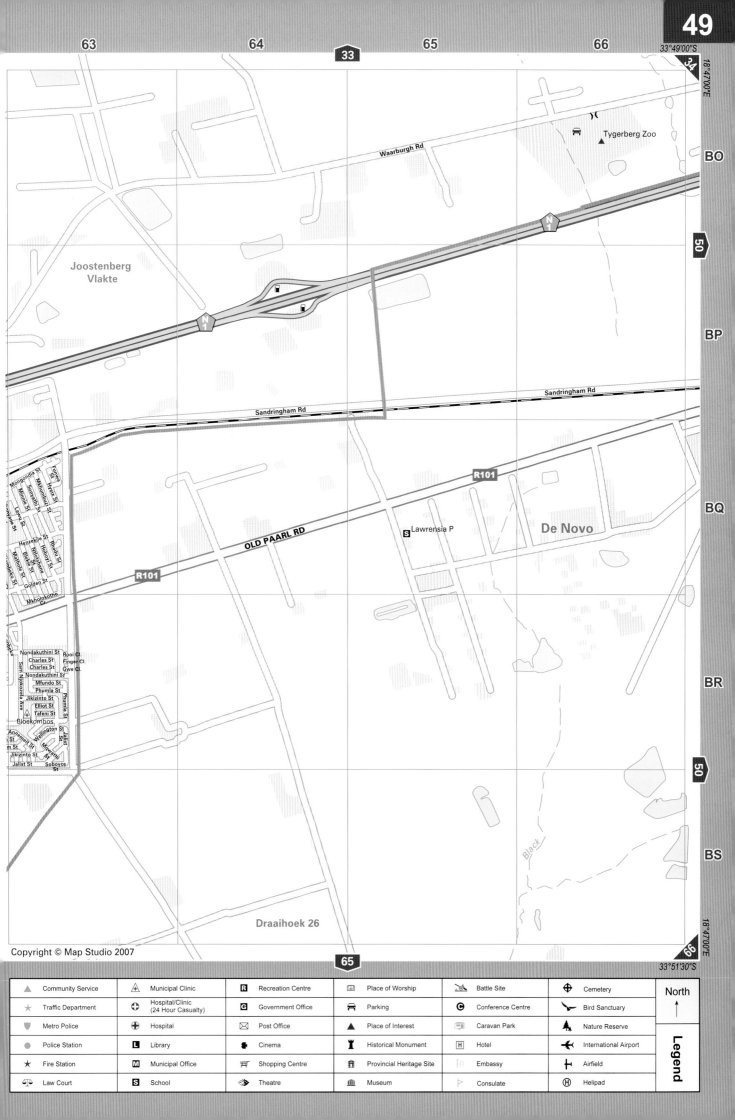

Map labels

Waarburgh Rd

N1

Joostenberg
Vlakte

Tygerberg Zoo

Sandringham Rd

Sandringham Rd

R101

Lawrensia P

De Novo

OLD PAARL RD

R101

Mongondia St
Funwa St
Mhleli St
Mhlanhluli St
Minnie St
Sonyathi St
Layu St
Henzekile St
Phadi St
Ngoshane
Mothole St
Black St
Golden St
Mkholokotho Cr

Nondakuthini St
Charles St
Charles St
Nondakuthini St
Mfundo St
Phumla St
Jikizinto St
Elliot St
Tafeni St
Bloekombos
Annemeu St
m St
Jikizinto St
Jalist St

Rooi Cl.
Finger Cl.
Gwe Cl.

Phumla St
Jalist St
Wellington St
Mqwathi
St
Soboyce
St

Sam Nokozela Ave

Draaihoek 26

Black

North ↑

Legend

▲	Community Service	Ⓐ	Municipal Clinic	🅡	Recreation Centre		Place of Worship		Battle Site	⊕	Cemetery	
★	Traffic Department	⊕	Hospital/Clinic (24 Hour Casualty)	🅖	Government Office	🚗	Parking	Ⓒ	Conference Centre		Bird Sanctuary	
▼	Metro Police	✚	Hospital	✉	Post Office	▲	Place of Interest		Caravan Park	♠	Nature Reserve	
●	Police Station	🅛	Library		Cinema	♚	Historical Monument	H	Hotel	✈	International Airport	
★	Fire Station	Ⓜ	Municipal Office		Shopping Centre		Provincial Heritage Site		Embassy	⊢	Airfield	
⚖	Law Court	🅢	School		Theatre	🏛	Museum	▷	Consulate	Ⓗ	Helipad	

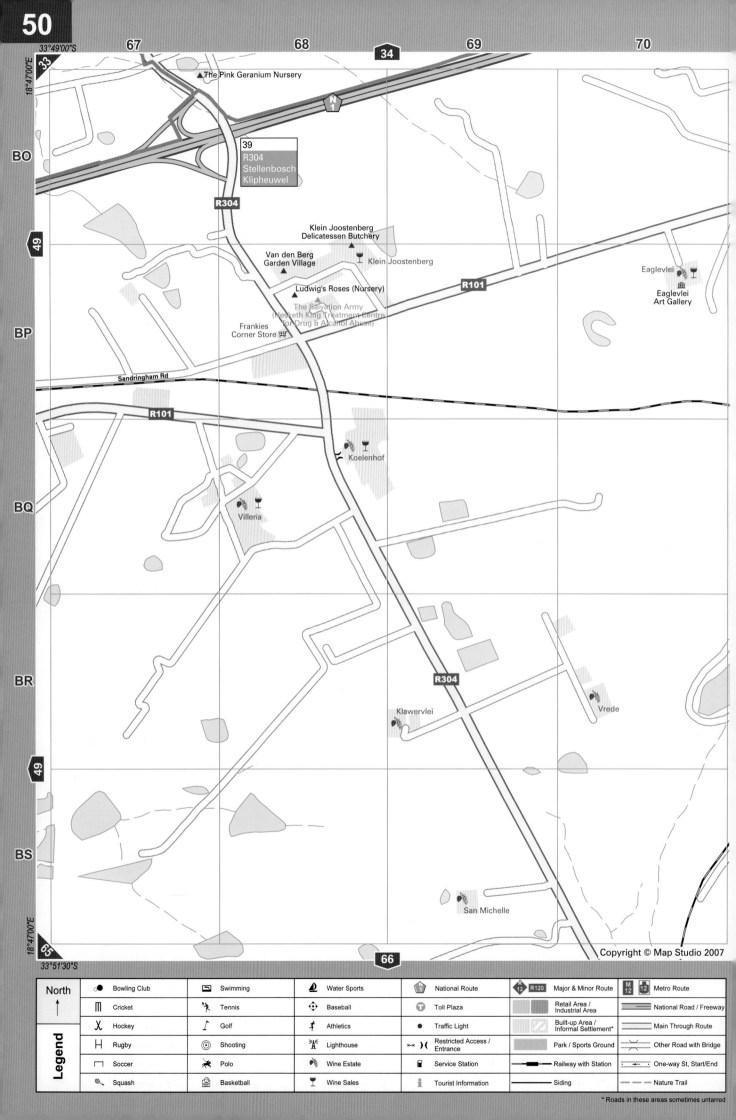

33°49'00"S
18°47'00"E

67 | 68 | 34 | 69 | 70

BO

39
R304
Stellenbosch
Klipheuwel

R304

▲ The Pink Geranium Nursery

N1

49

Klein Joostenberg
Delicatessen Butchery

Van den Berg
Garden Village

Klein Joostenberg

R101

Eaglevlei

Eaglevlei
Art Gallery

Ludwig's Roses (Nursery)

The Salvation Army
(Nesketh King Treatment Centre
for Drug & Alcohol Abuse)

Frankies
Corner Store

BP

Sandringham Rd

R101

Koelenhof

BQ

Villeria

BR

R304

Klawervlei

Vrede

49

BS

San Michelle

66

Copyright © Map Studio 2007

18°47'00"E
65

33°51'30"S

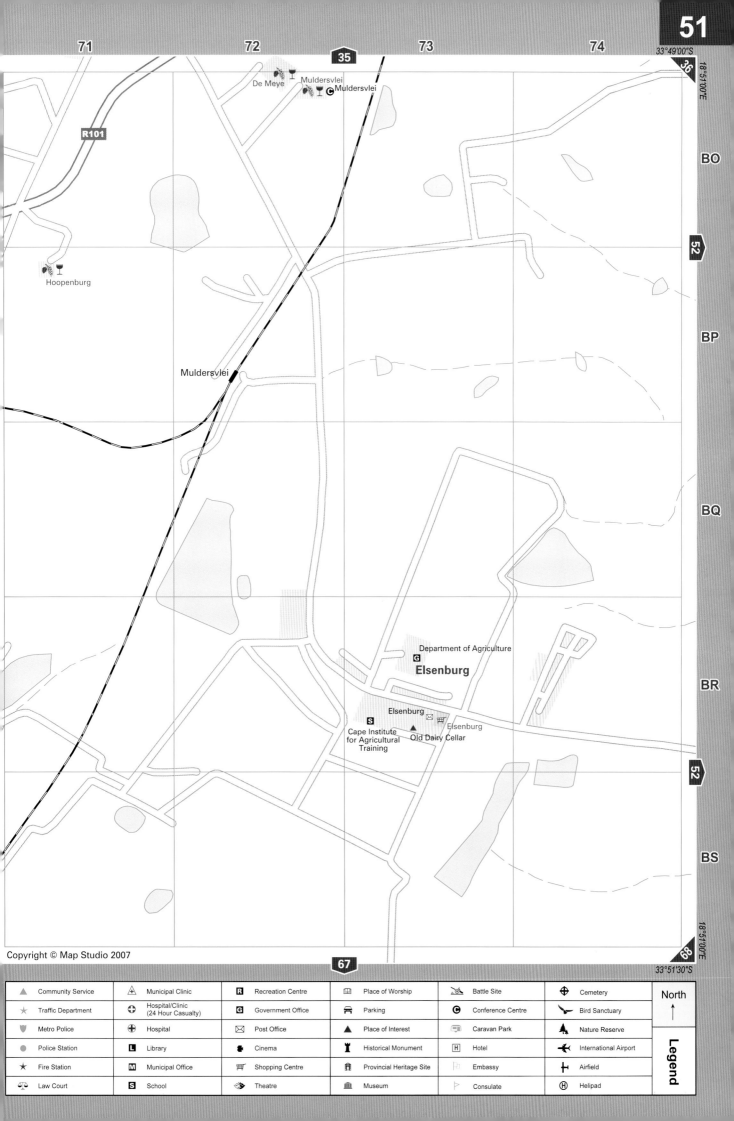

33°49'30"S

71　72　35　73　74　18°51'00"E

R101

De Meye　Muldersvlei

Muldersvlei

BO

52

Hoopenburg

BP

Muldersvlei

BQ

Department of Agriculture

Elsenburg

BR

Elsenburg

Elsenburg

Cape Institute
for Agricultural
Training

Old Dairy Cellar

52

BS

18°51'00"E

Copyright © Map Studio 2007

67

33°51'30"S

▲	Community Service	Ⓐ	Municipal Clinic	Ⓡ	Recreation Centre		Place of Worship		Battle Site	⊕	Cemetery
★	Traffic Department	⊕	Hospital/Clinic (24 Hour Casualty)	Ⓖ	Government Office		Parking	Ⓒ	Conference Centre		Bird Sanctuary
▼	Metro Police	⊕	Hospital	✉	Post Office	▲	Place of Interest		Caravan Park	♠	Nature Reserve
●	Police Station	Ⓛ	Library		Cinema	♛	Historical Monument	Ⓗ	Hotel	✈	International Airport
★	Fire Station	Ⓜ	Municipal Office		Shopping Centre	🏛	Provincial Heritage Site		Embassy	⊢	Airfield
⚖	Law Court	Ⓢ	School		Theatre	🏛	Museum	▷	Consulate	Ⓗ	Helipad

North
↑

Legend

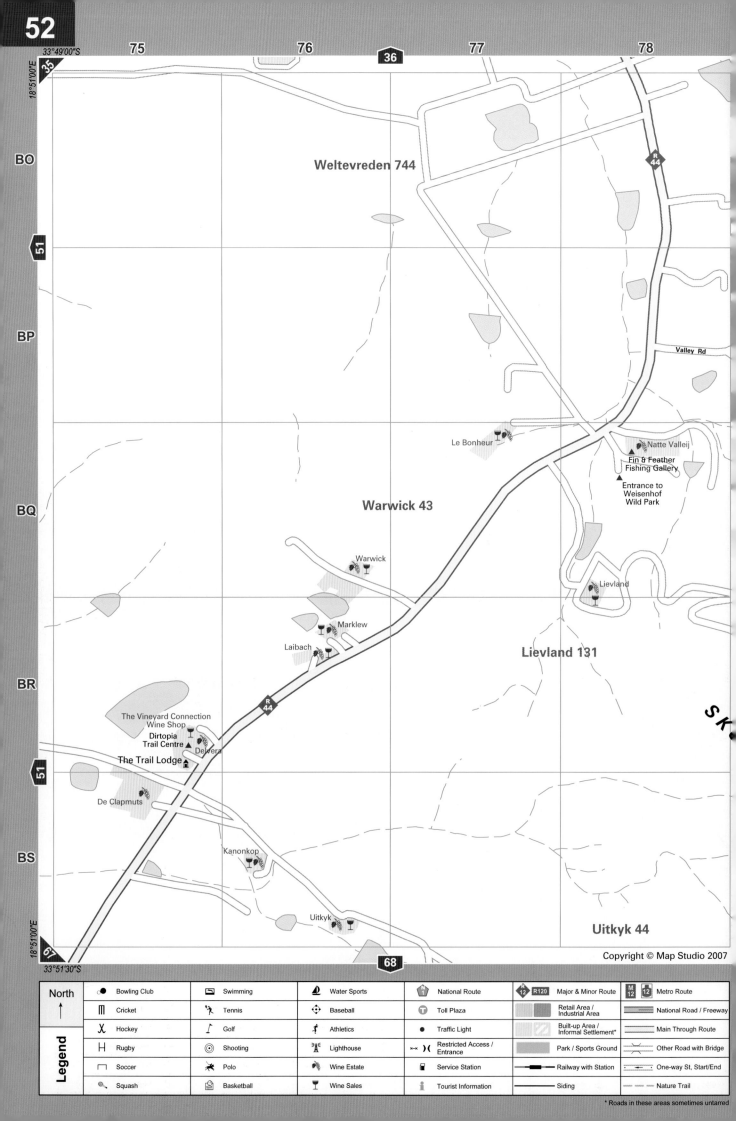

33°49'30"S
18°51'00"E

75 76 36 77 78

BO

Weltevreden 744

51

BP

Valley Rd

Le Bonheur
Natte Valleij
Fin & Feather
Fishing Gallery

BQ

Warwick 43

Entrance to
Weisenhof
Wild Park

Warwick

Lievland

Marklew

Lievland 131

Laibach

BR

S.K.

R44

The Vineyard Connection
Wine Shop
Dirtopia
Trail Centre
Delvera
The Trail Lodge

51

De Clapmuts

BS

Kanonkop

Uitkyk

Uitkyk 44

Copyright © Map Studio 2007

18°51'00"E
67
33°51'30"S
68

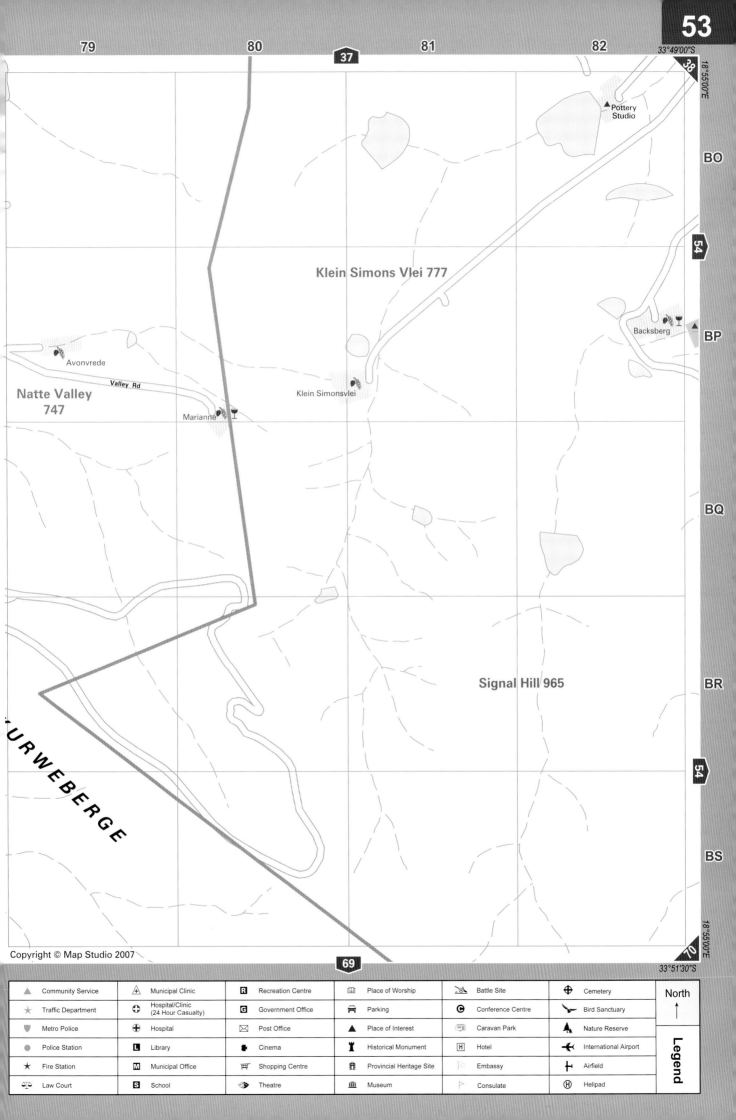

79　　　　80　　　　81　　　　82

37

33°49'30"S

18°55'00"E

38

BO

54

Klein Simons Vlei 777

Backsberg

BP

Avonvrede

Valley Rd

Natte Valley 747

Klein Simonsvlei

Marianne

Pottery Studio

BQ

Signal Hill 965

BR

54

BS

URWEBERGE

18°55'00"E

70

33°51'30"S

69

▲	Community Service	Ⓐ	Municipal Clinic	ℝ	Recreation Centre		Place of Worship		Battle Site	⊕	Cemetery
★	Traffic Department	⊕	Hospital/Clinic (24 Hour Casualty)	Ⓖ	Government Office	🚗	Parking	Ⓒ	Conference Centre		Bird Sanctuary
♦	Metro Police	✚	Hospital	✉	Post Office	▲	Place of Interest		Caravan Park	▲	Nature Reserve
●	Police Station	Ⓛ	Library		Cinema	Ⓧ	Historical Monument	Ⓗ	Hotel	✈	International Airport
★	Fire Station	Ⓜ	Municipal Office		Shopping Centre		Provincial Heritage Site		Embassy	⊢	Airfield
⚖	Law Court	Ⓢ	School		Theatre	🏛	Museum	▷	Consulate	Ⓗ	Helipad

North ↑

Legend

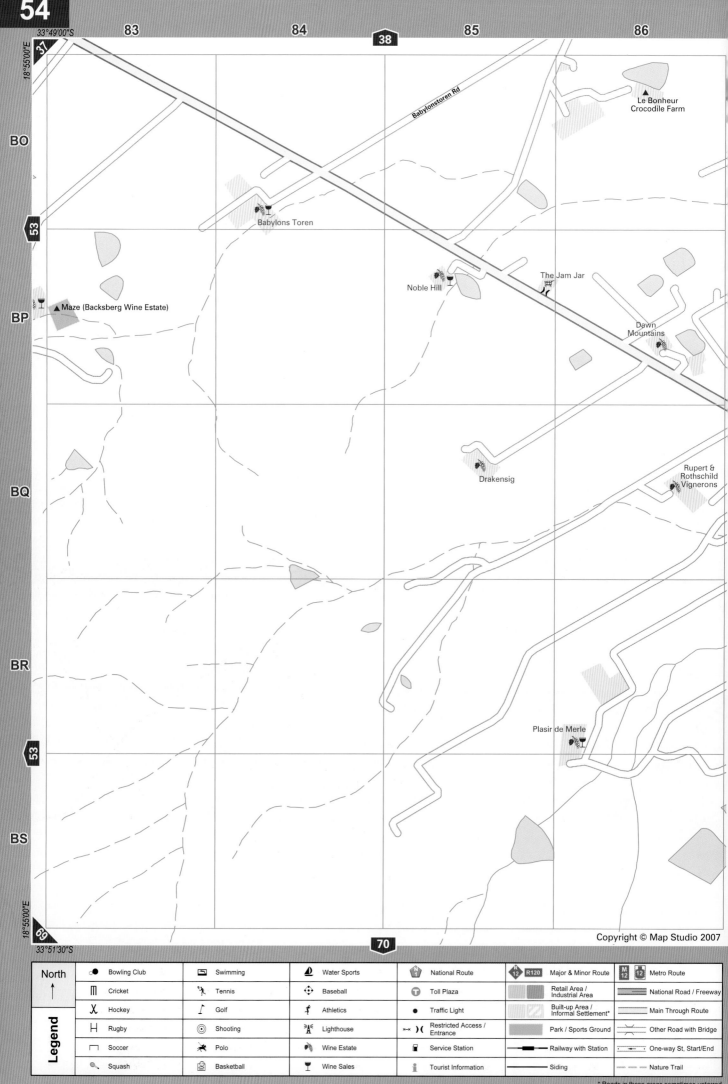

33°49'00"S
18°55'00"E

37
83
84
38
85
86

BO

Babylonstoren Rd

Le Bonheur
Crocodile Farm

53

Babylons Toren

The Jam Jar

Noble Hill

BP

Maze (Backsberg Wine Estate)

Dawn
Mountains

BQ

Drakensig

Rupert &
Rothschild
Vignerons

BR

Plasir de Merle

53

BS

69
70

33°51'30"S
18°55'00"E

Copyright © Map Studio 2007

North		Bowling Club		Swimming		Water Sports		National Route	R12 R120	Major & Minor Route	M12 12	Metro Route
		Cricket		Tennis		Baseball		Toll Plaza		Retail Area / Industrial Area		National Road / Freeway
		Hockey		Golf		Athletics		Traffic Light		Built-up Area / Informal Settlement*		Main Through Route
		Rugby		Shooting		Lighthouse		Restricted Access / Entrance		Park / Sports Ground		Other Road with Bridge
Legend		Soccer		Polo		Wine Estate		Service Station		Railway with Station		One-way St, Start/End
		Squash		Basketball		Wine Sales		Tourist Information		Siding		Nature Trail

* Roads in these areas sometimes untarred

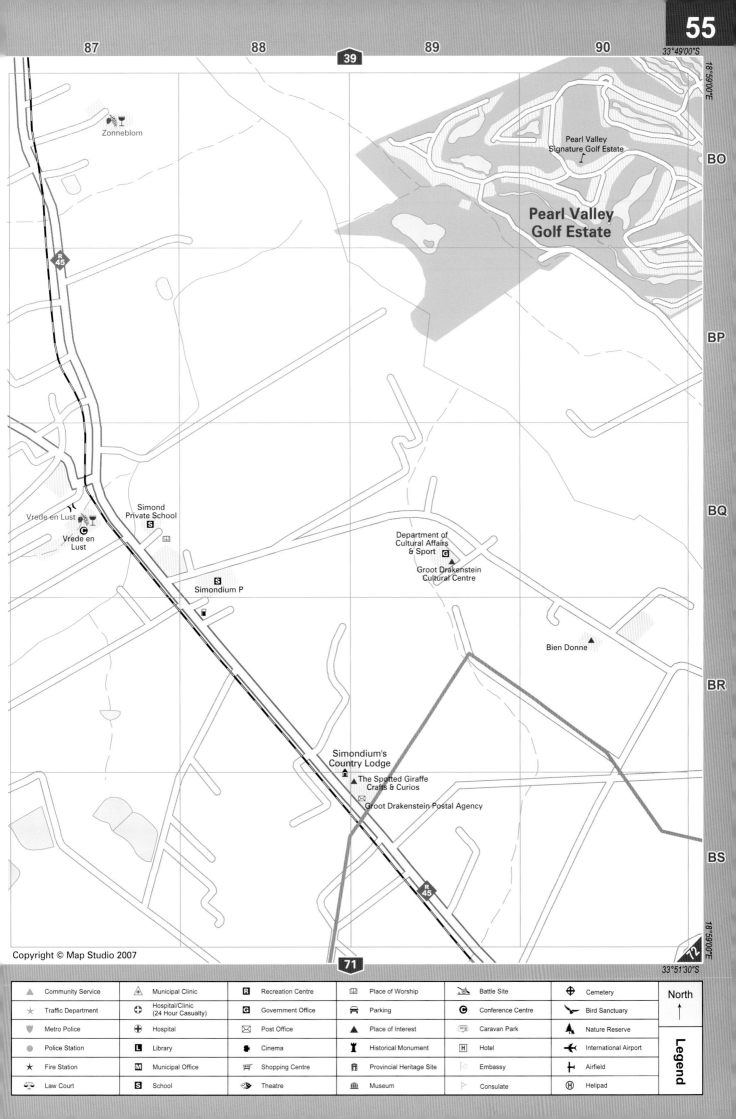

BO

BP

BQ

BR

BS

Zonneblom

Pearl Valley
Signature Golf Estate

**Pearl Valley
Golf Estate**

Vrede en Lust
Vrede en
Lust

Simond
Private School

Department of
Cultural Affairs
& Sport
Groot Drakenstein
Cultural Centre

Simondium P

Bien Donne

Simondium's
Country Lodge
The Spotted Giraffe
Crafts & Curios
Groot Drakenstein Postal Agency

71

18°59'00"E
33°51'30"S

▲	Community Service	⚕	Municipal Clinic	R	Recreation Centre	📖	Place of Worship	🗡	Battle Site	⊕	Cemetery
★	Traffic Department	⊕	Hospital/Clinic (24 Hour Casualty)	G	Government Office	🚗	Parking	C	Conference Centre	✈	Bird Sanctuary
▼	Metro Police	✚	Hospital	✉	Post Office	▲	Place of Interest	🚐	Caravan Park	▲	Nature Reserve
●	Police Station	L	Library	🎬	Cinema	⚱	Historical Monument	H	Hotel	✈	International Airport
★	Fire Station	M	Municipal Office	🛒	Shopping Centre	🏛	Provincial Heritage Site	⊢	Embassy	⊢	Airfield
⚖	Law Court	S	School	🎭	Theatre	🏛	Museum	▷	Consulate	H	Helipad

North
↑

Legend

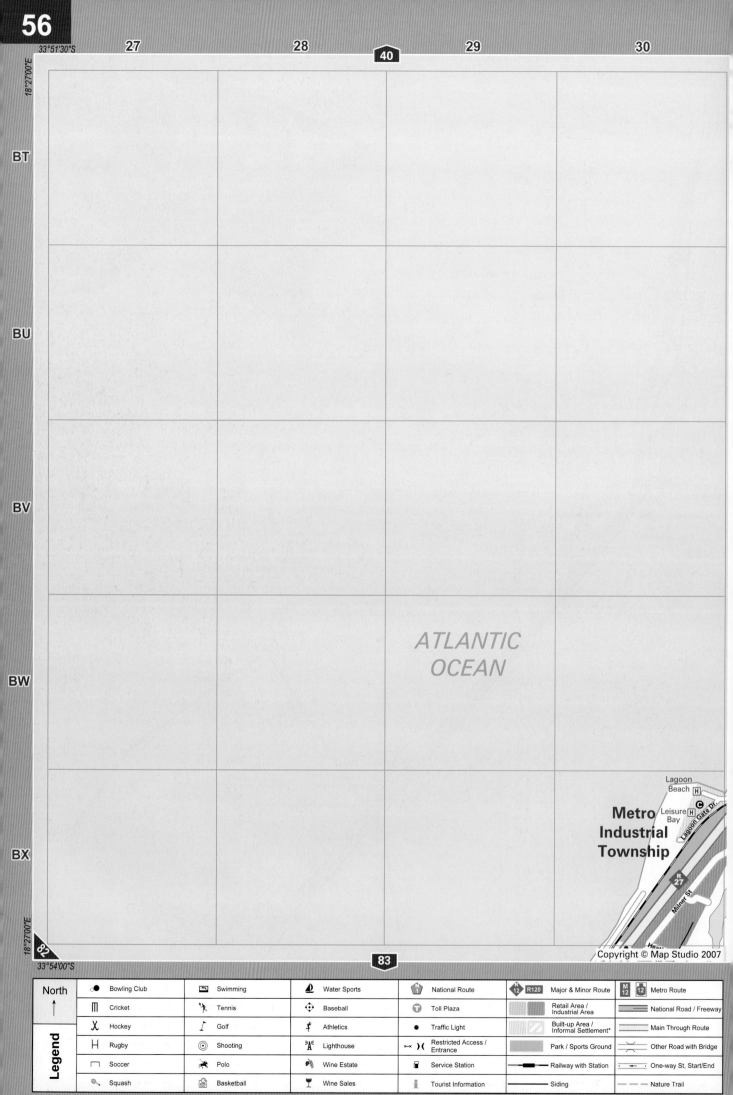

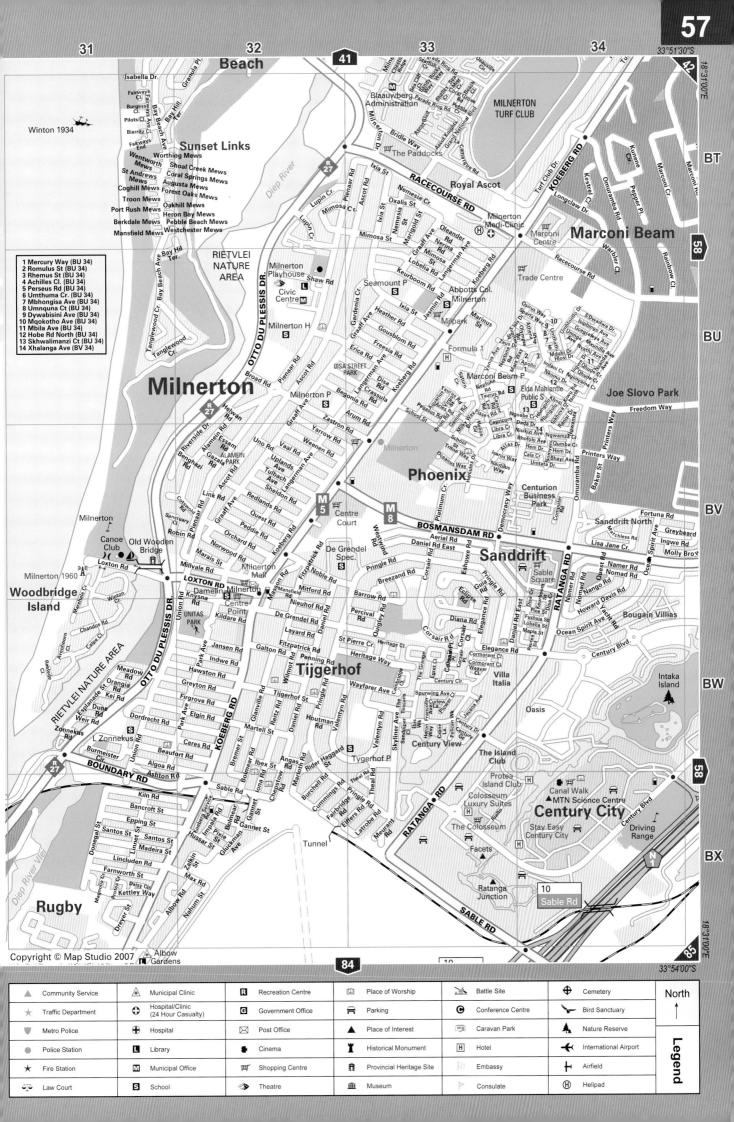

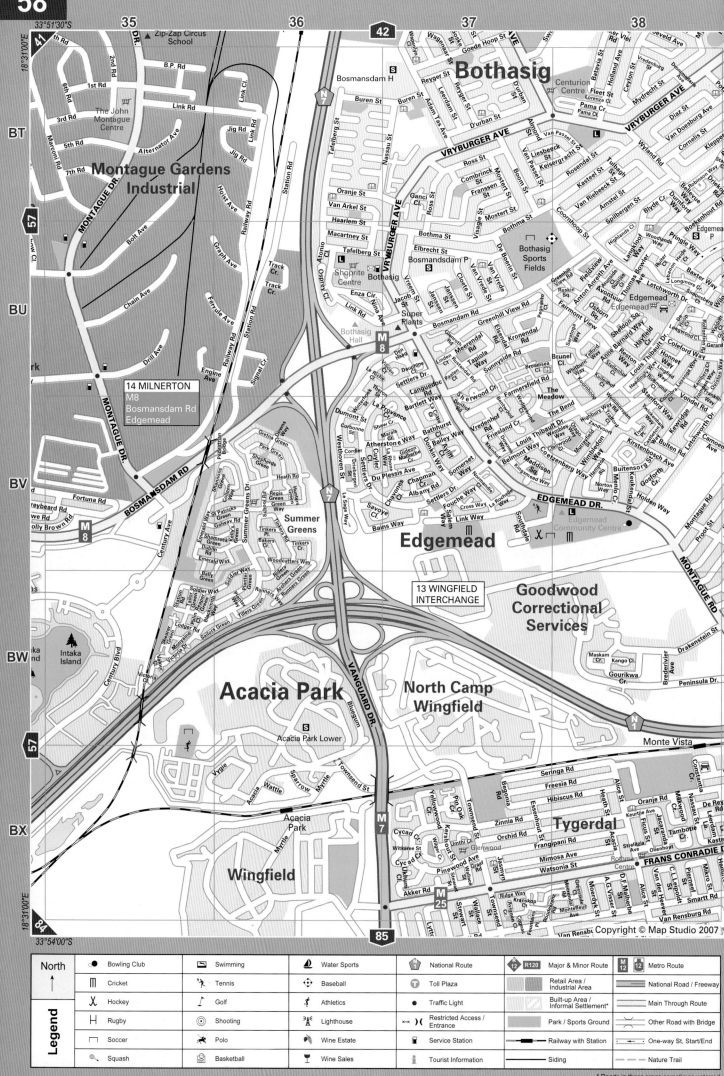

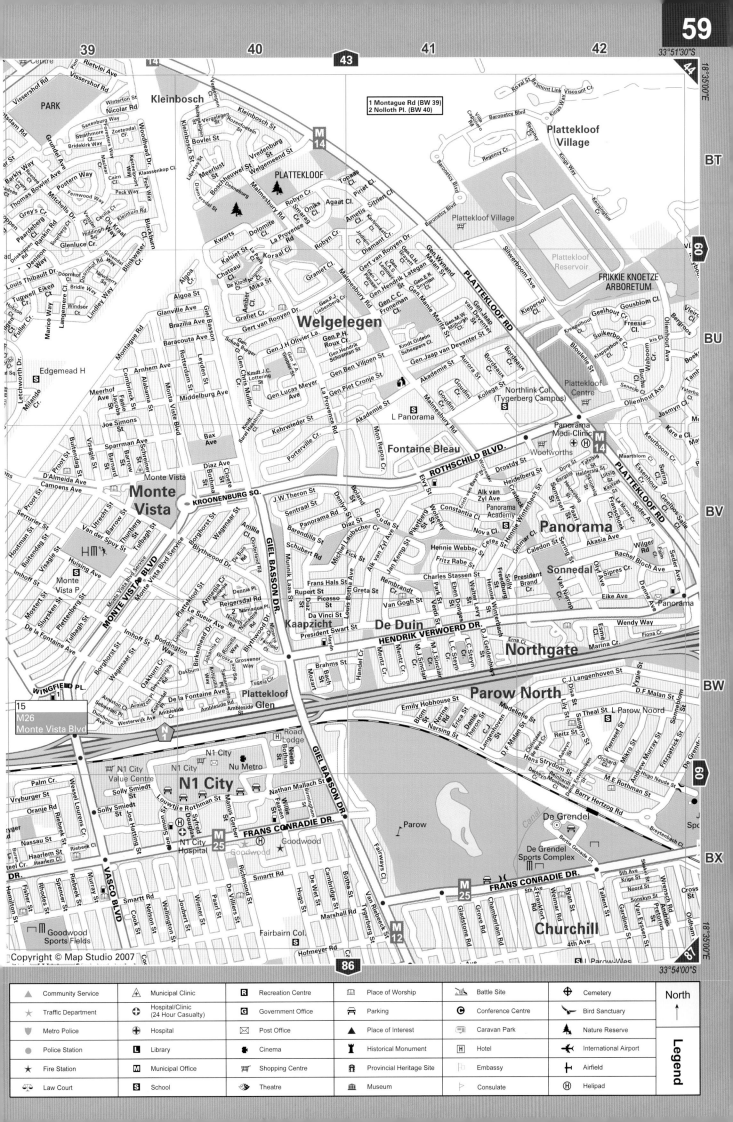

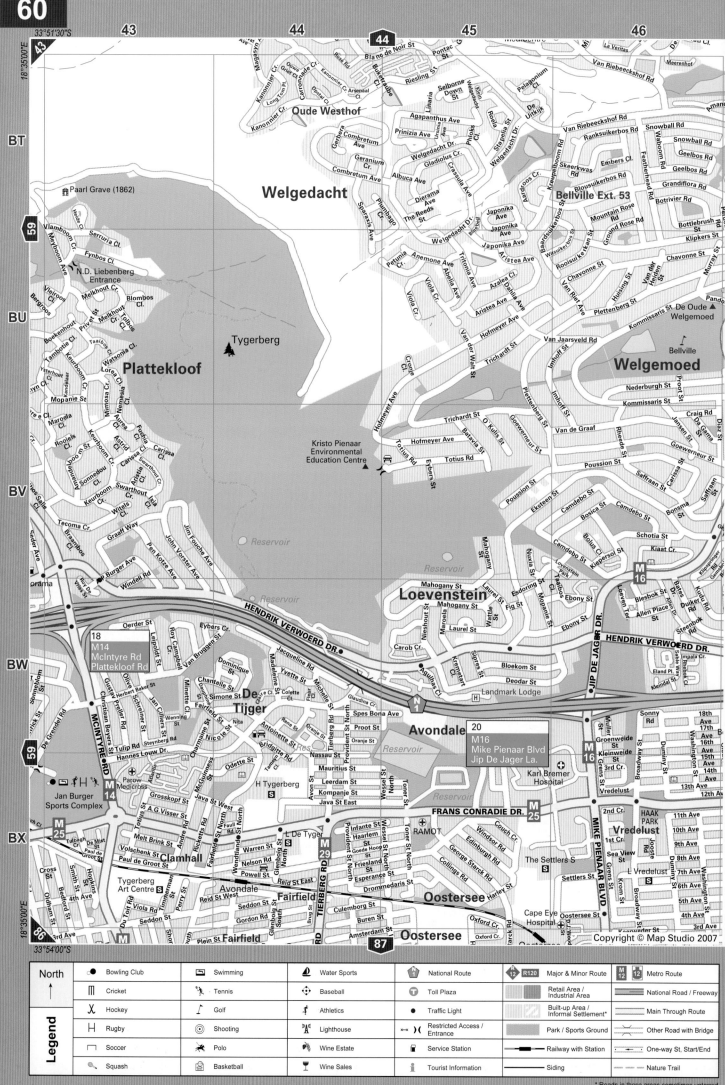

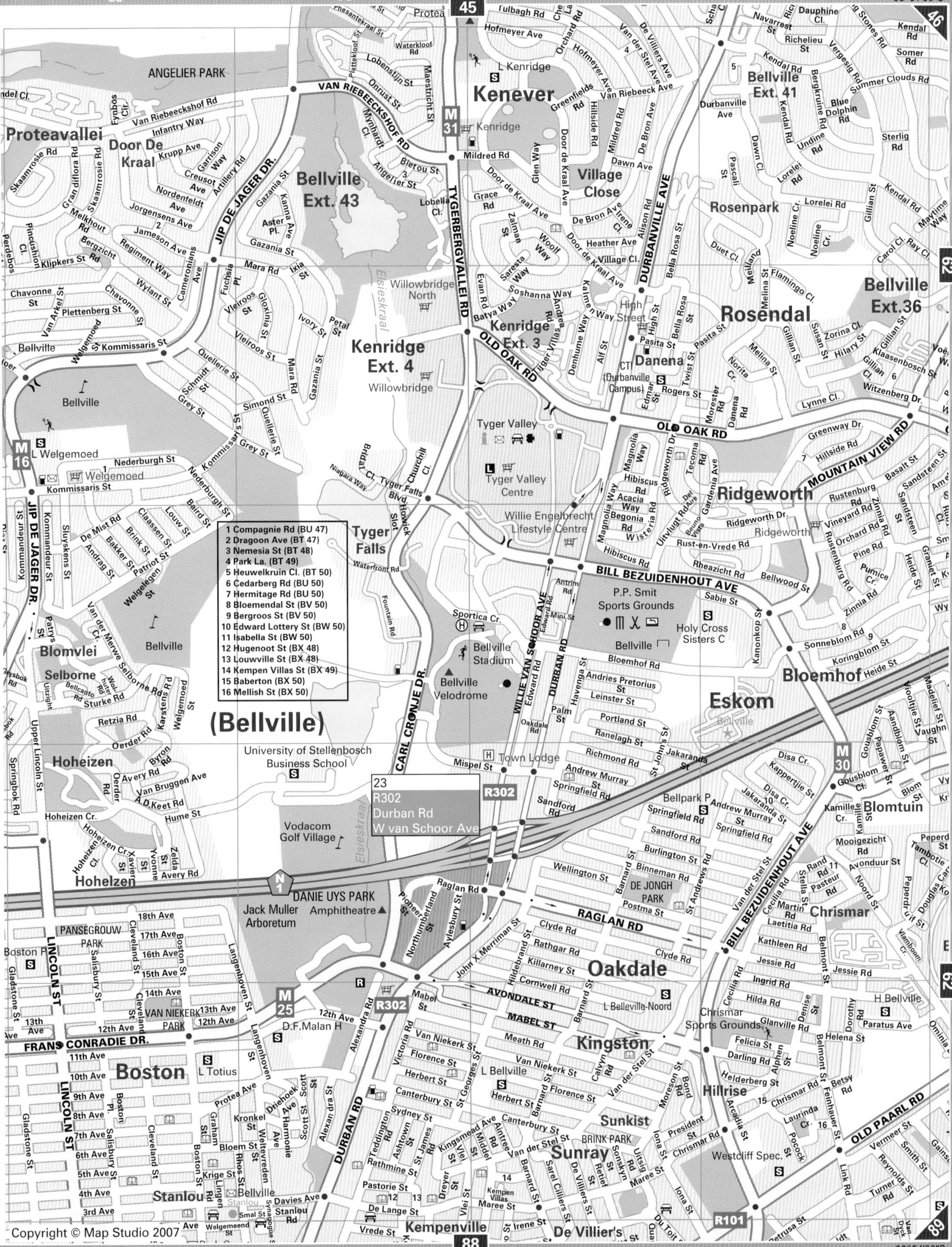

Place names

ANGELIER PARK
Proteavallei
Door De Kraal
Bellville Ext. 43
Kenever
Bellville Ext. 41
Rosenpark
Village Close
Bellville Ext. 36
Rosendal
Kenridge Ext. 4
Willowbridge
Kenridge Ext. 3
Danena
Bellville
Welgemoed
Tyger Valley
Tyger Valley Centre
Willie Engelbrecht Lifestyle Centre
Ridgeworth
Tyger Falls
Blomvlei
Selborne
(Bellville)
Bloemhof
Eskom
University of Stellenbosch Business School
Hoheizen
Vodacom Golf Village
Blomtuin
Danie Uys Park
Jack Muller Arboretum
Amphitheatre
DE JONGH PARK
Chrismar
PANSEGROUW PARK
VAN NIEKERK PARK
Oakdale
Boston
Kingston
Chrismar Sports Grounds
Hillrise
Sunkist
BRINK PARK
Stanlou
Sunray
Kempenville
De Villier's

Index box

1	Compagnie Rd (BU 47)
2	Dragoon Ave (BT 47)
3	Nemesia St (BT 48)
4	Park La. (BT 49)
5	Heuwelkruin Cl. (BT 50)
6	Cedarberg Rd (BU 50)
7	Hermitage Rd (BU 50)
8	Bloemendal St (BV 50)
9	Bergroos St (BV 50)
10	Edward Lottery St (BW 50)
11	Isabella St (BW 50)
12	Hugenoot St (BX 48)
13	Louuville St (BX 48)
14	Kempen Villas St (BX 49)
15	Baberton (BX 50)
16	Mellish (BX 50)

23
R302
Durban Rd
W van Schoor Ave

Legend

▲	Community Service	Ⓐ	Municipal Clinic	Ⓡ	Recreation Centre	🏛	Place of Worship		Battle Site	⊕	Cemetery
★	Traffic Department	✚	Hospital/Clinic (24 Hour Casualty)	Ⓖ	Government Office	🚍	Parking	Ⓒ	Conference Centre	⋌	Bird Sanctuary
⬇	Metro Police	✚	Hospital	✉	Post Office	▲	Place of Interest	🚐	Caravan Park	▲	Nature Reserve
●	Police Station	Ⓛ	Library	🎬	Cinema	♜	Historical Monument	Ⓗ	Hotel	✈	International Airport
★	Fire Station	Ⓜ	Municipal Office	🏬	Shopping Centre	🏛	Provincial Heritage Site		Embassy	✛	Airfield
⚖	Law Court	Ⓢ	School	◁	Theatre	🏛	Museum	▷	Consulate	Ⓗ	Helipad

North
↑

Legend

Copyright © Map Studio 2007

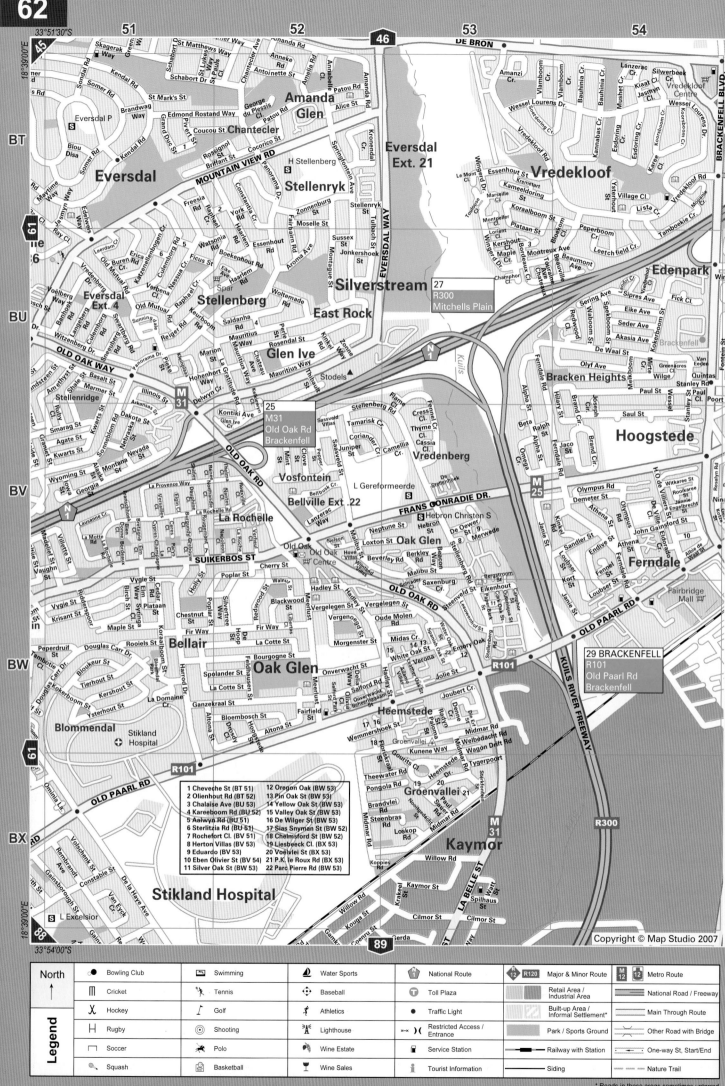

Legend

North

Bowling Club	Swimming	Water Sports	National Route	R120 Major & Minor Route	M12 Metro Route
Cricket	Tennis	Baseball	Toll Plaza	Retail Area / Industrial Area	National Road / Freeway
Hockey	Golf	Athletics	Traffic Light	Built-up Area / Informal Settlement*	Main Through Route
Rugby	Shooting	Lighthouse	Restricted Access / Entrance	Park / Sports Ground	Other Road with Bridge
Soccer	Polo	Wine Estate	Service Station	Railway with Station	One-way St, Start/End
Squash	Basketball	Wine Sales	Tourist Information	Siding	Nature Trail

* Roads in these areas sometimes untarred

Copyright © Map Studio 2007

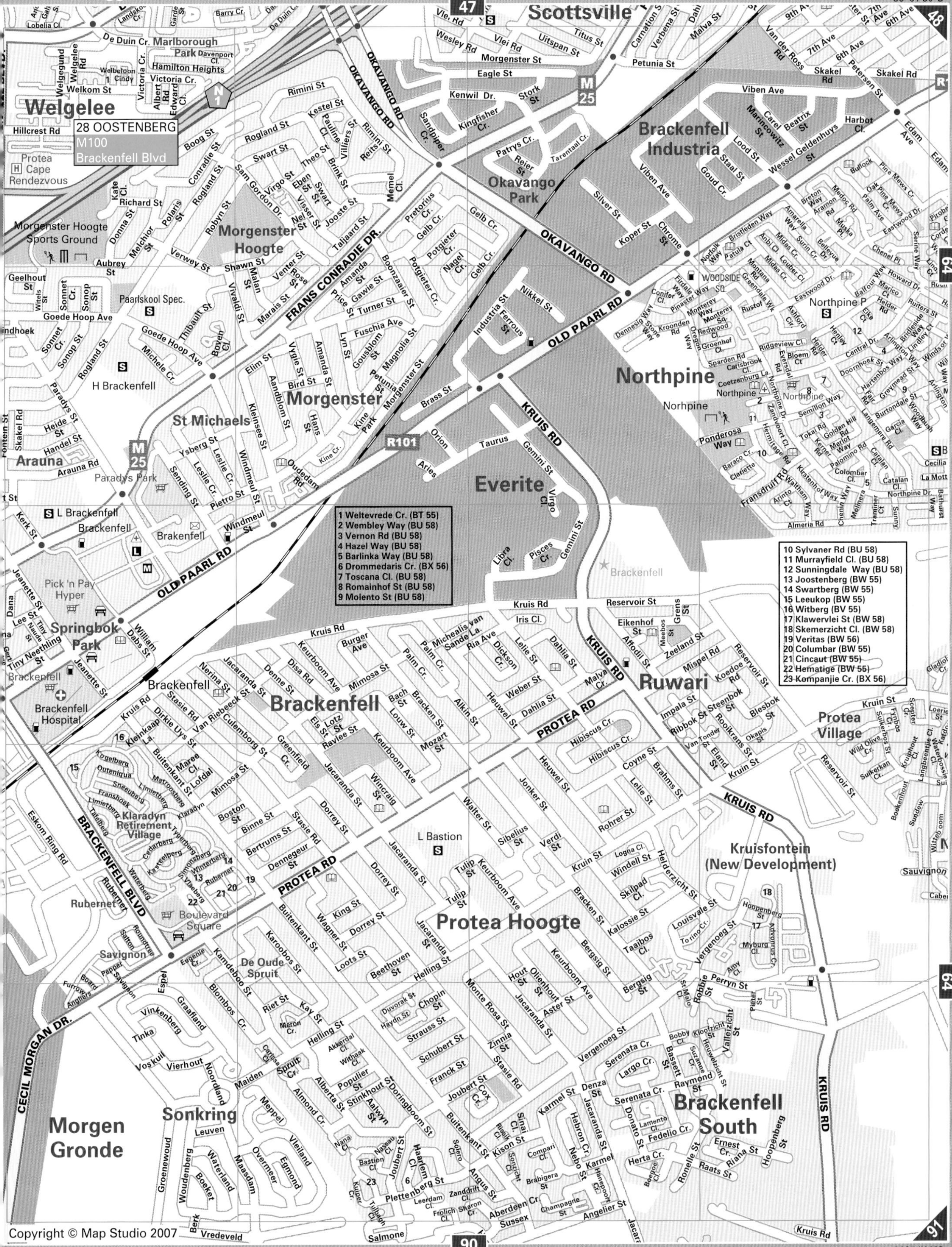

Map — Brackenfell area

33°51'30"S · 18°43'00"E · 33°54'00"S · 18°43'00"E

Grid references: 55, 56, 57, 58 / BT, BU, BV, BW, BX / 47, 48, 64, 90, 91

Areas / Places
Welgelee, Scottsville, Brackenfell Industria, Marlborough Park, Morgenster Hoogte, Morgenster, Okavango Park, Northpine, St Michaels, Arauna, Everite, Ruwari, Protea Village, Springbok Park, Brackenfell, Brackenfell South, Protea Hoogte, Kruisfontein (New Development), Morgen Gronde, Sonkring

Street index (left box)
1 Weltevrede Cr. (BT 55)
2 Wembley Way (BU 58)
3 Vernon Rd (BU 58)
4 Hazel Way (BU 58)
5 Barlinka Way (BU 58)
6 Drommedaris Cr. (BX 56)
7 Toscana Cl. (BU 58)
8 Romainhof St (BU 58)
9 Molento St (BU 58)

Street index (right box)
10 Sylvaner Rd (BU 58)
11 Murrayfield Cl. (BU 58)
12 Sunningdale Way (BU 58)
13 Joostenberg (BW 55)
14 Swartberg (BW 55)
15 Leeukop (BW 55)
16 Witberg (BV 55)
17 Klawervlei St (BW 58)
18 Skemerzicht Cl. (BW 55)
19 Veritas (BW 56)
20 Columbar (BW 55)
21 Cincaut (BW 55)
22 Hematige (BW 55)
23 Kompanjie Cr. (BX 56)

Legend
Symbol	Meaning	Symbol	Meaning
▲	Community Service	⬡	Place of Worship
Traffic Department		G	Government Office
Metro Police		✉	Post Office
Police Station		Cinema
Fire Station		Shopping Centre
Law Court		School
Municipal Clinic		Theatre
Hospital/Clinic (24 Hour Casualty)		Recreation Centre
Hospital		Parking
Library		Place of Interest
Municipal Office		Historical Monument
		Provincial Heritage Site
		Museum
Battle Site		Cemetery
Conference Centre		Bird Sanctuary
Caravan Park		Nature Reserve
Hotel		International Airport
Embassy		Airfield
Consulate		Helipad

North ↑ — Legend

Copyright © Map Studio 2007

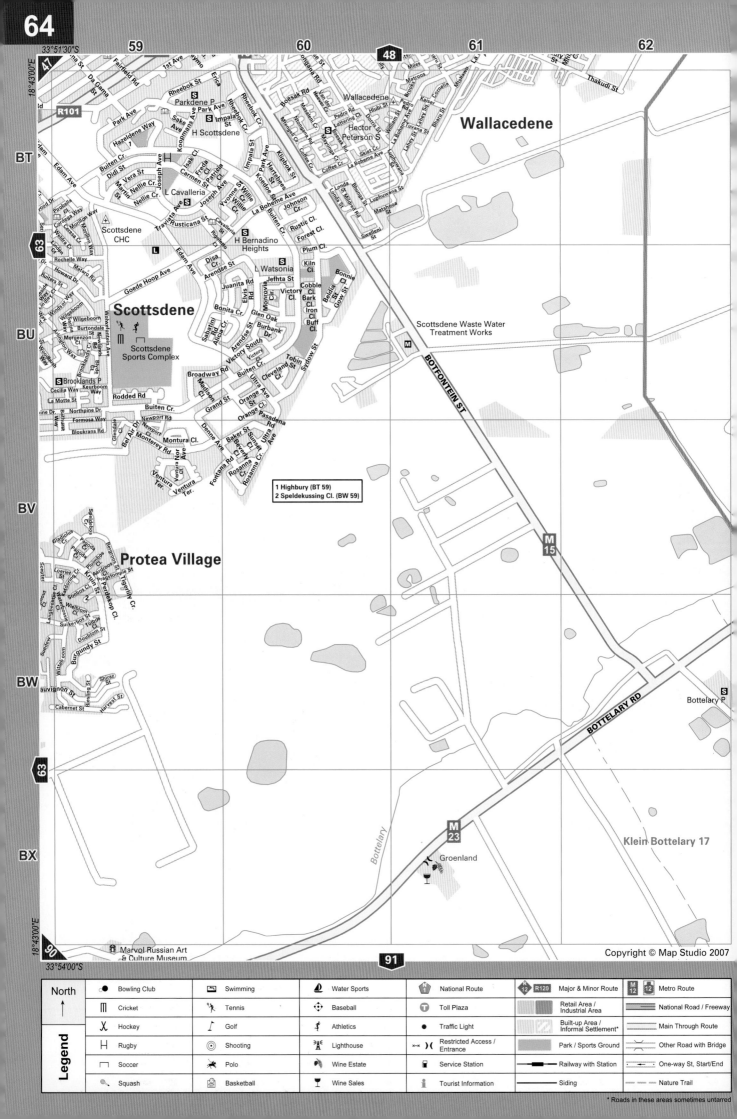

Wallacedene

Scottsdene

Scottsdene CHC

Scottsdene
Sports Complex

Scottsdene Waste Water
Treatment Works

Protea Village

1 Highbury (BT 59)
2 Speldekussing Cl. (BW 59)

Klein Bottelary 17

Groenland

BOTFONTEIN ST

BOTTELARY RD

Bottelary P

Bottelary

Marvol Russian Art
& Culture Museum

North

Legend

Bowling Club	Swimming	Water Sports	National Route	Major & Minor Route	Metro Route
Cricket	Tennis	Baseball	Toll Plaza	Retail Area / Industrial Area	National Road / Freeway
Hockey	Golf	Athletics	Traffic Light	Built-up Area / Informal Settlement*	Main Through Route
Rugby	Shooting	Lighthouse	Restricted Access / Entrance	Park / Sports Ground	Other Road with Bridge
Soccer	Polo	Wine Estate	Service Station	Railway with Station	One-way St, Start/End
Squash	Basketball	Wine Sales	Tourist Information	Siding	Nature Trail

* Roads in these areas sometimes untarred

63   64   **49**   65   66   18°47'00"E

50

BT

66

BU

Houd Den Beck 22

Bellevue

M 23

BV

BOTTELARY RD

Welgelegen 211

Koopmans Kloof Noord 216

BW

66

BX

18°47'00"E

93

92

33°54'00"S

▲	Community Service	⚠	Municipal Clinic	R	Recreation Centre	📖	Place of Worship	⚔	Battle Site	⊕	Cemetery		North ↑
★	Traffic Department	⊕	Hospital/Clinic (24 Hour Casualty)	G	Government Office	🚗	Parking	C	Conference Centre	⌇	Bird Sanctuary		
▼	Metro Police	✚	Hospital	✉	Post Office	▲	Place of Interest	🚐	Caravan Park	♣	Nature Reserve		
●	Police Station	L	Library	✦	Cinema	♟	Historical Monument	H	Hotel	✈	International Airport		Legend
★	Fire Station	M	Municipal Office	🛒	Shopping Centre	🏛	Provincial Heritage Site	E	Embassy	⊥	Airfield		
⚖	Law Court	S	School	🐟	Theatre	🏛	Museum	▷	Consulate	H	Helipad		

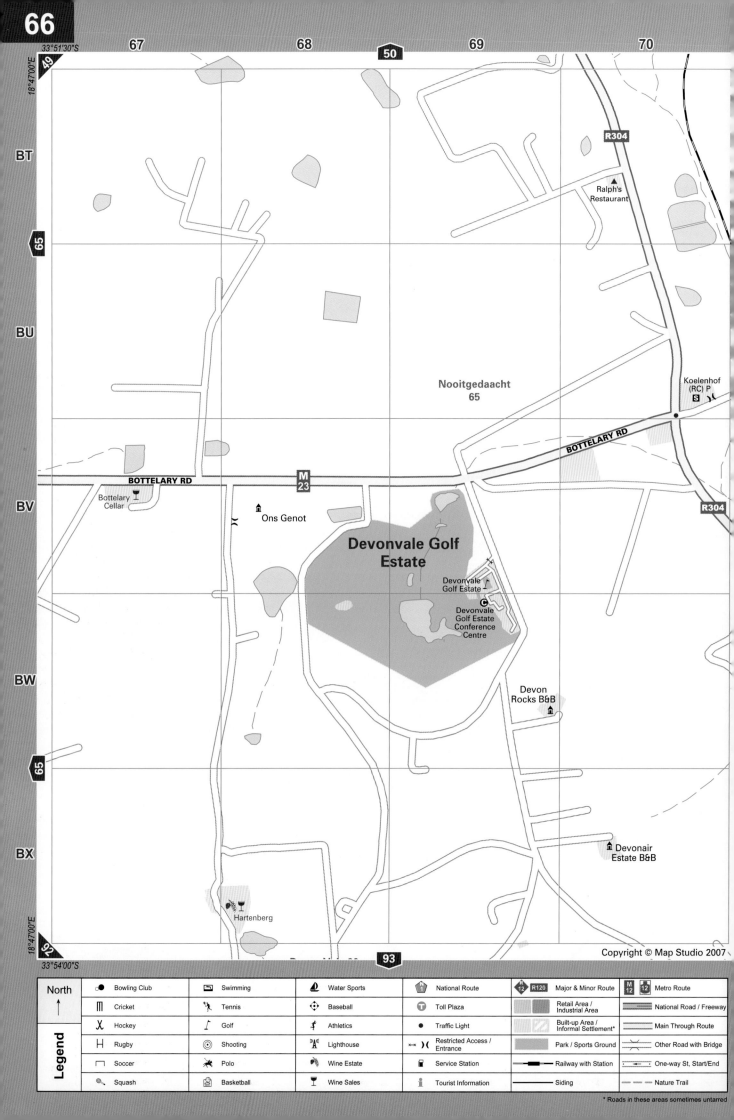

33°51'30"S

18°47'00"E

BT

BU

BV

BW

BX

67   68   50   69   70

49

65

65

R304

Ralph's
Restaurant

Koelenhof
(RC) P

Nooitgedaacht
65

BOTTELARY RD

R304

BOTTELARY RD

M
23

Bottelary
Cellar

Ons Genot

**Devonvale Golf
Estate**

Devonvale
Golf Estate

Devonvale
Golf Estate
Conference
Centre

Devon
Rocks B&B

Devonair
Estate B&B

Hartenberg

92

93

18°47'00"E

33°54'00"S

Copyright © Map Studio 2007

North	Bowling Club	Swimming	Water Sports	National Route	R120 Major & Minor Route	M 12 Metro Route
	Cricket	Tennis	Baseball	Toll Plaza	Retail Area / Industrial Area	National Road / Freeway
	Hockey	Golf	Athletics	Traffic Light	Built-up Area / Informal Settlement*	Main Through Route
Legend	Rugby	Shooting	Lighthouse	Restricted Access / Entrance	Park / Sports Ground	Other Road with Bridge
	Soccer	Polo	Wine Estate	Service Station	Railway with Station	One-way St, Start/End
	Squash	Basketball	Wine Sales	Tourist Information	Siding	Nature Trail

* Roads in these areas sometimes untarred

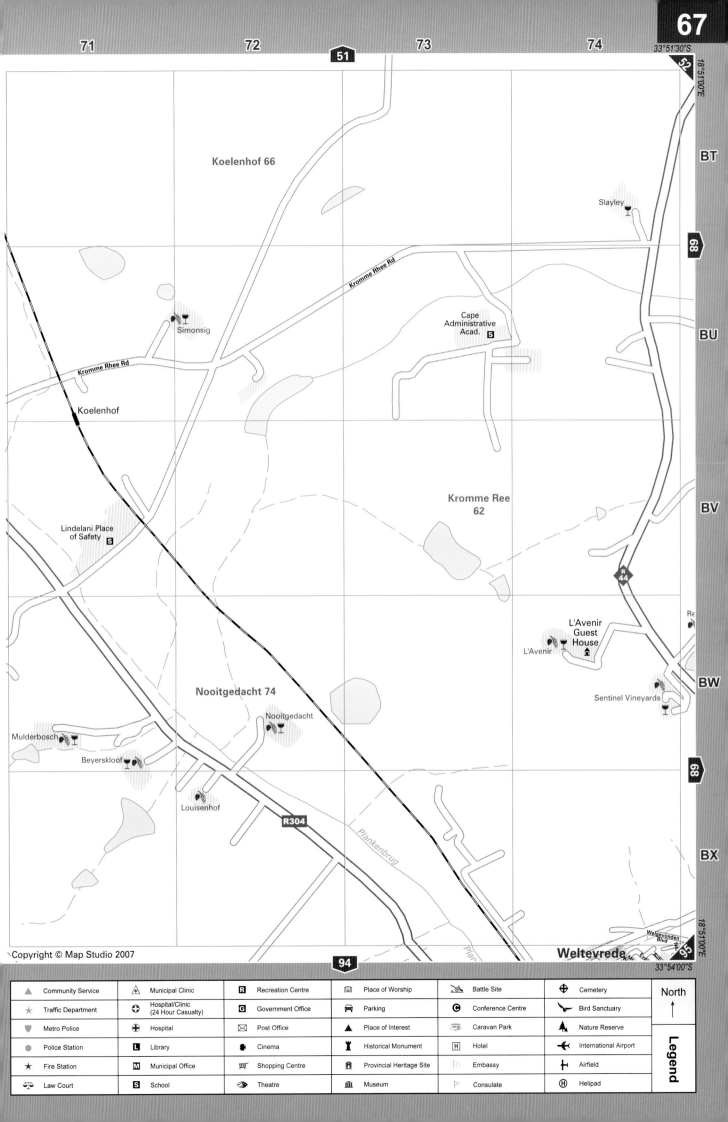

71   72   **51**   73   74

18°51'00"E

BT

Koelenhof 66

Slayley

68

Kromme Rhee Rd

Simonsig

Cape
Administrative
Acad. **S**

BU

Kromme Rhee Rd

Koelenhof

Kromme Ree
62

BV

Lindelani Place
of Safety **S**

R
44

L'Avenir
Guest
House

Re

L'Avenir

BW

Sentinel Vineyards

Nooitgedacht 74

Nooitgedacht

68

Mulderbosch

Beyerskloof

Louisenhof

R304

Plankenbrug

BX

18°51'00"E

Welgevonden
Blvd

Weltevrede

94

33°54'00"S

									North
▲ Community Service	Ⓐ Municipal Clinic	Ⓡ Recreation Centre	📖 Place of Worship	Battle Site	⊕ Cemetery	↑
★ Traffic Department	✛ Hospital/Clinic (24 Hour Casualty)	Ⓖ Government Office	🚗 Parking	Ⓒ Conference Centre	⤙ Bird Sanctuary	
⚕ Metro Police	✛ Hospital	✉ Post Office	▲ Place of Interest	Caravan Park	♣ Nature Reserve	
● Police Station	Ⓛ Library	✸ Cinema	👤 Historical Monument	Ⓗ Hotel	✈ International Airport	
★ Fire Station	Ⓜ Municipal Office	🛒 Shopping Centre	🏛 Provincial Heritage Site	Embassy	✈ Airfield	Legend
⚖ Law Court	Ⓢ School	Theatre	🏛 Museum	▷ Consulate	Ⓗ Helipad	

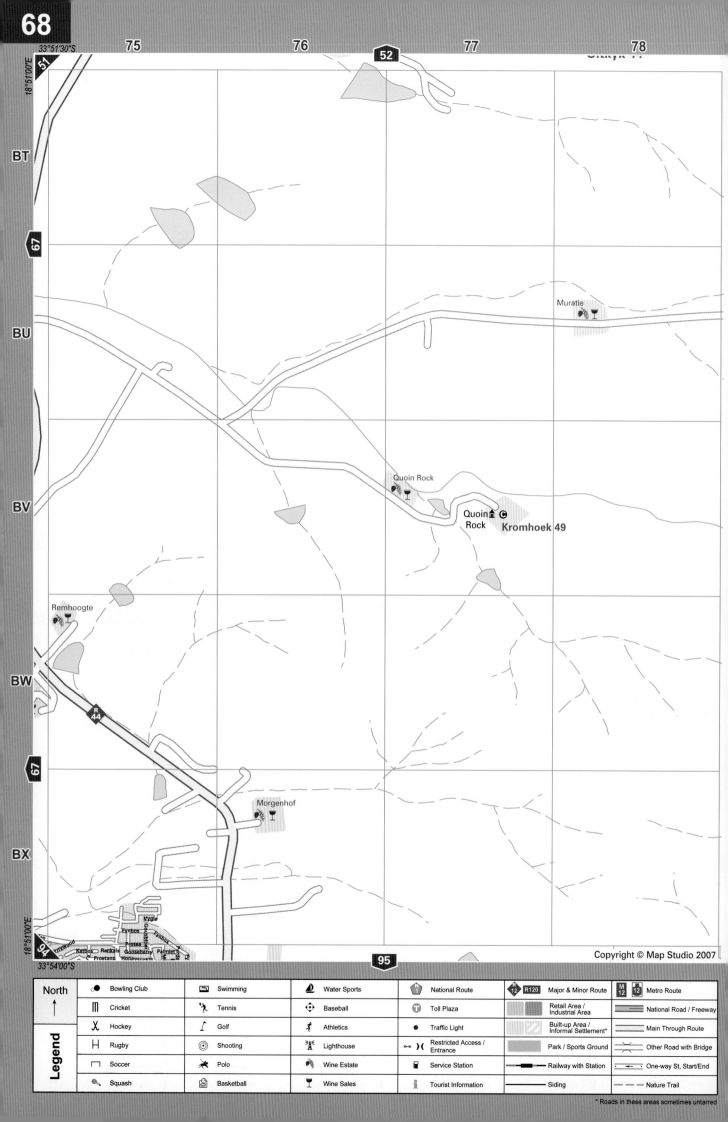

33°51'30"S
18°51'00"E

51
75
76
52
77
78
Uitkyk 4...

BT

67

BU
Muratie

BV
Quoin Rock
Quoin   C
Rock
Kromhoek 49

Remhoogte

BW

R44

67

Morgenhof

BX

18°51'00"E

Vygie
Fynbos Goudswm
Protea Fynbos
Karbos Rankals
Gooseberry Palmiet
Froetang Honeyweeth

94
95

33°54'00"S

Copyright © Map Studio 2007

North ↑	Bowling Club	Swimming	Water Sports	National Route	R120 Major & Minor Route	Metro Route
	Cricket	Tennis	Baseball	Toll Plaza	Retail Area / Industrial Area	National Road / Freeway
	Hockey	Golf	Athletics	Traffic Light	Built-up Area / Informal Settlement*	Main Through Route
Legend	Rugby	Shooting	Lighthouse	Restricted Access / Entrance	Park / Sports Ground	Other Road with Bridge
	Soccer	Polo	Wine Estate	Service Station	Railway with Station	One-way St, Start/End
	Squash	Basketball	Wine Sales	Tourist Information	Siding	Nature Trail

* Roads in these areas sometimes untarred

79　　　80　　　81　　　82

53

BT

70

Kanonkop
957m

Delheim

Delheim 1066

BU

Klippies Rivier 50

BV

Rustenburg 53

BW

Annexe
Schoongezicht 36

70

Rustenberg

Rustenburg 105

BX

96

▲	Community Service	Ⓐ	Municipal Clinic	Ⓡ	Recreation Centre	⌖	Place of Worship	⛷	Battle Site	⊕	Cemetery
★	Traffic Department	✚	Hospital/Clinic (24 Hour Casualty)	Ⓖ	Government Office	🚗	Parking	Ⓒ	Conference Centre	✎	Bird Sanctuary
▼	Metro Police	✚	Hospital	✉	Post Office	▲	Place of Interest	🚐	Caravan Park	♠	Nature Reserve
●	Police Station	Ⓛ	Library	✦	Cinema	⚱	Historical Monument	Ⓗ	Hotel	✈	International Airport
★	Fire Station	Ⓜ	Municipal Office	🎪	Shopping Centre	🏛	Provincial Heritage Site	🚩	Embassy	✛	Airfield
⚖	Law Court	Ⓢ	School	🎭	Theatre	🏛	Museum	▷	Consulate	Ⓗ	Helipad

North
↑

Legend

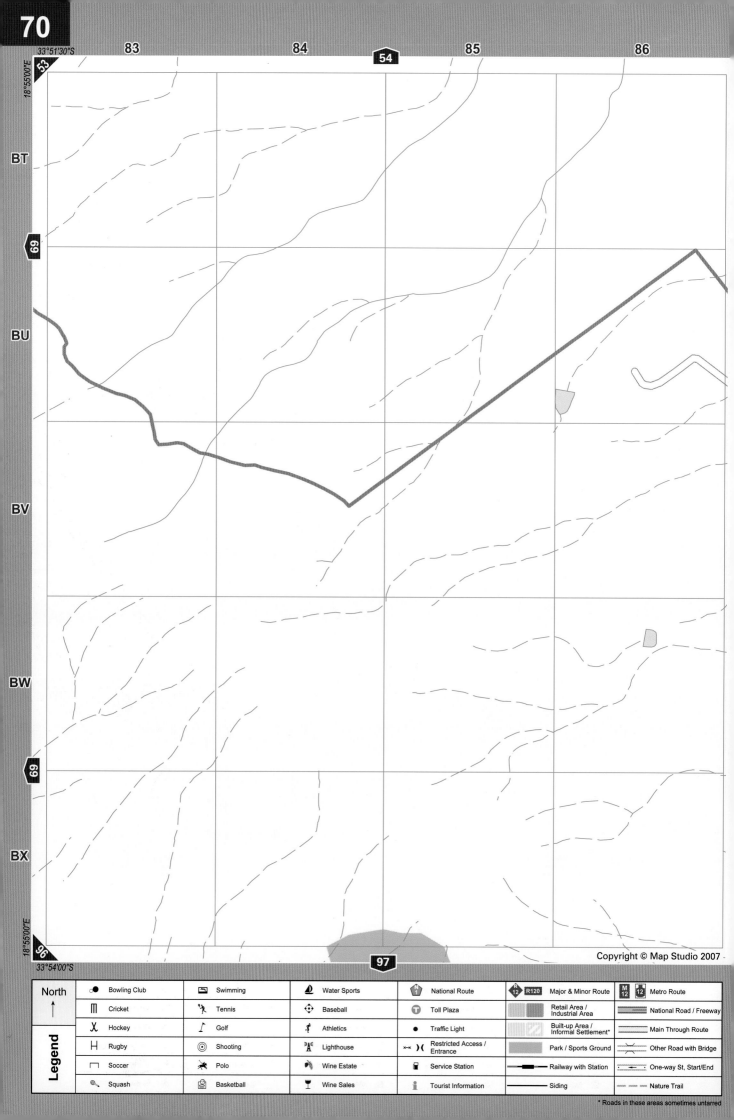

18°55'00"E 53

BT

69

BU

BV

BW

69

BX

18°55'00"E 96

33°54'00"S

97

Copyright © Map Studio 2007

North ↑		Bowling Club		Swimming		Water Sports		National Route	R120	Major & Minor Route	M 12	Metro Route
		Cricket		Tennis		Baseball		Toll Plaza		Retail Area / Industrial Area		National Road / Freeway
		Hockey		Golf		Athletics		Traffic Light		Built-up Area / Informal Settlement*		Main Through Route
Legend		Rugby		Shooting		Lighthouse		Restricted Access / Entrance		Park / Sports Ground		Other Road with Bridge
		Soccer		Polo		Wine Estate		Service Station		Railway with Station		One-way St, Start/End
		Squash		Basketball		Wine Sales		Tourist Information		Siding		Nature Trail

* Roads in these areas sometimes untarred

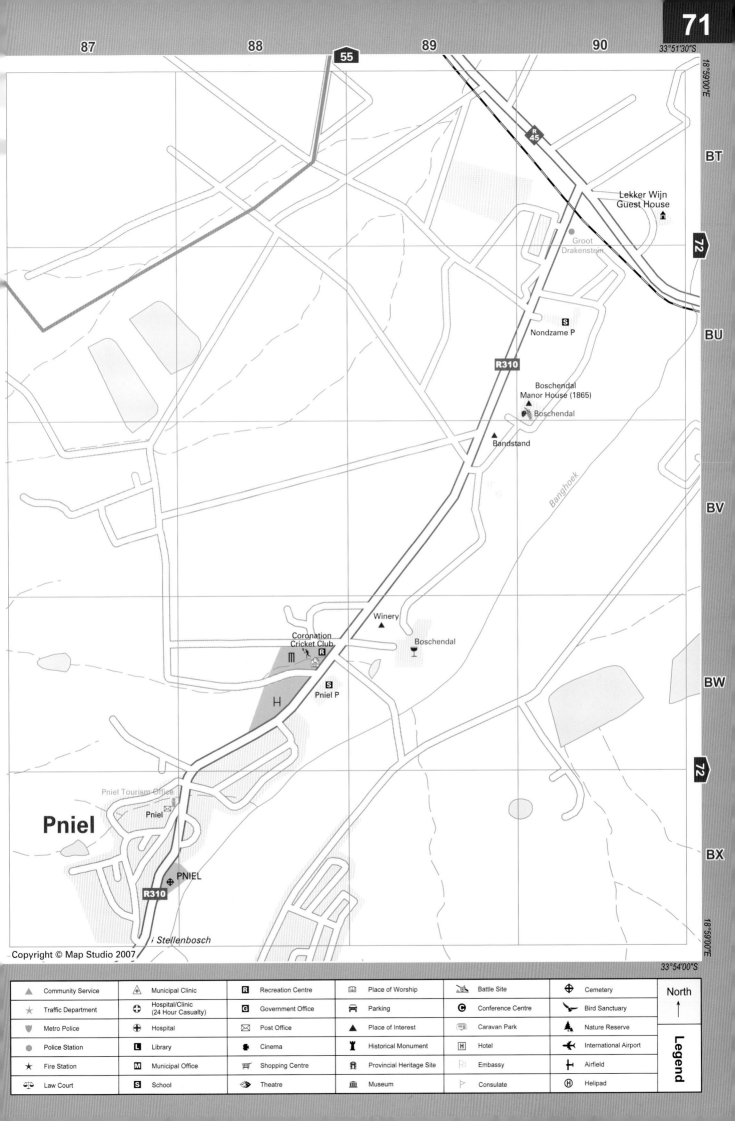

33°51'30"S

87 88 55 89 90

18°59'00"E

BT

R45

Lekker Wijn
Guest House

72

Groot
Drakenstein

BU

S
Nondzame P

R310

Boschendal
Manor House (1865)

Boschendal

Bandstand

Banghoek

BV

Winery

Coronation
Cricket Club

M R
R

Boschendal

BW

S
Pniel P

H

72

Pniel Tourism Office

Pniel

Pniel

BX

PNIEL

R310

Stellenbosch

Copyright © Map Studio 2007

33°54'00"S

18°59'00"E

▲ Community Service	Ⓐ Municipal Clinic	Ⓡ Recreation Centre	Place of Worship	Battle Site	⊕ Cemetery	**North** ↑
★ Traffic Department	⊕ Hospital/Clinic (24 Hour Casualty)	Ⓖ Government Office	Parking	Ⓒ Conference Centre	Bird Sanctuary	
Metro Police	⊕ Hospital	✉ Post Office	▲ Place of Interest	Caravan Park	Nature Reserve	
● Police Station	Ⓛ Library	Cinema	⚔ Historical Monument	Ⓗ Hotel	International Airport	**Legend**
★ Fire Station	Ⓜ Municipal Office	Shopping Centre	Provincial Heritage Site	Embassy	Airfield	
Law Court	Ⓢ School	Theatre	🏛 Museum	Consulate	Ⓗ Helipad	

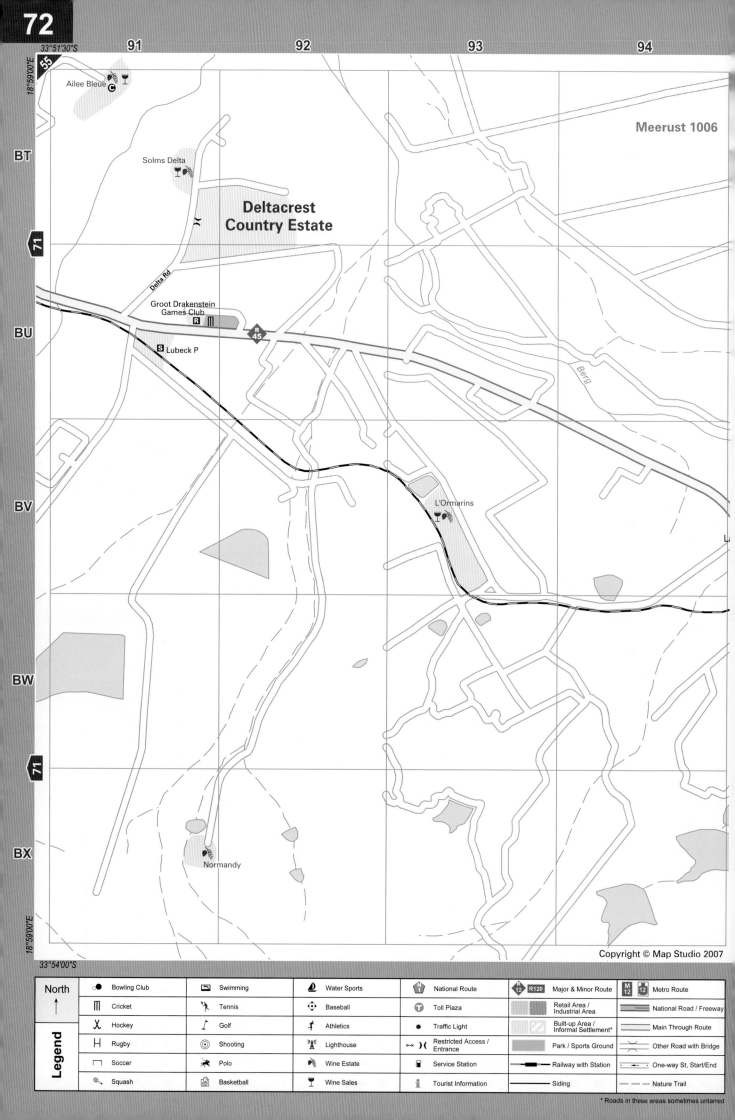

Meerust 1006

Ailee Bleue

Solms Delta

Deltacrest Country Estate

Delta Rd

Groot Drakenstein Games Club

Lubeck P

Berg

L'Ormarins

Normandy

Copyright © Map Studio 2007

North ↑	⊙● Bowling Club	⊡ Swimming	⛵ Water Sports	🛡 National Route	12 R120 Major & Minor Route	M12 12 Metro Route
	Ⅲ Cricket	🏃 Tennis	⊕ Baseball	Ⓣ Toll Plaza	Retail Area / Industrial Area	National Road / Freeway
	X Hockey	⌇ Golf	🏃 Athletics	● Traffic Light	Built-up Area / Informal Settlement*	Main Through Route
Legend	H Rugby	◎ Shooting	🗼 Lighthouse	✕)(Restricted Access / Entrance	Park / Sports Ground	Other Road with Bridge
	⊡ Soccer	🐎 Polo	🍷 Wine Estate	⛽ Service Station	▬▬ Railway with Station	One-way St, Start/End
	⊛ Squash	🏀 Basketball	🍷 Wine Sales	ℹ Tourist Information	─── Siding	Nature Trail

* Roads in these areas sometimes untarred

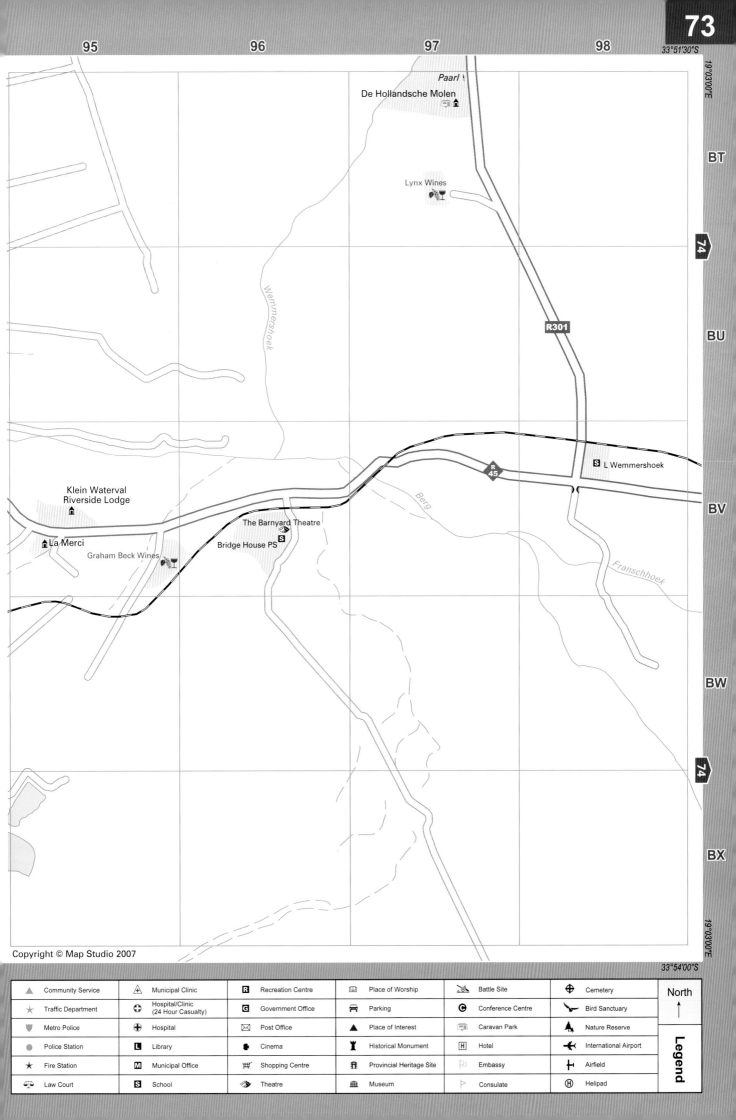

Paarl

De Hollandsche Molen

Lynx Wines

R301

L Wemmershoek

Wemmershoek

Berg

Franschhoek

Klein Waterval
Riverside Lodge

La Merci

Graham Beck Wines

The Barnyard Theatre

Bridge House PS

R45

▲ Community Service	Ⓐ Municipal Clinic	Ⓡ Recreation Centre	Place of Worship	Battle Site	⊕ Cemetery
★ Traffic Department	⊕ Hospital/Clinic (24 Hour Casualty)	Ⓖ Government Office	🚗 Parking	Ⓒ Conference Centre	Bird Sanctuary
▼ Metro Police	⊕ Hospital	✉ Post Office	▲ Place of Interest	Caravan Park	Nature Reserve
● Police Station	Ⓛ Library	Cinema	Ⓨ Historical Monument	Ⓗ Hotel	International Airport
★ Fire Station	Ⓜ Municipal Office	🛒 Shopping Centre	Provincial Heritage Site	Embassy	Airfield
⚖ Law Court	Ⓢ School	Theatre	🏛 Museum	▷ Consulate	Ⓗ Helipad

North
↑

Legend

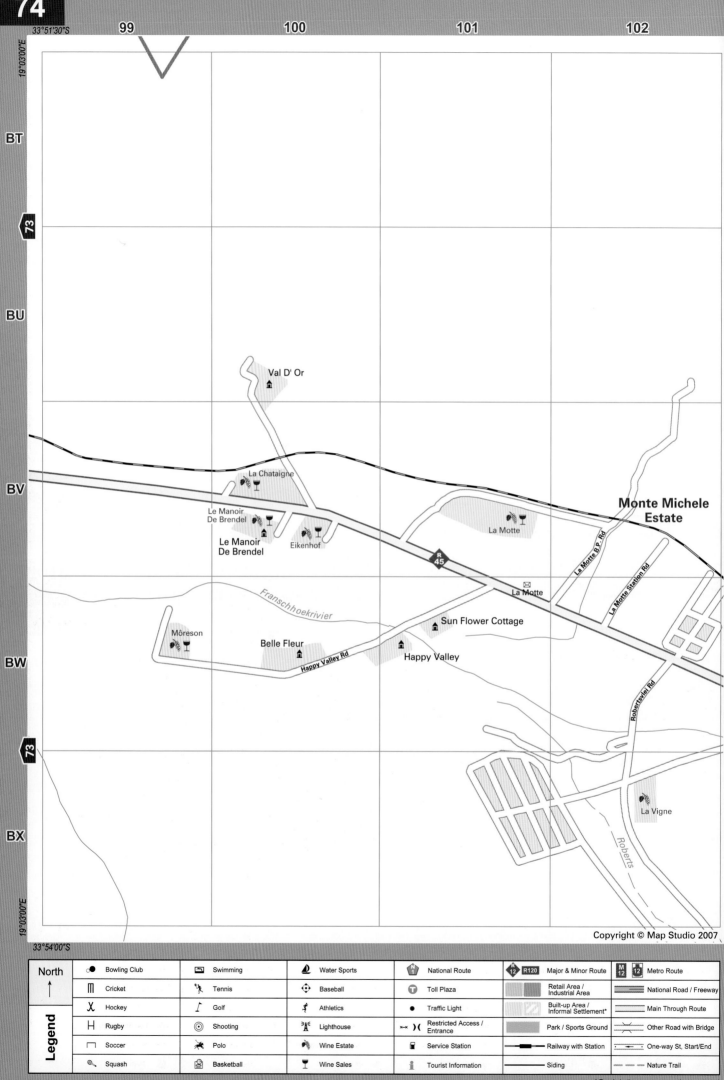

Val D' Or

La Chataigne

Le Manoir
De Brendel

Le Manoir
De Brendel

Eikenhof

La Motte

Monte Michele
Estate

La Motte B.P. Rd

La Motte Station Rd

Franschhoekrivier

La Motte

Môreson

Belle Fleur

Sun Flower Cottage

Happy Valley Rd

Happy Valley

Robertsvlei Rd

Roberts

La Vigne

R45

R120

Legend

North ↑

⌀ Bowling Club	⛱ Swimming	⛵ Water Sports	National Route	R12 R120 Major & Minor Route	M12 12 Metro Route
Ⅲ Cricket	Tennis	Baseball	Toll Plaza	Retail Area / Industrial Area	National Road / Freeway
Hockey	Golf	Athletics	● Traffic Light	Built-up Area / Informal Settlement*	Main Through Route
H Rugby	◎ Shooting	Lighthouse	Restricted Access / Entrance	Park / Sports Ground	Other Road with Bridge
Soccer	Polo	Wine Estate	Service Station	Railway with Station	One-way St, Start/End
Squash	Basketball	Wine Sales	Tourist Information	Siding	Nature Trail

* Roads in these areas sometimes untarred

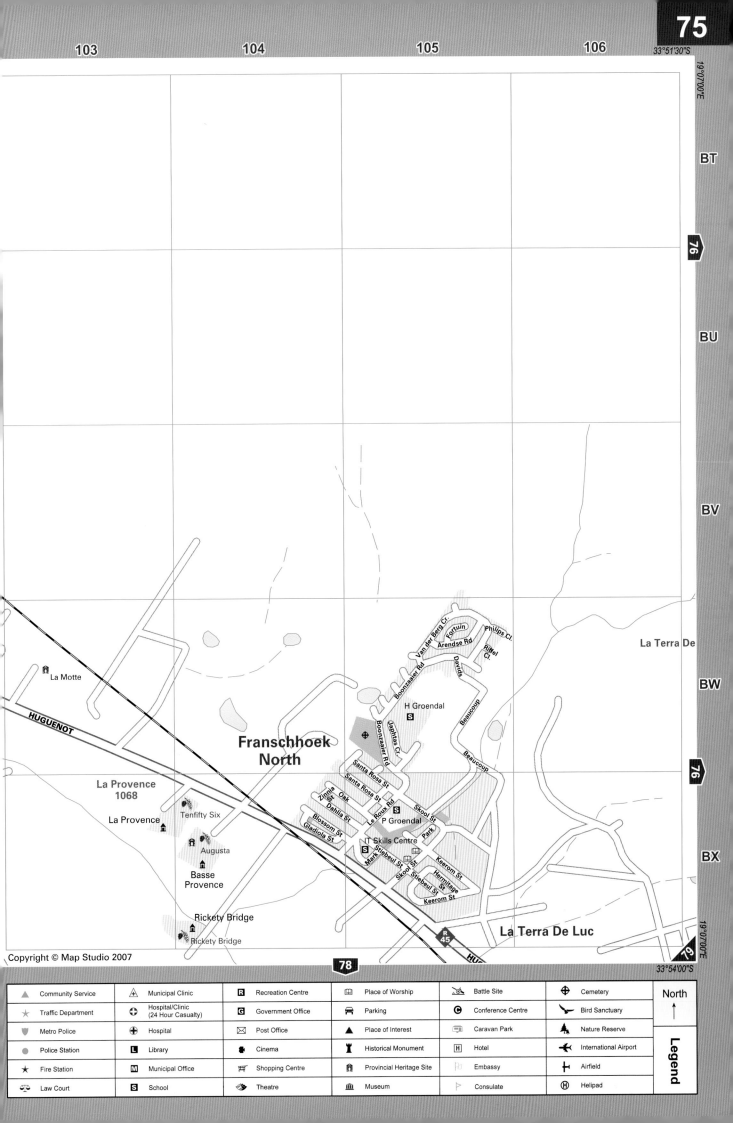

19°07'00"E

BT

76

BU

BV

La Terra De

BW

La Motte

HUGUENOT

Franschhoek North

Van der Berg Cr.
Fortwin
Arendse Rd
Philips Cl.
Riffel Cl.
Davids

Boonzaaier Rd

H Groendal
S

Japhtas Cr.
Boonzaaier Rd

Beaucoup

Beaucoup

La Provence
1068

Santa Rosa St

Santa Rosa St

La Provence

Tenfifty Six

Zinnia St
Oak
Dahlia St

Le Roux Rd
S
P Groendal

Skool St

76

Blossom St

Gladiola St

IT Skills Centre
S

Park

Augusta

Mark
Stiebeul St
Skool St
Stiebeul St

Keerom St

Hermitage St

BX

Basse Provence

Keerom St

Rickety Bridge

Rickety Bridge

La Terra De Luc

R45

HU

19°07'00"E

79

33°54'00"S

Symbol	Legend	Symbol	Legend	Symbol	Legend	Symbol	Legend	Symbol	Legend	Symbol	Legend
▲	Community Service	Ⓐ	Municipal Clinic	Ⓡ	Recreation Centre		Place of Worship		Battle Site	⊕	Cemetery
★	Traffic Department	✚	Hospital/Clinic (24 Hour Casualty)	Ⓖ	Government Office	🚗	Parking	Ⓒ	Conference Centre	⌖	Bird Sanctuary
▼	Metro Police	✚	Hospital	✉	Post Office	▲	Place of Interest		Caravan Park	▲	Nature Reserve
●	Police Station	Ⓛ	Library		Cinema		Historical Monument	Ⓗ	Hotel	✈	International Airport
★	Fire Station	Ⓜ	Municipal Office		Shopping Centre	🏛	Provincial Heritage Site		Embassy	⊦	Airfield
⚖	Law Court	Ⓢ	School		Theatre	🏛	Museum	▷	Consulate	Ⓗ	Helipad

North
↑

Legend

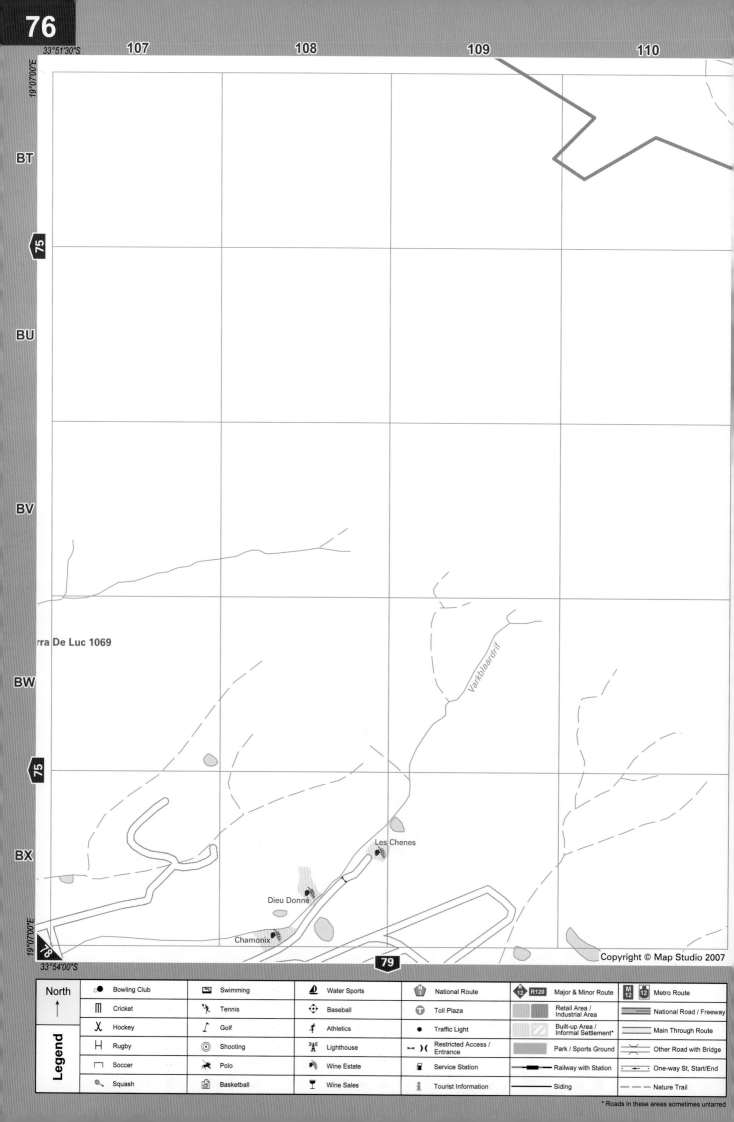

33°51'30"S
19°07'00"E

107   108   109   110

BT

75

BU

BV

rra De Luc 1069

Varkblaardrif

BW

75

BX

Les Chenes

Dieu Donné

Chamonix

19°07'00"E
33°54'00"S

79

Copyright © Map Studio 2007

North								
↑	⊶● Bowling Club	⊟ Swimming	⚓ Water Sports	🛡 National Route	◆ R120 Major & Minor Route	M12 12 Metro Route
	Ⓜ Cricket	🎾 Tennis	✛ Baseball	Ⓣ Toll Plaza	Retail Area / Industrial Area	National Road / Freeway
Legend	✗ Hockey	⌐ Golf	⚐ Athletics	● Traffic Light	Built-up Area / Informal Settlement*	Main Through Route
	Ⱶ Rugby	⊙ Shooting	⚞ Lighthouse	⤬)(Restricted Access / Entrance	Park / Sports Ground	Other Road with Bridge
	⊏⊐ Soccer	🐎 Polo	⚘ Wine Estate	⬣ Service Station	Railway with Station	One-way St, Start/End
	🎾 Squash	🏀 Basketball	⚍ Wine Sales	🛈 Tourist Information	Siding	Nature Trail

* Roads in these areas sometimes untarred

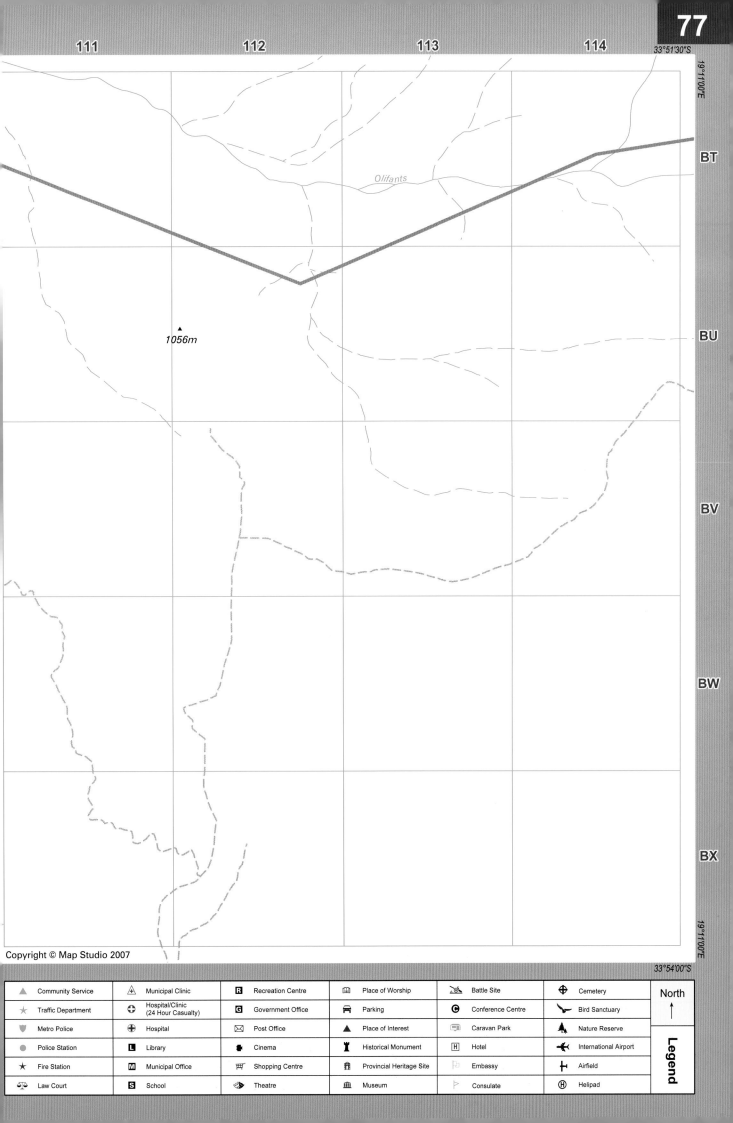

Olifants

1056m

▲	Community Service	Ⓐ	Municipal Clinic	Ⓡ	Recreation Centre		Place of Worship		Battle Site	⊕	Cemetery
★	Traffic Department	⊕	Hospital/Clinic (24 Hour Casualty)	Ⓖ	Government Office	🚗	Parking	Ⓒ	Conference Centre		Bird Sanctuary
🛡	Metro Police	⊕	Hospital	✉	Post Office	▲	Place of Interest		Caravan Park	🌲	Nature Reserve
●	Police Station	Ⓛ	Library		Cinema	♟	Historical Monument	Ⓗ	Hotel	✈	International Airport
★	Fire Station	Ⓜ	Municipal Office	🛒	Shopping Centre	🏛	Provincial Heritage Site		Embassy	⊦	Airfield
⚖	Law Court	Ⓢ	School		Theatre	🏛	Museum	▷	Consulate	Ⓗ	Helipad

North
↑

Legend

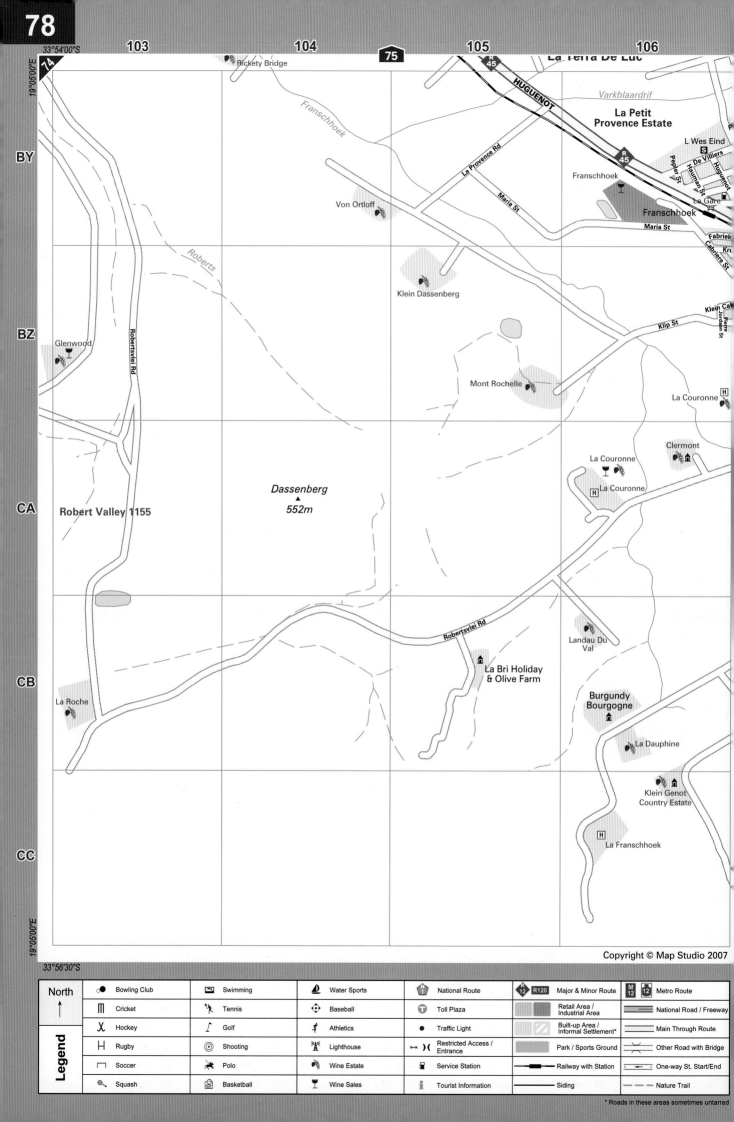

North ↑		Bowling Club		Swimming		Water Sports		National Route		Major & Minor Route
		Cricket		Tennis		Baseball		Toll Plaza		Retail Area / Industrial Area
		Hockey		Golf		Athletics		Traffic Light		Built-up Area / Informal Settlement*
Legend		Rugby		Shooting		Lighthouse		Restricted Access / Entrance		Park / Sports Ground
		Soccer		Polo		Wine Estate		Service Station		Railway with Station
		Squash		Basketball		Wine Sales		Tourist Information		Siding

Metro Route
National Road / Freeway
Main Through Route
Other Road with Bridge
One-way St, Start/End
Nature Trail

* Roads in these areas sometimes untarred

Chamonix

Franschhoek South

Roux Malherbe
Akademie St.
Dikkie Uys St.
De Wet St.
Uitkyk St.
Naude St.
La Cotta St.
Franschhoek Inn
Louis Botha St.
NGK Church Cemetery
La Cotte
uger St.
De la Rey St.
Huguenot
La Rochelle St.
Inn
Cabriere St.
Bordeaux St.
Huguenot
Daniel Hugo St.
Franschhoek
Cabriere
Reservoir St.
Wilhelmina St.
Berg St.
Cabriere St.
HUGUENOT

Reservoir St.
H Franschhoek
Union St.
Akademie St.
Dirkie Uys St.
Heide St.
Van Riebeeck St.
Nerina St.
Erica St.
Disa St.
Freesia St.
Tuin St.
Aalwyn St.
Protea
Fransche Hoek Estate (New Development)

LAMBRECHT ST.

Eagles Nest

Huguenot

Haute Cabrière

Huguenot Monument

R45

La Cabriere Country House

La Providance

Robertsvlei Rd
Cape Vineyard

Mount Martre Lodge

R45

La Petite Fermé

R45

Franschhoek Pass

La Bri

Colmant Cap Classique & Champagne

Klein Dauphine

Auberge La Dauphine

Lavande De Franschhoek

La Bourgogne

Verdun

LAMBRECHTS ST.

Riverside Cottages

Steinmetz Arabians

Le Domaine Charmant

Keerweder

La Petite Dauphine

Stony Brook

Villiersdorp

79

Legend

▲ Community Service	Ⓐ Municipal Clinic	ℝ Recreation Centre	🕍 Place of Worship	Battle Site	⊕ Cemetery	**North** ↑
★ Traffic Department	⊕ Hospital/Clinic (24 Hour Casualty)	Ⓖ Government Office	🚗 Parking	Ⓒ Conference Centre	Bird Sanctuary	
Metro Police	⊕ Hospital	✉ Post Office	▲ Place of Interest	Caravan Park	⚲ Nature Reserve	
● Police Station	Ⓛ Library	Cinema	Ⓨ Historical Monument	Ⓗ Hotel	✈ International Airport	
★ Fire Station	Ⓜ Municipal Office	🛒 Shopping Centre	🏛 Provincial Heritage Site	Embassy	⊢ Airfield	
⚖ Law Court	Ⓢ School	🐟 Theatre	🏛 Museum	⚐ Camp Site	Ⓗ Helipad	

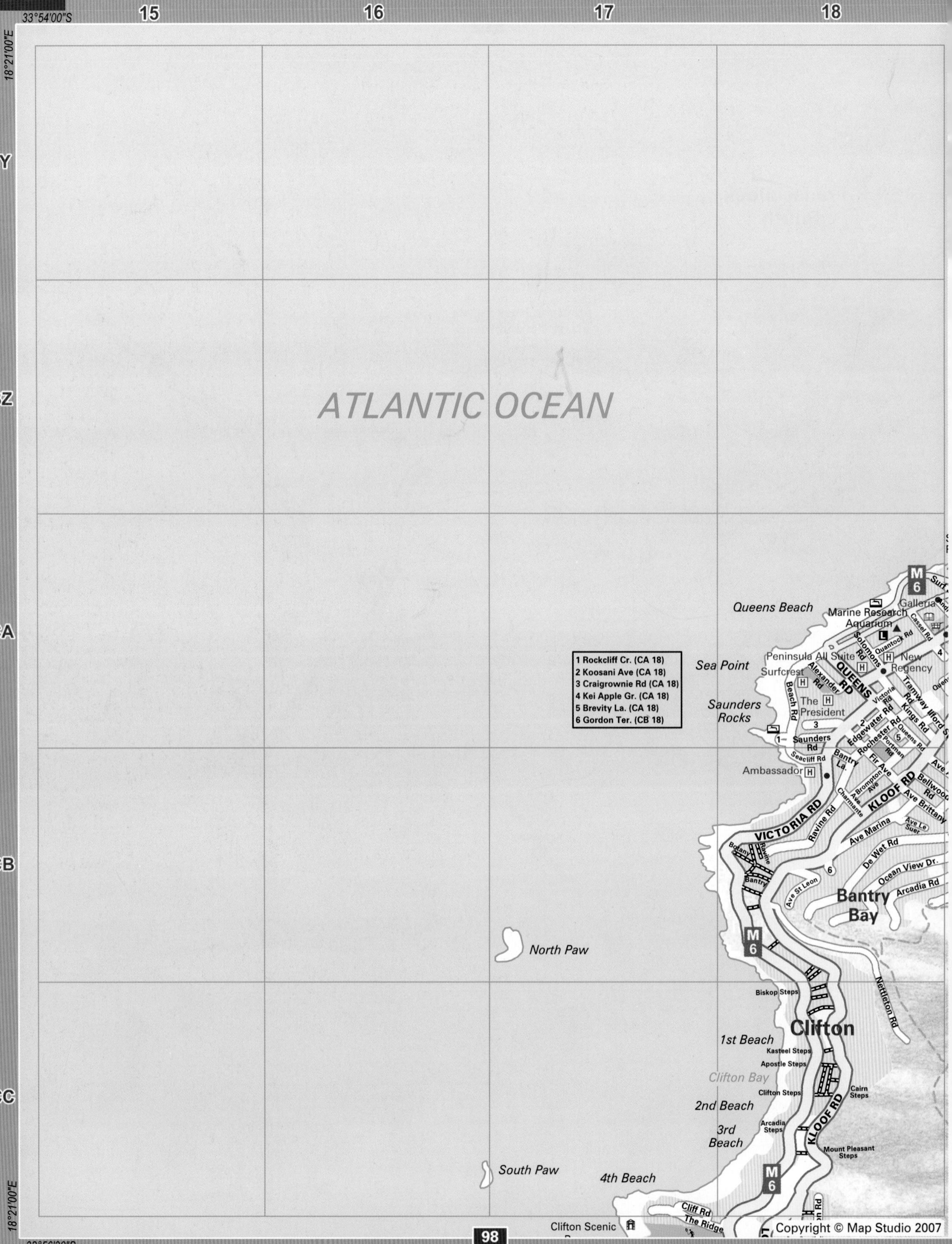
33°54'00"S
15
16
17
18
18°21'00"E
BY
BZ
CA
CB
CC
ATLANTIC OCEAN
1 Rockcliff Cr. (CA 18)
2 Koosani Ave (CA 18)
3 Craigrownie Rd (CA 18)
4 Kei Apple Gr. (CA 18)
5 Brevity La. (CA 18)
6 Gordon Ter. (CB 18)
Queens Beach
Marine Research Aquarium
Galleria
Sea Point
Peninsula All Suite
Surfcrest
New Regency
QUEENS RD
The President
Saunders Rocks
Saunders Rd
Seacliff Rd
Ambassador
Beach Rd
Alexander Rd
Victoria Rd
Edgewater Rd
Rochester Rd
Kings Rd
Tramway Rd
Queens Rd
Portman Rd
Fir Ave
Bantry La.
Brompton Ave
Charmante Ave
KLOOF RD
Bellwood Rd
Ave Brittany
Ave Le Suer
Ave Marina
VICTORIA RD
Ravine Rd
Botany
De Wet Rd
Ocean View Dr.
Arcadia Rd
Ave St Leon
Bantry Bay
North Paw
Nettleton Rd
Biskop Steps
Clifton
1st Beach
Kasteel Steps
Apostle Steps
Clifton Bay
Clifton Steps
Cairn Steps
2nd Beach
3rd Beach
Arcadia Steps
KLOOF RD
Mount Pleasant Steps
South Paw
4th Beach
Cliff Rd
The Ridge
Clifton Scenic
Copyright © Map Studio 2007
33°56'30"S
98

North ↑ / Legend						
	Bowling Club	Swimming	Water Sports	National Route	R120 Major & Minor Route	Metro Route
	Cricket	Tennis	Baseball	Toll Plaza	Retail Area / Industrial Area	National Road / Freeway
	Hockey	Golf	Athletics	Traffic Light	Built-up Area / Informal Settlement*	Main Through Route
	Rugby	Shooting	Lighthouse	Restricted Access / Entrance	Park / Sports Ground	Other Road with Bridge
	Soccer	Polo	Wine Estate	Service Station	Railway with Station	One-way St, Start/End
	Squash	Basketball	Wine Sales	Tourist Information	Siding	Nature Trail

* Roads in these areas sometimes untarred

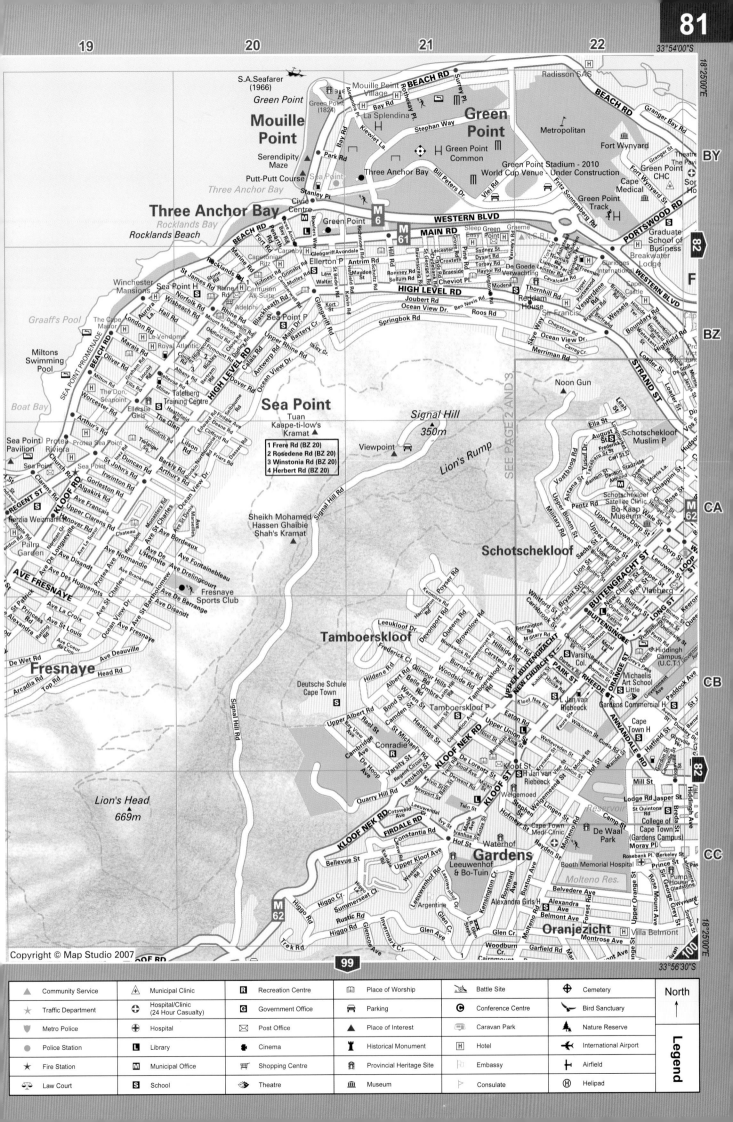

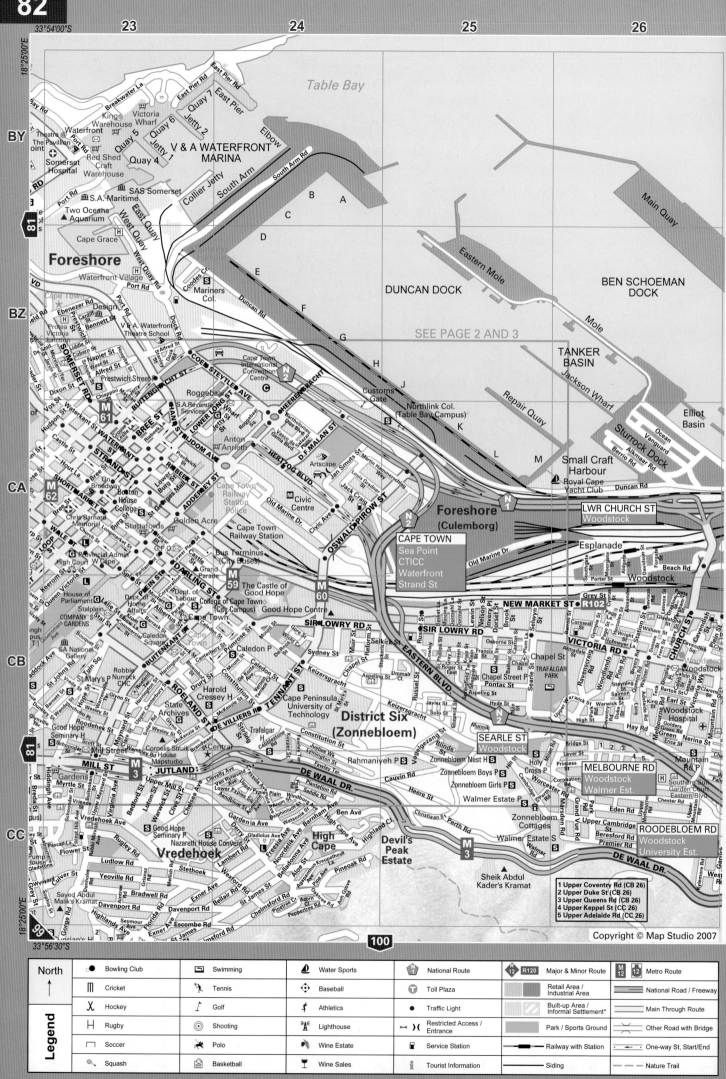

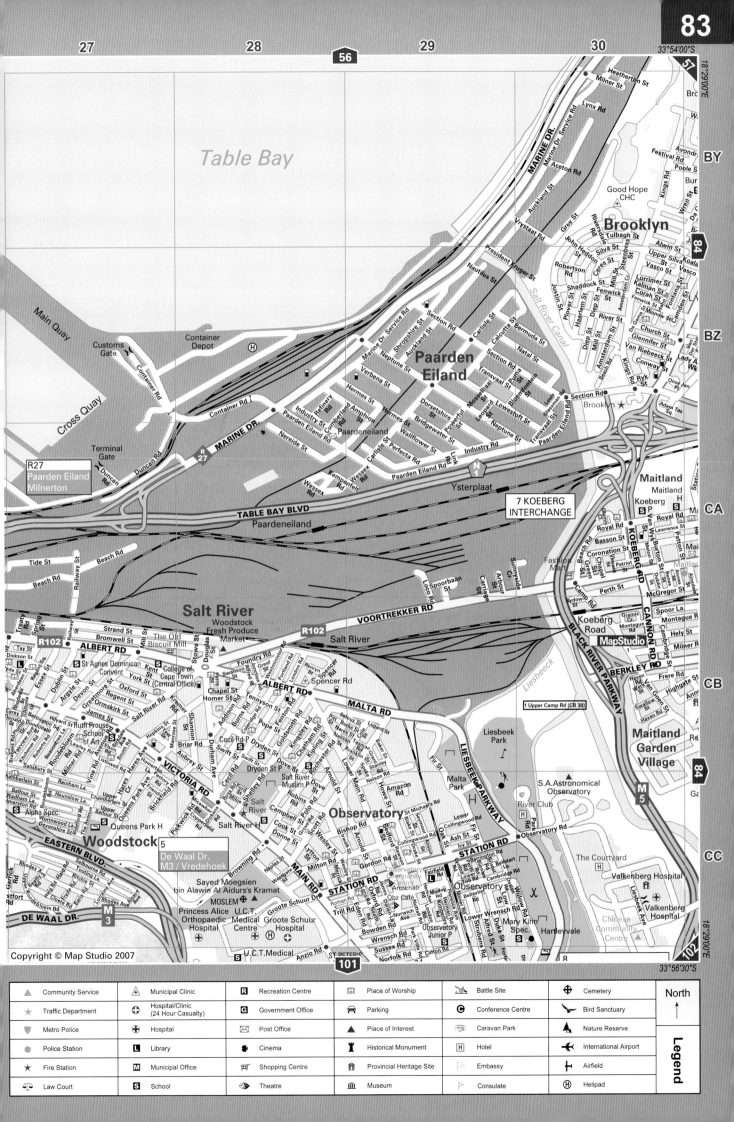

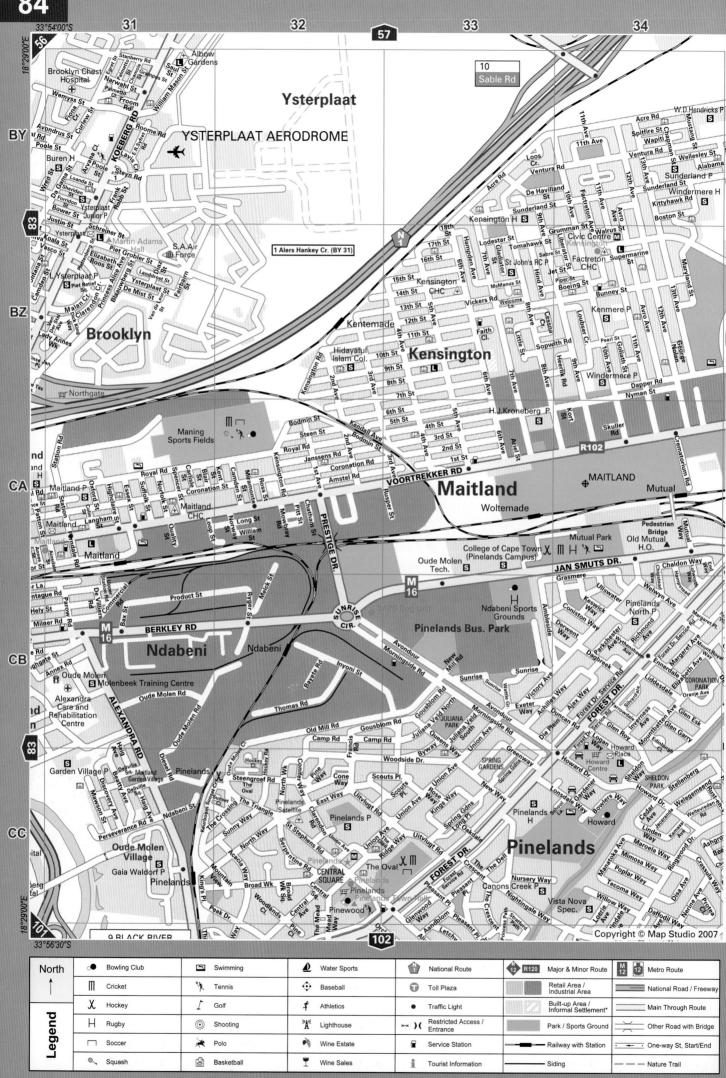

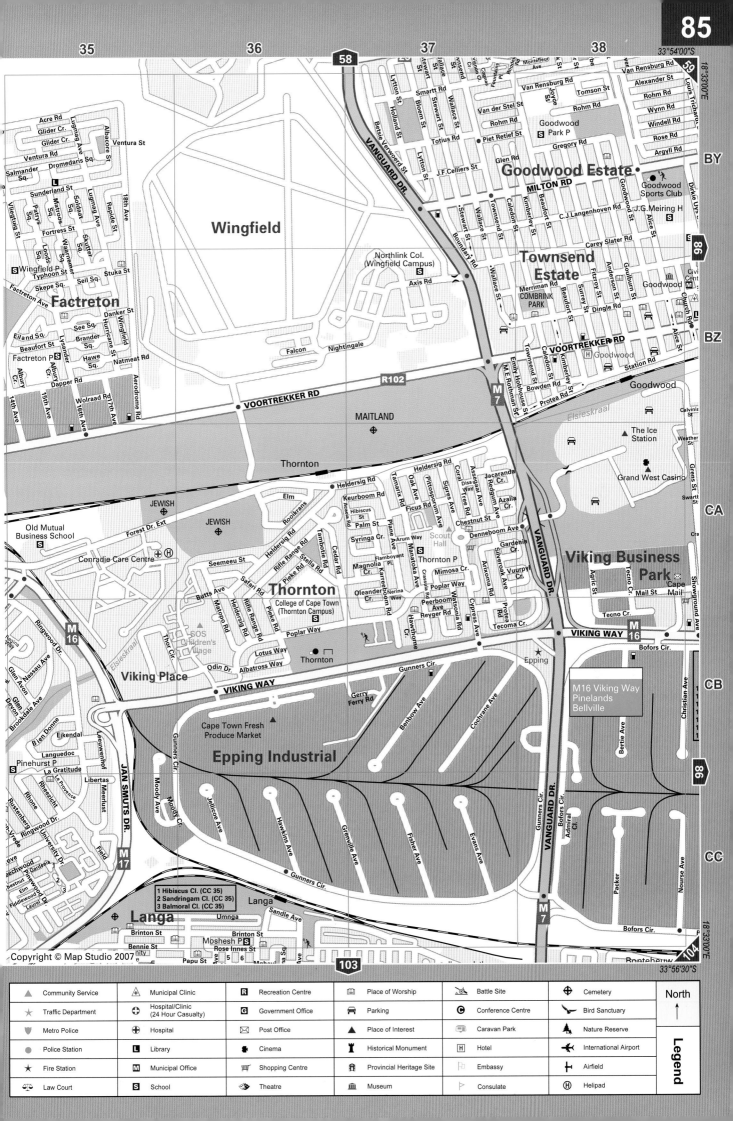

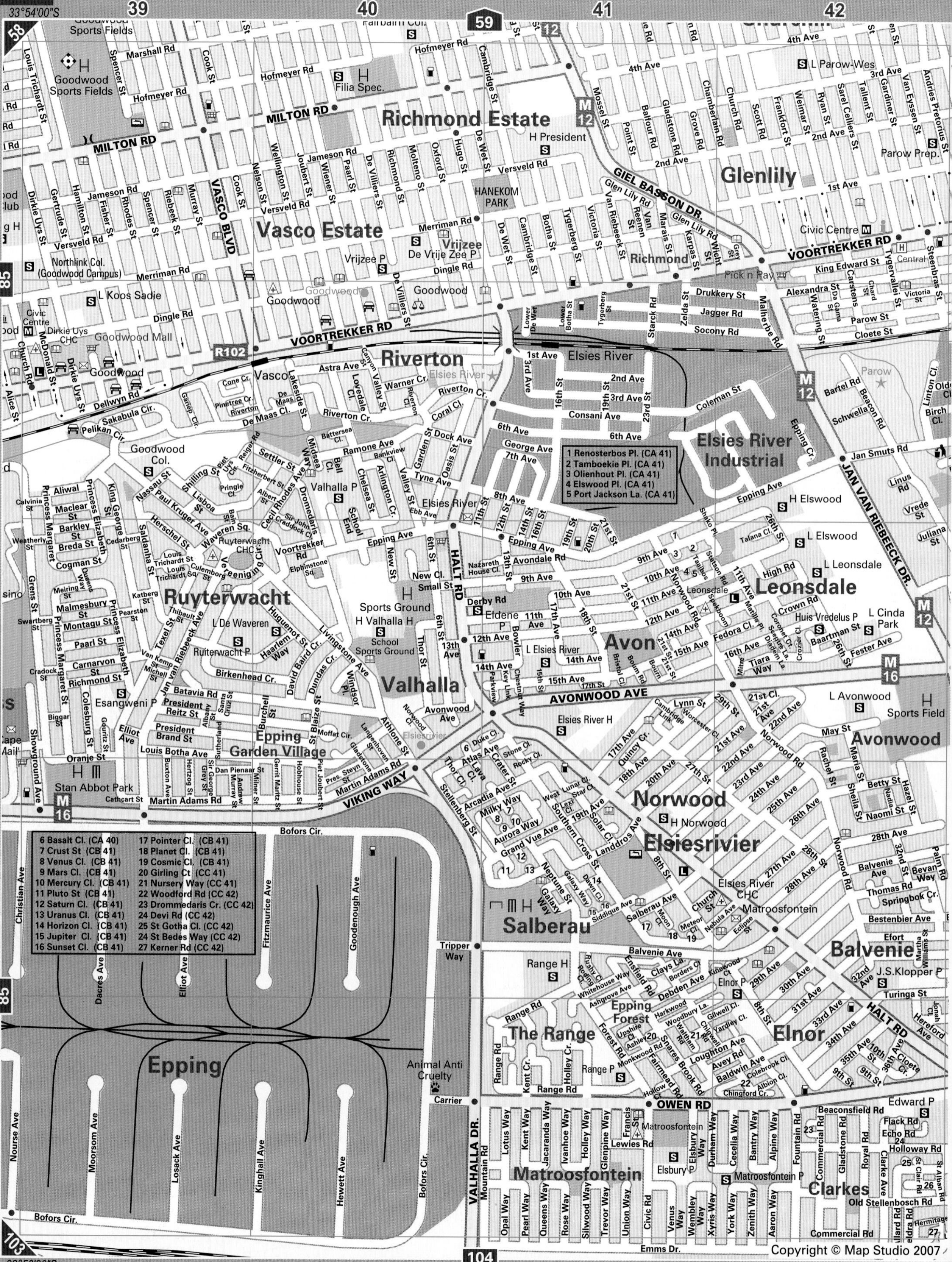
33°54'00"S
18°33'00"E
39
40
41
42
59
58
85
104
103
BY
BZ
CA
CB
CC
Richmond Estate
Vasco Estate
Glenlily
Vrijzee
Goodwood
Richmond
Riverton
Elsies River
Elsies River Industrial
Ruyterwacht
Valhalla
Avon
Leonsdale
Avonwood
Epping Garden Village
Norwood
Elsiesrivier
Salberau
Balvenie
The Range
Epping Forest
Elnor
Epping
Matroosfontein
Clarkes
MILTON RD
VOORTREKKER RD
GIEL BASSON DR.
VASCO BLVD
HALT RD
AVONWOOD AVE
VIKING WAY
VALHALLA DR.
JAN VAN RIEBEECK DR.
OWEN RD
Goodwood Sports Fields
Goodwood Mall
Stan Abbot Park
Sports Ground
School Sports Ground
Animal Anti Cruelty
1 Renosterbos Pl. (CA 41)
2 Tamboekie Pl. (CA 41)
3 Olienhout Pl. (CA 41)
4 Elswood Pl. (CA 41)
5 Port Jackson La. (CA 41)
6 Basalt Cl. (CA 40)
7 Crust St (CB 41)
8 Venus Cl. (CB 41)
9 Mars Cl. (CB 41)
10 Mercury Cl. (CB 41)
11 Pluto St (CB 41)
12 Saturn Cl. (CB 41)
13 Uranus Cl. (CB 41)
14 Horizon Cl. (CB 41)
15 Jupiter Cl. (CB 41)
16 Sunset Cl. (CB 41)
17 Pointer Cl. (CB 41)
18 Planet Cl. (CB 41)
19 Cosmic Cl. (CB 41)
20 Girling Ct (CC 41)
21 Nursery Way (CC 41)
22 Woodford Rd (CC 42)
23 Drommedaris Cr. (CC 42)
24 Devi Rd (CC 42)
25 St Gotha Cl. (CC 42)
26 St Bedes Way (CC 42)
27 Kerner Rd (CC 42)
18°33'00"E
33°56'30"S
Copyright © Map Studio 2007

North ↑

Legend

Bowling Club	Swimming	Water Sports	National Route	Major & Minor Route	Metro Route
Cricket	Tennis	Baseball	Toll Plaza	Retail Area / Industrial Area	National Road / Freeway
Hockey	Golf	Athletics	Traffic Light	Built-up Area / Informal Settlement*	Main Through Route
Rugby	Shooting	Lighthouse	Restricted Access / Entrance	Park / Sports Ground	Other Road with Bridge
Soccer	Polo	Wine Estate	Service Station	Railway with Station	One-way St, Start/End
Squash	Basketball	Wine Sales	Tourist Information	Siding	Nature Trail

* Roads in these areas sometimes untarred

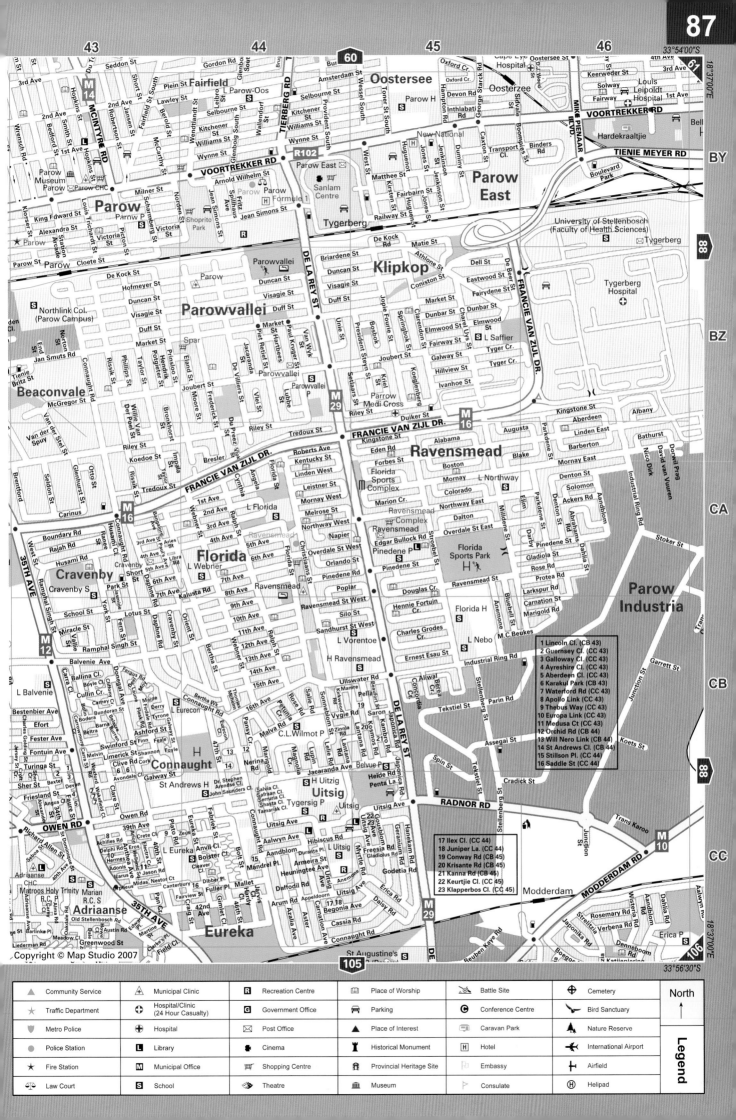

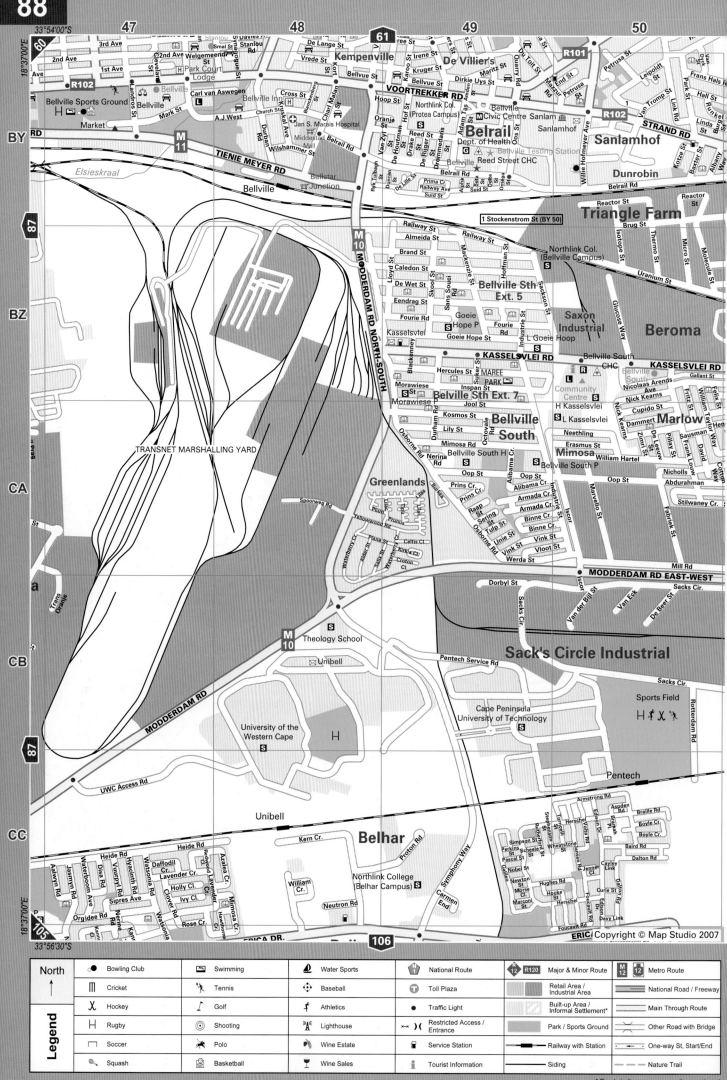

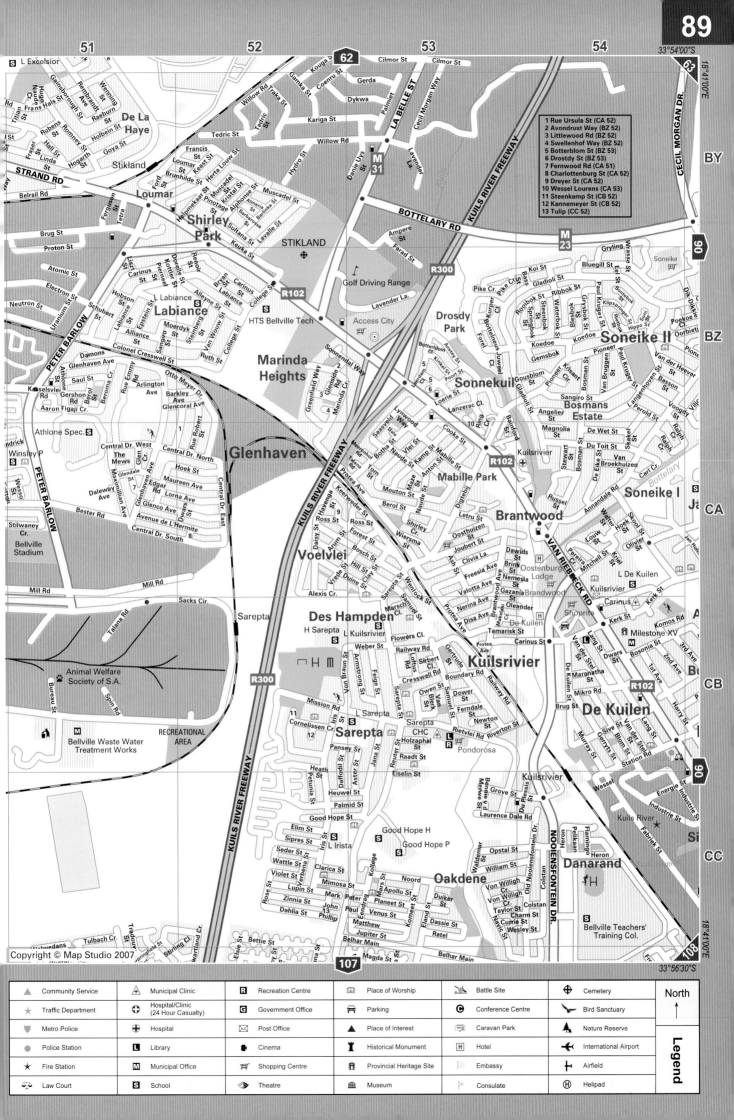

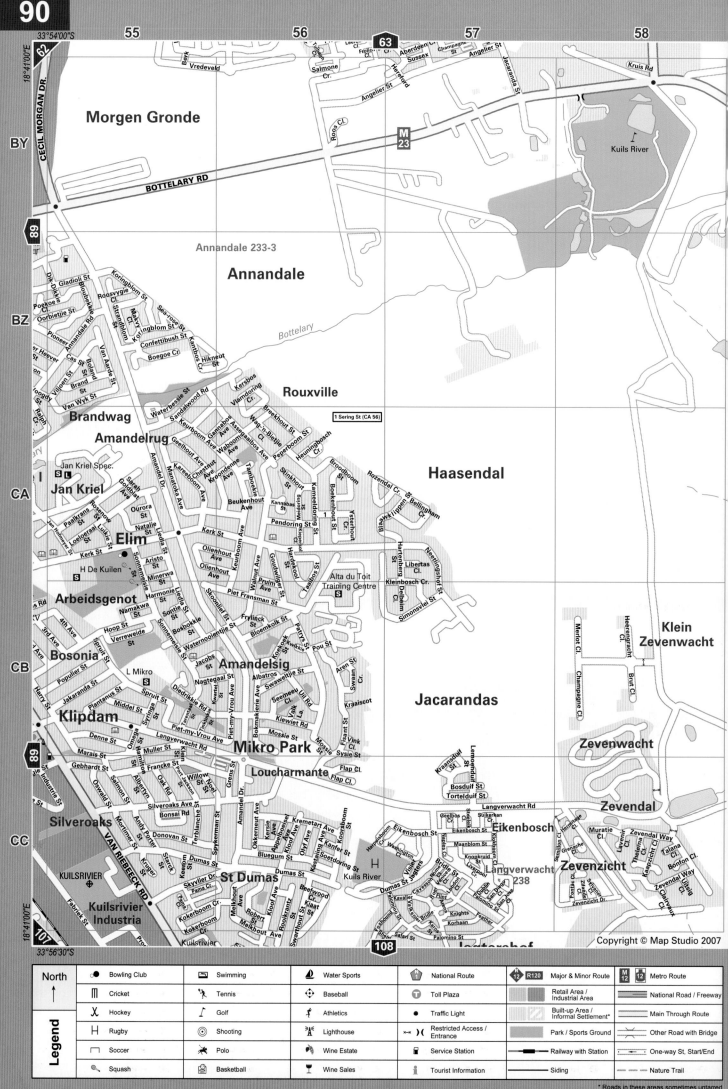

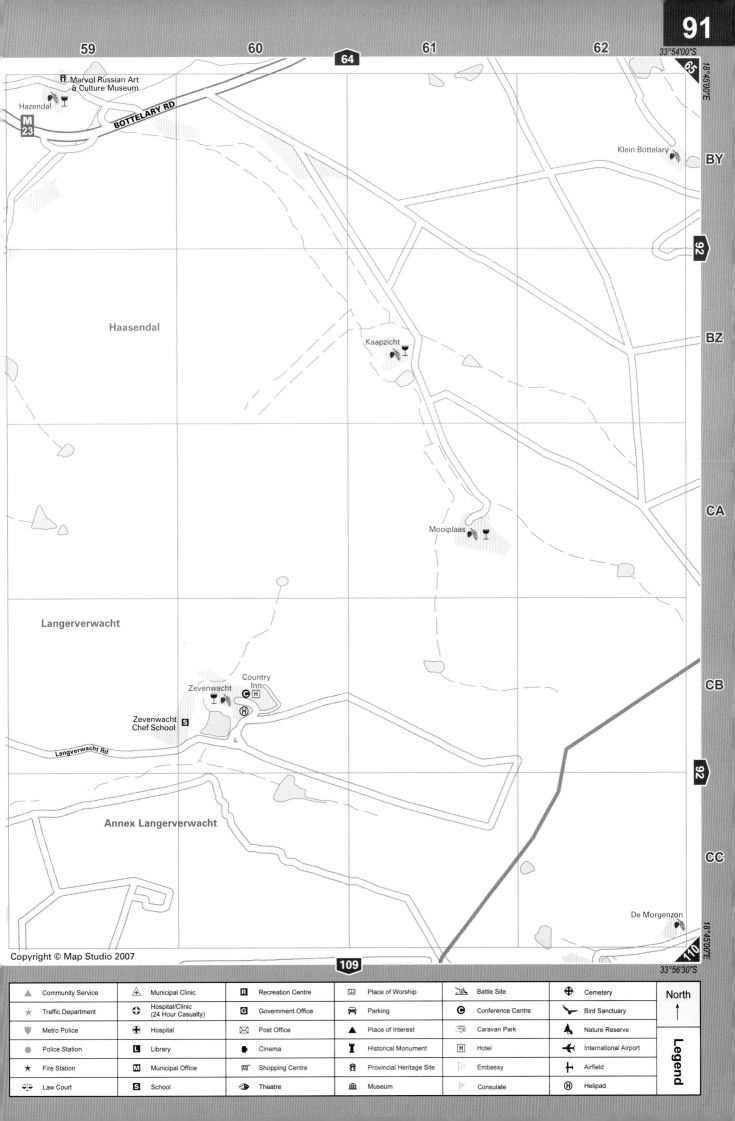

59　60　64　61　62　65

BY

92

BZ

CA

CB

92

CC

18°45'00"E

33°56'30"S

Marvol Russian Art
& Culture Museum

Hazendal

M
23

BOTTELARY RD

Klein Bottelary

Haasendal

Kaapzicht

Mooiplaas

Langerverwacht

Country
Inn

Zevenwacht

Zevenwacht
Chef School

Langverwacht Rd

Annex Langerverwacht

De Morgenzon

109

Symbol	Name	Symbol	Name	Symbol	Name	Symbol	Name	Symbol	Name	Symbol	Name
▲	Community Service	Ⓐ	Municipal Clinic	Ⓡ	Recreation Centre		Place of Worship		Battle Site	⊕	Cemetery
★	Traffic Department	⊕	Hospital/Clinic (24 Hour Casualty)	Ⓖ	Government Office		Parking	Ⓒ	Conference Centre		Bird Sanctuary
▼	Metro Police	✚	Hospital	✉	Post Office	▲	Place of Interest		Caravan Park	▲	Nature Reserve
●	Police Station	Ⓛ	Library		Cinema	♛	Historical Monument	Ⓗ	Hotel		International Airport
★	Fire Station	Ⓜ	Municipal Office		Shopping Centre	🏛	Provincial Heritage Site		Embassy	✈	Airfield
⚖	Law Court	Ⓢ	School		Theatre	🏛	Museum	▷	Consulate	Ⓗ	Helipad

North
↑

Legend

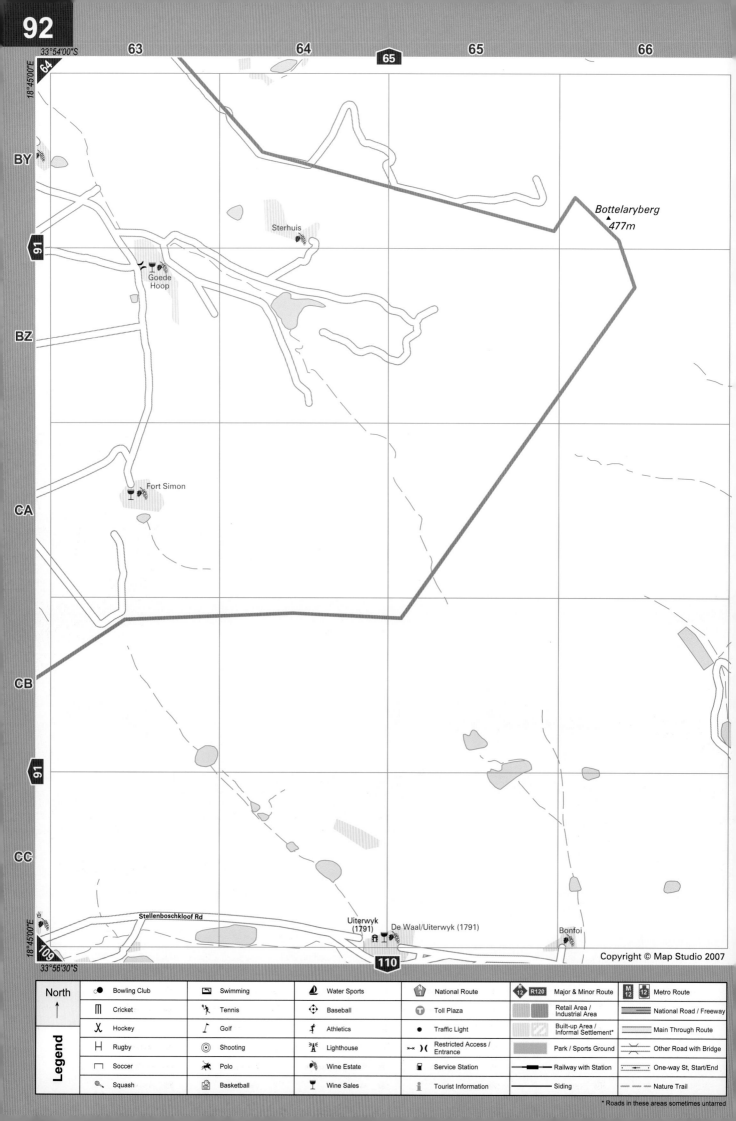

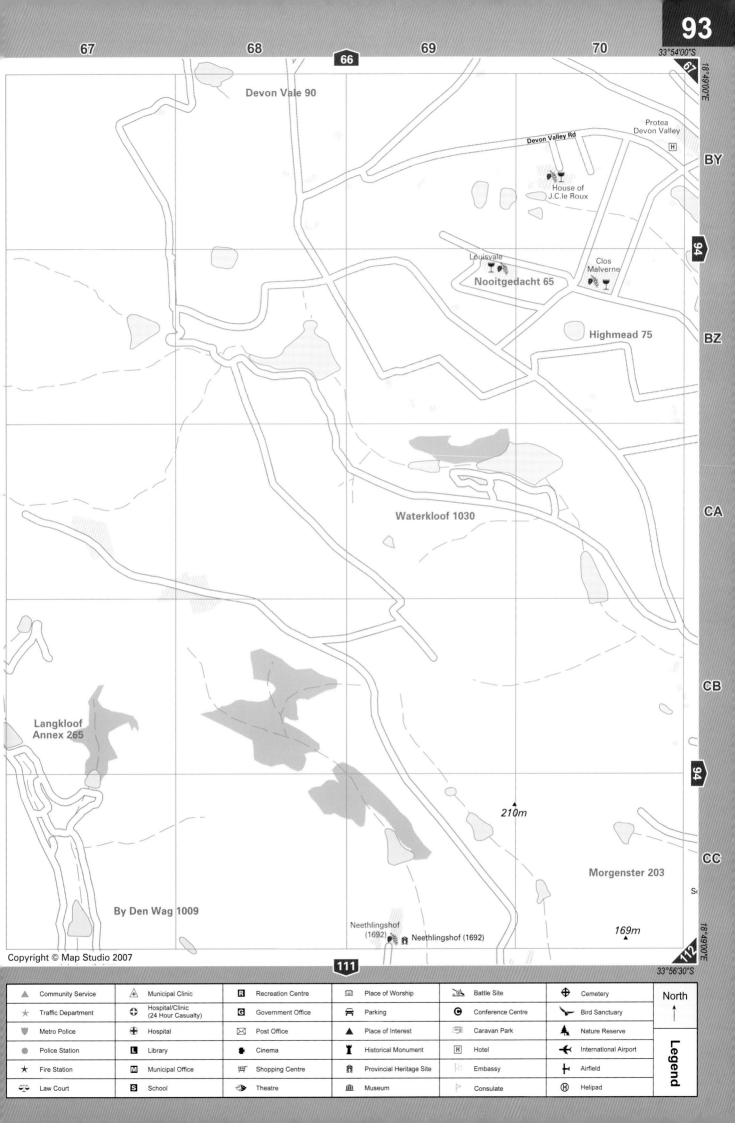

BY

94

BZ

CA

CB

94

CC

Devon Vale 90

Protea
Devon Valley

Devon Valley Rd

House of
J.C.le Roux

Louisvale

Nooitgedacht 65

Clos
Malverne

Highmead 75

Waterkloof 1030

Langkloof
Annex 265

210m

Morgenster 203

By Den Wag 1009

Neethlingshof
(1692)   Neethlingshof (1692)

169m

111

33°56'30"S   18°49'00"E   112

▲ Community Service	Ⓐ Municipal Clinic	Ⓡ Recreation Centre	Place of Worship	Battle Site	⊕ Cemetery	**North** ↑
★ Traffic Department	✚ Hospital/Clinic (24 Hour Casualty)	Ⓖ Government Office	🚗 Parking	Ⓒ Conference Centre	✈ Bird Sanctuary	
Metro Police	✚ Hospital	✉ Post Office	▲ Place of Interest	Caravan Park	♠ Nature Reserve	
● Police Station	Ⓛ Library	Cinema	Historical Monument	Ⓗ Hotel	✈ International Airport	**Legend**
★ Fire Station	Ⓜ Municipal Office	Shopping Centre	Provincial Heritage Site	Embassy	✈ Airfield	
Law Court	Ⓢ School	Theatre	🏛 Museum	Consulate	Ⓗ Helipad	

33°54'00"S

71   72   67   73   74

18°49'00"E   66

BY

Weltevrede

Waterboom

Sports
Fields

93

Devon
Valley

Sylvanvale

Nooitgedacht
Annex 72

▲ 215m

R304

BZ

1 Blinkblaar (BY 74)
2 Waboom (BY 74)
3 Hercules (BY 74)

Hidden Valley

▲ 246m

Luxolo
Luyolo
Cedile
Masithandane
Mengo
Manyano
Kayamandi
Ndumela
Mdala

8th Ave
7th Ave
6th Ave
5th Ave
4th Ave
14th Cl.
Retreat
Forest
School
School

▲ Kayamandi

Kayamandi

CA

Devon Vallei

Papegaaiberg
Industrial Park

Middelvlei

CB

▲ 168m

Flamingo   Kakelaar

Pelikaan

Dagbreek

Loerie

PAPEGAAIBERG

Patrys   Kiewiet

Hamerkop

Pikkewyn

Kleinvallei

Loerie

The Bergkelder

93

Uil

Troupant

Jan Frederick

Kleinvallei

Fisant

Flamingo

Bokmakierie

Bosman's
Crossing

Adelaar

Kokkewiet

Stellekaya

Tarentaal

Jan Pierewiet

Torteltuif

Kanarie

Flamingo

Pistol
Club

CC

Animal Welfare
Society Stellenbosch

Devon Vallei

Kwikstert

Piet-my-Vrou

Jan Fiskaal

Swawel

Tinktinkie

Oude Libertas

Oude Libertas
Distillery

Geological
Reserve

Distillery

ADAM TAS ST

Onderpapegaaiberg

Hoep-Hoep

Devon
Park

Tiptol

Nagtegaal

Santhagen   112   Devonvallei P

Copyright © Map Studio 2007

18°49'00"E   111

33°56'30"S

Legend

North ↑

⊙●	Bowling Club	🏊	Swimming	⛵	Water Sports	🛡	National Route	R120	Major & Minor Route	M12	Metro Route
Ⅲ	Cricket	🎾	Tennis	⬦	Baseball	Ⓣ	Toll Plaza		Retail Area / Industrial Area		National Road / Freeway
X	Hockey	⛳	Golf	🏃	Athletics	●	Traffic Light		Built-up Area / Informal Settlement*		Main Through Route
H	Rugby	◎	Shooting	⋝ᴇ	Lighthouse	⤫)(	Restricted Access / Entrance		Park / Sports Ground		Other Road with Bridge
▱	Soccer	🐎	Polo	🍷	Wine Estate	ⓢ	Service Station		Railway with Station		One-way St, Start/End
🔍	Squash	🏀	Basketball	🍷	Wine Sales	ℹ	Tourist Information		Siding		Nature Trail

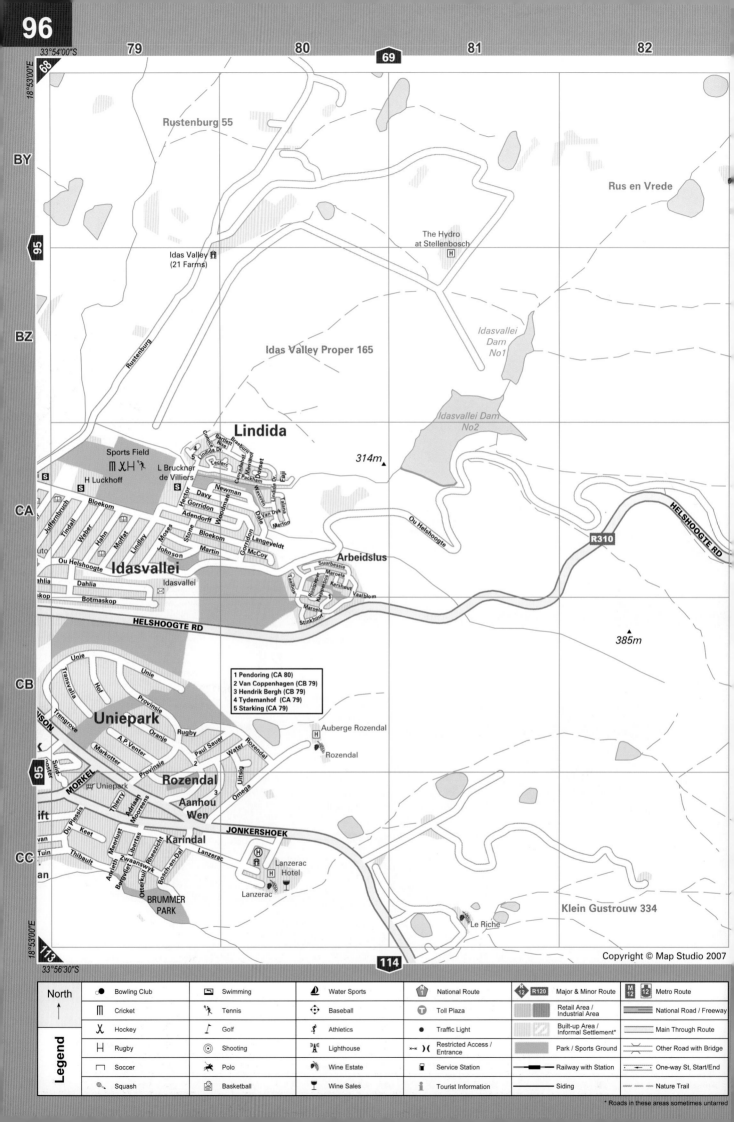

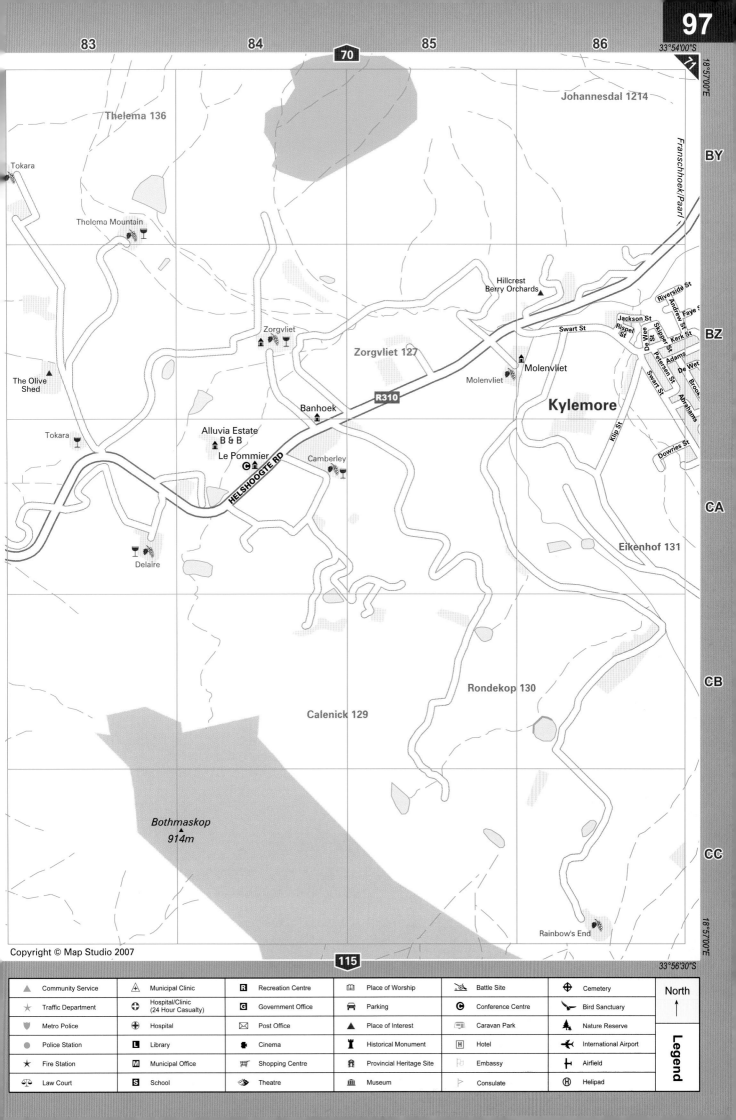

83 84 70 85 86 71

18°57'00"E

Johannesdal 1214

Thelema 136

Tokara

Thelema Mountain

BY

Hillcrest
Berry Orchards

Riverside St
Andrew St
Faye St
Jackson St
Rispel St
De Wee St
Skipper St
Kerk St

Zorgvliet

Zorgvliet 127

Molenvliet
Molenvliet

Petersen St
De Wet St
Swart St
Abrahams
Brook

BZ

The Olive
Shed

R310

Swart St

Kylemore

Banhoek

Tokara

Alluvia Estate
B & B
Le Pommier

Camberley

HELSHOOGTE RD

Dowries St
Klip St

CA

Eikenhof 131

Delaire

CB

Rondekop 130

Calenick 129

Bothmaskop
914m

CC

Rainbow's End

18°57'00"E
33°56'30"S

115

Legend

▲	Community Service	Ⓐ	Municipal Clinic	Ⓡ	Recreation Centre		Place of Worship		Battle Site	⊕	Cemetery
★	Traffic Department	⊕	Hospital/Clinic (24 Hour Casualty)	Ⓖ	Government Office	🚗	Parking	Ⓒ	Conference Centre		Bird Sanctuary
▼	Metro Police	⊕	Hospital	✉	Post Office	▲	Place of Interest		Caravan Park	♠	Nature Reserve
●	Police Station	Ⓛ	Library		Cinema	🎻	Historical Monument	Ⓗ	Hotel	✈	International Airport
★	Fire Station	Ⓜ	Municipal Office		Shopping Centre		Provincial Heritage Site		Embassy		Airfield
⚖	Law Court	Ⓢ	School		Theatre	🏛	Museum	▷	Consulate	Ⓗ	Helipad

North
↑

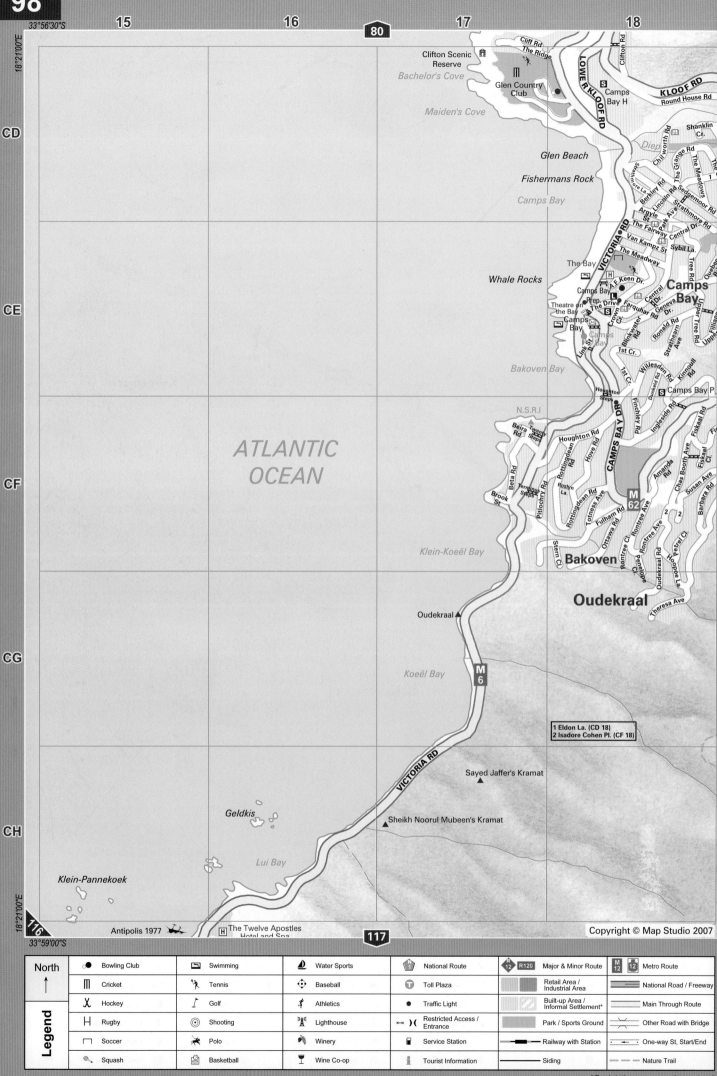

ATLANTIC
OCEAN

Clifton Scenic
Reserve
Bachelor's Cove

Glen Country
Club

Maiden's Cove

Glen Beach

Fishermans Rock

Camps Bay

Whale Rocks

Camps
Bay

Bakoven Bay

N.S.R.I

Klein-Koeël Bay

Bakoven

Oudekraal

Oudekraal ▲

Koeël Bay

1 Eldon La. (CD 18)
2 Isadore Cohen Pl. (CF 18)

VICTORIA RD

Sayed Jaffer's Kramat ▲

Geldkis

Sheikh Noorul Mubeen's Kramat ▲

Klein-Pannekoek

Lui Bay

Antipolis 1977

The Twelve Apostles
Hotel and Spa

Copyright © Map Studio 2007

33°56'30"S
18°21'00"E
18°21'00"E
33°59'00"S

15   16   17   18
CD
CE
CF
CG
CH

80   116   117

North ↑	Legend	
● Bowling Club	▭ Swimming	⛵ Water Sports
Ⅲ Cricket	🏃 Tennis	◈ Baseball
Ⅹ Hockey	Ⲋ Golf	🏃 Athletics
H Rugby	◉ Shooting	⚓ Lighthouse
▭ Soccer	🐎 Polo	🍷 Winery
◠ Squash	🏢 Basketball	🍷 Wine Co-op

🏛 National Route	
Ⓣ Toll Plaza	
● Traffic Light	
×—× Restricted Access / Entrance	
🏪 Service Station	
ℹ Tourist Information	

12 R120 Major & Minor Route	M12 12 Metro Route
Retail Area / Industrial Area	National Road / Freeway
Built-up Area / Informal Settlement*	Main Through Route
Park / Sports Ground	Other Road with Bridge
Railway with Station	One-way St, Start/End
Siding	Nature Trail

* Roads in these areas sometimes untarred

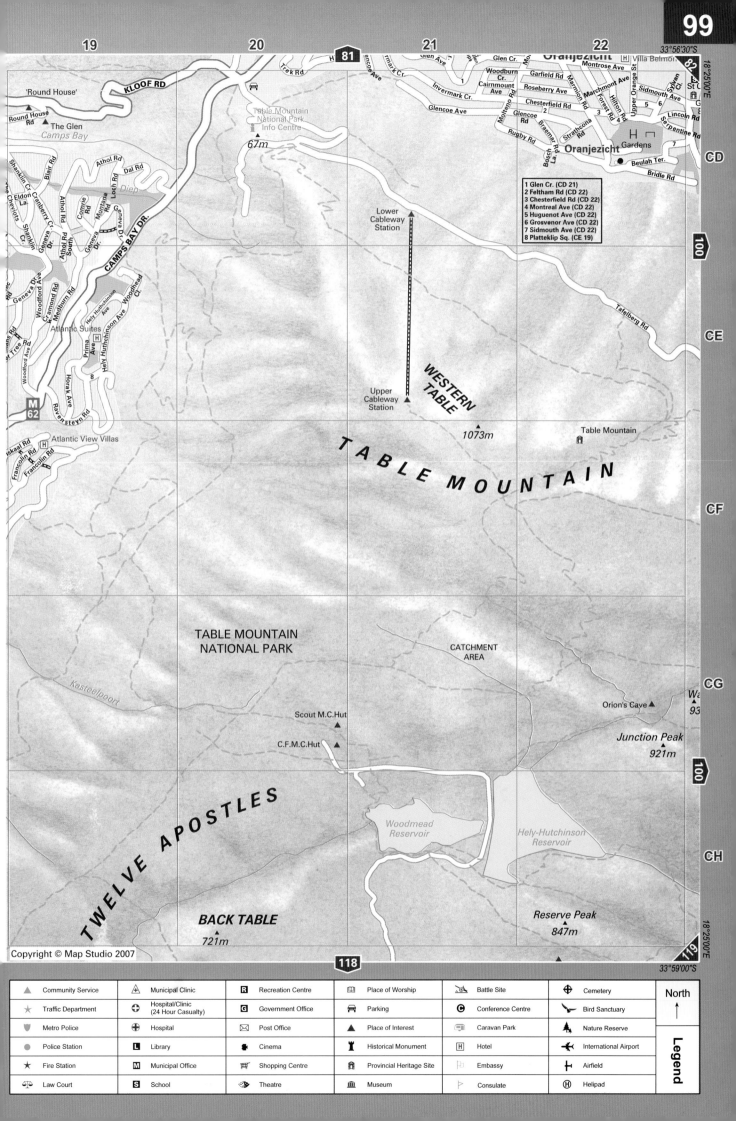

19 20 81 21 22 33°56'30"S 18°25'00"E

KLOOF RD

'Round House'
Round House Rd
The Glen
Camps Bay
Trek Rd
Table Mountain National Park Info Centre
67m

Shanklin Cr.
Blair Rd
Athol Rd
Comrie Rd
Montana Rd
Geneva Dr.
Dal Rd
Loch Rd
Athol Rd
Eldon La.
Cranberry Cr.
The Cheviots
Shanklin Cr.
Geneva Dr.
Geneva Ave
Woodford Rd
Medburn Rd
Cramond Rd
Hely Huthchinson
Hely Huthchinson Ave
Woodhead Cl.
CAMPS BAY DR.
Atlantic Suites
Prima Ave
Horak Ave
Ravensteyn Rd
M 62
Skaal Rd
Atlantic View Villas
Francolin Rd
Francolin Rd
Tree Tree Rd
Woodford Ave

Oranjezicht
Glen Cr.
Glen Ave
Montrose Ave
Villa Belmont
Invermark Cr.
Woodburn Cr.
Garfield Rd
Cairnmount Ave
Marmion Rd
Sidmouth Ave
Glencoe Ave
Moteno Rd
Roseberry Ave
Chesterfield Rd
Marchmont Rd
Forest Rd
Upper Orange St
Sylvan Rd
Lincoln Rd
Hilton Rd
5
Glencoe Rd
Strathcona Rd
Braemar Rd
Rugby Ave
Bosch Ave
Oranjezicht
Gardens
Serpentine Rd
4
7
Beulah Ter.
Bridle Rd

1 Glen Cr. (CD 21)
2 Feltham Rd (CD 22)
3 Chesterfield Rd (CD 22)
4 Montreal Ave (CD 22)
5 Huguenot Ave (CD 22)
6 Grosvenor Ave (CD 22)
7 Sidmouth Ave (CD 22)
8 Platteklip Sq. (CE 19)

Lower Cableway Station

WESTERN TABLE

Upper Cableway Station

1073m

Table Mountain

T A B L E   M O U N T A I N

TABLE MOUNTAIN NATIONAL PARK

CATCHMENT AREA

Kasteelpoort

Scout M.C.Hut
C.F.M.C.Hut

Orion's Cave
Wa 93

Junction Peak
921m

T W E L V E   A P O S T L E S

Woodmead Reservoir

Hely-Hutchinson Reservoir

BACK TABLE
721m

Reserve Peak
847m

CD
100
CE
CF
CG
100
CH
119
18°25'00"E
33°59'00"S

Copyright © Map Studio 2007

118

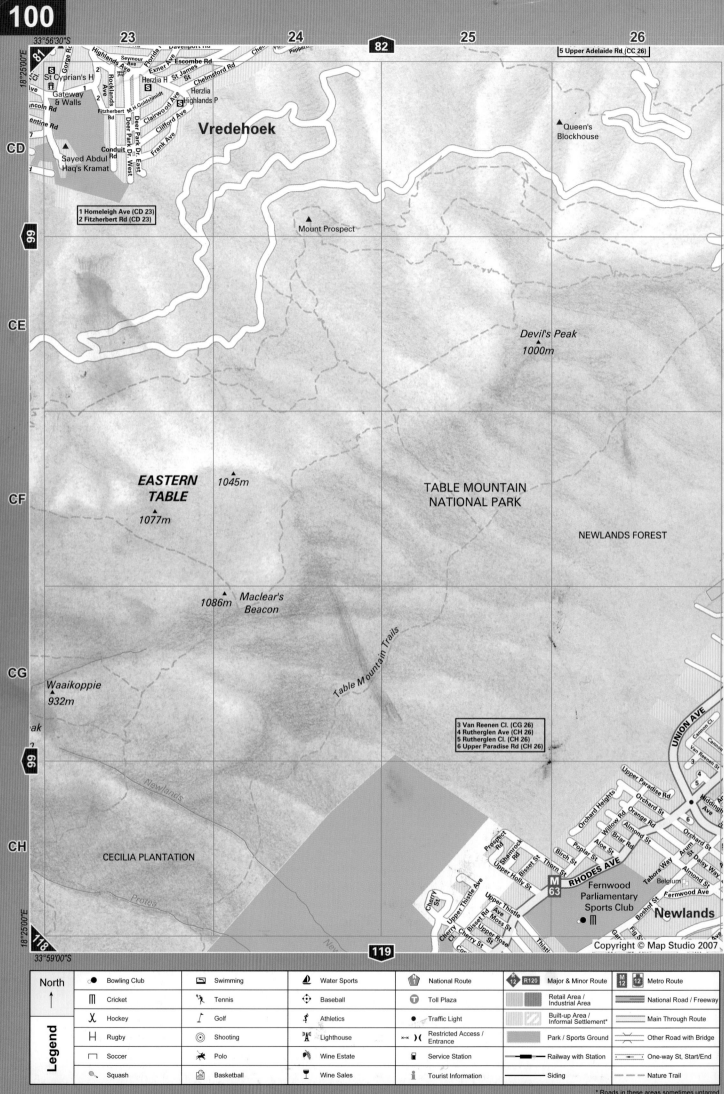

33°56'30"S
18°25'00"E

81

99

CD

CE

CF

CG

CH

5 Upper Adelaide Rd (CC 26)

St Cyprian's H
Gateway & Walls
Highlands Ave
Seymour Ave
Florida Rd
Davenport Rd
Escombe Rd
Exner St
St James St
Chelmsford Rd
Herzlia H
M H Goldschmidt
Clairwood Ave
Herzlia Highlands P
Rocklands Ave
Clifford Ave
Fitzherbert Rd
Deer Park Dr East
Deer Park Dr West
Frank Ave
Conduit Rd
Lincoln Rd
entine Rd

Vredehoek

Sayed Abdul Haq's Kramat

▲ Queen's Blockhouse

1 Homeleigh Ave (CD 23)
2 Fitzherbert Rd (CD 23)

▲ Mount Prospect

Devil's Peak
1000m

▲ 1045m

EASTERN TABLE
▲ 1077m

TABLE MOUNTAIN NATIONAL PARK

NEWLANDS FOREST

▲ 1086m Maclear's Beacon

Table Mountain Trails

Waaikoppie
932m

3 Van Reenen Cl. (CG 26)
4 Rutherglen Ave (CH 26)
5 Rutherglen Cl. (CH 26)
6 Upper Paradise Rd (CH 26)

66

Newlands

UNION AVE
Van Reenen St
Cannon Cl
Upper Paradise Rd
Orchard St
Orchard Heights
Orchard Rd
Willow Rd
Orange Rd
Almond St
iddingh Ave
Orchard St
Almond St
Prospect Rd
Shamrock Rd
Upper Holly Rd
Bisset St
Birch St
Thorn St
Poplar St
Aloe St
Briar Rd
Tabora Way
Arum St
Daisy Way
Belgium
Fernwood Ave
Boshof St

CECILIA PLANTATION

Protea

M 63 **RHODES AVE**

Fernwood Parliamentary Sports Club

Newlands

Cherry St
Upper Thistle Ave
Upper Thistle Ave
Bisset Rd
Moss St
Upper Rose St
Cherry Cl
Cherry St
Thistle
Figs

118
33°59'00"S
18°25'00"E

119

Copyright © Map Studio 2007

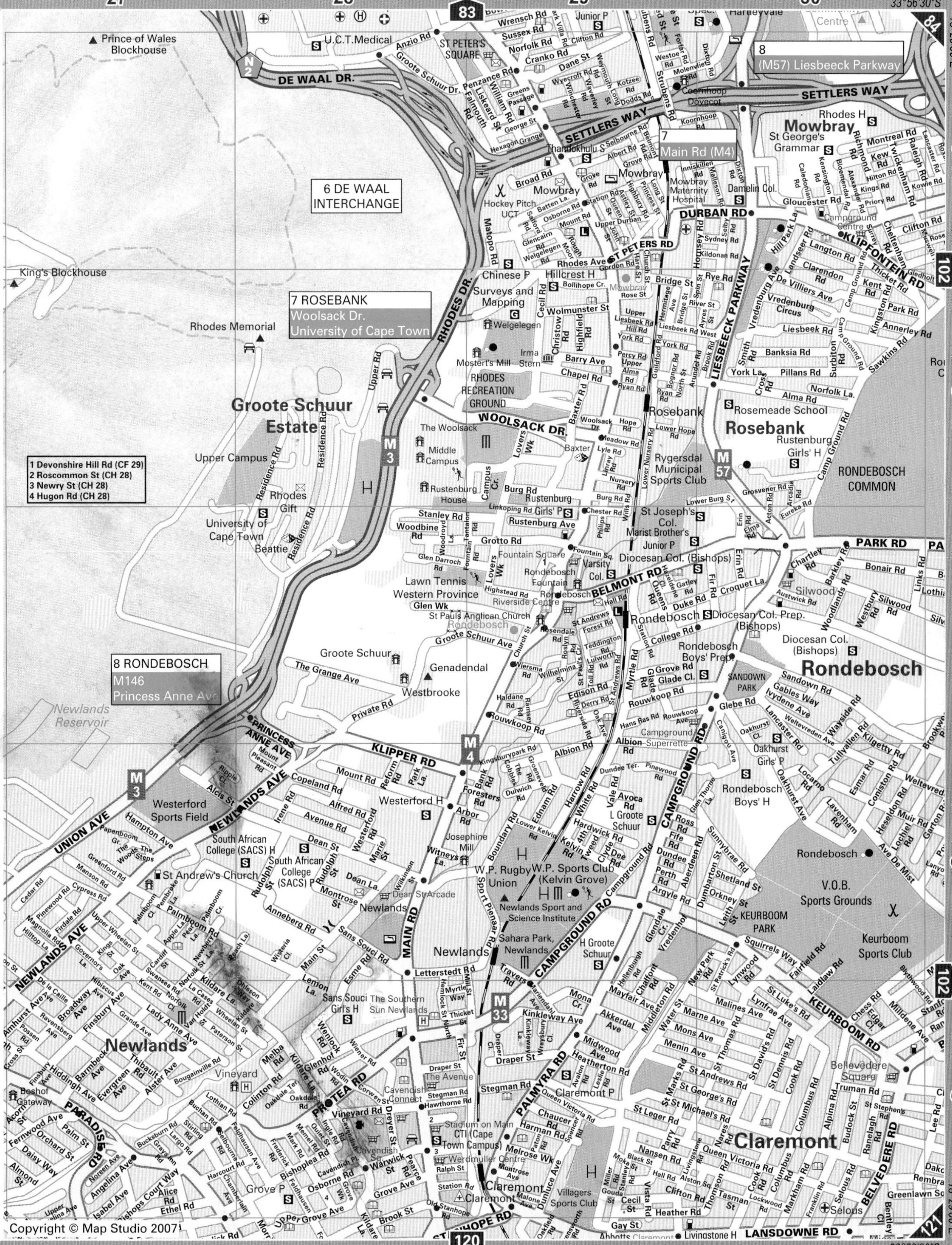

27 28 83 29 30 84

33°56'30"S
18°29'00"E

Map labels

Prince of Wales Blockhouse
U.C.T. Medical
ST PETER'S SQUARE
DE WAAL DR.
N2
8 (M57) Liesbeeck Parkway
SETTLERS WAY
Mowbray
Rhodes H
St George's Grammar
7 Main Rd (M4)
Mowbray Maternity Hospital
Mowbray
DURBAN RD
KLIPFONTEIN RD
102
6 DE WAAL INTERCHANGE
King's Blockhouse
Rhodes Memorial
7 ROSEBANK
Woolsack Dr.
University of Cape Town
RHODES DR.
Surveys and Mapping
Mostert's Mill
RHODES RECREATION GROUND
Rosebank
Rosebank
Rosemeade School
Rustenburg Girls' H
CE
Groote Schuur Estate
WOOLSACK DR.
The Woolsack
Middle Campus
Rustenburg House
RONDEBOSCH COMMON
Upper Campus
1 Devonshire Hill Rd (CF 29)
2 Roscommon St (CH 28)
3 Newry St (CH 28)
4 Hugon Rd (CH 28)
Rhodes Gift
University of Cape Town
Beattie
Lawn Tennis Western Province
Rondebosch Fountain
St Pauls Anglican Church
Rondebosch
BELMONT RD
Diocesan Col. (Bishops)
St Joseph's Col.
Marist Brother's Junior P
Rygersdal Municipal Sports Club
M57
PARK RD
Rondebosch Boys' Prep
Diocesan Col. Prep. (Bishops)
CF
Diocesan Col. (Bishops)
Rondebosch
8 RONDEBOSCH
M146
Princess Anne Ave
Groote Schuur
Westbrooke
Genadendal
The Grange Ave
Groote Schuur Ave
Sandown Park
Gables Way
Iydene Ave
KLIPPER RD
M4
Rouwkoop Rd
Rondebosch Boys' H
Oakhurst Girls' P
Oakhurst
Newlands Reservoir
Newlands Ave
PRINCESS ANNE AVE
M3
Westerford Sports Field
Westerford H
CAMPGROUND RD
V.O.B. Sports Grounds
Rondebosch
CG
UNION AVE
Hampton Ave
South African College (SACS) H
South African College (SACS)
W.P. Rugby Union
W.P. Sports Club (Kelvin Grove)
Newlands Sport and Science Institute
Keurboom Park
Keurboom Sports Club
NEWLANDS AVE
MAIN RD
Newlands
Sahara Park, Newlands
Groote Schuur
102
KEURBOOM RD
Newlands
M33
Letterstedt Rd
The Southern Sun Newlands
Sans Souci Girls' H
Vineyard
PARADISE RD
PROTEA RD
The Avenue
CTI (Cape Town Campus)
Werdmuller Centre
Cavendish Connect
PALMYRA RD
Claremont
CH
Boshof Gateway
Newlands
Vineyard
Cavendish
Stadium on Main
Villagers Sports Club
Claremont
120
LANSDOWNE RD
121
BELVEDERE RD
33°59'00"S
18°29'00"E

Copyright © Map Studio 2007

Legend

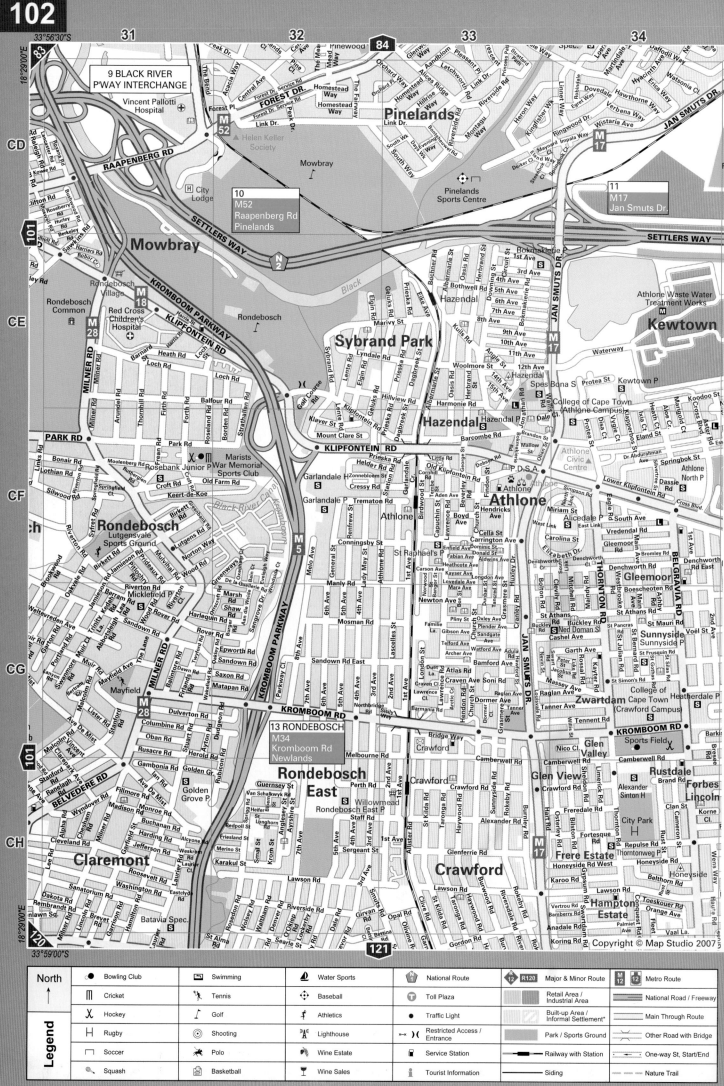

Map Studio 2007 – Page 102. Cape Town area map showing Pinelands, Mowbray, Rondebosch, Sybrand Park, Hazendal, Kewtown, Athlone, Gleemoor, Rondebosch East, Crawford, Claremont, Frere Estate, Forbes Lincoln, Hampton Estate and surrounding suburbs.

Legend

North ↑

Bowling Club	Swimming	Water Sports
Cricket	Tennis	Baseball
Hockey	Golf	Athletics
Rugby	Shooting	Lighthouse
Soccer	Polo	Wine Estate
Squash	Basketball	Wine Sales

National Route	Major & Minor Route
Toll Plaza	Metro Route
Traffic Light	Retail Area / Industrial Area
Lighthouse	Built-up Area / Informal Settlement*
Restricted Access / Entrance	Park / Sports Ground
Service Station	National Road / Freeway
Railway with Station	Main Through Route
Siding	Other Road with Bridge
Tourist Information	One-way St, Start/End
	Nature Trail

* Roads in these areas sometimes untarred

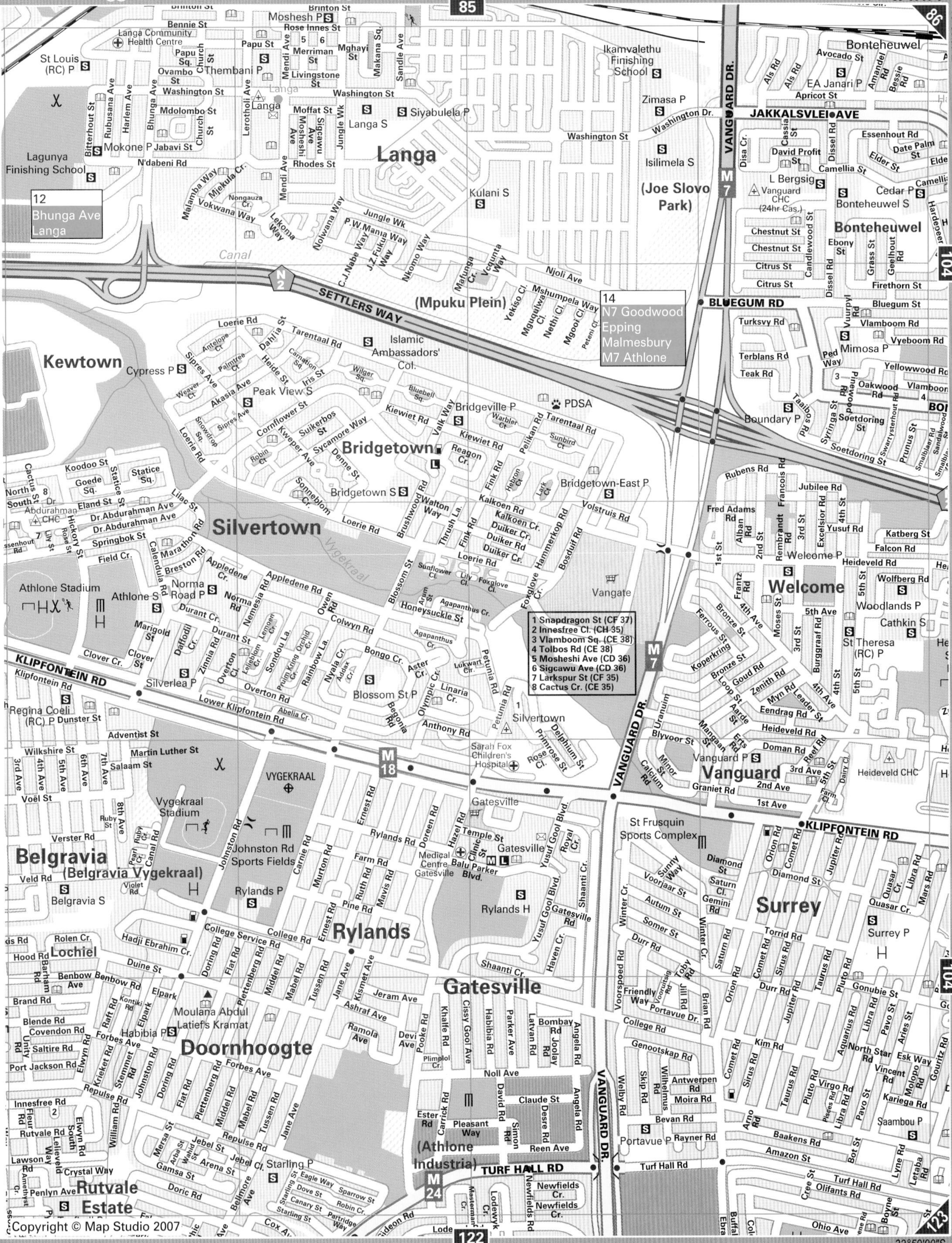

35 **36** **37** **38**

33°56'30"S
18°33'00"E
18°33'00"E
33°59'00"S

CD
CE
CF
CG
CH

104
103

Place names

Langa
(Joe Slovo Park)
Jakkalsvlei Ave
Bonteheuwel
Bonteheuwel S
Bluegum Rd
Kewtown
Bridgetown
Silvertown
Athlone Stadium
Vangate
Welcome
Vanguard
Surrey
Belgravia
(Belgravia Vygekraal)
Vygekraal
Rylands
Gatesville
Lochiel
Doornhoogte
(Athlone Industria)
Rutvale Estate
Klipfontein Rd
Settlers Way
Turf Hall Rd

12
Bhunga Ave
Langa

14
N7 Goodwood
Epping
Malmesbury
M7 Athlone

1 Snapdragon St (CF 37)
2 Innesfree Cl. (CH 35)
3 Vlamboom Sq. (CE 38)
4 Tolbos Rd (CE 38)
5 Mosheshi Ave (CD 36)
6 Sigcawu Ave (CD 36)
7 Larkspur St (CF 35)
8 Cactus Cr. (CE 35)

Legend

Symbol	Description	Symbol	Description	Symbol	Description
▲	Community Service	Ⓐ	Municipal Clinic	R	Recreation Centre
★	Traffic Department	✚	Hospital/Clinic (24 Hour Casualty)	G	Government Office
	Metro Police	✚	Hospital	✉	Post Office
●	Police Station	L	Library		Cinema
★	Fire Station	M	Municipal Office		Shopping Centre
	Law Court	S	School		Theatre
	Place of Worship		Battle Site	✚	Cemetery
	Parking	Ⓒ	Conference Centre		Bird Sanctuary
▲	Place of Interest		Caravan Park		Nature Reserve
	Historical Monument	H	Hotel	✈	International Airport
	Provincial Heritage Site		Embassy	✈	Airfield
🏛	Museum		Consulate	Ⓗ	Helipad

North ↑

Legend

Copyright © Map Studio 2007

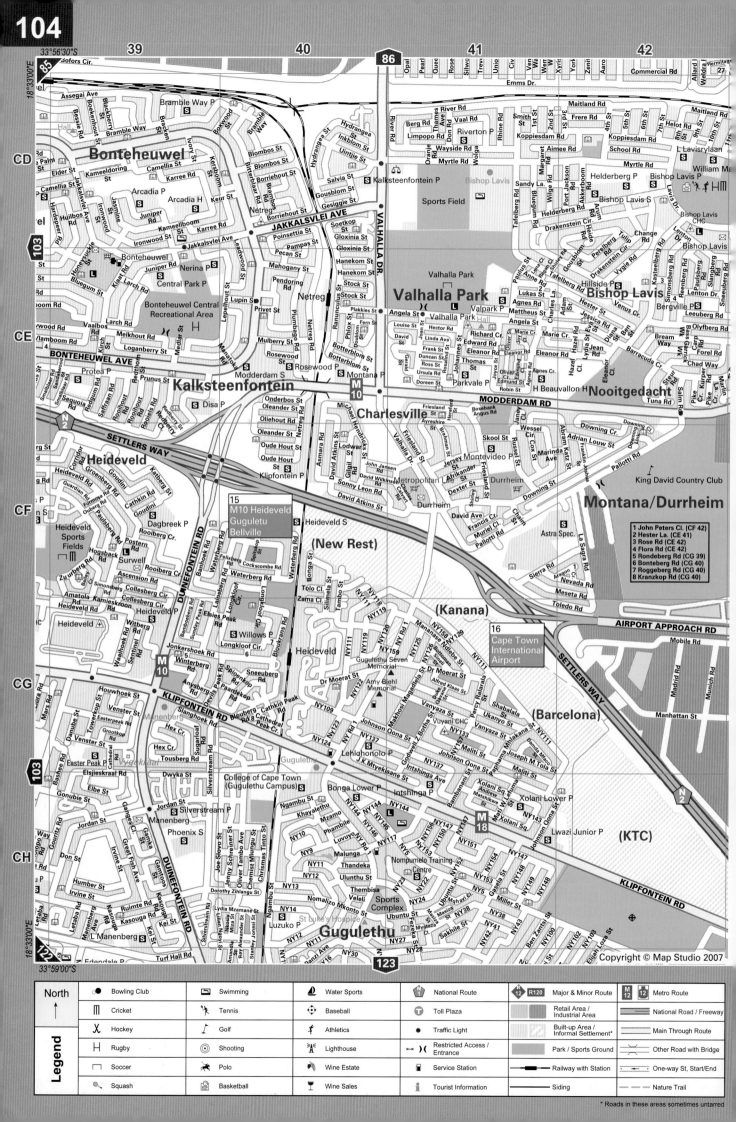

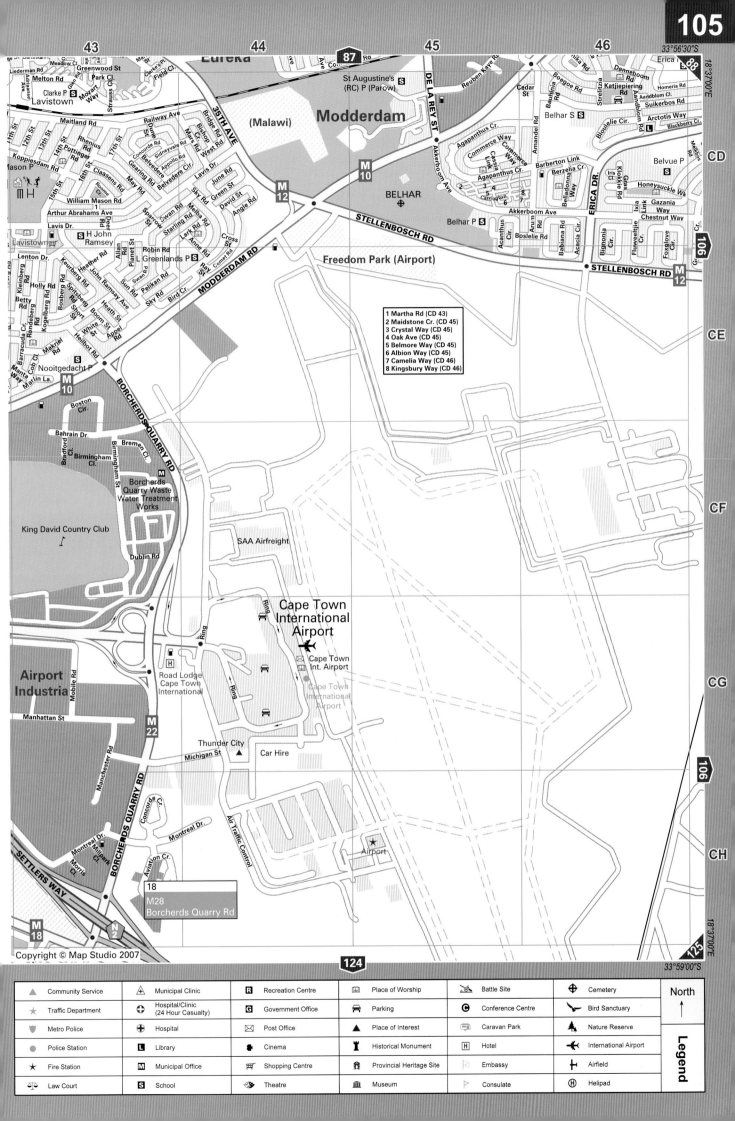

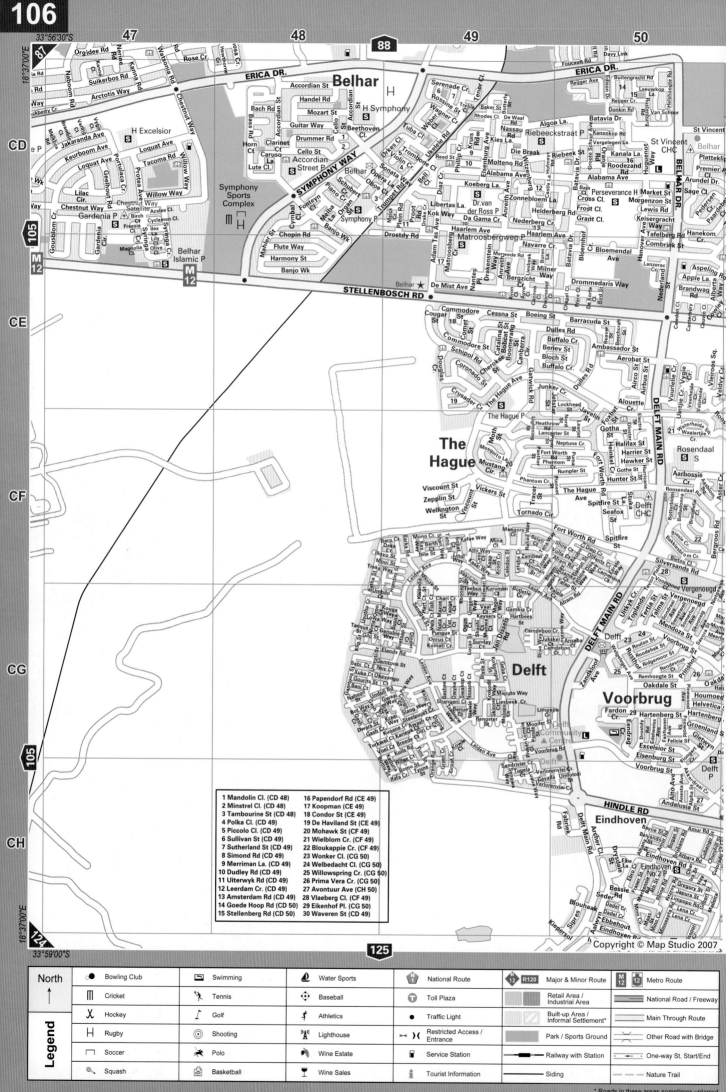

Grid references:
- 33°56'30"S · 18°37'00"E (top)
- 33°59'00"S · 18°37'00"E (bottom)
- Columns: 47, 48, 49, 50
- Rows: CD, CE, CF, CG, CH
- Route markers: 87, 88, 124, 125, 105, M12

Place names: Belhar, Symphony Sports Complex, The Hague, Delft, Voorbrug, Eindhoven, Rosendaal

Street index

1 Mandolin Cl. (CD 48)
2 Minstrel Cl. (CD 48)
3 Tambourine St (CD 48)
4 Polka Cl. (CD 49)
5 Piccolo Cl. (CD 49)
6 Sullivan St (CD 49)
7 Sutherland St (CD 49)
8 Simond Rd (CD 49)
9 Merriman La. (CD 49)
10 Dudley Rd (CD 49)
11 Uiterwyk Rd (CD 49)
12 Leerdam Cr. (CD 49)
13 Amsterdam Rd (CD 49)
14 Goede Hoop Rd (CD 50)
15 Stellenberg Rd (CD 50)
16 Papendorf Rd (CE 49)
17 Koopman (CE 49)
18 Condor St (CE 49)
19 De Haviland St (CE 49)
20 Mohawk St (CF 49)
21 Wielblom Cr. (CF 49)
22 Bloukappie Cr. (CF 49)
23 Wonker Cl. (CG 50)
24 Welbedacht Cl. (CG 50)
25 Willowspring Cr. (CG 50)
26 Prima Vera Cr. (CG 50)
27 Avontuur Ave (CH 50)
28 Vlaeberg Cl. (CF 50)
29 Eikenhof Pl. (CG 50)
30 Waveren St (CD 49)

Legend

North ↑

Bowling Club	
Cricket	
Hockey	
Rugby	
Soccer	
Squash	
Swimming	
Tennis	
Golf	
Shooting	
Polo	
Basketball	
Water Sports	
Baseball	
Athletics	
Lighthouse	
Wine Estate	
Wine Sales	
National Route	
Toll Plaza	
Traffic Light	
Restricted Access / Entrance	
Service Station	
Tourist Information	
Major & Minor Route	
Retail Area / Industrial Area	
Built-up Area / Informal Settlement*	
Park / Sports Ground	
Railway with Station	
Siding	
Metro Route	
National Road / Freeway	
Main Through Route	
Other Road with Bridge	
One-way St, Start/End	
Nature Trail	

* Roads in these areas sometimes untarred

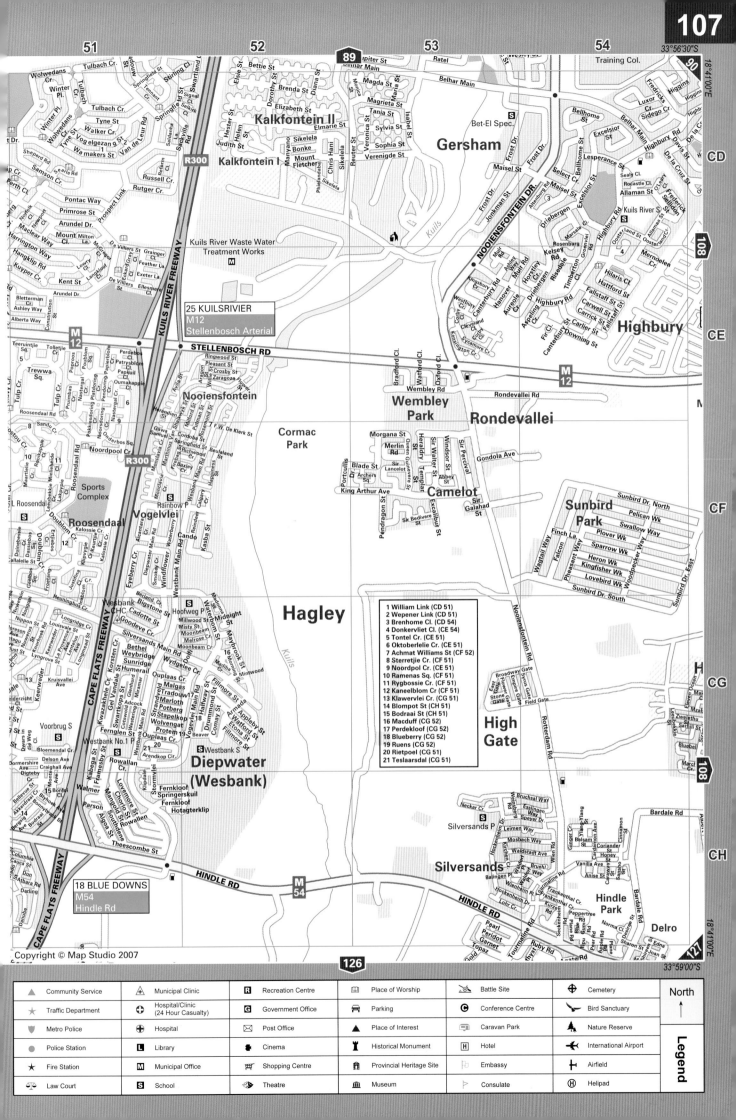

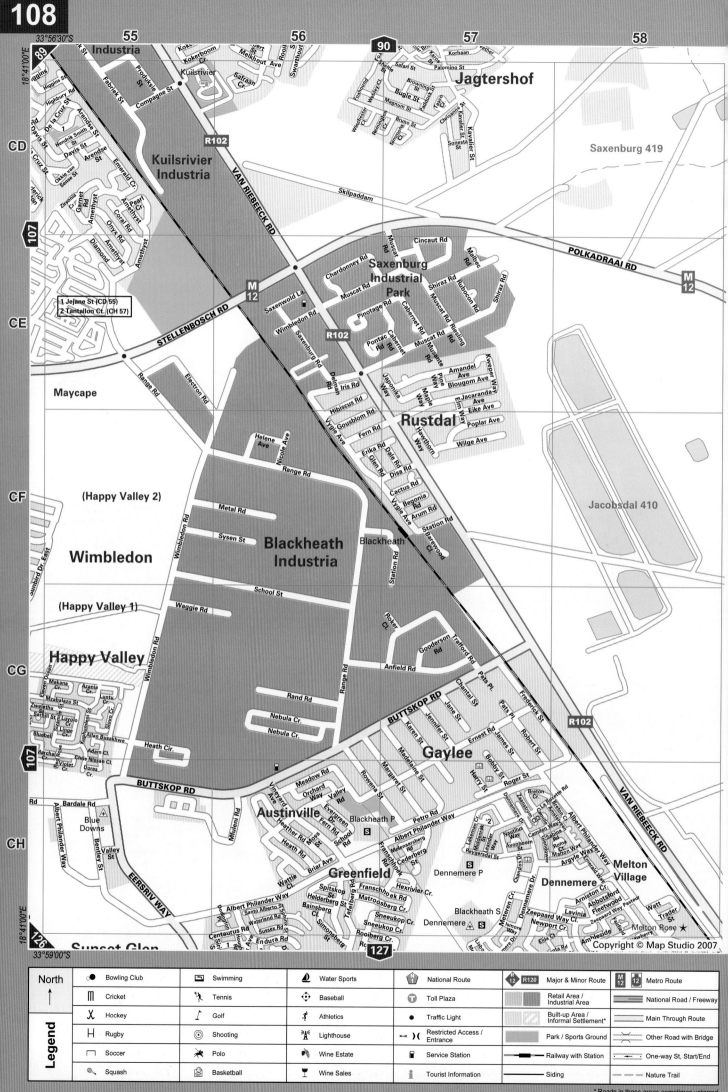

33°56'30"S

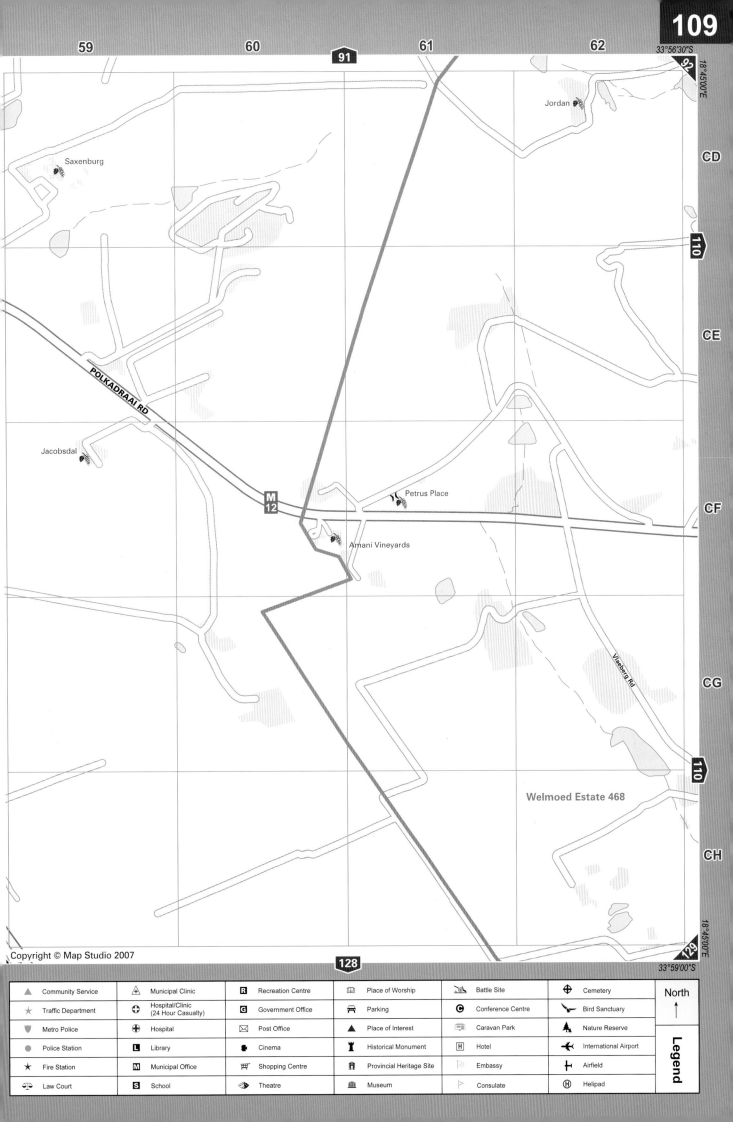

18°45'00"E

18°45'00"E

91

92

110

110

128

CD

CE

CF

CG

CH

Jordan

Saxenburg

POLKADRAAI RD

Jacobsdal

M12

Petrus Place

Amani Vineyards

Vlaeberg Rd

Welmoed Estate 468

Copyright © Map Studio 2007

128

33°59'00"S

▲ Community Service	⚕ Municipal Clinic	R Recreation Centre	⛪ Place of Worship	⚔ Battle Site	✠ Cemetery	**North** ↑
★ Traffic Department	✚ Hospital/Clinic (24 Hour Casualty)	G Government Office	🚗 Parking	C Conference Centre	🦅 Bird Sanctuary	
⛨ Metro Police	✚ Hospital	✉ Post Office	▲ Place of Interest	🚐 Caravan Park	🌲 Nature Reserve	
● Police Station	L Library	♣ Cinema	⚱ Historical Monument	H Hotel	✈ International Airport	**Legend**
★ Fire Station	M Municipal Office	🛒 Shopping Centre	🏛 Provincial Heritage Site	Embassy	✛ Airfield	
⚖ Law Court	S School	Theatre	🏛 Museum	▷ Consulate	Ⓗ Helipad	

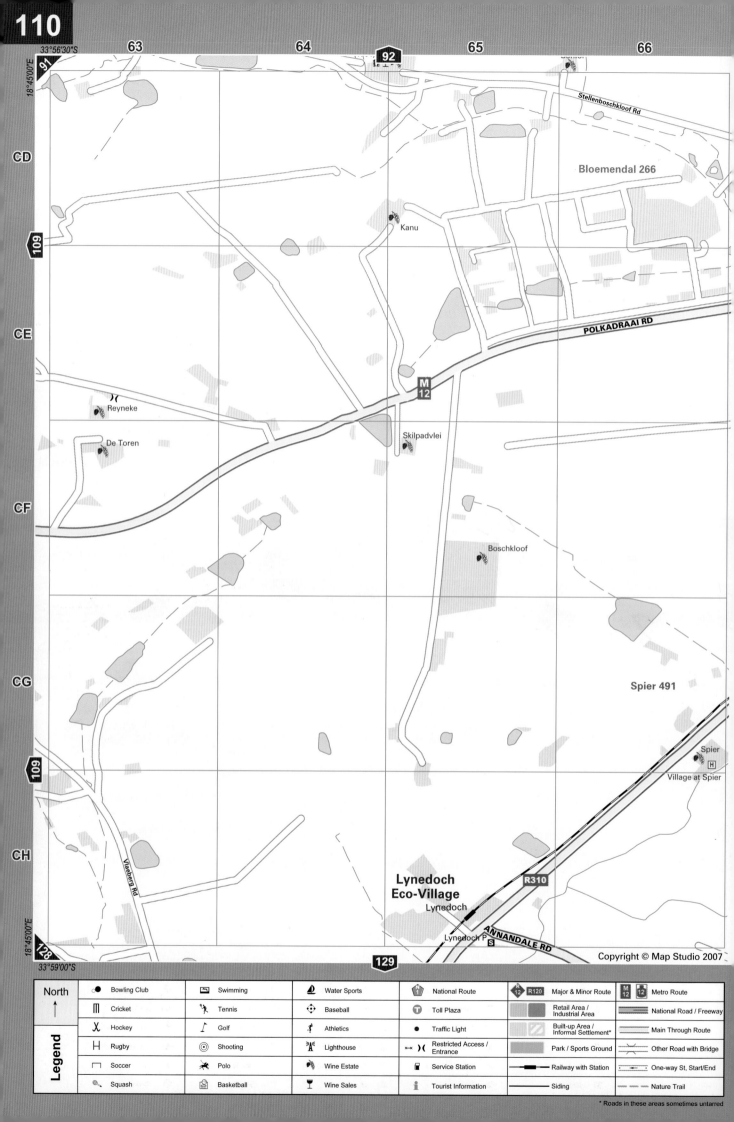

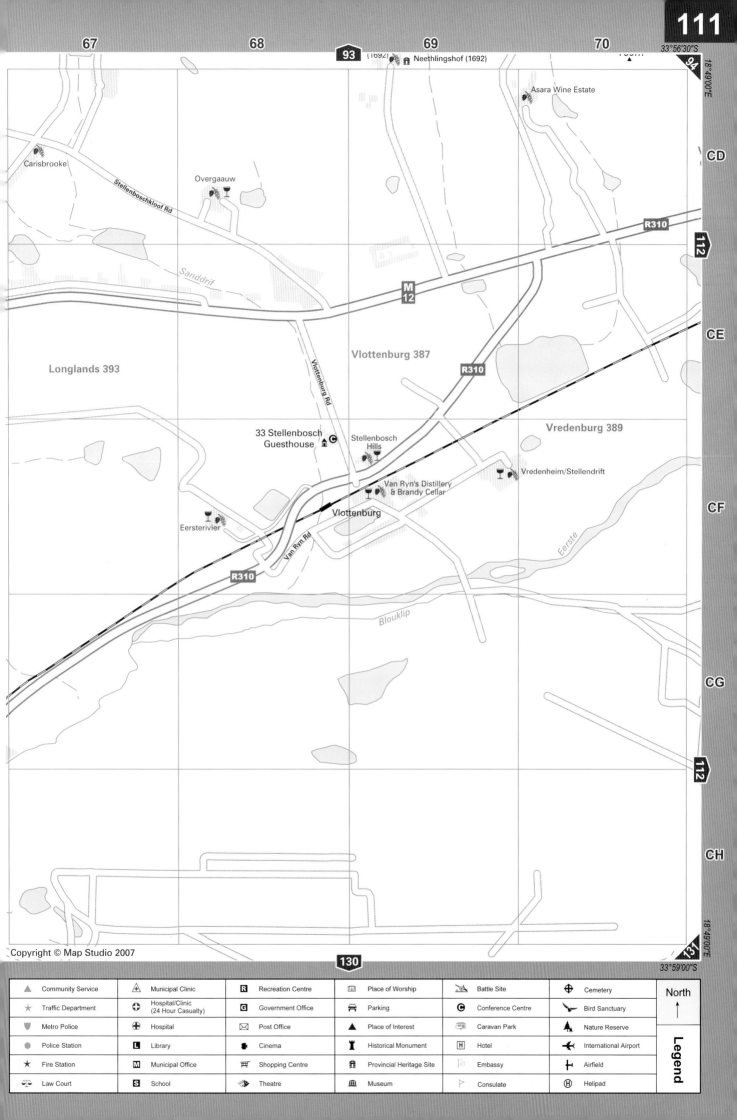

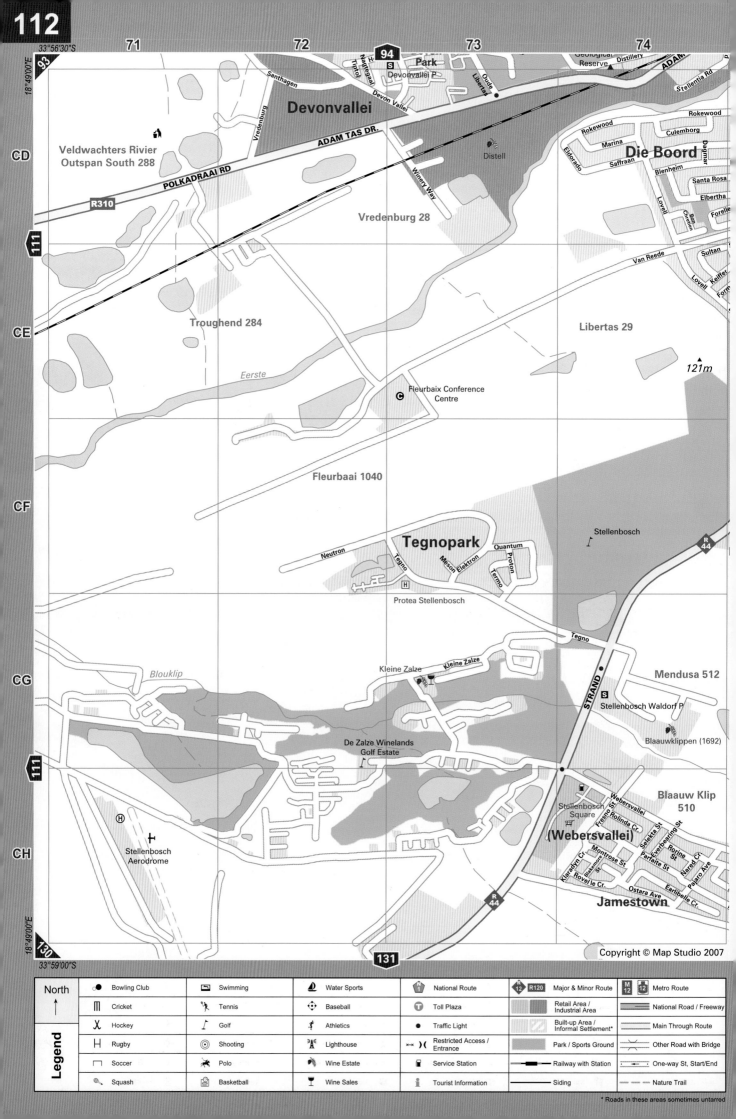

North						
↑	ᵒ● Bowling Club	⌐ Swimming	⚓ Water Sports	⚑ National Route	12 R120 Major & Minor Route	M 12 Metro Route
	�III Cricket	Tennis	◈ Baseball	T Toll Plaza	Retail Area / Industrial Area	National Road / Freeway
	X Hockey	Golf	Athletics	● Traffic Light	Built-up Area / Informal Settlement*	Main Through Route
Legend	H Rugby	◎ Shooting	Lighthouse	⨯)(Restricted Access / Entrance	Park / Sports Ground	Other Road with Bridge
	⊏ Soccer	Polo	Wine Estate	Service Station	Railway with Station	One-way St, Start/End
	Squash	Basketball	Y Wine Sales	i Tourist Information	Siding	Nature Trail

*Roads in these areas sometimes untarred

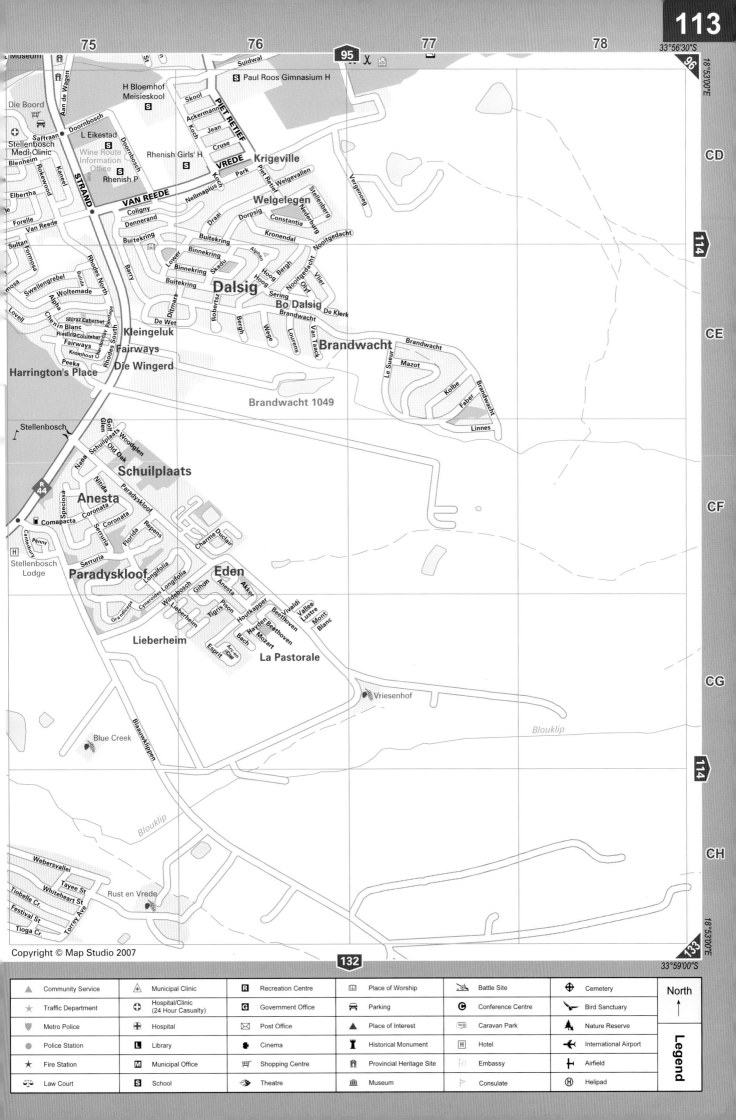

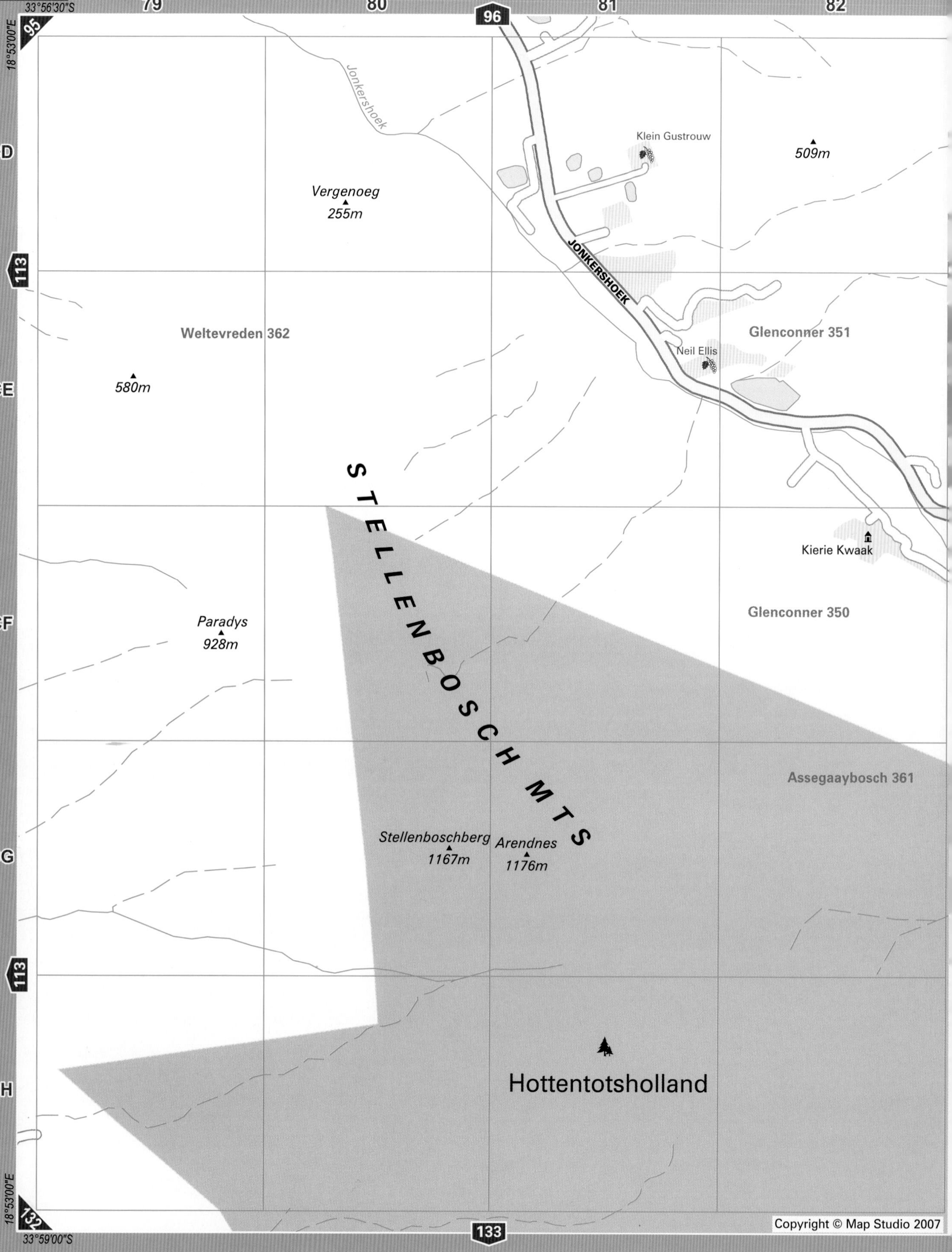

33°56'30"S

18°53'00"E

95

79   80   96   81   82

CD

Klein Gustrouw

509m

Jonkershoek

Vergenoeg
255m

113

Weltevreden 362

Glenconner 351

Neil Ellis

CE

580m

S T E L L E N B O S C H   M T S

Kierie Kwaak

CF

Paradys
928m

Glenconner 350

Assegaaybosch 361

JONKERSHOEK

CG

Stellenboschberg
1167m

Arendnes
1176m

113

CH

Hottentotsholland

18°53'00"E

132

133

33°59'00"S

Copyright © Map Studio 2007

North ↑	⊙ Bowling Club	▭ Swimming	⛵ Water Sports	National Route	12 R120 Major & Minor Route	M12 12 Metro Route
	Ⅲ Cricket	✗ Tennis	Golf	Baseball	Retail Area / Industrial Area	National Road / Freeway
	✗ Hockey	Golf	Athletics	Ⓣ Toll Plaza	Built-up Area / Informal Settlement*	Main Through Route
Legend	⊢ Rugby	◎ Shooting	Lighthouse	● Traffic Light	Park / Sports Ground	Other Road with Bridge
	▭ Soccer	Polo	Wine Estate	Restricted Access / Entrance	Railway with Station	One-way St, Start/End
	Squash	Basketball	♀ Wine Sales	Service Station	Siding	Nature Trail
				ℹ Tourist Information		

* Roads in these areas sometimes untarred

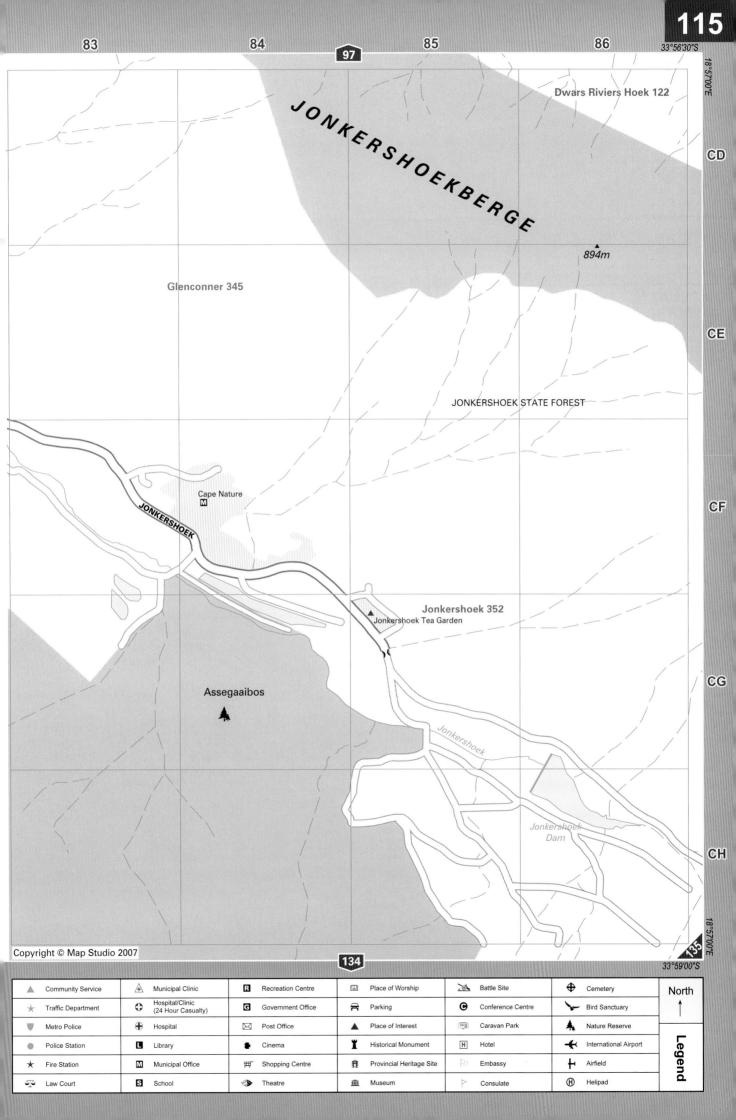

83 84 97 85 86

18°57'00"E
33°56'30"S

JONKERSHOEKBERGE

Dwars Riviers Hoek 122

CD

▲ 894m

Glenconner 345

CE

JONKERSHOEK STATE FOREST

Cape Nature
M

JONKERSHOEK

CF

Jonkershoek 352
▲
Jonkershoek Tea Garden

Assegaaibos
🌲

Jonkershoek

CG

Jonkershoek
Dam

CH

18°57'00"E
33°59'00"S

134

135

▲	Community Service	⚕	Municipal Clinic	R	Recreation Centre	⛪	Place of Worship	⚔	Battle Site	⊕	Cemetery
★	Traffic Department	⊕	Hospital/Clinic (24 Hour Casualty)	G	Government Office	🚗	Parking	C	Conference Centre	🦅	Bird Sanctuary
▼	Metro Police	✚	Hospital	✉	Post Office	▲	Place of Interest	🚐	Caravan Park	🏕	Nature Reserve
●	Police Station	L	Library	✠	Cinema	🏛	Historical Monument	H	Hotel	✈	International Airport
★	Fire Station	M	Municipal Office	🛍	Shopping Centre	🏛	Provincial Heritage Site	E	Embassy	⊢	Airfield
⚖	Law Court	S	School	🎭	Theatre	🏛	Museum	▷	Consulate	Ⓗ	Helipad

North
↑

Legend

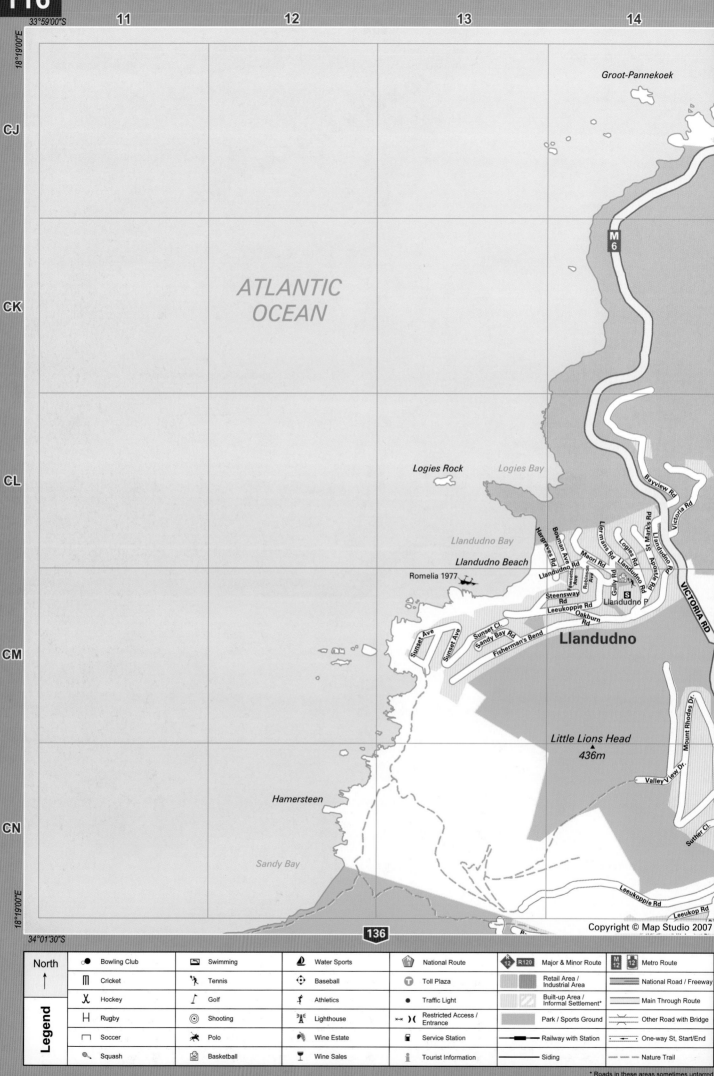

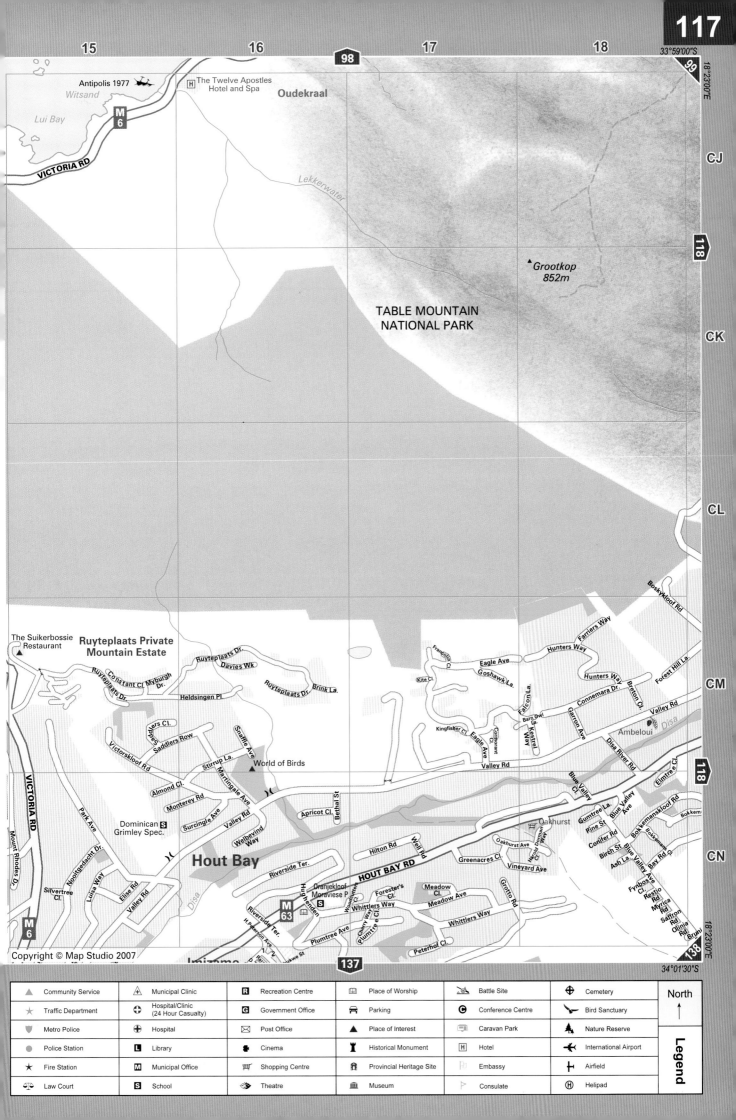

33°59'00"S
18°23'00"E
99
CJ
118
CK
CL
CM
118
CN
138
18°23'00"E
34°01'30"S

15   16   98   17   18

Antipolis 1977
Witsand
Lui Bay
M 6
The Twelve Apostles Hotel and Spa
Oudekraal
VICTORIA RD
Lekkerwater

▲ *Grootkop 852m*

TABLE MOUNTAIN NATIONAL PARK

The Suikerbossie Restaurant
Ruyteplaats Private Mountain Estate
Ruyteplaats Dr.
Davies Wk.
Ruyteplaats Dr.
Constant Cl. Myburgh Dr.
Heldsingen Pl.
Brink La.
Ruyteplaats Dr.
Kite Cl.
Francolin Cl.
Eagle Ave
Goshawk La.
Hunters Way
Farriers Way
Hunters Way
Forest Hill La.
Breton Cl.
Connemara Dr.
Valley Rd
Falcon La.
Kingfisher Cl.
Eagle Ave
Barn Owl La.
Kestrel Way
Cormorant Cl.
Garron Ave
Ambeloui
Disa
Spiders Cl.
Saddlers Row
Victorskloof Rd
Snaffle Ave
Stirrup La.
Valley Rd
Disa River Rd
Blue Valley Cl.
Elmtree Cl.
Almond Cl.
Martingale Ave
▲ **World of Birds**
Monterey Rd
Surcingle Ave
Apricot Cl.
Bethal St
Oakhurst
Blue Valley Cl.
Gumtree La.
Pine St
Conifer Rd
Birch St
Bokkemanskloof Rd
Bokkem
Park Ave
Dominican S Grimley Spec.
Welbewind Way
Hilton Rd
Well Rd
HOUT BAY RD
Greenacres Cl.
Oakhurst Ave
Hood Dorman Way
Vineyard Ave
Ash La. Blue Valley Ave
Fynbos Cl.
Restio Rd
Myrica Rd
VICTORIA RD
Mount Rhodes Dr.
Silvertree Cl.
Nooitgedacht Dr.
Luisa Way
Elise Rd
Valley Rd
Hout Bay
Riverside Ter.
Oranjekloof Moraviese P
Hughenden
S
Forester's Cl.
Meadow Cl.
Meadow Ave
Grotto Rd
Whittlers Way
Saffron Rd
Olinia Rd
M 6
M 63
Riverside Ter.
H Peterson Ave
Plumtree Ave
Cherry Way
Plumtree Cl.
Whittlers Way
Peterhof Cl.
Bruni
Imizamo
137

▲	Community Service	Ⓐ	Municipal Clinic	R	Recreation Centre	🕮	Place of Worship	Battle Site	⊕ Cemetery
★	Traffic Department	⊕	Hospital/Clinic (24 Hour Casualty)	G	Government Office	🚗	Parking	C Conference Centre	Bird Sanctuary
▼	Metro Police	✚	Hospital	✉	Post Office	▲	Place of Interest	Caravan Park	Nature Reserve
●	Police Station	L	Library	✦	Cinema	⚔	Historical Monument	H Hotel	✈ International Airport
★	Fire Station	M	Municipal Office	🛒	Shopping Centre	🏛	Provincial Heritage Site	Embassy	Airfield
⚖	Law Court	S	School	🎭	Theatre	🏛	Museum	Consulate	Ⓗ Helipad

North ↑

Legend

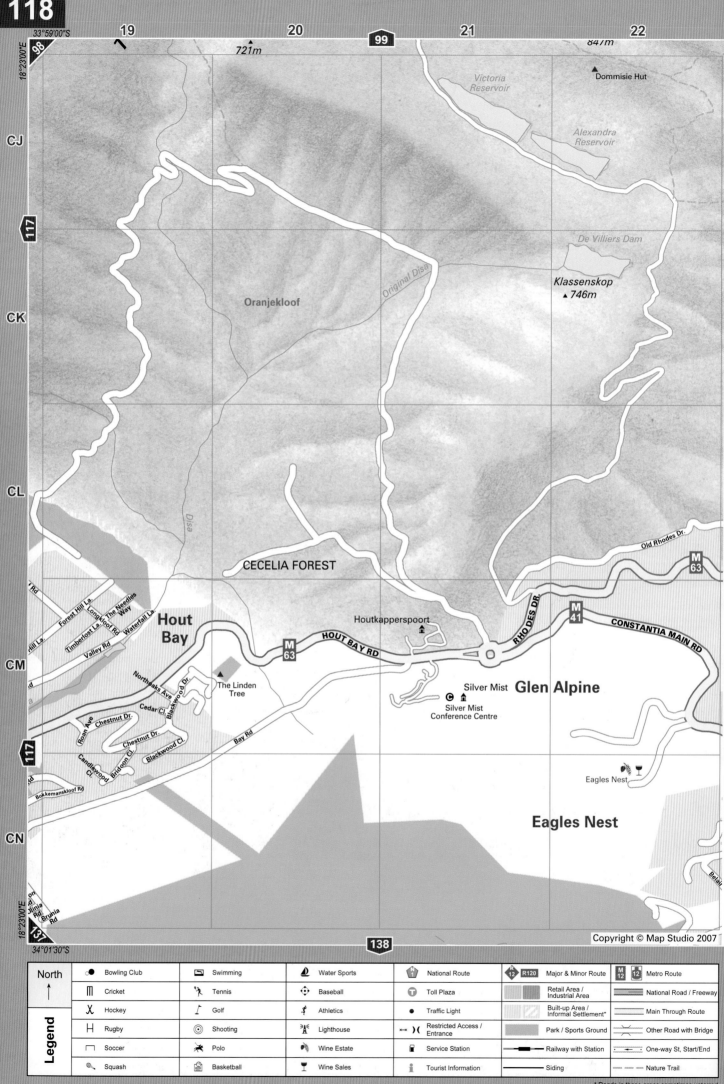

33°59'00"S
18°23'00"E

19 **20** 99 **21** **22**

847m

CJ

117

CK

CL

M 63

M 41

CM

117

CN

18°23'00"E
34°01'30"S

138

Victoria Reservoir

Alexandra Reservoir

▲ Dommisie Hut

De Villiers Dam

Klassenskop
▲ 746m

Oranjekloof

Original Disa

Disa

CECELIA FOREST

Houtkappersspoort

Old Rhodes Dr.

RHODES DR.

CONSTANTIA MAIN RD

Hout Bay

HOUT BAY RD

Silver Mist

Glen Alpine

Silver Mist
Conference Centre

Forest Hill La.
Longkloof Rd
The Needles Way
Waterfall La.
Timberlost La.
Hill La.
Valley Rd
Northpeaks Ave
Blackwood Dr.
Cedar Cl.
Roan Ave
Chestnut Dr.
Chestnut Dr.
Candlewood Cl.
Bridoon Cl.
Blackwood Cl.
Bay Rd
Bokkemanskloof Rd

The Linden
Tree

Eagles Nest

Eagles Nest

721m

Brunia Rd
Olinia Rd

Belair

Copyright © Map Studio 2007

North												
	Bowling Club		Swimming		Water Sports		National Route	R120	Major & Minor Route	M 12	Metro Route
	Cricket		Tennis		Baseball		Toll Plaza		Retail Area / Industrial Area		National Road / Freeway
	Hockey		Golf		Athletics		Traffic Light		Built-up Area / Informal Settlement*		Main Through Route
	Rugby		Shooting		Lighthouse		Restricted Access / Entrance		Park / Sports Ground		Other Road with Bridge
	Soccer		Polo		Wine Estate		Service Station		Railway with Station		One-way St, Start/End
	Squash		Basketball		Wine Sales		Tourist Information		Siding		Nature Trail

Legend

* Roads in these areas sometimes untarred

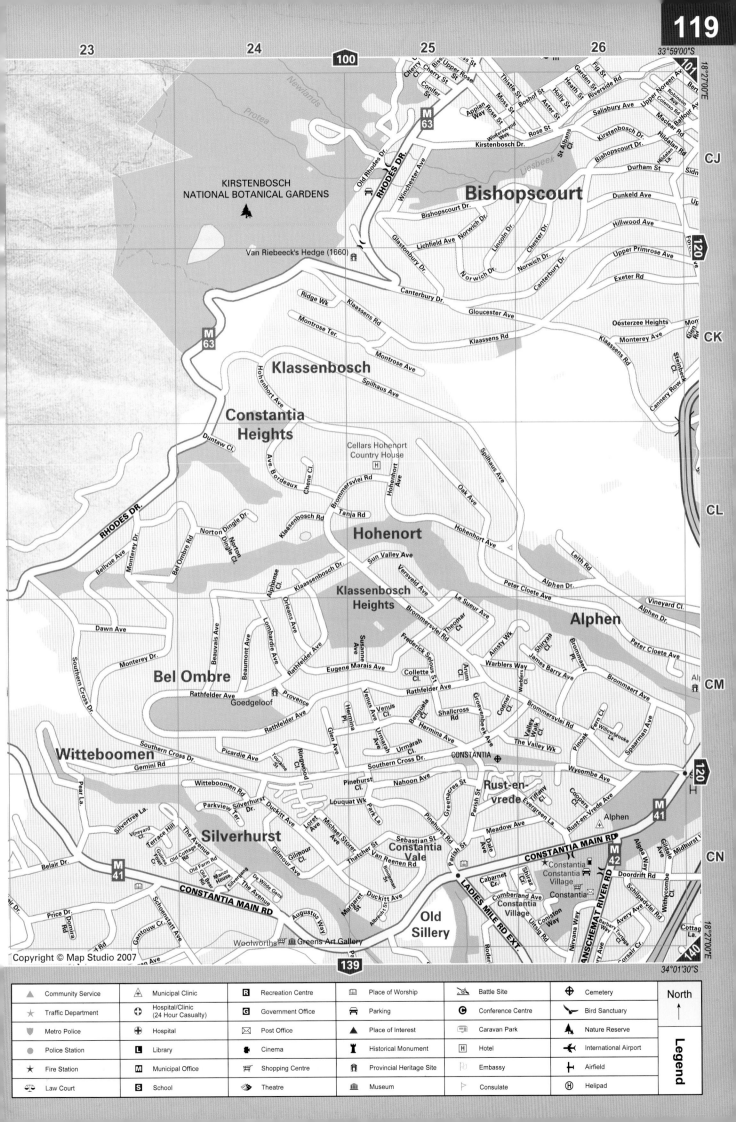

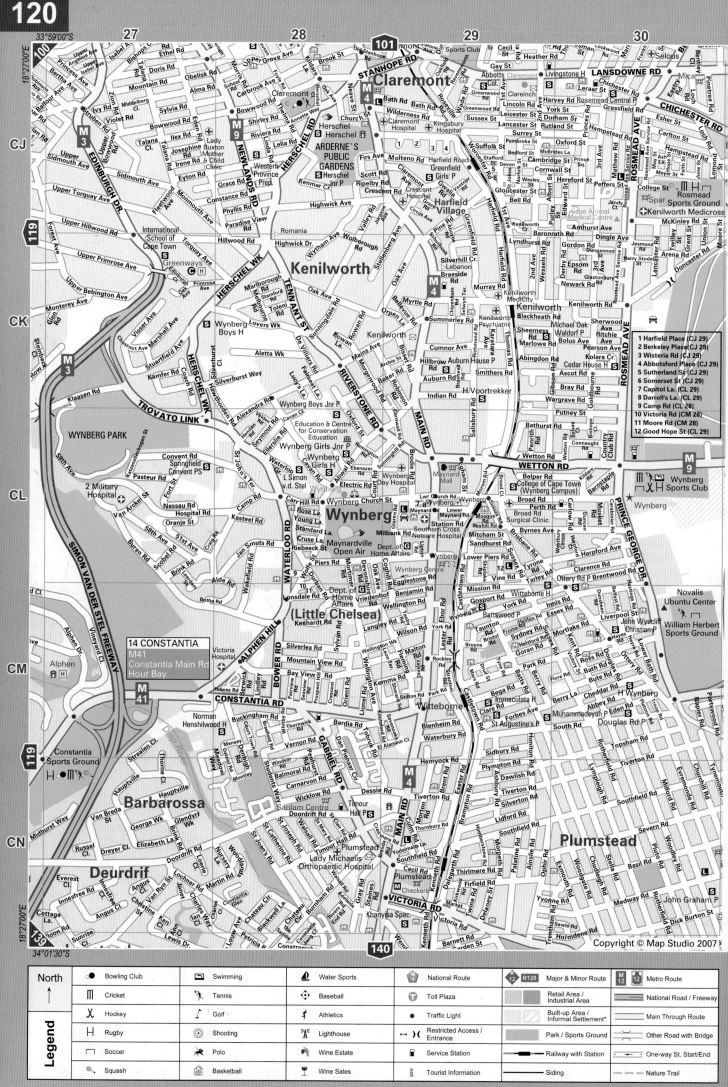

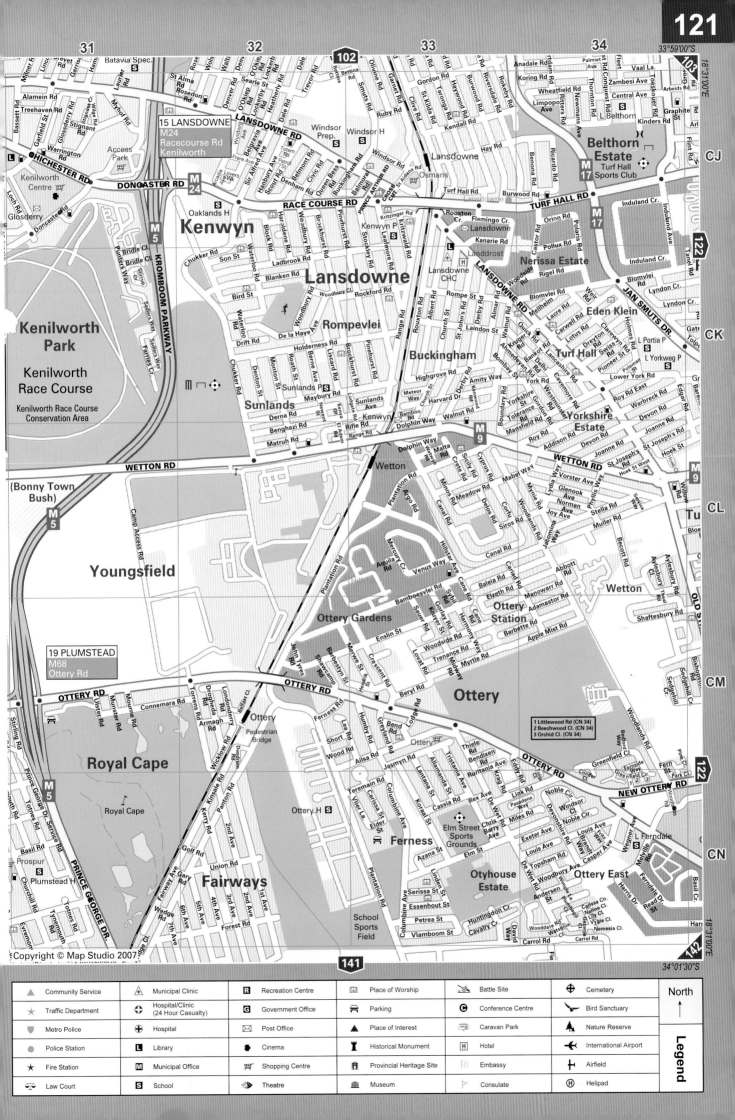

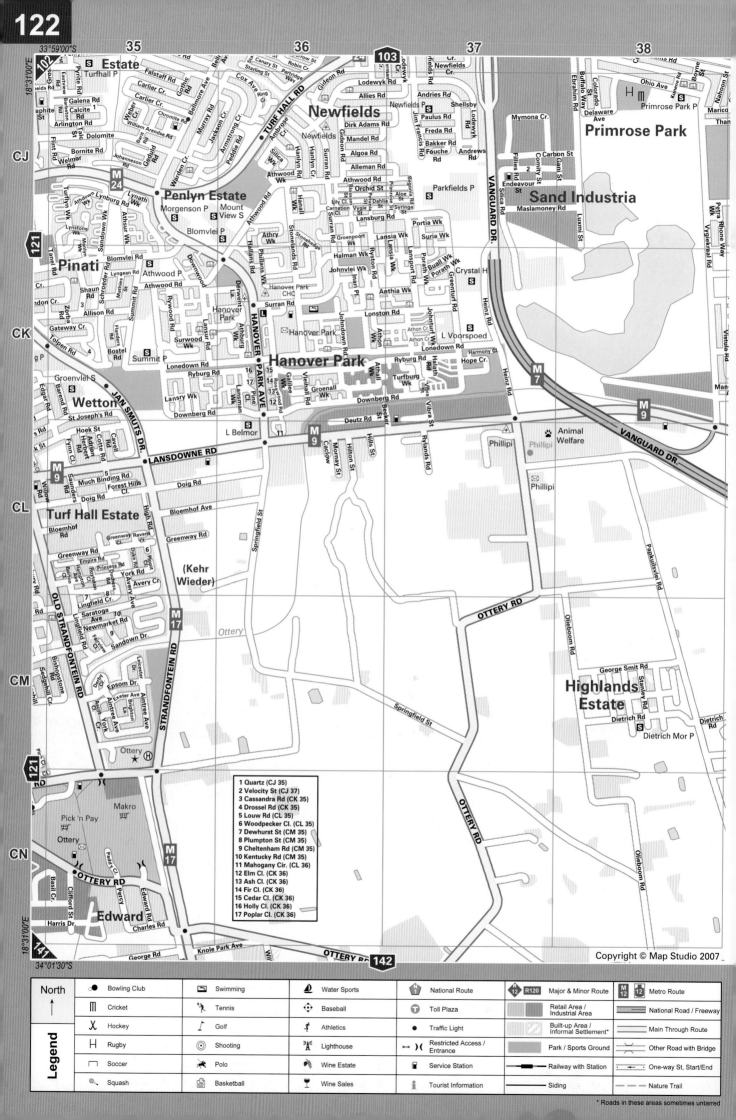

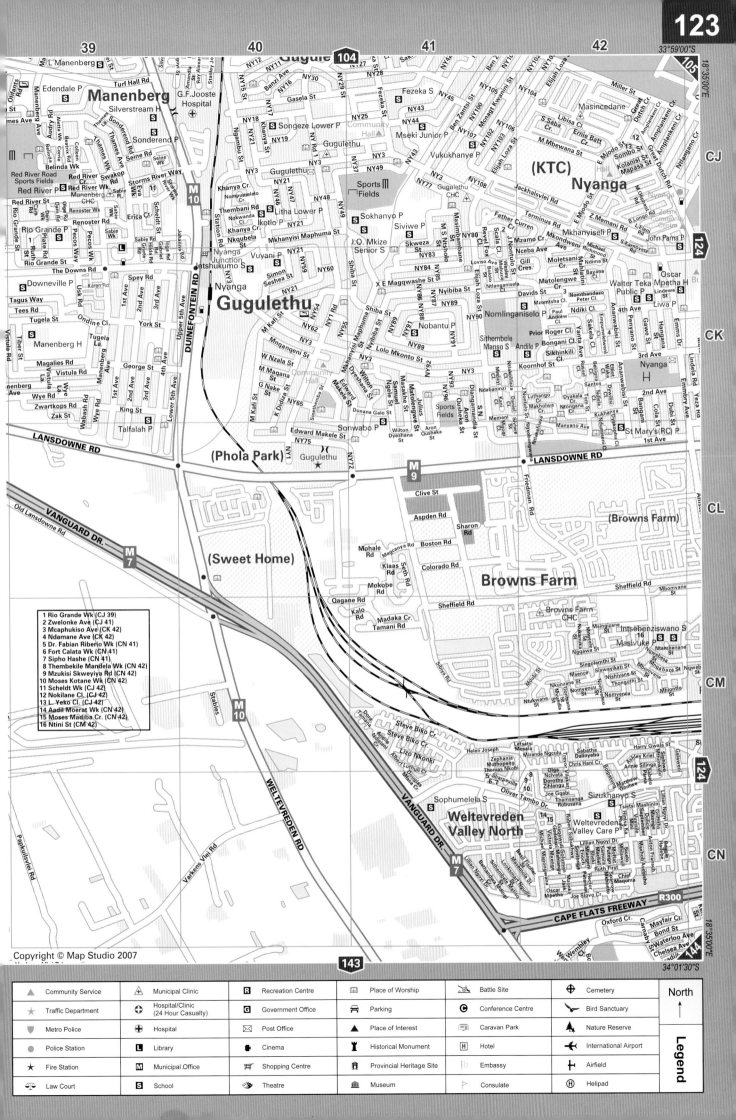

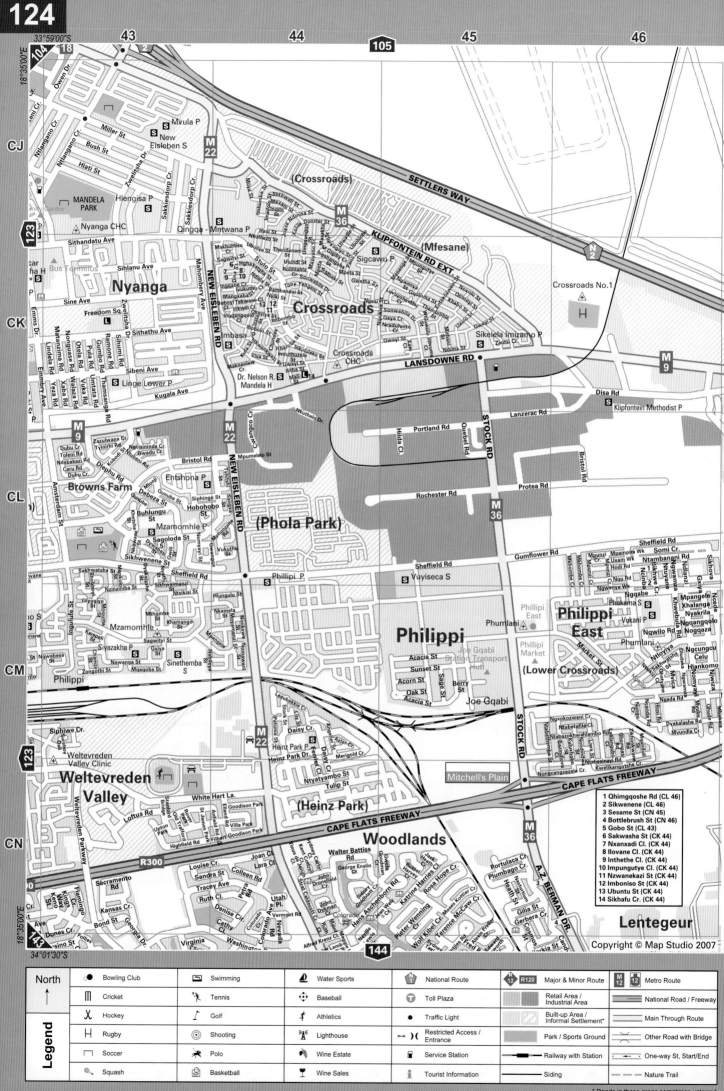

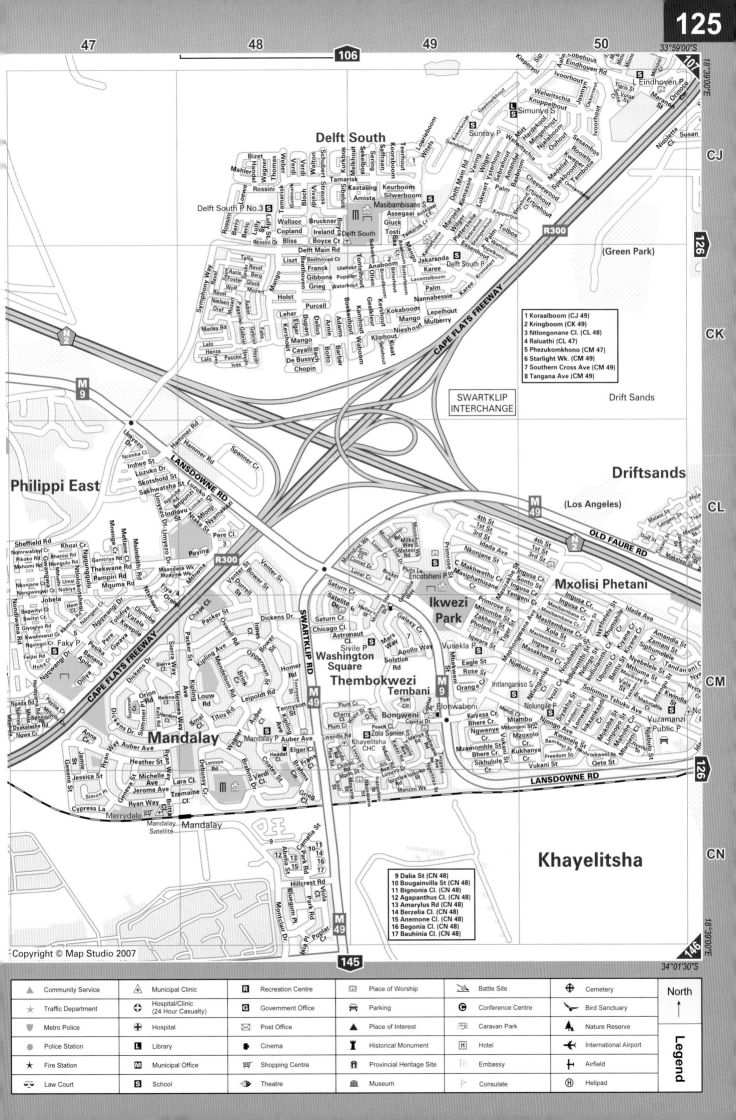

Legend

▲	Community Service	Ⓐ	Municipal Clinic	Ⓡ	Recreation Centre	⊞	Place of Worship	⚔	Battle Site	⊕	Cemetery
★	Traffic Department	⊕	Hospital/Clinic (24 Hour Casualty)	Ⓖ	Government Office	🚗	Parking	Ⓒ	Conference Centre	🦅	Bird Sanctuary
▼	Metro Police	✚	Hospital	✉	Post Office		Place of Interest	🚐	Caravan Park	▲	Nature Reserve
●	Police Station	Ⓛ	Library	✸	Cinema	♛	Historical Monument	Ⓗ	Hotel	✈	International Airport
★	Fire Station	Ⓜ	Municipal Office	🏬	Shopping Centre	🏛	Provincial Heritage Site		Embassy	⊢	Airfield
⚖	Law Court	Ⓢ	School	🎭	Theatre	🏛	Museum	▷	Consulate	Ⓗ	Helipad

North

Legend

Copyright © Map Studio 2007

Brentwood Park

Fairdale

Fountain Village

1 Zambezi St (CK 54)
2 Elsies St (CK 53)
3 Kaap St (CK 54)
4 Iligwa St (CK 54)
5 Incora St (CK 53)
6 Nsikazi St (CK 53)
7 Umbashe St (CK 53)
8 Botletle St (CK 53)
9 Bot St (CK 53)
10 Blyde St (CK 53)
11 Dutywa St (CK 53)
12 Gqora St (CK 53)
13 Nqabara St (CK 53)
14 Mbashe St (CK 53)

Mfuleni No. 3 P

(Ezindlovini)

Mfuleni

(Malindi)

Driftsands

(Ekuphumleni)

Mfuleni CHC

Mfuleni P

Manzomthombo S

OLD FAURE RD

OLD FAURE RD

25 TYGERBERG
M44
Mew Way

MEW WAY

Oliver Tambo
Sports Centre

LANSDOWNE RD

(Bongani)

Khayelitsha

(Trevor Vilakazi)

BONGA DR

Barnet Molokwana Corner

Nonqubela

Victoria Mxenge

Mfesane School for the Deaf Spec.

(Victoria Mxenge)

The Ark Christian School PS

Copyright © Map Studio 2007

North	Bowling Club	Swimming	Water Sports	National Route	R120	Major & Minor Route	Metro Route
Legend	Cricket	Tennis	Baseball	Toll Plaza		Retail Area / Industrial Area	National Road / Freeway
	Hockey	Golf	Athletics	Traffic Light		Built-up Area / Informal Settlement*	Main Through Route
	Rugby	Shooting	Lighthouse	Restricted Access / Entrance		Park / Sports Ground	Other Road with Bridge
	Soccer	Polo	Wine Estate	Service Station			Railway with Station
	Squash	Basketball	Wine Sales	Tourist Information			Siding	One-way St, Start/End
							Nature Trail

* Roads in these areas sometimes untarred

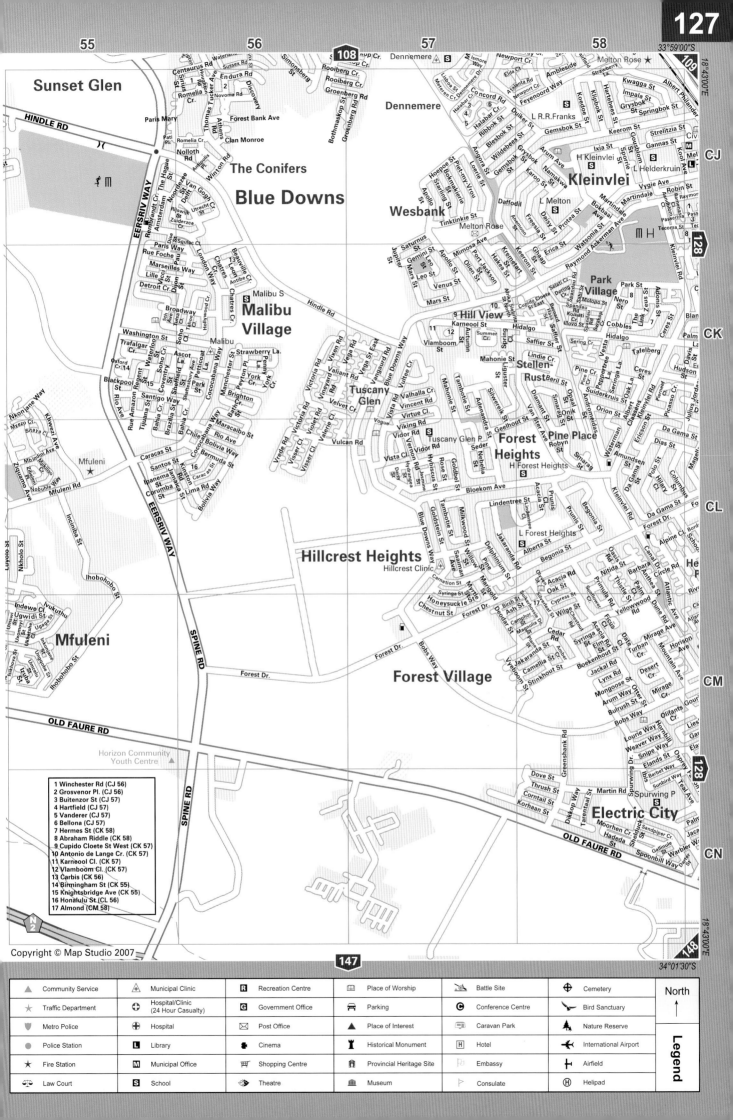

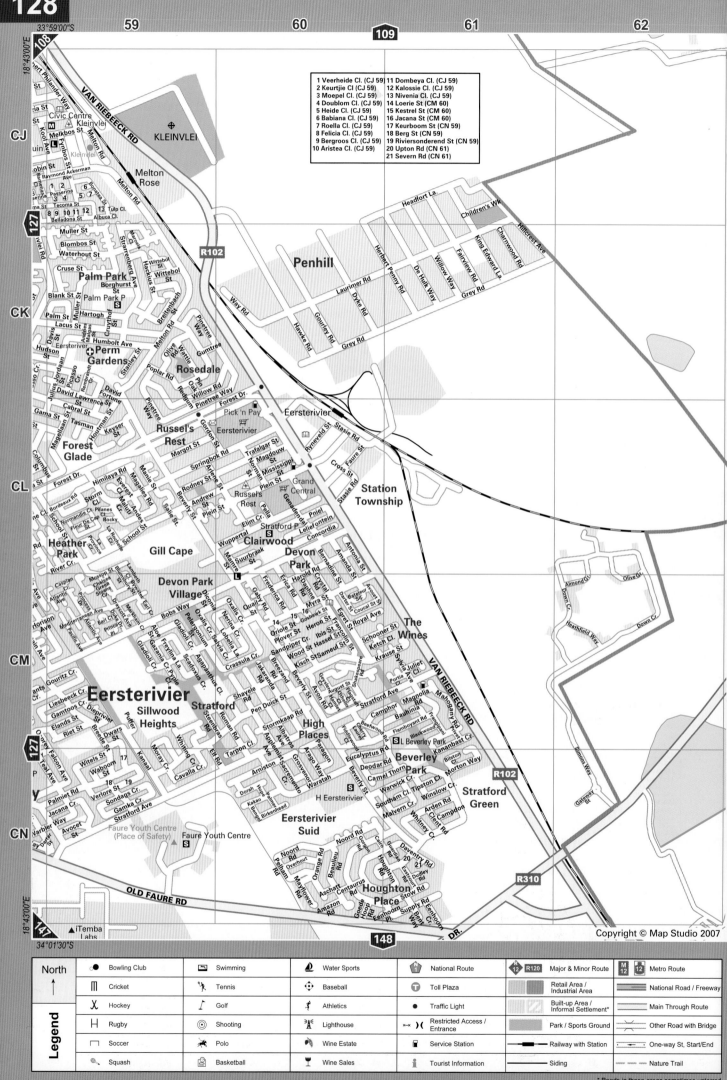

Index of streets:

1 Veerheide Cl. (CJ 59)
2 Keurtjie Cl. (CJ 59)
3 Moepel Cl. (CJ 59)
4 Doublom Cl. (CJ 59)
5 Heide Cl. (CJ 59)
6 Babiana Cl. (CJ 59)
7 Roella Cl. (CJ 59)
8 Felicia Cl. (CJ 59)
9 Bergroos Cl. (CJ 59)
10 Aristea Cl. (CJ 59)
11 Dombeya Cl. (CJ 59)
12 Kalossie Cl. (CJ 59)
13 Nivenia Cl. (CJ 59)
14 Loerie St (CM 60)
15 Kestrel St (CM 60)
16 Jacana St (CM 60)
17 Keurboom St (CN 59)
18 Berg St (CN 59)
19 Riviersonderend St (CN 59)
20 Upton Rd (CN 61)
21 Severn Rd (CN 61)

Legend

North ↑

Bowling Club		Swimming		Water Sports		National Route
Cricket		Tennis		Baseball		Toll Plaza
Hockey		Golf		Athletics		Traffic Light
Rugby		Shooting		Lighthouse		Restricted Access / Entrance
Soccer		Polo		Wine Estate		Service Station
Squash		Basketball		Wine Sales		Tourist Information

R120 Major & Minor Route
Retail Area / Industrial Area
Built-up Area / Informal Settlement*
Park / Sports Ground
Railway with Station
Siding

M12 / 12 Metro Route
National Road / Freeway
Main Through Route
Other Road with Bridge
One-way St, Start/End
Nature Trail

* Roads in these areas sometimes untarred

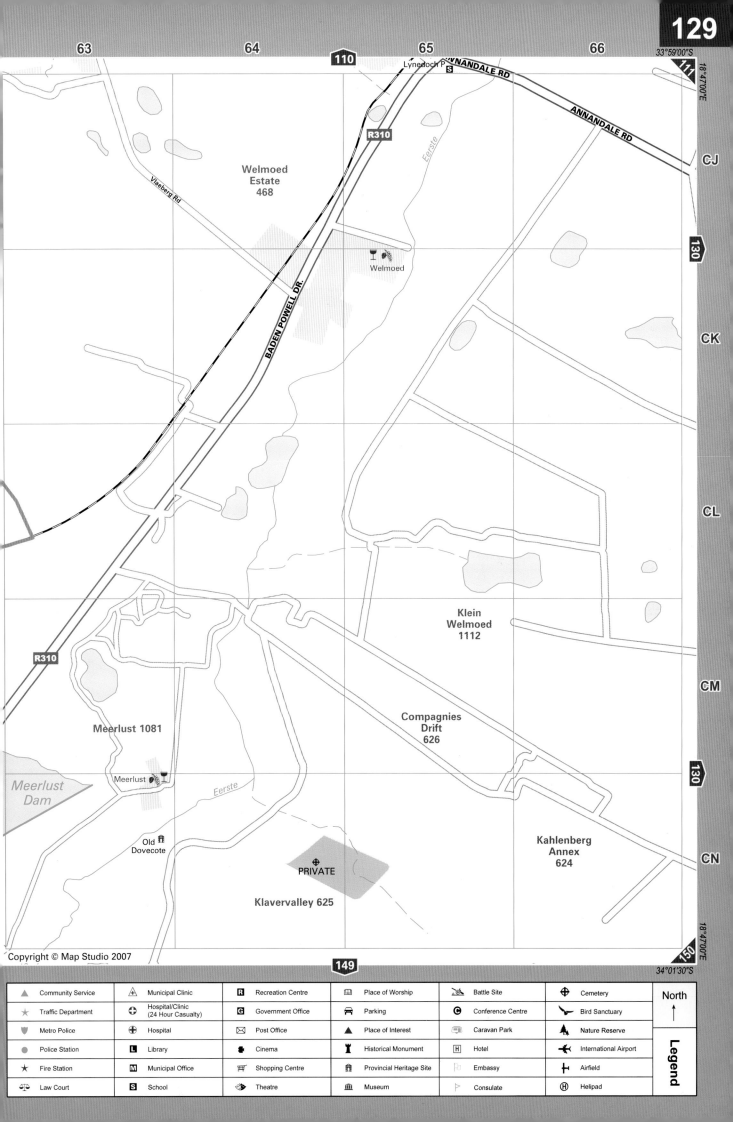

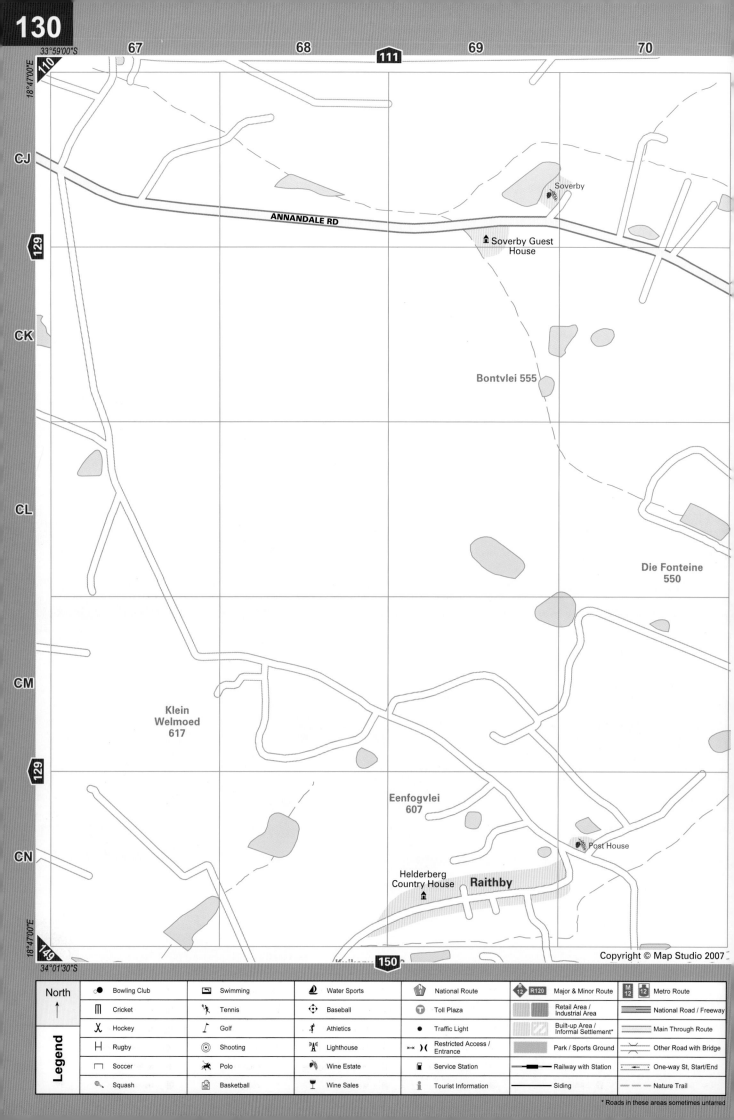

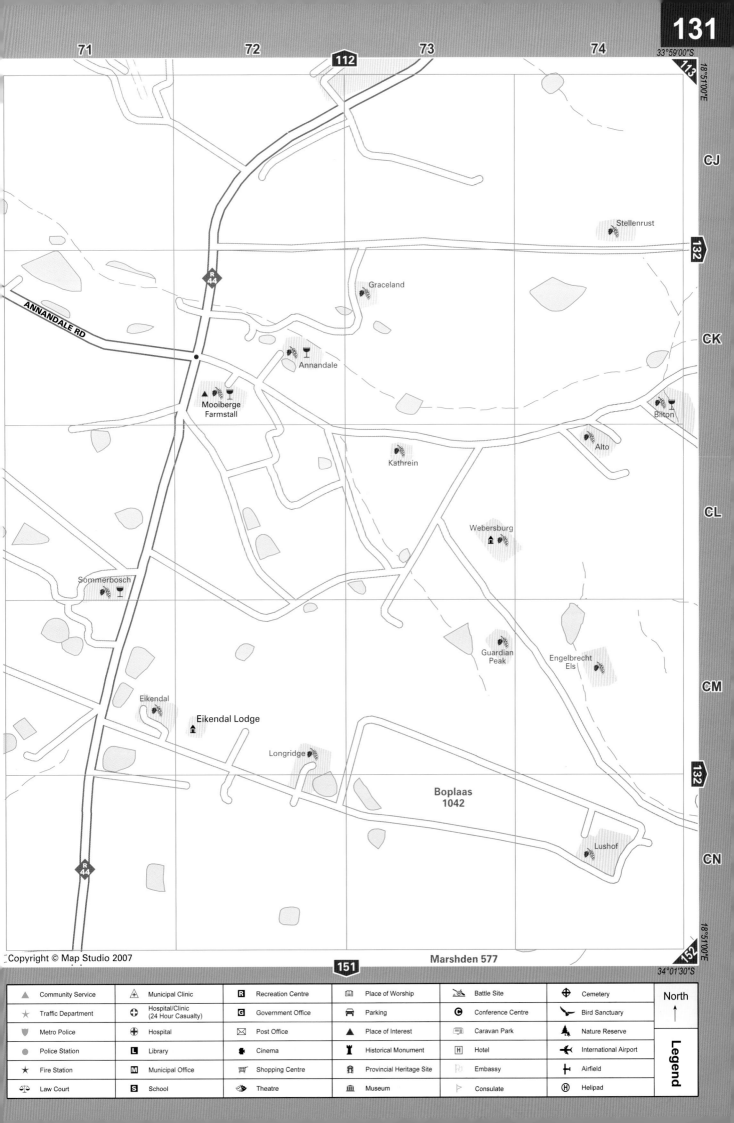

Legend

▲	Community Service	⚕	Municipal Clinic	R	Recreation Centre		Place of Worship		Battle Site	⊕	Cemetery
★	Traffic Department	✚	Hospital/Clinic (24 Hour Casualty)	G	Government Office	🚗	Parking	C	Conference Centre		Bird Sanctuary
▼	Metro Police	✚	Hospital	✉	Post Office	▲	Place of Interest		Caravan Park	▲	Nature Reserve
●	Police Station	L	Library		Cinema	Y	Historical Monument	H	Hotel	✈	International Airport
★	Fire Station	M	Municipal Office	🛒	Shopping Centre	🏛	Provincial Heritage Site		Embassy	⊢	Airfield
⚖	Law Court	S	School		Theatre	🏛	Museum	▷	Consulate	Ⓗ	Helipad

North
↑

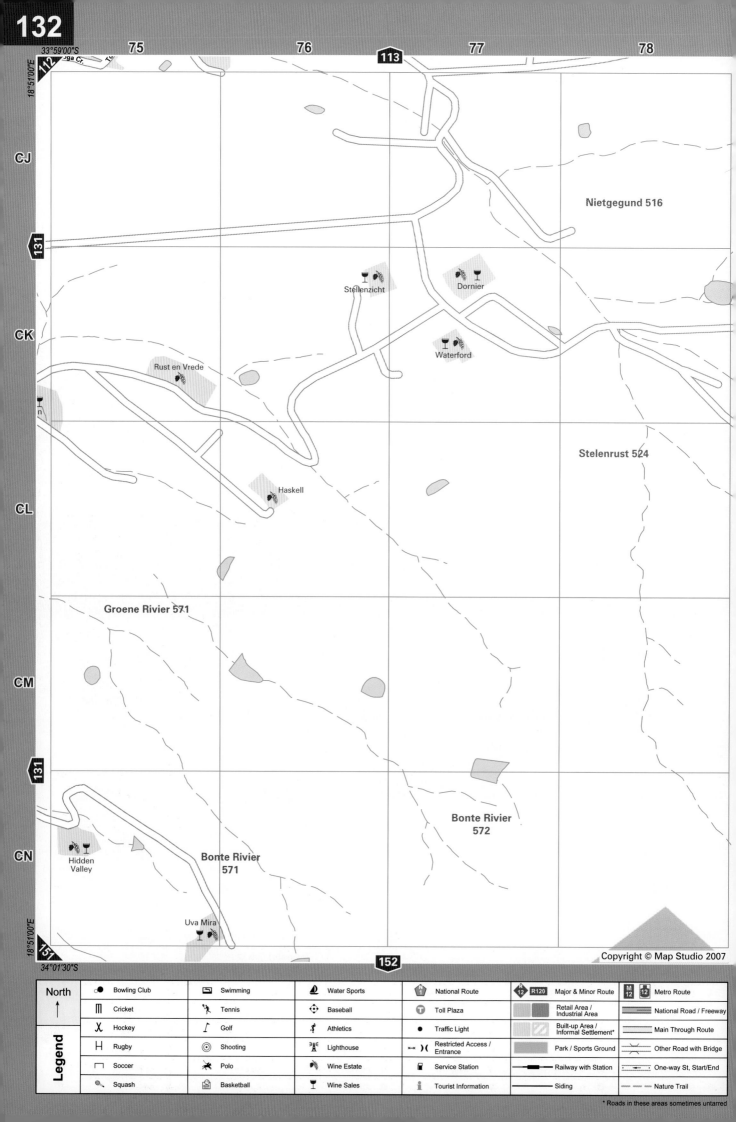

33°59'00"S
18°51'00"E
112

75   76   113   77   78

CJ

Nietgegund 516

131

Stellenzicht   Dornier

CK

Waterford

Rust en Vrede

Stelenrust 524

CL

Haskell

Groene Rivier 571

CM

131

Bonte Rivier
572

CN

Hidden
Valley

Bonte Rivier
571

Uva Mira

18°51'00"E
151
152
34°01'30"S

Copyright © Map Studio 2007

North	Legend					
⊙ Bowling Club	⌷ Swimming	⛵ Water Sports	🏛 National Route	12 R120 Major & Minor Route	M12 12 Metro Route	
Ⅲ Cricket	🏃 Tennis	✦ Baseball	T Toll Plaza	Retail Area / Industrial Area	National Road / Freeway	
⅄ Hockey	⌁ Golf	🏃 Athletics	● Traffic Light	Built-up Area / Informal Settlement*	Main Through Route	
H Rugby	◎ Shooting	⧖ Lighthouse	Restricted Access / Entrance	Park / Sports Ground	Other Road with Bridge	
⊓ Soccer	🐎 Polo	🍇 Wine Estate	⛽ Service Station	▬ Railway with Station	One-way St, Start/End	
🎾 Squash	🏀 Basketball	♈ Wine Sales	ℹ Tourist Information	Siding	Nature Trail	

* Roads in these areas sometimes untarred

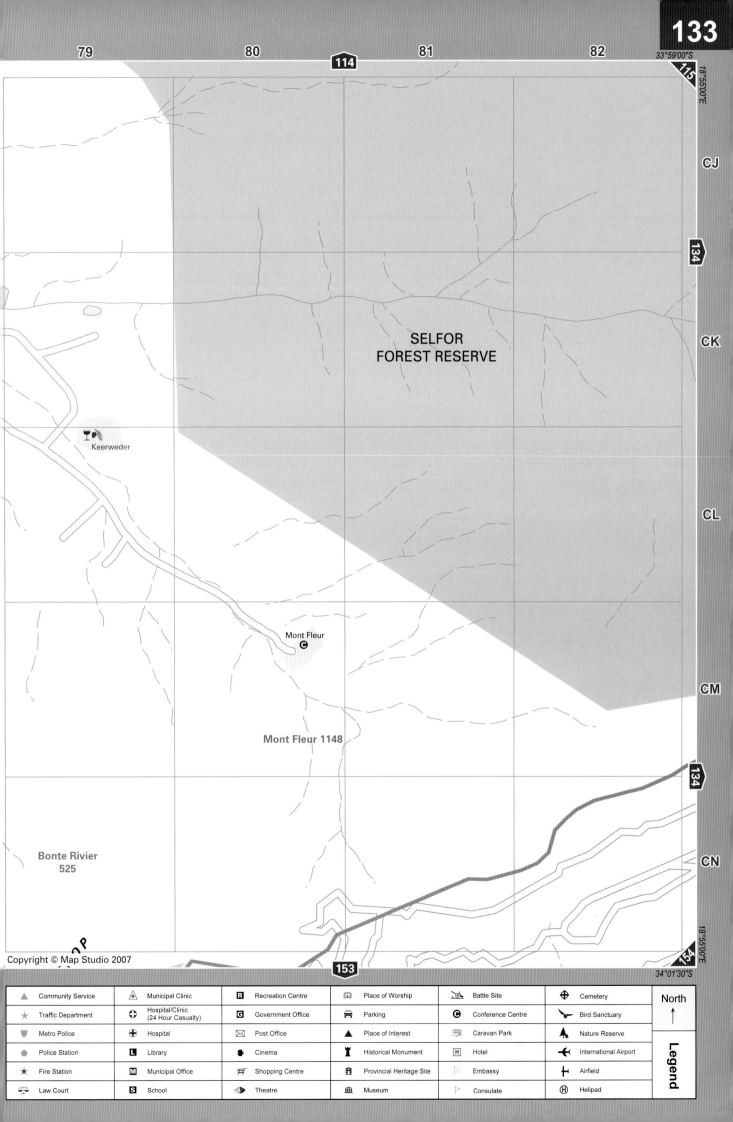

79
80
81
82

114

33°59'30"S
18°55'00"E

CJ

115

134

CK

SELFOR
FOREST RESERVE

CL

Keerweder

CM

Mont Fleur
C

134

Mont Fleur 1148

CN

Bonte Rivier
525

18°55'00"E
154

153

33°01'30"S

Copyright © Map Studio 2007

										North
▲	Community Service	Ⓐ	Municipal Clinic	ℝ	Recreation Centre		Place of Worship		Battle Site	⊕	Cemetery	↑
★	Traffic Department	✛	Hospital/Clinic (24 Hour Casualty)	Ⓖ	Government Office		Parking	Ⓒ	Conference Centre		Bird Sanctuary	
♥	Metro Police	✚	Hospital	✉	Post Office	▲	Place of Interest		Caravan Park	♠	Nature Reserve	
●	Police Station	Ⓛ	Library		Cinema	Ⓨ	Historical Monument	Ⓗ	Hotel		International Airport	Legend
★	Fire Station	Ⓜ	Municipal Office		Shopping Centre		Provincial Heritage Site		Embassy	╅	Airfield	
⚖	Law Court	Ⓢ	School		Theatre	🏛	Museum	▷	Consulate	Ⓗ	Helipad	

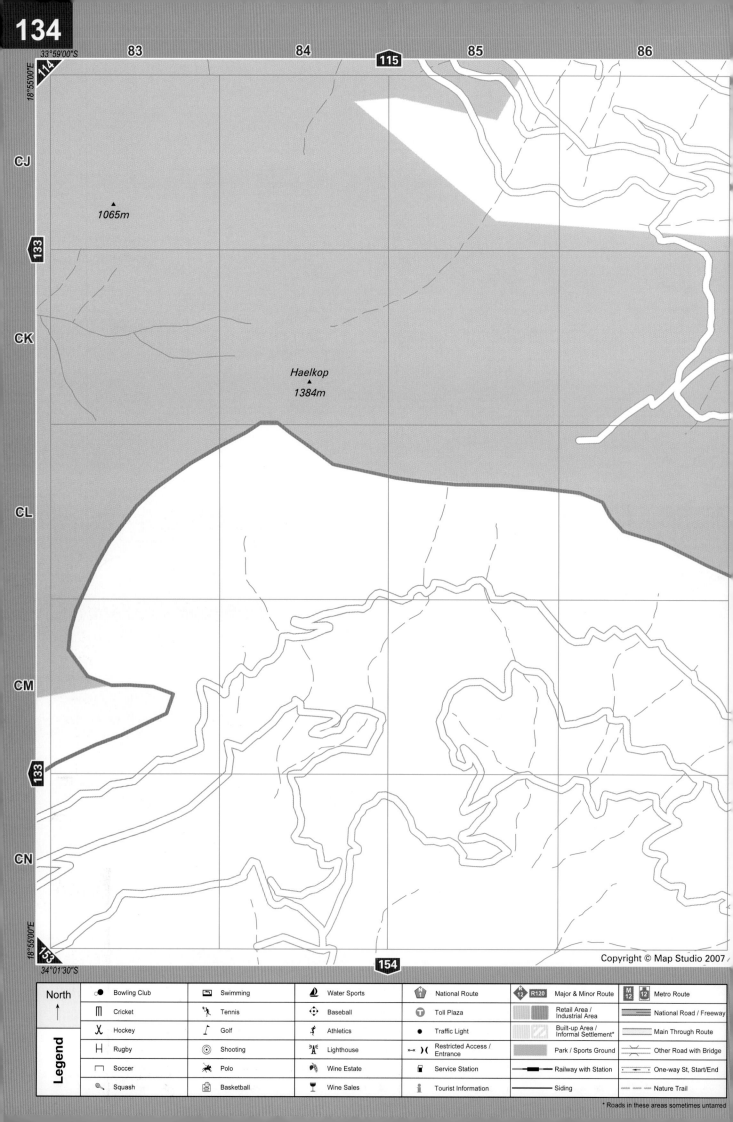

CJ

▲
1065m

133

CK

Haelkop
▲
1384m

CL

CM

133

CN

North ↑								
Bowling Club	Swimming	Water Sports	National Route	Major & Minor Route	Metro Route
Cricket	Tennis	Baseball	Toll Plaza	Retail Area / Industrial Area	National Road / Freeway
Hockey	Golf	Athletics	Traffic Light	Built-up Area / Informal Settlement*	Main Through Route
Rugby	Shooting	Lighthouse	Restricted Access / Entrance	Park / Sports Ground	Other Road with Bridge
Soccer	Polo	Wine Estate	Service Station	Railway with Station	One-way St, Start/End
Squash	Basketball	Wine Sales	Tourist Information	Siding	Nature Trail

Legend

* Roads in these areas sometimes untarred

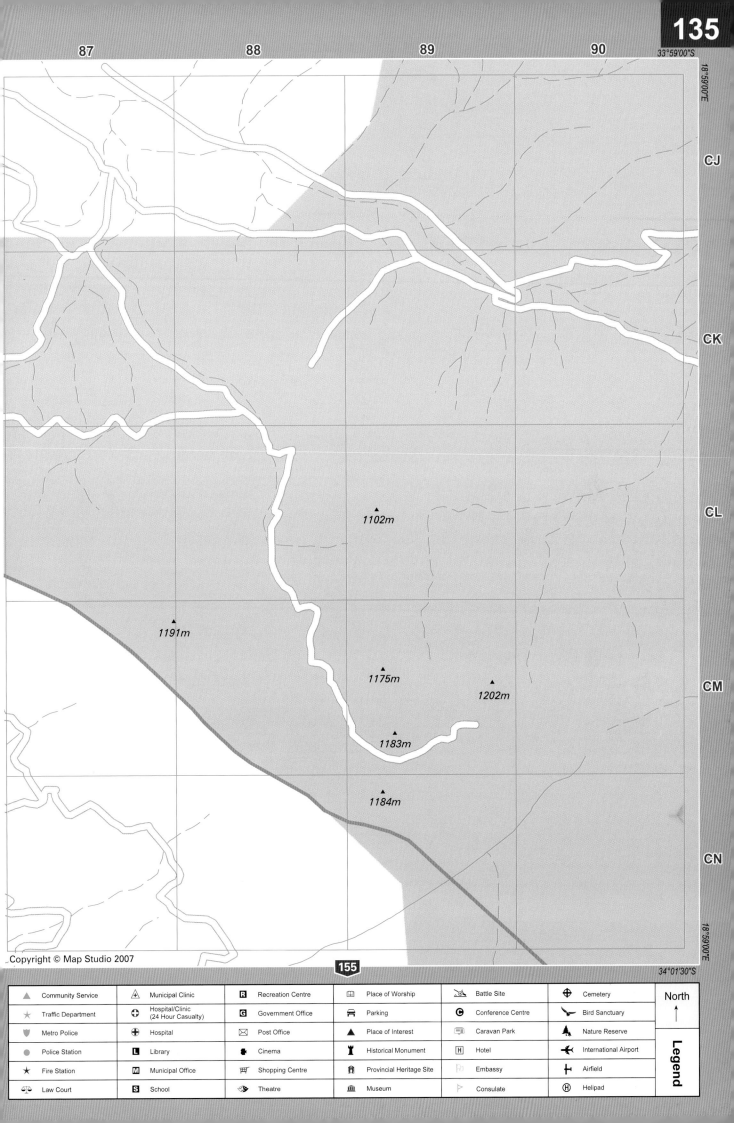

33°59'30"S

18°59'00"E

87 88 89 90

CJ

CK

CL

1102m

1191m

1175m

1202m

CM

1183m

1184m

CN

18°59'00"E

Copyright © Map Studio 2007

155

34°01'30"S

▲	Community Service	Ⓐ	Municipal Clinic	Ⓡ	Recreation Centre		Place of Worship		Battle Site	⊕	Cemetery	North ↑
★	Traffic Department	✚	Hospital/Clinic (24 Hour Casualty)	Ⓖ	Government Office	🚌	Parking	Ⓒ	Conference Centre	✈	Bird Sanctuary	
▼	Metro Police	✚	Hospital	✉	Post Office	▲	Place of Interest		Caravan Park	♣	Nature Reserve	Legend
●	Police Station	Ⓛ	Library	✦	Cinema	♟	Historical Monument	Ⓗ	Hotel	✈	International Airport	
★	Fire Station	Ⓜ	Municipal Office		Shopping Centre	🏛	Provincial Heritage Site		Embassy	✚	Airfield	
⚖	Law Court	Ⓢ	School		Theatre	🏛	Museum	▷	Consulate	Ⓗ	Helipad	

34°01'30"S
18°19'00"E

11 12 116 13 14

Langrots

CO

Suther Peak
▲
614m

CP

Karbonkelberg
▲
594m

▲
653m

**TABLE MOUNTAIN
NATIONAL PARK**

Kronenzicht

Brunia Way
Cynthia Cl.
Edmondia Cl.
Euclea Cl.
Eustegia Way
Doris Rd
Sheeda Rd
Helgarda Estate
Edgar Rd
Helgarda Rd
Karakal Rd
Bisschop Rd
Governor's Wk
Leeukop Rd
Lair Ave
Bisschop Rd
Leeukoop Rd

M 6

Laurentia Way
Orbea Cl.
Printzia Cl.
Ursinia Cl.
Rochea Cl.
Perrault Rd
Henschell Rd
M 6
Linda Cl.
Linda St
Mountain St
Daphne St
Worcester St
Victor St

Albert St
Gordon Rd
Pondicherry Ave
Sandpiper Cl.
Sandpiper Cl.
Albert Cr.
Norman St
VICTORIA AVE
Lancaster St
Cecil St

Gilquin Cr.
Liverpool St
Clyde St
Oxford St
Pondicherry Ave
Edward St
Earl St
Albert Rd
Princess St

Gilquin Cl.
Pondicherry Cl.
Lichtenstein Castle ♠
Harbour Lights
Zoutman Rd
Zoutman Rd
Edward St

1	Bayview Rd (CR 13)
2	Blanberg St (CR 14)
3	Corvina Link (CR 14)
4	Bell Capri Link (CR 14)
5	Blomberg Rd (CR 14)

Westford Rd
Gibraltar Rd
Sluysken Rd
Northshore Dr.

CQ

Badsampie

Kapteinspiek
▲
414m

Seacliffe Rd
Harbour Dr.
Fishmarket St
N.S.R.I
SA Fisheries
Museum
Mariners
Wharf

North Mole

Hout Bay Trail

Braco

CR

Bayview Rd
Flora Cl.
Sentinel Cl.
Sandy Cl.
Dolphin St
Duiker St
Bayview Rd
Canon
Neptune St
Seagull Cl.
York Cl.
Martin Cr.
Spinner Cl.
Fishing Harbour

Medina Cl.
Hangberg
Harbour Rd
S
H Houtbaai
Sentinel P

East Fort
Lions Paw
Oude Skip Rd
Anvil Cl.
Roman La.
Kingfisher La.
Vulcan La.
Karbonkel Rd
S
Oceana
Sapphire
Hout Bay
Harbour
CHC
York
Point

Rhode Vos Rd

South Mole

Hout Bay Harbour

Oceana Ruby Way
Oceana Emerald Way
Oceana Amethyst Way
Atlantic Skipper Rd

Hangberg

The Sentinel
▲
331m

Duiker Island

Badtamboer

CS

Copyright © Map Studio 2007

34°04'00"S
18°19'00"E

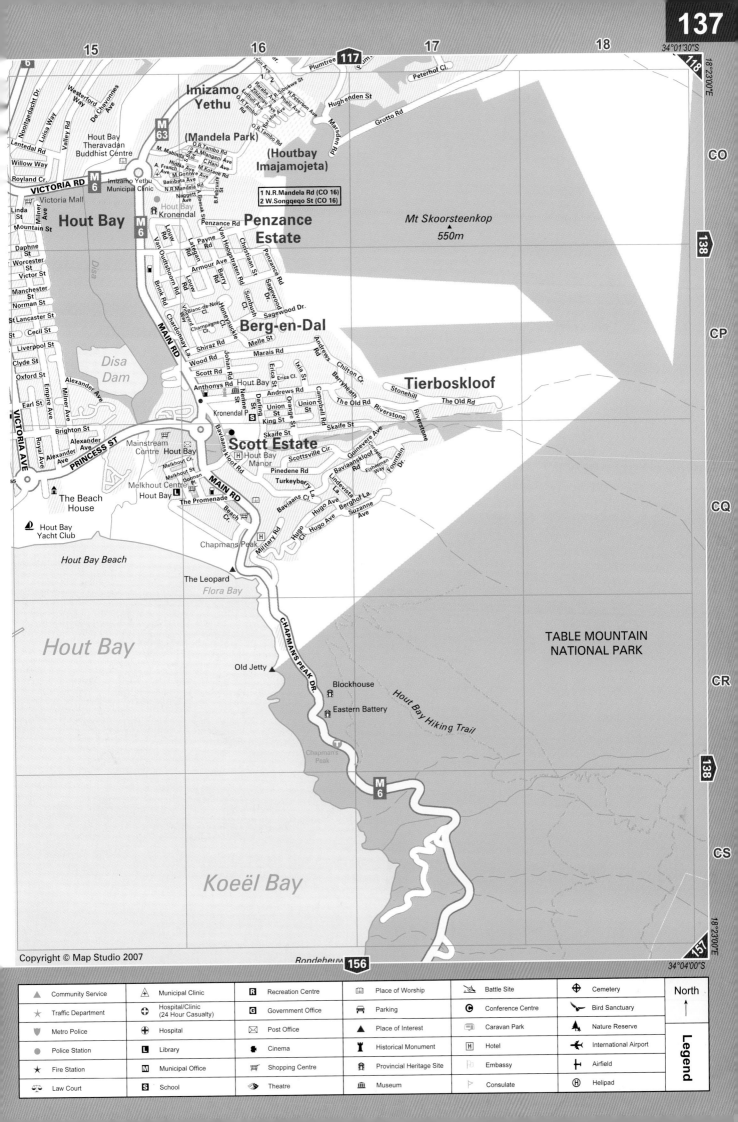

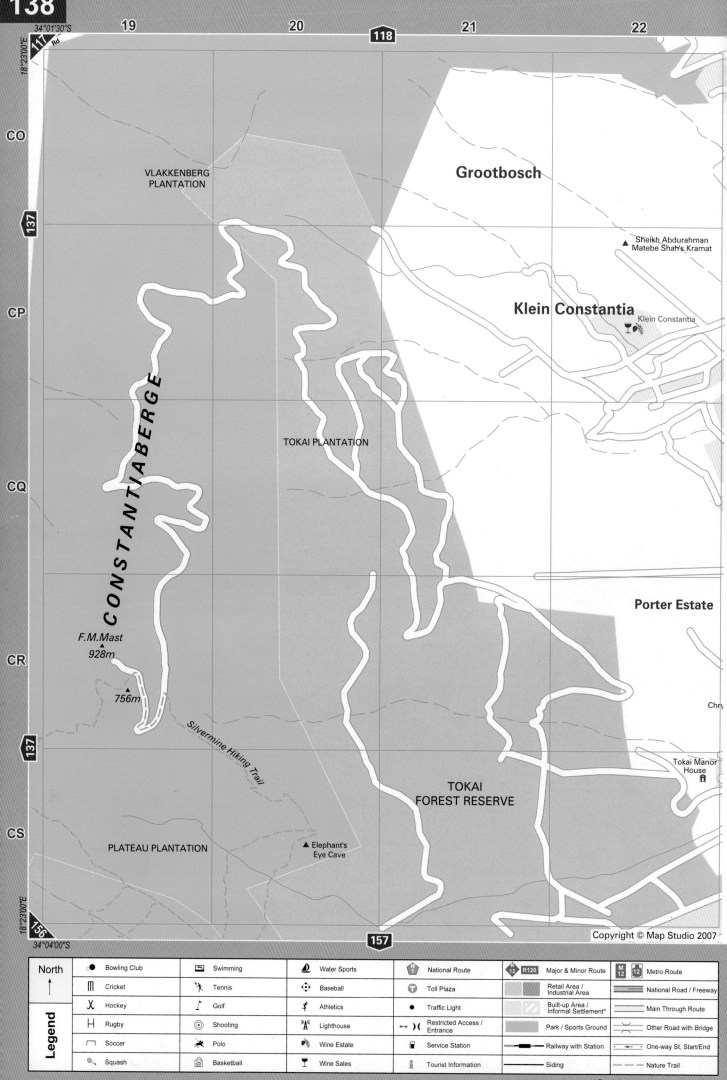

CO

VLAKKENBERG
PLANTATION

Grootbosch

137

▲ Sheikh Abdurahman
Matebe Shah's Kramat

CP

Klein Constantia

Klein Constantia

C O N S T A N T I A B E R G E

TOKAI PLANTATION

CQ

Porter Estate

F.M.Mast
▲
928m

CR

▲
756m

Silvermine Hiking Trail

Chry

137

Tokai Manor
House

TOKAI
FOREST RESERVE

CS

PLATEAU PLANTATION

▲ Elephant's
Eye Cave

156

North
↑

Legend

⚲ Bowling Club	⊟ Swimming	⛵ Water Sports	National Route	R120 Major & Minor Route	M 12 Metro Route
Ⅲ Cricket	Tennis	Baseball	Ⓣ Toll Plaza	Retail Area / Industrial Area	National Road / Freeway
X Hockey	Golf	Athletics	● Traffic Light	Built-up Area / Informal Settlement*	Main Through Route
H Rugby	◉ Shooting	Lighthouse	Restricted Access / Entrance	Park / Sports Ground	Other Road with Bridge
⊡ Soccer	Polo	Wine Estate	Service Station	Railway with Station	One-way St, Start/End
Squash	Basketball	Wine Sales	Tourist Information	Siding	Nature Trail

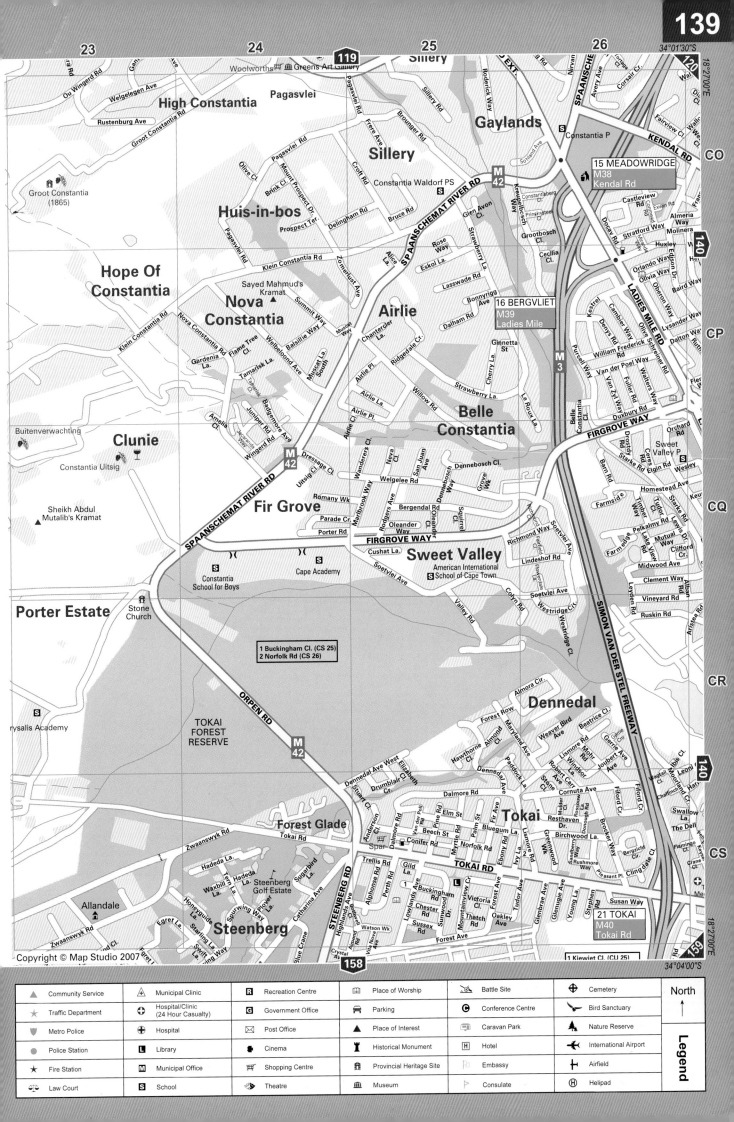

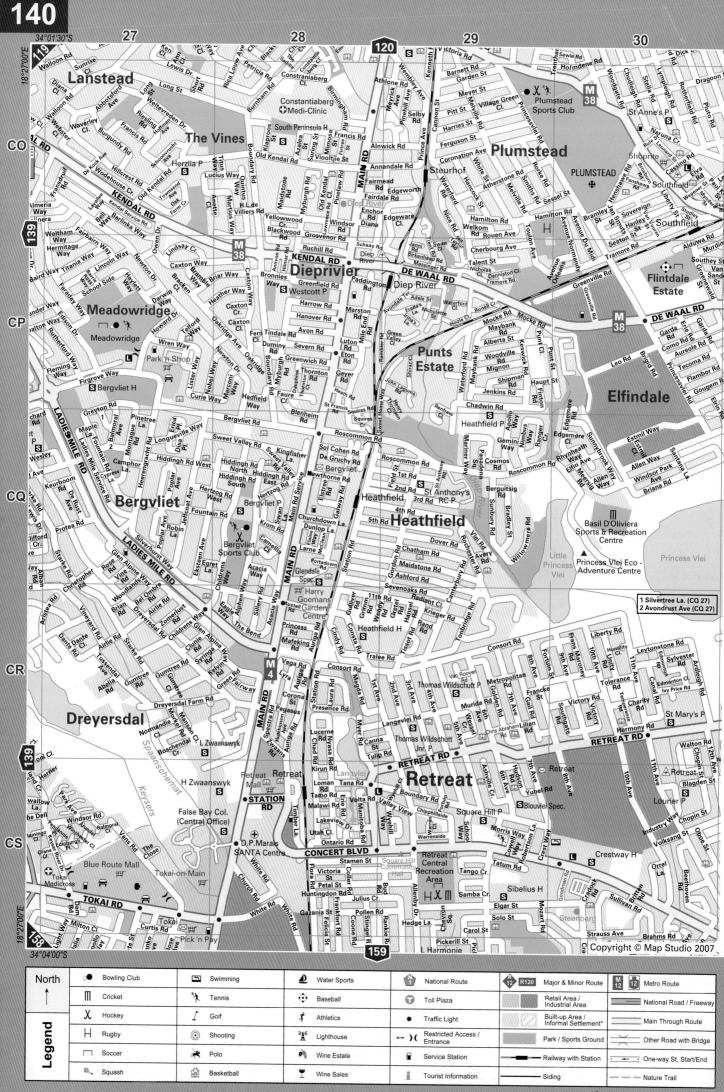

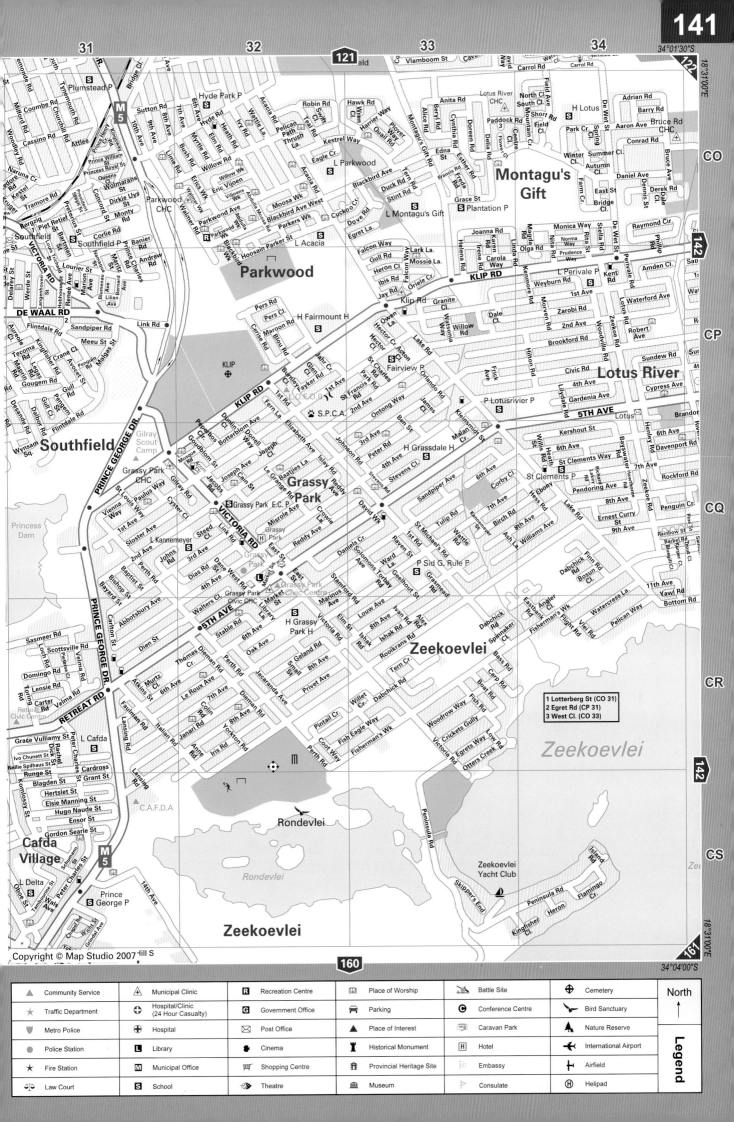

Legend

▲	Community Service	⚕	Municipal Clinic	R	Recreation Centre	⌂	Place of Worship	⚔	Battle Site	⊕	Cemetery
★	Traffic Department	⊕	Hospital/Clinic (24 Hour Casualty)	G	Government Office	🚗	Parking	C	Conference Centre	⚓	Bird Sanctuary
▽	Metro Police	✚	Hospital	✉	Post Office	▲	Place of Interest	🚐	Caravan Park	🌲	Nature Reserve
●	Police Station	L	Library	🎬	Cinema	♛	Historical Monument	H	Hotel	✈	International Airport
★	Fire Station	M	Municipal Office	🛒	Shopping Centre	🏛	Provincial Heritage Site	⚑	Embassy	✛	Airfield
⚖	Law Court	S	School	◁▷	Theatre	🏛	Museum	⚑	Consulate	Ⓗ	Helipad

North ↑

1 Lotterberg St (CO 31)
2 Egret Rd (CP 31)
3 West Cl. (CO 33)

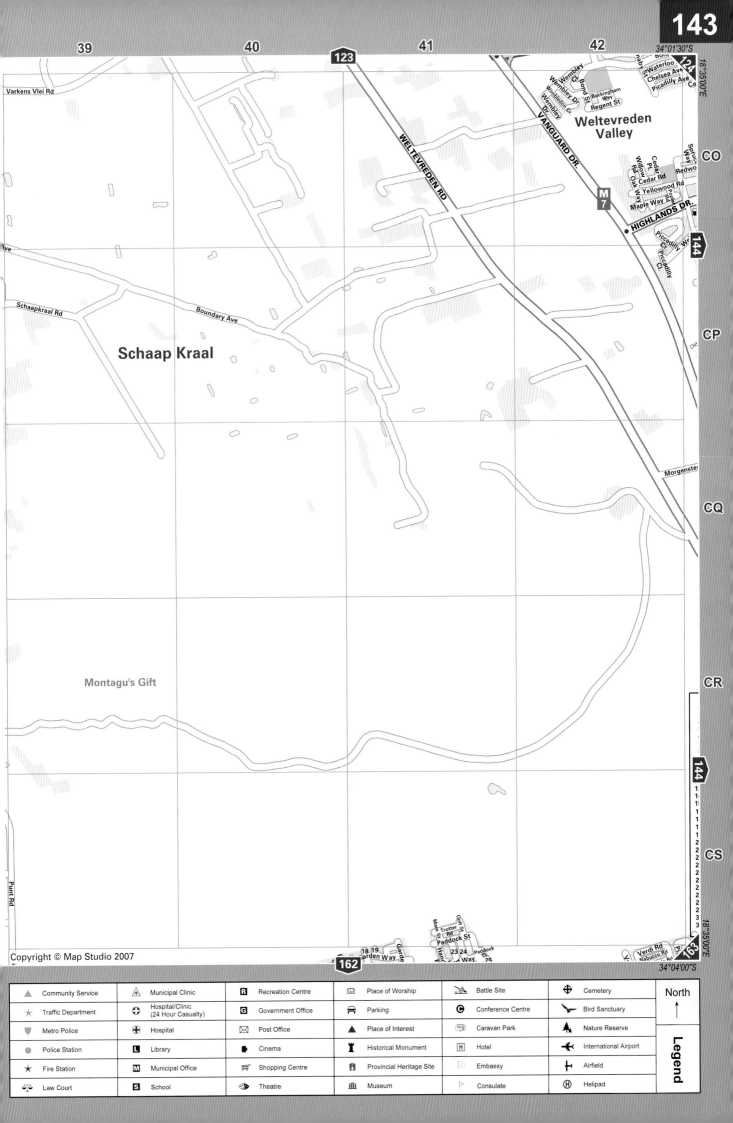

Varkens Vlei Rd

Schaapkraal Rd

Boundary Ave

Schaap Kraal

Montagu's Gift

Punt Rd

34°01'30"S
18°35'00"E

WELTEVREDEN RD

VANGUARD DR.

Weltevreden Valley

Wembley Ct
Wembley Wy
Wimbledon Ct
Wembley
Bond St
Buckingham
Regent St
Waterloo
Chelsea Ave
Picadilly Ave

Cedar Pl.
Willow Rd
Oak Way
Cedar Rd
Yellowood Rd
Maple Way
Redwo

Spruce Way

Piccadilly Wr
Piccadilly Ct.
Piccadilly Ct.

HIGHLANDS DR.

Morgenster

Mare St
Trotter Rd
Colt Rd
Paddock St
Paddock St
Hand Way
Garden Way

162

18 19
23 24
25

Verdi Rd
Nabucco Rd

CO

CP

CQ

CR

CS

34°04'00"S
18°35'00"E

39 40 41 42

123 124 144 162 163

M7

▲ Community Service	Ⓐ Municipal Clinic	Ⓡ Recreation Centre	Place of Worship	Battle Site	✛ Cemetery
★ Traffic Department	⊕ Hospital/Clinic (24 Hour Casualty)	Ⓖ Government Office	Parking	Ⓒ Conference Centre	Bird Sanctuary
▼ Metro Police	⊕ Hospital	✉ Post Office	▲ Place of Interest	Caravan Park	Nature Reserve
● Police Station	Ⓛ Library	Cinema	Historical Monument	Ⓗ Hotel	International Airport
★ Fire Station	Ⓜ Municipal Office	Shopping Centre	Provincial Heritage Site	Embassy	Airfield
Law Court	Ⓢ School	Theatre	🏛 Museum	▷ Consulate	Ⓗ Helipad

North
↑

Legend

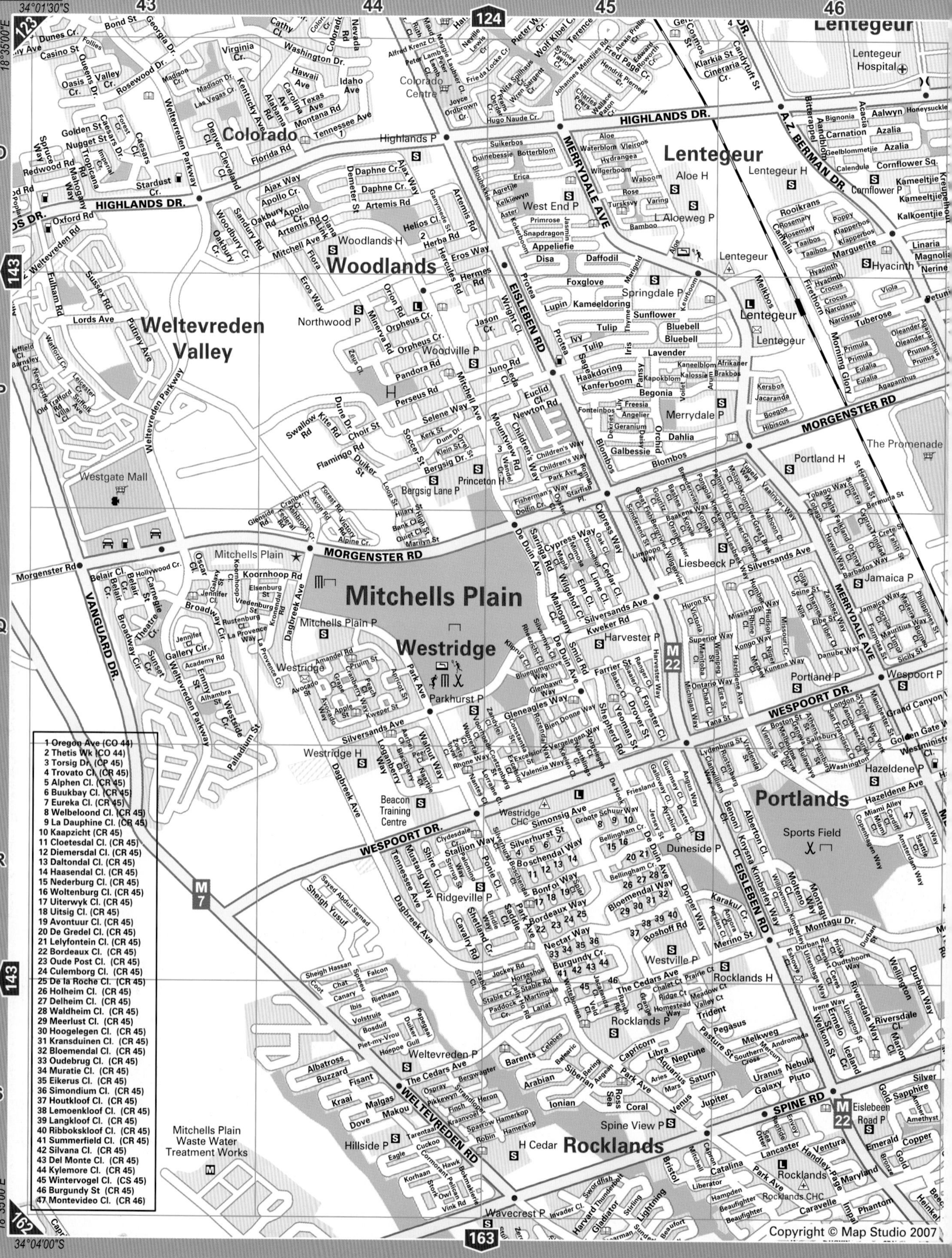

34°01'30"S
18°35'00"E
43
44
45
46
124
123
143
163
162
CO
CP
CQ
CR
CS
Colorado
Colorado Centre
Lentegeur
Lentegeur Hospital
Woodlands
Weltevreden Valley
Westgate Mall
Mitchells Plain
Westridge
Merrydale
Portlands
Rocklands
The Promenade
Sports Field
Mitchells Plain Waste Water Treatment Works
Beacon Training Centre
Westridge CHC
Rocklands CHC
HIGHLANDS DR.
MORGENSTER RD
WESPOORT DR.
SPINE RD
VANGUARD DR.
WELTEVREDEN RD
EISLEBEN RD
MERRYDALE AVE
A.Z. BERMAN DR.
Weltevreden Parkway
1 Oregon Ave (CO 44)
2 Thetis Wk (CO 44)
3 Torsig Dr. (CP 45)
4 Trovato Cl. (CR 45)
5 Alphen Cl. (CR 45)
6 Buukbay Cl. (CR 45)
7 Eureka Cl. (CR 45)
8 Welbeloond Cl. (CR 45)
9 La Dauphine Cl. (CR 45)
10 Kaapzicht (CR 45)
11 Cloetesdal Cl. (CR 45)
12 Diemersdal Cl. (CR 45)
13 Daltondal Cl. (CR 45)
14 Haasendal Cl. (CR 45)
15 Nederburg Cl. (CR 45)
16 Woltenburg Cl. (CR 45)
17 Uiterwyk Cl. (CR 45)
18 Uitsig Cl. (CR 45)
19 Avontuur Cl. (CR 45)
20 De Gredel Cl. (CR 45)
21 Lelyfontein Cl. (CR 45)
22 Bordeaux Cl. (CR 45)
23 Oude Post Cl. (CR 45)
24 Culemborg Cl. (CR 45)
25 De la Roche Cl. (CR 45)
26 Holheim Cl. (CR 45)
27 Delheim Cl. (CR 45)
28 Waldheim Cl. (CR 45)
29 Meerlust Cl. (CR 45)
30 Hoogelegen Cl. (CR 45)
31 Kransduinen Cl. (CR 45)
32 Bloemendal Cl. (CR 45)
33 Oudebrug Cl. (CR 45)
34 Muratie Cl. (CR 45)
35 Eikerus Cl. (CR 45)
36 Simondium Cl. (CR 45)
37 Houtkloof Cl. (CR 45)
38 Lemoenkloof Cl. (CR 45)
39 Langkloof Cl. (CR 45)
40 Ribbokskloof Cl. (CR 45)
41 Summerfield Cl. (CR 45)
42 Silvana Cl. (CR 45)
43 Del Monte Cl. (CR 45)
44 Kylemore Cl. (CR 45)
45 Wintervogel Cl. (CS 45)
46 Burgundy St (CR 45)
47 Montevideo Cl. (CR 46)
34°04'00"S
Copyright © Map Studio 2007

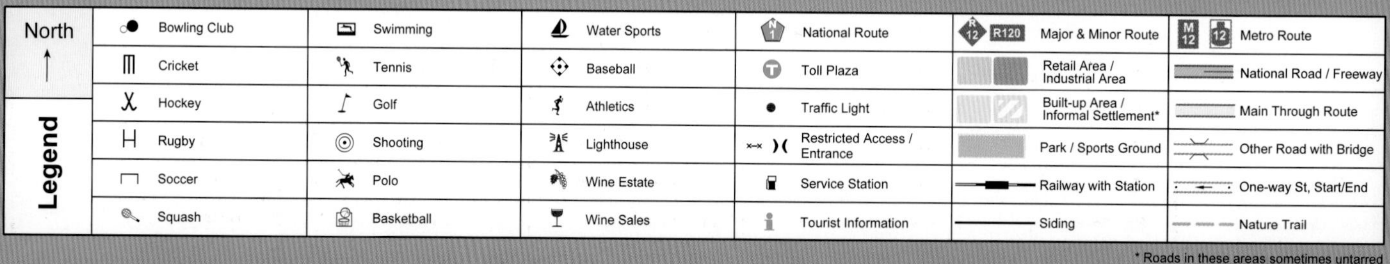

North
Legend
Bowling Club
Cricket
Hockey
Rugby
Soccer
Squash
Swimming
Tennis
Golf
Shooting
Polo
Basketball
Water Sports
Baseball
Athletics
Lighthouse
Wine Estate
Wine Sales
National Route
Toll Plaza
Traffic Light
Restricted Access / Entrance
Service Station
Tourist Information
Major & Minor Route
Retail Area / Industrial Area
Built-up Area / Informal Settlement*
Park / Sports Ground
Railway with Station
Siding
Metro Route
National Road / Freeway
Main Through Route
Other Road with Bridge
One-way St, Start/End
Nature Trail

* Roads in these areas sometimes untarred

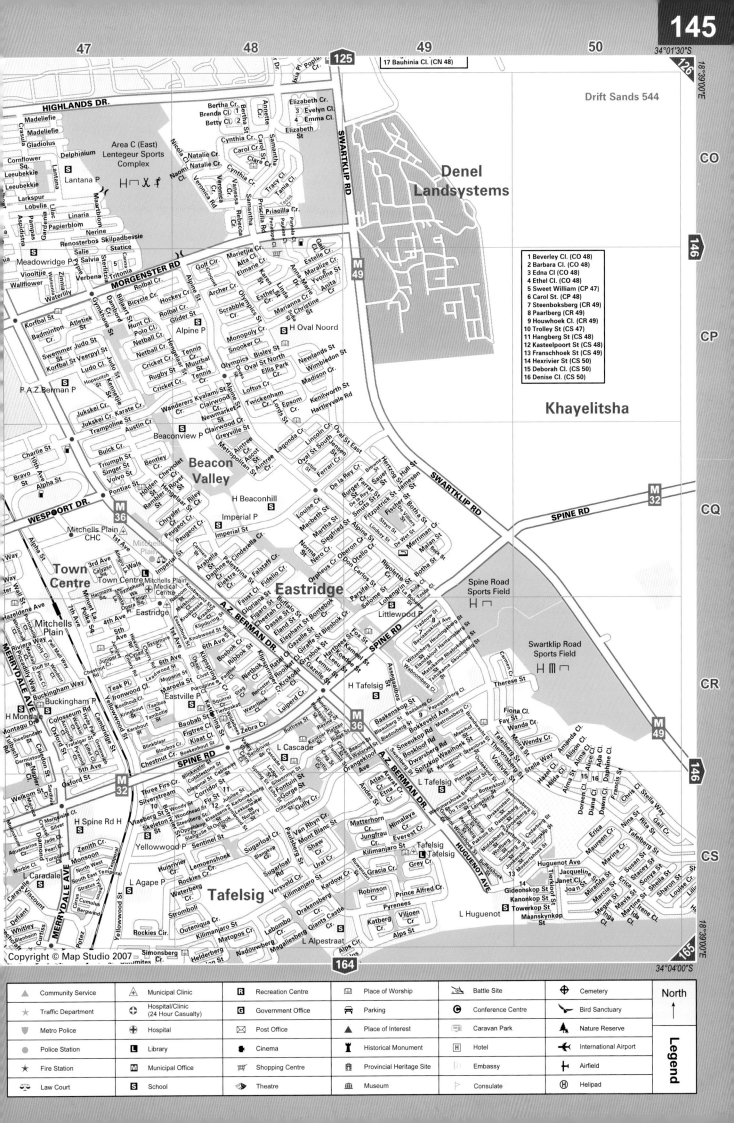

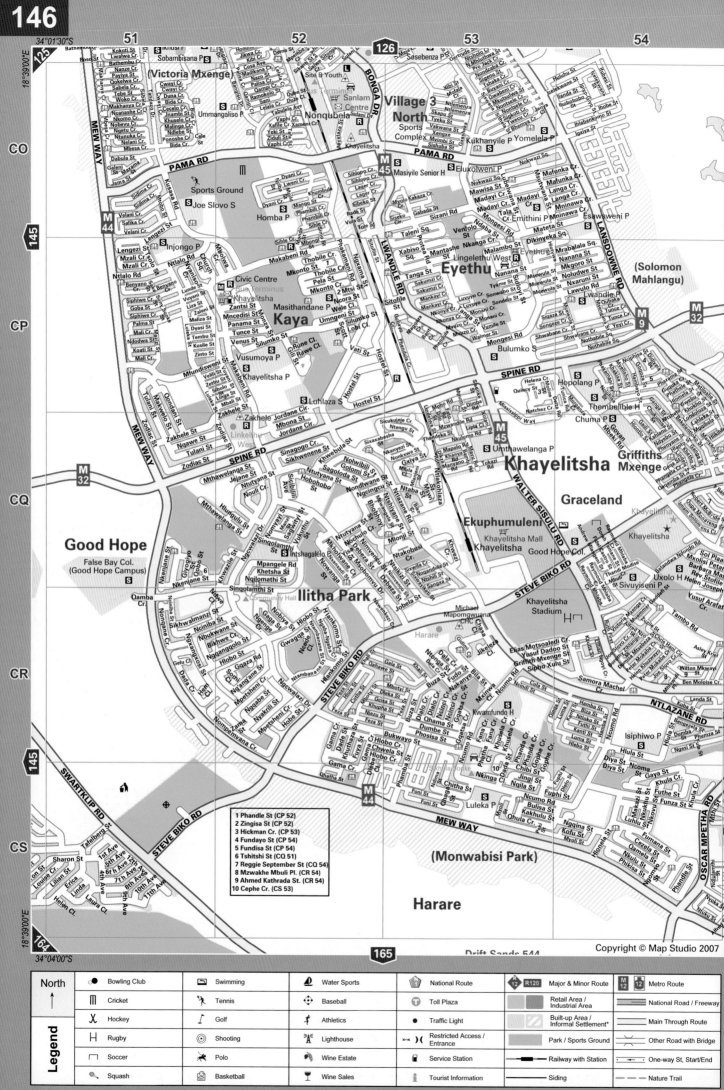

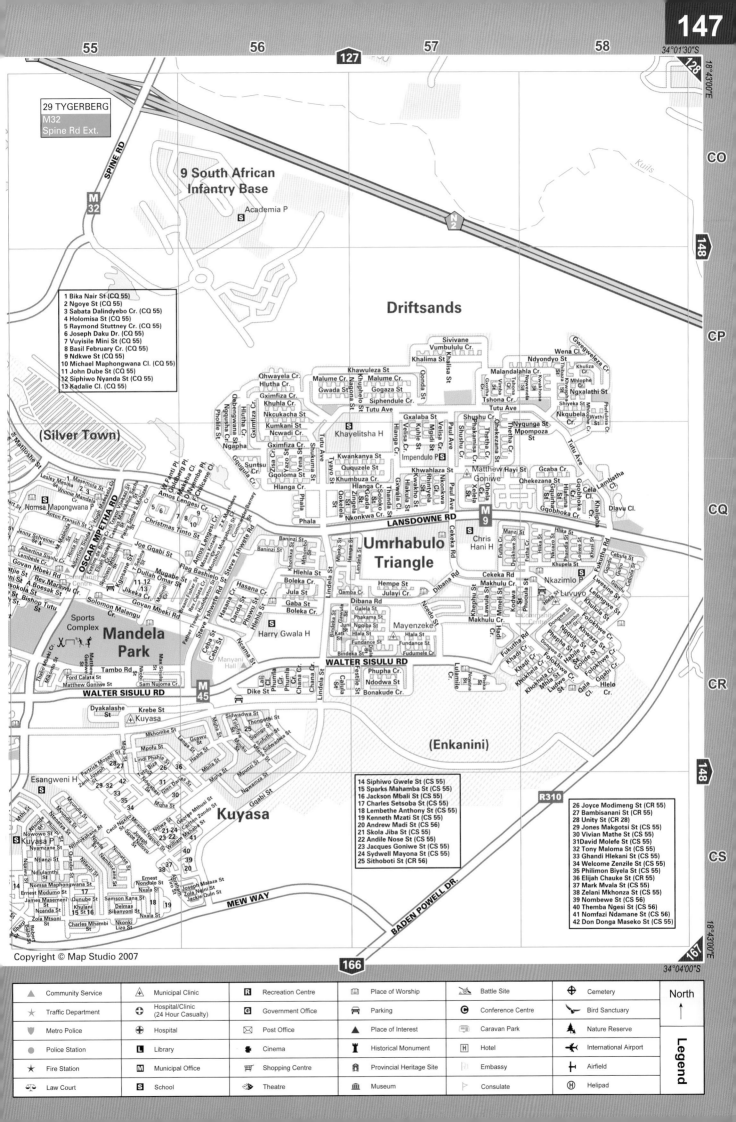

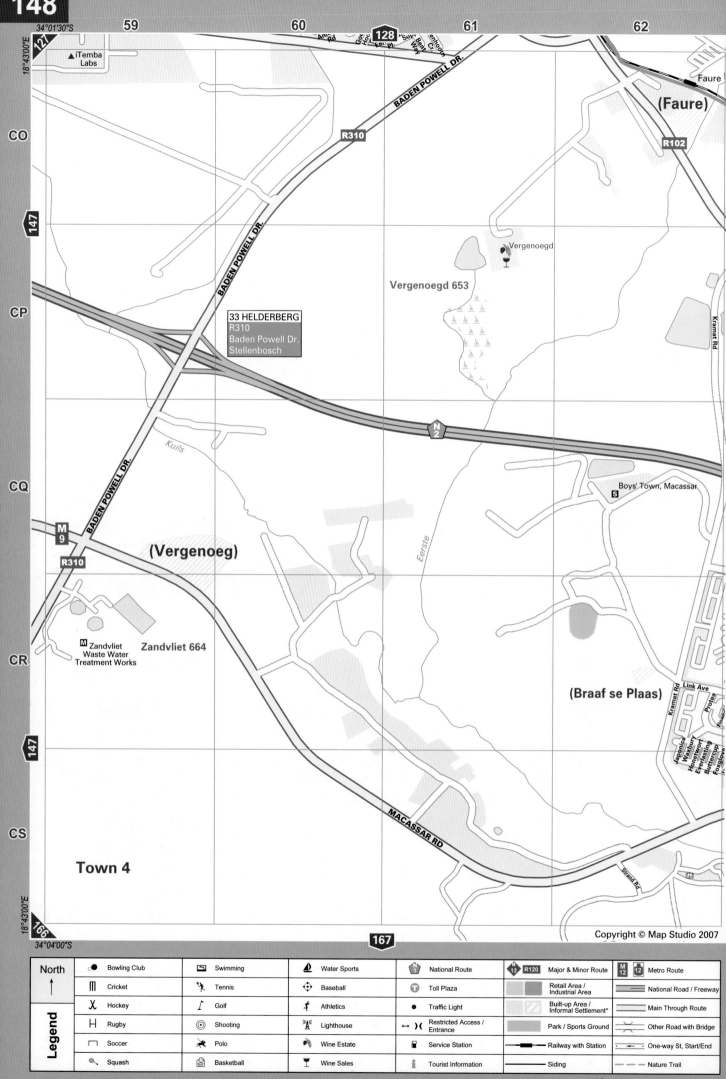

Town 4

(Vergenoeg)

(Faure)

Vergenoegd 653

33 HELDERBERG
R310
Baden Powell Dr.
Stellenbosch

▲iTemba Labs

Zandvliet 664

Ⓜ Zandvliet
Waste Water
Treatment Works

Boys' Town, Macassar

(Braaf se Plaas)

BADEN POWELL DR.

MACASSAR RD

Kuils

Eerste

Strand Rd

Kramat Rd

Link Ave

Protea

Japonica Waxbury Honeywort Everlasting Buttercup Foxglove

Copyright © Map Studio 2007

North ↑	◉ Bowling Club	▭ Swimming	⛵ Water Sports	🏛 National Route	🅜🅡 12 R120 Major & Minor Route
	🏛 Cricket	🏃 Tennis	◈ Baseball	Ⓣ Toll Plaza	M 12 Metro Route
Legend	✗ Hockey	⛳ Golf	🏃 Athletics	● Traffic Light	Retail Area / Industrial Area
	H Rugby	◉ Shooting	🗼 Lighthouse	)(Restricted Access / Entrance	Built-up Area / Informal Settlement*
	▭ Soccer	🐎 Polo	🍷 Wine Estate	⛽ Service Station	Park / Sports Ground
	✎ Squash	🏀 Basketball	🍷 Wine Sales	ℹ Tourist Information	Railway with Station · Siding · National Road / Freeway · Main Through Route · Other Road with Bridge · One-way St, Start/End · Nature Trail

* Roads in these areas sometimes untarred

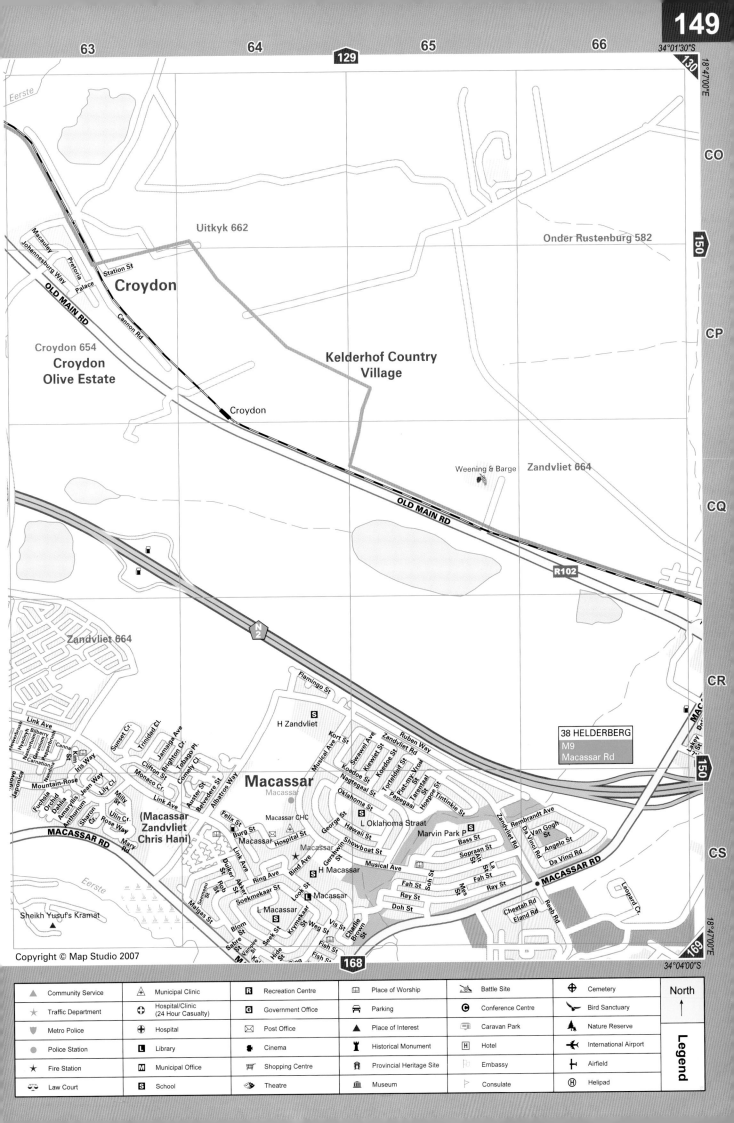

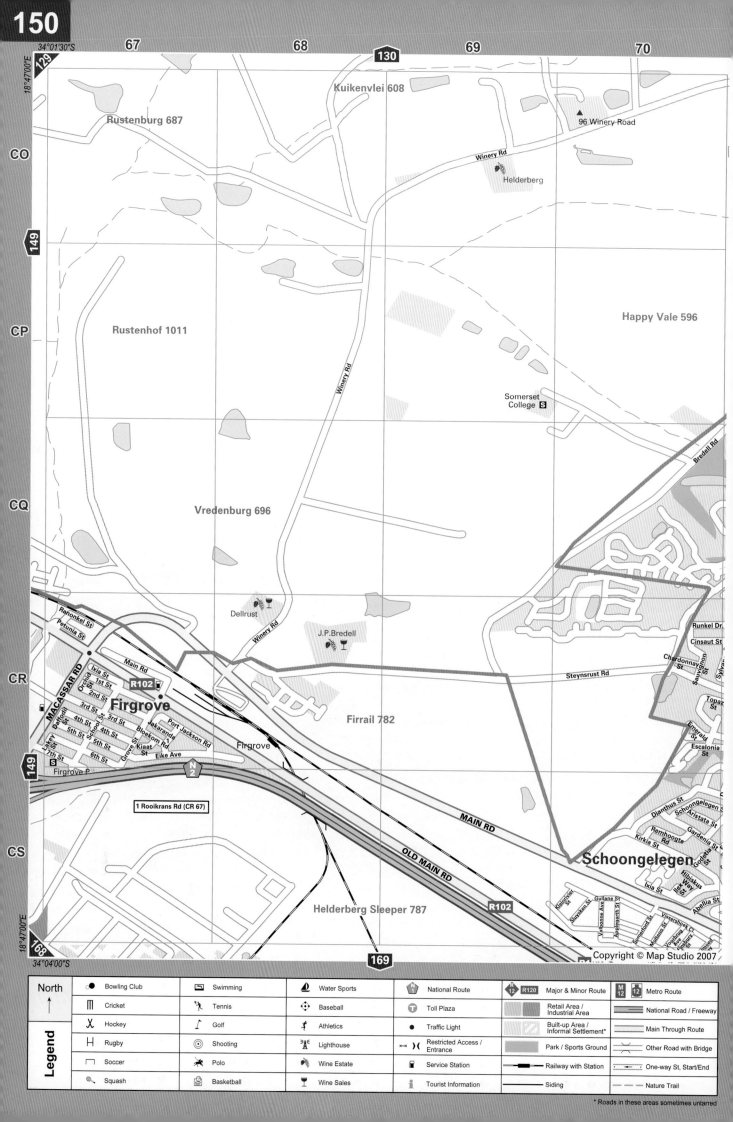

North ↑	Legend				
● Bowling Club	⊡ Swimming	⛵ Water Sports	⬠ National Route	R120 Major & Minor Route	Metro Route
Ⅲ Cricket	Tennis	Baseball	Ⓣ Toll Plaza	Retail Area / Industrial Area	National Road / Freeway
Hockey	Golf	Athletics	● Traffic Light	Built-up Area / Informal Settlement*	Main Through Route
Rugby	◎ Shooting	Lighthouse	⊶)(Restricted Access / Entrance	Park / Sports Ground	Other Road with Bridge
⬚ Soccer	Polo	Wine Estate	Service Station	Railway with Station	One-way St, Start/End
Squash	Basketball	Wine Sales	ℹ Tourist Information	Siding	Nature Trail

* Roads in these areas sometimes untarred

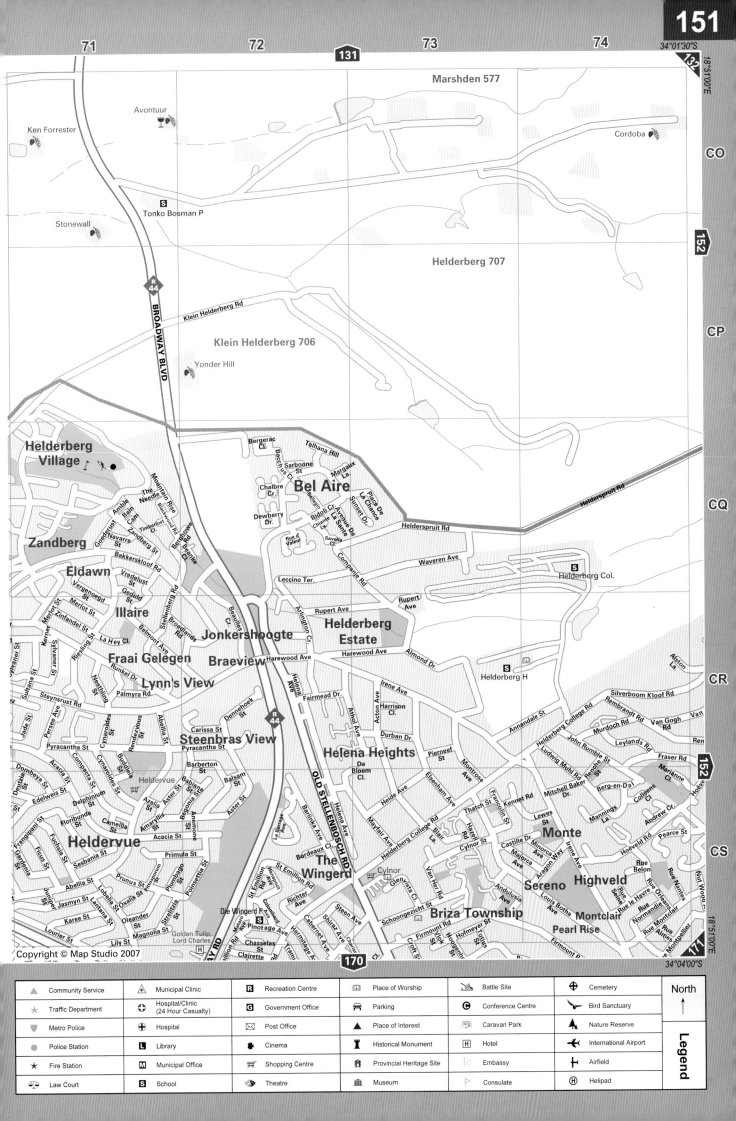

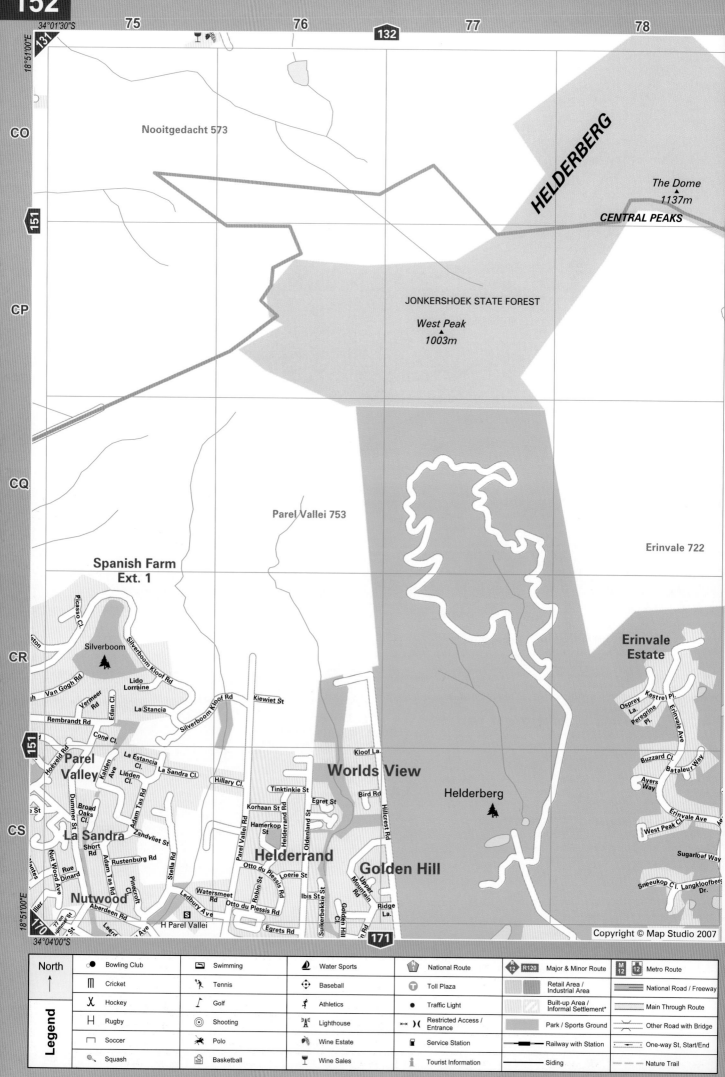

CO

Nooitgedacht 573

HELDERBERG

151

The Dome
1137m

CENTRAL PEAKS

CP

JONKERSHOEK STATE FOREST

West Peak
1003m

CQ

Parel Vallei 753

Erinvale 722

Spanish Farm
Ext. 1

Silverboom
Picasso Cl.
Silverboom Kloof Rd
Lido
Lorraine
Van Gogh Rd
Vermeer
Rd
Edan Cl.
La Stancia
Silverboom Kloof Rd
Kiewiet St

CR

Erinvale
Estate

Osprey
La.
Kestrel Pl.
Peregrine
Pl.
Erinvale Ave

Rembrandt Rd
Cone Cl.
Buzzard Cl.
Bateleur Way
Ayers
Way

151
Hoeveld Rd
Parel
Valley
La Estancia
Cl.
Kaldan
Ave
Linden
Cl.
La Sandra Cl.
Hillary Cl.
Kloof La.
Worlds View

Erinvale Ave

West Peak Cl.

Tinktinkie St
Bird Rd
Helderberg
Sugarloaf Way

CS

Broad
Oaks
Cl.
Dummer St
Adam Tas Rd
Zandvliet St
Korhaan St
Parel Vallei Rd
Helderrand Rd
Oldenland St
Egret St
Hamerkop
St
Hillcrest Rd

La Sandra
Short
Rd
Adam Tas Rd
Rustenburg Rd
Stella Rd
Otto du Plessis St
Loerie St
Helderrand
Upper
Mountain
Rd
Golden Hill

Nut Wood Ave
Rue Dinard
Pinecroft
Cl.
Ledbury Ave
Watersmeet
Rd
Otto du Plessis Rd
Robin St
Ibis St
Suikerbekkie St
Golden Hill
Cl.
Ridge
La.

Nutwood
Aberdeen Rd
H Parel Vallei
Egrets Rd
171

Sneeukop Cl. Langkloofberg
Dr.

18°51'00"E
170
34°04'00"S

Copyright © Map Studio 2007

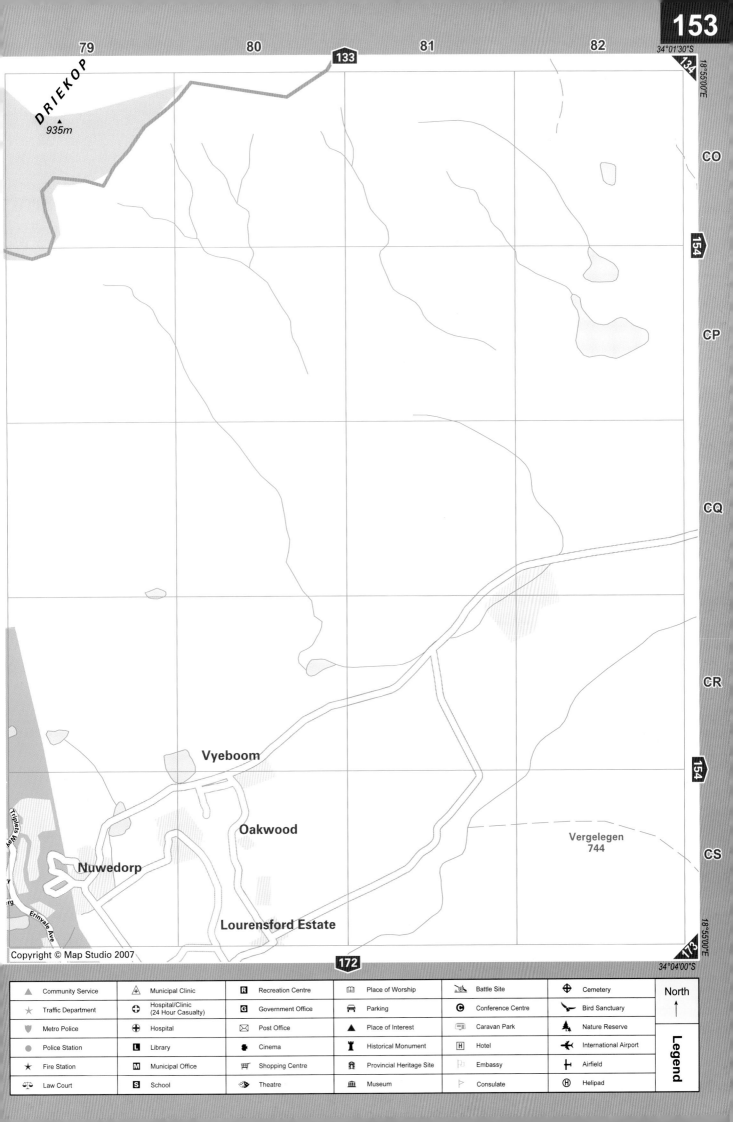

DRIEKOP
▲ 935m

CO

CP

CQ

CR

CS

Vyeboom

Oakwood

Nuwedorp

Lourensford Estate

Vergelegen
744

133

172

79   80   81   82

34°01'30"S

18°55'00"E

18°55'00"E

34°04'00"S

134

154

154

173

▲ Community Service	Ⓐ Municipal Clinic	Ⓡ Recreation Centre	Place of Worship	Battle Site	⊕ Cemetery
★ Traffic Department	⊕ Hospital/Clinic (24 Hour Casualty)	Ⓖ Government Office	🚗 Parking	Ⓒ Conference Centre	Bird Sanctuary
▼ Metro Police	⊕ Hospital	✉ Post Office	▲ Place of Interest	Caravan Park	🌲 Nature Reserve
● Police Station	Ⓛ Library	Cinema	Historical Monument	Ⓗ Hotel	✈ International Airport
★ Fire Station	Ⓜ Municipal Office	Shopping Centre	Provincial Heritage Site	Embassy	Airfield
Law Court	Ⓢ School	Theatre	🏛 Museum	▷ Consulate	Ⓗ Helipad

North
↑

Legend

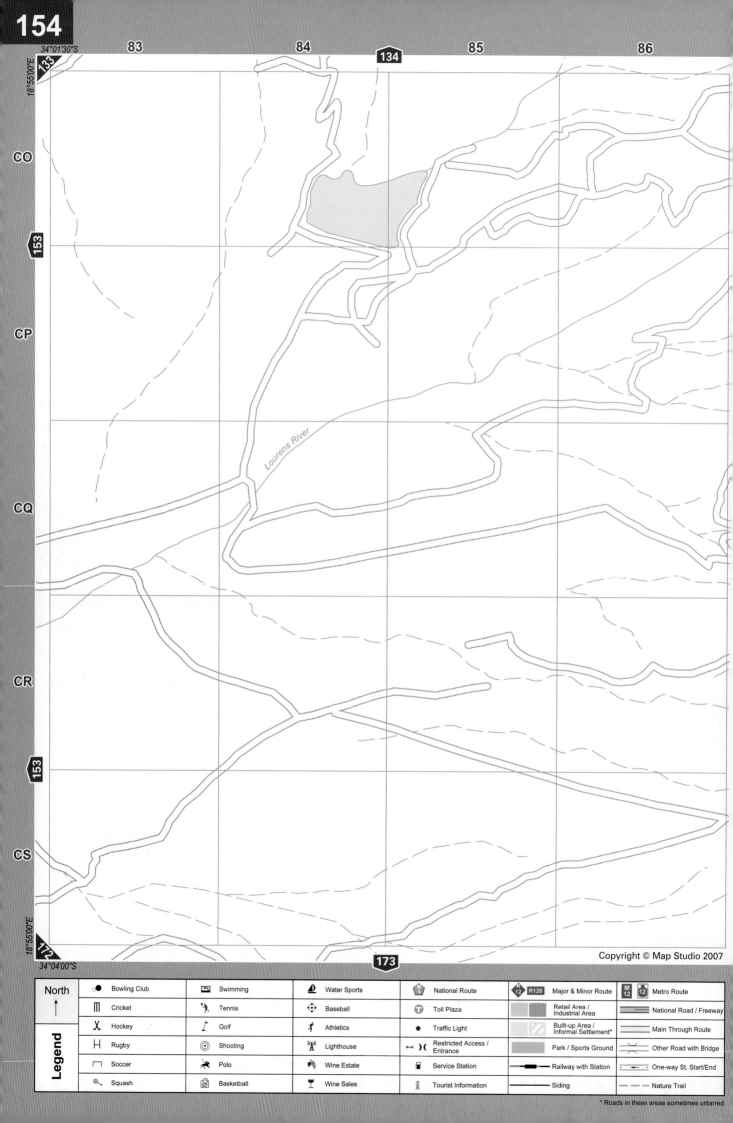

Lourens River

North										
Legend	⊙ Bowling Club	▭ Swimming	⛵ Water Sports	National Route	R12 R120 Major & Minor Route	M12 12 Metro Route
	⊞ Cricket	🏃 Tennis	Baseball	Toll Plaza	Retail Area / Industrial Area	National Road / Freeway
	✗ Hockey	Golf	Athletics	● Traffic Light	Built-up Area / Informal Settlement*	Main Through Route
	H Rugby	◎ Shooting	Lighthouse	⤫)(Restricted Access / Entrance	Park / Sports Ground	Other Road with Bridge
	▭ Soccer	Polo	Wine Estate	Service Station	Railway with Station	One-way St, Start/End
	Squash	Basketball	▼ Wine Sales	i Tourist Information	Siding	Nature Trail

* Roads in these areas sometimes untarred

34°01'30"S
18°59'00"E
34°04'00"S
18°59'00"E

87   88   135   89   90

CO
CP
CQ
CR
CS

1261m
1349m
1196m
1346m
505m

▲ Community Service	⚕ Municipal Clinic	R Recreation Centre	⌖ Place of Worship	⚔ Battle Site	✛ Cemetery	North
★ Traffic Department	✛ Hospital/Clinic (24 Hour Casualty)	G Government Office	🚗 Parking	C Conference Centre	✈ Bird Sanctuary	↑
▼ Metro Police	✛ Hospital	✉ Post Office	▲ Place of Interest	🚐 Caravan Park	🌲 Nature Reserve	
● Police Station	L Library	🎬 Cinema	♟ Historical Monument	H Hotel	✈ International Airport	
★ Fire Station	M Municipal Office	🛒 Shopping Centre	🏛 Provincial Heritage Site	Embassy	✠ Airfield	Legend
⚖ Law Court	S School	🎭 Theatre	🏛 Museum	▷ Consulate	Ⓗ Helipad	

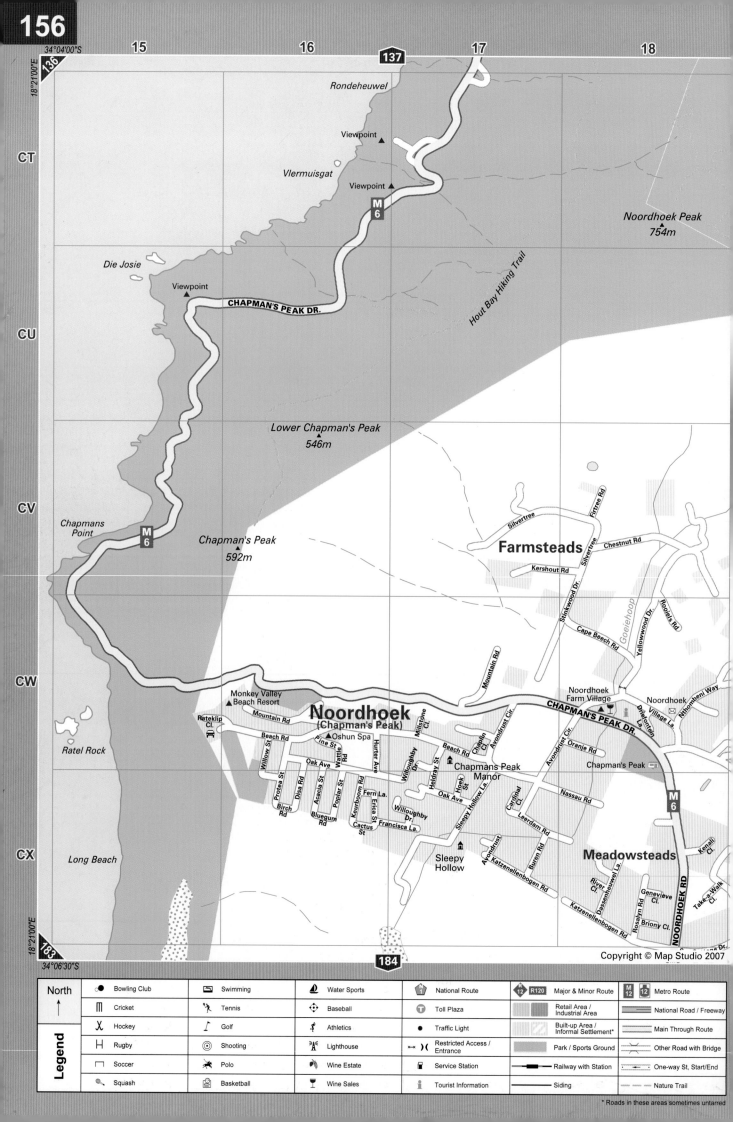

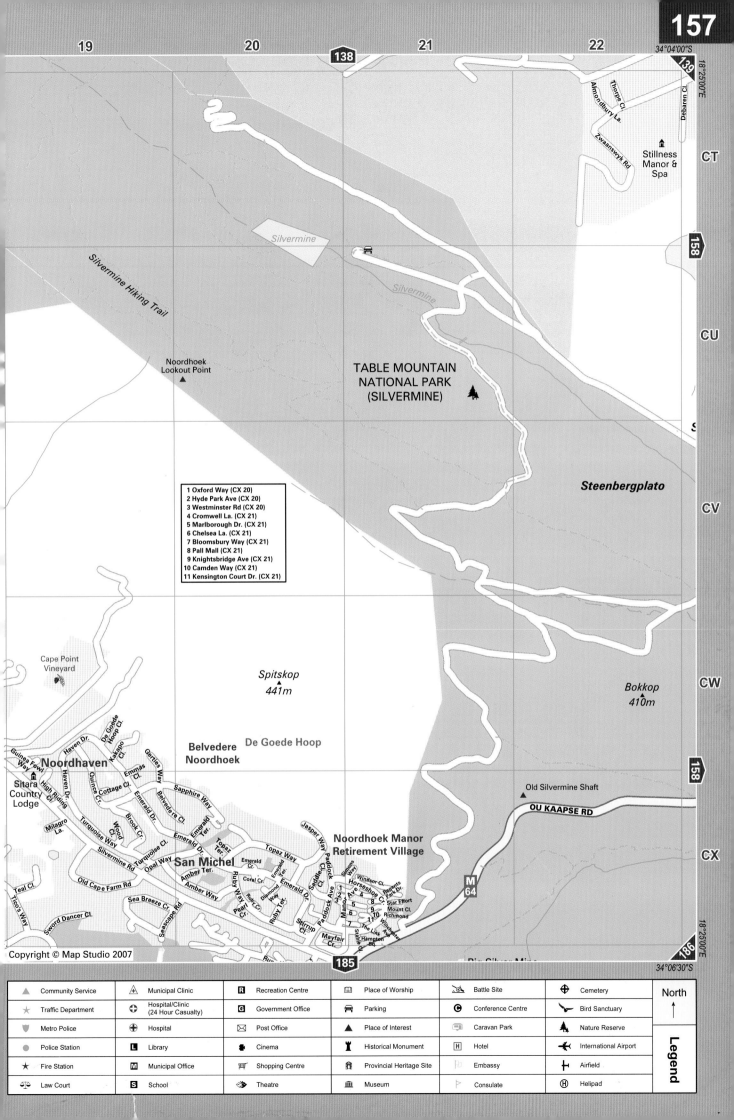

19　20　138　21　22

34°04'30"S
18°25'00"E
139

CT

158

CU

Silvermine Hiking Trail

Noordhoek Lookout Point ▲

Silvermine

Silvermine

Stillness Manor & Spa ⌂

TABLE MOUNTAIN
NATIONAL PARK
(SILVERMINE) 🌲

Steenbergplato

CV

1 Oxford Way (CX 20)
2 Hyde Park Ave (CX 20)
3 Westminster Rd (CX 20)
4 Cromwell La. (CX 21)
5 Marlborough Dr. (CX 21)
6 Chelsea La. (CX 21)
7 Bloomsbury Way (CX 21)
8 Pall Mall (CX 21)
9 Knightsbridge Ave (CX 21)
10 Camden Way (CX 21)
11 Kensington Court Dr. (CX 21)

Cape Point Vineyard

Spitskop
▲
441m

Bokkop
▲
410m

CW

Belvedere
Noordhoek

De Goede Hoop

158

Noordhaven

Sitara Country Lodge

Old Silvermine Shaft ▲

OU KAAPSE RD

Guinea Fowl Way
Haven Dr.
De Goede Hoop Cl.
Kakapo Cl.
Emmas Cl.
Gerties Way
Belvedere Cl.
Sapphire Way
Quince Cr.
Haven Dr.
High Riding
Wood Cl.
Brook Cr.
Emerald Dr.
Emerald Ter.
Milagro La.
Turquoise Way
Opal Way
Silvermine Rd
Emerald Dr.
Topaz Ter.
Topaz Way
Jasper Way
Paddock Cl.
Sapphire Way
Emerald Cl.
Amber Ter.
San Michel
Coral Cr.
Emerald Dr.
Emerald Cl.
Amber Way
Ruby Way
Pearl Cl.
Diamond Way
Ruby Ter.
Saddleleigh Cl.
Simons Way
Windsor Cl.
Horseshoe Cl.
Regents Park Dr.
Star Effort
Mount Cl.
Richmond
Manor Ave
Winchester
Old Cape Farm Rd
Teal Cl.
Sea Breeze Cr.
Seascape Rd
Stirrup Cl.
Mayfair Cr.
The Link
Hampton Sq.
Tico's Way
Sword Dancer Cl.

Noordhoek Manor
Retirement Village

M 64

CX

185

34°06'30"S
18°25'00"E
186

Copyright © Map Studio 2007

Big Silver Mine

▲ Community Service	⚕ Municipal Clinic	R Recreation Centre	📖 Place of Worship	Battle Site	⊕ Cemetery
★ Traffic Department	⊕ Hospital/Clinic (24 Hour Casualty)	G Government Office	🚗 Parking	C Conference Centre	Bird Sanctuary
Metro Police	⊕ Hospital	✉ Post Office	▲ Place of Interest	Caravan Park	🌲 Nature Reserve
Police Station	L Library	Cinema	Ⓨ Historical Monument	H Hotel	International Airport
★ Fire Station	M Municipal Office	Shopping Centre	Provincial Heritage Site	Embassy	Airfield
Law Court	S School	Theatre	🏛 Museum	Consulate	Ⓗ Helipad

North
↑

Legend

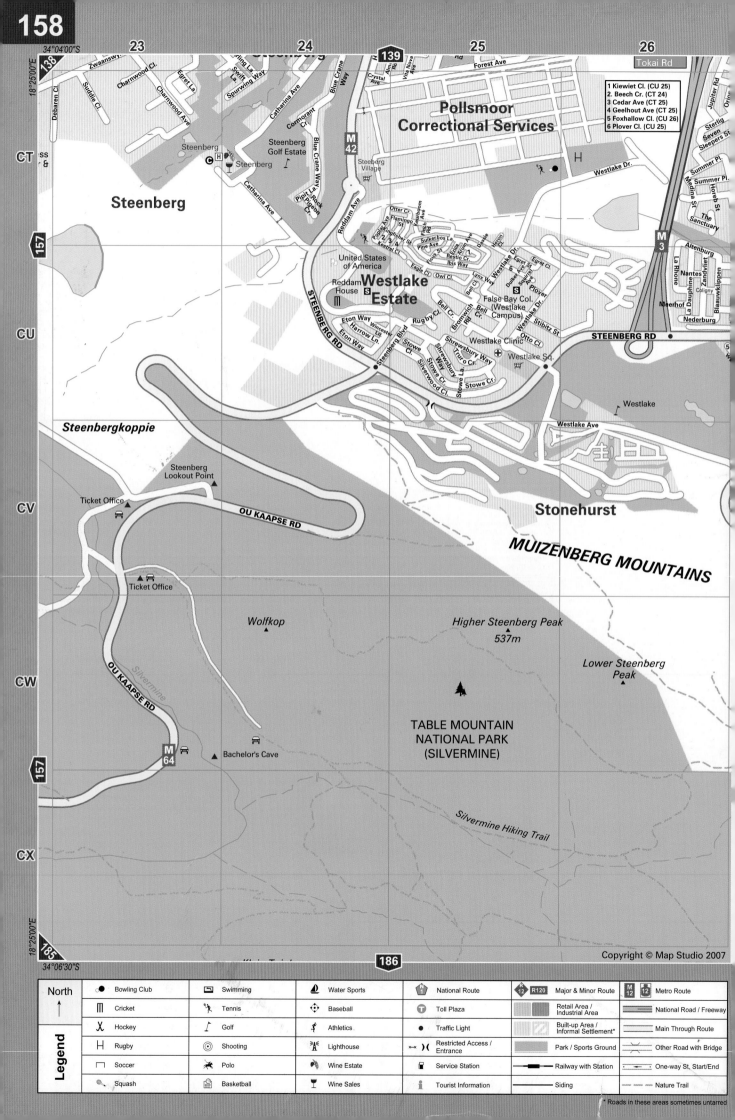

34°04'00"S
18°25'00"E

23 24 25 26

138 139 Tokai Rd

1 Kiewiet Cl. (CU 25)
2 Beech Cr. (CT 24)
3 Cedar Ave (CT 25)
4 Geelhout Ave (CT 25)
5 Foxhallow Cl. (CU 26)
6 Plover Cl. (CU 25)

**Pollsmoor
Correctional Services**

M 42

Westlake Dr.

CT

Zwaanswyk
Charnwood Cl.
Charnwood
Egret La.
Spurwing Way
Catharina Ave
Cormorant Cr.
Swift La.
Swift La.
ling La.
Blue Crane Way
Crystal Ave
Vita Nova
Forest Ave
Alma Rd

Suddie Cl.
Debaren Cl.

Steenberg
Steenberg
Steenberg
Golf Estate
Blue Crane Way
Pigeon Cr.
Pipit La.
Rock Cr.
Steenberg
Village

Steenberg

157

Catharina Ave
Reddam Ave

Otter Cr.
Flamingo
Flamingo La.
Poplar Ave
Kingfisher La.
Keurboom
Suikerbos La.
Finch
Pine Ave
Fiscal St.
Restio Cr.
Ibis Way
Daisie
Higon
Egret St.
Egret Cl.
Westlake Dr.
Westlake Dr.

United States
of America
Reddam
House
**Westlake
Estate**

Eagle Cr.
Owl Cl.
Bell Cl.
Lynx Way
Squirrel Cl.
Duiker Cl.
Plover

CU

STEENBERG RD

Eton Way
Eton Way
Harrow Ln.
Wincaster Ln.
Rugby Cl.
Bell Cr.
Bronwich
Bell
Bell
Bell
Shrewsbury Way
Shrewsbury
Truro Cr.
Otto Cl.
Stibitz St.

False Bay Col.
(Westlake
Campus)

Westlake Clinic

STEENBERG RD

Meerhof
Nederburg
Altenburg
La Rhone
Nantes
Zandvliet
Blaauwklippen
Cbligny
Dauphine

M 3

The
Sanctuary
Horeb St.
Medina St.
Summer Pl.
Summer Pl.
Sterlig
Seven
Sleepers St.
Jupiter Rd
Orion

Steenberg Blvd
Stowe Cl.
Silverwood Cl.
Stowe Way
Stowe Cr.
Stowe La.
Stowe Cr.

Westlake Sq.

Westlake

Westlake Ave

Steenbergkoppie

Steenberg
Lookout Point

Ticket Office

CV

OU KAAPSE RD

Stonehurst

MUIZENBERG MOUNTAINS

Ticket Office

Wolfkop

Higher Steenberg Peak
537m

*Lower Steenberg
Peak*

CW

157

OU KAAPSE RD

Silvermine

M 64

Bachelor's Cave

**TABLE MOUNTAIN
NATIONAL PARK
(SILVERMINE)**

Silvermine Hiking Trail

CX

18°25'00"E
34°06'30"S

185

186

Klein Tuin

North ↑

Legend

🎳	Bowling Club	🏊	Swimming	⛵	Water Sports	🛡	National Route	R120	Major & Minor Route	M 12	Metro Route
🏛	Cricket	🎾	Tennis	⚾	Baseball	T	Toll Plaza		Retail Area / Industrial Area		National Road / Freeway
X	Hockey	⛳	Golf	🏃	Athletics	●	Traffic Light		Built-up Area / Informal Settlement*		Main Through Route
H	Rugby	⊙	Shooting	🗼	Lighthouse	⊶ (	Restricted Access / Entrance		Park / Sports Ground		Other Road with Bridge
☐	Soccer	🐎	Polo	🍇	Wine Estate	🛢	Service Station		Railway with Station		One-way St, Start/End
🔍	Squash	🏀	Basketball	🍷	Wine Sales	ℹ	Tourist Information		Siding		Nature Trail

* Roads in these areas sometimes untarred

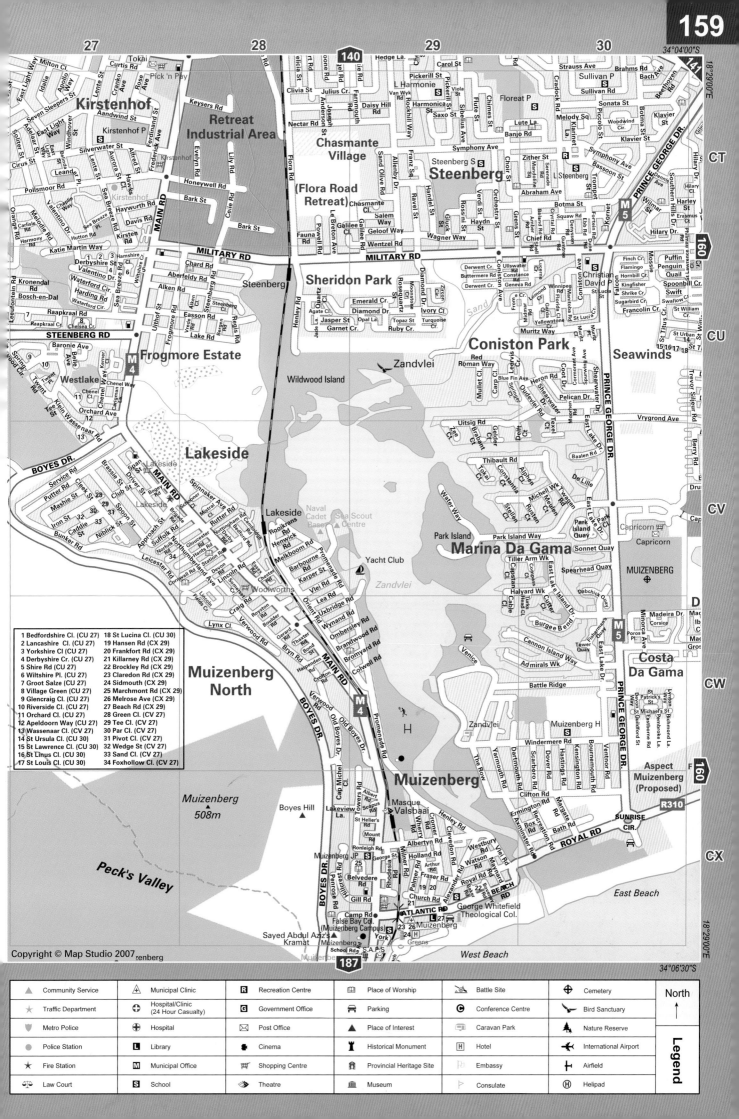

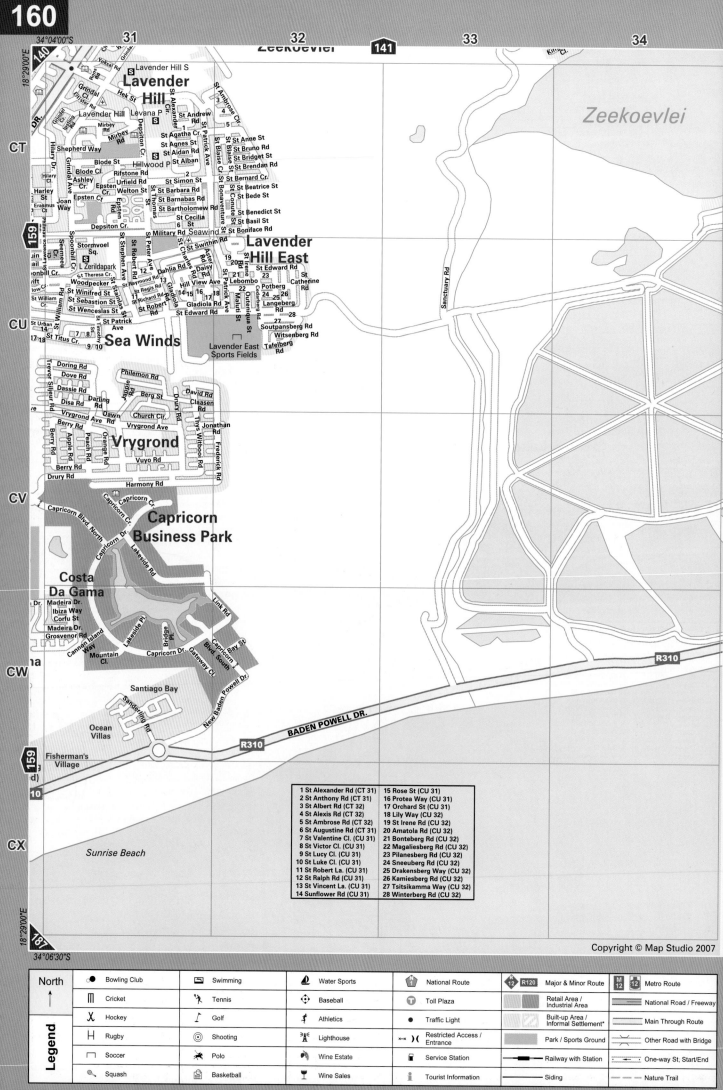

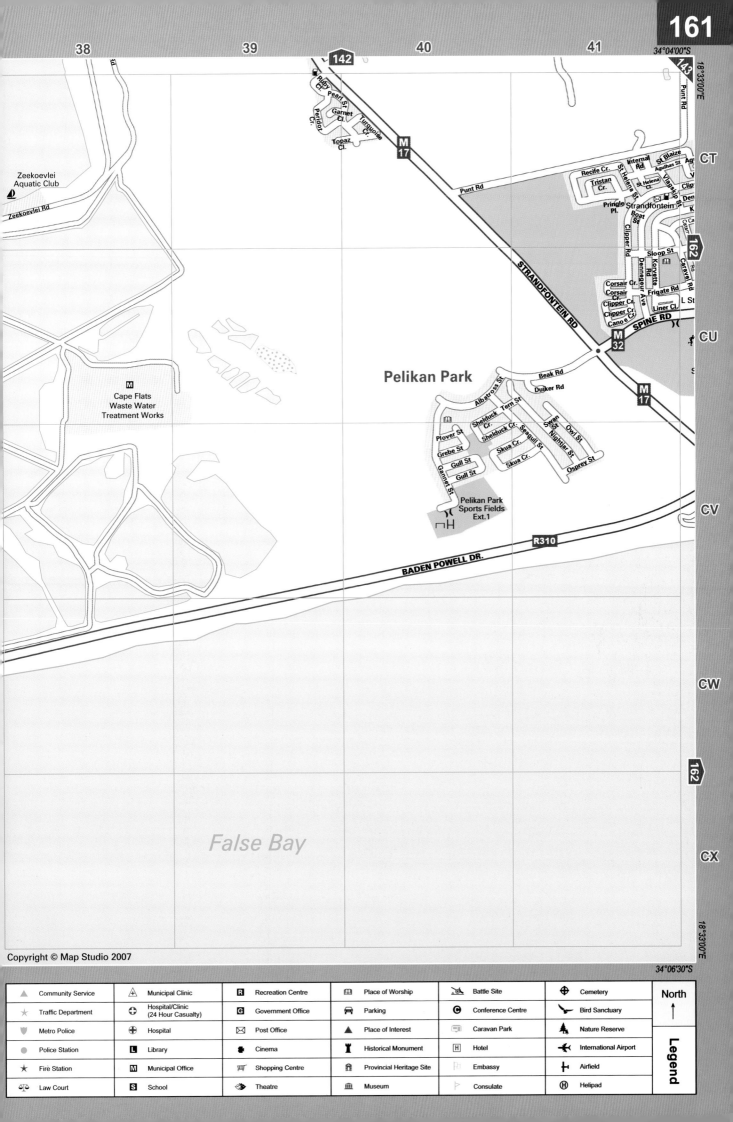

Zeekoevlei
Aquatic Club

Zeekoevlei Rd

142

Ruby Cl.
Pearl St
Garnet Cl.
Peridot Cr.
Turquoise Cr.
Topaz Cl.

M 17

Punt Rd

Recife Cr.
Tristan Cr.
St Helena St
Internal Rd
St Blaize
Agulhas St
St Helena St
Pringle Pl.
Strandfontein
Boat St
Clipper Rd
Sloop St
Dennegeur Ave
Korvette Rd
Frigate Rd
Corsair Cr.
Corsair Cr.
Clipper Cr.
Clipper Cr.
Cano e Cr.
Liner Cl.
L St

162

CT

STRANDFONTEIN RD

M 32
SPINE RD
CU

M 17

M
Cape Flats
Waste Water
Treatment Works

Pelikan Park

Beak Rd
Duiker Rd

Albatross St
Plover St
Grebe St
Gull St
Gannet St
Gull St

Shelduck Cr.
Tern St
Shelduck Cr.
Skua Cr.
Seagull St
Skua Cr.
Swan St
Nightjar St
Owl St
Osprey St

Pelikan Park
Sports Fields
Ext.1
H

R310
CV

BADEN POWELL DR.

CW

162

False Bay

CX

34°04'00"S
18°33'00"E
18°33'00"E
34°06'30"S

						North
▲ Community Service	Ⓐ Municipal Clinic	Ⓡ Recreation Centre	Place of Worship	Battle Site	⊕ Cemetery	↑
★ Traffic Department	✚ Hospital/Clinic (24 Hour Casualty)	Ⓖ Government Office	Parking	▲ Place of Interest	Bird Sanctuary	
Metro Police	✚ Hospital	✉ Post Office	▲ Place of Interest	Caravan Park	Nature Reserve	
● Police Station	Ⓛ Library	Cinema	Ⓨ Historical Monument	H Hotel	International Airport	Legend
★ Fire Station	Ⓜ Municipal Office	Shopping Centre	Provincial Heritage Site	Embassy	Airfield	
Law Court	Ⓢ School	Theatre	Museum	▷ Consulate	Ⓗ Helipad	

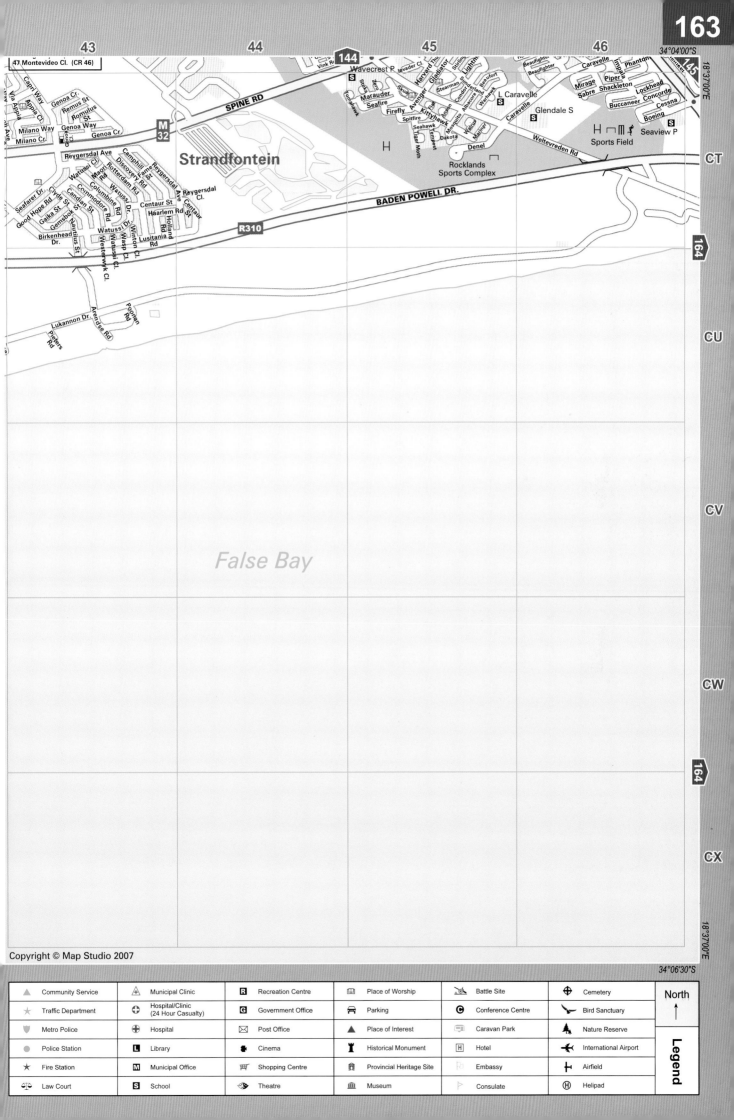

Strandfontein

False Bay

SPINE RD · BADEN POWELL DR. · R310 · M32 · R145 · R144 · R164

Rocklands Sports Complex · Sports Field · Seaview P · Wavecrest P · Glendale S · Weltevreden Rd · Reygersdal Ave · Lukannon Dr.

47 Montevideo Cl. (CR 46)

34°04'30"S · 18°37'00"E · 34°06'30"S

Legend — North

Symbol	Description	Symbol	Description
▲	Community Service	🏛	Place of Worship
★	Traffic Department	🚗	Parking
▼	Metro Police	▲	Place of Interest
●	Police Station	♜	Historical Monument
★	Fire Station	🏛	Provincial Heritage Site
⚖	Law Court	🏛	Museum
⚕	Municipal Clinic	⚔	Battle Site
⊕	Hospital/Clinic (24 Hour Casualty)	ⓒ	Conference Centre
✚	Hospital	🚐	Caravan Park
L	Library	🏨	Hotel
M	Municipal Office		Embassy
S	School	⚑	Consulate
R	Recreation Centre	⊕	Cemetery
G	Government Office	✈	Bird Sanctuary
✉	Post Office	🌲	Nature Reserve
🎬	Cinema	✈	International Airport
🛒	Shopping Centre	✈	Airfield
🎭	Theatre	Ⓗ	Helipad

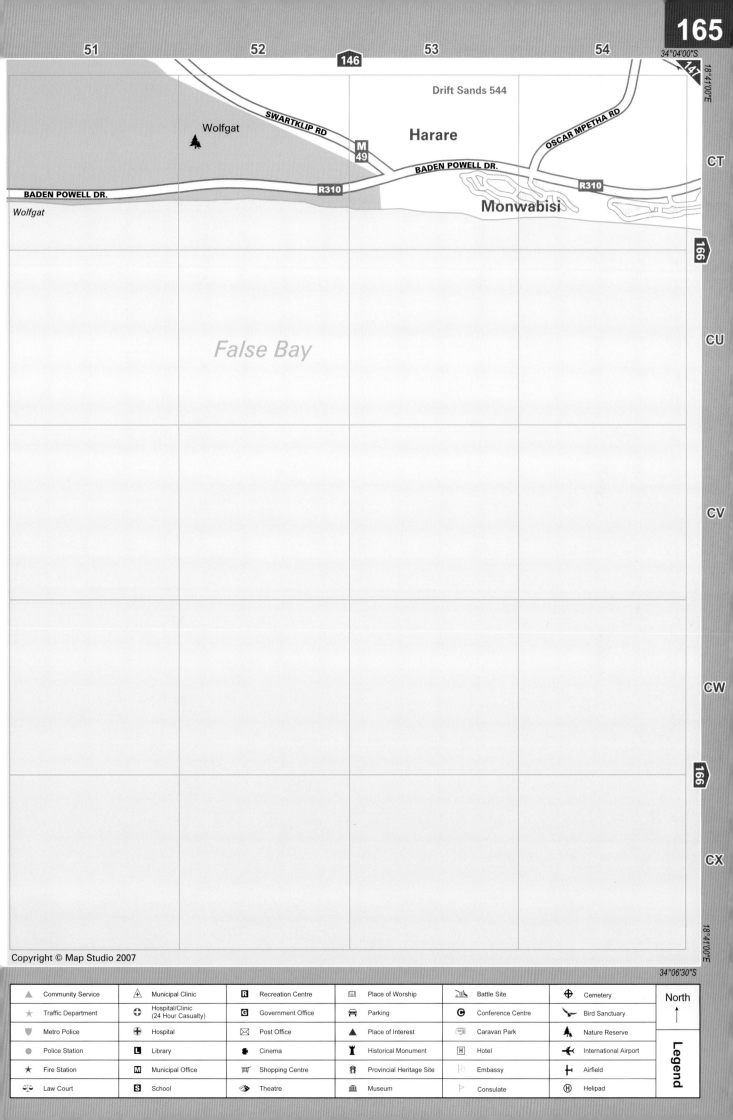

34°04'30"S

51 52 146 53 54 141 18°41'00"E

Drift Sands 544

Wolfgat

SWARTKLIP RD

Harare

OSCAR MPETHA RD

M 49

BADEN POWELL DR.

CT

BADEN POWELL DR. R310 R310

Monwabisi

Wolfgat

166

False Bay

CU

CV

CW

166

CX

18°41'00"E

34°06'30"S

▲ Community Service	Ⓐ Municipal Clinic	Ⓡ Recreation Centre	Place of Worship	Battle Site	⊕ Cemetery	**North** ↑
★ Traffic Department	Hospital/Clinic (24 Hour Casualty)	Ⓖ Government Office	Parking	Ⓒ Conference Centre	Bird Sanctuary	
Metro Police	✚ Hospital	✉ Post Office	▲ Place of Interest	Caravan Park	Nature Reserve	
● Police Station	Ⓛ Library	Cinema	Historical Monument	Ⓗ Hotel	✈ International Airport	**Legend**
★ Fire Station	Ⓜ Municipal Office	Shopping Centre	Provincial Heritage Site	Embassy	Airfield	
Law Court	Ⓢ School	Theatre	Museum	Consulate	Ⓗ Helipad	

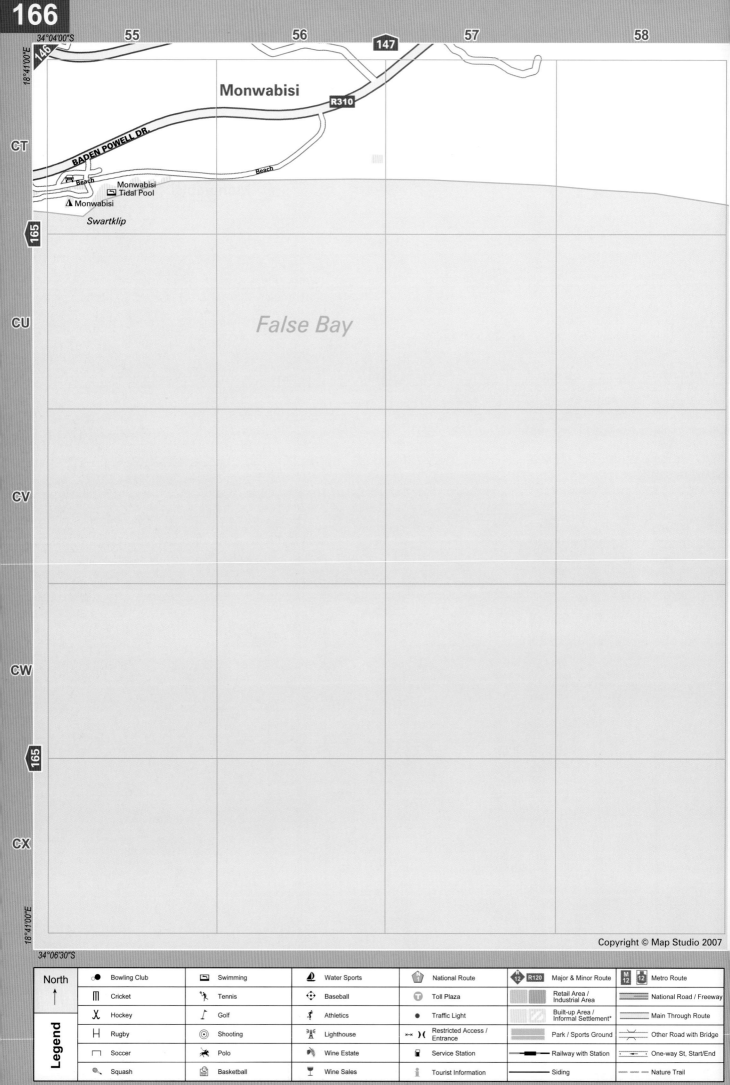

55   56   **147**   57   58

146

Monwabisi

R310

CT

BADEN POWELL DR.

Beach

Beach

Monwabisi
Tidal Pool

▲ Monwabisi

Swartklip

165

CU

False Bay

CV

CW

165

CX

Copyright © Map Studio 2007

34°06'30"S
18°41'00"E

North ↑		Bowling Club		Swimming		Water Sports		National Route	R120	Major & Minor Route	M 12	12	Metro Route
	Ⅲ	Cricket		Tennis		Baseball	Ⓣ	Toll Plaza		Retail Area / Industrial Area			National Road / Freeway
	Ⅹ	Hockey		Golf		Athletics	●	Traffic Light		Built-up Area / Informal Settlement*			Main Through Route
Legend	Ⱶ	Rugby	⊙	Shooting		Lighthouse	⤬)(	Restricted Access / Entrance		Park / Sports Ground			Other Road with Bridge
		Soccer		Polo		Wine Estate		Service Station		Railway with Station			One-way St, Start/End
		Squash		Basketball		Wine Sales	ℹ	Tourist Information		Siding			Nature Trail

* Roads in these areas sometimes untarred

34°04'30"S

59 60 61 62

148

149

18°45'00"E

Macassar Beach

CT

168

Macassar Beach

CU

False Bay

CV

CW

168

CX

18°45'00"E

34°06'30"S

▲ Community Service	Ⓐ Municipal Clinic	Ⓡ Recreation Centre	🕮 Place of Worship	Battle Site	⊕ Cemetery
★ Traffic Department	✛ Hospital/Clinic (24 Hour Casualty)	Ⓖ Government Office	🚗 Parking	Ⓒ Conference Centre	Bird Sanctuary
♥ Metro Police	✚ Hospital	✉ Post Office	▲ Place of Interest	Caravan Park	♠ Nature Reserve
● Police Station	Ⓛ Library	✦ Cinema	♟ Historical Monument	Ⓗ Hotel	✈ International Airport
★ Fire Station	Ⓜ Municipal Office	🛒 Shopping Centre	🏛 Provincial Heritage Site	Embassy	┿ Airfield
⚖ Law Court	Ⓢ School	Theatre	🏛 Museum	▷ Consulate	Ⓗ Helipad

North
↑

Legend

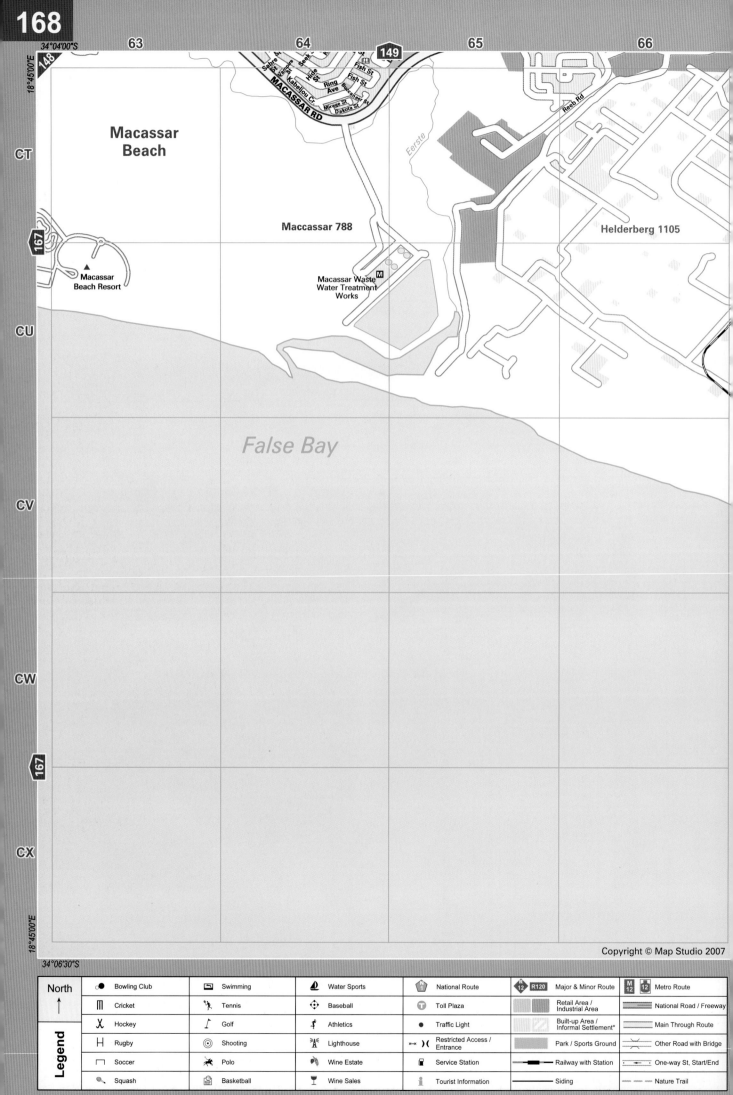

34°04'00"S

18°45'00"E

148

63

64

149

65

66

167

CT

Macassar
Beach

167

148

Maccassar 788

Helderberg 1105

Eerste

Macassar
Beach Resort

Macassar Waste
Water Treatment
Works

M

CU

CV

False Bay

CW

167

CX

18°45'00"E

34°06'30"S

North ↑		Bowling Club		Swimming		Water Sports		National Route		R120	Major & Minor Route			Metro Route
		Cricket		Tennis		Baseball		Toll Plaza			Retail Area / Industrial Area			National Road / Freeway
		Hockey		Golf		Athletics		Traffic Light			Built-up Area / Informal Settlement*			Main Through Route
Legend		Rugby		Shooting		Lighthouse		Restricted Access / Entrance			Park / Sports Ground			Other Road with Bridge
		Soccer		Polo		Wine Estate		Service Station			Railway with Station			One-way St, Start/End
		Squash		Basketball		Wine Sales		Tourist Information			Siding			Nature Trail

* Roads in these areas sometimes untarred

34°04'00"S
18°49'00"E

150
R102
N2
CT
Olive Grove Industrial Estate
Kynoch Rd
Olive Way
151
170
Helderberg Community Care Centre
Blue Crane Park
4 S
CU

Paarde Vlei
CV

CW

BEACH RD
170
LOURENS RIVER PICNIC AREA
De Ruyter D
Cook
Thomp
Waterworld
Van
CX

False Bay

18°49'00"E
34°06'30"S

Community Service	Municipal Clinic	Recreation Centre	Place of Worship	Battle Site	Cemetery
Traffic Department	Hospital/Clinic (24 Hour Casualty)	Government Office	Parking	Conference Centre	Bird Sanctuary
Metro Police	Hospital	Post Office	Place of Interest	Caravan Park	Nature Reserve
Police Station	Library	Cinema	Historical Monument	Hotel	International Airport
Fire Station	Municipal Office	Shopping Centre	Provincial Heritage Site	Embassy	Airfield
Law Court	School	Theatre	Museum	Consulate	Helipad

North

Legend

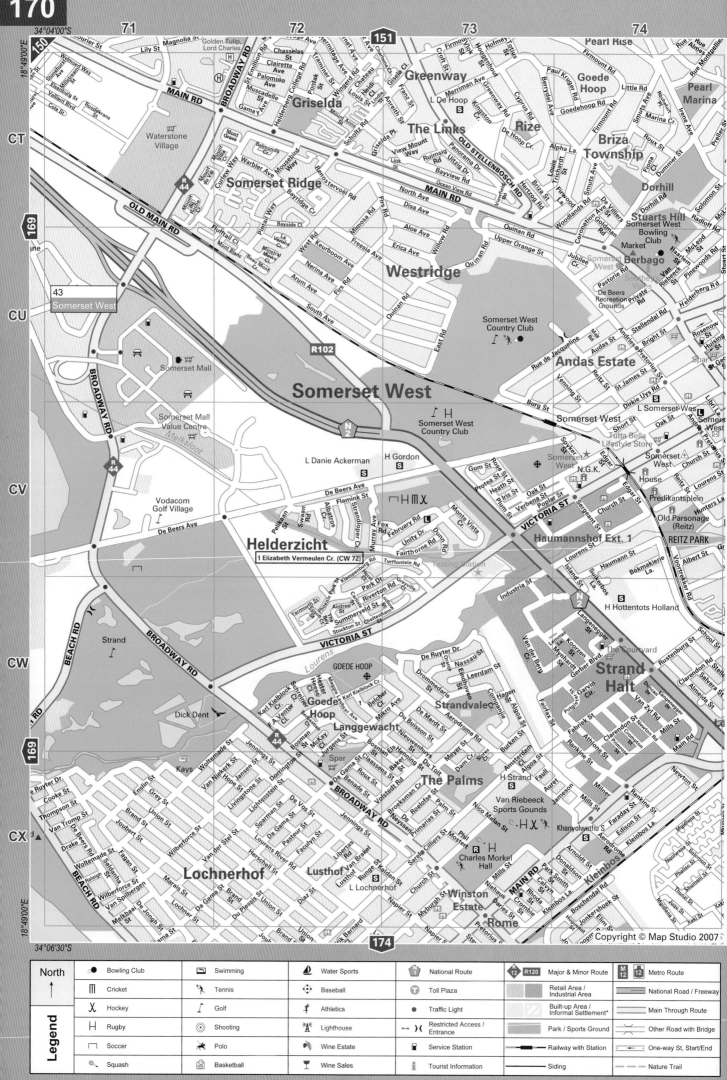

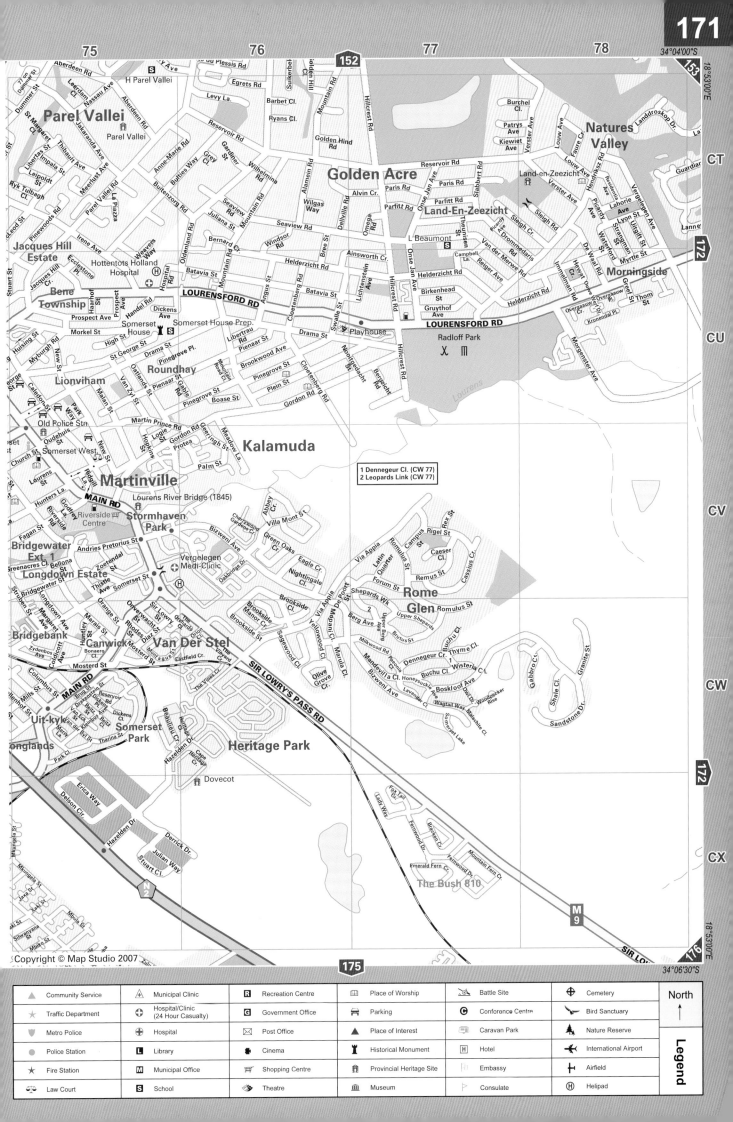

34°04'00"S
18°53'00"E
152
171
18°53'00"E
173
34°06'30"S

79   80   153   81   82

153
176

CT
CU
CV
CW
CX
171
171

Landdroskop Dr.
Erinvale Ave
Ave
Guardian Cr.
Guardian Cr.
Lanner Cl.
Erinvale [H] [C] Erinvale
Fleur Du Cap
Lourensford
Vergelegen
Rooiland Dam
Myrtle Grove 824

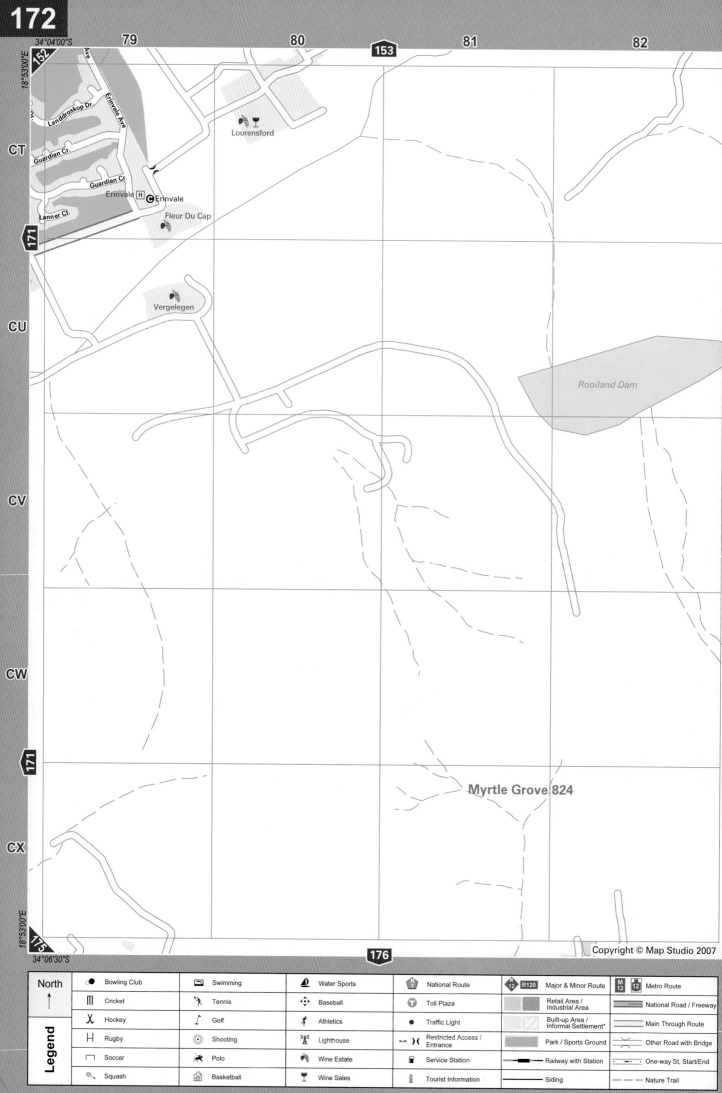

Copyright © Map Studio 2007

83   84   **154**   85   86

18°57'00"E

CT

CU

18°57'30"E

CV

CW

Wedderwill Country Estate

CX

Wedderwill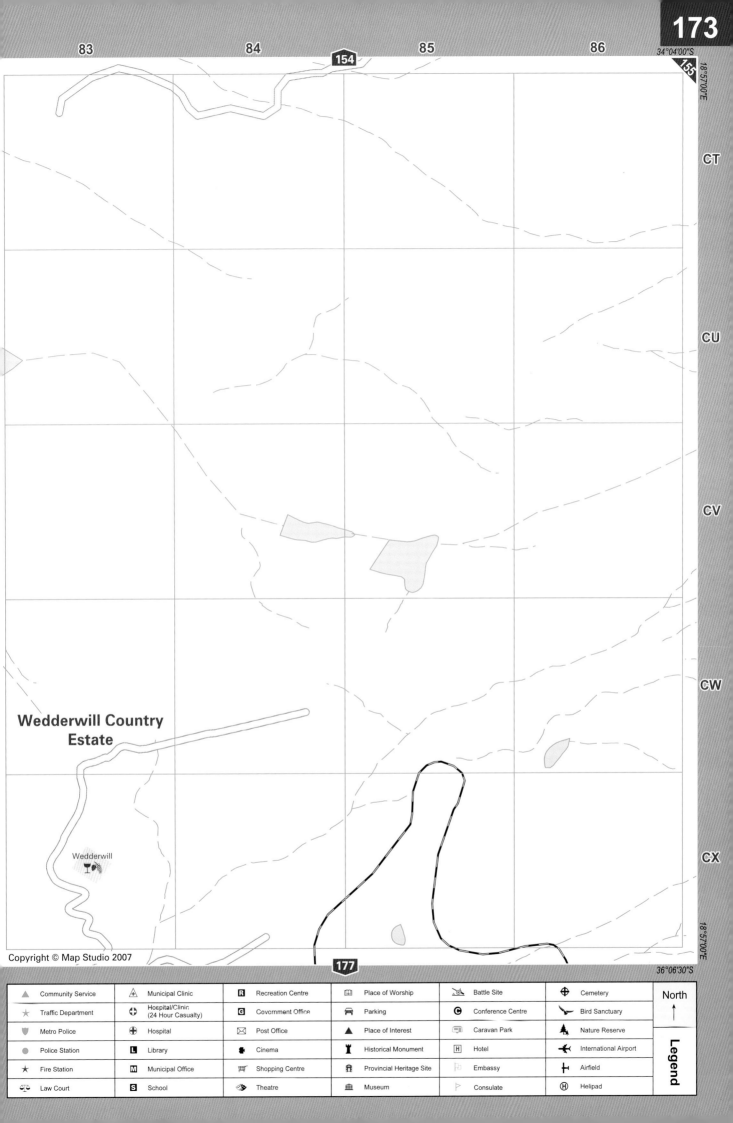

18°57'00"E

177

36°06'30"S

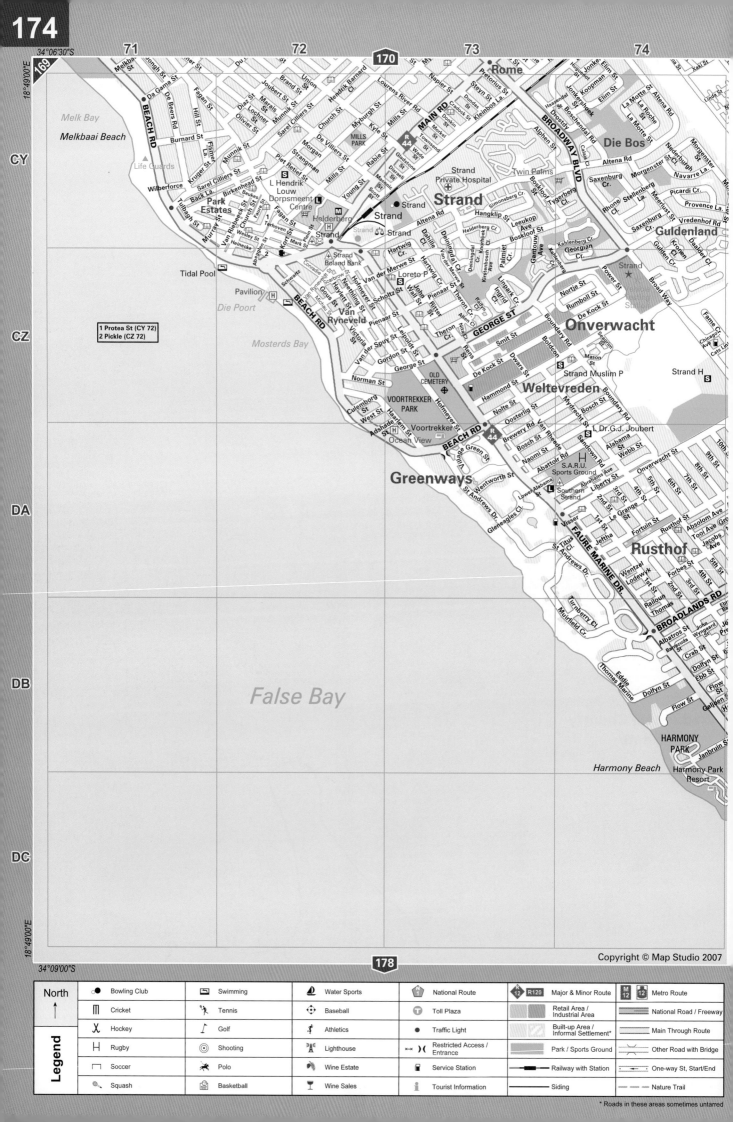

Legend

North ↑

•	Bowling Club	⌷	Swimming	⚓	Water Sports	⌂	National Route	R120	Major & Minor Route	Metro Route
Ⅲ	Cricket	🤾	Tennis	◈	Baseball	Ⓣ	Toll Plaza		Retail Area / Industrial Area	National Road / Freeway
Ⅹ	Hockey	⛳	Golf	🏃	Athletics	●	Traffic Light		Built-up Area / Informal Settlement*	Main Through Route
H	Rugby	◉	Shooting	🎿	Lighthouse	⤬	Restricted Access / Entrance		Park / Sports Ground	Other Road with Bridge
☐	Soccer	🐎	Polo	🍇	Wine Estate	▪	Service Station		Railway with Station	One-way St, Start/End
🎾	Squash	🏀	Basketball	🍷	Wine Sales	ⓘ	Tourist Information		Siding	Nature Trail

* Roads in these areas sometimes untarred

Grid references: 71, 72, 170, 73, 74

Row labels: CY, CZ, DA, DB, DC

Coordinates: 34°06'30"S, 18°49'00"E, 34°09'00"S, 169, 170, 178

Place names and features:

Melk Bay
Melkbaai Beach
Park Estates
Life Guards
Tidal Pool
Pavilion
Die Poort
Mosterds Bay
Van Ryneveld
Rome
Strand
Strand Private Hospital
Twin Palms
MILLS PARK
Helderberg
Broadway Blvd
Die Bos
Guldenland
Onverwacht
Weltevreden
Strand Muslim P
Strand H
George St
Old Cemetery
Voortrekker Park
Ocean View
Greenways
S.A.R.U. Sports Ground
Southern Strand
Rusthof
Broadlands Rd
Faure Marine Dr
False Bay
Harmony Park
Harmony Beach
Harmony Park Resort

1 Protea St (CY 72)
2 Pickle (CZ 72)

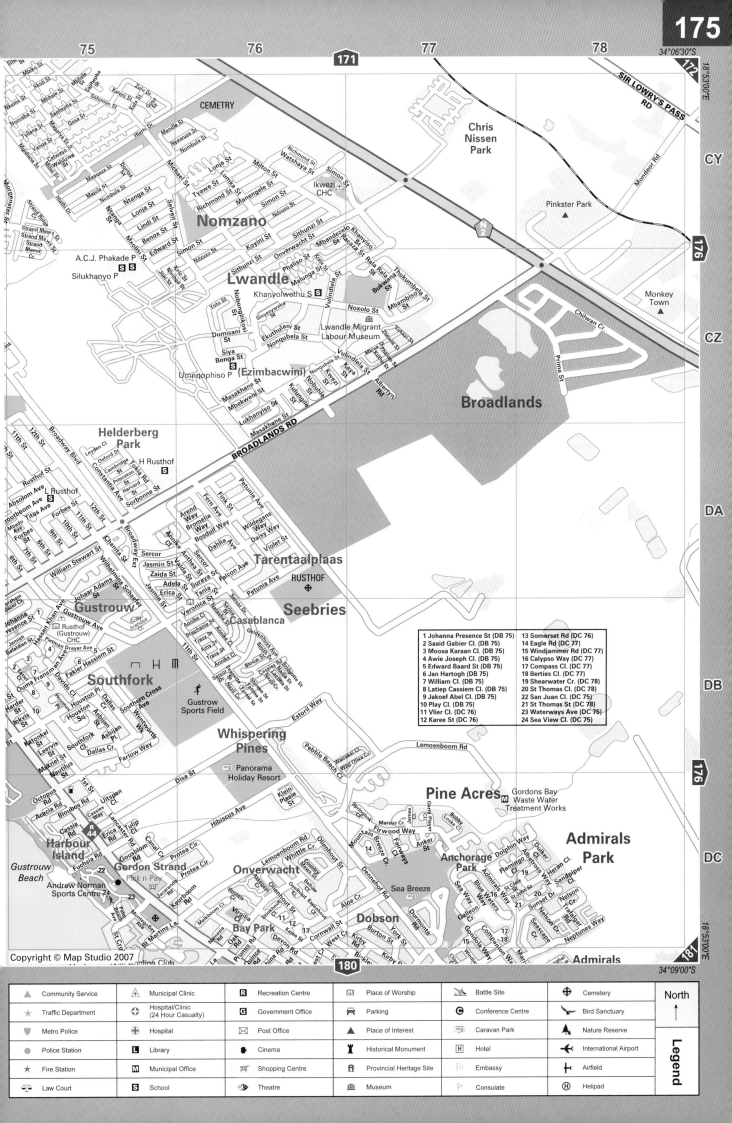

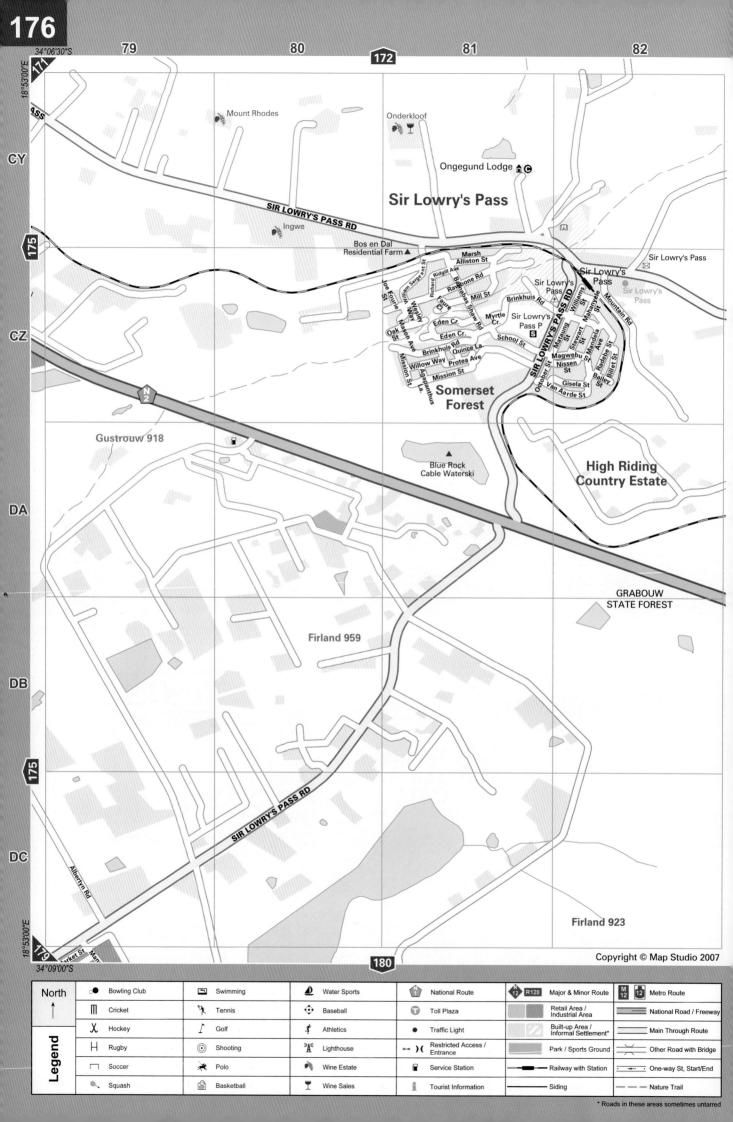

34°06'30"S
18°53'00"E

79
80
172
81
82

171
PASS
CY
175
CZ
DA
DB
175
DC
179

34°09'00"S
18°53'00"E

Mount Rhodes

Onderkloof

Ongegund Lodge

Sir Lowry's Pass

SIR LOWRY'S PASS RD

Ingwe

Bos en Dal
Residential Farm

Marsh
Alliston St
Richard Ridgill Ave
Barbone Rd
Mill St
Rev Sam Sergeant St
Joe Kourie St
Faure Ct
Wesley Way
Oak St
Mason Ave
Brinkhuis Rd
Eden Cr.
Eden Cr.
Brinkhuis Rd
Quince La.
Willow Way
Agapanthus La.
Protea Ave
Mission St
Mission St

Barnabas Shaw Rd

Myrtle
Cr.

Brinkhuis Rd

Sir Lowry's
Pass P
S

School St

Sir Lowry's
Pass

Sir Lowry's
Pass

SIR LOWRY'S PASS RD

Oktober St

Matang
Nissen
St

Magwebu
St

Van Aarde St

Gisela St

Williams
St

Stewart
St

Mahanyele
St

Mandela
Ave

Radeba St

Bailey
St

Billet St

Mountain Rd

Sir Lowry's
Pass

**Somerset
Forest**

Gustrouw 918

Blue Rock
Cable Waterski

**High Riding
Country Estate**

N2

GRABOUW
STATE FOREST

Firland 959

SIR LOWRY'S PASS RD

Alberlyn Rd

Firland 923

Market St

180

Copyright © Map Studio 2007

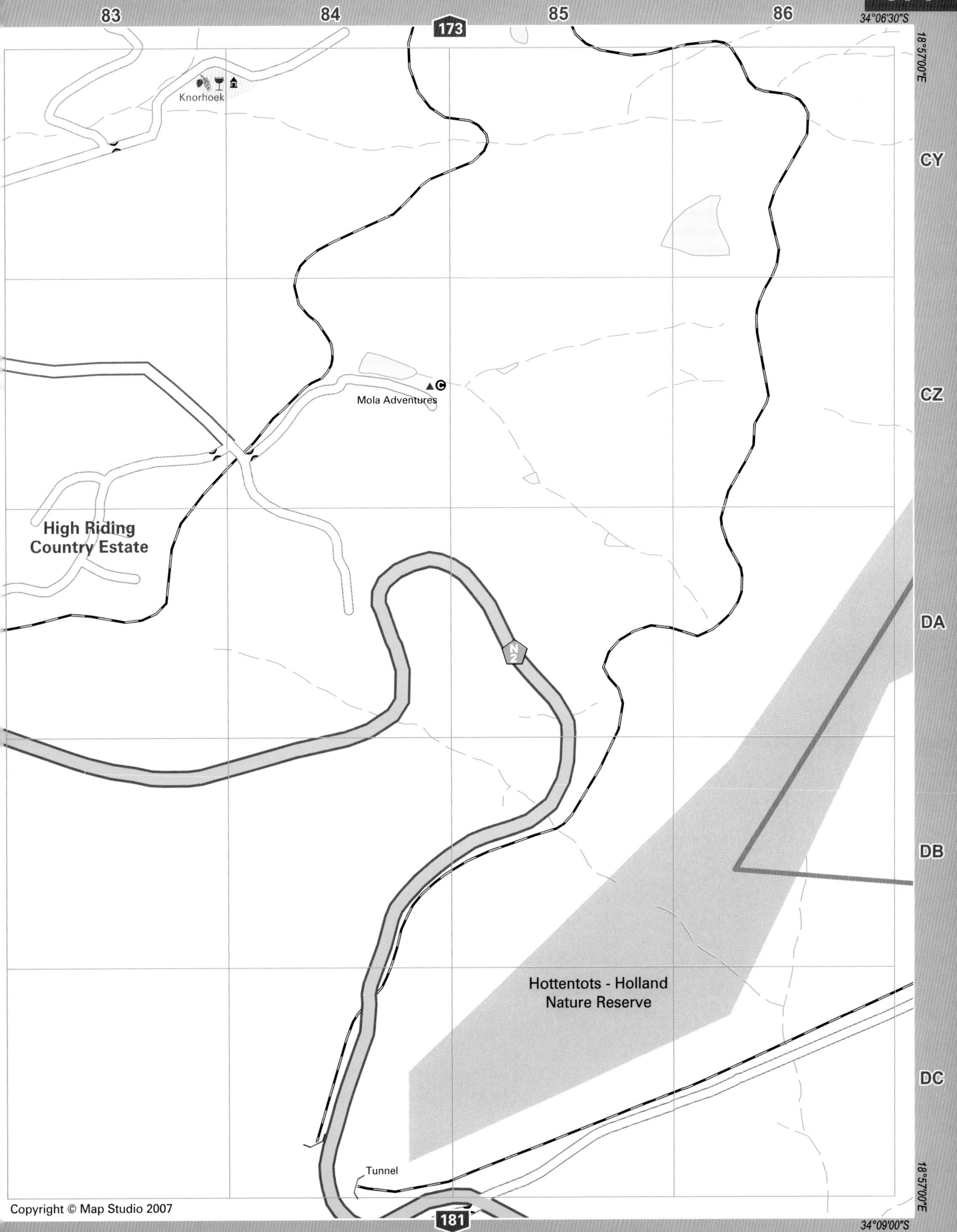

83 84 173 85 86

18°57'00"E

CY

Knorhoek

CZ

Mola Adventures ▲C

High Riding
Country Estate

DA

N2

DB

Hottentots - Holland
Nature Reserve

DC

Tunnel

181

18°57'00"E

34°09'00"S

▲	Community Service	Ⓐ	Municipal Clinic	Ⓡ	Recreation Centre		Place of Worship		Battle Site	⊕	Cemetery		North	
★	Traffic Department	✚	Hospital/Clinic (24 Hour Casualty)	Ⓖ	Government Office	🚗	Parking	Ⓒ	Conference Centre		Bird Sanctuary		↑	
▼	Metro Police	✚	Hospital	✉	Post Office	▲	Place of Interest		Caravan Park	♠	Nature Reserve			
●	Police Station	Ⓛ	Library		Cinema	♟	Historical Monument	Ⓗ	Hotel	✈	International Airport			
★	Fire Station	Ⓜ	Municipal Office		Shopping Centre	🏛	Provincial Heritage Site		Embassy	✈	Airfield		Legend	
⚖	Law Court	Ⓢ	School		Theatre	🏛	Museum	▷	Consulate	Ⓗ	Helipad			

False Bay

Platbank No. 1

Pofadderkloof

Nerina Rd

Bird Rock

Blushing Bride

Protea Dr.

Protea Dr.

Koei-en-Kalf

Hamerkop

Platbank No. 2

Roman Point

Hottentotsvis Bank

▲ 459m

The Cave

Faure Marine Drive
933

Steenbras Catchment Area
306

Ruigtevlei

Die Rakke

▲ 415m

Steenbras

DD
DE
DF
DG
DH

Die Kamer
Sunbird Guest Lodge

34°09'00"S
18°49'00"E
18°49'00"E
34°11'30"S

71   72   174   73   74

Copyright © Map Studio 2007

North ↑	●○ Bowling Club	Swimming	Water Sports	National Route	R120 12 Major & Minor Route	M12 12 Metro Route
Legend	Ⅲ Cricket	Tennis	Baseball	Toll Plaza	Retail Area / Industrial Area	National Road / Freeway
	Hockey	Golf	Athletics	● Traffic Light	Built-up Area / Informal Settlement*	Main Through Route
	H Rugby	Shooting	Lighthouse	Restricted Access / Entrance	Park / Sports Ground	Other Road with Bridge
	Soccer	Polo	Wine Estate	Service Station	Railway with Station	One-way St, Start/End
	Squash	Basketball	Wine Sales	Tourist Information	Siding	Nature Trail

* Roads in these areas sometimes untarred

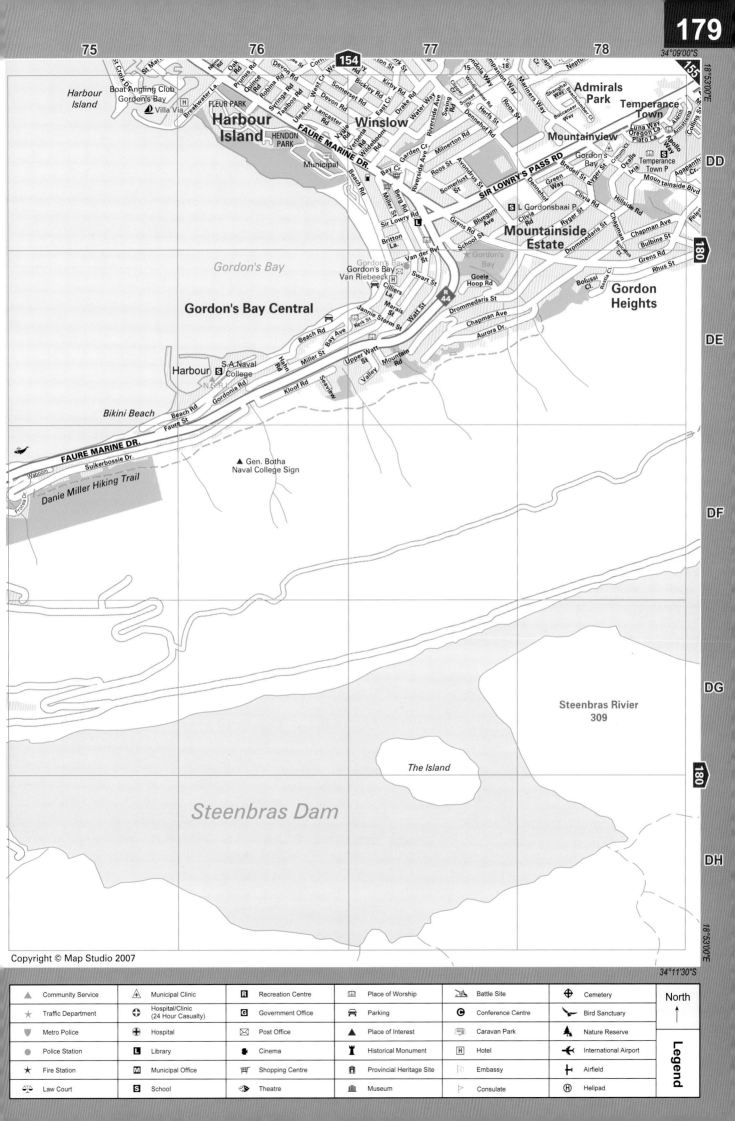

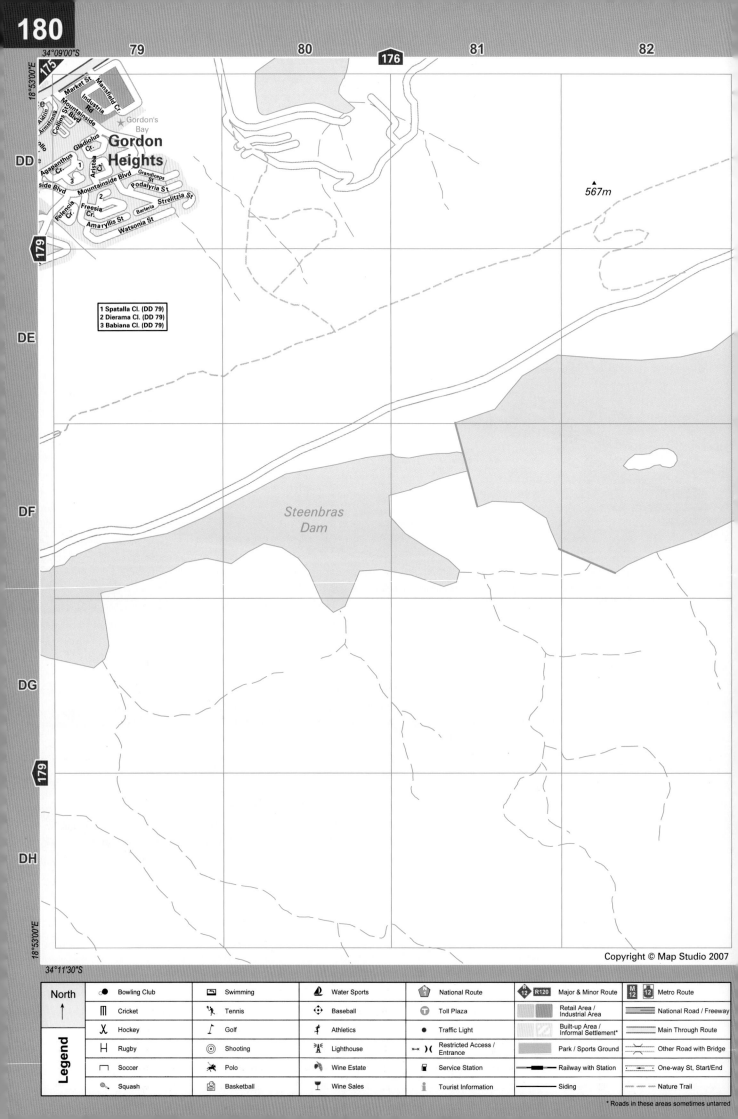

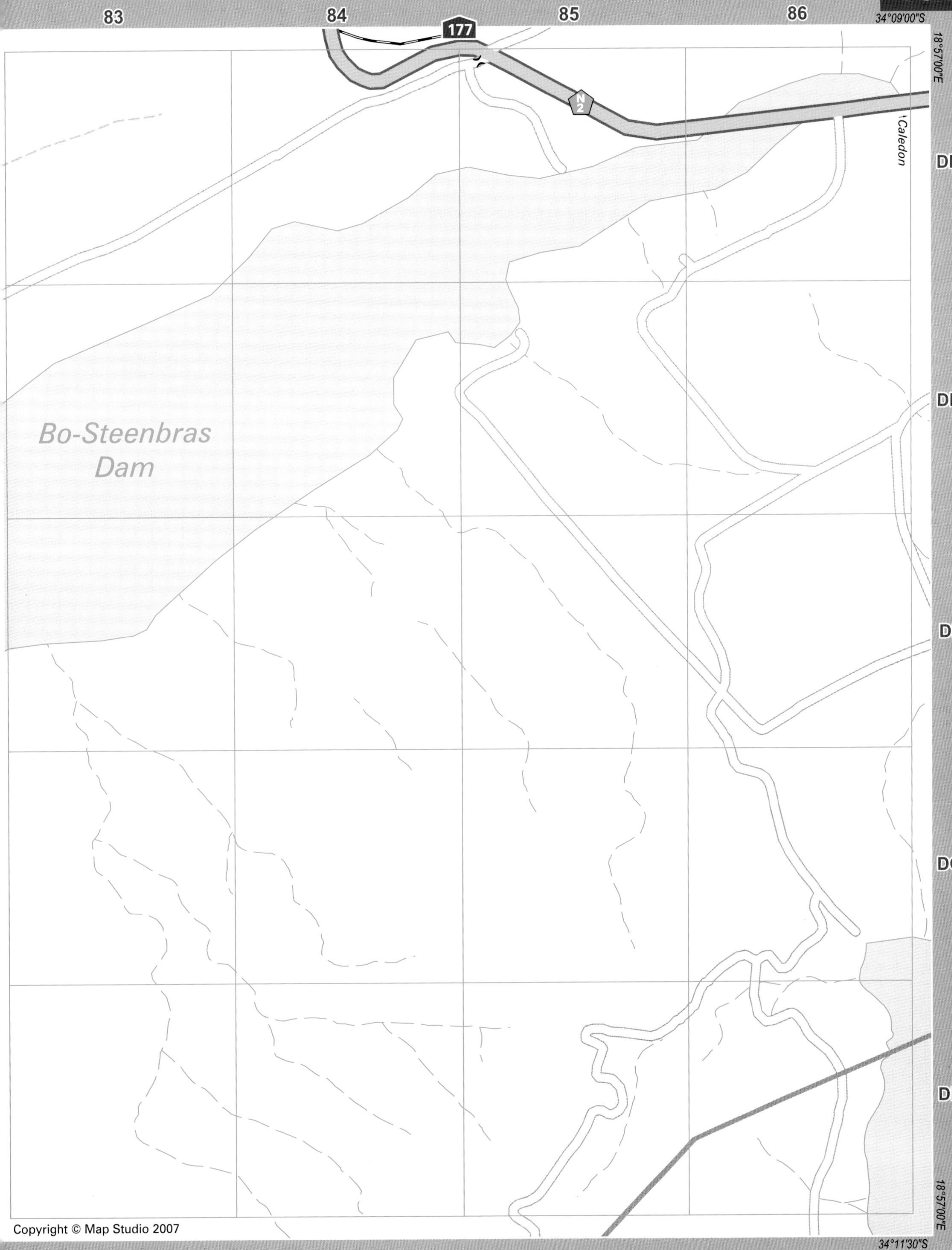

34°09'00"S

18°57'00"E

DD

DE

DF

DG

DH

Bo-Steenbras Dam

177

N2

Caledon

34°11'30"S

18°57'00"E

▲	Community Service	Ⓐ	Municipal Clinic	Ⓡ	Recreation Centre		Place of Worship		Battle Site	⊕	Cemetery
★	Traffic Department	✛	Hospital/Clinic (24 Hour Casualty)	Ⓖ	Government Office		Parking	Ⓒ	Conference Centre		Bird Sanctuary
▼	Metro Police	✚	Hospital	✉	Post Office	▲	Place of Interest		Caravan Park	♠	Nature Reserve
●	Police Station	Ⓛ	Library		Cinema	♜	Historical Monument	Ⓗ	Hotel	✈	International Airport
★	Fire Station	Ⓜ	Municipal Office		Shopping Centre		Provincial Heritage Site		Embassy	⊢	Airfield
⚖	Law Court	Ⓢ	School		Theatre	🏛	Museum	▷	Consulate	Ⓗ	Helipad

North
↑

Legend

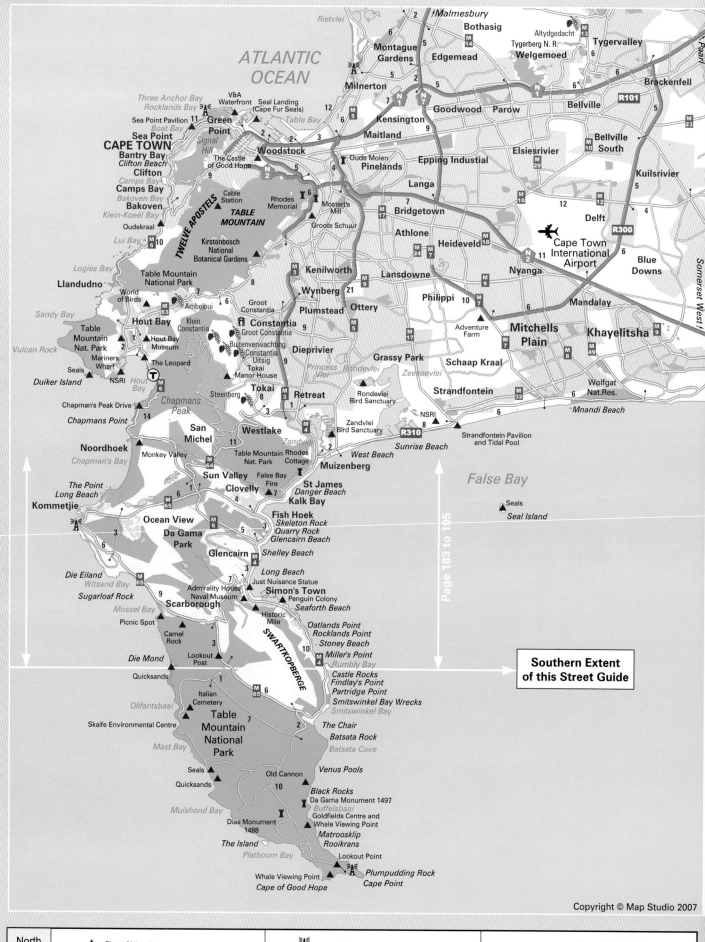

0   2.5   5   7.5   10km

ATLANTIC OCEAN

Malmesbury
Bothasig
Montague Gardens
Edgemead
Altydgedacht
Tygerberg N. R.
Welgemoed
Tygervalley
Milnerton
Brackenfell
Rietvlei
Three Anchor Bay
Rocklands Bay
Sea Point Pavilion
Boat Bay
Green Point
V&A Waterfront
Seal Landing (Cape Fur Seals)
Table Bay
Woodstock
Goodwood
Parow
Bellville
R101
Kensington
Maitland
CAPE TOWN
Sea Point
Bantry Bay
Clifton Beach
Clifton
Camps Bay
Bakoven Bay
Bakoven
Klein-Koeël Bay
Signal Hill
The Castle of Good Hope
Oude Molen
Pinelands
Epping Industial
Langa
Elsiesrivier
Bellville South
Kuilsrivier
Oudekraal
Cable Station
Rhodes Memorial
TABLE MOUNTAIN
Mostert's Mill
Groote Schuur
Bridgetown
Athlone
Heideveld
Delft
R300
Lui Bay
Logies Bay
Llandudno
Sandy Bay
Kirstenbosch National Botanical Gardens
Kenilworth
Wynberg
Lansdowne
Cape Town International Airport
Blue Downs
Nyanga
Table Mountain National Park
World of Birds
Ambeloui
Groot Constantia
Plumstead
Ottery
Philippi
Mitchells Plain
Khayelitsha
Hout Bay
Klein Constantia
Constantia
Groot Constantia
Dieprivier
Grassy Park
Adventure Farm
Schaap Kraal
Table Mountain Nat. Park
Hout Bay Museum
Butenverwachting
Constantia Uitsig
Tokai Manor House
Steenberg
Tokai
Retreat
Princess Vlei
Bondevlei
Zeekoevlei
Rondevlei Bird Sanctuary
Strandfontein
Mariners Wharf
The Leopard
Westlake
Table Mountain Nat. Park
Rhodes Cottage
Zandvlei
Zandvlei Bird Sanctuary
Wolfgat Nat.Res.
Seals
NSRI
Hout Bay
Chapman's Peak Drive
Chapmans Peak
Chapmans Point
Duiker Island
Vulcan Rock
Noordhoek
San Michel
Monkey Valley
Sun Valley
Muizenberg
West Beach
Sunrise Beach
NSRI
Strandfontein Pavilion and Tidal Pool
Mnandi Beach
False Bay
Chapman's Bay
The Point
Long Beach
Kommetjie
Ocean View
Da Gama Park
Clovelly
St James
Danger Beach
Kalk Bay
Fish Hoek
Skeleton Rock
Quarry Rock
Glencairn Beach
False Bay Fire
Seals
Seal Island
Die Eiland
Witsand Bay
Sugarloaf Rock
Mossel Bay
Glencairn
Shelley Beach
Scarborough
Picnic Spot
Camel Rock
Long Beach
Just Nuisance Statue
Admiralty House Naval Museum
Simon's Town
Penguin Colony
Seaforth Beach
Historic Mile
SWARTKOPBERGE
Oatlands Point
Rocklands Point
Stoney Beach
Miller's Point
Rumbly Bay
Die Mond
Quicksands
Lookout Post
Castle Rocks
Findlay's Point
Partridge Point
Smitswinkel Bay Wrecks
Smitswinkel Bay
Olifantsbaai
Italian Cemetery
Table Mountain National Park
Skaife Environmental Centre
The Chair
Batsata Rock
Batsata Cove
Mast Bay
Seals
Quicksands
Old Cannon
Venus Pools
Black Rocks
Da Gama Monument 1497
Buffelsbaai
Goldfields Centre and Whale Viewing Point
Matroosklip
Rooikrans
Muishond Bay
Dias Monument 1488
The Island
Platboom Bay
Whale Viewing Point
Cape of Good Hope
Lookout Point
Plumpudding Rock
Cape Point

Southern Extent of this Street Guide

Page 183 to 195

TWELVE APOSTELS

Copyright © Map Studio 2007

North ↑		Legend	
▲	Place of Interest	⚓ Lighthouse	▬▬▬ Freeway / National Road
🏛	National Monument	ⓣ Toll Route	▭▭▭ Through Route
⚎	Historical Site	✈ International Airport	▭▭▭ Other Road
🍇	Wine Estate	M12 🏛 R120 Route Markers	**Muizenberg** Suburb

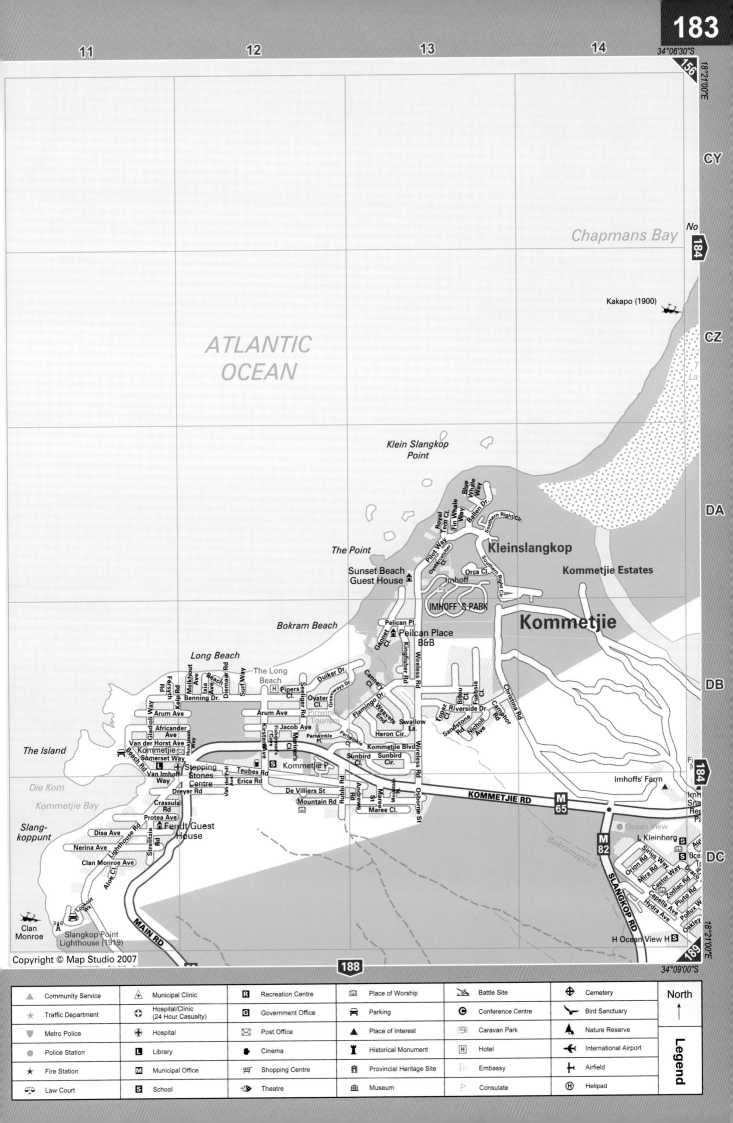

ATLANTIC
OCEAN

Chapmans Bay

Kakapo (1900)

Klein Slangkop
Point

Blue Whale Way
Fin Whale Way
Royal Tern Cl.
Pilot Way
Oystercatcher Cl.
Ballen Dr.
Southern Right Cir.

Kleinslangkop

Kommetjie Estates

The Point

Sunset Beach
Guest House

Imhoff
Orca Cl.
Southern Right Cir.

IMHOFF'S PARK

Kommetjie

Bokram Beach

Pelican Pl.
Pelican Place
B&B

Gannet Cl.
Kingfisher Rd.
Wireless Rd.

Long Beach

Malkhout Ave
Ixia Ave
Beach Ave
Diemaar Rd
Surf Way
Forsyth Rd
Kelp Rd

Benning Dr.

The Long
Beach

Pipers Cl.
Seeliger Rd
Duiker Dr.
Greenways Dr.
Oyster Cl.
Weavers End
Cannery Cl.
Flamingo Dr.
Swallow La.
Heron Cir.

Arum Ave

Arum Ave

Jacob Ave
Periwinkle Pl.
Periwinkle Cl.

Birds Cl.
Topaz Cl.
Riverside Dr.
Fuchsia Cl.
Camphor Rd.
Christina Rd.

Africander
Ave
Gladioli Way
Van der Horst Ave

Huskisson Way

Kirsten Ave
Mariner's Cl.
Fishermans Cl.

Sandstone Rd.
Nicholi Ave

The Island

Kommetjie
Somerset Way

Stepping
Stones
Centre

Van Imhoff
Way

Teubes Rd
Erica Rd
De Villiers St
Mountain Rd

Rughi Rd
Andrews St
Maree St
Maree Cl.

Sunbird Cl.
Sunbird Cir.

Wireless Rd
Osborne St

Kommetjie Blvd

Imhoffs' Farm

Die Kom

Kommetjie Bay

Dreyer Rd

Crassula
Rd

KOMMETJIE RD

M65

Slang-
koppunt

Protea Ave

Fendt Guest
House

Disa Ave

Nerina Ave

Clan Monroe Ave

Strelitzia Rd
Lighthouse Rd
Aloe Cl.

M82

Ocean View

L Kleinberg

Bokramspruit

Orion Rd
Sirius Way
Mira Rd
Castor Way
Capella Ave
Zodiac Cl.
Pluto Rd
Hydra Ave

H Ocean View H

Clan
Monroe

Lookout Way

Slangkop Point
Lighthouse (1919)

SLANGKOP RD

Copyright © Map Studio 2007

MAIN RD

188

34°09'00"S

▲ Community Service	Ⓐ Municipal Clinic	ℝ Recreation Centre	📖 Place of Worship	⚔ Battle Site	✦ Cemetery
★ Traffic Department	⊕ Hospital/Clinic (24 Hour Casualty)	Ⓖ Government Office	🚗 Parking	Ⓒ Conference Centre	⌇ Bird Sanctuary
▼ Metro Police	✚ Hospital	✉ Post Office	▲ Place of Interest	🚐 Caravan Park	⛰ Nature Reserve
● Police Station	Ⓛ Library	♟ Cinema	♜ Historical Monument	Ⓗ Hotel	✈ International Airport
★ Fire Station	Ⓜ Municipal Office	🛒 Shopping Centre	🏛 Provincial Heritage Site	⌸ Embassy	⊢ Airfield
⚖ Law Court	Ⓢ School	⟁ Theatre	🏛 Museum	▷ Consulate	Ⓗ Helipad

North
↑

Legend

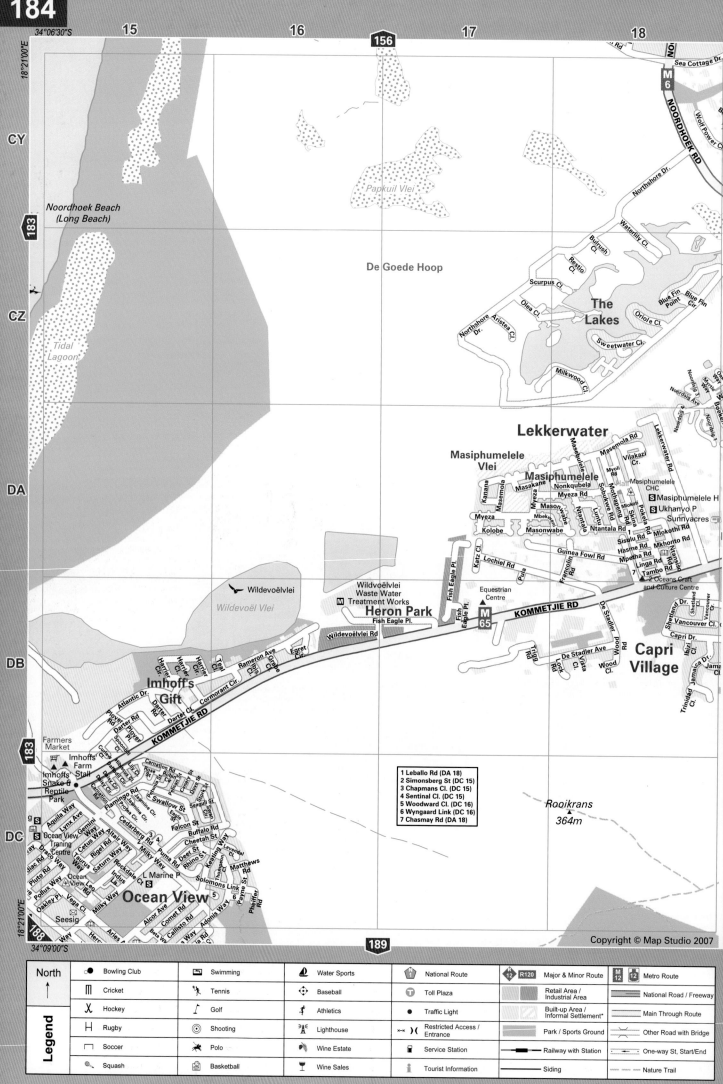

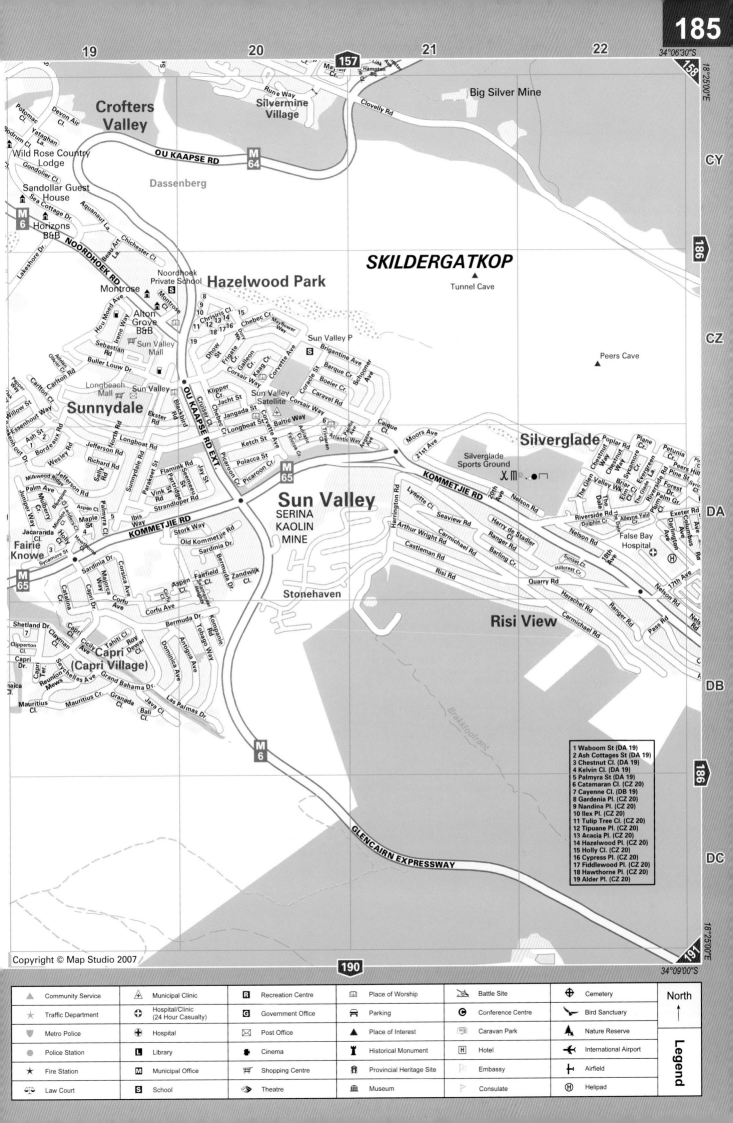

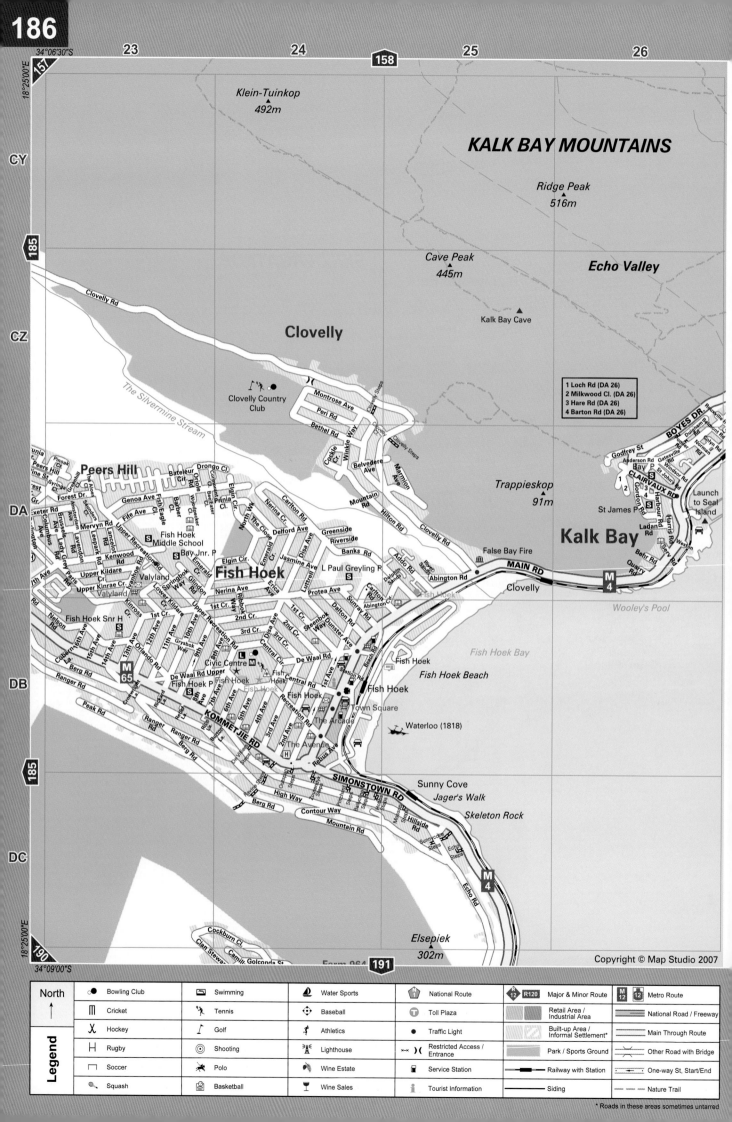

34°06'30"S
18°25'00"E
157

23 24 158 25 26

CY

KALK BAY MOUNTAINS

Klein-Tuinkop
492m

Ridge Peak
516m

Cave Peak
445m

Echo Valley

185

CZ

Clovelly Rd

The Silvermine Stream

Clovelly

Kalk Bay Cave

1 Loch Rd (DA 26)
2 Milkwood Cl. (DA 26)
3 Hare Rd (DA 26)
4 Barton Rd (DA 26)

Clovelly Country Club

Montrose Ave
Peri Rd
Bethel Rd
Cockle Cr.
Winkle Way
Belvedere Ave
Marmion

Clovelly Steps

BOYES DR.

Godfrey St
Anderson Rd
St John's
CLAIRVAUX RD
Harbour Rd
Gordon Rd

Launch to Seal Island

DA

Peers Hill
Pinoak Ct.
Drongo Cl.
Bateleur Cir.
Oriole Ave
Prinia Cl.
Elgin Cir.
Genoa Ave
Fish Eagle
Fife Ave
Barber Cl.

Mountain Rd
Hilton Rd
Clovelly Rd

Trappieskop
91m

St James P

Kalk Bay

Ladan Rd
Behr Rd

Mervyn Rd
Kenwood
Upper Kildare
Upper Kinrae Cr.
Valyland

Fish Hoek Middle School
Bay Jnr. P

Nerina Cr.
Carlton Rd
Delford Ave
Greenside
Riverside
Banks Rd

Addo Rd

False Bay Fire

MAIN RD

Clovelly

M 4

Wooley's Pool

DB

Fish Hoek Snr H

Nelson Rd
Coburn
16th Ave
15th Ave
14th Ave
13th Ave
12th Ave
11th Ave
10th Ave

Fish Hoek

Elgin Cir.
Emerald
Jasmine Cl.
L Paul Greyling P

Protea Ave

Fish Hoek

Fish Hoek Bay

Valyland
Kinross
1st Cr.
Grysbok Way
9th Ave

Civic Centre
M
L

Fish Hoek P
Fish Hoek
De Waal Rd Upper

De Waal Rd
Central Cir.

Dalton Rd
Sunray Rd

Fish Hoek

Fish Hoek Beach

Berg Rd
Ranger Rd
Peak Rd
Ranger Rd

M 65

Fish Hoek Recreation Rd

Fish Hoek

Waterloo (1818)

DC

KOMMETJIE RD

The Arcade
Town Square
The Avenue
Rebus Ave

SIMONSTOWN RD

Sunny Cove
Jager's Walk
Skeleton Rock

High Way
Contour Way
Mountain Rd
Hillside Rd
Sunnycove Steps
Echo Steps

Elsepiek
302m

Echo Rd
M 4

Cockburn Cl.
Clan Stewa
Golconda St

18°25'00"E
190

34°09'00"S

Form 964 191

Legend

North

Bowling Club	Swimming	Water Sports	National Route	Major & Minor Route	Metro Route
Cricket	Tennis	Baseball	Toll Plaza	Retail Area / Industrial Area	
Hockey	Golf	Athletics	Traffic Light	Built-up Area / Informal Settlement*	National Road / Freeway
Rugby	Shooting	Lighthouse	Restricted Access / Entrance	Park / Sports Ground	Main Through Route
Soccer	Polo	Wine Estate	Service Station	Railway with Station	Other Road with Bridge
Squash	Basketball	Wine Sales	Tourist Information	Siding	One-way St, Start/End
					Nature Trail

* Roads in these areas sometimes untarred

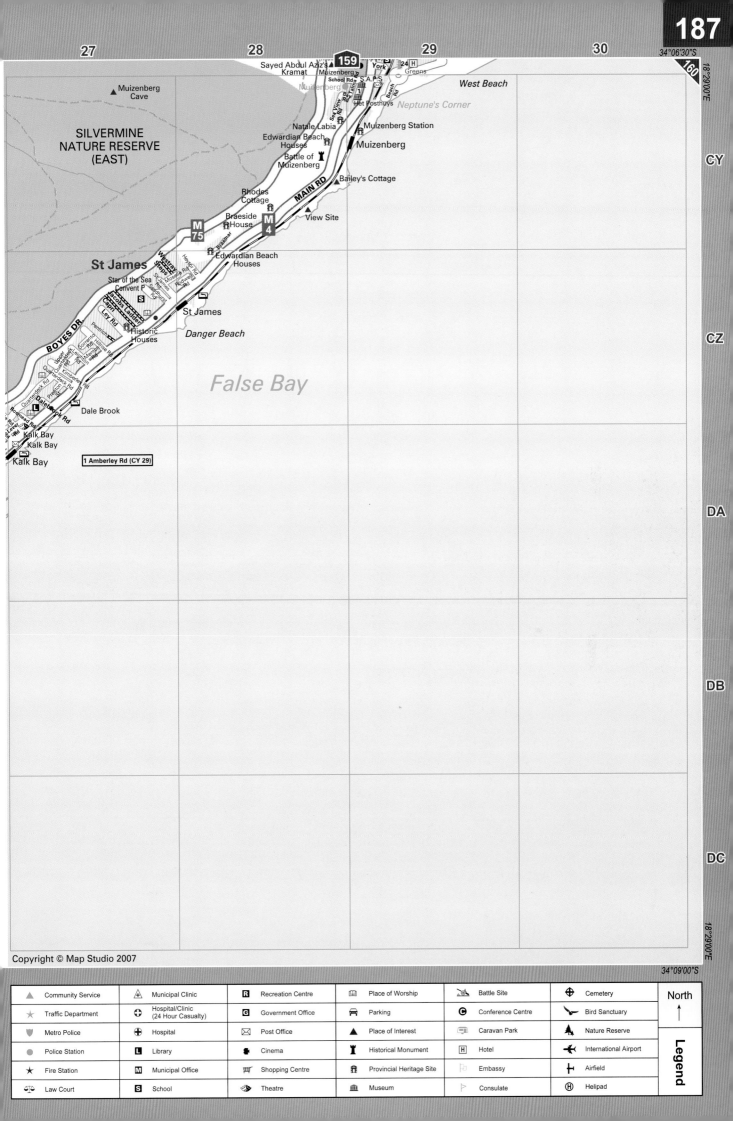

27   28   29   30

34°06'30"S

18°29'00"E
159
160

18°29'00"E

34°09'00"S

CY

CZ

DA

DB

DC

Muizenberg Cave

SILVERMINE NATURE RESERVE (EAST)

Sayed Abdul Aziz's Kramat

York

West Beach

School Rd
S.A.P.S

Muizenberg

Het Posthuys

Neptune's Corner

Natale Labia

Muizenberg Station

Edwardian Beach Houses

Battle of Muizenberg

Muizenberg

Bailey's Cottage

Rhodes Cottage

Braeside House

M 75   M 4

Braehar

View Site

St James

Edwardian Beach Houses

Star of the Sea Convent P

Westral Steps

St James

Jacobs Ladder

Capri

Ley Rd

Historic Houses

Danger Beach

False Bay

BOYES DR

Dale Brook

Kalk Bay

Kalk Bay

Kalk Bay

1 Amberley Rd (CY 29)

Copyright © Map Studio 2007

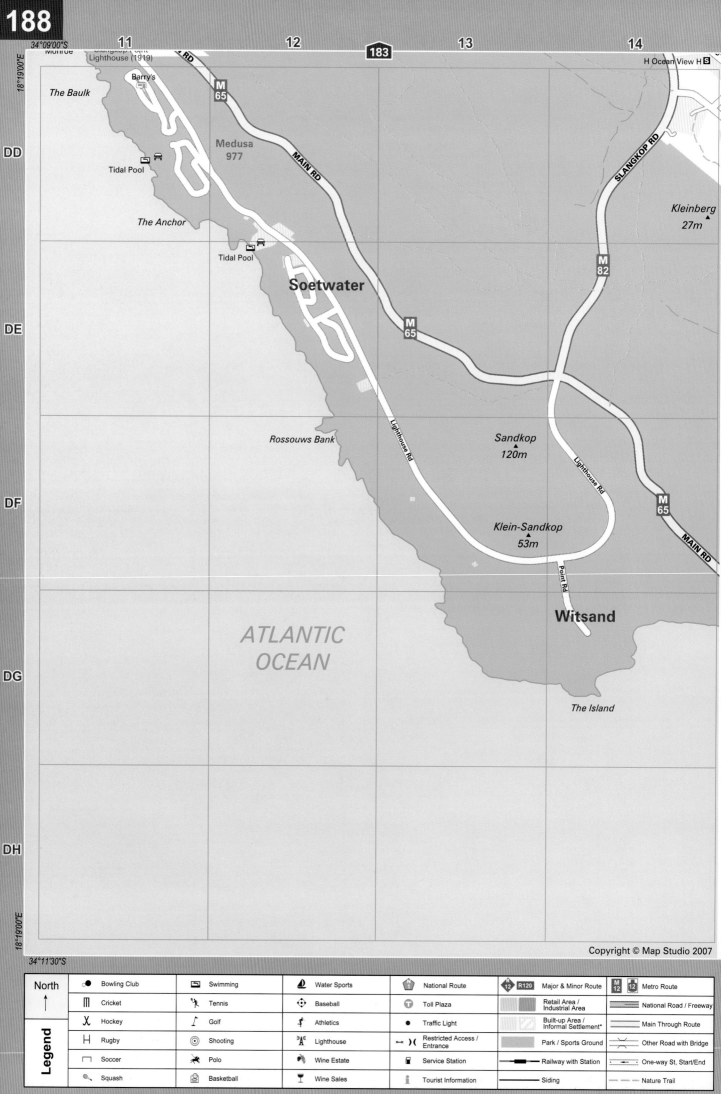

ATLANTIC
OCEAN

Soetwater

Witsand

The Island

Medusa
977

The Baulk

The Anchor

Rossouws Bank

Sandkop
▲
120m

Klein-Sandkop
▲
53m

Kleinberg
▲
27m

Monroe

Slangkop Point
Lighthouse (1919)

Barry's

Tidal Pool

Tidal Pool

H Ocean View H S

MAIN RD

SLANGKOP RD

Lighthouse Rd

Lighthouse Rd

Point Rd

MAIN RD

M 65
M 65
M 65
M 82
183

34°09'00"S
18°19'00"E
18°19'00"E
34°11'30"S

Copyright © Map Studio 2007

North						
↑	● Bowling Club	🏊 Swimming	Water Sports	🏛 National Route	12 R120 Major & Minor Route	M12 Metro Route
	Ⅲ Cricket	🎾 Tennis	Baseball	T Toll Plaza	Retail Area / Industrial Area	National Road / Freeway
Legend	✗ Hockey	⛳ Golf	🏃 Athletics	● Traffic Light	Built-up Area / Informal Settlement*	Main Through Route
	H Rugby	◎ Shooting	🗼 Lighthouse	⊁‒(Restricted Access / Entrance	Park / Sports Ground	Other Road with Bridge
	⬜ Soccer	🐎 Polo	🍷 Wine Estate	🏛 Service Station	Railway with Station	One-way St, Start/End
	✎ Squash	Basketball	🍸 Wine Sales	ℹ Tourist Information	Siding	Nature Trail

* Roads in these areas sometimes untarred

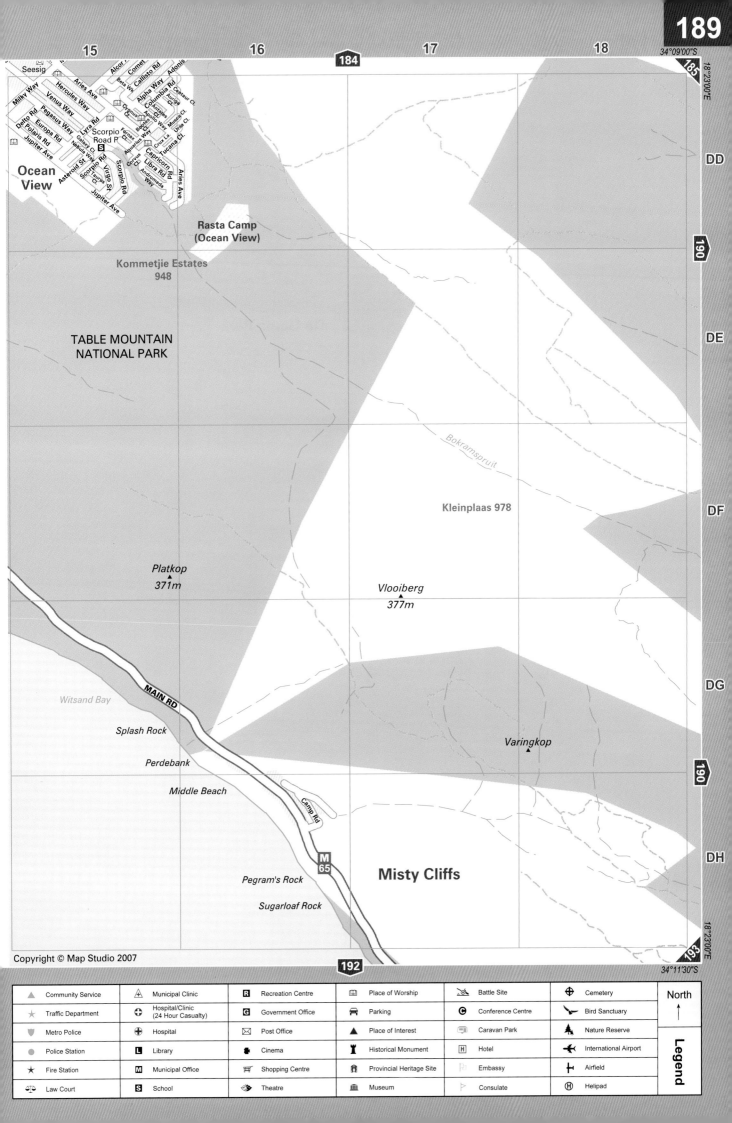

Ocean View

Seesig

Milky Way
Aries Ave
Hercules Way
Venus Way
Pegasus Way
Europa Rd
Delta Rd
Polaris Rd
Jupiter Ave
Galaxy Cl
Nebula Way
Asteroid St
Scorpio Rd
Taurus Cl
Virgo St
Scorpio Rd
Jupiter Ave

Alcor
Comet
Callisto Rd
Adonis
Beta Way
Alpha Way
Columbia Rd
Cygnus
Lyra Rd
Aquarius Way
Capricorn Rd
Libra Rd
Andromeda Way

Centaur Ct
Auriga
Apollo Way
Fornax
Muscat Cl
Ursa Cl
Crux La
Cantres
Baxters Way

Scorpio
Road P
S
Aries Ave

**Rasta Camp
(Ocean View)**

**Kommetjie Estates
948**

**TABLE MOUNTAIN
NATIONAL PARK**

Bokramspruit

Kleinplaas 978

Platkop
▲
371m

Vlooiberg
▲
377m

Witsand Bay

MAIN RD

Splash Rock

Perdebank

Varingkop
▲

Middle Beach

Camp Rd

**M
65**

Misty Cliffs

Pegram's Rock

Sugarloaf Rock

184　　**185**　　**190**　　**190**　　**192**　　**193**

DD　DE　DF　DG　DH

18°23'00"E

34°11'30"S

▲ Community Service	Ⓐ Municipal Clinic	Ⓡ Recreation Centre	📖 Place of Worship	Battle Site	⊕ Cemetery
★ Traffic Department	✚ Hospital/Clinic (24 Hour Casualty)	Ⓖ Government Office	🚗 Parking	Ⓒ Conference Centre	Bird Sanctuary
Metro Police	✚ Hospital	✉ Post Office	▲ Place of Interest	Caravan Park	Nature Reserve
Police Station	Ⓛ Library	Cinema	Historical Monument	Ⓗ Hotel	International Airport
★ Fire Station	Ⓜ Municipal Office	⊞ Shopping Centre	Provincial Heritage Site	Embassy	Airfield
Law Court	Ⓢ School	Theatre	Museum	Consulate	Ⓗ Helipad

North
↑

Legend

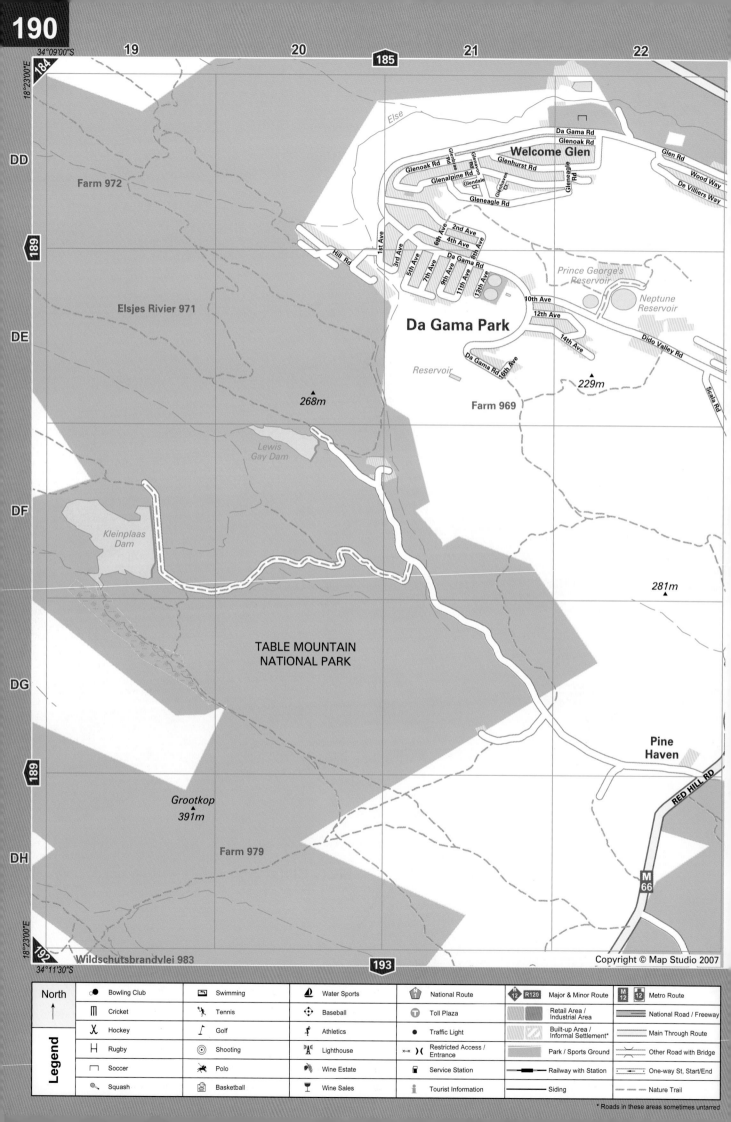

34°09'00"S
18°23'00"E

19 20 185 21 22

DD

Farm 972

189

Elsjes Rivier 971

DE

18°23'00"E

Else

Da Gama Rd
Glenoak Rd
Welcome Glen
Glen Rd
Glenoak Rd
Glenhurst Rd
Wood Way
Glenalpine Rd
De Villiers Way
Glendale Ct.
Gleneagle Rd
Gleneagle Rd

2nd Ave
4th Ave
1st Ave
6th Ave
8th Ave
3rd Ave
5th Ave
Da Gama Rd
7th Ave
9th Ave
11th Ave
13th Ave

Prince George's Reservoir

Neptune Reservoir

Da Gama Park

10th Ave
12th Ave
14th Ave
Dido Valley Rd

Reservoir

Da Gama Rd 16th Ave

▲ 229m

Farm 969

Scala Rd

268m ▲

Lewis Gay Dam

DF

Kleinplaas Dam

▲ 281m

TABLE MOUNTAIN NATIONAL PARK

DG

Pine Haven

189

RED HILL RD

Grootkop
▲
391m

M 66

DH

34°11'30"S
18°23'00"E

192

Wildschutsbrandvlei 983

193

Copyright © Map Studio 2007

North
↑

Legend

⊙●	Bowling Club	🏊	Swimming	⚓	Water Sports	🏛	National Route	12 R120	Major & Minor Route	M 12 / 12	Metro Route
Ⅲ	Cricket	🎾	Tennis	✛	Baseball	Ⓣ	Toll Plaza		Retail Area / Industrial Area		National Road / Freeway
🏑	Hockey	⛳	Golf	🏃	Athletics	●	Traffic Light		Built-up Area / Informal Settlement*		Main Through Route
H	Rugby	◉	Shooting	🗼	Lighthouse	✕—✕)(	Restricted Access / Entrance		Park / Sports Ground		Other Road with Bridge
☐	Soccer	🐎	Polo	🍇	Wine Estate	🏬	Service Station	▬▬	Railway with Station		One-way St, Start/End
🔍	Squash	🏀	Basketball	🍷	Wine Sales	ℹ	Tourist Information		Siding		Nature Trail

* Roads in these areas sometimes untarred

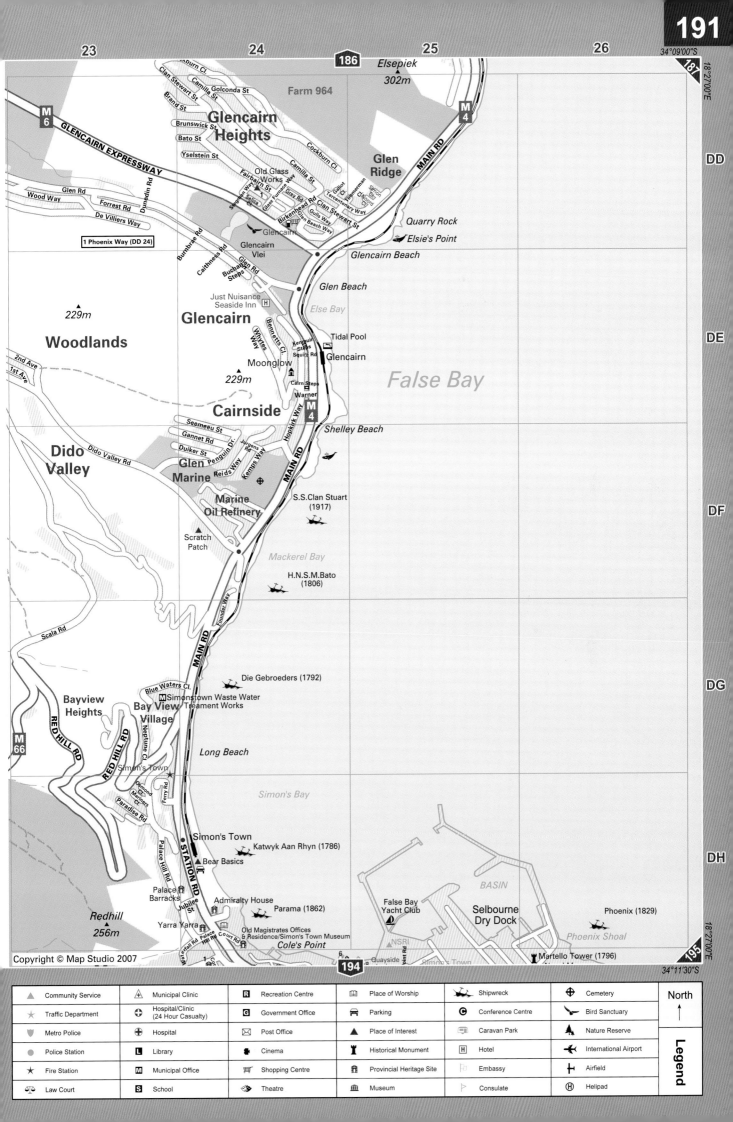

34°09'30"S
18°27'00"E

23 24 186 25 26 187

Elsepiek
302m

DD

M6 GLENCAIRN EXPRESSWAY

Sackburn Cl
Camilla St
Golconda St
Clan Stewart St
Brand St
Brunswick St
Bato St
Yselstein St

Glencairn Heights

Farm 964

M4

Glencairn Cl

Fairbairn St
Stephens Way
Selica
Glass Furnace Way
Grey Rd
Birkenhead Rd Clan Stewart St
Galjot
Camilla St
Cockburn Cl
Tercentenary Way
Timmerman Cl
Simon
Noord
Gulls Way
Glen Beach Way

Glen Ridge

Old Glass Works

MAIN RD

Wood Way
Glen Rd
Forrest Rd
De Villiers Way

Dunedin Rd

Glencairn

Quarry Rock
Elsie's Point

1 Phoenix Way (DD 24)

Bumbrae Rd
Caithness Rd

Glencairn
Vlei
Glen Rd
Buchanan Steps

Glencairn Beach

DE

229m

Woodlands

Just Nuisance
Seaside Inn H

Glencairn

Glen Beach

Else Bay

Whyres Way
Bennetts Cl

Kenguin Steps
Squire Rd
Tidal Pool
Glencairn

False Bay

Moonglow
229m

Cairn Steps
Warner

Cairnside

M4

2nd Ave
1st Ave

Seemeeu St
Gannet Rd
Duiker St
Penguin Dr

Jurgens Rd
Kemps Way

Hopkirk Way

Shelley Beach

Dido Valley

Dido Valley Rd

Reids Way

Glen Marine

MAIN RD

DF

Marine Oil Refinery

S.S.Clan Stuart
(1917)

Scratch
Patch

Mackerel Bay

H.N.S.M.Bato
(1806)

Founder Way

Scala Rd

Die Gebroeders (1792)

DG

Blue Waters Cl
M Simonstown Waste Water
Treament Works

Bayview Heights

RED HILL RD

Bay View Village

M66

Neptune Cl

Long Beach

Simon's Town

Ferry Rd

Ormond
Marners Cl
Paradise Rd

Simon's Bay

Simon's Town

MAIN RD

STATION RD

Simon's Town
Bear Basics

Katwyk Aan Rhyn (1786)

DH

Palace Hill Rd

Palace
Barracks
Jubilee St

Admiralty House

Parama (1862)

BASIN

False Bay
Yacht Club

Selbourne Dry Dock

Phoenix (1829)

Redhill
256m

Yarra Yarra

Waterfall Rd
Palace
Court Rd

Old Magistrates Offices
& Residence/Simon's Town Museum

Cole's Point

NSRI

Point Rd
Quayside

Phoenix Shoal

Martello Tower (1796)

194

18°27'00"E

195

34°11'30"S

Copyright © Map Studio 2007

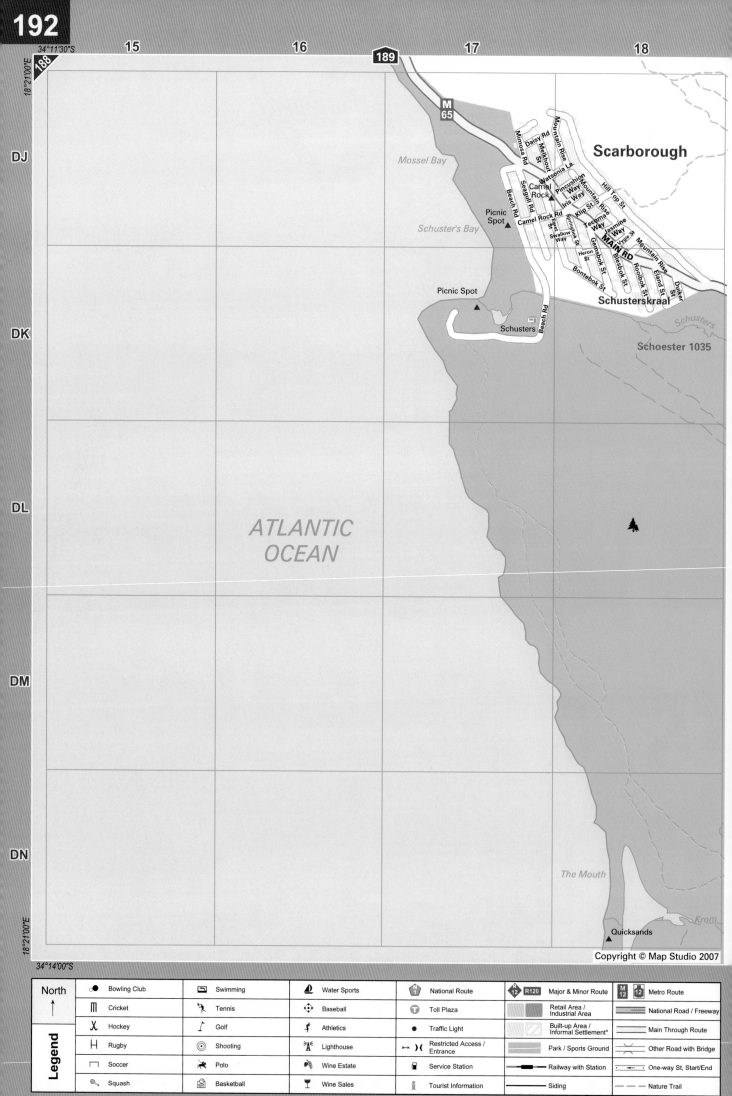

Legend

North ↑

⊙ Bowling Club	🏊 Swimming	⛵ Water Sports	🏛 National Route	12 R120 Major & Minor Route	M12 12 Metro Route
Ⅲ Cricket	🎾 Tennis	⚾ Baseball	Ⓣ Toll Plaza	Retail Area / Industrial Area	National Road / Freeway
X Hockey	⛳ Golf	🏃 Athletics	● Traffic Light	Built-up Area / Informal Settlement*	Main Through Route
H Rugby	⊙ Shooting	🗼 Lighthouse	⤬—)(Restricted Access / Entrance	Park / Sports Ground	Other Road with Bridge
☐ Soccer	🐎 Polo	🍇 Wine Estate	Service Station	Railway with Station	One-way St, Start/End
🔍 Squash	🏀 Basketball	🍷 Wine Sales	ℹ Tourist Information	Siding	Nature Trail

* Roads in these areas sometimes untarred

Copyright © Map Studio 2007

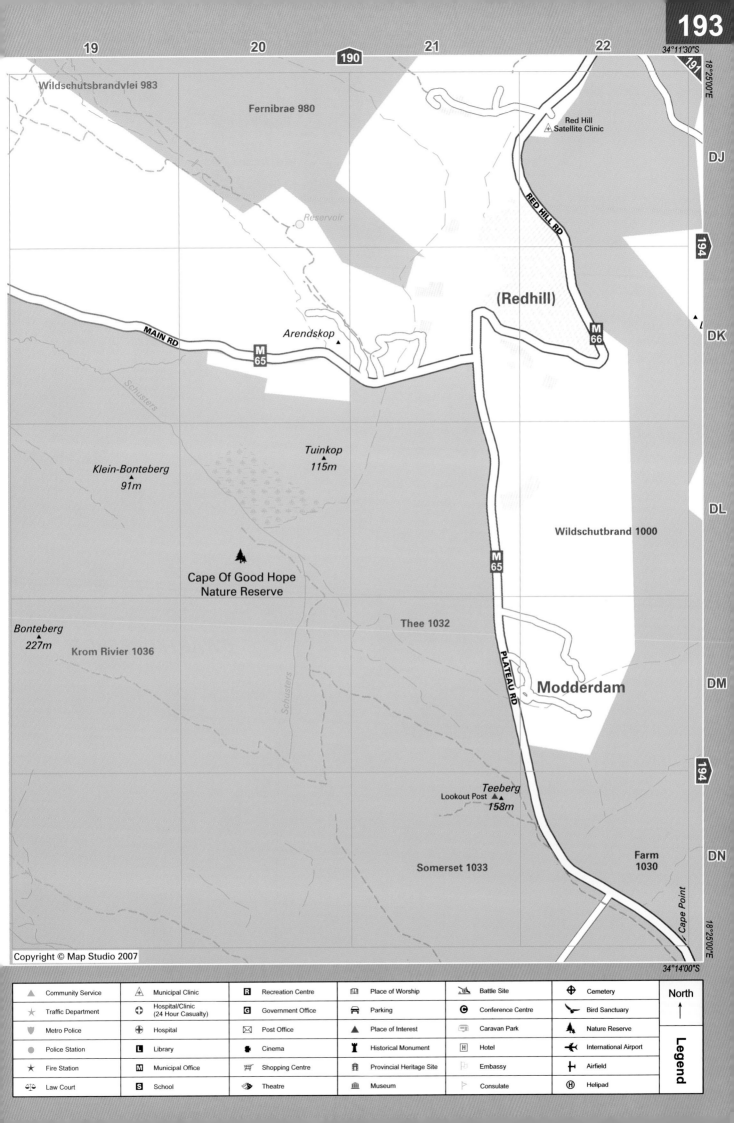

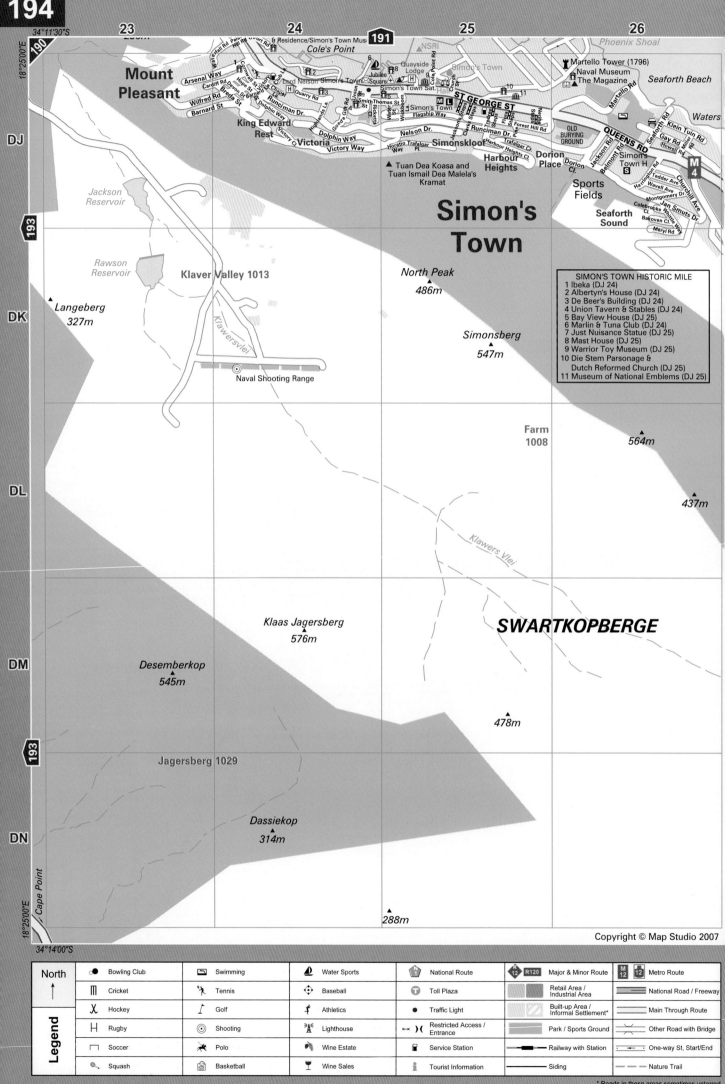

34°11'30"S
18°25'00"E

Mount Pleasant

Cole's Point

Mount Pleasant

King Edward Rest

Jackson Reservoir

Rawson Reservoir

Klaver Valley 1013

▲ Langeberg 327m

Naval Shooting Range

Simon's Town

▲ North Peak 486m

▲ Simonsberg 547m

Farm 1008

▲ 564m

▲ 437m

Klawers Vlei

SWARTKOPBERGE

Klaas Jagersberg 576m

▲ Desemberkop 545m

▲ 478m

Jagersberg 1029

▲ Dassiekop 314m

▲ 288m

Martello Tower (1796)
Naval Museum
The Magazine

Seaforth Beach

Waters

Seaforth Sound

Sports Fields

SIMON'S TOWN HISTORIC MILE
1 Ibeka (DJ 24)
2 Albertyn's House (DJ 24)
3 De Beer's Building (DJ 24)
4 Union Tavern & Stables (DJ 24)
5 Bay View House (DJ 25)
6 Marlin & Tuna Club (DJ 24)
7 Just Nuisance Statue (DJ 25)
8 Mast House (DJ 25)
9 Warrior Toy Museum (DJ 25)
10 Die Stem Parsonage & Dutch Reformed Church (DJ 25)
11 Museum of National Emblems (DJ 25)

Copyright © Map Studio 2007

North									
Cricket		Bowling Club		Swimming		Water Sports		National Route		Major & Minor Route		Metro Route

North ↑								
Legend	Bowling Club	Swimming	Water Sports	National Route	Major & Minor Route R120	Metro Route M
	Cricket	Tennis	Baseball	Toll Plaza	Retail Area / Industrial Area	National Road / Freeway
	Hockey	Golf	Athletics	Traffic Light	Built-up Area / Informal Settlement*	Main Through Route
	Rugby	Shooting	Lighthouse	Restricted Access / Entrance	Park / Sports Ground	Other Road with Bridge
	Soccer	Polo	Wine Estate	Service Station	Railway with Station	One-way St, Start/End
	Squash	Basketball	Wine Sales	Tourist Information	Siding	Nature Trail

* Roads in these areas sometimes untarred

34°14'00"S
18°25'00"E

Cape Point

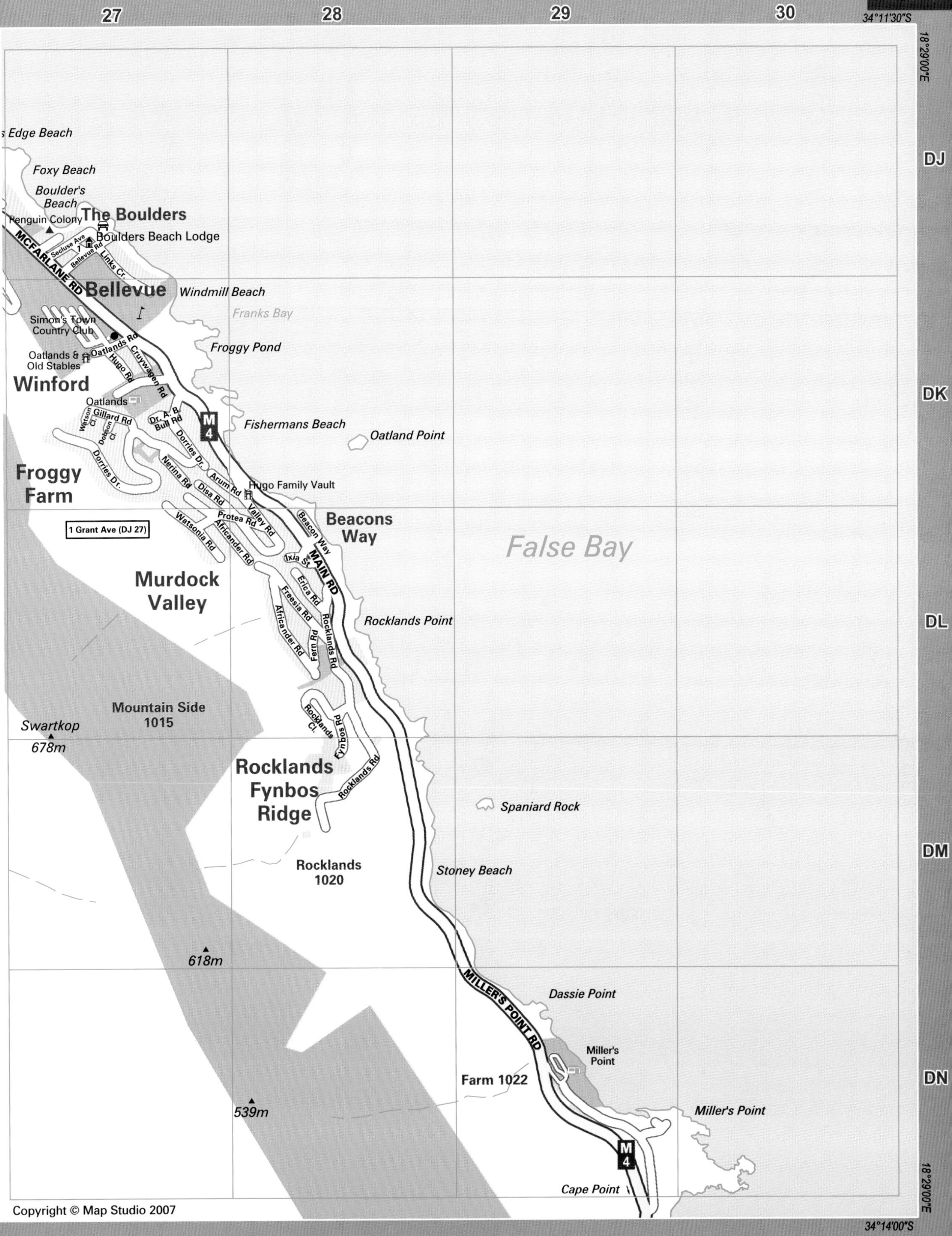

27 28 29 30 34°11'30"S

18°29'00"E

DJ

s Edge Beach

Foxy Beach

Boulder's Beach

Penguin Colony

The Boulders

Boulders Beach Lodge

MCFARLANE RD

Secluse Ave

Bellevue Cr.

Links Cr.

Bellevue

Windmill Beach

Franks Bay

Simon's Town Country Club

Oatlands Rd

Crutwagen Rd

Froggy Pond

Oatlands & Old Stables

Hugo Rd

Winford

Oatlands

DK

Watson Cl.

Gillard Rd

Dr. A. B. Bull Rd

Dobson Cl.

Dorries Dr.

M4

Fishermans Beach

Oatland Point

Froggy Farm

Dorries Dr.

Nertina Rd

Arum Rd

Disa Rd

Valley Rd

Hugo Family Vault

1 Grant Ave (DJ 27)

Watsonia Rd

Protea Rd

Africander Rd

Beacon Way

Ixia St

MAIN RD

Beacons Way

False Bay

Murdock Valley

Freesia Rd

Erica Rd

Fern Rd

Africander Rd

Rocklands Rd

Rocklands Point

DL

Mountain Side 1015

Swartkop 678m

Rocklands Cr.

Rocklands Rd

Rocklands Fynbos Ridge

Rocklands 1020

Spaniard Rock

DM

618m

Stoney Beach

MILLER'S POINT RD

Dassie Point

Farm 1022

Miller's Point

DN

539m

Miller's Point

M4

Cape Point

18°29'00"E

34°14'00"S

▲	Community Service	Ⓐ	Municipal Clinic	Ⓡ	Recreation Centre	🕮	Place of Worship
★	Traffic Department	✛	Hospital/Clinic (24 Hour Casualty)	Ⓖ	Government Office	🚗	Parking
🛡	Metro Police	✚	Hospital	✉	Post Office	▲	Place of Interest
●	Police Station	Ⓛ	Library	✦	Cinema	🏛	Historical Monument
★	Fire Station	Ⓜ	Municipal Office	🏬	Shopping Centre	🏠	Provincial Heritage Site
⚖	Law Court	Ⓢ	School	◈	Theatre	🏛	Museum

⚓	Battle Site	⊕	Cemetery
Ⓒ	Conference Centre	✈	Bird Sanctuary
🚐	Caravan Park	♣	Nature Reserve
Ⓗ	Hotel	✈	International Airport
Ⓔ	Embassy	⊢	Airfield
▷	Consulate	Ⓗ	Helipad

North ↑

Legend

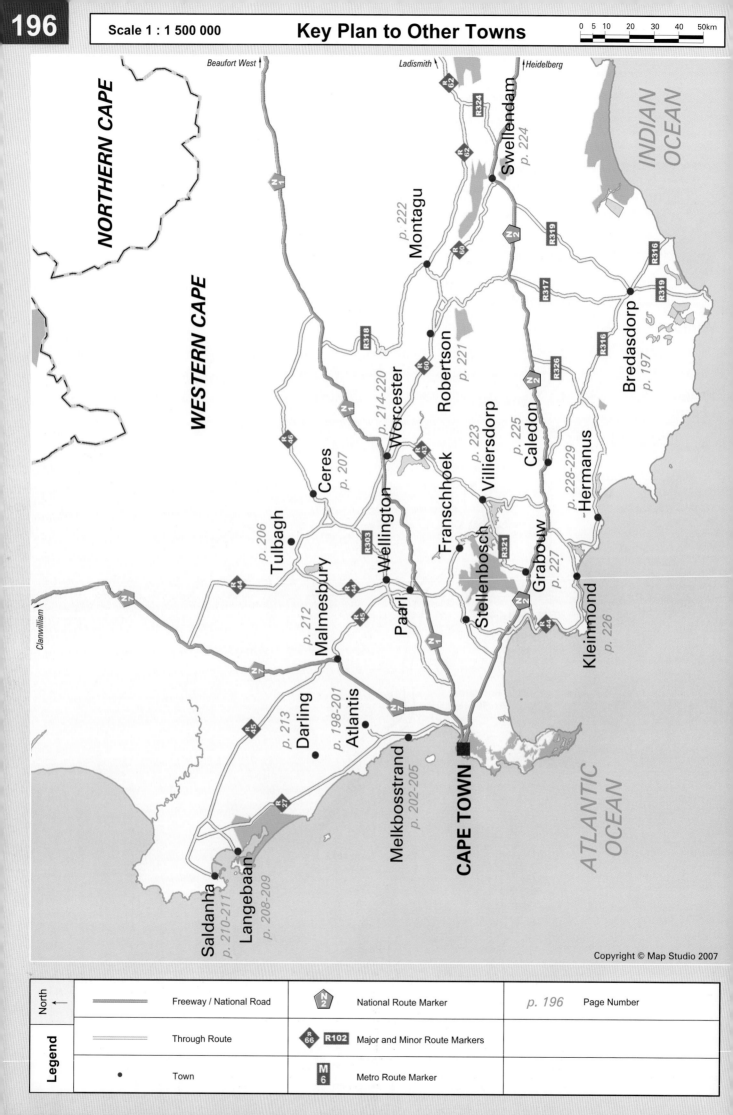

0 100 200 400 600m

33°31'30"S

18°27'00"E

18°27'00"E

33°34'00"S

| 27 | 28 | 29 | 30 |

AD

AE

R307

Mexican St
Montagu St
Nimrod St
Nautilus St
Nieuw Pl.
Namaqua Pl.
Napole...
Cr...

DASSENBERG RD

AF

Holle... St

▲ 216m R307

Hoog Ct.

Hoog...

Helen St

AG

1 Zoetendal Pl. (AG 30)

Zeelan Cir.
1

Wesfleur

DASSENBERG RD

AH

Gouda St

200

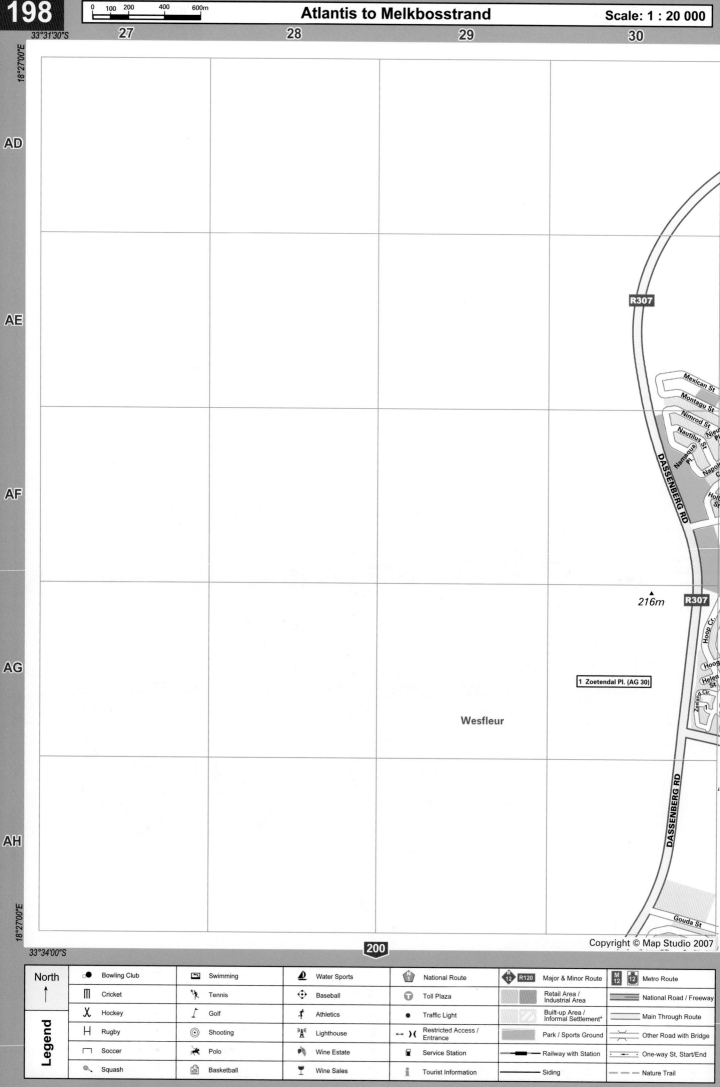

North ↑					
Legend	⊶● Bowling Club	⊟ Swimming	⛵ Water Sports	⬠ National Route	🛣 R120 Major & Minor Route · Ⓜ Metro Route
	⫼ Cricket	🎾 Tennis	⊕ Baseball	Ⓣ Toll Plaza	Retail Area / Industrial Area · National Road / Freeway
	𐤕 Hockey	⌁ Golf	🏃 Athletics	● Traffic Light	Built-up Area / Informal Settlement* · Main Through Route
	H Rugby	◎ Shooting	🗼 Lighthouse	⤬)(Restricted Access / Entrance	Park / Sports Ground · Other Road with Bridge
	▱ Soccer	🐎 Polo	🍾 Wine Estate	⛽ Service Station	Railway with Station · One-way St, Start/End
	🎾 Squash	🏀 Basketball	🍷 Wine Sales	ℹ Tourist Information	Siding · Nature Trail

* Roads in these areas sometimes untarred

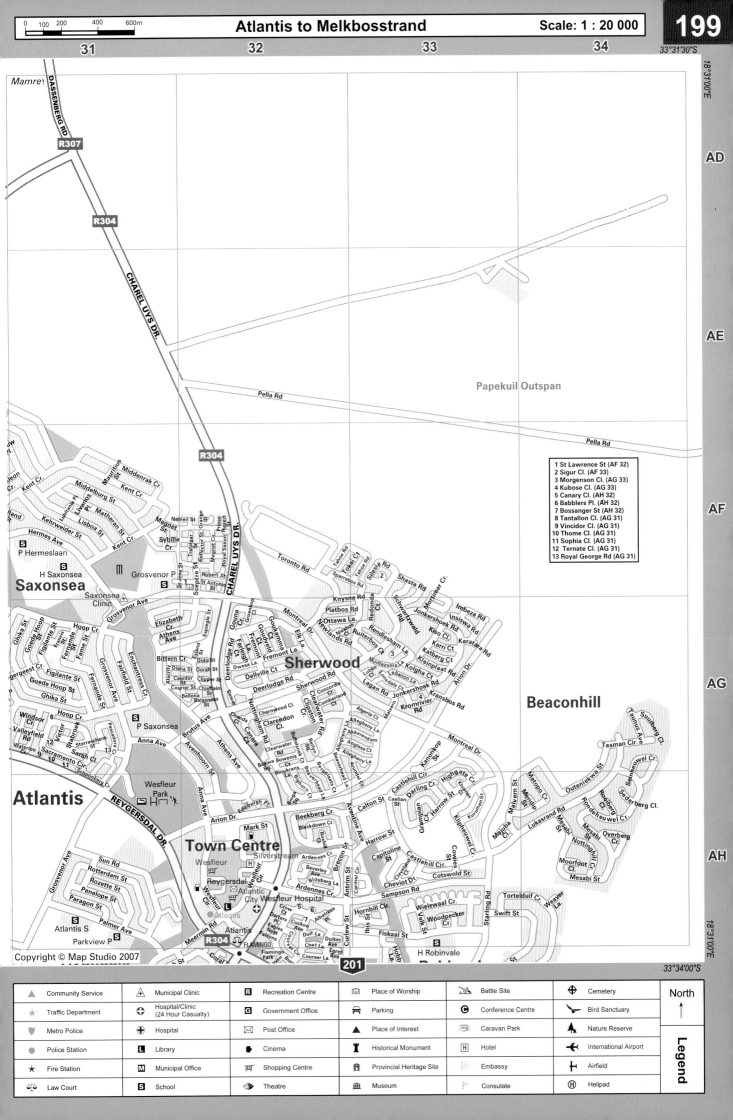

0 100 200 400 600m

33°31'30"S

31 32 33 34

18°31'00"E

Mamre

DASSENBERG RD

R307

R304

CHAREL UYS DR.

AD

AE

Papekuil Outspan

Pella Rd

Pella Rd

AF

1 St Lawrence St (AF 32)
2 Sigur Cl. (AF 33)
3 Morgenson Cl. (AG 33)
4 Kubose Cl. (AG 33)
5 Canary Cl. (AH 32)
6 Babblers Pl. (AH 32)
7 Bossanger St (AH 32)
8 Tantallon Cl. (AG 31)
9 Vincidor Cl. (AG 31)
10 Thome Cl. (AG 31)
11 Sophia Cl. (AG 31)
12 Ternate Cl. (AG 31)
13 Royal George Rd (AG 31)

R304

Saxonsea

Sherwood

Beaconhill

AG

Atlantis

REYGERSDAL DR.

Town Centre

AH

FLAMINGO

R304

201

33°34'00"S

18°31'00"E

Copyright © Map Studio 2007

	Community Service		Municipal Clinic		Recreation Centre		Place of Worship		Battle Site		Cemetery	**North**
	Traffic Department		Hospital/Clinic (24 Hour Casualty)		Government Office		Parking		Conference Centre		Bird Sanctuary	
	Metro Police		Hospital		Post Office		Place of Interest		Caravan Park		Nature Reserve	
	Police Station		Library		Cinema		Historical Monument		Hotel		International Airport	**Legend**
	Fire Station		Municipal Office		Shopping Centre		Provincial Heritage Site		Embassy		Airfield	
	Law Court		School		Theatre		Museum		Consulate		Helipad	

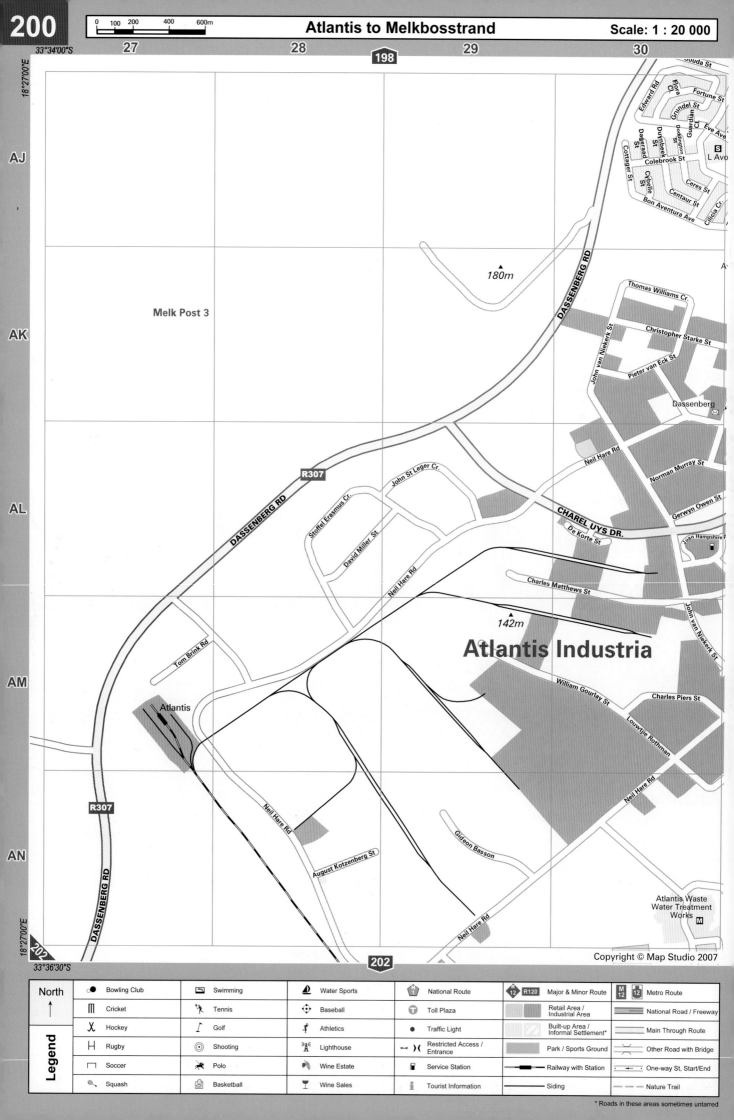

198

33°34'00"S
18°27'00"E

27 28 29 30

AJ

AK

AL

AM

AN

Melk Post 3

180m

Dassenberg Rd

Gouda St
Edward Rd
Flora Ct.
Fortune St
Grundel St
Guardian Ct.
Eve Ave.
Dageraad St
Duynbeek St
Doddington St
Colebrook St
Cottager St
Cybelle St
Ceres St
Centaur St
Cilicia Ct.
Bon Aventura Ave

S
L Ave.

Thomas Williams Cr.

Christopher Starke St

John van Niekerk St

Pieter van Eck St

Dassenberg

Neil Hare Rd

Norman Murray St

Gerwyn Owen St

Juan Hampshire St

R307

Dassenberg Rd

Stoffel Erasmus Cr.

John St Leger Cr.

David Miller St

Neil Hare Rd

CHAREL UYS DR.

De Korte St

Charles Matthews St

142m

Atlantis Industria

William Gourlay St

Charles Piers St

Louwtjie Rothman

Neil Hare Rd

Tom Brink Rd

Atlantis

Neil Hare Rd

August Kotzenberg St

Gideon Basson

Neil Hare Rd

Atlantis Waste
Water Treatment
Works   M

R307

Dassenberg Rd

202

33°36'30"S
18°27'00"E

202

North ↑	Legend							
⦾ Bowling Club	🏊 Swimming	⛵ Water Sports	🛡 National Route	12 R120 Major & Minor Route	M12 Metro Route
Ⅲ Cricket	🎾 Tennis	⚾ Baseball	T Toll Plaza	Retail Area / Industrial Area	National Road / Freeway
X Hockey	Golf	Athletics	● Traffic Light	Built-up Area / Informal Settlement*	Main Through Route
H Rugby	◎ Shooting	Lighthouse	⨯⟩(Restricted Access / Entrance	Park / Sports Ground	Other Road with Bridge
⊓ Soccer	🐎 Polo	🍇 Wine Estate	Service Station	Railway with Station	One-way St, Start/End
Squash	🏀 Basketball	🍷 Wine Sales	ℹ Tourist Information	Siding	Nature Trail

* Roads in these areas sometimes untarred

0 100 200 400 600m

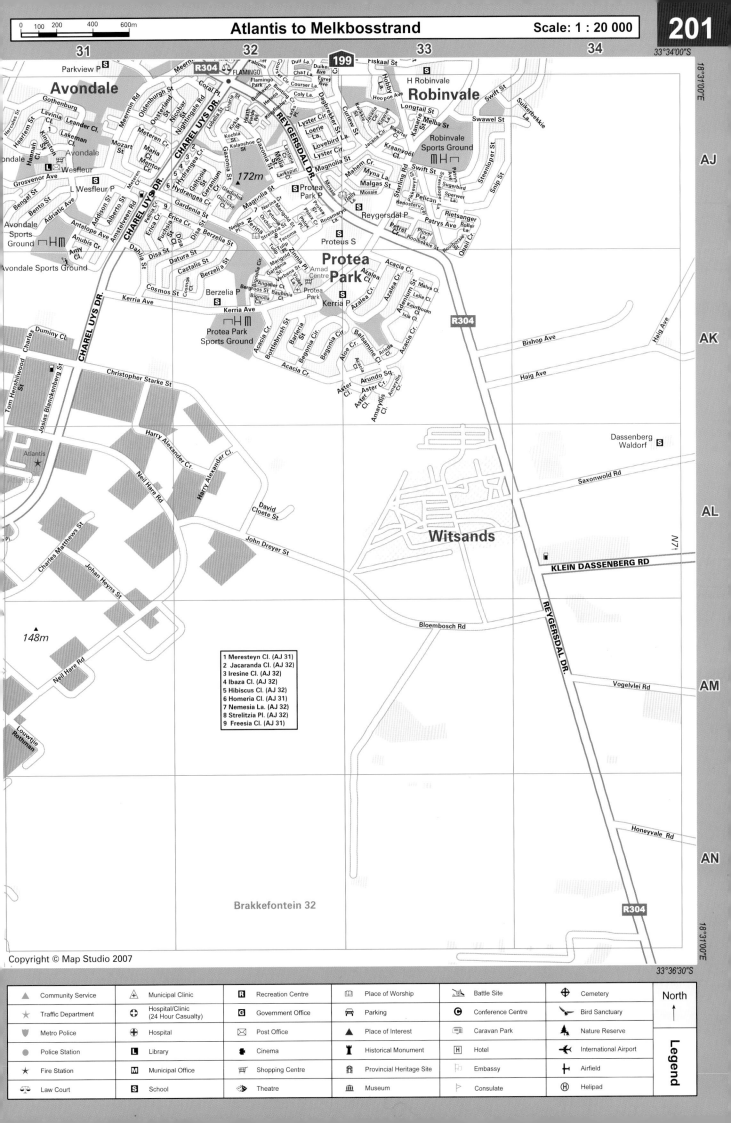

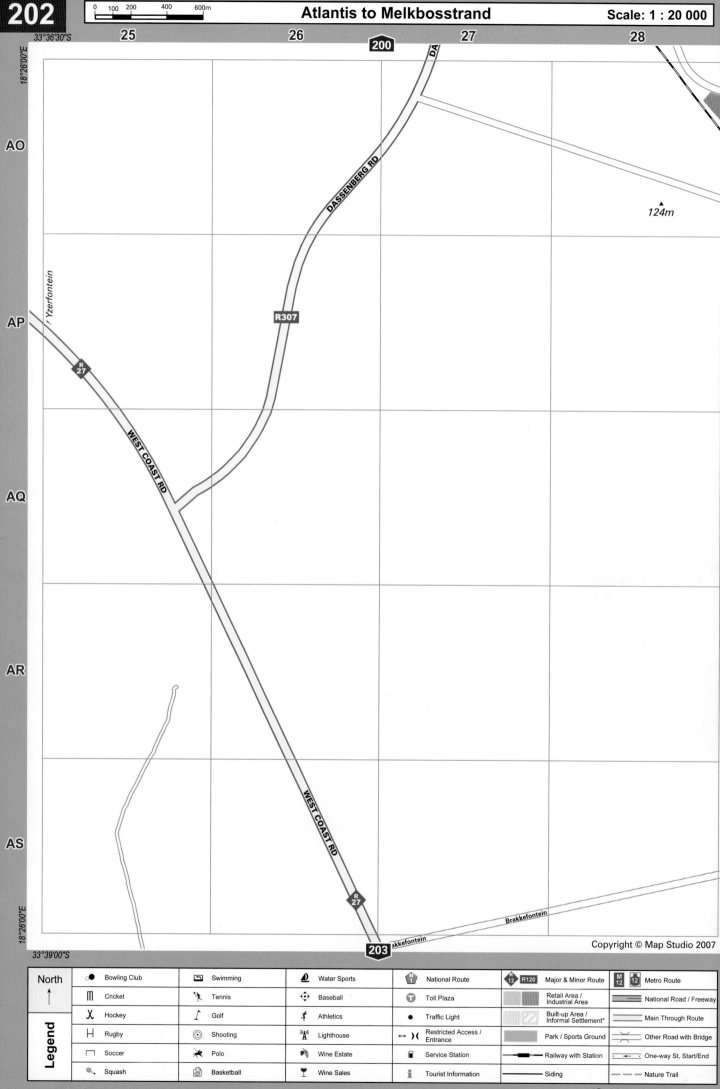

Atlantis to Melkbosstrand

Scale: 1 : 20 000

0   100   200   400   600m

33°36'30"S

18°26'00"E

25   26   **200**   27   28

AO

DASSENBERG RD

124m

Yzerfontein

AP

R307

R
27

WEST COAST RD

AQ

AR

WEST COAST RD

AS

R
27

Brakkefontein

Brakkefontein

203

18°26'00"E

33°39'00"S

Copyright © Map Studio 2007

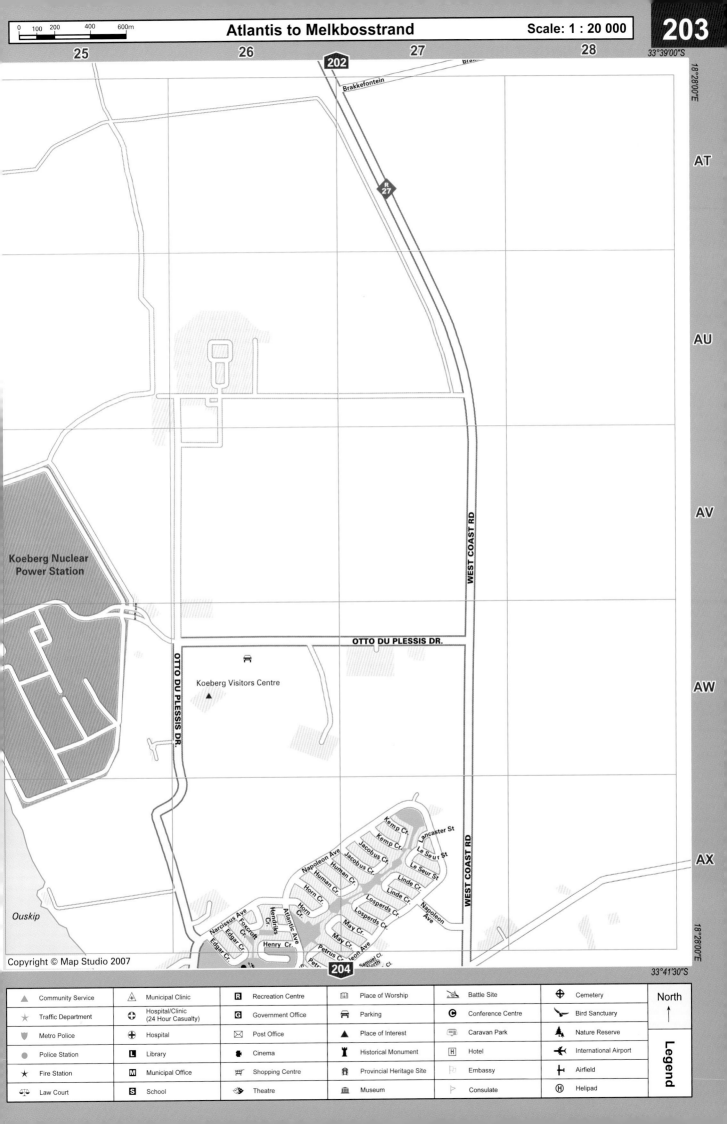

33°39'00"S

18°28'00"E

AT

AU

AV

AW

AX

18°28'00"E

33°41'30"S

Koeberg Nuclear Power Station

Koeberg Visitors Centre

Ouskip

OTTO DU PLESSIS DR.

OTTO DU PLESSIS DR.

WEST COAST RD

WEST COAST RD

Brakkefontein

Narcissus Ave
Foxcroft Cr.
Hendriks Cr.
Atlantic Ave
Edgar Cr.
Edgar Cr.
Henry Cr.
Napoleon Ave
Human Cr.
Horn Cr.
Horn Cr.
Jacobus Cr.
Jacobus Cr.
Kemp Cr.
Kemp Cr.
Lancaster St
Le Seur St
Le Seur St
Linde Cr.
Linde Cr.
Losperds Cr.
Losperds Cr.
May Cr.
May Cr.
Petrus Cr.
Napoleon Ave
Samuel Cl.

25   26   27   28

202
R27
204

Copyright © Map Studio 2007

North
↑

Legend

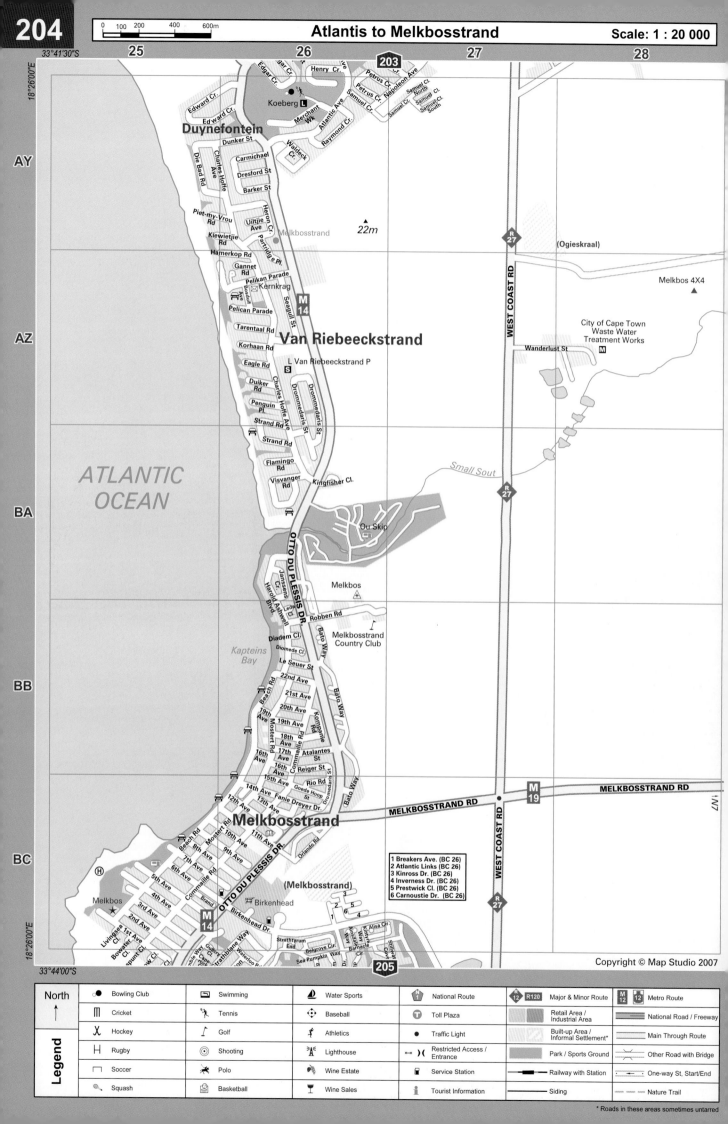

0 100 200 400 600m

33°41'30"S

18°26'00"E

25   **26**   203   **27**   **28**

AY

Duynefontein

Koeberg L

Edgar Cr.
Henry Cr.
Petrus Cr.
Napoleon Ave
Samuel Cr.
Edward Cr.
Edward Cr.
Merchant Wk
Atlantic Ave
Raymond Cr.
Samuel Ct.
Samuel Cl. North
Samuel Cl.
Samuel Cl. South

Dunker St
Waldeck Cr.
Carmichael
Charles Hoffe Ave
Die Bad Rd
Dresford St
Barker St

22m

Piet-my-Vrou Rd
Heron Cr.
Uiltjie Ave
Partridge Pl.
Melkbosstrand

AZ

Van Riebeeckstrand

(Ogieskraal)

R 27

WEST COAST RD

Kiewietjie Rd
Hamerkop Rd
Gannet Rd
Pelikan Parade
Kernkrag
Pelican Parade
M 14
Seagull St

Melkbos 4X4

City of Cape Town
Waste Water
Treatment Works

Wanderlust St
M

Tarentaal Rd
Korhaan Rd
Eagle Rd
L Van Riebeeckstrand P
S
Duiker Rd
Charles Hoffe Ave
Dronmedaris St
Penguin Pl.
Strand Rd
Strand Rd

BA

ATLANTIC
OCEAN

Flamingo Rd
Visvanger Rd
Kingfisher Cl.

Small Sout

R 27

Ou Skip

OTTO DU PLESSIS DR.

Janssens Cr.
Harold Ashwell Blvd
Ladu
Diadem Cl.
Diomede Cl.
Le Seuer St
22nd Ave
Bato Way

Melkbos

Robben Rd
Melkbosstrand
Country Club

BB

Beach Rd
21st Ave
20th Ave
19th Ave
19th Ave
Mostert Rd
18th Ave
17th Ave
16th Ave
16th Cr.
15th Ave
Kompanie Rd
Atalantes St
C Reiger St
Rio Rd
Goeda Hoop
Dronmedaris St
Bato Way

14th Ave
Fanie Dreyer Dr.
12th Ave
13th Ave

Melkbosstrand

11th Ave

MELKBOSSTRAND RD
M 19
MELKBOSSTRAND RD
N7

BC

H
Melkbos

Beach Rd
10th Ave
8th Ave
9th Ave
7th Ave
6th Ave
Commaille Rd
5th Ave
Mostert Rd
Orlando Rd

(Melkbosstrand)

1 Breakers Ave. (BC 26)
2 Atlantic Links (BC 26)
3 Kinross Dr. (BC 26)
4 Inverness Dr. (BC 26)
5 Prestwick Cl. (BC 26)
6 Carnoustie Dr. (BC 26)

WEST COAST RD

R 27

4th Ave
3rd Ave
2nd Ave
Livingsea Cl.
1st Ave
Bowater Cl.
M 14
Brand
Birkenhead
Birkenhead Dr.

Strathtyrum End
Belgrove Cir.
Sea Pumpkin Way
Alisa Cr.
Strathblane Way
Waterloo Rd
Kintrol
Ainsdale Cl.
Barnacle
Stilivar Cl.

205

Copyright © Map Studio 2007

North							
⚬● Bowling Club	🏊 Swimming	🏄 Water Sports	National Route	12 R120 Major & Minor Route	M-12 Metro Route
Ⅲ Cricket	🎾 Tennis	⚾ Baseball	Ⓣ Toll Plaza	Retail Area / Industrial Area	National Road / Freeway
Hockey	🏌 Golf	🏃 Athletics	● Traffic Light	Built-up Area / Informal Settlement*	Main Through Route
H Rugby	◉ Shooting	🗼 Lighthouse	⤬)(Restricted Access / Entrance	Park / Sports Ground	Other Road with Bridge
Soccer	🐎 Polo	🍷 Wine Estate	Service Station	Railway with Station	One-way St, Start/End
Squash	🏀 Basketball	🍷 Wine Sales	Tourist Information	Siding	Nature Trail

* Roads in these areas sometimes untarred

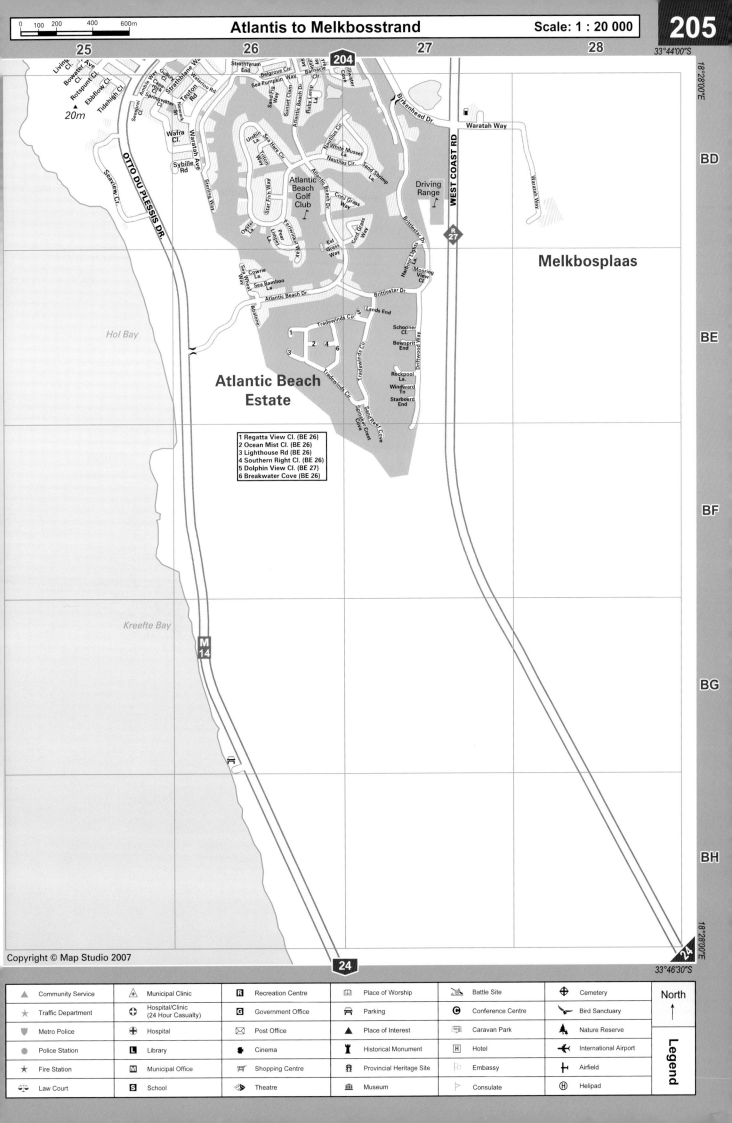

Melkbosplaas

Atlantic Beach Estate

Hol Bay

Kreefte Bay

1 Regatta View Cl. (BE 26)
2 Ocean Mist Cl. (BE 26)
3 Lighthouse Rd (BE 26)
4 Southern Right Cl. (BE 26)
5 Dolphin View Cl. (BE 27)
6 Breakwater Cove (BE 26)

Atlantic Beach Golf Club

Driving Range

										North
▲ Community Service	Ⓐ Municipal Clinic	Ⓡ Recreation Centre	Place of Worship	Battle Site	✚ Cemetery	↑
★ Traffic Department	Hospital/Clinic (24 Hour Casualty)	Ⓖ Government Office	🚗 Parking	Ⓒ Conference Centre	✈ Bird Sanctuary	
🛡 Metro Police	Hospital	✉ Post Office	▲ Place of Interest	Caravan Park	▲ Nature Reserve	
● Police Station	Ⓛ Library	Cinema	Historical Monument	Ⓗ Hotel	✈ International Airport	Legend
★ Fire Station	Ⓜ Municipal Office	Shopping Centre	Provincial Heritage Site	Embassy	Airfield	
Law Court	Ⓢ School	Theatre	Museum	Consulate	Ⓗ Helipad	

Tulbagh

Scale: 1 : 20 000

Tulbagh

Obiqua Correctional Facility

Nieuwe Helpmekaar

1 Patrys St (TW 13)
2 Meeu St (TW 13)

Chris Hani

Sports Ground

Kliprivier Park

Kruisvlei St

Karee St

Waveren St

Wilger La.

De Wet Huis (1812)

Rooiels La.

Tulbagh H

Eike La.

Market St

Steinthal Rd

Tulbagh

Waterkant St

Library (1785)

Museum St

Oude Kerk (1743)

Rossouw St

L H Waveren

Obiqua Cr.

6th Ave

5th Ave

4th Ave

3rd Ave

2nd Ave

1st Ave

Olifant St

Tier St

Arend St

Duif St

Kasuur St

Klapper St

Safraan St

East St

Meiring St

Freesia St

Nerina St

Dieset St

West St

High St

Protea St

Maroela St

Magnolia

VAN DER STEL ST

Gouda

Klip

Wolseley

Copyright © Map Studio 2007

33°15'49"S

19°0743"E

33°18'19"S

19°0743"E

10   11   12   13

TU

TV

TW

TX

TY

Legend

North

Bowling Club	Swimming	Water Sports	National Route	R120 Major & Minor Route	Metro Route
Cricket	Tennis	Baseball	Toll Plaza	Retail Area / Industrial Area	National Road / Freeway
Hockey	Golf	Athletics	Traffic Light	Built-up Area / Informal Settlement*	Main Through Route
Rugby	Shooting	Lighthouse	Restricted Access / Entrance	Park / Sports Ground	Other Road with Bridge
Soccer	Polo	Wine Estate	Service Station	Railway with Station	One-way St, Start/End
Squash	Basketball	Wine Sales	Tourist Information	Siding	Nature Trail

* Roads in these areas sometimes untarred

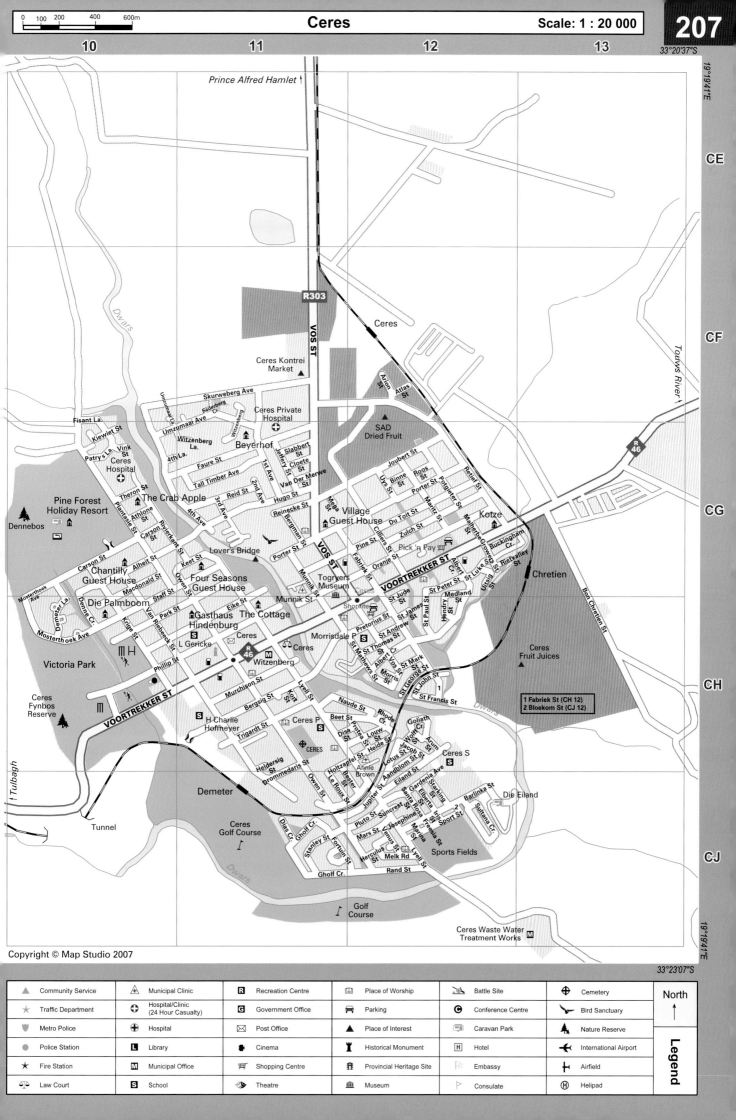

Saldanha

Summerveld

Adderly Rd

Summerveld

Strand

Ascot Pl.

Ascot Cir.

Ascot Cir.

Newmarket St

Loop St

Aintree

Newmarket St

Strand

Areos
Adonis
Elara
Delphi
Pegasus
Zeus
Asteria
Icarus
Orpheus
Odysseus
Artemis

Club
Mykonos

N.S.R.I 4

Club Mykonos
Resort

Club Mykonos
Casino

Santorini St
Naxos Cl.
Los Cl.
Amorgos St
Kimolos Cl.
Mykonos
Seritos
Thio
Delos Cl.
St
Kea Cl.
Syros St
Kythnos
Naxos
St

Loop St

Epson St

Scotsville Rd

Kenilworth

Casos Rd
Calithea Rd
Thera Rd
Samos Rd
Chios Cl.
Melos Cl.
Cleon Cl.
Tenos Rd
Casos Rd

Saldanha
Bay

Loop St

R27/Hopefield

Kraalbaai
Cl.
Leentjiesklip
Cl.
Seeberg
Cl.
Schaapenoest
Cl.
Rietbaai
Cl.
Pelican St
Pinkler
Cl. Osprey

Kingfisher
St

Batavier Cir.

Goede Hoop Dr.

Batavier
Cir.

Langebaan Counry Estate
(Under Construction)

Leentjiesklip

Wolraad Dr.
Jag.
Cl.

Robbejacht
Cir.

Wapen
Cl.

Fregat
Cl.

Van Breda Dr.

Brik Cl.

Van Breda
Dr.

Galjoot
Cl.

Tamboer
Cl.
Schapejacht
Cl.
De Swantje
Cl.
'Kalft Cl.

Heerengraaf Dr.

Aletta Van
As Cl.
Goede Hoop
Cl.

Willem
Eksteen Cl.

Muelen
Hoeks Cl.
Voorhoutin
Cl.
ngraaf Dr.
Alde

Copyright © Map Studio 2007

North

Legend

●| Bowling Club	Swimming	Water Sports	National Route	R120 Major & Minor Route	M12 / 12 Metro Route
Ⅲ	Cricket	Tennis	Baseball	Toll Plaza	Retail Area / Industrial Area	National Road / Freeway
X	Hockey	Golf	Athletics	Traffic Light	Built-up Area / Informal Settlement*	Main Through Route
H	Rugby	Shooting	Lighthouse	Restricted Access / Entrance	Park / Sports Ground	Other Road with Bridge
□	Soccer	Shipwreck	Wine Estate	Service Station	Railway with Station	One-way St, Start/End
	Squash	Basketball	Wine Sales	Tourist Information	Siding	Nature Trail

* Roads in these areas sometimes untarred

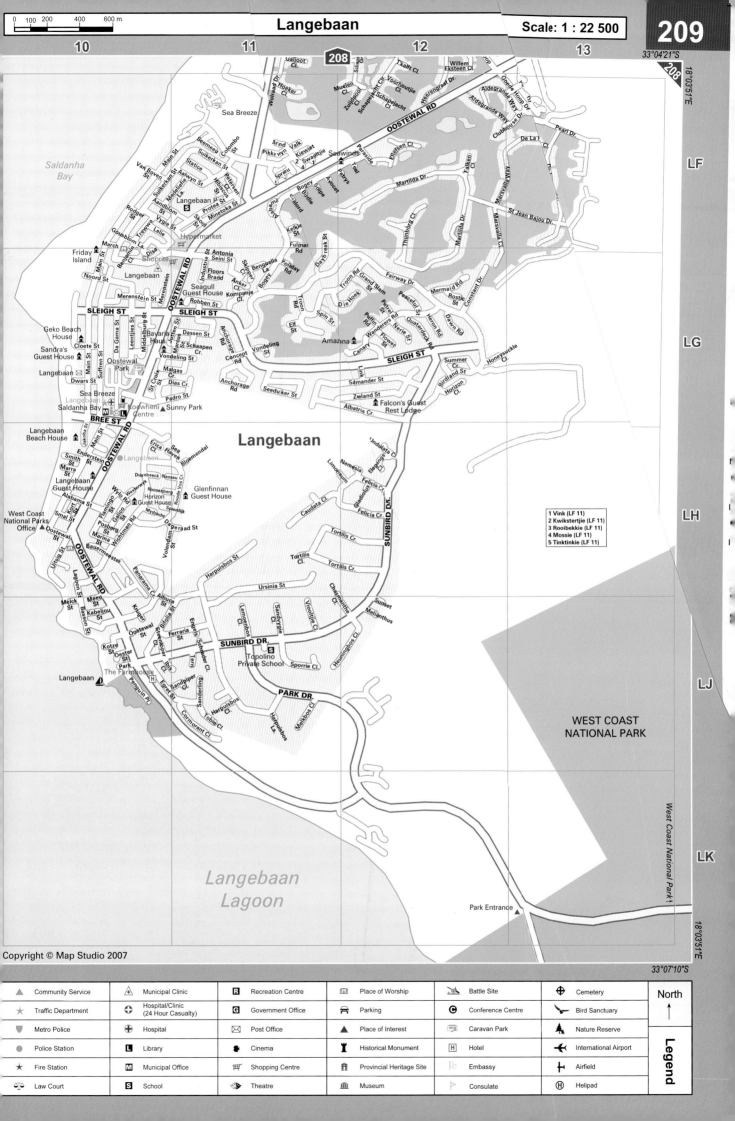

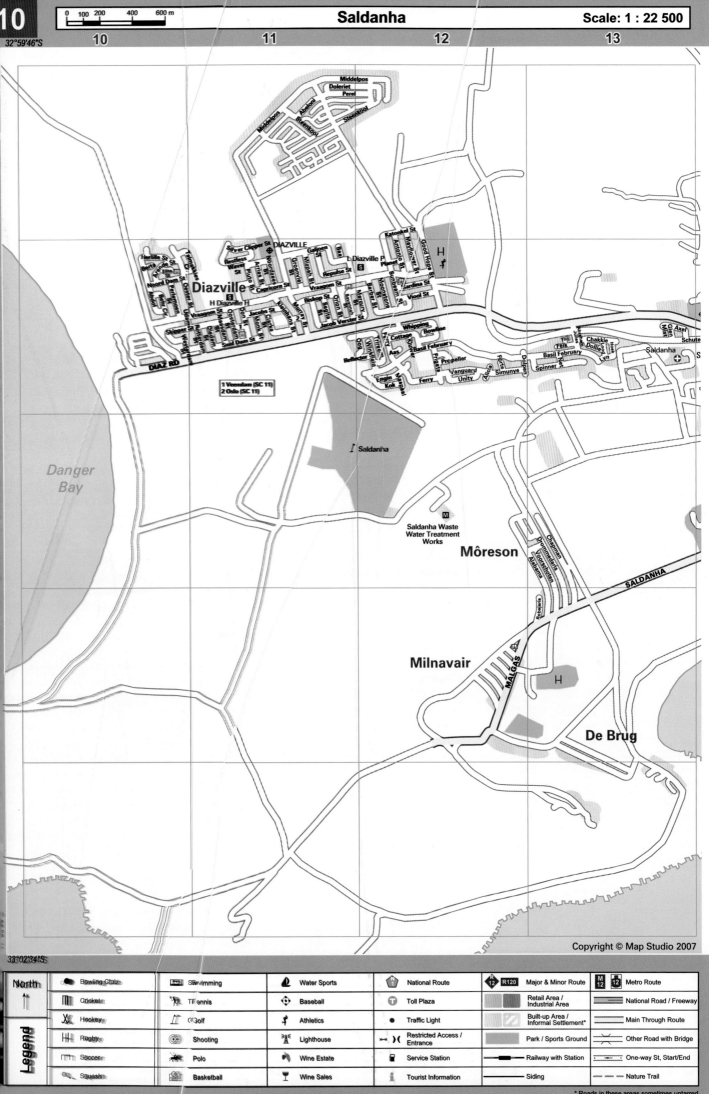

Middelpos
Doleriet
Perel

Middelpos
Steenkool
Steenkool
Abeloni

Silver Clipper St DIAZVILLE
Reckless Waves
Katonkel St
Diazville P
Good Hope St

Diazville

DIAZ RD

1 Veendam (SC 11)
2 Oslo (SC 11)

Saldanha

Danger Bay

Saldanha Waste
Water Treatment
Works

Môreson

SALDANHA

MALGAS

Milnavair

H

De Brug

Copyright © Map Studio 2007

33°02'34"S

North

Legend

Bowling Club		Swimming		Water Sports		National Route		Major & Minor Route	R120	Metro Route
Cricket		Tennis		Baseball		Toll Plaza		Retail Area / Industrial Area		National Road / Freeway
Hockey		Golf		Athletics		Traffic Light		Built-up Area / Informal Settlement*		Main Through Route
Rugby		Shooting		Lighthouse		Restricted Access / Entrance		Park / Sports Ground		Other Road with Bridge
Soccer		Polo		Wine Estate		Service Station		Railway with Station		One-way St, Start/End
Squash		Basketball		Wine Sales		Tourist Information		Siding		Nature Trail

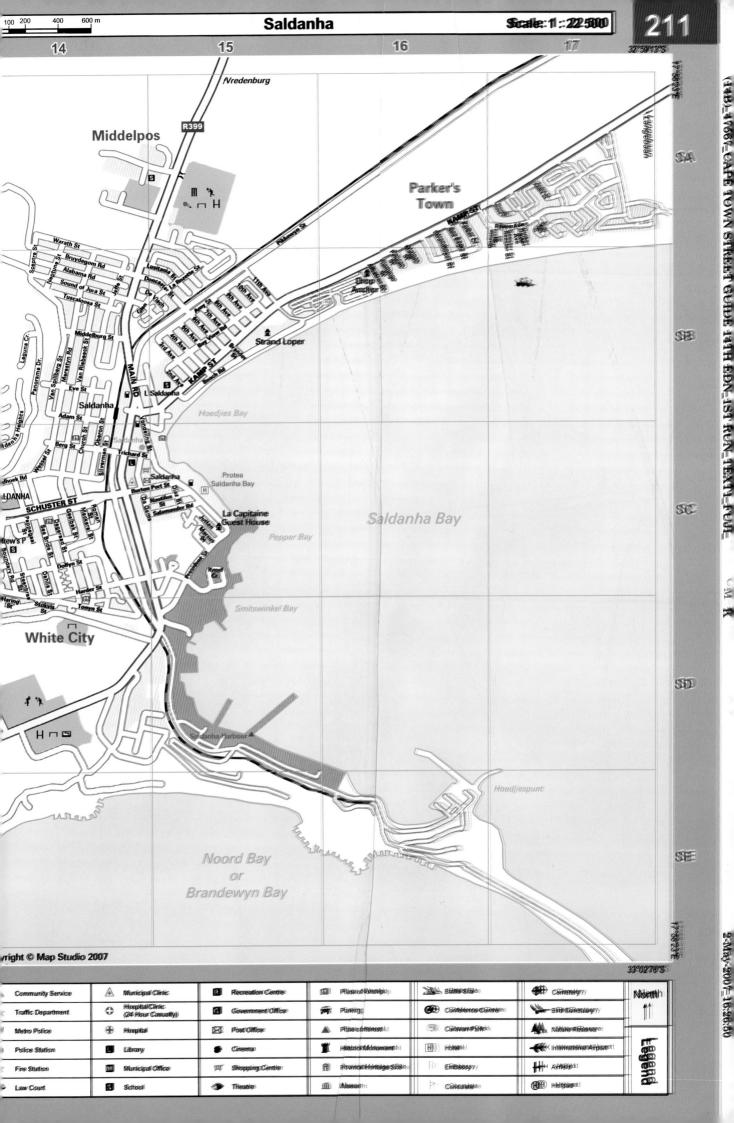

100 200 400 600 m

14   15   16   17

Nredenburg

R399

Middelpos

Parker's Town

Warath St
Sopra St
Bruydegom Rd
Neptune St
Alabama Rd
Sound of Jua St
Tuscaloosa St
Lusitania St
Dorceria La
De Visch
Middelburg St
Van Riebeeck Rd
Maradyn Rd
Eve St
Panorama Dr.
Laguna Cr.
Idana Heights

Saldanha
L.Saldanha
Adam St
Berg St
Church St
Oberon St
Silverman St
Trichard St

Strand Loper

Drop Anchor

MAIN RD
KAMP ST
Beach Rd

Hoedjies Bay

Saldanha

Protea Saldanha Bay

La Capitaine Guest House

Saldanha Bay

Pepper Bay

SCHUSTER ST

Berton Port St

Salamander Rd

Smitswinkel Bay

White City

Harder St
Haring St
Stokvis St
Tonyn St

Hoedjiespunt

Saldanha Harbour

Noord Bay or Brandewyn Bay

Legend

Community Service	Municipal Clinic	Recreation Centre	Place of Worship	Battle Site	Cemetery
Traffic Department	Hospital/Clinic (24 Hour Casualty)	Government Office	Parking	Conference Centre	Bird Sanctuary
Metro Police	Hospital	Post Office	Place of Interest	Caravan Park	Nature Reserve
Police Station	Library	Cinema	Historical Monument	Hotel	International Airport
Fire Station	Municipal Office	Shopping Centre	Provincial Heritage Site	Embassy	Airfield
Law Court	School	Theatre	Museum	Consulate	Helipad

North

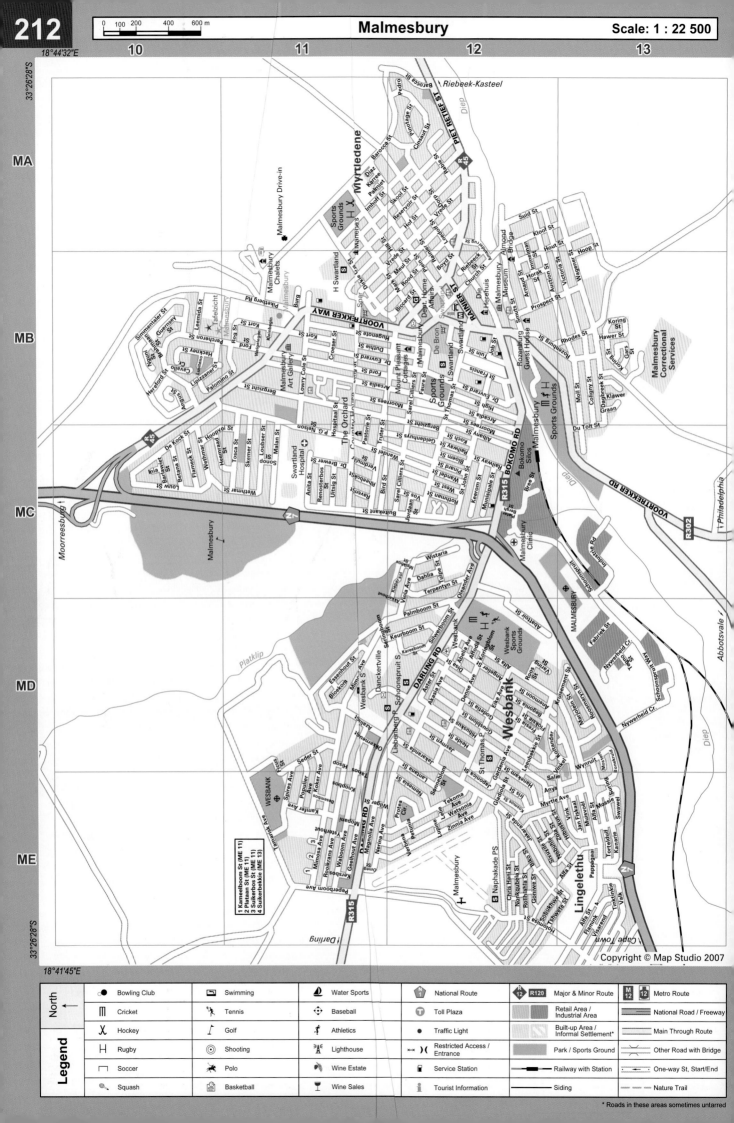

Copyright © Map Studio 2007

North			

Legend

●● Bowling Club	🏊 Swimming	⛵ Water Sports	National Route	12 R120 Major & Minor Route	M12 Metro Route
Cricket	Tennis	Baseball	Toll Plaza	Retail Area / Industrial Area	National Road / Freeway
✗ Hockey	⌐ Golf	Athletics	Traffic Light	Built-up Area / Informal Settlement*	Main Through Route
H Rugby	◉ Shooting	Lighthouse	Restricted Access / Entrance	Park / Sports Ground	Other Road with Bridge
☐ Soccer	Polo	Wine Estate	Service Station	Railway with Station	One-way St, Start/End
Squash	Basketball	Wine Sales	Tourist Information	Siding	Nature Trail

* Roads in these areas sometimes untarred

0 100 200 400 600m

10   11   12   13

33°21'00"S

18°24'00"E

DA

Malmesbury / R45 / Hopefield

Sports Ground

17th Ave
16th Ave
15th Ave
14th Ave
13th Ave
Clarendon
12th Ave
11th Ave
10th Ave
9th Ave
8th Ave
7th Ave
Loop
Vlei
Grey St
Durban St
Smith St

EVITA BEZUIDENHOUT BLVD

R307

DB

Nuwedorp

L Vooruitsig
S
6th Ave
5th Ave
4th Ave
3rd Ave
2nd Ave
1st Ave
Maitland St
Durban St
Donkin
Somerset St
Somerset Cr.
Cole

YZERFONTEIN RD

Yzerfontein / R27

R315

Wild Flower Reserve

DARLING

S.P.C.A.

Park Cl.

Fabriek St

Caledon St

DC

Old Darling Rd
Evita se Perron
Voortrekker St
Darling

The Granary

Spar
Darling
Queen Victoria St
Church St
Darling

Arcadia St
Voortrekker St

Darling Sports Club
R

Darling

Trinity Guest Lodge
H
Darling
Van Riebeeck St
Tulbagh St
Nerissa St
Mimosa Cl.
Van Der Stel St

Fountain St
Darling Lodge
Protea St
Delphinium St
Nerina St
Jakaranda St
S
Darling Col.

Buitekant St
High St
Mt Pleasant St
Prospect St
Long St
Hill St
Darling Museum & Information Centre
Fountain St

Garden St
Church St
Station St
Hildabrand St
Petunia St
Watsonia St

Darling

OLD DARLING RD

DD

Ormonde
Langfontein St

De Gans Guest House

L Darling Sports Ground
S
Kalkoentjie St

Ixia St
Vigie St
Botterblom St
Vigie St

R315
R307

Renosterveld
Wild Flower Reserve

Mamre / Atlantis

DE

18°24'00"E

33°23'30"S

Legend					
▲ Community Service	Ⓐ Municipal Clinic	Ⓡ Recreation Centre	Place of Worship	Battle Site	⊕ Cemetery
★ Traffic Department	✛ Hospital/Clinic (24 Hour Casualty)	Ⓖ Government Office	Parking	Ⓒ Conference Centre	Bird Sanctuary
▼ Metro Police	✚ Hospital	✉ Post Office	▲ Place of Interest	Caravan Park	Nature Reserve
● Police Station	Ⓛ Library	Cinema	Historical Monument	H Hotel	International Airport
★ Fire Station	Ⓜ Municipal Office	Shopping Centre	Provincial Heritage Site	Embassy	Airfield
Law Court	Ⓢ School	Theatre	Museum	Consulate	Ⓗ Helipad

North ↑

Legend

Touwsrivier

Robertson

217

220

Industrial Area

Sports Ground

Zwelletemba

ROBERTSON DR.

Hex Industria

Melrings Park

R 60

KLEINPLASIE SHOWGROUNDS

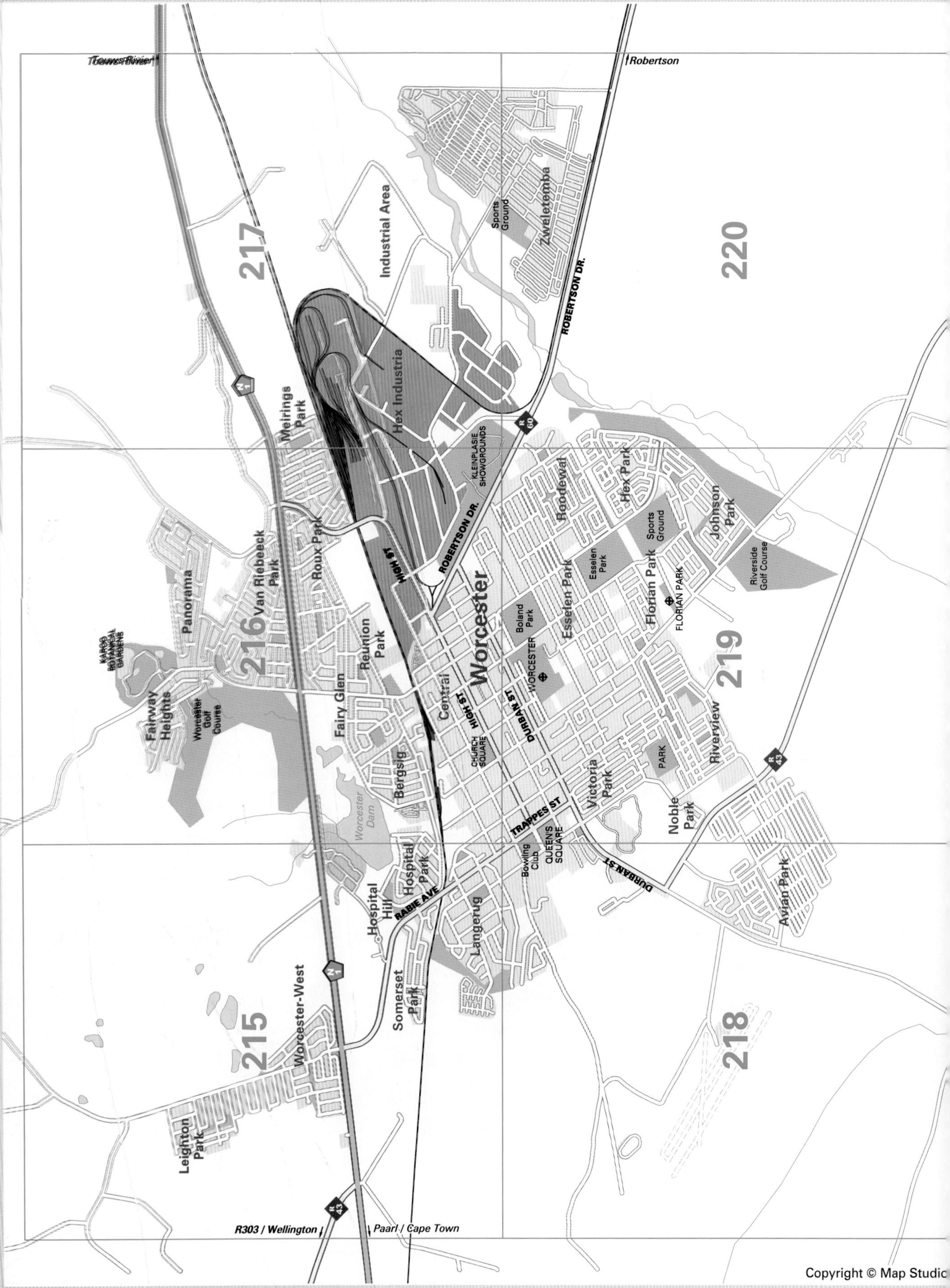

Roodewal

Hex Park

Johnson Park

ROBERTSON DR.

Van Riebeeck Park

Roux Park

HIGH ST

Sports Ground

Riverside Golf Course

Panorama

KAROO BOTANICAL GARDENS

216

Fairy Glen

Reunion Park

Worcester

Esselen Park

Esselen Park

Florian Park

FLORIAN PARK

219

Fairway Heights

Worcester Golf Course

Boland Park

WORCESTER

DURBAN ST

HIGH ST

Central

Bergsig

CHURCH SQUARE

PARK

Riverview

R 43

Worcester Dam

Victoria Park

Noble Park

DURBAN ST

Hospital Hill

Hospital Park

RABIE AVE

Langerug

TRAPPES ST

Bowling Club

QUEEN'S SQUARE

Avian Park

Somerset Park

215

Worcester-West

218

Leighton Park

R303 / Wellington

Paarl / Cape Town

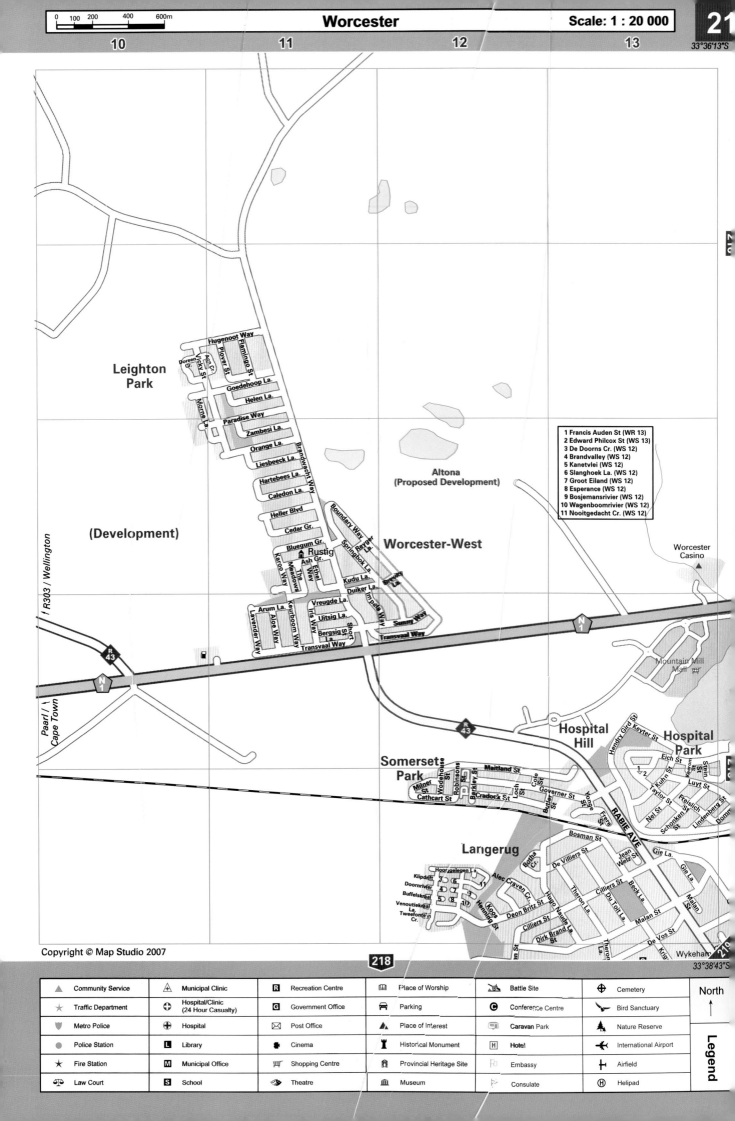

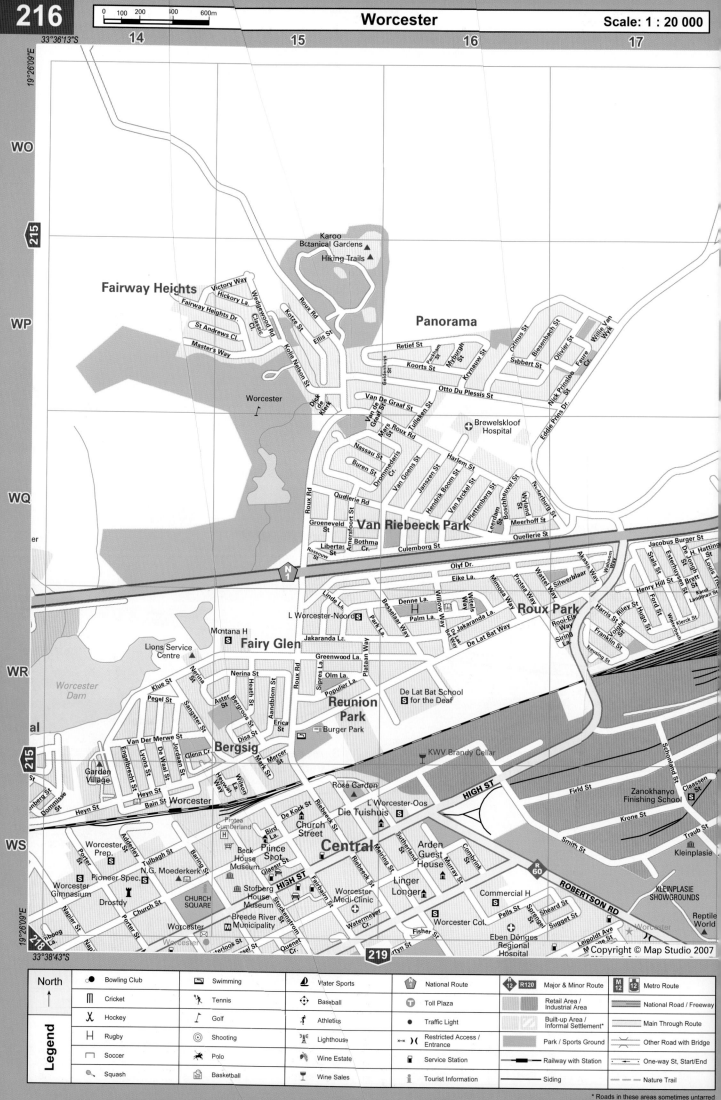

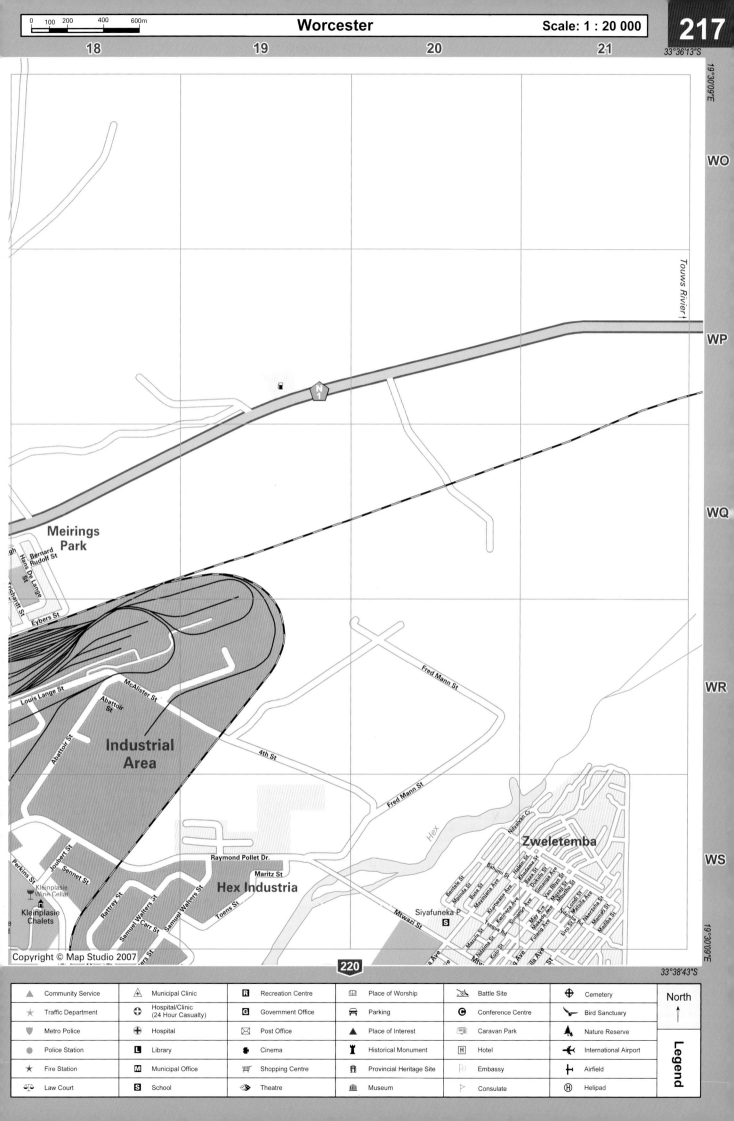

0 100 200   400   600m

10   11   215   12   13

WT

WU

WV

WW

WX

Worcester Race Track

Worcester

Breë

Distillery Rd

Pionier Institute
for the Blind

The Barn Arts &
Glass Gallery

L Worcester

Dirk Brand St
De Vos St
Marius Smit St
Van Rensburg Cr.
Malan St
Theron La.
De Vos St
Kriga St
Wyk

DURBAN ST

Aviar
Park

Kwikkie St
Kraai St
Makou St

Robin St
Kingfisher St
Swallow St
Eagle St
Mossie St
Finch St
Kwarter St
Pigeon St
Pelikaan St
Nightingale St
Myna St
Meeu St
Mannikin St
Penguin St
Parakeet St
Osprey St
Tortelduif St
Katlagter
Kalkoen

V Parrot St
Crane St
Lark St
Byvanger St
Bromvoël St
Blashoender St
Albat

Katlagter

Copyright © Map Studio

Legend

North ↑

Bowling Club	Swimming	Water Sports	National Route	Major & Minor Route	Metro Route
Cricket	Tennis	Baseball	Toll Plaza	Retail Area / Industrial Area	National Road
Hockey	Golf	Athletics	Traffic Light	Built-up Area / Informal Settlement*	Main Through R
Rugby	Shooting	Lighthouse	Restricted Access / Entrance	Park / Sports Ground	Other Road with
Soccer	Polo	Wine Estate	Service Station	Railway with Station	One-way St, Sta
Squash	Basketball	Wine Sales	Tourist Information	Siding	Nature Trail

* Roads in these areas sometimes

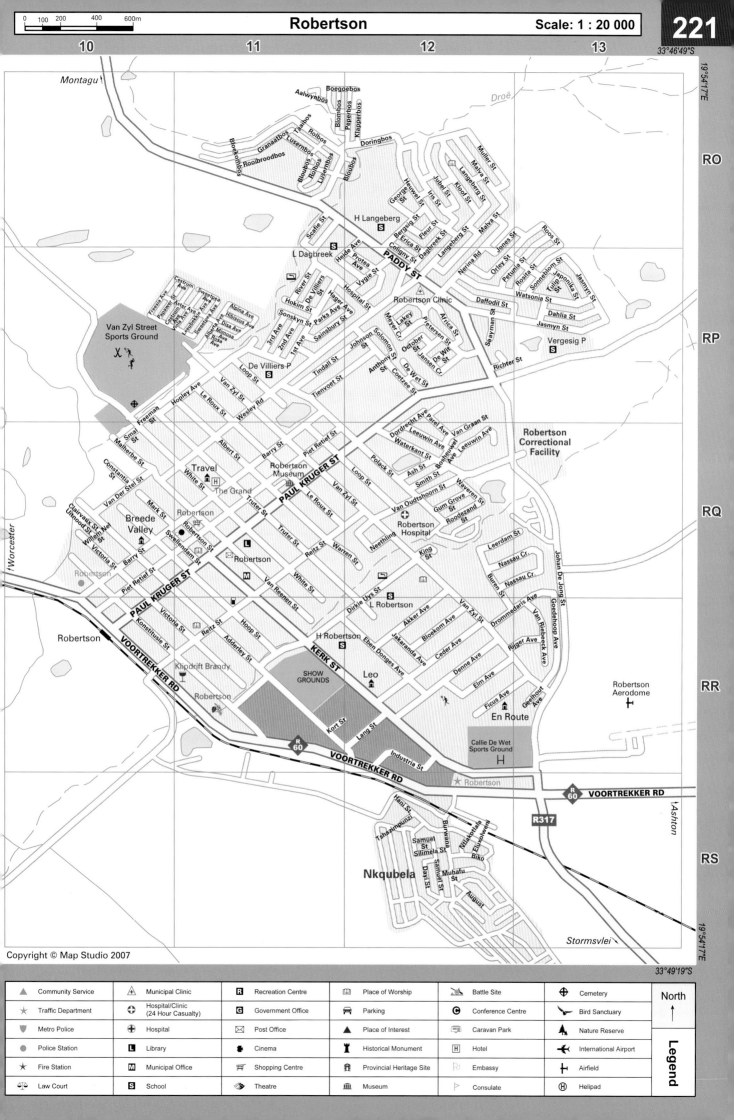

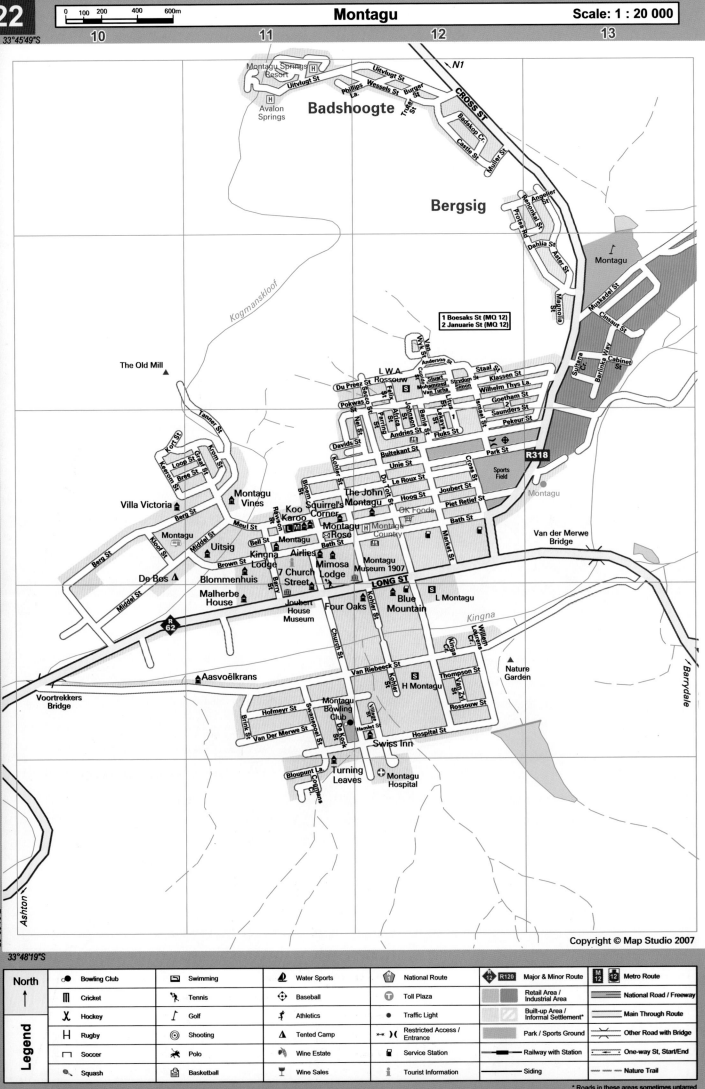

33°45'49"S

0   100 200   400   600m

10   11   12   13

N1

Montagu Springs Resort
Uitvlugt St
Uitvlugt St
Wessels St
Phillips La.
Burger St
Trader St
Badshoogte
Avalon Springs

CROSS ST
Badskop Cr.
Castle St
Muller St

Bergsig
Angelier St
Renonkel St
Protea Rd
Dahlia St
Aster St
Magnolia St
↟ Montagu

Muskadel St
Cinsaut St
Sultana Cr.
Berlinta Way
Cabinet St

Kogmanskloof

1 Boesaks St (MQ 12)
2 Januarie St (MQ 12)

The Old Mill ▲

Van Wyk St
Anderson St
L W A
Du Preez St
Rossouw St
Staal St
Klassen St
Stuart
Mohammed Simon
Van Turha
Strijdom St
Wilhelm Thys La.
Felix St
Pokwas St
Sacco St
Africa St
Parring St
Johnson St
Licius St
Lekays St
Goetham St
2
Saunders St
Banie St
Fluks St
1
Pekeur St
Tanner St
Nel St
Andries St
Davids St

Kort St
Krom St
Great St
Loop St
Bree St
Keerom St

Buitekant St
Park St
R318

Unie St
Kohler St
Le Roux St
Hoog St
Joubert St
Piet Retief St
Sports Field

Villa Victoria ▲
Montagu Vines
Berg St
Koo Squirrel's Corner
Karoo
The John Montagu
● Montagu

Meul St
Réyson St
Montagu Rosé
Montagu Country
Bath St

Montagu
Middel St
Uitsig
Bell St
Kingna Lodge
Airlies
Mimosa Lodge
Montagu Museum 1907
Market St
Van der Merwe Bridge

Berg St
Brown St
Berry St
7 Church Street
Blommenhuis
LONG ST
L Montagu

De Bos ▲
Malherbe House
Joubert House Museum
Four Oaks
Blue Mountain
Kingna

Middel St
R62
Church St
Van Riebeeck St
Kohler St
Kingna Ct.
William Loureng Cr.
Nature Garden ↟

Aasvoëlkrans ▲
Thompson St
Van Zyl St
H Montagu
Rossouw St

Voortrekkers Bridge
Hofmeyr St
Montagu Bowling Club
Village St
Hamlet St
Hospital St

Brink St
Van Der Merwe St
Swaepoel St
De Kock St
Swiss Inn

Bloupunt La.
Turning Leaves
Cougans Ct.
Montagu Hospital

Ashton

Copyright © Map Studio 2007

33°48'19"S

North ↑

Legend

Bowling Club	Swimming	Water Sports	National Route
Cricket	Tennis	Baseball	Toll Plaza
Hockey	Golf	Athletics	Traffic Light
Rugby	Shooting	Tented Camp	Restricted Access / Entrance
Soccer	Polo	Wine Estate	Service Station
Squash	Basketball	Wine Sales	Tourist Information

Major & Minor Route — Metro Route
Retail Area / Industrial Area — National Road / Freeway
Built-up Area / Informal Settlement* — Main Through Route
Park / Sports Ground — Other Road with Bridge
Railway with Station — One-way St, Start/End
Siding — Nature Trail

19°18'40"E

100 200 400 600m

10   11   12   13

34°00'16"S

VJ

Worcester

VK

R43

MAIN RD

Elands

De Villiers Graaff

De Villiers Graaff (1907)

Villiersdorp

Showgrounds

Van Riebaeck St

Reats St

Caledon St

Upington St

Waste Water Treatment Works

Church St

Vert Coppenhagen

Malherbe

Union Ave

Voortrekker St

Prins Albert St

Upington St

Villiersdorp St

Van Riebaeck St

Caledon

Mosko St

H De Villiers Graaff

Graaff St

Ham St

Du Toit St

Victoria St

Muller St

VL

Stadium

Lambrecht St

Coetzee St

Spring St

Street St

Spar

Roland St

Roux St

Huis de Villiers

Upper Union Ave

Berg St

Barnard St

Gunter St

Meyer St

O.K. Centre

MAIN RD

R43

VM

Ham St

Villiersdorp

Buitenkant St

Protea St

L Kosie De Wet

Nuwedorp

H Villiersdorp

Diaz St

Brown St

Ram St

Protea St

Wassonia St

Serruria St

Amarnta St

Buitenkant St

Protea St

Willem St

Memoria St

Erica St

Goniwe Park

Grabouw

VN

34°00'16"S

19°16'10"E

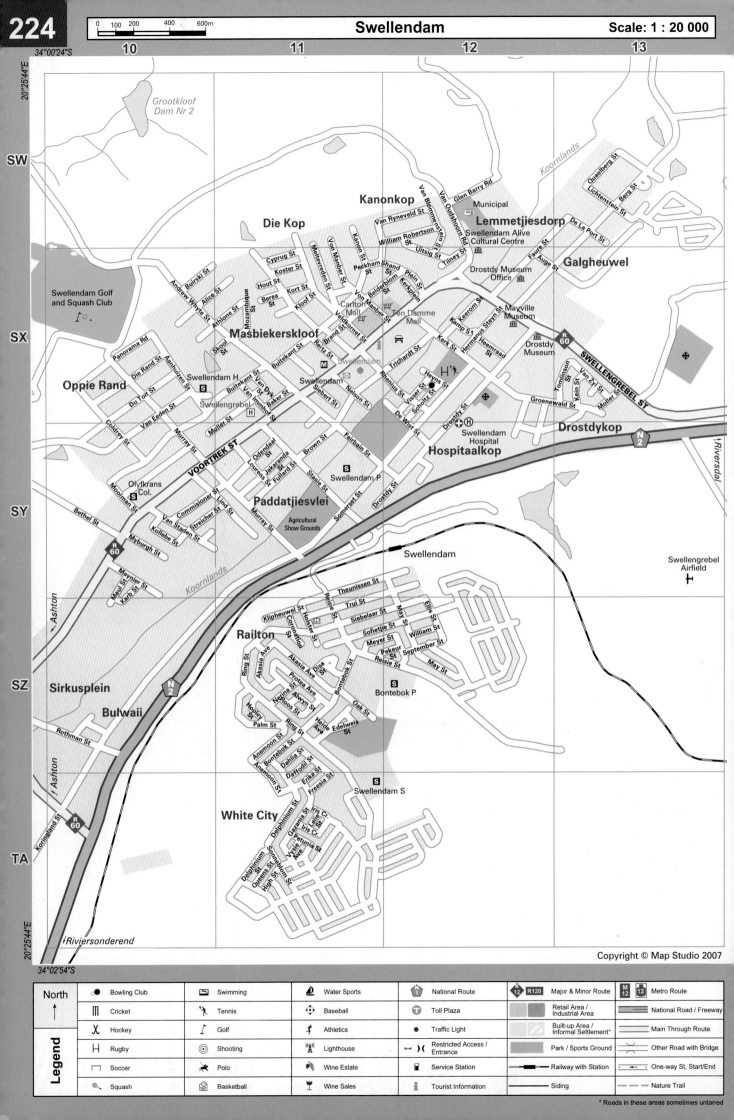

Swellendam

Scale: 1 : 20 000

0 100 200 400 600m

34°00'24"S
20°25'44"E

10   11   12   13

SW
SX
SY
SZ
TA

Grootkloof Dam Nr 2

Kanonkop

Die Kop

Municipal

Lemmetjiesdorp

Swellendam Alive Cultural Centre

Galgheuwel

Glen Barry Rd

Van Oudtshoorn Rd

Van Blommenstein St

Van Ryneveld St

William Robertson St

Uitsig St

Tilney

Peckham Shand Plein St

Faure St

Auge St

De La Port St

Quaelberg St

Lichtenstein St

Berg St

Koornlands

Swellendam Golf and Squash Club

Cyprug St

Koster St

Meitevreden St

Hout St

Von Manber St

Kanon St

Kerkplein

Drostdy Museum Office

Von Belderblom

Kamp St

Keerom St

Mayville Museum

R60

Andrew Whyte St

Alice St

Athlone St

Mozambique St

Berea St

Kloof St

Brand St

Veldkornet St

Carlton Mall

Ten Damme Mall

Hermanus Steyn St

Heemraad St

Drostdy Museum

Masbiekerskloof

Skool St

Reitz St

Buitekant St

Swellendam

Trichardt St

Hevns St

Kerk St

SWELLENGREBEL ST

Tomlinson

Van Zyl St

Kein St

Moller St

Panorama Rd

Die Rand

Aanhuizen St

Swellendam H

Buitekant St

Van Dyk St

Swellendam

Nelson St

Rhenius St

Visser St

Scholtz St

Groenewald St

Oppie Rand

Du Toit St

Van Eeden St

Baker St

Siebert St

De Wet St

Drostdy St

Swellendam Hospital

Drostdykop

N2

Riversdal

Coldrey St

Murray St

Moller St

Swellengrebel

Fairbain St

Brown St

Swellendam P

Hospitaalkop

VOORTREK ST

Odendaal St

Lind St

Jakaranda St

Staise St

Drostdy St

Olyfkrans Col.

Moolman St

Commissioner St

Streicher St

Lourens St

Fullard St

Murray St

Somerset St

Bethel St

Myburgh St

Kollebe St

Van Staden St

Paddatjiesvlei

Agricultural Show Grounds

R60

Maynier St

Meul St

Karb St

Koornlands

Ashton

Swellendam

Swellengrebel Airfield

Theunissen St

Klipheuwel St

Reisie St

Trui St

Ellis St

May St

William St

Railton

Coronation St

Hoister St

Siebelaar St

Sofietjie St

September St

May St

Sirkusplein

N2

Ring St

Akasia Ave

Akasia Ave

Disa St

Meyer St

Pekeur St

Reisie St

Oak St

Bontebok P

S

Bulwaii

Rothman St

Ashton

Negina St

Protea Ave

Alwyn St

Roos St

Bontebok St

Haide Ave

Edelweis St

Hopley St

Palm St

Ring St

Anemoon St

Bontebok St

Dahlia St

Daffodil St

Erika St

Freesia St

Swellendam S

S

R60

Kortjeland St

White City

Delphinium St

Gazania St

Iris Cr.

Vyfie Ave

Petunia Ave

Delphinium St

Queens St

Sommblom St

High St

Riviersonderend

34°02'54"S
20°25'44"E

Copyright © Map Studio 2007

North						
↑	Bowling Club	Swimming	Water Sports	National Route	12 R120 Major & Minor Route	M12 Metro Route
	Cricket	Tennis	Baseball	Toll Plaza	Retail Area / Industrial Area	National Road / Freeway
	Hockey	Golf	Athletics	Traffic Light	Built-up Area / Informal Settlement*	Main Through Route
Legend	Rugby	Shooting	Lighthouse	Restricted Access / Entrance	Park / Sports Ground	Other Road with Bridge
	Soccer	Polo	Wine Estate	Service Station	Railway with Station	One-way St, Start/End
	Squash	Basketball	Wine Sales	Tourist Information	Siding	Nature Trail

* Roads in these areas sometimes untarred

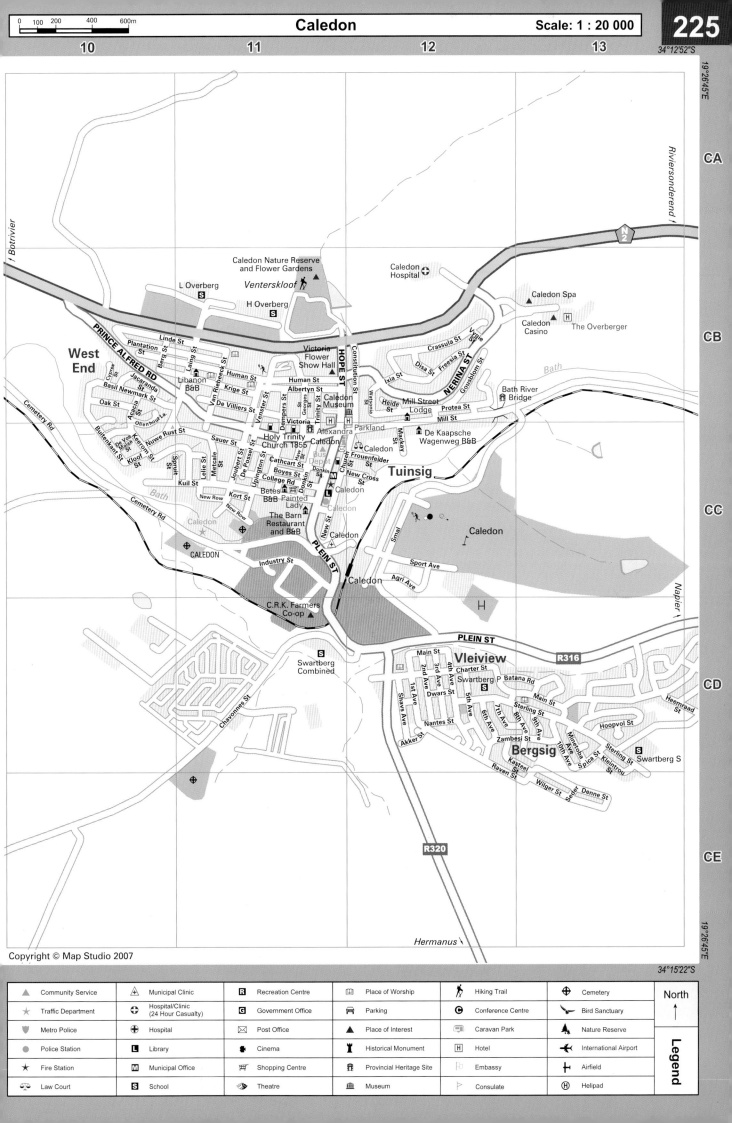

Caledon

Scale: 1 : 20 000

225

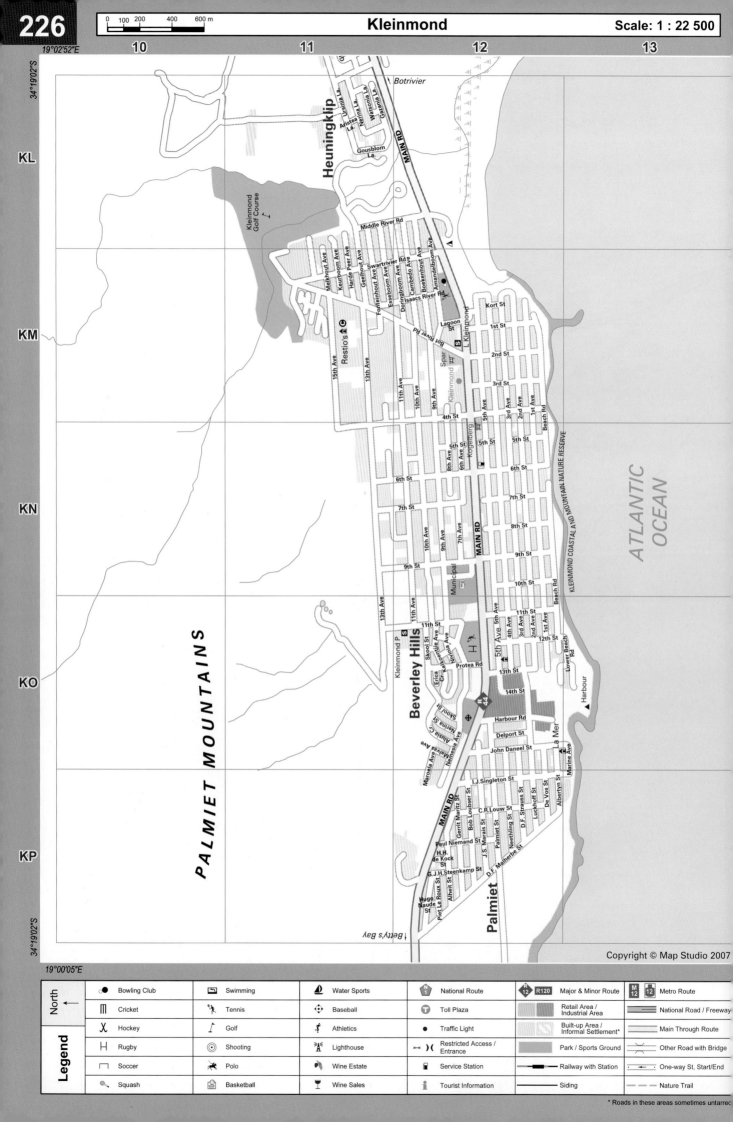

Legend									
● Bowling Club	Swimming	Water Sports	National Route	Major & Minor Route	Metro Route
Cricket	Tennis	Baseball	Toll Plaza	Retail Area / Industrial Area	National Road / Freeway
Hockey	Golf	Athletics	Traffic Light	Built-up Area / Informal Settlement*	Main Through Route
Rugby	Shooting	Lighthouse	Restricted Access / Entrance	Park / Sports Ground	Other Road with Bridge
Soccer	Polo	Wine Estate	Service Station	Railway with Station	One-way St, Start/End
Squash	Basketball	Wine Sales	Tourist Information	Siding	Nature Trail

North

* Roads in these areas sometimes untarred

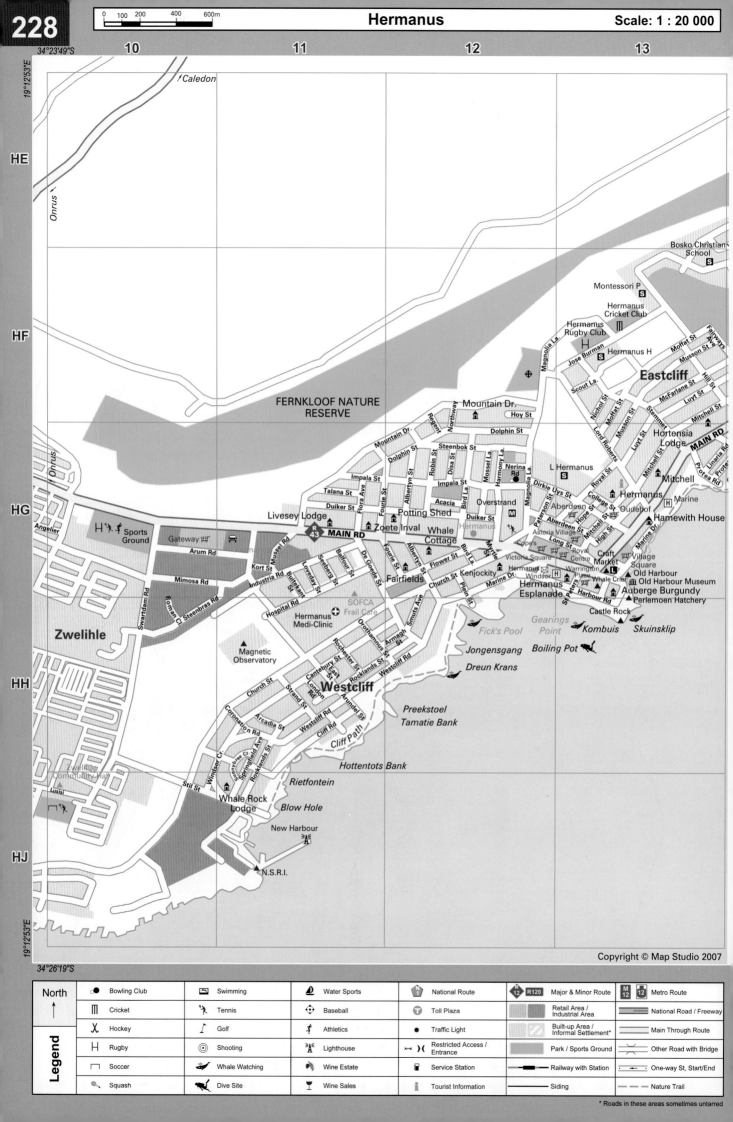

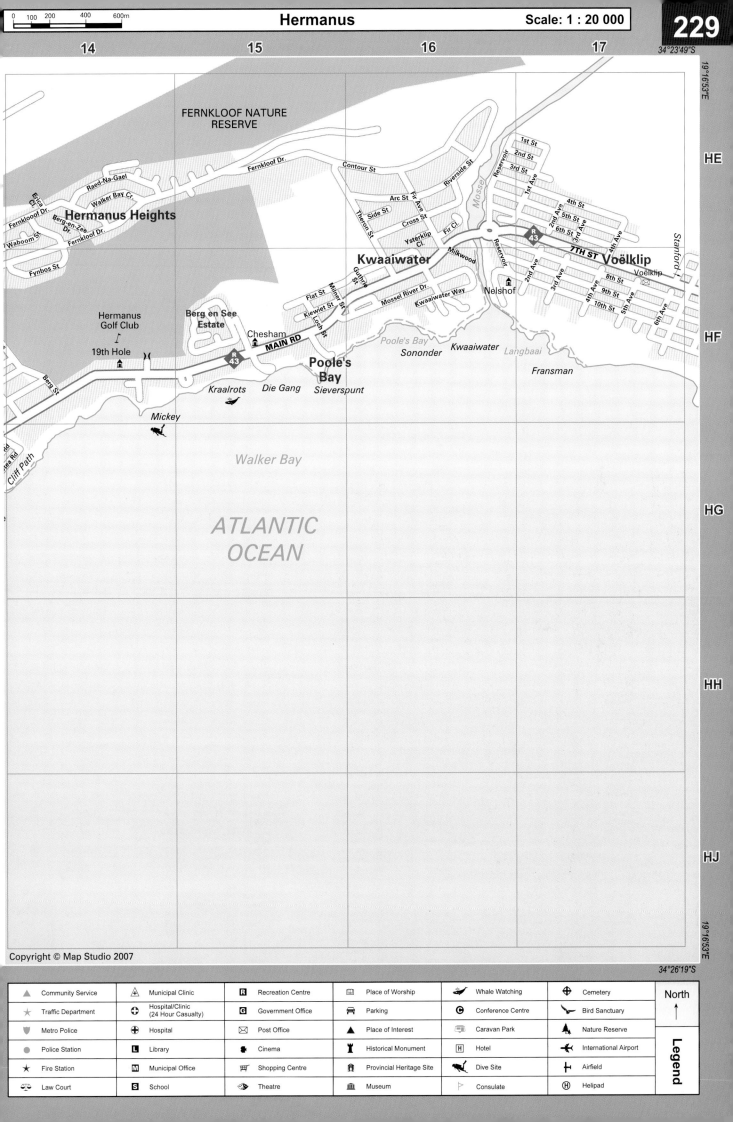

STREET NAME	SUBURB NAME	PG	GRID	
A				
A. Franch Ave	Hout Bay	137	CO	15
A.Boesak St	Hout Bay	137	CO	16
A.Boesak St	Mandela Pk	147	CQ	55
A.D.Keet Rd	Hohelzen	61	BW	47
A.F.Keen Dr.	Camps Bay	98	CE	18
A.G.Visser St	Clamhall	60	BX	43
A.G.Visser St	Townsend Est.	58	BX	38
A.J.West	Bellville	88	BY	48
A.Mlangeni Ave	Hout Bay	137	CO	16
A.P.Burger Ave	Plattekloof	60	BV	43
A.P.Venter	Uniepark	96	CB	79
A.Z. Berman Dr.	Eastridge (M.Plain)	145	CR	48
A.Z. Berman Dr.	Lentegeur (M.Plain)	124	CN	46
A.Z. Berman Dr.	Lentegeur (M.Plain)	144	CO	46
A.Z. Berman Dr.	Tafelsig (M.Plain)	145	CS	49
Aachen	Strandfontein	162	CT	40
Aadil Moerat Wk	Weltevreden Val. (M.Plain)	123	CN	42
Aadil Moerat Wk	Weltevreden Val. (M.Plain)	123	CM	39
Aalwyn	Delft Sth	106	CH	50
Aalwyn	Lentegeur (M.Plain)	144	CO	46
Aalwyn Ave	Uitsig	87	CC	44
Aalwyn Rd	Belhar	88	CC	47
Aalwyn Rd	Sonstraal	46	BR	52
Aalwyn Rd	Stellenberg	62	BU	51
Aalwyn Rd	Stellenberg	62	BX	52
Aalwyn St	Die Oude Spruit	63	BX	56
Aalwyn St	Franschhoek Sth	79	BZ	108
Aalwyn St	Parow Nth	59	BW	42
Aan de Wagen	Stellenbosch	113	CD	75
Aan die Weide	Rondebosch	102	CG	32
Aandblom	Lentegeur (M.Plain)	144	CO	46
Aandblom	Pinelands	102	CD	33
Aandblom	Ravensmead	87	CA	46
Aandblom	Uitsig	87	CC	44
Aandblom Cl.	Belhar	105	CD	46
Aandblom Cl.	Perm Gdns	127	CJ	58
Aandblom Rd	Belhar	87	CC	46
Aandblom Rd	Belhar	105	CD	46
Aandblom Rd	Durbanville	45	BQ	50
Aandblom St	Blomtuin	61	BV	50
Aandblom St	Devil's Peak Est.	82	CC	24
Aandblom St	Groenvlei	18	BA	89
Aandblom St	Morgenster	63	BU	56
Aandblom St	Peerless Pk East	47	BS	58
Aandblom St	Wellington	15	AT	92
Aandwind St	Kirstenhof	159	CT	27
Aarbei Cl.	Mitchells Plain	144	CQ	44
Aarbossie Cr.	Roosendaal	106	CF	50
Aarde St	Vanguard	103	CF	38
Aardroos Cl.	Protea Village	64	BV	59
Aardroos Cr.	Bellville Ext. 53	60	BT	45
Aaron Ave	Montagu's Gift	141	CO	34
Aaron Figaji Cr.	Beroma	89	BZ	51
Aaron Way	Matroosfontein	86	CC	42
Aasblom Sq.	Roosendaal	106	CF	50
Abalone Rd	Richwood	42	BP	38
Abattoir Rd	Greenways	174	DA	73
Abattoir St	Paarlzicht	19	BC	91
Abbey Cr.	Rome Glen	171	CV	76
Abbey Rd	Parklands	25	BM	32
Abbey Rd	Wynberg	120	CM	30
Abbey St	Camelot	107	CF	53
Abbotsbury Ave	Grassy Pk	141	CR	31
Abbotsford	Dennemere	108	CH	58
Abbotsford Ave	Barbarossa	140	CO	27
Abbotsford Pl.	Claremont	120	CJ	29
Abbotsford Pl.	Claremont	120	CK	30
Abbotsleigh Rd	Rondebosch	102	CG	31
Abbott Rd	Wetton	121	CL	34
Abdulla Moosa Rd	Parkwood	141	CO	32
Abdulla Wk	Parkwood	141	CO	32
Abdurahman	Bellville Sth Ind.	88	CA	50
Abegglen St	Park Estates	174	CZ	72
Abelia Ave	Welgedacht	60	BU	45
Abelia Cr.	Silvertown	103	CF	36
Abelia Rd	Dreyersdal	140	CR	27
Abelia St	Mandalay	125	CN	48
Abellia St	Somerset West	150	CS	70
Abellia St	Somerset West	151	CR	71
Abellia St	Somerset West	151	CS	71
Aberdeen	Ravensmead	87	CA	46
Aberdeen Cl.	Balvenie	87	CC	43
Aberdeen Cl.	Balvenie	87	CB	46
Aberdeen Cr.	Brackenfell Sth	63	BX	57
Aberdeen Rd	Rondebosch	101	CG	29
Aberdeen Rd	Somerset West	152	CS	75
Aberdeen Rd	Somerset West	171	CT	75
Aberdeen St	Woodstock	83	CB	27
Aberfeldy Rd	Frogmore Est.	159	CU	28
Abingdon Rd	Kenilworth	120	CK	29
Abington Cir.	Fish Hoek	186	DB	25
Abington Rd	Fish Hoek	186	DA	25
Aboyne Rd	Kenilworth	120	CJ	29
Abraham Ave	Steenberg	159	CT	30
Abraham Riddle	Park Village	127	CK	58
Abraham Riddle	Park Village	127	CN	55
Abraham Tiro St	Kuyasa	147	CS	55
Abrahams	Kylemore	97	BZ	86
Abrahams Ave	Greenways	174	DA	74
Abrahams Rd	Ravensmead	87	CA	46
Abrahams St	Wellington	10	AS	92
Abram Katz St	Montana/Durrheim	104	CF	42
Abrema Cl.	Northern Paarl	18	AZ	89
Absolom Ave	Rusthof	174	DA	74
Absolom Ave	Rusthof	175	DA	75
Acacia	Acacia Pk	58	BX	36
Acacia	Lentegeur (M.Plain)	144	CO	46
Acacia Ave	Bergsig	46	BO	51
Acacia Ave	Durbanville	46	BO	51
Acacia Cir.	Belhar	105	CD	46
Acacia Pl.	Hazelwood Pk	185	CZ	20
Acacia Pl.	Hazelwood Pk	185	DC	22
Acacia Rd	Forest Village	127	CL	58
Acacia Rd	Forest Village	127	CM	58
Acacia Rd	Harbour Island	175	DC	75
Acacia Rd	Kraaifontein Ind.	48	BQ	60
Acacia Rd	Parkwood	141	CO	32
Acacia Rd	Thornton	85	CA	37
Acacia St	Chapman's Peak	156	CX	16
Acacia St	Forest Hgts	127	CL	58
Acacia St	Philippi	124	CM	45
Acacia St	Somerset West	151	CS	71
Acacia St	Tygerdal	58	BX	38
Acacia Way	Bergvliet	140	CQ	28
Acacia Way	Bergvliet	140	CR	28
Acacia Way	Pinelands	84	CC	32
Acacia Way	Pinelands	102	CD	32
Acacia Way	Ridgeworth	61	BV	49
Academy Rd	Weltevreden Val. (M.Plain)	144	CQ	43
Acanthus Cir.	Belhar	105	CD	45
Accordian St	Belhar	106	CD	48
Aceton Rd	Paarden Eiland	83	BY	30
Achilles	Cloetesville	95	BZ	75
Achilles Cl.	Joe Slovo Pk	57	BU	34
Achilles Cl.	Joe Slovo Pk	57	BU	31
Achilles Rd	Eureka	87	CC	43
Achilles Way	Pinelands	84	CB	34
Achmat Williams St	Wesbank	107	CF	52
Achmat Williams St	Wesbank	107	CG	53
Ackermann	Krigeville	113	CD	76
Ackers Rd	Ravensmead	87	CA	46
Acopulco Cl.	Blouberg Sands	24	BM	29
Acorn Cl.	Devil's Peak Est.	82	CC	24
Acorn Cl.	Grassy Pk	141	CQ	32
Acorn St	Newlands	101	CH	27
Acorn St	Philippi	124	CM	45
Acre Rd	Factreton	84	BY	34
Acre Rd	Factreton	85	BY	35
Acre Rd	Kensington	84	BY	33
Acropolis Cl.	Portlands (M.Plain)	145	CR	47
Acton Ave	Somerset West	171	CR	73
Acton Cl.	Grassy Pk	141	CP	33
Acton Rd	Rosebank	101	CF	30
Ada	Lotus River	142	CQ	35
Ada Cl.	Tafelsig (M.Plain)	145	CR	50
Adagio	Sonstraal Hgts	46	BR	53
Adam Cl.	Wimbledon	108	CG	55
Adam St	Valhalla Pk	104	CE	42
Adam Tas Ave	Belhar	106	CE	49
Adam Tas Ave	Bothasig	42	BS	37
Adam Tas Ave	Bothasig	58	BT	37
Adam Tas Dr.	Devonvallei	112	CD	72
Adam Tas Rd	Somerset West	152	CS	75
Adam Tas Sq.	Brooklyn	83	BZ	30
Adam Tas St	Belrail	88	BY	49
Adam Tas St	Bosman's Crossing	94	CC	74
Adam Tas St	Klapmuts	36	BM	77
Adam Tas St	Stellenbosch	95	CC	75
Adam Tas St	Wellington	13	AU	85
Adamastor Rd	Ottery	121	CM	34
Adamo Villas	Oak Glen	62	BW	53
Adams	Delft Sth	125	CK	48
Adams	Kylemore	97	BZ	86
Adams St	Wellington	15	AV	93
Adcock	Wesbank	107	CG	51
Add van der Byl Ext	Durbanville	46	BP	52
Addax Cr.	Silvertown	103	CF	36
Adderley Rd	D'urbanvale	29	BL	50
Adderley St	Foreshore	82	CA	23
Addison Rd	Lansdowne	121	CL	34
Addison Rd	Salt River	83	CB	28
Addo Rd	Fish Hoek	186	DA	25
Addy	Wellington	10	AR	93
Addy	Wellington	10	AO	93
Adela St	Casablanca	175	DA	75
Adelaar	Onderpapegaaiberg	94	CC	72
Adelaar St	Kirstenhof	159	CT	27
Adelaide Rd	Plumstead	120	CN	28
Adelaide Rd	Woodstock	82	CB	26
Adele St	Plumstead	140	CP	29
Aden Ave	Athlone	102	CF	33
Adenandra St	Forest Hgts	127	CL	57
Adendorff	Idasvallei	96	CA	79
Aderem Cl.	West Beach	24	BM	29
Admiral Cl.	Epping Ind.	85	CC	38
Admirals Dr.	Strandfontein	162	CT	40
Admirals Way	Anchorage Pk	175	DC	77
Admirals Wk	Marina Da Gama	159	CW	30
Adonis Cl.	Eureka	87	CC	43
Adonis St	Park Village	127	CK	58
Adonis Way	Ocean View	184	DC	16
Adri Faas St	Klein Nederburg	19	BB	93
Adriaan Mooreens	Karindal	96	CC	79
Adriaanse Ave	Clarkes	87	CC	43
Adriaanse Ave	Clarkes	105	CD	43
Adrian	Dalvale	19	AZ	92
Adrian Herbert Rd	Lansdowne	122	CL	35
Adrian Louw St	Montana/Durrheim	104	CF	42
Adrian Olivier Cr.	Sunnydale	185	CZ	19
Adrian Rd	Montagu's Gift	141	CO	34
Adriatic Cl.	Sun Valley	185	DA	20
Adrienne St	Bonnie Brook	47	BQ	58
Adshade St	Park Estates	174	DA	73
Adula Rd	Athlone	102	CG	33
Adventist St	Belgravia	103	CF	35
Advonrus Cr.	Brackenfell Sth	63	BW	58
Aegean	Rocklands (M.Plain)	144	CS	45
Aegean Ave	Sun Valley	185	DA	21
Aerial Rd	Sanddrift	57	BV	33
Aerobat St	The Hague	106	CE	50
Aerodrome Rd	Maitland	85	BZ	35
Aerodrome Rd	Rome	170	CX	74
Aerodrome Rd	The Palms	170	CW	73
Affodil St	Ruwari	63	BV	57
Affodil St	Wellington	15	AT	92
Afram Rd	Delft	106	CF	50
Afram Rd	Delft	106	CG	50
Africana Cl.	Vredekloof Hgts	47	BS	55
Africander Ave	Kommetjie	183	DB	11
Africander Rd	Murdock Valley	195	DL	27
Africander Rd	Murdock Valley	195	DL	28
Afrika	Cloetesville	95	BZ	75
Afrika Siebritz St Nth	Hill View	127	CK	57
Afrikander St	Montana/Durrheim	104	CF	41
Afrikaner	Lentegeur (M.Plain)	144	CP	46
Afrikaner St	Halalie	46	BO	52
Afsaal	D'urbanvale	29	BN	50
Agaat Cl.	Welgelegen	59	BT	40
Agapanthus	Lentegeur (M.Plain)	144	CP	46
Agapanthus Ave	Devil's Peak Est.	82	CC	24
Agapanthus Ave	Welgedacht	60	BT	45
Agapanthus Cl.	Eersterivier	128	CM	59
Agapanthus Cl.	Mandalay	125	CN	48
Agapanthus Cl.	Mandalay	125	CN	49
Agapanthus Cr.	Belhar	105	CD	45
Agapanthus Cr.	Bridgetown	103	CF	36
Agapanthus Cr.	Gordon Hgts	180	DD	79
Agapanthus Cr.	Silvertown	103	CF	36
Agapanthus La.	Sir Lowry's Pass	176	CZ	81
Agate Cl.	Sheridon Pk	159	CU	28
Agate Rd	Fairdale	126	CJ	54
Agate St	Bellville	62	BV	51
Agincourt Way	Strandfontein	162	CT	40
Agnes Cr.	Valhalla Pk	104	CE	41
Agnes Rd	Valhalla Pk	104	CE	41
Agretjie	Lentegeur (M.Plain)	144	CO	45
Agric St	Epping Ind.	85	CA	38
Agulhas Cl.	Plattekloof	60	BW	45
Agulhas Cr.	Skoongesig	45	BO	50
Agulhas St	Strandfontein	161	CT	38
Agulhas St	Strandfontein	162	CT	39
Ahmed Kathrada St	Mandela Pk	146	CR	54
Ahmed Kathrada St	Mandela Pk	146	CS	52
Ahmedeyan Rd	Lansdowne	121	CK	33
Aida Cl.	Eastridge (M.Plain)	145	CQ	49
Ailsa Rd	Ottery	121	CM	33
Aimee Rd	Bishop Lavis	104	CD	42
Ainsdale St	Maitland	84	CA	31
Ainslie Rd	Plumstead	120	CN	29
Ainsty Wk	Alphen	119	CM	25
Ainsworth Cr.	Somerset West	171	CU	77
Aintree Ave	Ottery	122	CM	35
Aintree Cr.	Beacon Valley (M.Plain)	145	CQ	48
Aintree Rd	Kingston	61	BX	49
Aintree Rd	Vredehoek	82	CC	23
Aintree St	Somerset West	170	CW	72
Air Traffic Control	Airport Ind.	105	CH	44
Airbus St	The Hague	106	CE	50
Airco St	The Hague	106	CE	50
Airlie Cl.	Airlie	139	CQ	25
Airlie La.	Airlie	139	CP	25
Airlie Pl.	Airlie	139	CP	25
Airlie Rd	Bergvliet	140	CR	27
Airlie Rd	Dreyersdal	140	CR	27
Airport Approach Rd	Airport Ind.	104	CG	42
Ajax Way	Pinelands	84	CB	34
Ajax Way	Woodlands (M.Plain)	144	CO	44
Akademie St	Franschhoek Sth	79	BY	107
Akademie St	Franschhoek Sth	79	BZ	107
Akademie St	Welgelegen	59	BU	41
Akasia Ave	Bridgetown	103	CE	35
Akasia Ave	Edenpark	62	BU	54
Akasia Ave	Sonnedal	59	BV	42
Akasia Ave	Wellington	10	AS	94
Akker	Eden	113	CF	76
Akker Rd	Tygerdal	58	BX	37
Akker St	Macassar	149	CS	64
Akkerboom	Dunoon	42	BO	37
Akkerboom Ave	Belhar	105	CD	45
Akkerboom Ave	Belhar	105	CD	46
Akkerboom Rd	Bishop Lavis	104	CD	42
Akkerdal Ave	Claremont	101	CH	29
Akkerdal Cl.	Die Oude Spruit	63	BX	56
Akkerdraai Cr.	Voorbrug	106	CH	50
Akkerdraai Cr.	Voorbrug	107	CH	51
Akobo Ct	Delft	106	CF	48
Akron	Sunningdale	25	BN	31
Alabama	Factreton	84	BY	34
Alabama	Ravensmead	87	CA	45
Alabama Ave	Belhar	106	CD	49
Alabama Ave	Belhar	106	CD	50
Alabama Rd	Colorado (M.Plain)	144	CO	44
Alabama St	Greenways	174	DA	74
Alabama St	Monte Vista	59	BU	39
Alacrity Rd	Strandfontein	162	CT	42
Alamein Rd	Claremont	121	CJ	31
Alamein Rd	Milnerton	57	BV	32
Alamein Rd	Somerset West	171	CT	76
Alamo	Strandfontein	162	CU	40
Alan St	Vredekloof Hgts	47	BQ	56
Alant St	Groenvlei	18	BA	89
Alaska St	Stellenridge	62	BV	51
Alastair St	Bloekombos	48	BR	62
Albacore	Rocklands (M.Plain)	163	CT	45
Albacore St	Factreton	85	BY	35
Alban Rd	Bergvliet	139	CQ	26
Alban Rd	Welcome	103	CF	38
Albany	Ravensmead	87	BZ	46
Albany Cl.	Parklands	41	BO	32
Albany Cr.	Parklands	41	BO	32
Albany Rd	Edgemead	58	BV	37
Albany Rd	Sea Point	81	BZ	20
Albany St	Eindhoven	106	CH	50
Albany St	Ruyterwacht	86	CA	39
Albany Way	Stikland Hospital	89	BY	51
Albatros	Amandelsig	90	CB	56
Albatros Ave	Eersterivier	128	CM	60
Albatros Cr.	Somerset West	170	CV	72
Albatros St	Gustrow	174	DB	74
Albatros St	Wellington	11	AR	95
Albatros Way	Macassar	149	CS	64
Albatross	Rocklands (M.Plain)	144	CS	44
Albatross Ave	Bloubergrant	40	BO	30
Albatross St	Pelikan Pk	161	CU	37
Albatross Way	Admirals Pk	175	DC	78
Albatross Way	Thornton	85	CB	36
Albermarle St	Hazendal	102	CE	33
Albert Claasens	Forest Glade	127	CK	58
Albert Cr.	Hout Bay	136	CP	14
Albert Luthuli Cr.	Weltevreden Val. (M.Plain)	123	CM	41
Albert Luthuli St	Fisantekraal	31	BK	58
Albert Philander Way	Blue Downs	108	CH	56
Albert Philander Way	Dennemere	108	CH	58
Albert Philander Way	Greenfield	108	CH	57
Albert Philander Way	Kleinvlei	128	CJ	59
Albert Philander Way	Sunset Glen	108	CH	55
Albert Rd	Hout Bay	136	CP	14
Albert Rd	Hout Bay	136	CQ	14
Albert Rd	Lansdowne	121	CK	33
Albert Rd	Marlborough Pk	63	BT	55
Albert Rd	Mowbray	101	CD	29
Albert Rd	Muizenberg	159	CX	29
Albert Rd	Salt River	83	CB	28
Albert Rd	Tamboerskloof	81	CB	21
Albert Rd	Woodstock	83	CB	27
Albert St	Claremont	120	CJ	29
Albert St	Ruyterwacht	86	BZ	40
Albert St	Somerset West	170	CV	74
Albert St	Vierlanden	30	BM	52
Albert St	Wellington	10	AS	93
Alberta St	Die Oude Spruit	63	BX	56
Alberta St	Flintdale Est.	140	CP	29
Alberta St	Forest Hgts	127	CL	58
Alberta Way	Belhar	106	CE	50
Alberta Way	Belhar	107	CE	51
Albertina Sisulu Cr.	Mandela Pk	147	CQ	55
Alberton Cl.	Portlands (M.Plain)	144	CR	46
Alberts St	Klippiesdal	19	BC	91
Albertus St	Cape Town Cen.	82	CB	23
Albertyn Rd	Broadlands	175	CZ	77
Albertyn Rd	Muizenberg	159	CX	29
Albertyn Rd	Sir Lowry's Pass	176	DC	79
Albertyn St	Silveroaks	90	CC	55
Albertyn St	Wellington	10	AR	92
Albie de Waal St	Springbok Pk	62	BV	54
Albie Sachs St	Mandela Pk	147	CQ	55
Albion Cl.	Epping Forest	86	CC	42
Albion Rd	Rondebosch	101	CG	29
Albion Way	Belhar	105	CD	45
Albion Way	Belhar	105	CE	45
Albourne Cr.	Sonstraal Hgts	46	BQ	54
Albow Rd	Rugby	57	BX	32
Albrecht St	Constantia Vale	119	CN	25
Albuca Ave	Welgedacht	60	BT	45
Albuca Cl.	Perm Gdns	128	CJ	59
Albury Cr.	Factreton	85	BZ	35
Albus Dr.	Sunset Beach	41	BR	31
Alcantara Cr.	Wesbank	107	CF	51
Alcis St	Newlands	101	CG	27
Alcor Ave	Ocean View	184	DC	15
Alcyone Rd	Rondebosch	102	CH	31
Alde Rd	Wynberg	120	CM	28
Alder Pl.	Sun Valley	185	CZ	20
Alder Pl.	Sun Valley	185	DC	22
Alder St	Greenlands	88	CA	48
Aldgate St	Woodstock	82	CA	26
Aldrin	Temperance Town	179	DD	78
Alduwa Rd	Flintdale Est.	140	CP	30
Aldwins Ave	Athlone	102	CF	33
Alers Hankey Cr.	Brooklyn	84	BY	31
Alers Hankey Cr.	Brooklyn	84	BZ	32
Aletta Wk	Manenberg	123	CJ	39
Aletta Wk	Wynberg	120	CK	28
Alex Rd	Grassy Pk	141	CR	33
Alexa	Dalvale	19	AY	93
Alexander Ave	Hout Bay	137	CP	15
Alexander Ave	Hout Bay	137	CQ	15
Alexander Rd	Crawford	102	CH	33

Abbreviations used: Ave – Avenue, A.H. – Agricultural Holding, A.L.– Algemene Landgoed, Blvd – Boulevard, Cen. – Central, Cir. – Circle, Cl. – Close, Cr. – Crescent, Ct – Court, Dr. – Drive, Est. – Estate, Ext. – Extension, Hgts – Heights, Ind. – Industrial, Gdns – Gardens, Gr. – Grove, La. – Lane, (M.Plain) - Mitchells Plain, Nth – North, Pl. – Place, Pk – Park, Rd – Road, Rdg. – Ridge, S.H.– Small Holding, Sq. – Square, St – Street, Sth – South, Ter. – Terrace, Tn – Turn, Val. – Valley, Wk – Walk

STREET NAME	SUBURB NAME	PG	GRID
Alexander Rd	Mowbray	101	CD 30
Alexander Rd	Muizenberg	159	CX 29
Alexander Rd	Sea Point	80	CA 18
Alexander St	Balvenie	87	CC 43
Alexander St	Goodwood Est.	85	BY 38
Alexander St	Lemoenkloof	18	BC 88
Alexander St	Stellenbosch	95	CC 75
Alexander St	Wellington	15	AT 92
Alexander St	Woodstock	82	CB 26
Alexandra Ave	Oranjezicht	81	CC 22
Alexandra Pl.	Mouille Point	81	BY 21
Alexandra Rd	Maitland Gdn Village	84	CB 31
Alexandra Rd	Oakdale	61	BX 48
Alexandra Rd	Wynberg	120	CL 28
Alexandra St	Oakdale	61	BX 48
Alexandra St	Parow	86	BZ 42
Alexandra St	Parow	87	BY 43
Alexis Cr.	Sarepta	89	CB 52
Alexis Preller Cr.	Woodlands (M.Plain)	124	CN 45
Alf de Vine La.	Boschenmeer Est.	22	BG 90
Alf St	Kenridge	61	BU 49
Alfonso St	Denneburg	22	BD 90
Alfred Klaas St	Gugulethu	104	CG 41
Alfred Krenz Cl.	Woodlands (M.Plain)	144	CO 44
Alfred Nzo St	Mandela Pk	146	CR 54
Alfred Rd	Rondebosch	101	CG 28
Alfred Sharp St	Khayelitsha	147	CS 55
Alfred St	Cape Town Cen.	82	BZ 23
Alfred St	Kirstenhof	159	CT 27
Alfred St	Observatory	83	CC 29
Alfred St	Scottsville	47	BS 57
Alfred St	Windsor Pk	47	BS 57
Alfred St	Woodstock	83	CB 28
Algakirk Rd	Sea Point	81	CA 19
Algoa Cr.	Monte Vista	59	BU 40
Algoa La.	Belhar	106	CD 49
Algoa Rd	Milnerton	57	BW 31
Algoa Rd	Newfields	122	CJ 36
Algoa Rd	Skilpadvlei	45	BO 50
Algoa St	Monte Vista	59	BU 40
Algoa St	Strand Halt	170	CX 73
Algoa St	Strandvale	170	CW 73
Algoa St	Wesbank	107	CH 51
Algoa Way	Barbarossa	119	CN 26
Alhambra St	Weltevreden Val. (M.Plain)	144	CQ 43
Aliam Dr.	Victoria Mxenge	126	CN 52
Alibama Cr.	Bellville Sth	88	CA 49
Alicante Ave	Table View	41	BO 33
Alice Cl.	Tafelsig (M.Plain)	145	CR 50
Alice La.	Huis-in-bos	139	CP 25
Alice Rd	Claremont	101	CH 27
Alice Rd	Eikendal	48	BS 59
Alice Rd	Montagu's Gift	141	CO 33
Alice St	Amanda Glen	62	BT 52
Alice St	Goodwood Est.	58	BX 38
Alice St	Goodwood Est.	85	BY 38
Alice St	Townsend Est.	85	BZ 38
Alice St	Tygerdal	58	BX 38
Alices Ridge	Pinelands	102	CD 33
Alicia	Dalvale	19	AY 92
Alicia Cr.	Scottsdene	64	BU 60
Alima Ct	Delft	106	CG 48
Alison Cl.	Tafelsig (M.Plain)	145	CR 50
Alison Rd	Kenever	61	BT 49
Aliwal	Ravensmead	87	CB 45
Aliwal	Ruyterwacht	86	BZ 39
Aliwal Rd	Wynberg	120	CL 28
Alk van Zyl Ave	Panorama	59	BV 41
Alk van Zyl Ave	Panorama	59	BV 41
Alken Cl.	Frogmore Est.	159	CU 28
Alken Rd	Frogmore Est.	159	CU 27
Alkin St	Brackenfell	63	BV 56
Alkmaar Cr.	Uitzicht	31	BN 55
Alkmaar Rd	Foreshore	82	CA 26
Alkmaar St	Dal Josafat Ind.	18	BA 90
Allaman St	Highbury	107	CD 54
Allamanda St	Ottery	121	CN 33
Allan Busakhwe	Wimbledon	108	CG 55
Allan Rd	Bishop Lavis	105	CE 43
Allard Rd	Clarkes	86	CC 42
Allegra	Dalvale	19	AY 91
Allegro	Sonstraal Hgts	46	BR 53
Allegro La.	Mitchells Plain Cen.	145	CQ 47
Alleman Rd	Newfields	122	CJ 36
Alleman St	KWV	22	BG 88
Allen Dr.	Loevenstein	60	BW 46
Allen Place St	Loevenstein	60	BW 46
Allen Way	Elfindale	140	CQ 30
Allenby Dr.	Retreat	140	CS 29
Allenby Dr.	Steenberg	159	CT 29
Alleyne St	Labiance	89	BZ 52
Alleyne Yeld Cr.	Fish Hoek	185	DA 22
Alliance St	Labiance	89	BZ 51
Allies Rd	Newfields	122	CJ 36
Allison Rd	Pinati	122	CK 35
Allister Rd	Crawford	102	CH 33
Alma Cl.	Tafelsig (M.Plain)	145	CR 50
Alma Rd	Adriaanse	87	CC 43
Alma Rd	Claremont	120	CJ 27
Alma Rd	Kenridge Hgts	45	BR 48
Alma Rd	Kenridge Hgts	45	BS 49
Alma Rd	Rosebank	101	CE 30
Alma St	Tafelsig (M.Plain)	145	CS 50
Almar Rd	Lansdowne	121	CK 33
Almeida St	Bellville Sth	88	BZ 49

STREET NAME	SUBURB NAME	PG	GRID
Almeida St	Somerset West	170	CW 74
Almeria Rd	Northpine	63	BV 58
Almeria Rd	Sonstraal	46	BR 52
Almeria St	Paarl	22	BF 87
Almeria St	Shirley Pk	89	BY 52
Almeria Way	Meadowridge	139	CO 26
Almond	Forest Village	127	CM 58
Almond	Forest Village	127	CN 55
Almond Cl.	Dennedal	139	CR 25
Almond Cl.	Hout Bay	117	CN 15
Almond Cr.	Die Oude Spruit	63	BX 56
Almond Dr.	Somerset West	151	CR 73
Almond Gr.	Eersterivier	128	CM 62
Almond La.	Big Bay	24	BK 28
Almond La.	Big Bay	24	BL 29
Almond Rd	Tokai	139	CS 25
Almond St	Bothasig	58	BT 37
Almond St	Newlands	100	CH 26
Almond St	Newlands	101	CH 27
Almond Ter.	Schotsche Kloof	81	CA 22
Almondbury La.	Steenberg	157	CT 22
Almora Cir.	Dennedal	139	CR 26
Alnwick Rd	Dieprivier	140	CO 29
Aloe	Lentegeur (M.Plain)	144	CO 45
Aloe Ave	Somerset West	170	CU 73
Aloe Cl.	Kommetjie	183	DC 11
Aloe Cr.	Admirals Pk	175	DC 77
Aloe Cr.	Kewtown	102	CF 34
Aloe St	Devil's Peak Est.	82	CC 24
Aloe St	Dunoon	42	BO 37
Aloe St	Eersterivier	128	CM 59
Aloe St	Hanover Pk	122	CJ 37
Aloe St	Newlands	100	CH 26
Aloha Cl.	Windsor Est.	47	BQ 58
Alouette Cr.	The Hague	106	CF 50
Alpha	Die Boord	113	CE 75
Alpha La.	Somerset West	170	CT 74
Alpha Rd	Claremont	102	CH 31
Alpha St	Beacon Valley (M.Plain)	145	CQ 47
Alpha St	Belrail	88	BY 49
Alpha St	Eastridge (M.Plain)	145	CQ 47
Alpha St	Hoogstede	62	BV 53
Alpha St	Hoogstede	62	BU 53
Alpha St	Voorbrug	106	CH 50
Alpha Way	Ocean View	189	DD 15
Alphen	Dalsig	113	CE 76
Alphen Cl.	Marina Da Gama	159	CV 30
Alphen Cl.	Mitchells Plain	144	CR 45
Alphen Cl.	Mitchells Plain	144	CR 43
Alphen Cl.	Richwood	42	BP 38
Alphen Dr.	Alphen	119	CL 26
Alphen Dr.	Alphen	119	CM 26
Alphen Dr.	Alphen	120	CM 27
Alphen Hill	Wynberg	120	CM 28
Alphen Rd	Table View	41	BO 32
Alphen St	Chrismar	61	BX 50
Alphen St	Die Bos	174	CY 73
Alphen Way	Bergvliet	140	CR 28
Alphonse Cl.	Bel Ombre	119	CL 24
Alphonse Rd	Tokai	139	CS 25
Alphonse St	Shirley Pk	89	BY 52
Alphonse St	Sonstraal	46	BR 52
Alphorex St	Groenvlei	18	BA 88
Alpina Rd	Claremont	101	CH 30
Alpine Cl.	Eersterivier	127	CL 58
Alpine Cr.	Woodlands (M.Plain)	144	CQ 44
Alpine St	Beacon Valley (M.Plain)	145	CP 48
Alpine St	Eastridge (M.Plain)	145	CQ 49
Alpine Way	Matroosfontein	86	CC 42
Alps Cir.	Strandfontein	164	CT 49
Alps Cir.	Tafelsig (M.Plain)	164	CT 49
Alps St	Tafelsig (M.Plain)	145	CS 49
Als Ave	Groenvlei	18	BA 89
Als Rd	Bonteheuwel	103	CD 38
Alsace Ave	Woodstock	83	CC 27
Alster Ave	Newlands	101	CH 27
Alston La.	Somerset West	151	CR 74
Alston Sq.	Claremont	101	CH 29
Alt St	Macassar	149	CS 65
Alta Cl.	Beacon Valley (M.Plain)	145	CP 48
Altair Way	Ocean View	184	DC 15
Alten Cl.	Strand	174	CZ 73
Altena Rd	Die Bos	174	CY 74
Altena Rd	Strand	174	CY 73
Altenburg	Kirstenhof	158	CU 26
Altenburg Ave	Courtrai	22	BH 87
Altenburg Rd	Highbury	107	CD 54
Alternator Ave	Montague Gdns Ind.	58	BT 35
Alto Ave	Voorbrug	106	CH 50
Altona Gr.	Woodstock	83	CB 27
Altona St	Oak Glen	62	BW 51
Altona St	Oak Glen	62	BW 52
Altydbos Cl.	Vierlanden	30	BN 51
Altydgedacht Cr.	Kenridge Hgts	45	BR 48
Altydgedacht Cr.	Kenridge Hgts	45	BP 47
Alveni St	Victoria Mxenge	126	CN 51
Alvin Cr.	Somerset West	171	CT 77
Alwin St	Brooklyn	83	BZ 30
Alwyn St	Wellington	15	AT 92
Amafu	Mbekweni	15	AW 92
Amalfi Cl.	Durbanville	46	BP 51
Amalinde Way	Strandfontein	162	CT 41
Amanda Cl.	Tafelsig (M.Plain)	145	CR 50
Amanda Rd	Amanda Glen	46	BS 52
Amanda Rd	Amanda Glen	62	BT 52

STREET NAME	SUBURB NAME	PG	GRID
Amanda Rd	Bakoven	98	CF 18
Amanda St	Devon Pk	128	CL 60
Amanda St	Morgenster	63	BU 56
Amandel	Delft Sth	125	CJ 49
Amandel Ave	Rusdal	108	CE 57
Amandel Cl.	Proteavallei	61	BT 47
Amandel Cl.	Wellington	15	AT 92
Amandel Dr.	Amandelrug	90	CA 55
Amandel Dr.	Silveroaks	90	CC 56
Amandel Rd	Belhar	105	CD 46
Amandel Rd	Bonteheuwel	103	CD 38
Amandel Rd	Mitchells Plain	144	CQ 44
Amandel St	Dunoon	26	BN 37
Amandel St	Sonstraal Hgts	46	BS 52
Amandel St	William Lloyd	23	BD 93
Amandelboom St	Plattekloof	60	BV 43
Amandla St	Manenberg	123	CJ 40
Amandla St	Mxolisi Phetani	125	CM 50
Amanzi Cr.	Vredekloof	62	BT 53
Amarella Way	Northpine	63	BT 58
Amaryllis	Macassar	149	CS 63
Amaryllis St	Dalvale	19	AY 91
Amaryllis St	Gordon Hgts	180	DD 79
Amaryllis St	Somerset West	151	CS 71
Amarylus Rd	Mandalay	125	CN 48
Amarylus Rd	Mandalay	125	CN 49
Amatola Rd	Heideveld	104	CG 39
Amatola Rd	Lavender Hill East	160	CU 32
Amatola Rd	Lavender Hill East	160	CX 33
Amaza	Mbekweni	15	AW 92
Amazon Rd	Eersterivier	128	CN 60
Amazon Rd	Observatory	83	CC 29
Amazon St	Primrose Pk	103	CH 38
Ambagsvallei	Huguenot	18	BC 90
Ambagsvallei	Paarlzicht	19	BC 91
Ambassador	Fairyland	19	AZ 93
Ambassador St	The Hague	106	CE 50
Amber	Rocklands (M.Plain)	144	CS 46
Amber Cl.	Welgelegen	59	BU 40
Amber Cr.	Forest Village	127	CM 58
Amber Rd	Steenberg	159	CT 30
Amber Ter.	San Michel	157	CX 20
Amber Way	San Michel	157	CX 20
Amberley Rd	Muizenberg	187	CY 29
Amberley Rd	Muizenberg	187	DA 27
Amble	Somerset West	151	CQ 71
Ambleside	Dennemere	127	CJ 58
Ambleside	Pinelands	84	CB 33
Ambleside	Sonstraal Hgts	46	BQ 54
Ambleside Cl.	Parklands	41	BO 34
Ambleside Cr.	Plattekloof Glen	59	BW 39
Ambleside Rd	Plattekloof Glen	59	BW 40
Ambleside St	Plattekloof Glen	59	BW 40
Ambrose Cr.	Newfields	122	CJ 36
Amden Cl.	Lotus River	141	CP 34
Amden St	Kempenville	88	BY 49
Amelia Cl.	Clunie	139	CQ 24
Amelia Rd	Amanda Glen	62	BT 52
Amella	Dalvale	19	AY 92
Amethyst	Highbury	108	CD 55
Amethyst	Highbury	108	CE 55
Amethyst	Rocklands (M.Plain)	144	CS 46
Amethyst Cr.	Belthorn Est.	103	CH 35
Amethyst Rd	Fairdale	126	CJ 54
Amethyst St	Bellville	62	BU 51
Ametis Cl.	Welgelegen	59	BT 41
Amhurst Ave	Kenilworth	120	CJ 30
Amhurst Ave	Newlands	101	CH 27
Amiens Way	Strandfontein	162	CT 41
Amigo's	Sonstraal Hgts	46	BR 54
Amilia Cl.	Plattekloof Glen	59	BV 40
Amista	Delft Sth	125	CJ 49
Amity Way	Lansdowne	121	CK 33
Amos Lengesi Cr.	Mandela Pk	147	CQ 56
Amp St	Dal Josafat Ind.	19	AY 91
Ampere St	Kaymor	89	BY 53
Amphion St	Paarden Eiland	83	CA 29
Amplankeni Cr.	Nyanga	123	CJ 42
Amstel Rd	Maitland	84	CA 32
Amstel St	Bothasig	58	BT 38
Amstelhof Ave	Amstelhof	23	BD 93
Amstelveen	Dennemere	108	CH 58
Amsterdam	Malibu Village	127	CJ 55
Amsterdam Ave	Fish Hoek	186	DA 23
Amsterdam Cl.	Strandvale	170	CX 73
Amsterdam Cr.	Brooklyn	83	BZ 30
Amsterdam Rd	Belhar	106	CD 49
Amsterdam Rd	Belhar	106	CH 48
Amsterdam St	Avondale	87	BY 44
Amsterdam St	Brooklyn	83	BZ 30
Amsterdam St	Brown's Farm	124	CL 43
Amsterdam Way	Portlands (M.Plain)	144	CR 46
Amundsen St	Forest Glade	127	CL 58
Amur Rd	Eindhoven	106	CH 50
Amy Cl.	Brackenfell Sth	63	BW 58
Amy St	Casablanca	175	DB 76
Anaboom	Delft Sth	125	CK 49
Anaboom Ct	Delft Sth	125	CK 49
Anadale Rd	Belthorn Est.	102	CH 34
Ananwabisi St	Nyanga	123	CK 42
Anbi Cl.	Northpine	63	BT 58
Anchor Cl.	Blouberg Sands	24	BM 30
Anchor Cl.	Strandfontein	162	CT 39
Anchor Cl.	Strandfontein	162	CT 41
Anchusa Cl.	Vredekloof Hgts	47	BS 55

STREET NAME	SUBURB NAME	PG	GRID
Andalusia St	Voorbrug	106	CH 50
Andante	D'urbanvale	45	BO 49
Andersen St	Ottery East	121	CN 34
Anderson Cl.	Tokai	139	CS 25
Anderson Rd	Kalk Bay	186	DA 26
Anderson Rd Nth	Joostenberg	48	BP 60
Anderson Rd Sth	Joostenberg	48	BQ 60
Anderson Rd West	Joostenberg	48	BP 60
Anderson St	Townsend Est.	85	BZ 38
Andes	Eersterivier	128	CL 59
Andes St	Tafelsig (M.Plain)	145	CS 49
Andile Ndleleni Cr.	Weltevreden Val. (M.Plain)	123	CM 41
Andile Nose St	Kuyasa	147	CS 55
Andile Nose St	Kuyasa	147	CS 57
Andrag St	Vierlanden	30	BN 51
Andrag St	Welgemoed	61	BV 47
Andre Rd	Clamhall	60	BX 43
Andrea Rd	Kenridge	61	BU 49
Andrew Cr.	Somerset West	151	CS 74
Andrew Foster St	Bloubergstrand	24	BM 28
Andrew Madi St	Kuyasa	147	CS 56
Andrew Madi St	Kuyasa	147	CS 57
Andrew Matshikwe St	Gugulethu	104	CH 41
Andrew Mlangeni St	Graceland	146	CQ 54
Andrew Murray St	Oakdale	61	BW 49
Andrew Murray St	Oakdale	61	BW 50
Andrew Murray St	Parow Nth	59	BW 42
Andrew Murray St	Ruyterwacht	86	CB 39
Andrew Rd	Flintdale Est.	141	CP 31
Andrew St	Kylemore	97	BZ 86
Andrew St	Russel's Rest	128	CL 59
Andrews Rd	Hout Bay	137	CP 16
Andrews Rd	Kommetjie	183	DC 12
Andrews Rd	Newfields	122	CJ 37
Andries Malgas St	Perm Gdns	128	CK 59
Andries Pretorius St	Churchill	59	BX 42
Andries Pretorius St	Glenlily	86	BY 42
Andries Pretorius St	Somerset West	170	CV 74
Andries Pretorius St	Somerset West	171	CV 75
Andries Rd	Newfields	122	CJ 37
Andringa St	Stellenbosch	95	CB 76
Andringa St	Stellenbosch	95	CC 76
Andromeda	Rocklands (M.Plain)	144	CS 46
Andromeda Way	Ocean View	189	DD 15
Andromeidas St	Forest Hgts	127	CK 58
Andulusia Ave	Somerset West	151	CS 73
Andy Porter St	Silveroaks	90	CC 55
Aneisberg Rd	Bonnie Brae	47	BP 57
Anemone	Ravensmead	87	CB 45
Anemone	Uitsig	87	CC 44
Anemone Ave	Devil's Peak Est.	82	CC 24
Anemone Ave	Welgedacht	60	BU 45
Anemone Cl.	Mandalay	125	CN 48
Anemone Cl.	Mandalay	125	CN 49
Anemone St	Somerset West	151	CS 72
Anemoon St	Kleinvlei	127	CJ 57
Anesta	Eden	113	CF 76
Anesta Ave	Voorbrug	106	CH 50
Anette Cl.	The Vines	140	CO 27
Anfield Rd	Blackheath Ind.	108	CG 57
Anfield Rd	Weltevreden Val. (M.Plain)	124	CN 44
Angas Rd	Tijgerhof	57	BW 32
Angel	Mbekweni	15	AV 91
Angela	Florida	87	CA 44
Angela Cr.	Brentwood Pk	126	CJ 51
Angela Rd	Gatesville	103	CH 37
Angela Rd	Newfields	103	CH 37
Angela St	Valhalla Pk	104	CE 41
Angelier	Lentegeur (M.Plain)	144	CP 45
Angelier Cl.	Wellington	15	AT 92
Angelier St	Bellville	61	BT 48
Angelier St	Brackenfell Sth	63	BX 57
Angelier St	Brackenfell Sth	90	BY 56
Angelier St	Sonnekuil	89	CA 54
Angelier St	Weltevreden Val. (M.Plain)	124	CM 44
Angelina Ave	Claremont	101	CH 27
Angelique Pl.	Dalvale	19	AY 92
Angelique Pl.	Dalvale	19	BA 94
Angelo St	Macassar	149	CS 66
Angle Rd	Bishop Lavis	105	CD 44
Angle St	Hazendal	102	CE 33
Angler Cl.	Pelikan Pk	141	CR 34
Anglesey St	Rondebosch East	102	CH 32
Angliers	Morgen Gronde	63	BX 55
Angora Cl.	Mitchells Plain	144	CR 46
Angora St	Somerset Hgts	127	CJ 57
Angus Cl.	Balvenie	87	CC 43
Angus Cl.	Barbarossa	120	CN 27
Angus St	Brackenfell Sth	63	BX 57
Angus St	Durbanville	46	BP 53
Angus St	Somerset West	171	CU 76
Angus Way	Mitchells Plain	144	CR 45
Anise St	Sunset Glen	107	CH 54
Anita Cr.	Beacon Valley (M.Plain)	145	CP 48
Anita Rd	Montagu's Gift	141	CO 33
Anker Cr.	Strandfontein	162	CT 42
Anker St	Paarl	22	BF 88
Anker St	Pine Acres	175	DC 77
Ann Cl.	Barbarossa	140	CO 27
Annabelle Cl.	Amanda Glen	62	BT 52
Anna-Marie Dr.	Beacon Valley (M.Plain)	145	CP 48
Annandale Dr.	Richwood	42	BP 38
Annandale Rd	Bontvlei	131	CK 71
Annandale Rd	Brandwag	90	BZ 55
Annandale Rd	Cape Town Cen.	81	CB 22

Index to Street Names

Annandale Rd — Barbourne Rd

STREET NAME	SUBURB NAME	PG	GRID	
Annandale Rd	Dieprivier	140	CO	29
Annandale Rd	Lynedoch Eco-Village	110	CH	65
Annandale Rd	Soneike I	89	CA	54
Annandale Rd	Soverby	130	CJ	68
Annandale Rd	Welmoed Est.	129	CJ	66
Annandale St	Somerset West	151	CR	74
Anne Barnard Way	Edgemead	58	BU	38
Anne Cr.	Mandalay	125	CM	47
Anne Rd	Bishop Lavis	105	CE	44
Anne Rd	Grassy Pk	141	CR	32
Anne Rd	Valhalla Pk	104	CE	41
Anneberg Rd	Newlands	101	CG	28
Anneke Rd	Amanda Glen	62	BT	52
Anne-Marie Rd	Somerset West	171	CT	75
Annemeit St	Bloekombos	49	BR	63
Annerley Rd	Rosebank	101	CE	30
Annes St	Maitland	83	CA	30
Annette Cr.	Lentegeur (M.Plain)	145	CO	48
Annette Way	Claremont	120	CJ	28
Annex Rd	Maitland Gdn Village	84	CB	31
Annie Benjamin St	Rabiesdale	19	BC	92
Annie Silinga	Weltevreden Val. (M.Plain)	123	CM	42
Annike Cl.	Casablanca	175	DA	75
Annike Cl.	Casablanca	175	DB	76
Annvon Rd	Dieprivier	140	CP	28
Anreith Ave	Belhar	106	CD	49
Anreith Ave	Belhar	106	CE	49
Anreith St	Somerset West	170	CT	73
Anrieth	Karindal	96	CC	79
Anseba Cl.	Delft	106	CG	50
Anson	Rocklands (M.Plain)	163	CT	45
Anson St	Observatory	83	CC	29
Anstey St	Sonnekuil	89	BZ	53
Antares Cl.	Ocean View	189	DD	15
Antares La.	Fairdale	126	CJ	54
Antelope	Uitzicht	46	BO	54
Antelope Ct	Bridgetown	103	CE	35
Antelope Rd	Lotus River	142	CP	35
Anthea	Dalvale	19	AZ	92
Anthea Ave	Eureka	87	CC	43
Anthea St	Casablanca	175	DA	76
Anthea St	Eersterivier	127	CL	58
Anthia Wk	Hanover Pk	122	CK	37
Anthony	Cloetesville	95	BZ	75
Anthony Rd	Bridgetown	103	CF	36
Anthonys Rd	Hout Bay	137	CP	16
Anthurium	Macassar	149	CS	63
Antibe	Malibu Village	127	CK	56
Antigua Ave	Capri	185	DB	20
Antigua Cl.	Bloubergstrand	24	BM	29
Antipolis Pl.	Blue Downs	127	CJ	56
Antipolis Way	Plattekloof Glen	59	BW	40
Antlers	Wellington	15	AU	91
Antoinette St	Amanda Glen	62	BT	52
Antoinette St	De Tijger	60	BW	44
Antoinette St	Denneburg	23	BD	91
Anton Anreith Ave	Edgemead	58	BU	38
Anton Fransch	Weltevreden Val. (M.Plain)	123	CN	42
Anton Fransch St	Mandela Pk	147	CQ	55
Anton St	Mabille Pk	89	CA	53
Antonia St	Devon Pk	128	CL	60
Antrim Rd	Oakdale	61	BV	49
Antrim Rd	Three Anchor Bay	81	BZ	21
Antwerp Rd	Sea Point	81	CB	20
Antwerpen Rd	Surrey	103	CH	37
Anvil Cl.	Eureka	87	CC	44
Anvil Cl.	Hout Bay Harbour	136	CR	13
Anysberg Rd	Heideveld	104	CG	39
Anzio	Strandfontein	162	CU	40
Anzio Rd	Observatory	101	CD	28
Apeldoorn St	Uitzicht	31	BN	55
Apeldoorn Way	Westlake	159	CU	27
Apeldoorn Way	Westlake	159	CW	27
Apile	Philippi East	125	CM	47
Apollo	Wellington	15	AU	91
Apollo Cr.	Woodlands (M.Plain)	144	CO	44
Apollo Cr.	Woodlands (M.Plain)	144	CO	44
Apollo Link	Eureka	87	CC	43
Apollo Link	Eureka	87	CB	46
Apollo St	Sarepta	89	CC	53
Apollo St	Somerset Hgts	127	CJ	57
Apollo St	Somerset Hgts	127	CK	57
Apollo Way	Elfindale	140	CQ	29
Apollo Way	Joe Slovo Pk	57	BU	34
Apollo Way	Kirstenhof	159	CT	27
Apollo Way	Ocean View	189	DD	15
Apollo Way	Temperance Town	179	DD	78
Apollo Way	Thembokwezi	125	CM	49
Apostle Rd	Hout Bay	116	CM	14
Apostle Steps	Clifton	80	CC	18
Appaloosa Cr.	West Riding	41	BO	34
Appaloosa Rd	Milnerton	41	BS	34
Appel Rd	Nooitgedacht	105	CE	43
Appelboeisel Ave	Silveroaks	90	CC	56
Appeldoorn St	Uitsig	87	CC	44
Appeliefie	Lentegeur (M.Plain)	144	CO	45
Appelkoos	Delft Sth	125	CK	49
Appelkoos St	Wellington	15	AU	92
Appia Cl.	Strandfontein	163	CT	43
Appian Way	Bishopscourt	119	CJ	25
Apple Cl.	Thembokwezi	125	CM	49
Apple La.	Belhar	106	CE	50
Apple La.	Newlands	101	CG	27
Apple Mist Rd	Ottery	121	CM	34
Apple Rd	Capricorn	160	CV	31
Apple Rd	Hindle Pk	107	CH	54
Apple St	Mitchells Plain	144	CQ	44
Appleby St	Wesbank	107	CG	52
Appledene Cr.	Silvertown	103	CF	35
Appledene Rd	Silvertown	103	CF	36
Applegarth St	Somerset West	150	CS	70
Applemist Ave	Eersterivier	128	CN	60
Appollis St	Wellington	15	AV	93
Appollo Rd	Bishop Lavis	105	CD	43
Approach St	Lakeside	159	CV	27
Apricot Cl.	Hout Bay	117	CN	16
Apricot St	Bonteheuwel	103	CD	38
Apricot St	Mitchells Plain	144	CQ	44
April Ave	Wellington	15	AV	92
Aquamarine Cr.	Rocklands (M.Plain)	145	CS	47
Aquanaut La.	Crofters Valley	185	CY	19
Aquarius	Rocklands (M.Plain)	144	CS	45
Aquarius Rd	Phoenix	57	BU	33
Aquarius Rd	Surrey	103	CH	38
Aquarius Way	Ocean View	189	DD	15
Aquila Cl.	Fairdale	126	CJ	54
Aquila Rd	Ottery	121	CL	33
Aquila Way	Ocean View	184	DC	15
Arabella St	Eastridge (M.Plain)	145	CQ	48
Arabian	Rocklands (M.Plain)	144	CS	45
Arago Way	Eersterivier	128	CN	60
Aragon Cr.	Montana/Durrheim	104	CF	42
Aragon St	Wesbank	107	CE	52
Aragon Way	Somerset West	151	CS	74
Aramon Cr.	Groenvlei	18	BA	87
Aramon Rd	Northpine	63	BT	58
Ararat Cr.	Tafelsig (M.Plain)	145	CS	49
Arauna Rd	Arauna	63	BU	55
Arba St	Penlyn Est.	103	CH	35
Arbeids Rd	Belthorn Est.	121	CJ	34
Arbor Rd	Newlands	101	CG	28
Arboretum Ave	KWV	22	BG	90
Arbour St	Woodstock	83	CA	29
Arcadia Ave	Lansdowne	121	CJ	32
Arcadia Ave	Salberau	86	CB	41
Arcadia Rd	Bantry Bay	80	CB	18
Arcadia Rd	Fresnaye	81	CB	19
Arcadia Rd	Rosebank	101	CE	30
Arcadia St	Chrismar	61	BX	50
Arcadia Steps	Clifton	80	CC	18
Arc-en-Ciel	Schuilplaats	113	CG	76
Archer Ave	Athlone	102	CG	33
Archer Cl.	Eindhoven	106	CH	50
Archer Cr.	Beacon Valley (M.Plain)	145	CP	48
Archers Green	Summer Greens	58	BW	36
Archers Sq.	Hagley	107	CF	53
Archie St	Kenilworth	120	CK	29
Arctic Cr.	Athlone	102	CG	33
Arctotis Way	Belhar	105	CD	46
Arctotis Way	Belhar	106	CD	47
Arden Rd	Eersterivier	128	CN	61
Ardennes	Strandfontein	162	CT	40
Ardleigh Rd	Retreat	140	CR	30
Aren St	Amandelsig	90	CB	56
Arena	Jagtershof	90	CC	57
Arena Rd	Kenilworth Pk	120	CK	30
Arena St	Penlyn Est.	103	CH	35
Arend Cr.	Flamingo Vlei	41	BP	32
Arend St	Morningstar	46	BP	51
Arend St	Morningstar	46	BS	54
Arend St	Wellington	15	AT	92
Arend Way	Tarentaalplaas	175	DA	76
Arendkop Cir.	Wesbank	107	CG	51
Arendse Rd	Franschhoek Nth	75	BW	105
Arendse Rd	Strandfontein	163	CU	43
Arendse St	Highbury	108	CD	55
Arendse St	Scottsdene	64	BU	59
Arendse St	Scottsdene	64	BU	60
Argo Rd	Ottery	121	CL	33
Argonaut St	Strandfontein	162	CT	42
Argyl St	Wellington	11	AQ	95
Argyle Rd	Rondebosch	101	CG	29
Argyle St	Camps Bay	98	CE	18
Argyle St	Woodstock	83	CB	27
Argyle Way	Dennemere	108	CH	58
Argyll Rd	Goodwood Est.	85	BY	38
Aria St	Dalvale	19	AZ	92
Ariel St	Maitland	84	CA	33
Aries	Everite	63	BU	56
Aries	Rocklands (M.Plain)	144	CS	45
Aries Ave	Ocean View	189	DD	15
Aries Rd	Phoenix	57	BU	33
Aries St	Cravenby	87	CA	43
Aries St	Manenberg	103	CH	38
Arinto Ct	Northpine	63	BV	58
Arion Cl.	Eureka	87	CC	43
Aristata St	Somerset West	150	CS	70
Aristea Ave	Welgedacht	60	BU	45
Aristea Cl.	Perm Gdns	128	CJ	59
Aristea Cl.	Perm Gdns	128	CJ	60
Aristea Cl.	The Lakes	184	CZ	17
Aristea Cr.	Gordon Hgts	180	DD	79
Aristea Rd	Dreyersdal	140	CR	27
Aristea Rd	Durbanville	45	BQ	50
Aristea St	Vredekloof Hgts	47	BS	55
Aristia Cl.	Plattekloof	60	BV	43
Aristo St	Elim	90	CA	55
Arixoma Rd	Thornton	85	CA	37
Arkansas St	Stellenridge	62	BV	51
Arlene St	Russel's Rest	128	CL	59
Arlington Ave	Glenhaven	89	BZ	51
Arlington Cr.	Riverton	86	BZ	40
Arlington Cr.	Somerset West	151	CR	72
Arlington Place	Everglen	45	BS	50
Arlington Rd	Belthorn Est.	122	CJ	35
Arlington Rd	Everglen	46	BS	51
Arlington Way	Milnerton Rdg	41	BR	34
Arlington Way	Northpine	63	BU	58
Arlington Way	Northpine	64	BU	59
Armada	Wesbank	107	CG	52
Armada Cr.	Bellville Sth	88	CA	49
Armadale St	Woodstock	82	CB	26
Armagh Rd	Royal Cape	121	CM	32
Armdale Rd	West Beach	24	BM	29
Armeira St	Uitsig	87	CC	44
Armenia Cr.	Plattekloof Glen	59	BV	40
Armenia Pl.	Plattekloof Glen	59	BV	40
Armon Ave	Wellington	15	AT	94
Armour Ave	Hout Bay	137	CP	16
Armstrong	Temperance Town	179	DD	78
Armstrong Cr.	Penlyn Est.	122	CJ	36
Armstrong Rd	Belhar	88	CC	50
Armstrong St	Sarepta	89	CB	53
Arnhem Ave	Monte Vista	59	BU	39
Arnhem Cl.	Strandfontein	162	CT	40
Arnie	Delft Sth	125	CK	48
Arniston	Eersterivier	128	CN	60
Arniston Cl.	Monte Vista	59	BW	38
Arniston Cr.	Dennemere	108	CH	58
Arniston Pl.	Plattekloof Glen	59	BW	39
Arno Rd	Primrose Pk	103	CH	38
Arnold Rd	Table View	42	BP	35
Arnold Rd	Windsor Park Est.	47	BQ	58
Arnold St	Bonnie Brook	47	BQ	57
Arnold St	Observatory	83	CC	28
Arnold St	Observatory	83	CC	29
Arnold Wilhelm St	Parow East	87	BY	44
Arnolds	Cloetesville	95	BZ	75
Arnoldt St	Rome	170	CX	74
Aroma Ave	Stellenryk	62	BU	52
Aron Qusheka St	Guguletu	123	CK	41
Aron Qusheka St	Guguletu	123	CL	41
Aros Cl.	West Beach	24	BM	29
Arosi Cr.	Wallacedene	48	BS	60
Arrabella	Sunningdale	25	BM	31
Arsenaal Cl.	Oude Westhof	60	BT	44
Arsenal St	Dunoon	42	BO	37
Arsenal Way	Simon's Town	194	DJ	23
Artemis Rd	Woodlands (M.Plain)	144	CO	44
Arthur Abrahams Ave	Bishop Lavis	105	CD	43
Arthur Rd	Muizenberg	159	CX	29
Arthur Wright Rd	Fish Hoek	185	DA	21
Arthur's Rd	Sea Point	81	CA	19
Artillery Rd	Door De Kraal	61	BT	47
Arum	Lentegeur (M.Plain)	144	CP	45
Arum Ave	Kleinvlei	127	CJ	58
Arum Ave	Kommetjie	183	DB	11
Arum Ave	Kommetjie	183	DB	12
Arum Ave	Somerset West	170	CU	72
Arum Ave	Westlake Est.	158	CT	25
Arum Cl.	Bel Ombre	119	CM	25
Arum Pl.	D'urbanvale	45	BO	50
Arum Rd	Belhar	105	CD	46
Arum Rd	Bishop Lavis	104	CD	42
Arum Rd	Blackheath Ind.	108	CF	57
Arum Rd	Durbanville	45	BQ	50
Arum Rd	Durbanville	45	BP	47
Arum Rd	Milnerton	57	BU	33
Arum Rd	Murdock Valley	195	DK	27
Arum Rd	Table View	40	BO	30
Arum Rd	Table View	41	BO	31
Arum Rd	Table View	41	BP	32
Arum Rd	Table View	41	BP	33
Arum Rd	Uitsig	87	CC	44
Arum St	Bridgetown	103	CF	36
Arum St	Devil's Peak Est.	82	CC	24
Arum St	Klein Nederburg	19	BC	93
Arum St	Newlands	100	CH	26
Arum St	Voelvlei	89	CA	52
Arum Way	Electric City	127	CM	58
Arum Way	Thornton	85	CA	37
Arundel	Dreyersdal	140	CS	27
Arundel Dr.	Belhar	106	CD	50
Arundel Dr.	Belhar	107	CD	51
Arundel Dr.	Belhar	107	CE	51
Arundel Rd	Rondebosch	102	CE	31
Arundel Rd	Rosebank	101	CE	29
Arundel Rd	West Beach	24	BM	29
Arunside Cl.	Edgemead	58	BU	38
Arvana Cl.	Brooklyn	84	BY	31
Asalea	Ex-skool	95	CA	75
Asbijan Pl.	Southfork	175	DB	75
Asbijan St	Southfork	175	DB	75
Ascension Rd	Bloubergstrand	24	BM	29
Ascension Rd	Heideveld	104	CF	39
Aschatt	Eersterivier	128	CN	60
Ascot Blvd	Milnerton	57	BT	33
Ascot Cl.	Ottery	122	CM	35
Ascot Knights	Milnerton	57	BT	33
Ascot La.	Malibu Village	127	CK	56
Ascot Rd	Kenilworth	120	CK	30
Ascot Rd	Milnerton	57	BT	33
Ascot Rd	Milnerton	57	BU	32
Ascot Rd	Milnerton	57	BV	32
Ascot St	Beacon Valley (M.Plain)	145	CQ	48
Ascot St	Bonnie Brook	47	BQ	57
Ascot St	Windsor Park Est.	47	BQ	58
Ascot St	Windsor Park Est.	47	BR	58
Ash Cl.	Hanover Pk	122	CK	36
Ash Cl.	Hanover Pk	122	CN	36
Ash Cottages Cl.	Wellway Pk	46	BO	52
Ash Cottages St	Sun Valley	185	DA	19
Ash Cottages St	Sun Valley	185	DB	22
Ash Grove Rd	Devil's Peak Est.	82	CC	24
Ash La.	Claremont	120	CJ	30
Ash La.	Grassy Pk	141	CQ	33
Ash La.	Hout Bay	117	CN	18
Ash St	Brantwood	89	CA	53
Ash St	Forest Village	127	CM	58
Ash St	Observatory	83	CC	29
Ash St	Sunnydale	185	DA	19
Ashbrook Cr.	Woodlands (M.Plain)	144	CQ	44
Ashbury Rd	Plumstead	120	CN	29
Ashby Rd	Athlone	102	CG	34
Ashdown Cl.	Sunningdale	25	BM	31
Ashford Cir.	Northpine	63	BU	58
Ashford Cl.	Parklands	25	BN	32
Ashford Rd	Heathfield	140	CQ	29
Ashford St	Connaught	87	CB	43
Ashgrove	Pinelands	84	CC	34
Ashgrove Ave	Epping Forest	86	CB	41
Ashley Cl.	Epping Forest	86	CC	41
Ashley Cr.	Lavender Hill	160	CT	31
Ashley Kriel	Weltevreden Val. (M.Plain)	123	CM	42
Ashley Way	Belhar	107	CE	51
Ashley Way	Highbury	107	CE	53
Ashraf Ave	Gatesville	103	CH	36
Ashstead Rd	Green Point	81	BZ	22
Ashton Rd	Milnerton	57	BX	31
Ashtown St	Oakdale	61	BX	48
Ashville Cr.	Retreat	140	CS	29
Asley Kriel St	Mandela Pk	146	CR	54
Asmara Rd	Charlesville	104	CF	40
Aspden Rd	Belhar	88	CC	50
Aspden Rd	Brown's Farm	123	CL	41
Aspeling Cr.	Highbury	107	CE	54
Aspeling Rd	Belhar	106	CE	50
Aspeling St	District Six	82	CB	25
Aspeling St	District Six	82	CB	24
Aspen Cl.	Fairie Knowe	185	DA	19
Aspen Cl.	Sunnydale	185	DA	20
Aspidistra	Lentegeur (M.Plain)	145	CO	47
Assegaai	Delft Sth	125	CJ	49
Assegaai Ave	Thornton	85	CA	37
Assegaai Cr.	Onverwacht	175	DC	76
Assegaai Ct	Delft Sth	125	CJ	49
Assegaai Rd	Kraaifontein Ind.	48	BQ	61
Assegaaibos Ave	Rouxville	90	CA	56
Assegaaibos St	Tafelsig (M.Plain)	145	CR	49
Assegai Ave	Bonteheuwel	104	CD	39
Assegai St	Parow Ind.	87	CB	45
Astana St	Schotsche Kloof	81	CA	22
Aster	Lentegeur (M.Plain)	144	CO	45
Aster	Uitsig	87	CC	44
Aster Cr.	Roosendaal	107	CF	51
Aster Cr.	Silvertown	103	CF	36
Aster Cr.	Weltevreden Val. (M.Plain)	124	CM	44
Aster La.	Big Bay	24	BK	28
Aster La.	Big Bay	24	BL	29
Aster Pl.	Bellville	61	BT	48
Aster Rd	Kewtown	102	CF	34
Aster Rd	Lavender Hill East	160	CU	31
Aster St	Bishopscourt	119	CJ	26
Aster St	Protea Hoogte	63	BX	57
Aster St	Sarepta	89	CC	53
Aster St	Somerset West	151	CS	71
Aster St	Somerset West	151	CS	72
Aster St	Wellington	15	AT	92
Asteroid St	Ocean View	189	DD	15
Astley St	Mowbray	101	CD	29
Astra Ave	Riverton	86	BZ	40
Astrid Cl.	Plattekloof	60	BV	43
Astrid Cr.	Dalvale	19	AY	93
Astronaut Cl.	Thembokwezi	125	CM	48
Atalanta Rd	Dennemere	127	CJ	58
Atbara Rd	Eindhoven	106	CH	50
Atbara Rd	Eindhoven	107	CH	51
Athall Wk	Hanover Pk	122	CK	36
Athan St	Bonnie Brook	47	BQ	57
Athburg Wk	Hanover Pk	122	CK	36
Athdown Wk	Pinati	122	CJ	35
Athena Cl.	Phoenix	57	BU	34
Athena St	Ferndale	62	BV	54
Athens Rd	Blue Downs	127	CJ	56
Athens Rd	Table View	40	BO	30
Athens Rd	Table View	41	BO	31
Athens Rd	Table View	41	BP	32
Athens Rd	Table View	41	BP	33
Athens St	Portlands (M.Plain)	144	CQ	46
Athens St	Uitzicht	47	BO	56
Atherstone Rd	Plumstead	140	CO	29
Atherstone Way	Edgemead	58	BV	37
Athi Way	Delft	106	CF	49
Athlone Rd	Athlone	102	CF	33
Athlone Rd	Plumstead	140	CO	29
Athlone St	Beroma	89	BZ	51
Athlone St	Klipkop	87	BZ	45
Athlone St	Ruyterwacht	86	CA	40
Athlone St	Strand Halt	170	CW	74
Athol Ave	Somerset West	151	CR	72

Abbreviations used: Ave – Avenue, A.H. – Agricultural Holding, A.L.– Algemene Landgoed, Blvd – Boulevard, Cen. – Central, Cir. – Circle, Cl. – Close, Cr. – Crescent, Ct – Court, Dr. – Drive, Est. – Estate, Ext. – Extension, Hgts – Heights, Ind. – Industrial, Gdns – Gardens, Gr. – Grove, La. – Lane, (M.Plain) - Mitchells Plain, Nth – North, Pl. – Place, Pk – Park, Rd – Road, Rdg. – Ridge, S.H.– Small Holding, Sq. – Square, St – Street, Sth – South, Ter. – Terrace, Tn – Turn, Val. – Valley, Wk – Walk

STREET NAME	SUBURB NAME	PG	GRID
Athol Rd	Camps Bay	99	CD 19
Athol Rd South	Camps Bay	99	CE 19
Athon Cr.	Hanover Pk	122	CK 37
Athon Wk	Hanover Pk	122	CK 36
Athry Wk	Hanover Pk	122	CJ 36
Athsur Wk	Pinati	122	CJ 35
Athwood Rd	Hanover Pk	122	CJ 36
Athwood Rd	Hanover Pk	122	CK 35
Athwood Wk	Newfields	122	CJ 36
Atkins St	Grassy Pk	141	CR 31
Atlantic Ave	Eersterivier	127	CM 58
Atlantic Ave	Eersterivier	128	CM 59
Atlantic Dr.	Imhoff's Gift	184	DB 15
Atlantic Rd	Muizenberg	159	CX 29
Atlantic Skipper Rd	Hout Bay Harbour	136	CR 14
Atlantic Way	Sun Valley	185	DA 20
Atlantis Cl.	Parow Nth	60	BX 43
Atlas Ave	Salberau	86	CA 41
Atlas Cr.	Tafelsig (M.Plain)	145	CS 49
Atlas Dr.	Phoenix	57	BV 33
Atlas Rd	Athlone	102	CG 33
Atletiek St	Beacon Valley (M.Plain)	145	CP 47
Atomic St	Triangle Farm	89	BZ 51
Atonio Cl.	Bothasig	58	BU 36
Atrina Way	Sunset Beach	41	BR 31
Attie Bas St	Paarl	22	BE 88
Attlee	Plumstead	141	CO 31
Auber	Delft Sth	125	CK 48
Auber Ave	Mandalay	125	CM 47
Auber Ave	Mandalay	125	CM 48
Auber Cl.	Mandalay	125	CM 48
Aubrey St	Morgenster Hoogte	63	BU 55
Aubrey St	Salt River	83	CB 28
Auburn Rd	Kenilworth	120	CK 29
Auburn St	Denneburg	22	BD 90
Auckland St	Paarden Eiland	83	BY 30
Auckland St	Paarden Eiland	83	BZ 29
Audas St	Somerset West	170	CU 74
Audry Rd	Manenberg	123	CJ 39
August St	Eersterivier	128	CM 60
August St	Schotsche Kloof	81	CA 22
Augusta	Ravensmead	87	CA 45
Augusta Mews	Milnerton	57	BT 32
Augusta Rd	Sunningdale	25	BM 31
Augusta Rd	Sunningdale	25	BN 31
Augusta Rd	Sunningdale	25	BN 32
Augustus Way	Constantia Vale	119	CN 24
Aulax Cl.	Eversdal Hgts	45	BS 50
Aurea Cl.	Plattekloof	60	BV 43
Aureole Cl.	Flintdale Est.	141	CP 31
Aureole Cr.	Highbury	107	CE 53
Aureole Rd	Flintdale Est.	140	CP 30
Auret	Strand Halt	170	CX 74
Auret St	Paarl	22	BD 88
Auric	Delft Sth	125	CK 48
Auriga Cl.	Ocean View	189	DD 15
Auriga Rd	Retreat	140	CR 28
Aurora Dr.	Mountainside Est.	179	DE 77
Aurora La.	Sea Point	81	BZ 19
Aurora St	Bellavista	22	BD 90
Aurora St	Durbanville	45	BQ 49
Aurora St	Kirstenhof	159	CT 27
Aurora St	Welgelegen	59	BU 41
Aurora St	Wellington	15	AV 93
Aurora St	Wellington	15	AW 93
Aurora Way	Salberau	86	CB 41
Austell Rd	Retreat	140	CR 28
Auster St	Macassar	149	CS 64
Austin Cr.	Beacon Valley (M.Plain)	145	CQ 47
Austin Rd	Adriaanse	87	CC 43
Austwick Rd	Rondebosch	101	CF 30
Autum St	Surrey	103	CG 37
Autumn	Green Oaks	94	BY 74
Autumn Cl.	Montagu's Gift	141	CO 34
Autumn St	Hill View	127	CK 57
Avalon Rd	Claremont	101	CH 29
Ave Alexandra	Fresnaye	81	CB 19
Ave Bordeaux	Sea Point	81	CA 20
Ave Branksome	Fresnaye	81	CA 19
Ave Brittany	Fresnaye	80	CB 18
Ave Charmante	Bantry Bay	80	CB 18
Ave Coeur de Lion	Fresnaye	81	CB 19
Ave De Berrange	Fresnaye	81	CB 20
Ave De L'Hermite	Fresnaye	81	CA 19
Ave De Longueville	Fresnaye	81	CA 19
Ave De Mist	Claremont	102	CH 31
Ave De Mist	Rondebosch	101	CG 30
Ave De Mist	Rondebosch	102	CG 31
Ave Deauville	Fresnaye	81	CB 19
Ave Des Huguenots	Fresnaye	81	CA 19
Ave Disandt	Fresnaye	81	CA 19
Ave Disandt	Fresnaye	81	CB 19
Ave Drelingcourt	Fresnaye	81	CA 20
Ave Du Midi	Plumstead	140	CP 30
Ave Fontainebleau	Sea Point	81	CA 20
Ave Francais	Fresnaye	81	CA 19
Ave Fresnaye	Fresnaye	81	CA 19
Ave Fresnaye	Fresnaye	81	CB 19
Ave La Croix	Fresnaye	81	CB 19
Ave Le Suer	Fresnaye	80	CB 18
Ave Le Sueur	Fresnaye	81	CA 19
Ave Marina	Bantry Bay	80	CB 18
Ave Marseilles	Sea Point	81	CA 20
Ave Normandy	Plumstead	140	CP 30
Ave Orleans	Plumstead	140	CP 30

STREET NAME	SUBURB NAME	PG	GRID
Ave St Bartholomew	Fresnaye	81	CB 19
Ave St Charles	Fresnaye	81	CB 19
Ave St Charles	Sea Point	81	CA 19
Ave St Denis	Sea Point	81	CA 20
Ave St Leon	Bantry Bay	80	CB 18
Ave St Louis	Fresnaye	81	CB 19
Ave. Bordeaux	Hohenort	119	CL 24
Avebury	Sonstraal Hgts	46	BR 54
Avenger	Rocklands (M.Plain)	163	CT 45
Avenhoorn Cl.	Woodbridge Island	57	BW 31
Avenue De La Sante	Somerset West	151	CQ 72
Avenue de L'Hermite	Glenhaven	89	CA 51
Avenue Rd	Rondebosch	101	CG 28
Avenue Rd	Woodstock	83	CB 27
Avenue St	Cape Town Cen.	81	CB 22
Avery Ave	Barbarossa	119	CN 26
Avery Ave	Ottery	122	CL 35
Avery Ave	Silverhurst	139	CO 26
Avery Cr.	Ottery	122	CL 35
Avery Rd	Heathfield	140	CQ 29
Avery Rd	Hohelzen	61	BW 47
Avey Rd	Epping Forest	86	CC 42
Aviation Cr.	Airport Ind.	105	CH 43
Avignon Cl.	Welgelegen	59	BU 40
Avignon Cr.	Townsend Est.	58	BX 37
Avila St	Wesbank	107	CE 52
Avion St	Windsor Est.	47	BQ 58
Avoca Rd	Rondebosch	101	CG 29
Avocado St	Bonteheuwel	103	CD 38
Avocado St	Mitchells Plain	144	CQ 44
Avocado Way	Mitchells Plain	144	CQ 44
Avocet Cr.	Pelikan Pk	142	CQ 35
Avocet St	Eersterivier	128	CM 60
Avocet St	Electric City	128	CN 59
Avocet St	Flamingo Vlei	41	BQ 32
Avocet St	Flintdale Est.	141	CP 31
Avon Cl.	Belhar	106	CE 49
Avon Rd	Dieprivier	140	CP 28
Avon Rd	Eersterivier	128	CM 60
Avon Rd	Woodlands (M.Plain)	144	CQ 44
Avon St	Avondale	60	BX 44
Avondale Cl.	Connaught	87	CC 43
Avondale Cr.	West Beach	24	BM 30
Avondale Rd	Avon	86	CA 41
Avondale Rd	Three Anchor Bay	81	BZ 21
Avondale St	Oakdale	61	BX 49
Avondale Ter.	Plumstead	140	CP 29
Avondrus St	Brooklyn	84	BY 31
Avondrus St	Winslow	179	DD 77
Avondrust	Chapman's Peak	156	CX 17
Avondrust Ave	Bergvliet	140	CQ 27
Avondrust Ave	Bergvliet	140	CR 30
Avondrust Cir.	Chapman's Peak	156	CW 17
Avondrust Cir.	Chapman's Peak	156	CW 18
Avondrust Way	Marinda Hgts	89	BZ 52
Avondrust Way	Marinda Hgts	89	BY 54
Avonduur	Ndabeni	84	CB 33
Avonduur	Pinelands	84	CB 33
Avonduur St	Chrismar	61	BW 50
Avonhoorn St	Dennemere	108	CH 57
Avonlea Cl.	Parklands	25	BM 33
Avonmouth Ave	Parklands	25	BM 34
Avontuur	Voorbrug	106	CH 50
Avontuur	Voorbrug	106	CH 48
Avontuur Cl.	Mitchells Plain	144	CR 45
Avontuur Cl.	Mitchells Plain	144	CR 43
Avontuur Rd	Edgemead	58	BU 38
Avonwood Ave	Norwood	86	CA 41
Avonwood Ave	Valhalla	86	CA 40
Avro Ave	Kensington	84	BY 34
Awash Ct	Delft	106	CG 49
Awie Joseph Cl.	Gustrow	175	DB 75
Awie Joseph Cl.	Gustrow	175	DB 77
Axis Rd	Wingfield	85	BZ 37
Axminster Rd	Muizenberg	159	CX 30
Ayers Way	Somerset West	152	CS 78
Aylesbury Cl.	Wetton	121	CL 34
Aylesbury Rd	Wetton	121	CL 34
Aylesbury St	Oakdale	61	BW 48
Ayliff Cl.	Edgemead	58	BV 37
Ayre Cl.	Belhar	106	CE 49
Ayres St	Rosebank	101	CE 30
Ayreshire Cl.	Balvenie	87	CC 43
Ayreshire Cl.	Balvenie	87	CB 46
Ayreshire St	Montana/Durrheim	104	CF 41
Ayrshire Cl.	Mitchells Plain	144	CR 45
Ayrshire St	Rondebosch East	102	CH 32
Ayton Rd	Rondebosch	102	CG 31
Azalea Cl.	Belhar	106	CD 47
Azalea Cl.	Welgedacht	60	BU 45
Azalea Cr.	Belhar	88	CC 48
Azalea Rd	Durbanville	45	BQ 50
Azalea St	Plumstead	140	CO 28
Azalea St	Vredekloof Hgts	47	BS 55
Azalia	Lentegeur (M.Plain)	144	CO 46
Azalia Ave	Uitsig	87	CC 44
Azalia Cr.	Thornton	85	CA 37
Azalia St	Klein Nederburg	19	BC 93
Azana St	Ottery	121	CN 33
Azania Cr.	Wimbledon	108	CG 55
Azelia St	Somerset West	151	CS 71
B			
B.February St	Hout Bay	137	CO 16
B.Longo Rd	Nyanga	123	CJ 42

STREET NAME	SUBURB NAME	PG	GRID
B.P. Rd	Montague Gdns Ind.	58	BT 35
Baakens Rd	Primrose Pk	103	CH 38
Baakens Way	Portlands (M.Plain)	144	CP 45
Baakenskop St	Tafelsig (M.Plain)	145	CR 49
Baalen Rd	Marina Da Gama	159	CV 30
Baardsuikerbos St	Bellville Ext. 53	60	BT 46
Baartman St	Leonsdale	86	CA 42
Baatjies La.	Grassy Pk	141	CQ 32
Baberton	Chrismar	61	BX 50
Baberton	Chrismar	61	BV 48
Babiana Cl.	Gordon Hgts	180	DD 79
Babiana Cl.	Gordon Hgts	180	DE 79
Babiana Cl.	Perm Gdns	128	CJ 59
Babiana Cl.	Perm Gdns	128	CJ 60
Babiana Rd	Belhar	105	CD 46
Babiana St	Somerset West	151	CS 72
Babylonstoren Rd	Babylons Toren	54	BO 85
Babylonstoren Rd	Paarl	38	BN 86
Baca Ave	Victoria Mxenge	126	CN 51
Baca Ave	Victoria Mxenge	126	CN 52
Bacchos Rd	Table View	41	BO 33
Bacchus Cl.	Somerset West	151	CQ 72
Bach	Delft Sth	125	CK 48
Bach	Schuilplaats	113	CG 76
Bach Ave	Retreat	159	CT 30
Bach Cl.	Sonstraal Hgts	46	BQ 53
Bach Rd	Belhar	106	CD 48
Bach St	Brackenfell	63	BV 56
Bach St	Groenheuwel	19	AY 91
Bach St	Kaapzicht	59	BW 40
Bach Villas	Sonstraal Hgts	46	BQ 53
Back Cl.	Strandfontein	162	CT 40
Back La.	Park Estates	174	CY 71
Back Rd	Strandfontein	162	CT 40
Baden Powell Dr.	Capricorn	160	CW 32
Baden Powell Dr.	Khayelitsha	147	CS 57
Baden Powell Dr.	Khayelitsha	165	CT 53
Baden Powell Dr.	Khayelitsha	166	CT 55
Baden Powell Dr.	Pelikan Pk	161	CV 37
Baden Powell Dr.	Santiago Bay	161	CV 36
Baden Powell Dr.	Strandfontein	162	CU 41
Baden Powell Dr.	Strandfontein	163	CT 45
Baden Powell Dr.	Strandfontein	164	CT 50
Baden Powell Dr.	Strandfontein	165	CT 51
Baden Powell Dr.	Vergenoeg	148	CQ 53
Baden Powell Dr.	Welmoed Est.	129	CK 64
Badgemore Ave	Nova Constantia	139	CQ 24
Badgers	Wellington	15	AU 91
Badi Cr.	Nonqubela	126	CN 52
Badminton Cr.	Beacon Valley (M.Plain)	145	CP 47
Badsberg Cr.	Tafelsig (M.Plain)	145	CR 49
Bahia Cr.	Malibu Village	127	CK 55
Bahia Cr.	Malibu Village	127	CL 56
Bahrain Dr.	Airport Ind.	105	CF 43
Bailey	Tennantville	95	CA 75
Bailey Ave	Wellington	15	AV 91
Bailey Cr.	Heideveld	104	CF 39
Bailey St	Sir Lowry's Pass	176	CZ 82
Bailey Way	Edgemead	58	BV 37
Bain	Somerset West	151	CQ 71
Bain Cl.	Belhar	106	CD 50
Bain Ct	Rondebosch	102	CF 32
Bain St	Ruyterwacht	86	BZ 39
Bain St	Wellington	10	AR 94
Baines Rd	Richwood	42	BQ 38
Bainford St	Sonnekuil	89	CA 53
Bains Way	Edgemead	58	BV 37
Bainsberg Cl.	Greenfield	108	CH 56
Bainskloof St	Tafelsig (M.Plain)	145	CS 49
Baird Rd	Belhar	88	CC 50
Baird St	Dal Josafat Ind.	19	AY 91
Baird St	Welgemoed	61	BV 47
Baird Way	Meadowridge	140	CP 27
Baker Cl.	Mitchells Plain	144	CQ 45
Baker Rd	Kenilworth	120	CK 30
Baker Rd	Muizenberg	159	CX 29
Baker St	Belhar	106	CD 49
Baker St	Marconi Beam	57	BV 34
Baker St	Observatory	83	CB 29
Baker St	Scottsdene	64	BV 60
Baker St	The Palms	170	CX 73
Bakers Cr.	Summer Greens	58	BV 36
Bakersfield	Vredekloof Hgts	47	BS 55
Bakker	Idasvallei	95	CA 78
Bakker Rd	Newfields	122	CJ 37
Bakker St	Welgemoed	61	BV 47
Bakkerskloof Rd	Somerset West	151	CQ 71
Bakkiesblom Cr.	Roosendaal	106	CF 50
Bakoven Cl.	Simon's Town	194	DJ 26
Balalaika	Sonstraal Hgts	46	BR 53
Baldwin Ave	Epping Forest	86	CC 42
Balearic	Rocklands (M.Plain)	144	CS 45
Baleia Rd	Ottery	121	CL 33
Balers Way	Sunset Beach	41	BS 32
Balfour Ave	Bishopscourt	120	CJ 27
Balfour Rd	Glenlily	86	BY 41
Balfour Rd	Rondebosch	102	CE 32
Balfour Rd	Windsor Pk	47	BS 56
Balfour St	District Six	82	CB 25
Balfour St	Woodstock	83	CC 27
Balfour Way	Northpine	63	BU 58
Bali Cl.	Capri	185	DB 19
Bali Cr.	Bloubergstrand	24	BK 27
Balingen Pl.	Silversands	107	CH 53
Balintore Rd	Rondebosch	102	CG 31

STREET NAME	SUBURB NAME	PG	GRID
Ballen Dr.	Kommetjie	183	DA 13
Ballina Cl.	Connaught	87	CB 43
Bally Green	Summer Greens	58	BW 35
Ballycline Steps	Fish Hoek	186	DC 24
Balmoral Ave	Bergvliet	140	CQ 27
Balmoral Cl.	Dreyersdal	140	CS 27
Balmoral Cl.	Pinelands	85	CC 35
Balmoral Cl.	Pinelands	85	CC 36
Balmoral Rd	Lansdowne	121	CJ 33
Balmoral Rd	Plumstead	120	CN 28
Balmoral Rd	West Beach	24	BM 29
Baloyi Ave	Nonqubela	126	CN 52
Balsam St	Silversands	107	CH 54
Balsam St	Somerset West	151	CS 72
Balsillie Way	Nova Constantia	139	CP 24
Baltic Way	Sun Valley	185	CZ 20
Balu Parker Blvd.	Gatesville	103	CG 37
Balvenie Ave	Balvenie	86	CB 42
Balvenie Ave	Connaught	87	CB 43
Balvenie Ave	Epping Forest	86	CB 41
Bambanani St	Crossroads	124	CK 44
Bambanani St	Gugulethu	104	CH 41
Bambapho	Mbekweni	15	AW 92
Bambata Ave	Hout Bay	137	CO 16
Bambayi St	Mxolisi Phetani	125	CM 50
Bamberry Rd	Belthorn Est.	102	CH 34
Bambi Rd	Ekuphumuleni	146	CQ 53
Bambisanani St	Kuyasa	147	CR 55
Bambisanani St	Kuyasa	147	CS 58
Bamboeberg Rd	Heideveld	104	CG 39
Bamboesberg	Wellington	15	AV 91
Bamboesberg	Wellington	15	AU 94
Bamboesvlei Rd	Ottery	121	CM 33
Bamboo	Lentegeur (M.Plain)	144	CO 45
Bamboo Rd	Lansdowne	121	CK 33
Bamford Ave	Athlone	102	CG 33
Bamsley St	Dunoon	42	BO 37
Banana	Philippi East	125	CM 47
Bancroft St	Rugby	57	BX 31
Bangalore Ave	Cravenby	87	CA 43
Bangani St	Nyanga	123	CK 42
Banghoek	Stellenbosch	95	CB 76
Banghoek	Universiteits-oord	95	CB 77
Bangiso Dr.	Victoria Mxenge	126	CN 51
Bangiso Dr.	Victoria Mxenge	126	CN 52
Bangiso Dr.	Victoria Mxenge	146	CO 52
Bangor St	Athlone	102	CG 33
Banhoek Cl.	Richwood	42	BP 37
Banhoek Cl.	Richwood	42	BQ 37
Banhoek Rd	Eversdal	62	BU 51
Banhoek Rd	Heideveld	104	CF 39
Bani Ct	Delft	106	CG 48
Banier Rd	Flintdale Est.	141	CP 31
Baninzi St	Umrhabulo Triangle	147	CQ 56
Banjo Rd	Retreat	159	CT 29
Banjo Wk	Belhar	106	CE 48
Bank Cl.	Woodlands (M.Plain)	144	CQ 44
Bank Rd	Rondebosch	101	CG 29
Bank St	Kenridge Hgts	45	BR 49
Bankberg	Wellington	15	AV 91
Bankberg	Wellington	15	AU 94
Bankot Rd	Lansdowne	121	CK 34
Banks Rd	Fish Hoek	186	DA 24
Banksia Rd	Rosebank	101	CE 30
Bankview Cl.	Riverton	86	BZ 40
Bannockburn Cr.	Strandfontein	162	CT 40
Bantam St	Dal Josafat Ind.	18	BA 90
Bantam St	Schotsche Kloof	81	CA 22
Banti Cr.	Eyethu	146	CP 53
Bantry La.	Bantry Bay	80	CB 18
Bantry Steps	Bantry Bay	80	CB 18
Bantry Way	Matroosfontein	86	CC 42
Bantu St	Mxolisi Phetani	125	CM 50
Banzi Ave	Gugulethu	123	CJ 40
Banzi St	Victoria Mxenge	126	CN 51
Baobab St	Eastridge (M.Plain)	145	CR 48
Baptist St	Grassy Pk	141	CQ 31
Baraco Cr.	Northpine	63	BU 58
Baracouta Ave	Monte Vista	59	BU 40
Barbados Way	Portlands (M.Plain)	144	CQ 46
Barbara	Eersterivier	127	CL 58
Barbara Cl.	Lentegeur (M.Plain)	145	CO 48
Barbara Cl.	Lentegeur (M.Plain)	145	CP 50
Barbara Cr.	Dalvale	19	AZ 92
Barbara Cr.	Dalvale	19	BA 94
Barbara Masokola St	Mandela Pk	146	CQ 54
Barbara Rd	Bakoven	98	CF 18
Barbarossa Rd	Sonstraal	46	BR 52
Barbarossa St	Paarlzicht	19	BC 91
Barbarossa St	Shirley Pk	89	BY 52
Barbary Way	Barbarossa	119	CN 26
Barbel Rd	Pelikan Pk	141	CQ 34
Barber	Delft Sth	125	CK 48
Barber Cl.	Fish Hoek	186	DA 23
Barberton	Ravensmead	87	CA 46
Barberton Link	Belhar	105	CD 46
Barberton St	Somerset West	151	CS 72
Barbestyn St	Ottery	121	CM 32
Barbet Cl.	D'urbanvale	29	BN 49
Barbet Cl.	Somerset West	171	CT 76
Barbet Rd	Pelikan Pk	142	CS 36
Barbet Way	Electric City	127	CN 58
Barbeton Rd	Belthorn Est.	122	CJ 35
Barbette Rd	Ottery	121	CM 34
Barbourne Rd	Muizenberg Nth	159	CV 28

Index to Street Names

Barcelona — Bisset Rd

STREET NAME	SUBURB NAME	PG	GRID	
Barcelona	D'urbanvale	45	BO	49
Barcelona St	Uitzicht	47	BO	55
Barcelona St	Uitzicht	47	BO	55
Barcombe Rd	Hazendal	102	CF	33
Bardale Rd	Sunset Glen	107	CH	54
Bardale Rd	Sunset Glen	108	CH	55
Bardia	Strandfontein	162	CU	40
Bardia Rd	Plumstead	120	CM	28
Barend Rd	Lansdowne	122	CK	35
Barendilla St	Kaapzicht	59	BV	40
Barents	Rocklands (M.Plain)	144	CS	45
Barewood Cl.	Blackheath Ind.	108	CF	57
Barham Rd	Belgravia	103	CG	35
Baris Rd	Woodstock	83	CC	27
Barit Rd	Penlyn Est.	122	CJ	35
Bark Cl.	Scottsdene	64	BU	60
Bark St	Retreat Ind. Area	159	CT	28
Bark St	Retreat Ind. Area	159	CT	28
Barka Rd	Delft	106	CF	49
Barker St	William Lloyd	19	BC	92
Barkis Rd	Belgravia	103	CG	35
Barkley Ave	Glenhaven	89	BZ	52
Barkley Rd	Rondebosch	101	CF	30
Barkley St	Ruyterwacht	86	CA	39
Barkly Rd	Sea Point	81	CA	19
Barkly Way	Edgemead	59	BT	39
Barleria	Gordon Hgts	180	DD	79
Barling Cr.	Fish Hoek	185	DA	21
Barlinka Ave	Somerset West	151	CS	72
Barlinka Ave	Table View	41	BP	33
Barlinka Pl.	Adriaanse	87	CC	43
Barlinka Rd	Sonstraal	46	BR	52
Barlinka St	Paarl	22	BF	87
Barlinka St	Shirley Pk	89	BY	52
Barlinka St	Welgedacht	44	BS	45
Barlinka St	Wellington	11	AR	95
Barlinka Way	Meadowridge	140	CO	27
Barlinka Way	Northpine	63	BU	58
Barlinka Way	Northpine	63	BV	56
Barlow St	William Lloyd	23	BD	92
Barmania Rd	Athlone	102	CG	33
Barmbeck Ave	Newlands	101	CH	27
Barn Owl La.	Hout Bay	117	CM	18
Barn Rd	Bergvliet	139	CQ	26
Barna Cl.	Connaught	87	CB	43
Barnabas Shaw Rd	Sir Lowry's Pass	176	CZ	81
Barnabas St	Gardens	81	CB	21
Barnacle La.	Big Bay	24	BL	28
Barnard St	Kempenville	61	BX	49
Barnard St	Kingston	61	BX	49
Barnard St	Monte Vista	59	BV	39
Barnard St	Oakdale	61	BW	49
Barnard St	Oakdale	61	BX	49
Barnard St	Rondebosch	102	CE	31
Barnard St	Simon's Town	194	DJ	23
Barnard St	Simon's Town	194	DJ	24
Barnet St	Mountain View	19	BB	91
Barnett Rd	Plumstead	140	CO	29
Barnett St	Gardens	82	CB	23
Barnham Ave	Devil's Peak Est.	82	CC	24
Barnsley Cl.	Weltevreden Val. (M.Plain)	143	CP	42
Barnstaple Rd	Wynberg	120	CL	30
Baro Cr.	Delft	106	CF	49
Baroe	Green Oaks	95	BY	75
Baroe	Green Oaks	95	BY	77
Baronetcy Blvd	Plattekloof Village	59	BT	41
Baronie Ave	Westlake	159	CU	27
Baronrath Rd	Kenilworth	120	CK	29
Barque Cl.	Strandfontein	162	CU	39
Barque Cr.	Sun Valley	185	CZ	20
Barrack St	Cape Town Cen.	82	CB	23
Barrack St	District Six	82	CB	23
Barracuda Cr.	Nooitgedacht	104	CE	42
Barracuda Cr.	Nooitgedacht	105	CE	43
Barracuda St	Gustrow	174	DB	74
Barracuda St	The Hague	106	CE	50
Barracuda Way	Strandfontein	162	CT	39
Barrie Ross Way	Meadowridge	140	CP	27
Barrington Rd	Observatory	83	CC	29
Barron St	Woodstock	82	CB	26
Barrow Rd	Tijgerhof	57	BW	33
Barrow St	Monte Vista	59	BV	39
Barrowdale Cl.	Parklands	25	BM	33
Barry	Dalsig	113	CE	75
Barry Ave	Rosebank	101	CE	29
Barry Cr.	De Tuin	47	BS	55
Barry Hertzog Rd	Parow Nth	59	BX	42
Barry Rd	Hout Bay	137	CP	16
Barry Rd	Montagu's Gift	141	CO	34
Bartel Rd	Beaconvale	86	BZ	42
Bartholomeu Dias Blvd.	Cape Town Cen.	82	CA	24
Bartholomeu St	Dalvale	19	AY	92
Bartlett Rise	Lindida	96	CA	80
Bartlett Way	Edgemead	58	BV	37
Bartman St	Flintdale Est.	141	CO	31
Barton Rd	Kalk Bay	186	DA	26
Barton Rd	Kalk Bay	186	CZ	26
Barton St	Woodstock	82	CB	26
Basalt Cl.	Salberau	86	CA	40
Basalt Cl.	Salberau	86	CB	39
Basalt St	Bellville	61	BU	50
Basalt St	Bellville	62	BU	51
Basboom	Delft Sth	125	CJ	50
Bashee Ave	Bonnie Brook	47	BQ	57
Bashee Cl.	Portlands (M.Plain)	144	CP	45

STREET NAME	SUBURB NAME	PG	GRID	
Bashee Ct	Delft	106	CG	49
Bashee Rd	Manenberg	104	CG	39
Basil Cr.	Ottery East	122	CN	35
Basil February Cr.	Mandela Pk	147	CQ	56
Basil February Cr.	Mandela Pk	147	CP	55
Basil Fischer St	Weltevreden Val. (M.Plain)	123	CN	42
Basil Rd	Plumstead	120	CN	30
Basil Rd	Plumstead	121	CN	31
Basket La.	Foreshore	82	CB	25
Bass Rd	Belhar	106	CD	48
Bass Rd	Pelikan Pk	141	CR	33
Bass St	Macassar	149	CS	65
Bass St	Soneike II	89	BZ	53
Bass Wk	Nooitgedacht	104	CE	42
Basset	Strandfontein	162	CT	40
Bassett Rd	Claremont	121	CJ	31
Bassett St	Brackenfell Sth	63	BX	57
Bassi	Kayamandi	94	CA	74
Basson Rd	Durbanville	45	BQ	50
Basson St	Groenvlei	18	BA	88
Basson St	Maitland	83	CA	30
Basson St	Soneike I	89	BZ	54
Bassoon St	Steenberg	159	CT	30
Bastiaan St	Wellington	15	AV	93
Bastille St	Klein Parys	23	BE	91
Bastion Cl.	Brackenfell Sth	63	BX	56
Bata St	Strandfontein	162	CT	42
Bataleur Way	Somerset West	152	CS	78
Batandwa Ndondo Rd	Mandela Pk	146	CQ	54
Batavia Dr.	Belhar	106	CD	50
Batavia Dr.	Belhar	106	CE	50
Batavia Rd	Bloubergstrand	24	BM	28
Batavia Rd	Ruyterwacht	86	CA	39
Batavia St	Bothasig	42	BS	38
Batavia St	Bothasig	58	BT	38
Batavia St	Somerset West	171	CU	76
Batavia St	Welgemoed	60	BV	45
Bateleur Cir.	Fish Hoek	186	DA	23
Bateleur Cr.	Sunridge	41	BO	34
Bateleur Cr.	Sunridge	41	BP	34
Bateleur Rd	Klein Nederburg	46	BP	53
Bateleur Rd	Sunridge	42	BP	35
Bateleur Sq.	Eersterivier	128	CM	60
Bates Dr.	Loevenstein	60	BW	46
Bath Rd	Claremont	120	CJ	29
Bath Rd	Muizenberg	159	CX	30
Bath Rd	Wynberg	120	CM	30
Bath St	Gardens	81	CC	21
Bath St	Malibu Village	127	CK	56
Batha St	Delft	106	CF	48
Batha St	Mfuleni	126	CK	53
Bathandwa Mdingi Cr.	Weltevreden Val. (M.Plain)	123	CN	41
Bathembu Cr.	Bongani	126	CN	51
Bathembu Cr.	Victoria Mxenge	126	CN	51
Bathembu Cr.	Victoria Mxenge	146	CO	51
Bathhurst Cl.	Edgemead	58	BV	37
Bathurst	Ravensmead	87	CA	46
Bathurst Rd	Kenilworth	120	CL	29
Bathurst Way	Northpine	64	BV	59
Batis Rd	Die Wingerd	46	BP	53
Batis Rd	Durbanville	46	BQ	53
Batis Rd	Klein Nederburg	46	BP	53
Batiso St	Bloekombos	48	BR	62
Bato St	Glencairn Hgts	191	DD	24
Batten Bend	Blouberg Sands	24	BM	30
Batten La.	Mowbray	101	CD	29
Battersea	Parklands	25	BN	33
Battersea	Parklands	41	BO	33
Battersea Cl.	Riverton	86	BZ	40
Battery Cr.	Sea Point	81	BZ	20
Battle Ridge	Marina Da Gama	159	CW	30
Batts Rd	Wynberg	120	CM	29
Batya Way	Kenridge	61	BU	49
Bauhinia	Eersterivier	128	CM	61
Bauhinia Cl.	Mandalay	125	CN	48
Bauhinia Cl.	Mandalay	125	CN	49
Bauhinia Cr.	Vredekloof	62	BT	54
Bauhinia Rd	Belhar	105	CD	46
Bauhinia Rd	Halalie	46	BO	52
Bauhinia St	Klein Nederburg	19	BC	92
Baviaans Cl.	Hout Bay	137	CQ	16
Baviaanskloof Ave	Tafelsig (M.Plain)	145	CR	48
Baviaanskloof Rd	Hout Bay	137	CQ	16
Baviaanskloof Rd	Hout Bay	137	CQ	17
Bawa St	Mfuleni	126	CJ	53
Bax	Delft Sth	125	CJ	49
Bax Ave	Monte Vista	59	BV	40
Bax St	Bothasig	42	BS	37
Bax St	Ndabeni	84	CB	31
Baxley Cr.	Wesbank	107	CF	52
Baxter Ave	Durbanville	46	BQ	51
Baxter Rd	Rosebank	101	CE	29
Baxter St	Sanlamhof	88	BY	50
Baxter Way	Edgemead	58	BU	38
Bay Ave	Harbour Island	179	DE	76
Bay Beach Ave	Sunset Beach	41	BR	32
Bay Beach Ave	Sunset Beach	41	BS	32
Bay Beach Ave	Sunset Beach	57	BT	31
Bay Beach Ave	Sunset Links	57	BU	31
Bay Cr.	Gordon Strand	179	DD	77
Bay Cr.	West Riding	41	BO	34
Bay Cr.	West Riding	41	BO	34
Bay Hill Ter.	Milnerton	57	BU	32
Bay Hill Ter.	Sunset Beach	57	BT	32
Bay Rd	Green Point	81	BY	21

STREET NAME	SUBURB NAME	PG	GRID	
Bay Rd	Hout Bay	117	CN	18
Bay Rd	Hout Bay	118	CM	20
Bay Rd	Muizenberg	187	CY	28
Bay St	Capricorn	160	CW	32
Bay View Ave	Tamboerskloof	81	CB	21
Bay View Rd	Wynberg	120	CM	28
Bayana Ave	Victoria Mxenge	126	CN	52
Bayana Cl.	Nyanga	123	CK	42
Bayard St	Grassy Pk	141	CQ	31
Bayete Rd	Ndabeni	84	CB	32
Bayne St	Eindhoven	106	CH	50
Bayridge Cr.	Somerset West	170	CT	72
Bayside Cl.	Somerset West	170	CT	72
Bayside Ter.	Parklands	41	BO	32
Bayswater	Parklands	41	BO	33
Bayswater Rd	Lotus River	141	CQ	34
Bayview Rd	Hout Bay	116	CL	14
Bayview Rd	Hout Bay Harbour	136	CR	13
Bayview Rd	Hout Bay Harbour	136	CQ	13
Bayview Rd	Somerset West	170	CT	73
Baywater Cr.	Strandfontein	162	CT	42
Bazindlovu Cl.	Philippi East	124	CM	46
Beach	Khayelitsha	166	CT	55
Beach	Khayelitsha	166	CT	56
Beach	Kommetjie	183	DB	12
Beach Blvd	Table View	24	BN	29
Beach Blvd	Table View	40	BO	30
Beach Cl.	Milnerton	57	BT	33
Beach Cr.	Hout Bay	137	CQ	16
Beach Cr.	Table View	24	BN	29
Beach Rd	Brooklyn	83	BZ	30
Beach Rd	Chapman's Peak	156	CW	16
Beach Rd	Chapman's Peak	156	CW	17
Beach Rd	Fish Hoek	186	DB	24
Beach Rd	Green Point	81	BY	22
Beach Rd	Greenways	174	DA	73
Beach Rd	Harbour Island	179	DD	77
Beach Rd	Harbour Island	179	DE	76
Beach Rd	Kommetjie	183	DB	11
Beach Rd	Maitland	83	CA	30
Beach Rd	Misty Cliffs	192	DJ	17
Beach Rd	Mouille Point	81	BY	21
Beach Rd	Muizenberg	159	CW	27
Beach Rd	Muizenberg	159	CX	29
Beach Rd	Muizenberg	187	CY	29
Beach Rd	Park Estates	169	CW	70
Beach Rd	Park Estates	170	CW	71
Beach Rd	Park Estates	170	CX	71
Beach Rd	Park Estates	174	CY	71
Beach Rd	Park Estates	174	CZ	72
Beach Rd	Scarborough	192	DK	17
Beach Rd	Sea Point	80	CA	18
Beach Rd	Sea Point	81	BZ	19
Beach Rd	Three Anchor Bay	81	BY	20
Beach Rd	Woodstock	82	CA	26
Beach Rd	Woodstock	83	CA	27
Beachcomber Cl.	Admirals Pk	179	DD	78
Beacon Rd	Beaconvale	86	BZ	42
Beacon St	Tafelsig (M.Plain)	145	CR	49
Beacon Way	Bellair	62	BV	53
Beacon Way	Murdock Valley	195	DL	28
Beaconsfield Rd	Clarkes	86	CC	42
Beacontree La.	Woodstock	83	CB	27
Beagle	Strandfontein	162	CT	40
Beak Rd	Pelikan Pk	142	CS	36
Beak Rd	Pelikan Pk	161	CU	38
Beanke Cl.	Somerset West	151	CQ	72
Bear La.	Zoo Pk	47	BQ	56
Beatrice Cl.	Dennedal	139	CR	26
Beatrix Rd	Manenberg	123	CJ	39
Beatrix St	Brackenfell Ind.	63	BT	58
Beatty Ave	Maitland Gdn Village	84	CC	31
Beatty Rd	Woodstock	83	CC	27
Beau Art La.	Crofters Valley	185	CZ	19
Beau Monde Cr.	Everglen	45	BS	50
Beau Monde Cr.	Everglen	45	BP	47
Beau Mont Cr.	Somerset Rdg	170	CU	72
Beaucoup	Franschhoek Nth	75	BW	105
Beaufighter	Rocklands (M.Plain)	144	CS	46
Beaufort	Rocklands (M.Plain)	163	CT	45
Beaufort Rd	Milnerton	57	BW	31
Beaufort St	Factreton	85	BZ	35
Beaufort St	Ravensmead	87	CB	45
Beaufort St	Townsend Est.	85	BY	38
Beaufort St	Townsend Est.	85	BZ	38
Beaulieu Cr.	Somerset West	171	CW	75
Beaulieu Rd	Eersterivier	128	CN	60
Beaulles Cr.	Somerset West	151	CR	72
Beaumont Ave	Bel Ombre	119	CM	24
Beaumont Ave	Vredekloof	62	BU	54
Beaumont Cottages	Green Point	81	BZ	22
Beauvais Ave	Bel Ombre	119	CM	24
Beauville	Vredekloof	62	BU	54
Beauville Cr.	Malibu Village	127	CK	56
Beaver	Wellington	15	AU	91
Beaver	Wellington	15	AT	94
Beaver	Wesbank	107	CG	52
Beaver Rd	Zoo Pk	47	BR	56
Beaver St	The Hague	106	CE	50
Beck St	Durbanville	45	BQ	50
Beck St	Eastridge (M.Plain)	145	CQ	49
Becker St	Hanover Pk	122	CK	36
Beckham St	Gardens	81	CB	22
Becott Rd	Wetton	121	CL	34
Bedford Rd	Lakeside	159	CV	28

STREET NAME	SUBURB NAME	PG	GRID	
Bedford St	Churchill	60	BX	43
Bedford St	Claremont	120	CJ	29
Bedford St	Glenlily	87	BY	43
Bedford St	Observatory	83	CC	29
Bedford St	Vredehoek	82	CC	23
Bedford Way	Ottery	121	CM	34
Bedfordshire Cl.	Kirstenhof	159	CU	27
Bedfordshire Cl.	Kirstenhof	159	CW	27
Bee Eater Cl.	Fish Hoek	186	DA	23
Beech Cr.	Westlake Est.	158	CT	24
Beech Cr.	Westlake Est.	158	CT	26
Beech St	Tokai	139	CS	25
Beechcraft	Rocklands (M.Plain)	145	CS	47
Beechcraft St	The Hague	106	CE	50
Beechwood	Pinelands	85	CC	35
Beechwood Cl.	Ottery East	121	CN	34
Beechwood Cl.	Ottery East	121	CM	34
Beefwood Cr.	St Dumas	90	CC	56
Beefwood Rd	Eersterivier	128	CM	60
Beethoven	Delft Sth	125	CK	48
Beethoven	La Pastorale	113	CG	76
Beethoven	Schuilplaats	113	CG	76
Beethoven Cl.	Belhar	106	CD	48
Beethoven Cr.	Sonstraal Hgts	46	BQ	54
Beethoven Ct	Delft Sth	125	CK	48
Beethoven Rd	Cafda Village	140	CS	30
Beethoven Rd	Retreat	159	CT	30
Beethoven St	Groenheuwel	19	AZ	91
Beethoven St	Protea Hoogte	63	BW	56
Beets St	Wellington	15	AV	93
Bega Rd	Wynberg	120	CM	29
Begonia	Lentegeur (M.Plain)	144	CP	45
Begonia Ave	Uitsig	87	CC	44
Begonia Cl.	Mandalay	125	CN	48
Begonia Cl.	Mandalay	125	CN	49
Begonia Rd	Blackheath Ind.	108	CF	57
Begonia Rd	Hanover Pk	122	CJ	37
Begonia Rd	Milnerton	57	BU	33
Begonia Rd	Ridgeworth	61	BV	49
Begonia Rd	Silvertown	103	CF	36
Begonia Rd	Tygerdal	58	BX	37
Begonia St	Dalvale	19	AY	91
Begonia St	Forest Hgts	127	CL	58
Begonia St	Somerset West	151	CS	72
Behr Rd	Kalk Bay	186	DA	26
Beighton Rd	Kraaifontein	47	BQ	58
Beira Rd	Bakoven	98	CF	17
Bekelentloko St	Griffiths Mxenge	146	CQ	54
Bel Air Dr.	Scottsdene	64	BV	59
Bel Ombre Rd	Bel Ombre	119	CL	24
Bel Ombre Rd	Bergvliet	140	CR	27
Belacre Cl.	Connaught	87	CB	43
Belair Cr.	Weltevreden Val. (M.Plain)	144	CQ	43
Belair Dr.	Witteboomen	118	CN	22
Belair Dr.	Witteboomen	119	CN	23
Belami Dr.	Sonstraal Hgts	46	BR	54
Belami Dr.	Uitzicht	47	BR	55
Belcher Cl.	Langgewacht	170	CW	73
Beldia St	Scottsdene	64	BU	60
Belfast Cl.	Royal Cape	121	CM	32
Belfast Rd	Wynberg	120	CM	30
Belgravia Ave	Lansdowne	121	CJ	32
Belgravia Rd	Athlone	102	CF	34
Belhar Dr.	Belhar	106	CD	50
Belhar Main	Highbury	107	CD	54
Belhar Main	Kalkfontein II	89	CC	53
Belhar Main	Kalkfontein II	107	CD	53
Belinda	Dalvale	19	AY	93
Belinda Rd	Manenberg	123	CJ	39
Belinda St	Kirstenhof	159	CT	27
Belinda Wk	Manenberg	123	CJ	39
Bell	Stellenbosch	95	CA	75
Bell Capri Link	Hout Bay Harbour	136	CR	14
Bell Capri Link	Hout Bay Harbour	136	CQ	13
Bell Cl.	Belhar	106	CD	49
Bell Cl.	Riverton	86	BZ	40
Bell Cl.	Westlake Est.	158	CU	25
Bell Cr.	Westlake Est.	158	CU	25
Bell Rd	Kenilworth	120	CJ	29
Bell St	Paarl	22	BF	88
Bell Way	Meadowridge	140	CO	27
Bella Mare	Sunningdale	25	BM	31
Bella Ria	Welgedacht	44	BS	46
Bella Rosa St	Rosendal	61	BU	49
Bella Rosa St	Rosendal	61	BT	49
Belladona St	Perm Gdns	128	CJ	59
Belladonna	Cloetesville	95	BY	75
Belladonna Ave	Devil's Peak Est.	82	CC	24
Belladonna La.	Big Bay	24	BK	28
Belladonna St	Roosendaal	106	CF	50
Belladonna Way	Belhar	105	CD	46
Bellagio	Somerset West	151	CQ	72
Bellair Rd	Vredehoek	82	CC	24
Bellbusk Cr.	Bellville	62	BV	52
Bellcanto Rd	Selborne	61	BV	47
Belle Ave	Westlake	159	CU	27
Belle Constantia Cl.	Bergvliet	139	CP	26
Belle Ombre Rd	Tamboerskloof	81	CB	21
Bellevliet Rd	Observatory	83	CC	29
Bellevliet St	Bothasig	42	BS	38
Bellevue	Green Oaks	95	BY	75
Bellevue	Green Oaks	95	BY	77
Bellevue Dr.	Northpine	63	BT	58
Bellevue Rd	Kenilworth	120	CK	29
Bellevue Rd	Sea Point	81	BZ	19

Abbreviations used: Ave – Avenue, A.H. – Agricultural Holding, A.L.– Algemene Landgoed, Blvd – Boulevard, Cen. – Central, Cir. – Circle, Cl. – Close, Cr. – Crescent, Ct – Court, Dr. – Drive, Est. – Estate, Ext. – Extension, Hgts – Heights, Ind. – Industrial, Gdns – Gardens, Gr. – Grove, La. – Lane, (M.Plain) - Mitchells Plain, Nth – North, Pl. – Place, Pk – Park, Rd – Road, Rdg. – Ridge, S.H.– Small Holding, Sq. – Square, St – Street, Sth – South, Ter. – Terrace, Tn – Turn, Val. – Valley, Wk – Walk

STREET NAME	SUBURB NAME	PG	GRID
Bellevue Rd	Simon's Town	195	DJ 27
Bellevue St	Gardens	81	CC 20
Bellevue St	Voorbrug	107	CH 51
Bellevue Way	Edgemead	58	BT 38
Bellhome St	Highbury	107	CD 54
Bellingham Cr.	Haasendal	90	CA 57
Bellingham Cr.	Mitchells Plain	144	CR 45
Bellingham Rd	Table View	41	BO 32
Bellini Cl.	Sonstraal Hgts	46	BR 54
Bellmore Ave	Penlyn Est.	103	CH 36
Bellmore Ave	Penlyn Est.	122	CJ 35
Bellona	Dennemere	127	CJ 57
Bellona	Dennemere	127	CN 55
Bellona St	Somerset West	171	CV 75
Bellow Cl.	Admirals Pk	175	DC 76
Bellows Cl.	Hout Bay Harbour	136	CR 13
Belloy St	Bloubergstrand	24	BM 28
Bellstart La.	Observatory	83	CC 29
Bellview St	Wellington	15	AT 92
Bellvue Ave	Bel Ombre	119	CL 23
Bellvue St	Kempenville	88	BY 48
Bellvue St	Kempenville	88	BY 49
Bellvue St	Lemoenkloof	18	BC 87
Bellwood Rd	Fresnaye	80	CB 18
Bellwood St	Ridgeworth	61	BV 50
Belmondo Cr.	Somerset Rdg	170	CT 72
Belmont Ave	Oranjezicht	81	CC 22
Belmont Ave	Somerset West	151	CR 71
Belmont Link	Plattekloof Village	59	BT 42
Belmont Rd	Kalk Bay	186	DA 26
Belmont Rd	Lansdowne	121	CJ 32
Belmont Rd	Mowbray	101	CD 29
Belmont Rd	Rondebosch	101	CF 29
Belmont Rd	Simon's Town	194	DJ 26
Belmont St	Bellavista	18	BC 90
Belmont St	Chrismar	61	BW 50
Belmont St	Chrismar	61	BX 50
Belmont Way	Edgemead	58	BV 37
Belmore Way	Belhar	105	CD 45
Belmore Way	Belhar	105	CE 45
Belper Rd	Wynberg	120	CL 29
Belrail Rd	Belrail	88	BY 48
Belrail Rd	Belrail	88	BY 49
Belrail Rd	Sanlamhof	88	BY 50
Belrail Rd	Stikland Hospital	89	BY 51
Belsay Cl.	Kenilworth	120	CL 30
Belthorn Rd	Belthorn Est.	102	CH 34
Beltra Cl.	Connaught	87	CB 43
Belvedere Ave	Clovelly	186	DA 24
Belvedere Ave	Oranjezicht	81	CC 22
Belvedere Cir.	Bishop Lavis	105	CD 43
Belvedere Cl.	Belvedere Noordhoek	157	CX 19
Belvedere Cl.	Parklands	25	BN 32
Belvedere End	Parklands	25	BN 32
Belvedere Mews	Skilpadvlei	45	BP 49
Belvedere Rd	Claremont	101	CH 30
Belvedere Rd	Claremont	102	CH 31
Belvedere Rd	Muizenberg	159	CX 29
Belvedere St	Macassar	149	CS 64
Belvedere St	Skilpadvlei	45	BP 49
Belyando St	Eindhoven	106	CH 50
Ben Ave	Devil's Peak Est.	82	CC 24
Ben Moloise Cr.	Mandela Pk	146	CR 54
Ben Nevis Rd	Sea Point	81	BZ 21
Ben St	Grassy Pk	141	CQ 33
Ben St	Nooitgedacht	104	CE 42
Ben Zantsi St	Gugulethu	104	CH 41
Ben Zantsi St	Gugulethu	123	CJ 41
Benade St	The Palms	170	CX 72
Benbow Ave	Belgravia	103	CH 35
Benbow Ave	Epping Ind.	85	CB 37
Benbow Rd	Penlyn Est.	103	CH 35
Bend Rd	Ottery	121	CM 33
Bendixen Rd	Ottery East	121	CM 33
Benes St	Maitland	83	CA 30
Bengel	Eersterivier	128	CN 60
Bengezela St	Harare	146	CR 54
Benghazi Rd	Lansdowne	121	CL 32
Benghazi Rd	Milnerton	57	BV 32
Benguela Cl.	Bel Ombre	119	CM 25
Benigna Cl.	Nyanga	123	CK 42
Benjamin Rd	Wynberg	120	CM 29
Benjamin St	Wellington	15	AU 92
Bennett St	Cape Town Cen.	82	BZ 23
Bennetts Cl.	Simon's Town	191	DE 24
Bennie St	Langa	103	CD 35
Bennie v d Merwe St	Oakdene	89	CC 53
Benning Dr.	Kommetjie	183	DB 12
Bennington Rd	Tamboerskloof	81	CB 22
Benona Rd	Lansdowne	121	CJ 34
Benoni Cl.	Mitchells Plain	144	CR 46
Benox St	Nomzano	175	CY 75
Bent Way	Eersterivier	128	CN 61
Bentley Cl.	Claremont	120	CJ 30
Bentley Cr.	Beacon Valley (M.Plain)	145	CQ 47
Bentley St	Sunset Glen	108	CH 55
Bentwood Cl.	Edgemead	58	BV 37
Benue Ct	Delft	106	CG 49
Benurban Rd	Valmary Pk	46	BR 51
Benyano Cr.	Kaya	146	CP 51
Berea Cr.	Ravensmead	87	CB 45
Berea St	Paarl	22	BD 88
Beresford Rd	Bloubergstrand	24	BM 28
Beresford Rd	Woodstock	82	CC 26
Berg	Delft Sth	125	CK 48
Berg Ave	Somerset West	171	CW 77
Berg Rd	Bishop Lavis	104	CD 41
Berg Rd	Fish Hoek	186	DB 23
Berg Rd	Fish Hoek	186	DC 24
Berg Rd	Harbour Island	179	DD 77
Berg River Blvd	Paarl	22	BE 89
Berg River Blvd Nth	Lemoenkloof	18	BB 89
Berg River St	Lemoenkloof	18	BC 89
Berg St	Capricorn	160	CU 31
Berg St	Eersterivier	128	CN 59
Berg St	Eersterivier	128	CJ 61
Berg St	Franschhoek Sth	79	BZ 107
Berg St	Paarl	22	BE 88
Berg St	Wellington	10	AR 94
Berg St	Wellington	10	AS 94
Berg St	Wellington	11	AS 95
Bergen Rd	Frogmore Est.	159	CU 28
Berg-en-Dal	Somerset West	151	CS 74
Bergendal Rd	Fir Grove	139	CQ 25
Berg-en-Dal St	Lemoenkloof	18	BB 87
Berg-en-Dal St	Wellington	10	AR 94
Berg-en-Dal St	Wellington	11	AQ 95
Bergerac Cl.	Somerset West	151	CQ 72
Bergh	Brandwacht	113	CE 76
Bergh	Dalsig	113	CE 76
Berghof La.	Hout Bay	137	CQ 17
Berghowe Rd	Somerset West	151	CQ 72
Bergkruine Rd	Eversdal Hgts	61	BT 50
Bergpypie St	Groenvlei	18	BA 89
Bergrivier Cl.	Portlands (M.Plain)	144	CQ 45
Bergrivier Rd	Wellington	15	AU 92
Bergrivier St	Welgevonden	30	BN 53
Bergrivier St	Welgevonden	30	BM 53
Bergroos	Plattekloof	59	BU 42
Bergroos Cl.	Perm Gdns	128	CJ 59
Bergroos Cl.	Perm Gdns	128	CJ 60
Bergroos Rd	Roosendaal	106	CF 50
Bergroos St	Bloemhof	61	BV 50
Bergroos St	Bloemhof	61	BV 48
Bergroos St	Protea Village	64	BV 59
Bergshoop	Langeberg Rdg	47	BQ 55
Bergshoop	Sonstraal Hgts	46	BQ 54
Bergsicht Rd	Bergsig	46	BO 52
Bergsig	Panorama	59	BV 42
Bergsig Ave	Paarl	22	BE 88
Bergsig Ave	Voorbrug	107	CH 51
Bergsig Dr.	Woodlands (M.Plain)	144	CP 44
Bergsig St	Protea Hoogte	63	BX 57
Bergsig St	Protea Hoogte	63	BW 57
Bergsipres	Cloetesville	94	BY 74
Bergsipres	Weltevrede	94	BY 74
Bergstedt	Cloetesville	95	BZ 75
Bergstroom St	Bellair	62	BW 53
Berguitsig Rd	Elfindale	140	CQ 29
Bergvliet	Karindal	96	CC 79
Bergvliet Rd	Bergvliet	140	CQ 28
Bergwagter	Rocklands (M.Plain)	144	CS 44
Bergwind	Rocklands (M.Plain)	145	CS 47
Bergzicht	Paarl	22	BE 88
Bergzicht	Stellenbosch	95	CC 75
Bergzicht Cir.	Tokai	139	CS 26
Bergzicht Cr.	Belhar	106	CE 49
Bergzicht Rd	Proteavallei	61	BT 47
Bergzicht Rd	Richwood	42	BP 38
Bergzicht Rd	Somerset West	171	CU 77
Bergzig	Flintdale Est.	141	CO 31
Beriev St	The Hague	106	CE 50
Beril St	Forest Hgts	127	CK 58
Bering	Rocklands (M.Plain)	144	CS 45
Berio	Delft Sth	125	CJ 48
Berk	Morgen Gronde	63	BX 55
Berkdale Mews	Sunset Links	57	BT 31
Berkeley Pl.	Claremont	120	CJ 29
Berkeley Pl.	Claremont	120	CK 30
Berkeley Rd	Mowbray	102	CE 31
Berkeley St	Oranjezicht	81	CC 22
Berkley Rd	Bellair	62	BV 53
Berkley Rd	Camps Bay	98	CD 18
Berkley Rd	Ndabeni	83	CB 30
Berkley Rd	Ndabeni	84	CB 31
Berland Cr.	Wesbank	107	CG 51
Berlin Sq.	Strandfontein	162	CT 41
Berlin Sq.	Strandfontein	162	CT 41
Berlioz St	Dalvale	19	AY 91
Berlyn St	Lemoenkloof	18	BB 89
Berman Rd	Peerless Pk East	48	BR 59
Berman St	De Zoete Inval	22	BH 88
Bermuda Cr.	Blouberg Sands	24	BL 30
Bermuda Dr.	Capri	185	DB 20
Bermuda Dr.	Sunnydale	185	DA 20
Bermuda St	Malibu Village	127	CL 56
Bermuda St	Paarden Eiland	83	BZ 30
Bermuda St	Portlands (M.Plain)	144	CP 46
Bernadine St	Devon Pk	128	CL 60
Bernard Ave	Flintdale Est.	141	CP 31
Bernard Cr.	Somerset West	171	CT 76
Bernard Hass St	Hill View	127	CK 58
Berne Ave	Lansdowne	121	CK 32
Bernhardi St	Paarl	22	BD 88
Bernice	Dalvale	19	AY 93
Bernice	Dalvale	19	BA 94
Berol St	Beroma	89	BZ 51
Berol St	Mabille Pk	89	CA 53
Berold St	Fairfield	87	BY 43
Beroma Cr.	Glenhaven	89	BZ 51
Berram Rd	Rondebosch	102	CG 31
Berriedale Cr.	Sonstraal Hgts	46	BQ 54
Berrio Rd	Foreshore	82	CA 26
Berry La.	Wynberg	120	CM 30
Berry Rd	Capricorn	160	CV 31
Berry Rd	Wynberg	120	CM 29
Berry St	Philippi	124	CM 45
Berrydel Ave	Somerset West	170	CT 73
Berryheath	Hout Bay	137	CP 16
Berth Ct	Delft	106	CF 49
Bertha Ave	Bishopscourt	120	CJ 27
Bertha St	Florida	87	CB 44
Bertha St	Lentegeur (M.Plain)	145	CO 48
Bertha Wk	Cravenby	87	CB 44
Bertie Ave	Epping Ind.	85	CB 38
Bertie Genade St	De Grendel	59	BX 42
Berties Cl.	Anchorage Pk	175	DC 77
Berties Cl.	Anchorage Pk	175	DB 78
Bertram Cr.	Rondebosch	102	CG 31
Bertram Rd	Sea Point	81	BZ 20
Bertrand Rd	Green Point	81	BZ 22
Bertrums St	Brackenfell	63	BW 56
Berwick Cr.	West Beach	24	BN 30
Berwick Rd	Wynberg	120	CM 28
Beryl	Dalvale	19	AY 93
Beryl Rd	Montagu's Gift	141	CO 33
Beryl Rd	Ottery	121	CM 33
Berzelia Cl.	Mandalay	125	CN 48
Berzelia Cl.	Mandalay	125	CN 49
Berzelia Cr.	Belhar	105	CD 46
Bessie Rd	Bonteheuwel	103	CD 38
Bessie Rd	Bonteheuwel	104	CD 39
Bessie Rd	Delft Sth	106	CH 50
Bestenbier Ave	Balvenie	86	CB 42
Bestenbier Ave	Balvenie	87	CB 43
Bester Rd	Bellville Sth Ind.	89	CA 51
Beta	Cloetesville	94	BY 74
Beta	Hoogstede	62	BV 53
Beta Rd	Bakoven	98	CF 17
Beta St	Belrail	88	BY 49
Beta Wk	Ocean View	189	DD 15
Beth St	Mfuleni	126	CJ 53
Bethal St	Hout Bay	117	CN 16
Bethanie Rd	Sonstraal	46	BR 52
Bethanie Rd	Sonstraal Hgts	46	BS 51
Bethanie Rd	Wellway Pk	46	BO 52
Bethel	Wesbank	107	CG 51
Bethel Rd	Clovelly	186	DA 24
Bethel St	Lemoenkloof	18	BC 88
Betsie Verwoerd St	Townsend Est.	85	BY 37
Betsy Rd	Stikland Hospital	61	BX 50
Bettie St	Kalkfontein II	89	CC 52
Bettina Cl.	Lansdowne	121	CJ 32
Bettina Rd	Lansdowne	121	CJ 33
Bettington Sq.	Woodstock	83	CB 27
Betty Cl.	Lentegeur (M.Plain)	145	CO 48
Betty Rd	Bishop Lavis	105	CE 43
Betty St	Avonwood	86	CB 42
Betty St	De Zoete Inval	39	BJ 87
Beukenhout Ave	Amandelrug	90	CA 56
Beukes	Park Estates	174	CY 72
Beukes St	William Lloyd	19	BC 92
Beulah Ter.	Oranjezicht	99	CD 22
Beulaland St	Wesbank	107	CF 52
Beuno Vista	Ridgeworth	61	BV 50
Bevan Rd	Surrey	103	CH 37
Bevan Way	Balvenie	86	CB 42
Beveland St	Dal Josafat Ind.	18	AZ 90
Beverely Rd	Montague Gdns Ind.	42	BS 35
Beverley Cl.	Lentegeur (M.Plain)	145	CO 48
Beverley Cl.	Lentegeur (M.Plain)	145	CP 50
Beverley Rd	Athlone	102	CF 33
Beverley Rd	Bellair	62	BV 53
Beverly Cl.	Montague Gdns Ind.	42	BS 35
Beverly Cl.	Scottsdene	64	BV 60
Beverly St	Eersterivier	128	CN 60
Beverly St	Eersterivier	128	CL 59
Beverly St	Eersterivier	128	CM 60
Bewitched	Fairyland	19	AZ 92
Bewitched	Fairyland	19	BA 94
Bexhill Rd	Wynberg	120	CL 29
Bexter Cl.	Balvenie	87	CC 43
Beyers Rd	Woodstock	82	CB 26
Beyers St	Stellenbosch	95	CC 76
Bezuidenhout St	Scottsville	47	BR 58
Bezuidenhout St	Scottsville	47	BP 58
Bhabhalaza St	Bloekombos	48	BR 62
Bhaqolo	Mbekweni	15	AW 91
Bharu St	Scottsdene	48	BS 61
Bharu St	Scottsdene	64	BT 61
Bhayi Ave	Joe Slovo Pk	57	BV 34
Bheki Mlangeni	Weltevreden Val. (M.Plain)	123	CN 44
Bhemya Cr.	Nonqubela	146	CO 53
Bhengu St	Dunoon	42	BO 38
Bhere Cr.	Mxolisi Phetani	125	CM 47
Bhobhoyi St	Brown's Farm	124	CM 43
Bhobhoyi St	Ilitha Pk	146	CQ 52
Bhofolo Ave	Joe Slovo Pk	57	BV 34
Bhompasi Rd	Philippi East	124	CM 46
Bhongweni	Wellington	15	AV 91
Bhthwali St	Crossroads	124	CJ 44
Bhunga Ave	Langa	103	CD 35
Bhunga St	Scottsdene	64	BT 60
Biarritz Cl.	Sunset Beach	57	BT 31
Biccard St	Bloubergstrand	24	BM 28
Biccard St	Durbanville	45	BP 50
Bickley Rd	Sea Point	81	BZ 20
Bickley Rd	Winslow	179	DD 77
Bicycle Cr.	Beacon Valley (M.Plain)	145	CP 47
Bida Cr.	Victoria Mxenge	146	CO 51
Bideford Rd	Woodstock	83	CC 27
Bidoli Cr.	Somerset West	151	CQ 72
Biedouberg St	Tafelsig (M.Plain)	145	CR 49
Bien Donne	Pinelands	85	CB 35
Bien Donne Cl.	La Rochelle	62	BV 51
Bien Donne Rd	Sonstraal Hgts	46	BP 54
Bien Donne Way	Mitchells Plain	144	CQ 45
Biesie Cr.	Roosendaal	106	CF 50
Bietou Cl.	Roosendaal	106	CF 50
Bietou St	Bellville	61	BT 48
Big Bay Blvd	Big Bay	24	BL 28
Big Bay Blvd	Big Bay	24	BK 29
Biggar St	Ruyterwacht	86	CA 39
Bignonia	Lentegeur (M.Plain)	144	CO 46
Bignonia Cir.	Belhar	105	CD 46
Bignonia Cl.	Mandalay	125	CN 48
Bignonia Cl.	Mandalay	125	CN 49
Bigonia St	Vygeboom	46	BR 51
Bigstone St	Wesbank	107	CG 51
Bika Nair St	Mandela Pk	147	CQ 55
Bika Nair St	Mandela Pk	147	CP 55
Bikhwe Cr.	Ilitha Pk	146	CR 52
Bikhwe Cr.	Philippi East	124	CL 46
Biko Cr.	Ilitha Pk	146	CQ 53
Bila St	Harare	146	CR 53
Bilberry	Macassar	149	CR 63
Biljaart St	Beacon Valley (M.Plain)	145	CP 47
Bill Bezuidenhout Ave	Chrismar	61	BW 50
Bill Peters Dr.	Green Point	81	BY 21
Billet St	Sir Lowry's Pass	176	CZ 82
Billy	Scottsdene	48	BS 60
Bilston Cl.	Eersterivier	128	CN 61
Bilston Rd	Crawford	102	CH 34
Bind Ave	Macassar	149	CS 64
Bind St	Northern Paarl	18	AZ 89
Bindeka St	Umrhabulo Triangle	147	CR 56
Binders Rd	Parow East	87	BY 46
Binne Cr.	Bellville Sth	88	CA 49
Binne St	Brackenfell	63	BW 56
Binnekant St	Paarl	22	BF 88
Binnekring	Dalsig	113	CE 76
Binneman Rd	Oakdale	61	BW 49
Binneman St	Constantia Vale	119	CN 25
Birch Cl.	Beaconvale	86	BZ 42
Birch Ct	Belhar	106	CD 47
Birch Rd	Chapman's Peak	156	CX 16
Birch Rd	Grassy Pk	141	CQ 33
Birch St	Bellair	62	BW 51
Birch St	Forest Village	127	CM 57
Birch St	Hout Bay	117	CN 18
Birch St	Newlands	100	CH 26
Birchwood La.	Tokai	139	CS 26
Bird Cr.	Bishop Lavis	105	CE 44
Bird Rd	Somerset West	152	CS 76
Bird St	Belhar	106	CE 50
Bird St	Lansdowne	121	CK 32
Bird St	Morgenster	63	BU 56
Bird St	Stellenbosch	95	CB 75
Birdwood St	Athlone	102	CF 33
Birkdale Ave	Woodstock	83	CB 27
Birkdale Village	Milnerton	41	BS 33
Birkenhead	Eersterivier	128	CN 60
Birkenhead Cr.	Ruyterwacht	86	CA 39
Birkenhead Dr.	Plattekloof Glen	59	BW 40
Birkenhead Dr.	Strandfontein	162	CT 42
Birkenhead Dr.	Strandfontein	163	CT 43
Birkenhead Rd	Dolphin Beach	40	BP 30
Birkenhead Rd	Glencairn Hgts	191	DD 24
Birkenhead Rd	Plumstead	140	CP 29
Birkenhead Rd	Table View	41	BP 32
Birkenhead St	Park Estates	174	CY 72
Birkenhead St	Somerset West	171	CU 77
Birkett Rd	Rondebosch	102	CF 31
Birmingham Cl.	Airport Ind.	105	CF 43
Birmingham Rd	Plumstead	140	CO 28
Birmingham St	Airport Ind.	105	CF 43
Birmingham St	Malibu Village	127	CK 55
Birmingham St	Malibu Village	127	CN 55
Birmingham St	N1 City	59	BX 40
Bishop Cr.	Bishop Lavis	105	CD 44
Bishop Cr.	D'urbanvale	29	BN 49
Bishop Cr.	Mbekweni	15	AX 91
Bishop Rd	Observatory	83	CC 29
Bishop St	Grassy Pk	141	CQ 31
Bishop Tutu St	Mandela Pk	147	CR 55
Bishoplea Rd	Claremont	101	CH 28
Bishops Cl.	Kenilworth	120	CL 27
Bishops Court Cl.	Fisantekraal	31	BK 58
Bishops Court Way	Claremont	101	CH 27
Bishops End	Parklands	25	BM 33
Bishopscourt Dr.	Bishopscourt	119	CJ 26
Bishopscourt Dr.	Bishopscourt	119	CJ 25
Bishopstone Rd	Wetton	122	CM 35
Biskop Steps	Clifton	80	CC 18
Bisley St	Beacon Valley (M.Plain)	145	CP 48
Bisschop Rd	Hout Bay	136	CO 14
Bisset Rd	Kenilworth	120	CK 29
Bisset Rd	Newlands	100	CH 25
Bisset Rd	Windsor Pk	47	BS 57
Bisset Rd	Windsor Pk	47	BR 56

Abbreviations used: Ave – Avenue, A.H. – Agricultural Holding, A.L. – Algemene Landgoed, Blvd – Boulevard, Cen. – Central, Cir. – Circle, Cl. – Close, Cr. – Crescent, Ct – Court, Dr. – Drive, Est. – Estate, Ext. – Extension, Hgts – Heights, Ind. – Industrial, Gdns – Gardens, Gr. – Grove, La. – Lane, (M.Plain) - Mitchells Plain, Nth – North, Pl. – Place, Pk – Park, Rd – Road, Rdg. – Ridge, S.H.– Small Holding, Sq. – Square, St – Street, Sth – South, Ter. – Terrace, Tn – Turn, Val. – Valley, Wk – Walk

STREET NAME	SUBURB NAME	PG	GRID
Bordeaux Cl.	Mitchells Plain	144	CR 43
Bordeaux Cl.	Somerset West	151	CS 72
Bordeaux Cl.	Vredekloof	62	BU 53
Bordeaux Cr.	Welgelegen	59	BU 41
Bordeaux Rd	Eersterivier	128	CL 59
Bordeaux Rd	Sunnydale	185	DA 19
Bordeaux St	Franschhoek Sth	79	BZ 107
Bordeaux St	Wellington	11	AQ 95
Bordeaux St	William Lloyd	23	BE 92
Bordeaux Way	Mitchells Plain	144	CR 45
Borden Rd	Rondebosch	102	CF 32
Borders Cl.	Epping Forest	86	CB 41
Boreham Cr.	Durbanville Hills	45	BR 50
Borghorst St	Monte Vista	59	BV 40
Borghorst St	Monte Vista	59	BW 39
Borghurst St	Perm Gdns	128	CK 59
Borneo Cl.	Portlands (M.Plain)	144	CQ 46
Borneo St	Bloubergstrand	24	BJ 27
Bornite Rd	Belthorn Est.	122	CJ 35
Borok St	Durbanville	46	BQ 51
Borriehout St	Bonteheuwel	104	CD 40
Borssenberg St	Dal Josafat Ind.	18	BA 90
Borzoi Cr.	Strandfontein	162	CT 40
Bosberg Rd	Bishop Lavis	105	CE 43
Bosbok	Klipkop	87	BZ 45
Bosbok Cr.	Eastridge (M.Plain)	145	CR 48
Bosbok Rd	Lotus River	142	CP 36
Bosbok Rd	Phumlani	142	CQ 35
Bosbok Rd	Skilpadvlei	45	BP 49
Bosbok St	New Orleans	19	BB 92
Bosbokkie St	Elim	90	CB 55
Bosch La.	Oranjezicht	99	CD 22
Bosch St	Greenways	174	CZ 74
Bosch St	Greenways	174	DA 73
Bosch St	Groenvlei	18	BA 88
Bosch St	Voelvlei	89	CA 53
Bosch-en-Dal	Karindal	96	CC 79
Bosch-en-Dal	Kirstenhof	159	CU 27
Boschendal Cl.	Mitchells Plain	144	CR 45
Boschendal Cl.	Welgedacht	44	BS 45
Boschendal Cr.	Dreyersdal	140	CR 27
Boschendal Mews	Welgedacht	44	BS 45
Boschendal Rd	Die Bos	170	CX 74
Boschendal Rd	Die Bos	174	CY 74
Boschendal St	Welgedacht	44	BS 45
Boschendal St	Welgedacht	44	BS 46
Boschendal Ter.	Welgedacht	44	BS 45
Boschendal Way	Mitchells Plain	144	CR 45
Boschenvale	D'urbanvale	45	BO 49
Boschenvale Cl.	Langeberg Rdg	47	BR 55
Boschheuwel St	Kleinbosch	59	BT 40
Bosduif	Rocklands (M.Plain)	144	CS 44
Bosduif Cr.	Flamingo Vlei	41	BQ 33
Bosduif Rd	Bridgetown	103	CF 37
Bosduif St	Jacarandas	90	CC 57
Bosduif Way	Tarentaalplaas	175	DA 76
Bosheuwel Rd	Bothasig	42	BS 37
Boshof St	Bishopscourt	119	CJ 26
Boshof St	Newlands	100	CH 26
Boshoff Rd	Mitchells Plain	144	CR 45
Boshoff St	Skilpadvlei	45	BP 49
Bosica St	Loevenstein	60	BV 46
Boskloof Ave	Somerset West	171	CW 77
Boskloof Rd	Tafelsig (M.Plain)	145	CR 49
Boskloof St	Strand	174	CY 73
Boskykloof Rd	Hout Bay	117	CM 18
Boslelie Rd	Belhar	105	CD 46
Bosman	Paarl	22	BF 88
Bosman	Peerless Pk East	48	BR 59
Bosman	Stellenbosch	95	CB 77
Bosman Ave	Hout Bay	116	CL 14
Bosman St	Langgewacht	170	CW 72
Bosman St	Peerless Pk Nth	48	BQ 59
Bosman St	Soneike I	89	BZ 54
Bosman St	Soneike I	89	CA 54
Bosman St	The Palms	170	CX 72
Bosmandam Rd	Edgemead	58	BU 37
Bosmansdam Rd	Century City	58	BV 35
Bosmansdam Rd	Sanddrift	57	BV 33
Boso St	Victoria Mxenge	126	CN 51
Bosonia St	Bosonia	89	CB 54
Bostel Rd	Hanover Pk	122	CK 35
Boston	Ravensmead	87	CA 45
Boston Cir.	Airport Ind.	105	CE 43
Boston Pl.	Boston	61	BX 47
Boston Rd	Brown's Farm	123	CL 41
Boston St	Boston	61	BW 47
Boston St	Boston	61	BX 47
Boston St	Brackenfell	63	BW 56
Boston St	Factreton	84	BY 34
Boston St	Portlands (M.Plain)	144	CQ 46
Bosun Cl.	Pelikan Pk	141	CQ 34
Bosuns Cl.	Strandfontein	162	CT 40
Bosuns Rd	Strandfontein	162	CT 40
Bot St	Mfuleni	126	CK 53
Bot St	Mfuleni	126	CK 52
Bot St	Primrose Pk	103	CH 38
Bot Way	Delft	106	CG 48
Botany Steps	Bantry Bay	80	CB 18
Botfontein St	Wallacedene	64	BU 61
Botha Rd	Wynberg	120	CM 27
Botha St	Eastridge (M.Plain)	145	CQ 49
Botha St	Lemoenkloof	18	BB 88
Botha St	Mabille Pk	89	CA 53
Botha St	Richmond Est.	59	BX 40
Botha St	Richmond Est.	86	BY 41
Bothma St	Bothasig	58	BU 37
Bothma St	Monte Vista	59	BV 40
Bothman St	William Lloyd	19	BC 93
Bothmaskop St	Blue Downs	127	CJ 56
Bothwell Cl.	Tokai	139	CS 24
Bothwell Rd	Hazendal	102	CE 33
Botlelte Cr.	Delft	106	CG 49
Botlelte St	Mfuleni	126	CK 53
Botlelte St	Mfuleni	126	CK 52
Botma St	Retreat	159	CT 30
Botma St	Steenberg	159	CT 30
Botmaskop	Idasvallei	95	CB 78
Botmaskop	Idasvallei	96	CB 79
Botrivier Rd	Proteavallei	60	BT 46
Botrivier St	Tafelsig (M.Plain)	145	CS 47
Bottelary Rd	Annandale	90	BY 55
Bottelary Rd	Devondale Golf Est.	66	BV 67
Bottelary Rd	Hazendal	91	BY 59
Bottelary Rd	Kaymor	89	BY 53
Bottelary Rd	Koopmanskloof Noord	65	BV 64
Bottelary Rd	Scottsdene	64	BW 62
Bottelneus	Soneike II	89	BZ 53
Botterblom	Lentegeur (M.Plain)	144	CO 45
Botterblom Ave	Grassy Pk	141	CQ 32
Botterblom Cl.	Sonnekuil	89	BZ 53
Botterblom Cr.	Roosendaal	106	CF 50
Botterblom St	Bonteheuwel	104	CE 40
Botterblom St	Sonnekuil	89	BZ 53
Botterblom St	Sonnekuil	89	BY 54
Botterblom St	Vierlanden	30	BM 51
Botterblom St	Vierlanden	30	BM 52
Botterblom St	Vierlanden	30	BN 51
Botterboom	Delft Sth	125	CK 49
Botterboom Ave	New Orleans	19	BA 91
Botterkloof St	Tafelsig (M.Plain)	145	CS 49
Botterly St	Belhar	106	CD 49
Bottlebrush St	Lentegeur (M.Plain)	124	CN 46
Bottlebrush St	Proteavallei	60	BU 46
Bottom Rd	Pelikan Pk	141	CR 34
Bottoman Sineli St	Guguletu	104	CG 41
Boucher Rd	Durbanville	45	BQ 50
Bougaard St	Rabiesdale	19	BC 92
Bougainvilla St	Bongani	125	CN 49
Bougainvilla St	Mandalay	125	CN 48
Bougainvilla Rd	Newlands	101	CH 27
Bougainvillea Cl.	Skilpadvlei	45	BP 50
Bougainvillea St	Klein Nederburg	19	BC 93
Boulder Rd	Muizenberg Nth	159	CW 28
Boulevard Park	Hardekraaltjie	87	BY 46
Boum Rd	Avon	86	CA 41
Boundary Ave	Knole Pk	142	CO 36
Boundary Ave	Schaap Kraal	142	CO 38
Boundary Ave	Schaap Kraal	143	CP 40
Boundary Rd	Cravenby	87	CA 43
Boundary Rd	Des Hampden	89	CB 53
Boundary Rd	Green Point	81	BZ 22
Boundary Rd	Greenways	174	CZ 74
Boundary Rd	Lansdowne	121	CK 33
Boundary Rd	Meadowridge	140	CP 28
Boundary Rd	Milnerton	57	BX 31
Boundary Rd	Newlands	101	CG 29
Boundary Rd	Onverwacht	174	CZ 73
Boundary Rd	Retreat	140	CS 29
Boundary Rd	The Vines	140	CO 28
Boundary Rd	Townsend Est.	85	BZ 37
Bouquet St	Cape Town Cen.	82	CB 23
Bourbon St	Everglen	46	BS 51
Bourbon St	Paarl	22	BE 88
Bourgogne St	Oak Glen	62	BW 52
Bourn	Avon	86	CA 41
Bournemouth Bend	Parklands	25	BN 34
Bournemouth Rd	Muizenberg	159	CW 30
Boven Cl.	Morgenster Hoogte	63	BU 55
Boveney Rd	Muizenberg	159	CX 29
Bovlei St	Kleinbosch	59	BT 40
Bow Bend	Blouberg Sands	24	BM 30
Bowden Rd	Observatory	83	CC 29
Bowden Rd	Townsend Est.	85	BZ 38
Bower Rd	Wynberg	120	CM 28
Bower St	Brooklyn	84	BY 31
Bower St	Mandalay	125	CL 48
Bower St	Mandalay	125	CM 48
Bowler	Avon	86	CA 41
Bowlers Ave	Durbanville	45	BR 49
Bowlers Way	Pinelands	84	CC 34
Bowlers Way	Three Anchor Bay	81	BY 20
Bowspirit	Strandfontein	162	CT 41
Bowsprit St	Strandfontein	162	CT 41
Bowwood Rd	Claremont	120	CJ 27
Bowwood Rd	Claremont	120	CJ 28
Box Rd	Muizenberg	159	CX 30
Boxwood St	Bonteheuwel	104	CD 40
Boy Briers Rd	Fisantekraal	31	BK 58
Boy Briers Rd	Joostenberg	32	BN 59
Boy Briers Rd	Joostenberg	48	BO 60
Boy de Goede Cir.	Table View	41	BP 34
Boyce	Delft Sth	125	CJ 48
Boyce Ct	Delft Sth	125	CJ 48
Boyd Ave	Athlone	102	CF 33
Boyes Dr.	Kalk Bay	186	CZ 26
Boyes Dr.	Lakeside	159	CV 27
Boyes Dr.	Muizenberg	159	CX 28
Boyes Dr.	Muizenberg	159	CW 28
Boyes Dr.	St James	187	CZ 27
Boyle Cl.	Connaught	87	CB 43
Boyle Cr.	Belhar	88	CC 50
Boyne St	Manenberg	103	CH 38
Braam Fisher St	Mandela Pk	147	CQ 56
Braambos Cl.	Plattekloof	60	BV 43
Brabant Ct	Marina Da Gama	159	CV 29
Brabant Rd	Woodstock	83	CB 27
Brabigera St	Brackenfell Sth	63	BX 57
Bracken Cl.	Meadowridge	140	CP 27
Bracken Cr.	Somerset West	171	CX 77
Bracken St	Bonteheuwel	104	CD 39
Bracken St	Brackenfell	63	BV 56
Bracken St	Protea Hoogte	63	BW 57
Brackenfell Blvd	Morgen Gronde	63	BW 55
Brackenfell Blvd	Sonstraal Hgts	46	BS 54
Brackenfell Blvd	The Crest	30	BN 53
Brackenfell Blvd.	Welgelee	63	BT 55
Bradford Cl.	Airport Ind.	105	CF 43
Bradford Cl.	Parklands	41	BO 34
Bradford Cl.	Wembley Pk	107	CE 53
Bradley St	Elfindale	140	CQ 29
Bradwell Rd	Vredehoek	82	CC 23
Braeburn	Lindida	96	CA 80
Braefield Rd	Plumstead	120	CM 28
Braehead Rd	Kenilworth	120	CK 29
Braemar	Muizenberg	187	CY 28
Braemar Rd	Green Point	81	BZ 22
Braemar Rd	Oranjezicht	99	CD 22
Braeside	Green Point	81	BZ 21
Braeside Rd	Kenilworth	120	CK 29
Brahman St	Montana/Durrheim	104	CF 41
Brahms Cir.	Mandalay	125	CN 48
Brahms Cr.	Dalvale	19	AY 92
Brahms Dr.	Mandalay	125	CN 48
Brahms Rd	Retreat	159	CT 30
Brahms St	Kaapzicht	59	BW 40
Brahms St	Protea Hoogte	63	BW 57
Braille Rd	Belhar	88	CC 50
Brak Ct	Delft	106	CG 49
Brak St	Mfuleni	126	CK 53
Brakbos	Lentegeur (M.Plain)	144	CP 46
Bramah Pl.	Belhar	88	CC 50
Bramble Cl.	Belhar	106	CD 47
Bramble Way	Bonteheuwel	104	CD 39
Bramble Way	Bonteheuwel	104	CD 40
Bramble Way	Meadowridge	140	CP 27
Brambos Rd	Bonteheuwel	104	CD 40
Bramley	Sunningdale	24	BL 30
Bramley St	Plumstead	140	CO 30
Brampton Rd	Plumstead	120	CN 29
Brand Cir.	Hoogstede	62	BV 54
Brand Rd	Belgravia	102	CH 34
Brand Rd	Belgravia	103	CH 35
Brand St	Bellville Sth Ext. 5	88	BZ 49
Brand St	Brandwag	90	BZ 55
Brand St	Glencairn Hgts	191	DD 23
Brand St	Lochnerhof	170	CX 71
Brand St	Lochnerhof	170	CX 72
Brand St	Lochnerhof	174	CY 72
Brandberg	Wellington	15	AV 91
Brandberg	Wellington	15	AU 94
Brander Ave	Bloubergrant	24	BN 30
Brander Ave	Bloubergrant	40	BO 30
Brander Ave	Table View	40	BO 30
Brander Sq.	Factreton	85	BZ 35
Brandlelie Cl.	Roosendaal	106	CF 50
Brandon	Lotus River	142	CP 35
Brandon St	Hazendal	102	CF 33
Brands Hatch	Killarney Gdns	42	BP 36
Brandt Way	Ottery East	121	CN 34
Brandvlei Rd	Groenvallei	62	BX 53
Brandwacht	Brandwacht	113	CE 76
Brandwacht	Brandwacht	113	CE 77
Brandwacht St	Tafelsig (M.Plain)	145	CR 49
Brandwag Rd	Belhar	106	CE 50
Brandwag Rd	Durbanville Hills	45	BS 49
Brandwag Way	Eversdal	62	BT 51
Brandweer St	Gardens	82	CB 23
Brandwood Rd	Muizenberg Nth	159	CW 29
Brantwood Ave	Brantwood	89	CA 53
Brass St	Brackenfell Ind.	63	BU 56
Brassie St	Lakeside	159	CV 27
Bratton Way	West Beach	25	BN 31
Bravo St	Beacon Valley (M.Plain)	145	CQ 47
Bray Rd	Kenilworth	120	CK 30
Brazilia Ave	Monte Vista	59	BU 40
Brazilia St	Malibu Village	127	CL 55
Breakwater La.	Foreshore	82	BY 23
Breakwater La.	Harbour Island	179	DD 76
Bream Way	Nooitgedacht	104	CE 42
Breamar Rd	Parklands	25	BN 34
Breda St	Lemoenkloof	18	BC 89
Breda St	Oranjezicht	81	CC 22
Breda St	Ruyterwacht	86	CA 39
Breda St	Simon's Town	194	DJ 24
Bredell Rd	Somerset West	150	CQ 70
Bredell St	Mountainside Est.	179	DD 78
Brederivier Ave	Wingfield Nth Camp	58	BW 38
Bree St	Cape Town Cen.	81	CA 22
Bree St	Cape Town Cen.	82	CA 23
Bree St	Somerset West	171	CT 76
Bree St	Peerless Pk East	48	BR 59
Breë St	Peerless Pk Nth	48	BQ 59
Breede Ct	Delft	106	CG 49
Breede St	Eersterivier	128	CM 59
Breede St	Mfuleni	126	CJ 53
Breede St	Mfuleni	126	CK 53
Breederivier Cl.	Portlands (M.Plain)	144	CP 45
Breedt St	Wellington	10	AS 93
Breekhout St	Rouxville	90	CA 56
Breërivier St	Welgevonden	30	BN 54
Breërivier St	Welgevonden	30	BM 53
Breezand Rd	Eersterivier	128	CM 60
Breezand Rd	Tijgerhof	57	BV 33
Breitenbach St	Rosedale	128	CK 59
Bremen Cl.	Airport Ind.	105	CF 43
Bremer St	Tijgerhof	57	BW 32
Brenda Cl.	Lentegeur (M.Plain)	145	CO 48
Brenda Rd	Plumstead	120	CN 29
Brenda St	Kalkfontein II	107	CD 52
Brenda Way	Sonstraal Hgts	46	BS 54
Brenham	Highbury	107	CD 54
Brenham	Highbury	107	CG 53
Brenham Cl.	Courtrai	22	BH 87
Brent Rd	Plumstead	120	CN 29
Brentford	Beaconvale	87	CA 43
Brenton Cr.	Skilpadvlei	45	BP 49
Brentwood Rd	Parklands	25	BN 34
Brentwood Rd	Wynberg	120	CL 30
Bresee Rd	Belgravia	102	CG 34
Bresler	Beaconvale	87	CA 44
Breston Rd	Silvertown	103	CF 35
Bretagne Cl.	La Rochelle	62	BV 51
Breton Cl.	Hout Bay	117	CM 18
Breton Cr.	Dennemere	108	CH 57
Breton Cr.	Dennemere	108	CH 58
Breton Way	Northpine	63	BT 58
Brevet Rd	Claremont	102	CH 31
Brevity La.	Sea Point	80	CA 18
Brevity La.	Sea Point	80	CA 17
Brewery Rd	Greenways	174	DA 73
Breytenbach Cl.	Parow Nth	59	BX 42
Brian Rd	Bergvliet	140	CR 27
Brian Rd	Surrey	103	CH 38
Briana Rd	Elfindale	140	CQ 30
Briar Ave	Austinville	108	CH 56
Briar Cl.	Silverglade	185	DA 22
Briar Rd	Newlands	100	CH 26
Briar Rd	Salt River	83	CB 28
Briar Way	Meadowridge	140	CP 28
Briard	Strandfontein	162	CT 40
Briardene St	Klipkop	87	BZ 44
Brickfield Rd	Salt River	83	CC 27
Bridal Cl.	Bellville	61	BU 48
Bridekirk Way	Edgemead	59	BT 39
Bridge	Papegaaiberg Ind. Pk	95	CB 75
Bridge Cl.	Fairways	141	CO 31
Bridge Cl.	Montagu's Gift	141	CO 34
Bridge Pl.	Capricorn	160	CW 31
Bridge Rd	Bishop Lavis	105	CD 44
Bridge St	District Six	82	CB 26
Bridge St	Rosebank	101	CE 29
Bridge Way	Crawford	102	CG 33
Bridgette	Dalvale	19	AY 93
Bridgewater St	Paarden Eiland	83	CA 29
Bridgewater St	Somerset West	171	CV 75
Bridgitte Rd	De Tijger	60	BX 44
Bridgotte St	Casablanca	175	DB 76
Bridle	Jagtershof	90	CC 57
Bridle Cl.	Kenilworth Pk	121	CK 31
Bridle Rd	Oranjezicht	99	CD 22
Bridle St	Eikenbosch	90	CC 57
Bridle Way	Edgemead	59	BU 39
Bridle Way	Milnerton	57	BT 33
Bridle Way	Mitchells Plain	144	CR 45
Bridleside Way	Northpine	63	BU 58
Bridoon Cl.	Hout Bay	118	CN 19
Briffant St	Chantecler	62	BT 52
Brigade Rd	Lakeside	159	CV 27
Brigadier Cr.	Langeberg Rdg	47	BR 55
Brigantine Ave	Sun Valley	185	CZ 20
Bright St	Somerset West	170	CU 74
Brighton Cr.	Macassar	149	CR 63
Brighton Cr.	Malibu Village	127	CK 56
Brighton La.	Ottery	122	CM 35
Brighton Rd	Zoo Pk	47	BQ 57
Brighton St	Hout Bay	137	CQ 15
Brigid Rd	Elfindale	140	CP 30
Brink Cl.	Huis-in-bos	139	CO 24
Brink Cr.	Mandalay	125	CM 48
Brink La.	Hout Bay	117	CM 16
Brink Rd	Barbarossa	120	CN 27
Brink Rd	Hout Bay	137	CP 15
Brink Rd	Wynberg	120	CL 27
Brink St	Brantwood	89	CA 53
Brink St	Morgenster Hoogte	63	BT 56
Brink St	Welgemoed	61	BV 47
Brink St	Wellington	11	AR 95
Brinkhuis Rd	Sir Lowry's Pass	176	CZ 81
Brinton St	Langa	85	CC 35
Brinton St	Langa	85	CC 36
Briony Cl.	Meadowsteads	156	CX 18
Brisbane Rd	Eindhoven	106	CH 50
Brisbane Rd	Wynberg	120	CL 29
Bristleden Way	Northpine	63	BT 58
Bristol	Rocklands (M.Plain)	144	CS 45
Bristol Cl.	Avon	86	CA 41
Bristol Rd	Brown's Farm	124	CL 43
Bristol Rd	Observatory	83	CC 29
Bristol Rd	Philippi East	124	CL 46

STREET NAME	SUBURB NAME	PG	GRID	
Bristol Rd	Wynberg	120	CM	29
Britain Way	Strandfontein	162	CT	41
Britta Cl.	Mandalay	125	CN	47
Britten Rd	Retreat	140	CS	30
Britton La.	Harbour Island	179	DD	77
Briza Rd	Table View	40	BO	30
Briza Rd	Table View	41	BO	31
Briza Rd	Table View	41	BO	32
Briza Rd	Table View	41	BP	33
Briza St	Somerset West	170	CT	73
Broad Cl.	Wynberg	120	CL	29
Broad Oaks Cl.	Somerset West	152	CS	75
Broad Rd	Milnerton	57	BU	32
Broad Rd	Mowbray	101	CD	29
Broad Rd	Wynberg	120	CL	29
Broad Way	Guldenland	174	CZ	74
Broad Wk	Pinelands	84	CC	32
Broad Wk Sq.	Pinelands	84	CC	32
Broadlands Rd	Gustrow	174	DB	74
Broadlands Rd	Lwandle	175	DA	76
Broadlands Rd	Somerset West	151	CR	71
Broadway	Malibu Village	127	CK	56
Broadway Ave	Newlands	101	CH	27
Broadway Blvd	Die Bos	174	CY	74
Broadway Blvd	Somerset West	151	CP	71
Broadway Blvd	Tarentaalplaas	175	DA	75
Broadway Cir.	Weltevreden Val. (M.Plain)	144	CQ	43
Broadway Ext	Casablanca	175	DA	75
Broadway Gate	High Gate	107	CG	53
Broadway Rd	Helderzicht	170	CV	71
Broadway Rd	Park Estates	170	CW	71
Broadway Rd	Park Estates	170	CX	72
Broadway Rd	Scottsdene	64	BU	59
Broadway Rd	Somerset West	170	CT	72
Broadway St	Mountain View	19	BB	91
Broadway St	Vredelust	60	BX	46
Brocker Way	Tokai	139	CS	26
Brockhurst Rd	Lansdowne	121	CJ	32
Brockhurst Rd	Lansdowne	121	CK	33
Brockley Rd	Muizenberg	159	CX	29
Brockley Rd	Muizenberg	159	CW	27
Brodie Rd	Wynberg	120	CL	29
Broeksman Cr.	The Palms	170	CX	73
Bromelia Way	Tarentaalplaas	175	DA	76
Bromley Rd	Athlone	102	CF	34
Bromley Rd	Parklands	25	BN	33
Brommaert Ave	Alphen	119	CM	26
Brommaert Pl.	Alphen	119	CM	26
Brommersvlei Rd	Bel Ombre	119	CM	26
Brommersvlei Rd	Hohenort	119	CL	25
Brommersvlei Rd	Hohenort	119	CM	25
Brompton Ave	Bantry Bay	80	CB	18
Bromwell St	Woodstock	83	CB	27
Bromwich Rd	Westlake Est.	158	CU	25
Bromyard Rd	Muizenberg Nth	159	CW	29
Bronkhorst St	Parowvallei	87	CA	43
Bronnies Way	Dieprivier	140	CP	28
Bronze	Rocklands (M.Plain)	144	CS	46
Bronze St	Vanguard	103	CF	38
Broodboom	Delft Sth	125	CK	49
Broodboom St	Rouxville	90	CA	56
Brook Cr.	San Michel	157	CX	19
Brook Rd	Rosebank	101	CE	30
Brook St	Camps Bay	98	CF	17
Brook St	Claremont	120	CJ	28
Brook St	Foreshore	82	CB	25
Brookdale Ave	Pinelands	85	CB	35
Brookford Rd	Lotus River	141	CP	34
Brooklands Cr.	Northpine	64	BU	58
Brooks	Scottsdene	64	BT	61
Brooks Ave	Groenheuwel	19	BA	91
Brookside Cl.	Somerset West	171	CW	76
Brookside Manor Cr.	Somerset West	171	CW	76
Brookside St	Somerset West	171	CW	76
Brookwood Ave	Somerset West	171	CU	76
Brookwood Rd	Rondebosch	102	CF	31
Brounger Rd	Sillery	139	CO	25
Browne St	Eastridge (M.Plain)	145	CQ	49
Browning Rd	Observatory	83	CC	28
Browning St	Jagtershof	108	CD	57
Brownlow Rd	Tamboerskloof	81	CB	21
Brownsea Cl.	Edgemead	58	BU	37
Broxburn Rd	Plumstead	140	CO	30
Bruce Ave	Montagu's Gift	141	CO	34
Bruce Rd	Sillery	139	CO	25
Bruchsal Way	Silversands	107	CH	54
Bruckner	Delft Sth	125	CJ	48
Bruehl Way	Silversands	107	CH	54
Brug St	De Kuilen	89	CB	54
Brug St	Fairfield	60	BX	44
Brug St	Paarl	22	BF	88
Brug St	Somerset Pk	171	CW	75
Brug St	Triangle Farm	88	BZ	50
Brug St	Triangle Farm	89	BY	51
Brunel Cl.	Edgemead	58	BU	38
Brunhilde St	Loumar	89	BY	52
Brunia Rd	Hout Bay	118	CN	19
Brunia Way	Hout Bay	136	CO	13
Bruno St	Jagtershof	108	CD	57
Brunswick Rd	Tamboerskloof	81	CB	21
Brunswick St	Glencairn Hgts	191	DD	24
Brushwood Rd	Bridgetown	103	CF	36
Brussels Ave	Fish Hoek	186	DA	23
Brussels Cl.	Uitzicht	47	BO	55
Brut	Durmonte	30	BN	53
Brut Cl.	Klein Zevenwacht	90	CB	58
Brutus St	Somerset West	171	CW	77
Bruyns Rd	Wynberg	120	CM	29
Bryan St	Labiance	89	BZ	52
Bryant St	Schotsche Kloof	81	CB	22
Bryn Rd	Muizenberg Nth	159	CW	28
Buall Wk	Hanover Pk	122	CK	37
Bubele	Mbekweni	15	AW	92
Bubele	Mbekweni	15	AT	94
Buccaneer	Rocklands (M.Plain)	163	CT	46
Buccaneer	Wellington	15	AU	91
Buccaneer St	Macassar	168	CT	64
Buccaneer Way	Admirals Pk	179	DD	78
Buchan Rd	Newlands	101	CH	27
Buchan Steps	Simon's Town	191	DE	24
Buchanan Rd	Claremont	102	CH	31
Buchner Rd	Hazendal	102	CE	33
Buchu	Stellenbosch	95	BY	75
Buchu Cl.	Plattekloof	59	BU	42
Buchu Cl.	Somerset West	171	CW	77
Buck Rd	Lotus River	142	CP	35
Buck Rd	Pelikan Pk	142	CQ	35
Buck Rd	Pelikan Pk	142	CR	35
Buckingham Cl.	Tokai	139	CS	25
Buckingham Cl.	Tokai	139	CR	24
Buckingham Rd	Lansdowne	121	CJ	33
Buckingham Rd	Plumstead	120	CM	28
Buckingham Rd	Tokai	139	CS	25
Buckingham Way	Portlands (M.Plain)	145	CR	47
Buckingham Way	Weltevreden Val. (M.Plain)	143	CO	42
Buckley Rd	Athlone	102	CG	33
Buckley Rd	Athlone	102	CG	34
Bucksburn Rd	Newlands	101	CH	27
Bud Rd	Retreat	140	CS	28
Buddleia St	Somerset West	151	CS	71
Budock St	Claremont	101	CH	30
Buff Cl.	Scottsdene	64	BU	60
Buffalo Cr.	The Hague	106	CE	50
Buffalo Rd	Langeberg Rdg	47	BR	56
Buffalo Rd	Langeberg Rdg	47	BP	58
Buffalo Rd	Ocean View	184	DC	15
Buffalo Rd	Vygeboom	46	BR	51
Buffalo St	Eastridge (M.Plain)	145	CR	48
Buffalo St	Mfuleni	126	CJ	53
Buffalo Way	Primrose Pk	122	CJ	38
Buffelsberg	Bonnie Brae	47	BP	57
Buffelsberg	Bonnie Brae	47	BO	58
Buffelshoek	Durbanville Hills	45	BS	49
Buffelshoek St	Tafelsig (M.Plain)	145	CS	49
Buffelsrivier Ave	Welgevonden	30	BN	54
Bugle St	Jagtershof	108	CD	57
Buhlungu St	Brown's Farm	124	CL	43
Buick Cr.	Beacon Valley (M.Plain)	145	CQ	47
Buitekant St	Paarl	22	BF	89
Buitekant St	Wellington	15	AV	93
Buitekring	Dalsig	113	CD	75
Buitekring	Dalsig	113	CD	76
Buitekring	Dalsig	113	CE	76
Buiten Cr.	Scottsdene	64	BT	59
Buiten Cr.	Scottsdene	64	BT	60
Buiten Cr.	Scottsdene	64	BU	59
Buiten Cr.	Scottsdene	64	BU	60
Buiten St	Cape Town Cen.	81	CB	22
Buiten St	Schotsche Kloof	81	CA	22
Buitendag St	Monte Vista	59	BV	39
Buitengracht Dr.	Richwood	42	BQ	38
Buitengracht Rd	Belhar	106	CD	50
Buitengracht St	Cape Town Cen.	81	CA	22
Buitengracht St	Cape Town Cen.	82	BZ	23
Buitenkant St	Brackenfell	63	BW	55
Buitenkant St	Die Oude Spruit	63	BW	56
Buitenkant St	Die Oude Spruit	63	BX	56
Buitenkant St	District Six	82	CB	23
Buitenkant St	Vredehoek	82	CC	23
Buitensingle St	Cape Town Cen.	81	CB	22
Buitensorg St	Edgemead	58	BV	38
Buitenzor St	Dennemere	127	CJ	57
Buitenzor St	Dennemere	127	CN	55
Buitenzorg Rd	Somerset West	171	CT	75
Bukaneni	Mbekweni	15	AX	91
Buketraube Cl.	Oude Westhof	60	BT	44
Bukwana St	Lwandle	175	CZ	77
Bukwayo St	Harare	146	CR	53
Bula St	Victoria Mxenge	126	CN	51
Bulawayo	Portlands (M.Plain)	144	CR	46
Bulawayo Ave	Kenridge Hgts	45	BS	49
Bulbine St	Gordon Hgts	179	DD	78
Bulbinella Cl.	Dunoon	42	BO	37
Bulelani St	Dunoon	26	BN	38
Bulida	Die Boord	113	CE	75
Bulisa St	Harare	146	CS	53
Buller Louw Dr.	Sunnydale	185	CZ	19
Bullock	Northpine	63	BT	58
Bulrush Cl.	The Lakes	184	CZ	18
Bulrush St	Electric City	127	CM	58
Bulten Rd	Edgemead	58	BV	38
Bulties Way	Somerset West	171	CT	76
Bundoran St	Connaught	87	CB	43
Bungalow Dr.	Strandfontein	162	CU	42
Bunker Rd	Lakeside	159	CV	27
Bunkers Hill	Strandfontein	162	CT	41
Bunkers Hill	Strandfontein	162	CV	42
Bunney St	Kensington	84	BZ	34
Buntu	Mbekweni	15	AX	91
Buoy Bend	Blouberg Sands	24	BM	30
Burbank Dr.	Scottsdene	64	BU	60
Burbank St	Bellavista	18	BC	90
Burchel Cl.	Somerset West	171	CT	78
Burchell Rd	Tijgerhof	57	BX	32
Burchell St	Ruyterwacht	86	CA	40
Bureau St	Sack's Circle Ind.	89	CB	51
Buren Cr.	Stellenberg	62	BU	51
Buren La.	Belhar	106	CE	49
Buren La.	Tygerdal	59	BX	39
Buren Rd	Chapman's Peak	156	CX	17
Buren Rd	Wynberg	120	CL	27
Buren St	Avondale	60	BX	44
Buren St	Bothasig	58	BT	36
Buren St	Bothasig	58	BT	37
Burg Rd	Rondebosch	101	CE	29
Burg Rd	Rosebank	101	CE	29
Burg St	Cape Town Cen.	82	CA	23
Burg St	De La Haye	89	BY	51
Burg St	Macassar	149	CS	64
Burg St	Somerset West	170	CV	73
Burgandy Cl.	Richwood	42	BP	37
Burgandy Cl.	Richwood	42	BR	37
Burgee Bend	Marina Da Gama	159	CW	30
Burgee Bend	Strandfontein	162	CT	41
Burger Ave	Brackenfell	63	BV	56
Burger Rd	Rondebosch	102	CG	32
Burger St	Eastridge (M.Plain)	145	CQ	49
Burger St	Wellington	10	AR	93
Burgess Cl.	Sunset Beach	57	BT	31
Burggraaf Rd	Welcome	103	CF	38
Burgundy Cl.	La Rochelle	62	BV	51
Burgundy Cr.	Mitchells Plain	144	CR	45
Burgundy Rd	The Vines	140	CO	27
Burgundy St	Mitchells Plain	144	CS	45
Burgundy St	Mitchells Plain	144	CS	43
Burgundy St	Normandie	64	BW	59
Burke St	Observatory	83	CB	29
Burkea	Sack's Circle Ind.	88	CA	49
Burken St	Strandvale	170	CW	72
Burlington St	Oakdale	61	BW	49
Burma La.	Strandfontein	162	CT	40
Burmeister Cir.	Milnerton	57	BW	31
Burnam Rd	Observatory	83	CC	29
Burnard St	Park Estates	174	CY	71
Burnbrae Rd	Simon's Town	191	DD	24
Burnham Rd	Plumstead	120	CN	28
Burnham Rd	Plumstead	140	CO	28
Burning Sky	Fairyland	19	AZ	92
Burnley Cl.	Grassy Pk	141	CP	32
Burnley Rd	Crawford	102	CH	33
Burns Rd	Salt River	83	CB	28
Burns St	Wellington	15	AV	93
Burnside Rd	Tamboerskloof	81	CB	21
Burren Cl.	Connaught	87	CB	43
Bursa Way	Sunset Beach	41	BS	31
Burton Cl.	Ottery	122	CL	35
Burton La.	Fish Hoek	186	DB	24
Burton St	Aurora	45	BP	48
Burton St	Durbanville	45	BP	48
Burton St	Maitland	83	CA	30
Burton St	Winslow	175	DC	77
Burtondale St	Northpine	63	BU	58
Burtondale St	Northpine	64	BU	59
Burwood Rd	Crawford	102	CH	33
Burwood Rd	Crawford	121	CJ	33
Burwood Rd	Lansdowne	121	CJ	34
Bush Rd	Parkwood	141	CO	32
Bush St	Nyanga	124	CJ	43
Bushwood Rd	Mowbray	102	CD	31
Busira Ct	Delft	106	CG	49
Buso Cr.	Wallacedene	48	BS	61
Busy St	Strandfontein	162	CT	41
Bute Rd	Wynberg	120	CM	30
Buti Ave	Victoria Mxenge	126	CN	51
Buttercup	Macassar	148	CS	62
Buttermere Rd	Coniston Pk	159	CU	29
Buttress St	Tafelsig (M.Plain)	145	CR	48
Butts Ave	Thornton	85	CA	36
Buttskop Rd	Gaylee	108	CG	57
Buttskop Rd	Sunset Glen	108	CH	55
Buukbay Cl.	Mitchells Plain	144	CR	45
Buukbay Cl.	Mitchells Plain	144	CR	43
Buxton Ave	Gardens	81	CC	22
Buxton Ave	Ruyterwacht	86	CB	39
Buyambo	Mbekweni	15	AW	92
Buyani Cr.	Nonqubela	146	CO	53
Buza St	Harare	146	CR	53
Buzzard	Rocklands (M.Plain)	144	CS	44
Buzzard Cl.	Somerset West	152	CS	78
Buzzard Rd	Phumlani	142	CQ	36
Byrnes Ave	Wynberg	120	CL	29
Byron Rd	Hohelzen	61	BW	47
Byron Rd	Table View	42	BP	35
Byron Rd	Windsor Pk	47	BR	57
Byron St	Tamboerskloof	81	CB	21
Bywater St	Eersterivier	128	CM	59
Byway	Pinelands	84	CC	33
C				
C.Hani Ave	Hout Bay	137	CO	16
C.J. Langenhoven Rd	Townsend Est.	85	BY	38
C.J. Langenhoven St	Parow Nth	59	BW	41
C.J. Langenhoven St	Parow Nth	59	BW	42
C.J. Nabe Way	Langa	103	CD	36
C.L.Leipoldt St	Goodwood Est.	58	BX	38
C.Makhwethu Cr.	Mxolisi Phetani	125	CL	49
C.Zweni St	Mfuleni	126	CL	53
Cabarnet Cr.	Constantia Village	119	CN	25
Cabernet	Kleingeluk	113	CE	75
Cabernet	Langeberg Rdg	47	BR	55
Cabernet Ave	Somerset West	151	CS	72
Cabernet Cl.	Table View	41	BO	33
Cabernet Cl.	Vergesig	45	BQ	48
Cabernet Rd	Saxenburg Ind. Pk	108	CE	57
Cabernet Rd	Table View	41	BO	33
Cabernet Souvignon St	Oude Westhof	44	BS	45
Cabernet St	Normandie	64	BW	59
Cabernet St	Paarlzicht	19	BC	91
Cabin Cl.	Blouberg Sands	24	BM	30
Cable Cl.	Marina Da Gama	159	CW	29
Cableway St	Tafelsig (M.Plain)	145	CS	48
Cabot Way	Strandfontein	162	CT	41
Cabral St	Forest Glade	128	CL	59
Cabriere St	Franschhoek Sth	78	BZ	106
Cabriere St	Franschhoek Sth	79	BZ	107
Caclow	Schaap Kraal	122	CL	36
Cactus Cr.	Kewtown	103	CE	35
Cactus Cr.	Kewtown	103	CF	37
Cactus Rd	Blackheath Ind.	108	CF	57
Cactus St	Chapman's Peak	156	CX	16
Cactus St	Eversdal Hgts	46	BS	51
Cactus St	Kewtown	103	CE	35
Caddie St	Lakeside	159	CV	27
Cadiz St	Uitzicht	46	BO	54
Cadiz St	Uitzicht	47	BO	55
Cadotte St	Wesbank	107	CG	51
Caen Rd	Strandfontein	162	CT	40
Caernarvon Cr.	Parklands	25	BM	33
Caesar St	Woodstock	82	CB	26
Caesars Cl.	Weltevreden Val. (M.Plain)	144	CO	43
Caesars Dr.	Weltevreden Val. (M.Plain)	144	CO	43
Caeser Cl.	Somerset West	171	CV	77
Cain St	Grassy Pk	141	CQ	32
Caique Cl.	Sun Valley	185	DA	21
Cairn Cl.	Edgemead	59	BT	39
Cairn Cl.	Tafelsig (M.Plain)	145	CR	48
Cairn Steps	Clifton	80	CC	18
Cairn Steps	Simon's Town	191	DE	24
Cairnmount Ave	Gardens	99	CD	21
Cairo	Eersterivier	128	CN	60
Caithness Rd	Simon's Town	191	DE	24
Cala Cr.	Joe Slovo Pk	57	BV	34
Calais	Groenvlei	18	BA	88
Calais	Strandfontein	162	CT	40
Calais Cl.	Die Bos	174	CY	74
Calais Rd	Sea Point	81	BZ	20
Calais St	Wellington	11	AQ	95
Calanda Cr.	Victoria Mxenge	126	CN	51
Calcite Rd	Belthorn Est.	122	CJ	35
Calcium Rd	Vanguard	103	CG	37
Calcutta St	Paarden Eiland	83	BZ	29
Caleb St	Woodstock	82	CB	26
Caledon Cl.	Belhar	106	CE	50
Caledon Rd	Vygeboom	46	BR	51
Caledon St	Bellville Sth Ext. 5	88	BZ	49
Caledon St	Delft	106	CF	49
Caledon St	District Six	82	CB	23
Caledon St	District Six	82	CB	24
Caledon St	Mfuleni	126	CK	53
Caledon St	Panorama	59	BV	42
Caledon St	Portlands (M.Plain)	145	CR	47
Caledon St	Somerset West	171	CU	75
Caledon St	Townsend Est.	85	BY	37
Caledon St	Townsend Est.	85	BZ	38
Caledonian Rd	Mowbray	101	CD	30
Calendula	Dalvale	19	AY	91
Calendula	Dalvale	19	AZ	94
Calendula	Lentegeur (M.Plain)	144	CO	46
Calendula Rd	Silvertown	103	CF	35
Calgary Cr.	Wesbank	107	CF	52
Callalelie St	Roosendaal	107	CF	51
Callington Cr.	Parklands	25	BM	34
Callisto Rd	Ocean View	189	DD	15
Calpe Cl.	Woodbridge Island	57	BW	31
Calula St	Umrhabulo Triangle	147	CR	56
Calvin St	Woodstock	82	CB	26
Calvinia St	Ruyterwacht	86	BZ	39
Calvyn Rd	Kingston	61	BX	49
Calvyn St	Rome	170	CX	73
Calypso Sq.	Mitchells Plain Cen.	145	CQ	47
Calypso Way	Anchorage Pk	175	DC	77
Calypso Way	Anchorage Pk	175	DB	78
Cam	Somerset West	151	CQ	71
Cam Rd	Manenberg	123	CJ	39
Camagu	Mbekweni	15	AW	92
Camargue	Groenvlei	18	BA	88
Camargue Rd	West Riding	41	BO	34
Cambelton Cr.	Parklands	25	BN	34
Camberwell Rd	Belgravia	102	CH	34
Camberwell Rd	Crawford	102	CH	33
Camberwell Rd	Crawford	102	CH	34
Camberwell Rd	Three Anchor Bay	81	BZ	20
Cambier Way	Bergvliet	139	CP	26
Cambra Verdun Way	Strandfontein	162	CT	40
Cambridge	Parklands	41	BO	33
Cambridge Ave	Tamboerskloof	81	CB	21
Cambridge Cl.	Villa Italia	57	BW	33
Cambridge Link	Norwood	86	CA	41
Cambridge Pl.	Durbanville	46	BP	51
Cambridge Rd	Lakeside	159	CV	28

Index to Street Names

STREET NAME	SUBURB NAME	PG	GRID
Cambridge Rd	Observatory	83	CC 29
Cambridge St	Claremont	120	CJ 29
Cambridge St	Helderberg Pk	175	DA 75
Cambridge St	Maitland	83	CB 30
Cambridge St	Portlands (M.Plain)	145	CR 47
Cambridge St	Richmond Est.	59	BX 40
Cambridge St	Richmond Est.	86	BY 40
Cambridge St	Richmond Est.	86	BY 41
Cambridge St	Woodstock	82	CC 25
Camdebo St	Loevenstein	60	BV 46
Camdeboo Cr.	Delft	106	CG 49
Camdeboo Cr.	Delft	106	CG 50
Camden Cl.	Skilpadvlei	45	BP 49
Camden St	Brooklyn	83	BZ 30
Camden St	Maitland	84	CA 32
Camden St	Tamboerskloof	81	CB 21
Camden Way	Dennemere	108	CH 57
Camden Way	Noordhoek Manor	157	CX 21
Camden Way	Noordhoek Manor	157	CV 20
Camden Wk	Parklands	25	BN 34
Camel Rock Rd	Scarborough	192	DJ 17
Camel Thorn	Eersterivier	128	CN 61
Camelia	Lentegeur (M.Plain)	144	CO 46
Camelia St	Mandalay	125	CN 48
Camelia Way	Belhar	105	CD 46
Camelia Way	Belhar	105	CE 45
Camelia Way	Wellway Pk East	46	BP 52
Camellia Cl.	Bergvliet	140	CQ 28
Camellia Cr.	Bellair	62	BV 53
Camellia St	Bonteheuwel	103	CD 38
Camellia St	Bonteheuwel	104	CD 39
Camellia St	Forest Village	127	CM 58
Camellia St	Klein Nederburg	19	BC 94
Camellia St	Somerset West	151	CS 71
Camelot	Sonstraal Hgts	46	BR 54
Cameron St	Belgravia	102	CH 34
Cameronians Ave	Door De Kraal	61	BU 47
Cameroon Ct	Delft	106	CF 50
Camilla St	Glencairn Hgts	191	DD 24
Camille Cl.	Dennemere	108	CH 57
Camoens Ave	Edgemead	58	BV 38
Camoens Ave	Monte Vista	59	BV 39
Camp	Strandfontein	162	CU 41
Camp Access Rd	Youngsfield	121	CL 31
Camp Ground Rd	Claremont	101	CG 29
Camp Ground Rd	Mowbray	101	CE 30
Camp Ground Rd	Rondebosch	101	CE 30
Camp Ground Rd	Rondebosch	101	CG 29
Camp Ground Rd	Rosebank	101	CE 30
Camp Rd	Maitland	83	CB 30
Camp Rd	Misty Cliffs	189	DH 16
Camp Rd	Muizenberg	159	CX 29
Camp Rd	Pinelands	84	CB 32
Camp Rd	Wynberg	120	CL 28
Camp Rd	Wynberg	120	CK 30
Camp Rd	Wynberg	120	CL 28
Camp St	Oranjezicht	81	CC 22
Campbell La.	Somerset West	171	CU 77
Campbell Rd	Hout Bay	137	CP 16
Campbell St	Observatory	83	CC 28
Campdon	Eersterivier	128	CN 61
Campground Rd	Newlands	101	CG 29
Camphill	Strandfontein	163	CT 43
Camphor	Eersterivier	128	CM 61
Camphor La.	Bergvliet	140	CQ 27
Camphor Rd	Kommetjie	183	DB 13
Camphor St	Bellair	62	BW 53
Camphor St	Forest Village	127	CM 58
Camps Bay Dr.	Camps Bay	98	CF 18
Camps Bay Dr.	Camps Bay	99	CE 19
Campus Cr.	Rondebosch	101	CE 29
Campus St	Somerset West	171	CV 77
Canal Cl.	Kraaifontein	47	BP 57
Canal Cr.	Whispering Pines	175	DC 75
Canal Dr.	Eersterivier	127	CL 58
Canal Rd	Belgravia	103	CG 35
Canal Rd	Ottery	121	CL 33
Canal Rd	Retreat	140	CR 30
Canary	Rocklands (M.Plain)	144	CS 44
Canary Cr.	Sunridge	41	BP 34
Canary St	Joostenberg	48	BP 59
Canary St	Ocean View	184	DC 15
Canary St	Penlyn Est.	103	CH 36
Canberra Cir.	The Hague	106	CE 49
Cancer Rd	Joe Slovo Pk	57	BU 33
Canda Cr.	Victoria Mxenge	126	CN 51
Candelabra	Stellenbosch	95	BY 75
Candian St	Strandfontein	163	CT 43
Candice	Dalvale	19	AY 93
Candlewood Cl.	Hout Bay	118	CN 19
Candlewood St	Bonteheuwel	103	CD 38
Cando	Wesbank	107	CF 52
Candytuft St	Lentegeur (M.Plain)	144	CO 46
Cane Rd	Ottery	121	CL 33
Cane Rd	Ottery	121	CM 33
Canigou Ave	Rondebosch	101	CF 30
Canna	Lentegeur (M.Plain)	145	CP 47
Canna	Macassar	149	CR 63
Canna St	Retreat	140	CR 28
Cannery Cl.	Kommetjie	183	DB 13
Cannery Row	Bishopscourt	119	CK 26
Cannes St	Uitzicht	31	BN 56
Cannon Cl.	Belhar	106	CE 49
Cannon Cl.	Newlands	100	CG 26
Cannon Island Way	Capricorn	160	CW 31
Cannon Island Way	Marina Da Gama	159	CW 30
Cannon Rd	Croydon	149	CP 63
Cannon Rd	Maitland	83	CB 30
Cannon St	Newlands	100	CG 26
Cannon St	Plumstead	140	CO 29
Canoe Cr.	Strandfontein	161	CU 38
Canon Cl.	Hout Bay Harbour	136	CR 13
Canterbury	Anesta	113	CF 75
Canterbury Cl.	Belhar	106	CE 50
Canterbury Cr.	Table View	41	BO 34
Canterbury Dr.	Bishopscourt	119	CK 25
Canterbury Dr.	Bishopscourt	119	CK 26
Canterbury Rd	Heathfield	140	CQ 29
Canterbury Rd	Highbury	107	CE 53
Canterbury St	District Six	82	CB 23
Canterbury St	Eureka	87	CC 43
Canterbury St	Highbury	107	CE 54
Canterbury St	Kingston	61	BX 49
Canterbury St	Oakdale	61	BX 48
Cantor St	Courtrai	39	BJ 87
Canvadahof	Lindida	96	CA 80
Canyon St	Riverton	86	BZ 40
Canzibe	Mbekweni	15	AV 91
Cap Michel Cl.	Muizenberg	159	CX 29
Cape Beech Rd	Noordhoek	156	CW 18
Cape Flats Freeway	Delft Sth	125	CK 49
Cape Flats Freeway	Mandalay	124	CN 46
Cape Flats Freeway	Mandalay	125	CM 47
Cape Flats Freeway	Weltevreden Val. (M.Plain)	123	CN 42
Cape Flats Freeway	Woodlands (M.Plain)	124	CN 44
Cape Heritage Cr.	Somerset West	171	CW 76
Cape Verde Dr.	Bloubergstrand	24	BM 29
Capella Ave	Ocean View	183	DC 14
Capital Dr.	Thembokwezi	125	CM 49
Capital Pl.	Thembokwezi	125	CM 49
Capitol La.	Wynberg	120	CL 29
Capitol La.	Wynberg	120	CK 30
Capri	St James	187	CZ 27
Capri Cl.	Capri	185	DB 19
Capri Dr.	Capri	184	DB 18
Capri Dr.	Capri	185	DA 19
Capri Dr.	Capri	185	DB 19
Capri Ter.	Capri	185	DB 19
Capri Way	Strandfontein	163	CT 43
Capricorn	Rocklands (M.Plain)	144	CS 45
Capricorn Blvd. North	Capricorn	160	CV 31
Capricorn Blvd. South	Capricorn	160	CW 32
Capricorn Cr.	Capricorn	160	CV 31
Capricorn Dr.	Capricorn	160	CV 31
Capricorn Dr.	Capricorn	160	CW 31
Capricorn Rd	Ocean View	189	DD 15
Capricorn Way	Joe Slovo Pk	57	BU 33
Capron	Rocklands (M.Plain)	144	CS 45
Capstan Cl.	Marina Da Gama	159	CV 29
Capuchin St	Athlone	102	CF 33
Carabinier Rd	Wynberg	120	CL 30
Cara-Cara Rd	Phumlani	142	CQ 36
Caracas St	Malibu Village	127	CL 55
Caracas St	Malibu Village	127	CL 56
Caravel Rd	Strandfontein	162	CU 39
Caravel Rd	Sun Valley	185	CZ 20
Caravelle	Rocklands (M.Plain)	144	CS 46
Caravelle	Rocklands (M.Plain)	145	CS 47
Caravelle	Rocklands (M.Plain)	163	CT 46
Caraway St	Sunset Glen	107	CH 54
Carbis	Malibu Village	127	CK 56
Carbis	Malibu Village	127	CN 55
Carbon St	Primrose Pk	122	CJ 38
Carbrook Ave	Claremont	120	CJ 28
Cardamon Ave	Sunset Glen	107	CH 54
Cardiff Cl.	Portlands (M.Plain)	144	CR 46
Cardiff Rd	Simon's Town	194	DJ 24
Cardiff St	Cape Town Cen.	82	BZ 23
Cardiff St	Newlands	101	CG 27
Cardiff St	Uitzicht	47	BO 56
Cardinal	Wellington	15	AU 91
Cardinal Cl.	Chapman's Peak	156	CX 17
Carditta Cir.	Sunset Beach	41	BS 32
Cardross Grant St	Cafda Village	141	CS 31
Carel Marincowitz St	Brackenfell Ind.	63	BT 58
Carey Cl.	Adriaanse	87	CC 43
Carey Slater Rd	Townsend Est.	85	BY 38
Carey St	Woodstock	83	CB 27
Cariad Rd	Ottery	121	CL 33
Carigman La.	Westlake	159	CU 27
Carinus	Beaconvale	87	CA 43
Carinus St	De Kuilen	89	CB 54
Carinus St	Labiance	89	BZ 51
Carinus St	Labiance	89	BZ 52
Carisbrook	Uitzicht	46	BO 54
Carisbrook Cl.	Blouberg Rise	24	BN 30
Carisbrook Cl.	Northpine	63	BU 58
Carisbrook St	Gardens	81	CB 22
Carisbrook St	Tamboerskloof	81	CB 22
Carissa Cir.	Ottery East	121	CN 34
Carissa Cl.	Die Oude Spruit	63	BX 56
Carissa Cl.	Plattekloof	60	BV 43
Carissa St	Eversdal Hgts	45	BS 50
Carissa St	Loevenstein	60	BV 46
Carissa St	Ottery	121	CN 33
Carissa St	Somerset West	151	CR 72
Carl Cr.	Soneike I	89	CA 54
Carl Cronje Dr.	Bellville	61	BV 48
Carl St	Schotsche Kloof	81	CA 22
Carl van Aswegen	Bellville	88	BY 48
Carla Cl.	Dalvale	19	AY 93
Carla Cl.	Dalvale	19	BA 94
Carletta St	Lemoenkloof	18	BC 87
Carlier Cr.	Penlyn Est.	122	CJ 35
Carlier St	Highbury	107	CE 54
Carlisle Cl.	West Beach	24	BN 29
Carlisle Rd	Kirstenhof	159	CT 27
Carlisle St	Maitland	84	CA 31
Carlisle St	Paarden Eiland	83	BZ 29
Carlisle St	Paarden Eiland	83	CA 29
Carlisle St	Somerset West	170	CW 72
Carlow Rd	Wynberg	120	CL 30
Carlton Cl.	Sunnydale	185	CZ 19
Carlton Cr.	Parklands	25	BN 33
Carlton Pl.	Parklands	25	BM 33
Carlton Rd	Fish Hoek	186	DA 24
Carlton Rd	Sunnydale	185	CZ 19
Carlton St	Claremont	120	CJ 30
Carlton St	Grassy Pk	141	CR 31
Carlton Zondo St	Kuyasa	147	CS 56
Carmen Cr.	Tafelsig (M.Plain)	145	CR 49
Carmen End	Belhar	88	CC 49
Carmen St	Eastridge (M.Plain)	145	CQ 48
Carmen St	Scottsdene	64	BT 59
Carmen St	Wellington	10	AS 92
Carmichael Rd	Fish Hoek	185	DA 21
Carmichael Rd	Fish Hoek	185	DB 22
Carnaby St	Parklands	25	BM 33
Carnaby St	Weltevreden Val. (M.Plain)	123	CN 42
Carnarvon Cl.	West Beach	24	BN 29
Carnarvon Rd	Plumstead	120	CN 28
Carnarvon St	Ruyterwacht	86	CA 39
Carnation	Dunoon	42	BO 37
Carnation	Dunoon	42	BO 36
Carnation	Lentegeur (M.Plain)	144	CO 46
Carnation	Macassar	149	CR 63
Carnation Ave	Uitsig	87	CC 44
Carnation Cl.	Hanover Pk	122	CJ 36
Carnation Cl.	Skilpadvlei	45	BP 50
Carnation Rd	Ocean View	184	DC 15
Carnation Rd	Ocean View	184	DC 15
Carnation Sq.	Bridgetown	103	CE 36
Carnation St	Hillcrest Hgts	127	CL 57
Carnation St	Peerless Pk East	63	BT 57
Carnation St	Ravensmead	87	CB 46
Carnegie St	Weltevreden Val. (M.Plain)	144	CQ 43
Carney Cl.	Connaught	87	CB 43
Carnie Rd	Doornhoogte	103	CG 36
Carnoustie	Sunningdale	25	BM 32
Carob Cr.	Loevenstein	60	BW 45
Carol Anne Way	Voorbrug	126	CJ 51
Carol Cl.	Bellville	61	BT 50
Carol Cr.	Lentegeur (M.Plain)	145	CO 48
Carol St	Beacon Valley (M.Plain)	145	CP 48
Carol St	Beacon Valley (M.Plain)	145	CP 50
Carol St	Lentegeur (M.Plain)	145	CO 48
Carol St	Retreat	140	CS 29
Carola Way	Montagu's Gift	141	CP 33
Carolina Ave	Colorado (M.Plain)	144	CO 44
Carolina St	Athlone	102	CF 34
Carolina St	Denneburg	23	BD 91
Carp Cl.	Marina Da Gama	159	CU 29
Carp Rd	Nooitgedacht	104	CE 42
Carp Rd	Pelikan Pk	141	CR 33
Carr Hill Rd	Wynberg	120	CL 28
Carra Cl.	Connaught	87	CB 43
Carra St	Connaught	87	CB 43
Carradale Rd	Sunningdale	25	BM 31
Carreg Cr.	Green Point	81	BZ 22
Carriage St	Woodstock	83	CA 29
Carrick Rd	Newfields	103	CH 36
Carrick St	Highbury	107	CE 54
Carriem	Cloetesville	95	BZ 75
Carrier	Epping Ind.	86	CC 40
Carrington	Belhar	105	CD 45
Carrington Ave	Athlone	102	CF 33
Carrol Rd	Montagu's Gift	141	CO 34
Carrol Rd	Ottery East	121	CN 34
Carronnade Cr.	Oude Westhof	60	BT 44
Carrowmore Cr.	Connaught	87	CB 43
Carrwell St	Highbury	107	CE 54
Carson Ave	Athlone	102	CF 33
Carstens	Parow	86	BZ 42
Carstens St	Tamboerskloof	81	CB 21
Carstens St	Wellington	10	AR 91
Carter Rd	Retreat	141	CR 31
Cartier	Durbanville	45	BR 49
Caruso La.	Belhar	106	CD 48
Carwell Rd	Lansdowne	121	CK 34
Cas St	Brandwag	90	BZ 55
Casa Bello Cr.	The Crest	46	BO 53
Casa Lingo Rd	Eversdal Hgts	46	BS 51
Casa Mia	Durbanville	46	BP 51
Casalino Cr.	Welgedacht	44	BS 46
Cascade St	Tafelsig (M.Plain)	145	CR 48
Cashel Ave	Athlone	102	CG 34
Casino	Strandfontein	162	CT 40
Casino St	Weltevreden Val. (M.Plain)	144	CO 43
Casper Ave	Ottery East	121	CN 34
Caspian Cl.	Eersterivier	128	CM 59
Cassandra Rd	Pinati	122	CK 35
Cassandra Rd	Pinati	122	CN 36
Cassel Rd	Sea Point	80	CA 18
Cassia Cl.	Vredenberg	62	BV 53
Cassia Link	Belhar	105	CD 45
Cassia Rd	Harbour Island	175	DC 75
Cassia Rd	Ottery	121	CN 33
Cassia Rd	Uitsig	87	CC 44
Cassia St	Bonteheuwel	103	CD 38
Cassies Rd	Casablanca	175	DB 76
Cassies Way	Gordon Strand	175	DC 75
Cassino Rd	Plumstead	140	CO 30
Cassino Rd	Plumstead	141	CO 31
Cassius Cr.	Somerset West	171	CV 77
Cassius Make St	Mandela Pk	147	CQ 55
Castille Dr.	Somerset West	151	CS 73
Castle	Dunoon	42	BO 37
Castle Bar Cl.	Parklands	25	BN 33
Castle Cl.	Summerville	48	BS 59
Castle La.	Belhar	106	CD 49
Castle St	Cape Town Cen.	82	CA 23
Castle St	Lemoenkloof	18	BC 89
Castleman Rd	Fish Hoek	185	DA 21
Castleton Way	Edgemead	58	BV 38
Castletown Rd	Plumstead	120	CM 29
Castletown Rd	Wynberg	120	CM 29
Castleview Rd	Meadowridge	139	CO 26
Castor	Fairdale	126	CJ 54
Castor Rd	Lansdowne	121	CJ 34
Castor Way	Ocean View	183	DC 14
Catalan Cl.	Northpine	63	BU 58
Catalina	Rocklands (M.Plain)	144	CS 46
Catalina Cr.	Capri	185	DA 19
Catalina St	The Hague	106	CE 49
Catamaran Cl.	Sun Valley	185	CZ 20
Catamaran Cl.	Sun Valley	185	DC 22
Catamaran Cr.	Strandfontein	162	CV 42
Catamaran Cr.	Strandfontein	162	CT 39
Catamaran Rd	Strandfontein	162	CT 39
Catharina Ave	Steenberg	139	CS 24
Catharina Ave	Steenberg	158	CT 24
Cathcart Rd	Kenridge	45	BS 49
Cathcart St	Ruyterwacht	86	CB 39
Cathedral Cr.	Tafelsig (M.Plain)	164	CT 48
Cathedral Peak Cr.	Heideveld	104	CG 40
Cathedral Rd	Manenberg	104	CG 39
Cathkin Cr.	Tafelsig (M.Plain)	164	CT 48
Cathkin Peak Rd	Heideveld	104	CG 40
Cathkin Rd	Heideveld	104	CF 39
Cathy Cl.	Weltevreden Val. (M.Plain)	124	CN 44
Cats Link	Tarentaalplaas	174	CZ 74
Cauca St	Eindhoven	107	CH 51
Cauvin Cl.	Belhar	106	CE 50
Cauvin Rd	District Six	82	CC 25
Cavalcade Rd	Green Point	81	BZ 22
Cavalla Cr.	Eersterivier	128	CN 59
Cavalla Ct	Delft	106	CH 49
Cavalleria St	Scottsdene	64	BT 60
Cavalry Cr.	Ottery East	121	CN 33
Cavalry Rd	Mitchells Plain	144	CR 44
Cavan Cl.	Wynberg	120	CL 28
Cavan Rd	Wynberg	120	CL 28
Cavell Rd	Lansdowne	122	CL 35
Cavemore Rd	Lansdowne	121	CK 34
Cavendish Pl.	Claremont	101	CH 28
Cavendish Rd	Claremont	101	CH 28
Cavendish Sq.	Woodstock	82	CB 26
Cavendish St	Woodstock	82	CB 26
Cavernelis St	Wellington	15	AT 92
Cavesson	Jagtershof	90	CC 57
Cawood Cir.	Wellington	15	AV 92
Caxton Cl.	Meadowridge	140	CP 28
Caxton Cr.	Meadowridge	140	CP 28
Caxton St	Foreshore	82	CB 25
Caxton St	Parow East	87	BY 45
Caxton Way	Meadowridge	140	CP 27
Caxton Way	Meadowridge	140	CP 28
Cayalli	Delft Sth	125	CK 48
Cayenne Cl.	Capri	185	DB 19
Cayenne Cl.	Capri	185	DC 22
Cayley Link	Belhar	88	CC 50
Ceba St	Umrhabulo Triangle	147	CR 56
Cebani St	Bloekombos	48	BR 62
Cebula St	Umrhabulo Triangle	147	CQ 58
Cecelia Way	Matroosfontein	86	CC 42
Cecelo Cr.	Victoria Mxenge	146	CO 51
Cecil Morgan Dr.	Morgen Gronde	63	BX 55
Cecil Morgan Dr.	Morgen Gronde	89	BY 54
Cecil Morgan Way	Kaymor	89	BY 53
Cecil Ngxito St	Kuyasa	147	CS 55
Cecil Rd	Mowbray	101	CE 29
Cecil Rd	Plumstead	120	CN 29
Cecil Rd	Salt River	83	CC 28
Cecil Rhodes Ave	Ruyterwacht	86	BZ 40
Cecil St	Claremont	101	CH 29
Cecil St	Hout Bay	136	CP 14
Cecil St	Hout Bay	137	CP 15
Cecilia Cl.	Belle Constantia	139	CP 26
Cecilia Ct	Edgemead	59	BT 39
Cecilia Rd	Chrismar	61	BW 50
Cecilia Rd	Chrismar	61	BX 50
Cecilia St	KWV	22	BF 88
Cecilia St	KWV	22	BG 89
Cecilia Way	Northpine	64	BU 59
Cedar Ave	New Orleans	19	BA 91
Cedar Ave	Pinelands	84	CC 34
Cedar Ave	Westlake Est.	158	CT 24
Cedar Ave	Westlake Est.	158	CT 26
Cedar Cl.	Hanover Pk	122	CK 36
Cedar Cl.	Hanover Pk	122	CN 36

Index to Street Names

Cedar Cl. — Consort Rd

STREET NAME	SUBURB NAME	PG	GRID	
Cedar Cl.	Hout Bay	118	CM	19
Cedar Cl.	Mitchells Plain	144	CQ	45
Cedar Pl.	Weltevreden Val. (M.Plain)	143	CO	42
Cedar Rd	Bellair	62	BW	51
Cedar Rd	Forest Village	127	CM	58
Cedar Rd	Newlands	101	CG	27
Cedar Rd	Thornton	85	CA	36
Cedar Rd	Weltevreden Val. (M.Plain)	143	CO	42
Cedar St	Belhar	105	CD	46
Cedarberg	Brackenfell	63	BW	55
Cedarberg Rd	Eversdal	61	BU	50
Cedarberg Rd	Eversdal	61	BV	48
Cedarberg Rd	Lavender Hill East	160	CU	32
Cedarberg Rd	Ocean View	184	DC	15
Cedarberg St	Durbanville Hills	45	BS	49
Cedarberg St	Tafelsig (M.Plain)	145	CS	50
Cedarwood St	Sonstraal Hgts	46	BQ	54
Cederberg St	Greenfield	108	CH	57
Cederberg St	Ruyterwacht	86	CA	39
Cedile	Kayamandi	94	BZ	74
Cekeka Rd	Umrhabulo Triangle	147	CQ	57
Cekeka Rd	Umrhabulo Triangle	147	CQ	57
Cekiso Cr.	Victoria Mxenge	126	CN	51
Cela Cl.	Umrhabulo Triangle	147	CQ	58
Cele St	Victoria Mxenge	146	CO	51
Celebes	Rocklands (M.Plain)	144	CS	45
Celebes St	Bloubergstrand	24	BJ	27
Celeste	Dalvale	19	AY	93
Celeste	Dalvale	19	BA	94
Celie Rd	Retreat Ind. Area	159	CT	28
Celiwe	Mbekweni	15	AV	91
Celizapholo	Mbekweni	15	AX	91
Cella St	Athlone	102	CF	33
Cello St	Belhar	106	CD	48
Celtis Cl.	Greenlands	88	CA	49
Celu	Philippi East	124	CM	46
Centaur Cl.	Ocean View	189	DD	16
Centaur St	Strandfontein	163	CT	43
Centaur St	Strandfontein	163	CT	44
Centaurus Rd	Blue Downs	127	CJ	56
Centaurus Rd	Eersterivier	128	CN	60
Centivres Cr.	Blouberg Rise	25	BN	31
Central Ave	Belthorn Est.	121	CJ	34
Central Ave	Pinelands	84	CC	32
Central Ave	Pinelands	102	CD	32
Central Ave	Wallacedene	48	BS	61
Central Cir.	Fish Hoek	186	DB	24
Central Dr.	Camps Bay	98	CE	18
Central Dr.	Northpine	63	BU	58
Central Dr. East	Glenhaven	89	CA	52
Central Dr. North	Glenhaven	89	CA	52
Central Dr. South	Bellville Sth Ind.	89	CA	51
Central Dr. West	Glenhaven	89	CA	51
Central Rd	Fish Hoek	186	DB	24
Central Rd	Sunset Beach	41	BR	31
Central Sq.	Pinelands	84	CC	32
Centre Cl.	Montagu's Gift	141	CO	33
Century Ave	Century City	58	BV	35
Century Blvd	Century City	57	BX	34
Century Blvd	Century City	57	BW	34
Century Blvd	Century City	58	BW	35
Century Cir.	Villa Italia	57	BW	33
Century Dr.	Villa Italia	57	BW	33
Century Gr.	Villa Italia	57	BW	33
Cephe Cr.	Harare	146	CS	53
Cephe Cr.	Harare	146	CS	52
Ceres Cl.	La Rochelle	62	BV	51
Ceres Cl.	Portlands (M.Plain)	144	CR	46
Ceres Rd	Bergvliet	139	CQ	26
Ceres Rd	Milnerton	57	BW	32
Ceres St	Brooklyn	83	BZ	30
Ceres St	Forest Glade	127	CK	58
Ceres St	Panorama	59	BV	41
Ceres St	Park Village	127	CK	58
Ceresa Cl.	Table View	41	BP	33
Ceresa Cr.	Northpine	64	BT	59
Cerise Rd	Parkwood	141	CP	32
Ceru Rd	Brown's Farm	124	CL	43
Cess Ct	Delft	106	CF	49
Cessna	Rocklands (M.Plain)	163	CT	46
Cessna Cr.	Kensington	84	BZ	33
Cessna St	The Hague	106	CE	49
Cestrum	Eversdal Hgts	45	BS	50
Cetus Way	Ocean View	184	DC	15
Cetwayo St	Tarentaalplaas	175	CY	75
Ceylon St	Bothasig	58	BT	38
Cezela St	Harare	146	CS	54
Chad Cl.	Portlands (M.Plain)	144	CQ	45
Chad Rd	Retreat	140	CR	28
Chad Way	Nooitgedacht	104	CE	42
Chadwin Rd	Elfindale	140	CP	29
Chaffinch	Dreyersdal	139	CS	26
Chaffinch Rd	Sunridge	41	BP	34
Chaim St	Montana/Durrheim	104	CF	41
Chain Ave	Montague Gdns Ind.	58	BU	35
Chalaise Ave	Vredekloof	62	BX	52
Chalbre Cr.	Somerset West	151	CQ	72
Chaldon Way	Pinelands	84	CA	34
Chalet Ct	Rocklands (M.Plain)	144	CS	45
Chalfont Rd	Claremont	101	CH	29
Chamberlain Ave	Claremont	101	CH	27
Chamberlain Rd	Churchill	59	BX	41
Chamberlain Rd	Glenlily	86	BY	41
Chamberlain Rd	Scottsville	47	BS	57
Chamberlain St	Woodstock	83	CC	27

STREET NAME	SUBURB NAME	PG	GRID	
Chameleon	Wellington	15	AU	91
Chamois St	Rugby	84	BY	31
Champagne Cl.	Klein Zevenwacht	90	CB	58
Champagne Cr.	Hout Bay	137	CP	16
Champagne St	Brackenfell Sth	63	BX	57
Champagne St	Wellington	9	AS	90
Champagne St	Wellington	10	AS	92
Champagne St	William Lloyd	19	BC	93
Champagne St	William Lloyd	19	BC	94
Champagne Way	Table View	41	BP	33
Champhor Cl.	Vredekloof	62	BU	53
Chamze St	Brown's Farm	124	CM	43
Chana Cr.	Umrhabulo Triangle	147	CR	56
Chandler Cl.	Sonstraal Hgts	46	BQ	54
Chandos Dr.	Dennemere	108	CH	57
Chandos Rd	Woodbridge Island	57	BW	31
Change Rd	Bishop Lavis	104	CD	42
Chanita St	Casablanca	175	DA	75
Chantal St	Gaylee	108	CG	57
Chantecler Ave	Chantecler	62	BT	52
Chantelle St	De Tijger	60	BW	44
Chantercler La.	Airlie	139	CP	25
Chantilly	D'urbanvale	45	BO	49
Chantilly Cl.	Sunningdale	25	BM	31
Chapel Cl.	Belhar	106	CE	50
Chapel La.	Simon's Town	194	DJ	24
Chapel Rd	Lavender Hill	141	CS	31
Chapel Rd	Rosebank	101	CE	29
Chapel St	District Six	82	CB	24
Chapel St	District Six	82	CB	25
Chapel St	Maitland	83	CA	30
Chapel St	Salt River	83	CB	28
Chapelle St	Courtrai	22	BH	87
Chaplin Cl.	Chapman's Peak	156	CW	17
Chaplin Way	Kirstenhof	159	CT	27
Chapman	Mountainside Est.	179	DD	78
Chapman Ave	Gordon Hgts	179	DD	78
Chapman Ave	Mountainside Est.	179	DE	77
Chapman Cr.	Edgemead	58	BV	37
Chapman St	Factreton	84	BY	34
Chapmans Cl.	Ocean View	184	DC	15
Chapmans Cl.	Ocean View	184	DC	16
Chapman's Peak Dr.	Hout Bay	137	CR	16
Chapman's Peak Dr.	Noordhoek	156	CU	16
Chapman's Peak Dr.	Noordhoek	156	CW	18
Chard Rd	Frogmore Est.	159	CU	28
Chard St	Parow	86	BZ	42
Chardonay Cl.	Uitzicht	47	BO	55
Chardonay Cl.	Uitzicht	47	BO	58
Chardonnay	Fairways	113	CE	75
Chardonnay	Vergesig	45	BQ	48
Chardonnay Ave	Durmonte	30	BM	52
Chardonnay La.	Hout Bay	137	CP	15
Chardonnay Rd	Table View	41	BP	33
Chardonnay St	Oude Westhof	44	BS	44
Chardonnay St	Somerset West	150	CR	70
Chardonney Rd	Saxenburg Ind. Pk	108	CE	56
Charel Uys St	Klipkop	87	BZ	45
Chari Cr.	Delft	106	CG	49
Chari St	Eindhoven	106	CH	50
Charisma Cl.	Somerset West	170	CT	73
Charity Rd	Retreat	140	CR	30
Charl Malan St	Belrail	88	BY	48
Charl Rd	William Lloyd	19	BC	93
Charles Calvert Rd	Charlesville	104	CF	42
Charles Cl.	Barbarossa	120	CN	28
Charles Dr.	Sonstraal Hgts	46	BS	54
Charles Golding St	Balvenie	87	CB	43
Charles Grodes Cr.	Ravensmead	87	CB	45
Charles La.	Valhalla Pk	104	CE	41
Charles Mhambi St	Kuyasa	147	CS	55
Charles Park	Sonstraal Hgts	46	BQ	53
Charles Peers Cl.	Woodlands (M.Plain)	144	CO	45
Charles Rd	Edward	122	CN	35
Charles Setsoba St	Kuyasa	147	CS	56
Charles Setsoba St	Kuyasa	147	CS	57
Charles St	Bloekombos	49	BR	63
Charles Stassen St	Panorama	59	BV	41
Charles Way	Barbarossa	120	CN	27
Charles Wqakula Cl.	Barnet Molokwana Cnr	126	CN	53
Charlesville	D'urbanvale	45	BO	49
Charlie	Cloetesville	94	BY	74
Charlie Brown St	Macassar	149	CS	65
Charlie St	Beacon Valley (M.Plain)	145	CQ	47
Charlottenburg St	Glenhaven	89	CA	52
Charlottenburg St	Glenhaven	89	BY	54
Charm St	Oakdene	89	CC	54
Charmaine St	De Tijger	60	BW	43
Charmaine St	Zoo Pk	47	BR	57
Charme	Schuilplaats	113	CF	76
Charnwood Ave	Steenberg	158	CT	25
Charnwood Cl.	Steenberg	158	CT	23
Charnwood Rd	Penhill	128	CK	61
Charon St	Wellington	10	AS	94
Chart Cl.	Blouberg Sands	24	BM	30
Chartley Rd	Rondebosch	101	CF	30
Chas Booth Ave	Bakoven	98	CF	18
Chasa Cl.	Harare	146	CR	53
Chase Cl.	Mandalay	125	CM	48
Chasmante Cl.	Steenberg	159	CT	29
Chasmay Rd	Lekkerwater	184	DA	18
Chasmay Rd	Lekkerwater	184	DC	17
Chasselas St	Somerset West	170	CT	72
Chat	Rocklands (M.Plain)	144	CS	44
Chateau	Somerset West	170	CT	72

STREET NAME	SUBURB NAME	PG	GRID	
Chateau Ave	Fresnaye	81	CA	19
Chateau Ave	Glen Ive	62	BU	52
Chateau Cir.	Barbarossa	120	CN	28
Chateau Cir.	Plumstead	120	CN	28
Chateau Cl.	Welgelegen	59	BU	40
Chateau St	Courtrai	22	BH	87
Chateaux	Vredekloof	62	BU	53
Chatham Rd	Heathfield	140	CQ	29
Chatham Rd	Salt River	83	CB	28
Chatham St	Maitland	84	CA	32
Chatres Cr.	Malibu Village	127	CK	56
Chaucer Rd	Claremont	101	CH	29
Chavones Cl.	Edgemead	58	BV	37
Chavonne St	Welgemoed	60	BU	46
Chavonne St	Welgemoed	61	BU	47
Chebec Cr.	Sun Valley	185	CZ	20
Cheddar Rd	Wynberg	120	CM	30
Cheesewood	Delft Sth	125	CJ	50
Cheetah Cl.	Eastridge (M.Plain)	145	CR	48
Cheetah Rd	Macassar	149	CS	65
Cheetah Rd	Zoo Pk	47	BR	56
Cheetah St	Ocean View	184	DC	15
Chelmsford Cr.	Parklands	25	BN	33
Chelmsford Rd	Vredehoek	82	CC	24
Chelmsford Rd	Vredehoek	100	CD	24
Chelmsford St	Heemstede	62	BW	52
Chelmsford St	Heemstede	62	BX	52
Chelmwood Pl.	Parklands	25	BN	33
Chelmwood Pl.	Parklands	25	BL	33
Chelsea Ave	Vredehoek	82	CC	23
Chelsea Ave	Weltevreden Val. (M.Plain)	143	CO	42
Chelsea Cr.	Kirstenhof	159	CU	27
Chelsea Cr.	Parklands	25	BM	34
Chelsea Green	Eersterivier	128	CM	59
Chelsea La.	Noordhoek Manor	157	CX	21
Chelsea La.	Noordhoek Manor	157	CV	20
Chelsea Sq.	Blouberg Sands	24	BL	30
Chelsea St	Dunoon	42	BP	37
Chelsea St	Riverton	86	BZ	40
Cheltenham Rd	Mowbray	101	CD	30
Cheltenham Rd	Ottery	122	CM	35
Cheltenham Rd	Ottery	122	CN	36
Cheltenham St	Somerset West	170	CW	72
Chemist Mlungu St	Manenberg	104	CH	40
Chené	Halalie	30	BN	52
Chene Cl.	Hohenort	119	CL	24
Chenel Cl.	Westlake	159	CU	27
Chenel Pl.	Northpine	63	BT	58
Chenel Way	Westlake	159	CU	27
Chenin Blanc	Fairways	113	CE	75
Chenin Way	Northpine	63	BV	58
Chenoweth St	Durbanville	46	BP	51
Chepstow Rd	Green Point	81	BZ	22
Chepstow Rd	Tijgerhof	57	BX	32
Cherbourg Ave	Plumstead	140	CP	29
Cherokee St	The Hague	106	CE	49
Cherry Cl.	Bishopscourt	119	CJ	25
Cherry Cl.	Thembokwezi	125	CM	48
Cherry Hills Cr.	Sunningdale	25	BN	31
Cherry La.	Belle Constantia	139	CP	25
Cherry La.	Kenridge	45	BS	49
Cherry Laurel	Eersterivier	128	CM	60
Cherry Rd	Eastridge (M.Plain)	145	CR	47
Cherry St	Bellair	62	BV	52
Cherry St	Bishopscourt	119	CJ	25
Cherry St	Newlands	100	CH	25
Cherry Way	Hout Bay	117	CN	17
Cherrywood	Stellenbosch	95	BY	75
Cherrywood Cr.	Parklands	25	BN	33
Cherrywood Gdns Cr.	Somerset West	171	CV	76
Cherrywood Rd	Parklands	25	BM	33
Chesham Rd	Claremont	102	CH	31
Chess Rd	Rondebosch	101	CH	30
Chess St	Beacon Valley (M.Plain)	145	CP	48
Chester Dr.	Bishopscourt	119	CJ	26
Chester Rd	Lakeside	159	CV	28
Chester Rd	Rosebank	101	CF	29
Chester Rd	Tokai	139	CS	25
Chester Rd	Woodstock	82	CC	26
Chesterfield Cl.	Parklands	25	BM	32
Chesterfield Rd	Oranjezicht	99	CD	22
Chesterfield Way	Parklands	25	BM	32
Chestnut	Green Oaks	94	BY	74
Chestnut	Pinelands	85	CC	35
Chestnut Ave	Amandelrug	90	CA	55
Chestnut Ave	New Orleans	19	BA	91
Chestnut Ave	Wynberg	120	CK	27
Chestnut Cl.	Fairie Knowe	185	DA	19
Chestnut Cl.	Fairie Knowe	185	DB	22
Chestnut Cr.	Eastridge (M.Plain)	145	CR	47
Chestnut Cr.	Parklands	25	BM	32
Chestnut Dr.	Hout Bay	118	CM	19
Chestnut La.	Durbanville	46	BO	51
Chestnut Rd	Eastridge (M.Plain)	145	CR	47
Chestnut Rd	Farmsteads	156	CV	18
Chestnut Rd	Forest Village	127	CM	58
Chestnut Ridge	Milnerton	41	BS	33
Chestnut St	Bellair	62	BW	51
Chestnut St	Bonteheuwel	103	CD	38
Chestnut St	Hillcrest Hgts	127	CM	57
Chestnut St	Thornton	85	CA	37
Chestnut Way	Avon	86	CA	41
Chestnut Way	Belhar	105	CD	46
Chestnut Way	Belhar	106	CD	47
Chestnut Way	Silverglade	185	DA	22

STREET NAME	SUBURB NAME	PG	GRID	
Cheve St	Lemoenkloof	18	BC	88
Cheveche St	Chantecler	62	BT	51
Cheveche St	Chantecler	62	BX	52
Cheviot Pl.	Green Point	81	BZ	21
Chevrolet Cr.	Beacon Valley (M.Plain)	145	CQ	48
Chevron Sq.	Retreat	140	CS	29
Chiante La.	Somerset West	151	CQ	72
Chiappini St	Cape Town Cen.	82	BZ	23
Chiappini St	Schotsche Kloof	81	CA	22
Chibi St	Harare	146	CS	53
Chibini Rd	Thembokwezi	125	CN	48
Chicago Ave	Tarentaalplaas	174	CZ	74
Chicago Cl.	Thembokwezi	125	CM	48
Chichester Cl.	Crofters Valley	185	CY	19
Chichester Rd	Claremont	120	CJ	30
Chichester Rd	Claremont	121	CJ	31
Chief Cl.	Bloekombos	48	BR	62
Chief Maqoma	Weltevreden Val. (M.Plain)	123	CN	42
Chief Rd	Steenberg	159	CT	30
Chigwell Rd	Epping Forest	86	CC	41
Childrens Rd	Strandfontein	162	CT	41
Childrens Way	Bergvliet	140	CQ	28
Childrens Way	Bergvliet	140	CR	27
Children's Way	Woodlands (M.Plain)	144	CP	45
Children's Wk	Penhill	128	CJ	61
Chile	Malibu Village	127	CL	56
Chilton Cr.	Hout Bay	137	CP	16
Chilwan Cr.	Broadlands	175	CZ	78
Chilworth Rd	Camps Bay	98	CD	18
Chimes St	Retreat	159	CT	29
Chin Blanc St	Oude Westhof	44	BS	44
Chingford Cr.	Epping Forest	86	CC	42
Chipenham Rd	Kenilworth	120	CK	29
Chippendale	Cloetesville	95	BY	75
Chippenham Cr.	Parklands	25	BM	34
Chipphillside	Retreat	140	CS	29
Chipstead Way	Pinelands	84	CB	34
Chitha St	Harare	146	CS	53
Chitten Way	Richwood	42	BP	38
Choir St	Steenberg	159	CT	29
Choir St	Woodlands (M.Plain)	144	CP	44
Chopin	Delft Sth	125	CK	48
Chopin Ave	Groenheuwel	19	AZ	92
Chopin Cl.	Sonstraal Hgts	46	BQ	54
Chopin Rd	Belhar	106	CE	48
Chopin St	Cafda Village	140	CR	30
Chopin St	Cafda Village	140	CS	30
Chopin St	Protea Hoogte	63	BX	56
Chorlo St	Wesbank	107	CH	51
Chris Abraham Rd	Retreat	140	CR	29
Chris Barry Ave	Ottery	121	CN	33
Chris Cl.	Tafelsig (M.Plain)	145	CS	50
Chris Hani	Kalkfontein I	107	CD	52
Chris Hani Cir.	Mandela Pk	146	CR	54
Chris Hani Cr.	Weltevreden Val. (M.Plain)	123	CM	42
Chris Hani St	Fisantekraal	31	BK	58
Chris Hani St	Fisantekraal	32	BK	59
Chris Nissan Cl.	Wimbledon	108	CH	55
Chrisanne St	Jagtershof	108	CD	57
Chrisiris Cl.	Hazelwood Pk	185	CZ	20
Chrismar Rd	Chrismar	61	BX	50
Chrismar Rd	Hillrise	61	BX	49
Chrismas Tinto St	Manenberg	104	CH	40
Christa Way	Sonstraal Hgts	46	BS	54
Christelle St	Denneburg	23	BD	91
Christiaan Beyers St	Parow Nth	60	BW	43
Christiaan de Wet Cr.	Parow Nth	59	BW	42
Christiaan St	District Six	82	CC	25
Christiaan St	Hout Bay	137	CP	16
Christiaans St	Ravensmead	87	CA	44
Christian Ave	Epping Ind.	86	CB	39
Christina Rd	Kommetjie	183	DB	13
Christine Cl.	Brentwood Pk	126	CJ	51
Christine St	Barbarossa	120	CN	27
Christine St	Beacon Valley (M.Plain)	145	CP	48
Christmas Tinto St	Mandela Pk	147	CQ	55
Christopher Rd	Bergvliet	140	CR	27
Christowi Rd	Rosebank	101	CE	29
Chrome St	Brackenfell Ind.	63	BT	57
Chromite Rd	Penlyn Est.	122	CJ	35
Chrysler Cr.	Beacon Valley (M.Plain)	145	CQ	48
Chudleigh Rd	Plumstead	120	CN	30
Chudleigh Rd	Plumstead	140	CO	30
Chukker Rd	Lansdowne	121	CK	32
Chukumisa St	Griffiths Mxenge	146	CQ	54
Chumisa St	Crossroads	124	CK	44
Church Cir.	Capricorn	160	CV	31
Church Rd	Glenlily	86	BY	42
Church Rd	Goodwood Est.	85	BZ	38
Church Rd	Muizenberg	159	CX	29
Church Rd	Retreat Ind. Area	140	CS	28
Church Rd	Sea Point	81	CA	19
Church Sq.	Kaya	146	CP	51
Church St	Athlone	102	CF	33
Church St	Athlone	102	CG	33
Church St	Brooklyn	83	BZ	30
Church St	Cape Town Cen.	81	CA	22
Church St	Cape Town Cen.	82	CA	23
Church St	Cape Town Cen.	88	BY	48
Church St	Claremont	120	CJ	28
Church St	Durbanville	45	BQ	50
Church St	Durbanville	46	BP	51
Church St	Langa	103	CD	35
Church St	Lansdowne	121	CK	33
Church St	Mfuleni	126	CL	54

Abbreviations used: Ave – Avenue, A.H. – Agricultural Holding, A.L. – Algemene Landgoed, Blvd – Boulevard, Cen. – Central, Cir. – Circle, Cl. – Close, Cr. – Crescent, Ct – Court, Dr. – Drive, Est. – Estate, Ext. – Extension, Hgts – Heights, Ind. – Industrial, Gdns – Gardens, Gr. – Grove, La. – Lane, (M.Plain) - Mitchells Plain, Nth – North, Pl. – Place, Pk – Park, Rd – Road, Rdg. – Ridge, S.H. – Small Holding, Sq. – Square, St – Street, Sth – South, Ter. – Terrace, Tn – Turn, Val. – Valley, Wk – Walk

STREET NAME	SUBURB NAME	PG	GRID
Church St	Morningstar	46	BP 51
Church St	Mowbray	101	CD 29
Church St	Park Estates	170	CX 73
Church St	Park Estates	174	CY 72
Church St	Rondebosch	101	CF 29
Church St	Salberau	86	CB 42
Church St	Simon's Town	194	DJ 25
Church St	Somerset West	170	CV 74
Church St	Somerset West	171	CV 75
Church St	Stellenbosch	95	CC 76
Church St	Strandfontein	162	CT 41
Church St	Wellington	10	AR 94
Church St	Woodstock	82	CB 26
Church St	Wynberg	120	CL 28
Churchdown La.	Heathfield	140	CQ 28
Churchill Ave	Simon's Town	194	DJ 26
Churchill Cl.	Bellville	61	BU 48
Churchill Rd	Plumstead	120	CN 30
Churchill Rd	Plumstead	121	CN 31
Churchill Rd	Plumstead	141	CO 31
Churchill St	Dal Josafat Ind.	22	BD 89
Churchill St	Eindhoven	106	CH 50
Chwela St	Harare	146	CR 53
Cicily Ave	Capri	185	DB 19
Ciko Ave	Victoria Mxenge	126	CN 51
Ciko Ave	Victoria Mxenge	126	CN 52
Cillie St	Wellington	10	AR 92
Cilliers La.	Harbour Island	179	DE 77
Cilmor St	Kaymor	62	BX 53
Cincaut	Brackenfell	63	BW 55
Cincaut	Brackenfell	63	BV 58
Cincaut Rd	Saxenburg Ind. Pk	108	CE 57
Cinderella Cr.	Eastridge (M.Plain)	145	CQ 48
Cindy	Welgelee	63	BT 55
Cindy Rd	Heathfield	140	CR 28
Cineraria Cr.	Lentegeur (M.Plain)	144	CO 46
Cinnamon St	Sunset Glen	107	CH 54
Cinsaut	Langeberg Rdg	47	BR 55
Cinsaut Cl.	William Lloyd	19	BC 94
Cinsaut St	Oude Westhof	44	BS 45
Cinsaut St	Somerset West	150	CR 70
Circle Rd	Eersterivier	127	CL 58
Circle Rd	Sunridge	41	BP 34
Circle Rd	West Riding	41	BO 34
Circle Rd	West Riding	42	BO 35
Circle Way	Strandfontein	162	CT 41
Circle Way	Strandfontein	162	CV 42
Circuit St	Hazendal	102	CE 33
Circus Ave	Claremont	120	CJ 29
Cirrus	Rocklands (M.Plain)	145	CS 47
Cirus St	Kirstenhof	159	CT 27
Cissy Gool Ave	Gatesville	103	CH 36
Citabatwe Cr.	Victoria Mxenge	126	CN 51
Citrus St	Bonteheuwel	103	CE 38
Civet	Eastridge (M.Plain)	145	CR 48
Civet Cl.	Langeberg Rdg	47	BR 56
Civet Cr.	Langeberg Rdg	47	BR 56
Civic Ave	Foreshore	82	CA 24
Civic Rd	Lansdowne	121	CJ 32
Civic Rd	Lotus River	141	CP 34
Civic Rd	Matroosfontein	86	CC 41
Claasen	Stellenbosch	95	CC 77
Claasen Rd	Capricorn	160	CV 31
Claasens Rd	Bishop Lavis	105	CD 43
Claasens Rd	Skoongesig	45	BO 50
Claassen St	Welgemoed	61	BV 47
Claassens St	The Palms	170	CX 72
Claire Cl.	De Tijger	60	BW 44
Clairette Ave	Somerset West	170	CT 72
Clairvaux Cl.	Zevendal	90	CC 58
Clairvaux Rd	Kalk Bay	186	DA 26
Clairwood Ave	Vredehoek	100	CD 23
Clairwood Cl.	Edgemead	58	BV 38
Clairwood Cr.	Beacon Valley (M.Plain)	145	CP 48
Clairwood Cr.	Beacon Valley (M.Plain)	145	CQ 48
Clairwood Cr.	Milnerton Rdg	41	BS 33
Clam La.	Big Bay	24	BL 28
Clam Rd	Dolphin Beach	40	BO 30
Clam Rd	Richwood	42	BP 38
Clan Monroe	Blue Downs	127	CJ 56
Clan Monroe Ave	Kommetjie	183	DC 11
Clan St	Belgravia	102	CH 34
Clan Stewart St	Glencairn Hgts	191	DD 23
Clan Stewart St	Glencairn Hgts	191	DD 24
Clanwilliam Way	Portlands (M.Plain)	144	CR 45
Clare Cr.	Lentegeur (M.Plain)	145	CO 48
Clare Rd	Wynberg	120	CM 29
Clare St	Connaught	87	CC 43
Clare St	Gardens	82	CB 23
Claremont Ave	Claremont	120	CJ 29
Clarence Rd	Wynberg	120	CL 30
Clarendon Cr.	Brooklyn	84	BZ 31
Clarendon Rd	Mowbray	101	CE 30
Clarendon Rd	Muizenberg	159	CX 29
Clarendon Rd	Muizenberg	159	CW 27
Clarendon Rd	Pinelands	84	CC 32
Clarendon Rd	Somerset West	170	CW 74
Clarendon St	Klipkop	87	BZ 45
Clarendon St	Strand Halt	170	CW 74
Clarens Rd	Sea Point	81	CA 19
Clarens St	Woodstock	82	CB 26
Clarepark Ave	Rondebosch	102	CH 31
Claret Rd	Table View	41	BO 33
Claret St	Oude Westhof	44	BS 45
Claret St	Wellington	10	AR 94
Claret St	William Lloyd	19	BC 94
Clarewyn Rd	Lansdowne	121	CK 34
Clarica St	Sarepta	89	CC 52
Clariette	Northpine	63	BU 58
Clarinet	Sonstraal Hgts	46	BR 53
Clarinet Ct	Belhar	106	CD 48
Clarissa Cl.	Dalvale	19	AY 93
Clark Rd	Killarney Gdns	42	BO 36
Clarke Ave	Clarkes	86	CC 42
Clarke's Pl.	Adriaanse	87	CC 43
Clarkia St	Wellway Pk East	46	BP 53
Clarks Steps	Simon's Town	194	DJ 25
Claude St	Newfields	103	CH 37
Clay Rd	Corobrik	31	BK 56
Clay St	Voelvlei	89	CA 53
Clayman Cl.	Capri	185	DB 19
Clays La.	Epping Forest	86	CB 41
Cleaver Cl.	Eureka	87	CC 44
Cleek St	Lakeside	159	CV 27
Clement Way	Bergvliet	139	CQ 26
Clent Rd	Eersterivier	128	CN 61
Clevedon Rd	Muizenberg	159	CX 29
Cleveland Cl.	Colorado (M.Plain)	144	CO 43
Cleveland Cl.	Highbury	107	CE 53
Cleveland Cl.	Scottsdene	64	BU 60
Cleveland Rd	Claremont	102	CH 31
Cleveland St	Boston	61	BW 47
Cleveland St	Boston	61	BX 47
Cleveland St	Boston	88	BY 47
Clevily Rd	Athlone	102	CG 34
Cliff Rd	Clifton	80	CC 17
Cliffony Cr.	Connaught	87	CB 43
Clifford Ave	Vredehoek	100	CD 23
Clifford Cr.	Bergvliet	139	CQ 26
Clifford Rd	Sea Point	81	CA 20
Clifford St	Ottery East	122	CN 35
Clift St	KWV	22	BG 88
Clifton Cr.	Parklands	25	BM 33
Clifton Rd	Camps Bay	98	CD 18
Clifton Rd	Claremont	101	CH 29
Clifton Rd	Mowbray	101	CH 30
Clifton Rd	Muizenberg	159	CX 30
Clifton Rd	Observatory	101	CD 29
Clifton St	Macassar	149	CS 63
Clifton Steps	Clifton	80	CC 18
Clingdale Cl.	Tokai	139	CS 26
Clinic St	Gatesville	103	CG 37
Clipper Cr.	Anchorage Pk	179	DD 77
Clipper Cr.	Strandfontein	161	CU 38
Clipper Rd	Strandfontein	161	CT 38
Clipper Rd	Strandfontein	162	CT 39
Clipperton Cl.	Capri	185	DB 19
Clive Rd	Connaught	87	CB 43
Clive Rd	Crawford	102	CH 33
Clive Rd	Crawford	121	CJ 33
Clive St	Brown's Farm	123	CL 41
Clive St	Vredehoek	82	CC 23
Clivia La.	Brantwood	89	CA 53
Clivia Rd	Mountainside Est.	179	DD 78
Clivia St	Retreat	159	CT 28
Cloete Cr.	Elnor	86	CC 42
Cloete Rd	Woodstock	83	CC 27
Cloete St	Beaconvale	86	BZ 42
Cloete St	Bothasig	58	BU 37
Cloete St	Monte Vista	59	BV 40
Cloete St	Parow	87	BZ 43
Cloete St	William Lloyd	23	BD 92
Cloetenberg Rd	Somerset West	171	CU 76
Cloetesdal Cl.	Mitchells Plain	144	CR 45
Cloetesdal Cl.	Mitchells Plain	144	CR 43
Clove St	Vosfontein	62	BV 52
Clovelly Ave	Devil's Peak Est.	82	CC 24
Clovelly Cl.	Clovelly	186	DA 24
Clovelly Rd	Clovelly	186	CZ 23
Clovelly Rd	Clovelly	186	DA 25
Clovelly Rd	Silvermine Village	185	CY 21
Clovelly Steps	Clovelly	186	CZ 24
Clovelly Steps	Clovelly	186	DA 25
Clover Cr.	Silvertown	103	CF 35
Clover Rd	Belhar	88	CC 47
Clover St	Silvertown	103	CF 35
Club La.	Simon's Town	194	DJ 24
Club St	Lakeside	159	CV 27
Clunie Rd	Bergvliet	140	CR 27
Cluver	Simonswyk	95	CB 78
Cluver	Stellenbosch	95	CB 77
Clyde Rd	Green Point	81	BZ 21
Clyde Rd	Oakdale	61	BW 49
Clyde Rd	Rondebosch	101	CG 29
Clyde St	Hout Bay	136	CP 14
Clyde St	Hout Bay	137	CP 15
Clyde St	Strandfontein	163	CT 43
Clyde St	Woodstock	83	CB 27
Clydebank Cr.	Parklands	25	BM 33
Clydebank Rd	Green Point	81	BZ 21
Clydesdale Cr.	Mitchells Plain	144	CR 44
Coach Rd	Wynberg	120	CK 27
Coatbridge Cr.	Parklands	25	BM 34
Coates St	Mandalay	125	CN 48
Coaton St	Wellington	15	AU 91
Cob Cl.	Nooitgedacht	105	CE 43
Cobble Cl.	Scottsdene	64	BU 60
Cobbles	Park Village	127	CK 58
Cobblestone Rd	District Six	82	CB 24
Cobblestone St	Tafelsig (M.Plain)	145	CS 48
Cobern La.	Fish Hoek	186	DB 23
Cobern St	Cape Town Cen.	82	BZ 23
Coceko Cr.	Mxolisi Phetani	126	CM 51
Cochrane Ave	Epping Ind.	85	CB 37
Cockburn Cl.	Glencairn Hgts	186	DC 24
Cockburn Cl.	Glencairn Hgts	191	DD 24
Cockle Cl.	Richwood	42	BP 38
Cockle Cl.	Richwood	42	BR 37
Cockle Cr.	Clovelly	186	DA 24
Cockscombe Rd	Heideveld	104	CF 40
Cocktail	Fairyland	19	AZ 93
Cococabana Way	Malibu Village	127	CK 56
Cococabana Way	Malibu Village	127	CL 56
Cocorico St	Chantecler	62	BT 52
Coen Steytler Ave	Cape Town Cen.	82	BZ 24
Coenru St	Kaymor	89	BY 52
Coetzee Ave	Lemoenkloof	18	BB 89
Coetzenberg St	Mitchells Plain	144	CR 45
Coetzenberg Way	Edgemead	58	BV 38
Coetzenburg	Stellenbosch	95	CC 77
Coetzenburg La.	Northpine	63	BU 58
Coetzer St	Vierlanden	30	BN 51
Coffee Cr.	Scottsdene	64	BT 60
Coghill Mews	Sunset Links	57	BT 31
Coghill Rd	Wynberg	120	CL 29
Cogman St	Ruyterwacht	86	CA 39
Cognac Cl.	Townsend Est.	85	BY 37
Cognac Rd	Table View	41	BO 33
Coimbra Cl.	Edgemead	58	BV 38
Cola St	Nyanga	123	CK 42
Colchester Cr.	Parklands	25	BM 32
Colchester End	Parklands	25	BM 32
Coldicott Ave	Somerset West	171	CW 75
Cole Point Rd	Simon's Town	194	DJ 25
Cole St	Observatory	83	CB 29
Cole St	Somerset West	169	CT 70
Cole St	Somerset West	170	CT 71
Colebrook Cl.	Elnor	86	CC 42
Colebrooke Cl.	Seaforth Sound	194	DJ 26
Coleford Way	Edgemead	58	BU 38
Coleman St	Elsies River Ind.	86	BZ 42
Colenso Rd	Bishopscourt	119	CJ 26
Coleridge Rd	Salt River	83	CB 28
Colesburg St	Ruyterwacht	86	CA 39
Colette Cl.	De Tijger	60	BW 44
Colibri St	Wellington	15	AU 91
Coligny	Dalsig	113	CD 75
Coligny	Kirstenhof	158	CU 26
Coligny St	Lemoenkloof	18	BB 89
Colin Cr.	Zoo Pk	47	BR 57
Colin Rd	Grassy Pk	141	CR 32
Colin St	Maitland	84	CA 31
Colinton Rd	Newlands	101	CH 28
Colleen Rd	Manenberg	123	CJ 39
Colleen Rd	Weltevreden Val. (M.Plain)	124	CN 44
Colleen Way	Summer Greens	58	BV 36
Colleens Cl.	Somerset West	151	CS 74
College Rd	Doornhoogte	103	CG 36
College Rd	Rondebosch	101	CF 29
College Rd	Surrey	103	CH 37
College Service Rd	Doornhoogte	103	CG 36
College St	Claremont	120	CJ 30
College St	Labiance	89	BZ 52
College St	Wellington	10	AR 94
Coller Rd	Retreat	140	CS 28
Collesberg Cir.	Heideveld	104	CF 39
Collesberg Cir.	Heideveld	104	CG 39
Collette Cl.	Bel Ombre	119	CM 25
Collette Cl.	Eversdal Hgts	45	BS 50
Collette Cr.	Dalvale	19	AY 92
Collette Cr.	Dalvale	19	BA 94
Collings Rd	Oostersee	60	BX 45
Collingwood Rd	Observatory	83	CC 29
Collins St	Temperance Town	180	DD 79
Colombar Cl.	Northpine	63	BU 58
Colombar St	Oude Westhof	44	BS 44
Colombard Ave	Somerset West	151	CS 72
Colombard Cl.	Richwood	42	BQ 38
Colonel Cresswell St	Glenhaven	89	BZ 51
Colorado	Ravensmead	87	CA 45
Colorado Ave	Colorado (M.Plain)	124	CN 44
Colorado Cr.	Colorado (M.Plain)	124	CN 44
Colorado Rd	Brown's Farm	123	CL 41
Colorado St	Eindhoven	107	CH 51
Colorado St	Primrose Pk	122	CJ 38
Colosseum Rd	Portlands (M.Plain)	145	CR 47
Colstan	Oakdene	89	CC 54
Colt St	Strandfontein	143	CS 41
Columbar	Brackenfell	63	BW 55
Columbar	Brackenfell	63	BV 58
Columbar	Fairways	113	CE 75
Columbia	Eindhoven	107	CH 50
Columbia Rd	Ocean View	189	DD 15
Columbia Way	Mxolisi Phetani	125	CM 49
Columbine Ave	Ottery	121	CN 33
Columbine Rd	Rondebosch	102	CG 31
Columbine Rd	Skoongesig	45	BO 50
Columbine Rd	Strandfontein	163	CT 43
Columbus Ave	Fish Hoek	185	DA 22
Columbus Rd	Claremont	101	CH 30
Columbus St	Forest Glade	127	CL 58
Columbus St	Somerset West	171	CW 75
Colwell Rd	Muizenberg Nth	159	CW 29
Colwyn Rd	Silvertown	103	CF 36
Colyn Rd	Kalk Bay	186	DA 26
Colyn Rd	Sweet Valley	139	CR 25
Comapacta	Anesta	113	CF 75
Comay St	Wesbank	107	CG 52
Combretum Ave	Welgedacht	60	BT 44
Combrinck St	Bothasig	58	BT 37
Combrinck St	Monte Vista	59	BV 39
Combrink St	Belhar	106	CE 50
Comely Cl.	Macassar	149	CR 64
Comet Dr.	Thembokwezi	125	CL 49
Comet Rd	Bishop Lavis	105	CE 44
Comet Rd	Ocean View	184	DC 15
Comet Rd	Surrey	103	CG 38
Comet Rd	Surrey	103	CH 38
Comet St	The Hague	106	CE 49
Comice	Lindida	96	CA 79
Comity St	Primrose Pk	122	CJ 37
Commander Barney St	Driftsands	147	CQ 56
Commerce Way	Belhar	105	CD 45
Commercial Rd	Clarkes	86	CC 42
Commercial Rd	Clarkes	104	CD 42
Commercial Rd	Ndabeni	84	CB 31
Commercial St	Cape Town Cen.	82	CB 23
Commercial St	Lemoenkloof	18	BC 88
Commissioner St	Wellington	10	AR 93
Commodore Rd	Strandfontein	163	CT 43
Commodore St	The Hague	106	CE 49
Common Rd	Strandfontein	162	CT 40
Como Rd	Flintdale Est.	140	CP 30
Compacta St	Somerset West	151	CS 71
Compagne St	Kuilsrivier Ind.	108	CD 55
Compagnie Rd	Welgemoed	61	BU 47
Compagnie Rd	Welgemoed	61	BV 48
Companion Way	Anchorage Pk	179	DD 77
Companje Rd	Somerset West	151	CQ 72
Companjie Cr.	Strandvale	170	CW 73
Compari Cl.	Brackenfell Sth	63	BX 57
Compass Cl.	Anchorage Pk	175	DC 77
Compass Cl.	Anchorage Pk	175	DB 78
Compass Cl.	Blouberg Sands	24	BM 30
Compass Cl.	Marina Da Gama	159	CV 30
Compassberg	Tafelsig (M.Plain)	164	CT 48
Computer Rd	Marconi Beam	57	BV 34
Comrie Rd	Camps Bay	99	CD 19
Cona St	Victoria Mxenge	126	CN 52
Concert Blvd	Retreat	140	CS 28
Concerto	Sonstraal Hgts	46	BQ 54
Concerto St	Dalvale	19	AZ 92
Concord Rd	Dennemere	127	CJ 57
Concord St	Flintdale Est.	141	CO 31
Concorde	Rocklands (M.Plain)	163	CT 46
Concorde Cr.	Airport Ind.	105	CH 43
Concorde Rd	Bishop Lavis	105	CD 43
Concordia	Eersterivier	128	CL 60
Concordia Cr.	Ravensmead	87	CB 45
Concordia St	KWV	22	BG 88
Conde	Kromrivier	95	CB 76
Condoba	Mbekweni	15	AW 92
Condor	Rocklands (M.Plain)	163	CT 45
Condor St	The Hague	106	CE 49
Condor St	The Hague	106	CH 48
Conduit Rd	Vredehoek	100	CD 23
Cone Cl.	Somerset West	152	CR 75
Cone Cr.	Ruyterwacht	86	BZ 39
Cone Way	Pinelands	84	CC 32
Confettibush St	Annandale	90	BZ 55
Congo Ct	Delft	106	CG 49
Conifer Cl.	Northpine	63	BU 57
Conifer Cl.	Ottery East	121	CN 34
Conifer Rd	Hout Bay	117	CN 18
Conifer Rd	Sea Point	81	BZ 20
Conifer Rd	Tokai	139	CS 25
Conifer St	Bishopscourt	119	CJ 25
Conifer Way	Pinelands	84	CC 32
Coniston Ave	Coniston Pk	159	CU 29
Coniston Ave	Coniston Pk	159	CU 30
Coniston Rd	Rondebosch	101	CG 30
Coniston St	Klipkop	87	BZ 45
Coniston Way	Pinelands	84	CB 34
Coniston Way	Silverhurst	119	CN 26
Conmead Rd	Meadowridge	139	CO 26
Connaught Rd	Beaconvale	87	BZ 43
Connaught Rd	Connaught	87	CB 44
Connaught Rd	Cravenby	87	CA 43
Connaught Rd	Eureka	87	CC 44
Connaught Rd	Kenilworth	120	CL 30
Connaught Rd	Modderdam	87	CC 45
Connemara Dr.	Hout Bay	117	CM 18
Connemara Rd	Royal Cape	121	CM 31
Conner Cl.	Bel Ombre	119	CM 26
Conningsby St	Athlone	102	CF 32
Connoisseur	D'urbanvale	29	BN 49
Conquest Rd	Belthorn Est.	102	CH 34
Conquest Rd	Belthorn Est.	121	CJ 34
Conrad Rd	Montagu's Gift	141	CO 34
Conrad St	William Lloyd	23	BD 94
Conradie	Van Ryneveld	174	CZ 72
Conradie St	Morgenster Hoogte	63	BT 55
Conradie St	Mountain View	19	BB 91
Conradie St	Mountain View	19	AZ 94
Conradie St	Scottsville	47	BS 58
Conroy St	Peerless Pk East	47	BR 58
Conroy St	Peerless Pk East	48	BR 59
Consani Ave	Elsies River Ind.	86	BZ 41
Consort Rd	Retreat	140	CR 28
Consort Rd	Retreat	140	CR 29

STREET NAME	SUBURB NAME	PG	GRID	
Consta Rd	Heathfield	140	CR	28
Constable St	De La Haye	62	BX	51
Constance Rd	Claremont	120	CJ	28
Constance Rd	Coniston Pk	159	CU	29
Constant Cl.	Hout Bay	117	CM	15
Constantia	Welgelegen	113	CD	76
Constantia Ave	Helderberg Pk	175	DA	75
Constantia Cl.	Panorama	59	BV	41
Constantia Cr.	Stellenryk	62	BT	52
Constantia Cr.	Tygerdal	58	BX	38
Constantia Ct	Marina Da Gama	159	CV	29
Constantia Glen	Barbarossa	120	CN	28
Constantia Main Rd	Barbarossa	119	CN	26
Constantia Main Rd	High Constantia	119	CN	24
Constantia Main Rd	Witteboomen	118	CM	22
Constantia Rd	Gardens	81	CC	21
Constantia Rd	Langeberg Village	46	BP	53
Constantia Rd	Plumstead	120	CM	28
Constantia Rd	Richwood	42	BP	38
Constantia St	Mitchells Plain	144	CQ	45
Constantia St	Paarl	22	BF	88
Constantiaberg Cl.	Belle Constantia	139	CO	26
Constantiaberg Cl.	Plumstead	140	CO	28
Constitution St	Belhar	107	CE	51
Constitution St	District Six	82	CB	24
Container Rd	Foreshore	83	BZ	27
Container Rd	Foreshore	83	BZ	28
Contermanskloof Rd	Dunoon	43	BO	39
Contermanskloof Rd	Montblanc	27	BK	42
Contour Way	Fish Hoek	186	DC	24
Convent Rd	Wynberg	120	CL	27
Conway Cl.	West Beach	24	BM	30
Conway Rd	Uitsig	87	CB	45
Conway Rd	Uitsig	87	CC	45
Conway St	Brooklyn	83	BZ	30
Coode St	Wellington	15	AU	92
Coodes Cr.	Foreshore	82	BZ	23
Cook Rd	Claremont	101	CH	30
Cook St	Bothasig	42	BS	38
Cook St	Observatory	83	CC	28
Cook St	Vasco Est.	59	BX	39
Cook St	Vasco Est.	86	BY	39
Cooke St	Mabille Pk	89	CA	53
Cooke St	Park Estates	170	CX	71
Coombe Rd	Plumstead	141	CO	31
Coone Rd	Retreat	140	CS	28
Cooper St	Aurora	45	BQ	48
Coopers Cl.	Rust-en-vrede	119	CN	26
Coornhoop St	Bothasig	58	BU	38
Coot	Rocklands (M.Plain)	144	CS	44
Coot Cr.	Flamingo Vlei	41	BQ	33
Coot Dr.	Marina Da Gama	159	CU	30
Coot Rd	Pelikan Pk	142	CS	36
Coot Way	Pelikan Pk	141	CR	32
Copeland Rd	Rondebosch	101	CG	28
Copenhagen Way	Portlands (M.Plain)	144	CR	46
Copland	Delft Sth	125	CJ	48
Copper	Rocklands (M.Plain)	144	CS	46
Copperfield Rd	Salt River	83	CC	28
Coprosma St	Klein Nederburg	19	BC	92
Coprosma St	Klein Nederburg	19	BA	94
Coprosma St	Skilpadvlei	45	BP	50
Coracle St	Sun Valley	185	CZ	20
Corah St	Brooklyn	83	BZ	30
Coral	Rocklands (M.Plain)	144	CS	45
Coral Cl.	Riverton	86	BZ	40
Coral Cr.	San Michel	157	CX	20
Coral Grove Rd	Milnerton	57	BT	33
Coral Rd	Highbury	108	CD	55
Coral Rd	Langeberg Rdg	47	BR	55
Coral Rd	Table View	24	BN	29
Coral Rd	Table View	40	BO	30
Coral Springs Mews	Milnerton	57	BT	32
Coral Tree Rd	Thornton	85	CA	37
Corbonne St	Edgemead	58	BV	36
Corby Cl.	Grassy Pk	141	CQ	33
Corby Cl.	Highbury	107	CE	53
Corby Cl.	Highbury	107	CE	53
Cordega Way	Northpine	64	BT	59
Cordelia	Hout Bay	137	CQ	17
Cordier St	Edgemead	58	BV	36
Cordier St	Lemoenkloof	18	BC	87
Cordoba Ave	Bloubergstrand	24	BJ	27
Cordoba St	Wesbank	107	CF	52
Corfu	Ottery	121	CL	33
Corfu Ave	Capri	185	DB	19
Corfu Ave	Sunnydale	185	DB	19
Corfu Cl.	Sunnydale	185	DA	19
Corfu St	Capricorn	160	CW	31
Corgi	Strandfontein	162	CT	40
Coriander Cr.	Vredenberg	62	BV	52
Coriander St	Sunset Glen	107	CH	54
Cork Oak Cl.	Green Oaks	95	BY	75
Cork Oak St	Bellair	62	BW	53
Cork St	Connaught	87	CB	43
Corlie Rd	Flintdale Est.	141	CO	31
Cormorant	Rocklands (M.Plain)	144	CS	44
Cormorant Ave	Big Bay	24	BK	28
Cormorant Ave	Marina Da Gama	159	CU	30
Cormorant Cir.	Imhoff's Gift	184	DB	16
Cormorant Cl.	Fish Hoek	186	DA	23
Cormorant Cl.	Hout Bay	117	CM	17
Cormorant Cl.	Villa Italia	57	BW	33
Cormorant Cr.	Steenberg	158	CT	24
Cormorants Cl.	D'urbanvale	45	BO	49

STREET NAME	SUBURB NAME	PG	GRID	
Cornelia	Scottsdene	64	BT	61
Cornelis St	Bothasig	58	BT	38
Cornelissen Cr.	Sarepta	89	CB	52
Cornelissen St	William Lloyd	19	BC	93
Cornelle	Groenvlei	18	BA	88
Cornelson	Cloetesville	95	BY	75
Cornelson	Cloetesville	95	BY	77
Cornflower Cr.	Dalvale	19	AY	92
Cornflower Sq.	Lentegeur (M.Plain)	144	CO	46
Cornflower Sq.	Lentegeur (M.Plain)	145	CO	47
Cornflower St	Bridgetown	103	CE	36
Cornhill Rd	Athlone	102	CF	33
Corntail St	Electric City	127	CN	58
Cornuta Ave	Tokai	139	CS	26
Cornwall Rd	Kenilworth	120	CL	29
Cornwall Rd	Lakeside	159	CV	28
Cornwall St	Claremont	120	CJ	29
Cornwall St	Simon's Town	194	DJ	24
Cornwall St	Winslow	175	DC	76
Cornwall St	Woodstock	82	CB	26
Cornway Cr.	Parklands	25	BM	32
Cornwell Rd	Oakdale	61	BX	49
Corona St	Retreat	140	CR	28
Coronado St	The Hague	106	CE	49
Coronata	Anesta	113	CF	75
Coronation Ave	Plumstead	140	CO	29
Coronation Ave	Somerset West	170	CT	74
Coronation Ave	Tamboerskloof	81	CB	21
Coronation Rd	Maitland	84	CA	32
Coronation Rd	Woodstock	82	CC	26
Coronation St	Maitland	83	CA	30
Coronation St	Maitland	84	CA	31
Coronet Ct	Leonsdale	86	CA	42
Corporal St	Bothasig	42	BS	38
Corporation St	Cape Town Cen.	82	CB	23
Corridor Rd	Heideveld	104	CF	39
Corridor St	Tafelsig (M.Plain)	145	CS	48
Corrie Rd	Manenberg	123	CJ	39
Corsair Cl.	Sanddrift	57	BW	33
Corsair Cl.	Barbarossa	139	CO	26
Corsair Cr.	Strandfontein	161	CU	38
Corsair Pl.	Villa Italia	57	BW	33
Corsair Rd	Sanddrift	57	BV	33
Corsair Rd	Sanddrift	57	BW	33
Corsair Way	Sun Valley	185	CZ	20
Corsica	Capricorn	159	CW	30
Corsica Ave	Capri	185	DA	19
Corsica Cl.	Portlands (M.Plain)	144	CQ	46
Cortryk St	De Zoete Inval	39	BJ	87
Corumba St	Malibu Village	127	CL	55
Corvette Ave	Sun Valley	185	CZ	20
Corvette Ave	Sun Valley	185	DA	20
Corvina Link	Hout Bay Harbour	136	CR	14
Corvina Link	Hout Bay Harbour	136	CQ	13
Corvus Cl.	Ocean View	189	DD	15
Corwen St	Claremont	101	CH	30
Cosa Ave	Victoria Mxenge	126	CN	52
Cosa Ave	Victoria Mxenge	146	CO	52
Cosmic Cl.	Salberau	86	CB	41
Cosmic Cl.	Salberau	86	CB	39
Cosmos Cl.	Dunoon	42	BO	37
Cosmos Cl.	Dunoon	42	BO	36
Cosmos Rd	Elfindale	140	CQ	29
Cosmos St	Lentegeur (M.Plain)	144	CO	45
Cosmos St	Peerless Pk East	47	BS	58
Costerton Ave	Courtrai	22	BH	87
Cotha St	Harare	146	CR	52
Cotswold	Wesbank	107	CG	51
Cotswold Ave	Gardens	81	CC	21
Cotswold Rd	Milnerton	57	BV	32
Cottage Cl.	Noordhaven	157	CX	19
Cottage La.	Barbarossa	120	CN	27
Cotte Rd	Lansdowne	122	CL	35
Cotton Way	Marlow	88	CA	50
Coucal St	Eersterivier	128	CM	60
Couch Cr.	Oostersee	60	BX	45
Coucou St	Chantecler	62	BT	51
Cougar St	The Hague	106	CE	49
Country Club Rd	Kenilworth	120	CL	30
Country Estates	Sonstraal Hgts	46	BQ	53
Country La.	Sonstraal Hgts	46	BQ	54
Country Mews St	Onverwacht	175	DC	76
Country Pl.	Sonstraal Hgts	46	BQ	54
Court Rd	Simon's Town	191	DH	24
Court Rd	Wynberg	120	CL	28
Court Town Rd	Plumstead	120	CM	28
Courtrai Cl.	Eversdal Hgts	46	BS	51
Courville St	Gardens	81	CB	22
Covendon Rd	Belgravia	103	CH	35
Covent	Parklands	41	BO	33
Coventry Rd	Woodstock	82	CB	26
Coventry St	Malibu Village	127	CK	55
Cowell Way	Retreat	140	CS	29
Cowley	District Six	82	CB	25
Cowley Cl.	Belhar	106	CE	50
Cowrie Cl.	Bloubergrant	24	BN	30
Cowrie Cr.	Sunset Beach	41	BR	32
Cowrie Cr.	Sunset Beach	41	BS	32
Cox Ave	Penlyn Est.	122	CJ	35
Cox Cr.	Protea Hoogte	63	BX	57
Cox St	Montana/Durrheim	104	CF	41
Coyne St	Protea Hoogte	63	BW	57
Crab St	Gustrow	174	DB	74
Cradick St	Parow Ind.	87	CC	45
Cradock	Panorama	59	BV	41

STREET NAME	SUBURB NAME	PG	GRID	
Cradock Rd	Retreat	140	CS	30
Cradock Rd	Retreat	159	CT	30
Cradock St	Rome	174	CY	73
Cradock St	Ruyterwacht	86	CA	39
Crag St	Tafelsig (M.Plain)	145	CR	48
Craig Rd	Muizenberg Nth	159	CW	28
Craig Rd	Welgemoed	60	BV	46
Craig Rd	Wynberg	120	CL	27
Craig St	Eureka	87	CC	44
Craighall Ave	Voorbrug	107	CG	51
Craigrownie Rd	Bantry Bay	80	CA	18
Craigrownie Rd	Bantry Bay	80	CA	17
Crake Cl.	Pelikan Pk	142	CQ	35
Cramond Rd	Camps Bay	99	CE	19
Cranberry Cr.	Camps Bay	99	CD	19
Cranberry Cr.	Woodlands (M.Plain)	144	CP	44
Cranberry Way	Mitchells Plain	144	CQ	44
Crane Cl.	Dreyersdal	140	CS	27
Crane Cl.	Flintdale Est.	141	CP	31
Crane Cr.	Pelikan Pk	142	CS	36
Crane La.	Villa Italia	57	BW	33
Crane St	Flamingo Vlei	41	BQ	32
Cranko Ave	Kirstenhof	159	CT	27
Cranko Rd	Observatory	101	CD	29
Cranley Rd	Athlone	102	CG	33
Cranmere Rd	Plumstead	120	CN	29
Crassula Ave	Devil's Peak Est.	82	CC	24
Crassula Ave	Welgedacht	60	BT	45
Crassula Cr.	Eersterivier	128	CM	60
Crassula Rd	Kommetjie	183	DC	11
Crassula Rd	Milnerton	57	BU	33
Crassula Rd	Table View	40	BO	30
Crassula Rd	Table View	41	BO	31
Crassula Rd	Table View	41	BO	32
Crassula Rd	Thornton	85	CA	37
Crassula Way	Pinelands	84	CC	34
Crasula	Lentegeur (M.Plain)	145	CO	47
Crater St	Salberau	86	CB	41
Craven Ave	Athlone	102	CG	33
Craven Cl.	Athlone	102	CG	33
Cravenby St	Cravenby	87	CB	43
Crawford Rd	Crawford	102	CH	33
Crawford Rd	Crawford	102	CH	34
Crawford St	Wellington	15	AV	92
Crawley Cr.	Parklands	25	BM	34
Crecy	Strandfontein	162	CT	40
Cree St	Primrose Pk	103	CH	38
Creek Cl.	Durbanville	45	BP	49
Crematorium Rd	Maitland	84	CA	34
Creon Cl.	Uitzicht	47	BO	56
Crescendo	Sonstraal Hgts	46	BR	53
Crescent Ave	Denneburg	23	BE	93
Crescent Rd	Claremont	120	CJ	28
Crescent Rd	Ottery	121	CM	33
Crescent Rd	Wynberg	120	CM	28
Cress Cl.	Vredenberg	62	BV	53
Cresswell Rd	Des Hampden	89	CB	53
Cressy Rd	Athlone	102	CF	32
Crest View Cl.	The Crest	46	BO	53
Crest Way	Retreat	140	CS	30
Crete	Strandfontein	162	CT	40
Crete Cl.	Eureka	87	CC	43
Crete Rd	Ottery	121	CL	33
Crete St	Portlands (M.Plain)	144	CQ	46
Creusot Ave	Door De Kraal	61	BT	47
Crevasse St	Tafelsig (M.Plain)	145	CR	48
Cricket Cr.	Beacon Valley (M.Plain)	145	CP	47
Crickets Gully	Pelikan Pk	141	CR	33
Crinum Cl.	Mountainview	179	DD	78
Crinum Rd	Table View	40	BO	30
Crocus	Lentegeur (M.Plain)	144	CP	46
Croft Cr.	Balvenie	87	CC	43
Croft Rd	Rondebosch	102	CF	31
Croft Rd	Sillery	139	CO	25
Croft St	Somerset West	170	CT	73
Crofton Rd	Muizenberg Nth	159	CW	28
Crombie St	Rome	170	CX	73
Cromer Rd	Muizenberg	159	CX	29
Crompton St	Strand Halt	170	CW	74
Cromwell La.	Noordhoek Manor	157	CX	21
Cromwell La.	Noordhoek Manor	157	CV	20
Cronje Cl.	Welgemoed	60	BU	45
Cronwright La.	Fish Hoek	186	DB	23
Croquet	Beacon Valley (M.Plain)	145	CP	48
Croquet La.	Rondebosch	101	CF	30
Crosby St	Wesbank	107	CE	52
Cross Blvd.	Kewtown	102	CF	34
Cross Blvd.	Silvertown	102	CF	34
Cross Cl.	Belhar	106	CD	50
Cross Cut	Lansdowne	121	CJ	33
Cross Rd	Rosebank	101	CE	30
Cross Rd	Sea Point	81	BZ	20
Cross Rd	Sunridge	41	BO	34
Cross St	Bishop Lavis	105	CE	44
Cross St	Cape Town Cen.	88	BY	48
Cross St	Churchill	60	BX	43
Cross St	Eersterivier	128	CL	60
Cross St	Newlands	101	CH	27
Cross Way	Edgemead	58	BV	37
Crossnie St	Wellington	15	AV	93
Croton Cl.	Greenlands	88	CA	49
Crouse La.	Cape Town Cen.	82	CA	23
Crow Cr.	Pelikan Pk	142	CS	36
Crowie La.	Grassy Pk	141	CQ	32
Crown Cr.	Camps Bay	98	CE	18

STREET NAME	SUBURB NAME	PG	GRID	
Crown Rd	Leonsdale	86	CA	42
Crown St	Vierlanden	30	BN	52
Croxteth Rd	Green Point	81	BZ	21
Crozier	Stellenbosch	95	CC	76
Crozier Cl.	Leonsdale	86	CA	42
Crudop St	Bothasig	42	BS	37
Cruiser Cl.	Sun Valley	185	CZ	20
Cruiser St	Strandfontein	162	CT	39
Crusader Cr.	The Hague	106	CE	49
Cruse	Krigeville	113	CD	76
Cruse La.	Wynberg	120	CL	28
Cruse St	Perm Gdns	128	CK	59
Crust St	Salberau	86	CB	41
Crust St	Salberau	86	CB	39
Crux La.	Ocean View	189	DD	15
Cruythof St	Perm Gdns	128	CK	59
Cruywagen Rd	Simon's Town	195	DK	27
Crystal	Rocklands (M.Plain)	145	CS	47
Crystal Ave	Pollsmoor	158	CT	24
Crystal Rd	Devon Pk	128	CM	60
Crystal Rd	Steenberg	159	CT	30
Crystal St	Groenvlei	18	BA	89
Crystal Way	Belhar	105	CD	45
Crystal Way	Belhar	105	CE	45
Crystal Way	Belthorn Est.	103	CH	35
Cubango St	Eindhoven	106	CH	50
Cuckoo	Rocklands (M.Plain)	144	CS	44
Cuckoo Cr.	Montagu's Gift	141	CO	33
Cuito St	Mfuleni	126	CJ	53
Cula St	Harare	146	CR	53
Culemborg	Die Boord	112	CD	74
Culemborg Cl.	Mitchells Plain	144	CR	45
Culemborg Cl.	Mitchells Plain	144	CR	43
Culemborg Rd	Eversdal	62	BU	51
Culemborg Rd	Stellenberg	62	BU	51
Culemborg St	Avondale	60	BX	44
Culemborg St	Brackenfell	63	BV	56
Culemborg St	Park Estates	174	CZ	72
Culemborg St	Ruyterwacht	86	CA	39
Cullin Cr.	Connaught	87	CB	43
Culloden	Strandfontein	162	CT	40
Culloden Cl.	Strandfontein	162	CT	40
Culloden Cl.	Strandfontein	162	CV	42
Culm Rd	Plumstead	120	CN	29
Culver St	Oranjezicht	82	CC	23
Cumberland Ave	Constantia Village	119	CN	25
Cumberland Cl.	Northern Paarl	18	AZ	88
Cumberland Rd	Paarden Eiland	83	CA	28
Cummings Rd	Tigerhof	57	BX	32
Cummings St	Wellington	10	AR	94
Cummings St	Wellington	11	AS	95
Cumnor Ave	Kenilworth	120	CK	29
Cumulus	Rocklands (M.Plain)	145	CS	47
Cupido	Cloetesville	95	BZ	75
Cupido Cloete St East	Hill View	127	CK	58
Cupido St	Marlow	88	CA	50
Cupido St	Northern Paarl	18	AZ	89
Curie St	Belhar	88	CC	50
Curie Way	Meadowridge	140	CP	27
Curlew Cl.	Imhoff's Gift	184	DC	15
Curlew La.	Villa Italia	57	BW	33
Curlew St	Brooklyn	84	BY	31
Curlew Way	Pelikan Pk	142	CQ	35
Curlew Way	Pelikan Pk	142	CR	35
Curlew Way	Somerset Rdg	170	CT	72
Curlewis Rd	Blouberg Rise	25	BN	31
Curlewis St	Bloomsburg	23	BD	92
Currie St	Oakdene	89	CC	53
Curry	Cloetesville	95	BZ	75
Curry	Dunoon	42	BO	37
Curtis Rd	Gardens	81	CB	22
Curtis Rd	Kirstenhof	140	CS	27
Curtiss	Rocklands (M.Plain)	145	CS	47
Cushat La.	Sweet Valley	139	CQ	25
Cuthbert St	Elriche	18	BB	90
Cutter Cl.	Blouberg Sands	24	BM	30
Cutter Cl.	Marina Da Gama	159	CW	30
Cutter Cl.	Strandfontein	162	CT	39
Cuttlefish La.	Big Bay	24	BL	28
Cuyler Cl.	Edgemead	58	BV	36
Cwangco Cr.	Philippi	124	CL	44
Cwangco St	Mxolisi Phetani	126	CM	51
Cwayi Cr.	Victoria Mxenge	146	CO	51
Cycad Cr.	Tygerdal	58	BX	37
Cycad St	Eastridge (M.Plain)	145	CR	47
Cyclamen Cl.	Belhar	106	CD	47
Cyclamen Rd	Wellway Pk East	46	BP	52
Cygnus Cl.	Ocean View	189	DD	15
Cylnor St	Somerset West	151	CS	73
Cymbal Cl.	Belhar	106	CD	48
Cynaroides	Anesta	113	CG	75
Cynaroides St	Somerset West	151	CR	71
Cynaroides St	Somerset West	151	CS	71
Cynthia	Florida	87	CA	44
Cynthia Cr.	Lentegeur (M.Plain)	145	CO	48
Cynthia Rd	Montagu's Gift	141	CO	33
Cyphia Cl.	Hout Bay	136	CO	13
Cypres	La Rochelle	62	BV	51
Cypress Ave	Lotus River	141	CP	34
Cypress Ave	New Orleans	19	BA	91
Cypress Ave	Thornton	85	CB	37
Cypress La.	Bergvliet	140	CQ	27
Cypress La.	Mandalay	125	CN	47
Cypress Pl.	Sun Valley	185	CZ	20
Cypress Pl.	Sun Valley	185	DC	22

Abbreviations used: Ave – Avenue, A.H. – Agricultural Holding, A.L.– Algemene Landgoed, Blvd – Boulevard, Cen. – Central, Cir. – Circle, Cl. – Close, Cr. – Crescent, Ct – Court, Dr. – Drive, Est. – Estate, Ext. – Extension, Hgts – Heights, Ind. – Industrial, Gdns – Gardens, Gr. – Grove, La. – Lane, (M.Plain) - Mitchells Plain, Nth – North, Pl. – Place, Pk – Park, Rd – Road, Rdg. – Ridge, S.H.– Small Holding, Sq. – Square, St – Street, Sth – South, Ter. – Terrace, Tn – Turn, Val. – Valley, Wk – Walk

STREET NAME	SUBURB NAME	PG	GRID	
Cypress Rd	Newlands	101	CG	27
Cypress St	Forest Village	127	CM	58
Cypress Way	Mitchells Plain	144	CQ	45
Cyprus Cl.	Portlands (M.Plain)	144	CQ	46
Cyprus Rd	Ottery	121	CL	33
Cyprus Rd	Somerset West	170	CT	73
Cyprus St	Woodstock	82	CB	26
Cyster Cl.	Grassy Pk	141	CQ	31
D				
D.F.Malan St	Cape Town Cen.	82	CA	24
D.F.Malan St	Parow Nth	59	BW	41
D.F.Malan St	Parow Nth	59	BW	42
D.F.Malherbe St	Townsend Est.	58	BX	38
D.J. Wood St	Oostersee	87	BY	46
D.J.Geldenhuys St	De Duin	59	BW	41
D.Nyembe Pl.	Driftsands	147	CQ	56
D.Zihlangu Ave	Hout Bay	137	CO	16
Da Gama Cr.	Belhar	106	CD	49
Da Gama Rd	Da Gama Pk	190	DE	21
Da Gama Rd	Welcome Glen	190	DD	22
Da Gama St	Brooklyn	83	BZ	30
Da Gama St	Brooklyn	84	BY	31
Da Gama St	Dal Josafat Ind.	18	BA	90
Da Gama St	Eikendal	47	BS	58
Da Gama St	Eikendal	48	BS	59
Da Gama St	Eikendal	64	BT	59
Da Gama St	Forest Glade	127	CL	58
Da Gama St	Lochnerhof	170	CX	71
Da Gama St	Park Estates	170	CX	72
Da Gama St	Park Estates	174	CY	71
Da Gama St	Parow	86	BZ	42
Da Gama St	The Palms	170	CX	72
Da Gama St	Welgemoed	60	BV	46
Da Gama St	Wellington	11	AQ	95
Da Vinci Rd	Macassar	149	CS	66
Da Vinci St	Kaapzicht	59	BW	40
Da Vinci St	Wellington	11	AQ	95
Daalder Cl.	Guldenland	174	CZ	74
Daalder St	Vierlanden	30	BN	51
Dabchick Quay	Marina Da Gama	159	CW	30
Dabchick Rd	Pelikan Pk	141	CQ	34
Dabchick Rd	Pelikan Pk	141	CR	33
Dabchick Rd	Pelikan Pk	142	CS	36
Dabhat Cl.	New Orleans	19	BB	91
Dabula St	Victoria Mxenge	146	CO	51
Dacres Ave	Epping Ind.	86	CB	39
Dada Cr.	Ilitha Pk	146	CR	51
Dada Dr.	Joe Slovo Pk	57	BV	34
Dada St	Harare	146	CS	53
Dade St	Harare	146	CR	52
Dadel Cr.	Delft Sth	106	CH	50
Daffodil	Kleinvlei	127	CJ	57
Daffodil	Lentegeur (M.Plain)	144	CO	45
Daffodil Cir.	Ocean View	184	DC	15
Daffodil Cr.	Belhar	88	CC	47
Daffodil Cr.	Silvertown	103	CF	35
Daffodil Rd	Uitsig	87	CC	44
Daffodil St	Firgrove	150	CR	67
Daffodil St	Sarepta	89	CB	52
Daffodil Way	Pinelands	84	CC	34
Dagbreek	Onderpapegaaiberg	94	CB	73
Dagbreek	Pinelands	84	CB	34
Dagbreek Ave	Durbanville Hills	45	BR	50
Dagbreek Ave	Mitchells Plain	144	CQ	44
Dagbreek Ave	Mitchells Plain	144	CR	44
Dagbreek St	Sybrand Pk	102	CE	33
Dagbreek St	Sybrand Pk	102	CF	33
Dageraad Rd	Strandfontein	162	CT	39
Dagmar	Die Boord	112	CD	74
Dahlle Cl.	Strand	174	CY	73
Dahlia	Idasvallei	95	CA	78
Dahlia	Idasvallei	96	CA	79
Dahlia	Lentegeur (M.Plain)	144	CP	45
Dahlia	Macassar	149	CS	63
Dahlia Ave	Tarentaalplaas	175	DA	76
Dahlia Ave	Welgedacht	60	BU	45
Dahlia Cl.	Wellway Pk East	46	BP	52
Dahlia Rd	Belhar	87	CC	46
Dahlia Rd	Lavender Hill East	160	CU	31
Dahlia St	Brackenfell	63	BV	57
Dahlia St	Bridgetown	103	CE	36
Dahlia St	Dalvale	19	AY	92
Dahlia St	Dunoon	42	BO	37
Dahlia St	Franschhoek Nth	75	BX	104
Dahlia St	Hanover Pk	122	CJ	36
Dahlia St	Peerless Pk East	47	BS	58
Dahlia St	Ravensmead	87	CA	46
Dahlia St	Sarepta	89	CC	52
Dahlia St	Wellington	10	AS	93
Dainfern Rd	Sunningdale	25	BL	31
Dairy Cl.	Heideveld	103	CG	38
Daisy	Lentegeur (M.Plain)	144	CP	45
Daisy Cir.	Ocean View	184	DC	15
Daisy Cir.	Rugby	57	BX	31
Daisy Cr.	Weltevreden Val. (M.Plain)	124	CM	44
Daisy Cr.	Weltevreden Val. (M.Plain)	124	CN	44
Daisy Hill Rd	Retreat	159	CT	29
Daisy Rd	Lavender Hill East	160	CU	31
Daisy Rd	Scarborough	192	DJ	17
Daisy Rd	Uitsig	87	CC	45
Daisy St	Dunoon	42	BO	37
Daisy St	Hillcrest Hgts	127	CL	57
Daisy St	Kleinvlei	127	CJ	58
Daisy St	Voelvlei	89	CA	52

STREET NAME	SUBURB NAME	PG	GRID	
Daisy Way	Newlands	100	CH	26
Daisy Way	Newlands	101	CH	27
Daisy Way	Tarentaalplaas	175	DA	76
Daka Ct	Delft	106	CF	49
Daka St	Mfuleni	126	CJ	53
Dakota	Rocklands (M.Plain)	163	CT	45
Dakota Rd	Claremont	102	CH	31
Dakota St	Macassar	168	CT	64
Dakota St	Stellenridge	62	BV	51
Dal Loop Rd	Wellington	15	AW	94
Dal Loop Rd	Wellington	15	AX	94
Dal Rd	Camps Bay	99	CD	19
Dala Cr.	Harare	146	CR	53
Dalbor Rd	Flintdale Est.	141	CP	31
Dale	Idasvallei	96	CA	80
Dale	Mabille Pk	89	CA	53
Dale Ave	Silverhurst	119	CN	25
Dale Cl.	Hazendal	102	CF	33
Dale Cl.	Lotus River	141	CP	33
Dale Cl.	Montagu's Gift	141	CO	34
Dale Cr.	Table View	41	BO	34
Dale Rd	Adriaanse	87	CC	43
Dale Rd	Blackheath Ind.	108	CF	57
Dale Rd	Lansdowne	102	CH	32
Dale Rd	Lansdowne	121	CJ	32
Dalebrook Rd	Kalk Bay	187	CZ	27
Dalegarth Rd	Plumstead	120	CN	29
Dalene	Dalvale	19	AY	93
Dalene	Dalvale	19	BA	94
Daleway Ave	Bellville Sth Ind.	89	CA	51
Dalham Rd	Belle Constantia	139	CP	25
Dalia St	Mandalay	125	CN	48
Dalia St	Mandalay	125	CN	49
Dallas Cr.	Southfork	175	DB	75
D'Almeida Ave	Monte Vista	59	BV	39
D'Almeida St	Dal Josafat Ind.	18	BA	90
Dalmore Rd	Dennedal	139	CS	25
Dalmore Rd	Tokai	139	CS	25
Dalsig Rd	Vygeboom	45	BR	50
Dalsig Way	Sonstraal	46	BR	52
Dalsig Way	Vygeboom	46	BR	51
Dalton	Ravensmead	87	CA	45
Dalton Rd	Belhar	88	CC	50
Dalton Rd	Fish Hoek	186	DB	24
Dalton Way	Meadowridge	140	CP	27
Daltondal Cl.	Mitchells Plain	144	CR	45
Daltondal Cl.	Mitchells Plain	144	CR	43
Dalvie Ave	Wellington	15	AV	92
Dalziel Rd	Plumstead	120	CN	28
Dam	Groot Phesantekraal	30	BM	54
Dam Cr.	The Palms	170	CX	73
Dam Rd	Kirstenhof	140	CS	27
Dam Rd	Manenberg	123	CJ	39
Dam Wk	Manenberg	123	CJ	39
Dambord Cr.	Beacon Valley (M.Plain)	145	CP	47
Dambuza Cr.	Victoria Mxenge	126	CN	52
Damda Mfaco St	Guguletu	104	CG	41
Dameni Cr.	Victoria Mxenge	126	CN	52
Dammert	Marlow	88	CA	50
Damons	Glenhaven	89	BZ	51
Dan King Rd	Bonnie Brook	47	BQ	57
Dan King Rd	Bonnie Brook	47	BQ	58
Dan King Rd	Windsor Park Est.	47	BQ	58
Dan Pienaar	Stellenbosch	95	CA	76
Dan Pienaar Cir.	Plumstead	120	CN	28
Dan Pienaar St	Ruyterwacht	86	CB	39
Dan Sohuwa St	Mfuleni	126	CK	53
Dana	Springbok Pk	63	BV	55
Dandelion	Pelikan Pk	142	CQ	36
Dane St	Grassy Pk	141	CQ	32
Dane St	Observatory	101	CD	29
Danena Rd	Rosendal	61	BU	50
Danie Esterhuizen St	Parow Nth	59	BX	42
Danie Theron St	Amanda Glen	46	BS	52
Danie Theron St	Parow Nth	59	BW	41
Danie Uys St	Kaymor	89	BY	53
Daniel	Northern Paarl	18	AY	89
Daniel Ave	Montagu's Gift	141	CO	34
Daniel Cl.	Nyanga	123	CK	41
Daniel Hugo St	Franschhoek Sth	79	BZ	107
Daniel Rd	Tijgerhof	57	BW	32
Daniel Rd East	Sanddrift	57	BV	33
Daniel Rd East	Sanddrift	57	BW	34
Daniel St	De Tuin	47	BS	56
Daniels Cr.	Grassy Pk	141	CQ	33
Danker St	Factreton	85	BZ	35
Danster Cr.	Victoria Mxenge	126	CN	51
Danster Rd	Wellington	15	AV	92
Danster Rd	Wellington	15	AU	94
Dante Cl.	Dreyersdal	140	CR	27
Dante Rd	Dreyersdal	140	CR	27
Danube	Eindhoven	107	CH	51
Danube St	Manenberg	123	CG	39
Danube Way	Portlands (M.Plain)	144	CQ	46
Daphine Ct.	Tafelsig (M.Plain)	145	CR	50
Daphne Cr.	Eastridge (M.Plain)	145	CQ	48
Daphne Cr.	Kraaifontein Ext. 17	47	BQ	58
Daphne Cr.	Woodlands (M.Plain)	144	CO	44
Daphne Rd	Cravenby	87	CA	43
Daphne Rd	Cravenby	87	CB	43
Daphne Rd	Devon Pk	128	CM	60
Daphne St	Hout Bay	136	CP	14
Daphne St	Hout Bay	137	CP	15
Daphne St	Klein Nederburg	19	BC	93
Dapper Rd	Maitland	84	BZ	34

STREET NAME	SUBURB NAME	PG	GRID	
Dapper Rd	Maitland	85	BZ	35
Darby	Ravensmead	87	CA	46
Darien La.	Observatory	83	CC	29
Daries St	Rome	170	CX	73
Darling	Eindhoven	107	CH	51
Darling Cl.	Vierlanden	30	BN	52
Darling Rd	Capricorn	160	CU	31
Darling Rd	Chrismar	61	BX	50
Darling St	Cape Town Cen.	82	CB	23
Darling St	Hout Bay	137	CP	16
Darlington Ave	Fish Hoek	185	DA	22
Darroll's La.	Wynberg	120	CL	29
Darroll's La.	Wynberg	120	CK	30
Darter Cl.	Imhoff's Gift	184	DB	15
Darter Cr.	Pelikan Pk	142	CQ	35
Darter Rd	Imhoff's Gift	184	DB	15
Darter Rd	Sunridge	41	BP	34
Darter St	Eersterivier	128	CM	60
Darter St	Electric City	128	CN	59
Darter's Rd	Gardens	81	CB	22
Dartmoor Cl.	Table View	41	BO	34
Dartmoor Rd	Parklands	25	BM	33
Dartmouth Rd	Muizenberg	159	CW	29
Darwin Rd	Kraaifontein Ext. 17	47	BQ	58
Darwin Rd	Tygerberg Ind. Pk	31	BL	56
Darwin Rd	Windsor Park Est.	47	BQ	58
Darwin Rd	Windsor Pk	47	BR	57
Darwin Way	Meadowridge	140	CP	27
Dassen Rd	Sea Point	81	CA	20
Dassen Way	Skoongesig	45	BO	50
Dassenberg St	Tafelsig (M.Plain)	145	CS	49
Dassenheuwel La.	Meadowsteads	156	CX	18
Dassie	Westlake Est.	158	CT	25
Dassie Cl.	Langeberg Rdg	47	BR	56
Dassie Rd	Capricorn	160	CU	31
Dassie Rd	Silvertown	102	CF	34
Dassie St	Eastridge (M.Plain)	145	CR	48
Dassie St	Sarepta	89	CC	53
Dassiebos Sq.	Roosendaal	107	CF	51
Date Cl.	Eersterivier	127	CM	58
Date Palm St	Bonteheuwel	103	CD	38
Datis St	De Zoete Inval	39	BJ	88
Dauphine Cl.	Edgemead	58	BU	37
Dauphine Cl.	Everglen	45	BS	50
Dauphine Cl.	La Rochelle	62	BV	51
Dauphine St	Courtrai	22	BH	87
Dauphine St	De Tijger	60	BW	43
Dauphine Way	Dieprivier	140	CP	28
Davenport Cl.	Marlborough Pk	63	BT	55
Davenport Rd	Lotus River	141	CQ	34
Davenport Rd	Vredehoek	82	CC	23
Daventry Rd	Eersterivier	128	CN	61
Davey St	William Lloyd	23	BD	94
David	Marlow	88	CA	50
David Atkins St	Charlesville	104	CF	40
David Ave	Montana/Durrheim	104	CF	41
David Baird Cr.	Ruyterwacht	86	CA	40
David Fortune St	Forest Glade	128	CL	59
David Lawrence St	Forest Glade	128	CL	59
David Molefe St	Kuyasa	147	CS	55
David Molefe St	Kuyasa	147	CS	58
David Profit St	Bonteheuwel	103	CD	38
David Rd	Capricorn	160	CU	31
David Rd	Newfields	103	CH	37
David St	Bishop Lavis	105	CD	44
David St	Valhalla Pk	104	CE	41
David St	Zoo Pk	47	BR	57
David St	Zoo Pk	47	BP	58
David van Vuuren	Parow Ind.	87	CA	46
David Way	Ottery East	121	CN	33
David Wilkinson Rd	Charlesville	104	CF	40
David Wk	Grassy Pk	141	CQ	33
Davids	Franschhoek Nth	75	BW	105
Davids Ave	Wellington	15	AU	92
Davids Cl.	Southfork	175	DB	75
Davids St	Nyanga	123	CK	41
Davidse	Cloetesville	95	BZ	75
Davidson St	Woodstock	82	CA	26
Davies Ave	Stanlou	61	BX	54
Davies Wk	Hout Bay	117	CM	16
Davis Rd	Kirstenhof	159	CT	27
Davis St	Highbury	107	CD	54
Davis St	Highbury	108	CD	55
Davis St	Perm Gdns	128	CK	59
Davison Rd	Woodstock	82	CB	26
Davy	Idasvallei	96	CA	79
Davy Link	Belhar	88	CC	50
Dawes St	Schotsche Kloof	81	CA	22
Dawids St	Brantwood	89	CA	54
Dawlish Rd	Plumstead	120	CN	29
Dawn	Dalvale	19	AY	92
Dawn Ave	Bel Ombre	119	CM	23
Dawn Ave	Kenever	61	BT	49
Dawn Cl.	Rosendal	61	BT	50
Dawn Cl.	Salberau	86	CB	41
Dawn Cl.	Tafelsig (M.Plain)	145	CS	50
Dawn Rd	Capricorn	160	CV	31
Dawn Rd	Montague Gdns Ind.	42	BS	35
Dawn Rd	Rondebosch	102	CG	31
Dawson St	Aurora	45	BP	49
Days Wk	Pinelands	102	CD	33
Dayspring Villas	Sonstraal Hgts	46	BQ	54
Daytona Cl.	Killarney Gdns	42	BP	37
Daza St	Bloekombos	48	BR	62
De Villiers	Stellenbosch	95	CB	76

STREET NAME	SUBURB NAME	PG	GRID	
De Anker	Durbanville	45	BQ	49
De Anker	Durbanville	45	BP	47
De Beer	Stellenbosch	95	CB	76
De Beer St	Klipkop	87	BZ	45
De Beer St	Sack's Circle Ind.	88	CB	50
De Beers Ave	Helderzicht	170	CV	71
De Beers Ave	Somerset West	170	CV	72
De Beers Rd	Park Estates	170	CX	71
De Beers Rd	Park Estates	174	CY	71
De Bloem Cl.	Somerset West	151	CS	73
De Boerin St	Bothasig	58	BU	37
De Bron	De Tuin	47	BS	55
De Bron	Vredekloof	46	BS	53
De Bron Ave	Kenever	61	BT	49
De Buis Rd	Plattekloof Glen	59	BV	40
De Bussy	Delft Sth	125	CK	48
De Chavonnes Ave	Hout Bay	137	CO	15
De Dam Rd	Vierlanden	30	BN	52
De Duin Ave	Mitchells Plain	144	CQ	45
De Duin Ave	Mitchells Plain	144	CR	45
De Duin Cr.	De Tuin	47	BS	56
De Duin Cr.	Welgelee	63	BT	55
De Eike St	Soneike I	89	CA	54
De Goede Hoop Cl.	Noordhaven	157	CW	19
De Gredel Cl.	Mitchells Plain	144	CR	45
De Gredel Cl.	Mitchells Plain	144	CR	43
De Grendel Ave	Bothasig	42	BS	37
De Grendel Rd	Parow Nth	60	BW	43
De Grendel Rd	Tijgerhof	57	BW	32
De Gruchy Rd	Heathfield	140	CQ	28
De Hague Cl.	Uitzicht	47	BO	56
De Haviland St	The Hague	106	CE	49
De Haviland St	The Hague	106	CH	48
De Havilland St	Kensington	84	BY	33
De Hoek	Mitchells Plain	144	CR	45
De Hoop Ave	Tamboerskloof	81	CC	21
De Hoop Cr.	Edgemead	58	BU	38
De Hoop Cr.	Somerset West	170	CT	73
De Hoop St	Oak Glen	62	BW	52
De Houtman St	Belrail	88	BY	49
De Hulk Way	Penhill	128	CK	61
De Jager St	Windsor Pk	47	BR	57
De Jongh St	Park Estates	170	CX	71
De Jonghs Ave	Paarl	22	BE	88
De Keur Ave	Proteaville	46	BO	51
De Keur Rd	Vierlanden	30	BN	51
De Keur Rd	Vierlanden	30	BN	52
De Klein Molen St	Paarl	18	BC	87
De Klerk	Bo Dalsig	113	CE	76
De Kloof Cl.	Welgelegen	59	BU	40
De Kock Ave	The Vines	140	CO	27
De Kock Rd	Klipkop	87	BZ	45
De Kock St	Onverwacht	174	CZ	73
De Kock St	Onverwacht	174	CZ	74
De Kock St	Parowvallei	87	BZ	43
De Korte Ave	District Six	82	CB	24
De Korte Cl.	Belhar	106	CE	50
De Kuilen St	De Kuilen	89	CB	54
De la Caille Ave	Newlands	101	CH	27
De la Cruz St	Highbury	107	CD	54
De la Cruz St	Highbury	108	CD	55
De la Fontaine Ave	Monte Vista	59	BW	39
De la Fontaine Ave	Plattekloof Glen	59	BW	40
De la Haye Ave	De La Haye	62	BX	51
De la Haye Ave	Lansdowne	121	CK	32
De la Quellerie Rd	Rondebosch	102	CG	32
De la Rey Cr.	Eastridge (M.Plain)	145	CQ	49
De la Rey St	Franschhoek Sth	79	BZ	107
De la Rey St	Modderdam	105	CD	45
De la Rey St	Parow Ind.	87	CB	45
De la Rey St	Parowvallei	87	BZ	44
De la Roche Cl.	Mitchells Plain	144	CR	45
De la Roche Cl.	Mitchells Plain	144	CS	43
De Lange St	Belrail	61	BX	48
De Leeuw St	Marlow	88	CA	50
De Lille	Marina Da Gama	159	CV	30
De Lille St	Belrail	88	BY	49
De Lorentz St	Gardens	81	CB	21
De Luc Cr.	Groenvlei	18	BA	88
De Maas Cl.	Ruyterwacht	86	BZ	40
De Maas Cr.	Ruyterwacht	86	BZ	40
De Marcy	Table View	41	BQ	33
De Mardt St	The Palms	170	CW	73
De Mist Ave	Belhar	106	CE	49
De Mist Rd	Welgemoed	61	BV	47
De Mist St	Bloubergstrand	24	BL	28
De Mist St	Brooklyn	84	BZ	31
De Mist St	Churchill	60	BX	43
De Neyssen	The Palms	170	CX	73
De Oewer St	Bellair	62	BV	53
De Olivier St	William Lloyd	23	BD	92
De Oude Schuur	Langeberg Rdg	47	BR	55
De Oude Werf Cl.	Vredekloof Hgts	47	BS	55
De Poort St	Somerset West	171	CW	77
De Re St	KWV	22	BG	88
De Reyger Rd	Tygerdal	58	BX	38
De Rijger St	Belrail	88	BY	49
De Roos St	District Six	82	CB	24
De Rust Ave	Bergvliet	140	CQ	27
De Ruyter Dr.	Park Estates	170	CX	71
De Ruyter Dr.	Strandvale	170	CW	73
De Smit St	Green Point	81	BZ	22
De Stadler Ave	Capri Village	184	DB	18
De Stellenhoek	Bellair	62	BV	53
De Tyger Rd	Skoongesig	46	BO	51

Index to Street Names

De Uitkijk — Duiker Rd

STREET NAME	SUBURB NAME	PG	GRID	
De Uitkijk	Welgedacht	60	BT	45
De Vijgen	Eversdal Hgts	46	BS	51
De Ville Cl.	Ferndale	62	BV	54
De Villiers	Franschhoek Sth	78	BY	106
De Villiers Ave	Kenridge	45	BS	49
De Villiers Ave	Kenridge	61	BT	49
De Villiers Ave	Kenridge Hgts	45	BR	48
De Villiers Ave	Kenridge Hgts	45	BS	48
De Villiers Ave	Rosebank	101	CE	30
De Villiers Dr.	Durbanville	46	BQ	51
De Villiers Dr.	Valmary Pk	46	BR	51
De Villiers Dr. Ext	Durbanville	46	BP	51
De Villiers Rd	District Six	82	CB	24
De Villiers Rd	Durbanville	46	BP	51
De Villiers Rd	Maitland	84	CB	31
De Villiers Rd	Sonstraal Hgts	46	BQ	53
De Villiers Rd	Sonstraal Hgts	46	BR	54
De Villiers Rd	Wynberg	120	CK	28
De Villiers St	Belhar	107	CE	51
De Villiers St	Eastridge (M.Plain)	145	CQ	49
De Villiers St	Kommetjie	183	DC	12
De Villiers St	Lemoenkloof	18	BC	89
De Villiers St	Park Estates	174	CY	72
De Villiers St	Somerset West	170	CT	74
De Villiers St	Sunray	61	BX	49
De Villiers St	Vasco Est.	59	BX	40
De Villiers St	Vasco Est.	86	BY	40
De Villiers St	Wellington	10	AS	93
De Villiers Steps	Fish Hoek	186	DB	24
De Villiers Way	Simon's Town	190	DD	22
De Villiers Way	Simon's Town	191	DD	23
De Vos	Stellenbosch	95	CC	75
De Vos St	Park Estates	170	CX	72
De Vreugde Cr.	Dal Josafat Ind.	18	BB	89
De Vries St	Wellington	15	AV	92
De Waal	Stellenbosch	95	CC	77
De Waal Dr.	Devil's Peak Est.	82	CC	24
De Waal Dr.	Newlands	101	CD	28
De Waal Dr.	Woodstock	82	CC	26
De Waal Dr.	Woodstock	83	CC	27
De Waal Rd	Belhar	106	CD	49
De Waal Rd	Fish Hoek	186	DB	24
De Waal Rd	Flintdale Est.	140	CP	30
De Waal Rd	Flintdale Est.	141	CP	31
De Waal Rd	Plumstead	140	CP	29
De Waal Rd	Somerset West	171	CU	78
De Waal Rd Upper	Fish Hoek	186	DB	23
De Waal St	Bracken Hgts	62	BU	54
De Waal St	Paarl	22	BF	88
De Wee St	Kylemore	97	BZ	86
De Wet	Brandwacht	113	CE	75
De Wet Marais	Peerless Pk East	48	BR	59
De Wet Rd	Bantry Bay	80	CB	18
De Wet Rd	Fresnaye	81	CB	19
De Wet Rd	Ottery	121	CN	33
De Wet Rd	Ottery East	121	CN	34
De Wet St	Bellville Sth Ext. 5	88	BZ	49
De Wet St	Eastridge (M.Plain)	145	CQ	49
De Wet St	Franschhoek Sth	79	BY	107
De Wet St	Montagu's Gift	141	CO	34
De Wet St	Richmond Est.	59	BX	40
De Wet St	Richmond Est.	86	BY	40
De Wet St	Richmond Est.	86	BY	41
De Wet St	Soneike I	89	CA	54
De Wilde Gans	Silverhurst	119	CN	24
De Wilger St	Heemstede	62	BW	52
De Wilger St	Heemstede	62	BX	52
Dean La.	Newlands	101	CG	28
Dean St	Cape Town Cen.	81	CB	22
Dean St	Newlands	101	CG	28
Deane Rd	Sea Point	81	CA	20
Deauville Cir.	Milnerton	41	BS	33
Debaren Cl.	Steenberg	158	CT	23
Debden Ave	Epping Forest	86	CB	41
Debeza St	Brown's Farm	124	CL	43
Debeza St	Ilitha Pk	146	CQ	52
Debeza St	Ilitha Pk	146	CR	53
Deborah	Dalvale	19	AY	92
Deborah	Dalvale	19	AY	93
Deborah Cl.	Tafelsig (M.Plain)	145	CS	50
Deborah Cl.	Tafelsig (M.Plain)	145	CP	50
Debussy Cr.	Mandalay	125	CN	48
Debussy St	Groenheuwel	19	AZ	91
Dee Rd	Newlands	101	CG	29
Deel Cl.	Connaught	87	CB	43
Deer Park Dr. East	Vredehoek	100	CD	23
Deer Park Dr. West	Vredehoek	100	CD	23
Deer Rd	Bishop Lavis	105	CD	43
Deer St	Durbanville	45	BP	49
Deer St	Ocean View	184	DC	15
Deerfield	Table View	25	BN	31
Defiant	Rocklands (M.Plain)	145	CS	47
Deiningdal Cr.	Strand	174	CZ	73
Dekriet	Lentegeur (M.Plain)	144	CP	45
Del Aire	Ridgeworth	61	BV	49
Del Monte Cl.	Mitchells Plain	144	CR	45
Del Monte Cl.	Mitchells Plain	144	CS	43
Del Valle	Sunningdale	25	BM	31
Delaire St	Welgedacht	44	BS	46
Delaney St	Plumstead	120	CN	29
Delarey St	Flintdale Est.	141	CP	31
Delaware Ave	Primrose Pk	122	CJ	38
Delen Dr.	Sonstraal Hgts	46	BS	54
Delford Ave	Fish Hoek	186	DA	24
Delft	Malibu Village	127	CJ	56
Delft Ct	Marina Da Gama	159	CV	30
Delft Main Rd	Delft	106	CH	50
Delft Main Rd	Delft Sth	125	CJ	49
Delft Main Rd	Delft Sth	125	CK	48
Delft Main Rd	The Hague	106	CF	50
Delft Main Rd	Voorbrug	106	CG	50
Delheim Cl.	Haasendal	90	CB	57
Delheim Cl.	Welgedacht	44	BS	45
Delheim Cl.	Weltevreden Val. (M.Plain)	144	CR	45
Delheim Cl.	Weltevreden Val. (M.Plain)	144	CS	43
Delheim Rd	Table View	41	BO	32
Delhi Rd	Lansdowne	121	CK	34
Delia Rd	Montagu's Gift	141	CO	33
Delia Way	Oak Glen	62	BW	52
Delingham Rd	Huis-in-bos	139	CO	25
Delius	Delft Sth	125	CK	48
Dell Cl.	Durbanville	45	BP	49
Dell St	Klipkop	87	BZ	45
Dellville Rd	Somerset West	171	CT	76
Dellville Sq.	Maitland Gdn Village	84	CC	31
Dellwyn Rd	Ruyterwacht	86	BZ	39
Delman Rd	Blackheath Ind.	108	CE	56
Delmas Sibanyoni St	Kuyasa	147	CS	55
Delos Rd	Ottery	121	CL	33
Delphi Rd	Eureka	87	CC	43
Delphinium	Lentegeur (M.Plain)	145	CO	47
Delphinium St	Devil's Peak Est.	82	CC	24
Delphinium St	Hillcrest Hgts	127	CL	57
Delphinium St	Somerset West	151	CS	73
Delphium St	Bridgetown	103	CG	37
Delson Ave	Voorbrug	107	CG	51
Delson Cir.	Somerset West	171	CV	75
Delta	Cloetesville	94	BY	74
Delta Rd	Deltacrest Country Est.	72	BU	91
Delta Rd	Graceland	146	CP	53
Delta St	Belrail	88	BY	54
Delto Rd	Ocean View	189	DD	15
Delwyn Cr.	Glen Ive	62	BU	51
Dema St	Victoria Mxenge	126	CN	52
Demeter St	Ferndale	62	BV	54
Demeter St	Woodlands (M.Plain)	144	CO	44
Demi-Sec	Durmonte	30	BN	52
Democracy Way	Marconi Beam	57	BV	33
Dempers St	Paarlzicht	19	BC	91
Den Haag	Edgemead	58	BU	37
Denbigh Rd	Plumstead	120	CN	28
Denchworth Cl.	Athlone	102	CF	34
Denchworth Cr.	Athlone	102	CF	33
Denchworth Rd	Athlone	102	CF	34
Denchworth Rd East	Belgravia	102	CF	34
Denel	Strandfontein	163	CT	45
Denham Rd	Lansdowne	121	CJ	34
Denhof Rd	Edgemead	58	BV	37
Denholm Rd	Vredehoek	82	CC	23
Denhume Way	Kenridge	61	BU	49
Denise Cir.	Weltevreden Val. (M.Plain)	124	CN	44
Denise Cl.	Dalvale	19	AY	93
Denise Cl.	Tafelsig (M.Plain)	145	CS	50
Denise Cl.	Tafelsig (M.Plain)	145	CP	50
Denise St	Chrismar	61	BX	50
Denison Way	Edgemead	59	BU	39
Denlyn St	Welgelegen	59	BV	40
Denne Ave	Scottsdene	64	BV	59
Denne Ave	Sonnedal	59	BV	42
Denne Cr.	Heemstede	62	BW	53
Denne St	Belmont Pk	48	BR	61
Denne St	Brackenfell	63	BV	56
Denne St	Bridgetown	103	CE	36
Denne St	Klipdam	90	CB	55
Denne St	Wellington	10	AS	92
Denne St	Wellway Pk	46	BO	52
Denneboom Ave	Thornton	85	CA	37
Denneboom Rd	Belhar	105	CD	46
Denneboom St	Dunoon	42	BO	37
Dennebosch Cl.	Fir Grove	139	CQ	25
Dennebosch Way	Fir Grove	139	CQ	25
Denneburg	Welgelegen	59	BT	40
Dennedal Ave	Dennedal	139	CS	25
Dennedal Ave West	Dennedal	139	CS	25
Dennegeur Ave	Strandfontein	161	CU	38
Dennegeur Ave	Strandfontein	162	CT	39
Dennegeur Ave	Strandfontein	162	CT	41
Dennegeur Cl.	Rome Glen	171	CW	77
Dennegeur Cl.	Rome Glen	171	CV	77
Dennegeur Cr.	Somerset West	171	CW	77
Dennegeur St	Brackenfell	63	BW	56
Dennehoek St	Somerset West	151	CR	72
Dennehof	Mitchells Plain	144	CQ	45
Dennehof	Mountainside Est.	179	DD	78
Dennehof Rd	Pine Acres	175	DC	77
Dennehof Rd	Winslow	179	DD	77
Dennemere Dr.	Dennemere	108	CH	57
Dennemere Dr.	Dennemere	127	CJ	57
Dennerand	Dalsig	113	CD	75
Dennesig St	Stellenbosch	95	CB	75
Dennesig Way	Northpine	63	BU	57
Dennia Pl.	Plattekloof Glen	59	BV	40
Dennis Ave	Lavender Hill	159	CT	30
Dennis St	Montagu's Gift	141	CO	34
Denniston Cl.	Plumstead	140	CP	29
Denton St	Lansdowne	121	CK	32
Denton St	Ravensmead	87	CA	46
Denton Ter.	Schotsche Kloof	81	CA	22
Denver Cl.	Colorado (M.Plain)	144	CO	43
Denver Cl.	Portlands (M.Plain)	144	CR	46
Denver Rd	Lansdowne	102	CH	32
Denver Rd	Lansdowne	121	CJ	32
Denys Rd	Bergvliet	139	CP	26
Denyssen Rd	Steenberg	159	CT	30
Denza St	Brackenfell Sth	63	BX	57
Deodar Rd	Eersterivier	128	CN	60
Deodar St	Forest Village	127	CM	57
Deodar St	Loevenstein	60	BW	45
Depsiton Cr.	Lavender Hill	160	CT	31
Derby Ave	Valmary Pk	46	BR	51
Derby Cl.	Milnerton Rdg	41	BS	34
Derby Cr.	Ottery	122	CM	35
Derby Rd	Avon	86	CA	41
Derby Rd	Kenilworth	120	CK	30
Derby Rd	Lakeside	159	CV	28
Derby Rd	Lansdowne	121	CK	33
Derbyshire Cr.	Kirstenhof	159	CU	27
Derbyshire Cr.	Kirstenhof	159	CW	27
Derbyshire St	Kirstenhof	159	CU	27
Derek Rd	Montagu's Gift	141	CO	34
Derheyn Cr.	Parow Nth	59	BX	42
Derna Rd	Lansdowne	121	CK	32
Derrick Cloete St	Fisantekraal	31	BK	58
Derrick Dr.	Somerset West	171	CX	75
Derry Cl.	Connaught	87	CB	43
Derry Rd	Rondebosch	101	CF	29
Derry St	Vredehoek	82	CC	24
Derwent Cr.	Coniston Pk	159	CU	29
Derwent La.	Hanover Pk	122	CK	36
Derwent Rd	Gardens	81	CC	21
Derwent Way	Pinelands	84	CB	34
Des Pres St	De Zoete Inval	22	BH	88
Des Pres St	De Zoete Inval	39	BJ	87
Desande Rd	Flintdale Est.	141	CP	31
Desch	Idasvallei	95	CA	78
Desere St	Delro	107	CH	54
Desert Cr.	Eersterivier	127	CM	58
Desiree Cl.	Dalvale	19	AY	93
Desmore St	Amstelhof	23	BD	93
Desmore St	Wellington	10	AS	92
Desmore St	William Lloyd	23	BD	92
Desre Rd	Newfields	103	CH	37
Dessie Rd	Plumstead	120	CN	28
Detroit Cr.	Malibu Village	127	CK	55
Deutz Rd	Hanover Pk	122	CL	36
Deutzia St	Somerset West	151	CS	71
Devi Ave	Gatesville	103	CH	36
Devi Rd	Clarkes	86	CC	42
Devi Rd	Clarkes	86	CB	39
Devils Peak Rd	Heideveld	104	CG	40
Devine St	Paarl	22	BD	88
Devon Air Cl.	Crofters Valley	185	CY	19
Devon Cl.	Balvenie	87	CC	43
Devon Park	Table View	41	BP	34
Devon Park	Table View	41	BQ	33
Devon Rd	Bay Pk	175	DC	76
Devon Rd	Lakeside	159	CV	28
Devon Rd	Lansdowne	121	CK	34
Devon Rd	Lansdowne	121	CL	34
Devon Rd	Oostersee	87	BY	45
Devon Rd	Winslow	179	DD	76
Devon St	Claremont	120	CJ	29
Devon St	Simon's Town	194	DJ	24
Devon St	Woodstock	83	CB	27
Devon Vallei	Devonvallei	112	CD	73
Devon Vallei	Stellenbosch	94	CA	71
Devon Vallei	Stellenbosch	94	CC	71
Devon Valley Rd	Nooitgedacht	93	BY	70
Devon Valley Way	Table View	41	BO	32
Devon Way	Capricorn	159	CW	30
Devonport Rd	Tamboerskloof	81	CB	21
Devonshire Cl.	Parklands	25	BN	32
Devonshire Hill Rd	Rondebosch	101	CF	29
Devonshire Hill Rd	Rondebosch	101	CE	27
Devonshire Rd	Ottery East	121	CN	34
Devonshire Rd	Wynberg	120	CL	28
Devonshire St	Woodstock	83	CC	27
Dewberry Dr.	Somerset West	151	CQ	72
Dewhurst St	Ottery	122	CM	35
Dewhurst St	Ottery	122	CN	36
Dexter Cl.	Mitchells Plain	144	CR	45
Dexter St	Durbanville	46	BP	53
Dexter St	Durbanville	46	BS	54
Dexter St	Montana/Durrheim	104	CF	41
Dhow St	Sun Valley	185	CZ	20
Di Rialto St	Mountain View	19	BB	91
Diadem La.	Leonsdale	86	CA	42
Diagonal St	Tafelsig (M.Plain)	145	CS	48
Diamant Cr.	Welgelegen	59	BT	41
Diamant St	Forest Hgts	127	CK	58
Diamond	Highbury	108	CE	55
Diamond	Rocklands (M.Plain)	145	CS	47
Diamond Dr.	Sheridon Pk	159	CU	29
Diamond St	Surrey	103	CG	38
Diamond Way	San Michel	157	CX	20
Diana	Dalvale	19	AY	92
Diana	Dalvale	19	AY	93
Diana	Dieprivier	140	CO	28
Diana Cl.	Barbarossa	140	CO	27
Diana Cl.	Dalvale	19	AY	93
Diana Cl.	Dalvale	19	BA	94
Diana Cl.	Tafelsig (M.Plain)	145	CS	50
Diana Link	Woodlands (M.Plain)	144	CO	44
Diana Rd	Sanddrift	57	BW	33
Diana St	Kalkfontein II	107	CD	52
Diana St	Valhalla Pk	104	CE	42
Dianthus St	Somerset West	150	CS	70
Dianthus St	Table View	41	BO	32
Dias Rd	Grassy Pk	141	CQ	32
Dias St	Dal Josafat Ind.	18	BA	90
Dias St	Forest Glade	127	CL	58
Diaz Ave	Monte Vista	59	BV	40
Diaz Cr.	Belhar	106	CD	49
Diaz St	Bothasig	58	BT	38
Diaz St	Brooklyn	84	BZ	31
Diaz St	Kaapzicht	59	BW	40
Diaz St	Lochnerhof	170	CX	72
Diaz St	Lochnerhof	174	CY	72
Diaz St	Panorama	59	BV	41
Diaz St	Somerset West	171	CW	75
Diaz St	Welgemoed	60	BV	46
Dibana Rd	Umrhabulo Triangle	147	CQ	57
Dibana Rd	Umrhabulo Triangle	147	CR	57
Dibber Pl.	Eureka	87	CC	44
Dick Burton St	Plumstead	120	CN	30
Dick King Way	Brooklyn	84	BZ	31
Dickens Ave	Somerset West	171	CU	75
Dickens Cl.	Somerset Pk	171	CW	75
Dickens Dr.	Mandalay	125	CM	47
Dickens Dr.	Mandalay	125	CM	48
Dickens Pl.	Somerset Pk	171	CW	75
Dickens Rd	Salt River	83	CC	28
Dickson Cr.	Brackenfell	63	BV	57
Dickson St	Woodstock	83	CB	27
Diconia St	Eersterivier	128	CM	59
Didi St	Scottsdene	64	BT	59
Didiyela St	Griffiths Mxenge	146	CP	54
Dido Valley Rd	Simon's Town	190	DE	22
Dido Valley Rd	Simon's Town	191	DF	23
Die Braak	Belhar	106	CD	49
Die Erf St	Heemstede	62	BW	53
Die Laan	Stellenbosch	95	CC	77
Die Plein	Pinelands	84	CB	34
Diedrikkie Rd	Mikro Pk	90	CB	55
Diemaar Rd	Kommetjie	183	DB	12
Dieman Rd	Grassy Pk	141	CR	32
Diemersdal Cl.	Mitchells Plain	144	CR	45
Diemersdal Cl.	Mitchells Plain	144	CR	43
Diemersdal Rd	De Bron	45	BS	48
Diemersdal St	Kleinbosch	59	BT	40
Dien St	Grassy Pk	141	CR	31
Diep Cr.	Delft	106	CF	50
Diep St	Brooklyn	83	BZ	30
Diep St	Mfuleni	126	CJ	53
Dieppe Rd	Strandfontein	162	CT	40
Dieppe St	Courtrai	22	BH	87
Dieprivier St	Eersterivier	128	CM	59
Diepwater Main Rd	Wesbank	107	CF	51
Dierama Ave	Welgedacht	60	BT	45
Dierama Cl.	Gordon Hgts	180	DD	79
Dierama Cl.	Gordon Hgts	180	DE	79
Diesel Rd	Ndabeni	84	CC	31
Dietmann St	Wellington	15	AU	91
Dietrich Rd	Highlands Est.	122	CM	38
Dietrich Rd	Schaap Kraal	122	CM	38
Dietrich St	William Lloyd	23	BD	94
Digtebij	Mabille Pk	89	CA	53
Digteby Cr.	Voorbrug	107	CH	51
Dijon	Groenvlei	18	BA	88
Dijon St	Malibu Village	127	CK	56
Dik-Dikkie	Soneike II	90	BZ	55
Dike St	Umrhabulo Triangle	147	CR	56
Dikinyeka Sq.	Eyethu	146	CP	53
Dikkop Cl.	Pelikan Pk	142	CQ	35
Dikkop Cr.	Sunridge	41	BP	34
Dikkop Way	Electric City	127	CN	58
Dikza Rd	Ilitha Pk	146	CQ	53
Diliya	Philippi East	125	CM	47
Dilo St	Ekuphumuleni	146	CQ	53
Diluta Dr.	Sunset Beach	41	BS	32
Diluta Dr.	Sunset Beach	41	BS	32
Dimba Rd	Ekuphumuleni	146	CP	53
Dinder Cr.	Delft	106	CG	49
Dinghie Cir.	Strandfontein	162	CT	39
Dingiso Cr.	Victoria Mxenge	126	CN	51
Dingiso St	Bloekombos	48	BQ	62
Dingle Ave	Kenilworth	120	CK	30
Dingle Rd	Goodwood Est.	86	BZ	39
Dingle Rd	Richmond Est.	86	BY	40
Dingle Rd	Townsend Est.	85	BZ	38
Diniso	Mbekweni	15	AV	91
Dinsley Rd	Wynberg	120	CM	29
Dipidax Rd	Table View	24	BN	30
Dirk Adams Rd	Newfields	122	CJ	36
Dirkie Uys Rd	Somerset West	170	CU	74
Dirkie Uys St	Amanda Glen	46	BS	52
Dirkie Uys St	Brackenfell	63	BV	55
Dirkie Uys St	Flintdale Est.	141	CO	31
Dirkie Uys St	Franschhoek Sth	79	BY	107
Dirkie Uys St	Franschhoek Sth	79	BZ	107
Dirkie Uys St	Goodwood Est.	86	BZ	39
Dirkie Uys St	Kempenville	88	BY	49
Disa	Lentegeur (M.Plain)	144	CO	45
Disa	Stellenbosch	95	BY	75
Disa Ave	Brantwood	89	CB	53
Disa Ave	Fish Hoek	186	DA	24
Disa Ave	Fish Hoek	186	DB	24
Disa Ave	Kommetjie	183	DC	11
Disa Ave	Pinelands	84	CC	34
Disa Ave	Somerset West	170	CT	73

Abbreviations used: Ave – Avenue, A.H. – Agricultural Holding, A.L.– Algemene Landgoed, Blvd – Boulevard, Cen. – Central, Cir. – Circle, Cl. – Close, Cr. – Crescent, Ct – Court, Dr. – Drive, Est. – Estate, Ext. – Extension, Hgts – Heights, Ind. – Industrial, Gdns – Gardens, Gr. – Grove, La. – Lane, (M.Plain) - Mitchells Plain, Nth – North, Pl. – Place, Pk – Park, Rd – Road, Rdg. – Ridge, S.H.– Small Holding, Sq. – Square, St – Street, Sth – South, Ter. – Terrace, Tn – Turn, Val. – Valley, Wk – Walk

STREET NAME	SUBURB NAME	PG	GRID	
Disa Cr.	Blomtuin	61	BW	50
Disa Cr.	Bonteheuwel	103	CD	38
Disa Cr.	Sanddrift	57	BW	34
Disa Cr.	Scottsdene	64	BU	59
Disa Ct	Kewtown	102	CF	34
Disa Pl.	Bergvliet	140	CQ	27
Disa Rd	Belhar	88	CC	47
Disa Rd	Blackheath Ind.	108	CF	57
Disa Rd	Brackenfell	63	BV	56
Disa Rd	Capricorn	160	CU	31
Disa Rd	Chapman's Peak	156	CX	16
Disa Rd	Milnerton	57	BU	33
Disa Rd	Murdock Valley	195	DK	27
Disa Rd	Philippi East	124	CK	46
Disa Rd	Table View	41	BO	31
Disa River Rd	Hout Bay	117	CM	18
Disa St	Crossroads	124	CK	44
Disa St	Durbanville	46	BO	51
Disa St	Franschhoek Sth	79	BZ	108
Disa St	Klein Nederburg	19	BC	93
Disa St	Klein Nederburg	19	BC	93
Disa St	Parow Nth	59	BW	42
Disa St	Wellington	10	AS	93
Disa St	Whispering Pines	175	DC	76
Disa Way	Delft	106	CF	50
Disa Way	Thornton	85	CA	37
Discovery	Blue Downs	127	CJ	56
Discovery Ave	Maitland Gdn Village	84	CC	31
Discovery Rd	Strandfontein	163	CT	43
Dise St	Malibu Village	127	CJ	55
Disraeli St	Rome	174	CY	73
Dissel Rd	Bonteheuwel	103	CD	38
Dissel Rd	Bonteheuwel	103	CE	38
Distillery	Stellenbosch	94	CC	73
Distillery	Stellenbosch	94	CC	74
Distillery St	Dal Josafat Ind.	18	BB	90
Distillery St	Dal Josafat Ind.	18	BC	90
Ditmars	Brandwacht	113	CE	75
Dixon St	Cape Town Cen.	82	BZ	23
Dixton Rd	Mowbray	101	CD	30
Dixton Rd	Observatory	101	CD	30
Diya St	Harare	146	CR	54
Diya St	Harare	146	CS	54
Dlala St	Umrhabulo Triangle	147	CR	57
Dlalo Cr.	Harare	146	CR	53
Dlavu Cl.	Umrhabulo Triangle	147	CQ	58
Dlayedwa St	Bloekombos	48	BQ	62
Dlebe Cl.	Harare	146	CS	52
Dleka St	Harare	146	CR	53
Dlelo St	Harare	146	CS	54
Dlephu Rd	Brown's Farm	124	CL	43
Dludaka	Philippi East	124	CM	46
Dobson Cl.	Simon's Town	195	DK	27
Dobson Rd	Athlone	102	CF	33
Docav Rd	Meadowridge	139	CO	26
Dock Ave	Riverton	86	BZ	40
Dock Rd	Cape Town Cen.	82	BZ	23
Dock Rd	Foreshore	82	BZ	23
Doddington Way	Plattekloof Glen	59	BW	39
Dodds Rd	Observatory	101	CD	29
Dodington Pl.	Blue Downs	108	CH	56
Doh St	Macassar	149	CS	65
Doig Rd	Ottery	122	CL	35
Doig Rd	Schaap Kraal	122	CL	35
Dolabella Dr.	Sunset Beach	41	BS	32
Dolfi	Wesbank	107	CG	52
Dolfin Cr.	Woodlands (M.Plain)	144	CP	45
Dolfyn St	Gustrow	174	DB	74
Dolfyn St	Southfork	174	DB	74
Dolomite	Belthorn Est.	122	CJ	35
Dolomite Cl.	Welgelegen	59	BT	40
Dolomites	Tafelsig (M.Plain)	164	CT	47
Dolomites	Tafelsig (M.Plain)	164	CT	48
Dolomites Cir.	Tafelsig (M.Plain)	164	CT	47
Dolphin Cr.	Fish Hoek	185	DA	22
Dolphin Cr.	Zoo Pk	47	BQ	56
Dolphin Dr.	Table View	24	BN	29
Dolphin Sands	Fish Hoek	186	DA	25
Dolphin St	Hout Bay Harbour	136	CR	13
Dolphin Ter.	Strandfontein	162	CT	39
Dolphin Way	Anchorage Pk	175	DC	77
Dolphin Way	Lansdowne	121	CL	33
Dolphin Way	Ottery	121	CL	33
Dolphin Way	Simon's Town	194	DJ	24
Dolphin Way	Victoria	194	DJ	24
Dolphini St	Wallacedene	48	BS	60
Dolphini St	Wallacedene	48	BS	61
Doman Rd	Vanguard	103	CG	38
Dombas St	Rabiesdale	19	BC	92
Dombeya Ave	Langeberg Rdg	47	BR	55
Dombeya Cl.	Perm Gdns	128	CJ	59
Dombeya Cl.	Perm Gdns	128	CJ	61
Dombeya St	Somerset West	151	CS	71
Domingo Rd	Retreat	141	CR	31
Dominic St	Athlone	102	CF	33
Dominica Ave	Capri	185	DB	19
Dominique St	De Tijger	60	BW	44
Domira Rd	High Constantia	119	CN	23
Don	Eindhoven	107	CH	51
Don Carlos St	Eastridge (M.Plain)	145	CQ	49
Don Rd	Bishop Lavis	104	CD	41
Don St	Manenberg	104	CH	39
Donald St	Athlone	102	CF	33
Donald St	Woodstock	83	CB	27
Donaldson St	Rome	170	CX	74
Donaldson St	Wellington	10	AR	94
Donana Galo St	Gugulethu	123	CK	41
Donato St	Brackenfell Sth	63	BX	57
Donax Dr.	Sunset Beach	41	BS	31
Doncaster Rd	Kenilworth Pk	120	CK	30
Doncaster Rd	Kenilworth Pk	121	CJ	31
Doncaster Rd	Lansdowne	121	CJ	31
Dondashe St	Victoria Mxenge	126	CN	51
Donegal Ave	Connaught	87	CB	43
Donegal St	Rugby	57	BX	31
Donell Way	Grassy Pk	141	CQ	32
Dongwe St	Umrhabulo Triangle	147	CR	58
Donkervliet	Highbury	107	CE	54
Donkervliet	Highbury	107	CG	53
Donkervliet St	Dal Josafat Ind.	19	AY	91
Donkin Ave	Table View	41	BO	32
Donkin Ave	Table View	41	BP	31
Donkin La.	Sea Point	81	CA	20
Donkin Rd	Belhar	106	CD	50
Donkin St	Rome	174	CY	73
Donkin Way	Edgemead	58	BV	37
Donna St	Morgenster Hoogte	63	BT	55
Donne St	Observatory	83	CC	28
Donnington Cl.	Parklands	25	BN	34
Donnington Rd	Killarney Gdns	42	BP	36
Donough Rd	Tokai	139	CS	26
Donovan St	Silveroaks	90	CC	55
Dontsa	Wellington	15	AU	91
Dontsa St	Tarentaalplaas	175	CY	75
Door de Kraal Ave	Kenever	61	BT	49
Door de Kraal Ave	Kenridge	61	BU	49
Doordrift Rd	Barbarossa	119	CN	26
Doordrift Rd	Barbarossa	120	CN	27
Doordrift Rd	Plumstead	120	CN	28
Doornbosch	Stellenbosch	113	CD	75
Doornhoek St	Northpine	63	BU	58
Doornhof Cl.	Edgemead	59	BU	39
Doornhof Rd	Edgemead	59	BU	39
Dora Tamana	Weltevreden Val. (M.Plain)	123	CM	41
Dorah	Eersterivier	128	CN	60
Dorah Tamane St	Mandela Pk	146	CQ	54
Doral	Sunningdale	25	BM	31
Dorbyl St	Sack's Circle Ind.	88	CB	49
Dorchester Dr.	Parklands	25	BM	33
Dorchester Dr.	Parklands	25	BN	34
Dorchester Pl.	Parklands	25	BM	34
Dordrecht Rd	Milnerton	57	BW	31
Doreen Cl.	Tafelsig (M.Plain)	145	CS	50
Doreen Rd	Doornhoogte	103	CG	36
Doreen Rd	Montagu's Gift	141	CO	33
Doreen St	Northern Paarl	18	AZ	89
Doreen St	Valhalla Pk	104	CE	41
Dorelle Rd	Labiance	89	BZ	51
Dores Cr.	Wimbledon	108	CH	55
Dorette St	Courtrai	22	BH	87
Dorhill Rd	Somerset West	170	CT	74
Doric Rd	Penlyn Est.	103	CH	35
Doring Cr.	Delft	106	CG	49
Doring Cr.	Park Village	127	CK	58
Doring Rd	Capricorn	160	CU	31
Doring Rd	Doornhoogte	103	CG	35
Doring Rd	Doornhoogte	103	CH	35
Doringboom St	Die Oude Spruit	63	BX	56
Dorion Cl.	Simon's Town	194	DJ	26
Doris Dr.	Wellington	10	AS	94
Doris Rd	Claremont	120	CJ	27
Doris Rd	Hout Bay	136	CO	14
Dorman Pl.	Hout Bay	137	CQ	16
Dorman St	Gardens	81	CB	22
Dorman Way	Hout Bay	117	CN	18
Dormehl La.	Foreshore	82	CB	25
Dormehl St	Foreshore	82	CB	25
Dormer Ave	Athlone	102	CG	33
Dormer Cl.	Athlone	102	CG	33
Dormershire Ave	Voorbrug	107	CG	51
Dorn Rosa St	Paarlzicht	19	BC	91
Dorothy Rd	Stikland Hospital	61	BX	50
Dorothy St	Kalkfontein II	107	CD	52
Dorothy Zihlangu	Weltevreden Val. (M.Plain)	123	CN	42
Dorothy Zihlangu St	Mandela Pk	146	CR	54
Dorothy Zihlangu St	Manenberg	104	CH	40
Dorp St	Cape Town Cen.	81	CA	22
Dorp St	Lemoenkloof	18	BC	88
Dorp St	Lemoenkloof	18	BC	89
Dorp St	Panorama	59	BV	42
Dorp St	Peerless Pk Nth	48	BQ	59
Dorp St	Stellenbosch	95	CC	75
Dorper Way	Mitchells Plain	144	CR	45
Dorpsig	Welgelegen	113	CD	76
Dorrey St	Brackenfell	63	BW	56
Dorrey St	Protea Hoogte	63	BW	56
Dorries Dr.	Simon's Town	195	DK	27
Dorrington St	Langgewacht	170	CX	72
Dorris St	Scottsdene	64	BT	60
Dorset	Lindida	96	CA	80
Dorset St	Foreshore	82	CB	25
Dorsetshire St	Paarden Eiland	83	BZ	29
Dorwil Prag	Parow Ind.	87	CA	46
Dory Wk	Sun Valley	185	CZ	20
Dosi Cr.	Victoria Mxenge	126	CN	51
Doublom Cl.	Perm Gdns	128	CJ	59
Doublom Cl.	Perm Gdns	128	CJ	60
Doublom Cr.	Roosendaal	107	CF	51
Doublom St	Bonteheuwel	104	CE	40
Doublom St	Protea Village	64	BW	59
Douglas Carr Dr.	Blommendal	62	BW	51
Douglas Cr.	Ravensmead	87	CA	45
Douglas Cr.	The Hague	106	CE	49
Douglas Mfaca Cr.	Weltevreden Val. (M.Plain)	123	CN	41
Douglas Pl.	Woodstock	82	CB	26
Douglas Rd	Wynberg	120	CM	30
Douglas St	Woodstock	83	CB	28
Dove	Rocklands (M.Plain)	144	CS	44
Dove Rd	Capricorn	160	CU	31
Dove Rd	Montagu's Gift	141	CO	33
Dove Rd	Pelikan Pk	142	CS	36
Dove St	Electric City	127	CN	58
Dove St	Observatory	83	CC	28
Dove St	Ocean View	184	DC	15
Dove St	Penlyn Est.	103	CH	36
Dove St	Salt River	83	CB	28
Dovedale	Pinelands	102	CD	34
Dover Rd	Heathfield	140	CQ	29
Dover Rd	Muizenberg	159	CW	30
Dover Rd	Sea Point	81	BZ	20
Dower St	Des Hampden	89	CB	53
Down Cr.	Eersterivier	128	CM	62
Downberg Rd	Hanover Pk	122	CK	35
Downberg Rd	Hanover Pk	122	CK	36
Downes Way	Edgemead	58	BV	37
Downing Cl.	Montana/Durrheim	104	CF	42
Downing Cr.	Montana/Durrheim	104	CF	42
Downing Link	Montana/Durrheim	104	CF	42
Downing St	Hazendal	102	CE	33
Downing St	Highbury	107	CE	54
Downing St	Montana/Durrheim	104	CF	41
Downs Way	Summer Greens	58	BV	36
Downwood	Hanover Pk	122	CK	35
Dowries St	Kylemore	97	CA	86
Dr Moerat St	Gugulethu	104	CG	40
Dr Moerat St	Gugulethu	104	CG	41
Dr. A.B. Bull Rd	Simon's Town	195	DK	27
Dr. Abdurahman Ave	Wellington	15	AU	92
Dr. Bester Ave	Boschenmeer Est.	22	BG	90
Dr. Malan	Stellenbosch	95	CA	76
Dr.Abdurahman Ave	Kewtown	102	CF	34
Dr.Abdurahman Ave	Kewtown	103	CF	35
Draa Way	Delft	106	CG	49
Draai	Dalsig	113	CD	76
Draai St	Paarl	22	BF	88
Draco Way	Ocean View	184	DC	15
Dragoon Ave	Door De Kraal	61	BT	47
Dragoon Ave	Door De Kraal	61	BV	48
Dragoon St	Plumstead	140	CO	30
Dragoon St	Plumstead	140	CO	30
Drake	Park Estates	170	CX	71
Drake Cr.	Belhar	106	CD	49
Drake Rd	Winslow	179	DD	77
Drake St	Belrail	88	BY	49
Drake St	Observatory	83	CC	29
Drakensberg	Wellington	15	AV	91
Drakensberg Cl.	Welgevonden	30	BN	54
Drakensberg Cr.	Tafelsig (M.Plain)	145	CS	48
Drakensberg Way	Lavender Hill East	160	CU	32
Drakensberg Way	Lavender Hill East	160	CT	33
Drakenstein Cir.	Bishop Lavis	104	CD	42
Drakenstein Cir.	Bishop Lavis	104	CE	42
Drakenstein Rd South	Paarl	23	BE	92
Drakenstein Rd South	Paarl	23	BF	93
Drakenstein Rd South	Paarl	23	BG	91
Drakenstein St	Durbanville Hills	45	BR	50
Drakenstein St	Durbanville Hills	45	BS	49
Drakenstein St	Somerset Pk	171	CW	75
Drakenstein St	Tafelsig (M.Plain)	145	CS	48
Drakenstein St	Wingfield Nth Camp	58	BW	38
Drakenstein Way	Belhar	106	CE	49
Draklow St	Woodstock	82	CB	26
Drama St	Somerset West	171	CU	75
Drama St	Somerset West	171	CU	76
Draper Cl.	Claremont	101	CH	29
Draper St	Claremont	101	CH	28
Draper St	Claremont	101	CH	29
Draycott Ave	Eersterivier	128	CM	59
Dressage Cl.	Fir Grove	139	CQ	24
Dreyden St	Wellington	15	AT	92
Dreyer Cl.	Barbarossa	120	CN	27
Dreyer Rd	Kommetjie	183	DC	12
Dreyer St	Claremont	101	CH	28
Dreyer St	Kempenville	61	BX	48
Dreyer St	Rugby	57	BX	31
Dreyer St	Voelvlei	89	CA	52
Dreyer St	Voelvlei	89	BY	54
Dreyersdal Farm Rd	Dreyersdal	140	CR	27
Dreyersdal Rd	Dreyersdal	140	CR	27
Dreyton Rd	Lansdowne	121	CK	34
Driebergen	Highbury	107	CD	54
Driebergen	Highbury	107	CE	54
Driebergen St	Dal Josafat Ind.	19	AZ	91
Driebergen St	Edgemead	58	BV	36
Driefontein La.	Farmsteads	156	CW	18
Driehoek Ave	Boston	61	BX	48
Driekoppen Rd	Edgemead	58	BT	38
Driekoppen Rd	Edgemead	59	BU	39
Drift Rd	Lansdowne	121	CK	33
Drill Ave	Montague Gdns Ind.	58	BU	35
Driver St	Lakeside	159	CV	27
Drogheda Rd	Royal Cape	121	CM	32
Dromedaris	Ruyterwacht	86	BZ	40
Dromedaris Sq.	Factreton	85	BY	35
Drommedaris	Simonswyk	95	CB	78
Drommedaris Ave	Bothasig	58	BT	38
Drommedaris Cr.	Brackenfell Sth	63	BX	56
Drommedaris Cr.	Brackenfell Sth	63	BV	56
Drommedaris Cr.	Clarkes	86	CC	42
Drommedaris Cr.	Clarkes	86	CB	39
Drommedaris Rd	Somerset West	171	CU	77
Drommedaris St	Avondale	60	BX	45
Drommedaris St	Belrail	88	BY	49
Drommedaris St	Dal Josafat Ind.	18	AZ	90
Drommedaris St	Dal Josafat Ind.	18	BA	90
Drommedaris St	Mountainside Est.	179	DD	78
Drommedaris St	Mountainside Est.	179	DE	77
Drommedaris St	Strandvale	170	CW	73
Drommedaris St	Wellington	15	AX	91
Drommedaris Way	Belhar	106	CE	50
Drongo Cl.	Fish Hoek	186	DA	23
Drongo St	Sonstraal	46	BS	52
Drosdy Cl.	Oak Glen	62	BW	52
Drossel Rd	Pinati	122	CK	35
Drossel Rd	Pinati	122	CN	36
Drostdy	Die Bos	174	CY	74
Drostdy	Stellenbosch	95	CC	76
Drostdy Rd	Belhar	106	CE	49
Drostdy Rd	Bergvliet	139	CQ	26
Drostdy Rd	Voorbrug	106	CG	50
Drostdy St	Panorama	59	BV	41
Drostdy St	Peerless Pk Nth	48	BQ	59
Drostdy St	Sonnekuil	89	BZ	53
Drostdy St	Sonnekuil	89	BY	54
Drover St	Mitchells Plain	144	CQ	45
Druif St	Wynberg	120	CM	29
Drukkers	Stellenbosch	95	CB	75
Drukkery St	Elsies River Ind.	86	BZ	42
Druk-my-Niet	Simonswyk	95	CB	78
Drumblair Cr.	Dennedal	139	CS	25
Drummer Rd	Belhar	106	CD	48
Drummond Rd	West Beach	24	BN	29
Drummond Rd	West Beach	24	BN	30
Drummond St	Wesbank	107	CG	52
Drury Rd	Capricorn	160	CU	31
Drury Rd	Capricorn	160	CV	31
Drury St	District Six	82	CB	23
Dryden St	Salt River	83	CB	28
Drysdale St	Delft Sth	106	CH	50
Ds. Botha	Stellenbosch	95	CB	76
Du Buisson St	The Palms	170	CW	73
Du Lot St	Groenvlei	18	BA	87
Du Plessis	Mostertsdrift	96	CC	79
Du Plessis Ave	Edgemead	58	BV	37
Du Plessis St	Lemoenkloof	18	BB	89
Du Plessis St	Lochnerhof	170	CX	72
Du Plessis St	Oakdene	89	CC	54
Du Preez St	Parowvallei	87	CA	44
Du Toit	The Palms	170	CX	73
Du Toit Rd	Clamhall	60	BX	43
Du Toit St	Bellville	88	BY	49
Du Toit St	Paarl	22	BD	88
Du Toit St	Paarl	22	BD	89
Du Toit St	Soneike I	89	CA	54
Du Toit St	Stellenbosch	95	CC	75
Du Toit St	Wellington	10	AS	93
Du Toits Kloof St	Tafelsig (M.Plain)	145	CS	49
Dube St	Victoria Mxenge	146	CO	52
Dubi St	Nyanga	123	CK	42
Dublin Cl.	Eikenbosch	90	CC	57
Dublin Rd	Airport Ind.	105	CF	43
Dublin Rd	Summer Greens	58	BV	35
Dublin St	Maitland	83	CA	30
Dublin St	Woodstock	83	CB	27
Dubu Cr.	Brown's Farm	124	CL	43
Duchess Rd	Ottery	122	CL	35
Duck Rd	Montagu's Gift	141	CO	33
Duck Rd	Pelikan Pk	142	CR	36
Duckitt Ave	Constantia Vale	119	CN	25
Duckitt Ave	Silverhurst	119	CN	24
Duclair	Schuilplaats	113	CF	76
Dudgeon Rd	Rondebosch	102	CG	32
Dudley Rd	Belhar	106	CD	49
Dudley Rd	Belhar	106	CH	48
Dudley Rd	Eersterivier	128	CN	61
Dudley Rd	Sea Point	81	BZ	20
Duet Cl.	Rosendal	61	BT	50
Duet Cr.	Sonstraal Hgts	46	BR	54
Duet La.	Athlone	102	CG	33
Duff St	Klipkop	87	BZ	44
Duff St	Parowvallei	87	BZ	43
Duff St	Parowvallei	87	BZ	44
Duif St	Driftsands	125	CL	50
Duif St	Driftsands	126	CL	51
Duif St	Peerless Pk Nth	48	BQ	59
Duignam Rd	Kalk Bay	186	DA	26
Duiker	Rocklands (M.Plain)	144	CS	44
Duiker Ave	Lotus River	142	CP	35
Duiker Ave	Westlake Est.	158	CU	25
Duiker Cl.	Admirals Pk	175	DC	78
Duiker Cl.	Pinelands	102	CD	33
Duiker Cl.	Wellington	15	AV	92
Duiker Cr.	Bridgetown	103	CF	37
Duiker Cr.	Flamingo Vlei	41	BQ	33
Duiker Dr.	Kommetjie	183	DB	12
Duiker Rd	Bridgetown	103	CF	37
Duiker Rd	Dunoon	26	BN	38
Duiker Rd	Goedemoed	46	BP	53
Duiker Rd	Langeberg Rdg	47	BR	56
Duiker Rd	Loevenstein	60	BW	46

Index to Street Names

Duiker Rd — Ester Rd

STREET NAME	SUBURB NAME	PG	GRID	
Duiker Rd	Pelikan Pk	161	CU	38
Duiker St	Beaconvale	87	BZ	45
Duiker St	Hout Bay Harbour	136	CR	13
Duiker St	Macassar	149	CS	64
Duiker St	New Orleans	19	BB	92
Duiker St	Sarepta	89	CC	53
Duiker St	Scarborough	192	DK	18
Duiker St	Simon's Town	191	DF	24
Duiker St	Somerset Hgts	127	CJ	58
Duiker St	Woodlands (M.Plain)	144	CP	44
Duiker Vlei Rd	Bothasig	42	BS	38
Duine Rd	Wellington	15	AU	92
Duine St	Penlyn Est.	103	CG	35
Duine St	Scottsville	47	BS	58
Duine St	Voelvlei	89	CA	53
Duinebessie	Lentegeur (M.Plain)	144	CO	45
Duinebessie Cr.	Roosendaal	107	CF	51
Duinefontein Rd	Heideveld	104	CF	39
Duinefontein Rd	Manenberg	104	CH	39
Duinefontein Rd	Manenberg	123	CK	40
Duinhoop Ave	Monte Vista	59	BW	39
Dukani St	Mfuleni	126	CK	54
Duke Cl.	Salberau	86	CA	41
Duke Dr.	Eersterivier	128	CM	59
Duke Qavane St	Guguletu	104	CG	41
Duke Rd	Ottery	122	CL	35
Duke Rd	Rondebosch	101	CF	29
Duke St	Observatory	83	CC	29
Duke St	Woodstock	82	CB	26
Dulah Omar St	Fisantekraal	31	BK	58
Dulah Omar St	Fisantekraal	32	BJ	59
Dulicie September	Weltevreden Val. (M.Plain)	123	CN	42
Dullah Omar St	Mandela Pk	147	CQ	55
Dulles Rd	The Hague	106	CE	50
Dulverton Rd	Rondebosch	102	CG	31
Dulwich Rd	Rondebosch	101	CG	29
Dumani	Dunoon	26	BN	37
Dumani	Dunoon	42	BO	38
Dumas St	Jagtershof	90	CC	57
Dumas St	St Dumas	90	CC	55
Dumas St	St Dumas	90	CC	56
Dumba St	Harare	146	CR	54
Dumbarton St	Rondebosch	101	CG	30
Dumbe St	Harare	146	CR	53
Duminy Rd	Dieprivier	140	CP	28
Duminy St	Parow East	87	BY	45
Duminy St	Vredelust	60	BX	46
Dumisa Mtsebeza St	Mandela Pk	146	CR	54
Dumisani	Wellington	15	AU	91
Dumisani St	Lwandle	175	CZ	76
Dummer St	Somerset West	152	CS	75
Dummer St	Somerset West	170	CT	74
Dummer St	Somerset West	171	CT	75
Dumont St	Courtrai	22	BH	87
Dumont St	Edgemead	58	BV	36
Duna Cr.	Victoria Mxenge	146	CO	51
Dunbar St	Athlone	102	CG	33
Dunbar St	Klipkop	87	BZ	45
Dunbar St	Table View	40	BO	30
Duncan Rd	Foreshore	82	BZ	24
Duncan Rd	Foreshore	82	CA	26
Duncan Rd	Foreshore	83	CA	27
Duncan Rd	Pinelands	84	CB	34
Duncan Rd	Sea Point	81	CA	19
Duncan Rd	Wynberg	120	CL	30
Duncan St	Belrail	88	BY	49
Duncan St	Klipkop	87	BZ	44
Duncan St	Parowvallei	87	BZ	43
Duncan St	Parowvallei	87	BZ	44
Duncan St	Strand Halt	170	CW	74
Duncan St	Valhalla Pk	104	CE	41
Dundas Cr.	Ruyterwacht	86	CA	40
Dundas St	Rome	174	CY	73
Dundee Rd	Rondebosch	101	CG	29
Dundee St	Uitzicht	47	BO	55
Dundee St	Uitzicht	47	BO	56
Dundee Ter.	Rondebosch	101	CG	29
Dundonald St	Woodstock	83	CB	27
Dundrum Rd	Fairways	121	CM	32
Dune Dr.	Woodlands (M.Plain)	144	CP	44
Dune Rd	Eersterivier	127	CM	58
Dune Rd	Milnerton	57	BW	31
Dune Rd	Steenberg	159	CT	30
Dune St	Bishop Lavis	105	CD	43
Dunedin Rd	Simon's Town	191	DD	23
Dunes Cr.	Weltevreden Val. (M.Plain)	144	CO	43
Dungannon St	Kenilworth	120	CK	30
Dunkeld Ave	Bishopscourt	119	CJ	26
Dunkeld Rd	Camps Bay	98	CE	18
Dunkirk Rd	Strandfontein	162	CT	40
Dunkley St	Gardens	82	CB	23
Dunlin Cl.	Grassy Pk	141	CQ	32
Dunlop La.	Heathfield	140	CQ	28
Dunluce Ave	Claremont	101	CH	29
Dunn Rd	Somerset West	170	CV	73
Dunrobin Rd	Sea Point	81	BZ	20
Dunsheen Rd	Wynberg	120	CM	30
Dunster Ave	Fish Hoek	186	DB	24
Dunster St	Belgravia	103	CF	35
Duntaw Cl.	Hohenort	119	CL	24
Duparc	Delft Sth	125	CK	48
Durant Cr.	Silvertown	103	CF	35
Durant St	Silvertown	103	CF	35
Duranta Pl.	Uitsig	87	CC	44
Durban Dr.	Somerset West	151	CR	73
Durban Rd	Bellville	88	BY	48
Durban Rd	Mowbray	101	CD	30
Durban Rd	Oakdale	61	BV	49
Durban Rd	Oakdale	61	BX	48
Durban Rd	Portlands (M.Plain)	144	CR	46
Durban Rd	Wynberg	120	CM	28
Durban St	Portlands (M.Plain)	144	CR	46
D'urban St	Bothasig	58	BT	37
Durban Way	Portlands (M.Plain)	144	CS	46
Durbanville Ave	Durbanville	45	BQ	50
Durbanville Ave	Durbell	45	BS	50
Durbanville Ave	Rosendal	61	BT	50
Durbanville Ave	Rosendal	61	BT	49
Durbanville Cr.	Milnerton Rdg	41	BS	34
Durbanville St	Peerless Pk East	48	BR	59
Durbell Rd	Durbell	45	BS	50
Durham Ave	Salt River	83	CB	28
Durham Cl.	West Beach	24	BM	30
Durham Rd	Bellville Sth	88	CA	49
Durham St	Bishopscourt	119	CJ	26
Durham St	Claremont	120	CJ	30
Durham Way	Matroosfontein	86	CC	42
Durmonté Rd	Dobson	175	DC	77
Durmonté St	Durmonte	30	BM	52
Durmonté St	Durmonte	30	BN	53
Durnford Way	Edgemead	58	BT	38
Durr Rd	Surrey	103	CG	37
Durr Rd	Surrey	103	CH	38
Durr St	Paarl	22	BD	88
Durrell St	Mandalay	125	CM	48
Durvale Cl.	D'urbanvale	45	BO	49
Dutywa St	Mfuleni	126	CK	53
Dutywa St	Mfuleni	126	CK	52
Duvorak St	Protea Hoogte	63	BX	56
Duxbury Rd	Bergvliet	139	CP	26
Duze Cl.	Victoria Mxenge	146	CO	52
Dwars in die Weg Cl.	Voorbrug	107	CG	51
Dwars St	De Kuilen	89	CB	54
Dwars St	Delft	106	CG	48
Dwars St	Eersterivier	128	CM	59
Dwars St	Glenhaven	89	CA	52
Dwars St	Northern Paarl	18	AZ	89
Dwars St	Onverwacht	174	CZ	73
Dwars St	Wellington	10	AS	93
Dwarsberg Rd	Tafelsig (M.Plain)	145	CR	49
Dwarseind Cl.	Belhar	106	CE	49
Dwyka Ct	Delft	106	CG	49
Dwyka St	Manenberg	104	CH	39
Dyakala Cr.	Nyanga	123	CK	42
Dyakalashe Rd	Philippi East	124	CM	46
Dyakalashe Rd	Philippi East	125	CM	47
Dyakalashe St	Brown's Farm	124	CL	43
Dyakalashe St	Kuyasa	147	CR	55
Dyakophu Cl.	Nyanga	123	CL	42
Dyalvane Cr.	Nonqubela	126	CN	52
Dyani Cr.	Kaya	146	CO	52
Dyasi St	Kaya	146	CP	51
Dyke Rd	Penhill	128	CK	60
Dykwa	Kaymor	89	BY	53
Dyokhwe St	Umrhabulo Triangle	147	CQ	57
Dysart Rd	Green Point	81	BZ	21
Dywabasi St	Brown's Farm	124	CL	43
Dywabisini Ave	Joe Slovo Pk	57	BU	34
Dywabisini Ave	Joe Slovo Pk	57	BU	31
Dywhi St	Bloekombos	48	BQ	62
Dywili Cr.	Wallacedene	48	BS	60
Dywilisi Cl.	Nyanga	123	CK	42
E				
E Mjodo St	Nyanga	123	CJ	42
E.K.Green	Huguenot	18	BB	90
E.R.Syfret Rd	Brooklyn	84	BY	31
E.Sula St	Mfuleni	126	CK	53
Eagle	Dunoon	42	BO	37
Eagle	Dunoon	42	BO	38
Eagle	Rocklands (M.Plain)	144	CS	44
Eagle Ave	Hout Bay	117	CM	17
Eagle Cl.	Westlake Est.	158	CU	25
Eagle Cr.	Montagu's Gift	141	CO	33
Eagle Cr.	Somerset West	171	CV	76
Eagle Cr.	Sunridge	41	BP	34
Eagle Rd	Athlone	102	CF	34
Eagle Rd	Pelikan Pk	142	CS	36
Eagle Rd	Pine Acres	175	DC	77
Eagle Rd	Pine Acres	175	DB	78
Eagle St	Morgenster Hoogte	63	BT	57
Eagle St	Mxolisi Phetani	125	CM	49
Eagle St	Ocean View	184	DC	15
Eagle Way	Bergvliet	140	CR	28
Eagle Way	Penlyn Est.	103	CH	36
Earl Cr.	Eersterivier	128	CM	59
Earl Cr.	Eersterivier	128	CM	60
Earl St	Hout Bay	136	CP	14
Earl St	Hout Bay	137	CP	15
Earl St	Woodstock	82	CB	26
Earlibelle Cr.	Jamestown	112	CH	74
Earlswood Cl.	Parklands	26	BN	35
Earlswood Rd	Parklands	26	BN	35
Easson Rd	Frogmore Est.	159	CU	28
East Cl.	Strandfontein	162	CT	41
East Cr.	Winslow	179	DD	77
East Fort	Hout Bay Harbour	136	CR	13
East Gate	High Gate	107	CG	53
East Lake Dr.	Marina Da Gama	159	CV	30
East Lake Dr.	Marina Da Gama	159	CW	30
East Lake Island Dr.	Marina Da Gama	159	CV	30
East Light Way	Kirstenhof	159	CT	27
East Link	Athlone	102	CF	34
East Mascalls	Durbanville	45	BP	49
East Pier Rd	Foreshore	82	BY	23
East Pier Rd	Foreshore	82	BY	24
East Rd	Somerset West	170	CU	73
East St	Grassy Pk	141	CQ	32
East St	Montagu's Gift	141	CO	34
East St	Strandfontein	162	CT	41
East St	Wellington	10	AR	94
East Way	Pinelands	84	CC	32
Eastbank Rd	Pelikan Pk	141	CR	34
Eastborne Rd	Capricorn	159	CW	30
Eastclyde Rd	Claremont	102	CH	31
Eastcourt Rd	Eersterivier	128	CN	61
Eastern Blvd	Woodstock	83	CC	27
Eastern Blvd.	District Six	82	CB	25
Easterpeak Rd	Manenberg	104	CG	39
Eastfield Cr.	Somerset West	171	CW	76
Eastry Rd	Claremont	120	CJ	30
Eastview Rd	Belthorn Est.	122	CJ	35
Eastwood Cl.	Sunningdale	25	BM	32
Eastwood Dr.	Northpine	63	BT	58
Eastwood Dr.	Northpine	63	BU	58
Eastwood St	Klipkop	87	BZ	45
Eaton Rd	Gardens	81	CB	21
Ebb Ave	Riverton	86	BZ	40
Ebb Rd	Steenberg	159	CT	30
Ebb St	Gustrow	174	DB	74
Ebbehout	Delft Sth	106	CH	50
Eben Donges St	De Duin	59	BW	41
Eben Olivier St	Springbok Pk	62	BV	54
Eben Olivier St	Springbok Pk	62	BX	52
Eben St	Morgenster Hoogte	63	BT	56
Ebenezer Rd	Cape Town Cen.	82	BZ	23
Ebenezer Rd	Wynberg	120	CL	28
Ebony	Grassy Pk	141	CQ	34
Ebony Rd	Tokai	139	CS	25
Ebony St	Bonteheuwel	103	CD	38
Ebony St	Loevenstein	60	BW	46
Ebor Rd	Wynberg	120	CM	29
Ebraham Bazer Cr.	Gustrow	175	DB	75
Ebrahim Rd	Primrose Pk	122	CJ	38
Ebro Cr.	Eindhoven	106	CH	50
Ecclestone Pl.	Somerset West	171	CU	75
Echium Rd	Table View	41	BO	32
Echo	Cloetesville	94	BY	74
Echo Rd	Clarkes	86	CC	40
Echo Rd	Fish Hoek	186	DC	25
Echo St	Tafelsig (M.Plain)	145	CS	48
Echo Steps	Fish Hoek	186	DC	25
Eckard Cl.	Belhar	107	CE	51
Eclipse Cl.	Sonstraal Hgts	46	BR	54
Eclipse Rd	Sanddrift	57	BW	33
Eclipse St	Salberau	86	CB	42
Ecole St	Klein Parys	23	BD	91
Edam Ave	Northpine	63	BT	58
Edam Ave	Northpine	64	BT	59
Edam Ave	Scottsdene	64	BU	59
Edan Cl.	Somerset West	152	CR	75
Eddie Thomas Marine	Southfork	174	DB	74
Eddy Rd	Ottery East	121	CN	33
Edelweis St	Somerset West	151	CS	71
Edelweis Way	Eversdal	62	BT	51
Edelweiss Ave	Voorbrug	106	CG	50
Eden Cr.	Sir Lowry's Pass	176	CZ	81
Eden Rd	Claremont	120	CJ	27
Eden Rd	Observatory	83	CC	29
Eden Rd	Ravensmead	87	CA	45
Eden Rd	Woodstock	82	CC	26
Eden Rd	Wynberg	120	CM	30
Edgar Bullock Rd	Ravensmead	87	CA	45
Edgar Cl.	Rondebosch	101	CH	30
Edgar Rd	Glenhaven	89	CA	51
Edgar Rd	Hout Bay	136	CO	14
Edgar Rd	Lansdowne	121	CK	34
Edgar St	Somerset West	170	CV	74
Edgemead Dr.	Edgemead	58	BV	38
Edgemere Cl.	Elfindale	140	CQ	30
Edgemere Rd	Elfindale	140	CQ	30
Edgeware Cl.	Dieprivier	140	CO	29
Edgewater Rd	Sea Point	80	CA	18
Edgeworth	Dieprivier	140	CO	29
Edinburgh Cl.	Claremont	120	CK	27
Edinburgh Cl.	Pinelands	84	CB	34
Edinburgh Dr.	Bishopscourt	120	CJ	27
Edinburgh Pl.	Dreyersdal	140	CS	27
Edinburgh Rd	Oostersee	60	BX	45
Edinburgh Rd	West Beach	24	BN	29
Edison Dr.	Belhar	88	CC	50
Edison Dr.	Belhar	106	CD	50
Edison Dr.	Meadowridge	139	CP	26
Edison Dr.	Meadowridge	140	CP	27
Edison Rd	Rondebosch	101	CF	29
Edison St	Dal Josafat Ind.	19	AY	91
Edison St	Tarentaalplaas	170	CX	74
Edmar St	Danena	61	BU	49
Edmond Rostand Way	Chantecler	62	BT	51
Edmondia Cl.	Hout Bay	136	CO	14
Edmonton Cl.	Retreat	140	CR	30
Edmonton Rd	Retreat	140	CR	30
Edmund Cl.	Valhalla Pk	104	CE	41
Edmund St	Valhalla Pk	104	CE	41
Edna	Delro	126	CJ	54
Edna Cl.	Lentegeur (M.Plain)	145	CO	48
Edna Cl.	Lentegeur (M.Plain)	145	CP	50
Edna St	Montagu's Gift	141	CO	33
Ednam Rd	Rondebosch	101	CG	29
Edrei St	Bonnie Brook	47	BQ	57
Eduardo	Bellair	62	BV	53
Eduardo	Bellair	62	BX	52
Edward Ave	Montagu's Gift	142	CO	35
Edward Baard St	Gustrow	175	DB	75
Edward Baard St	Gustrow	175	DB	77
Edward Cl.	Marlborough Pk	63	BT	55
Edward Lottery St	Blomtuin	61	BW	50
Edward Lottery St	Blomtuin	61	BV	48
Edward Makele St	Guguletu	123	CK	40
Edward Makele St	Guguletu	123	CL	40
Edward Pl.	Adriaanse	87	CC	43
Edward Rd	Edward	122	CN	35
Edward Rd	Oakdale	61	BV	49
Edward Rd	Sea Point	81	BZ	20
Edward Rd	Valhalla Pk	104	CE	41
Edward Rd	Windsor Pk	47	BR	57
Edward Roworth Cr.	Woodlands (M.Plain)	144	CO	45
Edward St	Claremont	120	CJ	30
Edward St	Hout Bay	136	CP	14
Edward St	Hout Bay	136	CQ	14
Edward St	Nomzano	175	CY	75
Edwards Rd	Vygeboom	46	BR	51
Edwina	Dalvale	19	AY	93
Eel St	Soneike II	89	BZ	54
Eendrag	Sarepta	89	CC	53
Eendrag Cr.	Voorbrug	106	CG	50
Eendrag Rd	Vanguard	103	CF	38
Eendrag St	Bellville Sth Ext. 5	88	BZ	49
Eenhoorn Cr.	Eersterivier	128	CN	61
Eenhoorn Pl.	Eersterivier	128	CN	61
Eenzaamheid Rd	Klapmuts	35	BJ	74
Eenzaamheid Rd	Klapmuts	36	BJ	75
Eenzaamheid Rd	Klapmuts	36	BK	75
Eersriv Way	Malibu Village	127	CJ	55
Eersriv Way	Malibu Village	127	CL	55
Eersriv Way	Sunset Glen	108	CH	55
Eerste Way	Delft	106	CF	50
Eeuwfees St	Paarl	22	BE	88
Efort	Balvenie	86	CB	42
Efort	Balvenie	87	CB	43
Egbert St	Northern Paarl	18	AZ	89
Egglestone Rd	Wynberg	120	CL	29
Egham St	Wynberg	120	CL	29
Egmond	Morgen Gronde	63	BX	56
Egret Cir.	Imhoff's Gift	184	DB	16
Egret Cl.	Sonstraal Hgts	46	BR	54
Egret Cl.	Villa Italia	57	BW	33
Egret Cl.	Westlake Est.	158	CU	25
Egret La.	Bergvliet	140	CQ	27
Egret La.	Montagu's Gift	141	CO	34
Egret La.	Steenberg	139	CS	23
Egret La.	Steenberg	158	CT	23
Egret Rd	Flintdale Est.	141	CP	31
Egret Rd	Parkwood	141	CR	34
Egret St	Eersterivier	128	CM	60
Egret St	Flamingo Vlei	41	BP	31
Egret St	Rugby	84	BY	31
Egret St	Scarborough	192	DJ	17
Egret St	Somerset West	152	CS	76
Egret St	Sonstraal Hgts	46	BR	53
Egret St	Westlake Est.	158	CU	25
Egret Way	Pinelands	102	CD	34
Egrets Rd	Somerset West	171	CT	76
Egrets Way	Pelikan Pk	141	CR	33
Eiffel Cl.	Portlands (M.Plain)	145	CR	47
Eighteenth Ave	Boston	60	BW	46
Eighteenth Ave	Boston	61	BW	47
Eighteenth Ave	Factreton	85	BY	35
Eighteenth Ave	Fish Hoek	185	DA	22
Eighteenth Ave	Norwood	86	CB	41
Eighteenth Ave	Schaap Kraal	142	CS	36
Eighteenth St	Avon	86	CA	41
Eighteenth St	Kensington	84	BZ	33
Eighth	De Oude Renbaan	22	BH	88
Eighth Ave	Belgravia	103	CG	35
Eighth Ave	Belmont Pk	48	BR	60
Eighth Ave	Belmont Pk	48	BR	61
Eighth Ave	Belmont Pk	48	BS	59
Eighth Ave	Boston	60	BX	46
Eighth Ave	Boston	61	BX	47
Eighth Ave	Da Gama Pk	190	DD	21
Eighth Ave	Eikendal	47	BS	58
Eighth Ave	Eikendal	48	BS	59
Eighth Ave	Elsies River Ind.	86	BZ	41
Eighth Ave	Fairways	141	CO	31
Eighth Ave	Fish Hoek	186	DB	23
Eighth Ave	Fish Hoek	186	DB	24
Eighth Ave	Florida	87	CA	44
Eighth Ave	Grassy Pk	141	CQ	34
Eighth Ave	Grassy Pk	141	CR	32
Eighth Ave	Grassy Pk	141	CR	33
Eighth Ave	Hazendal	102	CE	33
Eighth Ave	Kayamandi	94	CA	74
Eighth Ave	Kensington	84	BZ	33
Eighth Ave	Lotus River	141	CQ	34
Eighth Ave	Maitland	84	BZ	33
Eighth Ave	Retreat	140	CR	29
Eighth Ave	Retreat	140	CS	30
Eighth Ave	Rondebosch East	102	CG	32
Eighth Ave	Schaap Kraal	142	CQ	36

Abbreviations used: Ave – Avenue, A.H. – Agricultural Holding, A.L.– Algemene Landgoed, Blvd – Boulevard, Cen. – Central, Cir. – Circle, Cl. – Close, Cr. – Crescent, Ct – Court, Dr. – Drive, Est. - Estate, Ext. – Extension, Hgts – Heights, Ind. – Industrial, Gdns – Gardens, Gr. – Grove, La. – Lane, (M.Plain) - Mitchells Plain, Nth – North, Pl. – Place, Pk – Park, Rd – Road, Rdg. – Ridge, S.H.– Small Holding, Sq. – Square, St – Street, Sth – South, Ter. – Terrace, Tn – Turn, Val. – Valley, Wk – Walk

STREET NAME	SUBURB NAME	PG	GRID	
Eighth Ave	Tafelsig (M.Plain)	146	CS	51
Eighth St	Bishop Lavis	104	CD	42
Eighth St	Elnor	86	CC	42
Eighth St	Kensington	84	BZ	33
Eighth St	Rusthof	174	DA	74
Eighth St	Rusthof	175	DA	75
Eighth St	Salberau	86	CB	41
Eike	Cloetesville	95	BZ	75
Eike	New Orleans	19	BA	91
Eike	Stellenbosch	95	CA	75
Eike Ave	Edenpark	62	BU	54
Eike Ave	Firgrove	150	CR	67
Eike Ave	Rusdal	108	CF	57
Eike Ave	Sonnedal	59	BW	42
Eike Ave	Stellenberg	62	BU	52
Eike Ave	Sybrand Pk	102	CE	33
Eike Ave	Wellington	10	AS	94
Eike Ct	Northpine	63	BU	58
Eike St	Wellway Pk	46	BO	52
Eiken Ct	Edgemead	59	BU	39
Eikenbosch St	Eikenbosch	90	CC	57
Eikendal	Pinelands	85	CB	35
Eikendal Rd	Durbanville	46	BO	51
Eikenhof	Durbanville	46	BO	51
Eikenhof Pl.	Voorbrug	106	CG	50
Eikenhof Pl.	Voorbrug	106	CH	48
Eikenhof St	Ruwari	63	BV	57
Eikenhout	Bellair	62	BW	53
Eikerus Cl.	Mitchells Plain	144	CR	45
Eikerus Cl.	Mitchells Plain	144	CS	43
Eiland Sq.	Factreton	85	BZ	35
Eindhoven Rd	Delft Sth	125	CJ	50
Eindhoven Rd	Eindhoven	106	CH	50
Eindhoven St	Strandvale	170	CW	73
Eire St	Portlands (M.Plain)	144	CQ	46
Eiselin St	Sarepta	89	CC	53
Eisleben Rd	Mitchells Plain	144	CR	46
Eisleben Rd	Woodlands (M.Plain)	144	CP	45
Eksteen Ave	Bergvliet	140	CQ	27
Eksteen St	Loevenstein	60	BV	45
Ekster Rd	Sunnydale	185	CZ	19
Ekuphumleni	Dunoon	42	BO	37
Ekuphumleni	Mbekweni	15	AV	92
Ekuthuleni St	Lwandle	175	CZ	76
El Adem Rd	Lansdowne	121	CL	32
El Alamein Cl.	Plumstead	120	CM	29
El Camino	Peerless Pk East	48	BR	59
Elaine Way	Heathfield	140	CQ	28
Eland Ave	Lotus River	142	CP	35
Eland Pl.	Loevenstein	60	BW	46
Eland Rd	Macassar	149	CS	66
Eland Rd	Skoongesig	45	BO	50
Eland St	Eastridge (M.Plain)	145	CR	48
Eland St	Kewtown	102	CF	34
Eland St	Kewtown	103	CF	35
Eland St	Parowvallei	87	BZ	44
Eland St	Ruwari	63	BW	58
Eland St	Sarepta	89	CC	53
Eland St	Scarborough	192	DK	18
Eland St	Wellington	15	AU	92
Eland Way	Pinelands	102	CD	33
Elands Rd	Delft	106	CG	49
Elands St	Eersterivier	128	CM	59
Elands St	Electric City	127	CM	58
Elandskloof St	Tafelsig (M.Plain)	145	CR	49
Elba	Wellington	14	AT	89
Elba St	Paarl	22	BF	88
Elbe La.	Eindhoven	106	CH	50
Elbe St	Manenberg	104	CH	39
Elbe St	Portlands (M.Plain)	144	CQ	46
Elbertha	Die Boord	112	CD	74
Elbertha	Die Boord	113	CD	75
Elbrecht St	Bothasig	58	BU	37
Elda Ct	Dennemere	127	CJ	57
Elder St	Bonteheuwel	103	CD	38
Elder St	Bonteheuwel	104	CD	39
Elder St	Ottery	121	CN	33
Eldon La.	Camps Bay	98	CD	18
Eldon La.	Camps Bay	98	CG	18
Eldon La.	Camps Bay	99	CD	19
Eldorado	Die Boord	112	CD	74
Eldorado Cr.	Ferndale	62	BV	54
Eldorado Rd	Langeberg Village	46	BP	53
Eleanor Cl.	Nooitgedacht	104	CE	42
Eleanor Rd	Valhalla Pk	104	CE	41
Electra Cr.	Eureka	87	CC	43
Electra St	The Hague	106	CF	50
Electric Rd	Wynberg	120	CL	28
Electron Rd	Wimbledon	108	CE	55
Electron St	Triangle Farm	89	BZ	51
Elegance Rd	Sanddrift	57	BW	33
Elegance Rd	Villa Italia	57	BW	33
Elektra Cr.	Eastridge (M.Plain)	145	CQ	48
Elektron	Tegnopark	112	CF	73
Elephant St	Eastridge (M.Plain)	145	CR	48
Eleven Ocean	Wimbledon	108	CG	55
Eleventh	De Oude Renbaan	22	BH	88
Eleventh	Mxolisi Phetani	126	CM	51
Eleventh Ave	Avon	86	CA	41
Eleventh Ave	Belmont Pk	48	BR	59
Eleventh Ave	Belmont Pk	48	BR	60
Eleventh Ave	Boston	60	BX	46
Eleventh Ave	Boston	61	BX	47
Eleventh Ave	Cafda Village	140	CS	30
Eleventh Ave	Da Gama Pk	190	DE	21

STREET NAME	SUBURB NAME	PG	GRID	
Eleventh Ave	Eikendal	48	BS	59
Eleventh Ave	Fish Hoek	186	DB	23
Eleventh Ave	Florida	87	CB	44
Eleventh Ave	Hazendal	102	CE	33
Eleventh Ave	Kensington	84	BY	34
Eleventh Ave	Kensington	84	BZ	34
Eleventh Ave	Leonsdale	86	CA	41
Eleventh Ave	Leonsdale	86	CA	42
Eleventh Ave	Pelikan Pk	141	CQ	34
Eleventh Ave	Pelikan Pk	142	CQ	36
Eleventh Ave	Retreat	140	CR	30
Eleventh Ave	Schaap Kraal	142	CQ	36
Eleventh Ave	Tafelsig (M.Plain)	146	CS	51
Eleventh Cl.	Kayamandi	94	CA	74
Eleventh Rd	Heathfield	140	CR	28
Eleventh St	Bishop Lavis	105	CD	43
Eleventh St	Elsies River Ind.	86	BZ	41
Eleventh St	Kensington	84	BZ	33
Eleventh St	Rusthof	175	DA	75
Eleventh St	Southfork	175	DB	76
Elf Rd	Eersterivier	128	CN	59
Elffers Rd	Tijgerhof	57	BX	33
Elfin Ave	Elfindale	140	CQ	30
Elfrisco St	Wellington	10	AS	92
Elgar	Delft Sth	125	CK	48
Elgar Cl.	Mandalay	125	CM	48
Elgar St	Retreat	140	CS	29
Elgin Cir.	Fish Hoek	186	DA	24
Elgin Cl.	La Rochelle	62	BV	51
Elgin Rd	Bergvliet	139	CQ	26
Elgin Rd	Milnerton	57	BW	32
Elgin Rd	Sybrand Pk	102	CE	32
Elias Motsoaledi Cr.	Mandela Pk	146	CR	53
Elijah Barayi Cr.	Mandela Pk	147	CQ	55
Elijah Chauke St	Kuyasa	147	CR	55
Elijah Chauke St	Kuyasa	147	CS	58
Elijah Loza St	Gugulethu	123	CK	41
Elijah Loza St	Nyanga	104	CH	42
Elijah Loza St	Nyanga	123	CJ	41
Elim	Ravensmead	87	CA	45
Elim Cr.	Eersterivier	128	CL	60
Elim St	Die Bos	170	CX	74
Elim St	Die Bos	174	CY	74
Elim St	Morgenster	63	BU	56
Elim St	Sarepta	89	CC	52
Elisabet St	Paarl	22	BE	88
Elise Rd	Hout Bay	117	CN	15
Eliza	Dalvale	19	AY	93
Eliza	Dalvale	19	BA	94
Elizabeth Ave	Grassy Pk	141	CQ	32
Elizabeth Ave	Pinelands	84	CB	34
Elizabeth Cl.	Dennedal	139	CS	25
Elizabeth Cr.	Lentegeur (M.Plain)	145	CO	48
Elizabeth Dr.	Athlone	102	CF	34
Elizabeth La.	Barbarossa	120	CN	27
Elizabeth Roos St	Brooklyn	84	BZ	31
Elizabeth St	Bloekombos	48	BR	62
Elizabeth St	Kalkfontein II	107	CD	52
Elizabeth St	Lentegeur (M.Plain)	145	CO	48
Ella St	Schotsche Kloof	81	CA	22
Elland Rd	Weltevreden Val. (M.Plain)	124	CN	44
Ellerslie Rd	Wynberg	120	CL	28
Ellesmere Cl.	Belhar	107	CE	51
Elliot Ave	Epping Ind.	86	CB	39
Elliot Ave	Ruyterwacht	86	CA	39
Elliot St	Bloekombos	49	BR	63
Elliot Waka Cl.	Nyanga	123	CK	42
Ellis Park Cr.	Beacon Valley (M.Plain)	145	CP	48
Ellis Rd	Sea Point	81	BZ	19
Elm	Pinelands	85	CC	35
Elm	Thornton	85	CA	36
Elm Cl.	Hanover Pk	122	CK	36
Elm Cl.	Hanover Pk	122	CN	36
Elm Cl.	La Rochelle	62	BV	51
Elm Cl.	Mitchells Plain	144	CQ	45
Elm Cl.	Silverglade	185	DA	22
Elm Rd	Parkwood	141	CO	32
Elm St	Forest Village	127	CM	58
Elm St	Grassy Pk	141	CR	32
Elm St	Ottery East	121	CN	33
Elm St	Tokai	139	CS	25
Elm Way	Bellair	62	BW	51
Elm Way	Rusdal	108	CF	57
Elma Rd	Rosebank	101	CF	30
Elmarie Cr.	Beacon Valley (M.Plain)	145	CP	48
Elmarie St	Kalkfontein II	107	CD	52
Elmtree Cl.	Hout Bay	117	CN	18
Elmwood Cl.	Parklands	25	BM	32
Elmwood St	Klipkop	87	BZ	45
Eloff St	Portlands (M.Plain)	145	CR	47
Elonwabo	Mbekweni	15	AV	92
Elpark	Penlyn Est.	103	CH	35
Elphinstone Ave	Table View	41	BP	32
Elphinstone Sq.	Ruyterwacht	86	CA	40
Elriche Cl.	Elriche	19	BB	91
Elrin Rd	Flintdale Est.	140	CP	30
Els	The Palms	170	CW	73
Els St	Brackenfell	63	BV	56
Elsane Cl.	De Zoete Inval	22	BH	88
Elsbury Way	Matroosfontein	86	CC	41
Elsenburg Ave	Belhar	106	CD	49
Elsenburg St	Mitchells Plain	144	CQ	44
Elsenburg St	Somerset West	169	CT	70
Elsenburg St	Somerset West	170	CT	71
Elsenburg St	Voorbrug	106	CG	50

STREET NAME	SUBURB NAME	PG	GRID	
Elsendal Rd	Edgemead	58	BU	37
Elsenham Ave	Somerset West	151	CS	73
Elsie Manning St	Cafda Village	141	CS	31
Elsie St	Kalkfontein II	107	CD	52
Elsies Peak Rd	Heideveld	104	CG	39
Elsies St	Mfuleni	126	CK	53
Elsies St	Mfuleni	126	CK	52
Elsjieskraal Rd	Manenberg	104	CH	39
Elson Rd	Woodstock	83	CB	27
Elstree Rd	Heathfield	140	CQ	28
Elswood Pl.	Leonsdale	86	CA	41
Elswood Pl.	Leonsdale	86	BZ	41
Elterman	Windsor Pk	47	BR	58
Eltister Rd	Lavender Hill	160	CT	31
Eluxolweni	Wellington	15	AU	91
Eluxolweni	Wellington	15	AT	94
Elva Rd	Plumstead	140	CO	30
Elvis Rd	Scottsdene	64	BU	60
Elvy St	Panorama	59	BV	41
Elwyn Rd	Penlyn Est.	103	CH	35
Elwyn Rd South	Belthorn Est.	103	CH	35
Elzeth Rd	Ottery	121	CM	33
Embers Cl.	Welgedacht	60	BT	46
Emerald	Rocklands (M.Plain)	144	CS	46
Emerald Cr.	Fish Hoek	186	DA	23
Emerald Cr.	Fish Hoek	186	DA	24
Emerald Cr.	Highbury	108	CD	55
Emerald Cr.	San Michel	157	CX	20
Emerald Cr.	Sheridon Pk	159	CU	29
Emerald Dr.	Belvedere Noordhoek	157	CX	19
Emerald Dr.	San Michel	157	CX	20
Emerald Fern Cr.	Somerset West	171	CS	77
Emerald St	Somerset West	150	CR	70
Emerald Ter.	San Michel	157	CX	20
Emerald Way	Dennemere	108	CH	58
Emerald Way	Summer Greens	58	BV	35
Emerald Way	Summer Greens	58	BV	36
Emery Rd	Eastridge (M.Plain)	145	CR	47
Emilion Cl.	Uitzicht	31	BN	55
Emily Hobhouse St	Parow Nth	59	BW	41
Emily Hobhouse St	Townsend Est.	85	BZ	38
Emma Cl.	Lentegeur (M.Plain)	145	CO	48
Emmas Cl.	Belvedere Noordhoek	157	CX	19
Emmbry Ave	Nyanga	123	CK	42
Emms Dr.	Matroosfontein	104	CD	41
Emms Dr.	Nyanga	123	CK	42
Emmy St	Weltevreden Val. (M.Plain)	144	CQ	43
Emory Oak	Oak Glen	62	BW	53
Empire Ave	Hout Bay	137	CP	15
Empire Gate	High Gate	107	CG	53
Empire Rd	Ottery	122	CL	35
Empumelelweni Cl.	Nyanga	123	CK	43
Enchor Rd	Dieprivier	140	CO	28
End St	Beaconvale	87	BZ	43
End St	Belgravia	88	BY	50
End St	Wellington	10	AS	92
End Way	Pinelands	84	CA	34
Endeavour St	Sand Ind.	122	CJ	37
Endive St	Ferndale	62	BV	54
Endler	Stellenbosch	95	CB	78
Endura Rd	Blue Downs	127	CJ	56
Energie St	Kuilsrivier Ind.	89	CC	54
Enfield Ave	Athlone	102	CF	33
Engina Cr.	Sunset Beach	41	BS	32
Engine Ave	Montague Gdns Ind.	58	BU	35
Enkosi	Mbekweni	15	AW	92
Enkululekweni St	Mxolisi Phetani	125	CM	50
Ennerdale	Pinelands	84	CB	34
Enoch Sontonga	Weltevreden Val. (M.Plain)	123	CN	42
Enoller	Groenheuwel	19	AZ	92
Ensfield Rd	Epping Forest	86	CB	41
Enslin St	Lochnerhof	170	CX	71
Enslin St	Ottery	121	CM	33
Enslin St	Paarl	22	BF	88
Ensor St	Cafda Village	141	CS	31
Entabeni	Mbekweni	15	AV	92
Entokozweni St	Crossroads	124	CK	45
Envoy	Rocklands (M.Plain)	144	CS	46
Enza Cir.	Bothasig	58	BU	36
Epping Ave	Avon	86	CA	41
Epping Ave	Leonsdale	86	BZ	42
Epping Ave	Valhalla	86	CA	40
Epping Cr.	Elsies River Ind.	86	BZ	42
Epping St	Rugby	57	BX	31
Epsom Cl.	Milnerton Rdg	41	BS	34
Epsom Cr.	Beacon Valley (M.Plain)	145	CP	48
Epsom Dr.	Ottery	122	CM	35
Epsom Rd	Kenilworth	120	CK	30
Epson St	Somerset West	170	CW	72
Epstein St	Labiance	89	BZ	51
Epsten Cr.	Lavender Hill	160	CT	31
Epsten Ct	Lavender Hill	160	CT	31
Epsten Rd	Lavender Hill	160	CT	31
Epworth Rd	Rondebosch	102	CG	32
Erani Cl.	Kraaifontein Ext. 17	47	BQ	58
Erasmus Ct	Lavender Hill	159	CT	30
Erasmus Smit	Idasvallei	95	CA	78
Erasmus St	Mimosa	88	CA	50
Erasmus St	Scottsville	47	BS	57
Eric Vijoen	Parkwood	141	CO	32
Eric Way	Montagu's Gift	142	CO	35
Erica	Lentegeur (M.Plain)	144	CO	44
Erica	Summerville	64	BT	59
Erica	Tafelsig (M.Plain)	145	CS	50
Erica	Tafelsig (M.Plain)	146	CS	51

STREET NAME	SUBURB NAME	PG	GRID	
Erica	William Lloyd	23	BD	93
Erica Ave	Fish Hoek	186	DA	24
Erica Ave	Somerset West	170	CU	73
Erica Ave	Westlake Est.	158	CU	25
Erica Cl.	Hout Bay	137	CP	16
Erica Cl.	Table View	41	BO	32
Erica Cr.	Manenberg	123	CJ	39
Erica Dr.	Belhar	105	CD	46
Erica Dr.	Belhar	106	CD	48
Erica Dr.	Belhar	106	CD	50
Erica Pl.	Bergvliet	140	CQ	27
Erica Rd	Devon Pk	128	CM	60
Erica Rd	Durbanville Hills	45	BR	49
Erica Rd	Gordon Strand	175	DC	75
Erica Rd	Kommetjie	183	DC	12
Erica Rd	Milnerton	57	BU	33
Erica Rd	Murdock Valley	195	DL	28
Erica Rd	Stellenberg	62	BU	51
Erica Rd	Table View	41	BO	31
Erica Rd	Table View	41	BO	32
Erica Rd	Uitsig	87	CC	45
Erica St	Casablanca	175	DA	75
Erica St	Chapman's Peak	156	CX	16
Erica St	Franschhoek Sth	79	BZ	108
Erica St	Hout Bay	137	CP	16
Erica St	Kleinvlei	127	CK	58
Erica St	Parow Nth	59	BW	41
Erica St	Woodstock	82	CB	26
Erica Way	Pinelands	102	CD	34
Erica Way	Somerset West	171	CX	75
Erich von Bayer	Panorama	59	BV	41
Erics Wk	Parkwood	141	CO	32
Ericson St	Forest Glade	127	CL	58
Erie Rd	Flintdale Est.	140	CP	30
Erie Rd	Retreat	140	CS	28
Erika Rd	Blackheath Ind.	108	CF	56
Erika St	Wellington	15	AT	93
Erin Rd	Rondebosch	101	CF	30
Erin Rd	Rosebank	101	CF	30
Erinvale Ave	Somerset West	152	CR	78
Erinvale Ave	Somerset West	152	CS	78
Erinvale Ave	Somerset West	153	CS	79
Erinvale Ave	Somerset West	172	CT	79
Ermelo St	Portlands (M.Plain)	144	CS	46
Ermington Rd	Muizenberg	159	CX	30
Erna Cl.	Northgate	59	BW	42
Ernest Cr.	Brackenfell Sth	63	BX	58
Ernest Curry St	Lotus River	141	CQ	34
Ernest Esau St	Ravensmead	87	CB	45
Ernest Modumo St	Kuyasa	147	CS	55
Ernest Nondulo St	Kuyasa	147	CS	55
Ernest Rd	Doornhoogte	103	CG	36
Ernest Rd	Gaylee	108	CG	57
Ernie Batt Cr.	Nyanga	123	CJ	42
Erongo	Wellington	15	AV	91
Eros Cl.	Bonnie Brae	47	BP	57
Eros Cl.	Eureka	87	CC	43
Eros St	Wellington	15	AV	93
Eros Way	Woodlands (M.Plain)	144	CO	44
Eros Way	Woodlands (M.Plain)	144	CP	44
Ertjiebos Cr.	Roosendaal	107	CF	51
Ertjiehout	Delft Sth	125	CJ	50
Ertjiehout Ct	Delft Sth	125	CJ	50
Erts Rd	Vanguard	103	CG	38
Escalonia St	Somerset West	150	CR	70
Escombe Rd	Vredehoek	100	CD	23
Esdoring Cr.	Vredekloof	62	BT	54
Esdoring St	Loevenstein	60	BW	45
Esher St	Claremont	120	CJ	30
Eshowe Cl.	Portlands (M.Plain)	144	CR	46
Eshowe Rd	Sanddrift	57	BV	33
Esk Way	Manenberg	103	CH	38
Eskdale Rd	Gardens	81	CC	21
Eskol La.	Belle Constantia	139	CP	25
Eskom Ring Rd	Morgen Gronde	63	BW	55
Esmar Rd	Rondebosch	101	CG	30
Esme Cl.	Northgate	59	BW	42
Esme Rd	Newlands	101	CG	28
Espel	Morgen Gronde	63	BW	55
Esperance St	Avondale	60	BX	44
Esplanade St	Milnerton	57	BW	31
Esprit	Schuilplaats	113	CG	76
Essam Rd	Milnerton	57	BV	32
Essenhout	Delft Sth	125	CK	49
Essenhout	Weltevrede	94	BY	74
Essenhout Cl.	Onverwacht	175	DC	76
Essenhout Cr.	Plattekloof	59	BV	42
Essenhout Cr.	Wallacedene	48	BS	60
Essenhout Rd	Bonteheuwel	103	CD	38
Essenhout Rd	Silvertown	103	CF	35
Essenhout Rd	Stellenberg	62	BU	52
Essenhout St	Eastridge (M.Plain)	145	CR	48
Essenhout St	Ottery	121	CN	33
Essenhout St	Tygerdal	58	BX	37
Essenhout St	Vredekloof	62	BT	53
Essenhout Way	Sunnydale	185	CZ	19
Essex Rd	Lakeside	159	CV	28
Essex Rd	Wynberg	120	CM	30
Essex St	Maitland	84	CA	31
Essex St	Woodstock	83	CB	27
Esslingen Way	Silversands	107	CH	54
Esso Rd	Montague Gdns Ind.	42	BS	35
Estella	Dalvale	19	AY	93
Estelle Cr.	Beacon Valley (M.Plain)	145	CP	48
Ester Rd	Newfields	103	CH	36

Index to Street Names

Esther Cr. — Fountain Rd

STREET NAME	SUBURB NAME	PG	GRID	
Esther Cr.	Beacon Valley (M.Plain)	145	CP	48
Esther Rd	Montagu's Gift	141	CO	33
Estmil Cl.	Elfindale	140	CQ	30
Estmil Way	Elfindale	140	CQ	30
Estoril Rd	Killarney Gdns	42	BP	37
Estoril Way	Whispering Pines	175	DB	76
Ethel Cl.	Lentegeur (M.Plain)	145	CO	48
Ethel Cl.	Lentegeur (M.Plain)	145	CP	50
Ethel Rd	Claremont	101	CH	27
Etna Cr.	Tafelsig (M.Plain)	145	CS	49
Etna St	Lemoenkloof	18	BB	89
Eton Rd	Heathfield	140	CP	28
Eton Way	Westlake Est.	158	CU	24
Etona St	Wesbank	107	CG	52
Eucalyptus Rd	Eersterivier	128	CN	60
Euclea Cl.	Hout Bay	136	CO	14
Euclid Cl.	Woodlands (M.Plain)	144	CP	45
Eugene Marais Ave	Bel Ombre	119	CM	25
Eugenie Cr.	Die Oude Spruit	63	BW	55
Eulalia	Lentegeur (M.Plain)	144	CP	46
Eurecon Cl.	Connaught	87	CB	44
Eureka Cl.	Mitchells Plain	144	CR	45
Eureka Cl.	Mitchells Plain	144	CR	43
Eureka Rd	Rosebank	101	CF	30
Eureka St	Eureka	87	CC	44
Europa Link	Eureka	87	CC	43
Europa Link	Eureka	87	CB	46
Europa Rd	Ocean View	189	DD	15
Eustegia Way	Hout Bay	136	CO	14
Eva Paulse St	Bloomsburg	23	BD	92
Eva St	Valhalla Pk	104	CE	42
Eva Wk	Manenberg	123	CJ	39
Evan Rd	Kenridge	61	BU	49
Evans Ave	Epping Ind.	85	CC	37
Evans St	William Lloyd	19	BC	92
Evans St	William Lloyd	19	BC	93
Eveleigh Way	Rondebosch	102	CF	32
Eveline de Bruin Cr.	Mandela Pk	147	CQ	55
Evelyn	Dalvale	19	AY	93
Evelyn	Dalvale	19	BA	94
Evelyn Cl.	Lentegeur (M.Plain)	145	CO	48
Evelyn Rd	Retreat Ind. Area	159	CT	28
Evening Way	Pinelands	102	CD	33
Everbearing St	Jamestown	112	CH	74
Everest Cl.	Barbarossa	120	CN	27
Everest Cl.	Eersterivier	128	CL	59
Everest Cr.	Tafelsig (M.Plain)	145	CS	49
Everglen Manor	Everglen	45	BS	50
Evergreen	Green Oaks	94	BY	74
Evergreen Ave	Newlands	101	CH	27
Evergreen Dr.	Austinville	108	CH	56
Evergreen La.	Rust-en-vrede	119	CN	26
Evergreen La.	Silverglade	185	DA	22
Everlasting	Macassar	148	CS	62
Eversdal Rd	Amanda Glen	46	BS	52
Eversdal Rd	Eversdal Hgts	45	BS	50
Eversdal Rd	Northpine	63	BU	58
Eversdal Way	Stellenryk	62	BU	53
Eversham Rd	Parklands	25	BN	33
Evette	Dalvale	19	AY	92
Evremonde Rd	Plumstead	120	CN	30
Evremonde Rd	Plumstead	121	CN	31
Ewfield End	Parklands	25	BM	32
Excalibur St	Camelot	107	CF	53
Excelsior Cl.	Mitchells Plain	144	CR	45
Excelsior Rd	Welcome	103	CF	38
Excelsior St	Highbury	107	CD	54
Excelsior St	Mitchells Plain	144	CR	45
Excelsior St	Voorbrug	106	CG	50
Exeter Ave	Ottery	122	CM	35
Exeter Ave	Ottery East	121	CN	34
Exeter La.	Belhar	107	CE	51
Exeter Rd	Bishopscourt	119	CK	26
Exeter Rd	Fish Hoek	185	DA	22
Exeter Rd	Plumstead	120	CN	29
Exeter Way	Pinelands	84	CB	33
Exhibition Ter.	Green Point	81	BZ	22
Exmoor Cl.	Table View	41	BO	34
Exmouth Rd	Plumstead	120	CN	30
Exner Ave	Vredehoek	82	CC	23
Exner Ave	Vredehoek	100	CD	23
Exwin Rd	Meadowridge	139	CO	26
Eybers Cr.	Parow Nth	60	BW	44
Eybers St	Welgemoed	60	BV	45
Eyeberry Cr.	Wesbank	107	CF	51
Eyton Rd	Claremont	120	CJ	27

F

STREET NAME	SUBURB NAME	PG	GRID	
F. Boroch	Groenvlei	18	BA	88
F.A.Venter Cl.	Langgewacht	170	CW	72
F.Baart St	Mandela Pk	146	CQ	54
F.Chilcane Cl.	Driftsands	147	CQ	56
F.Dodovu St	Mfuleni	126	CL	53
F.W. De Klerk St	Wesbank	107	CF	52
Faber	Brandwacht	113	CE	77
Fabian Ave	Athlone	102	CF	33
Fabriek	Wellington	10	AR	92
Fabriek Rd	Eindhoven	106	CH	50
Fabriek St	Bellville Sth Ind.	88	CA	50
Fabriek St	Eureka	87	CC	44
Fabriek St	Franschhoek Sth	78	BY	106
Fabriek St	Kuilsrivier Ind.	89	CC	54
Fabriek St	Kuilsrivier Ind.	90	CC	55
Fabriek St	Kuilsrivier Ind.	108	CD	55
Fabriek St	Lemoenkloof	18	BC	88
Fabriek St	Peerless Pk East	47	BS	58
Fabriek St	Strand Halt	170	CW	74
Factory Rd	Salt River	83	CC	27
Factreton Ave	Factreton	85	BZ	35
Factreton Ave	Kensington	84	BY	34
Faculyn St	Park Estates	170	CX	72
Fafan St	Delft	106	CF	50
Fagan St	Park Estates	170	CX	71
Fagan St	Park Estates	174	CY	71
Fagan St	Park Estates	174	CY	72
Fagan St	Somerset West	171	CV	75
Fah St	Macassar	149	CS	65
Fair Rd	Northpine	63	BU	58
Fair Way	Table View	41	BQ	34
Fairbairn Rd	Stellenberg	62	BU	52
Fairbairn St	Glencairn Hgts	191	DD	24
Fairbairn St	Parow East	87	BY	45
Fairbairn St	Ysterplaat	84	BZ	31
Fairbairn Way	Meadowridge	140	CP	27
Fairbridge Rd	Table View	41	BQ	34
Fairbridge Rd	Tijgerhof	57	BX	32
Fairdale Rd	Dieprivier	140	CO	28
Fairfax St	Strand Halt	170	CW	73
Fairfield	Dennemere	108	CH	58
Fairfield Cl.	Plattekloof Glen	59	BW	40
Fairfield Cl.	Sunnydale	185	DA	20
Fairfield Cl.	Sweet Valley	139	CQ	26
Fairfield Rd	Eikendal	64	BT	59
Fairfield Rd	Observatory	83	CC	29
Fairfield Rd	Rondebosch	101	CG	30
Fairfield St	De Tijger	60	BW	43
Fairfield St	Oak Glen	62	BW	52
Fairfield St North	Fairfield	60	BX	44
Fairfield St South	Fairfield	87	BY	43
Fairhaven Ave	Voorbrug	106	CG	50
Fairmead Dr.	Somerset West	151	CR	72
Fairmead Rd	Dieprivier	140	CO	28
Fairmead Rd	Epping Forest	86	CC	41
Fairmont	Sunningdale	25	BN	31
Fairmont View	Edgemead	58	BU	38
Fairseat La.	Wynberg	120	CK	28
Fairthorne Rd	Somerset West	170	CV	73
Fairtrees Cl.	Durbanville	46	BP	52
Fairtrees Rd	Amanda Glen	46	BS	53
Fairtrees Rd	Durbanville	46	BQ	52
Fairtrees Rd	Sonstraal	46	BR	53
Fairview Ave	Woodstock	83	CB	27
Fairview Cl.	Barbarossa	139	CO	26
Fairview Cl.	Milnerton Rdg	41	BS	33
Fairview Cl.	Ottery	122	CM	35
Fairview Cl.	Richwood	42	BP	38
Fairview Cl.	Richwood	42	BP	37
Fairview Cr.	Milnerton Rdg	41	BS	33
Fairview End	Parklands	25	BM	32
Fairview Rd	Penhill	128	CK	61
Fairview Rd	Wynberg	120	CM	28
Fairview St	Bellavista	22	BD	90
Fairview St	Eureka	87	CC	44
Fairway	Bergvliet	140	CR	28
Fairway	Vredelust	87	BY	46
Fairway Ave	Fairways	121	CN	31
Fairway Cl.	Table View	41	BQ	34
Fairway St	Klipkop	87	BZ	45
Fairways	Die Wingerd	113	CE	75
Fairways Ave	Sunset Beach	57	BT	31
Fairways Cl.	N1 City	59	BX	41
Fairways Cl.	Pine Acres	175	DC	77
Fairways Cl.	Sunset Beach	57	BT	31
Fairways Cl.	Sunset Links	57	BT	31
Fairwinds Rd	Eversdal	46	BS	51
Fairwood Cl.	Parklands	25	BM	32
Fairwood Rd	Parklands	25	BM	32
Fairydene St	Klipkop	87	BZ	45
Faith Cl.	Kensington	84	BZ	33
Faith St	Claremont	120	CJ	27
Fakier Hassiem St	Gustrow	175	DB	75
Falaise St	Paarl	22	BD	88
Falcon	Dunoon	42	BO	37
Falcon	Dunoon	42	BO	38
Falcon	Rocklands (M.Plain)	144	CR	44
Falcon	Seawinds	159	CU	30
Falcon	Sunbird Pk	107	CF	54
Falcon	Wingfield	85	BZ	36
Falcon Ave	Electric City	128	CN	59
Falcon Ave	Tarentaalplaas	175	DA	76
Falcon Cr.	Parklands	25	BN	32
Falcon Cr.	Pelikan Pk	142	CS	36
Falcon Cr.	Sunridge	41	BP	34
Falcon La.	Hout Bay	117	CM	18
Falcon Rd	Heideveld	103	CF	38
Falcon St	D'urbanvale	29	BN	49
Falcon St	D'urbanvale	45	BO	49
Falcon St	Ocean View	184	DC	15
Falcon Way	Montagu's Gift	141	CP	33
Falcon's Crest	D'urbanvale	45	BO	49
Falia	Delft Sth	125	CK	48
Falkland Cl.	Portlands (M.Plain)	144	CQ	46
Fallstaff St	Highbury	107	CE	54
Falmouth Rd	Observatory	101	CD	28
Falstaff Cr.	Eastridge (M.Plain)	145	CQ	48
Falstaff Rd	Penlyn Est.	122	CJ	35
Falsterbo Cr.	Sunningdale	25	BL	31
Fame Cr.	Tarentaalplaas	174	CZ	74
Fame St	Strandfontein	163	CT	43
Familie La.	Athlone	102	CG	33
Fana Cr.	Harare	146	CR	53
Fanaphi St	Bloekombos	48	BR	62
Fancourt Cr.	Sunningdale	25	BM	31
Fanie Jacobs St	Monte Vista	59	BU	39
Fanshawe Rd	Plumstead	140	CO	30
Farad St	Kaymor	89	BZ	53
Faraday St	Tarentaalplaas	170	CX	74
Faraday Way	Meadowridge	140	CP	27
Fardon Cr.	Voorbrug	106	CG	50
Fareal St	Casablanca	175	DB	76
Fareham St	Woodstock	82	CB	26
Farlow Way	Southfork	175	DB	75
Farm Cl.	Heideveld	103	CG	38
Farm Cr.	Montagu's Gift	141	CO	34
Farm Field Rd	Knole Pk	142	CO	36
Farm Rd	Doornhoogte	103	CG	36
Farmedge	Bergvliet	139	CQ	26
Farmersfield Rd	Edgemead	58	BU	37
Farmside	Bergvliet	139	CQ	26
Farnmouth Rd	Retreat	159	CT	29
Farnworth St	Rugby	57	BX	31
Farquhar Rd	Camps Bay	98	CE	18
Farrar St	Eastridge (M.Plain)	145	CQ	49
Farrier St	Mitchells Plain	144	CQ	45
Farriers Way	Hout Bay	117	CM	18
Farries Cr.	Kenilworth Pk	121	CK	31
Farrington St	Bloekombos	48	BR	62
Father Curren Cr.	Nyanga	123	CJ	41
Father Trevor Huddleston St	Mandela Pk	147	CR	56
Fathom Rd	Bloubergrant	24	BN	30
Fatima St	Casablanca	175	DB	76
Fatima Way	Delft	106	CF	50
Fato Rd	Ekuphumuleni	146	CQ	53
Faull	Strand Halt	170	CX	73
Faull Rd	Fairfield	60	BX	44
Faulman Rd	Grassy Pk	141	CR	31
Fauna Rd	Steenberg	159	CT	28
Faure	Kromrivier	95	CB	75
Faure Cl.	Dieprivier	140	CP	28
Faure Cl.	Sir Lowry's Pass	176	CZ	81
Faure Cr.	Somerset West	171	CT	78
Faure Marine Dr.	Greenways	174	DA	74
Faure Marine Dr.	Harbour Island	179	DD	76
Faure Marine Dr.	Harbour Island	179	DF	75
Faure St	Balvenie	87	CC	43
Faure St	Eersterivier	128	CL	60
Faure St	Gardens	81	CB	22
Faure St	Harbour Island	179	DF	75
Faure St	Paarl	22	BD	88
Faure St	Park Estates	174	CY	72
Faure-Klipfontein Rd	Fairdale	126	CJ	54
Faust Cl.	Eastridge (M.Plain)	145	CR	48
Fawcett Way	Strandfontein	162	CT	41
Fawcetts Ave	Hout Bay	116	CM	14
Fawley Ter.	District Six	82	CB	24
Fawley Ter.	District Six	82	CC	24
Fay St	Tafelsig (M.Plain)	145	CR	49
Fayker Rd	Grassy Pk	141	CP	32
Faymo	Summerville	48	BS	59
Feale Cl.	Connaught	87	CB	43
Feather	Jagtershof	90	CC	57
Feather La.	Belhar	107	CE	51
Featherhead Rd	Proteavallei	60	BT	46
February	Cloetesville	94	BY	74
February	Cloetesville	95	BY	75
February Rd	Somerset West	170	CV	73
Fedelio Cr.	Brackenfell Sth	63	BX	57
Federal Rd	Woodlands (M.Plain)	144	CQ	44
Fedora Cl.	Leonsdale	86	CA	42
Feige St	Sarepta	89	CB	53
Feinhauer St	Stikland Hospital	61	BX	50
Feldhausen Ave	Claremont	101	CH	28
Feldhausen Rd	Claremont	101	CH	28
Feldhausen St	Oak Glen	62	BW	52
Felencia Cr.	Gordon Hgts	180	DD	79
Felicia Cl.	Perm Gdns	128	CJ	59
Felicia Cl.	Perm Gdns	128	CJ	60
Felicia St	Chrismar	61	BX	50
Felicia St	Durbanville	46	BP	52
Felicia St	Retreat	140	CS	28
Felicia St	Voorbrug	106	CG	50
Felix St	Macassar	149	CS	64
Felix St	Marlow	88	BZ	50
Felixberg Rd	Heideveld	104	CF	40
Feljisi Rd	Philippi East	125	CM	47
Fell Cl.	Table View	42	BO	35
Feltham Rd	Oranjezicht	99	CD	22
Felucca Cr.	Sun Valley	185	DA	20
Femela St	Victoria Mxenge	126	CN	51
Fennel Cr.	Vredenberg	62	BV	53
Fennel St	Ferndale	62	BV	54
Fenton Rd	Salt River	83	CB	28
Fenwick St	Brooklyn	83	BZ	30
Ferdinand St	Kirstenhof	159	CT	27
Fergus Rd	Connaught	87	CB	43
Ferguson St	Aurora	45	BP	48
Ferguson St	Bloubergstrand	24	BL	28
Ferguson St	Plumstead	140	CO	29
Ferguson St	Triangle Farm	89	BY	51
Fern Ave	Tarentaalplaas	175	DA	76
Fern Cl.	Alphen	119	CM	26
Fern Cl.	Meadowridge	140	CP	28
Fern La.	Chapman's Peak	156	CX	16
Fern La.	Grassy Pk	141	CP	32
Fern Rd	Austinville	108	CH	56
Fern Rd	Blackheath Ind.	108	CF	56
Fern Rd	Murdock Valley	195	DL	28
Fern St	Bonteheuwel	104	CE	40
Fern St	Cravenby	87	CB	43
Fern St	Ottery East	121	CN	34
Ferndale Dr.	Ottery East	121	CN	34
Ferndale Rd	Bracken Hgts	62	BU	53
Ferndale Rd	Ferndale	62	BV	54
Ferndale Rd	Hoogstede	62	BV	54
Ferndale Rd	Lotus River	142	CP	35
Ferndale Rd	Maitland	84	CA	31
Ferndale St	Des Hampden	89	CB	53
Ferness Rd	Ottery	121	CM	32
Fernglen St	Wesbank	107	CG	51
Fernkloof	Wesbank	107	CH	51
Fernside Way	Ottery East	121	CM	34
Fernwood Ave	Newlands	100	CH	26
Fernwood Ave	Newlands	101	CH	27
Fernwood Cl.	Parklands	26	BN	35
Fernwood Cl.	Richwood	42	BQ	38
Fernwood Dr.	Somerset West	171	CX	77
Fernwood Rd	Glenhaven	89	CA	51
Fernwood Rd	Glenhaven	89	BY	54
Fernwood St	Tafelsig (M.Plain)	145	CS	48
Fernwood Way	Edgemead	59	BT	39
Ferrari Cr.	Beacon Valley (M.Plain)	145	CQ	48
Ferrier Cl.	Weltevreden Val. (M.Plain)	124	CN	44
Ferrous St	Brackenfell Ind.	63	BU	57
Ferrous St	Vanguard	103	CF	38
Ferrule Ave	Montague Gdns Ind.	58	BU	36
Ferry Rd	Simon's Town	191	DH	23
Ferry Way	Strandfontein	162	CT	39
Fesi St	Victoria Mxenge	126	CN	51
Fester Ave	Balvenie	87	CB	43
Fester Ave	Leonsdale	86	CA	42
Festile St	Umrhabulo Triangle	147	CR	57
Festival Rd	Brooklyn	83	BY	30
Festival St	Jamestown	113	CH	75
Feyenoord Way	Somerset Hgts	127	CJ	58
Feza St	Harare	146	CR	52
Feza St	Harare	146	CR	53
Fezeka St	Gugulethu	104	CH	41
Fezeka St	Gugulethu	123	CJ	41
Fiat	Rocklands (M.Plain)	163	CT	45
Fick Cl.	Edenpark	62	BU	54
Fick Rd	Scottsville	47	BS	57
Fick St	Kaapzicht	59	BV	41
Ficus	Vygeboom	46	BR	51
Ficus Cl.	Forest Village	127	CM	58
Ficus Rd	Thornton	85	CA	37
Ficus St	Somerset West	151	CS	71
Ficus St	Stellenberg	62	BU	51
Ficus St	Tygerdal	58	BX	38
Ficus St	Westlake Est.	158	CU	25
Fiddlewood	Pinelands	85	CC	35
Fiddlewood Cl.	Eersterivier	128	CM	60
Fiddlewood Pl.	Sun Valley	185	CZ	20
Fiddlewood Pl.	Sun Valley	185	DC	22
Fidel Castro St	Mandela Pk	146	CQ	54
Fidelio Cr.	Eastridge (M.Plain)	145	CQ	48
Field	Epping Ind.	85	CC	35
Field Ave	Montagu's Gift	141	CO	34
Field Cl.	Adriaanse	105	CD	43
Field Cl.	Montagu's Gift	141	CO	34
Field Cl.	Strandfontein	162	CT	41
Field Cr.	Silvertown	103	CF	35
Field Gate	High Gate	107	CG	54
Field St	Heathfield	140	CQ	29
Field St	Strandfontein	162	CV	42
Field St	Strandfontein	162	CT	41
Field St	William Lloyd	23	BD	92
Fieldview	Edgemead	58	BU	38
Fife Ave	Fish Hoek	186	DA	23
Fife Rd	Rondebosch	101	CG	29
Fiford Cr.	Tokai	139	CS	26
Fifteenth Ave	Avon	86	CA	41
Fifteenth Ave	Boston	60	BX	46
Fifteenth Ave	Boston	61	BW	47
Fifteenth Ave	Fish Hoek	186	DB	23
Fifteenth Ave	Florida	87	CB	44
Fifteenth Ave	Hazendal	102	CE	33
Fifteenth Ave	Leonsdale	86	CA	41
Fifteenth Ave	Maitland	85	BZ	35
Fifteenth Ave	Schaap Kraal	142	CR	36
Fifteenth St	Avon	86	CA	41
Fifteenth St	Bishop Lavis	105	CD	43
Fifteenth St	Kensington	84	BZ	33
Fifth	De Oude Renbaan	22	BH	88
Fifth Ave	Athlone	102	CG	32
Fifth Ave	Belgravia	103	CG	35
Fifth Ave	Belmont Pk	48	BR	61
Fifth Ave	Belmont Pk	48	BS	60
Fifth Ave	Boston	60	BX	46
Fifth Ave	Boston	61	BX	47
Fifth Ave	Churchill	59	BX	42
Fifth Ave	Cravenby	87	CA	43
Fifth Ave	Da Gama Pk	190	DE	21
Fifth Ave	Eastridge (M.Plain)	145	CR	47
Fifth Ave	Eikendal	48	BS	59
Fifth Ave	Fairways	121	CN	32
Fifth Ave	Fish Hoek	186	DB	24
Fifth Ave	Florida	87	CA	44
Fifth Ave	Grassy Pk	141	CR	32
Fifth Ave	Hazendal	102	CE	33
Fifth Ave	Kayamandi	94	CA	74

Abbreviations used: Ave – Avenue, A.H. – Agricultural Holding, A.L. – Algemene Landgoed, Blvd – Boulevard, Cen. – Central, Cir. – Circle, Cl. – Close, Cr. – Crescent, Ct – Court, Dr. – Drive, Est. – Estate, Ext. – Extension, Hgts – Heights, Ind. – Industrial, Gdns – Gardens, Gr. – Grove, La. – Lane, (M.Plain) - Mitchells Plain, Nth – North, Pl. – Place, Pk – Park, Rd – Road, Rdg. – Ridge, S.H.– Small Holding, Sq. – Square, St – Street, Sth – South, Ter. – Terrace, Tn – Turn, Val. – Valley, Wk – Walk

STREET NAME	SUBURB NAME	PG	GRID	
Fifth Ave	Kensington	84	BZ	33
Fifth Ave	Kensington	84	CA	33
Fifth Ave	Lotus River	141	CP	34
Fifth Ave	Lotus River	142	CP	35
Fifth Ave	Malibu Village	127	CK	55
Fifth Ave	Portlands (M.Plain)	145	CR	47
Fifth Ave	Retreat	140	CR	29
Fifth Ave	Rondebosch East	102	CG	32
Fifth Ave	Rondebosch East	102	CH	32
Fifth Ave	Tafelsig (M.Plain)	146	CS	51
Fifth Ave	Welcome	103	CF	38
Fifth Ave	Wellington	10	AS	93
Fifth Rd	Heathfield	140	CQ	28
Fifth Rd	Montague Gdns Ind.	58	BT	35
Fifth St	Bishop Lavis	104	CD	42
Fifth St	Firgrove	150	CR	67
Fifth St	Heideveld	103	CF	38
Fifth St	Heideveld	103	CG	38
Fifth St	Kensington	84	CA	33
Fifth St	Rusthof	174	DA	74
Fifty-Eighth Ave	Wynberg	120	CL	27
Fifty-First Ave	Wynberg	120	CL	27
Fig	Dunoon	42	BO	37
Fig St	Loevenstein	60	BW	45
Fig St	Newlands	100	CH	26
Figaro Cr.	Kraaifontein	47	BQ	58
Figaro St	Eastridge (M.Plain)	145	CR	48
Figtree Cl.	Eastridge (M.Plain)	145	CR	48
Fikizolo St	Victoria Mxenge	126	CN	52
Filbert St	Weltevreden Val. (M.Plain)	124	CN	44
Filda Makkriel St	William Lloyd	19	BC	92
Fillians Rd	Camps Bay	99	CE	19
Fillies Rd	Primrose Pk	122	CJ	37
Fillmore Rd	Claremont	102	CH	31
Fillmore St	Wesbank	107	CG	52
Fimi St	Delft	106	CG	49
Fin Whale Way	Kommetjie	183	DA	13
Finch	Rocklands (M.Plain)	144	CS	44
Finch Cl.	Blouberg Rise	25	BN	31
Finch Cr.	Pelikan Pk	142	CS	36
Finch Cr.	Seawinds	159	CU	30
Finch La.	Sunbird Pk	107	CF	54
Finch Rd	Westlake Est.	158	CT	25
Finch Way	Blouberg Rise	25	BN	31
Finchley Rd	Camps Bay	98	CF	18
Findon St	Athlone	102	CF	33
Finger Cl.	Bloekombos	49	BR	63
Fink Rd	Bridgetown	103	CF	37
Fink St	Tarentaalplaas	175	DA	76
Finn Cl.	Connaught	87	CB	43
Finn Rd	Pelikan Pk	141	CQ	34
Finsbury Ave	Newlands	101	CH	27
Finsbury St	Somerset West	150	CS	70
Finton Rd	Elfindale	140	CP	29
Fiona Cl.	Somerset West	170	CT	74
Fiona Cl.	Tafelsig (M.Plain)	145	CR	50
Fiona Cr.	Brooklyn	84	BY	31
Fiona Cr.	Northgate	59	BW	42
Fiongart Cr.	Voorbrug	106	CH	50
Fir	Cloetesville	95	BZ	75
Fir Ave	Bantry Bay	80	CB	18
Fir Ave	Tokai	139	CS	25
Fir Cl.	Hanover Pk	122	CK	36
Fir Cl.	Hanover Pk	122	CN	36
Fir Cl.	Highbury	107	CE	54
Fir Rd	Rondebosch	101	CF	30
Fir St	Claremont	101	CH	28
Fir St	Observatory	83	CB	29
Fir St	Observatory	83	CC	29
Fir St	Tafelsig (M.Plain)	145	CS	48
Fir Way	Oak Glen	62	BW	51
Fir Way	Oak Glen	62	BW	52
Firans	Mbekweni	15	AW	92
Firdale Ave	Sea Point	81	BZ	20
Firdale Rd	Connaught	87	CB	43
Firdale Rd	Gardens	81	CC	21
Firdale Rd	Newlands	101	CG	27
Firdale Way	Northpine	63	BU	57
Firebag St	Wesbank	107	CF	51
Firefly	Rocklands (M.Plain)	163	CT	45
Firethorn	Lentegeur (M.Plain)	144	CP	46
Firethorn St	Bonteheuwel	103	CE	38
Firfield Rd	Plumstead	120	CN	29
Firgrove Rd	Milnerton	57	BW	32
Firgrove Way	Bergvliet	139	CQ	26
Firgrove Way	Bergvliet	140	CP	27
Firgrove Way	Sweet Valley	139	CQ	25
Firlands Rd	Rondebosch	102	CG	31
Firmount Rd	Sea Point	81	BZ	20
Firmount Rd	Somerset West	151	CS	73
Firmount Rd	Somerset West	170	CT	74
Firs Ave	Claremont	120	CJ	28
Firs Rd	Somerset West	170	CT	72
Firs Rd	Somerset West	170	CU	72
First	De Oude Renbaan	22	BH	88
First Ave	Athlone	102	CF	33
First Ave	Athlone	102	CG	33
First Ave	Belgravia	102	CF	34
First Ave	Bosonia	89	CB	54
First Ave	Boston	87	BY	46
First Ave	Boston	88	BY	47
First Ave	Claremont	120	CJ	29
First Ave	Da Gama Pk	190	DD	20
First Ave	Eastridge (M.Plain)	145	CQ	47
First Ave	Eastridge (M.Plain)	145	CR	47
First Ave	Elsies River Ind.	86	BZ	41
First Ave	Fairways	121	CN	32
First Ave	Fish Hoek	186	DB	24
First Ave	Florida	87	CA	44
First Ave	Glenlily	86	BY	42
First Ave	Glenlily	87	BY	43
First Ave	Grassy Pk	141	CP	32
First Ave	Grassy Pk	141	CQ	31
First Ave	Hazendal	102	CE	33
First Ave	Kayamandi	95	CA	75
First Ave	Kenilworth	120	CJ	29
First Ave	Klein Begin	48	BS	60
First Ave	Klein Begin	48	BS	61
First Ave	Knole Pk	142	CP	36
First Ave	Lotus River	141	CP	34
First Ave	Lotus River	142	CP	35
First Ave	Maitland	84	CA	32
First Ave	Manenberg	123	CK	39
First Ave	Nyanga	123	CL	42
First Ave	Paarl	22	BD	88
First Ave	Retreat	140	CR	28
First Ave	Rondebosch East	102	CH	33
First Ave	Scottsdene	48	BS	59
First Ave	Tafelsig (M.Plain)	146	CS	51
First Ave	Vanguard	103	CG	38
First Ave	Wellington	10	AS	93
First Ave	Woodlands	191	DE	23
First Cr.	Camps Bay	98	CE	18
First Cr.	Fish Hoek	186	DB	23
First Cr.	Fish Hoek	186	DB	24
First Cr.	Vredelust	60	BX	46
First Rd	Grassy Pk	141	CP	32
First Rd	Grassy Pk	141	CQ	33
First Rd	Heathfield	140	CQ	29
First Rd	Montague Gdns Ind.	58	BT	35
First St	Bishop Lavis	104	CD	41
First St	Firgrove	150	CR	67
First St	Gordon Strand	175	DC	75
First St	Maitland	84	CA	33
First St	Mxolisi Phetani	125	CL	49
First St	Mxolisi Phetani	125	CL	50
First St	Rusthof	174	DA	74
First St	Welcome	103	CF	38
First St	Wellington	10	AR	91
Firth Rd	Rondebosch	102	CE	31
Firtree Rd	Farmsteads	156	CV	18
Firtree St	Plumstead	140	CO	28
Firwood La.	Somerset West	170	CT	74
Firwood Way	Pine Acres	175	DC	77
Fisant	Onderpapegaaiberg	94	CC	73
Fisant	Rocklands (M.Plain)	144	CS	44
Fisant	William Lloyd	23	BD	94
Fisant St	Amanda Glen	46	BS	52
Fisant St	Loucharmante	90	CB	56
Fisant St	Wellington	15	AT	92
Fischer St	Eastridge (M.Plain)	145	CQ	49
Fish Ct	Delft	106	CG	49
Fish Eagle	Bonnie Brae	47	BP	57
Fish Eagle Cl.	Fish Hoek	186	DA	23
Fish Eagle Pl.	Heron Pk	184	DB	17
Fish Eagle Rd	Langeberg Rdg	47	BR	56
Fish Eagle Rd	Sunridge	42	BP	35
Fish Eagle Way	Pelikan Pk	141	CR	33
Fish Rd	Pelikan Pk	141	CR	33
Fish St	Macassar	168	CT	64
Fisher Ave	Epping Ind.	85	CC	37
Fisher St	Goodwood Est.	59	BX	38
Fisher St	Goodwood Est.	86	BY	39
Fisherman Way	Hout Bay	137	CQ	17
Fisherman's Bend	Hout Bay	116	CM	13
Fisherman's Cove	Kommetjie	183	DB	12
Fisherman's Quay	Marina Da Gama	159	CW	30
Fishermans Way	Parklands	26	BN	35
Fisherman's Way	Woodlands (M.Plain)	144	CP	45
Fishermans Wk	Parklands	42	BO	35
Fisherman's Wk	Pelikan Pk	141	CR	33
Fisherman's Wk	Pelikan Pk	141	CR	34
Fisherman's Wk	Pelikan Pk	142	CQ	35
Fishmarket St	Hout Bay	136	CQ	14
Fiskaal Cl.	Bakoven	98	CF	18
Fiskaal Rd	Bakoven	98	CF	18
Fiskaal Rd	Bakoven	99	CF	19
Fiskaal St	Wellington	15	AT	92
Fismer La.	Park Estates	174	CY	71
Fissant Cr.	Langeberg Rdg	47	BQ	56
Fitzherbert Rd	Vredehoek	100	CD	23
Fitzherbert St	Ruyterwacht	86	BZ	40
Fitzmaurice Ave	Epping Ind.	86	CB	40
Fitzpatrick Rd	Tijgerhof	57	BV	32
Fitzpatrick Rd	Tijgerhof	57	BW	32
Fitzpatrick St	Eastridge (M.Plain)	145	CQ	49
Fitzpatrick St	Parow Nth	59	BW	40
Fitzroy Rd	Eindhoven	106	CH	50
Fitzroy St	Townsend Est.	85	BZ	38
Fivaz St	Vergesig	45	BQ	49
Fivaz St	Vergesig	45	BR	48
Fiya	Philippi East	125	CL	47
Flack Rd	Clarkes	86	CC	42
Flag Bashielo St	Mandela Pk	147	CQ	56
Flagship Way	Simon's Town	194	DJ	25
Flagstaff Cl.	Eersterivier	128	CM	60
Flambeau St North	Courtrai	22	BH	87
Flambeau St South	Courtrai	22	BH	87
Flambor Rd	Flintdale Est.	140	CP	30
Flamboyant Pl.	Thornton	85	CA	37
Flamboyant Rd	Eersterivier	128	CM	61
Flame Cl.	Vredenberg	62	BV	53
Flame Tree Cl.	Nova Constantia	139	CP	24
Flamingo	Danarand	89	CC	54
Flamingo	Fairyland	19	AZ	93
Flamingo	Kleinvallei	94	CB	72
Flamingo	Kleinvallei	94	CC	73
Flamingo	Onderpapegaaiberg	94	CC	73
Flamingo	Seawinds	159	CU	30
Flamingo Cl.	Admirals Pk	175	DC	78
Flamingo Cl.	Dreyersdal	139	CS	26
Flamingo Cl.	Rosendal	61	BU	50
Flamingo Cr.	Lansdowne	121	CJ	33
Flamingo Cr.	Pelikan Pk	141	CS	34
Flamingo Cr.	Weltevreden Val. (M.Plain)	124	CN	43
Flamingo Dr.	Kommetjie	183	DB	13
Flamingo Rd	Ocean View	184	DC	15
Flamingo Rd	Woodlands (M.Plain)	144	CP	44
Flamingo St	Macassar	149	CR	64
Flamingo St	Westlake Est.	158	CT	25
Flamink Cl.	Morningstar	46	BP	51
Flamink Rd	Sunnydale	185	DA	19
Flamink St	Somerset West	170	CV	72
Flamink St	Wellington	15	AT	92
Flamink St	William Lloyd	23	BD	94
Flanders	Strandfontein	162	CT	40
Flanders Rd	Pinati	122	CK	35
Flap Cl.	Loucharmante	90	CC	56
Flat Rd	Doornhoogte	103	CG	35
Flat Rd	Doornhoogte	103	CH	35
Flax	Green Oaks	95	BY	75
Flax	Green Oaks	95	BY	77
Fleet	Belthorn Est.	102	CH	34
Fleet St	Bothasig	58	BT	38
Fleetwood	Dennemere	108	CH	58
Fleetwood Ave	Claremont	120	CJ	27
Fleming Rd	Wynberg	120	CM	29
Fleming Way	Meadowridge	140	CP	27
Flesk Rd	Connaught	87	CB	43
Fleur Cl.	De Tijger	60	BW	44
Fleur De Cap St	Eersterivier	128	CL	59
Fleur de Lis Cr.	Langeberg Rdg	47	BR	55
Fleur Rd	Belthorn Est.	103	CH	35
Flight Rd	Pelikan Pk	141	CR	34
Flint	Jagtershof	90	CC	57
Flint Rd	Belthorn Est.	122	CJ	35
Flintdale Rd	Flintdale Est.	141	CP	31
Flintdale Rd	Flintdale Est.	141	CQ	31
Flodden Way	Strandfontein	162	CT	41
Flodden Way	Strandfontein	162	CV	42
Flora	Woodlands (M.Plain)	144	CO	44
Flora Cl.	Hout Bay Harbour	136	CR	13
Flora Rd	Bishop Lavis	104	CE	42
Flora Rd	Bishop Lavis	104	CF	42
Flora Rd	Retreat	140	CS	29
Flora Rd	Retreat Ind. Area	159	CT	28
Flora Rd	Wynberg	120	CM	30
Flora Steps	Simon's Town	194	DJ	25
Florence Ave	Observatory	83	CC	29
Florence St	Kingston	61	BX	49
Florence St	Oakdale	61	BX	48
Flores St	Bloubergstrand	24	BK	28
Floribunda St	Somerset West	151	CS	71
Florida	Anesta	113	CF	75
Florida Cl.	Coniston Pk	159	CU	30
Florida Rd	Colorado (M.Plain)	144	CO	44
Florida Rd	Vredehoek	82	CC	23
Florida St	Durbanville	46	BO	51
Florida St	Florida	87	CA	44
Floriskraal St	Groenvallei	62	BX	52
Flounder	Wellington	15	AU	91
Flow St	Gustrow	174	DB	74
Flower Cl.	Montagu's Gift	141	CO	33
Flower Gate	High Gate	107	CG	53
Flower St	Oranjezicht	82	CC	23
Flower St	Wesbank	107	CE	52
Flowerbrush	Macassar	149	CR	63
Flowerdale La.	Sweet Valley	139	CQ	26
Flowers Cl.	Des Hampden	89	CB	53
Flufftail Cl.	Somerset Rdg	170	CU	72
Flute St	Retreat	159	CT	29
Flute Way	Belhar	106	CE	47
Fluweeltjie Cr.	Belhar	105	CD	46
Fluweeltjie Rd	Durbanville	46	BP	52
Foam Rd	Bloubergrant	40	BO	30
Fodo Cr.	Victoria Mxenge	126	CN	51
Folkert de Vries St	Bloomsburg	23	BD	91
Folkert de Vries St	Bloomsburg	23	BE	93
Folkestone Way	Parklands	25	BM	33
Follies St	Weltevreden Val. (M.Plain)	144	CO	43
Folokhwe Cr.	Umrhabulo Triangle	147	CR	58
Folosi St	Bloekombos	48	BR	62
Fondokop St	Fisantekraal	31	BK	58
Foni St	Harare	146	CS	53
Fontana Rd	Scottsdene	64	BV	60
Fontana St	Brooklyn	83	BZ	30
Fontein	Cloetesville	95	BZ	76
Fontein Rd	Steenberg	159	CT	30
Fontein St	Arauna	63	BU	55
Fontein St	Wellington	10	AS	93
Fonteinbos	Lentegeur (M.Plain)	144	CP	45
Fontenay	D'urbanvale	45	BO	48
Fonteyn Cl.	Belhar	106	CD	48
Fontuin Ave	Balvenie	87	CB	43
Fontuin St	Tafelsig (M.Plain)	145	CS	48
Forata	Sunset Beach	41	BS	31
Forbes Ave	Doornhoogte	103	CH	36
Forbes Ave	Penlyn Est.	103	CH	35
Forbes Ave	Wynberg	120	CM	29
Forbes St	Ravensmead	87	CA	45
Forbes St	Rusthof	174	DA	74
Forbes St	Rusthof	175	DA	75
Ford Calata St	Mandela Pk	147	CR	55
Ford St	Loumar	89	BY	51
Ford St	Salt River	83	CC	28
Forel	Soneike II	89	BZ	53
Forel	Wellington	10	AS	92
Forel Rd	Nooitgedacht	104	CE	42
Forelle	Die Boord	112	CD	74
Forelle	Die Boord	113	CD	75
Forest	Kayamandi	94	CA	74
Forest Ave	Bishopscourt	120	CK	27
Forest Ave	Pollsmoor	139	CS	25
Forest Ave	Tokai	139	CS	25
Forest Bank Ave	Blue Downs	127	CJ	56
Forest Cl.	Parklands	25	BN	33
Forest Cl.	Scottsdene	64	BT	60
Forest Cr.	Weltevreden Val. (M.Plain)	144	CO	43
Forest Dr.	Eersterivier	127	CL	58
Forest Dr.	Eersterivier	128	CL	59
Forest Dr.	Forest Village	127	CM	57
Forest Dr.	Forest Village	127	CM	56
Forest Dr.	Kraaifontein	47	BQ	57
Forest Dr.	Peers Hill	185	DA	22
Forest Dr.	Peers Hill	186	DA	23
Forest Dr.	Pinelands	84	CB	34
Forest Dr.	Pinelands	84	CC	33
Forest Dr.	Pinelands	102	CD	32
Forest Dr.	Russel's Rest	128	CL	60
Forest Dr. Ext	Thornton	85	CA	35
Forest Dr. Service Rd	Pinelands	84	CB	34
Forest Dr. Service Rd	Pinelands	84	CC	33
Forest Dr. Service Rd	Pinelands	102	CD	32
Forest Dr. Service Rd	Pinelands	102	CD	32
Forest Hill Ave	Oranjezicht	82	CC	23
Forest Hill La.	Hout Bay	117	CM	18
Forest Hill La.	Hout Bay	118	CM	19
Forest Hill Rd	Simon's Town	194	DJ	25
Forest Hills Cl.	Ottery	122	CL	35
Forest La.	Parklands	25	BN	33
Forest Oaks Mews	Milnerton	57	BT	32
Forest Pl.	Pinelands	102	CD	32
Forest Rd	Fairways	121	CN	32
Forest Rd	Oranjezicht	81	CC	22
Forest Rd	Oranjezicht	99	CD	22
Forest Rd	Rondebosch	101	CF	29
Forest Rd	The Range	86	CC	41
Forest Rd	Woodlands (M.Plain)	144	CP	44
Forest Row	Dennedal	139	CR	25
Forest St	Voelvlei	89	CA	53
Forester Cl.	Mitchells Plain	144	CQ	45
Forester's Cl.	Hout Bay	117	CN	17
Foresters Rd	Rondebosch	101	CG	29
Foresters Way	Edgemead	59	BT	39
Forfar Rd	Observatory	101	CD	29
Forgate St	Woodstock	82	CA	26
Formby	Sunningdale	25	BM	31
Formosa	Die Boord	113	CE	75
Formosa Rd	Heideveld	104	CF	39
Formosa St	Portlands (M.Plain)	144	CQ	46
Formosa Way	Northpine	64	BV	59
Fornax Cl.	Ocean View	189	DD	15
Forrest Rd	Simon's Town	191	DD	23
Forridon St	Brooklyn	84	BY	31
Forsyth Rd	Kommetjie	183	DB	11
Fort Calata Wk	Weltevreden Val. (M.Plain)	123	CN	41
Fort Calata Wk	Weltevreden Val. (M.Plain)	123	CM	39
Fort Rd	Three Anchor Bay	81	BY	20
Fort St	Wynberg	120	CL	27
Fort Worth Rd	Delft	106	CF	50
Fort Worth Rd	The Hague	106	CF	50
Fort Wynyard St	Green Point	81	BY	22
Fortesque Rd	Crawford	102	CH	34
Forth Rd	Rondebosch	102	CF	31
Fortieth Ave	Adriaanse	87	CC	43
Fortieth St	Eureka	87	CC	43
Fortress St	Factreton	85	BY	35
Fortuin	Franschhoek Nth	75	BW	105
Fortuin Rd	Retreat	140	CS	29
Fortuin St	Retreat	140	CR	29
Fortuin St	Rusthof	174	DA	74
Fortuna Rd	Sanddrift	57	BV	34
Fortuna Rd	Sanddrift	58	BV	35
Forty-Second Ave	Eureka	87	CC	44
Forty-Seventh St	Connaught	87	CB	44
Forty-Sixth St	Eureka	87	CC	44
Forum St	Somerset West	171	CV	77
Foster	Dalvale	19	AY	91
Foster	Delft Sth	125	CK	48
Foster St	Groenheuwel	19	AZ	91
Foucault Rd	Belhar	88	CC	50
Foucault Rd	Belhar	106	CD	50
Fouche Rd	Newfields	122	CJ	37
Fouche Way	Edgemead	58	BV	37
Founder Way	Simon's Town	191	DG	24
Foundry Rd	Woodstock	83	CB	28
Fountain Dr.	Hout Bay	137	CQ	17
Fountain Rd	Bellville	61	BV	48
Fountain Rd	Bergvliet	140	CQ	27
Fountain Rd	Clarkes	86	CC	42

Index to Street Names

Fountain Rd — Glencoral Ave

STREET NAME	SUBURB NAME	PG	GRID
Fountain Rd	Rondebosch	101	CF 29
Fountain Sq.	Rondebosch	101	CF 29
Fountains Pl.	Townsend Est.	85	BY 37
Fourie Rd	Bellville Sth	88	BZ 49
Fourie Rd	Bellville Sth Ext. 5	88	BZ 49
Fourie St	Wellington	11	AS 95
Fourteenth Ave	Avon	86	CA 41
Fourteenth Ave	Avon	86	CA 41
Fourteenth Ave	Boston	60	BX 46
Fourteenth Ave	Boston	61	BX 47
Fourteenth Ave	Da Gama Pk	190	DE 22
Fourteenth Ave	Fish Hoek	186	DB 23
Fourteenth Ave	Florida	87	CB 44
Fourteenth Ave	Hazendal	102	CE 33
Fourteenth Ave	Lavender Hill	141	CS 31
Fourteenth Ave	Leonsdale	86	CA 41
Fourteenth Ave	Maitland	85	BZ 35
Fourteenth Ave	Pelikan Pk	142	CR 36
Fourteenth Ave	Schaap Kraal	142	CR 36
Fourteenth Cl.	Kayamandi	94	CA 74
Fourteenth St	Bishop Lavis	105	CD 43
Fourteenth St	Elsies River Ind.	86	CA 41
Fourteenth St	Kensington	84	BZ 33
Fourth	De Oude Renbaan	22	BH 88
Fourth Ave	Athlone	102	CG 32
Fourth Ave	Belgravia	103	CG 35
Fourth Ave	Belmont Pk	48	BR 61
Fourth Ave	Belmont Pk	48	BS 60
Fourth Ave	Bosonia	90	CB 55
Fourth Ave	Boston	60	BX 46
Fourth Ave	Boston	61	BX 47
Fourth Ave	Churchill	59	BX 42
Fourth Ave	Churchill	60	BX 43
Fourth Ave	Churchill	86	BY 41
Fourth Ave	Cravenby	87	CA 43
Fourth Ave	Da Gama Pk	190	DD 21
Fourth Ave	Eastridge (M.Plain)	145	CR 47
Fourth Ave	Eikendal	48	BS 59
Fourth Ave	Fairways	121	CN 32
Fourth Ave	Fish Hoek	186	DB 24
Fourth Ave	Florida	87	CA 44
Fourth Ave	Grassy Pk	141	CQ 32
Fourth Ave	Grassy Pk	141	CQ 33
Fourth Ave	Hazendal	102	CE 33
Fourth Ave	Kayamandi	94	CA 74
Fourth Ave	Kensington	84	BZ 33
Fourth Ave	Lotus River	141	CP 34
Fourth Ave	Lotus River	142	CP 35
Fourth Ave	Maitland	84	CA 33
Fourth Ave	Manenberg	123	CK 39
Fourth Ave	Nyanga	123	CK 42
Fourth Ave	Paarl	22	BD 88
Fourth Ave	Retreat	140	CR 29
Fourth Ave	Rondebosch East	102	CG 32
Fourth Ave	Rondebosch East	102	CH 32
Fourth Ave	Schaap Kraal	142	CP 36
Fourth Ave	Tafelsig (M.Plain)	146	CS 51
Fourth Ave	Vanguard	103	CF 38
Fourth Ave	Wellington	10	AS 93
Fourth Rd	Heathfield	140	CQ 29
Fourth Rd	Montague Gdns Ind.	42	BS 35
Fourth Rd	Rondebosch	101	CG 29
Fourth St	Bishop Lavis	104	CD 42
Fourth St	Eindhoven	106	CH 50
Fourth St	Firgrove	150	CR 67
Fourth St	Kensington	84	CA 33
Fourth St	Mxolisi Phetani	125	CL 49
Fourth St	Mxolisi Phetani	125	CL 50
Fourth St	Rusthof	174	DA 74
Fourth St	Welcome	103	CF 38
Fourth St	Wellington	10	AR 91
Fox Rd	Somerset West	170	CV 72
Fox Rd	Strandfontein	162	CT 41
Fox St	Eastridge (M.Plain)	145	CR 49
Fox Tail Cr.	Somerset West	171	CX 77
Foxbat St	The Hague	106	CF 50
Foxglove	Lentegeur (M.Plain)	144	CP 45
Foxglove	Macassar	149	CS 63
Foxglove Cir.	Belhar	105	CD 46
Foxglove Cl.	Bridgetown	103	CF 37
Foxglove St	Groenvlei	18	BA 87
Foxglove St	Groenvlei	18	BA 88
Foxhallow Cl.	Lakeside	159	CV 27
Foxhallow Cl.	Lakeside	159	CW 27
Foxhallow Cl.	Westlake	158	CU 26
Foxhallow Cl.	Westlake	158	CT 26
Foxhound	Jagtershof	90	CC 57
Foxhound	Jagtershof	108	CD 56
Foxwold St	Voorbrug	106	CG 50
Foyle Cl.	Connaught	87	CB 43
Foyle Rd	Claremont	120	CJ 28
Framesby St	Wesbank	107	CG 51
Franc St	Vierlanden	30	BN 51
France St	Bloekombos	48	BQ 62
Francie van Zijl Dr.	Florida	87	CA 44
Francie van Zijl Dr.	Klipkop	87	BZ 46
Francie van Zijl Dr.	Ravensmead	87	CA 45
Francis Albert Ave	Durbanville	29	BN 50
Francis Albert Ave	Durbanville	30	BN 51
Francis Cr.	Montana/Durrheim	104	CF 41
Francis Rd	Montagu's Gift	141	CO 33
Francis Rd	Pinelands	84	CB 34
Francis Rd	Plumstead	140	CO 28
Francis Rd	The Vines	140	CO 27
Francis Server St	William Lloyd	23	BD 92
Francis St	District Six	82	CB 25
Francis St	Loumar	89	BY 52
Francis St	Matroosfontein	86	CC 41
Francis St	Tafelsig (M.Plain)	145	CS 50
Francisca La.	Chapman's Peak	156	CX 17
Franck	Delft Sth	125	CK 48
Franck St	Protea Hoogte	63	BX 56
Francke St	Retreat	140	CR 29
Francke St	Silveroaks	90	CC 55
Francois Rd	Welcome	103	CE 38
Francois St	Bonnie Brae	47	BP 57
Francolin Ave	Villa Italia	57	BW 33
Francolin Cl.	Hout Bay	117	CM 17
Francolin Cr.	Seawinds	159	CU 30
Francolin Rd	Bakoven	99	CF 19
Francolin Rd	Lekkerwater	184	DA 18
Francolin Rd	Pelikan Pk	142	CS 36
Francolin St	Eersterivier	128	CM 60
Francolin St	Somerset West	151	CS 73
Francolin Way	Pelikan Pk	142	CR 35
Frangipani	Eersterivier	128	CM 61
Frangipani Rd	Tygerdal	58	BX 38
Frangipani St	Klein Nederburg	19	BC 93
Frangipani St	Somerset West	151	CS 71
Frangipani St	Vredekloof Hgts	47	BS 55
Frank Ave	Vredehoek	100	CD 23
Frank Louw	Marlow	88	CA 50
Frank Robb St	Ysterplaat	84	BY 31
Frank St	Valhalla Pk	104	CE 41
Frank Way	Montagu's Gift	142	CO 35
Frankenthal Cr.	Silversands	107	CH 54
Frankfort Rd	Churchill	59	BX 42
Frankfort Rd	Muizenberg	159	CX 29
Frankfort Rd	Muizenberg	159	CW 27
Frankfort Rd	Retreat	140	CS 28
Frankfort St	Glenlily	86	BY 42
Franklin Joshua St	Montana/Durrheim	104	CF 42
Franklin Rd	Claremont	101	CH 30
Franklin St	Observatory	83	CB 29
Franklin Way	Edgemead	58	BV 38
Frans Cl.	Mandalay	125	CM 48
Frans Conradie Dr.	Avondale	60	BX 45
Frans Conradie Dr.	Bellair	62	BV 53
Frans Conradie Dr.	Boston	61	BX 47
Frans Conradie Dr.	Churchill	59	BX 42
Frans Conradie Dr.	Goodwood Est.	58	BX 38
Frans Conradie Dr.	Morgenster	63	BU 56
Frans Conradie Dr.	Peerless Pk East	47	BS 57
Frans Conradie Dr.	Richmond Est.	59	BX 40
Frans Hals Rd	De La Haye	88	BY 50
Frans Hals St	De La Haye	89	BY 51
Frans Hals St	Kaapzicht	59	BW 40
Frans Maroney Rd	Retreat	140	CR 30
Frans Oerder Cr.	Woodlands (M.Plain)	144	CO 45
Frans St	Paarlzicht	18	BC 90
Franschhoek Cl.	La Rochelle	62	BV 51
Franschhoek Cr.	Panorama	59	BV 42
Franschhoek Rd	Greenfield	108	CH 57
Franschhoek St	Tafelsig (M.Plain)	145	CS 49
Franschhoek St	Tafelsig (M.Plain)	145	CP 50
Fransdruif Rd	Meadowridge	140	CO 27
Fransdruif Rd	Northpine	63	BU 58
Franshoek	Brackenfell	63	BW 55
Franshoek Rd	Durbanville Hills	45	BR 49
Franssen St	Bothasig	58	BT 37
Frantz Rd	Vanguard	103	CF 38
Franz Sq.	Steenberg	159	CT 29
Franz St	Somerset West	170	CT 73
Fraser Rd	Muizenberg	159	CX 29
Fraser Rd	Somerset West	151	CR 74
Fraser St	De La Haye	89	BY 51
Fraser St	Eindhoven	106	CH 50
Frater St	De Zoete Inval	22	BH 88
Frean Rd	Rondebosch	102	CF 31
Fred Adams Rd	Welcome	103	CF 38
Fred Page Cr.	Woodlands (M.Plain)	144	CO 45
Freda Cl.	Scottsdene	64	BT 59
Freda Rd	Montagu's Gift	141	CO 33
Freda Rd	Newfields	122	CJ 37
Freda's La.	Plumstead	140	CP 29
Frederica Rd	Devon Pk	128	CM 60
Frederick	Durbanville	45	BQ 50
Frederick Ave	Kirstenhof	159	CT 27
Frederick Cl.	Tamboerskloof	81	CB 21
Frederick Rd	Capricorn	160	CV 30
Frederick Rd	Claremont	101	CH 28
Frederick Sellidon St	Highbury	107	CD 54
Frederick Selous St	Bel Ombre	119	CM 25
Frederick St	Gaylee	108	CG 57
Frederick St	Parowvallei	87	BZ 44
Frederick St	Schotsche Kloof	81	CA 22
Fredericks St	Wellington	15	AV 92
Fredricks	Highbury	107	CD 54
Freedom	Mbekweni	15	AW 91
Freedom	Wellington	15	AV 91
Freedom Sq.	Nyanga	124	CK 43
Freedom St	Fisantekraal	32	BJ 59
Freedom St	Mxolisi Phetani	125	CM 50
Freedom Way	Marconi Beam	57	BU 34
Freeman Rd	Green Point	81	BZ 22
Freeman St	Bothasig	43	BS 39
Freesia	Lentegeur (M.Plain)	144	CP 45
Freesia Ave	Brantwood	89	CA 53
Freesia Ave	Devil's Peak Est.	82	CC 24
Freesia Ave	Somerset West	170	CU 72
Freesia Cl.	Belhar	106	CD 47
Freesia Cl.	Plattekloof	59	BU 42
Freesia Cr.	Gordon Hgts	180	DD 79
Freesia Rd	Milnerton	57	BU 33
Freesia Rd	Murdock Valley	195	DL 28
Freesia Rd	Stellenberg	62	BT 51
Freesia Rd	Tygerdal	58	BX 38
Freesia Rd	Uitsig	87	CC 45
Freesia St	Franschhoek Sth	79	BZ 108
Freesia St	Kleinvlei	127	CJ 58
Freesia St	Wellington	15	AT 93
Freezia	Dalvale	19	AY 92
Freezia	Dalvale	19	AZ 94
Frere Ave	Flamingo Vlei	41	BP 32
Frere Ave	Lansdowne	121	CJ 32
Frere Ave	Sillery	139	CO 25
Frere Cl.	Belhar	106	CE 50
Frere Rd	Bishop Lavis	104	CD 42
Frere Rd	Ndabeni	83	CB 30
Frere Rd	Three Anchor Bay	81	BZ 20
Frere Rd	Three Anchor Bay	81	CA 20
Frere St	Woodstock	82	CB 26
Freredale Rd	Crawford	102	CH 34
Fresno St	Jamestown	112	CH 74
Freylina La.	Eersterivier	128	CM 59
Friars Rd	Sea Point	81	CA 20
Frick Ave	Lotus River	141	CP 33
Frieda Locke Cr.	Woodlands (M.Plain)	144	CO 45
Friedman Rd	Brown's Farm	123	CL 42
Friend St	Salt River	83	CC 27
Friendly Way	Surrey	103	CH 37
Friesland	Mitchells Plain	144	CR 45
Friesland Cr.	Edgemead	58	BV 37
Friesland St	Avondale	60	BX 44
Friesland St	Balvenie	87	CC 43
Friesland St	Montana/Durrheim	104	CE 41
Friesland St	Montana/Durrheim	104	CF 41
Friesland St	Rondebosch East	102	CH 32
Frigate Cl.	Strandfontein	162	CU 39
Frigate Cr.	Sun Valley	185	CZ 20
Frigate Rd	Strandfontein	161	CU 38
Frigate Rd	Strandfontein	162	CT 39
Frigate Rd	Strandfontein	162	CU 39
Fritz Rabe St	Panorama	59	BV 41
Fritz Sonnenberg Rd	Green Point	81	BY 22
Fritz Spillhaus Ave	Parow East	87	BY 44
Fritz St	Marlow	88	BZ 50
Fritz Way	Ottery East	121	CN 34
Froetang	Stellenbosch	95	BY 75
Froetang Cl.	Roosendaal	107	CF 51
Frogmore Rd	Frogmore Est.	159	CU 27
Frolich Cl.	Brackenfell Sth	90	BY 56
Frome Cr.	Coniston Pk	159	CU 29
Frome Rd	Wynberg	120	CM 29
Froom Rd	Rugby	84	BY 31
Frost Cl.	Belhar	106	CD 50
Frost Dr.	Gersham	107	CD 53
Frost Dr.	Gersham	107	CD 54
Fryde Rd	Woodstock	83	CC 27
Frylinck St	Elim	90	CB 56
Fuchia Cl.	Plattekloof	60	BV 43
Fuchia St	Wellway Pk East	46	BO 53
Fuchia St	Wellway Pk East	46	BP 53
Fuchsia	Macassar	149	CS 63
Fuchsia Cl.	Kommetjie	183	DB 13
Fuchsia Pl.	Bellville	61	BU 48
Fuchsia Rd	Harbour Island	175	DC 75
Fuchsia St	Sanddrift	57	BW 34
Fuchsia St	Somerset West	151	CS 71
Fudo St	Harare	146	CR 53
Fudumele Cr.	Umrhabulo Triangle	147	CR 57
Fuji	Lindida	96	CA 80
Fukuse St	Scottsdene	48	BS 60
Fukutha Rd	Umrhabulo Triangle	147	CQ 58
Fukutha Rd	Umrhabulo Triangle	147	CR 57
Fula St	Harare	146	CR 54
Fulham Rd	Bakoven	98	CF 18
Fulham Rd	Weltevreden Val. (M.Plain)	144	CP 43
Fuller Cr.	Edgemead	59	BU 39
Fuller Pl.	Eureka	87	CC 44
Fuller Rd	Bergvliet	139	CP 26
Fumana St	Harare	146	CS 54
Funani Cr.	Victoria Mxenge	126	CN 51
Funda	Mbekweni	15	AW 92
Fundance St	Umrhabulo Triangle	147	CR 57
Fundani	Mbekweni	15	AW 92
Fundani	Mbekweni	15	AT 94
Fundayo St	Griffiths Mxenge	146	CP 54
Fundayo St	Griffiths Mxenge	146	CS 52
Fundisa St	Griffiths Mxenge	146	CP 54
Fundisa St	Griffiths Mxenge	146	CS 52
Funwa St	Bloekombos	49	BQ 63
Funza St	Harare	146	CS 54
Fuphi St	Harare	146	CS 54
Furrow	Morgen Gronde	63	BX 55
Fuschia Ave	Morgenster	63	BU 56
Futha Cr.	Umrhabulo Triangle	147	CQ 57
Futha Cr.	Umrhabulo Triangle	147	CQ 58
Futhe St	Harare	146	CS 54
Futhi St	Harare	146	CR 54
Fuya St	Harare	146	CR 52
Fynbos	D'urbanvale	45	BO 49
Fynbos	Stellenbosch	95	BY 75
Fynbos	Weltevrede	68	BX 75
Fynbos Cir.	Door De Kraal	61	BT 47
Fynbos Cl.	Hout Bay	117	CN 18
Fynbos Cl.	Plattekloof	60	BU 43
Fynbos Cr.	Protea Village	63	BV 58
Fynbos Rd	Murdock Valley	195	DL 28
Fynbos St	Kleinvlei	128	CJ 59
Fynn Cl.	Lansdowne	122	CL 35
G			
G Nake St	Gugulethu	123	CK 40
Gaba St	Umrhabulo Triangle	147	CR 56
Gabada St	Eyethu	146	CO 53
Gabbema Doordrift	Courtrai	21	BH 86
Gabbema Doordrift	Courtrai	22	BH 87
Gabbro Cr.	Somerset West	171	CW 78
Gable Rd	Somerset West	171	CU 75
Gables Way	Rondebosch	101	CF 30
Gabon St	Delft	106	CF 50
Gabriel	Delft Sth	125	CK 48
Gabriel Rd	Manenberg	123	CK 39
Gabriel Rd	Plumstead	120	CN 28
Gabriels	Cloetesville	94	BY 74
Gabriels	Cloetesville	95	BY 75
Gaby Rd	Eersterivier	128	CM 60
Gadi St	Griffiths Mxenge	146	CQ 54
Gaff	Strandfontein	162	CT 41
Gaff Cl.	Strandfontein	162	CT 41
Gaga St	Ilitha Pk	146	CR 52
Gaika St	Strandfontein	163	CT 43
Gail Cl.	Beacon Valley (M.Plain)	145	CP 48
Gail Cr.	Tafelsig (M.Plain)	145	CS 50
Gail Rd	Retreat	140	CR 29
Gainsborough St	De La Haye	62	BX 51
Gainsborough St	De La Haye	89	BY 51
Gala St	Harare	146	CR 53
Galanga St	Bloekombos	48	BR 62
Galaweni	Weltevreden Val. (M.Plain)	123	CM 42
Galaxy	Rocklands (M.Plain)	144	CS 46
Galaxy Cl.	Ocean View	189	DD 15
Galaxy Cr.	Thembokwezi	125	CM 49
Galaxy St	Weltevreden Val. (M.Plain)	144	CQ 43
Galaxy Way	Salberau	86	CB 41
Galbessie	Lentegeur (M.Plain)	144	CP 45
Galela St	Umrhabulo Triangle	147	CR 57
Galena Rd	Belthorn Est.	122	CJ 35
Galeni St	Victoria Mxenge	146	CO 51
Galilee Cl.	Steenberg	159	CT 28
Galilee Rd	Steenberg	159	CT 29
Galilee Wk	Hanover Pk	122	CK 36
Galileo	Belhar	88	CC 49
Galiot Cl.	Glen Rdg	191	DD 24
Galjoen St	Gustrow	174	DB 74
Gallant St	Marlow	88	BZ 50
Galleon Cr.	Anchorage Pk	175	DC 77
Galleon Cr.	Sun Valley	185	CZ 20
Galleon Rd	Strandfontein	162	CT 39
Gallery Cir.	Weltevreden Val. (M.Plain)	144	CQ 43
Gallinule Cl.	Pelikan Pk	142	CQ 35
Gallinule St	Electric City	127	CN 58
Gallop Way	Strandfontein	162	CT 41
Gallop Way	Strandfontein	162	CV 42
Galloway Cl.	Balvenie	87	CC 43
Galloway Cl.	Balvenie	87	CB 46
Galloway Cl.	Mitchells Plain	144	CR 45
Galton Rd	Tijgerhof	57	BW 32
Galtonia St	Vredekloof Hgts	47	BS 55
Galway Rd	Heathfield	140	CQ 28
Galway Rd	Summer Greens	58	BV 36
Galway St	Connaught	87	CB 43
Galway St	Connaught	87	CC 43
Galway St	Klipkop	87	BZ 45
Gama	Mbekweni	15	AW 91
Gama Cr.	Harare	146	CR 52
Gama Cr.	Harare	146	CS 52
Gamay Ave	Somerset West	170	CT 72
Gamay Cl.	William Lloyd	19	BC 94
Gamay Cl.	William Lloyd	19	BA 94
Gamay St	Welgedacht	44	BS 45
Gambia Cr.	Delft	106	CG 49
Gambonia Rd	Rondebosch	102	CH 31
Gamka Cr.	Eersterivier	128	CN 59
Gamka St	Delft	106	CF 50
Gamka St	Kaymor	89	BY 52
Gamka St	Manenberg	104	CH 39
Gamka St	Mfuleni	126	CJ 53
Gamsa St	Penlyn Est.	103	CH 35
Gamtoos Cl.	Portlands (M.Plain)	144	CQ 46
Gamtoos Cr.	Eersterivier	128	CM 59
Gamtoos St	Delft	106	CG 49
Gamtoos St	Delft	106	CH 48
Gamtoos St	Manenberg	104	CH 39
Gamtoos St	Mfuleni	126	CK 53
Gamtriya Rd	Philippi East	125	CL 47
Ganci Cl.	Bothasig	58	BT 37
Ganga St	Griffiths Mxenge	146	CP 54
Ganga St	Griffiths Mxenge	146	CQ 54
Ganges Cl.	Manenberg	104	CH 39
Gani St	Primrose Pk	122	CJ 37
Gannabos Ave	Amandelrug	90	CA 56
Gannas St	Kleinvlei	127	CJ 58
Gannet Cl.	Kommetjie	183	DB 13
Gannet Rd	Simon's Town	191	DF 24
Gannet St	Pelikan Pk	161	CV 37
Gannet St	Rugby	57	BX 32
Gannet St	Ysterplaat	57	BX 32
Gans St	Wellington	15	AT 91

Abbreviations used: Ave – Avenue, A.H. – Agricultural Holding, A.L.– Algemene Landgoed, Blvd – Boulevard, Cen. – Central, Cir. – Circle, Cl. – Close, Cr. – Crescent, Ct – Court, Dr. – Drive, Est. – Estate, Ext. – Extension, Hgts – Heights, Ind. – Industrial, Gdns – Gardens, Gr. – Grove, La. – Lane, (M.Plain) - Mitchells Plain, Nth – North, Pl. – Place, Pk – Park, Rd – Road, Rdg. – Ridge, S.H.– Small Holding, Sq. – Square, St – Street, Sth – South, Ter. – Terrace, Tn – Turn, Val. – Valley, Wk – Walk

STREET NAME	SUBURB NAME	PG	GRID	
Gant St	De Zoete Inval	22	BH	89
Gantouw Ave	Strand	174	CZ	73
Gantouw Cr.	High Constantia	119	CN	23
Gantsho Cr.	Victoria Mxenge	126	CN	52
Ganymede St	Woodlands (M.Plain)	144	CO	44
Ganzekraal St	Oak Glen	62	BW	52
Gaqa St	Griffiths Mxenge	146	CQ	54
Gaqawuli Godolozi	Weltevreden Val. (M.Plain)	123	CN	42
Garcia Cl.	Northpine	63	BU	58
Garda Cl.	Coniston Pk	159	CU	30
Garda Rd	Flintdale Est.	140	CP	30
Garden Cl.	Strandfontein	162	CT	41
Garden Cl.	Strandfontein	162	CV	42
Garden Cr.	Winslow	179	DD	77
Garden Dr.	Sunningdale	25	BN	32
Garden La.	Strandfontein	162	CT	41
Garden La.	Strandfontein	162	CV	42
Garden St	Bishopscourt	119	CJ	26
Garden St	Klippiesdal	19	BC	91
Garden St	Plumstead	140	CO	29
Garden St	Riverton	86	BZ	40
Garden Way	Strandfontein	162	CT	41
Gardener St	De Tuin	47	BS	55
Gardener Way	Pinelands	84	CC	34
Gardenia	Lentegeur (M.Plain)	145	CO	47
Gardenia	Pinelands	85	CC	35
Gardenia Ave	Devil's Peak Est.	82	CC	24
Gardenia Ave	Lotus River	141	CP	34
Gardenia Ave	Ridgeworth	61	BU	50
Gardenia Cir.	Belhar	106	CE	47
Gardenia Cr.	Milnerton	57	BU	33
Gardenia Cr.	Thornton	85	CA	37
Gardenia La.	Nova Constantia	139	CP	24
Gardenia Pl.	Hazelwood Pk	185	CZ	20
Gardenia Pl.	Hazelwood Pk	185	DC	22
Gardenia St	Eversdal Hgts	46	BS	51
Gardenia St	Klein Nederburg	19	BB	92
Gardenia St	Somerset West	150	CS	70
Gardenia St	Somerset West	151	CS	71
Gardenia St	Wellington	10	AS	92
Gardens Cl.	Uitzicht	47	BO	55
Gardiner St	Churchill	59	BX	42
Gardiner St	Glenlily	86	BY	42
Gardiner St	Somerset West	171	CT	76
Garfield Rd	Oranjezicht	99	CD	22
Garfield St	Claremont	102	CH	31
Garfield St	Claremont	121	CJ	31
Gariep Cir.	Ruyterwacht	86	BZ	39
Garland St	Peerless Pk East	47	BS	58
Garlandale Cr.	Athlone	102	CF	33
Garnet	Fairdale	126	CJ	53
Garnet Cl.	Pelikan Pk	161	CT	36
Garnet Cr.	Sheridon Pk	159	CU	28
Garnet Rd	Highbury	108	CD	55
Garnet Rd	Lansdowne	121	CJ	33
Garonne	Groenvlei	18	BA	88
Garrett St	Parow Ind.	87	CB	46
Garrick Rd	Woodstock	83	CC	27
Garrick Wk	Nooitgedacht	104	CE	42
Garrison Rd	Claremont	102	CH	31
Garrison Way	Door De Kraal	61	BT	47
Garron Ave	Hout Bay	117	CM	18
Garry Player Cl.	Pine Acres	175	DC	77
Garth Ave	Athlone	102	CG	34
Garton Rd	Rondebosch	102	CG	31
Garvin Cir.	Strand Halt	170	CW	74
Gary Rd	Fairways	121	CN	32
Gasela St	Gugulethu	104	CH	41
Gasela St	Gugulethu	123	CJ	40
Gash Cr.	Delft	106	CG	48
Gatesville Rd	Gatesville	103	CG	37
Gatesville Rd	Kalk Bay	186	DA	26
Gateway Cl.	Capricorn	160	CW	31
Gateway Cr.	Pinati	122	CK	35
Gateway St	Eersterivier	128	CN	62
Gatley Rd	Rondebosch	101	CF	29
Gatwick Rd	The Hague	106	CE	49
Gavin St	Zoo Pk	47	BR	57
Gawa Samuel	Wesbank	107	CF	51
Gawe St	Nyanga	123	CK	42
Gawie St	Morgenster	63	BU	56
Gawula St	Umrhabulo Triangle	147	CR	56
Gay Rd	Simon's Town	194	DJ	26
Gay St	Claremont	120	CJ	29
Gaya St	Harare	146	CS	54
Gazala Cr.	Strandfontein	162	CT	40
Gazala Rd	Milnerton	57	BV	32
Gazania Cl.	Ottery East	121	CN	34
Gazania Cr.	Eersterivier	128	CM	59
Gazania St	Bellville	61	BT	48
Gazania St	Brantwood	89	CB	53
Gazania St	Kenridge	61	BU	48
Gazania St	Retreat	140	CS	28
Gazania Way	Belhar	105	CD	46
Gazelle	Uitzicht	46	BO	50
Gazelle Cl.	Lotus River	142	CP	35
Gazelle St	Eastridge (M.Plain)	145	CR	48
Gazi St	Victoria Mxenge	126	CN	51
Gcaba Cr.	Umrhabulo Triangle	147	CQ	58
Gcada St	Umrhabulo Triangle	147	CQ	57
Gcawu St	Kuyasa	147	CR	56
Gcegceleya Ave	Joe Slovo Pk	57	BU	34
Gcilishe Cr.	Victoria Mxenge	126	CN	51
Gcisa St	Harare	146	CR	53
Gcuwa St	Mfuleni	126	CK	53

STREET NAME	SUBURB NAME	PG	GRID	
Gearing Rd	Bishop Lavis	105	CD	43
Geba Cr.	Delft	106	CG	49
Geba St	Mfuleni	126	CK	53
Gebhardt St	Silveroaks	90	CC	55
Gecelo St	Wallacedene	48	BS	60
Gecelo St	Wallacedene	48	BS	61
Geduld Rd	Penlyn Est.	122	CJ	35
Geduld St	Somerset West	151	CR	71
Geelblommetjie	Lentegeur (M.Plain)	144	CO	46
Geelbos Cl.	Klein Begin	48	BS	60
Geelbos Cl.	Plattekloof	59	BV	42
Geelbos Cr.	Eikenbosch	90	CC	57
Geelbos Cr.	Vierlanden	30	BM	52
Geelbos Rd	Proteavallei	60	BT	46
Geelbos Sq.	Roosendaal	107	CF	51
Geelhout Ave	Amandelrug	90	CA	55
Geelhout Ave	New Orleans	19	BB	91
Geelhout Ave	Westlake Est.	158	CT	25
Geelhout Ave	Westlake Est.	158	CT	26
Geelhout Cl.	Onverwacht	175	DC	76
Geelhout Cr.	Plattekloof	59	BU	42
Geelhout Rd	Belhar	106	CD	47
Geelhout Rd	Bonteheuwel	103	CD	38
Geelhout St	Eversdal Hgts	46	BS	51
Geelhout St	Forest Hgts	127	CL	57
Geelhout St	Grassy Pk	141	CQ	33
Geelhout St	Morgenster Hoogte	63	BU	55
Geelkleur	Delft Sth	125	CK	49
Geelmelkhout	Delft Sth	125	CJ	49
Geeringh St	Somerset West	171	CV	76
Geffer St	Dal Josafat Ind.	18	BC	90
Gel Vandale St	Wesbank	107	CG	51
Geland Rd	Grassy Pk	141	CR	32
Gelb Cr.	Morgenster	63	BT	56
Gelb Cr.	Morgenster	63	BT	57
Gelb Cr.	Morgenster	63	BU	57
Geldenhuys Ave	Casablanca	175	DB	76
Gelder Ct	Marina Da Gama	159	CV	29
Gelem St	Bloekombos	48	BR	62
Gelmar Cl.	Panorama	59	BV	42
Geloof Way	Steenberg	159	CT	29
Gelu Cl.	Ilitha Pk	146	CR	51
Geluks Rd	Sybrand Pk	102	CE	32
Geluks Rd	Sybrand Pk	102	CE	33
Gem Rd	Fairdale	126	CJ	54
Gemane St	Victoria Mxenge	126	CN	51
Gemini Rd	Phoenix	57	BU	33
Gemini Rd	Surrey	103	CG	38
Gemini Rd	Witteboomen	119	CM	23
Gemini St	Everite	63	BU	57
Gemini St	Everite	63	BV	57
Gemini St	Somerset Hgts	127	CK	57
Gemini Way	Elfindale	140	CQ	29
Gemini Way	Ocean View	184	DC	15
Gemsbok	Soneike II	89	BZ	54
Gemsbok Ave	Lotus River	142	CP	35
Gemsbok Rd	Langeberg Rdg	47	BR	56
Gemsbok Rd	Loevenstein	61	BV	47
Gemsbok St	Kleinvlei	127	CJ	57
Gemsbok St	New Orleans	19	BA	92
Gemsbok St	Scarborough	192	DK	18
Gemsbok St	Somerset Hgts	127	CJ	58
Gemsbok St	Strandfontein	163	CT	43
Gemsbok St	Wellington	15	AV	92
Gemsbok St	Wellington	15	AU	94
Gen .F.A. Grobler St	Welgelegen	59	BU	40
Gen.Ben Viljoen St	Welgelegen	59	BU	41
Gen.Chris Muller Cr.	Welgelegen	59	BU	40
Gen.E.R. Snyman Cl.	Welgelegen	59	BU	41
Gen.G.H. Gravett Cl.	Welgelegen	59	BU	41
Gen.Hendrik Lategan St	Welgelegen	59	BU	41
Gen.Hendrik Schoeman St	Welgelegen	59	BU	40
Gen.Hertzog	Wellington	11	AQ	95
Gen.Hertzog Dr.	Wellington	10	AS	94
Gen.Hertzog Dr.	Wellington	11	AS	95
Gen.J.H.Olivier La.	Welgelegen	59	BU	40
Gen.J.J. Pienaar Cl.	Welgelegen	59	BU	41
Gen.Jaap van Deventer St	Welgelegen	59	BU	41
Gen.Janssens St	Bloubergstrand	24	BL	28
Gen.Janssens St	Bloubergstrand	24	BL	29
Gen.Lucas Meyer Ave	Welgelegen	59	BU	40
Gen.Manie Maritz St	Welgelegen	59	BU	41
Gen.P.H. Roux Cr.	Welgelegen	59	BU	40
Gen.Piet Cronje St	Welgelegen	59	BU	41
Gen.Wynand Malan St	Welgelegen	59	BU	41
Genadendal	Eersterivier	128	CL	60
Genene St	Mandalay	125	CN	47
General St	Athlone	102	CF	32
Geneva Cl.	Portlands (M.Plain)	144	CQ	46
Geneva Cr.	Uitzicht	47	BO	55
Geneva Dr.	Camps Bay	98	CE	18
Geneva Dr.	Camps Bay	99	CD	19
Geneva Dr.	Camps Bay	99	CE	19
Geneva Rd	Coniston Pk	159	CU	29
Geneva St	Mandalay	125	CN	47
Genevieve Cl.	Meadowsteads	156	CX	18
Genoa Ave	Fish Hoek	186	DA	23
Genoa Cl.	Strandfontein	163	CT	43
Genoa Cr.	Strandfontein	163	CT	43
Genoa Way	Strandfontein	163	CT	43
Genootskap Rd	Surrey	103	CH	37
Gents Cl.	Strandfontein	162	CT	41
Gents Mile	Strandfontein	162	CV	42
Gents Mile	Strandfontein	162	CT	41
Genubie Way	Delft	106	CG	49

STREET NAME	SUBURB NAME	PG	GRID	
George Ave	Elsies River Ind.	86	BZ	41
George Blake	Stellenbosch	95	CA	75
George Blake	Stellenbosch	95	CB	75
George Enslin Cr.	Woodlands (M.Plain)	124	CN	44
George Mthusi St	Kuyasa	147	CS	56
George Nolan	Factreton	84	BZ	34
George Rd	Montagu's Gift	142	CO	35
George Smit Rd	Highlands Est.	122	CM	38
George St	Athlone	102	CF	33
George St	Macassar	149	CS	64
George St	Manenberg	123	CK	39
George St	Muizenberg	159	CX	29
George St	Observatory	101	CD	29
George St	Onverwacht	174	CZ	73
George St	Park Estates	174	CZ	73
George Starck Rd	Oostersee	60	BX	45
George Starck Rd	Oostersee	87	BY	45
George Wk	Barbarossa	120	CN	27
Georgia Dr.	Weltevreden Val. (M.Plain)	144	CO	43
Georgia St	Stellenridge	62	BV	51
Georgian Cr.	Strand	174	CZ	74
Gerald St	Valhalla Pk	104	CE	41
Geranium	Lentegeur (M.Plain)	144	CP	45
Geranium	Macassar	149	CR	63
Geranium St	Dunoon	26	BN	37
Geranium Cr.	Welgedacht	60	BT	44
Geranium Rd	Uitsig	87	CC	45
Geranium St	Dalvale	19	AY	92
Gerard Rd	Muizenberg Nth	159	CW	28
Gerard Sq.	Edgemead	58	BU	38
Gerard Way	Montagu's Gift	142	CO	35
Gerber Blvd.	Strand Halt	170	CW	74
Gerbera	Welgedacht	60	BT	44
Gerbera Cr.	Lentegeur (M.Plain)	124	CN	45
Gerda	Kaymor	89	BY	53
Gericke St	Groenvlei	18	BA	89
Germain St	Klein Parys	23	BE	91
Germiston Rd	Portlands (M.Plain)	145	CR	47
Gerrie Ave	Dennedal	139	CR	26
Gerrie Cnr	Dennedal	139	CR	26
Gerrit Marits St	Ruyterwacht	86	CB	40
Gerrits St	Bothasig	42	BS	37
Gerry Ferry Rd	Epping Ind.	85	CB	37
Gerryts St	De Kuilen	89	CB	54
Gershon Rd	Beroma	89	BZ	51
Gershwin St	Macassar	149	CS	64
Gert Kotze St	Springbok Pk	62	BV	54
Gert Thomas St	Rabiesdale	19	BC	92
Gert van Rooyen Dr.	Welgelegen	59	BU	40
Gert van Rooyen Dr.	Welgelegen	59	BU	41
Gerties Way	Belvedere Noordhoek	157	CW	19
Gertrude Shope Cr.	Nonqubela	126	CN	53
Gertrude St	Des Hampden	89	CB	53
Gertrude St	Goodwood Est.	86	BY	39
Gerts Cl.	Sonstraal Hgts	46	BS	54
Gesiggie St	Bonteheuwel	104	CD	40
Gettys Cl.	Strandfontein	162	CT	40
Gettys Cl.	Strandfontein	162	CV	42
Geya Cr.	Crossroads	124	CK	45
Geyer Rd	Heathfield	140	CP	28
Geysler Cr.	Eersterivier	128	CM	60
Ghaap St	Kleinvlei	127	CK	58
Ghandi Hlekani St	Kuyasa	147	CS	55
Ghandi Hlekani St	Kuyasa	147	CS	56
Ghwarri Ave	New Orleans	18	BB	90
Giants Castle Cr.	Tafelsig (M.Plain)	145	CS	48
Gibbons	Delft Sth	125	CK	48
Gibraltar Rd	Hout Bay	136	CQ	14
Gibson Ave	Athlone	102	CG	33
Gibson Rd	Kenilworth	120	CK	30
Gideon Malherbe Cr.	Edgemead	58	BV	37
Gideon Rd	Newfields	122	CJ	36
Gideonskop St	Tafelsig (M.Plain)	145	CS	50
Gidimi Cl.	Harare	146	CR	53
Gie Rd	Parklands	25	BM	34
Gie Rd	Sunridge	41	BP	34
Gie Rd	Sunridge	42	BO	35
Gie Rd	Table View	42	BP	35
Giel Basson	Monte Vista	59	BU	40
Giel Basson Dr.	N1 City	59	BX	40
Giel Basson Dr.	Plattekloof Glen	59	BV	40
Giel Basson Dr.	Richmond	86	BY	41
Gifberg Cl.	Bonnie Brae	47	BP	57
Gihon	Eden	113	CF	76
Gilbert St	Eindhoven	106	CH	50
Gild La.	Tokai	139	CS	25
Gildale Ave	Barbarossa	119	CN	26
Gilfillan St	William Lloyd	23	BD	93
Gilgil Rd	Charlesville	104	CF	40
Gili St	Kaya	146	CP	52
Gilia St	Lentegeur (M.Plain)	124	CN	45
Gill Cres.	Nyanga	123	CK	42
Gill Rd	Muizenberg	159	CX	29
Gill Rd	Table View	42	BQ	35
Gillard Rd	Simon's Town	195	DK	27
Gillian Cl.	Bellville	61	BU	50
Gillian St	Bellville	61	BU	50
Gillian St	Eversdal	61	BT	50
Gillian St	Rosendal	61	BU	50
Gilmour Ave	Silverhurst	119	CN	24
Gilmour Cl.	Silverhurst	119	CN	24
Gilmour Hills Rd	Tamboerskloof	81	CB	21
Gilo St	Delft	106	CG	49
Gilquin Cr.	Hout Bay	136	CP	14
Gilray Rd	Grassy Pk	141	CQ	32

STREET NAME	SUBURB NAME	PG	GRID	
Gilwell Cl.	Epping Forest	86	CC	42
Gimlet Cl.	Eureka	87	CC	44
Gimnasium St	Paarl	18	BC	88
Ginger Cr.	Silversands	107	CH	54
Ginnetta St	Belle Constantia	139	CP	25
Giraffe Cr.	Goedemoed	46	BP	53
Giraffe St	Eastridge (M.Plain)	145	CR	48
Giri Ct	Delft	106	CG	49
Girling Ct	Epping Forest	86	CC	41
Girling Ct	Epping Forest	86	CB	39
Girvan Rd	Lansdowne	102	CH	32
Gisela Cl.	Somerset West	170	CT	73
Gisela St	Sir Lowry's Pass	176	CZ	82
Giyogiyo Rd	Philippi East	125	CM	47
Giyogiyo St	Ilitha Pk	146	CQ	51
Glade Cl.	Rondebosch	101	CF	29
Glade Rd	Rondebosch	101	CF	29
Gladiator	Rocklands (M.Plain)	144	CS	45
Gladiator St	Kensington	84	BZ	33
Gladiola Rd	Lavender Hill East	160	CU	31
Gladiola Rd	Seawinds	160	CU	31
Gladiola St	Franschhoek Nth	75	BX	104
Gladiola St	Ravensmead	87	CA	46
Gladioli Cr.	Dalvale	19	AY	92
Gladioli Cr.	Dalvale	19	BA	94
Gladioli Cr.	Eersterivier	128	CM	59
Gladioli St	Soneike II	89	BZ	54
Gladioli St	Soneike II	90	BZ	55
Gladioli St	Sonnekuil	89	BZ	54
Gladioli Way	Kommetjie	183	DB	11
Gladiolus	Lentegeur (M.Plain)	145	CO	47
Gladiolus Ave	Devil's Peak Est.	82	CC	24
Gladiolus Cr.	Gordon Hgts	180	DD	79
Gladiolus Cr.	Protea Village	64	BV	59
Gladiolus Cr.	Welgedacht	60	BT	45
Gladiolus Rd	Uitsig	87	CC	45
Gladstone	Ruyterwacht	86	CA	40
Gladstone Rd	Churchill	59	BX	41
Gladstone Rd	Clarkes	86	CC	42
Gladstone Rd	Glenlily	86	BY	41
Gladstone St	Boston	61	BX	47
Gladstone St	Durbanville	45	BP	50
Gladstone St	Oranjezicht	81	CC	22
Gladstone St	Rome	174	CY	73
Gladstone St	Woodstock	82	CB	26
Glamis Cl.	Maitland	83	CA	30
Glanville Ave	Monte Vista	59	BU	40
Glanville Rd	Chrismar	61	BX	50
Glanville Rd	Tijgerhof	57	BW	32
Glaren Rd	Wynberg	120	CL	29
Glass Furnace Way	Glencairn Hgts	191	DD	24
Glastonbury Dr.	Bishopscourt	119	CK	25
Glastonbury Rd	Kenilworth	120	CK	30
Glaudina Cr.	Avondale	60	BW	44
Glaze Rd	Corobrik	31	BK	55
Glebe Rd	Rondebosch	101	CF	30
Gledholdt St	Mountain View	19	BB	91
Gledholt Rd	Mowbray	102	CE	31
Gleemoor Rd	Athlone	102	CF	34
Glen Alpine Way	Bergvliet	140	CQ	27
Glen Alpine Way	Bergvliet	140	CR	27
Glen Ave	Bel Ombre	119	CM	24
Glen Ave	Gardens	81	CC	21
Glen Avon	Pinelands	85	CB	35
Glen Avon Cl.	Belle Constantia	139	CO	25
Glen Beach Way	Glencairn Hgts	191	DD	24
Glen Choral	Sonstraal Hgts	46	BQ	54
Glen Cl.	Grassy Pk	141	CP	32
Glen Cr.	Gardens	81	CC	21
Glen Cr.	Gardens	99	CD	22
Glen Cr.	Glenhaven	89	CA	51
Glen Daries St	Kuyasa	147	CS	55
Glen Darroch Rd	Rondebosch	101	CF	28
Glen Devon	Pinelands	85	CB	35
Glen Eagles	D'urbanvale	45	BO	49
Glen Esk	Pinelands	84	CB	34
Glen Garry	Pinelands	84	CB	34
Glen Ive Cr.	Glen Ive	62	BV	52
Glen Lily Rd	Richmond	86	BY	41
Glen Oak	Scottsdene	64	BU	60
Glen Rd	Adriaanse	105	CD	43
Glen Rd	Bishopscourt	120	CK	27
Glen Rd	Blackheath Ind.	108	CF	56
Glen Rd	Goodwood Est.	85	BY	37
Glen Rd	Simon's Town	190	DD	21
Glen Rd	Simon's Town	191	DD	23
Glen Rd	Simon's Town	191	DE	24
Glen Roy	Pinelands	84	CB	34
Glen Thorne La.	Rondebosch	101	CG	30
Glen Way	Kenever	61	BT	49
Glen Wk	Rondebosch	101	CF	28
Glenalpine Rd	Welcome Glen	190	DD	21
Glenavon Rd	Welcome Glen	190	DD	21
Glenbawn Way	Mitchells Plain	144	CQ	45
Glenboig South	Fairfield	87	BY	44
Glenboig St Nth	Fairfield	60	BX	44
Glenboig St Sth	Fairfield	60	BX	44
Glenbrae Ave	Tokai	139	CS	26
Glenbrae Rd	Welcome Glen	190	DD	21
Glencairn Rd	Mowbray	101	CD	29
Glenco Ave	Glenhaven	89	CA	51
Glencoe Ave	Gardens	81	CC	21
Glencoe Ave	Oranjezicht	99	CD	21
Glencoe Rd	Oranjezicht	99	CD	22
Glencoral Ave	Glenhaven	89	BZ	52

Index to Street Names
Glencraig Cl. — Harrier St

STREET NAME	SUBURB NAME	PG	GRID	
Glencraig Cl.	Westlake	159	CU	27
Glencraig Cl.	Westlake	159	CW	27
Glendale Cl.	Scottsdene	64	BV	59
Glendale Cl.	Simon's Town	190	DD	21
Glendale Cr.	Claremont	101	CG	29
Glendale St	Glenhaven	89	CA	51
Glendower	Dennemere	108	CH	57
Glendower	Sunningdale	25	BN	32
Glendyrr Wk	Barbarossa	120	CN	27
Gleneagle Cr.	Sunningdale	25	BN	31
Gleneagle Cr.	Sunningdale	25	BN	32
Gleneagle Rd	Simon's Town	190	DD	21
Gleneagle Rd	Welcome Glen	190	DD	22
Gleneagles Cl.	Greenways	174	DA	73
Gleneagles Way	Mitchells Plain	144	CQ	45
Glenferrie Rd	Crawford	102	CH	33
Glengariff Rd	Sea Point	81	BZ	20
Glengariff Ter.	Three Anchor Bay	81	BZ	20
Glenhaven Ave	Beroma	89	BZ	51
Glenhaven Ave	Glenhaven	89	CA	51
Glenhaven Cl.	Welcome Glen	190	DD	21
Glenhof Rd	Newlands	101	CH	28
Glenhurd	Wesbank	107	CG	51
Glenhurst Rd	Welcome Glen	190	DD	21
Glenhurst St	Beaconvale	87	CA	43
Glenluce Cr.	Edgemead	59	BT	39
Glennifer St	Brooklyn	83	BZ	30
Glenoak Rd	Welcome Glen	190	DD	21
Glenoak Rd	Welcome Glen	190	DD	22
Glenook Ave	Wetton	121	CL	34
Glenpine Way	Matroosfontein	86	CC	41
Glenroth Rd	Edgemead	58	BU	37
Glenside Rd	Green Point	81	BZ	22
Glenside Rd	Marinda Hgts	89	BZ	52
Glenside Rd	Woodlands (M.Plain)	144	CQ	44
Glenugie Ave	Tokai	139	CS	26
Glenvista Cl.	Somerset West	151	CS	73
Glenwood Cl.	Parklands	25	BN	32
Glenwood Way	Pinelands	84	CC	33
Gletwyn St	Voorbrug	106	CG	50
Glider Cr.	Factreton	85	BY	35
Glider St	Beacon Valley (M.Plain)	145	CP	48
Glindon Rd	Fish Hoek	186	DA	23
Gllo St	Mfuleni	126	CK	53
Gloriana St	Eastridge (M.Plain)	145	CR	48
Glossderry Rd	Claremont	121	CJ	31
Gloster St	The Hague	106	CF	50
Gloucester Ave	Bishopscourt	119	CK	25
Gloucester La.	Flamingo Vlei	41	BQ	33
Gloucester Rd	Lakeside	159	CV	28
Gloucester Rd	Mowbray	101	CD	30
Gloucester Rd	Table View	41	BQ	34
Gloucester St	Claremont	120	CJ	29
Gloxinia St	Bonteheuwel	104	CD	40
Gloxinia St	Bonteheuwel	104	CE	40
Gloxinia St	Kenridge	61	BU	48
Gluck	Delft Sth	125	CJ	49
Gluck	Delft Sth	125	CK	48
Gluck St	Steenberg	159	CT	29
Gluckman Ave	Rugby	57	BX	32
Glucose Way	Saxon Ind.	88	BZ	50
Glynn St	Cape Town Cen.	82	CB	23
Glynn St	Gardens	82	CB	23
Glynville Ter.	Gardens	81	CB	22
Glyogiyo St	Brown's Farm	124	CM	43
Goba St	Kaya	146	CP	51
Gobo St	Brown's Farm	124	CL	43
Gobo St	Brown's Farm	124	CN	46
Goda St	Mfuleni	126	CJ	53
Godetia Rd	Uitsig	87	CC	45
Godetia St	Somerset West	150	CS	70
Godfrey La.	Somerset West	171	CV	75
Godfrey St	Kalk Bay	186	DA	26
Godwell.Z.Botha St	Guguletu	104	CG	41
Goede Gift Rd	Simon's Town	194	DJ	24
Goede Hoop Ave	Morgenster Hoogte	63	BU	55
Goede Hoop Ave	Scottsdene	64	BU	59
Goede Hoop Rd	Belhar	106	CD	50
Goede Hoop Rd	Belhar	106	CH	48
Goede Hoop Rd	Eersterivier	128	CN	60
Goede Hoop St	Avondale	60	BX	44
Goede Hoop St	Bothasig	58	BT	37
Goede Sq.	Kewtown	103	CE	35
Goedehoop Rd	Somerset West	170	CT	74
Goedemoed Rd	Durbanville	46	BP	53
Goedemoed Rd	Goedemoed	46	BP	53
Goedemoed Rd	The Crest	46	BO	53
Goederust St	Somerset West	151	CQ	71
Goedverwacht St	Fisantekraal	31	BJ	58
Goeie Hoop Rd	Mountainside Est.	179	DE	77
Goeie Hope St	Bellville Sth Ext. 5	88	BZ	49
Goetham St	William Lloyd	23	BD	93
Goewerneur St	Welgemoed	60	BV	45
Goewerneur St	Welgemoed	60	BV	46
Gogaza St	Umrhabulo Triangle	147	CP	57
Golconda St	Glencairn Hgts	191	DD	24
Gold	Fairdale	126	CJ	53
Gold	Rocklands (M.Plain)	144	CS	46
Goldbel St	Hillcrest Hgts	127	CL	57
Goldberg Pl.	Driftsands	147	CQ	56
Goldbourne Rd	Kenilworth	120	CK	30
Golden Gate Way	Portlands (M.Plain)	144	CQ	46
Golden Gr.	Rondebosch	102	CH	31
Golden Hill Cl.	Somerset West	152	CS	76
Golden Hill Rd	Northpine	63	BU	58
Golden Hind Rd	Somerset West	171	CT	76
Golden Rd	Retreat	140	CR	29
Golden St	Bloekombos	49	BQ	63
Golden St	Weltevreden Val. (M.Plain)	144	CO	43
Golders Green Rd	Woodstock	82	CB	26
Goldman Rd	Somerset West	170	CU	74
Goldmark	Delft Sth	125	CJ	48
Goldsmith Rd	Salt River	83	CB	28
Goldstein St	Hillcrest Hgts	127	CL	57
Golf Cir.	Beacon Valley (M.Plain)	145	CP	48
Golf Course Rd	Sybrand Pk	102	CE	32
Golf Glen	Schuilplaats	113	CF	75
Golf Rd	Fairways	121	CN	32
Goliath St	Kensington	84	BZ	34
Golide	Mbekweni	15	AV	92
Golide	Wellington	15	AU	94
Golide St	Umrhabulo Triangle	147	CR	58
Golomi St	Ilitha Pk	146	CQ	52
Gondola Ave	Rondevallei	107	CF	53
Gondola Way	Anchorage Pk	175	DC	77
Gondolier Cl.	Crofters Valley	185	CY	19
Gongo St	Victoria Mxenge	126	CN	51
Goniwe St	Nonqubela	126	CN	52
Gonoti St	Nonqubela	126	CN	52
Gontsana St	Brown's Farm	123	CM	42
Gonubie St	Manenberg	104	CH	39
Gonubie St	Mfuleni	126	CK	53
Gonubie St	Surrey	103	CH	38
Gonzalves	Cloetesville	95	BZ	75
Good Hope Rd	Strandfontein	163	CT	43
Good Hope St	Sarepta	89	CC	52
Good Hope St	Wynberg	120	CL	29
Good Hope St	Wynberg	120	CL	30
Goodenough Ave	Epping Ind.	86	CB	40
Gooderson Rd	Blackheath Ind.	108	CG	57
Goodeve Cr.	Wesbank	107	CG	51
Goodison Park	Weltevreden Val. (M.Plain)	124	CN	44
Goodison Park	Weltevreden Val. (M.Plain)	124	CN	44
Goodman Rd	Retreat	140	CS	30
Goodwood St	Townsend Est.	85	BY	38
Goose Rd	Phumlani	142	CQ	36
Gooseberry	Stellenbosch	95	BY	75
Goosen St	Wellington	10	AR	91
Gophe Cr.	Harare	146	CR	53
Goqoza St	Griffiths Mxenge	146	CP	54
Goran Rd	Wynberg	120	CM	29
Gordon Rd	Crawford	121	CJ	33
Gordon Rd	Fairfield	60	BX	44
Gordon Rd	Heathfield	140	CQ	29
Gordon Rd	Hout Bay	136	CP	14
Gordon Rd	Kalk Bay	186	DA	26
Gordon Rd	Kenilworth	120	CK	30
Gordon Rd	Lansdowne	121	CK	34
Gordon Rd	Mowbray	101	CD	29
Gordon Rd	Observatory	83	CC	29
Gordon Rd	Somerset West	171	CU	76
Gordon Rd	Somerset West	171	CV	76
Gordon Searle St	Cafda Village	141	CS	31
Gordon St	Gardens	81	CB	22
Gordon St	Russel's Rest	128	CL	59
Gordon St	Van Ryneveld	174	CZ	73
Gordon Ter.	Bantry Bay	80	CB	18
Gordon Ter.	Bantry Bay	80	CA	17
Gordonia Rd	Harbour Island	179	DE	76
Gore St	District Six	82	CB	24
Gorge Rd	Vredehoek	82	CC	23
Gorge St	Tafelsig (M.Plain)	145	CS	48
Gorgon Rd	Eersterivier	128	CN	60
Gorlay Rd	Ottery	121	CM	33
Gorleston Rd	Sea Point	81	CA	19
Gorridon	Idasvallei	96	CA	79
Gorridon	Idasvallei	96	CA	80
Gosa St	Tarentaalplaas	175	CY	75
Gosforth Cr.	Edgemead	58	BV	38
Gosforthpark Way	Milnerton Rdg	41	BS	34
Goshawk La.	Hout Bay	117	CM	17
Goshawk Rd	Sunridge	42	BP	35
Goshawk St	Eersterivier	128	CM	60
Goske St	Bothasig	42	BS	37
Gosport Rd	Wynberg	120	CM	29
Gotha St	The Hague	106	CF	50
Gothic Rd	Penlyn Est.	122	CJ	35
Goud Cr.	Brackenfell Ind.	63	BT	58
Goud Rd	Vanguard	103	CF	38
Gouda St	Claremont	101	CH	29
Gouda St	Panorama	59	BV	41
Goudblom St	Grassy Pk	141	CQ	32
Goudini	Heideveld	104	CF	39
Goudini Cl.	Tafelsig (M.Plain)	145	CS	49
Goudini Cr.	Welgelegen	59	BU	41
Goudstad St	Fisantekraal	31	BK	58
Goudwilger St	Amandelrug	90	CA	56
Gougem Rd	Flintdale Est.	140	CP	30
Gougem Rd	Flintdale Est.	141	CP	31
Goulburn St	Townsend Est.	85	BZ	38
Gourikwa Cr.	Wingfield Nth Camp	58	BW	38
Gourits Cl.	Groenvallei	62	BX	53
Gourits St	Delft	106	CG	48
Gouritz St	Portlands (M.Plain)	144	CP	45
Gouritz Cr.	Eersterivier	128	CM	59
Gouritz Rd	Manenberg	104	CH	39
Gouritz St	Ruyterwacht	86	CA	39
Gourley Rd	Penhill	128	CK	60
Gourmand St	Peerless Pk East	47	BS	58
Gous St	Van Ryneveld	174	CZ	72
Gousblom	Weltevrede	68	BX	75
Gousblom Ave	Uitsig	87	CC	45
Gousblom Cl.	Blomtuin	61	BW	50
Gousblom Cl.	Plattekloof	59	BU	42
Gousblom Cr.	Belhar	106	CD	47
Gousblom Rd	Blackheath Ind.	108	CF	56
Gousblom Rd	Gordon Strand	175	DC	75
Gousblom Rd	Milnerton	57	BU	33
Gousblom Rd	Pinelands	84	CB	32
Gousblom Rd	Pinelands	84	CB	33
Gousblom St	Bishop Lavis	104	CE	42
Gousblom St	Blomtuin	61	BV	50
Gousblom St	Bonteheuwel	104	CD	40
Gousblom St	Dunoon	26	BN	37
Gousblom St	Kleinvlei	127	CJ	58
Gousblom St	Morgenster	63	BU	56
Gousblom St	Sonnekuil	89	BZ	54
Gousblom St	William Lloyd	19	BC	93
Gousblom St	William Lloyd	19	BA	94
Govan Mbeki Rd	Griffiths Mxenge	146	CQ	54
Govan Mbeki Rd	Mandela Pk	147	CQ	55
Govan Mbeki Rd	Mandela Pk	147	CR	55
Government Ave	Cape Town Cen.	81	CB	22
Government Ave	Cape Town Cen.	82	CB	23
Governor's La.	Newlands	101	CG	27
Governor's Wk	Hout Bay	136	CO	14
Gow St	Scottsdene	64	BU	60
Goya St	De La Haye	89	BY	51
Gqabi Cr.	Umrhabulo Triangle	147	CR	58
Gqabi St	Kuyasa	147	CS	56
Gqadu Cr.	Nonqubela	126	CN	53
Gqaji St	Nonqubela	126	CN	53
Gqatsa Cr.	Harare	146	CR	53
Gqaza Rd	Ilitha Pk	146	CR	52
Gqobhoka Cr.	Umrhabulo Triangle	147	CQ	57
Gqoloma St	Crossroads	124	CK	45
Gqoloma St	Umrhabulo Triangle	147	CQ	56
Gqora St	Mfuleni	126	CK	53
Gqora St	Mfuleni	126	CK	52
Gqudu	Umrhabulo Triangle	147	CQ	58
Gqugula Cr.	Umrhabulo Triangle	147	CQ	56
Gquirha St	Umrhabulo Triangle	147	CQ	58
Graaf Rd	Scottsville	47	BS	57
Graaf Rd	Tygerdal	58	BX	37
Graaff Ave	Milnerton	57	BT	33
Graaff Ave	Milnerton	57	BU	32
Graaff Ave	Milnerton	57	BU	33
Graaff Ave	Milnerton	57	BV	32
Graaff Way	Plattekloof	60	BV	43
Graafland	Morgen Gronde	63	BX	55
Grabouw Cl.	La Rochelle	62	BV	51
Grace Rd	Claremont	120	CJ	28
Grace Rd	Claremont	120	CJ	29
Grace Rd	Kenever	61	BT	49
Grace St	Montagu's Gift	141	CO	33
Grace Vulliamy St	Cafda Village	141	CR	31
Gracia Cr.	Tafelsig (M.Plain)	145	CS	49
Grafiet Cr.	Welgelegen	59	BU	40
Graham Rd	Sea Point	81	BZ	19
Graham St	Boston	61	BX	47
Grainger Cl.	Belhar	107	CE	51
Gramis Cr.	Maitland	83	CB	30
Grampus St	Rugby	84	BY	31
Granada	Fairyland	19	AZ	93
Granada Cl.	Capri	185	DB	19
Grand Bahama Dr.	Capri	185	DB	19
Grand Canyon Way	Portlands (M.Plain)	144	CQ	46
Grand Duc St	Chantecler	62	BT	51
Grand National Blvd	Milnerton	41	BS	34
Grand National Blvd	Milnerton	57	BT	33
Grand St	Scottsdene	64	BU	59
Grand Vue Ave	Salberau	86	CB	41
Grand Vue Rd	Woodstock	82	CC	26
Grande Ave	Newlands	101	CH	27
Grandiceps	Anesta	113	CG	75
Grandiceps St	Gordon Hgts	180	DD	79
Grandiflora	Dunoon	42	BO	37
Grandiflora Rd	Proteavallei	60	BT	46
Grandiflora Rd	Proteavallei	61	BT	47
Grange Ave	Observatory	101	CD	29
Grange Ct	Rocklands (M.Plain)	144	CS	45
Granger Bay Rd	Foreshore	81	BY	22
Granger St	Green Point	81	BY	22
Graniet Cl.	Welgelegen	59	BU	40
Graniet Rd	Vanguard	103	CG	38
Graniet St	Bellville	61	BV	50
Graniet St	Lemoenkloof	18	BB	87
Granite Cl.	Lotus River	141	CP	33
Granite St	Somerset West	171	CW	78
Grant Ave	Simon's Town	195	DJ	27
Grant Ave	Simon's Town	195	DL	27
Grant Cl.	Belhar	106	CD	50
Grant Rd	Windsor Pk	47	BS	56
Grant St	Kenilworth Pk	120	CK	30
Grant St	Observatory	83	CB	29
Granula Pl.	Sunset Beach	57	BT	32
Grape Cl.	Mitchells Plain	144	CQ	44
Graph Ave	Montague Gdns Ind.	58	BU	36
Graphite St	Belthorn Est.	121	CJ	34
Gras Klokkie Rd	Belhar	105	CD	46
Grasmead Rd	Grassy Pk	141	CQ	33
Grasmere	Pinelands	84	CB	34
Grasmere St	Athlone	102	CG	33
Grasmere St	Athlone	102	CG	33
Grass St	Bonteheuwel	103	CD	38
Grassfield Rd	Claremont	120	CJ	30
Grawe St	Groenvlei	18	BA	88
Gray Cl.	Belhar	107	CE	51
Gray Rd	Plumstead	120	CN	28
Gray St	District Six	82	CB	25
Grayhawk	Sunningdale	25	BL	31
Grayhawk Cr.	Sunningdale	25	BL	31
Graymaur St	Peerless Pk East	47	BS	58
Grays Inn Rd	Newlands	101	CH	27
Great Brak Cl.	Portlands (M.Plain)	144	CQ	46
Great Circle Rd	Fairdale	126	CJ	54
Great Dutch Cr.	Nyanga	123	CJ	42
Great Dutch Rd	Nyanga	123	CJ	42
Great Fish Ave	Manenberg	104	CH	39
Great Fish Cl.	Portlands (M.Plain)	144	CP	45
Greatmore St	Woodstock	83	CB	27
Grebe Cl.	Imhoff's Gift	184	DB	16
Grebe Cl.	Pelikan Pk	142	CQ	35
Grebe Rd	Table View	41	BQ	34
Grebe St	Pelikan Pk	161	CV	37
Grebe St	William Lloyd	19	BC	92
Greef St	Somerset West	171	CU	78
Greef St	Woodstock	83	CB	28
Green	Woodstock	82	CB	26
Green Cl.	Lakeside	159	CV	27
Green Cl.	Lakeside	159	CW	27
Green Dolphin	Wellington	15	AU	91
Green Oaks Cr.	Somerset West	171	CV	76
Green Rd	Bergvliet	140	CR	28
Green St	Bishop Lavis	105	CD	44
Green St	Cape Town Cen.	81	CB	22
Green St	Maitland	83	CA	30
Green St	Peerless Pk East	47	BS	58
Green Valley Cl.	Plumstead	140	CP	29
Green Way	Mountainside Est.	179	DD	78
Green Way	Strandfontein	162	CT	41
Green Way	Summer Greens	58	BV	36
Greenacres Cl.	Bracken Hgts	62	BU	54
Greenacres Cl.	Hout Bay	117	CN	17
Greenacres Cl.	Somerset West	171	CV	75
Greenacres St	Silverhurst	119	CN	25
Greenbank Rd	Rondebosch	102	CF	31
Greendale Wk	Northpine	63	BU	58
Greenfield Cir.	Ottery East	121	CN	34
Greenfield Cl.	Ottery East	121	CM	34
Greenfield Cr.	Brackenfell	63	BW	56
Greenfield Rd	Dieprivier	140	CP	28
Greenfield Rd	Kenilworth	120	CK	29
Greenfield Way	Marinda Hgts	89	BZ	52
Greenfields Rd	Kenever	61	BT	49
Greenford Rd	Newlands	101	CG	27
Greenhawk	Pelikan Pk	142	CQ	35
Greenhill Cl.	Peers Hill	186	DA	23
Greenhill View Rd	Edgemead	58	BU	37
Greenhill View Rd	Edgemead	58	BU	38
Greenhurst	Halalie	30	BN	52
Greenlawn Sq.	Claremont	101	CH	30
Greens Passage	Observatory	101	CD	29
Greenshank Rd	Electric City	127	CM	58
Greenside	Fish Hoek	186	DA	24
Greenside Cl.	Townsend Est.	58	BX	38
Greensleeves Way	Eversdal	46	BS	51
Greenturf Rd	Hanover Pk	122	CK	37
Greenville Rd	Flintdale Est.	140	CP	30
Greenway	Pinelands	84	CC	33
Greenway Cl.	Ottery	122	CL	35
Greenway Dr.	Ridgeworth	61	BU	50
Greenway Rd	Ottery	122	CL	35
Greenway Rd	Schaap Kraal	122	CL	35
Greenway Rd	Somerset West	170	CT	73
Greenways	Rondebosch	102	CF	32
Greenways Dr.	Kommetjie	183	DB	12
Greenwich Cl.	Portlands (M.Plain)	145	CR	47
Greenwich Rd	Dieprivier	140	CP	28
Greenwood Cr.	Parklands	25	BN	33
Greenwood Rd	Claremont	120	CJ	29
Greenwood St	Adriaanse	87	CC	43
Greenwood Way	Sonstraal Hgts	46	BQ	54
Greenwood Wk	Tokai	139	CS	26
Gregory Rd	Goodwood Est.	85	BY	38
Gregory St	Eindhoven	106	CH	50
Grenach St	Wellington	10	AS	94
Grenache Cl.	Zevenzicht	90	CC	58
Grenada Cl.	Bloubergstrand	24	BM	29
Grens Rd	Gordon Hgts	179	DE	78
Grens Rd	Mountainside Est.	179	DD	77
Grens St	Epping Ind.	86	CA	39
Grens St	Ruwari	63	BV	57
Grens St	Silveroaks	90	CC	56
Grens St	Steenberg	159	CT	29
Grens St	Vredelust	60	BX	46
Grenville Ave	Epping Ind.	85	CC	36
Greta St	De Duin	59	BV	41
Gretel Rd	Heathfield	140	CR	29
Gretna Green	Summer Greens	58	BV	36
Grey Ave	Flamingo Vlei	41	BP	32
Grey Ave	Flamingo Vlei	41	BQ	32
Grey Ave	Table View	41	BP	32
Grey Cl.	Somerset West	171	CT	76
Grey Cr.	Tafelsig (M.Plain)	145	CS	49
Grey Rd	Glencairn Hgts	191	DD	24
Grey Rd	Penhill	128	CK	60
Grey Rd	Penhill	128	CK	61
Grey St	Brooklyn	83	BY	30
Grey St	Lochnerhof	170	CX	71

Abbreviations used: Ave – Avenue, A.H. – Agricultural Holding, A.L.– Algemene Landgoed, Blvd – Boulevard, Cen. – Central, Cir. – Circle, Cl. – Close, Cr. – Crescent, Ct – Court, Dr. – Drive, Est. – Estate, Ext. – Extension, Hgts – Heights, Ind. – Industrial, Gdns – Gardens, Gr. – Grove, La. – Lane, (M.Plain) - Mitchells Plain, Nth – North, Pl. – Place, Pk – Park, Rd – Road, Rdg. – Ridge, S.H.– Small Holding, Sq. – Square, St – Street, Sth – South, Ter. – Terrace, Tn – Turn, Val. – Valley, Wk – Walk

STREET NAME	SUBURB NAME	PG	GRID	
Grey St	Richmond	86	BY	42
Grey St	Welgemoed	61	BU	47
Grey St	Welgemoed	61	BU	48
Grey St	Woodstock	82	CB	26
Greybeard Rd	Sanddrift	58	BV	35
Greyland Rd	Ottery	121	CM	33
Greyling St	Aurora	45	BP	48
Greymead St	Northpine	63	BU	58
Grey's Cr.	Edgemead	59	BT	39
Grey's Pass	Cape Town Cen.	81	CB	22
Greyton Rd	Bergvliet	140	CQ	27
Greyton Rd	Milnerton	57	BW	32
Greyvenstein Rd	Plattekloof Glen	59	BW	39
Greyville Cl.	Milnerton Rdg	41	BR	34
Greyville Cl.	Somerset West	170	CW	73
Greyville St	Beacon Valley (M.Plain)	145	CQ	48
Greyvillea St	Vredekloof Hgts	47	BS	55
Grieg	Delft Sth	125	CK	48
Grieg Cl.	Mandalay	125	CN	48
Grieg St	Groenheuwel	19	AZ	91
Grieta Rd	Manenberg	123	CK	39
Grieve Cr.	Durbanville	45	BQ	49
Griffith Mxenge St	Mandela Pk	146	CR	53
Griffiths Mxenge	Weltevreden Val. (M.Plain)	123	CN	42
Grimm Rd	Heathfield	140	CR	28
Grimsby Rd	Three Anchor Bay	81	BZ	20
Grindal Ave	Lavender Hill	141	CS	31
Grindal Ave	Lavender Hill	160	CT	31
Grindal Cl.	Lavender Hill	160	CT	31
Grindel Cr.	Lavender Hill	160	CT	31
Griselda Pl.	Somerset West	170	CT	73
Grisnez Rd	Vredehoek	82	CC	23
Grobler St	Aurora	45	BQ	48
Groenall Wk	Hanover Pk	122	CK	36
Groenberg	The Crest	46	BO	53
Groenberg	Wellington	15	AV	91
Groenberg	Wellington	15	AU	94
Groenberg Cr.	Greenfield	127	CJ	56
Groenberg Rd	Blue Downs	127	CJ	57
Groenberg Rd	Heideveld	104	CF	39
Groenberg St	Tafelsig (M.Plain)	145	CS	50
Groendal Way	Edgemead	59	BU	39
Groeneveld Rd	Rondebosch	101	CG	29
Groenewald St	Flintdale Est.	140	CP	30
Groenhof Cl.	Northpine	63	BU	58
Groenkloof St	Table View	41	BO	32
Groenland St	Voorbrug	106	CG	50
Groenleegte St	Groenvlei	18	BA	88
Groenpoort Wk	Hanover Pk	122	CJ	36
Groenvlei Ave	Groenvlei	18	BA	88
Groenvlei Rd	Highbury	107	CE	54
Groenweide	Universiteits-oord	95	CB	77
Groenweide St	Vredelust	60	BW	46
Groeveld Ave	Bothasig	42	BS	38
Groevenbeek Ave	Bel Ombre	119	CM	25
Groot Constantia Rd	High Constantia	139	CO	23
Groot Cr.	Delft	106	CG	49
Groot Cr.	Delft	106	CH	49
Groot Salze	Kirstenhof	159	CU	27
Groot Salze	Kirstenhof	159	CW	27
Grootboom Ave	Rusthof	175	DA	75
Grootboom St	Wallacedene	48	BS	60
Grootbosch Cl.	Belle Constantia	139	CO	26
Groote Schuur Ave	Belhar	106	CD	50
Groote Schuur Ave	Rondebosch	101	CF	29
Groote Schuur Dr.	Observatory	83	CC	28
Groote Schuur Dr.	Observatory	101	CD	28
Groote Schuur Way	Mitchells Plain	144	CR	45
Grootfontein Rd	Klapmuts	36	BL	75
Grootfontein Rd	Klapmuts	36	BM	76
Grootkop Rd	Manenberg	104	CG	39
Gross	Belthorn Est.	122	CJ	35
Gross St	Wellington	10	AS	93
Grosskopf St	Clamhall	60	BX	43
Grosvener Rd	Rosebank	101	CE	30
Grosvenor	Eersterivier	128	CN	60
Grosvenor Ave	Oranjezicht	99	CD	22
Grosvenor Ave	Oranjezicht	99	CD	22
Grosvenor Pl.	Blue Downs	127	CJ	56
Grosvenor Pl.	Blue Downs	127	CN	55
Grosvenor Rd	Capricorn	160	CW	31
Grosvenor Rd	Dieprivier	140	CP	28
Grosvenor Sq.	Plattekloof Glen	59	BW	40
Grosvenor Way	Plattekloof Glen	59	BW	40
Grotto Cr.	Tafelsig (M.Plain)	145	CR	48
Grotto Rd	Hout Bay	117	CN	17
Grotto Rd	Hout Bay	137	CO	17
Grotto Rd	Rondebosch	101	CF	29
Ground Rose Rd	Bellville Ext. 53	60	BT	46
Grove Ave	Claremont	101	CH	28
Grove Rd	Churchill	59	BX	41
Grove Rd	Glenlily	86	BY	41
Grove Rd	Green Point	81	BZ	21
Grove Rd	Mowbray	101	CD	29
Grove Rd	Observatory	83	CC	28
Grove Rd	Rondebosch	101	CF	29
Grove St	Firgrove	150	CR	67
Grove St	Oakdene	89	CC	53
Grove Wk	Claremont	101	CH	28
Grove Wk	Fir Grove	139	CQ	25
Gro-Villa	Bonnie Brae	47	BP	57
Grumman St	Kensington	84	BZ	34
Grundel Ave	Edgemead	59	BT	39
Gruythof Ave	Somerset West	171	CU	77
Gryling	Soneike II	89	BZ	54
Grysbok Rd	Durbanville	45	BP	49
Grysbok Rd	Loevenstein	61	BV	47
Grysbok Rd	Lotus River	142	CP	35
Grysbok St	Eastridge (M.Plain)	145	CR	48
Grysbok St	Kleinvlei	127	CJ	58
Grysbok St	New Orleans	19	BB	92
Grysbok St	Somerset Hgts	127	CJ	58
Grysbok St	Soneike II	89	BZ	54
Grysbok Way	Fish Hoek	186	DB	23
Guardian Cr.	Somerset West	172	CT	79
Guardian Rd	Eersterivier	128	CN	61
Guardian Rd	Heideveld	104	CF	39
Gubayo Cr.	Kaya	146	CP	53
Gubu St	Umrhabulo Triangle	147	CQ	58
Guernsey Cl.	Mitchells Plain	144	CR	45
Guernsey St	Rondebosch East	102	CH	32
Guernsley Cl.	Balvenie	87	CC	43
Guernsley Cl.	Balvenie	87	CB	46
Gufens Cl.	Parklands	25	BN	34
Guia Rd	Sanddrift	57	BV	33
Guildford Rd	Parklands	25	BN	34
Guildford Rd	Rosebank	101	CE	29
Guildford St	Capricorn	159	CW	30
Guinea Fowl Cr.	Silverhurst	119	CN	23
Guinea Fowl Rd	Lekkerwater	184	DA	18
Guinea Fowl Way	Noordhaven	157	CW	19
Guinevere Ave	Hout Bay	137	CQ	17
Guitar Way	Belhar	106	CD	48
Gulden Cr.	Guldenland	174	CZ	74
Gulden Rd	Vierlanden	30	BN	52
Gull	Rocklands (M.Plain)	144	CS	44
Gull Cl.	Flintdale Est.	141	CP	31
Gull Rd	Bloubergstrand	24	BM	29
Gull Rd	Flintdale Est.	141	CP	31
Gull Rd	Montagu's Gift	141	CP	33
Gull St	Pelikan Pk	161	CV	37
Gullane St	Somerset West	150	CS	70
Gulliver Rd	Heathfield	140	CR	28
Gulls Way	Glencairn Hgts	191	DD	24
Gully Cr.	Tafelsig (M.Plain)	145	CS	48
Gully Rd	Hout Bay	116	CM	14
Gum St	Somerset West	170	CV	73
Gumbe St	Nonqubela	126	CN	53
Gumbo Rd	Nyanga	124	CK	43
Gumflower Rd	Philippi East	124	CL	45
Gumtree	Rosedale	128	CK	59
Gumtree Cl.	Dreyersdal	140	CR	27
Gumtree La.	Hout Bay	117	CN	18
Gumtree Rd	Dreyersdal	140	CR	27
Gumtree Rd	Steenberg	159	CU	30
Gunners Cir.	Epping Ind.	85	CB	35
Gunners Cir.	Epping Ind.	85	CB	37
Gunners Cir.	Epping Ind.	85	CC	36
Gunners Cir.	Epping Ind.	85	CC	38
Gunnings St	Peerless Pk East	47	BS	58
Gunqwa St	Bloekombos	48	BR	62
Guqaka Cr.	Griffiths Mxenge	146	CP	54
Gustav Preller Rd	Parow Nth	60	BW	43
Gustrouw Ave	Gustrow	175	DB	75
Gwaai Way	Delft	106	CG	49
Gwabeni Cr.	Nonqubela	146	CO	53
Gwada St	Umrhabulo Triangle	147	CP	56
Gwadu Cr.	Philippi	124	CL	43
Gwagqa St	Ilitha Pk	146	CR	52
Gwalia Rd	Claremont	120	CJ	29
Gwam Cr.	Nonqubela	126	CN	53
Gwangqa	Brown's Farm	124	CL	44
Gwangwa	Philippi East	125	CL	47
Gwava	Philippi East	125	CM	47
Gwayi St	Crossroads	124	CK	44
Gwayi St	Crossroads	124	CK	45
Gwaza Cr.	Wallacedene	48	BS	60
Gwe Cl.	Bloekombos	49	BR	63
Gwebu St	Griffiths Mxenge	146	CP	54
Gwegweleza Cr.	Umrhabulo Triangle	147	CP	58
Gwelo Goodman Cr.	Woodlands (M.Plain)	124	CN	45
Gwetha St	Crossroads	124	CK	44
Gwili St	Brown's Farm	124	CL	43
Gxalaba St	Umrhabulo Triangle	147	CP	57
Gxasheka	Nonqubela	146	CO	53
Gximfiza Cr.	Umrhabulo Triangle	147	CP	56
Gximfiza Cr.	Umrhabulo Triangle	147	CQ	56
Gxiya	Philippi East	124	CL	46
Gxiya St	Brown's Farm	124	CM	43
Gxiya St	Ilitha Pk	146	CQ	53
Gxokwe Cr.	Victoria Mxenge	126	CN	51
Gxotha Cr.	Umrhabulo Triangle	147	CP	57
Gxwala Cl.	Umrhabulo Triangle	147	CQ	57
Gymkhana St	Beacon Valley (M.Plain)	145	CP	47
Gympie St	Woodstock	82	CB	26
Gypsum Rd	Crawford	102	CH	34
H				
H.L.de Villiers Rd	The Vines	140	CO	28
H.O.de Villiers St	Ferndale	62	BV	54
H.Peterson Ave	Hout Bay	117	CN	16
H.Peterson Ave	Hout Bay	137	CO	16
Haakdoring	Lentegeur (M.Plain)	144	CP	45
Haarhof St	Somerset West	171	CU	75
Haarlem Ave	Belhar	106	CD	49
Haarlem Ave	Belhar	106	CE	49
Haarlem Cl.	Brackenfell Sth	63	BX	56
Haarlem Cl.	Tygerdal	59	BX	39
Haarlem Rd	Stellenberg	62	BU	52
Haarlem Rd	Strandfontein	163	CT	43
Haarlem St	Avondale	60	BX	44
Haarlem St	Bothasig	58	BU	36
Haarlem St	Brooklyn	83	BZ	30
Haarlem St	Paarl	22	BE	88
Haarlem St	Park Estates	174	DA	73
Haarlem St	Somerset West	170	CU	74
Haarlem St	Tygerdal	59	BX	39
Haarlem Way	Ruyterwacht	86	CA	40
Haasendal Cl.	Mitchells Plain	144	CR	45
Haasendal Cl.	Mitchells Plain	144	CR	43
Haasendal St	Die Bos	174	CY	74
Habibia Rd	Gatesville	103	CH	37
Habile St	Umrhabulo Triangle	147	CR	58
Hackius St	Perm Gdns	128	CK	59
Hackney Cl.	Table View	42	BO	35
Hadeda	Klein Nederburg	46	BP	53
Hadeda La.	Steenberg	139	CS	24
Hadeda St	Electric City	127	CN	58
Hadfield Way	Meadowridge	140	CP	28
Hadi Cr.	Umrhabulo Triangle	147	CR	57
Hadji Ebrahim Cr.	Belgravia	103	CG	35
Hadley St	Bellair	62	BW	52
Hadley St	Oak Glen	62	BW	53
Hafele Rd	Durbanville	46	BP	51
Hagen St	Strandvale	170	CW	73
Hahn	Idasvallei	96	CA	79
Hahn Rd	Harbour Island	179	DE	76
Hahn St	Northern Paarl	18	AZ	88
Haig Ave	Maitland Gdn Village	84	CC	31
Haig Rd	Woodstock	83	CC	27
Hakea St	Somerset Hgts	127	CK	57
Halabar Cr.	Dennemere	127	CJ	57
Halath Rd	Hanover Pk	122	CK	37
Haldane Rd	Rondebosch	101	CF	29
Halfway St	Wesbank	107	CG	52
Halifax	Rocklands (M.Plain)	164	CT	47
Halifax Rd	Wynberg	120	CM	29
Halifax St	The Hague	106	CF	50
Hall Rd	Claremont	101	CH	29
Hall Rd	Rondebosch	101	CF	29
Hall Rd	Sea Point	81	BZ	19
Hall St	Bellville	88	BY	50
Hall St	De La Haye	89	BY	51
Hall St	District Six	82	CB	25
Hallans Rd	Hanover Pk	122	CK	36
Halley's St	Thembokwezi	125	CM	49
Hallwell End	Parklands	25	BM	32
Halman Wk	Hanover Pk	122	CK	36
Halmstead St	Sunningdale	25	BM	31
Halt Rd	Avon	86	CA	40
Halt Rd	Elnor	86	CC	42
Halyard Cl.	Blouberg Sands	24	BM	30
Halyard Wk	Marina Da Gama	159	CV	30
Hamba St	Harare	146	CR	54
Hambayo St	Griffiths Mxenge	146	CP	54
Hambo St	Umrhabulo Triangle	147	CR	58
Hamburg St	Portlands (M.Plain)	144	CR	46
Hamerkop	Onderpapegaaiberg	94	CC	72
Hamerkop	Rocklands (M.Plain)	144	CS	45
Hamerkop St	Somerset West	152	CS	76
Hamilton Cr.	Parklands	25	BN	32
Hamilton Hgts	Marlborough Pk	63	BT	55
Hamilton Rd	Claremont	102	CH	31
Hamilton Rd	Plumstead	140	CO	30
Hamilton Rd	Plumstead	140	CO	29
Hamilton St	Goodwood Est.	58	BX	38
Hamilton St	Goodwood Est.	86	BY	39
Hamilton St	Silveroaks	90	CC	55
Hamlet St	Eersterivier	128	CM	60
Hamlet's Pl.	Sonstraal Hgts	46	BR	54
Hamman	Stellenbosch	95	CC	75
Hamman St	Delft	106	CF	49
Hammanshand	Stellenbosch	95	CB	77
Hammer Rd	Philippi East	125	CL	48
Hammerkop Rd	Bridgetown	103	CF	37
Hammond St	Greenways	174	CZ	73
Hampden	Rocklands (M.Plain)	144	CS	46
Hampden Ave	Kensington	84	BZ	33
Hampstead	Pinelands	84	CB	34
Hampstead Cl.	Parklands	25	BN	33
Hampstead Rd	Claremont	120	CJ	30
Hampton Ave	Newlands	101	CG	27
Hampton Ave	Ottery	122	CL	35
Hampton Cl.	Parklands	25	BN	33
Hampton Cr.	Skilpadvlei	45	BP	49
Hampton Gate	Halalie	30	BN	52
Hampton Rd	Oostersee	87	BY	45
Hampton Sq.	Edgemead	58	BV	38
Hampton Sq.	Noordhoek Manor	157	CX	21
Hamshire Cl.	Kirstenhof	159	CU	27
Hanall Wk	Hanover Pk	122	CJ	36
Hanbury Ave	Lansdowne	121	CJ	33
Hancock St	Plumstead	140	CO	29
Handel	Delft Sth	125	CJ	48
Handel Cl.	Mandalay	125	CM	48
Handel Cr.	De Duin	59	BW	41
Handel Rd	Belhar	106	CD	48
Handel Rd	Somerset West	171	CU	75
Handel St	Arauna	63	BU	55
Handel St	Groenheuwel	19	AZ	91
Handel St	Steenberg	159	CT	29
Handicap Rd	Strandfontein	162	CT	41
Handley-Page	Rocklands (M.Plain)	144	CS	46
Hanekam Rd	Pelikan Pk	142	CQ	36
Hanekam Rd	Uitsig	87	CC	45
Hanekom Cr.	Belhar	106	CE	50
Hanekom St	Bonteheuwel	104	CE	40
Hanepoort Cr.	Brackenfell Sth	63	BX	57
Hanepoot Ave	Somerset West	151	CS	72
Hanepoot Cr.	Sonstraal	46	BR	52
Hanepoot St	Bellavista	18	BC	90
Hanepoot St	Wellington	15	AT	94
Hangana St	Nyanga	123	CK	42
Hangberg St	Tafelsig (M.Plain)	145	CS	48
Hangberg St	Tafelsig (M.Plain)	145	CP	50
Hangklip Rd	Belhar	107	CE	51
Hangklip Rd	Durbanville Hills	45	BS	50
Hangklip St	Strand	174	CY	73
Hangklip St	Tafelsig (M.Plain)	145	CS	50
Hani St	Crossroads	124	CJ	44
Hanley St	Plumstead	140	CO	30
Hanlyn Cr.	Newfields	122	CJ	36
Hanlyn Rd	Newfields	122	CJ	36
Hannes Louw Dr.	Parow Nth	60	BX	43
Hanover	Highbury	107	CE	53
Hanover Ave	Belhar	106	CE	50
Hanover Park Ave	Hanover Pk	122	CK	36
Hanover Rd	Dieprivier	140	CP	28
Hanover Rd	Fresnaye	81	CA	19
Hanover St	Wellington	15	AV	92
Hans Aschenborn Rd	Woodlands (M.Plain)	124	CN	45
Hans Ras Rd	Rondebosch	101	CF	29
Hans St	Morgenster	63	BU	56
Hans Strijdom Ave	Cape Town Cen.	82	CA	23
Hans Strydom St	Parow Nth	59	BW	42
Hansel Rd	Heathfield	140	CR	29
Hansen Rd	Muizenberg	159	CX	29
Hansen Rd	Muizenberg	159	CW	27
Hantamberg	Wellington	15	AU	91
Hantamberg Rd	Bonnie Brae	47	BP	57
Hantamberg Rd	Bonnie Brae	47	BO	58
Hantamsberg St	Tafelsig (M.Plain)	145	CR	49
Hants Rd	Lakeside	159	CV	28
Happiness St	Wesbank	107	CF	52
Happy Valley Rd	Franschhoek Nth	74	BW	100
Harbot Cl.	Brackenfell Ind.	63	BT	58
Harbour Cl.	Blouberg Sands	24	BM	30
Harbour Heights Cl.	Simon's Town	194	DJ	25
Harbour Lights	Hout Bay	136	CQ	14
Harbour Rd	Hout Bay	136	CQ	14
Harbour Rd	Hout Bay Harbour	136	CR	14
Harbour Rd	Kalk Bay	186	DA	26
Harcourt Rd	Claremont	101	CH	27
Hardekool	Delft Sth	125	CJ	50
Hardekool St	Rouxville	90	CA	56
Hardepeer Rd	Bonteheuwel	104	CD	39
Harder St	Gustrow	175	DB	75
Harding Rd	Claremont	102	CH	31
Harding Rd	Kirstenhof	159	CU	27
Hardwick Rd	Rondebosch	101	CG	29
Hardy Cl.	Eureka	87	CC	44
Hare Rd	Kalk Bay	186	DA	26
Hare Rd	Kalk Bay	186	CZ	26
Hare St	Mowbray	101	CD	29
Hares Ave	Salt River	83	CB	27
Hares Cr.	Salt River	83	CC	27
Harewood Ave	Somerset West	151	CR	72
Harewood Ave	Somerset West	151	CR	73
Harfield Pl.	Claremont	120	CJ	29
Harfield Pl.	Claremont	120	CK	30
Harfield Rd	Kenilworth	120	CJ	29
Harfield Rd	Kenilworth	120	CK	29
Hargraves Rd	Hout Bay	116	CL	13
Haring Rd	Strandfontein	162	CT	39
Harlem Ave	Langa	103	CD	35
Harlequin Rd	Rondebosch	102	CG	31
Harley St	Lavender Hill	159	CT	30
Harley St	Oostersee	60	BX	45
Harman Rd	Claremont	101	CH	29
Harman St	Bothasig	42	BS	38
Harman St	Bothasig	43	BS	39
Harmonica St	Retreat	159	CT	29
Harmonie Ave	Stanlou	61	BX	48
Harmonie Rd	Hazendal	102	CE	33
Harmonie St	Elim	90	CB	55
Harmony	Fairyland	19	AZ	92
Harmony	Fairyland	19	BA	94
Harmony Cl.	Hanover Pk	122	CK	37
Harmony Rd	Capricorn	160	CV	31
Harmony Rd	Kirstenhof	159	CT	27
Harmony Rd	Retreat	140	CR	30
Harmony Sq.	Mitchells Plain Cen.	145	CR	47
Harmony St	Belhar	106	CE	48
Harmony Way	Ottery	121	CM	33
Harold Cl.	Hout Bay	117	CN	18
Harold Rd	Devon Pk	128	CM	60
Harold St	Paarlzicht	19	BC	91
Haroldene Rd	Lansdowne	121	CJ	32
Harpenden Rd	Muizenberg Nth	159	CW	28
Harper St	William Lloyd	19	BC	89
Harpford Ave	Wynberg	120	CL	30
Harpford Cl.	Wynberg	120	CL	30
Harpuisboom Cr.	Eikenbosch	90	CC	56
Harrier	Dreyersdal	140	CS	27
Harrier Cir.	Imhoff's Gift	184	DB	15
Harrier Cl.	Imhoff's Gift	184	DB	15
Harrier Rd	Parklands	25	BN	32
Harrier Rd	Phumlani	142	CQ	36
Harrier St	Flamingo Vlei	41	BQ	32
Harrier St	The Hague	106	CF	50

Index to Street Names

Harrier Way — Hoog St

STREET NAME	SUBURB NAME	PG	GRID
Harrier Way	Montagu's Gift	141	CO 33
Harriers Rd	Mowbray	102	CE 31
Harries St	Plumstead	140	CO 29
Harrington Rd	Fish Hoek	185	DA 21
Harrington Rd	Simon's Town	194	DJ 26
Harrington Rd	Tamboerskloof	81	CB 21
Harrington St	District Six	82	CB 23
Harrington St	Gardens	82	CB 23
Harrington Way	Belhar	107	CE 51
Harris Dr.	Ottery East	121	CN 34
Harris Dr.	Ottery East	122	CN 35
Harris Rd	Kalk Bay	186	DA 26
Harris Rd	Rondebosch	102	CE 31
Harris St	Mowbray	102	CE 31
Harrison Cl.	Somerset West	151	CR 73
Harrod Dr.	Oak Glen	62	BW 51
Harrongate	Parklands	25	BM 34
Harrow Ln.	Westlake Est.	158	CU 24
Harrow Rd	Dieprivier	140	CP 28
Harrow Rd	Rondebosch	101	CG 29
Harry de Stadler Cl.	Fish Hoek	185	DA 21
Harry Gwala Cr.	Mxolisi Phetani	126	CM 51
Harry Gwala St	Weltevreden Val. (M.Plain)	123	CM 42
Harry St	Gaylee	108	CH 57
Harry St	Klipdam	89	CB 54
Harry Stodel St	Kenilworth Pk	120	CK 30
Hart Ct	Delft	106	CG 49
Hart Rd	Crawford	102	CH 33
Hartbees	Parowvallei	87	BZ 44
Hartbees St	Delft	106	CG 49
Hartbees St	Eastridge (M.Plain)	145	CR 48
Hartbees St	Mfuleni	126	CK 53
Hartebees Rd	Goedemoed	46	BP 53
Hartebees Rd	Goedemoed	46	BO 53
Hartebees St	Kleinvlei	127	CJ 58
Hartebees St	Scottsdene	64	BT 60
Hartenberg St	Haasendal	90	CA 57
Hartenberg St	Voorbrug	106	CG 50
Hartenbos Way	Northpine	63	BU 58
Hartfield	Dennemere	127	CJ 57
Hartfield	Dennemere	127	CN 55
Hartford St	KWV	22	BG 88
Hartleyvale Rd	Beacon Valley (M.Plain)	145	CP 48
Hartogh	Perm Gdns	128	CK 59
Hartwig Cr.	Strand	174	CZ 73
Harvard	Rocklands (M.Plain)	163	CT 45
Harvard Dr.	Lansdowne	121	CK 33
Harvard St	Helderberg Pk	175	DA 75
Harvest St	Normandie	64	BW 59
Harvester Way	Mitchells Plain	144	CQ 45
Harvey Rd	Claremont	120	CJ 30
Harwood End	Parklands	25	BM 34
Harwood End	Parklands	25	BL 33
Hasana Cr.	Umrhabulo Triangle	147	CQ 56
Hasana Cr.	Umrhabulo Triangle	147	CR 56
Hashe St	Kuyasa	147	CR 56
Hasme Rd	Masiphumelele	184	DA 18
Hassan Khan Ave	Gustrow	175	DB 75
Hassel St	Eersterivier	128	CM 60
Hastings Rd	Muizenberg	159	CW 30
Hastings Rd	Wynberg	120	CM 30
Hastings St	Tamboerskloof	81	CB 21
Hastula Way	Sunset Beach	41	BS 31
Hatfield Rd	Three Anchor Bay	81	BZ 21
Hatfield St	Gardens	81	CB 22
Hattford St	Highbury	107	CE 54
Hauman St	Franschhoek Sth	78	BY 106
Haumann St	Somerset West	170	CV 74
Haupt St	Flintdale Est.	140	CP 29
Hauptfleisch Cl.	Groenvlei	18	BA 88
Hauptville	Barbarossa	120	CN 27
Haute Rd	Belthorn Est.	102	CH 34
Haven Cr.	Gatesville	103	CG 37
Haven Dr.	Noordhaven	157	CW 19
Haven Dr.	Noordhaven	157	CX 19
Haven Rd	Maitland Gdn Village	83	CB 30
Haven Rd	Ndabeni	83	CB 30
Havenga St	Oakdale	61	BV 49
Havenga St	Voelvlei	89	CA 52
Hawaii Ave	Colorado (M.Plain)	144	CO 44
Hawaii St	Macassar	149	CS 65
Hawaii Way	Portlands (M.Plain)	144	CQ 46
Hawe Sq.	Factreton	85	BZ 35
Hawford St	Athlone	102	CG 33
Hawk	Rocklands (M.Plain)	144	CS 44
Hawk Cr.	Flamingo Vlei	41	BQ 33
Hawk Cr.	Pelikan Pk	142	CS 36
Hawk Rd	Langeberg Rdg	47	BR 55
Hawk Rd	Montagu's Gift	141	CO 33
Hawke Rd	Penhill	128	CK 60
Hawker St	The Hague	106	CF 50
Hawkins Ave	Epping Ind.	85	CC 36
Hawks Cl.	Kirstenhof	159	CT 27
Hawkwood La.	Epping Forest	86	CC 41
Hawston Rd	Milnerton	57	BW 32
Hawthorden Rd	Wynberg	120	CK 28
Hawthorn St	Klein Nederburg	19	BB 92
Hawthorn Way	Rusdal	108	CF 57
Hawthorne Cl.	Dennedal	139	CR 25
Hawthorne Cl.	Fairie Knowe	185	DA 19
Hawthorne Cr.	Belhar	106	CD 48
Hawthorne Cr.	Thornton	85	CB 37
Hawthorne Pl.	Sun Valley	185	CZ 20
Hawthorne Pl.	Sun Valley	185	DC 22
Hawthorne Rd	Claremont	101	CH 28

STREET NAME	SUBURB NAME	PG	GRID
Hawthorne Rd	Heathfield	140	CQ 28
Hawthorne Rd	Lotus River	141	CP 34
Hawthorne Way	Pinelands	102	CD 34
Hay La.	Eindhoven	106	CH 50
Hay Rd	Lansdowne	121	CJ 33
Hay Rd	Woodstock	82	CB 26
Hayan	Groenheuwel	19	AZ 91
Hayden	Schuilplaats	113	CG 76
Haydn	Delft Sth	125	CK 48
Haydn	Kaapzicht	59	BW 40
Haydn St	Protea Hoogte	63	BX 56
Haydn St	Steenberg	159	CT 29
Hayes Rd	Wynberg	120	CM 30
Hayfield Cr.	Edgemead	58	BU 38
Hayi St	Umrhabulo Triangle	147	CQ 57
Haylett St	Van Ryneveld	174	CZ 72
Haylett Way	Meadowridge	140	CP 27
Hayro Rd	Wynberg	120	CM 30
Haytor Rd	Green Point	81	BZ 21
Haywood Rd	Crawford	102	CH 33
Haywood Rd	Crawford	121	CJ 33
Hayworth Rd	Kirstenhof	159	CT 27
Hazel Cl.	Tafelsig (M.Plain)	145	CS 50
Hazel Cl.	Valhalla Pk	104	CE 42
Hazel Rd	Gatesville	103	CG 36
Hazel Rd	Valhalla Pk	104	CE 42
Hazel St	Avonwood	86	CB 42
Hazel Way	Northpine	63	BU 58
Hazel Way	Northpine	63	BV 56
Hazelden Dr.	Somerset West	171	CW 76
Hazelden Dr.	Somerset West	171	CX 75
Hazeldene Ave	Portlands (M.Plain)	144	CQ 46
Hazeldene Ave	Portlands (M.Plain)	144	CR 46
Hazeldene Ave	Portlands (M.Plain)	145	CR 47
Hazeldene Cl.	Rondebosch	101	CF 29
Hazeldene Way	Scottsdene	64	BT 59
Hazell Rd	Somerset West	151	CS 73
Hazelwood Cr.	Sunningdale	24	BM 30
Hazelwood Cr.	Sunningdale	24	BL 29
Hazelwood Pl.	Hazelwood Pk	185	CZ 20
Hazelwood Pl.	Hazelwood Pk	185	DC 22
Hazelwood Rd	Parklands	25	BM 33
Hazelwood Way	Sunningdale	24	BM 30
Head Rd	Fresnaye	81	CB 19
Headfort La.	Penhill	128	CJ 61
Headingly Way	Edgemead	58	BU 38
Heath Cir.	Blackheath Ind.	108	CG 55
Heath Ct	Kewtown	102	CF 34
Heath Rd	Austinville	108	CH 56
Heath Rd	Heathfield	140	CP 28
Heath Rd	Lotus River	141	CQ 34
Heath Rd	Parkwood	141	CO 32
Heath Rd	Rondebosch	102	CE 31
Heath Rd	Summer Greens	58	BV 36
Heath St	Bishop Lavis	105	CE 43
Heath St	Bishopscourt	119	CJ 26
Heath St	Lentegeur (M.Plain)	124	CN 45
Heath St	Sarepta	89	CC 52
Heath St	Somerset West	170	CV 73
Heath St	Tygerdal	58	BX 38
Heathcote Ave	Athlone	102	CF 33
Heather Ave	Kenever	61	BT 49
Heather Rd	Austinville	108	CH 56
Heather Rd	Bishop Lavis	105	CE 43
Heather Rd	Claremont	120	CJ 29
Heather Rd	Milnerton	57	BU 33
Heather St	Mandalay	125	CM 47
Heather Way	Meadowridge	140	CP 28
Heatherly Rd	Lansdowne	121	CJ 32
Heatherton Rd	Claremont	101	CH 29
Heatherton St	Metro Ind. Township	83	BY 30
Heathfield Rd	Sea Point	81	BZ 20
Heathfield Way	Eersterivier	128	CM 62
Heathrow Rd	The Hague	106	CF 49
Hebron Cr.	Brackenfell Sth	63	BX 57
Hebron Ct	Bridgetown	103	CE 37
Hebron St	Amanda Glen	46	BS 52
Hebron St	Bellair	62	BV 53
Hebron St	Sonstraal	46	BR 52
Hector	Idasvallei	96	CA 79
Hector Ave	Montagu's Gift	142	CO 35
Hector Cl.	Grassy Pk	141	CP 33
Hector Cr.	Grassy Pk	141	CP 33
Hector Petersen	Weltevreden Val. (M.Plain)	123	CN 42
Hector Rd	Valhalla Pk	104	CE 41
Hedge La.	Retreat	140	CS 29
Heemraden St	Somerset West	169	CT 70
Heemstede Dr.	Groenvallei	62	BX 53
Heere St	District Six	82	CC 25
Heerengracht	Cape Town Cen.	82	BZ 24
Heerengracht Cl.	Klein Zevenwacht	90	CB 58
Heerengracht Rd	Bergvliet	140	CQ 27
Heerengracht St	Skoongesig	45	BO 50
Heerenzicht	Vygeboom	45	BR 50
Heerlik Rd	Kensington	84	BZ 34
Heese St	Paarlzicht	19	BC 91
Heide Ave	Somerset West	151	CS 73
Heide Cl.	Perm Gdns	128	CJ 59
Heide Cl.	Perm Gdns	128	CJ 60
Heide Cl.	Plattekloof	60	BT 43
Heide Ct	Edgemead	58	BU 38
Heide Rd	Belhar	88	CC 47
Heide Rd	Bishop Lavis	104	CD 42
Heide Rd	Durbanville Hills	45	BR 49
Heide Rd	Uitsig	87	CC 45

STREET NAME	SUBURB NAME	PG	GRID
Heide St	Arauna	63	BU 55
Heide St	Bloemhof	61	BV 50
Heide St	Bridgetown	103	CE 36
Heide St	Franschhoek Sth	79	BZ 108
Heide St	Groenvlei	18	AZ 89
Heide St	Ridgeworth	61	BV 50
Heide St	Wellington	15	AT 92
Heidelberg St	Panorama	59	BV 42
Heideveld Rd	Heideveld	103	CF 38
Heideveld Rd	Heideveld	104	CF 39
Heideveld Rd	Heideveld	104	CG 39
Heideveld Rd	Vanguard	103	CF 38
Heidi Cl.	Somerset West	170	CT 72
Heifer St	Rondebosch East	102	CH 32
Heilbot Rd	Nooitgedacht	105	CE 43
Heinecke	Park Estates	174	CY 72
Heinkel	Rocklands (M.Plain)	144	CS 46
Heinkel Cr.	The Hague	106	CF 50
Heinz Park Dr.	Weltevreden Val. (M.Plain)	124	CN 44
Heinz Rd	Hanover Pk	122	CK 37
Hek St	Lavender Hill	160	CT 31
Helder Rd	Athlone	102	CF 32
Helder Rd	Northpine	63	BU 58
Helderberg	Stellenbosch	95	CC 76
Helderberg	Tafelsig (M.Plain)	164	CT 48
Helderberg Cl.	Richwood	42	BP 38
Helderberg Cl.	Richwood	42	BO 38
Helderberg Cl.	Strand	174	CY 73
Helderberg Cl.	Vredekloof Hgts	47	BS 55
Helderberg College Rd	Somerset West	151	CR 74
Helderberg College Rd	Somerset West	151	CS 73
Helderberg College Rd	Somerset West	170	CT 72
Helderberg Rd	Belhar	106	CD 49
Helderberg Rd	Bishop Lavis	104	CD 42
Helderberg Rd	Richwood	42	BQ 37
Helderberg Rd	Somerset West	170	CU 74
Helderberg Rd	Valmary Pk	46	BR 51
Helderberg St	Greenfield	108	CH 56
Helderberg St	Hillrise	61	BX 50
Helderrand Rd	Somerset West	152	CS 76
Heldersig Rd	Thornton	85	CA 36
Heldersig Rd	Thornton	85	CA 37
Heldersig Rd	Thornton	85	CB 36
Heldersig St	Panorama	59	BV 42
Helderspruit Rd	Somerset West	151	CQ 73
Helderspruit Rd	Somerset West	151	CQ 74
Helderview Cl.	Vredekloof Hgts	47	BS 55
Helderzicht Cl.	Voorbrug	107	CG 51
Helderzicht Rd	Somerset West	171	CU 76
Helderzicht Rd	Somerset West	171	CU 77
Helderzicht Rd	Somerset West	171	CU 78
Helderzicht St	Brackenfell Sth	63	BW 57
Heldray St	Chapman's Peak	156	CX 17
Heldsingen Pl.	Hout Bay	117	CM 16
Helen Cl.	Tafelsig (M.Plain)	146	CS 51
Helen Joseph	Weltevreden Val. (M.Plain)	123	CM 41
Helen Joseph St	Mandela Pk	146	CQ 54
Helen Khuzwayo St	Mandela Pk	146	CR 54
Helen St	Kalkfontein II	107	CD 52
Helena Ave	Somerset West	151	CR 72
Helena Ave	Somerset West	151	CS 72
Helena Cl.	Mandalay	125	CM 47
Helena Cr.	Graceland	146	CP 53
Helena Rd	Montagu's Gift	141	CP 33
Helena St	Chrismar	61	BX 50
Helene Ave	Blackheath Ind.	108	CF 56
Helgarda Rd	Hout Bay	136	CO 14
Helios Cir.	Phoenix	57	BV 33
Helios Cl.	Woodlands (M.Plain)	144	CO 44
Hella Cr.	Uitzicht	47	BO 55
Hellenburgh Rd	Claremont	101	CG 29
Hellenic Sq.	Eureka	87	CC 43
Helliger La.	Cape Town Cen.	81	CA 22
Helling St	Die Oude Spruit	63	BX 56
Helling St	Protea Hoogte	63	BW 56
Helmsley End	Parklands	26	BN 35
Helmsley Rd	Parklands	25	BN 34
Helot Rd	Bishop Lavis	104	CD 42
Helpmekaar St	Shirley Pk	89	BY 52
Helshoogte Rd	Belhar	106	CD 50
Helshoogte Rd	Die Rand	95	CA 76
Helshoogte Rd	Kylemore	97	CA 84
Helshoogte Rd	Stellenbosch	95	CB 78
Helshoogte Rd	Stellenbosch	96	CA 82
Helshoogte Rd	Stellenbosch	96	CB 79
Helvetica St	Voorbrug	106	CG 50
Helwan Rd	Milnerton	57	BU 32
Hely Hutchinson Ave	Bakoven	99	CE 18
Hely St	Maitland	83	CB 30
Hem Cl.	Ilitha Pk	146	CR 51
Hem Cl.	Philippi East	125	CM 47
Hem Dr.	Joe Slovo Pk	57	BV 34
Hematige	Brackenfell	63	BW 55
Hematige	Brackenfell	63	BV 58
Hemlock St North	Newlands	101	CH 28
Hempe St	Umrhabulo Triangle	147	CQ 57
Hemyock Rd	Plumstead	120	CN 29
Hendon	Parklands	25	BM 34
Hendon Rd	Athlone	102	CG 33
Hendon Rd	Wynberg	120	CL 28
Hendrick	Marlow	89	CA 51
Hendricks Ave	Athlone	102	CF 33
Hendricks Cl.	Mountain View	19	BB 92
Hendrik Barnard Cl.	Park Estates	174	CY 72
Hendrik Bergh	Rozendal	96	CC 79

STREET NAME	SUBURB NAME	PG	GRID
Hendrik Bergh	Rozendal	96	CB 80
Hendrik Pierneef Cr.	Woodlands (M.Plain)	144	CO 45
Hendrik Potgieter St	Parowvallei	87	BZ 43
Hendrik Smith St	Highbury	108	CD 55
Hendrik St	Ottery	121	CM 33
Hendrik Verwoerd Dr.	De Duin	59	BW 41
Hendrik Verwoerd Dr.	Plattekloof	60	BW 44
Hendrika St	Northern Paarl	18	AZ 89
Hendrikse	Cloetesville	95	BY 75
Hendriksz Rd	Somerset West	171	CT 78
Hengelaar St	Beacon Valley (M.Plain)	145	CP 48
Hengelaar St	Beacon Valley (M.Plain)	145	CQ 48
Henley Ct	Northpine	63	BU 58
Henley Rd	Lotus River	141	CQ 34
Henley Rd	Muizenberg	159	CX 29
Henley Rd	Sheridon Pk	159	CU 28
Henlo Park Cr.	Langeberg Glen	47	BQ 56
Hennie Fortuin Cr.	Ravensmead	87	CB 45
Hennie Webber St	Panorama	59	BV 41
Hennie Winterbach St	Panorama	59	BV 42
Hennie Winterbach St	Panorama	59	BW 41
Henning St	The Palms	170	CX 73
Hennop Rd	Langeberg Glen	47	BQ 56
Henry Thomson Cl.	Heathfield	140	CP 29
Henschell Rd	Hout Bay	136	CO 14
Henshawe Rd	Plumstead	140	CO 30
Henwick Rd	Muizenberg Nth	159	CV 28
Henze	Delft Sth	125	CK 48
Henzekile St	Bloekombos	48	BQ 62
Henzekile St	Bloekombos	49	BQ 63
Heraldry St	Camelot	107	CF 53
Herandien St	Wesbank	107	CF 51
Herba Rd	Woodlands (M.Plain)	144	CO 44
Herbert Baker St	Parow Nth	60	BW 43
Herbert Penny Rd	Penhill	128	CK 61
Herbert Rd	Sea Point	81	BZ 20
Herbert Rd	Sea Point	81	CA 20
Herbert St	Kingston	61	BX 49
Herbert St	Oakdale	61	BX 48
Herbert St	Paarlzicht	19	BB 91
Herbrand St	Hazendal	102	CE 33
Herbrand St	Hazendal	102	CE 33
Hercule St	De Zoete Inval	39	BJ 88
Hercules	Cloetesville	94	BZ 74
Hercules	Cloetesville	94	BZ 73
Hercules Dr.	Phoenix	57	BV 34
Hercules Pillar Rd	Joostenberg	33	BL 66
Hercules Pillar Rd	Joostenberg	34	BJ 68
Hercules Pillar Rd	Joostenberg	34	BK 67
Hercules Rd	Woodlands (M.Plain)	144	CO 44
Hercules St	Bellville Sth Ext. 5	88	BZ 49
Hercules St	Wellington	15	AV 93
Hercules St	Woodstock	82	CB 26
Hercules Way	Ocean View	189	DD 15
Here	Simonswyk	95	CB 78
Hereford	Brackenfell Sth	90	BY 57
Hereford	Durbanville	46	BP 53
Hereford Ave	Balvenie	86	CC 42
Hereford St	Claremont	120	CJ 30
Hereford St	Montana/Durrheim	104	CE 41
Herfs St	Anchorage Pk	179	DD 77
Heritage Cl.	Somerset West	171	CW 76
Heritage Cl.	Tijgerhof	57	BW 33
Heritage Way	Tijgerhof	57	BW 33
Herman Rd	Observatory	83	CC 29
Hermes Cl.	Mandalay	125	CM 47
Hermes Rd	Eureka	87	CC 43
Hermes Rd	Woodlands (M.Plain)	144	CP 44
Hermes St	Paarden Eiland	83	BZ 29
Hermes St	Park Village	127	CK 58
Hermes St	Park Village	127	CN 55
Hermes Way	Mandalay	125	CM 47
Hermina Ave	Bel Ombre	119	CM 25
Hermina Pl.	Bel Ombre	119	CM 24
Hermitage Ave	Rosebank	101	CE 29
Hermitage Ave	Somerset West	170	CT 72
Hermitage Cl.	Zevenzicht	90	CC 58
Hermitage Rd	Northpine	63	BU 58
Hermitage Rd	Ridgeworth	61	BU 50
Hermitage Rd	Ridgeworth	61	BV 48
Hermitage Rd	Sonstraal	46	BR 52
Hermitage St	Clarkes	86	CC 42
Hermitage St	Franschhoek Nth	75	BX 105
Hermitage St	Paarlzicht	18	BC 90
Hermitage Way	Meadowridge	140	CP 27
Hermon Cr.	Bonnie Brook	47	BQ 57
Hermon St	Vierlanden	30	BN 52
Herold Rd	Rondebosch	102	CH 31
Herold St	Stellenbosch	95	CC 75
Heron	Danarand	89	CC 53
Heron	Pelikan Pk	141	CS 34
Heron	Rocklands (M.Plain)	144	CS 45
Heron Bay Mews	Milnerton	57	BT 32
Heron Cir.	Kommetjie	183	DB 13
Heron Cl.	Admirals Pk	175	DC 78
Heron Cl.	D'urbanvale	29	BN 49
Heron Cl.	Montagu's Gift	141	CP 33
Heron Cl.	Westlake Est.	158	CT 25
Heron Pl.	D'urbanvale	45	BO 49
Heron Rd	Marina Da Gama	159	CU 30
Heron Rd	Pelikan Pk	142	CS 35
Heron St	D'urbanvale	29	BN 49
Heron St	D'urbanvale	29	BN 50
Heron St	Eersterivier	128	CM 60
Heron St	Flamingo Vlei	41	BP 32

Abbreviations used: Ave – Avenue, A.H. – Agricultural Holding, A.L.– Algemene Landgoed, Blvd – Boulevard, Cen. – Central, Cir. – Circle, Cl. – Close, Cr. – Crescent, Ct – Court, Dr. – Drive, Est. – Estate, Ext. – Extension, Hgts – Heights, Ind. – Industrial, Gdns – Gardens, Gr. – Grove, La. – Lane, (M.Plain) - Mitchells Plain, Nth – North, Pl. – Place, Pk – Park, Rd – Road, Rdg. – Ridge, S.H.– Small Holding, Sq. – Square, St – Street, Sth – South, Ter. – Terrace, Tn – Turn, Val. – Valley, Wk – Walk

STREET	SUBURB NAME	PG	GRID	
Heron St	Scarborough	192	DK	18
Heron Way	Pinelands	102	CD	33
Heron Way	Villa Italia	57	BW	33
Heron Wk	Sunbird Pk	107	CF	54
Heronsbrook Way	Somerset West	169	CT	70
Herschel	Belhar	88	CC	50
Herschel Cl.	Claremont	120	CJ	28
Herschel Rd	Claremont	120	CJ	28
Herschel Rd	Fish Hoek	185	DB	22
Herschel Rd	Observatory	83	CC	29
Herschel St	Ruyterwacht	86	CA	39
Herschel Wk	Kenilworth	120	CK	28
Herschel Wk	Wynberg	120	CK	27
Herschell St	Lochnerhof	170	CX	72
Hersham Cr.	Sunningdale	24	BM	30
Hersham Cr.	Sunningdale	24	BL	29
Hersham St	Sunningdale	24	BM	30
Hersham St	Sunningdale	24	BL	29
Herta Cr.	Brackenfell Sth	63	BX	57
Herta Erna Ave	Durbanville	46	BO	51
Herta Erna Ave	Skoongesig	29	BN	50
Herta Louw St	Shirley Pk	89	BY	52
Herte Rd	Peerless Pk Nth	48	BQ	59
Herte St	Stellenbosch	95	CC	75
Hertford Rd	Wynberg	120	CM	29
Herton Villas	Bellair	62	BV	53
Herton Villas	Bellair	62	BX	52
Hertslet St	Cafda Village	141	CS	31
Hertzog Blvd.	Foreshore	82	CA	24
Hertzog Rd	Bergvliet	140	CQ	28
Hertzog Rd	Somerset West	170	CT	73
Hertzog Rd West	Bergvliet	140	CQ	28
Hertzog St	Eastridge (M.Plain)	145	CQ	49
Hertzog St	Ruyterwacht	86	CB	39
Heseldon Rd	Rondebosch	101	CG	30
Hess Rd	Grassy Pk	141	CQ	34
Hester Heese Cl.	Langgewacht	170	CW	72
Hester La.	Valhalla Pk	104	CE	41
Hester La.	Valhalla Pk	104	CF	42
Hester St	Kalkfontein II	107	CD	52
Hester St	Valhalla Pk	104	CE	42
Heuningboom	Weltevrede	94	BY	74
Heuningbos Cr.	Roosendaal	107	CG	51
Heuningbosch Cr.	Rouxville	90	CA	56
Heuningsberg St	Tafelsig (M.Plain)	145	CR	49
Heuningtee Ave	Uitsig	87	CC	44
Heuwel St	Brackenfell	63	BV	57
Heuwel St	Protea Hoogte	63	BW	57
Heuwel St	Sarepta	89	CC	52
Heuwel St	Wellington	15	AV	93
Heuwelkruin Cl.	Bellville Ext. 41	61	BT	50
Heuwelkruin Cl.	Bellville Ext. 42	61	BV	48
Heuwelsig	D'urbanvale	45	BO	49
Heuwelsig St	Panorama	59	BV	42
Heuwelzicht St	Brackenfell Sth	63	BX	58
Hewat Cr.	Somerset West	171	CU	78
Hewett Ave	Epping Ind.	86	CC	40
Hewitt St	Aurora	45	BP	48
Hex Cr.	Manenberg	104	CG	39
Hex St	Mfuleni	126	CK	53
Hexagon Cr.	Observatory	101	CD	29
Hexberg	Wellington	10	AQ	94
Hexberg	Wellington	11	AQ	95
Hexrivier Cr.	Greenfield	108	CH	57
Hexrivier Rd	Bonnie Brae	47	BP	56
Hexrivier St	Tafelsig (M.Plain)	145	CS	50
Hexrivier St	Tafelsig (M.Plain)	145	CP	50
Heytor Rd	Muizenberg	187	CZ	28
Hghakatgha St	Crossroads	124	CK	44
Hibiscus	Lentegeur (M.Plain)	144	CP	46
Hibiscus Ave	Newlands	101	CH	27
Hibiscus Ave	Whispering Pines	175	DC	76
Hibiscus Cl.	Ocean View	184	DC	15
Hibiscus Cl.	Pinelands	85	CC	35
Hibiscus Cl.	Pinelands	85	CC	36
Hibiscus Cr.	Protea Hoogte	63	BV	57
Hibiscus Cr.	Protea Hoogte	63	BW	57
Hibiscus Park	Durbanville	46	BO	51
Hibiscus Rd	Blackheath Ind.	108	CE	56
Hibiscus Rd	Oakdale	61	BV	49
Hibiscus Rd	Ridgeworth	61	BU	49
Hibiscus Rd	Tygerdal	58	BX	38
Hibiscus Rd	Uitsig	87	CC	44
Hibiscus St	Klein Nederburg	19	BC	93
Hibiscus St	Thornton	85	CA	37
Hibiscus Way	Durbanville	46	BO	51
Hibiscus Way	Wellway Pk	46	BO	52
Hibiskus Way	Somerset West	150	CS	70
Hickman Cr.	Graceland	146	CP	53
Hickman Cr.	Graceland	146	CS	52
Hickory Rd	Eastridge (M.Plain)	145	CR	47
Hickory St	Kewtown	103	CF	35
Hidalgo	Hill View	127	CK	58
Hidalgo	Park Village	127	CK	58
Hiddingh Ave	Newlands	100	CH	26
Hiddingh Ave	Newlands	101	CH	27
Hiddingh Ave	Oranjezicht	82	CC	23
Hiddingh Rd East	Bergvliet	140	CQ	28
Hiddingh Rd North	Bergvliet	140	CQ	28
Hiddingh Rd South	Bergvliet	140	CQ	28
Hiddingh Rd West	Bergvliet	140	CQ	27
Hiddingh Sq.	Edgemead	59	BT	39
Hide St	Macassar	168	CT	64
Hiebner Cl.	Northern Paarl	18	AZ	89
Hiewele Cr.	Victoria Mxenge	126	CN	52
Higgins	Highbury	107	CD	54
Higgins St	Highbury	108	CD	55
Higgo Cr.	Gardens	81	CC	20
Higgo La.	Gardens	81	CC	21
Higgo Rd	Gardens	81	CC	20
Higgo St	Lemoenkloof	18	BC	88
High Cape Ave	Devil's Peak Est.	82	CC	24
High Court Cl.	Fisantekraal	32	BJ	59
High Level Rd	Green Point	81	BZ	21
High Level Rd	Paarl	22	BF	87
High Level Rd	Sea Point	81	BZ	20
High Rd	Leonsdale	86	CA	42
High Rd	Ottery	122	CL	35
High Riding Cl.	Noordhaven	157	CX	19
High St	Paarl	22	BE	88
High St	Rosendal	61	BU	49
High St	Somerset West	171	CU	75
High St	Wellington	10	AS	93
High St	Woodlands (M.Plain)	144	CQ	44
High St	Woodstock	82	CB	26
High Trees Way	Amanda Glen	46	BS	51
High Way	Fish Hoek	186	DC	24
Highbury	Scottsdene	64	BT	59
Highbury	Scottsdene	64	BV	60
Highbury Rd	Highbury	108	CD	55
Highbury Rd	Highbury	107	CD	54
Highbury Rd	Highbury	107	CE	54
Highbury Rd	Mowbray	101	CD	29
Highbury Way	Edgemead	58	BV	38
Highclaire St	Maitland	84	CA	31
Highcliffe Cr.	Sunningdale	25	BL	31
Highfield Rd	Green Point	81	BZ	22
Highfield Rd	Rosebank	101	CE	29
Highfield Rd	Weltevreden Val. (M.Plain)	124	CN	43
Highfield St	Green Point	81	BZ	22
Highfield St	Wellington	10	AR	92
Highgate St	Ndabeni	83	CB	30
Highgrove Rd	Lansdowne	121	CK	33
Highland Cl.	Devil's Peak Est.	82	CC	24
Highland Cl.	Table View	42	BO	35
Highlands Ave	Tokai	139	CS	24
Highlands Ave	Vredehoek	100	CD	23
Highlands Cl.	Edgemead	58	BU	38
Highlands Dr.	Lentegeur (M.Plain)	144	CO	45
Highlands Dr.	Lentegeur (M.Plain)	145	CO	47
Highlands Dr.	Weltevreden Val. (M.Plain)	143	CO	42
Highlands Dr.	Weltevreden Val. (M.Plain)	144	CO	43
Highlands La.	Simon's Town	194	DJ	24
Highstead Rd	Rondebosch	101	CF	29
Highwick Ave	Kenilworth	120	CJ	28
Highwick Dr.	Kenilworth	120	CK	28
Highworth Rd	Sea Point	81	BZ	20
Hikneut St	Amandelrug	90	BZ	56
Hilaris Ave	Elriche	18	BB	90
Hilaris Cl.	Highbury	107	CE	54
Hilary Cl.	Forest Glade	127	CL	58
Hilary Cl.	Lavender Hill	160	CT	31
Hilary Dr.	Lavender Hill	159	CT	30
Hilary Dr.	Lavender Hill	160	CT	31
Hilary St	Bellville	61	BU	50
Hilary St	Hoogstede	62	BV	54
Hilary St	Woodlands (M.Plain)	144	CQ	44
Hilda Cl.	Philippi	124	CL	45
Hilda Cl.	Tafelsig (M.Plain)	145	CS	50
Hilda Rd	Chrismar	61	BX	50
Hilda Rd	Manenberg	123	CK	39
Hildalan La.	Bishopscourt	119	CJ	26
Hildalan Rd	Bishopscourt	119	CJ	26
Hildebrand St	Oakdale	61	BW	49
Hildene Rd	Tamboerskloof	81	CB	21
Hill Rd	Da Gama Pk	190	DE	20
Hill Cl.	Kraaifontein	47	BQ	57
Hill Park La.	Mowbray	101	CD	30
Hill Rd	Green Point	81	BZ	21
Hill Rd	Rosebank	101	CE	29
Hill Rd	Table View	24	BN	29
Hill Rd	Windsor Pk	47	BR	56
Hill Rd	Windsor Pk	47	BR	57
Hill St	Park Estates	174	CY	71
Hill St	Voelvlei	89	CA	53
Hill St	Woodstock	82	CC	25
Hill Top St	Scarborough	192	DJ	18
Hill View Ave	Lavender Hill East	160	CU	31
Hillary Cl.	Somerset West	152	CS	76
Hillbrow Rd	Kenilworth	120	CK	29
Hillcrest Ave	Penhill	128	CK	61
Hillcrest Cr.	Fish Hoek	185	DA	22
Hillcrest Rd	Mandalay	125	CN	48
Hillcrest Rd	Muizenberg	159	CX	28
Hillcrest Rd	Somerset West	152	CS	77
Hillcrest Rd	Somerset West	171	CT	77
Hillcrest Rd	Somerset West	171	CU	77
Hillcrest Rd	The Vines	140	CO	27
Hillcrest Rd	Welgelee	63	BT	55
Hillrise Cr.	Durbell	45	BS	49
Hillrise Rd	St James	187	CZ	27
Hillrise Way	Pinelands	102	CD	33
Hills St	Schaap Kraal	122	CL	36
Hillside Rd	Fish Hoek	186	DC	25
Hillside Rd	Kenever	61	BT	49
Hillside Rd	Mountainside Est.	179	DD	78
Hillside Rd	Ridgeworth	61	BU	50
Hillside Rd	Tamboerskloof	81	CB	21
Hillside St	Groenvlei	18	BA	88
Hillside Ter.	Green Point	81	BZ	22
Hillstar Ave	Ottery	121	CL	33
Hilltop La.	Newlands	101	CG	27
Hillview Rd	Sybrand Pk	102	CE	33
Hillview St	Klipkop	87	BZ	45
Hillwood Ave	Bishopscourt	119	CJ	26
Hillwood Rd	Claremont	120	CK	28
Hilmar Rd	Dieprivier	140	CP	28
Hilton Rd	Clovelly	186	DA	25
Hilton Rd	Hout Bay	117	CN	17
Hilton Rd	Lotus River	141	CP	34
Hilton Rd	Mowbray	101	CD	30
Hilton Rd	Oranjezicht	99	CD	22
Hilton St	Schaap Kraal	122	CL	36
Hilyard St	Woodstock	83	CB	27
Himalaya Cr.	Tafelsig (M.Plain)	145	CS	49
Himilaya Rd	Eersterivier	128	CL	59
Hind Ave	Kensington	84	BZ	33
Hindle Rd	Eindhoven	106	CH	50
Hindle Rd	Fairdale	107	CH	53
Hindle Rd	Malibu Village	127	CK	56
Hindle Rd	Sunset Glen	127	CJ	55
Hindle Rd	Voorbrug	107	CH	52
Hine	Cloetesville	95	BY	75
Hinta St	Mandela Pk	147	CQ	55
Hintsa Ave	Hout Bay	137	CO	16
Hintsa Ka Phalo	Weltevreden Val. (M.Plain)	123	CN	42
Hippo Dr.	Zoo Pk	47	BR	57
Hippo St	Soneike II	89	BZ	54
Hlafuna St	Umrhabulo Triangle	147	CQ	58
Hlakula St	Umrhabulo Triangle	147	CQ	57
Hlala St	Umrhabulo Triangle	147	CR	57
Hlamba	Wellington	15	AU	91
Hlanga Cr.	Umrhabulo Triangle	147	CQ	56
Hlanga Cr.	Umrhabulo Triangle	147	CQ	57
Hlankomo	Philippi East	124	CM	46
Hlankomo St	Ilitha Pk	146	CR	52
Hlanto St	Griffiths Mxenge	146	CQ	54
Hlathi Dr.	Tarentaalplaas	175	CY	75
Hlati St	Nyanga	124	CJ	43
Hlebo St	Harare	146	CR	54
Hlehla St	Umrhabulo Triangle	147	CQ	56
Hlehla St	Umrhabulo Triangle	147	CR	56
Hlela St	Umrhabulo Triangle	147	CR	58
Hlelo Cr.	Kuyasa	147	CR	58
Hlengisa St	Victoria Mxenge	126	CN	51
Hlika St	Umrhabulo Triangle	147	CQ	58
Hlikihla St	Griffiths Mxenge	146	CQ	54
Hlobo Cr.	Harare	146	CR	53
Hlobo St	Ilitha Pk	146	CR	52
Hlola St	Harare	146	CR	52
Hlomela St	Griffiths Mxenge	146	CP	54
Hlonela St	Harare	146	CS	54
Hlongwana Cl.	Nonqubela	126	CN	53
Hlontlo St	Griffiths Mxenge	146	CQ	54
Hlosi Dr.	Joe Slovo Pk	57	BU	34
Hlosi Rd	Philippi East	124	CM	46
Hlotywa St	Eyethu	146	CP	53
Hlubi St	Scottsdene	64	BT	60
Hlula St	Harare	146	CR	54
Hlungulu Cr. East	Joe Slovo Pk	57	BU	34
Hlungulu Cr. West	Joe Slovo Pk	57	BU	34
Hlungulu Rd	Philippi East	125	CL	47
Hlungulu St	Brown's Farm	124	CM	44
Hlungulu St	Ilitha Pk	146	CQ	52
Hlutha Cr.	Umrhabulo Triangle	147	CP	56
Hobbs Steps	Fish Hoek	186	DC	25
Hobe	Wellington	15	AU	91
Hobe Cr.	Philippi East	125	CM	47
Hobe Rd North	Joe Slovo Pk	57	BU	34
Hobe Rd North	Joe Slovo Pk	57	BU	31
Hobe St	Ilitha Pk	146	CR	52
Hobhouse St	Flintdale Est.	141	CP	31
Hobhouse St	Ruyterwacht	86	CB	40
Hobohobo St	Brown's Farm	124	CL	43
Hobohobo St	Ilitha Pk	146	CQ	52
Hoboyi St	Bloekombos	49	BQ	63
Hobson Ct	Edgemead	59	BU	39
Hobson St	Labiance	89	BZ	51
Hockenheim Dr.	Silversands	107	CH	53
Hockey Cl.	Pinelands	84	CC	32
Hockey Cr.	Beacon Valley (M.Plain)	145	CP	48
Hockey Rd	Pinelands	84	CC	32
Hodgson St	Courtrai	22	BG	88
Hodgson St	Durbanville	45	BQ	49
Hodi Rd	Philippi East	124	CL	46
Hoebridge Cr.	Sunningdale	24	BM	30
Hoebridge Cr.	Sunningdale	24	BL	29
Hoek	Cloetesville	94	BY	74
Hoek Cl.	Lansdowne	121	CL	34
Hoek St	Chapman's Peak	156	CX	17
Hoek St	Elim	89	CA	54
Hoek St	Glenhaven	89	CA	52
Hoek St	Lansdowne	121	CL	34
Hoek St	Lansdowne	122	CL	35
Hoek St	Wellington	10	AS	92
Hoek St West	Lansdowne	121	CL	34
Hoep-Hoep	Devon Pk	94	CC	73
Hoepoe	Rocklands (M.Plain)	144	CS	44
Hoepoe St	Macassar	149	CS	65
Hoepoe St	Somerset Hgts	127	CJ	57
Hoëveld Rd	Somerset West	151	CS	74
Hoëveld Rd	Somerset West	152	CS	75
Hof	Uniepark	96	CB	79
Hof St	Belrail	88	BY	49
Hof St	Flamingo Vlei	41	BQ	34
Hof St	Gardens	81	CC	21
Hof St	Oranjezicht	81	CB	22
Hoff St	Peerless Pk East	47	BR	58
Hoff St	Peerless Pk East	48	BR	59
Hoffman Ave	The Vines	140	CO	27
Hoffman St	Bellville Sth	88	BZ	49
Hoffmann Ave	Paarl	22	BE	88
Hoffmeister St	William Lloyd	19	BC	92
Hofman	Stellenbosch	95	CB	75
Hofmeyer	Stellenbosch	95	CC	77
Hofmeyer Ave	Kenridge	61	BT	49
Hofmeyer Ave	Welgemoed	60	BU	45
Hofmeyer Ave	Welgemoed	60	BV	45
Hofmeyer La.	Woodstock	82	CB	26
Hofmeyer Rd	Richmond Est.	86	BY	40
Hofmeyer Rd	Vasco Est.	86	BY	39
Hofmeyer Rd	Vasco Est.	86	BY	40
Hofmeyer St	Park Estates	174	CZ	73
Hofmeyer St	Parowvallei	87	BZ	43
Hofmeyer St	Peerless Pk Nth	48	BQ	59
Hofmeyer St	Somerset West	151	CS	73
Hofmeyer St	Van Ryneveld	174	CZ	72
Hofmeyr Rd	Belhar	106	CD	49
Hofmeyr Rd	Three Anchor Bay	81	BZ	20
Hofmeyr St	Gardens	81	CC	21
Hofmeyr St	Wellington	11	AR	95
Hogarth St	De La Haye	89	BY	51
Hogsback Rd	Heideveld	104	CF	39
Hoheizen Cl.	Hohelzen	61	BW	47
Hoheizen Cr.	Hohelzen	61	BW	47
Hohenhort Ave	Hohenort	119	CK	24
Hohenhort Ave	Hohenort	119	CL	25
Hohenhort Way	Glen Ive	62	BU	51
Hoho Cl.	Victoria Mxenge	126	CN	51
Hoist Ave	Montague Gdns Ind.	58	BT	36
Holbein St	De La Haye	89	BY	51
Holden St	Beacon Valley (M.Plain)	145	CQ	47
Holden Way	Edgemead	58	BV	38
Holderness Rd	Lansdowne	121	CK	32
Holheim Cl.	Mitchells Plain	144	CR	45
Holheim Cl.	Weltevreden Val. (M.Plain)	144	CS	43
Holland Ave	Bothasig	42	BS	38
Holland Ave	Bothasig	58	BT	38
Holland Rd	Muizenberg	159	CX	29
Holland Rd	Strandfontein	163	CT	43
Holland St	Peerless Pk East	47	BR	58
Holland St	Peerless Pk East	48	BR	59
Holland St	Townsend Est.	85	BY	37
Holley Cr.	The Range	86	CC	41
Holley Way	Matroosfontein	86	CC	41
Hollow Ct	Epping Forest	86	CC	41
Holloway Rd	Clarkes	86	CC	42
Holly Cl.	Belhar	88	CC	47
Holly Cl.	Fairie Knowe	185	DA	19
Holly Cl.	Hanover Pk	122	CK	36
Holly Cl.	Hanover Pk	122	CN	36
Holly Cl.	Hazelwood Pk	185	CZ	20
Holly Cl.	Hazelwood Pk	185	DC	22
Holly Oak La.	Green Oaks	94	BY	74
Holly Rd	Bishop Lavis	105	CE	43
Holly St	Bellair	62	BW	51
Holly St	Bishopscourt	119	CJ	26
Hollywood Cr.	Malibu Village	127	CK	56
Hollywood Cr.	Weltevreden Val. (M.Plain)	144	CQ	43
Holmdene Rd	Plumstead	140	CO	30
Holmes Rd	Lansdowne	121	CK	34
Holmfirth Rd	Sea Point	81	CA	19
Holomisa St	Mandela Pk	147	CQ	55
Holomisa St	Mandela Pk	147	CP	55
Holst	Delft Sth	125	CK	48
Holzaphel St	Sarepta	89	CB	53
Homeleigh Ave	Vredehoek	100	CD	23
Homer Rd	Mandalay	125	CM	48
Homer St	Salt River	83	CB	28
Homeria Rd	Belhar	105	CD	46
Homerton La.	Salt River	83	CC	27
Homestead Ave	Bergvliet	139	CQ	26
Homestead Way	Pinelands	102	CD	32
Homestead Way	Pinelands	102	CD	33
Homestead Way	Rocklands (M.Plain)	144	CS	45
Homtini St	Delft	106	CF	49
Honalulu St	Malibu Village	127	CL	56
Honalulu St	Malibu Village	127	CN	55
Honetwort	Macassar	148	CS	62
Honey St	Sunset Glen	107	CH	54
Honeyguide La.	Steenberg	139	CS	24
Honeyside Rd	Belthorn Est.	102	CH	34
Honeyside Rd West	Crawford	102	CH	34
Honeysuckle	Lentegeur (M.Plain)	144	CO	46
Honeysuckle	Stellenbosch	95	BY	75
Honeysuckle Ave	Somerset West	171	CW	77
Honeysuckle Cl.	Hout Bay	137	CP	16
Honeysuckle St	Bonteheuwel	104	CE	39
Honeysuckle St	Bridgetown	103	CF	36
Honeysuckle St	Hillcrest Hgts	127	CM	57
Honeysuckle Wk	Belhar	105	CD	46
Honeywell Rd	Retreat Ind. Area	159	CT	28
Honiton Rd	Plumstead	120	CM	29
Honnet Way	Edgemead	58	BU	38
Honono Cr.	Victoria Mxenge	126	CN	52
Hood Rd	Belgravia	103	CG	35
Hoog	Dalsig	113	CE	76
Hoog	Dalsig	113	CE	76
Hoog St	Durbanville	45	BP	49
Hoog St	Durbanville	45	BQ	50

Index to Street Names

Hoogeberg — Jennifer St

STREET NAME	SUBURB NAME	PG	GRID	
Hoogeberg	De Bron	45	BS	48
Hoogeberg	De Bron	45	BP	47
Hoogekraal St	De Bron	45	BS	48
Hoogelegen Cl.	Weltevreden Val. (M.Plain)	144	CR	45
Hoogelegen Cl.	Weltevreden Val. (M.Plain)	144	CS	43
Hoogenhout St	Somerset West	170	CT	73
Hoogenhout St	Vredekloof Hgts	47	BS	55
Hoogenhout St	Wellington	11	AS	95
Hoogstede St	Oak Glen	62	BW	52
Hooke St	Belhar	88	CC	50
Hoole Cl.	Plumstead	140	CP	29
Hoop	Cloetesville	95	BZ	75
Hoop St	Belrail	88	BY	49
Hoop St	Elim	90	CB	55
Hoop St	Paarl	22	BE	88
Hoop St	Wellington	15	AV	93
Hoopenberg St	Brackenfell Sth	63	BW	58
Hoopenberg St	Brackenfell Sth	63	BX	58
Hoopoe La.	Bakoven	98	CG	18
Hoosain Parker St	Parkwood	141	CP	32
Hop Rd	Scottsville	47	BS	57
Hope	Eersterivier	128	CN	60
Hope Cr.	Hanover Pk	122	CK	37
Hope Rd	Rosebank	101	CE	29
Hope St	Cape Town Cen.	82	CB	23
Hope St	Claremont	120	CJ	30
Hope St	Park Estates	170	CX	72
Hope St	Simon's Town	194	DJ	24
Hope St	Thembokwezi	125	CM	49
Hope St	Wellington	10	AR	93
Hopeville St	Gardens	81	CB	22
Hopkins St	Churchill	60	BX	43
Hopkins St	Glenlily	87	BY	43
Hopkins St	Salt River	83	CB	27
Hopkins St	Somerset West	171	CV	75
Hopkirk Way	Simon's Town	191	DE	24
Hopley Rd	Table View	41	BQ	34
Hopley Rd	Table View	42	BQ	35
Hopscotch St	Beacon Valley (M.Plain)	145	CP	47
Horak Ave	Bakoven	99	CE	19
Horak St	Denneburg	23	BD	91
Horak St	Peerless Pk East	48	BR	59
Horak St	Peerless Pk East	48	BR	60
Horatio Way	Simonskloof	194	DJ	25
Horeb St	Kirstenhof	158	CT	26
Horison Ave	Eersterivier	128	CM	59
Horison St	Amanda Glen	46	BS	52
Horizon Cl.	Salberau	86	CB	41
Horizon Cl.	Salberau	86	CB	39
Horn Ct	Belhar	106	CD	48
Hornbill	Electric City	127	CM	58
Hornbill Cr.	Seawinds	159	CU	30
Hornbill Rd	Pelikan Pk	142	CS	35
Hornsey Rd	Mowbray	101	CD	30
Horseshoe Cl.	Mitchells Plain	144	CR	45
Horseshoe Cr.	Noordhoek Manor	157	CX	21
Horsham Bend	Parklands	25	BM	34
Horstley Cr.	Highbury	107	CE	54
Hospitaal	Universiteits-oord	95	CB	77
Hospital Rd	Somerset West	171	CU	75
Hospital Rd	Wynberg	120	CL	27
Hospital St	Cape Town Cen.	82	BZ	24
Hospital St	Lemoenkloof	18	BC	88
Hospital St	Lemoenkloof	18	BC	89
Hospital St	Macassar	149	CS	64
Hospital St	Wellington	10	AS	92
Hostel St	Kaya	146	CP	52
Hotagterklip	Wesbank	107	CH	52
Hou Moed Ave	Sunnydale	185	CZ	19
Houghton Cr.	Sunningdale	25	BM	31
Houghton Rd	Bakoven	98	CF	18
Houghton Rd	Blue Downs	127	CJ	56
Houghton Rd	Eersterivier	128	CN	60
Houghton Steps	Bakoven	98	CE	18
Houmoed St	Voorbrug	106	CG	50
Hounslow La.	Woodstock	83	CC	27
Houston Pl.	Southfork	175	DB	75
Houston Sq.	Southfork	175	DB	75
Hout Bay Rd	Hout Bay	116	CM	14
Hout Bay Rd	Hout Bay	117	CN	17
Hout Bay Rd	Hout Bay	118	CM	20
Hout La.	Cape Town Cen.	82	CA	23
Hout St	Paarl	22	BD	88
Hout St	Peerless Pk Nth	48	BQ	59
Hout St	Peerless Pk Nth	48	BR	59
Hout St	Protea Hoogte	63	BX	57
Houtkapper	Schuilplaats	113	CG	76
Houtkapper St	William Lloyd	23	BD	94
Houtkloof Cl.	Mitchells Plain	144	CR	45
Houtkloof Cl.	Mitchells Plain	144	CS	43
Houtman Rd	Tijgerhof	57	BW	32
Houtman St	Dal Josafat Ind.	18	BA	90
Houtman St	Forest Glade	128	CL	59
Houtman St	Monte Vista	59	BV	39
Houwhoek Cl.	Tafelsig (M.Plain)	145	CR	49
Houwhoek Cl.	Tafelsig (M.Plain)	145	CP	50
Houwhoek Rd	Durbanville Hills	45	BR	49
Houwhoek St	Manenberg	104	CG	39
Hove Rd	Bakoven	98	CF	18
Hove Villas	Bellair	62	BV	52
Howard Davis Rd	Sanddrift	57	BW	34
Howard Dr.	Meadowridge	140	CP	27
Howard Dr.	Northpine	63	BU	58
Howard Dr.	Northpine	64	BU	59
Howard Dr.	Pinelands	84	CC	34
Howe Cl.	Adriaanse	87	CC	43
Howe St	Observatory	83	CC	29
Howell Rd	Simon's Town	194	DJ	26
Howes Rd	Wynberg	120	CM	28
Howick Slot	Bellville	61	BV	48
Hudson Cl.	Portlands (M.Plain)	144	CQ	46
Hudson Rd	Retreat	140	CS	29
Hudson St	Perm Gdns	127	CK	58
Hudson St	Schotsche Kloof	82	CA	23
Hugenoot St	Belrail	61	BX	48
Hugenoot St	Belrail	61	BV	48
Hugenot Cr.	Richwood	42	BQ	38
Hugenot Cr.	Richwood	42	BQ	37
Hugh Masekela Cr.	Mandela Pk	147	CQ	55
Hughenden	Hout Bay	117	CN	16
Hughenden St	Hout Bay	137	CO	17
Hughes Rd	Belhar	88	CC	50
Hugo Ave	Hout Bay	137	CQ	16
Hugo Cl.	Hout Bay	137	CQ	16
Hugo Naude Cr.	De La Haye	89	BY	51
Hugo Naude Cr.	Woodlands (M.Plain)	144	CO	45
Hugo Naude St	Cafda Village	141	CS	31
Hugo Naude St	Parow Nth	59	BX	42
Hugo Rd	Montagu's Gift	142	CO	35
Hugo Rd	Simon's Town	195	DK	27
Hugo St	Durbanville	46	BQ	51
Hugo St	Richmond Est.	59	BX	40
Hugo St	Richmond Est.	86	BY	40
Hugon Rd	Claremont	101	CH	28
Hugon Rd	Claremont	101	CE	27
Huguenot	Franschhoek Nth	75	BW	103
Huguenot	Franschhoek Nth	78	BY	105
Huguenot	Franschhoek Sth	78	BY	106
Huguenot	Franschhoek Sth	79	BZ	107
Huguenot	Parow East	87	BY	45
Huguenot Ave	Everglen	45	BS	50
Huguenot Ave	Oranjezicht	99	CD	22
Huguenot Ave	Tafelsig (M.Plain)	145	CS	49
Huguenot Ave	Tafelsig (M.Plain)	145	CS	50
Huguenot Bypass	Huguenot	18	BC	90
Huguenot St	Die Bos	174	CY	74
Huguenot St	Ruyterwacht	86	CA	40
Huguenot Way	Belhar	106	CD	50
Huilboom Cr.	Vredekloof Hgts	47	BS	55
Huilbos Rd	Bonteheuwel	104	CD	39
Huising Ave	Monte Vista	59	BV	39
Huising St	Bothasig	42	BS	37
Huising St	Somerset West	170	CU	74
Huising St	Somerset West	171	CU	75
Huising St	Welgemoed	60	BU	46
Huisrivier Cr.	Tafelsig (M.Plain)	145	CS	48
Hulett	Papegaaiberg Ind. Pk	94	CB	74
Hull St	Eastridge (M.Plain)	145	CQ	49
Huluhu St	Village 3 Nth	146	CO	54
Humber Cl.	Portlands (M.Plain)	144	CQ	46
Humber St	Manenberg	104	CH	39
Humberstone Rd	Plumstead	120	CN	29
Humbolt Ave	Perm Gdns	128	CK	59
Humby Rd	Ottery	121	CM	33
Hume St	Hohelzen	61	BW	47
Humerail	Wesbank	107	CG	51
Humewood Dr.	Parklands	25	BM	32
Humewood Dr.	Parklands	25	BN	32
Humewood Dr.	Parklands	25	BN	33
Humility Cl.	Retreat	140	CR	30
Hunt Cl.	Beacon Valley (M.Plain)	145	CP	47
Hunt Rd	Killarney Gdns	42	BO	37
Hunter Ave	Strandfontein	162	CT	41
Hunter St	Table View	41	BO	34
Hunter St	Table View	42	BO	35
Hunter St	The Hague	106	CF	50
Hunters Green	Summer Greens	58	BV	36
Hunters La.	Somerset West	170	CV	74
Hunters La.	Somerset West	171	CV	75
Hunters Way	Hout Bay	117	CM	17
Huntingdon Cr.	Ottery East	121	CN	33
Huntingdon Rd	Retreat	140	CS	28
Huntley St	Somerset West	171	CW	75
Hurley Rd	Mowbray	102	CD	31
Huron St	Portlands (M.Plain)	144	CQ	45
Hurricane St	Factreton	85	BZ	35
Hurricane St	The Hague	106	CF	50
Hurst Cl.	Somerset West	170	CW	72
Hurter Ave	Chapman's Peak	156	CW	16
Husami Cl.	Cravenby	87	CA	43
Husami Rd	Cravenby	87	CA	43
Huskisson	Paarl	22	BF	88
Huskisson Way	Kommetjie	183	DB	12
Hussar St	Rugby	57	BX	32
Hutchinson Ave	Retreat	140	CR	28
Hutchinson Ave	Table View	41	BP	32
Hutton Rd	Kirstenhof	159	CT	27
Huxley Dr.	Athlone	102	CF	33
Huxley Dr.	Meadowridge	139	CP	26
Hyacinth	Lentegeur (M.Plain)	144	CO	46
Hyacinth	Lentegeur (M.Plain)	144	CP	46
Hyacinth Ave	Pinelands	102	CD	34
Hyacinth Rd	Belhar	88	CC	47
Hyacinth Rd	Durbanville	46	BP	51
Hyacinth St	Dalvale	19	AY	92
Hyacinyh	Macassar	149	CR	63
Hybiscus St	Hillcrest Hgts	127	CL	57
Hyde Park Ave	Noordhoek Manor	157	CX	20
Hyde Park Ave	Noordhoek Manor	157	CV	20
Hyde Park Cl.	Portlands (M.Plain)	145	CR	47
Hyde Rd	Parkwood	141	CO	32
Hyde St	District Six	82	CB	25
Hydra Ave	Ocean View	183	DC	14
Hydrangea	Lentegeur (M.Plain)	144	CO	45
Hydrangea St	Bonteheuwel	104	CD	40
Hydrangea St	Hillcrest Hgts	127	CL	57
Hydrangea St	Klein Nederburg	19	BB	92
Hydro St	Kaymor	89	BY	52
Hyeix St	Bloekombos	49	BQ	63
I				
Ian Cl.	Barbarossa	120	CN	27
Ian Rd	Rondebosch	102	CH	31
Ian Taylor Rd	Plumstead	140	CP	29
Ibali	Mbekweni	15	AV	92
Ibex St	Tijgerhof	57	BW	32
Ibis	Electric City	127	CN	58
Ibis	Rocklands (M.Plain)	144	CS	44
Ibis Cl.	Dreyersdal	139	CR	26
Ibis Cl.	Imhoff's Gift	184	DB	16
Ibis Rd	Montagu's Gift	141	CP	33
Ibis St	Eersterivier	128	CM	60
Ibis St	Flamingo Vlei	41	BQ	33
Ibis St	Pelikan Pk	142	CS	36
Ibis St	Somerset West	152	CS	76
Ibis St	Sonstraal Hgts	46	BR	53
Ibis Villas	Sonstraal Hgts	46	BR	53
Ibis Way	Sunnydale	185	DA	19
Ibis Way	Westlake Est.	158	CU	25
Ibis Wk	Villa Italia	57	BW	33
Ibiza Way	Capricorn	160	CW	31
Ibizi Cl.	Capri	184	DB	18
Ica La.	Eindhoven	106	CH	50
Icaneshini St	Thembokwezi	125	CN	49
Icarus Cl.	Eureka	87	CC	43
Icarus Way	Phoenix	57	BV	33
Iceland Cr.	Portlands (M.Plain)	144	CS	46
Icelekwane St	Village 3 Nth	146	CO	54
Icola St	Barnet Molokwana Cnr	126	CN	53
Ida Cl.	Tafelsig (M.Plain)	145	CS	50
Idada Ave	Mxolisi Phetani	125	CL	49
Idada Ave	Mxolisi Phetani	125	CM	50
Idada Ave	Mxolisi Phetani	126	CM	51
Idaho Ave	Colorado (M.Plain)	144	CO	44
Idaho St	Brooklyn	83	BZ	30
Idalia	Kirstenhof	159	CT	27
Idaliya St	Thembokwezi	125	CM	49
Iena Cl.	Strandfontein	162	CT	40
Ifafa Cr.	Delft	106	CH	49
Ifubesi St	Village 3 Nth	146	CO	54
Igiyogiyo St	Crossroads	124	CK	44
Igiyo-Giyo St	Village 3 Nth	146	CO	54
Igqili St	Mfuleni	126	CJ	53
Igxiya St	Village 3 Nth	146	CO	54
Ihlabankomo St	Village 3 Nth	146	CO	54
Ihluhluwe St	Mfuleni	126	CK	53
Ihobe St	Village 3 Nth	146	CO	54
Ihobohobo St	Mfuleni	127	CL	55
Ihobohobo St	Mfuleni	127	CM	55
Ihobohobo St	Village 3 Nth	146	CO	54
Ihobolo St	Crossroads	124	CK	44
Ikhaka	Mbekweni	15	AW	92
Ikwelera St	Mfuleni	126	CK	53
Ilanda St	Village 3 Nth	146	CO	54
Ilex La.	Belhar	106	CD	47
Ilex Ave	Ottery	121	CN	33
Ilex Cl.	Uitsig	87	CC	44
Ilex Cl.	Uitsig	87	CC	45
Ilex Pl.	Hazelwood Pk	185	CZ	20
Ilex Pl.	Hazelwood Pk	185	DC	22
Ilex Rd	Claremont	120	CJ	27
Ilex St	Somerset West	150	CS	70
Ilford St	Sea Point	80	CA	18
Iligwa St	Mfuleni	126	CK	54
Iligwa St	Mfuleni	126	CK	52
Ilili Ave	Thembokwezi	125	CN	49
Ilitha St	Crossroads	124	CK	44
Ilkley Cr.	Sea Point	81	BZ	20
Illinois St	Stellenridge	62	BU	51
Illovo Rd	Bonnie Brook	47	BQ	57
Illovo Rd	Bonnie Brook	47	BP	58
Illovo St	Delft	106	CF	49
Illovo St	Mfuleni	126	CJ	53
Illovo St	Park Village	127	CK	58
Ilovane Cl.	Crossroads	124	CK	44
Ilovane Cl.	Crossroads	124	CN	46
Imadolo St	Crossroads	124	CJ	44
Imali	Mbekweni	15	AW	91
Imam Solomons Cl.	Mandela Pk	146	CQ	54
Imbomiso St	Crossroads	124	CK	44
Imbomiso St	Crossroads	124	CN	46
Imbumba St	Crossroads	124	CJ	44
Imfeni Ct	Joe Slovo Pk	57	BU	34
Imhoff Ave	Table View	41	BP	32
Imhoff St	Monte Vista	59	BV	39
Imhoff St	Monte Vista	59	BW	39
Imhoff St	Welgemoed	60	BU	46
Imhoff St	Welgemoed	60	BV	46
Immelman Rd	Somerset West	171	CU	78
Immerzicht	D'urbanvale	29	BN	50
Imola	Killarney Gdns	42	BP	36
Impala	Rocklands (M.Plain)	144	CS	46
Impala Cl.	Lotus River	142	CP	35
Impala Cr.	Loevenstein	60	BW	46
Impala Rd	Langeberg Rdg	47	BR	56
Impala Rd	Rugby	57	BX	32
Impala Rd	Wellington	15	AU	92
Impala St	Durbanville	45	BP	49
Impala St	Kleinvlei	127	CJ	58
Impala St	Parowvallei	87	CA	43
Impala St	Ruwari	63	BV	57
Impala St	Scottsdene	64	BT	60
Impala St	Somerset West	171	CT	75
Impala Way	Pinelands	102	CD	34
Impepho	Mbekweni	15	AW	92
Imperial Cr.	Weltevreden Val. (M.Plain)	144	CO	43
Imperial St	Eastridge (M.Plain)	145	CQ	47
Imperial St	Eastridge (M.Plain)	145	CQ	48
Impunguye Cl.	Crossroads	124	CK	44
Impunguye Cl.	Crossroads	124	CN	46
Impunzi St	Philippi East	125	CL	48
Imtuthuzelo St	Crossroads	124	CK	44
Imvulo	Mbekweni	15	AW	92
Imvumu Cl.	Crossroads	124	CK	45
Inari Pl.	Hanover Pk	122	CK	36
Incholm Pl.	Cape Town Cen.	82	CB	23
Inciba St	Mfuleni	126	CJ	53
Inciniba St	Mfuleni	126	CM	54
Inciniba St	Mfuleni	127	CL	55
Incora St	Mfuleni	126	CK	53
Incora St	Mfuleni	126	CK	52
Indewe Cl.	Mfuleni	127	CM	55
Indian Rd	Kenilworth	120	CK	29
Indlovu St	Mfuleni	126	CJ	53
Indlovu St	Philippi East	125	CL	48
Indlulamthi Cr.	Mxolisi Phetani	125	CM	50
Indlulamthi St	Mxolisi Phetani	125	CM	50
Induland Ave	Pinati	121	CJ	33
Induland Cr.	Pinati	121	CJ	34
Induland Cr.	Pinati	121	CK	34
Induli	Mbekweni	15	AV	92
Indus La.	Ocean View	184	DC	15
Industria	Stellenbosch	95	CB	75
Industria Rd	Temperance Town	180	DD	79
Industria St	Brackenfell Ind.	63	BU	57
Industria St	Somerset West	170	CW	73
Industrial Rd	Kraaifontein Ind.	48	BQ	60
Industrial Ring Rd	Parow Ind.	87	CB	45
Industrial Ring Rd	Ravensmead	87	CA	46
Industrial St	Wellington	10	AR	92
Industrie St	Bellville Sth	88	CA	50
Industrie St	Bellville Sth	88	BZ	49
Industrie St	Kuilsrivier Ind.	89	CC	54
Industrie St	Kuilsrivier Ind.	90	CC	55
Industry Rd	Paarden Eiland	83	CA	29
Industry St	Paarden Eiland	83	BZ	28
Industry Way	Cafda Village	140	CS	30
Indwe Rd	Milnerton	57	BW	32
Indwe St	Mxolisi Phetani	125	CM	50
Indwe St	Philippi East	125	CL	47
Inez Ave	Brentwood Pk	126	CJ	51
Inez Rd	Sea Point	81	CA	19
Infanta Cr.	Strandfontein	162	CT	39
Infante St	Avondale	60	BX	44
Infantry Way	Door De Kraal	61	BT	47
Inga Cl.	Tafelsig (M.Plain)	145	CS	50
Inga Rd	Manenberg	123	CK	39
Ingabangaba St	Crossroads	124	CK	44
Ingle Rd	Claremont	101	CH	28
Ingleside Rd	Camps Bay	98	CF	18
Ingqabe Cr.	Crossroads	124	CK	44
Ingqangqolo Cl.	Crossroads	124	CK	44
Ingqura St	Mfuleni	126	CK	53
Ingrid Cl.	Strand	174	CZ	73
Ingrid Rd	Chrismar	61	BX	50
Ingrid Rd	Montague Gdns Ind.	42	BS	35
Ingulufe St	Brown's Farm	124	CM	43
Ingusa Cr.	Mxolisi Phetani	125	CL	50
Ingusa Cr.	Mxolisi Phetani	125	CM	50
Ingwe	Dunoon	42	BO	37
Ingwe Dr.	Joe Slovo Pk	57	BU	34
Ingwe Rd	Sanddrift	57	BV	34
Ingwe St	Mxolisi Phetani	125	CM	50
Inkblom Cr.	Roosendaal	107	CF	51
Inkblom St	Bonteheuwel	104	CD	40
Inkonjane St	Mfuleni	127	CM	55
Inkululeko St	Crossroads	124	CK	44
Inkvis St	Gustrow	175	DB	75
Inkwenkwezi St	Crossroads	124	CK	44
Inkwili Cl.	Crossroads	124	CK	44
Inkwili St	Mfuleni	126	CM	54
Inkxankxadi Cr.	Mxolisi Phetani	125	CM	50
Innes Cl.	Mandalay	125	CM	48
Innesfree Cl.	Barbarossa	120	CN	27
Innesfree Cl.	Belthorn Est.	103	CH	35
Innesfree Cl.	Belthorn Est.	103	CF	37
Innesfree Rd	Barbarossa	120	CN	27
Innesfree Rd	Belthorn Est.	103	CH	35
Innis Rd	Wynberg	120	CM	30
Inniskillen Rd	Mowbray	101	CD	30
Inqilo St	Crossroads	124	CJ	44
Inqilo St	Mfuleni	126	CM	54
Inqura St	Mfuleni	126	CK	53
Inspan St	Bellville Sth Ext. 5	88	BZ	49
Intengu St	Mxolisi Phetani	125	CM	50
Interlude Cr.	Dalvale	19	AZ	91
Intermezzo	Sonstraal Hgts	46	BR	53
Internal Rd	Strandfontein	161	CT	38
Intethe Cl.	Crossroads	124	CK	44
Intethe Cl.	Crossroads	124	CN	46

Abbreviations used: Ave – Avenue, A.H. – Agricultural Holding, A.L. – Algemene Landgoed, Blvd – Boulevard, Cen. – Central, Cir. – Circle, Cl. – Close, Cr. – Crescent, Ct – Court, Dr. – Drive, Est. – Estate, Ext. – Extension, Hgts – Heights, Ind. – Industrial, Gdns – Gardens, Gr. – Grove, La. – Lane, (M.Plain) - Mitchells Plain, Nth – North, Pl. – Place, Pk – Park, Rd – Road, Rdg. – Ridge, S.H.– Small Holding, Sq. – Square, St – Street, Sth – South, Ter. – Terrace, Tn – Turn, Val. – Valley, Wk – Walk

STREET NAME	SUBURB NAME	PG	GRID
Inthlabati Rd	Oostersee	87	BY 45
Intonga	Mbekweni	15	AW 92
Intonga	Wellington	15	AU 94
Intshinga Ave	Gugulethu	104	CH 41
Invader Cl.	Rocklands (M.Plain)	144	CS 45
Invermark Cr.	Gardens	81	CC 21
Invermark Cr.	Gardens	99	CD 21
Inverness Ave	Pinelands	84	CB 34
Invery Pl.	Foreshore	82	CB 25
Inyoka St	Mfuleni	126	CJ 53
Inyoni St	Ndabeni	84	CB 32
Iona Rd	Tijgerhof	57	BX 32
Iona St	Hillrise	61	BX 49
Iona St	Sunkist	61	BX 49
Ionian	Rocklands (M.Plain)	144	CS 45
Iowa St	Stellenridge	62	BV 51
Ipanema St	Malibu Village	127	CL 55
Ipikoko St	Thembokwezi	125	CN 49
Iprotiya Rd	Thembokwezi	125	CN 49
Ipsting Rd	Lavender Hill	160	CT 31
Iqwara St	Mxolisi Phetani	125	CM 49
Ireland	Delft Sth	125	CJ 48
Irene	Die Rand	95	CA 76
Irene Ave	Somerset West	151	CR 73
Irene Ave	Somerset West	151	CS 74
Irene Ave	Somerset West	170	CT 74
Irene Ave	Somerset West	171	CT 75
Irene Cl.	Kenever	61	BT 49
Irene Cl.	Tafelsig (M.Plain)	145	CS 50
Irene Rd	Claremont	120	CJ 27
Irene Rd	Montagu's Gift	141	CP 33
Irene Rd	Rondebosch	101	CG 28
Irene St	Kempenville	88	BY 49
Irene Way	Portlands (M.Plain)	144	CS 46
Irene Way	Sunnydale	185	CZ 19
Iris	Lentegeur (M.Plain)	144	CP 45
Iris Cl.	Belhar	105	CD 46
Iris Cl.	Brackenfell	63	BV 57
Iris Cl.	Plattekloof	59	BU 42
Iris Rd	Blackheath Ind.	108	CE 56
Iris Rd	Grassy Pk	141	CR 32
Iris St	Bridgetown	103	CE 36
Iris St	Dalvale	19	AY 92
Iris St	Sarepta	89	CB 52
Iris St	Sarepta	89	CC 52
Iris St	Skilpadvlei	45	BP 50
Iris St	Somerset West	170	CV 73
Iris Way	Macassar	149	CR 63
Iris Way	Scarborough	192	DJ 18
Irma's La.	Plumstead	140	CP 29
Iron Cl.	Scottsdene	64	BU 60
Iron St	Lakeside	159	CV 27
Ironwood Cl.	Eastridge (M.Plain)	145	CR 47
Ironwood Rd	Parklands	25	BN 34
Ironwood St	Bonteheuwel	104	CD 39
Irozi St	Thembokwezi	125	CN 48
Irvine St	Manenberg	104	CH 39
Irwell St	Observatory	83	CC 28
Irwinton Rd	Sea Point	81	CA 19
Isaac Rd	Montagu's Gift	142	CO 35
Isaac Way	Montagu's Gift	142	CO 35
Isaacs	Cloetesville	95	BY 75
Isaacs Cir.	Cloetesville	95	BY 75
Isabel Ave	Claremont	101	CH 27
Isabel St	Kalkfontein II	107	CD 53
Isabella Dr.	Sunset Beach	57	BT 31
Isabella St	Chrismar	61	BW 50
Isabella St	Chrismar	61	BV 48
Isabella St	Sonstraal	46	BR 53
Isadore Cohen Pl.	Bakoven	98	CF 18
Isadore Cohen Pl.	Bakoven	98	CG 18
Isak Cl.	Scottsdene	64	BT 59
Iscor	Bellville Sth	88	CA 50
Iscor	Sack's Circle Ind.	88	CB 50
Ishak Rd	Grassy Pk	141	CR 33
Isikhova St	Mfuleni	126	CM 54
Isikhova St	Mfuleni	127	CM 55
Isiphingo Ave	Joe Slovo Pk	57	BU 34
Isipingo St	Mfuleni	126	CK 53
Isis Dr.	Phoenix	57	BU 34
Island Rd	Pelikan Pk	141	CS 34
Island St	Dal Josafat Ind.	18	BC 89
Island St	Somerset West	170	CV 74
Island View	Bloubergstrand	24	BJ 27
Islay Rd	Grassy Pk	141	CQ 32
Ismail	Cloetesville	95	BY 75
Ismail	Cloetesville	95	BY 77
Ismore Way	Dennemere	108	CH 57
Isotope St	Triangle Farm	88	BZ 50
Italian Rd	Grassy Pk	141	CR 31
Ithekwana Rd	Thembokwezi	125	CM 49
Ithemba St	Crossroads	124	CK 44
Itsitsa St	Mfuleni	126	CJ 53
Itsomo St	Mfuleni	126	CJ 53
Ivan Rd	Grassy Pk	141	CR 33
Ivan Rd	Montagu's Gift	142	CO 35
Ivanhoe Rd	Fish Hoek	186	DA 23
Ivanhoe Rd	Scottsville	47	BS 57
Ivanhoe St	Gardens	81	CC 21
Ivanhoe St	Klipkop	87	BZ 45
Ivanhoe Way	Matroosfontein	86	CC 41
Ives	Delft Sth	125	CK 48
Ivo Chunett St	Cafda Village	141	CR 31
Ivoorhout	Delft Sth	125	CJ 50
Ivory Cl.	Sheridon Pk	159	CU 29

STREET NAME	SUBURB NAME	PG	GRID
Ivory St	Bonteheuwel	104	CD 39
Ivory St	Kenridge	61	BU 48
Ivukuthu	Mfuleni	127	CM 55
Ivukuthu Cl.	Crossroads	124	CK 44
Ivuzi Cr.	Mxolisi Phetani	125	CM 50
Ivy	Lentegeur (M.Plain)	144	CP 45
Ivy Cl.	Belhar	88	CC 47
Ivy La.	Tokai	139	CS 25
Ivy Price Rd	Retreat	140	CR 30
Ivy Rd	Claremont	120	CJ 27
Ivy Rd	Parkwood	141	CO 32
Ivy St	Gardens	81	CC 21
Ivy St	Observatory	83	CC 29
Ivy St	Wellway Pk East	46	BO 53
Ivydene Ave	Rondebosch	101	CF 30
Ixia	Mountainview	179	DD 78
Ixia Ave	Devil's Peak Est.	82	CC 24
Ixia Ave	Kommetjie	183	DB 12
Ixia Cl.	Plattekloof	60	BV 43
Ixia Ct	Kewtown	102	CF 34
Ixia Link	Belhar	105	CD 46
Ixia Pl.	Mandalay	145	CO 48
Ixia St	Bellville	61	BU 48
Ixia St	Durbanville	46	BO 51
Ixia St	Firgrove	150	CR 67
Ixia St	Hout Bay	137	CP 16
Ixia St	Kleinvlei	127	CJ 58
Ixia St	Milnerton	57	BT 33
Ixia St	Milnerton	57	BU 33
Ixia St	Murdock Valley	195	DL 28
Ixia St	Somerset West	150	CS 70
Izala St	Crossroads	124	CK 44
Izuba St	Mfuleni	127	CM 55
J			
J.F. Celliers St	Townsend Est.	85	BY 37
J.K.Mtyekisane St	Gugulethu	104	CG 40
J.Nontulo St	Nyanga	123	CK 41
J.Nontulo St	Nyanga	123	CK 42
J.W.Theron St	Welgelegen	59	BV 40
J.Z.Fuku Way	Langa	103	CD 36
Jabavi St	Langa	103	CD 35
Jabulani	Mbekweni	15	AW 91
Jacana Ave	Villa Italia	57	BW 33
Jacana Cr.	Electric City	128	CN 59
Jacana Cr.	Langeberg Rdg	47	BR 56
Jacana La.	Pelikan Pk	142	CR 35
Jacana St	Eersterivier	128	CM 60
Jacana St	Eersterivier	128	CJ 61
Jacaranda	Lentegeur (M.Plain)	144	CP 46
Jacaranda Ave	Grassy Pk	141	CR 32
Jacaranda Ave	New Orleans	18	BA 90
Jacaranda Ave	Pinelands	84	CC 34
Jacaranda Ave	Rusdal	108	CE 57
Jacaranda Ave	Uitsig	87	CC 44
Jacaranda Ave	Valmary Pk	46	BR 51
Jacaranda Cl.	Fairie Knowe	185	DA 19
Jacaranda Cl.	Mitchells Plain	144	CS 45
Jacaranda Cr.	Thornton	85	CA 37
Jacaranda Rd	Gordon Strand	175	DC 75
Jacaranda St	Brackenfell	63	BV 56
Jacaranda St	Brackenfell	63	BW 56
Jacaranda St	Brackenfell Sth	63	BX 57
Jacaranda St	Brackenfell Sth	90	BY 57
Jacaranda St	Parowvallei	87	BZ 44
Jacaranda St	Protea Hoogte	63	BW 56
Jacaranda St	Protea Hoogte	63	BX 57
Jacaranda St	Tygerdal	58	BX 38
Jacaranda Way	Matroosfontein	86	CC 41
Jacaranda Way	Nova Constantia	139	CQ 24
Jacht St	Sun Valley	185	CZ 20
Jack Craig St	Cape Town Cen.	82	CA 24
Jack Crow St	Scottsville	47	BR 58
Jack Crow St	Scottsville	47	BP 58
Jack Heath Cr.	Woodlands (M.Plain)	124	CN 45
Jackal Rd	Electric City	127	CM 58
Jackhalsvlei Rd	Nyanga	123	CJ 42
Jackie Quin St	Kuyasa	147	CS 56
Jackson Cr.	Penlyn Est.	122	CJ 36
Jackson Masala St	Bloekombos	48	BR 62
Jackson Mbali St	Kuyasa	147	CS 55
Jackson Mbali St	Kuyasa	147	CS 57
Jackson Rd	Simon's Town	194	DJ 26
Jackson St	Driftsands	125	CL 50
Jackson St	Kylemore	97	BZ 86
Jackson's Steps	Simon's Town	194	DJ 25
Jaco St	Hoogstede	62	BV 54
Jacob Ave	Kommetjie	183	DB 12
Jacob St	Bothasig	58	BU 37
Jacobs Ave	Rusthof	174	DA 74
Jacobs Ladder	St James	187	CZ 27
Jacobs Rd	Grassy Pk	141	CQ 32
Jacobs St	Amandelsig	90	CB 55
Jacobs St	William Lloyd	19	BC 93
Jacobus St	Athlone	102	CG 34
Jacomina Way	Wetton	121	CL 34
Jacqueline Rd	De Tijger	60	BW 44
Jacqueline St	Tafelsig (M.Plain)	145	CS 50
Jacques Ave	Wellington	15	AT 94
Jacques Goniwe St	Kuyasa	147	CS 55
Jacques Goniwe St	Kuyasa	147	CS 57
Jacques Hill Cr.	Somerset West	171	CU 75
Jacques St	Paarl	22	BD 88
Jade Cl.	Langeberg Rdg	47	BR 55
Jade Cl.	Rocklands (M.Plain)	145	CS 47

STREET NAME	SUBURB NAME	PG	GRID
Jade La.	Sheridon Pk	159	CU 28
Jade St	Somerset West	151	CR 71
Jafta St	Bloekombos	48	BQ 62
Jagger Rd	Elsies River Ind.	86	BZ 42
Jagger Rd	Halalie	46	BO 52
Jagger Wk	Vierlanden	30	BN 52
Jahr Cr.	Grassy Pk	141	CP 32
Jakaranda	Cloetesville	95	BZ 75
Jakaranda	Delft Sth	125	CK 49
Jakaranda	Firgrove	150	CR 67
Jakaranda Ave	Belhar	106	CD 47
Jakaranda Ave	Somerset West	171	CT 75
Jakaranda Rd	Eersterivier	128	CM 60
Jakaranda Rd	Hillcrest Hgts	127	CL 57
Jakaranda Rd	Scottsville	47	BS 57
Jakaranda St	Bellville	61	BW 49
Jakaranda St	Forest Village	127	CM 58
Jakaranda St	Klipdam	90	CB 55
Jakaranda St	Oakdale	61	BW 50
Jakkalsvlei Ave	Bonteheuwel	103	CD 38
Jakkalsvlei Ave	Bonteheuwel	104	CD 39
Jakkalsvlei Ave	Bonteheuwel	104	CD 40
Jakoef Abel Cl.	Gustrow	175	DB 75
Jakoef Abel Cl.	Gustrow	175	DB 77
Jali Cl.	Wallacedene	48	BS 60
Jali Cl.	Wallacedene	48	BS 61
Jalist St	Bloekombos	49	BR 63
Jama St	Victoria Mxenge	146	CO 51
Jamaica Cl.	Capri	184	DB 18
Jamaica Dr.	Capri	184	DB 18
Jamaica St	Malibu Village	127	CL 55
Jamaica Way	Portlands (M.Plain)	144	CQ 46
Jamaiga Ave	Macassar	149	CR 63
James Barry Ave	Alphen	119	CM 26
James Cl.	Grassy Pk	141	CP 33
James Cl.	Pine Acres	175	DC 77
James Cr.	De Tuin	47	BS 56
James Masemeni St	Kuyasa	147	CS 55
James Rd	Observatory	83	CC 29
James St	Gaylee	108	CG 57
James St	Woodstock	83	CB 27
James Walton Rd	Durbanville	45	BP 49
James Walton Rd	Durbanville	45	BP 47
Jameson	Strand Halt	170	CX 74
Jameson Ave	Door De Kraal	61	BT 47
Jameson Rd	Goodwood Est.	86	BY 39
Jameson Rd	Vasco Est.	86	BY 40
Jameson Rd	Windsor Pk	47	BS 56
Jameson St	Eastridge (M.Plain)	145	CQ 49
Jamiah Gafaldien St	Gustrow	175	DB 75
Jamie St	Mandalay	125	CM 47
Jamieson Rd	Rondebosch	102	CF 31
Jamieson Rd	Rondebosch	102	CG 31
Jamieson Rd	Table View	41	BQ 34
Jamieson St	Gardens	81	CB 22
Jan Celliers	Stellenbosch	95	CB 76
Jan Cilliers St	Parow Nth	60	BW 43
Jan Dissels Rd	Delft	106	CG 49
Jan Fiskaal	Onderpapegaaiberg	94	CC 72
Jan Fiskaal St	Amstelhof	23	BD 93
Jan Frederick	Onderpapegaaiberg	94	CC 73
Jan Groentjie St	Amstelhof	23	BD 93
Jan Hartogh	Gustrow	175	DB 75
Jan Hartogh	Gustrow	175	DB 77
Jan Hofmeyer St	Elim	90	CA 55
Jan Hofmeyr St	Denneburg	22	BD 90
Jan Kemp St	Panorama	59	BV 41
Jan Phillips Mountain Dr.	Paarl	17	BC 86
Jan Phillips Mountain Dr.	Paarl	18	AZ 87
Jan Phillips Mountain Dr.	Paarl	22	BG 87
Jan Phillips Mountain Dr.	Paarl	22	BG 88
Jan Phillips Mountain Dr.	Paarl	22	BE 87
Jan Pierewiet	Onderpapegaaiberg	94	CC 72
Jan Smuts Dr.	Athlone	102	CG 33
Jan Smuts Dr.	Epping Ind.	85	CC 35
Jan Smuts Dr.	Kewtown	102	CD 34
Jan Smuts Dr.	Kewtown	102	CE 34
Jan Smuts Dr.	Lansdowne	121	CK 34
Jan Smuts Dr.	Lansdowne	122	CL 35
Jan Smuts Dr.	Pinelands	84	CA 34
Jan Smuts Dr.	Seaforth Sound	194	DJ 26
Jan Smuts Rd	Beaconvale	86	BZ 42
Jan Smuts Rd	Beaconvale	87	BZ 43
Jan Smuts Rd	Wynberg	120	CL 28
Jan Smuts St	Cape Town Cen.	82	CA 24
Jan Smuts St	Dal Josafat Ind.	22	BD 89
Jan Smuts St	Plumstead	140	CO 30
Jan Steyn St	Northern Paarl	18	AZ 89
Jan van Riebeeck Ave	Ruyterwacht	86	CA 39
Jan van Riebeeck Dr.	Leonsdale	86	CA 42
Jan van Riebeeck Dr.	Wellington	15	AW 92
Jan van Riebeeck Rd	Groenheuwel	19	AZ 91
Jan van Riebeeck Rd	Paarl	22	BD 90
Jan van Riebeeck Rd	Paarl	22	BF 90
Jan van Riebeeck Rd	Paarlzicht	18	BC 90
Jan van Riebeeck St	Wellington	10	AR 93
Jana St	Sarepta	89	CB 53
Janari Rd	Grassy Pk	141	CQ 32
Janbruin St	Southfork	174	DB 74
Janda Cr.	Victoria Mxenge	126	CN 52
Jandy Cl.	Kenilworth	120	CJ 30
Jane Ave	Gatesville	103	CH 37
Jane St	Gaylee	108	CG 57
Janet	Barbarossa	120	CN 27
Janet Cl.	Tafelsig (M.Plain)	145	CS 50

STREET NAME	SUBURB NAME	PG	GRID
Janey Cl.	Montana/Durrheim	104	CE 41
Jangada St	Sun Valley	185	CZ 20
Janie St	Ferndale	62	BW 54
Janie St	Ferndale	62	BV 53
Jannasch	Mostertsdrift	95	CC 78
Jannasch	Stellenbosch	95	CB 78
Janni Rd	Plumstead	140	CP 29
Jannie Engelbrecht St	Springbok Pk	62	BV 54
Jannie Rossouw St	Windsor Pk	47	BS 57
Jannie Storm St	Harbour Island	179	DE 77
Jansen	William Lloyd	23	BD 94
Jansen	William Lloyd	23	BE 93
Jansen Rd	Belhar	88	CC 50
Jansen Rd	Milnerton	57	BW 32
Jansen St	Aurora	45	BP 48
Jansen St	Glenlily	87	BY 43
Jansen St	Park Estates	170	CX 72
Jansen St	Welgemoed	60	BV 46
Jansens Ave	Flamingo Vlei	41	BQ 33
Jansens Ave	Table View	41	BO 33
Jansens Ave	Table View	41	BP 33
Janssen St	Bothasig	58	BU 37
Janssens Rd	Maitland	84	CA 32
Jantjies	Mbekweni	15	AV 91
Jantjies	Mbekweni	15	AW 91
Janya Cl.	Nonqubela	146	CO 53
Japhtas Cr.	Franschhoek Nth	75	BW 105
Japonica	Macassar	148	CR 62
Japonica	Macassar	149	CS 63
Japonica Rd	Uitsig	87	CB 45
Japonica Rd	Uitsig	87	CC 45
Japonica St	Klein Nederburg	19	BC 93
Japonica St	Vredekloof Hgts	47	BS 55
Japonika Ave	Welgedacht	60	BT 45
Japonika Ave	Welgedacht	60	BU 45
Japonika Rd	Belhar	87	CC 46
Japonika Way	Rusdal	108	CE 57
Jappie Rd	Capricorn	160	CU 31
Japura St	Eindhoven	106	CH 50
Jardine St	Wellington	10	AS 92
Jarisch Rd	Scottsville	47	BS 57
Jarvis Cl.	Eureka	87	CC 44
Jarvis St	Green Point	82	BZ 23
Jarvis Way	Montagu's Gift	142	CO 35
Jasmin	Lentegeur (M.Plain)	144	CO 45
Jasmin Rd	Milnerton	57	BU 33
Jasmin St	Casablanca	175	DA 75
Jasmine Ave	Fish Hoek	186	DA 24
Jasmine Cir.	Ocean View	184	DC 15
Jasmine Cl.	Dunoon	42	BO 37
Jasmine Rd	Wellway Pk East	46	BO 53
Jasmine St	Bonteheuwel	104	CD 39
Jasmine St	Cravenby	87	CB 43
Jasmine St	Hillcrest Hgts	127	CL 57
Jasmine Way	Scarborough	192	DJ 18
Jasmyn	Delft Sth	125	CJ 50
Jasmyn Cl.	Plattekloof	59	BU 42
Jasmyn Cl.	Vredekloof	62	BT 54
Jasmyn Rd	Belhar	88	CC 47
Jasmyn Rd	Ottery	121	CM 33
Jasmyn St	Klein Nederburg	19	BB 92
Jasmyn St	Somerset West	151	CS 71
Jasmyn St	Tygerdal	58	BX 37
Jasmyn St	Wellington	10	AS 93
Jasmyn Way	Eversdal	62	BT 51
Jason Cr.	Woodlands (M.Plain)	144	CP 45
Jason Rd	Eureka	87	CC 43
Jasper St	Oranjezicht	81	CC 22
Jasper St	Sheridon Pk	159	CU 28
Jasper Way	San Michel	157	CX 20
Java Ave	Bloubergstrand	24	BK 27
Java Cl.	Capri	185	DB 19
Java St East	Avondale	60	BX 44
Java St West	Clamhall	60	BX 43
Javelin St	The Hague	106	CF 49
Javier St	District Six	82	CB 25
Jaxa St	Tarentaalplaas	171	CX 75
Jay Rd	Montagu's Gift	141	CP 33
Jay St	Sunnydale	185	DA 20
Jean	Krigeville	113	CD 76
Jean Rd	Strandfontein	162	CU 42
Jean Rd	Valhalla Pk	104	CE 42
Jean Simons St	Parow East	87	BY 44
Jean Way	Macassar	149	CS 63
Jean Welz Cr.	Woodlands (M.Plain)	124	CN 45
Jeanette St	Brackenfell	63	BV 55
Jeanette St	Springbok Pk	63	BV 55
Jebel Cl.	Penlyn Est.	103	CH 36
Jebel St	Penlyn Est.	103	CH 35
Jeffcoat Ave	Bergvliet	140	CQ 27
Jefferson Rd	Claremont	102	CH 31
Jefferson Rd	Sunnydale	185	DA 19
Jeffrey St	Northern Paarl	18	AZ 89
Jefhta St	Scottsdene	64	BU 60
Jeftha	Rusthof	174	DA 74
Jejane St	Highbury	108	CD 55
Jejane St	Highbury	108	CE 55
Jejane St	Ilitha Pk	146	CQ 52
Jellicoe Ave	Epping Ind.	85	CC 36
Jengoa Cr.	Victoria Mxenge	126	CN 51
Jenkins Rd	Elfindale	140	CP 29
Jenkinson St	Parow East	87	BY 45
Jenner Cl.	Belhar	88	CC 50
Jennifer Cl.	Weltevreden Val. (M.Plain)	144	CQ 43
Jennifer St	Gaylee	108	CG 57

Abbreviations used: Ave – Avenue, A.H. – Agricultural Holding, A.L. – Algemene Landgoed, Blvd – Boulevard, Cen. – Central, Cir. – Circle, Cl. – Close, Cr. – Crescent, Ct – Court, Dr. – Drive, Est. – Estate, Ext. – Extension, Hgts – Heights, Ind. – Industrial, Gdns – Gardens, Gr. – Grove, La. – Lane, (M.Plain) - Mitchells Plain, Nth – North, Pl. – Place, Pk – Park, Rd – Road, Rdg. – Ridge, S.H.– Small Holding, Sq. – Square, St – Street, Sth – South, Ter. – Terrace, Tn – Turn, Val. – Valley, Wk – Walk

STREET NAME	SUBURB NAME	PG	GRID	
Karoo St	Kempenville	88	BY	49
Karoo St	Kleinvlei	127	CJ	58
Karoobos St	Die Oude Spruit	63	BW	56
Karoopoort St	Tafelsig (M.Plain)	145	CR	49
Karos St	Jagtershof	108	CD	57
Karpas St	Richmond	86	BY	41
Karper St	Muizenberg Nth	159	CV	28
Karree Rd	Bonteheuwel	104	CD	39
Karreeboom Rd	Thornton	85	CA	37
Karstens Rd	Selborne	61	BV	47
Kasai Way	Delft	106	CF	49
Kasba St	Wesbank	107	CF	52
Kasouga Rd	Manenberg	104	CH	39
Kasselsvlei Rd	Bellville Sth Ext. 5	88	BZ	49
Kasselsvlei Rd	Beroma	89	BZ	51
Kasselsvlei Rd	Marlow	88	BZ	50
Kastaiing	Delft Sth	125	CJ	49
Kastaiing Ave	Silveroaks	90	CC	56
Kastaiinghout	Weltevrede	94	BY	74
Kastanje St	Vredekloof Hgts	47	BS	55
Kasteel Cr.	Tygerdal	59	BX	39
Kasteel Rd	Wynberg	120	CL	28
Kasteel St	Bothasig	58	BT	38
Kasteel St	Panorama	59	BV	42
Kasteel Steps	Clifton	80	CC	18
Kasteelberg	Brackenfell	63	BW	55
Kasteelberg Cl.	Bonnie Brae	47	BP	57
Kasteelberg Cl.	Bonnie Brae	47	BQ	58
Kasteelberg Rd	Bishop Lavis	104	CE	42
Kasteelberg Rd	The Crest	46	BO	53
Kasteelpoort St	Tafelsig (M.Plain)	145	CS	48
Kasteelpoort St	Tafelsig (M.Plain)	145	CP	50
Kasteelpoort Way	Edgemead	59	BT	39
Kat Ct	Delft	106	CG	48
Kat St	Mfuleni	126	CK	53
Katberg Cr.	Tafelsig (M.Plain)	145	CS	49
Katberg St	Heideveld	103	CF	38
Katberg St	Heideveld	104	CF	39
Katberg St	Ruyterwacht	86	CA	39
Katbos	Stellenbosch	95	BY	75
Katdoring Cr.	Protea Village	64	BV	59
Katdoring St	Eastridge (M.Plain)	145	CR	48
Kate Cl.	Morgenster Hoogte	63	BT	55
Kathleen Rd	Chrismar	61	BW	50
Kati St	Umrhabulo Triangle	147	CR	56
Katie Johannes	William Lloyd	23	BD	92
Katie Martin Way	Kirstenhof	159	CU	27
Katjiepiering Rd	Belhar	105	CD	46
Katonkel St	Gustrow	175	DB	75
Katrine Harries Cl.	Woodlands (M.Plain)	124	CN	45
Katz Cl.	Lekkerwater	184	DA	17
Katzenellenbogen Cr.	Stellenberg	62	BU	51
Katzenellenbogen Rd	Chapman's Peak	156	CX	17
Katzenellenbogen Rd	Meadowsteads	156	CX	18
Katzenellenbogen St	Wynberg	120	CL	27
Kauda St	Mandela Pk	146	CR	54
Kavalier	Jagtershof	90	CC	57
Kavalier St	Jagtershof	108	CD	57
Kay St	Die Oude Spruit	63	BX	56
Kaya St	Lwandle	175	CZ	76
Kayla Cl.	Sunningdale	25	BL	31
Kaymor St	Kaymor	62	BX	53
Kayser Ave	Athlone	102	CF	33
Kayter Rd	Athlone	102	CG	34
Kearns St	Rabiesdale	19	BC	92
Keast St	Loumar	89	BY	52
Keating Way	Ocean View	184	DC	16
Keats Rd	Table View	41	BP	34
Kedah Rd	Rondebosch	102	CG	31
Keel Cl.	Blouberg Sands	24	BM	30
Keerom	Stellenbosch	95	CC	76
Keerom	Wellington	10	AR	93
Keerom St	Cape Town Cen.	82	CB	23
Keerom St	Dal Josafat Ind.	18	BC	90
Keerom St	Franschhoek Nth	75	BX	105
Keerom St	Kleinvlei	127	CJ	58
Keerom St	Kleinvlei	127	CK	58
Keerom St	St Dumas	90	CC	55
Keeromsberg St	Tafelsig (M.Plain)	145	CS	50
Keert-de-Koe	Rondebosch	102	CF	31
Keerweder	Voorbrug	107	CG	51
Keerweder Rd	Vygeboom	46	BR	51
Keerweder St	Voelvlei	89	CA	53
Keerweder St	Vredelust	87	BY	46
Keet	Mostertsdrift	96	CC	79
Kehrwieder St	Welgelegen	59	BV	40
Kei Apple Gr.	Sea Point	80	CA	18
Kei Apple Gr.	Sea Point	80	CA	17
Kei Apple Rd	Sea Point	81	CA	19
Kei Rd	Milnerton	57	BW	31
Kei St	Manenberg	104	CH	39
Keiffer	Die Boord	112	CE	74
Keisergracht St	Bothasig	58	BT	38
Keisergracht Way	Belhar	106	CD	50
Keisi Cr.	Delft	106	CG	49
Keith Rd	Montagu's Gift	142	CO	35
Keizersgracht	District Six	82	CB	24
Keizersgracht	District Six	82	CB	25
Kelkiewyn	Lentegeur (M.Plain)	144	CO	45
Kelkiewyn Cl.	Glen Ive	62	BU	52
Kelly's Green	Summer Greens	58	BV	36
Kelp Rd	Kommetjie	183	DB	12
Kelsey Rd	Highbury	107	CE	54
Kelsey St	Bellavista	18	BC	90
Kelvin Cl.	Fairie Knowe	185	DA	19
Kelvin Cl.	Fairie Knowe	185	DC	22
Kelvin Rd	Bergvliet	140	CR	28
Kelvin Rd	Green Point	81	BZ	21
Kelvin Rd	Newlands	101	CG	29
Kelvin St	Gardens	81	CC	21
Kemms Rd	Wynberg	120	CM	29
Kempen St	Wellington	10	AS	94
Kempen Villas St	Kempenville	61	BX	49
Kempen Villas St	Kempenville	61	BV	48
Kempenfelt Rd	Paarden Eiland	83	CA	28
Kemps Way	Simon's Town	191	DF	24
Ken Cl.	Barbarossa	120	CN	27
Kenali Cl.	Noordhoek	156	CX	18
Kendal Rd	Diep River	140	CP	28
Kendal Rd	Eversdal	61	BT	50
Kendal Rd	Eversdal	62	BT	51
Kendal Rd	Eversdal Hgts	61	BT	50
Kendal Rd	Meadowridge	139	CO	26
Kendal Rd	Meadowridge	140	CO	27
Kendal Service Rd	Meadowridge	140	CO	27
Kendall Ave	Maitland	84	CA	32
Kendall Rd	Lansdowne	121	CJ	33
Kenhardt Rd	Wynberg	120	CM	28
Kenilworth Ave	Milnerton Rdg	41	BS	34
Kenilworth Cr.	Kenilworth	120	CJ	29
Kenilworth Rd	Kenilworth	120	CK	30
Kenilworth St	Beacon Valley (M.Plain)	145	CP	48
Kenjockity Cr.	Sonstraal Hgts	46	BQ	54
Kenmar Cr.	Claremont	120	CJ	28
Kenmore Rd	Lotus River	141	CP	34
Kenmore Rd	Tamboerskloof	81	CB	21
Kenmuir Steps	Simon's Town	191	DE	24
Kennermer Cl.	Sunningdale	25	BM	32
Kennet Rd	Somerset West	151	CS	73
Kenneth Mzati St	Kuyasa	147	CS	55
Kenneth Mzati St	Kuyasa	147	CS	57
Kenneth Rd	Plumstead	120	CN	29
Kennetjie St	Beacon Valley (M.Plain)	145	CP	47
Keno St	Weltevreden Val. (M.Plain)	124	CN	43
Kenridge Ave	Kenridge Hgts	45	BS	48
Kenridge Rd	Kenridge	45	BS	49
Kenridge Rd	Kenridge Hgts	45	BS	48
Kensal Cl.	Parklands	25	BN	32
Kensington	Parklands	41	BO	33
Kensington Cr.	Gardens	81	CC	21
Kensington Cr.	Highbury	107	CE	53
Kensington Cr.	Plattekloof Village	59	BT	42
Kensington Rd	Kensington	84	BZ	32
Kensington Rd	Maitland	84	CA	32
Kensington Rd	Mowbray	101	CD	30
Kensington Rd	Muizenberg	159	CW	30
Kent Cottrell Cl.	Woodlands (M.Plain)	124	CN	44
Kent Cr.	The Range	86	CC	41
Kent Rd	Lotus River	141	CP	34
Kent Rd	Mandalay	125	CM	47
Kent Rd	Newlands	101	CH	27
Kent Rd	Rosebank	101	CE	30
Kent Rd	Wynberg	120	CM	30
Kent St	Belhar	107	CE	51
Kent St	Maitland	84	CA	31
Kent St	Woodstock	83	CB	27
Kent Way	Matroosfontein	86	CC	41
Kentucky Ave	Colorado (M.Plain)	144	CO	43
Kentucky Rd	Ottery	122	CM	35
Kentucky Rd	Ottery	122	CN	36
Kentucky St	Ravensmead	87	CA	44
Kenwil Dr.	Morgenster Hoogte	63	BT	57
Kenwood Rd	Fish Hoek	186	DA	23
Kenwood Rd	Lansdowne	121	CK	33
Kenya Gr.	Lansdowne	121	CK	32
Kerk St	Amandelrug	90	CA	55
Kerk St	Arauna	63	BV	55
Kerk St	Belmont Pk	48	BR	59
Kerk St	Belmont Pk	48	BS	60
Kerk St	Bosonia	89	CB	54
Kerk St	Elim	90	CA	55
Kerk St	Fisantekraal	31	BK	58
Kerk St	Harbour Island	179	DE	77
Kerk St	Kylemore	97	BZ	86
Kerk St	Northern Paarl	18	AZ	88
Kerk St	Northern Paarl	18	AZ	89
Kerk St	Woodlands (M.Plain)	144	CP	44
Kern Cr.	Belhar	88	CC	48
Kerner	Somerset West	151	CR	71
Kerner Cl.	Westlake	159	CU	27
Kerner Rd	Clarkes	86	CC	42
Kerner Rd	Clarkes	86	CB	39
Kerner Rd	Northpine	63	BU	58
Kerry Rd	Fairways	121	CN	32
Kersboom St	Bonteheuwel	104	CD	39
Kersbos	Lentegeur (M.Plain)	144	CP	46
Kersbos	Rouxville	90	BZ	56
Kershout	Arbeidslus	96	CA	80
Kershout	Delft Sth	125	CK	48
Kershout	Delft Sth	125	CK	49
Kershout Cl.	Vredekloof	62	BU	53
Kershout Rd	Noordhoek	156	CV	17
Kershout St	Blommendal	62	BW	51
Kershout St	Eastridge (M.Plain)	145	CR	47
Kershout St	Lotus River	141	CQ	34
Kershout St	Tygerdal	58	BX	37
Kersie Ave	Silveroaks	90	CC	56
Kestel St	Morgenster Hoogte	63	BT	56
Kestel St	Plumstead	141	CO	31
Kestrel	Bergvliet	139	CP	26
Kestrel Cl.	Marconi Beam	57	BT	34
Kestrel Cl.	Westlake Est.	158	CU	24
Kestrel Pl.	Somerset West	152	CR	78
Kestrel St	Eersterivier	128	CM	60
Kestrel St	Eersterivier	128	CJ	61
Kestrel St	Joostenberg	48	BO	62
Kestrel St	Joostenberg	48	BP	61
Kestrel Way	Hout Bay	117	CM	18
Kestrel Way	Montagu's Gift	141	CO	32
Keswick Rd	Flintdale Est.	140	CP	29
Keswick Way	Pinelands	84	CB	34
Ketch Cl.	Eersterivier	128	CM	61
Ketch Cl.	Strandfontein	162	CU	39
Ketch Rd	Strandfontein	162	CU	39
Ketch St	Sun Valley	185	DA	20
Kethelo St	Bloekombos	48	BQ	62
Kettley Way	Rugby	57	BX	31
Keuka St	Shirley Pk	89	BZ	52
Keukendal St	Edgemead	58	BV	38
Keur St	Bonteheuwel	104	CD	40
Keurberg Rd	Bishop Lavis	105	CE	43
Keurboom	Delft Sth	125	CJ	49
Keurboom	Lentegeur (M.Plain)	144	CP	45
Keurboom	Pinelands	84	CC	31
Keurboom Ave	Amandelrug	90	CA	55
Keurboom Ave	Amandelrug	90	CA	56
Keurboom Ave	Belhar	106	CD	47
Keurboom Ave	Brackenfell	63	BV	56
Keurboom Ave	Brackenfell	63	BW	56
Keurboom Ave	New Orleans	18	BB	90
Keurboom Ave	Northpine	64	BU	59
Keurboom Ave	Protea Hoogte	63	BW	57
Keurboom Ave	Somerset West	170	CU	72
Keurboom Ave	Westlake Est.	158	CT	25
Keurboom Cr.	Plattekloof	59	BV	42
Keurboom Cr.	Plattekloof	60	BU	43
Keurboom Cr.	Plattekloof	60	BV	43
Keurboom Rd	Bergvliet	140	CQ	27
Keurboom Rd	Chapman's Peak	156	CX	16
Keurboom Rd	Claremont	101	CH	30
Keurboom Rd	Gordon Strand	175	DC	76
Keurboom Rd	Milnerton	57	BU	33
Keurboom Rd	Stellenberg	62	BU	51
Keurboom Rd	Thornton	85	CA	37
Keurboom St	Eersterivier	128	CN	59
Keurboom St	Eersterivier	128	CJ	61
Keurboom St	Sanddrift	57	BW	34
Keurboom St	Sonstraal	46	BS	52
Keurtjie Ave	Tygerdal	58	BX	38
Keurtjie Cl.	Durbanville	45	BQ	50
Keurtjie Cl.	Perm Gdns	128	CJ	59
Keurtjie Cl.	Perm Gdns	128	CJ	60
Keurtjie Cl.	Uitsig	87	CC	45
Keurtjie Cr.	Roosendaal	107	CF	51
Keurtjie St	Groenvlei	18	BA	89
Kevin Rd	Montagu's Gift	142	CO	35
Kew Rd	Gardens	81	CC	21
Kew Rd	Mowbray	101	CD	30
Kewridge Rd	Edgemead	58	BV	38
Kewuti Cr.	Victoria Mxenge	126	CN	51
Key Link	Avon	86	CA	41
Key Way	Delft	106	CF	49
Keyser River Dr.	Dreyersdal	140	CS	27
Keyser St	Forest Glade	128	CL	59
Keysers Cr.	Delft	106	CG	49
Keysers Rd	Retreat Ind. Area	159	CT	28
Kgosane St	Mandela Pk	147	CQ	55
Khabo St	Crossroads	124	CK	45
Khadi Cr.	Umrhabulo Triangle	147	CR	57
Khadi Cr.	Umrhabulo Triangle	147	CR	58
Khakisa St	Griffiths Mxenge	146	CP	54
Khala St	Wallacedene	48	BS	61
Khaleni	Wellington	15	AU	91
Khalfe Rd	Gatesville	103	CH	36
Khali St	Harare	146	CR	52
Khali St	Harare	146	CR	53
Khalima St	Umrhabulo Triangle	147	CP	57
Khalipha Cr.	Umrhabulo Triangle	147	CQ	58
Khalisa St	Umrhabulo Triangle	147	CP	57
Khamango St	Brown's Farm	124	CM	43
Khan St	Northern Paarl	18	AZ	89
Khanya Cr.	Gugulethu	123	CJ	40
Khanya Rd	Ekuphumuleni	146	CQ	53
Khanya St	Gugulethu	123	CJ	40
Khanyiso St	Lwandle	175	CY	77
Khawuleza St	Umrhabulo Triangle	147	CP	57
Khayalethu	Gugulethu	104	CH	40
Khephu St	Umrhabulo Triangle	147	CR	57
Khethelo Cr.	Nonqubela	126	CN	53
Khetho St	Griffiths Mxenge	146	CQ	54
Khetsha St	Brown's Farm	124	CL	43
Khetsha St	Ilitha Pk	146	CQ	52
Khetshe Rd	Philippi East	125	CM	47
Khokhela Cr.	Umrhabulo Triangle	147	CR	58
Khokho St	Griffiths Mxenge	146	CP	54
Kholosa	Mbekweni	15	AW	92
Khonkxa St	Umrhabulo Triangle	147	CQ	56
Khosi St	Nonqubela	126	CN	52
Khozi Cr.	Philippi East	125	CL	47
Khozi Dr.	Joe Slovo Pk	57	BU	34
Khuhla Cr.	Umrhabulo Triangle	147	CP	56
Khula Cr.	Harare	146	CS	54
Khulani St	Kuyasa	147	CS	55
Khuliza Cr.	Umrhabulo Triangle	147	CP	58
Khulula St	Umrhabulo Triangle	147	CR	58
Khumbula Cr.	Kaya	146	CO	52
Khumbulani St	Dunoon	42	BO	38
Khumbuza Cr.	Umrhabulo Triangle	147	CR	57
Khumshile Cr.	Mxolisi Phetani	125	CM	50
Khupela St	Umrhabulo Triangle	147	CQ	58
Khupha St	Harare	146	CR	52
Khuphelo St	Umrhabulo Triangle	147	CP	57
Khupiso St	Bloekombos	48	BR	62
Khusela Cr.	Harare	146	CR	53
Khuselo Cr.	Victoria Mxenge	146	CO	51
Khusi St	Umrhabulo Triangle	147	CQ	58
Khuthaza St	Harare	146	CR	52
Khwababa St	Bloekombos	48	BR	62
Khwahlaza St	Umrhabulo Triangle	147	CQ	57
Khwapha St	Umrhabulo Triangle	147	CP	58
Khwaza St	Umrhabulo Triangle	147	CR	58
Khwazile St	Ilitha Pk	146	CQ	52
Khwebula Rd	Philippi East	124	CM	46
Khwebula St	Ilitha Pk	146	CQ	52
Khwezi	Mbekweni	15	AW	91
Khwezi	Wellington	15	AU	91
Khwezi Ave	Mfuleni	127	CL	55
Khwezi Cr.	Ilitha Pk	146	CQ	53
Kiaat	Delft Sth	125	CK	49
Kiaat	Weltevrede	94	BY	74
Kiaat Cl.	Eastridge (M.Plain)	145	CR	48
Kiaat Cl.	Vredekloof	62	BT	54
Kiaat Cr.	Loevenstein	60	BV	46
Kiaat Rd	Bonteheuwel	104	CE	39
Kiaat Rd	Kraaifontein Ind.	48	BQ	60
Kiaat St	Firgrove	150	CR	67
Kiaat St	St Dumas	90	CC	56
Kibi Cr.	Victoria Mxenge	126	CN	52
Kiepersol	Delft Sth	106	CH	50
Kiepersol Cl.	Plattekloof	59	BU	42
Kiepersol Cl.	Rouxville	90	CA	56
Kiepersol St	Loevenstein	60	BV	46
Kies La.	Belhar	106	CD	49
Kieskamma Cl.	Portlands (M.Plain)	144	CQ	46
Kiewiet	Kleinvallei	94	CC	73
Kiewiet Ave	Somerset West	171	CT	77
Kiewiet Cl.	D'urbanvale	29	BN	49
Kiewiet Cl.	Westlake Est.	158	CU	25
Kiewiet Cl.	Westlake Est.	158	CT	26
Kiewiet La.	Green Point	81	BY	21
Kiewiet Rd	Bridgetown	103	CE	36
Kiewiet Rd	Bridgetown	103	CE	37
Kiewiet Rd	Mikro Pk	90	CB	56
Kiewiet Rd	Pelikan Pk	142	CS	35
Kiewiet Rd	Sonstraal	46	BS	52
Kiewiet St	Joostenberg	48	BP	60
Kiewiet St	Macassar	149	CR	65
Kiewiet St	Somerset West	152	CR	76
Kiewiet St	William Lloyd	23	BD	94
Kildare	Newlands	101	CH	28
Kildare Cl.	Parklands	25	BM	32
Kildare La.	Claremont	120	CJ	28
Kildare La.	Newlands	101	CH	27
Kildare La.	Newlands	101	CH	28
Kildare Rd	Milnerton	57	BW	32
Kildare Rd	Wynberg	120	CL	30
Kildonan Cl.	West Beach	25	BN	31
Kildonan Rd	Mowbray	101	CD	30
Kilgetty Rd	Rondebosch	101	CG	30
Kilimanjaro St	Tafelsig (M.Plain)	145	CS	48
Kilimanjaro St	Tafelsig (M.Plain)	145	CS	49
Killarney Rd	Killarney Gdns	42	BP	36
Killarney Rd	Killarney Gdns	42	BO	37
Killarney Rd	Muizenberg	159	CX	29
Killarney Rd	Muizenberg	159	CW	27
Killarney St	Oakdale	61	BW	49
Kiln Cl.	Scottsdene	64	BU	60
Kiln Rd	Corobrik	31	BL	55
Kiln Rd	Rugby	57	BX	31
Kim Rd	Surrey	103	CH	38
Kim St	Macassar	149	CR	63
Kimberley Rd	Observatory	83	CC	29
Kimberley Rd	St James	187	CZ	27
Kimberley St	Townsend Est.	85	BY	38
Kimberley St	Townsend Est.	85	BZ	38
Kimberley Way	Portlands (M.Plain)	144	CR	46
Kimberly St	Portlands (M.Plain)	144	CR	46
Kinaboom Cr.	Vredekloof Hgts	47	BS	55
Kinders Rd	Belthorn Est.	121	CJ	34
Kine Cr.	Morgenster	63	BU	56
Kine Park Cr.	Morgenster	63	BU	56
Kinewood Ct	Elnor	86	CB	42
King	Cloetesville	95	BY	75
King Arthur Ave	Hagley	107	CF	53
King Edward La.	Penhill	128	CK	61
King Edward St	Parow	86	BY	42
King Edward St	Parow	87	BY	43
King George St	Ruyterwacht	86	BZ	39
King St	Durbanville	45	BP	50
King St	Gardens	81	CB	21
King St	Hout Bay	137	CQ	16
King St	Manenberg	123	CK	39
King St	Protea Hoogte	63	BW	56
King St	Woodstock	82	CB	26
Kingfisher	Seawinds	159	CU	30
Kingfisher Cl.	Hout Bay	117	CM	17
Kingfisher Cl.	Pelikan Pk	141	CS	34
Kingfisher Cr.	Morgenster Hoogte	63	BT	57
Kingfisher Cr.	Sunridge	41	BP	34
Kingfisher La.	Bergvliet	140	CQ	28

Index to Street Names

Kingfisher La. — Langenhoven St

STREET NAME	SUBURB NAME	PG	GRID
Kingfisher La.	Hout Bay Harbour	136	CR 14
Kingfisher Rd	Flintdale Est.	141	CP 31
Kingfisher Rd	Kommetjie	183	DB 13
Kingfisher St	Durbanville	46	BP 52
Kingfisher St	Pelikan Pk	142	CS 36
Kingfisher St	Westlake Est.	158	CT 25
Kingfisher Wk	Pinelands	102	CD 33
Kingfisher Wk	Sunbird Pk	107	CF 54
Kinghall Ave	Epping Ind.	86	CC 40
Kings Manor	Sonstraal Hgts	46	BR 54
King's Pl.	Pinelands	84	CC 31
Kings Rd	Brooklyn	83	BY 30
Kings Rd	Brooklyn	83	BZ 30
Kings Rd	Mowbray	101	CD 30
Kings Rd	Sea Point	80	CA 18
Kings St	Newlands	101	CG 27
Kings Way	Pinelands	84	CC 33
Kings Way	Plattekloof Village	59	BT 42
Kings Way	Weltevreden Val. (M.Plain)	124	CN 43
Kingsbury Cr.	Highbury	107	CE 53
Kingsburypark Rd	Rondebosch	101	CG 29
Kingsley Rd	Salt River	83	CB 28
Kingsmead Ave	Kingston	61	BX 48
Kingsmead Cl.	The Crest	46	BO 53
Kingsmead Way	Edgemead	58	BV 37
Kingston Cl.	Sunningdale	25	BM 31
Kingston Cl.	Sunningdale	25	BL 33
Kingston Cr.	Somerset West	170	CT 73
Kingston Rd	Rosebank	101	CE 30
Kingstone St	Ravensmead	87	BZ 46
Kingstone St	Ravensmead	87	CA 45
Kingsway Rd	Flintdale Est.	141	CO 31
Kingswood Cl.	Richwood	42	BP 38
Kingswood Cl.	Richwood	42	BO 38
Kinkel Rd	East Rock	62	BU 52
Kinkel Rd	Ferndale	62	BV 53
Kinkel St	Sonnekuil	89	BZ 53
Kinkleway Ave	Claremont	101	CH 29
Kinkleway La.	Claremont	101	CH 29
Kinnoull Rd	Camps Bay	98	CE 18
Kinross Cr.	Fish Hoek	186	DB 23
Kinsale Rd	Fairways	121	CN 32
Kinston Rd	Malibu Village	127	CL 56
Kipling Ave	Mandalay	125	CM 48
Kipling Rd	Windsor Pk	47	BR 57
Kipling St	Bonnie Brae	47	BQ 57
Kipling St	Observatory	83	CB 28
Kirby Rd	Winslow	175	DC 77
Kirby Rd	Winslow	179	DD 77
Kirby Way	Parklands	25	BN 34
Kirch St	Bonteheuwel	104	CE 39
Kirchen Cr.	Silversands	107	CH 53
Kirkia Cl.	Greenlands	88	CA 49
Kirkia St	Somerset West	150	CS 70
Kirkwood Rd	Plumstead	120	CN 29
Kirkwood Rd	Uitsig	87	CB 44
Kirsten Ave	Kommetjie	183	DB 12
Kirsten Rd	Kirstenhof	159	CT 27
Kirsten St	Parow East	87	BY 45
Kirstenbosch Ave	Edgemead	58	BV 38
Kirstenbosch Ave	Strand	174	CZ 73
Kirstenbosch Dr.	Bishopscourt	119	CJ 26
Kirstenbosch Dr.	Bishopscourt	119	CJ 25
Kirstenhof Way	Northpine	63	BU 58
Kirun Rd	Retreat	140	CS 28
Kisch St	Eersterivier	128	CM 60
Kismet Ave	Gatesville	103	CH 36
Kison St	Brackenfell Sth	63	BX 57
Kitchener Rd	Windsor Pk	47	BS 56
Kitchener Rd	Woodstock	83	CB 27
Kitchener St	Avondale	87	BY 44
Kitchener St	Fairfield	87	BY 44
Kite Cl.	Hout Bay	117	CM 17
Kite Rd	Woodlands (M.Plain)	144	CP 44
Kitt St	Eversdal Hgts	45	BS 50
Kittyhawk	Rocklands (M.Plain)	163	CT 45
Kittyhawk Rd	Factreton	84	BY 34
Kiwu Rd North	Joe Slovo Pk	57	BU 34
Kiyane Cr.	Mxolisi Phetani	125	CM 50
Klaas Rd	Brown's Farm	123	CL 41
Klaasen Rd	Wynberg	120	CK 27
Klaasen St	Wellington	15	AT 92
Klaasenbosch Rd	Hohenort	119	CL 24
Klaasenbosch St	Eversdal	61	BU 50
Klaassenbosch Dr.	Hohenort	119	CL 24
Klaassenkop Cl.	Edgemead	59	BT 38
Klaassens Rd	Alphen	119	CK 25
Klaassens Rd	Alphen	119	CK 26
Klaassens Rd	Hohenort	119	CK 25
Klaassens St	Tafelsig (M.Plain)	145	CS 48
Klampenborg Rd	Somerset West	170	CV 72
Klapperbos	Arbeidslus	96	CA 80
Klapperbos	Lentegeur (M.Plain)	144	CO 46
Klapperbos Cl.	Plattekloof	59	BU 42
Klapperbos Cl.	Uitsig	87	CC 45
Klapperbos St	Kewtown	102	CF 34
Klappertjie St	William Lloyd	19	BC 93
Klaproos St	Plumstead	140	CO 28
Klaradyn	Brackenfell	63	BW 55
Klaradyn Cr.	Jamestown	112	CH 74
Klarinet La.	Retreat	159	CT 30
Klarkia St	Lentegeur (M.Plain)	144	CO 45
Klaver St	Sybrand Pk	102	CF 32
Klavier St	Retreat	159	CT 30
Klawervlei Cr.	Voorbrug	107	CG 51
Klawervlei Cr.	Voorbrug	107	CG 53
Klawervlei St	Brackenfell Sth	63	BW 58
Klawervlei St	Brackenfell Sth	63	BV 58
Klein Bron Ave	Vredekloof Hgts	47	BS 55
Klein Cabriere St	Franschhoek Sth	78	BZ 106
Klein Constantia Rd	Huis-in-bos	139	CP 24
Klein Constantia Rd	Nova Constantia	139	CP 23
Klein Drakenstein Rd	Huguenot	18	BC 90
Klein Drakenstein Rd	Paarlzicht	19	BC 91
Klein Drakenstein Rd	William Lloyd	23	BD 94
Klein Helderberg Rd	Somerset West	151	CP 72
Klein Meul St	Lemoenkloof	18	BC 87
Klein Parys Rd	Klein Parys	23	BD 91
Klein Parys Rd	Klein Parys	23	BE 91
Klein Plasie St	Whispering Pines	175	DC 76
Klein Reservoir St	Paarl	22	BE 88
Klein St	District Six	82	CB 25
Klein St	Lemoenkloof	18	BB 88
Klein St	Silveroaks	90	CB 55
Klein St	Woodlands (M.Plain)	144	CP 44
Klein Tuin Rd	Simon's Town	194	DJ 26
Klein Wassenaar Rd	Westlake	159	CV 27
Klein Welgedacht	Welgedacht	60	BT 45
Kleinberg Rd	Bishop Lavis	105	CE 43
Kleinbos Ave	Somerset Pk	171	CW 75
Kleinbos La.	Kleinbos	170	CX 74
Kleinbos La.	Kleinbos	174	CY 73
Kleinbosch Cl.	Langeberg Rdg	47	BR 55
Kleinbosch Cr.	Haasendal	90	CB 57
Kleinbosch St	Kleinbosch	59	BT 40
Kleindal St	Loevenstein	60	BW 46
Kleine Weide	Universiteits-oord	95	CB 77
Kleine Zalze	Stellenbosch	112	CG 73
Kleinhof	Edgemead	58	BV 37
Kleinkaap La.	Brackenfell	63	BV 55
Kleinplaas	Glen Ive	62	BU 51
Kleinrivier St	Somerset West	150	CS 70
Kleinsee St	St Michaels	63	BU 56
Kleinsmidt St	Grassy Pk	141	CQ 33
Kleintuin Rd	Edgemead	59	BT 39
Kleinvallei	Onderpapegaaiberg	94	CC 73
Kleinvlei Rd	Forest Glade	127	CK 58
Kleinvlei Rd	Forest Glade	127	CL 58
Kleinvlei Rd	Park Village	127	CK 58
Kleinweide St	Vredelust	60	BX 46
Klepper St	Bothasig	58	BT 38
Klienbegin Rd	Klein Begin	48	BS 60
Klip Rd	Grassy Pk	141	CP 32
Klip Rd	Knole Pk	142	CO 36
Klip Rd	Lotus River	141	CP 33
Klip Rd	Lotus River	142	CO 35
Klip St	Delft	106	CG 48
Klip St	Franschhoek Sth	78	BZ 106
Klip St	Klippiesdal	19	BC 91
Klip St	Kylemore	97	CA 86
Klip St	Scarborough	192	DJ 18
Klipbok St	Kleinvlei	127	CJ 58
Klipbok St	New Orleans	19	BB 92
Klipbok St	Scottsdene	64	BT 60
Klipdale	Wesbank	107	CH 51
Klipdoring St	Eastridge (M.Plain)	145	CR 48
Klipfontein Rd	Athlone	102	CF 32
Klipfontein Rd	Belgravia	103	CF 35
Klipfontein Rd	Manenberg	104	CG 39
Klipfontein Rd	Mowbray	101	CD 30
Klipfontein Rd	Nyanga	104	CH 42
Klipfontein Rd	Rondebosch	102	CE 31
Klipfontein Rd	Surrey	103	CG 38
Klipfontein Rd	Sybrand Pk	102	CF 32
Klipfontein Rd Ext.	Crossroads	124	CK 45
Klipheuwel Rd	Corobrik	31	BL 56
Klipheuwel Rd	Fisantekraal	31	BJ 57
Klipheuwel Rd	Welgevonden	30	BM 54
Kliphout	Delft Sth	125	CK 49
Klipkers St	Proteavallei	60	BU 46
Klipkers St	Proteavallei	61	BT 47
Klipper Cr.	Sun Valley	185	CZ 20
Klipper Rd	Rondebosch	101	CG 28
Kliprug Cl.	Mitchells Plain	144	CQ 45
Klipspringer Cr.	Eastridge (M.Plain)	145	CR 48
Klipspringer Rd	Loevenstein	60	BV 46
Klipspringer St	Soneike II	89	BZ 54
Klipvygie Cr.	Roosendaal	107	CF 51
Klokboom Cl.	Eikenbosch	90	CC 57
Kloof	Cloetesville	95	BZ 75
Kloof	Cloetesville	95	BZ 76
Kloof Ave	Gardens	81	CB 21
Kloof Ave	Silveroaks	90	CC 56
Kloof Ave	St Dumas	90	CC 56
Kloof La.	Somerset West	152	CS 76
Kloof Nek Rd	Gardens	81	CB 21
Kloof Nek Rd	Gardens	81	CB 22
Kloof Nek Rd	Gardens	81	CC 21
Kloof Rd	Camps Bay	98	CD 18
Kloof Rd	Clifton	80	CC 18
Kloof Rd	Fresnaye	80	CB 18
Kloof Rd	Fresnaye	81	CA 19
Kloof Rd	Harbour Island	179	DE 76
Kloof Rd	Oranjezicht	99	CD 21
Kloof St	Gardens	81	CC 21
Kloof St	Paarl	18	BC 87
Kloof St	Wellington	10	AS 92
Kloofzicht St	Brackenfell Sth	63	BX 58
Klosser St	Parow	87	BY 43
Klossie St	Groenvlei	18	BA 89
Kmdt.Gideon Scheepers Cl.	Welgelegen	59	BU 41
Knights	Jagtershof	90	CC 57
Knightsbridge Ave	Malibu Village	127	CK 55
Knightsbridge Ave	Malibu Village	127	CN 55
Knightsbridge Ave	Noordhoek Manor	157	CX 21
Knightsbridge Ave	Noordhoek Manor	157	CV 20
Knobwood St	Eastridge (M.Plain)	145	CQ 48
Knobwood St	Eastridge (M.Plain)	145	CR 48
Knokke Ave	Table View	41	BP 33
Knole Park Ave	Knole Pk	142	CO 36
Knolvlei St	William Lloyd	19	BC 94
Knoop St	Wellington	15	AT 92
Knopkruid St	Eikenbosch	90	CC 57
Knorhoek Cl.	Strand	174	CY 73
Knorhoek Rd	Voorbrug	107	CG 51
Knuppelhout	Delft Sth	125	CJ 50
Knutsford Rd	Plumstead	120	CM 29
Knysna Cl.	Mitchells Plain	144	CR 46
Knysna Rd	Milnerton	57	BW 32
Koala	Wellington	15	AU 91
Koala	Wellington	15	AT 94
Koala St	Brooklyn	84	BZ 31
Koati St	Kaya	146	CP 51
Kob Rd	Hout Bay Harbour	136	CR 13
Kobodi St	Brown's Farm	124	CL 43
Kobompo St	Delft	106	CG 49
Koch	Krigeville	113	CD 76
Koch	Stellenbosch	113	CD 76
Kodwa St	Umrhabulo Triangle	147	CR 58
Koeberg La.	Belhar	106	CD 49
Koeberg Rd	Brooklyn	84	BY 31
Koeberg Rd	Durbanville	45	BP 50
Koeberg Rd	Maitland	83	CA 30
Koeberg Rd	Marconi Beam	57	BT 34
Koeberg Rd	Milnerton	42	BQ 36
Koeberg Rd	Milnerton	42	BR 35
Koeberg Rd	Milnerton	57	BU 33
Koeberg Rd	Milnerton	57	BV 32
Koeberg Rd	Tijgerhof	57	BW 32
Koeberg Service Rd	Rugby	57	BX 32
Koedoe	Soneike II	89	BZ 54
Koedoe Rd	Ruwari	63	BV 58
Koedoe Rd	Skoongesig	29	BN 50
Koedoe St	Eastridge (M.Plain)	145	CR 49
Koedoe St	Kleinvlei	127	CJ 58
Koedoe St	Macassar	149	CR 65
Koedoe St	Macassar	149	CS 65
Koedoe St	Parowvallei	87	CA 43
Koedoe St	Scottsdene	64	BT 60
Koeglenberg	Klipkop	87	BZ 45
Koekoek St	Amandelsig	90	CB 56
Koekoes Nest	Eversdal Hgts	46	BR 48
Koelen Cl.	Mitchells Plain	144	CR 45
Koelenhof St	Welgedacht	44	BS 46
Koets St	Parow Ind.	87	CB 46
Koetser	Stellenbosch	95	CC 75
Kofu St	Harare	146	CS 54
Kogelberg	Brackenfell	63	BW 55
Kogelberg Cr.	Welgevonden	30	BN 54
Kogelberg Rd	Bishop Lavis	105	CE 43
Kohler St	KWV	22	BG 89
Kohling St	Gardens	81	CB 22
Koi St	Soneike II	89	BZ 54
Kok Way	Belhar	106	CD 49
Kokaboom	Delft Sth	125	CK 49
Kokerboom	Delft Sth	125	CJ 49
Kokerboom	Lentegeur (M.Plain)	144	CO 45
Kokerboom Cr.	St Dumas	90	CC 55
Kokerboom Cr.	St Dumas	108	CD 55
Kokerboom St	Blommendal	62	BW 51
Kokerboom St	Edenpark	62	BU 54
Kokkewiet	Onderpapegaaiberg	94	CC 72
Kokkewiet St	Morningstar	46	BP 51
Kokkewiet St	Morningstar	46	BS 54
Kokoti St	Victoria Mxenge	126	CN 51
Kolanisi St	Nyanga	123	CJ 42
Kolara Cr.	Kenilworth	120	CK 30
Kolbe	Brandwacht	113	CE 77
Kolbe St	William Lloyd	19	BC 92
Kolgaans Cl.	D'urbanvale	29	BN 50
Kollege	Sarepta	89	CC 53
Kollege St	Welgelegen	59	BU 41
Kolobe	Lekkerwater	184	DA 17
Komati Cr.	Bonnie Brook	47	BQ 57
Komati Cr.	Delft	106	CG 49
Komati Cr.	Park Village	127	CK 58
Komati St	Mfuleni	126	CK 53
Komatie Cl.	Portlands (M.Plain)	144	CQ 45
Kombela Cr.	Nonqubela	126	CN 52
Komeet St	Sarepta	89	CC 53
Komlossy St	Cafda Village	141	CS 31
Kommandeur	Simonswyk	95	CB 78
Kommandeur St	Welgemoed	61	BV 47
Kommetjie Blvd	Kommetjie	183	DB 13
Kommetjie Rd	Fish Hoek	186	DA 21
Kommetjie Rd	Fish Hoek	186	DB 24
Kommetjie Rd	Imhoff's Gift	184	DB 15
Kommetjie Rd	Kommetjie	183	DC 13
Kommetjie Rd	Lekkerwater	184	DB 17
Kommetjie Rd	Sunnydale	185	DA 19
Kommissaris St	Welgemoed	60	BU 46
Kommissaris St	Welgemoed	60	BV 46
Kommissaris St	Welgemoed	61	BU 47
Komos Rd	Bosonia	89	CB 54
Kompanie Rd	Capri	185	DB 20
Kompanje St	Avondale	60	BX 44
Kompanjie Cr.	Brackenfell Sth	63	BX 56
Kompanjie Cr.	Brackenfell Sth	63	BV 58
Kompanjie St	Bothasig	42	BS 37
Komsberg	Wellington	15	AV 91
Kongo Way	Portlands (M.Plain)	144	CQ 46
Koning St	Groenvlei	18	BA 88
Koning St	Groenvlei	18	BA 89
Kontiki Ave	Glen Ive	62	BV 52
Kontiki Rd	Penlyn Est.	103	CH 35
Kontoer St	Tafelsig (M.Plain)	145	CR 48
Koodoo St	Kewtown	102	CE 34
Koodoo St	Kewtown	103	CE 35
Kool Ave	Kleinvlei	127	CJ 58
Koolhout Cl.	Eastridge (M.Plain)	145	CR 47
Koonap St	Delft	106	CG 49
Koopman	Belhar	106	CE 49
Koopman	Belhar	106	CH 48
Koopman	Die Bos	174	CY 74
Koopman St	Wellington	15	AV 92
Koopmans Ave	Scottsdene	64	BT 59
Koor St	Dalvale	19	AZ 92
Koornhof St	Nyanga	123	CK 42
Koornhoop	Edgemead	58	BU 38
Koornhoop Cl.	Mitchells Plain	144	CQ 43
Koornhoop Rd	Mitchells Plain	144	CQ 44
Koornhoop Rd	Mowbray	101	CD 30
Koorsboom	Delft Sth	125	CJ 49
Koorsboom Cr.	Vredekloof	62	BT 54
Koorsboom St	St Dumas	90	CC 56
Koorzen St	Strand Halt	170	CW 74
Koos Faure	Boschenmeer Est.	22	BH 90
Koosani Ave	Sea Point	80	CA 18
Koosani Ave	Sea Point	80	CA 17
Koper St	Brackenfell Ind.	63	BT 57
Koperkring	Vanguard	103	CF 38
Koppel St	Northern Paarl	18	AZ 88
Koppies Rd	Groenvallei	62	BX 52
Koppiesdam Rd	Bishop Lavis	104	CD 41
Koppiesdam Rd	Bishop Lavis	104	CD 42
Koppiesdam Rd	Bishop Lavis	105	CD 43
Koraal Cl.	Welgelegen	59	BU 40
Koraal St	Ottery	121	CN 33
Koraalboom	Delft Sth	125	CJ 49
Koraalboom	Delft Sth	125	CK 50
Koraalboom St	Blommendal	62	BW 51
Koraalboom St	Vredekloof	62	BT 53
Korfbal St	Beacon Valley (M.Plain)	145	CP 47
Korhaan	Jagtershof	90	CC 57
Korhaan	Rocklands (M.Plain)	144	CS 44
Korhaan Rd	Durbanville	46	BP 52
Korhaan St	Electric City	127	CN 58
Korhaan St	Somerset West	152	CS 76
Koring Rd	Belthorn Est.	121	CJ 34
Koring Rd	Durbanville	45	BP 49
Koring Rd	Durbanville	45	BP 47
Koringblom St	Annandale	90	BZ 55
Koringblom St	Bloemhof	61	BV 50
Korne Cl.	Belgravia	102	CH 34
Kornet	Steenberg	159	CT 30
Korsten Cr.	Wesbank	107	CG 51
Kort St	Belrail	88	BY 48
Kort St	Ferndale	62	BW 54
Kort St	Green Point	81	BZ 20
Kort St	Lemoenkloof	18	BB 88
Kort St	Macassar	149	CR 64
Kort St	Maitland	84	CA 34
Kort St	Park Estates	174	CY 72
Kort St	Peerless Pk Nth	48	BQ 59
Kortgedacht Cl.	Kenridge Hgts	45	BS 48
Kortgedacht Cl.	Kenridge Hgts	45	BP 47
Korvette Cl.	Strandfontein	162	CT 39
Korvette Cl.	Strandfontein	162	CV 42
Korvette Rd	Strandfontein	161	CU 38
Korvette Rd	Strandfontein	162	CT 39
Korvette Rd	Strandfontein	162	CV 42
Kosmos Rd	Uitsig	87	CB 45
Kosmos St	Bellville Sth	88	CA 49
Kota Cl.	Nonqubela	126	CN 52
Kottler St	Labiance	89	BZ 51
Kotze Rd	Scottsville	47	BS 57
Kotze St	Denneburg	22	BD 90
Kotze St	Gardens	81	CC 21
Kotze St	Sanlamhof	88	BY 50
Kotzee Rd	Observatory	101	CD 29
Kouga St	Kaymor	62	BX 52
Kouga Way	Delft	106	CG 49
Kowie Cl.	Delft	106	CG 49
Kowie Cl.	Portlands (M.Plain)	144	CQ 45
Kowie Rd	Mowbray	102	CD 31
Koyini St	Nomzano	175	CY 76
Koyo Cr.	Nonqubela	126	CN 52
Koyo St	Wallacedene	48	BS 61
Kraai	Rocklands (M.Plain)	144	CS 44
Kraai St	Mfuleni	126	CJ 53
Kraai Way	Delft	106	CG 49
Kraaibos Cl.	Eastridge (M.Plain)	145	CR 48
Kraaiscot	Amandelsig	90	CB 56
Kraal Rd	Knole Pk	142	CO 37
Kraal Rd	Schaap Kraal	142	CQ 37
Kraansduif St	Jacarandas	90	CC 57
Kraanvoël	Rocklands (M.Plain)	144	CS 44
Kraanvoël St	William Lloyd	23	BD 94
Krag Rd	Ottery East	121	CN 33
Krakeel St	Kaymor	62	BX 53

Abbreviations used: Ave – Avenue, A.H. – Agricultural Holding, A.L. – Algemene Landgoed, Blvd – Boulevard, Cen. – Central, Cir. – Circle, Cl. – Close, Cr. – Crescent, Ct – Court, Dr. – Drive, Est. – Estate, Ext. – Extension, Hgts – Heights, Ind. – Industrial, Gdns – Gardens, Gr. – Grove, La. – Lane, (M.Plain) - Mitchells Plain, Nth – North, Pl. – Place, Pk – Park, Rd – Road, Rdg. – Ridge, S.H.– Small Holding, Sq. – Square, St – Street, Sth – South, Ter. – Terrace, Tn – Turn, Val. – Valley, Wk – Walk

STREET NAME	SUBURB NAME	PG	GRID	
Kramat Rd	Macassar	148	CR	62
Kramat Rd	Macassar	148	CP	62
Kransduinen Cl.	Mitchells Plain	144	CR	45
Kransduinen Cl.	Mitchells Plain	144	CS	43
Kranskop Ct	Townsend Est.	58	BX	37
Kranzkop Rd	Heideveld	104	CG	40
Kranzkop Rd	Heideveld	104	CF	42
Krause St	Eersterivier	128	CM	61
Krebe St	Kuyasa	147	CR	55
Krele St	Lwandle	175	CZ	76
Kremer Rd	Salt River	83	CB	27
Kremetart	Delft Sth	125	CK	49
Kremetart	Vredekloof	62	BT	53
Kremetart Ave	Silveroaks	90	CC	56
Kremetart Cl.	Loevenstein	60	BW	45
Kremetart St	Somerset Hgts	127	CK	57
Kreupelboom Rd	Welgedacht	60	BT	46
Kreupelbosch Way	Belle Constantia	139	CO	25
Kreupelhout	Lentegeur (M.Plain)	144	CO	46
Kreupelhout Cl.	Plattekloof	59	BU	42
Kreupelhout La.	Devil's Peak Est.	82	CC	24
Krieger Rd	Heathfield	140	CR	29
Krieket Rd	Penlyn Est.	103	CH	35
Kriel Rd	Aurora	45	BQ	48
Kriel St	Elim	89	CA	54
Kriel St	Klipkop	87	BZ	45
Kriel St	Wellington	10	AS	93
Krige St	Churchill	59	BX	42
Krige St	Peerless Pk Nth	48	BQ	59
Krige St	Stanlou	61	BX	47
Krige St	Stellenbosch	95	CC	75
Kringboom	Delft Sth	125	CK	49
Kringboom	Delft Sth	125	CK	50
Kringhout St	Eastridge (M.Plain)	145	CR	47
Krisant Cir.	Sonnekuil	89	BZ	54
Krisant Rd	Durbanville	46	BQ	53
Krisant St	Blomtuin	62	BW	51
Krisante Rd	Uitsig	87	CB	45
Krisante Rd	Uitsig	87	CC	45
Kristal Cr.	Wellington	15	AT	92
Kristal St	Shirley Pk	89	BY	52
Kristal St	Sonstraal	46	BR	52
Kritzinger Rd	Lansdowne	121	CJ	33
Kritzwald Rd	Lansdowne	121	CJ	33
Krokodil Cl.	Eastridge (M.Plain)	145	CR	48
Krokodil Way	Delft	106	CG	49
Krom	Wellington	10	AR	94
Krom Cr.	Delft	106	CF	49
Krom Elbow La.	Cape Town Cen.	82	CB	23
Krom Rd	Bergvliet	140	CQ	28
Krom St	Mfuleni	126	CJ	53
Krom St	Rondebosch East	102	CH	32
Krom St	Scottsville	47	BS	58
Krom St	Vredelust	60	BX	46
Kromboom Parkway	Lansdowne	121	CK	31
Kromboom Parkway	Mowbray	102	CE	31
Kromboom Parkway	Rondebosch East	102	CG	32
Kromboom Rd	Belgravia	102	CG	34
Kromboom Rd	Rondebosch East	102	CG	32
Kromhout	Die Wingerd	113	CE	75
Kromme Rhee Rd	Koelenhof	67	BU	71
Krommerivier	Stellenbosch	95	CB	76
Kromriver Cl.	Portlands (M.Plain)	144	CP	46
Kroneberg St	Wellington	10	AS	93
Kronen Cl.	Guldenland	174	CZ	74
Kronendal	Dalsig	113	CD	76
Kronendal Cr.	Eversdal	62	BT	52
Kronendal Pl.	Somerset West	171	CU	78
Kronendal Rd	Edgemead	58	BU	37
Kronendal Rd	Kirstenhof	159	CU	27
Kronendal Rd	Mitchells Plain	144	CQ	44
Kronkel St	Northern Paarl	18	AZ	88
Kronkel St	Stanlou	61	BX	48
Kroonden Rd	Northpine	63	BU	57
Kroondenne Ave	Amandelrug	90	CA	56
Kroonenburg Sq.	Monte Vista	59	BV	40
Kruger Rd	Lansdowne	121	CK	34
Kruger St	Franschhoek Sth	79	BZ	107
Kruger St	Kempenville	88	BY	49
Kruger St	Park Estates	174	CY	71
Kruger St	St Dumas	90	CC	55
Kruin St	Brackenfell Sth	63	BW	58
Kruin St	Protea Hoogte	63	BW	57
Kruin St	Protea Village	63	BV	58
Kruin St	Protea Village	64	BV	59
Kruinzicht Cr.	Uitzicht	47	BO	55
Kruiphout Cl.	Protea Village	63	BW	58
Kruis Rd	Belhar	106	CD	49
Kruis Rd	Brackenfell	63	BV	55
Kruis Rd	Brackenfell	63	BV	56
Kruis Rd	Brackenfell	63	BV	57
Kruis Rd	Brackenfell Sth	63	BW	58
Kruis Rd	Brackenfell Sth	63	BX	58
Kruis Rd	Brackenfell Sth	90	BY	58
Kruis Rd	Everite	63	BU	57
Kruis St	District Six	82	CB	25
Kruis St	Lemoenkloof	18	BB	88
Kruisbessie Cl.	Eastridge (M.Plain)	145	CR	48
Kruisrivier Cr.	Welgevonden	30	BN	54
Kruisvallei Ave	Voorbrug	107	CG	51
Kruitvat Ave	Nieuw Maastrecht	44	BS	44
Krupp Ave	Door De Kraal	61	BT	47
Kruskal Ave	Cape Town Cen.	88	BY	48
Kruyer St	Ottery	121	CM	33
Krymekaar St	Macassar	149	CS	64

STREET NAME	SUBURB NAME	PG	GRID	
Krynauw St	Gardens	81	CB	22
Kuba St	Harare	146	CR	54
Kubekuhle St	Mxolisi Phetani	126	CM	51
Kubusie St	Mfuleni	126	CJ	52
Kudido St	Nonqubela	126	CN	53
Kudu Ave	Lotus River	142	CP	35
Kudu Rd	Loevenstein	60	BW	46
Kudu St	New Orleans	19	BA	92
Kudu St	New Orleans	19	BB	92
Kudu Way	Zoo Pk	47	BR	56
Kufa St	Crossroads	124	CK	44
Kugala Ave	Nyanga	124	CK	43
Kuhle St	Umrhabulo Triangle	147	CQ	57
Kuilenhof Ct	Edgemead	58	BU	38
Kuils Rd	Delft	106	CG	49
Kuils Rd	Hazendal	102	CE	33
Kuils River Freeway	Belhar	107	CE	51
Kuils River Freeway	Kaymor	62	BW	54
Kuils River Freeway	Kaymor	89	BY	53
Kuils River Freeway	Sarepta	89	CC	52
Kuils River Freeway	Voelvlei	89	CA	52
Kuils River Freeway	Voorbrug	107	CH	51
Kuiper Cr.	Morgen Gronde	63	BX	56
Kuiperskraal St	De Bron	45	BS	48
Kukhanya Cr.	Mxolisi Phetani	125	CM	50
Kukhanya St	Nyanga	123	CK	42
Kula Cr.	Nonqubela	126	CN	53
Kula St	Tarentaalplaas	175	CY	75
Kulungile St	Lwandle	175	CZ	76
Kuluxhobo St	Philippi East	124	CM	46
Kume Cr.	Nonqubela	126	CN	53
Kumkani St	Umrhabulo Triangle	147	CQ	56
Kunene Cir.	Marconi Beam	57	BT	34
Kunene Cr.	Delft	106	CG	49
Kunene Rd	Bonnie Brook	47	BQ	56
Kunene Rd	Primrose Pk	122	CJ	38
Kunene St	Mfuleni	126	CJ	53
Kunene Way	Groenvallei	62	BX	53
Kunene Way	Portlands (M.Plain)	144	CQ	46
Kuphumleni St	Wimbledon	108	CG	55
Kurkbos	Delft Sth	125	CJ	48
Kurper Cl.	Pelikan Pk	141	CQ	34
Kurper Cl.	Soneike II	89	BZ	53
Kurper Rd	Nooitgedacht	104	CE	42
Kuruman Ct	Delft	106	CG	49
Kuruman St	Mfuleni	126	CJ	52
Kurze Rd	Silversands	107	CH	54
Kusasa Rd	Kaya	146	CO	51
Kusile St	Kaya	146	CP	51
Kuthu St	Lwandle	175	CZ	77
Kuyasa Cr.	Mxolisi Phetani	125	CM	49
Kuyper Cr.	Belhar	107	CE	51
Kuyper St	District Six	82	CB	24
Kwagga St	Goedemoed	46	BO	53
Kwagga St	Goedemoed	46	BO	54
Kwagga St	Kleinvlei	127	CJ	58
Kwakho St	Umrhabulo Triangle	147	CQ	57
Kwakhona St	Umrhabulo Triangle	147	CP	58
Kwalimanzi Cr.	Philippi East	125	CM	47
Kwando St	Delft	106	CG	49
Kwanele St	Mxolisi Phetani	125	CM	50
Kwankanya St	Umrhabulo Triangle	147	CQ	57
Kwartel St	Amandelsig	90	CB	56
Kwartel St	Morningstar	46	BP	51
Kwarts	Welgelegen	59	BT	40
Kwarts St	Bellville	62	BV	51
Kwazakhele Cr.	Wesbank	107	CG	51
Kweek St	Lemoenkloof	18	BB	89
Kweek St	Wellington	10	AR	91
Kweker Rd	Mitchells Plain	144	CQ	45
Kwelikangotshe Cr.	Philippi East	124	CN	46
Kwenxura St	Mfuleni	126	CK	53
Kwepeli St	Brown's Farm	124	CM	43
Kweper	Delft Sth	125	CJ	50
Kweper Ave	Bridgetown	103	CE	36
Kweper St	Mitchells Plain	144	CQ	44
Kweper Way	Rusdal	108	CE	57
Kwepile	Philippi East	125	CM	47
Kwezi	Dunoon	42	BO	37
Kwezi Rd	Thembokwezi	125	CM	49
Kwezi St	Lwandle	175	CZ	76
Kwikkie	Amandelsig	90	CB	56
Kwikkie St	Amstelhof	23	BD	93
Kwikkie St	Wellington	15	AT	92
Kwikstert	Onderpapegaaiberg	94	CC	72
Kwindla	Mbekweni	15	AV	91
Kwindla St	Mxolisi Phetani	125	CM	50
Kyalami Dr.	Killarney Gdns	42	BP	37
Kyalami Dr.	Killarney Gdns	42	BP	36
Kyalami St	Beacon Valley (M.Plain)	145	CP	48
Kylah Way	Durbanville	45	BQ	49
Kyle St	Park Estates	174	CY	72
Kylemore Cl.	Mitchells Plain	144	CR	45
Kylemore Cl.	Mitchells Plain	144	CS	43
Kylemore Rd	Woodstock	82	CC	26
Kynoch Rd	Somerset West	169	CT	70
L				
L.C.Steyn Cr.	De Duin	59	BW	41
L.Eleni Rd	Nyanga	123	CJ	42
L.Mbuli St	Mandela Pk	146	CQ	54
L.R. Glen Steps	Gardens	81	CC	21
L.Yeko Cl.	Nyanga	123	CJ	42
L.Yeko Cl.	Nyanga	123	CM	39
La Barrage Ave	Somerset West	151	CS	72

STREET NAME	SUBURB NAME	PG	GRID	
La Belle St	Kaymor	62	BX	53
La Belle St	Kaymor	89	BY	53
La Boheme Ave	Scottsdene	64	BT	60
La Boheme Ave	Scottsdene	64	BT	61
La Boheme Ave	Wallacedene	48	BS	61
La Boheme St	Eastridge (M.Plain)	145	CR	49
La Bri	Oude Westhof	44	BS	45
La Camargue Rd	Milnerton	57	BT	33
La Cases Rd	Newlands	101	CH	27
La Chalet	Parklands	25	BM	33
La Champagne Cl.	La Rochelle	62	BV	51
La Colline	Stellenbosch	95	CA	76
La Constance Cr.	Durmonte	30	BN	52
La Constance Cr.	Durmonte	30	BM	53
La Cotta St	Franschhoek Sth	79	BY	107
La Cotte Cr.	Edgemead	58	BV	37
La Cotte St	Oak Glen	62	BW	52
La Dauphine	Kirstenhof	158	CU	26
La Dauphine Cl.	Mitchells Plain	144	CR	45
La Dauphine Cl.	Mitchells Plain	144	CR	44
La Domaine Cr.	Stikland Hospital	62	BW	51
La Estancia Cl.	Somerset West	152	CS	75
La Gratitude	Pinelands	85	CB	35
La Gratitude Rd	Glen Ive	62	BU	52
La Hey Cl.	Somerset West	151	CR	71
La Meer	Sonstraal Hgts	46	BR	54
La Merci I	Sonstraal Hgts	46	BQ	53
La Merci II	Sonstraal Hgts	46	BQ	53
La Mode St	Paarl	22	BD	88
La Motte B.P. Rd	Franschhoek Nth	74	BV	102
La Motte Cl.	Richwood	42	BP	37
La Motte Cr.	Panorama	59	BV	42
La Motte Rd	La Rochelle	62	BV	51
La Motte St	Die Bos	174	CY	74
La Motte St	Northpine	64	BU	59
La Motte Station Rd	Franschhoek Nth	74	BW	102
La Paloma Blvd	Bloubergstrand	24	BJ	27
La Paris Cl.	Welgelegen	59	BU	40
La Piazza	Somerset West	171	CT	75
La Provence Ave	Voorbrug	107	CG	51
La Provence Cr.	Edgemead	58	BV	37
La Provence Cr.	Mitchells Plain	144	CQ	44
La Provence Rd	Franschhoek Sth	78	BY	105
La Provence Rd	Welgelegen	59	BT	40
La Provence Rd	Welgelegen	59	BU	40
La Provence Rd	William Lloyd	23	BE	92
La Provence Way	Everglen	46	BS	51
La Provence Way	La Rochelle	62	BV	51
La Provence Way	Mitchells Plain	144	CQ	43
La Province Cr.	Eersterivier	128	CL	59
La Rambla Ave	Bloubergstrand	24	BJ	27
La Rhone	D'urbanvale	45	BO	49
La Rhone	Kirstenhof	158	CU	26
La Rhone Way	Edgemead	58	BV	37
La Roche Cl.	La Rochelle	62	BV	52
La Roche St	Die Bos	174	CY	74
La Roche St North	Northern Paarl	18	AZ	88
La Roche St South	Northern Paarl	18	AZ	88
La Rochelle St	Wellington	11	AR	95
La Rochelle Cr.	Eersterivier	128	CL	59
La Rochelle Rd	Everglen	45	BS	50
La Rochelle Rd	La Rochelle	62	BV	51
La Rochelle Rd	La Rochelle	62	BV	52
La Rochelle St	Franschhoek Sth	79	BZ	107
La Rochelle Way	Edgemead	58	BV	37
La Rosera St	Sunningdale	25	BM	31
La Rozette Rd	Dennemere	108	CH	58
La Sagra Rd	Montana/Durrheim	104	CF	42
La Sandra Cl.	Somerset West	152	CS	75
La Scala Rd	Strandfontein	162	CT	42
La St	Macassar	149	CS	65
La Stancia	Somerset West	152	CR	75
La Veritas	Welgedacht	44	BS	46
La Verona	Skilpadvlei	45	BP	49
La Verona Cr.	Somerset Rdg	170	CU	72
La Vie Cr.	Groenvlei	18	BA	88
Laai	Cloetesville	95	BZ	75
Laban Van Rooi St	Wellington	15	AV	92
Labiance St	Labiance	89	BZ	51
Labiance St	Labiance	89	BZ	52
Laborie Ave	Somerset West	171	CT	78
Laborie St	Courtrai	22	BH	88
Labourere St	Oranjezicht	82	CC	23
Lacre Rd	Lansdowne	121	CK	34
Lacus St	Perm Gdns	128	CK	59
Ladan Rd	Kalk Bay	186	DA	26
Ladbrook Rd	Lansdowne	121	CK	32
Ladies Mile Rd	Bergvliet	139	CP	26
Ladies Mile Rd	Bergvliet	140	CQ	27
Ladies Mile Rd Ext.	Gaylands	119	CN	25
Ladies Mile Service Rd	Bergvliet	140	CQ	27
Lady Anne Ave	Newlands	101	CH	27
Lady Annes Wk	Brooklyn	84	BZ	31
Lady Grey Rd	Fish Hoek	186	DA	23
Lady Grey St	Paarl	18	BC	89
Lady Loch Rd	Wellington	9	AQ	90
Lady Loch Rd	Wellington	10	AQ	91
Lady May St	Athlone	102	CF	32
Lady Way	Somerset West	171	CX	77
Laetitia Rd	Chrismar	61	BW	50
Laetitia St	Casablanca	175	DB	76
Lafayette Ave	Klein Parys	23	BD	91
Lager Cr.	Eyethu	146	CO	53
Lagonda Cr.	Beacon Valley (M.Plain)	145	CQ	48
Lagoon Gate Dr.	Metro Ind. Township	56	BX	30

STREET NAME	SUBURB NAME	PG	GRID	
Laguna Rd	Killarney Gdns	42	BP	36
Lahey Sq.	Scottsdene	64	BT	61
Lahey St	Scottsdene	64	BT	61
Lahlangubo Cl.	Philippi East	124	CM	46
Lahleka St	Griffiths Mxenge	146	CQ	54
Laiaane Ave	Eversdal Hgts	45	BS	50
Laidlaw Rd	Rondebosch	101	CH	30
Laindon St	Lansdowne	121	CK	33
Lainsberg Rd	Heideveld	104	CF	40
Lair Ave	Hout Bay	136	CO	14
Lakay	Tennantville	95	CA	75
Lakay St	William Lloyd	23	BD	92
Lake Cl.	Kraaifontein	47	BQ	57
Lake Rd	Frogmore Est.	159	CU	28
Lake Rd	Grassy Pk	141	CP	33
Lake Rd	Grassy Pk	141	CQ	34
Lake View Rd	Bergvliet	139	CQ	26
Lakeman Cr.	Dennemere	108	CH	57
Lakeshore Dr.	The Lakes	185	CZ	19
Lakeside Pl.	Capricorn	160	CW	31
Lakeside Rd	Capricorn	160	CV	31
Lakeside St	Ruyterwacht	86	BZ	40
Lakeview Dr.	Retreat	140	CS	28
Lakeview La.	Muizenberg	159	CX	28
Lakey St	Firgrove	150	CR	67
Lakpypie Cl.	Roosendaal	107	CF	51
Lali Cl.	Umrhabulo Triangle	147	CR	56
Lali St	Victoria Mxenge	126	CN	52
Lalo	Delft Sth	125	CK	48
Lambatha Cl.	Umrhabulo Triangle	147	CQ	58
Lambert Rd	Vredehoek	82	CC	24
Lambeth Cl.	Eersterivier	128	CM	59
Lambrecht St	Huguenot	18	BB	90
Lambrechts St	Franschhoek Sth	79	BZ	108
Lambrechts St	Franschhoek Sth	79	CA	109
Lamento Cl.	Brackenfell Sth	63	BX	57
Lamla	Kayamandi	94	CA	74
Lamoderne St	Mountain View	19	BB	91
Lancashire Cl.	Kirstenhof	159	CU	27
Lancashire Cl.	Kirstenhof	159	CW	27
Lancashire Rd	Lansdowne	121	CK	34
Lancaster	Gordon Strand	179	DD	76
Lancaster	Rocklands (M.Plain)	144	CS	46
Lancaster Rd	Gordon Strand	175	DC	75
Lancaster Rd	Kenilworth Pk	120	CK	30
Lancaster Rd	Mowbray	102	CD	31
Lancaster Rd	Rondebosch	101	CF	30
Lancaster St	Claremont	120	CJ	29
Lancaster St	Hout Bay	136	CP	14
Lancaster St	Hout Bay	137	CP	15
Lancaster St	The Hague	106	CF	50
Lancelot Rd	Fish Hoek	186	DA	23
Lancelot Village	Sonstraal Hgts	46	BR	54
Lancer Cl.	Kraaifontein	47	BQ	58
Landa St	Harare	146	CR	54
Landani Cr.	Mxolisi Phetani	125	CM	50
Landdros Ave	Salberau	86	CB	41
Landdroskop Dr.	Somerset West	171	CT	78
Landdrost St	Brooklyn	84	BZ	31
Landela St	Umrhabulo Triangle	147	CQ	57
Landelani St	Dunoon	42	BO	38
Landers Cl.	Fairie Knowe	185	DA	19
Landri Cr.	Edenpark	62	BU	54
Landros St	Bellville	88	BY	47
Landroskop Dr.	Somerset West	172	CT	79
Landseer Rd	Mowbray	101	CD	30
Landskoon Cr.	De Tuin	47	BS	55
Landskroon	Vygeboom	46	BR	51
Landskroon Rd	Vygeboom	46	BR	51
Landskroon Rd	Vygeboom	46	BS	54
Landskroon St	Welgedacht	44	BS	45
Landzela Cr.	Victoria Mxenge	126	CN	51
Lane	Woodstock	83	CB	26
Lang	Cloetesville	94	BY	74
Lang	Cloetesville	95	BY	75
Lang	Cloetesville	95	BZ	75
Lang	Weltevrede	94	BY	74
Lang St	Belmont Pk	48	BR	60
Lang St	De Kuilen	89	CB	54
Lang St	Groenvlei	18	AZ	88
Lang St	Klein Begin	48	BS	60
Lang St	Northern Paarl	18	AZ	89
Lang St South	Stellenbosch	95	CA	75
Langa Cr.	Eyethu	146	CO	54
Langa St	Kuyasa	147	CR	56
Langbeentjie Cl.	Protea Village	64	BW	59
Langeberg Rd	Durbanville	46	BP	52
Langeberg Rd	Eversdal	62	BU	51
Langeberg Rd	Langeberg Rdg	47	BQ	56
Langeberg Rd	Lavender Hill East	160	CU	32
Langeberg St	Tafelsig (M.Plain)	145	CS	49
Langelier	Stellenbosch	95	BY	75
Langemere Cl.	Edgemead	59	BU	39
Langemere Rd	Northpine	63	BU	58
Langenegger St	Strand Halt	170	CW	74
Langenhoven	Stellenbosch	95	CB	75
Langenhoven Ave	Amstelhof	23	BD	93
Langenhoven Ave	Paarl	22	BD	89
Langenhoven Ave	Paarl	22	BD	90
Langenhoven St	Boston	61	BX	48
Langenhoven St	Boston	61	BW	47
Langenhoven St	Durbanville	45	BP	50
Langenhoven St	Flintdale Est.	141	CP	31
Langenhoven St	Ruyterwacht	86	CA	40
Langenhoven St	Soneike I	89	BZ	54

STREET NAME	SUBURB NAME	PG	GRID
Langeni	Mbekweni	15	AX 91
Langeni St	Driftsands	125	CL 50
Langeni St	Driftsands	126	CL 51
Langerman Ave	Milnerton	57	BU 33
Langerman Ave	Milnerton	57	BV 32
Langeveldt	Idasvallei	96	CA 80
Langevlei Rd	Retreat	140	CR 29
Langgedacht Cl.	Kenridge Hgts	45	BS 48
Langgedacht Cl.	Kenridge Hgts	45	BP 47
Langham St	Maitland	84	CA 31
Langham St	Wellington	10	AS 92
Langkloof Cl.	Belhar	107	CE 51
Langkloof Cl.	Mitchells Plain	144	CR 45
Langkloof Cl.	Mitchells Plain	144	CS 43
Langkloof Way	Edgemead	58	BU 38
Langkloofberg Dr.	Somerset West	152	CS 78
Langley Rd	Parklands	25	BN 34
Langley Rd	Wynberg	120	CM 28
Langton Rd	Mowbray	101	CD 30
Languedoc	Pinelands	85	CB 35
Languedoc Rd	Edgemead	58	BV 37
Langverwacht Rd	Eikenbosch	90	CC 57
Langverwacht Rd	Silveroaks	90	CB 55
Langverwacht Rd	Zevenwacht	91	CB 59
Langverwacht St	Fisantekraal	31	BJ 58
Laninch Rd	Sunningdale	25	BM 32
Lanner Cl.	Somerset West	172	CT 79
Lanquedoc	Groenvlei	18	BA 88
Lansburg Rd	Hanover Pk	122	CJ 36
Lansdowne Rd	Brown's Farm	123	CL 42
Lansdowne Rd	Claremont	120	CJ 30
Lansdowne Rd	Eyethu	146	CP 54
Lansdowne Rd	Lansdowne	121	CJ 32
Lansdowne Rd	Lansdowne	121	CK 33
Lansdowne Rd	Mxolisi Phetani	125	CN 50
Lansdowne Rd	Nonqubela	126	CM 52
Lansdowne Rd	Philippi	124	CK 45
Lansdowne Rd	Philippi East	125	CL 48
Lansdowne Rd	Schaap Kraal	122	CL 35
Lansdowne Rd	Schaap Kraal	123	CL 39
Lansdowne Rd	Umrhabulo Triangle	147	CQ 57
Lansia Wk	Hanover Pk	122	CJ 37
Lansia Wk	Hanover Pk	122	CK 37
Lansing Rd	Grassy Pk	141	CR 31
Lansing Rd	Pelikan Pk	141	CS 31
Lansman Wk	Hanover Pk	122	CK 36
Lansport Rd	Hanover Pk	122	CK 37
Lansry Wk	Hanover Pk	122	CK 35
Lansur Rd	Hanover Pk	122	CK 35
Lantana	Lentegeur (M.Plain)	145	CO 47
Lantana Rd	Uitsig	87	CB 44
Lantana Rd	Uitsig	87	CB 45
Lantana St	Klein Nederburg	19	BC 92
Lantana St	Ottery	121	CN 33
Lantana St	Somerset West	151	CS 71
Lantana St	William Lloyd	19	BC 93
Lanyon Rd	Rondebosch	102	CG 31
Lanzarac Cl.	Table View	41	BO 32
Lanzerac	Karindal	96	CC 79
Lanzerac Cl.	Sonnekuil	89	BZ 53
Lanzerac Cr.	Belhar	106	CE 50
Lanzerac Cr.	Vredekloof	62	BT 54
Lanzerac Rd	Philippi East	124	CL 45
Lanzerac Way	Bellair	62	BV 52
Lappen	Stellenbosch	95	CA 75
Lapperts St	Paarlzicht	19	BC 91
Lara Cl.	Mandalay	125	CN 48
Lara Cl.	Weltevreden Val. (M.Plain)	124	CN 44
Lara St	William Lloyd	23	BD 92
Larch Rd	Bonteheuwel	104	CE 39
Largo	Sonstraal Hgts	46	BR 53
Largo Cr.	Brackenfell Sth	63	BX 57
Largo Rd	Newlands	101	CH 27
Lariat	Mitchells Plain	144	CS 45
Lark Cr.	Flamingo Vlei	41	BP 33
Lark Cr.	Pelikan Pk	142	CS 36
Lark Ct	Bridgetown	103	CE 37
Lark La.	Montagu's Gift	141	CP 33
Lark Rd	Bishop Lavis	105	CD 44
Larkspur	Lentegeur (M.Plain)	145	CO 47
Larkspur Rd	Ravensmead	87	CA 46
Larkspur St	Kewtown	103	CF 35
Larkspur St	Kewtown	103	CF 37
Larne Rd	Heathfield	140	CQ 28
Las Palmas Dr.	Capri	185	DB 20
Las Vegas Cr.	Weltevreden Val. (M.Plain)	144	CO 43
Lascelles St	Rondebosch East	102	CG 33
Lasea St	Bonnie Brook	47	BQ 57
Lasswade Rd	Belle Constantia	139	CP 25
Last	Cloetesville	95	BZ 75
Lategan Rd	Hout Bay	137	CP 16
Latief Cl.	Gustrow	175	DB 75
Latiep Cassiem Cl.	Gustrow	175	DB 75
Latiep Cassiem Cl.	Gustrow	175	DB 77
Latin Quarter	Somerset West	171	CV 77
Latin St	Strandfontein	162	CT 42
Latrobe Rd	Tijgerhof	57	BX 33
Latsky	Stellenbosch	95	CB 75
Latvan Rd	Gatesville	103	CH 37
Lauda Rd	Killarney Gdns	42	BO 36
Lauda Rd	Killarney Gdns	42	BO 37
Lauda Rd	Killarney Gdns	42	BO 37
Laune Cl.	Connaught	87	CB 43
Laura Cl.	Tafelsig (M.Plain)	146	CS 51
Laura Rd	Retreat	140	CR 28
Laurel	Pinelands	85	CC 35
Laurel St	Loevenstein	60	BW 45
Laurence Dale Rd	Oakdene	89	CC 53
Laurentia Way	Hout Bay	136	CO 14
Laurier Cl.	Claremont	102	CH 31
Laurier Rd	Claremont	102	CH 31
Laurier Rd	Claremont	121	CJ 31
Laurimer Rd	Penhill	128	CK 60
Laurinda Cr.	Stikland Hospital	61	BX 50
Lausanne Cr.	La Rochelle	62	BV 51
Lava Cl.	Salberau	86	CB 40
Lavalle St	Shirley Pk	89	BY 52
Lavender	Lentegeur (M.Plain)	144	CP 45
Lavender Cl.	Somerset West	171	CW 77
Lavender Cl.	Vredekloof Hgts	47	BS 55
Lavender Cr.	Belhar	88	CC 47
Lavender La.	Halalie	30	BN 52
Lavender La.	Kaymor	89	BY 53
Lavender Pl.	Pelikan Pk	142	CR 36
Lavendon Rd	Fish Hoek	186	DA 23
Lavenham Rd	Rondebosch	101	CG 30
Lavenir Cl.	Zevendal	90	CC 58
Laventelboom	Delft Sth	125	CK 49
Lavinia Cl.	Dennemere	108	CH 58
Lavis Cr.	Brooklyn	84	BY 31
Lavis Dr.	Bishop Lavis	104	CD 42
Lavis Dr.	Bishop Lavis	105	CD 43
Lavis Dr.	Bishop Lavis	105	CD 44
Lavumo	Mbekweni	15	AV 91
Law Rd	Three Anchor Bay	81	BZ 20
Lawley Rd	Woodstock	83	CB 27
Lawley St	Fairfield	87	BY 43
Lawrence Cl.	Athlone	102	CG 33
Lawrence Rd	Athlone	102	CF 33
Lawrence Rd	Athlone	102	CG 33
Lawrence Rd	Dieprivier	140	CO 28
Lawrence St	Maitland	83	CA 30
Lawson Rd	Belthorn Est.	102	CH 34
Lawson Rd	Belthorn Est.	103	CH 35
Lawson Rd	Crawford	102	CH 33
Lawson Rd	Lansdowne	102	CH 32
Lawu St	Bloekombos	49	BQ 63
Lawula St	Umrhabulo Triangle	147	CR 57
Lawulo Rd	Eyethu	146	CP 54
Layallee Way	Meadowridge	140	CO 27
Layard Rd	Tijgerhof	57	BW 32
Lazola	Mbekweni	15	AW 91
Le Breton Ave	Steenberg	159	CT 28
Le Domaine	Durmonte	30	BN 53
Le Domaine	Durmonte	30	BM 53
Le Fleur Cl.	Wellington	15	AW 93
Le Grange Rd	Grassy Pk	141	CQ 32
Le Grange St	Rusthof	174	DA 74
Le Mans	Killarney Gdns	42	BP 37
Le Mont Cl.	Vredekloof	62	BT 53
Le Provence	Pinelands	85	CC 35
Le Riche Cl.	Edgemead	58	BU 36
Le Roux Ave	Grassy Pk	141	CR 32
Le Roux La.	Belle Constantia	139	CP 26
Le Roux Rd	Franschhoek Nth	75	BX 105
Le Roux St	Wellington	10	AR 92
Le Sage Way	Edgemead	58	BV 36
Le Sueur	Brandwacht	113	CE 77
Le Sueur Ave	Hohenort	119	CM 25
Le Sueur Ave	Plattekloof Glen	59	BW 40
Lea Rd	Muizenberg Nth	159	CW 28
Lea Rd	Ottery	121	CM 32
Lea Rd	Rondebosch	102	CG 31
Leader St	Vanguard	103	CF 38
Leadwood St	Bonteheuwel	104	CE 40
Leadwood St	Eastridge (M.Plain)	145	CR 47
Leafmore Rd	Lansdowne	121	CK 33
Leah St	Schotsche Kloof	81	BZ 22
Leander Pl.	Kirstenhof	159	CT 27
Leander Rd	Strandfontein	162	CT 42
Leander Way	Dennemere	108	CH 57
Learjet St	The Hague	106	CF 50
Learner St	Sonstraal Hgts	46	BR 54
Leather Oak St	Oak Glen	62	BW 53
Leballo Rd	Masiphumelele	184	DA 18
Leballo Rd	Masiphumelele	184	DC 17
Lebanon Way	Edgemead	58	BU 38
Lebombo	Lavender Hill East	160	CU 32
Lebombo	Wellington	15	AV 91
Lebombo Cr.	Tafelsig (M.Plain)	145	CS 48
Leccino Ter.	Somerset West	151	CQ 72
Leclerc	Lindida	96	CA 79
Leda Cl.	Woodlands (M.Plain)	144	CP 45
Ledbury Ave	Somerset West	152	CS 75
Ledge St	Tafelsig (M.Plain)	145	CS 48
Ledore Rd	Plumstead	141	CO 31
Lee Rd	Claremont	102	CH 31
Lee St	Springbok Pk	63	BV 55
Leeds St	Dunoon	42	BO 37
Leepark Rd	Fish Hoek	186	DA 23
Leerdam	Sonnekuil	89	BZ 53
Leerdam Cl.	Brackenfell Sth	63	BX 56
Leerdam Cl.	Somerset West	171	CT 75
Leerdam Cl.	Sonnekuil	89	BZ 52
Leerdam Cr.	Belhar	106	CD 49
Leerdam Cr.	Belhar	106	CH 48
Leerdam Cr.	Stellenberg	62	BU 51
Leerdam La.	Tygerdal	58	BX 38
Leerdam Rd	Chapman's Peak	156	CX 17
Leerdam St	Avondale	60	BX 44
Leerdam St	Bothasig	58	BT 37
Leerdam St	Strandvale	170	CW 73
Leerdam St	Wynberg	120	CL 27
Leervis Cr.	Marina Da Gama	159	CU 30
Leervis St	Gustrow	175	DB 75
Leetchfield Cr.	Vredekloof	62	BU 54
Leeu St	Eastridge (M.Plain)	145	CR 48
Leeubekkie	Lentegeur (M.Plain)	145	CO 47
Leeubekkie	Stellenbosch	95	CA 77
Leeubekkie Cr.	Roosendaal	107	CF 51
Leeubekkie Cr.	Weltevreden Val. (M.Plain)	124	CM 44
Leeubekkie St	Wimbledon	107	CG 54
Leeuberg Rd	Bishop Lavis	104	CE 42
Leeufontein Rd	Kirstenhof	159	CU 27
Leeukloof Dr.	Tamboerskloof	81	CB 21
Leeukop	Brackenfell	63	BW 55
Leeukop	Brackenfell	63	BV 58
Leeukop Ave	Strand	174	CY 73
Leeukop Rd	Hout Bay	116	CN 14
Leeukop Rd	Sunningdale	25	BM 31
Leeukop St	Tamboerskloof	81	CC 21
Leeukoppie Rd	Hout Bay	116	CM 14
Leeukoppie Rd	Hout Bay	116	CN 14
Leeuloop	Hout Bay	136	CO 14
Leeuwen St	Cape Town Cen.	81	CA 22
Leeuwendal St	Wellington	10	AR 94
Leeuwenhof	Pinelands	85	CB 35
Leeuwenhof Cr.	Gardens	81	CC 21
Leeuwenhof Cr.	Table View	41	BO 33
Leeuwenhof Rd	Gardens	81	CC 21
Leeuwenhof St	Oak Glen	62	BW 53
Leeuwenvoet Rd	Tamboerskloof	81	CB 21
Leeuwkop La.	Belhar	106	CD 50
Legas Rd	Flintdale Est.	141	CP 31
Lehana Cr.	Wallacedene	48	BS 60
Lehar	Delft Sth	125	CK 48
Leibro St	Fairfield	87	BY 44
Leicester Cr.	Weltevreden Val. (M.Plain)	144	CP 43
Leicester Dr.	Ottery	122	CM 35
Leicester Gr.	Green Point	81	BZ 21
Leicester Rd	Lakeside	159	CV 27
Leicester St	Claremont	120	CJ 29
Leiden Ave	Delft	106	CF 49
Leiden Ave	Delft	106	CG 49
Leiden Cr.	Uitzicht	31	BN 55
Leighton Rd	St James	187	CZ 27
Leimen Way	Silversands	107	CH 53
Leinster Rd	Green Point	81	BZ 22
Leinster St	Oakdale	61	BV 49
Leipoldt Rd	Mandalay	125	CM 48
Leipoldt St	Belgravia	88	BY 50
Leipoldt St	Parow Nth	60	BW 43
Leipoldt St	Somerset West	171	CT 75
Leipoldt St	Sonstraal	46	BR 52
Leipoldt St	Van Ryneveld	174	CZ 73
Leistner St	Ravensmead	87	CA 44
Leith Hill Rd	Tamboerskloof	81	CB 21
Leith Rd	Alphen	119	CL 26
Leith St	Rondebosch	101	CG 30
Lekkerwater Rd	Capri	184	DA 18
Lekkerwater St	Tafelsig (M.Plain)	145	CS 48
Lekoma Way	Langa	103	CD 36
Lelala Cr.	Victoria Mxenge	146	CO 52
Lelia Rd	Claremont	120	CJ 28
Lelie	Idasvallei	95	CA 78
Lelie Rd	Uitsig	87	CB 44
Lelie St	Brackenfell	63	BV 57
Lelie St	Cape Town Cen.	82	CB 23
Lelie St	Protea Hoogte	63	BW 57
Lelieblom Cr.	Silvertown	103	CF 36
Leliefontein	Eersterivier	128	CL 60
Lelieveld Way	Belthorn Est.	103	CH 35
Lelongwe St	Umrhabulo Triangle	147	CR 58
Lelyfontein Cl.	Mitchells Plain	144	CR 45
Lelyfontein Cl.	Mitchells Plain	144	CR 43
Lembede Cr.	Mandela Pk	147	CQ 55
Lemietberg	The Crest	46	BO 54
Lemietberg Cr.	Uitzicht	46	BO 54
Lemmer La.	Strand Halt	170	CW 74
Lemoen Cr.	Silvertown	103	CF 36
Lemoenboom Rd	Onverwacht	175	DC 76
Lemoenboom Rd	Whispering Pines	175	DB 77
Lemoenduif St	Jacarandas	90	CC 57
Lemoenkloof Cl.	Mitchells Plain	144	CR 45
Lemoenkloof Cl.	Mitchells Plain	144	CS 43
Lemoenkloof Rd	Lemoenkloof	18	BB 88
Lemoenshoek Cr.	Tafelsig (M.Plain)	145	CS 48
Lemon La.	Newlands	101	CH 28
Lemur St	Eastridge (M.Plain)	145	CR 48
Lena Cl.	Bishop Lavis	104	CE 41
Lena Cr.	Eindhoven	106	CH 50
Lengezi St	Kaya	146	CO 51
Lengezi St	Kaya	146	CP 51
Lennon Rd	Mandalay	125	CN 48
Lennox St	Woodstock	82	CB 26
Lens Rd	Observatory	83	CC 29
Lensie Rd	Retreat	141	CR 31
Lente Rd	Sybrand Pk	102	CE 32
Lente Rd	Sybrand Pk	102	CF 32
Lente St	Kirstenhof	159	CT 27
Lentedal Rd	Hout Bay	137	CO 15
Lentelus Ave	Voorbrug	107	CG 51
Lenton Dr.	Bishop Lavis	104	CD 42
Lenton Dr.	Bishop Lavis	104	CE 42
Lenton Dr.	Bishop Lavis	105	CE 43
Leo Rd	Elfindale	140	CP 30
Leo Rd	Joe Slovo Pk	57	BU 33
Leo Rd	Ocean View	184	DC 15
Leo St	Somerset Hgts	127	CK 57
Leon	Malibu Village	127	CK 56
Leon St	Bonnie Brae	47	BP 57
Leon St	Wellington	15	AU 92
Leon Ter.	Wynberg	120	CM 29
Leonard St	Plumstead	140	CO 30
Leoni Cl.	Dreyersdal	140	CS 27
Leopard Cl.	Strandfontein	162	CT 40
Leopard Cr.	Macassar	149	CS 66
Leopard St	Paarden Eiland	83	BZ 29
Leopards Link	Somerset West	171	CW 77
Leopards Link	Somerset West	171	CV 77
Lepanto	Strandfontein	162	CT 40
Lepanto Cl.	Strandfontein	162	CT 40
Lepanto Cl.	Strandfontein	162	CV 42
Lepelhout	Delft Sth	125	CK 49
Lepelhout St	Bonteheuwel	104	CE 40
Leraar St	Claremont	120	CJ 30
Lerato Ponoane St	Mfuleni	126	CK 53
Lerato Ponoane St	Mfuleni	126	CL 54
Lerotholi Ave	Langa	103	CD 36
Lesibane St	Bloekombos	48	BQ 62
Lesley Mesina St	Mandela Pk	147	CQ 55
Leslie Cr.	St Michaels	63	BU 55
Leslie La.	Cape Town Cen.	82	CA 23
Leslie Rd	Claremont	101	CH 29
Lesperance St	Highbury	107	CD 54
Lester Rd	Wynberg	120	CM 29
Letaba Cr.	Bonnie Brook	47	BQ 56
Letaba Cr.	Delft	106	CF 49
Letaba Rd	Manenberg	103	CH 38
Letaba Rd	Manenberg	104	CH 39
Letaba St	Mfuleni	126	CJ 53
Letchworth Dr.	Edgemead	58	BU 38
Letchworth Dr.	Edgemead	58	BV 38
Letchworth Dr.	Edgemead	59	BU 39
Letchworth Rd	Pinelands	102	CD 33
Letru St	Brantwood	89	CA 53
Letsatsi Mosala	Weltevreden Val. (M.Plain)	123	CM 42
Letterstedt Rd	Newlands	101	CG 28
Leucadendron Rd	Big Bay	24	BK 28
Leucadendron Rd	Big Bay	24	BL 29
Leuven	Morgen Gronde	63	BX 55
Levendal Cl.	Ocean View	184	DC 16
Lever Rd	Kalk Bay	187	DA 27
Lever St	District Six	82	CC 26
Levin St	Wellington	10	AS 92
Levy La.	Somerset West	171	CT 76
Lewes St	Somerset West	151	CS 74
Lewies Rd	Matroosfontein	86	CC 41
Lewin St	Foreshore	82	CB 25
Lewis Dr.	Barbarossa	140	CO 27
Lewis Dr.	Bergvliet	139	CQ 26
Lewis Rd	Belhar	106	CD 50
Lewis Rd	Table View	41	BP 34
Lexi Cl.	Salberau	86	CB 41
Ley Rd	St James	187	CZ 27
Leyden Cl.	Helderberg Pk	175	DA 75
Leyden Rd	Bergvliet	139	CR 26
Leyden St	Monte Vista	59	BU 40
Leylands Rd	Somerset West	151	CR 74
Leyte	Strandfontein	162	CU 40
Leytonstone Rd	Retreat	140	CR 30
Liberator	Rocklands (M.Plain)	144	CS 45
Liberator St	Kensington	84	BZ 34
Libertas	Karindal	96	CC 79
Libertas	Pinelands	85	CC 35
Libertas Ave	Table View	41	BO 32
Libertas Ave	Table View	41	BO 33
Libertas Cl.	Haasendal	90	CA 57
Libertas Cl.	Oak Glen	62	BW 52
Libertas La.	Belhar	106	CD 49
Libertas Rd	Park Estates	170	CX 72
Libertas St	Kleinbosch	59	BT 40
Libertas St	Somerset West	171	CT 75
Libertrau Rd	Somerset West	171	CU 76
Liberty Rd	Retreat	140	CR 30
Liberty St	Greenways	174	DA 74
Liberty St	Plumstead	140	CO 30
Libisa Cl.	Nyanga	123	CJ 42
Libra	Rocklands (M.Plain)	144	CS 45
Libra Cl.	Everite	63	BV 57
Libra Cr.	Phoenix	57	BV 33
Libra Rd	Cravenby	87	CA 43
Libra Rd	Ocean View	189	DD 15
Libra Rd	Surrey	103	CG 38
Libra Rd	Surrey	103	CH 38
Library La.	Grassy Pk	141	CR 32
Libri La.	Somerset West	170	CV 74
Lichfield Ave	Bishopscourt	119	CJ 25
Lichtenburg Rd	Fisantekraal	31	BJ 58
Lichtenburg Rd	Fisantekraal	32	BJ 60
Lichtenstein Ave	Somerset West	171	CU 77
Lichtenstein St	Park Estates	170	CX 72
Liddesdale	Pinelands	84	CB 34
Liddle St	Cape Town Cen.	82	BZ 23
L'Ideal St	Paarl	22	BE 88
Lidford Rd	Plumstead	120	CN 29
Lido Lorraine	Somerset West	152	CT 75
Liebenberg St	Wellington	10	AS 92
Lieberheim	Lieberheim	113	CG 76
Liederman Rd	Clarkes	87	CC 43

Abbreviations used: Ave – Avenue, A.H. – Agricultural Holding, A.L. – Algemene Landgoed, Blvd – Boulevard, Cen. – Central, Cir. – Circle, Cl. – Close, Cr. – Crescent, Ct – Court, Dr. – Drive, Est. – Estate, Ext. – Extension, Hgts – Heights, Ind. – Industrial, Gdns – Gardens, Gr. – Grove, La. – Lane, (M.Plain) - Mitchells Plain, Nth – North, Pl. – Place, Pk – Park, Rd – Road, Rdg. – Ridge, S.H.– Small Holding, Sq. – Square, St – Street, Sth – South, Ter. – Terrace, Tn – Turn, Val. – Valley, Wk – Walk

STREET NAME	SUBURB NAME	PG	GRID	
Liedla St	Elim	90	CA	55
Liedla St	Elim	90	CB	55
Liermans Rd	Hout Bay	116	CL	14
Liesbeeck Cl.	Groenvallei	62	BX	53
Liesbeeck Cl.	Groenvallei	62	BX	52
Liesbeeck Cr.	Eersterivier	128	CM	59
Liesbeeck Parkway	Rosebank	101	CE	30
Liesbeeck St	Bothasig	58	BT	37
Liesbeek Cr.	Delft	106	CG	49
Liesbeek Ave	Observatory	83	CC	30
Liesbeek Parkway	Observatory	83	CC	29
Liesbeek Rd	Rosebank	101	CE	30
Liesbeek Rd West	Rosebank	101	CE	29
Liesbeek Way	Belhar	106	CE	49
Liesbeek Way	Portlands (M.Plain)	144	CQ	46
Lighthouse Rd	Kommetjie	183	DC	11
Lighthouse Rd	Witsand	188	DF	13
Lighthouse Rd	Witsand	188	DF	14
Lightning	Rocklands (M.Plain)	144	CS	45
Lightning St	The Hague	106	CF	49
Liguster St	Forest Hgts	127	CK	57
Lilac	Greenlands	88	CA	49
Lilac	Lentegeur (M.Plain)	145	CO	47
Lilac Cir.	Belhar	106	CD	47
Lilac St	Dalvale	19	AY	92
Lilac St	Kewtown	103	CF	35
Lilian Ave	Flintdale Est.	141	CP	31
Lilian Ngoyi Cr.	Weltevreden Val. (M.Plain)	123	CN	42
Lilian Ngoyi St	Manenberg	104	CH	39
Lilian Rd	Retreat	140	CR	29
Lilian St	Tafelsig (M.Plain)	146	CS	51
Lilian St	Wellington	10	AS	92
Lilie St	Durbanville	46	BP	51
Lille	Malibu Village	127	CK	55
Lille St	Courtrai	22	BH	87
Lillian Ngoyi Cr.	Mandela Pk	146	CR	54
Lillian Ngoyi Dr.	Weltevreden Val. (M.Plain)	123	CN	41
Lillian Ngoyi Dr.	Weltevreden Val. (M.Plain)	123	CN	42
Lillie St	Wellington	15	AT	92
Lilson Rd	Sea Point	81	CA	20
Lily	Dunoon	42	BO	37
Lily	Lentegeur (M.Plain)	144	CP	45
Lily Cl.	Belhar	106	CE	47
Lily Cl.	Bridgetown	103	CF	36
Lily Cl.	Hanover Pk	122	CJ	36
Lily Cl.	Macassar	149	CS	63
Lily Cl.	Ocean View	184	DC	15
Lily Cl.	Ottery East	121	CN	34
Lily Rd	Retreat Ind. Area	159	CT	28
Lily St	Bellville Sth	88	CA	49
Lily St	Kewtown	103	CF	35
Lily St	Paarl	22	BD	88
Lily St	Parow Nth	59	BW	42
Lily St	Somerset West	170	CT	71
Lily St	Weltevreden Val. (M.Plain)	124	CM	44
Lily Way	Lavender Hill East	160	CU	32
Lily Way	Lavender Hill East	160	CX	33
Lilydale Rd	Lotus River	141	CP	34
Lima Rd	Malibu Village	127	CL	56
Lime Cl.	Mitchells Plain	144	CQ	45
Lime Rd	Parkwood	141	CO	31
Limerick Rd	Crawford	102	CH	34
Limerick St	Connaught	87	CB	43
Limietberg	Brackenfell	63	BW	55
Limonium St	Vredekloof Hgts	47	BS	55
Limousin	Groenvlei	18	BA	88
Limpet Cl.	Richwood	42	BP	38
Limpet La.	Big Bay	24	BL	28
Limpet St	Richwood	42	BP	38
Limpopo Ave	Belthorn Est.	121	CJ	34
Limpopo Cr.	Delft	106	CG	49
Limpopo Rd	Bishop Lavis	104	CD	41
Limpopo Rd	Bonnie Brook	47	BQ	57
Limpopo Rd	Eindhoven	106	CH	50
Limpopo St	Mfuleni	126	CJ	53
Limpopo St	Mxolisi Phetani	125	CM	50
Limpopo Way	Portlands (M Plain)	144	CQ	45
Linaria	Lentegeur (M.Plain)	144	CO	46
Linaria	Lentegeur (M.Plain)	145	CO	47
Linaria	Welgedacht	60	BT	45
Linaria Cr.	Bridgetown	103	CF	36
Lincluden Rd	Rugby	57	BX	31
Lincoln Cl.	Balvenie	87	CB	43
Lincoln Cl.	Balvenie	87	CB	46
Lincoln Cr.	Beacon Valley (M.Plain)	145	CQ	48
Lincoln Cr.	Dolphin Beach	40	BP	30
Lincoln Dr.	Bishopscourt	119	CJ	25
Lincoln Fields Cr.	Lakeside	159	CW	28
Lincoln Rd	Camps Bay	98	CD	18
Lincoln Rd	Claremont	102	CH	31
Lincoln Rd	Claremont	120	CJ	29
Lincoln Rd	Lakeside	159	CV	28
Lincoln Rd	Oranjezicht	99	CD	22
Lincoln Rd	Sea Point	81	BZ	19
Lincoln St	Boston	61	BW	47
Lincoln St	Boston	61	BX	47
Lincoln St	Klein Begin	48	BS	61
Lincoln Way	Meadowridge	140	CP	27
Linda	Tafelsig (M.Plain)	146	CS	51
Linda Ave	Valhalla Pk	104	CE	41
Linda Cl.	Hout Bay	136	CO	14
Linda Rd	Claremont	120	CJ	28
Linda Rd	Montagu's Gift	141	CP	33
Linda St	Beacon Valley (M.Plain)	145	CP	48
Linda St	Hout Bay	136	CO	14

STREET NAME	SUBURB NAME	PG	GRID	
Linda St	Hout Bay	137	CO	15
Linda St	Stikland Hospital	88	BY	50
Linda St	Stikland Hospital	89	BY	51
Linda St	Tarentaalplaas	174	CY	74
Linde Rd	Bloubergstrand	24	BL	28
Lindela Rd	Nyanga	124	CK	43
Lindela St	Griffiths Mxenge	146	CQ	54
Lindela St	Umrhabulo Triangle	147	CQ	56
Lindela St	Umrhabulo Triangle	147	CR	56
Lindelwa St	Ekuphumuleni	146	CQ	53
Linden Cl.	Somerset West	152	CS	75
Linden Ct	Edgemead	58	BU	37
Linden Ct	Northpine	63	BU	58
Linden East	Ravensmead	87	CA	46
Linden St	Ottery	121	CN	33
Linden Way	Pinelands	84	CC	34
Linden West	Ravensmead	87	CA	44
Lindenberg Ave	Durbanville	46	BQ	51
Lindentree Cl.	Forest Hgts	127	CL	58
Lindentree St	Forest Hgts	127	CL	57
Lindeshof Rd	Sweet Valley	139	CQ	26
Lindevista La.	Hout Bay	137	CQ	16
Lindewa St	Nyanga	123	CK	42
Lindi Phahle St	Kuyasa	147	CR	55
Lindi St	Nomzano	175	CY	75
Lindi Way	Delft	106	CF	49
Lindida Dr.	Lindida	96	CA	79
Lindida Dr.	Stellenbosch	96	CA	80
Lindie Cr.	Forest Hgts	127	CK	58
Lindie St	Somerset West	170	CT	72
Lindley	Idasvallei	96	CA	79
Lindley Ct	Northpine	63	BU	58
Lindley Rd	Wynberg	120	CM	28
Lindley Way	Edgemead	59	BU	39
Lindsay Cr.	Meadowridge	140	CP	27
Lindsay St	Eastridge (M.Plain)	145	CQ	49
Liner Cl.	Strandfontein	161	CU	38
Linga Rd	Masiphumelele	184	DA	18
Linga St	Kaya	146	CP	52
Linge Cr.	Wimbledon	108	CG	55
Lingelihle	Mbekweni	15	AW	92
Lingen Rd	Boston	61	BX	47
Lingen St	Gardens	81	CC	22
Lingfied Way	Edgemead	58	BU	38
Lingfield Cl.	Milnerton Rdg	41	BR	34
Lingfield Cr.	Ottery	122	CM	35
Lingfield Rd	Ottery	122	CM	35
Link	Strandfontein	162	CT	40
Link	Wellway Pk East	46	BO	52
Link Ave	Macassar	148	CR	62
Link Ave	Macassar	149	CR	63
Link Ave	Macassar	149	CS	63
Link Ave	Macassar	149	CS	64
Link Cl.	Montague Gdns Ind.	58	BT	36
Link Cr.	Montague Gdns Ind.	42	BS	36
Link Dr.	Mowbray	102	CD	32
Link Dr.	Pinelands	102	CD	33
Link Rd	Belgravia	61	BX	50
Link Rd	Belgravia	88	BY	50
Link Rd	Big Bay	24	BK	28
Link Rd	Big Bay	24	BL	29
Link Rd	Bothasig	58	BU	36
Link Rd	Capricorn	160	CW	32
Link Rd	Flintdale Est.	141	CP	31
Link Rd	Grassy Pk	141	CQ	32
Link Rd	Milnerton	57	BV	32
Link Rd	Montague Gdns Ind.	58	BT	35
Link Rd	Montague Gdns Ind.	58	BT	36
Link Rd	Ottery East	121	CN	34
Link Rd	Paarden Eiland	83	CA	29
Link Rd	Parklands	25	BN	32
Link Rd	Skoongesig	45	BO	50
Link Rd	Table View	25	BN	31
Link St	Bakoven	98	CE	18
Link St	Somerset West	170	CT	73
Link Way	Edgemead	58	BV	37
Linkoping Rd	Rondebosch	101	CF	29
Links Cr.	Simon's Town	195	DJ	27
Links Rd	Rondebosch	101	CF	30
Linmanie St	Langeberg Glen	47	BQ	55
Linnes	Brandwacht	113	CF	77
Linnet St	Rugby	57	BX	31
Linnet Way	Pinelands	102	CD	34
Linpark Cr.	Strand	174	CZ	73
Linray Rd	Rosebank	101	CE	29
Linschoten St	Dal Josafat Ind.	18	BA	90
Linton	Papegaaiberg Ind. Pk	95	CA	75
Linton Cl.	Beaconvale	86	BZ	42
Linus Rd	Beaconvale	86	BZ	42
Lion Cl.	Strandfontein	162	CT	40
Lion St	Schotsche Kloof	81	CA	22
Lionel Rd	Wynberg	120	CM	28
Lions Paw	Hout Bay Harbour	136	CR	13
Lions Way	Zoo Pk	47	BQ	57
Lions Way	Zoo Pk	47	BR	57
Lipla Cl.	Ekuphumuleni	146	CQ	53
Lipton Rd	Wynberg	120	CL	29
Liquat St	Vredekloof Hgts	47	BS	55
Lisa Jane Cr.	Sanddrift	57	BV	34
Lisboa St	Dennemere	127	CJ	57
Lisboa St	Ruyterwacht	86	BZ	39
Lisbon St	Uitzicht	47	BO	55
Liscard Rd	Lansdowne	121	CK	32
Liskeard St	Observatory	101	CD	29
Lismore Cl.	West Beach	25	BN	31

STREET NAME	SUBURB NAME	PG	GRID	
Lismore Rd	Dennedal	139	CR	26
Lismore Rd	Tokai	139	CS	26
Lismore Ter.	Green Point	81	BZ	22
Lista Cr.	Vredekloof	62	BT	54
Lister Rd	Rondebosch	102	CG	31
Lister Way	Meadowridge	140	CP	27
Listowell Rd	Woodstock	83	CB	27
Liszt	Delft Sth	125	CK	48
Liszt St	Labiance	89	BZ	51
Little Rd	Athlone	102	CF	33
Little Rd	Somerset West	170	CT	74
Little St	Kensington	84	BZ	33
Littlewood Rd	Marinda Hgts	89	BZ	52
Littlewood Rd	Marinda Hgts	89	BY	54
Littlewood Rd	Ottery East	121	CN	34
Littlewood Rd	Ottery East	121	CM	34
Liverpool Cr.	Eikenbosch	90	CC	57
Liverpool St	Dunoon	42	BO	37
Liverpool St	Hout Bay	136	CP	14
Liverpool St	Hout Bay	137	CP	15
Liverpool St	Wynberg	120	CM	30
Livingstone Ave	Ruyterwacht	86	CA	40
Livingstone Rd	Claremont	101	CH	30
Livingstone Rd	Windsor Pk	47	BR	57
Livingstone Rd	Zoo Pk	47	BR	57
Livingstone St	Langa	103	CD	36
Livingstone St	Park Estates	170	CX	72
Liwa St	Philippi East	124	CM	46
Liza St	Kaya	146	CP	51
Lizo Nkonki	Weltevreden Val. (M.Plain)	123	CM	41
Llandudno Rd	Hout Bay	116	CL	14
Llandudno Rd	Hout Bay	116	CM	14
Lloyd St	Bellville Sth Ext. 5	88	BZ	49
Lloyd St	William Lloyd	19	BC	94
Lloyd St	William Lloyd	23	BD	93
Loader St	Green Point	81	BZ	22
Loanda St	Brooklyn	84	BY	31
Loarti Rd	Kraaifontein	47	BQ	58
Lobelia	Lentegeur (M.Plain)	145	CO	47
Lobelia Cl.	Bellville	61	BT	48
Lobelia Cl.	Vredekloof Hgts	47	BS	55
Lobelia La.	Eersterivier	128	CM	60
Lobelia Rd	Milnerton	57	BU	33
Lobelia Rd	Wellway Pk East	46	BP	52
Lobelia St	Sanddrift	57	BW	34
Lobelia St	Somerset West	151	CS	71
Lobenstijn St	De Bron	61	BT	48
Lobi Cl.	Kaya	146	CP	52
Lobola	Mbekweni	15	AV	91
Locarno Rd	Rondebosch	101	CG	30
Loch Rd	Camps Bay	99	CD	19
Loch Rd	Claremont	120	CJ	30
Loch Rd	Claremont	121	CJ	31
Loch Rd	Kalk Bay	186	DA	26
Loch Rd	Kalk Bay	186	CZ	26
Loch Rd	Retreat	141	CR	31
Loch Rd	Rondebosch	102	CE	32
Loch St	Rondebosch	102	CE	31
Lochiel Rd	Lekkerwater	184	DA	17
Lochiel Rd	Rondebosch	101	CG	30
Lochner Rd	Barbarossa	120	CN	27
Lochner St	Lochnerhof	170	CX	71
Lochner St	Lochnerhof	174	CY	72
Lock Rd	Lekkerwater	184	DB	18
Lockerby Rd	Lansdowne	102	CH	32
Lockerby Rd	Lansdowne	121	CJ	32
Lockhead	Rocklands (M.Plain)	163	CT	46
Lockheed St	The Hague	106	CF	50
Lockwood Rd	Claremont	101	CH	30
Loco Rd	Woodstock	83	CA	29
Lodestar St	Kensington	84	BZ	33
Lodewyk	Rusthof	174	DA	74
Lodewyk Cr.	Newfields	103	CH	37
Lodewyk Rd	Newfields	122	CJ	36
Lodewyk Rd	Newfields	122	CJ	37
Lodge Ave	Wellington	10	AS	94
Lodge Rd	Oranjezicht	81	CC	22
Lodge Rd	Ottery	121	CM	33
Lodger Rd	Summer Greens	58	BW	35
Lodwar St	Charlesville	104	CF	40
Loeloeraai St	Elim	90	CA	55
Loerie	Onderpapegaaiberg	94	CB	73
Loerie	Onderpapegaaiberg	94	CC	73
Loerie Ave	Pinelands	84	CC	34
Loerie Cl.	Barbarossa	120	CN	27
Loerie Cl.	Langeberg Rdg	47	BR	56
Loerie Rd	Bridgetown	103	CE	35
Loerie Rd	Bridgetown	103	CE	36
Loerie Rd	Bridgetown	103	CF	37
Loerie Rd	Pelikan Pk	142	CS	35
Loerie Rd	Silvertown	103	CF	36
Loerie St	Dunoon	26	BN	37
Loerie St	Eersterivier	128	CM	60
Loerie St	Eersterivier	128	CJ	61
Loerie St	Morningstar	46	BP	51
Loerie St	Somerset Hgts	127	CJ	57
Loerie St	Somerset West	152	CS	76
Loerie St	Sonnekuil	89	BZ	53
Loerie St	Wellington	15	AT	92
Loerier St	Protea Village	64	BV	59
Loeven Ter.	Loevenstein	60	BW	46
Loewe	Delft Sth	125	CJ	48
Lofdal	Brackenfell	63	BW	55
Loftus Cr.	Beacon Valley (M.Plain)	145	CP	48
Loftus Rd	Des Hampden	89	CB	53

STREET NAME	SUBURB NAME	PG	GRID	
Loftus Rd	Weltevreden Val. (M.Plain)	124	CN	43
Logan Way	Pinelands	84	CB	34
Loganberry Cl.	Strandfontein	162	CT	41
Loganberry Cl.	Strandfontein	162	CV	42
Loganberry Pl.	Strandfontein	162	CT	41
Loganberry St	Bonteheuwel	104	CE	39
Loganberry Way	Mitchells Plain	144	CR	44
Logie St	Somerset West	171	CV	75
Logies Rd	Hout Bay	116	CL	14
Logna Cl.	Brackenfell Sth	63	BW	57
Lohengrin St	Eastridge (M.Plain)	145	CQ	49
Lohr Cr.	Silversands	107	CH	53
Loire	Groenvlei	18	BA	88
Loliwe	Mbekweni	15	AW	91
Loliwe St	Umrhabulo Triangle	147	CQ	58
Lolo Mkonto St	Gugulethu	123	CK	41
Loman Rd	Retreat	140	CS	28
Lombard St	Wellington	10	AR	92
Lombardie Ave	Bel Ombre	119	CM	24
Lomela Ct	Delft	106	CG	49
Lomond Cr.	Coniston Pk	159	CU	30
Lomond St	Claremont	120	CJ	30
Londa St	Scottsdene	64	BT	60
Londoloza St	Griffiths Mxenge	146	CP	54
London Cl.	Eikenbosch	90	CC	57
London Rd	Observatory	83	CC	29
London Rd	Sea Point	81	BZ	19
London Rd	Woodstock	83	CB	28
London St	Athlone	102	CG	33
London St	Portlands (M.Plain)	144	CQ	46
London Way	Malibu Village	127	CK	56
Londonderry Rd	Royal Cape	121	CM	32
Lonedown Rd	Hanover Pk	122	CK	35
Lonedown Rd	Hanover Pk	122	CK	37
Long Pl.	Pinelands	84	CC	33
Long St	Cape Town Cen.	81	CB	22
Long St	Kayamandi	94	CA	74
Long St	Maitland	84	CA	32
Long St	Mowbray	101	CD	29
Long St	Observatory	101	CD	29
Long St	The Vines	140	CO	27
Long Tom Pl.	Oude Westhof	60	BT	44
Longboat Rd	Sunnydale	185	DA	19
Longboat St	Sun Valley	185	DA	20
Longchamp Cl.	Milnerton Rdg	41	BS	33
Longchamp Way	Milnerton Rdg	41	BS	33
Longclaw Dr.	Marconi Beam	57	BT	34
Longdon Ave	Athlone	102	CF	33
Longdown Ave	Somerset West	171	CW	75
Longfellow Rd	Table View	41	BP	33
Longhorn Rd	Rondebosch East	102	CH	32
Longifolia	Anesta	113	CF	75
Longkloof Cir.	Heideveld	104	CG	40
Longkloof Rd	Hout Bay	118	CM	19
Longmarket St	Cape Town Cen.	82	CA	23
Longmarket St	Schotsche Kloof	81	CA	22
Longmead St	Voorbrug	107	CG	51
Longmore Cr.	Edgemead	58	BU	38
Longridge Cr.	Voorbrug	107	CG	51
Longueville Way	Bergvliet	140	CQ	27
Longwood Cl.	Edgemead	58	BU	38
Longwood Rd	Sonstraal Hgts	46	BP	54
Lonja St	Nomzano	175	CY	75
Lonja St	Nomzano	175	CY	76
Lonsdale Rd	Wynberg	120	CM	28
Lonsdale Way	Pinelands	84	CC	34
Lonston Rd	Hanover Pk	122	CK	36
Lonwabo St	Mxolisi Phetani	125	CM	50
Lood St	Brackenfell Ind.	63	BT	58
Loods Sq.	Factreton	85	BZ	35
Look St	Macassar	149	CS	64
Lookout Wk	Kommetjie	183	DC	11
Looksmart Ngudle St	Weltevreden Val. (M.Plain)	123	CN	41
Loop Rd	Scottsville	47	BS	57
Loop St	Cape Town Cen	82	CA	23
Loop St	Maitland	84	CA	31
Loop St	Paarl	18	BC	89
Loop St	Vanguard	103	CF	38
Loop St	Wellington	10	AS	92
Loop St	Woodlands (M.Plain)	144	CP	44
Loos Cr.	Kensington	84	BY	33
Loots St	Protea Hoogte	63	BW	56
Loquat Ave	Belhar	106	CD	47
Lords Ave	Weltevreden Val. (M.Plain)	144	CP	43
Lords St	Beacon Valley (M.Plain)	145	CP	48
Lords Wk	Durbanville	46	BP	52
Lords Wk	Fisantekraal	32	BJ	59
Lorea Cl.	Plattekloof	60	BU	43
Lorea St	Halalie	46	BO	52
Lorelei Rd	Bellville	61	BT	50
Lorelei Rd	Eversdal Hgts	61	BT	50
Lorenza Cl.	Bothasig	58	BT	38
Loret Ave	Silverhurst	119	CN	24
Lorient Cl.	Vredekloof	62	BU	53
Lorna Ave	Glenhaven	89	CA	52
Lorraine Ave	Woodstock	83	CC	27
Lorraine Cl.	Mitchells Plain	144	CR	45
Lorraine Cr	Courtrai	22	BH	88
Lorrimer St	Brooklyn	83	BZ	30
Losack Ave	Epping Ind.	86	CC	39
Loskop Rd	Groenvallei	62	BX	53
Lothian Rd	Newlands	101	CH	27
Lothian Rd	Rondebosch	102	CF	31
Lotterberg St	Flintdale Est.	141	CO	31
Lotterberg St	Parkwood	141	CR	34

Abbreviations used: Ave – Avenue, A.H. – Agricultural Holding, A.L. – Algemene Landgoed, Blvd – Boulevard, Cen. – Central, Cir. – Circle, Cl. – Close, Cr. – Crescent, Ct – Court, Dr. – Drive, Est. – Estate, Ext. – Extension, Hgts – Heights, Ind. – Industrial, Gdns – Gardens, Gr. – Grove, La. – Lane, (M.Plain) - Mitchells Plain, Nth – North, Pl. – Place, Pk – Park, Rd – Road, Rdg. – Ridge, S.H. – Small Holding, Sq. – Square, St – Street, Sth – South, Ter. – Terrace, Tn – Turn, Val. – Valley, Wk – Walk

STREET NAME	SUBURB NAME	PG	GRID
Maasdorp St	Wellington	15	AV 92
Maasdorp St	William Lloyd	23	BD 92
Mabel Rd	Doornhoogte	103	CH 36
Mabel St	Oakdale	61	BX 48
Mabel St	Oakdale	61	BX 49
Mabel Way	Wetton	121	CL 34
Mabille St	Mabille Pk	89	CA 53
Mabindisa Cr.	Bloekombos	48	BR 62
Macartney St	Bothasig	58	BU 36
Macassar Rd	Macassar	148	CS 61
Macassar Rd	Macassar	149	CS 66
Macassar Rd	Macassar	168	CT 64
Macassar Rd	Macassar Beach	149	CS 63
Macassar Rd	Somerset West	150	CR 67
Macauley	Croydon	149	CO 63
Macbeth St	Eastridge (M.Plain)	145	CQ 48
MacCrone St	Wellington	10	AR 92
Macduff	Wesbank	107	CG 52
Macduff	Wesbank	107	CG 53
Macebo	Mbekweni	15	AW 91
Machule	Mbekweni	15	AW 91
Mackensie Rd	Eindhoven	106	CH 50
Mackenzie St	Bellville Sth Ext. 5	88	BZ 49
Mackier St	William Lloyd	23	BD 92
Mackier St	William Lloyd	23	BD 93
Macko	Mbekweni	15	AW 91
Maclear Cr.	Edgemead	59	BT 39
Maclear Rd	Bishopscourt	119	CJ 26
Maclear St	Ruyterwacht	86	CA 39
Maclear Way	Belhar	107	CD 51
Mactra Way	Sunset Beach	41	BS 32
Madaka Cr.	Brown's Farm	123	CM 41
Madayi Cr.	Eyethu	146	CO 53
Maddison Sq.	Edgemead	58	BV 37
Madeira	Eindhoven	106	CH 50
Madeira Cl.	Portlands (M.Plain)	144	CQ 46
Madeira Dr.	Capricorn	159	CW 30
Madeira Dr.	Capricorn	160	CW 31
Madeira St	Rugby	57	BX 31
Madekane	Mbekweni	15	AW 92
Madelaine St	Gaylee	108	CH 57
Madeleine St	De Tijger	60	BW 44
Madelief	Delft Sth	125	CJ 50
Madelief St	Blomtuin	61	BV 50
Madelief St	Wellington	15	AT 92
Madeliefie	Ex-skool	95	CA 75
Madeliefie	Lentegeur (M.Plain)	145	CO 47
Madeliefie St	Die Wingerd	46	BP 53
Madeliefie St	Parow Nth	59	BW 41
Madiba Cr.	Wesbank	107	CG 52
Madikana Cr.	Victoria Mxenge	146	CO 52
Madison Cl.	Scottsdene	64	BU 59
Madison Cr.	Beacon Valley (M.Plain)	145	CP 48
Madison Cr.	Weltevreden Val. (M.Plain)	144	CO 43
Madison Dr.	Weltevreden Val. (M.Plain)	144	CO 43
Madison Rd	Claremont	102	CH 31
Madodana	Mbekweni	15	AV 91
Madonna St	Wesbank	107	CG 52
Madrid Rd	Airport Ind.	104	CG 42
Madrid St	Uitzicht	46	BO 54
Madrid St	Uitzicht	47	BO 55
Maestricht St	De Bron	61	BT 48
Mafeking Rd	Retreat	140	CR 28
Mafila St	Mbekweni	15	AV 91
Mafila St	Mbekweni	15	AV 92
Mafunga Cr.	Langa	103	CE 37
Mafunka Cr.	Eyethu	146	CO 54
Magalies Rd	Eersterivier	128	CL 59
Magalies Rd	Manenberg	123	CK 39
Magaliesberg	Tafelsig (M.Plain)	145	CS 48
Magaliesberg Rd	Lavender Hill East	160	CU 32
Magaliesberg Rd	Lavender Hill East	160	CX 33
Magaret St	Wallacedene	48	BS 61
Magasyn Ave	Nieuw Maastrecht	44	BS 44
Magatya St	Tarentaalplaas	175	CY 75
Magcanya Rd	Brown's Farm	123	CL 41
Magda Rd	Montagu's Gift	141	CO 34
Magda Rd	Retreat	140	CR 28
Magda St	Kalkfontein II	107	CD 53
Magdouw St	Russel's Rest	128	CL 60
Magellaan St	Forest Glade	128	CL 58
Magennis St	William Lloyd	23	BD 92
Maggie Laubser Ave	Langgewacht	170	CW 72
Maggie Laubser Cl.	Woodlands (M.Plain)	144	CO 44
Maghina	Mbekweni	15	AW 92
Magnolia	Lentegeur (M.Plain)	144	CO 46
Magnolia Ave	Wellington	10	AS 94
Magnolia Cl.	Belhar	106	CE 47
Magnolia Cr.	Rugby	57	BX 31
Magnolia Cr.	Thornton	85	CA 37
Magnolia Cr.	Uitsig	87	CB 44
Magnolia Cr.	Valmary Pk	46	BR 51
Magnolia Rd	Eersterivier	128	CM 61
Magnolia Rd	Newlands	101	CG 27
Magnolia St	Forest Village	127	CM 58
Magnolia St	Klein Nederburg	19	BB 92
Magnolia St	Klein Nederburg	19	BC 93
Magnolia St	Morgenster	63	BU 56
Magnolia St	Somerset West	151	CS 71
Magnolia St	Sonnekuil	89	CA 54
Magnolia Way	Ridgeworth	61	BU 49
Magnolia Way	Ridgeworth	61	BV 49
Magnum St	Jagtershof	108	CD 57
Magol Way	Delft	106	CG 49
Magqaza Cr.	Eyethu	146	CP 53
Magqaza St	Tarentaalplaas	175	CY 75
Magrieta St	Kalkfontein II	107	CD 53
Magubudela St	Bloekombos	48	BR 62
Magugu	Mbekweni	15	AW 92
Magwebu St	Sir Lowry's Pass	176	CZ 82
Magwentshu St	Wallacedene	48	BS 62
Magwentshu St	Wallacedene	48	BS 61
Mahanyele St	Sir Lowry's Pass	176	CZ 82
Mahlatini St	Nyanga	123	CK 42
Mahler	Delft Sth	125	CJ 48
Mahler St	Belhar	106	CE 48
Mahlombe	Mbekweni	15	AX 92
Mahobe Cir.	Mxolisi Phetani	125	CM 50
Mahogany Cir.	Hanover Pk	122	CL 36
Mahogany Cir.	Hanover Pk	122	CN 36
Mahogany Cl.	Mitchells Plain	144	CQ 45
Mahogany Rd	Eersterivier	128	CM 61
Mahogany St	Bonteheuwel	104	CE 40
Mahogany St	Loevenstein	60	BV 45
Mahogany St	Loevenstein	60	BW 45
Mahogany Way	Weltevreden Val. (M.Plain)	144	CO 43
Mahomba	Mbekweni	15	AX 91
Mahombery Ave	Nyanga	124	CK 43
Mahonie Ave	Vredekloof Hgts	47	BS 55
Mahonie St	Forest Hgts	127	CK 57
Maiden	Morgen Gronde	63	BX 56
Maidstone Cr.	Belhar	105	CD 45
Maidstone Cr.	Belhar	105	CE 45
Maidstone Rd	Dieprivier	140	CQ 28
Maidstone Rd	Heathfield	140	CQ 29
Mail St	Epping Ind.	85	CA 38
Main	Lemoenkloof	18	BC 88
Main	Northern Paarl	18	AZ 88
Main	Paarl	22	BD 88
Main Ave	Athlone	102	CF 34
Main Ave	Athlone	102	CG 34
Main Dr.	Sea Point	81	BZ 20
Main Rd	Clovelly	186	DA 25
Main Rd	De Oude Renbaan	22	BH 88
Main Rd	Dieprivier	140	CQ 28
Main Rd	Durbanville	45	BP 50
Main Rd	Firgrove	150	CR 67
Main Rd	Green Point	81	BY 21
Main Rd	Heathfield	140	CQ 28
Main Rd	Hout Bay	137	CP 15
Main Rd	Hout Bay	137	CQ 16
Main Rd	Kenilworth	120	CL 29
Main Rd	Kommetjie	183	DC 11
Main Rd	Lakeside	159	CV 27
Main Rd	Mfuleni	126	CL 54
Main Rd	Misty Cliffs	189	DG 15
Main Rd	Muizenberg	187	CY 28
Main Rd	Muizenberg Nth	159	CW 28
Main Rd	Murdock Valley	195	DL 28
Main Rd	Newlands	101	CG 28
Main Rd	Observatory	83	CC 28
Main Rd	Paarl	22	BF 88
Main Rd	Plumstead	120	CN 29
Main Rd	Redhill	193	DK 19
Main Rd	Retreat	140	CR 28
Main Rd	Retreat Ind. Area	159	CT 27
Main Rd	Rome	170	CX 73
Main Rd	Rome	174	CY 73
Main Rd	Scarborough	192	DK 18
Main Rd	Simon's Town	191	DD 25
Main Rd	Simon's Town	191	DF 24
Main Rd	Simon's Town	191	DG 24
Main Rd	Somerset Pk	171	CW 75
Main Rd	Somerset Rdg	170	CT 71
Main Rd	Somerset West	150	CS 69
Main Rd	Somerset West	170	CT 73
Main Rd	Somerset West	171	CV 75
Main Rd	Tarentaalplaas	170	CW 74
Main Rd	Witsand	188	DD 12
Main Rd	Witsand	188	DF 14
Main Rd Service	Bergvliet	140	CQ 28
Main St	Newlands	101	CG 28
Main St	Wellington	10	AR 92
Main St	Wellington	10	AR 93
Maindy Rd	Athlone	102	CG 34
Maine Cl.	Connaught	87	CB 43
Mains Ave	Kenilworth	120	CK 28
Mainstay	Strandfontein	162	CT 39
Maisel St	Gersham	107	CD 53
Maisel St	Highbury	107	CD 54
Maitland Rd	Bishop Lavis	104	CD 42
Maitland Rd	Bishop Lavis	105	CD 43
Majola St	Tarentaalplaas	175	CY 75
Majorca Ave	Somerset West	151	CS 73
Majorca Cr.	Portlands (M.Plain)	145	CS 47
Majorca Way	Capri	185	DA 19
Makabeni Rd	Kaya	146	CP 52
Makana Cr.	Wimbledon	108	CG 55
Makana Sq.	Langa	103	CD 36
Makazi St	Harare	146	CS 54
Makeba Cl.	Driftsands	147	CQ 56
Makelani Cr.	Brantwood	89	CB 53
Maketesi St	Driftsands	125	CL 50
Maketesi St	Driftsands	126	CL 51
Makhanya Cr.	Victoria Mxenge	146	CO 51
Makhelwa	Mbekweni	15	AW 92
Makhohliso Cr.	Crossroads	124	CK 44
Makholwa Cr.	Nyanga	123	CK 42
Makhosi Magadlela St	Guguletu	104	CG 41
Makhulu Cr.	Umrhabulo Triangle	147	CQ 57
Makhulu Cr.	Umrhabulo Triangle	147	CR 57
Maknanlela Cr.	Crossroads	124	CK 44
Makou	Rocklands (M.Plain)	144	CS 44
Makriel Rd	Nooitgedacht	105	CE 43
Makriel St	Gustrow	175	DB 75
Makupula	Kayamandi	94	BZ 74
Makvy Cl.	Annandale	90	BZ 55
Makwelo St	Kaya	146	CQ 51
Malachite Cl.	Somerset West	171	CW 77
Malaga Cr.	Table View	41	BO 32
Malamba Way	Langa	103	CD 35
Malambo St	Eyethu	146	CP 53
Malan Cr.	Brooklyn	84	BZ 31
Malan Cr.	Grassy Pk	141	CQ 33
Malan St	Durbanville	46	BQ 51
Malan St	Eastridge (M.Plain)	145	CQ 49
Malan St	Gardens	81	CC 21
Malan St	Lemoenkloof	18	BB 88
Malan St	Morgenster Hoogte	63	BU 56
Malan St	Somerset West	171	CU 75
Malan St	Wellington	10	AR 94
Malandalahla Cr.	Umrhabulo Triangle	147	CP 57
Malati Cr.	Victoria Mxenge	126	CN 51
Malawi Rd	Retreat	140	CS 28
Malbec Cl.	Table View	41	BO 33
Malbec Rd	Saxenburg Ind. Pk	108	CE 57
Malborough Way	Parklands	25	BM 32
Malcolm Rd	Rondebosch	102	CG 31
Malgas	Rocklands (M.Plain)	144	CS 44
Malgas	Wesbank	107	CG 51
Malgas Cl.	Durbanville	46	BP 52
Malgas Cl.	Durbanville	46	BS 54
Malgas Rd	Table View	41	BQ 32
Malgas Rd	Table View	41	BQ 33
Malgas St	Flintdale Est.	141	CP 31
Malgas St	Macassar	149	CS 64
Malherbe Rd	Elsies River Ind.	86	BZ 42
Malherbe St	Paarl	22	BD 88
Malherbe St	Paarl	22	BD 89
Malherbe St	Wellington	10	AR 93
Mali Cr.	Kaya	146	CP 51
Mali St	Crossroads	124	CK 44
Malibu St	Bellair	62	BV 52
Malibu St	Bellair	62	BV 53
Malifa St	Bloekombos	48	BR 62
Malindi Cr.	Mandela Pk	147	CQ 55
Malines Ave	Claremont	101	CH 30
Malinga Cr.	Victoria Mxenge	146	CO 51
Malio St	Driftsands	126	CL 51
Malithi Cl.	Bloekombos	48	BQ 62
Maliti St	Guguletu	104	CG 41
Maliti St	Guguletu	104	CH 41
Maliza St	Kaya	146	CP 51
Malleson Rd	Mowbray	101	CD 30
Mallet	Eureka	87	CC 44
Mallow St	Hazendal	102	CF 33
Malmesbury Rd	Paarl	18	AY 88
Malmesbury Rd	Welgelegen	59	BT 40
Malmesbury Rd	Welgelegen	59	BU 41
Malmesbury Rd	Wellington	14	AU 88
Malmesbury St	Ruyterwacht	86	CA 39
Malone Ave	Claremont	101	CH 29
Malta Cl.	Portlands (M.Plain)	144	CP 46
Malta Rd	Observatory	83	CB 29
Malta Rd	Ottery	121	CL 33
Malton Rd	Wynberg	120	CM 29
Malton Way	Dennemere	108	CH 58
Malume Cr.	Umrhabulo Triangle	147	CP 56
Malume Cr.	Umrhabulo Triangle	147	CP 57
Malunga	Guguletu	104	CH 40
Malunga St	Lwandle	175	CZ 76
Maluti Cr.	Eersterivier	128	CL 59
Maluti Rd	Bonnie Brae	47	BP 57
Maluti St	Lavender Hill East	160	CU 32
Malva Cr.	Brackenfell	63	BV 57
Malva Rd	Uitsig	87	CB 44
Malva St	Peerless Pk East	63	BT 58
Malva St	Wellington	15	AT 92
Malvern Cr.	Eersterivier	128	CN 61
Mamre	Ravensmead	87	CB 44
Mamre St	Eersterivier	128	CL 60
Mamre St	Northern Paarl	18	AZ 89
Mananase Ndlebe St	Guguletu	104	CG 41
Manatoka Ave	Amandelrug	90	CA 55
Manatoka Ave	Pinelands	84	CC 34
Manatoka Ave	Thornton	85	CA 37
Manatoka Rd	Bonteheuwel	104	CE 40
Manchester Rd	Airport Ind.	105	CG 43
Manchester St	Dunoon	42	BO 38
Manchester St	Hout Bay	137	CP 15
Manchester St	Malibu Village	127	CK 56
Manchester St	Portlands (M.Plain)	144	CQ 46
Manchester St	Uitzicht	31	BN 55
Mandel Rd	Newfields	122	CJ 36
Mandela Ave	Sir Lowry's Pass	176	CZ 82
Mandevilla Cl.	Somerset West	171	CW 77
Mandla Cr.	Nonqubela	126	CN 52
Mandla St	Tarentaalplaas	175	CY 75
Mandoleni	Sonstraal Hgts	46	BR 53
Mandolin Cl.	Belhar	106	CD 48
Mandolin Cl.	Belhar	106	CH 48
Mandoline Sq.	Steenberg	159	CT 30
Mandrel Pl.	Uitsig	87	CC 44
Manenberg Ave	Manenberg	104	CH 39
Manenberg Ave	Manenberg	123	CJ 39
Manenberg Ave	Manenberg	123	CK 39
Manengele St	Nomzamo	175	CY 76
Mangaan St	Vanguard	103	CG 38
Mango	Delft Sth	125	CK 48
Mango	Delft Sth	125	CK 49
Mango St	Dunoon	42	BO 37
Mango St	Kaya	146	CO 52
Mangold St	Wesbank	107	CH 51
Mangoro Cr.	Delft	106	CF 49
Mangxaba St	Crossroads	124	CK 44
Manhattan St	Airport Ind.	104	CG 42
Manhattan St	Airport Ind.	105	CG 43
Manie St	Eersterivier	128	CL 59
Manitoba Cl.	Portlands (M.Plain)	144	CQ 45
Manitoba Rd	Coniston Pk	159	CU 30
Manitoba Rd	Retreat	140	CS 28
Mankadam	Mostertsdrift	95	CC 78
Mankayi Cl.	Bloekombos	48	BR 62
Mankayi Cr.	Eyethu	146	CP 53
Manly Rd	Athlone	102	CG 32
Manlyn Wk	Pinati	122	CK 35
Mannings La.	Somerset West	151	CS 74
Mano St	Mfuleni	126	CJ 53
Manono	Mbekweni	15	AX 91
Manor Ave	Noordhoek Manor	157	CX 21
Manor House	Constantia Vale	119	CN 25
Manor House	Silverhurst	119	CN 24
Manowarr Rd	Ottery	121	CL 34
Manrose St	Salt River	83	CB 27
Mansell Rd	Killarney Gdns	42	BP 36
Mansfield Cr.	Gordon Hgts	180	DD 79
Mansfield Mews	Sunset Links	57	BT 31
Mansfield Rd	Lansdowne	121	CL 34
Mansfield Rd	Parklands	25	BN 34
Mansfield Rd	Tijgerhof	57	BV 32
Manson Cl.	Dreyersdal	140	CR 27
Manson Rd	Newlands	101	CG 27
Manta Way	Nooitgedacht	105	CE 43
Manta Way	Strandfontein	162	CT 39
Mantashe St	Eyethu	146	CP 53
Manuels St	Wallacedene	48	BS 60
Manus Fortein St	William Lloyd	19	BC 92
Manus Gerber St	N1 City	59	BX 40
Manyano	Kalkfontein I	107	CD 52
Manyano	Kayamandi	94	CA 74
Manyano Ave	Nyanga	123	CL 42
Manyano Rd	Ekuphumuleni	146	CQ 53
Manyano St	Crossroads	124	CK 44
Manyano St	Griffiths Mxenge	146	CQ 54
Manzi St	Ilitha Pk	146	CQ 52
Manzi St	Umrhabulo Triangle	147	CQ 57
Manzini Wk	Thembokwezi	125	CN 49
Maori Rd	Hout Bay	116	CL 14
Maori Rd	Strandfontein	163	CT 43
Mapasa St	Nyanga	123	CJ 42
Maphelo St	Mxolisi Phetani	126	CM 51
Maphongwana Ave	Mxolisi Phetani	125	CM 50
Maple Ave	Gardens	81	CC 21
Maple Cl.	Mitchells Plain	144	CQ 45
Maple Cr.	Vredekloof	62	BU 53
Maple Gr.	Parklands	25	BN 33
Maple La.	Bergvliet	140	CQ 27
Maple St	Bellair	62	BW 51
Maple St	Fairie Knowe	185	DA 19
Maple St	Sanddrift	57	BW 34
Maple Way	Rusdal	108	CE 57
Maple Way	Weltevreden Val. (M.Plain)	143	CO 42
Mapolo Rd	Ekuphumuleni	146	CQ 53
Maprin Rd	Flintdale Est.	141	CP 31
Maputo St	Mfuleni	126	CJ 53
Maputo Way	Delft	106	CG 49
Mara Ave	Athlone	102	CG 33
Mara Rd	Bellville	61	BU 48
Mara Rd	Kenridge	61	BU 48
Maracaibo St	Malibu Village	127	CL 56
Marais	Stellenbosch	95	CC 77
Marais Cr.	Durbanville	46	BP 51
Marais Cr.	Edgemead	58	BV 37
Marais Rd	Hout Bay	137	CP 16
Marais Rd	Sea Point	81	BZ 19
Marais St	De Zoete Inval	39	BJ 87
Marais St	Harbour Island	179	DE 77
Marais St	Klipdam	90	CC 55
Marais St	Lochnerhof	170	CX 71
Marais St	Lochnerhof	174	CY 72
Marais St	Milnerton	57	BV 32
Marais St	Morgenster Hoogte	63	BU 56
Marais St	Richmond	86	BY 41
Marais St	Somerset West	171	CW 75
Marais St	Wellington	10	AR 94
Maralize Cr.	Beacon Valley (M.Plain)	145	CP 48
Maranatha St	De Kuilen	89	CB 54
Maranon St	Eindhoven	125	CJ 50
Marathon Rd	Silvertown	103	CF 35
Marauder	Rocklands (M.Plain)	163	CT 45
Marbella	D'urbanvale	45	BO 49
Marble Cl.	Rocklands (M.Plain)	145	CS 47
Marbon Cl.	Voorbrug	107	CG 51
Marchal Cr.	Wimbledon	108	CH 55
Marchand St	Wellington	15	AT 91
Marchmont Ave	Oranjezicht	99	CD 22
Marchmont Rd	Muizenberg	159	CX 29
Marchmont Rd	Muizenberg	159	CW 27
Marcia St	Tafelsig (M.Plain)	145	CS 50
Marco Cl.	Uitzicht	47	BO 56

Index to Street Names

Marconi Cr. — Milner Way

STREET NAME	SUBURB NAME	PG	GRID
Marconi Cr.	Marconi Beam	57	BT 34
Marconi Rd	Montague Gdns Ind.	42	BS 35
Marconi Rd	Montague Gdns Ind.	58	BT 35
Marconi St	Belhar	88	CC 49
Marconi Way	Meadowridge	140	CP 28
Marcus Cr.	Pine Acres	175	DC 77
Mare St	Strandfontein	143	CS 41
Maree Cl.	Brackenfell	63	BW 55
Maree Cl.	Kommetjie	183	DC 13
Maree St	Kempenville	61	BX 49
Maree St	Kommetjie	183	DC 13
Maree St	Stanlou	61	BX 49
Marehale Cr.	Woodbridge Island	57	BW 31
Marela Cl.	Bloekombos	48	BR 62
Margaret Ave	Pinelands	84	CB 34
Margaret Ave	Somerset West	171	CW 75
Margaret Pl.	Pinelands	84	CB 34
Margaret Rd	Bishop Lavis	104	CD 41
Margaret St	Delro	126	CJ 54
Margaret St	Gaylee	108	CH 57
Margaret St	Silverhurst	119	CN 25
Margate Rd	Muizenberg	159	CX 30
Margaux La.	Somerset West	151	CQ 72
Margot St	Russel's Rest	128	CL 59
Marguerite	Lentegeur (M.Plain)	144	CO 46
Marhamncwa St	Bloekombos	48	BR 62
Maria St	Avonwood	86	CB 42
Maria St	Franschhoek Sth	78	BY 105
Maria St	Franschhoek Sth	78	BY 106
Maria St	Kalkfontein II	107	CD 53
Marianna Cr.	Beacon Valley (M.Plain)	145	CP 48
Marianne Cl.	Somerset West	151	CS 74
Marico Ct	Northpine	63	BU 58
Marico St	Manenberg	122	CJ 38
Marico Way	Edgemead	59	BU 39
Marie Cr.	Valhalla Pk	104	CE 41
Marie St	Rondebosch	101	CG 28
Mariendahl Ave	Claremont	101	CH 29
Mariete Cl.	Sonstraal Hgts	46	BR 53
Marietjie Cr.	Beacon Valley (M.Plain)	145	CP 48
Mariette Mews	Eversdal Hgts	45	BS 50
Marigold	Dunoon	42	BO 37
Marigold	Lentegeur (M.Plain)	144	CO 45
Marigold	Uitsig	87	CB 44
Marigold Ct	Kewtown	102	CF 34
Marigold Rd	Ravensmead	87	CB 46
Marigold St	Dalvale	19	AZ 92
Marigold St	Dalvale	19	BA 94
Marigold St	Hillcrest Hgts	127	CL 57
Marigold St	Milnerton	57	BT 33
Marigold St	Silvertown	103	CF 35
Marike de Klerk St	Fisantekraal	31	BK 58
Marilyn St	Woodlands (M.Plain)	144	CQ 44
Marimba Cr.	Sonstraal Hgts	46	BR 53
Marina	Die Boord	112	CD 74
Marina Cr.	Blouberg Sands	24	BL 30
Marina Cr.	Northgate	59	BW 42
Marina Cr.	Somerset West	170	CT 74
Marina Cr.	Tafelsig (M.Plain)	145	CS 50
Marina Rd	William Lloyd	19	BC 93
Marinda Ave	Montana/Durrheim	104	CF 41
Marinda Cr.	Marinda Hgts	89	BZ 52
Marine Cir.	Table View	40	BO 30
Marine Dr.	Dolphin Beach	40	BP 30
Marine Dr.	Paarden Eiland	83	BY 30
Marine Dr.	Table View	24	BN 29
Marine Dr.	Table View	40	BO 29
Marine Dr.	Woodstock	83	CA 28
Marine Dr. Service Rd	Paarden Eiland	83	BY 30
Marine Dr. Service Rd	Paarden Eiland	83	BZ 29
Marine Rd	Strandfontein	162	CT 40
Marine Rd	Three Anchor Bay	81	BZ 20
Mariner	Rocklands (M.Plain)	163	CT 45
Mariner Way	Heathfield	140	CQ 29
Mariners Cl.	Simon's Town	191	DH 23
Mariner's Cl.	Kommetjie	183	DB 12
Mariners Way	Anchorage Pk	179	DD 78
Marinus Ave	Grassy Pk	141	CR 32
Marinus Cl.	Wellington	15	AV 92
Marinus St	Marconi Beam	57	BU 33
Marion Ave	Flintdale Est.	141	CP 31
Marion Cl.	Portlands (M.Plain)	144	CS 46
Marion Cr.	Ravensmead	87	CA 45
Marion St	Glen Ive	62	BU 51
Maritime	Langeberg Rdg	47	BR 55
Maritz St	Aurora	45	BP 48
Maritz St	Flintdale Est.	141	CP 31
Maritz St	Kempenville	88	BY 49
Marius Rd	Montagu's Gift	142	CO 35
Marivy St	Sybrand Pk	102	CE 33
Mark	Franschhoek Nth	75	BX 105
Mark	Sarepta	89	CC 52
Mark Mvala St	Kuyasa	147	CS 55
Mark Mvala St	Kuyasa	147	CS 58
Mark Rd	Claremont	101	CH 28
Mark St	Bellville	88	BY 47
Mark St	Belmont Pk	48	BR 60
Mark St	Park Estates	174	CY 72
Mark St	Wellington	10	AR 92
Mark St	Wellington	10	AR 93
Market	Plumstead	120	CN 29
Market	Stellenbosch	95	CC 75
Market St	Philippi East	124	CM 46
Market Sq.	Grassy Pk	141	CQ 32
Market St	Belhar	106	CD 50

STREET NAME	SUBURB NAME	PG	GRID
Market St	Grassy Pk	141	CR 32
Market St	Klipkop	87	BZ 45
Market St	Paarl	22	BD 88
Market St	Parowvallei	87	BZ 43
Market St	Parowvallei	87	BZ 44
Market St	Temperance Town	180	DD 79
Markham Cr.	Eersterivier	128	CM 59
Markham Rd	Claremont	101	CH 30
Markotter	Uniepark	96	CB 79
Marlborough Dr.	Noordhoek Manor	157	CX 21
Marlborough Dr.	Noordhoek Manor	157	CV 20
Marlborough Rd	Kenilworth	120	CK 28
Marlborough St	Windsor Pk	47	BS 57
Marlbrook Way	Fir Grove	139	CQ 25
Marlin Cr.	Hout Bay Harbour	136	CR 14
Marlin Cr.	Hout Bay Harbour	136	CR 14
Marlin Cr.	Strandfontein	162	CT 39
Marlin La.	Nooitgedacht	104	CE 42
Marlin La.	Nooitgedacht	105	CE 43
Marlin St	Strandfontein	162	CT 39
Marloth	Wesbank	107	CG 51
Marloth Rd	Tijgerhof	57	BW 32
Marlowe Rd	Kenilworth	120	CK 29
Marmer St	Bellville	62	BU 51
Marmion Ave	Clovelly	186	DA 25
Marmion Rd	Oranjezicht	99	CD 22
Marne Ave	Claremont	101	CH 30
Marne Rd	Strandfontein	162	CU 42
Maroela	Arbeidslus	96	CA 80
Maroela	Arbeidslus	96	CB 80
Maroela	Delft Sth	125	CJ 49
Maroela	Loevenstein	60	BW 46
Maroela Ave	New Orleans	18	BB 90
Maroela Cl.	Perm Gdns	128	CK 59
Maroela Cl.	Plattekloof	60	BV 43
Maroela Rd	Kraaifontein Ind.	48	BQ 61
Maroela St	Eastridge (M.Plain)	145	CR 48
Maroela St	Vygeboom	45	BR 50
Maroela St	Wallacedene	48	BS 61
Maroela Way	Pinelands	84	CC 34
Maroon Rd	Parkwood	141	CP 32
Marquisite Cl.	Rocklands (M.Plain)	145	CS 47
Mars	Rocklands (M.Plain)	144	CS 45
Mars Cl.	Salberau	86	CB 41
Mars Cl.	Salberau	86	CB 39
Mars Rd	Bishop Lavis	105	CD 44
Mars Rd	Manenberg	104	CG 39
Mars Rd	Wynberg	120	CM 29
Mars St	Bothasig	42	BS 37
Mars St	Sarepta	89	CC 53
Mars St	Somerset Hgts	127	CK 57
Mars Way	Phoenix	57	BU 34
Mars Way	Thembokwezi	125	CM 49
Marsala Cl.	Highbury	107	CD 54
Marsala St	Bellavista	22	BD 90
Marsch Cl.	Des Hampden	89	CB 53
Marsden Rd	Hout Bay	137	CO 16
Marsden Rd	Woodstock	82	CC 26
Marseille Cl.	Vredekloof	62	BT 53
Marseilles St	Wellington	10	AR 94
Marseilles Way	Malibu Village	127	CK 55
Marsh Alliston St	Sir Lowry's Pass	176	CZ 81
Marsh Rd	Rondebosch	102	CG 32
Marsh St	Denneburg	22	BD 90
Marshall Ave	Wynberg	120	CK 27
Marshall Rd	Richmond Est.	59	BX 40
Marshall Rd	Vasco Est.	86	BY 39
Marston Rd	Dieprivier	140	CP 28
Martell St	Tijgerhof	57	BW 32
Martello Rd	Simon's Town	194	DJ 26
Marten Cr.	Sunridge	41	BO 34
Martha Rd	Bishop Lavis	105	CD 43
Martha Rd	Bishop Lavis	105	CE 45
Martha St	Eastridge (M.Plain)	145	CQ 48
Martha Williams St	Balvenie	86	CB 42
Marthinus Van Shalkwyk St	Wesbank	107	CF 51
Martin	Idasvallei	96	CA 79
Martin Adams Rd	Ruyterwacht	86	CB 39
Martin Adams Rd	Ruyterwacht	86	CB 40
Martin Cr.	Pelikan Pk	142	CS 35
Martin Hammerschlag Way	Cape Town Cen.	82	CA 25
Martin Luther St	Belgravia	103	CG 35
Martin Prince Rd	Somerset West	171	CV 75
Martin Rd	Barbarossa	120	CN 28
Martin Rd	Chrismar	61	BW 50
Martin Rd	Electric City	127	CN 58
Martin St	Northern Paarl	18	AZ 89
Martin St	Scottsdene	64	BT 58
Martindale	Kleinvlei	127	CJ 58
Martindale Ave	Pinelands	102	CD 34
Martine St	Adriaanse	87	CC 43
Martine St	Tafelsig (M.Plain)	145	CS 50
Martingale	Mitchells Plain	144	CS 45
Martingale Ave	Hout Bay	117	CN 16
Martinson	Stellenbosch	95	CB 78
Martius Way	The Vines	140	CO 28
Marula Cl.	Somerset West	171	CW 76
Marvello St	Bellville Sth Ind.	88	CA 49
Mary Rd	Macassar Beach	149	CS 63
Maryland	Rocklands (M.Plain)	144	CS 46
Maryland Ave	Dennedal	139	CR 25
Maryland St	Factreton	84	BZ 34
Masakane	Masiphumelele	184	DA 17
Masakhane	Mbekweni	15	AW 92
Masakhane Cr.	Mxolisi Phetani	125	CM 50

STREET NAME	SUBURB NAME	PG	GRID
Masakhane St	Lwandle	175	CZ 76
Masakhane St	Lwandle	175	DA 76
Masakhe St	Crossroads	124	CJ 44
Masakhe St	Gugulethu	123	CK 41
Masaleni Cr.	Scottsdene	64	BT 60
Masebulele	Masiphumelele	184	DA 18
Masele	Mbekweni	15	AX 92
Masemola Rd	Masiphumelele	184	DA 18
Masemola St	Mandela Pk	147	CQ 55
Masemola St	Weltevreden Val. (M.Plain)	123	CN 42
Mashie St	Lakeside	159	CV 27
Masibambane Cr.	Mxolisi Phetani	125	CM 50
Masimbambane St	Gugulethu	123	CJ 41
Masiphathisane Cr.	Mxolisi Phetani	125	CL 49
Masitembane Cr.	Mxolisi Phetani	125	CM 50
Masithandane	Kayamandi	94	BZ 74
Masiza St	Gugulethu	104	CH 41
Masizakhe St	Mxolisi Phetani	125	CL 49
Maskam Cr.	Wingfield Nth Camp	58	BW 38
Maslamoney Rd	Sand Ind.	122	CJ 37
Masoka St	Bloekombos	48	BR 62
Masomi	Mbekweni	15	AW 92
Mason Ave	Sir Lowry's Pass	176	CZ 81
Mason St	Onverwacht	174	CZ 74
Masonic St	Rome	174	CY 72
Masonwabe	Lekkerwater	184	DA 17
Masonwabe	Masiphumelele	184	DA 18
Massey Ave	Athlone	102	CG 34
Massinger Rd	Plumstead	140	CP 29
Masson Rd	Tijgerhof	57	BV 32
Mast Mews	Blouberg Sands	24	BM 30
Masterman Cr.	Newfields	103	CH 36
Masters Way	Strandfontein	162	CT 41
Matanzima Rd	Nyanga	124	CK 43
Matapan Ave	Strandfontein	162	CT 40
Matapan Rd	Rondebosch	102	CG 32
Mataro Ave	Somerset West	151	CS 72
Mataro Rd	Northpine	64	BU 59
Mataung St	Sir Lowry's Pass	176	CZ 82
Matchless Rd	Sanddrift	57	BV 34
Mateta St	Eyethu	146	CO 53
Mathaba Cr.	Nonqubela	126	CN 53
Mathanbeka St	Bloekombos	48	BR 62
Mathemba	Mbekweni	15	AW 91
Mathew Rd	Claremont	120	CJ 30
Mathies St	Pinati	122	CK 35
Mathole St	Bloekombos	49	BQ 63
Mati W.Lefuma St	Gugulethu	104	CH 41
Matie St	Klipkop	87	BY 45
Matilla Pl.	Leonsdale	86	CA 42
Matiloshe St	Griffiths Mxenge	146	CP 54
Matiloshe St	Griffiths Mxenge	147	CQ 55
Matolengwe Cr.	Nyanga	123	CK 42
Matomela St	Mxolisi Phetani	126	CM 51
Matopo Rd	Mowbray	101	CD 29
Matopo Rd	Thornton	85	CB 36
Matopos Cr.	Tafelsig (M.Plain)	145	CS 48
Matroos	Scottsdene	64	BT 61
Matroos Rd	Durbanville Hills	45	BR 49
Matroos Sq.	Factreton	85	BY 35
Matroosberg	Brackenfell	63	BW 55
Matroosberg	Wellington	15	AU 91
Matroosberg Cr.	Belhar	106	CE 49
Matroosberg Cr.	Bonnie Brae	47	BP 57
Matroosberg Cr.	Bonnie Brae	47	BP 58
Matroosberg Cr.	Greenfield	108	CH 57
Matroosberg Cr.	Tafelsig (M.Plain)	145	CR 49
Matruh Rd	Lansdowne	121	CL 32
Matshoba Cr.	Victoria Mxenge	126	CN 51
Matshoba St	Scottsdene	48	BS 61
Matshooa St	Scottsdene	64	BT 60
Matsikama St	Tafelsig (M.Plain)	145	CR 49
Matterhorn Cr.	Tafelsig (M.Plain)	145	CS 49
Matthee St	Parow East	87	BY 45
Mattheus St	Valhalla Pk	104	CE 41
Matthew	Sarepta	89	CC 53
Matthew Goniwe	Weltevreden Val. (M.Plain)	123	CN 42
Matthew Goniwe St	Mandela Pk	147	CR 55
Matthews Rd	Ocean View	184	DC 16
Matthews St	William Lloyd	23	BD 94
Matukata	Mbekweni	15	AW 92
Maud	Woodlands (M.Plain)	124	CN 44
Maui	kraaifontein	47	BQ 58
Maureen Ave	Glenhaven	89	CA 52
Maureen Cr.	Tafelsig (M.Plain)	145	CS 50
Maurice St	Wellington	15	AU 93
Mauritius Cl.	Capri	185	DB 19
Mauritius Cr.	Capri	185	DB 19
Mauritius Rd	Bothasig	42	BS 37
Mauritius St	Avondale	60	BX 44
Mauritius Way	Glen Ive	62	BU 52
Mauritius Way	Portlands (M.Plain)	144	CQ 46
Mavis Rd	Doornhoogte	103	CG 36
Mavis St	Tafelsig (M.Plain)	145	CS 50
Mavu Rd	Ekuphumuleni	146	CQ 53
Mawetu	Kayamandi	94	BZ 74
Mawisa St	Eyethu	146	CO 53
Mawson St	Maitland Gdn Village	84	CC 31
Max Rd	Rugby	57	BX 32
Max Sisulu St	Mandela Pk	147	CR 55
Maxama St	Victoria Mxenge	146	CO 51
Maxhob'Asebisho	Weltevreden Val. (M.Plain)	123	CN 42
Maximillian Ave	Glenhaven	89	CA 51
May Ave	Wellington	15	AV 92
May Rd	Bishop Lavis	105	CD 43

STREET NAME	SUBURB NAME	PG	GRID
May Rd	Somerset West	170	CU 74
May Rd	Sunridge	41	BP 34
May St	Avonwood	86	CA 42
May St	Claremont	120	CJ 30
May St	William Lloyd	19	BC 93
Mayande	Mbekweni	15	AW 91
Mayataza St	Nonqubela	146	CO 52
Maybank Rd	Flintdale Est.	140	CP 29
Maybrook St	Wesbank	107	CG 52
Maybury Rd	Lansdowne	121	CK 32
Maydon St	Three Anchor Bay	81	BZ 21
Mayekiso St	Nonqubela	126	CN 53
Mayezana St	Wallacedene	48	BS 60
Mayfair Ave	Claremont	101	CH 29
Mayfair Ave	Somerset West	151	CS 73
Mayfair Cl.	Portlands (M.Plain)	145	CR 47
Mayfair Cr.	Durbanville	45	BP 49
Mayfair Cr.	Durbanville	45	BP 47
Mayfair Cr.	Silvermine Village	185	CY 20
Mayfair Cr.	Weltevreden Val. (M.Plain)	123	CN 42
Mayfield Ave	Rondebosch	102	CG 31
Mayflower Rd	Eersterivier	128	CN 60
Mayflower Way	Sun Valley	185	CZ 20
Mayibuye	Mbekweni	15	AW 92
Mayibuye St	Mxolisi Phetani	125	CM 50
Maynard Cl.	Pinelands	102	CD 33
Maynard Feenstra Rd	Wellington	10	AR 94
Maynard Rd	Muizenberg	159	CX 29
Maynard Rd	Wynberg	120	CL 29
Maynard St	Gardens	82	CB 23
Mayonga Cr.	Scottsdene	64	BT 60
Maytime Way	Eversdal	62	BT 51
Mayville Rd	Sonstraal Hgts	46	BP 54
Maze St	Mabille Pk	89	CA 53
Mazizi St	Kaya	146	CP 51
Mazoe Ct	Delft	106	CG 49
Mazot	Brandwacht	113	CE 77
Mazzur Rd	Belgravia	88	BY 49
Mbabala	Philippi East	124	CM 46
Mbadu Ave	Rusthof	175	DA 75
Mbali St	Kaya	146	CP 52
Mbambiso St	Lwandle	175	CZ 77
Mbandezelo St	Lwandle	175	CY 76
Mbashe St	Mfuleni	126	CK 53
Mbashe St	Mfuleni	126	CK 52
Mbeki St	Crossroads	124	CK 44
Mbeko St	Umrhabulo Triangle	147	CQ 56
Mbekweni	Lekkerwater	184	DA 17
Mbekweni St	Lwandle	175	CZ 76
Mbekweni St	Mxolisi Phetani	125	CM 49
Mbeleko	Mbekweni	15	AV 91
Mbesa Cr.	Victoria Mxenge	146	CO 51
Mbhele St	Tarentaalplaas	175	CY 75
Mbhongisa Ave	Joe Slovo Pk	57	BU 34
Mbhongisa Ave	Joe Slovo Pk	57	BU 31
Mbiko St	Tarentaalplaas	171	CX 75
Mbila	Philippi East	125	CM 47
Mbila Ave	Joe Slovo Pk	57	BU 34
Mbila Ave	Joe Slovo Pk	57	BU 31
Mbila St	Kuyasa	147	CR 56
Mbindini Ave	Mfuleni	127	CL 55
Mbiso	Mbekweni	15	AW 91
Mbolwa Cr.	Kaya	146	CP 51
Mbomvane St	Brown's Farm	123	CL 42
Mbomvane St	Brown's Farm	123	CM 42
Mbona St	Kaya	146	CQ 52
Mbongi	Mbekweni	15	AV 91
Mbongi St	Kaya	146	CP 52
Mbotyi St	Harare	146	CR 52
Mbotyi St	Harare	146	CR 53
Mbula St	Tarentaalplaas	171	CX 75
Mbumba	Mbekweni	15	AW 92
Mcaphukiso Ave	Nyanga	123	CK 42
Mcaphukiso Ave	Nyanga	123	CM 39
McBrides La.	Claremont	120	CJ 30
McCarthy St	Fairfield	87	BY 43
McClean Rd	Heathfield	140	CQ 28
McCoy	Idasvallei	96	CA 80
Mcdonald	Stellenbosch	95	CC 77
McDonald St	Goodwood Est.	86	BZ 39
Mcewula St	Eyethu	146	CP 53
Mcewula St	Eyethu	146	CP 54
McFarlane Rd	Simon's Town	195	DJ 27
McFarlane St	Lemoenkloof	18	BB 88
McGregor Cl.	Belhar	107	CE 51
McGregor St	Beaconvale	87	BZ 43
McGregor St	Maitland	83	CA 31
McGuinness St	De Tijger	60	BX 44
McIntyre Rd	Glenlily	87	BY 43
McIntyre Rd	Parow Nth	60	BW 42
McKay Cl.	Langgewacht	170	CW 72
McKenzie St	District Six	82	CB 24
McKenzie St	Gardens	82	CB 23
McKinley Rd	Kenilworth Pk	120	CJ 30
McLachlan Sq.	Groenheuwel	19	AZ 91
McLeod St	Somerset West	170	CU 74
McLeod St	Somerset West	171	CT 75
McManus St	Kensington	84	BZ 33
Mcnagt Kwanini St	Gugulethu	123	CJ 41
Mcwangele St	Ilitha Pk	146	CQ 52
Mdala	Kayamandi	94	CA 74
Mdingi Cr.	Mxolisi Phetani	126	CM 51
Mdolombo St	Langa	103	CD 35
Mdubi Dr.	Joe Slovo Pk	57	BU 34
Mdubi St	Brown's Farm	123	CM 42

Abbreviations used: Ave – Avenue, A.H. – Agricultural Holding, A.L.– Algemene Landgoed, Blvd – Boulevard, Cen. – Central, Cir. – Circle, Cl. – Close, Cr. – Crescent, Ct – Court, Dr. – Drive, Est. – Estate, Ext. – Extension, Hgts – Heights, Ind. – Industrial, Gdns – Gardens, Gr. – Grove, La. – Lane, (M.Plain) - Mitchells Plain, Nth – North, Pl. – Place, Pk – Park, Rd – Road, Rdg. – Ridge, S.H.– Small Holding, Sq. – Square, St – Street, Sth – South, Ter. – Terrace, Tn – Turn, Val. – Valley, Wk – Walk

STREET NAME	SUBURB NAME	PG	GRID	
Mdumbi St	Mfuleni	126	CK	54
Mead Way	Pinelands	84	CC	32
Meadow Ave	Hout Bay	117	CN	17
Meadow Cl.	Adriaanse	87	CC	43
Meadow Cl.	Hout Bay	117	CN	17
Meadow Ct	Rocklands (M.Plain)	144	CS	45
Meadow La.	Somerset West	171	CV	76
Meadow Rd	Austinville	108	CH	56
Meadow Rd	Milnerton	57	BW	31
Meadow Rd	Ottery	121	CL	33
Meadow Rd	Rosebank	101	CE	29
Meadow Way	Plumstead	120	CN	27
Meaker St	New Orleans	19	BA	91
Meath Rd	Oakdale	61	BX	49
Mechau St	Cape Town Cen.	82	BZ	23
Medburn Rd	Camps Bay	99	CE	19
Medeira Cr.	Table View	41	BO	33
Medina St	Kirstenhof	158	CT	26
Mediterranean Ave	Eersterivier	128	CM	59
Medlar St	Bonteheuwel	104	CE	39
Medoc Rd	Northpine	63	BT	58
Medusa Ct	Eureka	87	CC	43
Medusa Ct	Eureka	87	CB	46
Medway Rd	Durbell	45	BS	49
Medway Rd	Durbell	45	BS	50
Medway Rd	Plumstead	120	CN	30
Meebos St	Ruwari	63	BV	57
Meeltou Rd	Durbanville	45	BP	49
Meeltou Rd	Durbanville	45	BP	47
Meent St	Wellington	14	AT	90
Meerenbosch	D'urbanvale	45	BO	49
Meerendal Rd	Edgemead	58	BU	37
Meerendal Rd	Meerendal	29	BM	47
Meerendal Rd	Townsend Est.	58	BX	38
Meerendal St	De Bron	45	BS	48
Meerenhof	Welgedacht	60	BT	46
Meerenhof Rd	Mabille Pk	89	CA	53
Meerhof	Kirstenhof	158	CU	26
Meerhof Ave	Monte Vista	59	BU	39
Meerhof St	Bothasig	42	BS	37
Meerhof St	Paarlzicht	19	BC	91
Meerhof St	Tafelsig (M.Plain)	145	CR	49
Meerlust	Bellair	62	BW	52
Meerlust	Karindal	96	CC	79
Meerlust	Oak Glen	62	BW	52
Meerlust	Pinelands	85	CC	35
Meerlust Ave	Somerset West	171	CT	75
Meerlust Cl.	Richwood	42	BP	38
Meerlust Cl.	Weltevreden Val. (M.Plain)	144	CR	45
Meerlust Cl.	Weltevreden Val. (M.Plain)	144	CS	43
Meerlust St	Die Bos	174	CY	74
Meerlust St	Kleinbosch	59	BT	40
Meerlust St	Table View	41	BO	32
Meerlust St	Voorbrug	106	CG	50
Meersig Rd	Elfindale	140	CQ	30
Meeu St	Flintdale Est.	141	CP	31
Megan St	Tafelsig (M.Plain)	145	CS	50
Meidoring St	Rouxville	90	CA	56
Meilland	Rosendal	61	BT	50
Meiring St	Denneburg	22	BD	90
Meiring St	Ruyterwacht	86	CA	39
Meja Cr.	Nonqubela	126	CN	53
Mela St	Bloekombos	48	BQ	62
Melani St	Driftsands	125	CL	50
Melani St	Driftsands	126	CL	51
Melba La.	Belhar	106	CD	48
Melba Rd	Bishop Lavis	105	CD	44
Melba Rd	Newlands	101	CH	28
Melbourne Cl.	Portlands (M.Plain)	144	CQ	46
Melbourne Rd	Kenilworth	120	CK	28
Melbourne Rd	Rondebosch East	102	CH	32
Melbourne Rd	Woodstock	82	CB	26
Melchior St	Morgenster Hoogte	63	BT	55
Melck Cr.	Belhar	106	CD	49
Melck St	Ndabeni	84	CB	32
Melina St	Rosendal	61	BU	50
Melkbaai St	Park Estates	170	CX	71
Melkboom	Bracken Hgts	62	BU	54
Melkboom Cl.	Gordon Strand	175	DC	76
Melkboom Rd	Muizenberg Nth	159	CV	28
Melkbos	Lentegeur (M.Plain)	144	CP	46
Melkbos	Stellenbosch	95	BY	75
Melkbos Rd	Belhar	105	CD	46
Melkbos St	Kleinvlei	128	CJ	59
Melkhout	Delft Sth	125	CJ	49
Melkhout	Weltevrede	94	BY	74
Melkhout Ave	Kommetjie	183	DB	12
Melkhout Ave	St Dumas	90	CC	56
Melkhout Ave	St Dumas	108	CD	56
Melkhout Cl.	Eastridge (M.Plain)	145	CR	48
Melkhout Cr.	Hout Bay	137	CQ	15
Melkhout Cr.	Plattekloof	60	BU	43
Melkhout Rd	Bonteheuwel	104	CE	39
Melkhout Rd	Proteavallei	61	BT	47
Melkhout St	Hout Bay	137	CQ	15
Melkhout St	Scarborough	192	DJ	17
Melkweg	Rocklands (M.Plain)	144	CS	46
Melle St	Hout Bay	137	CP	16
Mellheim	Lansdowne	121	CK	34
Melling St	Wellington	10	AR	93
Mellish Rd	Vredehoek	82	CC	23
Mellish St	Stikland Hospital	61	BX	50
Mellish St	Stikland Hospital	61	BV	48
Melo Ave	Athlone	102	CF	32
Melodie Rd	Kirstenhof	159	CT	27
Melody Sq.	Retreat	159	CT	30
Melon St	Maitland	83	CA	30
Melrose	Dunoon	42	BO	37
Melrose Ave	Muizenberg	159	CX	29
Melrose Ave	Muizenberg	159	CW	27
Melrose Cr.	Wesbank	107	CG	52
Melrose St	Ravensmead	87	CA	44
Melrose Wk	Claremont	101	CH	29
Melt Brink St	Clamhall	60	BX	43
Melton Rd	Adriaanse	105	CD	43
Melton Rd	Kleinvlei	128	CJ	59
Melton Rd	Perm Gdns	128	CJ	59
Melton St	Rosedale	128	CK	59
Melville Rd	Ottery East	121	CN	34
Melville Rd	Plumstead	140	CO	29
Melvin Cl.	Connaught	87	CB	43
Memani Ave	Nyanga	123	CK	41
Memani Cr.	Nonqubela	126	CN	53
Memel Cl.	Morgenster Hoogte	63	BT	56
Memel Rd	Claremont	101	CH	28
Memento Dr.	Langeberg Rdg	47	BR	55
Memento Dr.	Sonstraal Hgts	46	BR	54
Memeza St	Driftsands	126	CL	51
Mendelsohn	Groenheuwel	19	AZ	91
Mendelsohn	Groenheuwel	19	AZ	94
Mendelsohn Cr.	Sonstraal Hgts	46	BQ	54
Mendelson Rd	Mandalay	125	CM	48
Mendi	Kayamandi	94	CA	74
Mendi Ave	Langa	103	CD	36
Mendi Cl.	Mxolisi Phetani	125	CM	49
Mendoza St	Voorbrug	106	CG	50
Mene Cr.	Victoria Mxenge	126	CN	52
Menenge St	Crossroads	124	CK	45
Mengo	Kayamandi	94	CA	74
Menin Ave	Claremont	101	CH	29
Menlo Cr.	Edgemead	58	BV	38
Mensey Rd	Plumstead	120	CM	28
Menton Rd	St James	187	CZ	27
Mentz Cr.	De Duin	59	BW	41
Meppel	Morgen Gronde	63	BX	56
Mer St	Dolphin Beach	40	BP	30
Mercury	Rocklands (M.Plain)	144	CS	46
Mercury Cl.	Salberau	86	CB	41
Mercury Cl.	Salberau	86	CB	39
Mercury Cr.	Ottery	121	CL	33
Mercury Way	Joe Slovo Pk	57	BU	34
Mercury Way	Joe Slovo Pk	57	BU	31
Merigold Cr.	Weltevreden Val. (M.Plain)	124	CM	44
Merino St	Mitchells Plain	144	CR	46
Merino St	Rondebosch East	102	CH	32
Merion	Sunningdale	25	BL	31
Merlin Rd	Camelot	107	CF	53
Merlin Rd	Phumlani	142	CQ	36
Merlot	Langeberg Rdg	47	BR	55
Merlot Ave	Table View	41	BO	33
Merlot Cl.	Klein Zevenwacht	90	CB	58
Merlot Cl.	Vergesig	45	BQ	48
Merlot Cr.	Groenvlei	18	BA	88
Merlot Cr.	Groenvlei	18	BA	89
Merlot St	Oude Westhof	44	BS	45
Merlot St	Somerset West	151	CR	71
Merlot Way	Northpine	63	BU	58
Mermaid La.	Strandfontein	162	CT	39
Mernoelen Cr.	Highbury	107	CE	54
Meroleon	Lemoenkloof	18	BC	89
Meron Cr.	Die Oude Spruit	63	BX	56
Merrick St	Observatory	83	CC	28
Merrilhof	Lindida	96	CA	80
Merriman	Stellenbosch	95	CB	76
Merriman	Stellenbosch	95	CB	78
Merriman Ave	Somerset West	170	CT	73
Merriman Cr.	Eastridge (M.Plain)	145	CQ	49
Merriman La.	Belhar	106	CD	49
Merriman La.	Belhar	106	CH	48
Merriman Rd	Goodwood Est.	86	BY	39
Merriman Rd	Richmond Est.	86	BY	40
Merriman Rd	Sea Point	81	BZ	22
Merriman Rd	Townsend Est.	85	BZ	38
Merriman St	Langa	103	CD	36
Merriman St	Table View	41	BQ	34
Merry La.	Uit-kyk	171	CW	75
Merry Rocks	Durbanville	46	BQ	53
Merrydale Ave	Lentegeur (M.Plain)	144	CO	45
Merrydale Ave	Portlands (M.Plain)	144	CQ	46
Merrydale Ave	Portlands (M.Plain)	145	CR	47
Merrydale Ave	Rocklands (M.Plain)	145	CS	47
Mersa St	Penlyn Est.	103	CH	35
Mersey Cl.	Portlands (M.Plain)	144	CQ	46
Merten St	Groenvlei	18	BA	88
Merton	Lindida	96	CA	80
Mervyn Rd	Fish Hoek	186	DA	23
Merwe St	Ottery	121	CM	33
Merwede	Bellair	62	BV	53
Merwede Rd	Belhar	106	CE	49
Meryl Rd	Simon's Town	194	DK	26
Mes St	Macassar	149	CS	65
Mesani St	Crossroads	124	CJ	44
Meseta Rd	Montana/Durrheim	104	CF	42
Mesfort Cl.	Hout Bay Harbour	136	CR	13
Meson	Tegnopark	112	CF	73
Metal La.	Gardens	81	CB	22
Metal Rd	Blackheath Ind.	108	CF	56
Metallica Cr.	Groenvlei	18	BA	87
Meteor Cl.	Salberau	86	CB	41
Meteor Rd	Thembokwezi	125	CL	49
Meteor Way	Lansdowne	121	CK	33
Meteren Cr.	Dennemere	108	CH	57
Meteren Cr.	Dennemere	127	CJ	57
Metlane Cl.	Philippi East	125	CL	47
Metropolitan Rd	Retreat	140	CR	29
Metropolitan St	Beacon Valley (M.Plain)	145	CQ	48
Mettler St	Wellington	10	AS	92
Metzler St	Paarl	22	BE	88
Meulen Ct	Marina Da Gama	159	CV	30
Meurant Rd	Tijgerhof	57	BX	33
Mew Way	Bongani	126	CN	51
Mew Way	Bongani	146	CO	51
Mew Way	Driftsands	126	CM	51
Mew Way	Harare	146	CS	53
Mew Way	Kaya	146	CQ	51
Mew Way	Khayelitsha	147	CS	56
Meyboom Ave	Plattekloof	60	BU	43
Meyer Cl.	Langeberg Glen	47	BP	56
Meyer St	Claremont	120	CJ	30
Meyer St	Plumstead	140	CO	29
Meyer St	The Palms	170	CX	73
Meyer St	William Lloyd	23	BD	93
Meyrick Ave	Plumstead	140	CO	29
Mfene St	Kuyasa	147	CR	56
Mfula Cl.	Ilitha Pk	146	CQ	53
Mfuleni	Wellington	15	AU	91
Mfuleni Rd	Mfuleni	127	CL	55
Mfuleni Rd	Sunset Glen	108	CH	56
Mfundisweni St	Kaya	146	CP	51
Mfundo St	Bloekombos	49	BR	63
Mgabadeli Cr.	Kayamandi	94	BZ	74
Mganto	Philippi East	124	CM	46
Mghayi St	Langa	103	CD	36
Mghele Cl.	Bloekombos	48	BR	62
Mgidi St	Umrhabulo Triangle	147	CQ	57
Mgidlana St	Tarentaalplaas	170	CX	74
Mgidlana St	Tarentaalplaas	175	CY	75
Mgombothi	Mbekweni	15	AW	91
Mgooi Cl.	Langa	103	CE	37
Mgoqi Cl.	Nyanga	123	CL	41
Mgqibela St	Griffiths Mxenge	146	CQ	54
Mguqulwa Cl.	Langa	103	CE	37
Mguyo	Mbekweni	15	AV	91
Mgwanda St	Mfuleni	126	CK	53
Mhla St	Umrhabulo Triangle	147	CR	58
Mhlawuli Pl.	Mandela Pk	146	CR	54
Mhlazana Cr.	Wallacedene	48	BS	62
Mhlontlo St	Brown's Farm	123	CM	42
Mhlophe Cr.	Umrhabulo Triangle	147	CP	58
Miami Alley	Portlands (M.Plain)	144	CR	46
Miami Cl.	Portlands (M.Plain)	144	CR	46
Miami Way	Portlands (M.Plain)	144	CR	46
Micawber Rd	Salt River	83	CC	28
Michael Hendricks St	Charlesville	104	CF	40
Michael Mapongwana	Weltevreden Val. (M.Plain)	123	CN	42
Michael Richmond St	Nyanga	123	CK	42
Michael St	Nomzano	175	CY	75
Michael St	Northern Paarl	18	AZ	89
Michael Storer Ave	Silverhurst	119	CN	24
Michaels Rd	Strandfontein	162	CV	41
Michau St	Van Ryneveld	174	CZ	72
Michel du Toit	Boschenmeer Est.	39	BJ	90
Michele Cr.	Morgenster Hoogte	63	BU	55
Michele St	Klein Parys	23	BE	92
Michell St	Ruyterwacht	86	CA	39
Michell Wk	Marina Da Gama	159	CV	30
Michelle Ave	Mandalay	125	CN	47
Michelle St	De Tijger	60	BW	44
Michiel Laubscher Cr.	Panorama	59	BV	41
Michigan St	Airport Ind.	105	CG	44
Michigan Way	Portlands (M.Plain)	144	CQ	45
Micro St	Triangle Farm	88	BZ	50
Midas Cr.	Northpine	63	BT	58
Midas Cr.	Northpine	63	BU	58
Midas Cr.	Oak Glen	62	BW	53
Midas Ct	Eureka	87	CC	43
Middel	Cloetesville	95	BZ	75
Middel Rd	Doornhoogte	103	CG	36
Middel Rd	Doornhoogte	103	CH	35
Middel St	Kingston	61	BX	48
Middel St	Klipdam	90	CB	55
Middelbank Rd	Strandfontein	162	CU	42
Middelberg Cl.	Claremont	120	CJ	27
Middelberg St	Tafelsig (M.Plain)	145	CS	49
Middelburg Ave	Monte Vista	59	BU	40
Middelvlei St	Welgedacht	44	BS	46
Middenrak St	Dennemere	108	CH	57
Middle Ave	Schaap Kraal	142	CP	36
Middle Ave	Schaap Kraal	142	CP	37
Middleton Rd	Claremont	101	CH	29
Midhurst Way	Barbarossa	120	CN	27
Midmar Rd	Coniston Pk	159	CU	30
Midmar Rd	Groenvallei	62	BW	53
Midmar Rd	Groenvallei	62	BX	53
Midmar Rd	Kaymor	62	BX	53
Midmar Rd	Stikland Hospital	62	BX	52
Midnight St	Wesbank	107	CG	52
Midsea Way	Ruyterwacht	86	BZ	40
Midway Rd	Ottery	121	CM	33
Midway St	Scottsville	47	BS	57
Midwood Ave	Bergvliet	139	CQ	26
Midwood Ave	Claremont	101	CH	29
Midwood Ave	Richwood	42	BQ	38
Mielieheide Cl.	Roosendaal	107	CF	51
Mignon	Elfindale	140	CP	29
Mika St	Welgelegen	59	BU	40
Mike Pienaar Blvd	Vredelust	60	BX	46
Mike Pienaar Blvd.	Vredelust	87	BY	46
Mikonto St	Mandela Pk	147	CR	55
Mikro Ave	Langgewacht	170	CW	73
Mikro Rd	De Kuilen	89	CB	54
Mikro St	Goodwood Est.	58	BX	38
Mikro St	Parow Nth	59	BW	42
Milagro La.	Noordhaven	157	CX	19
Milan Rd	District Six	82	CB	25
Milando Cr.	Edgemead	59	BU	39
Milano Cr.	Strandfontein	163	CT	43
Milano Way	Strandfontein	163	CT	43
Milbank Rd	Wynberg	120	CL	29
Mildred Rd	Kenever	61	BT	49
Mildred Rd	Scottsdene	64	BT	60
Mildred St	Windsor Pk	47	BR	57
Mile End Rd	Dieprivier	140	CP	28
Miles	Scottsdene	48	BS	61
Miles Rd	Ottery East	121	CN	34
Milford Rd	Plumstead	120	CN	30
Milford Rd	Plumstead	141	CO	31
Milford St	Wesbank	107	CE	52
Milford Way	Sunningdale	24	BL	30
Milisi St	Tarentaalplaas	175	CY	75
Military Rd	Hout Bay	137	CQ	16
Military Rd	Lavender Hill East	160	CT	31
Military Rd	Retreat Ind. Area	159	CU	28
Military Rd	Schotsche Kloof	81	CA	22
Military Rd	Sheridon Pk	159	CU	29
Military Rd	Tamboerskloof	81	CB	22
Milkwood Cl.	Kalk Bay	186	DA	26
Milkwood Cl.	Kalk Bay	186	CZ	26
Milkwood Cl.	The Lakes	184	CZ	18
Milkwood Cr.	Big Bay	24	BK	28
Milkwood Cr.	Tygerdal	58	BX	38
Milkwood Rd	Somerset West	171	CW	77
Milkwood Ridge	Sunnydale	185	DA	19
Milkwood St	Hillcrest Hgts	127	CL	57
Milky Way	Ocean View	184	DC	15
Milky Way	Ocean View	189	DD	15
Milky Way	Salberau	86	CB	41
Milky Way	Thembokwezi	125	CL	49
Milky Way Dr.	Phoenix	57	BV	33
Mill Rd	Bellville Sth Ind.	88	CA	51
Mill Rd	Sack's Circle Ind.	88	CA	50
Mill Rd	Sack's Circle Ind.	89	CA	51
Mill St	Bothasig	42	BS	37
Mill St	Brooklyn	83	BZ	30
Mill St	Lemoenkloof	18	BC	88
Mill St	Newlands	101	CH	29
Mill St	Oranjezicht	81	CC	22
Mill St	Paarl	18	BC	88
Mill St	Sir Lowry's Pass	176	CZ	81
Mill St	Stellenbosch	95	CC	76
Mill St	Vredehoek	82	CC	23
Mill St	Woodstock	83	CB	27
Milldene Ave	Rondebosch	101	CH	30
Milldene St	Ravensmead	87	CA	45
Millenium Mews Rd	Oude Westhof	44	BS	44
Miller Rd	Claremont	101	CH	29
Miller Rd	Knole Pk	142	CP	36
Miller Rd	Simon's Town	194	DJ	26
Miller St	Gugulethu	104	CH	41
Miller St	Harbour Island	179	DD	77
Miller St	Harbour Island	179	DE	76
Miller St	Nyanga	123	CJ	42
Miller St	Nyanga	124	CJ	43
Miller's Point Rd	Simon's Town	195	DN	29
Millin Rd	Table View	41	BP	34
Millpark Cl.	Airport Ind.	105	CH	43
Mills St	Durbanville	45	BR	50
Mills St	Durbanville	46	BQ	51
Mills St	Park Estates	174	CY	72
Mills St	Park Estates	174	CY	73
Mills St	Somerset West	171	CW	75
Mills St	Strand Halt	170	CW	74
Mills St	Strand Halt	170	CX	74
Mills St	Winston Est.	170	CX	73
Millstone Cl.	Chapman's Peak	156	CW	17
Millstream St	Somerset West	170	CT	71
Millvale Rd	Milnerton	57	BV	32
Millwood St	Wesbank	107	CG	52
Milly St	Macassar	149	CS	63
Milne St	Salt River	83	CC	28
Milner	Strand Halt	170	CX	74
Milner	Wellington	10	AR	93
Milner Ave	Hout Bay	137	CO	15
Milner Ave	Hout Bay	137	CP	15
Milner Rd	Claremont	102	CH	31
Milner Rd	Maitland	84	CB	31
Milner Rd	Muizenberg	159	CX	29
Milner Rd	Observatory	83	CC	29
Milner Rd	Rondebosch	102	CE	31
Milner Rd	Rondebosch	102	CF	31
Milner Rd	Rondebosch	102	CG	31
Milner Rd	Scottsville	47	BS	57
Milner Rd	Sea Point	81	BZ	19
Milner Rd	Tamboerskloof	81	CB	22
Milner Rd	Woodstock	83	CB	27
Milner St	Metro Ind. Township	56	BX	30
Milner St	Paarden Eiland	83	BY	30
Milner St	Parow	87	BY	43
Milner St	Ruyterwacht	86	CB	40
Milner Way	Belhar	106	CE	49

Index to Street Names

Milnerton Cl. — N1 (Kraaifontein)

STREET NAME	SUBURB NAME	PG	GRID	
Milnerton Cl.	Milnerton Rdg	41	BS	34
Milnerton Dr.	Milnerton	41	BS	33
Milnerton Dr.	Milnerton	41	BS	34
Milnerton Dr.	Milnerton	57	BT	33
Milnerton Dr.	Milnerton Rdg	41	BS	34
Milnerton Rd	Winslow	179	DD	77
Milton Cl.	Kirstenhof	140	CS	27
Milton La.	Belhar	107	CD	51
Milton Rd	Goodwood Est.	86	BY	39
Milton Rd	Observatory	83	CC	28
Milton Rd	Sea Point	81	BZ	19
Milton Rd	Townsend Est.	85	BY	38
Milton Rd	Vasco Est.	86	BY	40
Milton St	Nomzano	175	CY	76
Milton St	Peerless Pk East	47	BR	58
Milton St	Peerless Pk Nth	47	BR	58
Milton St	Peerless Pk Nth	48	BQ	59
Milton St	Scottsville	47	BS	57
Milton St	Scottsville	47	BS	58
Mimosa Ave	Somerset Hgts	127	CK	57
Mimosa Ave	Tygerdal	58	BX	38
Mimosa Cl.	Fairie Knowe	185	DA	19
Mimosa Cl.	Mitchells Plain	144	CQ	45
Mimosa Cr.	Belhar	88	CC	48
Mimosa Cr.	Milnerton	57	BT	32
Mimosa Cr.	Plattekloof	60	BU	43
Mimosa Cr.	Thornton	85	CA	37
Mimosa Rd	Bellville Sth	88	CA	49
Mimosa Rd	Misty Cliffs	192	DJ	17
Mimosa Rd	Somerset West	170	CT	72
Mimosa Rd	Wellway Pk	46	BO	52
Mimosa St	Brackenfell	63	BV	56
Mimosa St	Brackenfell	63	BW	55
Mimosa St	Milnerton	57	BT	33
Mimosa St	Milnerton	57	BU	33
Mimosa St	Plumstead	140	CO	28
Mimosa St	Sarepta	89	CC	52
Mimosa St	Wellington	11	AS	95
Mimosa Way	Pinelands	84	CC	34
Mina Cr.	Delft	106	CF	49
Minaret	Stellenbosch	95	BY	75
Mincing La.	Foreshore	82	CB	25
Minerva Cr.	Plattekloof Glen	59	BW	40
Minerva Rd	Woodlands (M.Plain)	144	CP	44
Minerva St	Amanda Glen	46	BS	52
Minerwa St	Elim	90	CB	55
Minette Cl.	Parow Nth	60	BW	43
Mingerhout	Delft Sth	125	CJ	50
Mini St	Oakdale	61	BV	49
Minnaar St	Paarl	22	BF	88
Minnaar St	Wellington	10	AS	92
Minnesota Rd	Eindhoven	106	CH	50
Minnie St	Bloekombos	49	BQ	63
Minnie St	Wellington	10	AS	93
Minnow St	Brooklyn	83	BZ	30
Mino Cir.	Eindhoven	106	CH	50
Minor St	Vanguard	103	CG	37
Minorca Ave	Capricorn	159	CW	30
Minorca Ave	Somerset West	151	CS	74
Minos Rd	Ottery	121	CL	33
Minserie	Stellenbosch	95	CC	76
Minstral Mews Cl.	Somerset Rdg	170	CU	72
Minstrel Cl.	Belhar	106	CD	48
Minstrel Cl.	Belhar	106	CH	48
Mint St	Vosfontein	62	BV	52
Mintoor St	Wellington	10	AS	92
Mintwood	Wesbank	107	CG	52
Minuet La.	Mitchells Plain Cen.	145	CR	47
Mira Rd	Ocean View	183	DC	14
Miracle St	Cravenby	87	CB	43
Mirage	Rocklands (M.Plain)	163	CT	46
Mirage Ave	Eersterivier	127	CM	58
Mirage Cr.	Eersterivier	127	CM	58
Mirage Cr.	Kraaifontein	47	BQ	58
Mirage St	Macassar	168	CT	64
Miramar	Wesbank	107	CG	51
Miramonte St	Maitland	84	CA	32
Miranda Ngculu	Weltevreden Val. (M.Plain)	123	CM	42
Miranda Ngculu St	Kuyasa	147	CS	55
Miranda St	Tafelsig (M.Plain)	145	CS	50
Miranda Way	Meadowridge	139	CP	26
Mirbey Rd	Lavender Hill	160	CT	31
Miriam St	Athlone	102	CF	34
Mirt	Delft Sth	125	CJ	50
Mirte Cr.	Bracken Hgts	62	BU	54
Mispel Rd	Ruwari	63	BV	58
Mispel St	Bellville	61	BW	49
Misrole Ave	Grassy Pk	141	CQ	32
Mission Hills	Sunningdale	25	BM	31
Mission Rd	Sarepta	89	CB	52
Mission Rd	Wynberg	120	CM	29
Mission St	Sir Lowry's Pass	176	CZ	81
Mississippi Way	Graceland	146	CQ	53
Mississippi St	Eersterivier	128	CL	60
Mississippi Way	Portlands (M.Plain)	144	CQ	46
Missouri Cr.	Eindhoven	125	CJ	50
Missouri Cr.	Portlands (M.Plain)	144	CQ	46
Mistel	Cloetesville	95	BY	75
Mistel	Cloetesville	95	BY	77
Mistletoe Rd	Pelikan Pk	142	CQ	36
Mistral Cl.	Lakeside	159	CV	28
Misty St	Wesbank	107	CG	52
Mitcham St	Wynberg	120	CL	29
Mitchell	Rocklands (M.Plain)	144	CS	45
Mitchell Ave	Woodlands (M.Plain)	144	CO	44

STREET NAME	SUBURB NAME	PG	GRID	
Mitchell Ave	Woodlands (M.Plain)	144	CP	44
Mitchell Baker Dr.	Somerset West	151	CS	74
Mitchell Rd	Athlone	102	CG	34
Mitchell St	Elim	89	CA	54
Mitchells Dr.	Edgemead	59	BT	39
Mitford Rd	Tijgerhof	57	BV	32
Mithani St	Crossroads	124	CK	45
Mitre Cl.	Leonsdale	86	CA	42
Mjandana	Kayamandi	94	CA	74
Mjekula Cr.	Langa	103	CD	35
Mjikiliso Cr.	Mfuleni	127	CL	55
Mkgoro St	Eyethu	146	CP	54
Mkhanyisi Maphuma St	Guguletu	123	CJ	40
Mkhanyisi Maphuma St	Guguletu	123	CK	41
Mkholokotho Cr.	Bloekombos	49	BR	63
Mkholwane Cr.	Ilitha Pk	146	CQ	52
Mkhombe Cr.	Philippi East	124	CL	46
Mkhombe St	Kuyasa	147	CR	55
Mkhonto Rd	Masiphumelele	184	DA	18
Mkhumbuzi St	Bloekombos	49	BQ	63
Mkiva St	Lwandle	175	CZ	77
Mkondweni Ave	Nyanga	123	CK	42
Mkonto Cr.	Kaya	146	CP	52
Mkonto St	Kaya	146	CP	52
Mkungela St	Tarentaalplaas	171	CX	75
Mkutsulwa St	Nonqubela	146	CO	53
Mkuze St	Delft	106	CF	49
Mkuze St	Mfuleni	126	CJ	53
Mlambo St	Mxolisi Phetani	125	CM	50
Mlanjeni Cl.	Mxolisi Phetani	125	CM	50
Mlanjeni St	Ilitha Pk	146	CQ	53
Mlenzana St	Bloekombos	48	BQ	62
Mlokothi Rd	Capri	184	DA	18
Mlokoti	Masiphumelele	184	DA	18
Mlonji	Brown's Farm	124	CL	43
Mlonji Cr.	Mbekweni	15	AW	91
Mlonji Cr.	Mbekweni	15	AX	91
Mlonji St	Ilitha Pk	146	CQ	53
Mlonji St	Philippi East	125	CL	48
Mmeli St	Umrhabulo Triangle	147	CR	57
Mnandi	Dunoon	42	BO	37
Mnandi	Wellington	15	AU	91
Mnandi	Wellington	15	AT	94
Mncedisi St	Kaya	146	CP	52
Mndayi Cl.	Nyanga	123	CK	41
Mnenge Cr.	Philippi East	125	CL	47
Mngazi St	Mfuleni	126	CK	54
Mngeele St	Brown's Farm	123	CM	42
Mninawa Cr.	Eyethu	146	CO	54
Mnqabaza St	Brown's Farm	123	CM	42
Mnqanqeni St	Guguletu	123	CK	40
Mnquma St	Brown's Farm	124	CM	43
Mnyama St	Thembokwezi	125	CN	48
Mnyamanzi St	Brown's Farm	124	CM	44
Mobile Rd	Airport Ind.	104	CG	43
Mobile Rd	Airport Ind.	105	CG	43
Mocke Rd	Flintdale Est.	140	CP	29
Modderdam Rd	Belhar	88	CB	47
Modderdam Rd	Bishop Lavis	105	CE	44
Modderdam Rd	Montana/Durrheim	104	CE	41
Modderdam Rd	Parow Ind.	87	CC	46
Modderdam Rd East-West	Sack's Circle Ind.	88	CA	50
Modderdam Rd North-South	Belrail	88	BZ	48
Modena Rd	Green Point	81	BZ	21
Modern Art	Fairyland	19	AZ	92
Moederkappie St	Groenvlei	18	BA	89
Moepel Cl.	Perm Gdns	128	CJ	59
Moepel Cl.	Perm Gdns	128	CJ	60
Moerdyk St	Labiance	89	BZ	51
Moerdyk St	Townsend Est.	58	BX	38
Mofala Cr.	Nonqubela	146	CO	53
Moffat	Idasvallei	96	CA	79
Moffat Cir.	Ruyterwacht	86	CA	40
Moffat Putego	Weltevreden Val. (M.Plain)	123	CN	42
Moffat St	Langa	103	CD	36
Mohajane	Mbekweni	15	AW	92
Mohale Rd	Brown's Farm	123	CL	41
Mohawk St	The Hague	106	CF	49
Mohawk St	The Hague	106	CH	48
Mohr Rd	Dennedal	139	CR	26
Moira Rd	Surrey	103	CH	37
Moira St	Tafelsig (M.Plain)	145	CR	50
Moka St	Claremont	101	CH	29
Mokoba St	Mxolisi Phetani	125	CM	50
Mokobe Rd	Brown's Farm	123	CL	41
Molecule St	Triangle Farm	88	BZ	50
Molenaarsberg Rd	Greenfield	108	CH	57
Molento St	Northpine	63	BU	58
Molento St	Northpine	63	BV	56
Molenvliet Rd	Observatory	101	CD	29
Moletsani Cr.	Nyanga	123	CK	42
Moline St	Graceland	146	CP	53
Molinera	Northpine	63	BU	58
Molinera Way	Meadowridge	139	CO	26
Moll St	Northern Paarl	18	AZ	88
Moll St	Northern Paarl	18	AZ	89
Molly Brown Rd	Sanddrift	58	BV	35
Molopo Cl.	Portlands (M.Plain)	144	CP	46
Molopo Ct	Delft	106	CG	49
Molopo Rd	Manenberg	103	CH	38
Molopo St	Mfuleni	126	CJ	53
Molopo St	Park Village	127	CK	58
Molteno Cl.	Portlands (M.Plain)	144	CR	46
Molteno Rd	Belhar	106	CD	49
Molteno Rd	Claremont	120	CJ	29

STREET NAME	SUBURB NAME	PG	GRID	
Molteno Rd	Oranjezicht	81	CC	22
Molteno Rd	Oranjezicht	99	CD	21
Molteno Rd	Stellenbosch	95	CB	75
Molteno St	Richmond Est.	86	BY	40
Molteno St	Somerset West	150	CS	70
Mon Repo Cl.	D'urbanvale	45	BO	49
Mon Repo Cl.	Eversdal Hgts	45	BS	50
Mon Repos Cr.	Welgelegen	59	BV	41
Mona Cr.	Claremont	101	CH	29
Monaco	Killarney Gdns	42	BP	37
Monaco Cr.	Macassar	149	CS	63
Monaco St	Uitzicht	31	BN	56
Monani Cr.	Eyethu	146	CP	53
Monastery Rd	Fresnaye	81	CA	19
Monclavia Cr.	Wesbank	107	CF	51
Monde Cr.	Kayamandi	94	CA	74
Monde St	Kaya	146	CO	52
Mondeor Rd	Broadlands	175	CY	78
Mongesi Rd	Eyethu	146	CO	53
Mongesi Rd	Eyethu	146	CP	53
Mongondia St	Bloekombos	49	BQ	63
Mongoose St	Electric City	127	CM	58
Moni St	Dal Josafat Ind.	22	BD	89
Monica St	Kalkfontein II	107	CD	53
Monica Way	Montagu's Gift	141	CO	34
Monkwood Rd	Epping Forest	86	CC	41
Monmouth Ave	Claremont	120	CJ	27
Mono Cr.	Delft	106	CF	49
Monopoly Cr.	Beacon Valley (M.Plain)	145	CP	48
Monroe Rd	Claremont	102	CH	31
Monrovia Cir.	Scottsdene	64	BU	60
Mons Ave	Claremont	101	CH	29
Monsoon	Rocklands (M.Plain)	145	CS	47
Mont Blanc	La Pastorale	113	CG	76
Mont Blanc	Somerset Rdg	170	CU	72
Mont Blanc	Welgedacht	44	BS	45
Mont Blanc Cr.	Uitzicht	31	BN	56
Mont Blanc St	Tafelsig (M.Plain)	145	CS	48
Mont Bleu Cl.	Bloubergstrand	24	BL	28
Mont Grace	Somerset Rdg	170	CT	72
Mont Rose	Elriche	19	BB	91
Mont Vue Ave	Mountain View	19	BB	91
Montagu Ave	Voorbrug	106	CG	50
Montagu Dr.	Portlands (M.Plain)	144	CR	46
Montagu Dr.	Portlands (M.Plain)	145	CR	47
Montagu St	Ruyterwacht	86	CA	39
Montagu Way	Pinelands	102	CD	33
Montagu Way	Portlands (M.Plain)	144	CR	46
Montague Dr.	Marconi Beam	58	BV	35
Montague Dr.	Montague Gdns Ind.	42	BS	35
Montague Dr.	Montague Gdns Ind.	58	BT	35
Montague Rd	Bergvliet	140	CQ	27
Montague Rd	Maitland	83	CB	30
Montague Rd	Monte Vista	58	BV	38
Montague Rd	Monte Vista	59	BW	38
Montague Rd	Monte Vista	59	BT	41
Montague Rd	Monte Vista	59	BU	39
Montague Rd	Wingfield Nth Camp	58	BW	38
Montague St	Silverstream	62	BU	52
Montague St	Somerset West	171	CW	75
Montague St	Wellington	15	AU	92
Montagu's Gift Rd	Montagu's Gift	141	CO	33
Montana Rd	Camps Bay	99	CD	19
Montana Rd	Colorado (M.Plain)	144	CO	44
Montana Rd	Northpine	63	BU	58
Montana St	Stellenridge	62	BV	51
Montclair Dr.	Mandalay	125	CN	48
Monte Ave	Voorbrug	107	CH	51
Monte Carlo St	Uitzicht	31	BN	56
Monte Cristo Ave	Lemoenkloof	18	BC	87
Monte Pescali	Sonstraal Hgts	46	BR	54
Monte Rio Ave	Northern Paarl	18	AZ	89
Monte Rosa St	Protea Hoogte	63	BX	57
Monte Verdi	Eversdal Hgts	46	BR	54
Monte Verdi	Eversdal Hgts	46	BS	54
Monte Vista Blvd	Monte Vista	59	BV	39
Monte Vista Blvd	Monte Vista	59	BU	39
Monte Vista Blvd Service Rd	Monte Vista	59	BV	39
Monte Vista Cr.	Somerset West	170	CV	73
Montefleur Ave	Townsend Est.	58	BX	38
Montego Bay Ave	Harbour Island	175	DC	75
Montego Cl.	Sunningdale	25	BM	32
Monterey Ave	Bishopscourt	119	CK	26
Monterey Ave	Bishopscourt	120	CK	27
Monterey Dr.	Bel Ombre	119	CL	23
Monterey Dr.	Bel Ombre	119	CM	23
Monterey Rd	Hout Bay	117	CN	16
Monterey Rd	Scottsdene	64	BV	59
Monterey Sq.	Northpine	63	BU	58
Monterey Way	Northpine	63	BU	58
Montevideo Cl.	Portlands (M.Plain)	144	CR	46
Montevideo Cl.	Portlands (M.Plain)	144	CS	43
Montgomery Dr.	Simon's Town	194	DJ	26
Montley Rd	Plumstead	120	CN	28
Montmartre St	Klein Parys	23	BE	91
Monton St	Lansdowne	121	CK	32
Montpeller Cl.	Vredekloof	62	BT	53
Montpellier Ave	Wellington	15	AT	94
Montreal Ave	Oranjezicht	99	CD	22
Montreal Dr.	Airport Ind.	105	CH	43
Montreal Dr.	Airport Ind.	105	CH	44
Montreal Rd	Mowbray	101	CD	30
Montreaux St	Courtrai	22	BH	87
Montreux Ave	Vredekloof	62	BU	53
Montrose Ave	Claremont	101	CH	29

STREET NAME	SUBURB NAME	PG	GRID	
Montrose Ave	Clovelly	186	CZ	24
Montrose Ave	Hohenort	119	CK	25
Montrose Ave	Oranjezicht	81	CC	22
Montrose Ave	Somerset West	151	CS	73
Montrose Cl.	Sunnydale	185	CZ	19
Montrose St	Jamestown	112	CH	74
Montrose St	Newlands	101	CG	28
Montrose Ter.	Hohenort	119	CK	24
Montsho Mokgabudi St	Mandela Pk	147	CQ	56
Montura Cl.	Scottsdene	64	BV	59
Monty Rd	Flintdale Est.	141	CO	31
Monwabisi	Mbekweni	15	AV	91
Monyaine	Summer Greens	58	BW	35
Monza Rd	Killarney Gdns	42	BP	36
Monza St	Kaya	146	CP	52
Mooder St	Delft	106	CG	49
Moody Ave	Epping Ind.	85	CC	35
Moody Cr.	Epping Ind.	85	CC	35
Mooi St	Delft	106	CF	49
Mooi St	Mfuleni	126	CJ	52
Mooigezicht Rd	Chrismar	61	BW	50
Mooivlei St	Wellington	15	AV	92
Mooizicht Cl.	Uitzicht	47	BO	55
Moolenberg Rd	Rondebosch	102	CF	31
Moolman Cl.	Bloubergstrand	24	BM	28
Moolman St	Bloubergstrand	24	BL	28
Moolman St	Lemoenkloof	18	BC	88
Moon Cl.	Salberau	86	CB	41
Moonbeam	Wesbank	107	CG	52
Moonbeam Cr.	Wesbank	107	CG	52
Moondust Wk	Thembokwezi	125	CL	49
Moonlight	Mbekweni	15	AW	91
Moonstone	Rocklands (M.Plain)	145	CS	47
Moonstone Cr.	Sheridon Pk	159	CU	29
Moore Rd	Wynberg	120	CM	28
Moore Rd	Wynberg	120	CL	30
Moore St	Kenilworth Pk	120	CJ	30
Moore St	Parowvallei	87	BZ	44
Moorgate St	Woodstock	82	CA	26
Moorhen Cr.	Electric City	127	CN	58
Moorhen Rd	Marina Da Gama	159	CU	30
Moorhen Rd	Pelikan Pk	142	CQ	35
Moorland Cr.	Dreyersdal	139	CS	26
Moors Ave	Fish Hoek	185	DA	21
Moorsom Ave	Epping Ind.	86	CC	39
Moosa Karaan Cl.	Gustrow	175	DB	75
Moosa Karaan Cl.	Gustrow	175	DB	77
Moosa Wk	Parkwood	141	CO	32
Mopani Cl.	Somerset West	171	CW	76
Mopanie Ave	New Orleans	19	BB	91
Mopanie Cr.	Vredekloof	62	BT	54
Mopanie Rd	Amanda Glen	46	BS	51
Mopanie St	Eastridge (M.Plain)	145	CR	47
Mopanie St	Loevenstein	60	BW	45
Mopanie St	Plattekloof	60	BU	43
Morawiese St	Bellville Sth Ext. 5	88	BZ	49
Moray Cr.	Eersterivier	128	CN	59
Moray Pl.	Oranjezicht	81	CC	22
Moray Way	Strandfontein	162	CU	39
Morea St	Halalie	46	BO	52
Moredou St	Valmary Pk	45	BR	50
Moreland Ter.	Green Point	82	BZ	23
Môrelig St	Wellington	11	AS	95
Moreson Ave	Voorbrug	107	CG	51
Moreson St	Hillrise	61	BX	49
Morester Rd	Rosendal	61	BU	50
Morgan	Park Estates	174	CY	72
Morgana St	Camelot	107	CF	53
Morganza Cr.	Graceland	146	CP	54
Morgenrood Rd	Kenilworth	120	CK	28
Morgenster	Mostertsdrift	95	CC	78
Morgenster Ave	Somerset West	171	CU	78
Morgenster Cr.	Richwood	42	BQ	38
Morgenster Cr.	Richwood	42	BQ	37
Morgenster Rd	Beacon Valley (M.Plain)	145	CP	47
Morgenster Rd	Durbanville Hills	45	BR	49
Morgenster Rd	Durbanville Hills	45	BP	47
Morgenster Rd	Mitchells Plain	144	CQ	44
Morgenster Rd	Portlands (M.Plain)	144	CP	46
Morgenster Rd	Schaap Kraal	144	CQ	43
Morgenster St	Brackenfell Ind.	63	BU	56
Morgenster St	Die Bos	174	CY	74
Morgenster St	Die Bos	175	CY	75
Morgenster St	Morgenster Hoogte	63	BT	57
Morgenster St	Oak Glen	62	BW	52
Morgenster St	Table View	41	BO	32
Morgenzon Cl.	Northpine	64	BU	58
Morgenzon Cr.	Belhar	106	CD	50
Morgenzon St	Groenvlei	18	BA	88
Morillon Way	Northpine	64	BT	58
Morkel	Uniepark	96	CC	79
Morkel Rd	Dreyersdal	140	CR	27
Morkel St	Gardens	81	CB	22
Morkel St	Rome	174	CY	73
Morkel St	Somerset West	171	CU	75
Morley Rd	Delft Sth	125	CK	48
Morley Rd	Observatory	83	CC	29
Mornay	Ravensmead	87	CA	45
Mornay East	Ravensmead	87	CA	46
Mornay St	Schaap Kraal	122	CL	36
Mornay West	Ravensmead	87	CA	44
Mornimg Glory	Lentegeur (M.Plain)	144	CP	46
Morning St	Wesbank	107	CG	52
Morning Star Dr.	Thembokwezi	125	CL	49
Morning Star Dr.	Thembokwezi	125	CM	49

Abbreviations used: Ave – Avenue, A.H. – Agricultural Holding, A.L.– Algemene Landgoed, Blvd – Boulevard, Cen. – Central, Cir. – Circle, Cl. – Close, Cr. – Crescent, Ct – Court, Dr. – Drive, Est. – Estate, Ext. – Extension, Hgts – Heights, Ind. – Industrial, Gdns – Gardens, Gr. – Grove, La. – Lane, (M.Plain) - Mitchells Plain, Nth – North, Pl. – Place, Pk – Park, Rd – Road, Rdg. – Ridge, S.H.– Small Holding, Sq. – Square, St – Street, Sth – South, Ter. – Terrace, Tn – Turn, Val. – Valley, Wk – Walk

STREET NAME	SUBURB NAME	PG	GRID
Morningside Rd	Ndabeni	84	CB 33
Morningside Rd	Pinelands	84	CB 33
Morom Rd	Wynberg	120	CL 29
Morpeth Rd	Plumstead	120	CN 29
Morris Cl.	Airport Ind.	105	CH 43
Morris La.	Schotsche Kloof	81	CA 22
Morris Rd	Claremont	120	CJ 28
Morris Shell Dr.	Richwood	42	BP 38
Morris St	Bloekombos	48	BR 62
Morris Way	Retreat	140	CS 29
Morse Cl.	Belhar	88	CC 49
Mortimer Rd	Wynberg	120	CL 28
Mortimer St	Silveroaks	90	CC 55
Mortlake Rd	Wynberg	120	CM 30
Morton Rd	Plumstead	120	CN 29
Morton Way	Eersterivier	128	CN 61
Morven Rd	Lotus River	141	CP 34
Mosbach Way	Silversands	107	CH 54
Moselle	Groenvlei	18	BA 88
Moselle Rd	St James	187	CZ 28
Moselle St	Stellenryk	62	BT 52
Moser Rd	Strandfontein	162	CU 42
Moses	Idasvallei	96	CA 79
Moses Cr.	Wellington	15	AU 92
Moses Kotane Cr.	Mandela Pk	147	CQ 56
Moses Kotane Wk	Weltevreden Val. (M.Plain)	123	CN 42
Moses Kotane Wk	Weltevreden Val. (M.Plain)	123	CM 39
Moses Kottler Cr.	Woodlands (M.Plain)	124	CN 45
Moses Mabhida St	Fisantekraal	31	BK 58
Moses Madiba Cr.	Weltevreden Val. (M.Plain)	123	CN 45
Moses Madiba Cr.	Weltevreden Val. (M.Plain)	123	CM 39
Moses St	Welcome	103	CF 38
Mosheshi Ave	Langa	103	CF 37
Mosheshi Ave	Langa	103	CD 36
Mosman Rd	Athlone	102	CG 32
Mosque Rd	Grassy Pk	141	CQ 32
Mosque Rd	Wynberg	120	CL 29
Mosquito	Rocklands (M.Plain)	163	CT 45
Mosquito La.	The Hague	106	CF 49
Moss St	Austinville	108	CH 56
Moss St	Bishopscourt	119	CJ 25
Moss St	Newlands	100	CH 25
Mossel St	Bloubergrant	24	BN 30
Mossel St	Churchill	86	BY 41
Mosselbaai St	Paarden Eiland	83	BZ 29
Mosselbank	Kraaifontein	47	BQ 58
Mosselbankrivier Dr.	D'urbanvale	29	BN 50
Mosselbankrivier Dr.	D'urbanvale	45	BO 49
Mossie	Seawinds	159	CU 30
Mossie Cr.	Morningstar	46	BP 51
Mossie Cr.	Pelikan Pk	142	CS 35
Mossie La.	Montagu's Gift	141	CP 33
Mossie St	Amstelhof	23	BD 93
Mossie St	Loucharmante	90	CB 56
Mossie St	Peerless Pk Nth	48	BQ 59
Mossie St	Wellington	15	AT 92
Mossop St	De Zoete Inval	39	BJ 88
Mossop St	Eersterivier	128	CM 59
Mossop Steps	Fish Hoek	186	DC 25
Mosterd St	Somerset West	171	CW 75
Mostert St	Bothasig	58	BT 37
Mostert St	Cape Town Cen.	82	CB 23
Mostert St	Kraaifontein	47	BP 58
Mostert St	Monte Vista	59	BW 39
Mostert St	Peerless Pk Nth	48	BP 59
Mostertshoek St	Tafelsig (M.Plain)	145	CS 50
Moth St	The Hague	106	CF 49
Mothapeng	Masiphumelele	184	DA 18
Mount Albert	Kromrivier	95	CB 75
Mount Anna St	Somerset West	170	CT 72
Mount Cl.	Belhar	107	CD 51
Mount Cl.	Noordhoek Manor	157	CX 21
Mount Cl.	Uitzicht	47	BO 55
Mount Clare St	Sybrand Pk	102	CF 32
Mount du Roche Cr.	Somerset Rdg	170	CT 71
Mount du Val	Somerset Rdg	170	CT 71
Mount Fletcher	Kalkfontein I	107	CD 52
Mount Nelson Rd	Sea Point	81	BZ 20
Mount Pleasant Rd	Rondebosch	101	CG 28
Mount Pleasant Steps	Clifton	80	CC 18
Mount Prospect Dr.	Huis-in-bos	139	CO 24
Mount Rd	Mowbray	101	CD 29
Mount Rd	Muizenberg	159	CX 29
Mount Rd	Rondebosch	101	CG 28
Mount Rhodes Dr.	Hout Bay	116	CM 14
Mount Rhodes Dr.	Hout Bay	117	CN 15
Mount Royal Way	Pinelands	84	CB 34
Mount St	District Six	82	CB 24
Mount Villa Cr.	Somerset Rdg	170	CT 72
Mountain Ave	Eersterivier	127	CM 58
Mountain Breeze Cr.	Pine Acres	175	DC 77
Mountain Cl.	Capricorn	160	CW 31
Mountain Cr.	Kraaifontein	47	BQ 57
Mountain Cr.	Montagu's Gift	141	CO 34
Mountain Fern Cr.	Somerset West	171	CX 77
Mountain Pl.	Kommetjie	183	DC 13
Mountain Rd	Chapman's Peak	156	CW 16
Mountain Rd	Claremont	120	CJ 27
Mountain Rd	Clovelly	186	DA 24
Mountain Rd	Fish Hoek	186	DC 24
Mountain Rd	Harbour Island	179	DE 77
Mountain Rd	Kommetjie	183	DC 12
Mountain Rd	Matroosfontein	86	CC 41
Mountain Rd	Noordhoek	156	CW 17
Mountain Rd	Sir Lowry's Pass	176	CZ 82
Mountain Rd	Somerset West	171	CT 76
Mountain Rd	Somerset West	171	CU 76
Mountain Rd	Woodstock	82	CB 26
Mountain Rise	Scarborough	192	DJ 17
Mountain Rise	Scarborough	192	DJ 18
Mountain Rise	Scarborough	192	DK 18
Mountain Rise	Somerset West	151	CQ 71
Mountain Road Cl.	Somerset West	171	CU 76
Mountain Rose Rd	Bellville Ext. 53	60	BT 46
Mountain St	Hout Bay	136	CO 14
Mountain St	Hout Bay	137	CO 15
Mountain View	Parklands	41	BO 32
Mountain View	Pinelands	84	CC 32
Mountain View Cr.	Durbell	45	BS 50
Mountain View Rd	Ridgeworth	61	BU 50
Mountain View Rd	Stellenryk	62	BT 52
Mountain View Rd	Wynberg	120	CM 28
Mountain-Rose	Macassar	149	CS 63
Mountainside Blvd	Gordon Hgts	180	DD 79
Mountainside Blvd	Mountainside Est.	179	DD 78
Mountainside Blvd	Temperance Town	180	DD 79
Mountainview Cr.	Tokai	139	CS 25
Mountbatten Ave	Pinelands	84	CB 34
Mountview Rd	Woodlands (M.Plain)	144	CP 45
Mourne Rd	Royal Cape	121	CM 31
Mousebird Way	Somerset Rdg	170	CT 72
Mouton St	Mabille Pk	89	CA 53
Mowbray Rd	Maitland	84	CA 32
Moy Cl.	Connaught	87	CB 43
Moya St	Crossroads	124	CJ 44
Mozart	Delft Sth	125	CK 48
Mozart	Kaapzicht	59	BW 40
Mozart	Schuilplaats	113	CG 76
Mozart Cl.	Sonstraal Hgts	46	BQ 54
Mozart Rd	Retreat	140	CS 29
Mozart St	Belhar	106	CD 48
Mozart St	Brackenfell	63	BW 56
Mozart St	Groenheuwel	19	AZ 91
Mozart Way	Adriaanse	105	CD 43
Mpampira Wk	Philippi East	124	CL 46
Mpangele	Brown's Farm	124	CM 44
Mpangele	Philippi East	124	CM 46
Mpangele Rd	Ilitha Pk	146	CQ 52
Mpayina Wk	Philippi East	125	CL 47
Mpembe Cl.	Nonqubela	126	CN 52
Mpepho	Wellington	15	AU 91
Mpeta St	Crossroads	124	CK 44
Mpetha Rd	Masiphumelele	184	DA 18
Mpetsheni Cr.	Ilitha Pk	146	CR 52
Mphakalasi	Mbekweni	15	AV 92
Mphakalasi	Mbekweni	15	AW 92
Mpho Rd	Ekuphumuleni	146	CP 53
Mphunzane Rd	Brown's Farm	124	CL 44
Mpilo St	Kaya	146	CO 52
Mpilo St	Thembokwezi	125	CN 49
Mpilontle	Mbekweni	15	AW 92
Mpofu St	Kuyasa	147	CR 55
Mpompoza St	Umrhabulo Triangle	147	CQ 58
Mpuku St	Kuyasa	147	CR 56
Mpumelelo	Wellington	15	AV 91
Mpumelelo St	Philippi	124	CL 44
Mpumi St	Ekuphumuleni	146	CP 53
Mpumie St	Dunoon	42	BO 37
Mpumie St	Dunoon	42	BO 36
Mpungutye St	Crossroads	124	CK 45
Mpunzi Cr.	Philippi East	124	CL 46
Mpunzi St	Kuyasa	147	CR 56
Mqandane Wk	Philippi East	125	CL 47
Mqanduli St	Philippi East	124	CM 46
Mqaqoba St	Brown's Farm	124	CM 43
Mqayi Cl.	Guguletu	104	CH 41
Mqha St	Kuyasa	147	CR 55
Mqha St	Kuyasa	147	CR 56
Mqha St	Kuyasa	147	CS 55
Mqha St	Kuyasa	147	CS 56
Mqokolo St	Brown's Farm	124	CL 43
Mqokotho Ave	Joe Slovo Pk	57	BU 34
Mqokotho Ave	Joe Slovo Pk	57	BU 31
Mquma Rd	Philippi East	125	CL 47
Mqwathi St	Bloekombos	49	BR 63
Mrabalala Sq	Eyethu	146	CP 54
Mrabaraba	Mbekweni	15	AV 92
Msence	Brown's Farm	123	CM 42
Msengana St	Eyethu	146	CP 54
Mshumpela Way	Langa	103	CE 37
Msimbithi Rd	Philippi East	125	CL 47
Msingizane St	Brown's Farm	123	CM 42
Msobomvu	Mbekweni	15	AX 91
Msobomvu	Wellington	15	AU 91
Msobomvu Dr.	Ilitha Pk	146	CQ 52
Msutwana St	Eyethu	146	CO 53
Mswi St	Ilitha Pk	146	CQ 53
Mt Silver	Cloetesville	94	BY 74
Mt Silver	Cloetesville	94	BZ 74
Mt Silver Dr.	Green Oaks	95	BY 75
Mt Silver Dr.	Weltevrede	94	BY 74
Mt. Joy	Elriche	19	BB 91
Mtamvuna St	Mfuleni	126	CK 53
Mtati St	Nonqubela	126	CN 52
Mtembeko St	Bloekombos	48	BQ 62
Mtengeli Cr.	Scottsdene	64	BT 60
Mthathi	Philippi East	125	CL 47
Mthathi Cr.	Philippi East	125	CM 47
Mthawelanga St	Ilitha Pk	146	CQ 52
Mthi St	Kuyasa	146	CS 54
Mthi St	Kuyasa	147	CS 55
Mthobeli St	Wallacedene	48	BS 60
Mthombe St	Brown's Farm	124	CM 43
Mthombe St	Mxolisi Phetani	125	CM 49
Mthombo St	Umrhabulo Triangle	147	CQ 56
Mthonjeni	Wellington	15	AU 91
Mthonjeni St	Mxolisi Phetani	125	CM 49
Mthubi	Mbekweni	15	AW 91
Mthuma St	Mxolisi Phetani	125	CM 50
Mthunzini	Mbekweni	15	AX 91
Mthwna	Philippi East	125	CL 48
Mtobo St	Kaya	146	CO 51
Mtshato	Griffiths Mxenge	146	CQ 54
Mtshawu	Scottsdene	64	BT 61
Mtsi St	Kaya	146	CP 52
Muammer Gaddafi St	Mandela Pk	146	CR 54
Much Binding Rd	Wetton	122	CL 35
Mugabe St	Mandela Pk	147	CQ 55
Muir Cl.	Rondebosch	102	CG 31
Muir Rd	Highbury	107	CE 53
Muir Rd	Highbury	107	CE 54
Muir Rd	Rondebosch	101	CG 30
Muir Rd	Rondebosch	102	CG 31
Muir St	District Six	82	CB 24
Muirfield Cr.	Greenways	174	DB 74
Muirfield Cr.	Sunningdale	25	BM 31
Muirfield Cr.	Sunningdale	25	BL 31
Muisvoël St	D'urbanvale	29	BN 49
Mulberry	Delft Sth	125	CK 49
Mulberry Cr.	Fairie Knowe	185	DA 19
Mulberry St	Bonteheuwel	104	CE 40
Mulder Cl.	Tokai	139	CS 26
Mullberry Way	Strandfontein	162	CT 41
Muller Ave	Denneburg	23	BD 91
Muller Rd	Wetton	121	CL 34
Muller St	Denneburg	23	BD 91
Muller St	Peerless Pk East	47	BR 58
Muller St	Peerless Pk East	48	BQ 59
Muller St	Peerless Pk East	48	BR 59
Muller St	Perm Gdns	128	CK 59
Muller St	Silveroaks	90	CB 55
Muller St	Stellenbosch	95	CB 76
Muller St	Vredelust	60	BW 46
Mullet Cl.	Marina Da Gama	159	CU 29
Mulvihal Rd	Rondebosch	102	CF 31
Munich Rd	Airport Ind.	104	CG 42
Munnik	District Six	82	CB 25
Munnik Laas St	Kaapzicht	59	BV 40
Munnik St	Lochnerhof	174	CY 72
Munnik St	Park Estates	174	CY 72
Munro St	William Lloyd	23	BD 92
Munster Rd	Royal Cape	121	CM 31
Munt St	Vierlanden	30	BM 51
Munwa Ct	Delft	106	CG 49
Murati Cl.	Welgedacht	44	BS 46
Muratie Cl.	Mitchells Plain	144	CR 45
Muratie Cl.	Mitchells Plain	144	CS 43
Muratie Cl.	Richwood	42	BP 38
Muratie Cl.	Zevendal	90	CC 58
Murdine St	Flintdale Est.	140	CP 30
Murdoch Rd	Somerset West	151	CR 74
Murex St	Sunset Beach	41	BS 32
Murida Rd	Retreat	140	CR 29
Muriel Cl.	Montana/Durrheim	104	CF 41
Muritz Cl.	Coniston Pk	159	CU 30
Muritz Pl.	Coniston Pk	159	CU 30
Muritz Way	Coniston Pk	159	CU 30
Murray	Stellenbosch	95	CC 77
Murray Ave	Somerset West	170	CV 72
Murray Rd	Kenilworth	120	CK 29
Murray Rd	Penlyn Est.	122	CJ 35
Murray St	De Kuilen	89	CB 54
Murray St	Durbanville	30	BN 51
Murray St	Durbanville	45	BO 50
Murray St	Durbanville	46	BO 51
Murray St	Paarlzicht	19	BC 91
Murray St	Park Estates	174	CY 71
Murray St	Vasco Est.	59	BX 39
Murray St	Vasco Est.	86	BY 39
Murray St	Vierlanden	30	BM 52
Murray St	Vierlanden	30	BN 51
Murray St	Welgemoed	60	BU 46
Murray St	Wellington	10	AR 93
Murrayfield Cl.	Northpine	63	BU 58
Murrayfield Cl.	Northpine	63	BV 58
Murrayfield St	Edgemead	58	BV 38
Murton Rd	Doornhoogte	103	CG 36
Murtz Cl.	Grassy Pk	141	CR 31
Musante Rd	Rusdal	108	CE 57
Musca Cl.	Ocean View	189	DD 15
Muscadel Rd	Table View	41	BO 34
Muscadel St	Bellavista	18	BC 90
Muscadel St	Paarlzicht	18	BC 90
Muscadel St	Shirley Pk	89	BY 52
Muscadel St	Wellington	10	AS 94
Muscadelle St	Somerset West	170	CT 72
Muscat Cl.	Table View	41	BP 33
Muscat La. South	Nova Constantia	139	CP 24
Muscat Rd	Saxenburg Ind. Pk	108	CE 56
Muscat Rd	Saxenburg Ind. Pk	108	CE 57
Muscat Way	Huis-in-bos	139	CP 24
Mushet Cr.	Vredekloof	62	BT 54
Musical Ave	Macassar	149	CR 64
Musical Ave	Macassar	149	CS 65
Muska Pl.	Northpine	63	BT 58
Musket Rd	Wynberg	120	CL 30
Musketeer Rd	Bothasig	42	BS 38
Mussel Cr.	Kraaifontein	47	BQ 58
Mussel La.	Big Bay	24	BL 28
Mussel Rd	Richwood	42	BP 38
Mustang Cir.	The Hague	106	CF 49
Mustang Cl.	Kraaifontein	47	BQ 58
Mustang Rd	Milnerton	41	BS 34
Mustang St	Factreton	84	BY 34
Mustang Way	Mitchells Plain	144	CR 44
Muswell Rd	Mowbray	102	CD 31
Mutley Rd	Three Anchor Bay	81	BZ 20
Mutual Way	Bergvliet	139	CQ 26
Mutual Way	Pinelands	84	CA 34
Muurbal St	Beacon Valley (M.Plain)	145	CP 48
Mvambo	Mbekweni	15	AW 91
Mvelisho St	Griffiths Mxenge	146	CP 54
Mvica	Philippi East	124	CM 46
Mvimbi St	Nonqubela	146	CO 53
Mvubu Rd	Philippi East	124	CM 46
Mvulinile	Mbekweni	15	AX 91
Mvumvu St	Mfuleni	126	CL 53
Mvundla Ave	Joe Slovo Pk	57	BU 34
Mvundla Cr.	Philippi East	124	CM 46
Mvundla St	Brown's Farm	123	CM 42
Mvundla St	Kuyasa	147	CS 55
Mvuzo Cr.	Eyethu	146	CP 53
Mxhomi Rd	Philippi East	125	CL 47
Mxinwa Cl.	Harare	146	CR 53
Mxolisi Petani St	Mandela Pk	146	CQ 54
Mxolisi St	Nomzano	175	CZ 75
Myataza Cl.	Guguletu	104	CH 41
Myburg Cl.	Brackenfell Sth	63	BW 58
Myburgh Dr.	Hout Bay	117	CM 15
Myburgh Rd	Dieprivier	140	CO 28
Myburgh Rd	Dieprivier	140	CP 28
Myburgh Rd	Somerset West	171	CU 75
Myburgh St	Paarl	18	BC 87
Myburgh St	Park Estates	170	CX 73
Myburgh St	Park Estates	174	CY 72
Mydrecht St	Bothasig	42	BS 38
Mydrecht St	Bothasig	58	BT 38
Mydrecht St	Greenways	174	CZ 74
Myer Rd	Retreat	140	CR 28
Myeza	Lekkerwater	184	DA 17
Myeza Rd	Masiphumelele	184	DA 18
Myezo Cr.	Mfuleni	127	CL 55
Myhof Rd	Claremont	121	CJ 31
Mymona Cr.	Primrose Pk	122	CJ 37
Myn Rd	Vanguard	103	CF 38
Mynderd St	Plumstead	140	CO 30
Mynhardt Cl.	Bellville	61	BT 48
Mynhardt St	Strand Halt	170	CW 74
Mynie Rd	Wetton	121	CL 34
Myoli Rd	Masiphumelele	184	DA 18
Myoli St	Harare	146	CS 53
Myoli St	Harare	146	CS 54
Myolo Cr.	Eyethu	146	CO 53
Myra St	Eersterivier	128	CM 60
Myra St	Northern Paarl	18	AZ 88
Myrica Rd	Hout Bay	117	CN 18
Myrtle	Acacia Pk	58	BX 36
Myrtle	Wingfield	58	BX 36
Myrtle Cr.	Sir Lowry's Pass	176	CZ 81
Myrtle Rd	Bishop Lavis	104	CD 41
Myrtle Rd	Bishop Lavis	104	CD 42
Myrtle Rd	Kenilworth	120	CK 29
Myrtle Rd	Ottery	121	CM 33
Myrtle Rd	Parkwood	141	CO 32
Myrtle Rd	Rondebosch	101	CF 29
Myrtle Rd	Tokai	139	CS 25
Myrtle Rd	Uitsig	87	CC 45
Myrtle St	Eversdal Hgts	46	BS 51
Myrtle St	Eversdal Hgts	46	BS 54
Myrtle St	Hillcrest Hgts	127	CM 57
Myrtle St	Oranjezicht	82	CC 23
Myrtle St	Somerset West	171	CU 78
Myrtle Way	Lekkerwater	184	CZ 18
Myrtle Way	Newlands	101	CH 28
Mzabalazo St	Wimbledon	108	CG 55
Mzali Cr.	Kaya	146	CP 51
Mzamo	Guguletu	104	CH 40
Mzamo Cr.	Nyanga	123	CJ 42
Mzam-Omhle	Mbekweni	15	AW 92
Mzamomhle St	Mxolisi Phetani	125	CM 49
Mzimvubu St	Mfuleni	126	CK 53
Mzintlava St	Mfuleni	126	CK 53
Mzomhle	Mbekweni	15	AW 92
Mzomtsha Cl.	Nyanga	123	CK 42
Mzondi St	Dunoon	42	BO 38
Mzonke Jack	Weltevreden Val. (M.Plain)	123	CN 42
Mzoxolo Cr.	Mxolisi Phetani	125	CM 50
Mzuzu Cr.	Bloekombos	48	BR 62
Mzwakhe Mbuli Pl.	Mandela Pk	146	CR 54
Mzwakhe Mbuli Pl.	Mandela Pk	146	CS 52
Mzwandile Rd	Ekuphumuleni	146	CQ 53
N			
N.Hoboshe St	Mfuleni	126	CL 53
N.Mgogoshe St	Mfuleni	126	CL 53
N.Mhluthwa St	Nonqubela	126	CN 53
N.R. Mandela Rd	Hout Bay	137	CO 16
N1	Century City	57	BX 34
N1	Klapmuts	36	BL 76
N1	Kraaifontein	48	BR 59

Index to Street Names

N1 (Paarl) — Ntambanane St

STREET NAME	SUBURB NAME	PG	GRID
N1	Paarl	23	BF 91
N1	Foreshore	82	CA 25
N1 (Table Bay Blvd)	Salt River	83	CA 29
N2	Cape Town Cen.	82	BZ 24
N2	Macassar	148	CQ 61
N2	Sir Lowry's Pass	176	CZ 79
N2 (Eastern Blvd)	District Six	82	CB 25
N2 (Settlers Way)	Mowbray	102	CE 32
N7	Edgemead	58	BV 37
N7	Vissershok	26	BK 38
Naartjie Cl.	Mitchells Plain	144	CR 44
Nabileyo St	Brown's Farm	124	CM 43
Naboom Rd	Belhar	106	CD 47
Naboom St	Eastridge (M.Plain)	145	CQ 48
Nabucco Rd	Strandfontein	162	CT 42
Nabygelegen St	Kleinbosch	59	BT 40
Nadia	Avonwood	86	CB 42
Nadia St	Casablanca	175	DB 76
Nadouwberg	Tafelsig (M.Plain)	164	CT 49
Nagel Cr.	Morgenster	63	BU 56
Naggett Ave	Hout Bay	137	CO 16
Nagona St	Umrhabulo Triangle	147	CP 56
Nagtegaal	Devon Pk	112	CD 72
Nagtegaal St	Amandelsig	90	CB 55
Nagtegaal St	Macassar	149	CS 65
Naguil Cl.	D'urbanvale	29	BN 50
Nahoon Ave	Silverhurst	119	CN 25
Nahoon Cl.	Portlands (M.Plain)	144	CQ 46
Nahoon St	Delft	106	CG 48
Nahoon St	Manenberg	122	CJ 38
Nahoon St	Mfuleni	126	CJ 53
Nahum St	Ysterplaat	57	BX 32
Naidoo Cir.	Wellington	15	AV 92
Nakanye St	Harare	146	CR 53
Naledi Cr.	Mfuleni	126	CL 54
Naledi St	Mfuleni	126	CL 54
Namakwa St	Elim	90	CB 55
Namakwa St	Kleinvlei	127	CJ 58
Namaqua Pl.	Plattekloof Glen	59	BW 40
Namaqua Rd	Plattekloof Glen	59	BW 40
Namaqua St	Flintdale Est.	141	CP 31
Nambuzane St	Kuyasa	147	CS 55
Namer Rd	Sanddrift	57	BV 34
Nana	Anesta	113	CF 75
Nana Cl.	Brackenfell Sth	63	BX 56
Nanana St	Eyethu	146	CP 53
Nanana St	Eyethu	146	CP 54
Nandina	Macassar	149	CR 63
Nandina Pl.	Hazelwood Pk	185	CZ 20
Nandina Pl.	Hazelwood Pk	185	DC 22
Nango Rd	Sanddrift	57	BV 34
Nannabessie	Delft Sth	125	CK 49
Nansen Rd	Claremont	101	CH 29
Nansen St	Observatory	83	CB 28
Nantes	Kirstenhof	158	CU 26
Nantes	Stellenbosch	95	CB 76
Nantes Cl.	La Rochelle	62	BV 52
Nantes Cl.	Mitchells Plain	144	CR 44
Nantes Pl.	Belhar	106	CE 49
Nantes St	Lemoenkloof	18	BC 88
Nanze Cr.	Victoria Mxenge	146	CO 51
Naomi Cl.	Lentegeur (M.Plain)	145	CO 48
Naomi St	Avonwood	86	CB 42
Naomi St	Greenways	174	DA 73
Napier	Ravensmead	87	CA 44
Napier Cl.	Portlands (M.Plain)	145	CS 47
Napier Rd	Kenridge	45	BS 49
Napier Rd	Royal Cape	120	CM 30
Napier St	Cape Town Cen.	82	BZ 23
Napier St	Lemoenkloof	18	BB 87
Napier St	Lemoenkloof	18	BC 87
Napier St	Park Estates	170	CX 73
Napier St	Park Estates	174	CY 73
Naples Cl.	Eikenbosch	90	CC 57
Naples Cl.	Uitzicht	47	BO 55
Naples St	Observatory	83	CC 28
Napoleon Cl.	La Rochelle	62	BV 52
Napoli Ave	Strandfontein	162	CT 42
Narcissus	Lentegeur (M.Plain)	144	CP 46
Nared Cr.	Jamestown	112	CH 74
Nares Rd	Claremont	101	CH 30
Nares St	Observatory	83	CB 28
Narsing St	Parow Nth	59	BW 41
Naruna Cr.	Plumstead	140	CO 30
Naruna Cr.	Plumstead	141	CO 31
Narvik St	Uitzicht	47	BO 55
Narwahl St	Rugby	84	BY 31
Nassau Ave	Pinelands	85	CB 35
Nassau Ave	Somerset West	171	CT 75
Nassau Cl.	Brackenfell Sth	63	BX 56
Nassau Rd	Belhar	106	CD 49
Nassau Rd	Chapman's Peak	156	CX 18
Nassau Rd	Wynberg	120	CL 27
Nassau St	Avondale	60	BX 44
Nassau St	Bothasig	58	BT 37
Nassau St	Ruyterwacht	86	BZ 39
Nassau St	Strandvale	170	CW 73
Nassau St	Tygerdal	58	BX 38
Nassau St	Tygerdal	59	BX 39
Nassua Cr.	Stellenberg	62	BU 51
Nastergal Cr.	Roosendaal	107	CE 51
Nastergal Cr.	Roosendaal	107	CE 51
Nasturtium	Dunoon	42	BO 37
Nasturtium St	Lentegeur (M.Plain)	124	CN 45
Nasturuim	Macassar	149	CR 63

STREET NAME	SUBURB NAME	PG	GRID
Nata Cr.	Delft	106	CG 49
Natal St	Paarden Eiland	83	BZ 30
Natalie Cr.	Lentegeur (M.Plain)	145	CO 48
Natalie St	Elim	90	CA 55
Natasha St	Casablanca	175	DB 76
Natchez Cr.	Graceland	146	CP 53
Nathan Mallach St	N1 City	59	BX 40
Natmeat Rd	Factreton	85	BZ 35
Naude	Wellington	15	AW 93
Naude St	Franschhoek Sth	79	BY 107
Naude St	Mabille Pk	89	CA 53
Nautical Cr.	Strandfontein	162	CT 42
Nautilus Cr.	Big Bay	24	BL 28
Nautilus St	Gustrow	175	DC 75
Nautilus St	Paarden Eiland	83	BZ 29
Nautilus St	Strandfontein	163	CT 43
Nautilus Way	Dennemere	108	CH 57
Nautilus Way	Phoenix	57	BV 33
Navarre Cr.	Belhar	106	CE 49
Navarre La.	Die Bos	174	CY 74
Navarre St	Lemoenkloof	18	BB 89
Navarre St	Somerset West	151	CQ 71
Navarrest St	Everglen	61	BT 50
Navic St	Oakdene	89	CC 53
Nazareth House Cl.	Avon	86	CA 41
Nazli Cr.	Casablanca	175	DB 76
Nazo St	Victoria Mxenge	146	CO 52
Nbukwane St	Ilitha Pk	146	CR 52
Ncama St	Umrhabulo Triangle	147	CR 56
Ncanashe Cr.	Victoria Mxenge	146	CO 51
Ncanda Ave	Joe Slovo Pk	57	BU 34
Ncanda Rd	Philippi East	124	CM 46
Ncanda St	Kuyasa	147	CS 55
Nceba Ave	Nyanga	123	CK 42
Ncede	Philippi East	124	CM 46
Ncede Cl.	Ilitha Pk	146	CR 52
Ncedo St	Umrhabulo Triangle	147	CR 57
Nceduluntu Cr.	Crossroads	124	CK 45
Nciba St	Kaya	146	CO 52
Ncimba Cl.	Philippi East	125	CL 47
Ncinba	Philippi East	124	CL 46
Ncinci Cr.	Harare	146	CR 53
Ncindi St	Harare	146	CR 53
Nciniba St	Ilitha Pk	146	CR 51
Nciphisa St	Griffiths Mxenge	146	CP 54
Nciphisa St	Griffiths Mxenge	146	CP 54
Ncoma St	Harare	146	CS 54
Ncora St	Kaya	146	CP 52
Ncumo Rd	Harare	146	CR 53
Ncumo Rd	Harare	146	CR 54
Ncumo Rd	Harare	146	CS 53
Ncwadi Cr.	Umrhabulo Triangle	147	CQ 56
Ncwina St	Umrhabulo Triangle	147	CR 57
Ndaba St	Eyethu	146	CO 53
Ndabakazi Rd	Brown's Farm	124	CL 43
Ndabambi Cr.	Nonqubela	126	CN 53
Ndabaninzi Ave	Nyanga	123	CK 41
N'dabeni Rd	Langa	103	CD 35
Ndabeni St	Ndabeni	84	CC 31
Ndamane Ave	Nyanga	123	CK 42
Ndamane Ave	Nyanga	123	CM 39
Ndawo St	Bloekombos	48	BQ 62
Ndeleni St	Wallacedene	48	BS 61
Ndemba Cr.	Victoria Mxenge	126	CN 51
Ndiki Cl.	Nyanga	123	CK 42
Ndima St	Crossroads	124	CK 45
Ndima St	Harare	146	CS 53
Ndima St	Nyanga	123	CK 42
Ndingo St	Mxolisi Phetani	125	CM 50
Ndinisa St	Mfuleni	126	CK 53
Ndize	Mbekweni	15	AV 92
Ndkwe St	Mandela Pk	147	CQ 54
Ndkwe St	Mandela Pk	147	CP 55
Ndlalifa	Mbekweni	15	AW 92
Ndlanzi	Philippi East	124	CL 46
Ndlebe St	Victoria Mxenge	146	CO 51
Ndlela Cl.	Nyanga	123	CK 42
Ndlela St	Crossroads	124	CK 44
Ndleleni	Mbekweni	15	AW 92
Ndlovu	Philippi East	125	CM 47
Ndlovu Cr.	Victoria Mxenge	126	CN 51
Ndlulamthi St	Kuyasa	146	CS 54
Ndlulamthi St	Kuyasa	147	CS 55
Ndodwa St	Kaya	146	CP 51
Ndodwa St	Umrhabulo Triangle	147	CR 57
Ndolo Cr.	Victoria Mxenge	126	CN 52
Ndongeni Cr.	Philippi East	125	CM 47
Ndumela	Kayamandi	94	CA 74
Ndumiseni Cl.	Nyanga	123	CL 42
Ndum-ndum St	Wallacedene	48	BS 62
Ndum-ndum St	Wallacedene	48	BS 61
Nduna Rd	Thembokwezi	125	CM 49
Ndwabasi St	Kuyasa	147	CS 55
Ndwe Cl.	Ilitha Pk	146	CR 51
Ndyebo St	Griffiths Mxenge	146	CQ 54
Ndyondyo St	Umrhabulo Triangle	147	CP 58
Ndzawumdi	Kayamandi	94	BZ 74
Ndzuzo St	Nomzano	175	CY 76
Ndzuzo St	Nomzano	175	CZ 76
Neath Rd	Observatory	83	CC 29
Neave St	Claremont	120	CJ 28
Nebelia St	Forest Hgts	127	CL 57
Nebo St	Brackenfell Sth	63	BX 57
Nebraska St	Stellenridge	62	BV 51
Nebula	Rocklands (M.Plain)	144	CS 46

STREET NAME	SUBURB NAME	PG	GRID
Nebula Ave	Salberau	86	CB 42
Nebula Cr.	Blackheath Ind.	108	CG 56
Nebula St	Wellington	15	AV 93
Nebula Way	Ocean View	189	DD 15
Neckar Cr.	Silversands	107	CH 53
Nectar Rd	Steenberg	159	CT 28
Nectar Way	Mitchells Plain	144	CR 45
Nederberg Cr.	Belhar	106	CD 49
Nederberg Dr.	Richwood	42	BP 38
Nederberg Rd	Table View	41	BO 32
Nederburg	Kirstenhof	158	CU 26
Nederburg	Welgelegen	113	CD 76
Nederburg Cl.	Mitchells Plain	144	CR 45
Nederburg Cl.	Mitchells Plain	144	CR 43
Nederburgh Cl.	Die Bos	174	CY 74
Nederburgh St	Welgemoed	60	BU 46
Nederburgh St	Welgemoed	61	BU 47
Nederland St	Belhar	106	CE 50
Neels Bothma St	N1 City	59	BW 40
Neethling	Mimosa	88	CA 50
Neethling	Stellenbosch	95	CC 76
Neethling St	Somerset West	151	CR 71
Neethling St	Van Ryneveld	174	CZ 72
Neethlings Cl.	Mitchells Plain	144	CR 45
Neetlingshof St	Haasendal	90	CA 57
Neil Cl.	Montagu's Gift	142	CO 35
Neil Moses	Klein Nederburg	19	BB 93
Nel St	Morgenster Hoogte	63	BT 56
Nel St	Wellington	11	AR 95
Nelani Cr.	Victoria Mxenge	146	CO 51
Nellie Cr.	Scottsdene	64	BT 59
Nellie Spilhaus St	Cafda Village	141	CR 31
Nellmapius	Welgelegen	113	CD 76
Nelson Cr.	Admirals Pk	175	DC 78
Nelson Dr.	Simonskloof	194	DJ 25
Nelson Rd	Fairfield	60	BX 44
Nelson Rd	Fish Hoek	185	DA 22
Nelson Rd	Fish Hoek	186	DB 23
Nelson Rd	Observatory	83	CC 29
Nelson St	Bellair	62	BV 52
Nelson St	Foreshore	82	CB 25
Nelson St	Vasco Est.	59	BX 39
Nelson St	Vasco Est.	86	BY 40
Nelson St	Wellington	15	AV 92
Nemesia Cl.	Ottery East	121	CN 34
Nemesia Cl.	Plattekloof	60	BU 43
Nemesia Cr.	Milnerton	57	BT 33
Nemesia Rd	Gordon Strand	175	DC 76
Nemesia Rd	Silvertown	103	CF 36
Nemesia St	Bellville	61	BT 48
Nemesia St	Bellville	61	BV 48
Nemesia St	Brantwood	89	CA 53
Nemesia St	Halalie	46	BO 52
Nemesia St	Milnerton	57	BT 33
Nenta	Weltevrede	94	BY 74
Neptune	Rocklands (M.Plain)	144	CS 45
Neptune Cl.	Bay View Village	191	DG 23
Neptune Cr.	The Hague	106	CF 50
Neptune Rd	Joe Slovo Pk	57	BU 33
Neptune St	Bellair	62	BV 53
Neptune St	Hout Bay Harbour	136	CR 13
Neptune St	Paarden Eiland	83	BZ 29
Neptune St	Paarden Eiland	83	CA 29
Neptune St	Salberau	86	CB 41
Neptunes Way	Admirals Pk	175	DC 78
Nereide St	Woodstock	83	CA 28
Nerina Ave	Brantwood	89	CB 53
Nerina Ave	Fish Hoek	186	DA 24
Nerina Ave	Kommetjie	183	DC 11
Nerina Ave	Somerset West	170	CU 72
Nerina Cr.	Eersterivier	128	CM 60
Nerina Cr.	Fish Hoek	186	DA 24
Nerina Rd	Bellville Sth	88	CA 49
Nerina Rd	Durbanville	45	BR 50
Nerina Rd	Harbour Island	178	DF 74
Nerina Rd	Milnerton	57	BU 33
Nerina Rd	Parow Nth	59	BW 41
Nerina Rd	Simon's Town	195	DK 27
Nerina Rd	Uitsig	87	CC 44
Nerina St	Brackenfell	63	BV 55
Nerina St	Denneburg	23	BD 91
Nerina St	Franschhoek Sth	79	BZ 108
Nerina St	Wellington	11	AS 95
Nerina St	Woodstock	82	CB 26
Nerina Way	Thornton	85	CA 37
Nerine	Lentegeur (M.Plain)	144	CO 46
Nerine	Lentegeur (M.Plain)	145	CO 47
Nerine Ave	Pinelands	84	CC 34
Nerine Cl.	Ottery East	121	CN 34
Nerine Rd	Belhar	88	CC 47
Nerine St	Hout Bay	137	CP 16
Nerine Steps	Simon's Town	194	DJ 25
Nero Cl.	Kraaifontein	47	BQ 58
Nero Cr.	Eastridge (M.Plain)	145	CQ 48
Nero St	Park Village	127	CK 58
Nestor Ct	Eureka	87	CC 43
Netball Cr.	Beacon Valley (M.Plain)	145	CP 47
Nethi Cl.	Langa	103	CE 36
Netreg Rd	Bonteheuwel	104	CE 40
Nettleton Rd	Clifton	80	CC 18
Neutron	Tegnopark	112	CF 72
Neutron Rd	Belhar	88	CC 48
Neutron St	Triangle Farm	89	BZ 51
Neva Cl.	Fir Grove	139	CQ 25
Nevada Rd	Colorado (M.Plain)	124	CN 44

STREET NAME	SUBURB NAME	PG	GRID
Nevada Rd	Montana/Durrheim	104	CF 42
Nevada St	Stellenridge	62	BV 51
Neville Lewis Cr.	Woodlands (M.Plain)	144	CO 44
Nevin St	Athlone	102	CG 33
New Baden Powell Dr.	Capricorn	160	CW 32
New Church St	Cape Town Cen.	81	CA 22
New Church St	Gardens	81	CB 22
New Cl.	Valhalla	86	CA 40
New Cross St	Wellington	10	AS 94
New Eisleben Rd	Brown's Farm	124	CL 44
New Eisleben Rd	Nyanga	124	CK 43
New Eskdale St	De Zoete Inval	22	BH 88
New Eskdale St	De Zoete Inval	22	BH 89
New Forest Cr.	West Riding	42	BO 35
New Haven	Durbanville	46	BP 51
New Market St	Foreshore	82	CB 25
New Mill Rd	Ndabeni	84	CB 33
New Ottery Rd	Ottery East	121	CN 34
New Park Rd	Claremont	101	CD 30
New St	Durbanville	45	BP 50
New St	Durbanville	46	BP 51
New St	Paarl	18	BC 89
New St	Somerset West	171	CU 75
New St	Somerset West	171	CV 75
New St	Valhalla	86	CA 40
New Vlei St	De Zoete Inval	22	BH 88
New Vlei St	KWV	22	BH 88
New Vlei St	KWV	22	BH 89
New Way	Pinelands	84	CC 33
New York Cl.	Portlands (M.Plain)	144	CQ 46
Newark Rd	Kenilworth	120	CK 30
Newberry Sq.	Edgemead	59	BU 39
Newbery La.	Newlands	101	CG 27
Newbury Cl.	Parklands	25	BN 33
Newbury Cr.	Milnerton Rdg	41	BS 33
Newcastle Cl.	Weltevreden Val. (M.Plain)	143	CP 42
Newcastle St	Dunoon	42	BO 37
Newcross Way	Sonstraal	46	BR 52
Newell Cl.	Langeberg Glen	47	BQ 56
Newent St	Lansdowne	121	CK 32
Newfields Cr.	Newfields	103	CH 37
Newfields Cr.	Newfields	122	CJ 37
Newfields Rd	Newfields	103	CH 37
Newlands Ave	Newlands	101	CG 27
Newlands Ave	Rondebosch	101	CG 28
Newlands Rd	Claremont	120	CJ 28
Newlands Rd	Northpine	64	BU 59
Newlands St	Beacon Valley (M.Plain)	145	CP 48
Newman	Idasvallei	96	CA 80
Newman Rd	Aurora	45	BQ 48
Newman St	William Lloyd	23	BD 91
Newmans Ave	Belthorn Est.	121	CJ 34
Newmarket Rd	Ottery	122	CM 35
Newmarket St	Beacon Valley (M.Plain)	145	CQ 48
Newport Cl.	Belhar	107	CD 51
Newport Cl.	Scottsdene	64	BV 59
Newport Cr.	Dennemere	108	CH 57
Newport Cr.	Dennemere	127	CJ 58
Newport Rd	Scottsdene	64	BU 59
Newport St	Gardens	81	CC 21
Newry St	Claremont	101	CH 28
Newry St	Claremont	101	CE 27
Newton Ave	Athlone	102	CG 33
Newton Dr.	Meadowridge	140	CP 27
Newton Dr.	Meadowridge	140	CP 28
Newton Rd	Strand Halt	170	CW 74
Newton Rd	Woodlands (M.Plain)	144	CP 45
Newton St	Belhar	88	CC 49
Newton St	Des Hampden	89	CB 53
Newton St	Tarentaalplaas	170	CX 74
Newton St	Wellington	15	AV 93
Newton St	Wellington	15	AW 93
Ngaba-Ngaba Cr.	Ilitha Pk	146	CR 52
Ngacu Cr.	Nonqubela	126	CN 52
Ngada Rd	Philippi East	124	CM 46
Ngada Rd	Philippi East	125	CM 47
Ngada St	Kuyasa	147	CS 55
Ngambu St	Guguletu	104	CH 40
Ngambu St	Guguletu	123	CJ 40
Nganawa	Mbekweni	15	AW 91
Ng'ang'ane St	Ilitha Pk	146	CR 52
Ngapha	Umrhabulo Triangle	147	CQ 56
Ngcingci Cr.	Philippi East	125	CM 47
Ngcingcu St	Ilitha Pk	146	CQ 52
Ngcisininde Cr.	Philippi	124	CL 43
Ngcungcu	Philippi East	124	CM 46
Ngcwalazi Dr.	Ilitha Pk	146	CQ 52
Ngcwalazi Dr.	Ilitha Pk	146	CR 52
Ngena St	Dunoon	42	BO 38
Ngenge Cr.	Ilitha Pk	146	CR 52
Ngentla Cl.	Nonqubela	126	CN 52
Ngesi Cr.	Crossroads	124	CK 44
Ngesi St	Harare	146	CR 54
Ngetu Cr.	Victoria Mxenge	146	CO 51
Ngoabe Cr.	Joe Slovo Pk	57	BU 34
Ngomso St	Harare	146	CS 54
Ngonyama Cr.	Joe Slovo Pk	57	BU 34
Ngonyama Rd	Philippi East	125	CM 47
Ngoye St	Mandela Pk	147	CQ 55
Ngoye St	Mandela Pk	147	CP 55
Ngqabe	Philippi East	124	CM 46
Ngqabe St	Ilitha Pk	146	CR 52
Ngqangqolo	Philippi East	124	CM 46
Ngqangqolo St	Ilitha Pk	146	CR 52
Ngqasa Cr.	Nonqubela	126	CN 52

Abbreviations used: Ave – Avenue, A.H. – Agricultural Holding, A.L.– Algemene Landgoed, Blvd – Boulevard, Cen. – Central, Cir. – Circle, Cl. – Close, Cr. – Crescent, Ct – Court, Dr. – Drive, Est. – Estate, Ext. – Extension, Hgts – Heights, Ind. – Industrial, Gdns – Gardens, Gr. – Grove, La. – Lane, (M.Plain) - Mitchells Plain, Nth – North, Pl. – Place, Pk – Park, Rd – Road, Rdg. – Ridge, S.H. – Small Holding, Sq. – Square, St – Street, Sth – South, Ter. – Terrace, Tn – Turn, Val. – Valley, Wk – Walk

STREET NAME	SUBURB NAME	PG	GRID		STREET NAME	SUBURB NAME	PG	GRID
Ngqawa St	Brown's Farm	123	CM 42		Nisikizi Ave	Joe Slovo Pk	57	BV 34
Ngqayi	Mbekweni	15	AW 91		Nissen St	Sir Lowry's Pass	176	CZ 82
Ngqiba St	Umrhabulo Triangle	147	CR 57		Nita	De Tijger	60	BW 44
Ngqina St	Harare	146	CS 54		Nita	Strand	174	CZ 73
Ngquba St	Umrhabulo Triangle	147	CR 58		Nita Rd	Montagu's Gift	141	CP 34
Ngqungqulu	Philippi East	125	CL 47		Nita Spilhaus Cr.	Woodlands (M.Plain)	144	CO 45
Ngqusha Cr.	Umrhabulo Triangle	147	CQ 58		Nitida	Anesta	113	CF 75
Ngqwangi Dr.	Philippi East	125	CM 47		Nitida St	Eersterivier	127	CL 58
Ngulube Rd	Philippi East	125	CL 47		Nivenia Cl.	Perm Gdns	128	CJ 59
Ngwamza	Philippi East	124	CL 46		Nivenia Cl.	Perm Gdns	128	CJ 61
Ngwamza	Philippi East	124	CM 46		Njabulo St	Mxolisi Phetani	125	CM 50
Ngwamza	Joe Slovo Pk	57	BV 34		Njabulo St	Mxolisi Phetani	125	CM 50
Ngwamza St	Kuyasa	147	CS 56		Njala Cr.	Goedemoed	46	BP 54
Ngwe Cr.	Philippi East	125	CM 47		Njalaboom	Delft Sth	125	CJ 50
Ngwenya St	Crossroads	124	CK 45		Njelele Way	Belhar	106	CG 49
Ngwenya St	Thembokwezi	125	CN 49		Njenjese St	Bloekombos	48	BR 62
Ngwenya Wk	Philippi East	124	CM 46		Njezu St	Harare	146	CR 52
Ngwenye Cr.	Mxolisi Phetani	125	CM 49		Nimba Ave	Nonqubela	126	CN 52
Ngweventsha	Dunoon	42	BO 37		Njoli Ave	Langa	103	CE 36
Ngweventsha	Dunoon	42	BO 38		Njongo Ave	Mxolisi Phetani	125	CM 50
Ngxalathi St	Umrhabulo Triangle	147	CP 58		Njongo St	Dunoon	42	BO 38
Ngxama St	Kaya	146	CP 52		Njongo St	Dunoon	42	BO 36
Ngxangxosi St	Ilitha Pk	146	CR 51		Njwiza	Philippi East	124	CM 46
Ngxobongwana	Nyanga	123	CJ 42		Nkali Cr.	Nonqubela	126	CN 52
Ngxokozweni Cr.	Philippi East	124	CM 46		Nkamela St	Brown's Farm	124	CM 44
Ngxowa St	Nonqubela	126	CN 53		Nkanga Cr.	Eyethu	146	CP 53
Niagara Way	Bellville	61	BU 48		Nkanyezi St	Ilitha Pk	146	CQ 53
Niblick St	Lakeside	159	CV 27		Nkcazo St	Umrhabulo Triangle	147	CQ 58
Nice Rd	Plumstead	140	CO 29		Nkcukacha St	Umrhabulo Triangle	147	CP 56
Nice St	Uitzicht	31	BN 54		Nkenjane St	Ilitha Pk	146	CQ 51
Nicholas Cl.	Plumstead	140	CP 29		Nkholo St	Mfuleni	126	CM 54
Nicholette St	Plumstead	140	CP 29		Nkholo St	Mfuleni	127	CL 55
Nicholi Ave	Kommetjie	183	DB 13		Nkinga Cl.	Harare	146	CS 53
Nicholls	Bellville Sth Ind.	88	CA 50		Nkobi St	Mandela Pk	147	CR 55
Nicholls St	William Lloyd	23	BD 94		Nkohla Cr.	Nonqubela	126	CN 53
Nick Kearns	Marlow	88	BZ 50		Nkomo Cr.	Victoria Mxenge	146	CO 51
Nick Kearns	Marlow	88	CA 50		Nkomo Dr.	Joe Slovo Pk	57	BU 34
Nico Cl.	Crawford	102	CG 34		Nkomo Way	Langa	103	CD 36
Nico Dirk	Parow Ind.	87	CA 46		Nkonjane St	Philippi East	125	CL 47
Nico Malan St	Park Estates	170	CX 73		Nkonjane St	Mxolisi Phetani	125	CL 49
Nicol St	Gardens	81	CB 21		Nkonjane Way	Mfuleni	127	CK 55
Nicola Cl.	Lentegeur (M.Plain)	145	CO 48		Nkonki St	Khayelitsha	147	CS 55
Nicola St	Northern Paarl	18	AZ 89		Nkonkwa Cr.	Umrhabulo Triangle	147	CQ 57
Nicolaas Arends Ave	Marlow	88	BZ 50		Nkonya Cr.	Eyethu	146	CP 53
Nicolar Rd	Edgemead	59	BT 39		Nkosazana St	Thembokwezi	125	CN 49
Nicole Ave	Blackheath Ind.	108	CF 56		Nkosiy Miza St	Manenberg	104	CH 40
Nicole St	De Tijger	60	BW 44		Nkovu St	Harare	146	CS 54
Nicolette Cl.	Brentwood Pk	125	CJ 50		Nkowane St	Brown's Farm	124	CL 43
Niehaus	Winston Est.	170	CX 73		Nkqubela Cr.	Umrhabulo Triangle	147	CQ 58
Nielsen	Delft Sth	125	CK 48		Nkqubela St	Gugulethu	123	CK 40
Nieman St	Peerless Pk East	47	BS 58		Nkukhu St	Harare	146	CS 54
Nieshout	Delft Sth	125	CK 49		Nkulu St	Harare	146	CS 54
Nieshout St	Loevenstein	60	BW 41		Nkulumo Rd	Ekuphumuleni	146	CQ 53
Nietgewek Ave	Voorbrug	107	CG 51		Nkume St	Tarentaalplaas	175	CY 75
Nietvoorbij	Stellenbosch	95	BZ 76		Nkunkwana	Dunoon	42	BO 37
Nieuhof Rd	Tijgerhof	57	BW 32		Nkunkwana	Dunoon	42	BO 36
Nieuwenhuys St	The Palms	170	CW 73		Nkunzane St	Brown's Farm	123	CM 42
Niger Cl.	Portlands (M.Plain)	144	CQ 46		Nkuthalo Dr.	Philippi	124	CL 45
Nightingale Cl.	Somerset West	171	CV 76		Nkuthazo St	Crossroads	124	CK 45
Nightingale Rd	Pelikan Pk	142	CS 35		Nkwenkezi Cr.	Ilitha Pk	146	CR 52
Nightingale Rd	Wingfield	85	BZ 37		Nkwenkwezi	Mbekweni	15	AX 92
Nightingale Way	Pinelands	84	CC 33		Nobahle St	Bloekombos	48	BR 62
Nightjar St	Pelikan Pk	161	CV 38		Nobantu Cl.	Bloekombos	48	BR 62
Nikkel St	Brackenfell Ind.	63	BU 57		Nobel St	Belhar	88	CC 49
Nile	Portlands (M.Plain)	144	CQ 46		Nobel Way	Meadowridge	140	CP 28
Nile Rd	Fairdale	126	CJ 54		Nobevu Cr.	Victoria Mxenge	146	CO 51
Nile St	Delft	106	CF 49		Nobiya	Philippi East	125	CL 47
Nile St	District Six	82	CB 25		Nobiya St	Ilitha Pk	146	CR 52
Nimbus Way	Elfindale	140	CQ 29		Noble	Stellenbosch	95	CA 75
Nimvencu St	Ilitha Pk	146	CQ 52		Noble Cir.	Ottery East	121	CN 34
Nimvencu St	Ilitha Pk	146	CQ 53		Noble Rd	Tijgerhof	57	BV 32
Nina	Springbok Pk	62	BV 54		Nobom St	Dunoon	42	BO 37
Nina Ave	Bothasig	58	BU 36		Nobongile Cr.	Wallacedene	48	BS 61
Nina St	Tafelsig (M.Plain)	145	CS 50		Noboninkosi St	Lwandle	175	CZ 76
Nineteenth Ave	Salberau	86	CB 41		Nobuhle St	Lwandle	175	CZ 76
Nineteenth St	Elsies River Ind.	86	BZ 41		Nobuhle Way	Mfuleni	127	CL 55
Nineteenth St	Elsies River Ind.	86	CA 41		Nobula	Mbekweni	15	AW 91
Ninth	De Oude Renbaan	22	BH 88		Nochulo Cr.	Ilitha Pk	146	CQ 52
Ninth Ave	Avon	86	CA 41		Noel St	Silveroaks	90	CC 55
Ninth Ave	Belmont Pk	48	BR 60		Noeline Cr.	Bellville	61	BT 50
Ninth Ave	Belmont Pk	48	BR 61		Noggaza	Philippi East	124	CM 46
Ninth Ave	Belmont Pk	48	BS 59		Nokilane Cl.	Nyanga	123	CJ 42
Ninth Ave	Boston	60	BX 46		Nokilane Cl.	Nyanga	123	CM 39
Ninth Ave	Boston	61	BX 47		Nokwanda Cl.	Gugulethu	123	CJ 40
Ninth Ave	Da Gama Pk	190	DE 24		Nokwazi	Mbekweni	15	AW 92
Ninth Ave	Eikendal	47	BS 58		Nokwazi Sq.	Eyethu	146	CO 53
Ninth Ave	Fairways	141	CO 31		Nolali	Kayamandi	94	BZ 74
Ninth Ave	Fish Hoek	186	DA 23		Noll Ave	Newfields	103	CH 37
Ninth Ave	Florida	87	CB 44		Nolloth Pl.	Plattekloof Glen	59	BW 40
Ninth Ave	Hazendal	102	CE 33		Nolloth Pl.	Plattekloof Glen	59	BT 41
Ninth Ave	Kayamandi	94	CA 74		Nolloth Rd	Blue Downs	127	CJ 56
Ninth Ave	Kensington	84	BZ 33		Nolloth Rd	Plattekloof Glen	59	BW 40
Ninth Ave	Kensington	84	BZ 34		Nolte St	Greenways	174	CZ 73
Ninth Ave	Leonsdale	86	CA 41		Nolubabalo St	Mxolisi Phetani	125	CM 50
Ninth Ave	Pelikan Pk	141	CQ 34		Noludwe St	Eyethu	146	CP 54
Ninth Ave	Retreat	140	CR 30		Nolwana Way	Langa	103	CD 36
Ninth Ave	Schaap Kraal	142	CQ 36		Nolwibili St	Ilitha Pk	146	CQ 52
Ninth Ave	Tafelsig (M.Plain)	146	CS 51		Nomad Rd	Sanddrift	57	BV 34
Ninth St	Bishop Lavis	104	CD 42		Nomalizo Mkonto St	Gugulethu	104	CH 40
Ninth St	Elnor	86	CC 42		Nomasi St	Kuyasa	147	CS 55
Ninth St	Kensington	84	BZ 33		Nomatse St	Kuyasa	147	CS 55
Ninth St	Rusthof	174	DA 74		Nomaweni St	Brown's Farm	124	CM 44
Ninth St	Rusthof	175	DA 74		Nomazi St	Bloekombos	48	BR 62
Nippon St	Voorbrug	107	CG 51		Nombewe St	Kuyasa	147	CS 56
Nirvana Way	Silverhurst	119	CN 26		Nombewe St	Kuyasa	147	CS 58
					Nombula St	Nomzano	175	CY 75

STREET NAME	SUBURB NAME	PG	GRID		STREET NAME	SUBURB NAME	PG	GRID
Nombula St	Tarentaalplaas	175	CY 76		Norman St	Park Estates	174	CZ 72
Nomfazi Ndamane St	Mandela Pk	147	CS 56		Norman St	Russel's Rest	128	CL 60
Nomfazi Ndamane St	Mandela Pk	147	CS 58		Normandie Cl.	Dreyersdal	140	CR 27
Nompemvana Cr.	Ilitha Pk	146	CR 52		Normandie Cl.	Edgemead	58	BV 37
Nompumelelo	Dunoon	42	BO 37		Normandie Cl.	La Rochelle	62	BV 51
Nompumelelo	Dunoon	42	BO 38		Normandie Cr.	Eersterivier	128	CL 59
Nompumelelo	Dunoon	42	BO 36		Normandy Cl.	Lemoenkloof	18	BB 89
Nompumelelo Cr.	Gugulethu	123	CJ 40		North Ave	Kewtown	103	CE 35
Nomrwabayi Cr.	Philippi East	125	CL 47		North Ave	Klein Begin	48	BS 61
Nomsa Maphongwana St	Kuyasa	147	CS 55		North Ave	Somerset West	170	CT 73
Nomthandazo Peter Cl.	Nyanga	123	CK 42		North Cl.	Montagu's Gift	141	CO 34
Nomvencu St	Brown's Farm	123	CM 42		North End	Cloeteville	95	BZ 75
Nomyani Dr.	Joe Slovo Pk	57	BV 34		North End	Strandfontein	162	CT 41
Nomyayi	Philippi East	124	CM 46		North Link	Athlone	102	CF 34
Nomyayi St	Brown's Farm	124	CL 43		North Rd	Killarney Gdns	42	BQ 36
Nomyayi St	Ilitha Pk	146	CQ 52		North Rd	Sunnydale	185	DA 19
Nomzamo	Dunoon	42	BO 37		North Rd	Table View	41	BP 34
Non Pareille St	Paarl	22	BD 87		North St	Rosebank	101	CE 29
Nonceba St	Tarentaalplaas	175	CY 75		North Star Rd	Surrey	103	CH 38
Nondakuthini St	Bloekombos	49	BR 63		North Way	Pinelands	84	CC 32
Nondindwa St	Philippi East	124	CM 46		North West	Rocklands (M.Plain)	145	CS 47
Nondlwana Rd	Philippi East	125	CM 47		North Wk	Fish Hoek	186	DA 24
Nondlwane St	Ilitha Pk	146	CQ 52		North Wk	Pinelands	84	CC 32
Nondumiso St	Bloekombos	48	BR 62		Northbridge Rd	Rondebosch East	102	CG 32
Nondzaba Cr.	Nonqubela	146	CO 53		Northern Cr.	Fairdale	126	CJ 54
Nongauza Cr.	Langa	103	CD 36		Northfield End	Parklands	25	BM 33
Nongcazela Cr.	Philippi East	124	CN 46		Northoaks Ave	Hout Bay	118	CM 19
Nonggai	Voorbrug	107	CG 51		Northpine Dr.	Northpine	63	BU 58
Nonguase Rd	Nyanga	124	CK 43		Northpine Dr.	Northpine	64	BU 59
Nongwingwi Cr.	Philippi East	125	CL 47		Northridge Cr.	Parklands	25	BM 32
Nonkonyana St	Wallacedene	48	BS 60		Northshore Cl.	The Lakes	184	CZ 17
Nonkqubela	Masiphumelele	184	DA 18		Northshore Dr.	Hout Bay	136	CQ 14
Nonkxwe St	Brown's Farm	124	CM 44		Northshore Dr.	The Lakes	184	CY 18
Nonkxwe St	Ilitha Pk	146	CQ 53		Northumberland Ave	Lakeside	159	CV 28
Nonqane Cr.	Ilitha Pk	146	CR 51		Northumberland Cl.	Parklands	25	BN 33
Nonqubela St	Lwandle	175	CZ 76		Northumberland Rd	Oakdale	61	BW 48
Nonsele Cr.	Nonqubela	146	CO 53		Northumbria Rd	Sea Point	81	CA 20
Nooiensfontein Dr.	Oakdene	89	CC 54		Northway East	Ravensmead	87	CA 45
Nooiensfontein Rd	High Gate	107	CG 53		Northway West	Ravensmead	87	CA 44
Nooiensfontein Rd	Highbury	107	CD 53		Nortje	Onverwacht	174	CZ 74
Nooitgedacht	Bo Dalsig	113	CE 76		Norton Dingle Dr.	Bel Ombre	119	CL 24
Nooitgedacht	Hout Bay	117	CN 15		Norton Sq.	Table View	41	BO 32
Nooitgedacht Dr.	Hout Bay	137	CO 15		Norton St	Beaconvale	87	BZ 43
Nooitgedacht Rd	West Riding	42	BO 35		Norton Way	Edgemead	58	BV 38
Nooitgedacht St	Groenvallei	62	BX 53		Norton Way	Rondebosch	102	CF 31
Nooitgedacht St	Somerset West	171	CU 76		Norway St	Maitland	84	CA 32
Noord	Cloetesville	95	BZ 75		Norwich Ave	Observatory	83	CC 29
Noord	Sarepta	89	CC 53		Norwich Dr.	Bishopscourt	119	CK 25
Noord Agter Paarl	Wellington	13	AU 84		Norwich Dr.	Bishopscourt	119	CK 25
Noord Agter Paarl	Wellington	13	AW 85		Norwich Dr.	Bishopscourt	119	CK 26
Noord Agter Paarl	Wellington	14	AX 87		Norwood Cl.	Valhalla	86	CA 43
Noord Cl.	Glen Rdg	191	DD 25		Norwood Rd	Avonwood	86	CA 41
Noord Rd	Eersterivier	128	CN 60		Norwood Rd	Leonsdale	86	CA 41
Noord St	Chrismar	61	BW 50		Norwood Rd	Milnerton	57	BV 32
Noord St	Churchill	59	BX 42		Norwood Rd	Norwood	86	CB 42
Noordelik Ave	Devil's Peak Est.	82	CC 24		Norwood St	Athlone	102	CG 33
Noordezee St	Malibu Village	127	CJ 56		Nosibulele St	Wallacedene	48	BS 61
Noordhoek Rd	Noordhoek	156	CX 18		Nossob Ct	Delft	106	CG 49
Noordhoek Rd	Sun Valley	185	CY 19		Nothabile Sq.	Eyethu	146	CP 54
Noordhoek Rd	Sunnydale	185	CZ 19		Notre Dame St	Klein Parys	23	BB 91
Noordhoek Rd	The Lakes	184	CY 18		Nottingham Cl.	Parklands	25	BN 33
Noordland	Morgen Gronde	63	BX 55		Nottingham Ct	Parklands	25	BN 33
Noordpool Cr.	Roosendaal	107	CF 51		Nottingham Ct	Parklands	25	BL 33
Noordpool Cr.	Roosendaal	107	CG 53		Nottingham Rd	Lakeside	159	CV 28
Noordsig 1	Lekkerwater	184	DA 18		Nottinghill	Sonstraal Hgts	46	BR 54
Noordsig 3	Lekkerwater	184	CZ 18		Notwari St	Delft	106	CG 49
Noordsig 4	Lekkerwater	184	DA 18		Nouli Cl.	Ilitha Pk	146	CQ 52
Noordsig Ave	Lekkerwater	184	DA 18		Nourse Ave	Epping Ind.	85	CC 38
Noordsig Rd	Skoongesig	29	BN 50		Nouveau	Vergesig	45	BQ 49
Noordwal East	Stellenbosch	95	CC 77		Nova Cl.	Panorama	59	BV 41
Noordwal East	Stellenbosch	95	CC 78		Nova Constantia Rd	Nova Constantia	139	CP 24
Noordwal West	Stellenbosch	95	CC 76		Novonia Rd	Blue Downs	127	CJ 56
Noorsdoring Cr.	Roosendaal	107	CF 51		Nowanga St	Brown's Farm	124	CM 43
Noqandula St	Ilitha Pk	146	CQ 53		Nowanga St	Ilitha Pk	146	CQ 52
Nor Ave	Scottsdene	64	BV 59		Nowowo St	Kuyasa	147	CS 55
Nor St	The Hague	106	CF 50		Noxolo St	Crossroads	124	CK 45
Norden St	Parow	87	BY 43		Noxolo St	Lwandle	175	CZ 77
Nordenfeldt Ave	Door de Kraal	61	BT 47		Nozala	Mbekweni	15	AW 91
Noreen Ave	Claremont	101	CH 31		Nozamile	Mbekweni	15	AX 92
Norfolk Cl.	Belhar	107	CD 51		Nozolile	Mbekweni	15	AX 92
Norfolk Cl.	Newlands	101	CH 27		Nqabara St	Mfuleni	126	CK 52
Norfolk La.	Rosebank	101	CE 30		Nqabara St	Mfuleni	126	CK 52
Norfolk Rd	Lakeside	159	CV 27		Nqawe St	Kaya	146	CQ 52
Norfolk Rd	Observatory	101	CD 29		Nqawu St	Kuyasa	147	CS 55
Norfolk Rd	Sea Point	81	BZ 20		Nqcikiza St	Crossroads	124	CK 44
Norfolk Rd	Tokai	139	CS 26		Nqila St	Harare	146	CS 53
Norfolk Rd	Tokai	139	CR 24		Nqilomathi St	Ilitha Pk	146	CQ 52
Norfolk Rd	Tokai	139	CS 25		Nqolwana St	Tarentaalplaas	170	CX 74
Norfolk St	Claremont	120	CJ 29		Nqu Rd	Philippi East	124	CL 46
Norfolk St	Maitland	84	CA 31		Nqwebesa St	Brown's Farm	123	CM 42
Norfolk St	Newlands	101	CG 27		Nqwebesa St	Brown's Farm	124	CM 43
Norfolk Way	Northpine	63	BT 58		Nqwenela St	Umrhabulo Triangle	147	CP 58
Norita Cr.	Rosendal	61	BU 50		Nqwilo St	Philippi East	124	CM 46
Norma Cl.	Hindle Pk	107	CH 54		Nsikazi St	Mfuleni	126	CK 55
Norma Rd	Silvertown	103	CF 35		Nsikazi St	Mfuleni	126	CK 52
Norma St	Eastridge (M.Plain)	145	CQ 48		Ntaba St	Ilitha Pk	146	CQ 53
Norma Way	Montagu's Gift	141	CO 34		Ntabazokhwahlambo St	Philippi East	124	CM 46
Norman Ave	Wetton	121	CL 34		Ntabesinayi Rd	Philippi East	124	CM 46
Norman Cl.	Montagu's Gift	142	CO 35		Ntabetafile Cl.	Philippi East	124	CM 46
Norman Gr.	Fresnaye	81	CA 19		Ntabetafile St	Mxolisi Phetani	125	CM 50
Norman Rd	Green Point	81	BZ 22		Ntabethemba St	Philippi East	124	CM 45
Norman Rd	Kalk Bay	186	DA 26		Ntaka St	Philippi East	125	CL 46
Norman Rd	Hout Bay	136	CP 14		Ntakobusi Cr.	Ilitha Pk	146	CQ 52
Norman St	Hout Bay	137	CP 15		Ntambanane St	Brown's Farm	123	CM 44
					Ntambanane St	Ilitha Pk	146	CR 52

Index to Street Names

Ntambanani Rd — Oxford Cr.

STREET NAME	SUBURB NAME	PG	GRID	
Ntambanani Rd	Philippi East	124	CL	46
Ntanga St	Nomzano	175	CY	75
Ntansiso Rd	Masiphumelele	184	DA	18
Ntantala Rd	Masiphumelele	184	DA	18
Ntelezi	Mbekweni	15	AW	92
Ntenetya St	Kuyasa	147	CS	55
Ntengu St	Ilitha Pk	146	CQ	53
Nthombeni Way	Noordhoek	156	CW	18
Ntini St	Brown's Farm	123	CM	40
Ntini St	Brown's Farm	123	CM	39
Ntlakohlaza Cl.	Nyanga	123	CK	41
Ntlakohlaza Cl.	Nyanga	123	CL	42
Ntlakohlaza St	Ilitha Pk	146	CQ	53
Ntlalo Rd	Kaya	146	CP	51
Ntlanganisela Cl.	Nyanga	123	CK	41
Ntlanganiso Cr.	Mxolisi Phetani	125	CM	50
Ntlangano Cr.	Nyanga	124	CJ	43
Ntlanzi St	Kuyasa	147	CS	55
Ntlazane	Mbekweni	15	AX	92
Ntlazane	Wellington	15	AU	91
Ntlazane Rd	Harare	146	CR	54
Ntlazane Rd	Ilitha Pk	146	CQ	53
Ntlemenza	Nonqubela	146	CO	53
Ntloko St	Harare	146	CR	54
Ntlolokotsheni	Philippi East	125	CL	47
Ntlolokshane St	Kuyasa	147	CS	55
Ntlongonane Cl.	Philippi East	125	CL	48
Ntlongonane Cl.	Philippi East	125	CK	50
Ntlonipho	Mbekweni	15	AW	92
Ntlotshane St	Bloekombos	49	BQ	63
Ntloyiya	Philippi East	124	CM	46
Ntlwa St	Kuyasa	147	CS	55
Ntonga St	Harare	146	CR	53
Ntongana Cr.	Nyanga	123	CK	42
Ntongana Rd	Scottsdene	48	BS	60
Ntongana Rd	Scottsdene	64	BT	60
Ntonjane	Mbekweni	15	AW	91
Ntozethu	Mbekweni	15	AW	92
Ntsethe St	Bloekombos	48	BQ	62
Ntshamba	Mbekweni	15	AW	91
Ntshanga	Kayamandi	94	BZ	74
Ntshangase St	Mfuleni	126	CK	53
Ntshawu	Philippi East	125	CM	47
Ntshili St	Ilitha Pk	146	CQ	53
Ntshiyane St	Brown's Farm	123	CM	42
Ntshiyane St	Ilitha Pk	146	CQ	53
Ntsholo Cr.	Nonqubela	126	CN	53
Ntsikisi St	Brown's Farm	124	CM	43
Ntsikizi	Philippi East	124	CM	46
Ntsikizi St	Ilitha Pk	146	CQ	53
Ntsinde St	Kuyasa	147	CS	55
Ntsinga St	Nomzano	175	CZ	76
Ntsona St	Mxolisi Phetani	126	CM	51
Ntubeni Rd	Brown's Farm	124	CL	43
Ntuku St	Kuyasa	146	CS	54
Ntukwane St	Brown's Farm	123	CM	42
Ntungele Cr.	Nonqubela	126	CN	52
Ntunuka Cr.	Victoria Mxenge	146	CO	51
Ntutyana St	Ilitha Pk	146	CQ	52
Ntuyane	Philippi East	124	CL	46
Ntyatyambo St	Weltevreden Val. (M.Plain)	124	CN	44
Nugget St	Weltevreden Val. (M.Plain)	144	CO	43
Nukanuka St	Brown's Farm	123	CM	42
Nungu Cr.	Philippi East	124	CM	46
Nursery La.	Barbarossa	120	CN	28
Nursery Rd	Rosebank	101	CE	29
Nursery St	Tafelsig (M.Plain)	145	CS	48
Nursery Way	Epping Forest	86	CC	41
Nursery Way	Epping Forest	86	CB	39
Nursery Way	Pinelands	84	CC	33
Nut Wood Ave	Somerset West	152	CS	75
Nutans Ave	Proteaville	46	BO	51
Nuttall Rd	Observatory	83	CC	29
Nuwe Berg St	Paarl	22	BE	88
Nuwerus St	Voorbrug	107	CG	51
Nuwetuin	Voorbrug	107	CG	51
Nuweveld	Wellington	15	AV	91
Nuweveld	Wellington	15	AU	94
Nuxia St	Loevenstein	60	BV	45
Nuy Ct	Delft	106	CG	49
Nxala St	Kuyasa	147	CS	55
Nxanxadi Cl.	Crossroads	124	CK	44
Nxanxadi Cl.	Crossroads	124	CN	46
Nxanxadi St	Ilitha Pk	146	CQ	52
Nxaruni St	Eyethu	146	CP	54
NY Rd 1	Guguletu	104	CG	40
NY Rd 1	Guguletu	104	CG	41
NY Rd 1	Guguletu	104	CH	41
NY Rd 1	Guguletu	123	CJ	40
NY1	Guguletu	123	CL	40
NY10	Guguletu	104	CH	40
NY100	Guguletu	104	CH	41
NY100	Guguletu	123	CJ	41
NY102	Guguletu	104	CH	42
NY102	Guguletu	123	CJ	41
NY103	Guguletu	104	CH	42
NY103	Guguletu	123	CJ	41
NY104	Guguletu	123	CJ	42
NY105	Guguletu	123	CJ	41
NY106	Guguletu	123	CJ	41
NY107	Guguletu	123	CJ	41
NY108	Guguletu	123	CJ	41
NY109	Guguletu	104	CG	40
NY11	Guguletu	104	CH	40
NY111	Guguletu	104	CG	40
NY111	Gugulethu	104	CG	41
NY117	Gugulethu	104	CH	41
NY118	Gugulethu	104	CG	40
NY119	Gugulethu	104	CG	40
NY12	Gugulethu	104	CH	40
NY120	Gugulethu	104	CG	41
NY122	Gugulethu	104	CG	40
Ny123	Gugulethu	104	CG	40
NY124	Gugulethu	104	CG	40
NY125	Gugulethu	104	CG	41
NY126	Gugulethu	104	CG	41
NY129	Gugulethu	104	CG	41
NY13	Gugulethu	104	CH	40
NY133	Gugulethu	104	CG	41
NY137	Gugulethu	104	CG	40
NY137	Gugulethu	104	CG	41
NY14	Gugulethu	104	CH	40
NY143	Gugulethu	104	CH	41
NY144	Gugulethu	104	CH	40
NY144	Gugulethu	104	CH	41
NY145	Gugulethu	104	CH	40
NY146	Gugulethu	104	CH	40
NY147	Gugulethu	104	CH	41
NY148	Gugulethu	104	CH	41
NY149	Gugulethu	104	CH	41
NY15 St	Gugulethu	123	CJ	40
NY150	Gugulethu	104	CH	41
NY151	Gugulethu	104	CH	41
NY152	Gugulethu	104	CH	41
NY153	Gugulethu	104	CH	41
NY154	Gugulethu	104	CH	41
NY156	Gugulethu	104	CH	41
NY157	Gugulethu	104	CG	41
NY158	Gugulethu	104	CG	41
NY159	Gugulethu	104	CG	41
NY16	Gugulethu	123	CJ	40
NY17	Gugulethu	123	CJ	40
NY18	Gugulethu	123	CJ	40
NY19	Gugulethu	123	CJ	40
NY21	Gugulethu	123	CJ	40
NY21	Gugulethu	123	CK	40
NY22	Gugulethu	104	CH	41
NY23	Gugulethu	104	CH	41
NY24	Gugulethu	104	CH	41
NY25	Gugulethu	123	CJ	41
NY27	Gugulethu	104	CH	41
NY28	Gugulethu	123	CJ	41
NY29 St	Gugulethu	123	CJ	40
NY3	Gugulethu	123	CJ	40
NY3	Gugulethu	123	CJ	41
NY3	Gugulethu	123	CK	40
NY3	Gugulethu	123	CK	41
NY30	Gugulethu	123	CJ	40
NY37	Gugulethu	123	CJ	41
NY38	Gugulethu	104	CH	41
NY38	Gugulethu	104	CH	41
NY41	Gugulethu	104	CH	41
NY42	Gugulethu	104	CH	41
NY43	Gugulethu	104	CH	41
NY43	Gugulethu	123	CJ	41
NY44	Gugulethu	123	CJ	41
NY45	Gugulethu	123	CJ	41
NY46	Gugulethu	123	CJ	40
NY47	Gugulethu	123	CJ	40
NY48	Gugulethu	123	CJ	40
NY49	Gugulethu	123	CJ	40
NY49	Gugulethu	123	CJ	41
NY5	Gugulethu	104	CH	41
NY5	Gugulethu	104	CH	41
NY54	Gugulethu	123	CK	40
NY55	Gugulethu	123	CK	40
NY59	Gugulethu	123	CK	40
NY60	Gugulethu	123	CK	40
NY62	Gugulethu	123	CK	40
NY65	Gugulethu	123	CK	40
NY72	Gugulethu	123	CL	40
NY75	Gugulethu	123	CL	40
NY77	Gugulethu	123	CJ	41
NY80	Gugulethu	123	CJ	41
NY83	Gugulethu	123	CK	41
NY84	Gugulethu	123	CK	41
NY85	Gugulethu	123	CK	41
NY86	Gugulethu	123	CK	41
NY87	Gugulethu	123	CK	41
NY88	Gugulethu	123	CK	41
NY89	Gugulethu	123	CK	41
NY9	Gugulethu	104	CH	40
NY90	Gugulethu	123	CK	41
NY91	Gugulethu	123	CK	41
NY92	Gugulethu	123	CK	41
NY93	Gugulethu	123	CK	41
NY96	Gugulethu	123	CK	41
Nyakrila	Philippi East	124	CM	46
Nyakrili St	Ilitha Pk	146	CR	52
Nyala Cr.	Silvertown	103	CF	36
Nyala Rd	Pelikan Pk	142	CQ	35
Nyamakazi	Dunoon	42	BO	37
Nyamakazi St	Philippi East	125	CL	48
Nyamende Cl.	Nonqubela	126	CN	52
Nyamzane St	Kuyasa	147	CS	55
Nyandeni Cr.	Mxolisi Phetani	126	CM	51
Nyaniso Cr.	Kaya	146	CP	51
Nyasa Rd	Retreat	140	CR	28
Nyathi Ave	Joe Slovo Pk	57	BU	34
Nyathi Ave	Nonqubela	126	CN	53
Nyathi St	Brown's Farm	124	CL	43
Nyathi St	Mxolisi Phetani	125	CM	50
Nyatyambo Cr.	Mxolisi Phetani	126	CM	51
Nyawuza St	Tarentaalplaas	175	CY	76
Nyebelele St	Mxolisi Phetani	125	CM	50
Nyebelele St	Mxolisi Phetani	126	CM	51
Nyhila St	Driftsands	126	CL	51
Nyhundu St	Wallacedene	48	BS	60
Nyhundu St	Wallacedene	48	BS	61
Nyibiba St	Gugulethu	123	CK	41
Nyiki St	Crossroads	124	CK	44
Nyman St	Maitland	84	BZ	34
Nyoka St	Kuyasa	146	CS	54
Nyqunga St	Umrhabulo Triangle	147	CQ	58
Nyuthu Cr.	Mxolisi Phetani	126	CM	51
Nzhelele St	Mfuleni	126	CJ	53
Nzinziniba St	Brown's Farm	124	CM	43
Nzolo	Mbekweni	15	AW	92
Nzoto Cl.	Mxolisi Phetani	126	CM	51
Nzuzo	Mbekweni	15	AV	91
Nzwana	Mbekweni	15	AV	91
Nzwanekazi St	Crossroads	124	CK	44
Nzwanekazi St	Crossroads	124	CN	46
O				
O.Nqubelani St	Mfuleni	126	CJ	53
O.Nqubelani St	Mfuleni	126	CK	54
O.R.Tambo Rd	Hout Bay	137	CO	16
O'Kulis St	Welgemoed	60	BV	45
Oak	Franschhoek Nth	75	BX	104
Oak	Northpine	63	BT	58
Oak Ave	Belhar	105	CD	45
Oak Ave	Belhar	105	CE	45
Oak Ave	Chapman's Peak	156	CW	16
Oak Ave	Chapman's Peak	156	CX	17
Oak Ave	Claremont	120	CJ	28
Oak Ave	Claremont	120	CK	27
Oak Ave	Grassy Pk	141	CR	32
Oak Ave	Hohenort	119	CL	25
Oak Ave	Kenilworth	120	CK	28
Oak Ave	Kenilworth	120	CK	29
Oak Ave	Newlands	101	CG	27
Oak Ave	Rondebosch	101	CF	29
Oak Ave	Thornton	85	CA	37
Oak Ave	Wynberg	120	CL	28
Oak Cl.	Mitchells Plain	144	CQ	45
Oak Farm Cr.	The Vines	140	CO	27
Oak La.	Forest Glade	127	CK	58
Oak Rd	Gordon Strand	175	DC	76
Oak Rd	Kenridge	45	BS	48
Oak Rd	Silveroaks	90	CC	56
Oak St	Forest Village	127	CL	58
Oak St	Observatory	83	CC	29
Oak St	Philippi	124	CM	45
Oak St	Sir Lowry's Pass	176	CZ	81
Oak St	Somerset West	170	CV	73
Oak St	Somerset West	170	CV	74
Oak Way	Lekkerwater	184	CZ	18
Oak Way	Weltevreden Val. (M.Plain)	143	CO	42
Oakbridge Dr.	Somerset West	171	CV	76
Oakburn	Plattekloof Glen	59	BW	40
Oakburn Cr.	Plattekloof Glen	59	BW	39
Oakburn Rd	Hout Bay	116	CM	14
Oakbury Cr.	Weltevreden Val. (M.Plain)	144	CO	44
Oakbury Rd	Woodlands (M.Plain)	144	CO	44
Oakdale	Pinelands	84	CC	33
Oakdale	Voorbrug	106	CG	50
Oakdale Cir.	Parklands	25	BN	34
Oakdale Rd	Adriaanse	87	CC	43
Oakdale Rd	Newlands	101	CH	28
Oakdale Rd	Oakdale	61	BW	48
Oakdale St	Voorbrug	106	CG	50
Oakdale Ter.	Newlands	101	CH	28
Oakdale Way	Parklands	25	BN	34
Oakdene	Wellington	10	AP	93
Oakfield Rd	Claremont	120	CJ	29
Oakglen	Wellington	10	AR	92
Oakhill Mews	Milnerton	57	BT	32
Oakhurst Ave	Hout Bay	117	CN	17
Oakhurst Ave	Rondebosch	101	CG	30
Oakhurst Cl.	Rondebosch	101	CF	30
Oakland Hills	Sunningdale	25	BL	31
Oakley Ave	Tokai	139	CS	25
Oakley Pl.	Ocean View	184	DC	15
Oakley Rd	Rondebosch	102	CG	32
Oakmont	Sunningdale	25	BM	32
Oakridge Ave	Meadowridge	140	CP	28
Oakridge Cl.	Meadowridge	140	CP	28
Oaktree Rd	Devil's Peak Est.	82	CC	24
Oakvale Rd	Rondebosch	102	CG	31
Oakwood Cl.	Richwood	42	BQ	38
Oakwood Rd	Bonteheuwel	103	CE	38
Oasis Cr.	Weltevreden Val. (M.Plain)	144	CO	43
Oasis Rd	Eersterivier	127	CL	58
Oasis Rd	Hazendal	102	CE	33
Oasis St	Riverton	86	BZ	40
Oatlands Rd	Simon's Town	195	DK	27
Oatlands St	Somerset West	171	CU	75
Oban Rd	Rondebosch	102	CG	31
Oban St	Hazendal	102	CF	33
Obelisk Rd	Claremont	120	CJ	27
Oberlander Cr.	Boschenmeer Est.	39	BJ	90
Oberon Cr.	Eastridge (M.Plain)	145	CQ	49
Oberon Way	Meadowridge	139	CP	26
Oboe Cl.	Belhar	106	CD	48
Oboe St	Cafda Village	140	CS	30
Oboe St	Cafda Village	141	CS	31
Obol St	Vierlanden	30	BN	51
Observatory Rd	Observatory	83	CC	30
Ocean	Foreshore	82	CA	26
Ocean Cl.	Uitzicht	47	BO	55
Ocean Spirit Ave	Sanddrift	57	BV	34
Ocean Spirit Ave	Sanddrift	57	BW	34
Ocean View Dr.	Bantry Bay	80	CB	18
Ocean View Dr.	Dolphin Beach	40	BP	30
Ocean View Dr.	Fresnaye	81	CB	19
Ocean View Dr.	Green Point	81	BZ	22
Ocean View Dr.	Sea Point	81	BZ	21
Ocean View Dr.	Sea Point	81	CA	20
Ocean View Rd	Somerset West	170	CT	73
Ocean Way	Sunset Beach	41	BS	31
Oceana Amethyst Way	Hout Bay Harbour	136	CR	14
Oceana Emerald Way	Hout Bay Harbour	136	CR	14
Oceana Ruby Way	Hout Bay Harbour	136	CR	14
Oceana Sapphire	Hout Bay Harbour	136	CR	14
Oceanus Way	Phoenix	57	BV	33
October St	Sir Lowry's Pass	176	CZ	81
October St	Wellington	15	AV	92
Octopus Rd	Harbour Island	175	DC	75
Octovale Rd	Bellville Sth	88	CA	49
Odendaal Rd	Aurora	45	BP	48
Odendaal Rd	Aurora	45	BQ	48
Odette St	De Tijger	60	BX	44
Odin Dr.	Thornton	85	CB	36
Oefenbach Cl.	Sonstraal Hgts	46	BQ	53
Oerder Rd	Hohelzen	61	BW	47
Oerder St	Parow Nth	60	BW	43
Ogun Ct	Delft	106	CG	49
Ohio Ave	Primrose Pk	122	CJ	38
Ohlsson Way	Newlands	101	CH	28
Okapi Cl.	Eastridge (M.Plain)	145	CR	48
Okapis St	Ruwari	63	BW	58
Okavango Ct	Delft	106	CG	49
Okavango Rd	Brackenfell Ind.	63	BT	57
Okavango Rd	Langeberg Glen	47	BP	56
Okavango Rd	Langeberg Rdg	47	BR	56
Okavango Rd	Morgenster Hoogte	63	BT	56
Okavango Rd	Uitzicht	47	BO	56
Okinawa Cl.	Strandfontein	162	CT	40
Okinawa Cl.	Strandfontein	162	CV	42
Okkerneut	Delft Sth	125	CJ	50
Okkerneut Ave	New Orleans	19	BA	91
Okkerneut Ave	Silveroaks	90	CC	56
Okkie van Sense St	Highbury	108	CD	55
Oklahoma St	Macassar	149	CS	65
Oktaaf	Dalvale	19	AZ	92
Oktoberlelie Cr.	Roosendaal	107	CE	51
Oktoberlelie Cr.	Roosendaal	107	CG	53
Old Bear Rd	Silverhurst	119	CN	25
Old Boyes Dr.	Muizenberg	159	CW	28
Old Boyes Dr.	Muizenberg	159	CW	29
Old Cape Farm Rd	Noordhaven	157	CX	19
Old Cottage Rd	Silverhurst	119	CN	24
Old Farm Rd	Dunoon	26	BN	37
Old Farm Rd	Rondebosch	102	CF	32
Old Farm Rd	Silverhurst	119	CN	24
Old Faure Rd	Driftsands	125	CL	50
Old Faure Rd	Driftsands	126	CM	51
Old Faure Rd	Eersterivier	128	CN	59
Old Faure Rd	Electric City	127	CN	58
Old Faure Rd	Mfuleni	126	CM	52
Old Faure Rd	Mfuleni	127	CM	55
Old Kendal Cl.	Dieprivier	140	CO	28
Old Kendal Rd	Dieprivier	140	CO	28
Old Kendal Rd	The Vines	140	CO	27
Old Klipfontein Rd	Athlone	102	CF	33
Old Kommetjie Rd	Sunnydale	185	DA	20
Old Lansdowne Rd	Schaap Kraal	123	CL	39
Old Main Rd	Croydon	149	CP	63
Old Main Rd	Macassar	149	CQ	65
Old Main Rd	Somerset West	150	CS	69
Old Main Rd	Somerset West	170	CU	71
Old Main Rd	Somerset West	170	CT	71
Old Main Rd	Somerset West	170	CU	74
Old Marine Dr.	Foreshore	82	CA	24
Old Marine Dr.	Foreshore	82	CA	25
Old Mill Rd	Pinelands	84	CB	32
Old Mutual Rd	Stellenberg	62	BU	51
Old Nectar Rd	Richwood	42	BQ	37
Old Nooiensfontein Dr.	Oakdene	89	CC	54
Old Oak	Schuilplaats	113	CF	75
Old Oak Rd	Bellair	62	BW	52
Old Oak Rd	La Rochelle	62	BV	52
Old Oak Rd	Ridgeworth	61	BU	49
Old Oak Rd	Rosendal	61	BU	50
Old Oak Way	Bellville	62	BU	51
Old Paarl Rd	Bloekombos	49	BQ	64
Old Paarl Rd	De La Haye	61	BX	50
Old Paarl Rd	Everite	63	BU	57
Old Paarl Rd	Everite	63	BV	55
Old Paarl Rd	Ferndale	62	BW	54
Old Paarl Rd	Klein Begin	48	BS	60
Old Paarl Rd	Stikland Hospital	62	BX	51
Old Rhodes Dr.	Bishopscourt	119	CJ	25
Old Rhodes Dr.	Witteboomen	118	CL	22
Old Stanhope Rd	Claremont	101	CH	28
Old Stellenbosch Rd	Adriaanse	87	CC	43
Old Stellenbosch Rd	Clarkes	86	CC	42
Old Stellenbosch Rd	Somerset West	151	CS	72
Old Strandfontein Rd	Wetton	122	CM	35

Abbreviations used: Ave – Avenue, A.H. – Agricultural Holding, A.L.– Algemene Landgoed, Blvd – Boulevard, Cen. – Central, Cir. – Circle, Cl. – Close, Cr. – Crescent, Ct – Court, Dr. – Drive, Est. – Estate, Ext. – Extension, Hgts – Heights, Ind. – Industrial, Gdns – Gardens, Gr. – Grove, La. – Lane, (M.Plain) - Mitchells Plain, Nth – North, Pl. – Place, Pk – Park, Rd – Road, Rdg. – Ridge, S.H.– Small Holding, Sq. – Square, St – Street, Sth – South, Ter. – Terrace, Tn – Turn, Val. – Valley, Wk – Walk

STREET NAME	SUBURB NAME	PG	GRID
Old Trafford	Weltevreden Val. (M.Plain)	124	CN 43
Old Trafford Cr.	Uitzicht	31	BN 56
Old Trafford Rd	Weltevreden Val. (M.Plain)	144	CP 43
Olden Cl.	Beaconvale	87	BZ 43
Oldenland Rd	Somerset West	171	CT 76
Oldenland St	Bothasig	42	BS 37
Oldenland St	Somerset West	152	CS 76
Oldfield Rd	Sea Point	81	BZ 20
Oldham St	Churchill	60	BX 43
Olea Cl.	The Lakes	184	CZ 17
Oleander	Brantwood	89	CB 54
Oleander	Lentegeur (M.Plain)	144	CP 46
Oleander Cl.	Fir Grove	139	CQ 25
Oleander Cr.	Thornton	85	CB 37
Oleander Rd	Milnerton	57	BT 33
Oleander St	Bonteheuwel	104	CE 40
Oleander St	Bonteheuwel	104	CF 40
Oleander St	Klein Nederburg	19	BC 92
Oleander St	Somerset West	151	CS 71
Oleander Way	Sweet Valley	139	CQ 25
O'Leary Cl.	Highbury	107	CD 54
Olga Ncivata	Weltevreden Val. (M.Plain)	123	CN 42
Olga Rd	Manenberg	123	CJ 39
Olga Rd	Montagu's Gift	141	CP 34
Olieboom Rd	Schaap Kraal	122	CM 38
Olieboom Rd	Schaap Kraal	122	CN 38
Olieboom Rd	Schaap Kraal	142	CP 38
Olieboom Rd	Schaap Kraal	142	CQ 37
Oliehout Rd	Bonteheuwel	104	CF 40
Olien	Delft Sth	125	CK 49
Olien St	Somerset Hgts	127	CK 57
Olienhout	Stellenbosch Cen.	95	CB 76
Olienhout Ave	Amandelrug	90	CA 55
Olienhout Ave	New Orleans	19	BA 91
Olienhout Ave	Plattekloof	59	BU 42
Olienhout Ave	Tygerdal	58	BX 38
Olienhout Pl.	Leonsdale	86	CA 41
Olienhout Pl.	Leonsdale	86	BZ 41
Olienhout Rd	Stellenberg	62	BT 52
Olienhout Rd	Stellenberg	62	BX 52
Olienhout St	Onverwacht	175	DC 76
Olienhout St	Protea Hoogte	63	BX 57
Olifants Cr.	Delft	106	CF 50
Olifants Cr.	Eersterivier	127	CM 58
Olifants Rd	Manenberg	123	CJ 39
Olifants Rd	Primrose Pk	103	CH 38
Olifants St	Mfuleni	126	CJ 53
Olifantsberg Cl.	Bonnie Brae	47	BP 57
Olifantsberg Cl.	Bonnie Brae	47	BO 58
Olifantsoog St	Tafelsig (M.Plain)	145	CS 48
Olifantsrivier Cl.	Portlands (M.Plain)	144	CQ 46
Olinia Rd	Hout Bay	117	CN 18
Oliphant St	Bothasig	42	BS 38
Olive	Stellenbosch	95	BY 75
Olive Cl.	Belhar	106	CE 47
Olive Cl.	Huis-in-bos	139	CO 24
Olive Gr.	Eersterivier	128	CM 62
Olive Gr.	Vredekloof Hgts	47	BS 55
Olive Grove Cr.	Somerset West	171	CW 76
Olive Rd	Rosedale	128	CK 59
Olive Rd	Sunridge	41	BP 34
Olive Schreiner Rd	Bergvliet	139	CP 26
Olive Schreiner St	Parow Nth	60	BW 43
Olive Way	Somerset West	169	CT 70
Oliver Cr.	Valhalla Pk	104	CE 41
Oliver Rd	Sea Point	81	BZ 19
Oliver St	Valhalla Pk	104	CE 41
Oliver Tambo Ave	Manenberg	104	CH 40
Oliver Tambo Dr.	Weltevreden Val. (M.Plain)	123	CN 42
Olivia Cl.	Oak Glen	62	BW 52
Olivia Way	Meadowridge	139	CP 26
Olivier St	Elim	89	CA 54
Olivier St	Lochnerhof	174	CY 72
Olivine Rd	Lansdowne	121	CJ 33
Olyf	Bo Dalsig	113	CE 76
Olyf Ave	Bracken Hgts	62	BU 54
Olyf Ave	Silveroaks	90	CC 56
Olyf Ave	Sonnedal	59	BV 42
Olyfberg Rd	Nooitgedacht	104	CE 42
Olympia Rd	Joe Slovo Pk	57	BU 34
Olympic Cr.	Bridgetown	103	CF 36
Olympics St	Beacon Valley (M.Plain)	145	CP 48
Olympus Rd	Ferndale	62	BV 54
Olyven St	Forest Village	127	CL 58
Olyven St	Lemoenkloof	18	BB 88
Ombersley Rd	Muizenberg Nth	159	CW 29
Omega	Rozendal	96	CC 80
Omega Cr.	Hoogstede	62	BV 53
Omega Rd	Somerset West	171	CT 77
Omega St	Belrail	88	BY 49
Omega St	Klipdam	90	CB 55
Ominia La.	Stikland Hospital	62	BX 51
Omo Ct	Delft	106	CG 48
Omsambeet	Delft Sth	125	CJ 50
Omuramba Rd	Marconi Beam	57	BT 34
Omuramba Rd	Marconi Beam	57	BV 34
Onderbos Sq.	Roosendaal	107	CF 51
Onderbos St	Bonteheuwel	104	CE 40
Ondine Cl.	Manenberg	123	CK 39
Ongegund St	De Bron	45	BS 48
Onik St	Forest Hgts	127	CL 58
Oniks Cl.	Welgelegen	59	BT 40
Onrus Ct	Delft	106	CG 49
Onrust St	De Bron	61	BT 48
Onse Jan Ave	Somerset West	171	CT 77
Onse Jan Ave	Somerset West	171	CU 77
Onse Jan Pl.	Brooklyn	83	BZ 30
Ontario Rd	Retreat	140	CS 28
Ontario Way	Portlands (M.Plain)	144	CQ 45
Ontong Way	Grassy Pk	141	CP 33
Onverwacht Beheerliggaam St	Oak Glen	62	BW 52
Onverwacht St	Lwandle	175	CZ 76
Onverwacht St	Oak Glen	62	BW 52
Onverwacht St	Rusthof	174	DA 74
Onverwacht St	Somerset West	171	CW 75
Onyx Rd	Highbury	108	CD 55
Onze Molen Rd	Durbanville	45	BP 49
O'Okiep Rd	Lansdowne	102	CH 32
O'Okiep Rd	Lansdowne	121	CJ 32
Oop St	Bellville Sth	88	CA 49
Oop St	Bellville Sth Ind.	88	CA 50
Oorbietjie St	Soneike I	90	BZ 55
Oortjie Rd	Vierlanden	30	BN 52
Oos St	Belrail	88	BY 49
Oosbosch St	Dal Josafat Ind.	18	BA 89
Oosterland Cr.	Highbury	107	CD 54
Oosterland Rd	Plattekloof Glen	59	BV 40
Oosterland St	Dal Josafat Ind.	19	AZ 91
Oosterland St	Highbury	107	CD 54
Oosterlig St	Greenways	174	CZ 73
Oostersee St	Oostersee	60	BX 46
Oosterzee Heights	Bishopscourt	119	CK 26
Oosthuizen St	Brantwood	89	CA 53
Opaal St	Forest Hgts	127	CK 58
Opal La.	Sheridon Pk	159	CU 29
Opal Rd	Lansdowne	102	CH 33
Opal Way	Matroosfontein	86	CC 41
Opal Way	San Michel	157	CX 19
Opera La.	Belhar	106	CD 48
Opera Pl.	Mitchells Plain Cen.	145	CR 47
Ophir Rd	Plumstead	120	CN 29
Oppelskop Cr.	Tafelsig (M.Plain)	145	CS 48
Opperman St	Mandalay	125	CM 48
Opstal Cl.	Oude Westhof	60	BT 44
Opstal St	Oakdene	89	CC 53
Optenhorst St	Lemoenkloof	18	BB 88
Orange Ave	Belthorn Est.	102	CH 34
Orange Cl.	Scottsdene	64	BU 60
Orange Cr.	Eversdal Hgts	46	BR 51
Orange Cr.	Mxolisi Phetani	125	CM 49
Orange Cr.	Vygeboom	46	BR 51
Orange Rd	Capricorn	160	CV 31
Orange Rd	Delft	106	CH 49
Orange Rd	Eersterivier	128	CN 60
Orange Rd	Kirstenhof	159	CT 27
Orange Rd	Newlands	100	CH 26
Orange St	Cape Town Cen.	81	CB 22
Orange St	Hout Bay	137	CP 16
Orange St	Scottsdene	64	BU 60
Orange St	Somerset West	171	CW 75
Orangekloof Ave	Tafelsig (M.Plain)	145	CR 49
Orangia Rd	Milnerton	57	BW 31
Oranje	Uniepark	96	CB 79
Oranje Ave	Pinelands	84	CB 34
Oranje Rd	Belhar	106	CD 50
Oranje Rd	Bishop Lavis	104	CD 41
Oranje Rd	Chapman's Peak	156	CW 18
Oranje Rd	Tygerdal	58	BX 38
Oranje Rd	Tygerdal	59	BX 39
Oranje St	Avondale	60	BW 44
Oranje St	Belrail	88	BY 49
Oranje St	Bothasig	58	BT 36
Oranje St	De Tijger	60	BW 44
Oranje St	Paarl	22	BD 88
Oranje St	Ruyterwacht	86	CB 39
Oranje St	Strandvale	170	CW 73
Oranje St	Wynberg	120	CL 27
Oranjerivier Cl.	Portlands (M.Plain)	144	CQ 45
Orbea Cl.	Hout Bay	136	CO 14
Orca Cl.	Kommetjie	183	DA 13
Orchard	Dunoon	42	BO 37
Orchard Ave	Westlake	159	CU 27
Orchard Cl.	Parow Nth	59	BW 42
Orchard Cl.	Westlake	159	CU 27
Orchard Cl.	Westlake	159	CW 27
Orchard Heights	Newlands	100	CH 26
Orchard Pl.	Pinelands	102	CD 33
Orchard Rd	Bergvliet	139	CQ 26
Orchard Rd	Kenridge	61	BT 49
Orchard Rd	Milnerton	57	BV 32
Orchard Rd	Ridgeworth	61	BV 50
Orchard St	Lavender Hill East	160	CU 31
Orchard St	Lavender Hill East	160	CX 33
Orchard St	Newlands	100	CH 26
Orchard St	Newlands	101	CH 27
Orchard Way	Austinville	108	CH 56
Orchard Way	Pinelands	102	CD 33
Orchestra St	Steenberg	159	CT 29
Orchid	Lentegeur (M.Plain)	144	CP 45
Orchid	Macassar	149	CS 63
Orchid Cl.	Peerless Pk East	47	BS 57
Orchid Cr.	Silvertown	103	CF 36
Orchid Cr.	Vredekloof Hgts	47	BS 55
Orchid Rd	Tygerdal	58	BX 37
Orchid Rd	Uitsig	87	CB 44
Orchid Rd	Uitsig	87	CB 46
Orchid St	Firgrove	150	CR 67
Orchid St	Hanover Pk	122	CJ 36
Orchio Cl.	Ottery East	121	CN 34
Orchio Cl.	Ottery East	121	CM 34
Oref	Delft Sth	125	CK 48
Oregon Ave	Colorado (M.Plain)	144	CO 44
Oregon Ave	Colorado (M.Plain)	144	CR 43
Oregon La.	Temperance Town	179	DD 78
Oregon Oak	Oak Glen	62	BW 53
Oregon Oak	Oak Glen	62	BX 52
Oregon Way	Northpine	63	BU 57
Orenji	Philippi East	125	CM 47
Organ St	Belhar	106	CD 48
Orgidee Rd	Belhar	88	CC 47
Oribi Ave	Lotus River	142	CP 35
Oribi Cl.	Edgemead	59	BU 39
Oribie Rd	Skoongesig	45	BO 50
Oriele Cr.	Montagu's Gift	141	CP 33
Orient Rd	Muizenberg Nth	159	CW 28
Orient Rd	Wynberg	120	CM 28
Orient St	Cravenby	87	CB 44
Orinoco Cir.	Eindhoven	126	CJ 51
Oriole Cl.	The Lakes	184	CZ 18
Oriole Rd	Fish Hoek	186	DA 23
Oriole Rd	Klein Nederburg	46	BP 53
Oriole St	Eersterivier	128	CM 60
Orion	Everite	63	BU 56
Orion Cl.	Somerset West	171	CW 76
Orion Rd	Lansdowne	121	CJ 34
Orion Rd	Mandalay	125	CM 47
Orion Rd	Ocean View	183	DC 14
Orion Rd	Phoenix	57	BU 33
Orion Rd	Surrey	103	CG 38
Orion Rd	Surrey	103	CH 38
Orion Rd	Woodlands (M.Plain)	144	CP 44
Orion St	Forest Glade	127	CK 58
Orion St	Kirstenhof	159	CT 27
Orkes Cl.	Belhar	106	CD 49
Orkney Cl.	Portlands (M.Plain)	144	CQ 46
Orkney St	Rondebosch	101	CG 30
Orlando Rd	Fish Hoek	186	DB 23
Orlando Rd	Grassy Pk	141	CP 33
Orlando St	Ravensmead	87	CA 44
Orlando Way	Meadowridge	139	CP 26
Orleans Ave	Bel Ombre	119	CM 24
Orleans Ave	New Orleans	19	BA 91
Orleans Ave	New Orleans	19	BB 92
Orly Cl.	Portlands (M.Plain)	145	CR 47
Ormskirk St	Woodstock	83	CB 27
Ornata St	Sunset Beach	41	BS 32
Orpen La.	Kenilworth	120	CK 29
Orpen Rd	Steenberg	159	CT 24
Orphan La.	Cape Town Cen.	81	CB 22
Orphan La.	Schotsche Kloof	81	CA 22
Orphan St	Cape Town Cen.	81	CB 22
Orpheus Cr.	Eastridge (M.Plain)	145	CQ 48
Orpheus Cr.	Woodlands (M.Plain)	144	CP 44
Orpheus Ct	Eureka	87	CC 43
Orrel La.	Cafda Village	140	CS 30
Orrel St	Woodlands (M.Plain)	144	CP 44
Orrscroft Rd	Rondebosch	102	CG 32
Ortell	Cloetesville	95	BY 75
Oryx Rd	Goedemoed	46	BP 53
Oryx Rd	Sonstraal Hgts	46	BP 54
Osborn Sq.	Edgemead	58	BU 38
Osborne Rd	Bellville Sth	88	CA 49
Osborne Rd	Claremont	101	CH 28
Osborne Rd	Mowbray	101	CD 29
Osborne Rd	Sack's Circle Ind.	88	CA 49
Osborne St	Foreshore	82	CB 25
Osborne St	Kommetjie	183	DC 13
Oscar Cl.	Weltevreden Val. (M.Plain)	144	CQ 43
Oscar Mpetha	Weltevreden Val. (M.Plain)	123	CN 42
Oscar Mpetha Rd	Khayelitsha	165	CT 54
Oscar Mpetha Rd	Kuyasa	146	CS 54
Oscar Mpetha Rd	Mandela Pk	147	CQ 55
Osirus Way	Phoenix	57	BU 34
Oslo Cr.	Uitzicht	47	BO 56
Osmond Cl.	Simon's Town	191	DH 23
Ospray	Rocklands (M.Plain)	144	CS 44
Osprey	Electric City	127	CM 58
Osprey Cl.	Bothasig	58	BU 36
Osprey Cl.	Sunridge	42	BP 35
Osprey La.	Somerset West	152	CR 78
Osprey St	Pelikan Pk	161	CV 38
Ossian Rd	Observatory	83	CC 29
Ostara Ave	Jamestown	112	CH 74
Osterley Rd	Crawford	102	CH 34
Ostrich Rd	Phumlani	142	CQ 36
Oswald Pirow St	Foreshore	82	CA 24
Oswald St	Silveroaks	90	CC 55
Oswell Rd	Mandalay	125	CM 48
Otago Way	Edgemead	58	BV 38
Otela Rd	Nyanga	124	CK 43
Otello Cr.	Eastridge (M.Plain)	145	CQ 49
Othello Cl.	Eersterivier	128	CM 60
Ottawa Rd	Bakoven	98	CF 18
Ottawa St	Lemoenkloof	18	BC 88
Otter Cl.	Table View	41	BQ 34
Otter Cr.	Langeberg Rdg	47	BR 56
Otter Cr.	Westlake Est.	158	CT 25
Otter Rd	Goedemoed	46	BP 54
Otter St	Electric City	127	CM 58
Otterkuil	Karindal	96	CC 79
Otters Creek	Pelikan Pk	141	CR 33
Ottery Rd	Ottery	121	CM 32
Ottery Rd	Ottery East	121	CN 34
Ottery Rd	Ottery East	122	CN 35
Ottery Rd	Royal Cape	121	CM 31
Ottery Rd	Schaap Kraal	122	CM 37
Ottery Rd	Schaap Kraal	122	CN 37
Ottery Rd	Schaap Kraal	142	CO 36
Ottery Rd	Wynberg	120	CM 30
Otto Cl.	Westlake Est.	158	CU 25
Otto du Plessis Dr.	Blouberg Rise	25	BN 31
Otto du Plessis Dr.	Bloubergstrand	24	BK 27
Otto Du Plessis Dr.	Milnerton	57	BU 32
Otto Du Plessis Dr.	Milnerton	57	BW 31
Otto du Plessis Dr.	Sunningdale	24	BM 30
Otto du Plessis Dr.	Table View	41	BO 31
Otto du Plessis Rd	Somerset West	152	CS 76
Otto Meyer Dr.	Glenhaven	89	BZ 52
Otto St	Beaconvale	87	CA 43
Ou Helshoogte	Arbeidslus	96	CA 81
Ou Helshoogte	Idasvallei	96	CA 79
Ou Kaapse Rd	Crofters Valley	185	CY 20
Ou Kaapse Rd	Noordhoek Manor	157	CX 22
Ou Kaapse Rd	Silvermine	158	CW 23
Ou Kaapse Rd	Steenberg	158	CV 24
Ou Kaapse Rd Ext.	Sunnydale	185	DA 20
Ou Kraal Way	Edgemead	59	BT 39
Ou Wingerd Rd	High Constantia	139	CO 23
Ouberg Rd	Heideveld	104	CF 39
Oude Hout St	Bonteheuwel	104	CF 40
Oude Libertas	Devon Pk	94	CC 73
Oude Libertas	Devonvallei	112	CD 73
Oude Molen Cl.	Pinelands	84	CC 32
Oude Molen Rd	Ndabeni	84	CB 31
Oude Molen Rd	Oak Glen	62	BW 53
Oude Post Cl.	Mitchells Plain	144	CR 45
Oude Post Cl.	Mitchells Plain	144	CR 43
Oude Renbaan Dr.	De Oude Renbaan	22	BH 88
Oude Skip Rd	Hout Bay Harbour	136	CR 13
Oudebrug	Wellington	14	AT 89
Oudebrug Cl.	Mitchells Plain	144	CR 45
Oudebrug Cl.	Mitchells Plain	144	CS 43
Oudedam Rd	Morgenster	63	BU 56
Oudehuis St	Somerset West	171	CV 75
Oudekloof St	Tafelsig (M.Plain)	145	CR 49
Oudekraal Rd	Bakoven	98	CF 18
Oudepont	Wellington	14	AT 90
Oudevlei Rd	Marina Da Gama	159	CU 30
Oudewerf Cl.	Durbanville	46	BP 52
Oudtshoorn Rd	Flamingo Vlei	41	BP 32
Oudtshoorn Way	Portlands (M.Plain)	144	CR 46
Ouhout	Delft Sth	125	CJ 50
Oukraal St	Lemoenkloof	18	BC 87
Ouma Fransman Ave	Gustrow	175	DB 75
Oumakappie Cl.	Roosendaal	107	CE 51
Oupa Monareng St	Mandela Pk	146	CQ 54
Ouplaas Cr.	Wesbank	107	CG 51
Ourora St	Elim	90	CA 55
Outeniekwa	Bonnie Brae	47	BP 57
Outeniqua	Brackenfell	63	BW 55
Outeniqua Cr.	Durbanville Hills	45	BR 50
Outeniqua Cr.	Tafelsig (M.Plain)	145	CS 48
Outeniqua St	Bellair	62	BW 52
Outeniqua St	Lavender Hill East	160	CU 32
Outhie St	Somerset West	169	CT 70
Outlook St	Tafelsig (M.Plain)	145	CS 48
Outspan Steps	Fish Hoek	186	DC 24
Ouwe Griet Cl.	Oude Westhof	60	BT 44
Ouwe Werf Dr.	Somerset West	171	CU 78
Oval St East	Beacon Valley (M.Plain)	145	CQ 48
Oval St North	Beacon Valley (M.Plain)	145	CP 48
Oval St South	Beacon Valley (M.Plain)	145	CQ 48
Ovambo St	Langa	103	CD 35
Overbosch Cl.	Blouberg Sands	24	BL 30
Overdale St East	Ravensmead	87	CA 45
Overdale St West	Ravensmead	87	CA 44
Overgaauw Cr.	Somerset West	171	CU 78
Overgaauw Pl.	Somerset West	171	CU 78
Overhout	Eersterivier	128	CN 60
Overmeer	Morgen Grove	63	BX 56
Overton Cl.	Silvertown	103	CF 36
Overton Rd	Silvertown	103	CF 36
Oviston Way	Edgemead	58	BU 38
Owen Dr.	Meadowridge	140	CP 27
Owen Dr.	Nyanga	124	CJ 43
Owen La.	Grassy Pk	141	CP 33
Owen Rd	Adriaanse	87	CC 43
Owen Rd	Eureka	87	CC 43
Owen Rd	Matroosfontein	86	CC 41
Owen Rd	Silvertown	103	CF 36
Owen St	Bloekombos	48	BR 62
Owen St	Des Hampden	89	CB 53
Owen St	Northern Paarl	18	AZ 89
Owl	Rocklands (M.Plain)	144	CS 44
Owl Cl.	Westlake Est.	158	CU 25
Owl Cr.	Somerset West	171	CW 77
Owl St	Pelikan Pk	161	CV 38
Owl St East	Joostenberg	48	BP 61
Owl St West	Joostenberg	48	BP 60
Oxalis	Mountainview	179	DD 78
Oxalis Cr.	Eersterivier	128	CM 59
Oxalis Cr.	Eersterivier	128	CM 60
Oxalis St	Milnerton	57	BT 33
Oxalis St	Somerset West	151	CS 71
Oxenham Ct	Rondebosch	102	CF 32
Oxford	Parklands	41	BO 33
Oxford Cl.	Wembley Pk	107	CE 53
Oxford Cr.	Malibu Village	127	CK 55
Oxford Cr.	Oostersee	60	BX 45
Oxford Cr.	Oostersee	87	BY 45

Index to Street Names

Oxford Cr. — Pilanesberg Rd

STREET NAME	SUBURB NAME	PG	GRID	
Oxford Cr.	Weltevreden Val. (M.Plain)	123	CN	42
Oxford Rd	Durbanville	46	BP	51
Oxford Rd	Observatory	83	CC	29
Oxford Rd	Weltevreden Val. (M.Plain)	144	CO	43
Oxford St	Claremont	120	CJ	30
Oxford St	Helderberg Pk	175	DA	75
Oxford St	Hout Bay	136	CP	14
Oxford St	Hout Bay	137	CP	15
Oxford St	Maitland	84	CA	31
Oxford St	Portlands (M.Plain)	145	CR	47
Oxford St	Portlands (M.Plain)	145	CS	47
Oxford St	Richmond Est.	86	BY	40
Oxford St	Skilpadvlei	45	BP	50
Oxford St	Wellington	10	AR	92
Oxford St	Woodstock	83	CB	27
Oxford St	Wynberg	120	CL	28
Oxford Way	Noordhoek Manor	157	CX	20
Oxford Way	Noordhoek Manor	157	CV	20
Oxley Ave	Athlone	102	CG	33
Oyster Cl.	Kommetjie	183	DB	12
Oyster Cl.	Mitchells Plain	144	CP	45
Oyster La.	Big Bay	24	BL	28
Oyster St	Richwood	42	BP	38
Oystercatcher Cl.	Kommetjie	183	DA	13
P				
P.K.le Roux Rd	Groenvallei	62	BX	53
P.K.le Roux Rd	Groenvallei	62	BX	52
P.Ndleko St	Mfuleni	126	CK	53
P.W.Mama Way	Langa	103	CD	36
Paalen Ct	Edgemead	58	BU	37
Paalkrans St	Elim	90	CA	55
Paardeberg Cl.	Edgemead	59	BT	39
Paardeberg Cr.	Belhar	107	CD	51
Paardeberg Rd	Durbanville Hills	45	BR	49
Paardeberg Rd	Durbanville Hills	45	BP	47
Paardekop Rd	Heideveld	104	CG	40
Paardekraal Cl.	Somerset West	169	CT	70
Paarden Eiland Rd	Paarden Eiland	83	CA	28
Paarden Eiland Rd	Paarden Eiland	83	CA	29
Paarden Eiland Rd	Paarden Eiland	83	CA	30
Paarl St	Panorama	59	BV	42
Paarl St	Ruyterwacht	86	CA	39
Paarl St	Vasco Est.	59	BX	40
Paarl St	Vasco Est.	86	BY	40
Paarlberg	Tafelsig (M.Plain)	145	CR	49
Paarlberg	Tafelsig (M.Plain)	145	CP	50
Paarlberg	The Crest	46	BO	53
Paarlberg Cl.	Vredekloof Hgts	47	BS	55
Pacific Ave	Eersterivier	128	CM	59
Pacific Ave	Sun Valley	185	DA	21
Pacific St	Strandfontein	162	CT	42
Packer	Epping Ind.	85	CC	38
Packer St	Mandalay	125	CM	48
Packham	Lindida	96	CA	80
Paddington Rd	Dieprivier	140	CP	28
Paddock Ave	Cape Town Cen.	81	CB	22
Paddock Ave	Noordhoek Manor	157	CX	20
Paddock Cl.	Noordhoek Manor	157	CX	20
Paddock Cl.	Strandfontein	162	CT	41
Paddock Cr.	Mitchells Plain	144	CS	45
Paddock La.	Dennedal	139	CS	25
Paddock Pl.	Milnerton Rdg	41	BS	34
Paddock Rd	Montagu's Gift	141	CO	33
Paddock St	Jagtershof	108	CD	57
Paddock St	Strandfontein	143	CS	41
Paddy Cl.	Ottery East	122	CN	35
Padrone	Strandfontein	162	CT	39
Paeonia Cl.	Somerset West	171	CW	77
Paganini	Delft Sth	125	CK	48
Paganini Cl.	Sonstraal Hgts	46	BQ	54
Pagasvlei Rd	Huis-in-bos	139	CO	24
Pagasvlei Rd	Sillery	139	CO	25
Page La.	Woodstock	82	CB	26
Page St	Woodstock	82	CB	26
Pagoda Cr.	Protea Village	64	BV	59
Pajaro Ave	Jamestown	112	CH	74
Pakhuis St	Tafelsig (M.Plain)	145	CS	49
Palace	Croydon	149	CP	63
Palace Hill Rd	Simon's Town	191	DH	23
Palace Hill Rd	Simon's Town	191	DH	24
Palala Cr.	Delft	106	CG	50
Palatine Rd	Plumstead	120	CN	29
Palermo Cr.	Strandfontein	162	CT	42
Palestrina St	Eastridge (M.Plain)	145	CQ	48
Palidor	Dunoon	42	BO	37
Palimino	Durbanville	30	BN	51
Palisa Cr.	Victoria Mxenge	146	CO	52
Pall Mall	Noordhoek Manor	157	CX	21
Pall Mall	Noordhoek Manor	157	CV	20
Pall Mall Way	Portlands (M.Plain)	145	CR	47
Palladium St	Weltevreden Val. (M.Plain)	144	CR	43
Pallotti Rd	Montana/Durrheim	104	CF	41
Pallotti Rd	Montana/Durrheim	104	CF	42
Palm	Delft Sth	125	CJ	49
Palm	Delft Sth	125	CK	49
Palm Ave	Fairie Knowe	185	DA	19
Palm Ave	Northpine	63	BT	58
Palm Ave	Wellington	10	AS	94
Palm Beach Ave	Harbour Island	175	DC	75
Palm Cl.	Eersterivier	127	CM	58
Palm Cl.	Parklands	25	BM	34
Palm Cl.	Sonnedal	59	BV	42
Palm Cl.	Summer Greens	58	BW	35
Palm Cr.	Brackenfell	63	BV	56
Palm Cr.	Tygerdal	59	BX	39
Palm Gr.	Peers Hill	185	DA	22
Palm Rd	Balvenie	86	CB	42
Palm St	Newlands	101	CH	27
Palm St	Oakdale	61	BV	49
Palm St	Perm Gdns	128	CK	59
Palm St	Somerset West	171	CV	76
Palm St	The Palms	170	CX	73
Palm St	Thornton	85	CA	37
Palm St	Tokai	139	CS	25
Palma St	Kaya	146	CP	51
Palmboom Cl.	Newlands	101	CG	27
Palmboom Cr.	Newlands	101	CG	27
Palmboom Rd	Newlands	101	CG	27
Palmer	Eersterivier	128	CN	60
Palmer Rd	Muizenberg	159	CX	29
Palmerston Rd	Woodstock	83	CC	27
Palmetto Cl.	Rugby	84	BY	31
Palmetto St	Rugby	84	BY	31
Palmid St	Sarepta	89	CC	53
Palmiet	Kaymor	89	BY	53
Palmiet	Stellenbosch	95	BY	75
Palmiet Ave	Belthorn Est.	102	CH	34
Palmiet Cl.	Portlands (M.Plain)	144	CP	45
Palmiet Cr.	Strand	174	CZ	73
Palmiet La.	William Lloyd	23	BD	94
Palmiet Rd	Electric City	128	CN	59
Palmtree Ct	Bridgetown	103	CE	35
Palmyra Cl.	Sunnydale	185	DA	19
Palmyra Rd	Claremont	101	CH	29
Palmyra Rd	Somerset West	151	CR	71
Palmyra St	Sunnydale	185	DA	19
Palmyra St	Sunnydale	185	DC	22
Paloma St	Heemstede	62	BW	53
Palomino Ave	Somerset West	170	CT	72
Palomino Rd	Milnerton	41	BS	34
Palomino Rd	Northpine	63	BU	58
Palomino Rd	West Riding	41	BO	34
Palomino St	Eikenbosch	90	CC	57
Palomino St	Jagtershof	90	CC	57
Palomino St	Jagtershof	108	CD	57
Palomino St	Paarlzicht	18	BC	90
Palomino Way	Mitchells Plain	144	CR	44
Pama Cl.	Bothasig	58	BT	38
Pama Cl.	St Dumas	90	CC	55
Pama Cr.	Bothasig	58	BT	38
Pama Cr.	St Dumas	90	CC	55
Pama Rd	Eyethu	146	CO	53
Pama Rd	Kaya	146	CO	51
Pamela Cl.	Lentegeur (M.Plain)	145	CO	48
Pampas	Lentegeur (M.Plain)	145	CO	47
Pampas St	Bonteheuwel	104	CD	40
Pampiri Rd	Philippi East	125	CL	47
Pan Cr.	Eureka	87	CC	43
Panama St	Kaya	146	CP	52
Panda Pl.	Zoo Pk	47	BR	56
Pandoer	Welgemoed	60	BU	46
Pandora Rd	Woodlands (M.Plain)	144	CP	44
Pangwa Cr.	Victoria Mxenge	126	CN	51
Pani St	Victoria Mxenge	126	CN	51
Panorama Ave	Valmary Pk	45	BR	50
Panorama Dr.	Eversdal	62	BU	51
Panorama Dr.	Somerset West	170	CT	73
Panorama Dr.	Stellenryk	62	BT	52
Panorama Rd	Panorama	59	BV	40
Panorama St	Denneburg	22	BD	90
Pansey St	Sarepta	89	CB	52
Pansy	Cloetesville	95	BZ	75
Pansy	Lentegeur (M.Plain)	144	CP	45
Pansy Cr.	Uitsig	87	CB	44
Panther Cl.	Eastridge (M.Plain)	145	CR	48
Panther St	The Hague	106	CF	49
Panton Rd	Fairways	121	CN	32
Papawer St	Blomtuin	61	BW	50
Papegaai	Macassar	149	CS	65
Papegaai	Rocklands (M.Plain)	144	CS	44
Papegaai St	Stellenbosch	95	CC	75
Papegaaiberg Cl.	Tafelsig (M.Plain)	145	CR	49
Papegaairand	Stellenbosch	95	CB	75
Papenboom Gr.	Newlands	101	CG	27
Papendorf Rd	Belhar	106	CD	50
Papendorf Rd	Belhar	106	CH	48
Paper Bark St	Bellair	62	BW	53
Paphama Mhlakana St	Guguletu	104	CG	41
Papierblom	Lentegeur (M.Plain)	145	CO	47
Papierblom Cr.	Roosendaal	107	CE	51
Papillon Rd	Strandfontein	162	CT	40
Papkuil Cl.	Roosendaal	107	CE	51
Papkuilsvlei Rd	Schaap Kraal	122	CL	38
Papkuilsvlei Rd	Schaap Kraal	123	CN	39
Papu Sq.	Langa	103	CD	35
Papu St	Langa	103	CD	36
Par Cl.	Lakeside	159	CV	27
Par Cl.	Lakeside	159	CW	27
Parade Cr.	Fir Grove	139	CQ	24
Parade Ring Rd	Milnerton	41	BS	33
Parade Ring Rd	Milnerton	57	BT	33
Parade St	Cape Town Cen.	82	CB	23
Paradise Cl.	Blouberg Sands	24	BL	30
Paradise Rd	Newlands	101	CH	27
Paradise Rd	Simon's Town	191	DH	23
Paradise View Rd	Claremont	120	CJ	28
Paradys St	Amanda Glen	46	BS	52
Paradys St	Arauna	63	BU	55
Paradyskloof	Anesta	113	CF	75
Paragon	Eersterivier	128	CN	60
Parakeet St	Sunnydale	185	DA	19
Parakeet St	Wellington	15	AT	92
Paratus Ave	Stikland Hospital	61	BX	50
Parc Pierre Rd	Oak Glen	62	BW	53
Parc Pierre Rd	Oak Glen	62	BX	52
Parel Vallei Rd	Somerset West	152	CS	76
Parel Vallei Rd	Somerset West	171	CT	75
Parfaite St	Jamestown	112	CH	74
Parfitt Rd	Somerset West	171	CT	77
Parin Rd	Parow Ind.	87	CB	45
Paris Mary	Sunset Glen	127	CJ	55
Paris Rd	Fish Hoek	186	DA	23
Paris Rd	Somerset West	171	CT	77
Paris St	Uitzicht	47	BO	56
Paris Way	Malibu Village	127	CK	55
Parish St	Constantia Vale	119	CN	25
Parish St	Rust-en-vrede	119	CN	25
Park	Franschhoek Nth	75	BX	105
Park	Krigeville	113	CD	76
Park Ave	Camps Bay	98	CD	18
Park Ave	Dreyersdal	140	CS	27
Park Ave	Hout Bay	117	CN	15
Park Ave	Milnerton	57	BW	32
Park Ave	Milnerton	57	BW	32
Park Ave	Mitchells Plain	144	CQ	44
Park Ave	Mitchells Plain	144	CR	45
Park Ave	Rocklands (M.Plain)	144	CS	45
Park Ave	Rocklands (M.Plain)	144	CS	46
Park Ave	Scottsdene	64	BT	59
Park Ave	Scottsdene	64	BT	60
Park Ave	Summerville	64	BT	59
Park Ave	Sunridge	41	BP	34
Park Ave	Woodlands (M.Plain)	144	CP	45
Park Cl.	Adriaanse	105	CD	43
Park Cl.	Marina Da Gama	159	CV	30
Park Cl.	Milnerton	41	BR	34
Park Cl.	Ottery East	121	CN	34
Park Cl.	Somerset West	171	CW	75
Park Cr.	Montagu's Gift	141	CO	34
Park Dr.	Somerset West	170	CW	72
Park Dr.	Table View	25	BN	32
Park Dr.	Table View	41	BO	32
Park Green	Summer Greens	58	BV	36
Park House Rd	Gardens	81	CB	22
Park Island Quay	Marina Da Gama	159	CV	30
Park Island Way	Marina Da Gama	159	CV	29
Park La.	Kenridge	61	BT	49
Park La.	Kenridge	61	BV	48
Park La.	Rondebosch	101	CG	28
Park La.	Silverhurst	119	CN	25
Park Rd	Durbanville	45	BP	50
Park Rd	Grassy Pk	141	CP	33
Park Rd	Green Point	81	BY	20
Park Rd	Mandalay	125	CN	48
Park Rd	Observatory	83	CC	30
Park Rd	Rondebosch	101	CF	30
Park Rd	Rondebosch	102	CF	31
Park Rd	Rosebank	101	CE	30
Park Rd	Woodstock	82	CB	26
Park Rd	Woodstock	82	CC	26
Park Rd	Wynberg	120	CM	29
Park Smith St	Rome	170	CX	73
Park St	Cravenby	87	CA	43
Park St	De Duin	59	BV	41
Park St	Gardens	81	CB	22
Park St	Malibu Village	127	CK	56
Park St	Park Village	127	CK	58
Park St	Stikland Hospital	88	BY	50
Park St	Wellington	10	AR	93
Park St	Wellington	10	AS	92
Park Villa Rd	Observatory	83	CC	29
Park Way	Somerset West	171	CU	75
Parkchester Ave	Pinelands	84	CB	34
Parkdene St	Ravensmead	87	CA	46
Parker	Stellenbosch	95	CA	75
Parker Ave	Gatesville	103	CH	37
Parker St	Vergesig	45	BQ	48
Parkers Wk	Parkwood	141	CO	32
Parkiet Rd	Morningstar	46	BP	51
Parklands	Parklands	41	BO	33
Parklands Main Rd	Parklands	25	BN	32
Parklands Main Rd	Parklands	25	BN	33
Parklands Main Rd	Parklands	25	BN	34
Parklands Main Rd	Parklands	41	BO	32
Parkview	Sunningdale	25	BN	32
Parkview Cl.	Milnerton	41	BS	34
Parkview Pl.	Avon	86	CA	41
Parkview Ter.	Silverhurst	119	CN	24
Parkway Cl.	Rondebosch East	102	CG	32
Parkwood Ave	Parkwood	141	CO	32
Parkwood Wk	Parkwood	141	CO	32
Parkzicht	The Crest	46	BO	54
Parkzicht Cl.	Uitzicht	31	BN	56
Parliament St	Cape Town Cen.	82	CA	23
Parow Rd	Maitland	84	CB	31
Parow St	Parow	86	BZ	42
Parow St	Parow	87	BZ	43
Parry Rd	Claremont	101	CH	29
Parsifal Cr.	Eastridge (M.Plain)	145	CR	49
Parson Cr.	Wesbank	107	CH	51
Partrick Mosedi St	Kuyasa	147	CR	55
Partridge St	Sunnydale	185	DA	19
Partridge Way	Penlyn Est.	122	CJ	36
Parys Cl.	La Rochelle	62	BV	51
Pasadena Rd	Scottsdene	64	BV	60
Pasadena Sq.	Heathfield	140	CQ	29
Pasadena Way	Ottery East	121	CN	34
Pascal St	Belhar	88	CC	49
Pascali Cl.	Sonstraal Hgts	46	BR	54
Pascali St	Rosendal	61	BT	50
Pascali St	Sonstraal Hgts	46	BR	54
Pascall La.	Oranjezicht	82	CC	23
Pasita St	Danena	61	BU	49
Pasita St	Rosendal	61	BU	50
Pass Rd	Fish Hoek	185	DB	22
Pass St	Klippiesdal	19	BC	91
Passerina	Perm Gdns	127	CJ	58
Passerina	Perm Gdns	128	CJ	59
Pasteur	Dennemere	108	CH	58
Pasteur Rd	Chrismar	61	BW	50
Pasteur Rd	Wynberg	120	CL	27
Pasteur St	Park Estates	170	CX	72
Pastorale Ave	Tygerberg Ind. Pk	31	BL	57
Pastorie Ave	Paarl	22	BD	88
Pastorie Rd	Somerset West	170	CU	74
Pastorie St	Belrail	61	BX	48
Pasture St	Rocklands (M.Plain)	144	CS	46
Paterson St	Newlands	101	CH	27
Pati Pl.	Blue Downs	127	CJ	55
Paton Rd	Claremont	101	CH	29
Patou Rd	Amanda Glen	62	BT	52
Patou Rd	Chantecler	62	BT	52
Patricia Cl.	Scottsdene	64	BT	60
Patriot St	Bellville	61	BV	47
Patriot St	Maitland	83	CA	30
Patriot St	Paarl	22	BE	88
Patrol St	Lansdowne	121	CJ	32
Patrys	Onderpapegaaiberg	94	CB	72
Patrys	Onderpapegaaiberg	94	CC	72
Patrys Ave	Somerset West	171	CT	77
Patrys Cr.	Okavango Pk	63	BT	57
Patrys Rd	Morningstar	46	BP	51
Patrys Rd	Morningstar	46	BS	54
Patrys Sq.	Factreton	85	BY	35
Patrys St	Amandelsig	90	CB	56
Patrys St	Blomvlei	61	BV	47
Patrys St	Wellington	15	AT	91
Patrys St	Wellington	15	AU	91
Patrys St	William Lloyd	23	BD	94
Patrysblom Cl.	Roosendaal	107	CE	51
Pats Pl.	Gaylee	108	CG	57
Patterson Rd	Aurora	45	BP	48
Patton St	Maitland	83	CA	30
Patula Cr.	Langeberg Rdg	47	BR	55
Patula Ct	Northpine	63	BT	58
Pau	Malibu Village	127	CK	56
Paul	Sarepta	89	CC	53
Paul Andrew Cl.	Nyanga	123	CK	42
Paul Ave	Umrhabulo Triangle	147	CQ	57
Paul Cl.	Hoogstede	62	BU	54
Paul de Groot St	Churchill	60	BX	43
Paul de Groot St	Clamhall	60	BX	43
Paul Kruger Ave	Ruyterwacht	86	BZ	39
Paul Kruger Rd	Somerset West	170	CT	74
Paul Kruger St	Dal Josafat Ind.	22	BD	89
Paul Kruger St	Durbanville	46	BO	51
Paul Kruger St	Parowvallei	87	BZ	44
Paul Kruger St	Plumstead	140	CO	30
Paul Kruger St	Soneike I	89	BZ	54
Paul Kruger St	Soneike II	89	BZ	54
Paul Kruger St	Stellenbosch	95	CB	75
Paul Roos	Stellenbosch	95	CA	76
Paul Sauer	Rozendal	96	CB	79
Paul Sauer Rd	Groenvallei	62	BX	53
Paul St	Hoogstede	62	BU	54
Pauli St	Crossroads	124	CK	44
Pauline Cl.	Lentegeur (M.Plain)	145	CO	48
Pauline Cl.	Morgenster Hoogte	63	BT	56
Paulsberg Rd	Bishop Lavis	104	CE	42
Paulsberg Rd	Heideveld	104	CF	39
Paulsberg St	Tafelsig (M.Plain)	145	CS	48
Paulus Rd	Newfields	122	CJ	37
Paulus St	Valhalla Pk	104	CE	41
Paulus St	William Lloyd	19	BC	92
Paulus St	William Lloyd	19	BC	93
Paulus Way	Grassy Pk	141	CQ	31
Pavo St	Surrey	103	CH	38
Payina	Philippi East	125	CL	48
Payina Cr.	Philippi East	125	CM	47
Payiya St	Victoria Mxenge	146	CO	51
Payne Rd	Hout Bay	137	CP	16
Payne St	Ocean View	184	DC	16
Peace	Fairyland	19	AZ	92
Peace St	Schotsche Kloof	81	CB	22
Peach Cl.	Mitchells Plain	144	CQ	44
Peach Cl.	Thembokwezi	125	CM	49
Peach La.	Newlands	101	CG	28
Peach Rd	Capricorn	160	CV	31
Peach Tree Cr.	Sunningdale	25	BM	31
Peacock Rd	Phumlani	142	CQ	36
Peak Dr.	Pinelands	84	CC	32
Peak Dr.	Pinelands	102	CD	32
Peak Rd	Devil's Peak Est.	82	CC	24
Peak Rd	Fish Hoek	186	DB	23
Pear Cir.	Thembokwezi	125	CM	49
Pear La.	Newlands	101	CG	27
Pear La.	Witteboomen	119	CN	23
Pear La.	Witteboomen	119	CN	23
Pear Rd	Hindle Pk	107	CH	54

Abbreviations used: Ave – Avenue, A.H. – Agricultural Holding, A.L.– Algemene Landgoed, Blvd – Boulevard, Cen. – Central, Cir. – Circle, Cl. – Close, Cr. – Crescent, Ct – Court, Dr. – Drive, Est. – Estate, Ext. – Extension, Hgts – Heights, Ind. – Industrial, Gdns – Gardens, Gr. – Grove, La. – Lane, (M.Plain) - Mitchells Plain, Nth – North, Pl. – Place, Pk – Park, Rd – Road, Rdg. – Ridge, S.H.– Small Holding, Sq. – Square, St – Street, Sth – South, Ter. – Terrace, Tn – Turn, Val. – Valley, Wk – Walk

STREET NAME	SUBURB NAME	PG	GRID	
Pearce Rd	Claremont	101	CH	28
Pearce St	Somerset West	151	CS	74
Pearl	Fairdale	107	CH	53
Pearl Cl.	Rocklands (M.Plain)	145	CS	47
Pearl Cr.	Belgravia	103	CG	35
Pearl Cr.	Highbury	108	CD	55
Pearl Cr.	San Michel	157	CX	20
Pearl St	Kensington	84	BZ	34
Pearl St	Pelikan Pk	161	CT	36
Pearl Way	Matroosfontein	86	CC	41
Pearly Shell Rd	Strandfontein	162	CV	39
Pearson Ave	Kenilworth	120	CK	30
Pearson Rd	Table View	42	BQ	35
Pearston St	Ruyterwacht	86	CA	39
Pebble Beach	West Beach	24	BM	29
Pebble Beach Cl.	Whispering Pines	175	DB	76
Pebble Beach Mews	Milnerton	57	BT	32
Pebble Cr.	Milnerton	57	BT	33
Pecan St	Bonteheuwel	104	CE	40
Peck Way	Edgemead	59	BT	39
Pecos Way	Manenberg	123	CJ	39
Pecos Wk	Manenberg	123	CJ	39
Ped Way	Bonteheuwel	103	CE	38
Peddie Rd	Milnerton	57	BV	32
Peddie Rd	Penlyn Est.	122	CJ	36
Pedersen Cr.	Belhar	106	CD	50
Pedro Rd	Scottsdene	64	BT	60
Pedro Rd	Scottsdene	64	BT	61
Pedro St	Paarlzicht	19	BC	91
Peeka	Harrington's Place	113	CE	75
Peer Cl.	Mitchells Plain	144	CR	44
Peerboom Ave	Thornton	85	CB	37
Peers Hill	Peers Hill	186	DA	23
Peffers St	Kenilworth	120	CJ	30
Pegasus	Retreat	140	CR	28
Pegasus	Rocklands (M.Plain)	144	CS	46
Pegasus Rd	Phoenix	57	BU	33
Pegasus Way	Ocean View	189	DD	15
Pegnanto Cl.	Edgemead	58	BU	37
Peki St	Harare	146	CS	53
Pela St	Kaya	146	CP	52
Pelagonium Cl.	Welgedacht	60	BT	45
Pelegrini St	Bloubergstrand	24	BL	28
Pelergonium St	Eersterivier	128	CM	59
Pelham Rd	Eersterivier	128	CN	60
Pelican	Rocklands (M.Plain)	144	CS	44
Pelican Cl.	Langeberg Rdg	47	BR	56
Pelican Dr.	Marina Da Gama	159	CU	30
Pelican Path	Montagu's Gift	141	CO	32
Pelican Pl.	Kommetjie	183	DB	13
Pelican St	Ocean View	184	DC	15
Pelican Way	Pelikan Pk	141	CR	34
Pelican Way	Skoongesig	45	BO	50
Pelican Wk	Sunbird Pk	107	CF	54
Pelican Wk	Villa Italia	57	BW	33
Pelikaan	Danarand	89	CC	54
Pelikaan	Onderpapegaaiberg	94	CB	73
Pelikaan St	Somerset West	170	CV	72
Pelikaan St	Wellington	15	AT	92
Pelikaan St	William Lloyd	23	BD	94
Pelikan Cir.	Ruyterwacht	86	BZ	39
Pelikan Rd	Bishop Lavis	105	CE	43
Pelikan Rd	Bridgetown	103	CE	37
Pelkalmy Rd	Bergvliet	139	CQ	26
Pella	Eersterivier	128	CL	60
Pella	Ravensmead	87	CB	45
Pembroke La.	Capricorn	159	CW	30
Pembroke La.	Newlands	101	CG	27
Pembroke St	Claremont	120	CJ	29
Pembury	Parklands	25	BM	33
Pembury Cr.	Parklands	25	BM	33
Pen Duick St	Eersterivier	128	CM	60
Pen Kotze Ave	Plattekloof	60	BV	43
Penarth Rd	Three Anchor Bay	81	BY	20
Pende St	Delft	106	CG	49
Pendennis Pl.	Dreyersdal	140	CS	27
Pendennis Rd	West Beach	24	BN	29
Pendoring	Arbeidslus	96	CB	80
Pendoring Ave	Lotus River	141	CQ	34
Pendoring Cr.	Roosendaal	107	CE	51
Pendoring Rd	Bonteheuwel	104	CE	40
Pendoring St	Rouxville	90	CA	56
Pendragon St	Camelot	107	CF	53
Penelope Cl.	Bakoven	98	CF	18
Penelope Cl.	Lentegeur (M.Plain)	145	CO	48
Pengem St	Flintdale Est.	141	CP	31
Penguin	Seawinds	159	CU	30
Penguin Cr.	Lotus River	141	CQ	34
Penguin Dr.	Simon's Town	191	DF	24
Penguin Rd	Flintdale Est.	141	CP	31
Penhurst Rd	Plumstead	120	CN	28
Peninsula Dr.	Wingfield Nth Camp	58	BW	38
Peninsula Rd	Pelikan Pk	141	CS	33
Peninsula Rd	Pelikan Pk	141	CS	34
Penlyn Ave	Belthorn Est.	103	CH	35
Pennant Cl.	Blouberg Sands	24	BM	30
Penning Rd	Tijgerhof	57	BW	32
Penny	Anesta	113	CF	75
Penny Cl.	Vierlanden	30	BN	51
Penny La.	Malibu Village	127	CK	56
Penrith Rd	Kenilworth	120	CL	29
Penrose Rd	Muizenberg	159	CX	28
Penryn St	Woodstock	83	CB	28
Penta La.	Uitsig	87	CC	45
Pentech Service Rd	Belhar	88	CB	49

STREET NAME	SUBURB NAME	PG	GRID	
Pentrich	St James	187	CZ	27
Pentz	Wellington	10	AS	91
Pentz Dr.	Table View	41	BP	31
Pentz Dr.	Table View	41	BQ	32
Pentz Dr.	Table View	41	BQ	33
Pentz La.	Flamingo Vlei	41	BQ	34
Pentz Rd	Schotsche Kloof	81	CA	22
Pentz St	Wellington	10	AR	93
Pentz St	Wellington	10	AR	94
Pentz St	Wellington	10	AS	92
Penyano St	Nyanga	123	CK	42
Penzance Rd	Hout Bay	137	CO	16
Penzance Rd	Hout Bay	137	CP	16
Penzance Rd	Observatory	101	CD	29
Peperboom Cr.	Vredekloof	62	BU	54
Peperboom St	Rouxville	90	CA	56
Peperbos Cir.	Grassy Pk	141	CQ	32
Peperdruif St	Blommendal	61	BW	50
Peperdruif St	Blommendal	62	BW	51
Pepler St	Franschhoek Sth	78	BY	106
Pepper	Morgen Gronde	63	BW	55
Pepper Pl.	Marconi Beam	57	BT	34
Pepper St	Cape Town Cen.	81	CA	22
Pepper St	Vosfontein	62	BV	52
Pepper Way	Sunnydale	185	CZ	19
Pepperbrush	Macassar	149	CR	63
Peppertree La.	Forest Glade	127	CK	58
Peppertree Rd	Devil's Peak Est.	82	CC	24
Peppertree Rd	Hindle Pk	107	CH	54
Percival Rd	Tijgerhof	57	BW	33
Percy	Edward	122	CN	35
Percy Ralarala St	Guguletu	104	CG	41
Percy Rd	Rosebank	101	CE	29
Percy St	Salt River	83	CB	28
Perdeberg Cl.	Bonnie Brae	47	BP	57
Perdeberg Cl.	Bonnie Brae	47	BO	58
Perdeberg St	Tafelsig (M.Plain)	145	CS	49
Perdebos Cl.	Roosendaal	107	CE	51
Perdebos Rd	Proteavallei	60	BT	46
Perdekloof	Wesbank	107	CG	52
Perdekloof	Wesbank	107	CG	53
Perdekop Cl.	Protea Village	64	BW	59
Perdevy	Stellenbosch	95	BY	75
Pere	Philippi East	125	CM	47
Pere Cl.	Philippi East	125	CL	48
Peregrine Pl.	Somerset West	152	CR	78
Pereira Cr.	Elim	89	CA	54
Perelberg Rd	Bishop Lavis	104	CE	42
Perfecta Rd	Paarden Eiland	83	CA	29
Peri Rd	Clovelly	186	CZ	24
Peridot	Fairdale	107	CH	53
Peridot Cr.	Pelikan Pk	161	CT	36
Perivale Rd	Lotus River	141	CP	34
Periwinkle Cl.	Kommetjie	183	DB	13
Periwinkle La.	Big Bay	24	BL	28
Periwinkle Pl.	Kommetjie	183	DB	12
Periwinkle Rd	Richwood	42	BP	38
Periwinkle Rd	Richwood	42	BO	38
Perkins St	Belhar	88	CC	49
Perla St	Sunset Beach	41	BS	32
Perle St	Glen Ive	62	BU	52
Perlemoen Rd	Bloubergstrand	24	BM	28
Perold St	Paarl	22	BF	88
Perold St	Soneike I	89	BZ	54
Perrault Rd	Hout Bay	136	CO	14
Perry St	Clamhall	60	BX	43
Perryn St	Brackenfell Sth	63	BX	58
Pers Cl.	Parkwood	141	CP	32
Pers Rd	Parkwood	141	CP	32
Persee Ave	Somerset West	151	CR	71
Perseus Rd	Joe Slovo Pk	57	BU	34
Perseus Rd	Joe Slovo Pk	57	BU	35
Perseus Rd	Woodlands (M.Plain)	144	CP	44
Perseverance Rd	Maitland Gdn Village	84	CC	31
Persian Cl.	Mitchells Plain	144	CR	46
Perth Cl.	Belhar	107	CD	51
Perth Rd	Cape Town Cen.	81	CB	22
Perth Rd	District Six	82	CC	25
Perth Rd	Eikendal	48	BS	59
Perth Rd	Grassy Pk	141	CQ	31
Perth Rd	Grassy Pk	141	CR	32
Perth Rd	Observatory	83	CC	29
Perth Rd	Pelikan Pk	141	CR	32
Perth Rd	Rondebosch	101	CG	29
Perth Rd	Rondebosch East	102	CH	32
Perth Rd	Tokai	139	CS	25
Perth Rd	Woodstock	82	CC	25
Perth Rd	Wynberg	120	CL	29
Perth St	Maitland	83	CA	30
Pesika	Philippi East	125	CM	47
Petal St	Kenridge	61	BU	48
Petal St	Retreat	140	CS	28
Peteni Cl.	Langa	103	CE	37
Peter	Sarepta	89	CC	53
Peter Barlow	Glenhaven	89	BZ	51
Peter Barlow	Marlow	89	CA	51
Peter Charles St	Cafda Village	141	CR	31
Peter Charles St	Cafda Village	141	CS	31
Peter Cloete Ave	Alphen	119	CL	26
Peter Cloete Ave	Alphen	119	CM	26
Peter Lamb	Woodlands (M.Plain)	144	CO	44
Peter Lamb Cl.	Woodlands (M.Plain)	144	CO	44
Peter Mokaba Cr.	Mandela Pk	146	CR	54
Peter Mokaba St	Fisantekraal	32	BJ	59
Peter Rd	Grassy Pk	141	CQ	33

STREET NAME	SUBURB NAME	PG	GRID	
Peter St	Athlone	102	CG	34
Peter St	Northern Paarl	18	AZ	88
Peterfield Rd	Parklands	25	BM	34
Peterfield Rd	Parklands	25	BL	33
Peterhof Cl.	Hout Bay	137	CO	17
Petersen St	Bloekombos	48	BR	62
Petersen St	Brackenfell Ind.	63	BT	58
Petersen St	Kylemore	97	BZ	86
Petra Rd	Weltevreden Val. (M.Plain)	124	CN	44
Petra St	Denneburg	23	BD	91
Petra Wk	Manenberg	122	CJ	38
Petrea St	Ottery	121	CN	33
Petrel Cl.	Bakoven	98	CF	18
Petrel Way	Pelikan Pk	142	CR	35
Petricia Rd	Barbarossa	140	CO	28
Petro Rd	Gaylee	108	CH	57
Petrusa St	Belgravia	88	BY	50
Petticoat La.	Malibu Village	127	CK	56
Petunia	Dunoon	42	BO	37
Petunia	Lentegeur (M.Plain)	144	CP	46
Petunia Ave	Tarentaalplaas	175	DA	76
Petunia Ave	Tarentaalplaas	175	DA	75
Petunia Cl.	Peers Hill	185	DA	22
Petunia Cr.	Uitsig	87	CB	44
Petunia Cr.	Welgedacht	60	BU	45
Petunia Rd	Bridgetown	103	CF	37
Petunia Rd	Silvertown	103	CF	37
Petunia St	Dalvale	19	AY	92
Petunia St	Firgrove	150	CR	67
Petunia St	Hanover Pk	122	CJ	36
Petunia St	Morgenster	63	BU	56
Petunia St	Morgenster Hoogte	63	BT	57
Petunia St	Ocean View	184	DC	15
Petunia St	Peerless Pk East	47	BS	58
Petunia St	Peerless Pk East	47	BS	58
Petunia St	Sarepta	89	CC	52
Petunia St	Weltevreden Val. (M.Plain)	124	CM	44
Peugeot Cr.	Beacon Valley (M.Plain)	145	CQ	48
Peyton Pl.	Malibu Village	127	CK	56
Phakama St	Umrhabulo Triangle	147	CR	57
Phakamani Rd	Kaya	146	CP	52
Phakamani St	Griffiths Mxenge	146	CP	54
Phakamisa Cr.	Umrhabulo Triangle	147	CQ	57
Phala	Umrhabulo Triangle	147	CQ	56
Phala	Umrhabulo Triangle	147	CQ	56
Phaliso St	Lwandle	175	CZ	76
Phaliso St	Lwandle	175	CZ	77
Phaliso St	Tarentaalplaas	170	CX	74
Phalo Ave	Hout Bay	137	CO	16
Phamba St	Harare	146	CS	53
Phambile	Guguletu	104	CH	40
Phambili Cr.	Kaya	146	CO	52
Phanda Cr.	Harare	146	CR	53
Phandla St	Umrhabulo Triangle	147	CQ	58
Phandle St	Harare	146	CS	53
Phandle St	Kaya	146	CP	52
Phandle St	Kaya	146	CS	52
Phangela Cr.	Griffiths Mxenge	146	CQ	54
Phantom	Rocklands (M.Plain)	144	CS	46
Phantom Cr.	The Hague	106	CF	49
Phantom Cr.	The Hague	106	CF	50
Phaphani St	Mxolisi Phetani	126	CM	51
Phatha Cl.	Harare	146	CR	53
Phathele St	Griffiths Mxenge	146	CP	54
Phawu St	Umrhabulo Triangle	147	CR	56
Phazama St	Griffiths Mxenge	146	CP	54
Pheasant Way	Sunbird Pk	107	CF	54
Phefulma Cr.	Umrhabulo Triangle	147	CP	58
Pheiffer Rd	Ocean View	184	DC	16
Pheka St	Umrhabulo Triangle	147	CR	57
Phendula Cr.	Eyethu	146	CP	53
Phenyane St	Griffiths Mxenge	146	CQ	54
Pheonix	Sunningdale	25	BM	31
Phepha St	Umrhabulo Triangle	147	CR	58
Phesantekraal St	De Bron	45	BS	48
Phezukomkhono	Philippi East	125	CM	47
Phezukomkhono	Philippi East	125	CK	50
Phielandaba	Kalkfontein I	107	CD	52
Phikisa St	Harare	146	CS	54
Phil Mostert	Park Estates	170	CX	73
Philander	Stellenbosch	95	CA	75
Philemon Rd	Capricorn	160	CU	31
Philimon Biyela St	Kuyasa	147	CS	55
Philimon Biyela St	Kuyasa	147	CS	58
Philippines St	Portlands (M.Plain)	144	CQ	46
Philips Cl.	Franschhoek Nth	75	BW	105
Philips Rd	Rondebosch	101	CF	29
Phillans Wk	Hanover Pk	122	CK	36
Phillip	Sarepta	89	CC	52
Phillip Cr.	Belhar	106	CD	49
Phillip Rd	Montagu's Gift	141	CP	34
Phillips St	Parowvallei	87	BZ	43
Philmau Rd	Lavender Hill	159	CT	30
Phimpi St	Kuyasa	147	CS	55
Phloks Cl.	Welgedacht	60	BT	45
Phlox St	Bonteheuwel	104	CE	40
Phoenix Cr.	Bonnie Brook	47	BQ	58
Phoenix Park St	Somerset West	170	CW	72
Phoenix Way	Glencairn Hgts	191	DD	24
Phoenix Way	Glencairn Hgts	191	DD	23
Phokeng	Mbekweni	15	AW	91
Phokeng	Mbekweni	15	AW	92
Pholani	Mbekweni	15	AW	92
Pholani	Mbekweni	15	AT	94
Pholani	Wellington	15	AU	91

STREET NAME	SUBURB NAME	PG	GRID	
Pholani St	Mxolisi Phetani	125	CM	49
Pholile St	Umrhabulo Triangle	147	CQ	56
Phosisa St	Harare	146	CR	53
Phucula St	Umrhabulo Triangle	147	CQ	58
Phumla Cr.	Umrhabulo Triangle	147	CR	56
Phumla Cr.	Umrhabulo Triangle	147	CR	56
Phumla St	Bloekombos	49	BR	63
Phumlani	Mbekweni	15	AX	92
Phumza St	Harare	146	CR	54
Phupha Cr.	Umrhabulo Triangle	147	CR	57
Phyllis Rd	Claremont	120	CJ	28
Phyllis Way	Wetton	121	CL	34
Piano Cr.	Belhar	106	CD	48
Piazza Cr.	Sonstraal Hgts	46	BQ	54
Picardi Cr.	Die Bos	174	CY	74
Picardi Rd	Hartebeeskraal	23	BH	91
Picardie Ave	Bel Ombre	119	CM	24
Picardie St	Courtrai	22	BH	88
Picardy Ave	Somerset West	171	CT	77
Picardy Ave	Somerset West	171	CT	78
Picardy Way	Everglen	46	BS	51
Picaroon Cr.	Sun Valley	185	DA	20
Picasso Cl.	Somerset West	152	CR	75
Picasso Cr.	Forest Glade	127	CK	58
Picasso Cr.	Forest Glade	128	CK	59
Picasso St	Kaapzicht	59	BW	40
Piccadilly Ave	Weltevreden Val. (M.Plain)	143	CO	42
Piccadilly Cl.	Weltevreden Val. (M.Plain)	143	CP	42
Piccadilly Cr.	Weltevreden Val. (M.Plain)	143	CP	42
Piccadilly Way	Portlands (M.Plain)	145	CR	47
Piccolo Cl.	Belhar	106	CD	49
Piccolo Cl.	Belhar	106	CH	48
Piccolo St	Retreat	159	CT	30
Pickerill St	Retreat	159	CT	29
Picketberg St	Tafelsig (M.Plain)	145	CS	49
Pickle	Park Estates	174	CZ	72
Pickle	Park Estates	174	CZ	71
Pickwick Rd	Salt River	83	CC	28
Picton St	Parow	87	BY	43
Piebald Rd	Milnerton	41	BS	34
Pieke Rd	Thornton	85	CA	36
Pieke Rd	Thornton	85	CB	36
Pieke St	Glen Ive	62	BU	51
Pienaar Rd	Milnerton	57	BT	33
Pienaar Rd	Milnerton	57	BU	32
Pienaar Rd	Milnerton	57	BV	32
Pienaar St	Aurora	45	BP	48
Pienaar St	Somerset West	171	CU	75
Pienaar St	Somerset West	171	CU	76
Pienaar St	Strand	174	CZ	73
Pienaar St	Van Ryneveld	174	CZ	73
Pienaar St	William Lloyd	23	BD	92
Pierneef Cl.	Forest Glade	127	CK	58
Pierneef Rd	Sonstraal	46	BR	52
Pierneef St	Goodwood Est.	58	BX	38
Pierneef St	Labiance	89	BZ	51
Pierneef St	Parow Nth	59	BW	42
Pierneef St	Somerset West	151	CR	73
Pierre Jordaan St	Franschhoek Sth	78	BZ	106
Piers Rd	Wynberg	120	CL	28
Piet Fransman St	Elim	90	CB	56
Piet Grobler St	Brooklyn	84	BZ	31
Piet Joubert St	Ruyterwacht	86	CB	40
Piet Retief	Krigeville	113	CD	76
Piet Retief Sq.	Brooklyn	84	BZ	31
Piet Retief St	Flintdale Est.	141	CO	31
Piet Retief St	Goodwood Est.	85	BY	37
Piet Retief St	Park Estates	174	CY	72
Piet Retief St	Parowvallei	87	BZ	44
Piet Retief St	Wellington	10	AS	93
Piet Retief St	Wellington	15	AU	93
Piet Uys Cir.	Ruyterwacht	86	BZ	39
Pieter Hugo St	Courtrai	39	BJ	87
Pieter Roux St	Paarl	22	BE	88
Pieter St	Brackenfell Sth	63	BX	58
Pieter Wenning Cr.	Woodlands (M.Plain)	124	CN	45
Pieter Wium	Northern Paarl	18	AZ	88
Pieter Wium	Northern Paarl	18	AZ	89
Pieters Rd	Strandfontein	163	CU	43
Pieterse Cl.	Retreat	141	CR	31
Pietersen St	William Lloyd	23	BD	94
Pietersielie	Delft Sth	125	CJ	49
Pieterson Rd	Scottsdene	48	BS	61
Pietman Dreyer Ave	Gustrow	175	DB	75
Piet-my-Vrou	Onderpapegaaiberg	94	CC	72
Piet-my-Vrou	Rocklands (M.Plain)	144	CS	44
Piet-my-Vrou	Somerset Hgts	127	CJ	57
Piet-my-Vrou Ave	Mikro Pk	90	CB	55
Piet-my-Vrou Ave	Mikro Pk	90	CB	56
Piet-my-Vrou St	Amstelhof	23	BD	93
Piet-my-Vrou St	Macassar	149	CS	65
Piet-my-Vrou St	Sonstraal Hgts	46	BR	53
Pietro St	St Michaels	63	BU	55
Pike Cr.	Nooitgedacht	104	CE	42
Pike Cr.	Soneike II	89	BZ	53
Piketberg Cl.	Welgevonden	46	BO	54
Piketberg St	Panorama	59	BV	41
Pikkewyn	Onderpapegaaiberg	94	CC	73
Pikkewyn	Rocklands (M.Plain)	144	CS	44
Pikkewyn Rd	Bloubergstrand	24	BM	29
Pikkewyn St	Durbanville	46	BP	52
Pikoko Rd	Philippi East	125	CL	47
Pilanes Cl.	Eersterivier	128	CL	59
Pilanesberg Rd	Lavender Hill East	160	CU	32
Pilanesberg Rd	Lavender Hill East	160	CX	33

Index to Street Names

Pillans Rd — Raats Dr.

STREET NAME	SUBURB NAME	PG	GRID	
Pillans Rd	Rosebank	101	CE	30
Pillay St	Marlow	88	CA	50
Pilot Cl.	Blouberg Sands	24	BM	29
Pilot Way	Kommetjie	183	DA	13
Pilot Way	Strandfontein	162	CT	40
Pilot Way	Strandfontein	162	CV	42
Pilot Way	Strandfontein	162	CU	40
Pilots Cl.	Sunset Beach	57	BT	31
Pin Oak	Rosedale	128	CK	59
Pin Oak Cr.	Tygerdal	58	BX	37
Pin Oak La.	Green Oaks	95	BY	75
Pin Oak St	Oak Glen	62	BW	53
Pin Oak St	Oak Glen	62	BX	52
Pinaster Way	Northpine	63	BU	57
Pincushion Cl.	Proteavallei	61	BT	47
Pincushion Way	Scarborough	192	DJ	18
Pine	Cloetesville	95	BZ	75
Pine	De Oude Renbaan	22	BH	88
Pine	Simon's Town	194	DJ	25
Pine Ave	Devil's Peak Est.	82	CC	24
Pine Ave	Table View	41	BO	32
Pine Ave	Westlake Est.	158	CT	25
Pine Cl.	Hanover Pk	122	CK	36
Pine Cl.	Ottery East	121	CM	34
Pine Cl.	Pinelands	102	CD	32
Pine Cr.	Forest Glade	127	CK	58
Pine Mews Cr.	Northpine	63	BT	58
Pine Rd	Doornhoogte	103	CG	36
Pine Rd	Green Point	81	BZ	21
Pine Rd	Kenilworth	120	CJ	29
Pine Rd	Ridgeworth	61	BV	50
Pine Rd	Thembokwezi	125	CM	48
Pine Rd	Tokai	139	CS	25
Pine Rd	Woodstock	82	CB	26
Pine St	Amanda Glen	46	BS	52
Pine St	Chapman's Peak	156	CW	16
Pine St	Courtrai	22	BH	88
Pine St	Hillcrest Hgts	127	CL	57
Pine St	Hout Bay	117	CN	18
Pine St	Peers Hill	185	DA	22
Pine St	Pelikan Pk	142	CQ	35
Pine St	Sanddrift	57	BW	34
Pine St	Wellington	10	AS	93
Pine Way	Pinelands	84	CC	32
Pine Way	Rusdal	108	CE	57
Pinecroft Cl.	Somerset West	152	CS	75
Pinedene Rd	Hout Bay	137	CQ	16
Pinedene Rd	Ravensmead	87	CA	44
Pinedene St	Ravensmead	87	CA	45
Pinedene St	Ravensmead	87	CA	46
Pinegrove Pl.	Somerset West	171	CU	76
Pinegrove St	Somerset West	171	CU	76
Pinehill Ave	Plumstead	140	CO	29
Pinehurst	Eversdal Hgts	46	BS	51
Pinehurst Cl.	Silverhurst	119	CN	25
Pinehurst Rd	Constantia Vale	119	CN	25
Pinehurst Rd	Lansdowne	121	CJ	32
Pinehurst Rd	Lansdowne	121	CK	33
Pinelaw Rd	Dieprivier	140	CO	28
Pineoak Rd	Devil's Peak Est.	82	CC	24
Pinetree Cr.	Ruyterwacht	86	BZ	39
Pinetree Cr.	Vredehoek	82	CC	24
Pinetree La.	Bergvliet	140	CQ	27
Pinetree Rd	Claremont	120	CJ	30
Pinetree Way	Rosedale	128	CK	59
Pinetree Way	Rosedale	128	CL	59
Pinewood Ave	Tygerdal	58	BX	37
Pinewood Ave	Voorbrug	106	CG	50
Pinewood Cr.	Langeberg Rdg	47	BR	55
Pinewood Dr.	Pinelands	85	CC	35
Pinewood Rd	Bonteheuwel	103	CE	38
Pinewood Rd	Newlands	101	CG	27
Pinewood Rd	Rondebosch	101	CG	29
Pinewoods Rd	Somerset West	170	CU	74
Pinewoods Rd	Somerset West	171	CT	75
Pinnacle Cr.	Strandfontein	162	CT	40
Pinnacle Cr.	Strandfontein	162	CV	42
Pinnotage St	Paarlzicht	19	BC	91
Pinoak	Alphen	119	CM	26
Pinoak Cr.	Peers Hill	186	DA	23
Pinotage	Kleingeluk	113	CE	75
Pinotage	Langeberg Rdg	47	BR	55
Pinotage Ave	Somerset West	151	CS	72
Pinotage Cl.	Uitzicht	47	BO	55
Pinotage Rd	Saxenburg Ind. Pk	108	CE	56
Pinotage St	Oude Westhof	44	BS	45
Pinotage St	Shirley Pk	89	BY	52
Pinscher	Strandfontein	162	CT	41
Pintail Cr.	Pelikan Pk	141	CR	32
Pintail Way	Somerset Rdg	170	CT	72
Pinto Rd	Milnerton	41	BS	34
Pinto Rd	West Riding	42	BO	35
Pinzi	Mbekweni	15	AX	91
Pioneer	Soneike I	89	BZ	54
Pioneer	Soneike I	90	BZ	55
Pioneer	Sonnekuil	89	BZ	54
Pioneer Rd	Durbanville	46	BQ	53
Pioneer St	Lansdowne	121	CK	34
Pioneer St	Oakdale	61	BW	48
Pioneer St	Scottsville	47	BS	57
Pioneer St	The Hague	106	CF	49
Pionier St	Bothasig	43	BS	39
Piper	Rocklands (M.Plain)	163	CT	46
Piper St	Kensington	84	BZ	34
Piper St	The Hague	106	CF	49
Pipers Cl.	Kommetjie	183	DB	12
Pipit La.	Steenberg	158	CT	24
Pippit Cl.	Ottery	122	CL	35
Pinet Cl.	Welgelegen	59	BT	41
Pirobella Cl.	Northpine	64	BT	59
Pisa Cl.	Portlands (M.Plain)	145	CR	47
Pisa Way	Strandfontein	162	CT	42
Pisces Cr.	Everite	63	BV	57
Pisces Rd	Phoenix	57	BU	33
Pisces Rd	Surrey	103	CH	38
Pison	Eden	113	CG	76
Pitlochry Rd	Bakoven	98	CF	17
Pitlochry Rd	Rondebosch	102	CF	31
Pitt St	Maitland	84	CA	32
Pitt St	Observatory	83	CB	28
Pitt St	Plumstead	140	CO	29
Pittisporum St	Amanda Glen	46	BS	52
Pittosporum Ave	Thornton	85	CA	37
Pittosporum St	Somerset West	151	CS	71
Pittosporum St	William Lloyd	19	BC	93
Pivaan Cl.	Delft	106	CG	49
Pivert St	Chantecler	62	BT	51
Pivot Cl.	Lakeside	159	CV	27
Pivot Cl.	Lakeside	159	CW	27
Pixie St	Rugby	57	BX	32
Pixley Seme St	Mandela Pk	147	CQ	55
Place De La Chance	Somerset West	151	CQ	73
Plakkaten Rd	Bothasig	42	BS	38
Plakkies St	Bonteheuwel	104	CE	40
Plane Ave	Thornton	85	CA	37
Plane Cr.	Silverglade	185	DA	22
Plane Rd	Hindle Pk	107	CH	54
Plane Rd	Hindle Pk	126	CJ	54
Plane St	Forest Village	127	CM	58
Plane St	Greenlands	88	CA	48
Planeet St	Sarepta	89	CC	53
Planet Cl.	Salberau	86	CB	41
Planet Cl.	Salberau	86	CB	39
Planet St	Bishop Lavis	105	CE	43
Planken	Papegaaiberg Ind. Pk	95	CA	75
Plantanus St	Klipdam	90	CB	55
Plantasie St	Belmont Pk	48	BR	61
Plantasie St	Paarl	22	BF	88
Plantasie St	Tafelsig (M.Plain)	145	CR	48
Plantation Rd	Devil's Peak Est.	82	CC	24
Plantation Rd	Ottery	121	CL	32
Plantation Rd	Ottery	121	CL	33
Plantation Rd	Ottery	121	CN	33
Planter Green	Summer Greens	58	BW	36
Planter Way	Summer Greens	58	BW	36
Plataan Rd	Skilpadvlei	45	BP	50
Plataan St	Bellair	62	BW	51
Plataan St	Vredekloof	62	BU	53
Platdoring Cr.	Roosendaal	107	CE	51
Plate Rd	Manenberg	123	CJ	39
Plateau Rd	Modderdam	193	DM	21
Plateau St	Tafelsig (M.Plain)	145	CR	48
Platinum Cr.	Marconi Beam	57	BV	33
Plato La.	Mountainview	179	DD	78
Plato Rd	Eureka	87	CC	43
Platoon Rd	Wynberg	120	CM	30
Platteklip Cr.	Belhar	106	CD	50
Platteklip Sq.	Bakoven	99	CE	19
Platteklip Sq.	Bakoven	99	CD	22
Plattekloof Rd	Bothasig	42	BR	37
Plattekloof Rd	Bothasig	43	BS	39
Plattekloof Rd	Montague Gdns Ind.	42	BR	36
Plattekloof Rd	Plattekloof	59	BU	41
Plattekloof Rd	Plattekloof	59	BV	42
Plattekloof St	De Bron	61	BT	48
Plattekloof St	Plattekloof Glen	59	BW	40
Plattekloof St	Tafelsig (M.Plain)	145	CS	49
Play Cl.	Gustrow	175	DB	75
Play Cl.	Gustrow	175	DB	77
Play St	Klippiesdal	19	BC	91
Play St	Strandfontein	162	CT	41
Pleasant Pl.	Pinelands	84	CC	33
Pleasant Pl.	Pinelands	102	CD	33
Pleasant Pl.	Tokai	139	CS	26
Pleasant St	Wesbank	107	CE	52
Pleasant Way	Newfields	103	CH	36
Plein	Stellenbosch	95	CC	76
Plein Rd	Belhar	106	CD	49
Plein St	Belmont Pk	48	BS	59
Plein St	Cape Town Cen.	82	CB	23
Plein St	Durbanville	45	BP	50
Plein St	Eersterivier	128	CL	59
Plein St	Eersterivier	128	CL	60
Plein St	Fairfield	87	BY	43
Plein St	Lemoenkloof	18	BC	88
Plein St	Lemoenkloof	18	BC	89
Plein St	Park Estates	174	CY	72
Plein St	Somerset West	171	CU	76
Plein St	Summerville	48	BS	60
Plein St	Wellington	11	AS	95
Plein St	Woodstock	82	CB	26
Plender Ave	Athlone	102	CG	33
Plettenberg Rd	Doornhoogte	103	CH	35
Plettenberg Rd	Doornhoogte	103	CH	36
Plettenberg St	Brackenfell Sth	63	BX	56
Plettenberg St	Brooklyn	84	BZ	31
Plettenberg St	Monte Vista	59	BW	39
Plettenberg St	Welgemoed	60	BU	46
Plettenberg St	Welgemoed	60	BV	45
Plettenberg St	Welgemoed	61	BU	47
Plimplol Cr.	Gatesville	103	CH	36
Pliny St	Athlone	102	CG	33
Plnot Cl.	William Lloyd	19	BC	94
Plnot Cl.	William Lloyd	19	BA	94
Plover	Westlake Est.	158	CU	25
Plover Cl.	Westlake Est.	158	CU	25
Plover Cl.	Westlake Est.	158	CT	26
Plover La.	Steenberg	139	CS	24
Plover Pl.	Imhoff's Gift	184	DB	15
Plover Rd	Imhoff's Gift	184	DB	15
Plover St	Brooklyn	83	BZ	30
Plover St	Eersterivier	128	CM	60
Plover St	Flamingo Vlei	41	BP	32
Plover St	Pelikan Pk	161	CV	37
Plover Way	Montagu's Gift	141	CO	33
Plover Wk	Sunbird Pk	107	CF	54
Plower Cl.	Villa Italia	57	BW	33
Plumbos Cl.	Protea Village	64	BV	59
Plum	Greenlands	88	CA	48
Plum Cl.	Peers Hill	185	DA	22
Plum Cl.	Scottsdene	64	BU	60
Plum Cr.	Thembokwezi	125	CM	48
Plum La.	District Six	82	CB	25
Plum St	Somerset West	170	CV	73
Plumbago Cl.	Ottery East	121	CN	34
Plumbago Cr.	Lentegeur (M.Plain)	124	CN	45
Plumbago Cr.	Welgedacht	60	BT	44
Plumbago Rd	Bonteheuwel	104	CE	40
Plumbago St	Klein Nederburg	19	BC	92
Plumbago St	Somerset West	151	CS	72
Plumer Gr.	Woodstock	83	CB	27
Plumpton Rd	Ottery	122	CM	35
Plumpton St	Ottery	122	CN	36
Plumtree Ave	Hout Bay	117	CN	16
Plumtree Cl.	Hout Bay	117	CN	17
Pluto	Rocklands (M.Plain)	144	CS	46
Pluto La.	Thembokwezi	125	CL	49
Pluto Rd	Ocean View	184	DC	15
Pluto Rd	Plumstead	120	CN	30
Pluto Rd	Plumstead	140	CO	30
Pluto Rd	Surrey	103	CH	38
Pluto St	Salberau	86	CB	41
Pluto St	Salberau	86	CB	39
Plympton Rd	Plumstead	120	CN	29
Pniel	Eersterivier	128	CL	60
Pochard Rd	Pelikan Pk	142	CR	35
Pocock St	Stikland Hospital	61	BX	50
Podalyria St	Gordon Hgts	180	DD	79
Poekoe Cl.	Soneike II	89	BZ	54
Poets Cnr	Woodstock	82	CB	26
Poffertjie Rd	Vissershok	28	BM	44
Poinsettia St	Bonteheuwel	104	CD	40
Poinsettia St	Somerset West	151	CS	72
Point Rd	Witsand	188	DF	14
Point St	Glenlily	86	BY	41
Pointer Cl.	Salberau	86	CB	41
Pointer Cl.	Salberau	86	CB	39
Pointer Way	Strandfontein	162	CT	40
Pointsettia St	Klein Nederburg	19	BC	93
Pokela Rd	Masiphumelele	184	DA	18
Pokkiesdoring Cr.	Roosendaal	107	CE	51
Polacca St	Sun Valley	185	DA	20
Polaris Rd	Lansdowne	121	CJ	34
Polaris Rd	Ocean View	189	DD	15
Polaris St	Morgenster Hoogte	63	BT	55
Poleman St	Lansdowne	121	CK	34
Polka Cl.	Voorbrug	106	CD	49
Polka Cl.	Voorbrug	106	CH	48
Polka Sq.	Mitchells Plain Cen.	145	CR	47
Polkadraai Rd	Bloemendal	110	CE	66
Polkadraai Rd	Devonvallei	112	CD	71
Polkadraai Rd	Jacobsdal	109	CE	59
Polkadraai Rd	Saxenburg Ind. Pk	108	CE	58
Pollen Rd	Retreat	140	CS	28
Pollock St	William Lloyd	23	BD	92
Pollsmoor Rd	Kirstenhof	159	CT	27
Pollux Rd	Lansdowne	121	CK	34
Pollux Way	Ocean View	184	DC	15
Polo Cl.	Beacon Valley (M.Plain)	145	CP	47
Polo Rd	Observatory	83	CC	28
Polo St	Forest Glade	127	CL	58
Polonaise St	Dalvale	19	AY	92
Pomela Cr.	Vredekloof Hgts	47	BS	55
Ponder Rd	Kalk Bay	186	DA	26
Ponderosa Way	Northpine	63	BU	58
Pondicherry Ave	Hout Bay	136	CP	14
Pondicherry Cl.	Hout Bay	136	CP	14
Pongola Cl.	Portlands (M.Plain)	144	CP	45
Pongola Cr.	Bonnie Brook	47	BQ	57
Pongola Rd	Groenvallei	62	BX	53
Ponie Cl.	Mitchells Plain	144	CR	45
Ponoshe Cr.	Victoria Mxenge	146	CO	51
Pontac Cl.	Zevenzicht	90	CC	58
Pontac Rd	Saxenburg Ind. Pk	108	CE	56
Pontac St	District Six	82	CB	25
Pontac St	Oude Westhof	60	BT	45
Pontac St	Paarl	22	BD	88
Pontac Way	Belhar	107	CD	51
Pontak St	Somerset West	170	CT	72
Pontiac St	Beacon Valley (M.Plain)	145	CQ	47
Pooke Rd	Gatesville	103	CH	36
Pool	Cloetesville	95	BZ	75
Poole Rd	Wellington	15	AV	92
Poole St	Brooklyn	84	BY	31
Poonan Rd	Strandfontein	163	CU	43
Poort St	Arauna	62	BU	54
Poort St	Sonnekuil	89	BZ	53
Pope St	Salt River	83	CB	28
Popham St	Bloubergstrand	24	BL	28
Popham St	Dolphin Beach	40	BP	30
Popham St	Table View	41	BO	31
Poplar	Ravensmead	87	CA	44
Poplar Ave	Bergvliet	140	CQ	27
Poplar Ave	Rusdal	108	CF	57
Poplar Ave	Westlake Est.	158	CT	24
Poplar Cl.	Hanover Pk	122	CK	36
Poplar Cl.	Hanover Pk	122	CN	36
Poplar Cr.	Mandalay	125	CN	48
Poplar Rd	Rosedale	128	CK	59
Poplar Rd	Silverglade	185	DA	22
Poplar Rd	Weltevreden Val. (M.Plain)	143	CO	42
Poplar St	Bellair	62	BW	51
Poplar St	Bellair	62	BW	52
Poplar St	Chapman's Peak	156	CX	16
Poplar St	Newlands	100	CH	26
Poplar St	Somerset West	170	CV	73
Poplar Way	Pinelands	84	CC	34
Poplar Way	Thornton	85	CA	37
Poplar Way	Thornton	85	CB	36
Poponi Cr.	Nonqubela	126	CN	52
Poppy	Lentegeur (M.Plain)	144	CO	46
Poproos Cr.	Roosendaal	107	CE	51
Populier	Delft Sth	125	CK	49
Populier St	Die Oude Spruit	63	BX	56
Populier St	Klipdam	90	CB	55
Porath Wk	Hanover Pk	122	CK	37
Porcupine Cl.	Eastridge (M.Plain)	145	CR	48
Porcupine Way	Table View	41	BQ	34
Poros Pl.	Capricorn	159	CW	30
Port Cl.	Blouberg Sands	24	BM	29
Port Cl.	Table View	41	BO	33
Port Jackson La.	Leonsdale	86	CA	41
Port Jackson La.	Leonsdale	86	BZ	41
Port Jackson Rd	Belgravia	103	CH	35
Port Jackson Rd	Bishop Lavis	104	CD	42
Port Jackson Rd	Firgrove	150	CR	67
Port Jackson St	Silveroaks	90	CC	55
Port Jackson St	Somerset Hgts	127	CK	57
Port Pl.	Blouberg Sands	24	BM	30
Port Rd	Cape Town Cen.	82	BZ	23
Port Rd	Foreshore	82	BY	23
Port Rd	Foreshore	82	BY	23
Port Rush Mews	Sunset Links	57	BT	31
Portadown Rd	Heathfield	140	CQ	28
Portavue Dr.	Surrey	103	CH	37
Portcullis Dr.	Hagley	107	CF	53
Porter	Stellenbosch	95	CA	75
Porter Rd	Fir Grove	139	CQ	24
Porter St	Woodstock	82	CB	26
Porterfield Rd	Blouberg Rise	25	BN	31
Porterfield Rd	Table View	40	BO	30
Porterville Cr.	Welgelegen	59	BV	40
Portford Rd	Parklands	25	BN	34
Portia Cl.	Eersterivier	128	CM	61
Portia Wk	Hanover Pk	122	CJ	37
Portland Cr.	Bonnie Brae	47	BQ	57
Portland Rd	Philippi	124	CL	45
Portland Rd	Rondebosch	102	CG	31
Portland Rd	Woodstock	83	CB	28
Portland St	Oakdale	61	BV	49
Portman Rd	Sea Point	80	CB	18
Portobello Cl.	Portlands (M.Plain)	145	CR	47
Portswood Rd	Foreshore	82	BY	22
Portswood Rd	Royal Cape	120	CM	30
Portulaca Ave	Wellway Pk East	46	BO	53
Portulaca Cr.	Belhar	106	CD	47
Portulaca Cr.	Lentegeur (M.Plain)	124	CN	45
Posmansdam Rd	Dunoon	27	BM	39
Possen Rd	Newlands	101	CH	27
Postern Rd	Heideveld	104	CF	39
Postern Way	Edgemead	59	BT	39
Postma St	Oakdale	61	BW	49
Potberg	Lavender Hill East	160	CU	32
Potberg	Wesbank	107	CG	51
Potez	Rocklands (M.Plain)	145	CS	47
Potgieter Cr.	Morgenster	63	BT	56
Potgieter Cr.	Morgenster	63	BU	56
Potgieter St	Strand Halt	170	CW	74
Potomac Cl.	Crofters Valley	185	CY	19
Potsdam Rd	Bothasig	59	BT	39
Potsdam Rd	Dunoon	26	BN	37
Potsdam Rd	Killarney Gdns	42	BO	36
Pottinger Rd	Bishop Lavis	105	CD	43
Pou St	Amandelsig	90	CB	56
Poublom Sq.	Roosendaal	107	CE	51
Poussion St	Loevenstein	60	BV	45
Poussion St	Loevenstein	60	BV	46
Powell Rd	Steenberg	159	CT	28
Powell St	Fairfield	60	BX	44
Powell St	Wellington	10	AS	92
Power St	Onverwacht	174	CZ	74
Powerful St	Paarden Eiland	83	CA	29
Poyser Rd	Tamboerskloof	81	CA	21
Pragstompie St	Protea Village	64	BV	59
Prairie Ct	Rocklands (M.Plain)	144	CR	45
Preller St	Somerset West	170	CT	74
Prelude Ave	Dalvale	19	AZ	92
Premier Cl.	Belhar	106	CD	50
Premier Rd	Woodstock	82	CC	26
Premier St	Northern Paarl	18	AZ	89

Abbreviations used: Ave – Avenue, A.H. – Agricultural Holding, A.L.– Algemene Landgoed, Blvd – Boulevard, Cen. – Central, Cir. – Circle, Cl. – Close, Cr. – Crescent, Ct – Court, Dr. – Drive, Est. – Estate, Ext. – Extension, Hgts – Heights, Ind. – Industrial, Gdns – Gardens, Gr. – Grove, La. – Lane, (M.Plain) - Mitchells Plain, Nth – North, Pl. – Place, Pk – Park, Rd – Road, Rdg. – Ridge, S.H.– Small Holding, Sq. – Square, St – Street, Sth – South, Ter. – Terrace, Tn – Turn, Val. – Valley, Wk – Walk

STREET NAME	SUBURB NAME	PG	GRID	
Prenton St	St James	187	CZ	27
Presence Rd	Retreat	140	CR	28
Present St	Wellington	15	AV	92
President Brand Cr.	Panorama	59	BV	42
President Brand St	Ruyterwacht	86	CA	39
President Kruger St	Paarden Eiland	83	BZ	29
President Reitz St	Ruyterwacht	86	CA	39
President St	Hillrise	61	BX	49
President Steyn St	Flintdale Est.	141	CO	31
President Steyn St	Klipkop	87	BZ	45
President Steyn St	Ruyterwacht	86	CB	40
President Swart St	Kaapzicht	59	BW	40
Prestige Dr.	Ndabeni	84	CA	32
Prestwich St	Cape Town Cen.	82	BZ	23
Prestwich St	Cape Town Cen.	82	CA	23
Pretoria	Croydon	149	CP	63
Pretorius Cr.	Morgenster	63	BT	56
Pretorius Rd	Aurora	45	BP	48
Pretorius St	Flintdale Est.	141	CO	31
Pretorius St	Rome	174	CY	73
Price Dr.	High Constantia	119	CN	23
Price St	Morgenster	63	BU	56
Prideaux Rd	Rondebosch	102	CF	31
Prieska Rd	Athlone	102	CF	33
Prieska Rd	Sybrand Pk	102	CE	33
Prieska Rd	Sybrand Pk	102	CF	33
Prima Ave	Bakoven	99	CE	19
Prima Cr.	Belrail	88	BY	49
Prima St	Broadlands	175	CZ	78
Prima Vera Cr.	Voorbrug	106	CG	50
Prima Vera Cr.	Voorbrug	106	CH	48
Primarias St	The Palms	170	CX	73
Primrose	Cloetesville	95	BZ	75
Primrose	Lentegeur (M.Plain)	144	CO	45
Primrose Ave	Claremont	120	CK	27
Primrose Cr.	Skoongesig	45	BO	50
Primrose St	Belhar	107	CD	51
Primrose St	Bridgetown	103	CG	37
Primrose St	District Six	82	CB	24
Primrose St	Groenvlei	18	BA	88
Primrose St	Hanover Pk	122	CJ	37
Primrose St	Mxolisi Phetani	125	CL	49
Primrose St	Mxolisi Phetani	125	CM	49
Primrose St	Strand Halt	170	CX	74
Primula	Lentegeur (M.Plain)	144	CP	46
Primula Ave	Wellway Pk East	46	BO	52
Primula Rd	Eersterivier	127	CL	58
Primula St	Somerset West	151	CS	71
Prince Alfred Cr.	Tafelsig (M.Plain)	145	CS	49
Prince Arthur Rd	Lansdowne	121	CJ	33
Prince Ave	Plumstead	140	CO	29
Prince Charles Rd	Flintdale Est.	141	CP	31
Prince George Dr.	Lavender Hill	159	CT	30
Prince George Dr.	Marina Da Gama	159	CU	30
Prince George Dr.	Muizenberg	159	CW	30
Prince George Dr.	Parkwood	141	CQ	31
Prince George Dr.	Plumstead	121	CN	31
Prince George Dr.	Retreat	141	CR	31
Prince George Dr.	Wynberg	120	CL	30
Prince George Dr. Service Rd	Plumstead	121	CN	31
Prince Henry Cr.	Flintdale Est.	141	CO	31
Prince Pl.	Eersterivier	128	CM	59
Prince Sq.	Claremont	120	CJ	30
Prince St	Oranjezicht	81	CC	22
Prince William St	Flintdale Est.	141	CO	31
Princes Rd	Claremont	120	CJ	30
Princess Alice Ave	Brooklyn	84	BZ	31
Princess Anne Ave	Rondebosch	101	CF	28
Princess Ave	Bishopscourt	120	CJ	27
Princess Dr.	Eersterivier	128	CM	59
Princess Margaret St	Ruyterwacht	86	CA	39
Princess Path	Pinelands	84	CC	33
Princess Rd	Fresnaye	81	CB	19
Princess Rd	Ottery	122	CL	35
Princess Rd	Retreat	140	CR	28
Princess Royal St	Flintdale Est.	141	CO	31
Princess St	Hout Bay	136	CQ	14
Princess St	Hout Bay	137	CQ	15
Princess St	Mowbray	101	CD	29
Princess St	Woodstock	82	CC	26
Princessvlei Rd	Elfindale	140	CP	30
Princessvlei Rd	Plumstead	140	CO	29
Princeton St	Helderberg Pk	175	DA	75
Pringle Cl.	Ruyterwacht	86	BZ	39
Pringle Pl.	Strandfontein	161	CT	38
Pringle Rd	Richwood	42	BQ	37
Pringle Rd	Sanddrift	57	BV	33
Pringle Rd	Tijgerhof	57	BV	33
Pringle Rd	Tijgerhof	57	BW	32
Pringle Rd	Tijgerhof	57	BX	33
Pringle Way	Edgemead	58	BU	38
Prinia Cl.	Fish Hoek	186	DA	24
Prinizia Ave	Welgedacht	60	BT	45
Prins Cr.	Bellville Sth	88	CA	49
Prins Fortuin St	William Lloyd	19	BC	92
Prins St	Groenvlei	18	BA	88
Prins St	Wellington	10	AR	93
Prinshof	Voorbrug	106	CG	50
Prinskasteel Cl.	Belle Constantia	139	CO	26
Prinsloo St	Parowvallei	87	BZ	43
Printers Way	Marconi Beam	57	BV	34
Printzia Cl.	Hout Bay	136	CO	14
Prion Way	Pelikan Pk	142	CR	35
Prior Roger Cl.	Nyanga	123	CK	42
Priory Rd	Mowbray	101	CD	30
Priscilla Cr.	Lentegeur (M.Plain)	145	CO	48
Priscilla Rd	Lentegeur (M.Plain)	145	CO	48
Priska Cl.	Portlands (M.Plain)	144	CR	46
Pritchard Steps	Fish Hoek	186	DC	24
Private Rd	Courtrai	39	BJ	87
Private Rd	Somerset West	170	CU	74
Privateer Rd	Strandfontein	162	CU	39
Privet	Eersterivier	128	CM	61
Privet Ave	Grassy Pk	141	CR	32
Privet St	Bonteheuwel	104	CE	40
Privet St	Plattekloof	60	BU	43
Pro Jack Cr.	Nonqubela	146	CO	53
Product St	Ndabeni	84	CB	31
Produksie St	Kuilsrivier Ind.	108	CD	55
Promenade Rd	Muizenberg	159	CW	29
Promenade Rd	Muizenberg Nth	159	CV	28
Proot Rd	Belhar	106	CD	49
Proot St	Avondale	60	BW	44
Proot St	Monte Vista	58	BV	38
Proot St	Monte Vista	59	BV	39
Proot St	Welgemoed	60	BU	46
Prospect Ave	Somerset West	171	CU	75
Prospect Hill Rd	Wynberg	120	CM	28
Prospect Link	Belhar	107	CD	51
Prospect Rd	Newlands	100	CH	25
Prospect Ter.	Huis-in-bos	139	CO	24
Protea	Dunoon	42	BO	37
Protea	Dunoon	42	BO	36
Protea	Franschhoek Sth	79	BZ	108
Protea	Idasvallei	95	CA	78
Protea	Lentegeur (M.Plain)	144	CP	45
Protea	Macassar	148	CR	62
Protea	Paarl	22	BD	88
Protea	Somerset West	171	CV	76
Protea	Stellenbosch	95	BY	75
Protea Ave	Belhar	106	CD	47
Protea Ave	Brantwood	89	CB	53
Protea Ave	De Kuilen	89	CB	53
Protea Ave	Fish Hoek	186	DA	24
Protea Ave	Fresnaye	81	CA	19
Protea Ave	Kommetjie	183	DC	11
Protea Ave	Sir Lowry's Pass	176	CZ	81
Protea Ave	Stanlou	61	BX	47
Protea Ave	Voelvlei	89	CA	53
Protea Cir.	Ocean View	184	DC	15
Protea Cir.	Whispering Pines	175	DC	76
Protea Cl.	Pinelands	84	CC	34
Protea Cr.	Rugby	57	BX	31
Protea Dr.	Harbour Island	178	DF	74
Protea Dr.	Harbour Island	179	DF	75
Protea Rd	Bergsig	30	BN	52
Protea Rd	Bergsig	46	BO	51
Protea Rd	Bergvliet	140	CQ	27
Protea Rd	Claremont	101	CH	28
Protea Rd	Durbanville	45	BO	50
Protea Rd	Durbanville	46	BO	51
Protea Rd	Eyethu	146	CP	53
Protea Rd	Klapmuts	35	BL	74
Protea Rd	Klapmuts	35	BM	71
Protea Rd	Klapmuts	36	BK	76
Protea Rd	Klapmuts	36	BL	77
Protea Rd	Murdock Valley	195	DL	28
Protea Rd	Philippi East	124	CL	45
Protea Rd	Protea Hoogte	63	BV	57
Protea Rd	Protea Hoogte	63	BW	56
Protea Rd	Ravensmead	87	CA	46
Protea Rd	Thornton	85	CB	37
Protea Rd	Townsend Est.	85	BZ	38
Protea St	Chapman's Peak	156	CX	16
Protea St	Kewtown	102	CE	34
Protea St	Kewtown	102	CF	34
Protea St	Kleinvlei	127	CJ	58
Protea St	Park Estates	174	CY	72
Protea St	Park Estates	174	CZ	71
Protea St	Sanddrift	57	BW	34
Protea St	Somerset West	170	CV	73
Protea St	Wellington	11	AS	95
Protea Way	Lavender Hill East	160	CU	31
Protea Way	Lavender Hill East	160	CX	33
Protem	Wesbank	107	CG	51
Proton	Tegnopark	112	CF	73
Proton Rd	Belhar	88	CC	49
Proton St	Triangle Farm	89	BZ	51
Provance Cr.	Langeberg Rdg	47	BR	55
Provence	Bel Ombre	119	CM	24
Provence	Groenvlei	18	BA	88
Provence La.	Die Bos	174	CY	74
Provident South	Avondale	87	BY	44
Provident St North	Avondale	60	BW	44
Provident St North	Avondale	60	BX	44
Province	Skilpadvlei	45	BO	49
Provinsie	Rozendal	96	CB	79
Provinsie	Uniepark	96	CB	79
Pru Way	Delft	106	CG	49
Prudence Way	Montagu's Gift	141	CP	34
Pruim Ave	Amandelrug	90	CB	56
Pruim Kring Cr.	Silvertown	103	CF	36
Pruim St	Mitchells Plain	144	CQ	44
Pruimbas Cr.	Roosendaal	107	CE	51
Prunis Cl.	Forest Hgts	127	CL	58
Prunis St	Forest Hgts	127	CL	58
Prunus	Greenlands	88	CA	49
Prunus	Lentegeur (M.Plain)	144	CP	46
Prunus Rd	Gordon Strand	179	DD	76
Prunus St	Bonteheuwel	103	CE	38
Prunus St	Bonteheuwel	104	CE	39
Prunus St	Somerset West	151	CS	71
Puca	Mbekweni	15	AV	92
Puccini	Delft Sth	125	CK	48
Puffer	Eersterivier	128	CM	59
Puffin	Seawinds	159	CU	30
Pula	Lekkerwater	184	DA	17
Pula Rd	Nyanga	124	CK	43
Puma Rd	Ocean View	184	DC	15
Puma St	Paarden Eiland	83	BZ	30
Puma St	The Hague	106	CF	50
Pumice Cr.	Ridgeworth	61	BV	50
Pungue St	Delft	106	CG	49
Punt	Wellington	10	AS	92
Punt Cl.	Flintdale Est.	140	CP	29
Punt Rd	Schaap Kraal	142	CR	38
Punt Rd	Schaap Kraal	142	CS	38
Punt Rd	Schaap Kraal	161	CT	38
Punt Rd	Strandfontein	161	CT	37
Punt St	Flintdale Est.	140	CP	29
Punters Way	Kenilworth Pk	121	CK	31
Pupil St	Strandfontein	162	CT	41
Purcell	Delft Sth	125	CK	48
Purcell Way	Bergvliet	139	CP	26
Purley St	Kenilworth	120	CJ	30
Putman St	Wesbank	107	CE	52
Putney Ave	Weltevreden Val. (M.Plain)	144	CP	43
Putney St	Kenilworth	120	CL	30
Putter Rd	Lakeside	159	CV	27
Pypie	Lentegeur (M.Plain)	145	CP	47
Pypie Cl.	Eersterivier	128	CM	59
Pyracantha St	Somerset West	151	CR	71
Pyracantha St	Somerset West	151	CR	72
Pyramid Cl.	Portlands (M.Plain)	145	CR	47
Pyramid St	Fairdale	126	CJ	54
Pyrenees	Tafelsig (M.Plain)	145	CS	49
Pyrite Rd	Belthorn Est.	122	CJ	35
Q				
Qagane Rd	Brown's Farm	123	CM	40
Qahawe St	Harare	146	CR	52
Qala Cl.	Kuyasa	147	CR	58
Qamba Cr.	Good Hope	146	CR	51
Qamba Cr.	Umrhabulo Triangle	147	CQ	57
Qamela St	Harare	146	CS	54
Qampi Cr.	Victoria Mxenge	146	CO	52
Qanda St	Umrhabulo Triangle	147	CR	56
Qaqamba St	Griffiths Mxenge	146	CQ	54
Qebengwana St	Umrhabulo Triangle	147	CP	56
Qete St	Mxolisi Phetani	125	CM	50
Qhaga St	Harare	146	CS	53
Qhama St	Harare	146	CR	53
Qhatha St	Harare	146	CS	52
Qhayiya St	Crossroads	124	CK	44
Qhekezana St	Umrhabulo Triangle	147	CQ	57
Qhekezana St	Umrhabulo Triangle	147	CQ	58
Qhela Cr.	Umrhabulo Triangle	147	CQ	57
Qhimgqoshe Rd	Philippi East	124	CL	46
Qhimgqoshe Rd	Philippi East	124	CN	46
Qhotyane Cl.	Philippi East	124	CM	46
Qhude Cr.	Joe Slovo Pk	57	BU	34
Qhude Rd	Philippi East	124	CM	46
Qhula Cr.	Harare	146	CS	53
Qhwayela Cr.	Umrhabulo Triangle	147	CP	56
Qinqa St	Harare	146	CR	54
Qobo St	Ilitha Pk	146	CQ	51
Qokelela St	Umrhabulo Triangle	147	CQ	56
Qokelwa Cr.	Victoria Mxenge	146	CO	51
Qomiliso Cr.	Nonqubela	126	CN	54
Qomoyi St	Crossroads	124	CK	45
Qonda St	Umrhabulo Triangle	147	CP	57
Qondani St	Kaya	146	CP	52
Qoqonga St	Mfuleni	126	CK	53
Quail	Seawinds	159	CU	30
Quail Rd	Montagu's Gift	141	CO	33
Quail St	Eersterivier	128	CM	60
Quality St	Maitland	84	CA	31
Quantock Rd	Sea Point	80	CA	18
Quantum	Tegnopark	112	CF	73
Quarry	Cloetesville	95	CA	75
Quarry Hill Rd	Tamboerskloof	81	CC	21
Quarry Rd	Belrail	88	BY	49
Quarry Rd	Fish Hoek	185	DA	22
Quarry Rd	Kalk Bay	186	DA	26
Quarry Rd	Simon's Town	194	DJ	24
Quarterdeck Rd	Kalk Bay	187	CZ	27
Quarterdeck Rd	St James	187	CZ	27
Quartz	Belthorn Est.	122	CJ	35
Quartz	Belthorn Est.	122	CN	36
Quartz Cl.	Sheridon Pk	159	CU	28
Quasar Cr.	Surrey	103	CG	38
Qubaka Cr.	Eyethu	146	CP	54
Quebec Rd	Camps Bay	99	CE	19
Quebel Rd	Philippi	124	CL	45
Queen Bess Rd	Lansdowne	121	CJ	32
Queen Guinevere St	Camelot	107	CF	53
Queen St	District Six	82	CB	25
Queen St	Durbanville	45	BP	50
Queen St	Mowbray	101	CD	29
Queen St	Paarl	22	BF	87
Queen St	Wellington	15	AT	93
Queen Victoria Rd	Claremont	101	CH	29
Queen Victoria Rd	Claremont	101	CH	30
Queen Victoria St	Cape Town Cen.	82	CB	23
Queens Cl.	Flintdale Est.	141	CO	31
Queens Cl.	Parklands	25	BN	34
Queens Dr.	Weltevreden Val. (M.Plain)	144	CO	43
Queens Park Ave	Salt River	83	CC	27
Queens Rd	Parklands	25	BN	34
Queens Rd	Rondebosch	101	CF	29
Queens Rd	Sea Point	80	CA	18
Queens Rd	Simon's Town	194	DJ	26
Queens Rd	Tamboerskloof	81	CB	21
Queens Rd	Woodstock	82	CB	26
Queens Way	Matroosfontein	86	CC	41
Queens Way	Pinelands	84	CB	33
Queens Way	Ruyterwacht	86	CA	39
Quellerie St	Welgemoed	61	BU	47
Quellerie St	Welgemoed	61	BU	48
Quendon Rd	Sea Point	81	CA	19
Quercus	Cloetesville	95	BY	75
Querus Ave	Vredekloof Hgts	47	BS	55
Quest Rd	Milnerton	57	BV	32
Quest Rd	Sanddrift	57	BV	34
Quick Rd	Lansdowne	121	CK	34
Quiet Cl.	Woodlands (M.Plain)	144	CQ	44
Quiet St	Claremont	101	CH	28
Quigley Rd	Tijgerhof	57	BW	33
Quinan Rd	Somerset West	170	CU	73
Quince Cr.	Noordhaven	157	CX	19
Quince La.	Sir Lowry's Pass	176	CZ	81
Quince Rd	Gordon Strand	179	DD	76
Quincy Cr.	Norwood	86	CA	41
Quincy St	Graceland	146	CP	53
Quintas	Bracken Hgts	62	BU	54
Quintus Way	The Vines	140	CO	28
Quiver St	Vredekloof Hgts	47	BS	55
Qumanco St	Mfuleni	126	CK	53
Qumatana	Mbekweni	15	AV	91
Qumba Cr.	Joe Slovo Pk	57	BV	34
Qumbra St	Mfuleni	126	CK	53
Qumra St	Mfuleni	126	CK	53
Qunube	Brown's Farm	124	CL	43
Qunube	Philippi East	125	CM	47
Qunube St	Brown's Farm	124	CL	43
Qunube St	Kuyasa	147	CS	55
Quoin Cr.	Strandfontein	162	CT	39
Ququzele St	Umrhabulo Triangle	147	CQ	57
Qwabe St	Victoria Mxenge	126	CN	51
Qwesha St	Nonqubela	126	CN	53
R				
R.First St	Mfuleni	126	CK	54
R.Sibukwe St	Hout Bay	137	CO	16
R101 (Klein Drakenstein Rd)	Rabiesdale	19	BC	91
R101 (Lady Grey St)	Lemoenkloof	18	BC	89
R101 (Old Paarl Rd)	Brackenfell	63	BU	56
R101 (Old Paarl Rd)	Kraaifontein	48	BS	59
R102 (New Market St)	District Six	82	CB	26
R102 (Old Main Rd)	Croydon	149	CQ	66
R102 (Strand Rd)	Sanlamhof	88	BY	50
R102 (Van Riebeeck Rd)	De Kuilen	89	CB	54
R102 (Van Riebeeck Rd)	Penhill	128	CK	59
R102 (Voortrekker Rd)	Salt River	83	CB	28
R27 (Marine Dr.)	Milnerton	41	BR	31
R27 (Marine Dr.)	Paarden Eiland	83	CA	28
R27 (Otto Du Plessis Dr.)	Milnerton	57	BW	31
R27 (Otto Du Plessis Dr.)	Sunningdale	25	BN	31
R27 (West Coast Rd)	Blouberg Sands	24	BK	29
R300 (Kuils River Freeway)	Kuilsrivier	89	CB	62
R300 (Kuils River Freeway)	Roosendaal	107	CF	51
R300 (Kuils River Way)	Kaymor	62	BX	54
R302 (Durban Rd)	Bellville	61	BW	49
R302 (Durbanville Ave)	Kenridge	45	BS	50
R302 (Klipheuwel Rd)	Welgevonden	30	BM	54
R302 (Wellington Rd)	Durbanville	46	BP	51
R303	Wellington	11	AR	96
R303 (Church St)	Wellington	10	AR	94
R303 (Jan van Riebeeck Rd)	Huguenot	18	BB	90
R303 (Piet Retief St)	Wellington	15	AT	93
R304	Kayamandi	94	BZ	74
R304	Klein Joostenberg	50	BO	68
R304	Koelenhof	66	BV	70
R310	Lynedoch Eco-Village	110	CH	65
R310	Pniel	71	BX	87
R310	Vlottenburg	111	CF	68
R310 (Baden Powel Dr.)	Muizenberg	159	CX	30
R310 (Baden Powell Dr.)	Eersterivier	128	CN	61
R310 (Helshoogte Rd)	Stellenbosch	95	CA	77
R312 (Lichtenburg Rd)	Fisantekraal	31	BK	57
R44	Harbour Island	178	DF	74
R44	Remhoogte	67	BV	74
R44 (Adam Tas St)	Stellenbosch	95	CC	75
R44 (Adam Tas St)	Wellington	13	AU	84
R44 (Broadway Blvd)	Somerset West	151	CP	71
R44 (Faure Marine Dr.)	Greenways	174	DA	73
R44 (Stokery Rd)	Wellington	10	AP	91
R44 (Strand)	Jamestown	112	CH	73
R45	Groot Drakenstein	71	BT	90
R45	Simondium	55	BS	88
R45 (Main)	Northern Paarl	18	AZ	88
R45 (Malmesbury Rd)	Wellington	14	AV	45
Raadt St	Sarepta	89	CB	53
Raan St	Peerless Pk East	47	BR	58
Raap St	Bellville Sth	88	CA	49
Raapenberg Rd	Mowbray	102	CD	31
Raapkraal Cr.	Kirstenhof	159	CU	27
Raapkraal Rd	Kirstenhof	159	CU	27
Raats Dr.	Table View	41	BO	31
Raats Dr.	Table View	41	BO	32

STREET NAME	SUBURB NAME	PG	GRID
Raats Dr.	Table View	41	BO 34
Raats Dr.	Table View	42	BO 35
Raats St	Brackenfell Sth	63	BX 58
Rabbi Mirvish Ave	Vredehoek	82	CC 23
Rabie St	Paarl	22	BE 88
Rabie St	Park Estates	174	CY 72
Rabinowitz St	De Zoete Inval	22	BH 88
Racaza St	Lwandle	175	CY 77
Race Course Rd	Durbanville	45	BQ 50
Race Course Rd	Lansdowne	121	CJ 32
Racecourse Rd	Marconi Beam	57	BU 34
Racecourse Rd	Milnerton	57	BT 33
Rachel Bloch Ave	Sonnedal	59	BV 42
Rachel Dick St	Cafda Village	141	CR 31
Rachel St	Avonwood	86	CB 42
Rada St	Eyethu	146	CO 52
Radar Cl.	Blouberg Sands	24	BL 30
Radar Rd	Blouberg Sands	24	BL 30
Radebe St	Sir Lowry's Pass	176	CZ 82
Radial Rd	Fairdale	126	CJ 54
Radiant Cl.	Heathfield	140	CR 29
Radloff Rd	Somerset West	170	CT 74
Radnor Rd	Parow Ind.	87	CC 45
Radyn Cl.	Strand	174	CZ 73
Radyn St	Heemstede	62	BW 53
Raeburn St	De La Haye	89	BY 51
Rael St	Tamboerskloof	81	CB 21
Rael St	Uitzicht	46	BO 54
Raft Rd	Penlyn Est.	103	CH 35
Raglan Ave	Athlone	102	CG 33
Raglan Ave	Athlone	102	CG 34
Raglan Rd	Oakdale	61	BW 48
Raglan Rd	Oakdale	61	BW 49
Rahad Way	Delft	106	CF 49
Railoun	Rusthof	174	DB 74
Railway Ave	Belrail	88	BY 49
Railway Ave	Bishop Lavis	105	CD 43
Railway Rd	Des Hampden	89	CB 53
Railway Rd	Montague Gdns Ind.	58	BT 36
Railway Rd	Montague Gdns Ind.	58	BU 36
Railway St	Bellville Sth	88	BZ 49
Railway St	Parow East	87	BY 45
Railway St	Wellington	10	AR 92
Railway St	Woodstock	83	CA 27
Railway St	Woodstock	83	CB 27
Rainbow Cl.	Marconi Beam	57	BU 34
Rainbow La.	Silvertown	103	CF 36
Rainbow St	Pelikan Pk	141	CQ 34
Rainbows End	Fairyland	19	AZ 93
Rainham La.	Woodstock	83	CC 27
Rajah Rd	Cravenby	87	CA 43
Rala Rala St	Lwandle	175	CZ 77
Raleigh	Park Estates	170	CX 71
Raleigh Rd	Mowbray	101	CD 30
Ralph Cr.	Soneike I	89	CA 54
Ralph St	Claremont	101	CH 28
Ralph St	Florida	87	CA 44
Ralph St	Florida	87	CB 44
Ralph St	Hoogstede	62	BV 53
Raluathi	Philippi East	125	CM 47
Raluathi	Philippi East	125	CK 50
Rambler Rd	Plumstead	140	CP 28
Rambler St	Beacon Valley (M.Plain)	145	CQ 47
Ramenas Cl.	Perm Gdns	127	CJ 58
Ramenas Sq.	Roosendaal	107	CF 51
Ramenas Sq.	Roosendaal	107	CG 53
Rameron Ave	Imhoff's Gift	184	DB 16
Ramokolo St	Victoria Mxenge	146	CO 52
Ramola Ave	Gatesville	103	CH 36
Ramone Ave	Riverton	86	BZ 40
Ramone Rd	Nyanga	124	CK 43
Ramphal Singh St	Cravenby	87	CB 43
Ramsey Rd	Rondebosch	101	CF 29
Ramsgate Rd	Parklands	25	BM 33
Ranch Rd	Rocklands (M.Plain)	144	CS 45
Rancke Rd	Bloubergstrand	24	BL 28
Rand	Stellenbosch	95	CB 75
Rand Park Cr.	Sunningdale	25	BM 31
Rand Rd	Blackheath Ind.	108	CG 56
Rand Rd	Chrismar	61	BW 50
Rand Rd	Heathfield	140	CR 29
Rand Rd	Vierlanden	46	BO 51
Rand St	Wellington	15	AW 93
Ranee St	Cravenby	87	CA 43
Ranelagh Rd	Claremont	101	CH 30
Ranelagh Rd	Rondebosch	102	CH 31
Ranelagh St	Oakdale	61	BW 49
Range Rd	Blackheath Ind.	108	CF 56
Range Rd	Blackheath Ind.	108	CG 56
Range Rd	Lansdowne	121	CK 33
Range Rd	Lansdowne	121	CL 33
Range Rd	The Range	86	CC 41
Range Rd	Wimbledon	108	CE 55
Ranger Cl.	Mitchells Plain	144	CQ 45
Ranger Cr.	Elfindale	140	CQ 29
Ranger Rd	Fish Hoek	185	DA 21
Ranger Rd	Fish Hoek	185	DB 22
Ranger Rd	Fish Hoek	186	DB 23
Ranisi Dr.	Joe Slovo Pk	57	BU 34
Rankals	Stellenbosch	95	BY 75
Rankie Rd	Retreat	140	CS 29
Rankin Rd	Edgemead	59	BT 39
Rankine St	Strand Halt	170	CX 74
Rankine St	Tarentaalplaas	170	CX 74
Ranksuikerbos Rd	Welgedacht	60	BT 46

STREET NAME	SUBURB NAME	PG	GRID
Ranonkel St	Firgrove	150	CR 67
Ranonkel St	Wellington	15	AT 92
Ranunculus St	Bonteheuwel	104	CE 40
Ranzadale St	Wellington	11	AS 95
Raphael Cr.	Stellenberg	62	BT 51
Raphael Cr.	Stellenberg	62	BU 51
Rapide St	Factreton	85	BY 35
Raptide	Rocklands (M.Plain)	144	CS 46
Rarabe Ave	Hout Bay	137	CO 16
Rascke	Paarlzicht	19	BB 91
Rastede Cl.	Woodbridge Island	57	BW 31
Ratanga Rd	Century City	57	BX 33
Ratanga Rd	Sanddrift	57	BV 34
Rateklip Cl.	Chapman's Peak	156	CW 15
Ratel	Sarepta	89	CC 53
Ratel Cl.	Eastridge (M.Plain)	145	CR 48
Rathfelder Ave	Bel Ombre	119	CM 24
Rathfelder Ave	Bel Ombre	119	CM 25
Rathgar Rd	Oakdale	61	BW 49
Rathmine St	Oakdale	61	BX 48
Ratling Rd	Fresnaye	81	CB 19
Rattray	Stellenbosch	95	CC 77
Ravel	Delft Sth	125	CK 48
Ravel St	Steenberg	159	CT 29
Raven Cl.	Blouberg Rise	24	BN 30
Raven St	Blouberg Rise	24	BN 30
Raven St	Grassy Pk	141	CQ 33
Raven St	West Beach	24	BN 30
Ravens Cl.	Ottery	122	CL 35
Ravensberg Ave	Newlands	101	CH 27
Ravenscourt	Parklands	25	BN 32
Ravenscourt Cl.	Parklands	25	BN 32
Ravenscraig Rd	Green Point	81	BZ 21
Ravenscraig Rd	Woodstock	82	CB 26
Ravensmead St	Ravensmead	87	CA 45
Ravensmead St West	Ravensmead	87	CB 44
Ravensteyn Rd	Bakoven	99	CF 19
Ravenswood Cl.	Parklands	25	BN 33
Ravenswood Rd	Parklands	25	BM 34
Ravenswood Rd	Parklands	25	BN 33
Ravensworth Rd	Claremont	120	CJ 29
Ravine Rd	Bantry Bay	80	CB 18
Ravine St	Tafelsig (M.Plain)	145	CR 48
Ravine Steps	Bantry Bay	80	CB 18
Ravine Steps	Fish Hoek	186	DC 24
Ravlee St	Brackenfell	63	BV 56
Rawbone Rd	Sir Lowry's Pass	176	CZ 81
Rawbone St	Green Point	81	BZ 22
Rawe Cl.	Kaya	146	CP 52
Rawson St	Observatory	83	CC 29
Ray Alexander St	Manenberg	104	CH 40
Ray Cl.	Bellville	61	BT 50
Ray Cl.	Bellville	62	BU 51
Ray St	Bishop Lavis	105	CE 44
Ray St	Macassar	149	CS 65
Ray St	Macassar	149	CS 65
Rayden St	Gardens	81	CC 22
Raymond Ackerman Ave	Kleinvlei	128	CJ 59
Raymond Ackerman Ave	Park Village	127	CK 58
Raymond Cir.	Montagu's Gift	141	CO 34
Raymond Mhlaba Cr.	Mandela Pk	146	CQ 54
Raymond St	Brackenfell Sth	63	BX 57
Rayner Rd	Surrey	103	CH 37
Raziet	Cloetesville	95	BZ 75
Reactor St	Triangle Farm	88	BY 50
Read St	Ottery East	121	CN 34
Reagon Cr.	Bridgetown	103	CE 36
Reaper Street	Summer Greens	58	BW 35
Rebecca Cl.	Langeberg Glen	47	BP 56
Rebecca Cr.	De Tuin	47	BS 56
Rebecca Cr.	Lentegeur (M.Plain)	145	CO 48
Rebus Ave	Fish Hoek	186	DB 24
Recife Cr.	Strandfontein	161	CT 38
Recreation Rd	Eikendal	48	BS 59
Recreation Rd	Fish Hoek	186	DB 24
Recreation Rd	Muizenberg	159	CX 30
Red Cross Dr.	Strandfontein	162	CU 41
Red Globe St	Wellington	15	AT 94
Red Hill Rd	Redhill	193	DJ 22
Red Hill Rd	Simon's Town	190	DH 22
Red Hill Rd	Simon's Town	191	DG 23
Red Oak La.	Green Oaks	95	BY 75
Red River Cr.	Manenberg	123	CJ 39
Red River St	Manenberg	123	CJ 39
Red River Wk	Manenberg	123	CJ 39
Red Roman Way	Marina Da Gama	159	CU 29
Red Rose	Wimbledon	108	CG 55
Redberry Cl.	Bonteheuwel	104	CF 39
Redberry St	Bonteheuwel	104	CE 39
Redcliffe	Parklands	25	BN 33
Redcliffe Cl.	Parklands	25	BN 32
Redcliffe Cr.	Sunningdale	25	BM 31
Reddam Ave	Westlake Est.	158	CT 24
Reddy Ave	Grassy Pk	141	CQ 32
Reddy Ave	Grassy Pk	141	CQ 32
Redgum	Rosedale	128	CL 59
Redgum Ave	Thornton	85	CA 37
Redgum Rd	Bonteheuwel	104	CE 39
Redhawk	Pelikan Pk	142	CQ 35
Redlands Rd	Milnerton	57	BV 32
Redpoll St	Rondebosch East	102	CH 32
Redthorn St	Bonteheuwel	104	CE 39
Redwood Cl.	Belhar	88	CC 47
Redwood Cl.	Edenpark	62	BU 54
Redwood Cl.	Northpine	63	BU 58

STREET NAME	SUBURB NAME	PG	GRID
Redwood Rd	Weltevreden Val. (M.Plain)	144	CO 43
Redwood St	Bellair	62	BW 52
Reeb Rd	Macassar	149	CS 66
Reeb Rd	Macassar	168	CT 66
Reed St	Belhar	106	CD 49
Reed St	Belrail	88	BY 49
Reef Rd	Vanguard	103	CG 38
Reen Ave	Newfields	103	CH 37
Reenberg Rd	Bishop Lavis	104	CE 42
Reenen Ct	Edgemead	59	BT 39
Reenen La.	Table View	41	BP 33
Reenen La.	Table View	41	BQ 33
Refinery Rd	Paarden Eiland	83	BZ 28
Reform Cl.	Belhar	107	CD 51
Reform Rd	Rondebosch	101	CG 28
Reform St	District Six	82	CB 24
Regan Cl.	Bishop Lavis	104	CE 41
Regency Cl.	Plattekloof Village	59	BT 42
Regency Cr.	Plattekloof Village	59	BT 41
Regent Circus	Tamboerskloof	81	CB 21
Regent Rd	Parklands	25	BN 33
Regent Rd	Parklands	41	BO 33
Regent Sq.	Woodstock	83	CB 27
Regent St	Durbanville	45	BP 49
Regent St	Klippiesdal	19	BC 91
Regent St	Malibu Village	127	CK 55
Regent St	Sea Point	81	CA 19
Regent St	Wellington	10	AR 92
Regent St	Weltevreden Val. (M.Plain)	143	CO 42
Regent St	Woodstock	83	CB 27
Regents Park Dr.	Noordhoek Manor	157	CX 21
Reggie Hadebe	Weltevreden Val. (M.Plain)	123	CN 42
Regiment Way	Door De Kraal	61	BT 47
Regina Way	Pinelands	85	CB 35
Regis Green	Summer Greens	58	BV 36
Regis Rd	Frogmore Est.	159	CU 28
Reid St East	Fairfield	60	BX 44
Reid St West	Fairfield	60	BX 44
Reids Way	Simon's Town	191	DF 24
Reier St	Okavango Pk	63	BT 57
Reiger Ave	Somerset West	171	CU 77
Reiger Rd	Ruyterwacht	86	BZ 39
Reiger Rd	Stellenberg	62	BU 51
Reigersdal Rd	Plattekloof Glen	59	BW 40
Reijger Ave	Belhar	106	CD 50
Reijger Cr.	Belhar	106	CD 50
Reindeer	Wesbank	107	CF 52
Reinders St	Wellington	11	AR 95
Reinhardt Moolman Cl.	Parow Nth	59	BX 42
Reits	Morgenster Hoogte	63	BT 56
Reitz Cl.	Somerset Pk	171	CW 75
Reitz Rd	Tijgerhof	57	BW 33
Reitz St	Northern Paarl	18	AY 89
Reitz St	Parow Nth	59	BW 42
Reitz St	Somerset Pk	171	CW 75
Reitz St	Somerset West	170	CU 74
Reitz St	Somerset West	170	CV 74
Rembrandt Ave	De La Haye	62	BX 51
Rembrandt Ave	De La Haye	89	BY 51
Rembrandt Ave	Macassar	149	CS 66
Rembrandt Cr.	De Duin	59	BV 41
Rembrandt Cr.	Forest Glade	128	CK 59
Rembrandt Cr.	Malibu Village	127	CJ 55
Rembrandt Rd	Claremont	102	CH 31
Rembrandt Rd	Somerset West	151	CR 74
Rembrandt Rd	Somerset West	152	CR 75
Rembrandt Rd	Sonstraal	46	BR 52
Rembrandt Rd	Welcome	103	CF 38
Rembrandt St	Scottsville	47	BS 57
Remhoogte Rd	Somerset West	150	CS 70
Remhoogte St	Voorbrug	106	CG 50
Remington Cr.	Jagtershof	108	CD 57
Remington Rd	Wynberg	120	CL 28
Remus St	Somerset West	171	CV 77
Remus St	Strandfontein	163	CT 43
Renche St	Somerset West	151	CS 74
Rendevous Cr.	Voorbrug	106	CG 50
Rendezvous St	Somerset West	151	CR 71
Rene St	Courtrai	22	BH 87
Rene St	De Tijger	60	BW 44
Reneé Ave	Flintdale Est.	141	CP 31
Renee Cl.	Bellville	62	BV 51
Renfrew Cl.	Heathfield	140	CQ 29
Renfrew St	Athlone	102	CF 32
Renoir St	Labiance	89	BZ 52
Renoster Cr.	Eastridge (M.Plain)	145	CR 48
Renoster Rd	Manenberg	123	CJ 39
Renoster St	Delft	106	CG 49
Renoster Wk	Manenberg	123	CJ 39
Renosterbos	Lentegeur (M.Plain)	145	CO 47
Renosterbos Pl.	Leonsdale	86	CA 41
Renosterbos Pl.	Leonsdale	86	BZ 41
Renostervoël Rd	Somerset West	170	CT 72
Rens St	Onverwacht	174	CZ 73
Rentia St	Northern Paarl	18	AZ 89
Repens	Anesta	113	CF 75
Repulse Rd	Belgravia	102	CH 34
Repulse Rd	Penlyn Est.	103	CH 35
Repulse Rd	Penlyn Est.	103	CH 36
Resandon Ave	Fresnaye	81	CA 19
Reservoir Rd	Kenridge Hgts	45	BS 49
Reservoir Rd	Somerset Pk	171	CW 75
Reservoir Rd	Somerset West	171	CT 76
Reservoir Rd	Somerset West	171	CT 77
Reservoir St	Brackenfell Sth	63	BW 58

STREET NAME	SUBURB NAME	PG	GRID
Reservoir St	Franschhoek Sth	79	BZ 107
Reservoir St	Franschhoek Sth	79	BZ 108
Reservoir St	Ruwari	63	BV 57
Reservoir St	Ruwari	63	BV 58
Residence Rd	Rondebosch	101	CE 28
Residence Rd	Rondebosch	101	CF 28
Residentia Ave	Somerset West	171	CT 78
Resthaven Dr.	Tokai	139	CS 26
Restia Cl.	Gordon Hgts	179	DE 78
Restio	Stellenbosch	95	BY 75
Restio Cl.	The Lakes	184	CZ 18
Restio Cr.	Westlake Est.	158	CU 25
Restio Rd	Big Bay	24	BK 28
Restio Rd	Hout Bay	117	CN 18
Reston Way	Edgemead	58	BU 38
Retief La.	Fish Hoek	186	DB 23
Retief St	Northern Paarl	18	AY 89
Retief St	Northern Paarl	18	AZ 88
Retief St	Sunray	62	BX 49
Retreat	Kayamandi	94	CA 74
Retreat Rd	Cafda Village	141	CR 31
Retreat Rd	Retreat	140	CR 30
Retreat Rd	Retreat	140	CS 29
Retzia Rd	Hohelzen	61	BV 47
Reuben Kaye Rd	Parow Ind.	105	CD 45
Reunion Mews	Capri	185	DB 19
Reuter St	Kalkfontein II	107	CD 53
Reuter St	Sarepta	89	CB 53
Rev.Calata Cr.	Mandela Pk	147	CQ 56
Rev.Marawu Cr.	Mandela Pk	147	CQ 55
Rev.Stofile St	Mandela Pk	146	CQ 54
Revel Fox Cl.	Gugulethu	123	CJ 41
Rex St	Somerset West	171	CV 77
Reyger	Simonswyk	95	CB 78
Reyger Rd	Thornton	85	CB 37
Reyger St	Bothasig	58	BT 37
Reygersdal Ave	Strandfontein	163	CT 43
Reygersdal Cl.	Strandfontein	163	CT 44
Reygersdal St	Dennemere	108	CH 57
Reyneke St	Lemoenkloof	18	BC 88
Reynolds St	De La Haye	61	BX 50
Rhaboksberg St	Tafelsig (M.Plain)	145	CR 49
Rhadu St	Bloekombos	49	BQ 63
Rhanisi Rd	Philippi East	125	CL 47
Rhapsody St	Dalvale	19	AZ 92
Rhapsody St	Dalvale	19	BA 94
Rheazicht Rd	Ridgeworth	61	BV 50
Rhebok Cl.	Loevenstein	60	BW 46
Rheebok Cr.	Scottsdene	64	BT 60
Rheebok St	Scottsdene	64	BT 59
Rheebok St	Wellington	9	AS 90
Rheede La.	Flamingo Vlei	41	BP 33
Rheede St	Gardens	81	CB 22
Rheede St	Welgemoed	60	BV 46
Rheezicht	Karindal	96	CC 79
Rheezicht	Pinelands	85	CC 35
Rheezicht Cl.	Mitchells Plain	144	CQ 45
Rhemus St	Joe Slovo Pk	57	BU 34
Rhemus St	Joe Slovo Pk	57	BU 31
Rhenius Rd	Bishop Lavis	105	CD 43
Rhigala St	Bloekombos	48	BQ 62
Rhine Cl.	Portlands (M.Plain)	144	CQ 46
Rhine Rd	Bishop Lavis	104	CD 41
Rhine Rd	Eindhoven	106	CH 50
Rhine Rd	Sea Point	81	BZ 20
Rhino St	Ocean View	184	DC 15
Rhintyela St	Umrhabulo Triangle	147	CQ 57
Rhoda St	Rome	170	CX 73
Rhode	Cloetesville	95	BY 75
Rhode Vos Rd	Hout Bay Harbour	136	CR 14
Rhodes	Kenridge	45	BS 48
Rhodes Ave	Mowbray	101	CD 29
Rhodes Ave	Newlands	100	CH 26
Rhodes Ave	Woodstock	83	CC 27
Rhodes Cl.	Belhar	106	CD 49
Rhodes Dr.	Bel Ombre	119	CL 23
Rhodes Dr.	Bishopscourt	119	CJ 25
Rhodes Dr.	Glen Alpine	118	CM 21
Rhodes Dr.	Mowbray	101	CE 28
Rhodes North	Die Boord	113	CE 75
Rhodes South	Fairways	113	CE 75
Rhodes St	Goodwood Est.	59	BX 39
Rhodes St	Goodwood Est.	86	BY 39
Rhodes St	Langa	103	CD 36
Rhodes St	Somerset West	171	CW 75
Rhodesia Rd	Muizenberg	159	CX 29
Rhodesia St	Woodstock	83	CB 27
Rhone	Pinelands	85	CC 35
Rhone Cl.	Die Bos	174	CY 74
Rhone St	Lemoenkloof	18	BB 89
Rhone Way	Manenberg	122	CJ 38
Rhone Way	Mitchells Plain	144	CQ 44
Rhos St	Stanlou	61	BX 47
Rhus St	Gordon Hgts	179	DE 78
Rhynheath Way	Elfindale	140	CQ 30
Ria Ave	Brackenfell	63	BV 57
Ria St	Bonnie Brae	47	BP 57
Rialto	Century City	57	BX 33
Riana St	Brackenfell Sth	63	BX 58
Ribbok Rd	Uitzicht	46	BO 54
Ribbok St	Eastridge (M.Plain)	145	CR 48
Ribbok St	New Orleans	19	BB 92
Ribbok St	Ruwari	63	BV 57
Ribbok St	Somerset Hgts	127	CJ 57
Ribbok St	Soneike II	89	BZ 54

Abbreviations used: Ave – Avenue, A.H. – Agricultural Holding, A.L.– Algemene Landgoed, Blvd – Boulevard, Cen. – Central, Cir. – Circle, Cl. – Close, Cr. – Crescent, Ct – Court, Dr. – Drive, Est. – Estate, Ext. – Extension, Hgts – Heights, Ind. – Industrial, Gdns – Gardens, Gr. – Grove, La. – Lane, (M.Plain) - Mitchells Plain, Nth – North, Pl. – Place, Pk – Park, Rd – Road, Rdg. – Ridge, S.H.– Small Holding, Sq. – Square, St – Street, Sth – South, Ter. – Terrace, Tn – Turn, Val. – Valley, Wk – Walk

STREET NAME	SUBURB NAME	PG	GRID	
Ribbok Way	Fish Hoek	186	DB	24
Ribbokskloof Cl.	Mitchells Plain	144	CR	45
Ribbokskloof Cl.	Mitchells Plain	144	CS	43
Rica Louw Ave	Barbarossa	140	CO	28
Ricardo Rd	Lansdowne	121	CJ	34
Rice La.	Fish Hoek	186	DB	23
Rice St	William Lloyd	23	BD	92
Richard Allen St	Adriaanse	87	CC	43
Richard Cr.	Valhalla Pk	104	CE	41
Richard Lakey Rd	Lotus River	141	CQ	34
Richard Rd	Sunnydale	185	DA	19
Richard Ridgill Ave	Sir Lowry's Pass	176	CZ	81
Richard St	Groenvlei	18	BA	88
Richard St	Morgenster Hoogte	63	BT	55
Richelieu St	Courtrai	22	BH	87
Richelieu St	Everglen	45	BS	50
Richelieu St	Eversdal Hgts	61	BT	50
Richelieu St	Wellington	10	AR	94
Richelieu St	Wellington	11	AR	95
Richmond	Noordhoek Manor	157	CX	21
Richmond Ave	Elriche	18	BB	90
Richmond Ave	Pinelands	84	CB	34
Richmond Cl.	Edgemead	58	BU	38
Richmond Cl.	Sweet Valley	139	CQ	26
Richmond La.	Capricorn	159	CW	30
Richmond Pl.	West Beach	24	BN	30
Richmond Rd	Kenilworth	120	CK	29
Richmond Rd	Mowbray	101	CD	30
Richmond Rd	Oakdale	61	BW	49
Richmond Rd	Three Anchor Bay	81	BY	21
Richmond Rd	West Beach	24	BN	30
Richmond St	Nomzano	175	CY	76
Richmond St	Richmond Est.	59	BX	40
Richmond St	Richmond Est.	86	BY	40
Richmond St	Ruyterwacht	86	CA	39
Richmond Way	Sweet Valley	139	CQ	26
Richter Ave	Somerset West	151	CS	72
Richter Ave	Wellington	15	AT	94
Richter St	Uitzicht	47	BO	55
Richwood Ave	Richwood	42	BP	38
Richwood Cr.	Wesbank	107	CF	52
Rickard La.	Fish Hoek	186	DB	23
Ricketts Cl.	Simon's Town	194	DJ	24
Ricketts Rd	Clamhall	60	BX	43
Ridderspoor	Blomtuin	62	BW	51
Rider Haggard St	Tijgerhof	57	BW	32
Riders Green	Summer Greens	58	BW	36
Ridge Ct	Rocklands (M.Plain)	144	CS	45
Ridge La.	Somerset West	152	CS	77
Ridge Rd	Bergsig	46	BO	51
Ridge Rd	Langeberg Rdg	47	BR	56
Ridge Rd	Langeberg Rdg	47	BQ	56
Ridge St	Tafelsig (M.Plain)	145	CR	48
Ridge Way	Pinelands	84	CC	33
Ridge Way	Townsend Est.	58	BX	37
Ridge Wk	Hohenort	119	CK	24
Ridgedale Cr.	Airlie	139	CP	25
Ridgemoor St	Voorbrug	106	CG	50
Ridgeview Cl.	Northpine	63	BU	58
Ridgeworth Dr.	Ridgeworth	61	BU	49
Ridgeworth Dr.	Ridgeworth	61	BV	50
Ridgill La.	Somerset West	171	CV	75
Riebeeck St	Wynberg	120	CL	28
Riebeek Cl.	Tygerdal	59	BX	39
Riebeek La.	Cape Town Cen.	82	CA	23
Riebeek St	Belhar	106	CD	50
Riebeek St	Cape Town Cen.	82	CA	23
Riebeek St	Goodwood Est.	59	BX	39
Riebeek St	Goodwood Est.	86	BY	39
Riebeek St	Tygerdal	59	BX	39
Riesling	Durmonte	30	BN	53
Riesling	Fairways	113	CE	75
Riesling Rd	Saxenburg Ind. Pk	108	CE	57
Riesling Rd	The Vines	140	CO	27
Riesling St	Normandie	64	BW	59
Riesling St	Oude Westhof	60	BT	45
Riesling St	Paarl	22	BE	88
Riesling St	Somerset West	151	CR	71
Riesling St	Wellington	15	AT	94
Riet Cl.	Delft	106	CG	49
Riet St	Die Oude Spruit	63	BX	56
Riet St	Eersterivier	128	CM	59
Rietbok Ave	Lotus River	142	CQ	35
Rietbok Cr.	Eastridge (M.Plain)	145	CR	48
Rietbok Rd	Langeberg Rdg	47	BR	56
Rietbok St	Durbanville	45	BQ	49
Rietbok St	New Orleans	19	BB	92
Rietbok St	Soneike II	89	BZ	54
Riethaan	Rocklands (M.Plain)	144	CS	44
Rietpoel	Wesbank	107	CG	51
Rietpoel	Wesbank	107	CG	52
Rietvlei Ave	Bothasig	43	BS	39
Rietvlei Rd	Sarepta	89	CB	53
Riffel Cl.	Franschhoek Nth	75	BW	105
Rifle Range Rd	Thornton	85	CA	36
Rifle Range Rd	Thornton	85	CB	36
Rifle Rd	Lansdowne	121	CL	33
Rifstone Rd	Lavender Hill	160	CT	31
Rigel Rd	Lansdowne	121	CK	34
Rigel Rd	Ocean View	184	DC	15
Rigel St	Somerset West	171	CV	77
Rigoletto Cl.	Scottsdene	64	BT	59
Rigoletto Cr.	Eastridge (M.Plain)	145	CQ	49
Rijswijk St	Malibu Village	127	CJ	56
Riley Cr.	Beacon Valley (M.Plain)	145	CQ	48
Riley St	Beaconvale	87	CA	44
Riley St	Klipkop	87	BZ	45
Riley St	Parowvallei	87	CA	43
Rimini St	Morgenster Hoogte	63	BT	56
Ring	Airport Ind.	105	CG	44
Ring	Airport Ind.	105	CG	44
Ring	Airport Ind.	105	CG	44
Ring Ave	Macassar	149	CS	64
Ring Ave	Macassar	168	CT	64
Ring Cr.	Penlyn Est.	122	CJ	36
Ring Cr.	Sonnekuil	89	CA	53
Ring Rd	Refinery	42	BR	38
Ring Rd	Refinery	42	BS	38
Ring Rd	Refinery	43	BR	39
Ring Rd	Refinery	43	BS	39
Ringwood Cl.	Bel Ombre	119	CM	24
Ringwood Dr.	Parklands	25	BM	33
Ringwood Dr.	Parklands	25	BN	32
Ringwood Dr.	Pinelands	84	CC	34
Ringwood Dr.	Pinelands	85	CB	35
Ringwood Dr.	Pinelands	85	CC	35
Ringwood Dr.	Pinelands	102	CD	34
Ringwood St	Wesbank	107	CE	52
Rinquest	William Lloyd	23	BD	92
Rio Ave	Malibu Village	127	CK	55
Rio Ave	Malibu Village	127	CL	56
Rio Grande St	Manenberg	123	CJ	39
Rio Grande St	Manenberg	123	CK	39
Rio Grande Wk	Manenberg	123	CJ	39
Rio Grande Wk	Manenberg	123	CM	39
Riparia St	Groenvlei	18	BA	88
Ripelby Rd	Claremont	120	CJ	28
Ripple Cl.	Rondebosch	101	CG	27
Risedale	Highbury	107	CE	54
Risedale	Paarl	22	BE	88
Risi Rd	Fish Hoek	185	DA	21
Rispel St	Kylemore	97	BZ	86
Rissik Cl.	Brackenfell Sth	63	BX	57
Rissik St	Beaconvale	87	CA	43
Rissik St	Parowvallei	87	BZ	43
Rita St	Montagu's Gift	141	CO	34
Rita St	Tafelsig (M.Plain)	145	CS	50
Ritchie Ave	Kenilworth	120	CK	30
Ritchie St	Woodstock	83	CC	27
Ritter St	Strand	174	CZ	73
Ritters Rd	Belthorn Est.	121	CJ	34
River Cl.	Meadowsteads	156	CX	18
River Cr.	Eersterivier	128	CL	59
River Rd	Bishop Lavis	104	CD	41
River Rd	Paarl	23	BD	94
River Sands	Fish Hoek	186	DA	25
River St	Brooklyn	83	BZ	30
River St	Rosebank	101	CE	30
Riverine Cl.	Parklands	25	BN	34
Rivers Edge Cl.	Sunridge	42	BP	35
Rivers End Rd	Plumstead	120	CN	28
Riversdale Cl.	Portlands (M.Plain)	144	CS	46
Riversdale Rd	Brooklyn	83	BY	30
Riversdale Rd	Crawford	102	CH	33
Riversdale Rd	Crawford	121	CJ	33
Riversdale Way	Portlands (M.Plain)	144	CS	46
Riverside	Fish Hoek	186	DA	24
Riverside Ave	Winslow	179	DD	77
Riverside Cl.	Westlake	159	CU	27
Riverside Cl.	Westlake	159	CW	27
Riverside Dr.	Kommetjie	183	DB	13
Riverside Dr.	Milnerton	57	BV	32
Riverside Rd	Bishopscourt	119	CJ	26
Riverside Rd	Fish Hoek	185	DA	22
Riverside Rd	Lansdowne	102	CH	32
Riverside Rd	Lotus River	142	CQ	35
Riverside Rd	Peers Hill	185	DA	22
Riverside Rd	Pinelands	102	CD	33
Riverside Rd	Rondebosch	101	CF	29
Riverside Rd	Somerset West	171	CV	75
Riverside St	Kylemore	97	BZ	86
Riverside St	William Lloyd	23	BD	94
Riverside Ter.	Hout Bay	117	CN	16
Riverstone	Hout Bay	137	CP	17
Riverstone	Hout Bay	137	CQ	17
Riverstone Rd	Wynberg	120	CK	28
Riverton Cl.	Riverton	86	BZ	40
Riverton Cl.	Rondebosch	102	CG	31
Riverton Cr.	Riverton	86	BZ	40
Riverton Cr.	Ruyterwacht	86	BZ	39
Riverton Rd	Rondebosch	102	CF	31
Riverton Rd	Rondebosch	102	CG	31
Riverton Rd	Somerset West	170	CW	72
Riverton St	Des Hampden	89	CB	53
Riviera Rd	Claremont	120	CJ	28
Riviera Way	Portlands (M.Plain)	145	CR	47
Riviersonderend St	Eersterivier	128	CN	59
Riviersonderend St	Eersterivier	128	CJ	61
Roan Ave	Hout Bay	118	CM	19
Roan Rd	Lotus River	142	CQ	35
Roath St	Lansdowne	121	CK	32
Rob St	Macassar	149	CS	64
Robbie Robertson La.	Boschenmeer Est.	22	BG	90
Robbie St	Brackenfell Sth	63	BX	58
Robert Ave	Lotus River	141	CP	34
Robert Baloi St	Kuyasa	147	CS	55
Robert Carr Ave	Dennedal	139	CS	26
Robert McBride St	Mandela Pk	146	CQ	54
Robert Rd	Windsor Pk	47	BS	56
Robert Sobukhwe	Weltevreden Val. (M.Plain)	123	CN	42
Robert St	Gaylee	108	CG	57
Robert St	St Dumas	90	CC	56
Roberts Ave	Ravensmead	87	CA	44
Roberts Rd	Woodstock	83	CB	27
Robertson La.	Retreat	140	CS	29
Robertson Rd	Brooklyn	83	BZ	30
Robertson St	Glenlily	87	BY	43
Robertson St	Mountain View	19	BB	91
Robertsvlei Rd	Franschhoek	78	BZ	103
Robertsvlei Rd	Franschhoek	78	CB	105
Robertsvlei Rd	Franschhoek Nth	74	BW	102
Robertsvlei Rd	Franschhoek Sth	79	CA	107
Robertsz	Brandwacht	113	CE	76
Robin	Rocklands (M.Plain)	144	CS	45
Robin Cir.	Ocean View	184	DC	15
Robin Cr.	Penlyn Est.	103	CH	36
Robin Ct	Bridgetown	103	CE	36
Robin La.	Bergvliet	140	CQ	27
Robin Rd	Bishop Lavis	105	CE	43
Robin Rd	Langeberg Rdg	47	BR	56
Robin Rd	Milnerton	57	BV	32
Robin Rd	Montagu's Gift	141	CO	32
Robin St	Kleinvlei	127	CJ	58
Robin St	Somerset West	152	CS	76
Robin St	Valhalla Pk	104	CE	41
Robina Rd	Gordon Strand	179	DD	76
Robindale	Pinelands	102	CD	34
Robins Rd	Observatory	83	CC	28
Robinson Ave	Bishopscourt	119	CJ	26
Robinson Ave	Hout Bay	116	CM	14
Robinson Cr.	Tafelsig (M.Plain)	145	CS	49
Robinson Rd	Kenilworth	120	CK	29
Robinson St	Vergesig	45	BQ	48
Robinson Way	Edgemead	58	BT	38
Robor Cr.	Mowbray	102	CE	31
Robsend St	The Crest	46	BO	53
Robyn Cr.	Welgelegen	59	BT	40
Robyn Park Cl.	Langeberg Rdg	47	BR	55
Robyn Rd	Langeberg Rdg	47	BR	55
Robyn Rd	Langeberg Rdg	47	BR	56
Robyn St	Forest Hgts	127	CL	58
Robyn St	Morgenster Hoogte	63	BT	55
Rocastle Cl.	Highbury	107	CD	54
Rochea	Hout Bay	136	CO	14
Rochefort Cl.	La Rochelle	62	BV	51
Rochefort Cl.	La Rochelle	62	BX	52
Rochefort Pl.	Somerset West	170	CT	74
Rochelle Way	Northpine	64	BU	59
Rochester La.	Heathfield	140	CQ	29
Rochester Rd	Observatory	83	CB	28
Rochester Rd	Philippi	124	CL	45
Rochester Rd	Sea Point	80	CA	19
Rochester Rd	West Beach	24	BM	29
Rock Pigeon Cr.	Steenberg	158	CT	24
Rockcliff Cr.	Bantry Bay	80	CA	18
Rockcliff Cr.	Bantry Bay	80	CA	17
Rockdale Ct	Ocean View	184	DC	15
Rocket La.	Thembokwezi	125	CL	49
Rockford Rd	Lansdowne	121	CK	33
Rockford Rd	Lotus River	141	CQ	34
Rockhill Way	Retreat	159	CT	29
Rockies Cir.	Tafelsig (M.Plain)	145	CS	47
Rockies Cr.	Tafelsig (M.Plain)	145	CS	48
Rocklands Ave	Vredehoek	100	CD	23
Rocklands Cl.	Murdock Valley	195	DL	28
Rocklands Rd	Murdock Valley	195	DL	28
Rocklands Rd	Murdock Valley	195	DM	28
Rocklands Rd	Sea Point	81	BZ	20
Rockley Rd	Wynberg	120	CM	29
Rocktree Cl.	Sonstraal Hgts	46	BQ	54
Rocky	Eersterivier	128	CL	59
Rocky Cl.	Salberau	86	CA	41
Rocky Way	Milnerton	57	BT	33
Rod La.	Lotus River	142	CP	35
Rodded Rd	Scottsdene	64	BU	59
Roderick Way	Gaylands	139	CO	25
Rodger St	Durbanville	46	BQ	51
Rodgers Ave	Fir Grove	139	CQ	25
Rodgers St	Wellington	15	AU	92
Roding Cl.	Epping Forest	86	CB	41
Rodney St	Russel's Rest	128	CL	59
Rodwell Rd	St James	187	CZ	28
Roela	Welgedacht	60	BT	45
Roeland St	Gardens	82	CB	23
Roeland Ter.	Cape Town Cen.	82	CB	23
Roella Cl.	Perm Gdns	128	CJ	59
Roella Cl.	Perm Gdns	128	CJ	60
Roelofse St	The Palms	170	CX	73
Roer	Jagtershof	90	CC	57
Roger St	Gaylee	108	CH	57
Roger St East	District Six	82	CB	25
Rogers St	Danena	61	BU	49
Roggebaai Sq.	Cape Town Cen.	82	CA	24
Roggeberg Rd	Heideveld	104	CG	40
Roggeberg Rd	Heideveld	104	CF	42
Roggeland Rd	Wellington	15	AX	93
Rogland St	Morgenster Hoogte	63	BT	55
Rogland St	Morgenster Hoogte	63	BT	56
Rogland St	Morgenster Hoogte	63	BU	55
Rohm Rd	Goodwood Est.	85	BY	37
Rohm Rd	Goodwood Est.	85	BY	38
Rohrer St	Protea Hoogte	63	BW	57
Rokeby Rd	Crawford	102	CH	33
Rokeby Rd	Crawford	121	CJ	33
Roker Cl.	Blackheath Ind.	108	CG	57
Rokewood	Die Boord	112	CD	74
Rokewood	Die Boord	113	CD	75
Rolbal Cr.	Beacon Valley (M.Plain)	145	CP	47
Rolbal Cr.	Beacon Valley (M.Plain)	145	CP	48
Rolen Cr.	Belgravia	103	CG	35
Rolfontien Rd	Edgemead	58	BU	38
Rolihlahla Cr.	Crossroads	124	CK	44
Rolinda Cr.	Jamestown	112	CH	74
Rolisusu Cr.	Nonqubela	126	CN	52
Roma Ct.	Dennemere	108	CH	58
Romainhof St	Northpine	63	BU	58
Romainhof St	Northpine	63	BV	56
Roman La.	Hout Bay Harbour	136	CR	13
Roman Pl.	Woodlands (M.Plain)	144	CP	45
Roman Rd	Eersterivier	128	CM	60
Roman Rd	Observatory	83	CC	28
Roman Rd	Skoongesig	45	BO	50
Romany Wk	Fir Grove	139	CQ	24
Rome Cl.	Eikenbosch	90	CC	57
Romelia Cr.	Blue Downs	127	CJ	56
Romelia Cr.	Blue Downs	127	CJ	56
Romelia Way	Plattekloof Glen	59	BW	40
Romeo St	Fisantekraal	32	BJ	59
Romney Rd	Green Point	81	BZ	21
Romney St	De La Haye	89	BY	51
Rompe St	Lansdowne	121	CK	33
Romulus St	Joe Slovo Pk	57	BU	31
Romulus St	Joe Slovo Pk	57	BU	34
Romulus St	Somerset West	171	CV	77
Romulus St	Somerset West	171	CW	77
Romulus St	Strandfontein	163	CT	43
Ronald Rd	Camps Bay	98	CE	18
Rondeberg Cr.	Bonnie Brae	47	BP	57
Rondeberg Rd	Bishop Lavis	105	CE	43
Rondeberg Rd	Heideveld	104	CG	39
Rondeberg Rd	Heideveld	104	CF	42
Rondevallei Rd	Rondevallei	107	CE	53
Ronell Cr.	Plumstead	140	CP	29
Ronelle St	Brackenfell Sth	63	BX	57
Ronleigh Rd	Muizenberg	159	CX	29
Rontree Ave	Bakoven	98	CF	18
Rontree Cl.	Bakoven	98	CF	18
Roodeberg Ave	KWV	22	BF	88
Roodeberg St	Tafelsig (M.Plain)	145	CS	49
Roodebloem Rd	Woodstock	83	CB	27
Roodebloem Rd	Woodstock	83	CC	27
Roodehek St	Gardens	82	CB	23
Roodehek St	Voorbrug	106	CG	50
Roodekrans St	Somerset West	170	CT	71
Roodekranz Rd	Townsend Est.	58	BX	38
Roodezand Rd	Belhar	106	CD	50
Roodt	Aurora	45	BO	49
Rooi Cl.	Bloekombos	49	BR	63
Rooi Els Ave	New Orleans	18	BA	90
Rooibekkie	Joostenberg	48	BQ	60
Rooiberg	Wellington	15	AV	91
Rooiberg	Wellington	15	AT	94
Rooiberg Cr.	Bonnie Brae	47	BP	57
Rooiberg Cr.	Greenfield	127	CJ	56
Rooiberg Cr.	Heideveld	104	CF	39
Rooibok St	Scarborough	192	DK	18
Rooibok St	Soneike II	89	BZ	54
Rooibok St	Wellington	15	AU	92
Rooibok St	Wellington	15	AU	94
Rooiborsie St	Amstelhof	23	BD	93
Rooiels	Delft Sth	125	CJ	50
Rooiels Cl.	Plattekloof	60	BV	43
Rooiels Cr.	Bay Pk	175	DC	76
Rooiels Rd	Bonteheuwel	104	CE	39
Rooiels Rd	Noordhoek	156	CW	18
Rooiels St	Blommendal	62	BW	51
Rooihout Rd	Bonteheuwel	104	CE	39
Rooikappie Cl.	Roosendaal	107	CF	51
Rooikaree St	Springbok Pk	62	BV	54
Rooikat Cl.	Eastridge (M.Plain)	145	CR	48
Rooikrans	Lentegeur (M.Plain)	144	CO	46
Rooikrans	Simonswyk	95	CB	78
Rooikrans	Thornton	85	CA	36
Rooikrans Ave	New Orleans	19	BB	91
Rooikrans Rd	Firgrove	150	CR	67
Rooikrans Rd	Firgrove	150	CS	67
Rooikrans Rd	Muizenberg Nth	159	CV	28
Rooikrans Rd	Pelikan Pk	141	CR	33
Rooikrans St	Ruwari	63	BV	58
Rooikrantz St	St Dumas	90	CC	56
Rooipeper	Arbeidslus	96	CA	80
Rooisuikerkan St	Bellville Ext. 53	60	BU	46
Rooivalk Cl.	D'urbanvale	29	BN	48
Roome Cr.	Bishop Lavis	105	CD	43
Roome Rd	Brooklyn	84	BY	31
Roos Cl.	Brackenfell Sth	90	BY	57
Roos Rd	Lavender Hill	160	CT	31
Roos Rd	Sea Point	81	BZ	21
Roos St	Anchorage Pk	179	DD	77
Roos St	Winslow	179	DD	77
Rooseboom St	Bothasig	42	BS	37
Roosendaal Rd	Roosendaal	106	CF	50
Roosendaal Rd	Roosendaal	107	CE	51
Roosendaal Rd	Roosendaal	107	CF	51
Roosevelt Rd	Claremont	102	CH	31
Roosevelt St	Dal Josafat Ind.	22	BD	88
Roosmaryn Rd	Durbanville	46	BQ	53
Roostou Cr.	Roosendaal	107	CF	51
Roosvygie Cl.	Annandale	90	BZ	55
Roozenboom	De Bron	45	BS	48

Index to Street Names

Rorine St — Seagull St

STREET NAME	SUBURB NAME	PG	GRID	
Rorine St	Jamestown	112	CH	74
Rorke Rd	Plumstead	140	CO	29
Rosa Hope Cr.	Woodlands (M.Plain)	124	CN	45
Rosaki St	Paarlzicht	19	BC	91
Rosalind St	Valhalla Pk	104	CE	41
Rosalyn Rd	Meadowsteads	156	CX	18
Rosalyn Rd	Springbok Pk	62	BV	54
Rosamond St	Wesbank	107	CF	52
Rosanna Cr.	Scottsdene	64	BV	60
Rosary St	Mountain View	19	BB	91
Rosary St	Paarlzicht	19	BC	91
Roscommon Rd	Elfindale	140	CQ	29
Roscommon Rd	Heathfield	140	CQ	28
Roscommon Rd	Heathfield	140	CQ	29
Roscommon St	Claremont	101	CH	28
Roscommon St	Claremont	101	CE	27
Rose	Dunoon	42	BO	37
Rose	Lentegeur (M.Plain)	144	CO	45
Rosé	Durmonte	30	BN	53
Rose Ave	Kirstenhof	159	CT	27
Rose Cl.	Bridgetown	103	CG	37
Rose Cr.	Belhar	106	CD	47
Rose Innes St	Langa	103	CD	36
Rose La.	Wynberg	120	CL	28
Rose Mount Ave	Oranjezicht	81	CC	22
Rose Rd	Bergvliet	140	CQ	27
Rose Rd	Bishop Lavis	104	CE	42
Rose Rd	Bishop Lavis	104	CF	42
Rose Rd	Goodwood Est.	85	BY	38
Rose Rd	Ravensmead	87	CA	46
Rose Rd	Uitsig	87	CB	44
Rosé Rd	Oude Westhof	60	BT	46
Rose St	Bishopscourt	119	CJ	26
Rose St	Bishopscourt	119	CJ	25
Rose St	Cape Town Cen.	81	CA	22
Rose St	Hillcrest Hgts	127	CL	57
Rose St	Kewtown	103	CF	35
Rose St	Lavender Hill East	160	CU	31
Rose St	Lavender Hill East	160	CX	33
Rose St	Morgenster Hoogte	63	BU	56
Rose St	Mowbray	101	CE	29
Rose St	Mxolisi Phetani	125	CM	49
Rose St	Ocean View	184	DC	15
Rose St	Paarl	22	BE	88
Rose St	Sarepta	89	CC	52
Rose St	Somerset West	170	CV	73
Rose St	Wellington	10	AR	94
Rose Way	Belle Constantia	139	CP	25
Rose Way	Macassar	149	CS	63
Rose Way	Matroosfontein	86	CC	41
Rose Way	Pinelands	84	CC	33
Rosebank Angus Rd	Montana/Durrheim	104	CE	42
Rosebank Pl.	Oranjezicht	81	CC	22
Roseberry Ave	Oranjezicht	99	CD	22
Roseberry Cl.	Sonstraal Hgts	46	BQ	54
Roseberry Rd	Mowbray	102	CD	31
Rosedene Rd	Sea Point	81	BZ	20
Rosedene Rd	Sea Point	81	CA	20
Rosedon Rd	Lansdowne	102	CH	32
Rosedon Rd	Lansdowne	121	CJ	32
Rose-Innes	William Lloyd	23	BD	92
Rose-Innes Rd	Table View	41	BO	31
Roseland Rd	Rondebosch	102	CF	31
Rosemary	Lentegeur (M.Plain)	144	CO	46
Rosemary Rd	Belhar	87	CC	46
Rosenburg	Highbury	107	CE	54
Rosendal St	Bothasig	58	BT	38
Rosendal St	Glen Ive	62	BU	52
Rosendal St	Paarl	22	BF	88
Rosendale Rd	Rondebosch	101	CF	29
Rosenow St	Elim	90	CA	55
Rosenow St	Somerset West	170	CU	74
Rosequartz St	Sheridon Pk	159	CU	29
Roseville Rd	Claremont	120	CJ	29
Rosewood Dr.	Weltevreden Val. (M.Plain)	144	CO	44
Rosewood Rd	Hanover Pk	122	CK	36
Rosewood St	Bonteheuwel	104	CE	40
Roslin Cl.	West Beach	24	BN	30
Roslyn La.	Bakoven	98	CF	18
Roslyn Rd	Rondebosch	101	CF	29
Rosmead Ave	Claremont	120	CJ	30
Rosmead Ave	Gardens	81	CC	22
Rosmead Ave	Kenilworth Pk	120	CK	30
Rosmead Ave Service Rd	Claremont	120	CJ	30
Rosmead Ave Service Rd	Kenilworth	120	CK	30
Rosmead Rd	Kalk Bay	187	CZ	27
Ross Rd	Rondebosch	101	CG	29
Ross Rd	Salt River	83	CC	28
Ross Rd	Wynberg	120	CM	30
Ross Sea	Rocklands (M.Plain)	144	CS	45
Ross St	Bothasig	58	BT	37
Ross St	Maitland	84	CA	32
Ross St	Valhalla Pk	104	CE	41
Ross St	Voelvlei	89	CA	52
Ross St	Voelvlei	89	CA	53
Rossal Rd	Athlone	102	CG	34
Rossignol St	Chantecler	62	BT	52
Rossine St	Belhar	106	CD	49
Rossini	Delft Sth	125	CJ	48
Rossini Ct	Delft Sth	125	CJ	48
Rossini St	Steenberg	159	CT	29
Rossiter St	Wellington	10	AR	92
Rossouw	Wellington	15	AV	93
Rossouw La.	Tokai	139	CS	26
Rotherfield Rd	Plumstead	120	CN	30
Rotherfield Rd	Plumstead	140	CO	30
Rothesay Pl.	Green Point	81	BY	21
Rothesay Rd	West Beach	24	BN	30
Rothschild Blvd.	Panorama	59	BV	41
Rotsho St	Victoria Mxenge	126	CN	51
Rotterdam Cr.	Uitzicht	47	BO	56
Rotterdam Rd	High Gate	107	CG	54
Rotterdam Rd	Sack's Circle Ind.	88	CB	50
Rotterdam Rd	Strandfontein	163	CT	43
Rotterdam St	Monte Vista	59	BU	40
Rottingdean Rd	Bakoven	98	CF	18
Rouen Ave	Plumstead	140	CO	29
Rouge Cl.	Uitzicht	47	BO	56
Rougemont Cl.	La Rochelle	62	BV	51
Rough Moor Rd	Mowbray	101	CD	29
Roulon St	Voorbrug	106	CG	50
Round House Rd	Camps Bay	98	CD	18
Round House Rd	Camps Bay	99	CD	19
Roundtree	Morgen Gronde	63	BW	55
Rouwkoop Ave	Rondebosch	101	CF	29
Rouwkoop Rd	Rondebosch	101	CF	29
Roux	Universiteits-oord	95	CB	77
Roux Malherbe	Franschhoek Sth	79	BY	107
Roux St	Langgewacht	170	CX	72
Roux St	Peerless Pk East	48	BR	59
Roux St	Peerless Pk Nth	47	BR	58
Roux St	Somerset West	170	CT	74
Rouxton Cr.	Lansdowne	121	CJ	33
Rouxton Rd	Lansdowne	121	CK	33
Rouxville Cl.	La Rochelle	62	BV	52
Rouxville Rd	Kalk Bay	186	CZ	26
Rovelle Cr.	Jamestown	112	CH	74
Rover Park	Weltevreden Val. (M.Plain)	124	CN	43
Rover Rd	Rondebosch	102	CG	31
Rover St	Beacon Valley (M.Plain)	145	CQ	48
Rowallan Cr.	Wesbank	107	CH	51
Rowallan Cr.	West Beach	24	BN	30
Rowallan Rd	West Beach	24	BN	30
Rowan	Dr Malan	95	CC	78
Rowan	Mostertsdrift	95	CC	78
Rowan La.	Kenilworth	120	CK	28
Rowan Rd	Kenilworth	120	CK	28
Rowena St	Gaylee	108	CH	56
Roxana Rd	Mowbray	102	CD	31
Roy Campbell Cr.	Parow Nth	60	BW	43
Roy De Vries St	Plattekloof	60	BW	43
Roy Dewar Cl.	Capri	185	DB	19
Roy Rd	Lansdowne	121	CL	34
Roy Rd East	Lansdowne	121	CK	34
Royal Ave	Eersterivier	128	CM	60
Royal Ave	Hout Bay	137	CQ	15
Royal Cr.	Gatesville	103	CG	37
Royal Rd	Clarkes	86	CC	42
Royal Rd	Maitland	83	CA	30
Royal Rd	Maitland	84	CA	31
Royal Rd	Maitland	84	CA	32
Royal Rd	Muizenberg	159	CX	29
Royal Rd	Muizenberg	159	CX	30
Royal St	Plattekloof Village	59	BT	42
Royal Tern Cl.	Kommetjie	183	DA	13
Royland Cr.	Hout Bay	137	CO	15
Royston Rd	Muizenberg Nth	159	CW	28
Roytston Cl.	Ottery	122	CL	35
Rozenburg St	Paarl	22	BF	88
Rozenburg St	Paarl	22	BF	87
Rozendal	Rozendal	96	CB	80
Rozendal Cr.	Haasendal	90	CA	56
Rozendal Way	Mitchells Plain	144	CQ	45
Rozenfontein St	Kleinbosch	59	BT	40
Rubbi Rd	Kommetjie	183	DC	12
Ruben Way	Macassar	149	CR	65
Rubens Rd	Table View	41	BP	31
Rubens Rd	Welcome	103	CE	38
Rubens St	De La Haye	89	BY	51
Rubernet	Brackenfell	63	BW	55
Rubernet	Morgen Gronde	63	BW	55
Rubicon Rd	Rondebosch	102	CH	32
Rubocon Rd	Saxenburg Ind. Pk	108	CE	57
Rubusana Ave	Langa	103	CD	35
Ruby Cl.	Bellville	62	BV	51
Ruby Cl.	Pelikan Pk	161	CT	36
Ruby Cr.	Belgravia	103	CG	35
Ruby Cr.	San Michel	157	CX	20
Ruby Cr.	Sheridon Pk	159	CU	29
Ruby Rd	Fairdale	126	CJ	54
Ruby Rd	Lansdowne	121	CJ	33
Ruby St	Belgravia	103	CG	35
Ruby Way	Noordhoek Manor	157	CX	20
Ruby Way	San Michel	157	CX	20
Ruchill Rd	Dieprivier	140	CP	28
Rudolph St	Newlands	101	CG	28
Rudolph St	Wellington	15	AV	92
Rue Almes	Somerset West	151	CS	74
Rue Amazon	Malibu Village	127	CK	55
Rue Belon	Somerset West	151	CS	74
Rue d' Valeur	Somerset West	151	CQ	72
Rue de Jacqueline	Somerset West	170	CU	74
Rue de la Bri Cl.	Richwood	42	BQ	38
Rue Dinard	Somerset West	152	CS	75
Rue Emmy Rd	Glenhaven	89	BZ	51
Rue Foche	Malibu Village	127	CK	55
Rue le Havre	Somerset West	151	CS	74
Rue Montclair	Somerset West	151	CS	74
Rue Montpellier	Somerset West	170	CT	74
Rue Nantes	Somerset West	151	CS	74
Rue Normandie	Somerset West	151	CS	74
Rue Orleans	Somerset West	151	CS	74
Rue Robert St	Glenhaven	89	CA	52
Rue Seine	Somerset West	151	CS	74
Rue Ursula St	Glenhaven	89	CA	52
Rue Ursula St	Glenhaven	89	BY	54
Ruens	Wesbank	107	CG	52
Ruens	Wesbank	107	CG	53
Ruff Cr.	Pelikan Pk	142	CR	35
Rugby	Uniepark	96	CB	79
Rugby Cl.	Westlake Est.	158	CU	25
Rugby Park Cr.	Belmont Pk	48	BS	60
Rugby Rd	Oranjezicht	99	CD	22
Rugby St	Beacon Valley (M.Plain)	145	CP	47
Rugley Rd	Vredehoek	82	CC	23
Ruimsig Rd	Somerset West	170	CT	73
Ruimte Rd	Manenberg	104	CH	39
Ruiter Ct	Edgemead	58	BU	38
Ruiters St	Northpine	63	BU	58
Ruitershoogte Ave	Durbanville	30	BN	51
Rule St	Plumstead	140	CO	30
Rumboll St	Onverwacht	174	CZ	74
Rumpler St	The Hague	106	CF	50
Runciman Dr.	Simon's Town	194	DJ	24
Runciman Dr.	Simon's Town	194	DJ	25
Rune Cl.	Kaya	146	CP	52
Rune Way	Silvermine Village	185	CY	20
Runelli St	William Lloyd	19	BC	93
Runge St	Cafda Village	141	CS	31
Runge St	Park Estates	170	CX	72
Runkel Dr.	Somerset West	150	CR	70
Runkel Dr.	Somerset West	151	CR	71
Runkel St	De La Haye	88	BY	50
Runners Green	Summer Greens	58	BW	36
Runners Way	Summer Greens	58	BW	36
Rupert Ave	Somerset West	151	CR	72
Rupert Ave	Somerset West	151	CR	73
Rupert St	Kaapzicht	59	BV	40
Rupestris St	Groenvlei	18	BA	88
Ruritania Ave	Ottery East	121	CN	33
Rus Cr.	Northern Paarl	18	AZ	88
Rusacre Rd	Rondebosch	102	CG	31
Rushmore Way	Tokai	139	CS	26
Rushy Cl.	Epping Forest	86	CB	41
Ruskin	Parklands	25	BM	33
Ruskin Rd	Dreyersdal	139	CR	26
Ruskin Sq.	Edgemead	58	BU	38
Rusper St	Maitland	84	CA	33
Russel	Groenvlei	18	BA	88
Russel Cl.	Barbarossa	120	CN	27
Russel Cl.	Nyanga	123	CK	42
Russel Harvey Cr.	Woodlands (M.Plain)	124	CN	45
Russel St	District Six	82	CB	25
Russel St	Foreshore	82	CB	25
Russel St	Montana/Durrheim	104	CF	41
Russel St	Soneike I	89	CA	54
Russel St	Wellington	15	AU	92
Russel Cr.	Belhar	107	CD	51
Rust en Vrede Cl.	Welgedacht	44	BS	46
Rust St	Belgravia	102	CH	34
Rust St	Belthorn Est.	102	CH	34
Rusten Ct	Marina Da Gama	159	CV	30
Rustenberg	Pinelands	85	CC	35
Rustenburg	Idasvallei	95	CA	78
Rustenburg	Idasvallei	96	BZ	79
Rustenburg Ave	High Constantia	139	CO	23
Rustenburg Ave	Rondebosch	101	CF	29
Rustenburg Cl.	Mitchells Plain	144	CQ	43
Rustenburg Cl.	Portlands (M.Plain)	144	CR	46
Rustenburg Rd	Belhar	106	CD	50
Rustenburg Rd	Richwood	42	BQ	38
Rustenburg Rd	Ridgeworth	61	BV	50
Rustenburg Rd	Somerset West	152	CS	75
Rustenburg St	Somerset West	170	CW	74
Rustendal Rd	Edgemead	58	BU	37
Rust-en-Vrede	Pinelands	84	CC	34
Rust-en-Vrede Ave	Alphen	119	CN	26
Rust-en-Vrede Rd	Ridgeworth	61	BV	50
Rusthof	Voorbrug	106	CG	50
Rusthof St	Rusthof	174	DA	74
Rusthof St	Rusthof	175	DA	75
Rustic Cl.	Scottsdene	64	BT	60
Rustic Rd	Gardens	81	CC	21
Rusticana St	Scottsdene	64	BT	59
Rustig St	Durbanville	45	BP	49
Rustof	Northpine	63	BU	58
Rutger Cr.	Belhar	107	CD	51
Ruth Cl.	Weltevreden Val. (M.Plain)	124	CN	44
Ruth Cl.	Woodlands (M.Plain)	124	CN	44
Ruth First	Fisantekraal	31	BK	58
Ruth First	Weltevreden Val. (M.Plain)	123	CN	42
Ruth First Cr.	Mandela Pk	146	CR	54
Ruth Rd	Doornhoogte	103	CG	36
Ruth St	Labiance	89	BZ	52
Ruth St	Manenberg	123	CK	39
Rutherford St	Belhar	88	CC	49
Rutherford Way	Meadowridge	140	CP	27
Rutherglen Ave	Newlands	100	CH	26
Rutherglen Ave	Newlands	100	CG	25
Rutherglen Cl.	Newlands	100	CH	26
Rutherglen Cl.	Newlands	100	CG	25
Rutherglen Rd	Rondebosch	102	CF	31
Rutland St	Claremont	120	CJ	30
Rutter Rd	Lakeside	159	CV	28
Rutvale Rd	Belthorn Est.	103	CH	35
Ruwenzori St	Tafelsig (M.Plain)	145	CS	49
Ruyteplaats Dr.	Hout Bay	117	CM	15
Ruyteplaats Dr.	Hout Bay	117	CM	16
Ryan Rd	Rosebank	101	CE	29
Ryan St	Churchill	59	BX	42
Ryan St	Glenlily	86	BY	42
Ryan Way	Mandalay	125	CM	47
Ryan Way	Mandalay	125	CN	47
Ryans Cl.	Somerset West	171	CT	76
Ryburg Rd	Hanover Pk	122	CK	35
Ryburg Rd	Hanover Pk	122	CK	37
Rye Rd	Mowbray	101	CE	30
Rygbossie Cr.	Roosendaal	107	CF	51
Rygbossie Cr.	Roosendaal	107	CG	53
Ryger	Dal Josafat Ind.	18	BA	90
Ryger St	Mountainside Est.	179	DD	78
Ryger St	Ndabeni	84	CB	32
Ryk St	Brooklyn	83	BZ	30
Ryk Tulbagh Cl.	Somerset West	171	CT	75
Ryk Tulbagh St	Belrail	88	BY	48
Rylands Rd	Doornhoogte	103	CG	36
Rylands Rd	Schaap Kraal	122	CL	37
Ryneveld	Stellenbosch	95	CB	76
Ryneveld	Stellenbosch	95	CC	76
Ryneveld St	Eersterivier	128	CL	60
Ryston Rd	Hanover Pk	122	CK	36
Rywood Rd	Hanover Pk	122	CK	35
S				
S N Dlangamandla St	Guguletu	123	CK	41
S.Biko St	Hout Bay	137	CO	16
S.Biko St	Mfuleni	126	CK	54
S.Jama St	Mfuleni	126	CK	53
S.Jama St	Mfuleni	126	CK	54
S.Karnovetz Rd	Nyanga	123	CK	42
S.Lindi St	Mfuleni	126	CK	53
S.Mabizela Cr.	Mandela Pk	147	CQ	55
S.Saba Cr.	Nyanga	123	CJ	42
Saaid Gabier Cl.	Gustrow	175	DB	75
Saaid Gabier Cl.	Gustrow	175	DB	77
Saaier Cl.	Mitchells Plain	144	CQ	45
Saaiman Ave	Hillcrest Hgts	127	CL	57
Saartjie Baartman	Fisantekraal	31	BK	58
Saartjie Baartman	Fisantekraal	31	BJ	57
Saasveld	Mabille Pk	89	CA	53
Saasveld Rd	Table View	41	BO	32
Saasveld St	Vosfontein	62	BV	52
Sabatha Dalinyebo	Weltevreden Val. (M.Plain)	123	CM	42
Sabatini Rd	Scottsdene	64	BU	59
Sabela Cr.	Victoria Mxenge	146	CO	51
Sabelo Pama	Weltevreden Val. (M.Plain)	123	CN	42
Sabi Ct	Delft	106	CG	48
Sabi St	Mfuleni	126	CK	54
Sabi St	Park Village	127	CK	58
Sabie Pl.	Manenberg	123	CJ	39
Sabie Rd	Manenberg	123	CJ	39
Sabie St	Bloemhof	61	BV	50
Sabie Wk	Manenberg	123	CJ	39
Sabina Rd	Dennemere	108	CH	58
Sable Cr.	Goedemoed	46	BO	53
Sable Rd	Lotus River	142	CP	35
Sable Rd	Rugby	57	BX	32
Sable Rd	Ysterplaat	57	BX	33
Sable Way	Loevenstein	60	BW	46
Sabre	Rocklands (M.Plain)	163	CT	46
Sabre St	Kensington	84	BZ	33
Sabre St	Macassar	168	CT	64
Sachs St	Schotsche Kloof	81	CA	22
Sacks Cir.	Sack's Circle Ind.	88	CB	49
Sacks Cir.	Sack's Circle Ind.	88	CB	50
Sacks Cir.	Sack's Circle Ind.	89	CB	52
Sackson St	Bellville Sth	88	BZ	49
Sackville Rd	Kalkfontein II	107	CD	52
Sacramento Pl.	Plattekloof Glen	59	BW	40
Sacramento Rd	Weltevreden Val. (M.Plain)	124	CN	43
Sacremento Cr.	Eersterivier	128	CN	60
Sadaf St	Parklands	25	BN	33
Saddle Cl.	Mitchells Plain	144	CR	45
Saddle Cl.	Noordhoek Manor	157	CX	20
Saddle Rd	Devil's Peak Est.	82	CC	24
Saddle St	Eureka	87	CC	44
Saddle St	Eureka	87	CB	46
Saddlers Cl.	Hout Bay	117	CM	15
Saddlers Row	Hout Bay	117	CM	15
Sadlers Way	Kenilworth Pk	121	CK	31
Safari Rd	Thornton	85	CA	36
Safari St	Jagtershof	108	CD	57
Saffier St	Hill View	127	CK	58
Saffraan	Delft Sth	125	CJ	49
Saffraan	Die Boord	112	CD	74
Saffraan	Die Boord	113	CD	75
Saffraan Ave	New Orleans	18	BA	90
Saffraan Rd	Bonteheuwel	104	CE	39
Saffraan St	Loevenstein	60	BV	46
Saffron Rd	Hout Bay	117	CN	18
Safika Cr.	Kaya	146	CO	51
Safraan Cl.	Langeberg Rdg	47	BR	55
Safraan Cl.	Uitsig	87	CC	44
Safraan Cr.	St Dumas	108	CD	56
Sage	Lentegeur (M.Plain)	144	CP	45
Sage Cl.	Belhar	106	CD	50
Sage St	Philippi	124	CM	45
Sagewood Cl.	Langeberg Rdg	47	BR	55
Sagewood Cl.	Somerset West	171	CW	76
Sagewood Dr.	Hout Bay	137	CP	16

Abbreviations used: Ave – Avenue, A.H. – Agricultural Holding, A.L. – Algemene Landgoed, Blvd – Boulevard, Cen. – Central, Cir. – Circle, Cl. – Close, Cr. – Crescent, Ct – Court, Dr. – Drive, Est. – Estate, Ext. – Extension, Hgts – Heights, Ind. – Industrial, Gdns – Gardens, Gr. – Grove, La. – Lane, (M.Plain) - Mitchells Plain, Nth – North, Pl. – Place, Pk – Park, Rd – Road, Rdg. – Ridge, S.H. – Small Holding, Sq. – Square, St – Street, Sth – South, Ter. – Terrace, Tn – Turn, Val. – Valley, Wk – Walk

STREET NAME	SUBURB NAME	PG	GRID	
Sagoloda St	Brown's Farm	124	CL	43
Sagoloda St	Ilitha Pk	146	CQ	52
Sagwityi	Wellington	15	AU	91
Sagwityi Cr.	Philippi East	125	CM	47
Sagwityi St	Brown's Farm	124	CM	43
Sagwityi St	Crossroads	124	CK	44
Sagwityi St	Ilitha Pk	146	CQ	52
Sail	Strandfontein	162	CT	41
Sail St	Blouberg Sands	24	BM	30
Sailors Green	Summer Greens	58	BW	36
Saint	Delft Sth	125	CK	48
Sajini Cr.	Nonqubela	126	CN	52
Sakabula Cir.	Ruyterwacht	86	BZ	39
Sake Ave	Scottsdene	64	BT	59
Sake St	Kaya	146	CP	51
Sakela Cl.	Nyanga	123	CK	42
Sakhelwe	Mbekweni	15	AW	92
Sakhelwe	Mbekweni	15	AU	94
Sakhile St	Guguletu	104	CH	41
Sakhwatsha St	Brown's Farm	124	CL	43
Sakhwatsha St	Philippi East	124	CM	46
Sakhwatsha St	Philippi East	125	CL	47
Sakkiesdorp Cr.	Nyanga	124	CJ	43
Sakrivier St	Delft	106	CF	49
Sakumzi Cr.	Eyethu	146	CP	53
Sakwasha St	Crossroads	124	CK	44
Sakwasha St	Crossroads	124	CN	46
Salaam St	Belgravia	103	CG	35
Salamander Hghts	Sunnydale	185	DA	20
Salazar Plain	Cape Town Cen.	82	CA	24
Salberau Ave	Salberau	86	CB	41
Saldanha La.	Belhar	107	CD	51
Saldanha Rd	Stellenberg	62	BU	52
Saldanha St	Park Estates	170	CX	71
Saldanha St	Ruyterwacht	86	CA	39
Salem Way	Edgemead	58	BV	37
Salem Way	Steenberg	159	CT	29
Salerna Way	Strandfontein	162	CT	41
Salford Park St	Oak Glen	62	BW	52
Salford Rd	Mowbray	101	CD	29
Salford Rd	Oak Glen	62	BW	52
Salie	Lentegeur (M.Plain)	145	CP	47
Salie Cl.	Plattekloof	59	BV	42
Salie Rd	Uitsig	87	CB	44
Salie St	Eersterivier	128	CL	59
Saliehout	Delft Sth	125	CK	49
Salieri Way	Sonstraal Hgts	46	BQ	54
Salisbury Ave	Bishopscourt	119	CJ	26
Salisbury Ave	Kenridge Hgts	45	BS	49
Salisbury Rd	Kenilworth	120	CL	29
Salisbury St	Boston	61	BW	47
Salisbury St	Boston	61	BX	47
Salisbury St	Parklands	25	BM	34
Salisbury St	Woodstock	83	CB	27
Salisbury Way	Portlands (M.Plain)	144	CQ	46
Salix St	Greenlands	88	CA	49
Sally Rd	Sunnydale	185	DA	19
Salm Rd	Nooitgedacht	104	CE	42
Salmander Sq.	Factreton	85	BY	35
Salmon Rd	Pelikan Pk	142	CQ	35
Salmon St	Silveroaks	90	CC	55
Salmon St	Woodstock	82	CB	26
Salmon Way	Strandfontein	162	CT	39
Salmone Cr.	Brackenfell Sth	90	BY	56
Salome St	Eastridge (M.Plain)	145	CR	49
Salt River Rd	Salt River	83	CB	27
Salt St	Mfuleni	126	CK	54
Saltire Rd	Belgravia	103	CH	35
Salton	Morgen Gronde	63	BW	55
Salvera St	Somerset West	170	CW	74
Salvia	Lentegeur (M.Plain)	145	CP	47
Salvia	Stellenbosch	95	BY	75
Salvia Cl.	Uitsig	87	CC	44
Salvia Cr.	Eersterivier	128	CM	60
Salvia St	Bonteheuwel	104	CD	40
Salwe Cr.	Nonqubela	146	CO	52
Sam Gordon Dr.	Morgenster Hoogte	63	BT	56
Sam Njokozela Ave	Bloekombos	48	BR	62
Sam Njokozela Ave	Bloekombos	49	BR	63
Sam Nujoma Cr.	Mandela Pk	147	CR	55
Samantha	Lentegeur (M.Plain)	145	CO	48
Samba Cr.	Retreat	140	CS	29
Sameul St	Eersterivier	128	CM	60
Samora Machel	Weltevreden Val. (M.Plain)	123	CN	42
Samora Machel Cr.	Mandela Pk	146	CR	54
Sampson St	William Lloyd	19	BC	93
Sampson St	William Lloyd	19	BA	94
Sampson St	William Lloyd	19	BC	94
Samson Cr.	Belhar	107	CD	51
Samson Kana St	Kuyasa	147	CS	55
Samson St	Wellington	10	AS	92
Samuel Ngele St	Guguletu	123	CK	41
Samuel St	Des Hampden	89	CB	53
San Diego Cl.	Eikenbosch	90	CC	57
San Francisco Cl.	Portlands (M.Plain)	144	CQ	46
San Jose Cl.	Eikenbosch	90	CC	57
San Juan Ave	Fir Grove	139	CQ	25
San Juan Cl.	Harbour Island	175	DC	75
San Marino Cl.	Uitzicht	47	BO	55
San Martine Cr.	West Beach	24	BN	29
San Remo Ave	Strandfontein	162	CT	42
San Rogue	Sunningdale	25	BM	31
San Rogue Cl.	Sunningdale	25	BM	31
Sanatorium Rd	Claremont	102	CH	31
Sanctuary Cl.	Milnerton	57	BV	32
Sanctuary Rd	Pelikan Pk	160	CU	33
Sand Cl.	Lakeside	159	CV	27
Sand Cl.	Lakeside	159	CW	27
Sand Olive Rd	Steenberg	159	CT	29
Sand St	Mbekweni	15	AV	91
Sand St	Mbekweni	15	AV	92
Sandalwood Rd	Amandelrug	90	CA	55
Sandalwood St	Bonteheuwel	104	CE	39
Sandberry Way	Tokai	139	CS	26
Sandbury Rd	Weltevreden Val. (M.Plain)	144	CO	43
Sanddrift St	Lemoenkloof	18	BB	88
Sandelhout	Delft Sth	125	CJ	49
Sanderling Rd	Capricorn	160	CW	31
Sandford Rd	Oakdale	61	BW	49
Sandgate Ave	Athlone	102	CG	33
Sandhurst Rd	St James	187	CZ	27
Sandhurst Rd	Wynberg	120	CL	29
Sandhurst St West	Ravensmead	87	CB	44
Sandile	Mbekweni	15	AX	91
Sandla St	Nonqubela	126	CN	53
Sandle Ave	Langa	85	CC	36
Sandle Ave	Langa	103	CD	36
Sandler St	Ferndale	62	BV	54
Sandown Cr.	Milnerton Rdg	41	BS	34
Sandown Dr.	Ottery	122	CM	35
Sandown Mews	West Beach	24	BM	30
Sandown Rd	Blouberg Sands	24	BL	30
Sandown Rd	Blouberg Sands	24	BM	30
Sandown Rd	Greenways	174	DA	74
Sandown Rd	Rondebosch	101	CF	30
Sandown Rd	Rondebosch	102	CG	31
Sandown Rd	Rondebosch	102	CG	32
Sandown Rd	West Beach	24	BM	30
Sandown Rd East	Rondebosch East	102	CG	32
Sandown Rd East	Sunningdale	25	BM	31
Sandpiper Ave	Grassy Pk	141	CQ	33
Sandpiper Ave	Table View	41	BQ	32
Sandpiper Ave	Table View	41	BQ	33
Sandpiper Cl.	Admirals Pk	175	DC	78
Sandpiper Cl.	Hout Bay	136	CP	14
Sandpiper Cl.	Villa Italia	57	BW	33
Sandpiper Cr.	Eersterivier	128	CM	60
Sandpiper Cr.	Electric City	127	CN	58
Sandpiper Cr.	Morgenster Hoogte	63	BT	56
Sandpiper Rd	Flintdale Est.	141	CP	31
Sandpiper Way	Big Bay	24	BL	28
Sandra St	Weltevreden Val. (M.Plain)	124	CN	44
Sandrif Cl.	Welgevonden	30	BN	54
Sandringham Cl.	Pinelands	85	CC	35
Sandringham Cl.	Pinelands	85	CC	36
Sandringham Rd	Bloekombos	48	BQ	62
Sandringham Rd	Bloekombos	49	BP	64
Sandringham Rd	Bloekombos	49	BP	66
Sandringham Rd	Klein Joostenberg	50	BP	67
Sandrivier Cr.	Delft	106	CH	49
Sandrivier St	Tafelsig (M.Plain)	145	CR	48
Sandsteen St	Bellville	62	BU	51
Sandsteen St	Ridgeworth	61	BV	50
Sandstone Dr.	Somerset West	171	CW	78
Sandstone Rd	Kommetjie	183	DB	13
Sandu Cr.	Roosendaal	107	CF	51
Sandwyk St	Klein Draken	38	BJ	86
Sandy Bay Rd	Hout Bay	116	CM	13
Sandy Cl.	Hout Bay Harbour	136	CR	13
Sandy La.	Bishop Lavis	104	CD	41
Sandy Way	Milnerton	57	BT	33
Sangiro St	Labiance	89	BZ	51
Sangiro St	Parow Nth	59	BW	42
Sangiro St	Soneike I	89	BZ	54
Sangoba	Mbekweni	15	AW	92
Sangoma	Mbekweni	15	AV	91
Sangrove Dr.	Rondebosch	102	CG	32
Sangxa St	Brown's Farm	124	CL	44
Sangxa St	Ilitha Pk	146	CQ	53
Sani	Victoria Mxenge	146	CQ	51
Sans Souci Rd	Bellville Sth Ext. 5	88	BZ	49
Sans Souci Rd	Newlands	101	CG	28
Sansho St	Sunset Glen	107	CH	54
Santa Cruz Cr.	Bloubergstrand	24	BJ	27
Santa Cruz St	Ruyterwacht	86	CA	39
Santa Fe Cr.	Bloubergstrand	24	BJ	27
Santa Rosa	Die Boord	112	CD	74
Santa Rosa St	Bellavista Ext.1	18	BC	90
Santa Rosa St	Franschhoek Nth	75	BX	105
Santana	Fairyland	19	AZ	93
Santana La.	Elfindale	140	CQ	30
Santenay	Oude Westhof	44	BS	45
Santhagen	Devonvallei	112	CD	72
Santigo Way	Malibu Village	127	CK	55
Santo Alberto St	Blue Downs	108	CH	56
Santos Ave	Nyanga	123	CK	42
Santos St	Malibu Village	127	CL	55
Santos St	Rugby	57	BX	31
Santraline St	Denneburg	23	BD	91
Saphepha St	Tarentaalplaas	175	CY	75
Sapphire	Rocklands (M.Plain)	144	CS	46
Sapphire Way	Belvedere Noordhoek	157	CX	20
Sara Cir.	Langeberg Glen	47	BQ	56
Sarah Goldblat Ave	Elim	90	CA	55
Sarasota Cl.	Parklands	25	BM	32
Saratoga Ave	Ottery	122	CM	35
Saratoga Way	Edgemead	58	BU	38
Sarazen	Sunningdale	25	BL	33
Sarazen Cr.	Sunningdale	25	BL	31
Sarbonne St	Somerset West	151	CQ	72
Sardinia Cr.	Portlands (M.Plain)	145	CS	47
Sardinia Cr.	Uitzicht	31	BN	56
Sardinia Dr.	Capri	185	DA	19
Sardinia Dr.	Sunnydale	185	DA	20
Sardyn Rd	Strandfontein	162	CU	39
Sarel Celliers St	Glenlily	86	BY	42
Sarel Cilliers St	Kempenville	61	BX	49
Sarel Cilliers St	Park Estates	170	CX	73
Sarel Cilliers St	Park Estates	174	CY	72
Sarel van Deventer Rd	Bonnie Brae	47	BP	57
Sarembock St	Wellington	11	AR	95
Sarepta Cr.	Des Hampden	89	CA	53
Sarepta St	Sarepta	89	CB	53
Saresta Way	Kenridge	61	BU	49
Sarhili St	Wimbledon	108	CG	55
Sarina Way	Northpine	64	BU	59
Saringa Rd	Mitchells Plain	144	CQ	45
Saron	Uitsig	87	CB	45
Sasmeer Rd	Retreat	141	CR	30
Sassveld Villas	Vredenberg	62	BV	52
Satelite Dr.	Thembokwezi	125	CM	48
Sati Rd	Killarney Gdns	42	BO	36
Saturn	Rocklands (M.Plain)	144	CS	45
Saturn Cir.	Phoenix	57	BU	33
Saturn Cl.	Salberau	86	CB	41
Saturn Cl.	Salberau	86	CB	39
Saturn Cl.	Surrey	103	CG	38
Saturn Cr.	Thembokwezi	125	CL	48
Saturn Cr.	Thembokwezi	125	CM	48
Saturn Rd	Surrey	103	CG	38
Saturn Way	Ocean View	184	DC	15
Saturnus St	Somerset Hgts	127	CK	57
Sauer Rd	Ottery	121	CM	33
Sauer St	Eastridge (M.Plain)	145	CQ	49
Saul St	Beroma	89	BZ	51
Saul St	Hoogstede	62	BV	54
Saul St	Rugby	84	BY	31
Saunders Cl.	Fish Hoek	186	DA	23
Saunders Rd	Aurora	45	BP	48
Saunders Rd	Bantry Bay	80	CB	18
Saunders Rd	Wetton	122	CL	35
Sausman	Marlow	88	CA	50
Sauvignon Blanc St	Oude Westhof	44	BS	44
Sauvignon St	Normandie	64	BW	59
Sauvignon St	Somerset West	150	CR	70
Savanna Cl.	Durbanville	45	BP	49
Savella Cl.	Somerset West	151	CQ	72
Savignon	Morgen Gronde	63	BX	55
Savignon Cl.	Courtrai	22	BH	87
Savora St	Voorbrug	106	CG	50
Savoy St	Courtrai	22	BH	87
Savoye Cl.	Edgemead	58	BV	36
Sawkins Rd	Mowbray	102	CE	31
Sawkins Rd	Rondebosch	101	CE	30
Sawle Rd	Plumstead	120	CN	30
Saxenburg Cr.	Bellair	62	BW	53
Saxenburg Cr.	Die Bos	174	CY	74
Saxenburg Rd	Blackheath Ind.	108	CE	56
Saxenburg Way	Edgemead	59	BT	39
Saxenwold La.	Blackheath Ind.	108	CE	56
Saxo St	Retreat	159	CT	29
Saxon Cl.	West Beach	24	BN	30
Saxon Cr.	West Beach	24	BN	30
Saxon Rd	Rondebosch	102	CG	32
Sayed Abdul Samad	Weltevreden Val. (M.Plain)	144	CR	44
Scadoxus Cr.	Eersterivier	128	CM	59
Scala Cl.	Nyanga	123	CJ	41
Scala Rd	Simon's Town	190	DE	22
Scala Rd	Simon's Town	191	DG	23
Scarboro Rd	Muizenberg	159	CW	30
Scarbrow St	Van Ryneveld	174	CZ	72
Scarlet Cr.	Weltevrede	94	BY	74
Scepter Cr.	Protea Village	63	BV	58
Sceptre Cr.	Dolphin Beach	41	BP	31
Sceptre La.	Leonsdale	86	CA	42
Schaap Rd	Knole Pk	142	CP	36
Schaap Rd	Schaap Kraal	142	CQ	36
Schaapkraal Rd	Schaap Kraal	142	CP	36
Schaapkraal Rd	Schaap Kraal	142	CP	38
Schaapkraal Rd	Schaap Kraal	143	CP	39
Schaay Rd	Diepriver	140	CP	28
Schabort Dr.	Amanda Glen	46	BS	51
Schabort Dr.	Eversdal	62	BT	51
Scharbort Cr.	Durbell	45	BS	50
Scharnberg St	Parow	87	BY	43
Scheckter Rd	Killarney Gdns	42	BO	37
Scheele St	Belhar	88	CC	49
Schelde St	De Zoete Inval	39	BJ	88
Scheldt St	Manenberg	123	CJ	39
Scheldt Wk	Manenberg	123	CJ	39
Scheldt Wk	Manenberg	123	CM	39
Scheneider	Paarl	18	BC	88
Scher La.	Groenheuwel	19	BA	91
Schiebe St	Cape Town Cen.	82	BZ	23
Schilpadvlei Rd	Barbarossa	119	CN	26
Schipol Rd	The Hague	106	CE	49
Schmidt St	Welgemoed	61	BU	47
Schoenstatt Ave	High Constantia	119	CN	23
Scholtz Ave	Wellington	15	AV	92
Scholtz Rd	Somerset West	170	CT	72
Scholtz Rd	Three Anchor Bay	81	BZ	21
Scholtz St	Van Ryneveld	174	CZ	73
School	Kayamandi	94	CA	74
School Cl.	Strandfontein	162	CT	41
School End	Riverton	86	CA	40
School Rd	Austinville	108	CH	56
School Rd	Bishop Lavis	104	CD	42
School Rd	Claremont	120	CJ	28
School Rd	Muizenberg	187	CY	28
School Rd	Summer Greens	58	BV	36
School Side	Meadowridge	140	CP	27
School St	Blackheath Ind.	108	CG	56
School St	Cravenby	87	CB	43
School St	Eersterivier	128	CL	59
School St	Firgrove	150	CR	67
School St	Marconi Beam	57	BU	33
School St	Mountainside Est.	179	DD	77
School St	Northern Paarl	18	AZ	88
School St	Northern Paarl	18	AZ	89
School St	Phoenix	57	BV	33
School St	Sir Lowry's Pass	176	CZ	81
School St	Somerset West	170	CW	74
School St	Strandfontein	162	CT	41
School Way	Retreat	140	CS	29
Schools La.	Pinelands	84	CC	34
Schoonder St	Gardens	82	CB	23
Schoonder St	Oranjezicht	82	CC	23
Schooner Ave	Sun Valley	185	CZ	21
Schooner Cl.	Lakeside	159	CV	28
Schooner Rd	Strandfontein	162	CT	40
Schooner St	Eersterivier	128	CM	60
Schoongelegen St	Somerset West	150	CS	70
Schoongezicht	Groenvlei	18	BA	88
Schoongezicht	Simonswyk	95	CB	78
Schoongezicht Cl.	Richwood	42	BP	38
Schoongezicht St	Somerset West	151	CS	73
Schoongezicht St	Wellington	10	AS	92
Schoongezigt Rd	Skoongesig	45	BO	50
Schoongezigt Rd	Skoongesig	46	BO	51
Schoonvrucht Ave	The Vines	140	CO	27
Schotia St	Loevenstein	60	BV	46
Schrader Cl.	Bellair	62	BW	53
Schreiner Cl.	Langgewacht	170	CW	72
Schreiner Rd	Table View	41	BQ	34
Schreiner St	Brooklyn	84	BZ	31
Schreiner St	Monte Vista	59	BV	39
Schroder St	Stellenbosch	95	CC	75
Schroeder Rd	Pinati	122	CK	35
Schubert	Delft Sth	125	CJ	48
Schubert Ave	Sonstraal Hgts	46	BR	54
Schubert Cr.	Belhar	106	CD	48
Schubert Rd	Kaapzicht	59	BV	40
Schubert St	Groenheuwel	19	AZ	92
Schubert St	Labiance	89	BZ	51
Schubert St	Protea Hoogte	63	BX	56
Schuilhoek Rd	Kenilworth	120	CK	29
Schuilplaats	Schuilplaats	113	CF	75
Schumann St	Cafda Village	141	CS	31
Schus St	Durbanville	45	BP	50
Schwartz	Van Ryneveld	174	CZ	72
Schwartz St	Wellington	10	AR	92
Schwella	Beaconvale	86	BZ	42
Scobel Rd	Wynberg	120	CL	27
Scopus Rd	Muizenberg	159	CX	29
Scorpio Rd	Ocean View	189	DD	15
Scott Rd	Claremont	120	CJ	28
Scott Rd	Glenlily	86	BY	42
Scott Rd	Hout Bay	137	CP	16
Scott Rd	Observatory	83	CC	28
Scott St	Gardens	82	CB	23
Scott St	Kaya	146	CP	52
Scott St	Oakdale	61	BX	48
Scott St	Park Estates	174	CY	72
Scott St	Stanlou	61	BX	48
Scottsville Cir.	Hout Bay	137	CQ	16
Scottsville Rd	Retreat	141	CR	31
Scottsville Way	Milnerton Rdg	41	BS	34
Scout Rd	Lansdowne	121	CJ	32
Scouts Pl.	Pinelands	84	CC	33
Scrabble Cr.	Beacon Valley (M.Plain)	145	CP	48
Scuba Cl.	Strandfontein	162	CT	42
Scurpus Cl.	The Lakes	184	CZ	17
S'Dwadwa Dr.	Joe Slovo Pk	57	BU	34
Sea Breeze Pl.	Kirstenhof	159	CT	27
Sea Breeze Cr.	San Michel	157	CX	19
Sea Breeze Rd	Kirstenhof	159	CT	27
Sea Breeze Rd	Kirstenhof	159	CU	27
Sea Cliff Cl.	Milnerton	57	BT	33
Sea Cottage Dr.	Crofters Valley	184	CY	18
Sea Cottage Dr.	Crofters Valley	185	CY	19
Sea Mist Cr.	Milnerton	57	BT	33
Sea Otter	Rocklands (M.Plain)	144	CS	46
Sea View Cl.	Harbour Island	175	DC	75
Sea View Rd	Muizenberg	187	CY	28
Sea View St	Vredelust	60	BX	46
Sea Way	Anchorage Pk	175	DC	77
Seacliff Rd	Bantry Bay	80	CB	18
Seacliffe Rd	Hout Bay	136	CQ	14
Seafarer Cr.	Parklands	26	BN	35
Seafarer Dr.	Strandfontein	162	CT	42
Seafarer Dr.	Strandfontein	163	CT	43
Seafire	Rocklands (M.Plain)	163	CT	45
Seaforth Rd	Simon's Town	194	DJ	26
Seafox St	The Hague	106	CE	50
Seagrim St	Onverwacht	174	CZ	74
Seagull Cl.	Hout Bay Harbour	136	CR	14
Seagull Cl.	Kraaifontein	47	BQ	58
Seagull Rd	Scarborough	192	DJ	17
Seagull St	Ocean View	184	DC	15
Seagull St	Pelikan Pk	161	CV	38

Index to Street Names

Seahawk — Skutter Sq.

STREET NAME	SUBURB NAME	PG	GRID
Seahawk	Rocklands (M.Plain)	163	CT 45
Seahorse La.	Big Bay	24	BM 28
Seal Rd	Table View	24	BN 29
Sealy Cl.	Highbury	107	CD 54
Searle Rd	Belhar	107	CD 51
Searle St	Lansdowne	121	CJ 32
Searle St	Woodstock	82	CB 25
Sea-rose St	Annandale	90	BZ 55
Seascape Cr.	Anchorage Pk	175	DC 78
Seascape Rd	San Michel	157	CX 19
Seaton St	Parklands	25	BN 34
Seaton St	Plumstead	140	CP 30
Seattle Cl.	Portlands (M.Plain)	144	CR 46
Seaview	Harbour Island	179	DE 76
Seaview Rd	Fish Hoek	185	DA 21
Seaview Rd	Somerset West	171	CT 76
Seaview Rd	Wynberg	120	CM 28
Sebastian Cr.	Skilpadvlei	45	BP 49
Sebastian Cr.	Skilpadvlei	45	BP 47
Sebastian Pl.	Monte Vista	59	BW 39
Sebastian Rd	Sunnydale	185	CZ 19
Sebastian St	Constantia Vale	119	CN 25
Seboa St	Adriaanse	87	CC 43
Sebrahout	Delft Sth	125	CJ 49
Seckenheim Rd	Hindle Pk	107	CH 54
Secluse Ave	Simon's Town	195	DJ 27
Second	De Oude Renbaan	22	BH 88
Second	Mxolisi Phetani	126	CM 51
Second Ave	Belgravia	102	CG 34
Second Ave	Bellville	88	BY 47
Second Ave	Boston	88	BY 47
Second Ave	Claremont	120	CJ 29
Second Ave	Da Gama Pk	190	DD 21
Second Ave	Elsies River Ind.	86	BZ 41
Second Ave	Fairways	121	CN 32
Second Ave	Fish Hoek	186	DB 24
Second Ave	Florida	87	CA 44
Second Ave	Glenlily	86	BY 41
Second Ave	Glenlily	86	BY 42
Second Ave	Glenlily	87	BY 43
Second Ave	Grassy Pk	141	CP 33
Second Ave	Grassy Pk	141	CQ 31
Second Ave	Green Oaks	95	CA 75
Second Ave	Kayamandi	95	CA 75
Second Ave	Kenilworth	120	CK 29
Second Ave	Kensington	84	BZ 32
Second Ave	Klein Begin	48	BS 60
Second Ave	Klein Begin	48	BS 61
Second Ave	Knole Pk	142	CP 36
Second Ave	Lotus River	141	CP 34
Second Ave	Lotus River	142	CP 35
Second Ave	Maitland	84	CA 32
Second Ave	Manenberg	123	CK 39
Second Ave	Marinda Hgts	89	CB 54
Second Ave	Nyanga	123	CK 42
Second Ave	Paarl	22	BD 88
Second Ave	Paarl	22	BE 88
Second Ave	Retreat	140	CR 29
Second Ave	Rondebosch East	102	CG 33
Second Ave	Rondebosch East	102	CH 33
Second Ave	Vanguard	103	CG 38
Second Ave	Wellington	10	AS 93
Second Ave	Woodlands	191	DE 23
Second Cr.	Fish Hoek	186	DB 24
Second Cr.	Vredelust	60	BX 46
Second Gate Green	Strandfontein	162	CU 41
Second Rd	Heathfield	140	CQ 29
Second Rd	Montague Gdns Ind.	42	BS 35
Second Rd	Montague Gdns Ind.	58	BT 35
Second St	Bishop Lavis	104	CD 41
Second St	Firgrove	150	CR 67
Second St	Maitland	84	CA 33
Second St	Park Estates	174	DA 74
Second St	Rusthof	174	DA 74
Second St	Welcome	103	CF 38
Second St	Wellington	10	AR 91
Section Rd	Brooklyn	83	BZ 30
Section Rd	Paarden Eiland	83	BZ 29
Seddon St	Fairfield	60	BX 44
Seddon St	Glenlily	60	BX 43
Seder	Delft Sth	106	CH 50
Seder	Forest Hgts	127	CL 57
Seder Ave	Edenpark	62	BU 54
Seder Ave	Panorama	59	BV 42
Seder Ave	Sonnedal	59	BV 42
Seder St	Sarepta	89	CC 52
Sederberg	Wellington	15	AV 91
Sederberg Rd	Bonnie Brae	47	BP 57
Sedgehill Cr.	Wetton	121	CM 34
Sedgemoor Rd	Camps Bay	98	CD 18
See Sq.	Factreton	85	BZ 35
See St	Bothasig	42	BS 37
Seek St	Macassar	149	CS 64
Seeliger Rd	Kommetjie	183	DB 12
Seemeeu Cl.	Mikro Pk	90	CB 56
Seemeeu Cr.	Seawinds	160	CU 31
Seemeeu St	Bloubergrant	24	BN 30
Seemeeu St	Macassar	149	CS 64
Seemeeu St	Simon's Town	191	DF 24
Seemeeu St	Sunnydale	185	DA 20
Seemeeu St	Thornton	85	CA 36
Seil Sq.	Factreton	85	BZ 35
Seine Cr.	Eindhoven	125	CJ 50
Seine Rd	Manenberg	123	CJ 39
Seine St	Klein Parys	23	BD 91
Seine St	Portlands (M.Plain)	144	CQ 46
Seine Wk	Manenberg	123	CJ 39
Sekelbos	Delft Sth	125	CJ 49
Selati Cr.	Park Village	127	CK 58
Selati Ct	Delft	106	CF 49
Selba St	Wellington	15	AT 93
Selborne Down St	Welgedacht	60	BT 45
Selborne Rd	Selborne	61	BV 47
Selbourne Rd	Claremont	101	CH 27
Selbourne Rd	Mowbray	101	CD 29
Selbourne Rd	Sea Point	81	BZ 20
Selbourne Rd	Windsor Pk	47	BR 57
Selbourne Rd	Woodstock	83	CC 27
Selbourne St	Avondale	87	BY 44
Selbourne St	Fairfield	87	BY 44
Selby Rd	Mowbray	101	CD 30
Selby Rd	Plumstead	140	CO 29
Seldon St	Beaconvale	87	CA 43
Select Cr.	Highbury	107	CD 54
Selekta St	Jamestown	112	CH 74
Selene Way	Woodlands (M.Plain)	144	CP 44
Selesho St	Nonqubela	126	CN 53
Selica Cl.	Glencairn Hgts	191	DD 24
Selkirk Cl.	Belhar	107	CD 52
Selkirk St	District Six	82	CB 25
Selous Rd	Claremont	101	CH 30
Selous St	Observatory	83	CB 29
Selven St	Nomzano	175	CY 75
Selwyn St	Foreshore	82	CB 25
Selwyn Ter.	Kenilworth	120	CK 29
Semillon Cl.	Zevenzicht	90	CC 58
Semillon Way	Northpine	63	BU 58
Sending St	Eikendal	47	BS 58
Sending St	St Michaels	63	BU 55
Senecio Cl.	Plattekloof	59	BU 42
Senegal St	Delft	106	CG 49
Sengwa Way	Delft	106	CH 49
Senna Rd	Killarney Gdns	42	BP 36
Sentinal Cl.	Ocean View	184	DC 15
Sentinal Cl.	Ocean View	184	DC 17
Sentinel Cl.	Hout Bay Harbour	136	CR 13
Sentinel Rd	Durbanville Hills	45	BR 50
Sentinel Rd	Heideveld	104	CG 39
Sentinel St	Tafelsig (M.Plain)	145	CS 48
Sentraal St	Welgelegen	59	BV 40
September	Cloetesville	95	BY 75
September St	Wellington	15	AV 92
Septimus St	Paarl	22	BD 88
Sequoia Rd	Bonteheuwel	104	CE 39
Serangetti St	Welgevonden	30	BN 54
Serangetti St	Welgevonden	30	BM 53
Serbastian Cl.	Langgewacht	170	CW 72
Sercor	Casablanca	175	DA 75
Sercor	Casablanca	175	DA 76
Sercor Dr.	Casablanca	175	DB 76
Serenade Cr.	Belhar	106	CD 49
Serenade Rd	Steenberg	159	CT 30
Serenata Cr.	Brackenfell Sth	63	BX 57
Sergeant St	Rondebosch East	102	CH 32
Sergeant St	Somerset West	170	CV 74
Serina St	Casablanca	175	DB 76
Serine Way	Northpine	63	BT 58
Sering	Bo Dalsig	113	CE 76
Sering	Delft Sth	125	CJ 49
Sering Ave	Edenpark	62	BU 54
Sering Cr.	Park Village	127	CK 58
Sering St	Bellville Sth	88	CA 49
Sering St	Paarl	22	BF 88
Sering St	Panorama	59	BV 42
Sering St	Rouxville	90	CA 56
Seringa La.	Forest Glade	127	CK 58
Seringa Rd	Tygerdal	58	BX 38
Serissa St	Ottery	121	CN 33
Serpentine Rd	Oranjezicht	99	CD 22
Serpentine Rd	Pinelands	84	CC 32
Serruria	Anesta	113	CF 75
Serruria Cl.	Plattekloof	60	BU 43
Serruria Cl.	Uitsig	87	CC 44
Serrurier St	Monte Vista	59	BV 39
Serv Rd	Kalk Bay	186	DA 26
Serval	Goedemoed	46	BO 53
Service Rd	Lakeside	159	CV 27
Service Way	Wetton	121	CL 34
Sesambos	Delft Sth	125	CJ 50
Sesame St	Lentegeur (M.Plain)	124	CN 45
Sesame St	Lentegeur (M.Plain)	124	CN 46
Sesbania St	Somerset West	151	CS 71
Sesibhozo	Kayamandi	94	BZ 74
Sesibini	Kayamandi	94	BZ 74
Sesihlanu	Kayamandi	94	BZ 74
Sesine	Kayamandi	94	BZ 74
Sesithoba	Kayamandi	94	BZ 74
Sesixhenxe	Kayamandi	94	BZ 74
Sessel St	Plumstead	140	CO 30
Sesthathu	Kayamandi	94	BZ 74
Seth Rd	Brown's Farm	123	CL 41
Setlaars Rd	Bothasig	43	BS 39
Setlaars St	Klipkop	87	BZ 45
Setona St	Kayamandi	94	CA 74
Settler St	Ruyterwacht	86	BZ 40
Settlers Dr.	Edgemead	58	BU 37
Settlers Dr.	Edgemead	58	BV 36
Settlers Dr.	Edgemead	58	BV 37
Settlers St	Oostersee	60	BX 46
Settlers Way	Bridgetown	103	CE 36
Settlers Way	Gugulethu	104	CG 42
Settlers Way	Gugulethu	105	CH 43
Settlers Way	Heideveld	104	CF 39
Settlers Way	Kewtown	102	CE 34
Settlers Way	Mowbray	101	CD 29
Settlers Way	Mowbray	101	CD 30
Settlers Way	Mowbray	102	CE 32
Settlers Way	Philippi East	124	CJ 45
Seven Sleepers St	Kirstenhof	158	CT 26
Seven Sleepers St	Kirstenhof	159	CT 27
Sevenoaks Rd	Heathfield	140	CR 29
Sevenoaks Rd	Plumstead	120	CM 29
Seventeenth Ave	Avon	86	CA 41
Seventeenth Ave	Boston	60	BW 46
Seventeenth Ave	Boston	61	BW 47
Seventeenth Ave	Fish Hoek	185	DA 22
Seventeenth Ave	Maitland	85	BZ 35
Seventeenth Ave	Norwood	86	CA 39
Seventeenth Ave	Schaap Kraal	142	CR 36
Seventeenth St	Avon	86	CA 41
Seventeenth St	Bishop Lavis	105	CD 43
Seventeenth St	Kensington	84	BZ 33
Seventh	De Oude Renbaan	22	BH 88
Seventh Ave	Belgravia	103	CG 35
Seventh Ave	Belmont Pk	48	BR 60
Seventh Ave	Belmont Pk	48	BR 61
Seventh Ave	Belmont Pk	48	BS 60
Seventh Ave	Boston	60	BX 46
Seventh Ave	Boston	61	BX 47
Seventh Ave	Cravenby	87	CA 43
Seventh Ave	Da Gama Pk	190	DE 21
Seventh Ave	Eikendal	47	BS 58
Seventh Ave	Eikendal	48	BS 59
Seventh Ave	Eikendal	63	BT 58
Seventh Ave	Elsies River Ind.	86	BZ 41
Seventh Ave	Fairways	121	CN 31
Seventh Ave	Fairways	141	CO 32
Seventh Ave	Fish Hoek	186	DB 24
Seventh Ave	Florida	87	CA 44
Seventh Ave	Grassy Pk	141	CQ 33
Seventh Ave	Grassy Pk	141	CR 32
Seventh Ave	Hazendal	102	CE 33
Seventh Ave	Kayamandi	94	CA 74
Seventh Ave	Kensington	84	BZ 33
Seventh Ave	Lotus River	141	CQ 34
Seventh Ave	Lotus River	142	CQ 35
Seventh Ave	Maitland	84	BZ 33
Seventh Ave	Mitchells Plain Cen.	145	CR 47
Seventh Ave	Retreat	140	CR 29
Seventh Ave	Retreat	140	CS 29
Seventh Ave	Rondebosch East	102	CG 32
Seventh Ave	Rondebosch East	102	CH 32
Seventh Ave	Schaap Kraal	142	CQ 36
Seventh Ave	Tafelsig (M.Plain)	146	CS 51
Seventh La.	Fisantekraal	31	BJ 58
Seventh La.	Fisantekraal	32	BJ 59
Seventh Rd	Montague Gdns Ind.	58	BT 35
Seventh St	Bishop Lavis	104	CD 42
Seventh St	Firgrove	150	CR 67
Seventh St	Kensington	84	BZ 33
Seventh St	Rusthof	174	DA 74
Seventh St	Rusthof	175	DA 75
Seventy-Seventh on Dummer St	Somerset West	171	CT 75
Severn Rd	Dieprivier	140	CP 28
Severn Rd	Eersterivier	128	CN 61
Severn Rd	Eersterivier	128	CJ 61
Severn Rd	Plumstead	120	CN 30
Sextet Cl.	Dalvale	19	AZ 92
Seychelles Ave	Capri	185	DB 19
Seymour Ave	Vredehoek	100	CD 23
Seymour Rd	Wynberg	120	CL 28
Seymour St	Observatory	83	CC 29
Shaanti Cr.	Gatesville	103	CG 37
Shabalala St	Gugulethu	104	CG 41
Shackelton Cr.	Kraaifontein	47	BQ 58
Shackelton Cr.	Kraaifontein	47	BQ 58
Shackleton	Rocklands (M.Plain)	163	CT 46
Shaddock St	Brooklyn	83	BZ 32
Shaftesbury Ave	Malibu Village	127	CK 56
Shaftesbury Rd	Wetton	121	CM 34
Shakespeare Rd	Eersterivier	128	CM 60
Shako Pl.	Leonsdale	86	CA 41
Shale Cl.	Somerset West	171	CW 78
Shale St	Bellville	62	BU 51
Shallcross Rd	Bel Ombre	119	CM 25
Shamrock Green	Summer Greens	58	BV 36
Shamrock Rd	Newlands	100	CH 25
Shangani Cr.	Delft	106	CG 49
Shangani St	Mfuleni	126	CK 53
Shanghai Way	Admirals Pk	179	DD 78
Shanklin Cr.	Camps Bay	98	CD 18
Shanklin Cr.	Camps Bay	99	CD 19
Shannon St	Connaught	87	CB 43
Shannon St	Salt River	83	CB 28
Shannons Green	Summer Greens	58	BV 36
Shari Way	Delft	106	CF 49
Sharon Cr.	Brackenfell Sth	63	BX 57
Sharon Cr.	Macassar	149	CS 63
Sharon Rd	Brown's Farm	123	CL 41
Sharon St	Delro	107	CH 54
Sharon St	Tafelsig (M.Plain)	145	CS 50
Sharon St	Tafelsig (M.Plain)	146	CS 51
Sharp Cl.	Dalvale	19	AZ 92
Sharpeville	Weltevreden Val. (M.Plain)	123	CN 41
Shashi Ct	Delft	106	CG 49
Shashi St	Mfuleni	126	CJ 54
Shasta Cl.	Uitsig	87	CC 44
Shaun Rd	Pinati	122	CK 35
Shaw Cr.	Edgemead	58	BV 37
Shaw Cr.	Tafelsig (M.Plain)	145	CS 48
Shaw Rd	Milnerton	57	BU 32
Shaw Rd	Rondebosch	102	CG 32
Shawcamp Rd	Ottery	121	CM 32
Shawn St	Morgenster Hoogte	63	BU 56
Shayele Rd	Eersterivier	128	CM 60
Shearer Green	Summer Greens	58	BW 35
Shearwater Cr.	Admirals Pk	175	DC 78
Shearwater Cr.	Admirals Pk	175	DB 78
Shearwater Dr.	Marina Da Gama	159	CU 30
Sheba St	Vredekloof Hgts	47	BS 55
Sheeda Rd	Hout Bay	136	CO 10
Sheerness Rd	Kenilworth	120	CK 29
Sheffield Cl.	Parklands	25	BN 34
Sheffield Cl.	Weltevreden Val. (M.Plain)	143	CP 42
Sheffield Rd	Brown's Farm	123	CL 42
Sheffield Rd	Brown's Farm	123	CM 41
Sheffield Rd	Brown's Farm	124	CL 43
Sheffield Rd	Philippi	124	CL 45
Sheffield Rd	Philippi East	124	CL 46
Sheffield Rd	Philippi East	125	CL 47
Sheffield St	Malibu Village	127	CK 56
Sheigh Hassan	Weltevreden Val. (M.Plain)	144	CR 44
Sheigh Yusuf	Weltevreden Val. (M.Plain)	144	CR 44
Sheila St	Avonwood	86	CB 42
Sheila St	Tafelsig (M.Plain)	145	CS 50
Sheldon Rd	Crawford	102	CH 34
Sheldon Rd	Milnerton	57	BV 32
Sheldon Sq.	Edgemead	58	BU 38
Sheldon Way	Pinelands	84	CC 34
Shelduck Cr.	Pelikan Pk	161	CV 37
Shelduck Rd	Pelikan Pk	142	CR 36
Shelduck St	Electric City	127	CN 58
Shell Rd	Steenberg	159	CU 30
Shell Rd	Table View	24	BN 29
Shelley Cr.	Milnerton	57	BT 33
Shelley Rd	Salt River	83	CC 28
Shelley Rd	Table View	41	BP 34
Shelley St	Windsor Pk	47	BR 57
Shelley St	Zoo Pk	47	BQ 57
Shellsby	Newfields	122	CJ 37
Sheltie St	Jagtershof	108	CD 56
Sheny Cl.	Vredekloof Hgts	47	BS 55
Shepards Wk	Somerset West	171	CV 77
Sheperd Rd	Belhar	107	CD 51
Sheperd St	District Six	82	CB 25
Shepherd Rd	Mitchells Plain	144	CQ 45
Shepherd Way	Lavender Hill	160	CT 31
Shepherds Green	Summer Greens	58	BV 36
Sheppard St	District Six	82	CB 25
Sher Cr.	Balvenie	87	CC 43
Sher St	Balvenie	87	CC 43
Sher St	Durbanville	45	BP 50
Sherard Sq.	Wynberg	120	CM 29
Sheridan St	Brooklyn	84	BY 31
Sheringham St	Parklands	25	BM 34
Sherry Cl.	Table View	41	BO 33
Sherry Rd	Table View	41	BO 33
Sherry Way	Table View	41	BO 33
Sherwood Ave	Kenilworth	120	CK 30
Sherwood Cl.	Parklands	25	BN 32
Sherwood Cl.	Parklands	25	BN 33
Sherwood Cl.	Sonstraal Hgts	46	BQ 53
Sherwood Cr.	Edgemead	58	BV 37
Shetland Cl.	Capri	184	DB 18
Shetland Cr.	Mitchells Plain	144	CR 44
Shetland Dr.	Capri	184	DB 18
Shetland Dr.	Capri	185	DB 19
Shetland Rd	West Riding	42	BO 35
Shetland St	Rondebosch	101	CG 30
Shiba St	Gugulethu	123	CK 41
Shiba St	Gugulethu	123	CK 41
Shilling St	Ruyterwacht	86	BZ 39
Shilling St	Vierlanden	30	BN 51
Shingle	Green Oaks	95	BY 75
Shiplake Rd	Wynberg	120	CL 29
Shipman Rd	Elfindale	140	CP 29
Shiraz	Kleingeluk	113	CE 75
Shiraz Cr.	Constantia Village	119	CN 26
Shiraz Ave	Somerset West	151	CS 72
Shiraz Cl.	Elfindale	140	CP 29
Shiraz Cl.	Table View	41	BO 33
Shiraz Ebrahim St	Fisantekraal	31	BK 58
Shiraz Ebrahim St	Fisantekraal	32	BK 59
Shiraz Rd	Hout Bay	137	CP 16
Shiraz Rd	Saxenburg Ind. Pk	108	CE 57
Shiraz St	Normandie	64	BW 59
Shiraz St	Oude Westhof	44	BS 44
Shiraz St	William Lloyd	19	BC 94
Shire Cl.	Mitchells Plain	144	CR 44
Shire Ct	Delft	106	CF 50
Shire Rd	Kirstenhof	159	CU 27
Shire Rd	Kirstenhof	159	CW 27
Shire Rd	West Riding	41	BO 34
Shire St	Mfuleni	126	CK 54
Shireen St	Casablanca	175	DB 76
Shireen St	Delro	126	CJ 54
Shirley Cl.	Bellville	62	BV 51
Shirley Cl.	Montana/Durrheim	104	CF 41
Shirley Cr.	Mabille Pk	89	CA 53
Shirley Rd	Bishop Lavis	104	CE 42

Abbreviations used: Ave – Avenue, A.H. – Agricultural Holding, A.L.– Algemene Landgoed, Blvd – Boulevard, Cen. – Central, Cir. – Circle, Cl. – Close, Cr. – Crescent, Ct – Court, Dr. – Drive, Est. – Estate, Ext. – Extension, Hgts – Heights, Ind. – Industrial, Gdns – Gardens, Gr. – Grove, La. – Lane, (M.Plain) - Mitchells Plain, Nth – North, Pl. – Place, Pk – Park, Rd – Road, Rdg. – Ridge, S.H.– Small Holding, Sq. – Square, St – Street, Sth – South, Ter. – Terrace, Tn – Turn, Val. – Valley, Wk – Walk

STREET NAME	SUBURB NAME	PG	GRID	
Shirley Rd	Claremont	120	CJ	28
Shiryan Cl.	Alphen	119	CM	26
Shiyeka St	Umrhabulo Triangle	147	CP	58
Shoal Creek Mews	Milnerton	57	BT	32
Short	Cloetesville	95	CA	75
Short	Durbanville	45	BQ	50
Short	Ottery	121	CM	32
Short Rd	Barbarossa	140	CO	27
Short Rd	Montagu's Gift	141	CO	34
Short Rd	Somerset West	152	CS	75
Short St	Bishop Lavis	105	CE	43
Short St	Cravenby	87	CA	43
Short St	Glenlily	87	BY	43
Short St	Somerset West	170	CV	74
Short St	Table View	41	BO	31
Short St	Wellington	10	AR	93
Shortmarket St	Cape Town Cen.	82	CA	23
Shoveller Way	Pelikan Pk	142	CR	36
Showboat St	Macassar	149	CS	65
Showground Ave	Epping Ind.	86	CB	39
Shrewsbury Way	Westlake Est.	158	CU	25
Shrike Cr.	Seawinds	159	CU	30
Shropshire St	Paarden Eiland	83	BZ	29
Shukuma St	Umrhabulo Triangle	147	CQ	56
Shumani St	Tarentaalplaas	170	CX	74
Shushu Cr.	Umrhabulo Triangle	147	CP	57
Shushu Cr.	Umrhabulo Triangle	147	CQ	57
Shwabane Cr.	Eyethu	146	CP	53
Shwabane Cr.	Eyethu	146	CP	54
Sias Snyman St	Heemstede	62	BW	52
Sias Snyman St	Heemstede	62	BX	52
Sibeko St	Eyethu	146	CO	52
Sibelius Ave	Retreat	159	CT	29
Sibelius St	Protea Hoogte	63	BW	57
Sibeluis	Delft Sth	125	CJ	48
Sibeni Ave	Nyanga	124	CK	43
Siberian	Rocklands (M.Plain)	144	CS	45
Sibiya Rd	Brown's Farm	123	CM	41
Sibolo St	Kaya	146	CP	52
Sicelo Mhlawuli	Weltevreden Val. (M.Plain)	123	CN	42
Sicibilili Ave	Ilitha Pk	146	CQ	52
Sicily Rd	Ottery	121	CL	33
Sicily St	Portlands (M.Plain)	144	CQ	46
Sicily Way	Rondebosch East	102	CG	33
Sicukujeje Cr.	Ilitha Pk	146	CQ	53
Sidbury Rd	Plumstead	120	CM	29
Siddique Ave	Salberau	86	CB	41
Sidego Cr.	Highbury	107	CD	54
Sidima Cr.	Kaya	146	CO	51
Sidloyi St	Eyethu	146	CP	53
Sidmouth	Muizenberg	159	CX	29
Sidmouth	Muizenberg	159	CW	27
Sidmouth Ave	Claremont	120	CJ	27
Sidmouth Ave	Oranjezicht	99	CD	22
Sidneyvale Rd	Bishop Lavis	105	CD	43
Sidon Cl.	Bonnie Brook	47	BQ	57
Sidvale St	Oostersee	87	BY	45
Sidwadwa St	Kuyasa	147	CR	56
Siebbritz St	Rabiesdale	19	BC	92
Siegfried St	Eastridge (M.Plain)	145	CQ	48
Sierra Cl.	Mandalay	125	CM	47
Sierra Rd	Montana/Durrheim	104	CF	41
Sierra St	Fisantekraal	32	BJ	59
Sierra Way	Mandalay	125	CM	47
Sigcawu Ave	Langa	103	CF	37
Sigcawu Ave	Langa	103	CD	36
Sigenu St	Nonqubela	146	CO	53
Sigkoti Cr.	Nonqubela	146	CO	53
Signal Cl.	Belhar	107	CD	52
Signal Cr.	Montague Gdns Ind.	58	BU	36
Signal Hill Rd	Tamboerskloof	81	CA	20
Signal Hill Rd	Tamboerskloof	81	CB	20
Signal St	Schotsche Kloof	81	CA	22
Sigutya St	Nonqubela	126	CN	53
Sigwele Ave	Victoria Mxenge	126	CN	51
Sihawu Cr.	Nonqubela	126	CN	53
Sihlanu Ave	Nyanga	124	CK	43
Sihle Cr.	Kaya	146	CO	52
Sihle Cr.	Kaya	146	CP	52
Sihlopo Cr.	Eyethu	146	CO	52
Sihumi Rd	Nyanga	124	CK	43
Sikade St	Mfuleni	126	CL	53
Sikanti St	Nonqubela	146	CO	52
Sikelela	Kalkfontein I	107	CD	52
Sikhafu Cr.	Crossroads	124	CK	44
Sikhafu Cr.	Crossroads	124	CN	46
Sikhawini	Wellington	15	AU	91
Sikhinkili Cl.	Nyanga	123	CK	42
Sikhobongela St	Wallacedene	48	BS	62
Sikhova	Philippi East	124	CL	46
Sikhova Cr.	Joe Slovo Pk	57	BU	34
Sikhulule Cr.	Mxolisi Phetani	125	CN	49
Sikhwalmanzi St	Brown's Farm	124	CM	43
Sikhwalmanzi St	Ilitha Pk	146	CR	51
Sikhwenene St	Brown's Farm	124	CL	43
Sikhwenene St	Ilitha Pk	146	CQ	52
Sikwenene	Philippi East	124	CL	46
Sikwenene	Philippi East	124	CN	46
Silica Rd	Sand Ind.	122	CJ	37
Silica Wk	Newfields	122	CJ	36
Silimela	Mbekweni	15	AX	91
Silimela St	Gugulethu	104	CF	40
Silivere	Mbekweni	15	AV	92
Silivere	Mbekweni	15	AU	94
Sillery Rd	Bergvliet	140	CR	28
Sillery Rd	Sillery	139	CO	25
Sillery St	Somerset West	169	CT	70
Silo St	Ravensmead	87	CB	44
Silumko St	Kaya	146	CP	52
Silva St	Brooklyn	83	BZ	30
Silvana Cl.	Mitchells Plain	144	CR	45
Silvana Cl.	Mitchells Plain	144	CS	43
Silver	Rocklands (M.Plain)	144	CS	46
Silver	Rocklands (M.Plain)	145	CS	47
Silver Leaves Way	Eversdal	46	BS	51
Silver Mist Rd	Sunridge	42	BP	35
Silver Oak La.	Green Oaks	94	BY	74
Silver Oak St	Bellair	62	BW	53
Silver Oak St	Bellair	62	BX	52
Silver Sands	Parklands	25	BN	34
Silver St	Brackenfell Ind.	63	BT	57
Silverboom Kloof Rd	Somerset West	151	CR	74
Silverboom Kloof Rd	Somerset West	152	CR	75
Silverdale	Pinelands	84	CB	34
Silverdale St	Wellington	11	AQ	96
Silvergang	Silverhurst	119	CN	24
Silverhill Cr.	Kenilworth	120	CK	29
Silverhill Rd	Courtrai	39	BJ	87
Silverhurst Cl.	Mitchells Plain	144	CR	45
Silverhurst Cl.	Wynberg	120	CK	28
Silverhurst Dr.	Silverhurst	119	CN	24
Silverhurst St	Mitchells Plain	144	CR	45
Silverhurst Way	Bergvliet	140	CQ	27
Silverhurst Way	Wynberg	120	CK	28
Silverlea Rd	Wynberg	120	CM	28
Silverleaf	Dunoon	42	BO	37
Silverleaf St	Forest Village	127	CM	58
Silvermine Rd	San Michel	157	CX	19
Silvermyn Cl.	Mitchells Plain	144	CQ	45
Silveroak Ave	Thornton	85	CA	37
Silveroaks Ave	Silveroaks	90	CC	55
Silversands Ave	Mitchells Plain	144	CQ	44
Silversands Ave	Mitchells Plain	144	CQ	45
Silversands Ave	Portlands (M.Plain)	144	CQ	46
Silversands Main Rd	Wesbank	107	CG	51
Silversands Rd	Voorbrug	106	CF	50
Silverstone Rd	Killarney Gdns	42	BP	37
Silverstream	Tafelsig (M.Plain)	145	CS	47
Silverstream Rd	Manenberg	104	CG	39
Silverstream Rd	Manenberg	104	CH	39
Silverton Rd	Plumstead	120	CN	29
Silvertree	Noordhoek	156	CV	17
Silvertree	Noordhoek	156	CV	18
Silvertree Cl.	Hout Bay	117	CN	15
Silvertree La.	Bergvliet	140	CQ	27
Silvertree La.	Bergvliet	140	CR	30
Silvertree La.	Silverhurst	119	CN	23
Silvertree St	Silvertown	102	CF	34
Silvertree Way	Bellair	62	BW	52
Silverwater St	Kirstenhof	159	CT	27
Silverwood Cl.	Westlake Est.	158	CU	25
Silwanyana St	Tarentaalplaas	171	CX	75
Silwerbeek Cr.	Vredekloof	62	BT	54
Silwerboom	Delft Sth	125	CJ	49
Silwerboom Ave	Plattekloof	59	BU	42
Silwereik St	Forest Hgts	127	CK	57
Silwermyn Cl.	Tafelsig (M.Plain)	145	CS	48
Silwood Rd	Rondebosch	101	CF	30
Silwood Rd	Rondebosch	102	CF	31
Silwood Way	Matroosfontein	86	CC	41
Simanga St	Bloekombos	48	BQ	62
Simmons Cl.	Jagtershof	108	CD	57
Simo St	Kaya	146	CO	52
Simon Cl.	Glen Rdg	191	DD	25
Simon Pl.	Mandalay	125	CN	47
Simon Rd	Montagu's Gift	142	CO	35
Simon Rd	Newfields	103	CH	37
Simon Seshea St	Gugulethu	123	CK	40
Simon St	Nomzano	175	CY	76
Simon St	Nomzano	175	CZ	76
Simon van der Stel Freeway	Dennedal	139	CR	26
Simond Rd	Belhar	106	CD	49
Simond Rd	Belhar	106	CH	48
Simond St	Welgemoed	61	BU	48
Simondium Cl.	Mitchells Plain	144	CR	45
Simondium Cl.	Mitchells Plain	144	CS	43
Simone St	De Tijger	60	BW	44
Simons Way	Eersterivier	128	CN	62
Simons Way	Noordhoek Manor	157	CX	21
Simonsberg	Brackenfell	63	BW	55
Simonsberg	Simonswyk	95	CB	78
Simonsberg	Wellington	10	AS	92
Simonsberg Cr.	Strand	174	CY	73
Simonsberg Cr.	Tafelsig (M.Plain)	164	CT	47
Simonsberg Ct	Edgemead	58	BU	38
Simonsberg Rd	Bishop Lavis	104	CE	42
Simonsberg Rd	Heideveld	104	CF	39
Simonsberg Rd	Valmary Pk	46	BR	51
Simonsberg St	Blue Downs	127	CJ	56
Simonsberg St	Bonnie Brae	47	BQ	57
Simonsberg St	Ocean View	184	DC	15
Simonsberg St	Ocean View	184	DC	17
Simonsig	De Bron	45	BS	48
Simonsig	Oude Westhof	44	BS	45
Simonsig Ave	Mitchells Plain	144	CR	45
Simonstown Rd	Fish Hoek	186	DC	24
Simonsvlei Rd	Simonsvlei	37	BN	82
Simonsvlei Rd	Simonsvlei	38	BL	84
Simonsvlei St	Haasendal	90	CB	57
Simpson Rd	Athlone	102	CF	34
Simpson St	Belhar	88	CC	49
Sinagogo Cr.	Ilitha Pk	146	CQ	52
Sinai Cl.	Brackenfell Sth	63	BX	57
Sine Ave	Nyanga	124	CK	43
Sinethemba St	Gugulethu	123	CK	40
Singer St	Beacon Valley (M.Plain)	145	CQ	47
Singolamthi St	Brown's Farm	123	CM	42
Singolamthi St	Ilitha Pk	146	CQ	52
Sinqolamthi St	Ilitha Pk	146	CR	52
Sinyenyweba St	Lwandle	175	CZ	76
Siphendule Cr.	Umrhabulo Triangle	147	CP	57
Siphingo St	Brown's Farm	124	CL	43
Siphiwe Cr.	Kaya	146	CP	51
Siphiwe Cr.	Weltevreden Val. (M.Plain)	124	CM	43
Siphiwo Gwele St	Kuyasa	147	CS	55
Siphiwo Gwele St	Kuyasa	147	CS	57
Siphiwo Mthimkulu	Weltevreden Val. (M.Plain)	123	CM	42
Siphiwo Mthmkulu St	Mandela Pk	147	CQ	55
Siphiwo Nyanda St	Mandela Pk	147	CQ	55
Siphiwo Nyanda St	Mandela Pk	147	CP	55
Sipho Hashe	Weltevreden Val. (M.Plain)	123	CN	41
Sipho Hashe	Weltevreden Val. (M.Plain)	123	CM	39
Sipho Xulu St	Mandela Pk	146	CR	53
Siphumelele Cr.	Mxolisi Phetani	125	CM	50
Sipingo St	Kuyasa	147	CR	56
Sipres	Delft Sth	106	CH	50
Sipres Ave	Belhar	88	CC	47
Sipres Ave	Bridgetown	103	CE	35
Sipres Ave	Edenpark	62	BU	54
Sipres Ave	Thornton	85	CA	37
Sipres Cl.	The Palms	170	CX	73
Sipres Cr.	Sonnedal	59	BV	42
Sipres Cr.	Wellington	10	AS	94
Sipres Rd	Halalie	46	BO	52
Sipres St	Bridgetown	103	CE	35
Sipres St	Loevenstein	60	BW	45
Sipres St	Sarepta	89	CC	52
Siqaza St	Eyethu	146	CP	53
Sir Alfred Ave	Lansdowne	121	CJ	32
Sir Bedivere St	Camelot	107	CF	53
Sir David Baird Dr.	Bloubergstrand	24	BL	28
Sir Galahad St	Camelot	107	CF	53
Sir George Grey St	Oranjezicht	81	CC	22
Sir George Grey St	Ruyterwacht	86	CB	39
Sir Lancelot	Camelot	107	CF	53
Sir Lowry Rd	District Six	82	CB	24
Sir Lowry Rd	Foreshore	82	CB	25
Sir Lowry Rd	Harbour Island	179	DD	77
Sir Lowry St	Somerset West	171	CW	75
Sir Lowry's Pass Rd	Mountainside Est.	179	DD	78
Sir Lowry's Pass Rd	Sir Lowry's Pass	175	CY	78
Sir Lowry's Pass Rd	Sir Lowry's Pass	176	CY	80
Sir Lowry's Pass Rd	Sir Lowry's Pass	176	CZ	80
Sir Lowry's Pass Rd	Sir Lowry's Pass	176	DC	80
Sir Lowry's Pass Rd	Somerset West	171	CW	76
Sir Percival	Camelot	107	CF	53
Sir Walter St	Camelot	107	CF	53
Sirbert Cl.	Des Hampden	89	CB	53
Sirius St	Blue Downs	127	CJ	55
Sirius Way	Ocean View	183	DC	14
Sirkel St	Wellington	10	AS	91
Siros Rd	Ottery	121	CL	33
Sirus Rd	Surrey	103	CG	38
Sirus Rd	Surrey	103	CH	38
Siseko Cir.	Eyethu	146	CO	53
Sishuba St	Nonqubela	146	CO	53
Sisonke St	Ekuphumuleni	146	CP	53
Sisulu Rd	Masiphumelele	184	DA	18
Siswana	Nonqubela	146	CO	53
Sitaya Cl.	Mfuleni	127	CL	55
Sithandatu Ave	Nyanga	124	CK	43
Sithathu Ave	Nyanga	124	CK	43
Sithela St	Nonqubela	146	CO	53
Sithembele Matiso St	Weltevreden Val. (M.Plain)	123	CN	41
Sithoboti St	Kuyasa	147	CR	56
Sithoboti St	Kuyasa	147	CS	57
Sithunzi St	Lwandle	175	CZ	76
Sithunzi St	Nomzano	175	CY	76
Sitofile St	Eyethu	146	CP	52
Sitofile St	Eyethu	146	CP	53
Sitonga Cr.	Nonqubela	126	CN	52
Sitrien Cl.	Welgelegen	59	BT	41
Sitrus St	Lemoenkloof	18	BB	88
Sive St	De Kuilen	89	CB	54
Sivivana	Mbekweni	15	AX	91
Sivivane	Umrhabulo Triangle	147	CP	57
Siviwe St	Nyanga	123	CL	41
Sivuyile Cr.	Kayamandi	94	CA	74
Sixaxabesha St	Ilitha Pk	146	CQ	52
Sixteenth Ave	Boston	60	BW	46
Sixteenth Ave	Boston	61	BW	47
Sixteenth Ave	Da Gama Pk	190	DE	22
Sixteenth Ave	Fish Hoek	186	DB	23
Sixteenth Ave	Leonsdale	86	CA	42
Sixteenth Ave	Maitland	85	BZ	35
Sixteenth Ave	Schaap Kraal	142	CR	36
Sixteenth Ave	Uitsig	87	CB	44
Sixteenth St	Bishop Lavis	105	CD	43
Sixteenth St	Elsies River Ind.	86	BZ	41
Sixteenth St	Elsies River Ind.	86	CA	41
Sixteenth St	Kensington	84	BZ	33
Sixth	De Oude Renbaan	22	BH	88
Sixth Ave	Athlone	102	CG	32
Sixth Ave	Belgravia	103	CG	35
Sixth Ave	Belmont Pk	48	BR	60
Sixth Ave	Belmont Pk	48	BS	60
Sixth Ave	Bloekombos	48	BR	61
Sixth Ave	Boston	60	BX	46
Sixth Ave	Boston	61	BX	47
Sixth Ave	Cravenby	87	CA	43
Sixth Ave	Da Gama Pk	190	DD	21
Sixth Ave	Eastridge (M.Plain)	145	CR	47
Sixth Ave	Eastridge (M.Plain)	145	CR	48
Sixth Ave	Eikendal	47	BS	58
Sixth Ave	Eikendal	48	BS	59
Sixth Ave	Eikendal	63	BT	58
Sixth Ave	Elsies River Ind.	86	BZ	41
Sixth Ave	Fairways	121	CN	32
Sixth Ave	Fairways	141	CO	32
Sixth Ave	Fish Hoek	186	DB	24
Sixth Ave	Florida	87	CA	44
Sixth Ave	Grassy Pk	141	CQ	33
Sixth Ave	Grassy Pk	141	CR	31
Sixth Ave	Grassy Pk	141	CR	32
Sixth Ave	Hazendal	102	CE	33
Sixth Ave	Kayamandi	94	CA	74
Sixth Ave	Kensington	84	BZ	33
Sixth Ave	Lotus River	141	CQ	34
Sixth Ave	Lotus River	142	CP	35
Sixth Ave	Maitland	84	CA	33
Sixth Ave	Retreat	140	CR	29
Sixth Ave	Retreat	140	CS	29
Sixth Ave	Rondebosch East	102	CG	32
Sixth Ave	Schaap Kraal	142	CP	36
Sixth Ave	Tafelsig (M.Plain)	146	CS	51
Sixth Ave	Wellington	10	AS	93
Sixth Rd	Montague Gdns Ind.	58	BT	37
Sixth St	Bishop Lavis	104	CD	42
Sixth St	Firgrove	150	CR	67
Sixth St	Kensington	84	CA	33
Sixth St	Rusthof	174	DA	74
Sixth St	Rusthof	175	DA	75
Sixth St	Valhalla	86	CA	40
Sixth St	Valhalla	86	CA	40
Sixwayikati St	Brown's Farm	123	CM	42
Sixwayikati St	Ilitha Pk	146	CQ	53
Sixwila Cr.	Ilitha Pk	146	CQ	53
Siya Bonga St	Lwandle	175	CZ	76
Siyabonga	Dunoon	26	BN	38
Siyabonga St	Dunoon	42	BO	37
Siyakha St	Mxolisi Phetani	125	CM	50
Siyaya Ave	Nonqubela	126	CN	52
Sizakhele Cr.	Mfuleni	126	CL	54
Sizamile St	Wimbledon	108	CG	55
Sizani Rd	Eyethu	146	CO	53
Skaamrosie Rd	Proteavallei	61	BT	47
Skadu	Dalsig	113	CE	76
Skagerak Way	Eversdal	62	BT	51
Skaife St	Hout Bay	137	CQ	16
Skakel Rd	Arauna	63	BU	55
Skakel Rd	Brackenfell Ind.	63	BT	58
Skakel St	Churchill	59	BX	42
Skakel St	Paarl	22	BF	88
Skakel St	Soneike I	89	CA	54
Skapenberg Cr.	Welgevonden	46	BO	54
Skapu St	Nonqubela	146	CO	53
Skeerkwas Rd	Welgedacht	60	BT	46
Skeleton St	Tafelsig (M.Plain)	145	CS	47
Skemerzicht Cl.	Brackenfell Sth	63	BW	58
Skemerzicht Cl.	Brackenfell Sth	63	BV	58
Skepe Sq.	Factreton	85	BZ	35
Skew St	Plumstead	140	CO	30
Skewbald Rd	Milnerton	41	BS	34
Skewbald Rd	Milnerton	41	BS	33
Skhwalimanzi Ct	Joe Slovo Pk	57	BU	34
Skhwalimanzi Ct	Joe Slovo Pk	57	BU	31
Skiet Cr.	Scottsdene	64	BT	60
Skilpad Cl.	Protea Hoogte	63	BW	57
Skilpadbessie	Lentegeur (M.Plain)	145	CO	47
Skilpaddam	Jagtershof	108	CD	56
Skilpadvlei Way	Skilpadvlei	45	BO	50
Skina Rd	Masiphumelele	184	DA	18
Skinner Ct	Delft	106	CG	49
Skip Rd	Surrey	103	CH	37
Skipper St	Kylemore	97	BZ	86
Skipper's End	Pelikan Pk	141	CS	33
Skoenmaker St	Dal Josafat Ind.	18	BA	90
Skoji St	Tarentaalplaas	175	CY	75
Skola Jiba St	Kuyasa	147	CS	55
Skola Jiba St	Kuyasa	147	CS	57
Skool	Krigeville	113	CD	76
Skool St	Bellville Sth Ext. 5	88	BZ	49
Skool St	Belmont Pk	48	BS	60
Skool St	Elim	89	CA	54
Skool St	Franschhoek Nth	75	BX	105
Skool St	Mfuleni	126	CL	54
Skool St	Montana/Durrheim	104	CF	41
Skool St	Morningstar	46	BP	52
Skool St	Wellington	15	AV	93
Skoongesig St	Tafelsig (M.Plain)	145	CR	49
Skoonlief St	Elim	90	CB	55
Skoonsig Ave	Voorbrug	106	CG	50
Skoonsig St	Panorama	59	BV	42
Skotshold St	Philippi East	125	CL	47
Skua	Rocklands (M.Plain)	163	CT	45
Skua Cr.	Pelikan Pk	161	CV	37
Skua Cr.	Pelikan Pk	161	CV	38
Skuins St	Paarlzicht	19	BC	91
Skuller Rd	Maitland	84	CA	34
Skutter Sq.	Factreton	85	BY	35

Index to Street Names

Skweza St — Steenbok Way

STREET NAME	SUBURB NAME	PG	GRID	
Skweza St	Gugulethu	123	CK	41
Sky Rd	Bishop Lavis	105	CD	44
Sky Rd	Bishop Lavis	105	CE	43
Skye Way	Sea Point	81	BZ	22
Skyliner Ave	Villa Italia	57	BW	33
Skyvlier Dr.	St Dumas	90	CC	55
Slabbert Rd	Somerset West	171	CT	77
Slang Way	Delft	106	CG	49
Slangberg Rd	Bishop Lavis	104	CE	42
Slanghoek Rd	Manenberg	104	CG	39
Slanghoek St	Welgevonden	46	BO	54
Slangkop Cr.	Tafelsig (M.Plain)	145	CS	48
Slangkop Rd	Kommetjie	183	DC	14
Slangkop Rd	Witsand	188	DD	14
Slangkop Way	Skoongesig	45	BO	50
Slangolie St	Tafelsig (M.Plain)	145	CS	48
Sleepy Hollow La.	Chapman's Peak	156	CX	17
Sleigh Cr.	Somerset West	171	CT	78
Sleigh Rd	Somerset West	171	CT	78
Sloane Cr.	Eersterivier	128	CM	59
Sloane Sq.	Parklands	25	BM	33
Sloop St	Strandfontein	161	CU	38
Sloster Ave	Grassy Pk	141	CQ	31
Slovo Cr.	Wimbledon	108	CG	55
Sluysken Rd	Hout Bay	136	CQ	14
Sluysken St	Monte Vista	59	BW	39
Sluysken St	Somerset West	150	CS	70
Sluyskens St	Welgemoed	61	BV	47
Smal Cl.	Mandalay	125	CM	48
Smal St	Rondebosch East	102	CH	32
Smal St	Stanlou	61	BX	48
Smalblaar Rd	Bonteheuwel	104	CE	39
Small St	Grassy Pk	141	CR	32
Small St	Valhalla	86	CA	40
Smarag Cr.	Welgelegen	59	BT	40
Smarag St	Bellville	62	BV	51
Smarag St	Forest Hgts	127	CK	58
Smarag St	Forest Hgts	127	CL	58
Smartt Rd	Goodwood Est.	58	BX	38
Smartt Rd	Richmond Est.	59	BX	40
Smartt Rd	Townsend Est.	85	BY	37
Smartt Rd	Vasco Est.	59	BX	39
Smid Rd	Mitchells Plain	144	CQ	45
Smit St	Onverwacht	174	CZ	73
Smith Cr.	Groenheuwel	19	BA	91
Smith Rd	Rosebank	101	CE	30
Smith St	Bishop Lavis	104	CD	41
Smith St	Casablanca	175	DB	76
Smith St	Churchill	60	BX	43
Smith St	De La Haye	61	BX	50
Smith St	Glenlily	87	BY	43
Smith St	Simon's Town	194	DJ	24
Smith St	Wellington	11	AR	95
Smithers Rd	Kenilworth	120	CK	29
Smiths Rd	Plumstead	140	CO	29
Smokey Cr.	Wesbank	107	CF	51
Smook	Paarl	22	BE	87
Smuts	Stellenbosch	95	CB	76
Smuts Ave	Somerset West	170	CT	74
Smuts Rd	Lansdowne	102	CH	32
Smuts Rd	Lansdowne	121	CJ	33
Smuts St	Eastridge (M.Plain)	145	CQ	49
Snaffle Ave	Hout Bay	117	CM	16
Snapdragon	Lentegeur (M.Plain)	144	CO	45
Snapdragon St	Bridgetown	103	CF	37
Snares Brook Rd	Epping Forest	86	CC	41
Sneeuberg	Brackenfell	63	BW	55
Sneeuberg	Wellington	15	AV	91
Sneeuberg Cr.	Bonnie Brae	47	BQ	57
Sneeuberg Cr.	Bonnie Brae	47	BP	58
Sneeuberg Rd	Bishop Lavis	104	CE	42
Sneeuberg Rd	Durbanville Hills	45	BR	49
Sneeuberg Rd	Eversdal	62	BU	51
Sneeuberg Rd	Heideveld	104	CG	40
Sneeuberg Rd	Lavender Hill East	160	CU	32
Sneeuberg Rd	Lavender Hill East	160	CS	33
Sneeukop Cl.	Somerset West	152	CS	78
Sneeukop Cr.	Greenfield	108	CH	57
Sneeukop Rd	Tafelsig (M.Plain)	145	CR	49
Snell St	Scottsville	47	BS	57
Snipe Rd	Pelikan Pk	142	CR	35
Snipe Way	Electric City	127	CM	58
Snooker Cl.	Beacon Valley (M.Plain)	145	CP	48
Snowball Rd	Proteavallei	60	BT	46
Snowdon St	Tafelsig (M.Plain)	164	CT	48
Snowdrop Sq.	Bridgetown	103	CE	35
Sobat Ct	Delft	106	CF	49
Sobers St	William Lloyd	23	BD	92
Soboyce St	Bloekombos	49	BS	63
Sobukwe Rd	Masiphumelele	184	DA	18
Soccer St	Woodlands (M.Plain)	144	CP	44
Socony Rd	Elsies River Ind.	86	BZ	42
Soekmekaar St	Macassar	149	CS	64
Soetdoring Cr.	Vredekloof	62	BT	53
Soetdoring St	Bonteheuwel	103	CE	38
Soetdoring St	Silveroaks	90	CC	56
Soeteweide	Universiteits-oord	95	CB	77
Soeteweide St	Amanda Glen	46	BS	52
Soetkop St	Bonteheuwel	104	CD	40
Soetrivier St	Bothasig	42	BS	37
Soetvlei Ave	Porter Est.	139	CQ	25
Soetvlei Ave	Sweet Valley	139	CQ	26
Soetvlei Ave	Sweet Valley	139	CR	26
Sofia St	Beacon Valley (M.Plain)	145	CP	48
Sofutho St	Kuyasa	147	CR	56
Sofy St	Wallacedene	48	BS	61
Soh St	Macassar	149	CS	65
Sohland Ave	Belle Constantia	139	CO	26
Soho Cl.	Malibu Village	127	CK	56
Soho Cr.	Malibu Village	127	CK	55
Sokuqala	Kayamandi	94	BZ	74
Sol Cohen Rd	Heathfield	140	CQ	28
Sol Plaatjie St	Mandela Pk	146	CQ	54
Solan Rd	Gardens	82	CB	23
Solar Cl.	Salberau	86	CB	41
Solara Cr.	Sonstraal Hgts	46	BR	53
Soldaat Sq.	Factreton	85	BY	35
Soldier Way	Summer Greens	58	BW	35
Soldier Way	Summer Greens	58	BW	36
Soleil	Sonstraal Hgts	46	BR	53
Solero Cl.	Brackenfell Sth	63	BX	56
Soliter St	Kirstenhof	159	CT	27
Sollum Rd	Green Point	81	BZ	21
Solly Arendse Cl.	Gustrow	175	DB	75
Solly Freedburg St	Panorama	59	BV	41
Solly Smiedt St	N1 City	59	BX	39
Solo St	District Six	82	CB	25
Solo St	Retreat	140	CS	29
Soloko St	Umrhabulo Triangle	147	CQ	57
Solomans Cr.	Wellington	10	AR	92
Solomon	Ravensmead	87	CA	46
Solomon Mahlangu	Weltevreden Val. (M.Plain)	123	CN	42
Solomon Malangu Cr.	Mandela Pk	147	CR	55
Solomon St	Somerset West	170	CT	74
Solomon St	Tarentaalplaas	170	CX	74
Solomon St	Tarentaalplaas	175	CY	75
Solomon St	William Lloyd	19	BC	93
Solomon St	William Lloyd	23	BD	93
Solomon Tshuku Ave	Mxolisi Phetani	125	CM	50
Solomons Ave	Grassy Pk	141	CQ	33
Solomons Link	Ocean View	184	DC	16
Solomons Rd	Sea Point	80	CA	18
Solonis Cr.	Groenvlei	18	BA	87
Solstice Rd	Thembokwezi	125	CM	49
Soluta St	Sunset Beach	41	BS	31
Solway	Vredelust	87	BY	46
Sombo St	Nyanga	123	CJ	42
Somer Rd	Eversdal	61	BT	50
Somer Rd	Eversdal	62	BT	51
Somer St	Surrey	103	CG	37
Somerford St	Somerset West	150	CS	70
Somerlus Ave	Voorbrug	106	CG	50
Somerlust St	Winslow	179	DD	77
Somerset Cl.	Parklands	25	BN	33
Somerset Cr.	Lakeside	159	CV	28
Somerset Cr.	Wellway Pk	46	BP	51
Somerset Lake	Somerset West	171	CW	77
Somerset Rd	Green Point	82	BZ	23
Somerset Rd	Onverwacht	175	DC	76
Somerset Rd	Onverwacht	175	DB	78
Somerset Rd	Richwood	42	BQ	37
Somerset Rd	Winslow	179	DD	76
Somerset St	Claremont	120	CJ	29
Somerset St	Claremont	120	CK	30
Somerset St	Panorama	59	BV	42
Somerset St	Somerset West	171	CV	75
Somerset Way	Edgemead	58	BV	37
Somerset Way	Kommetjie	183	DB	11
Somi Cl.	Ilitha Pk	146	CR	52
Somi Cr.	Philippi East	124	CL	46
Somme Cl.	Strandfontein	162	CT	40
Somme Cl.	Strandfontein	162	CV	42
Sommerville Rd	Blouberg Sands	24	BL	30
Son St	Lansdowne	121	CK	32
Sonata Ave	Dalvale	19	AY	92
Sonata La.	Mitchells Plain Cen.	145	CR	47
Sonata St	Retreat	159	CT	27
Sonata Way	Belhar	106	CD	49
Sonbos Cl.	Protea Village	64	BV	59
Sondags Cr.	Eersterivier	128	CN	59
Sondal Cr.	Sonstraal Hgts	46	BR	53
Sondal Rd	Eversdal	46	BS	51
Sondal Rd	Eversdal	62	BT	51
Sondela St	Eyethu	146	CP	53
Sonderend Rd	Manenberg	123	CJ	39
Sonderend St	Mfuleni	126	CJ	53
Sonderend St	Portlands (M.Plain)	144	CQ	45
Sondou La.	Silvertown	103	CF	36
Sondraai Ave	Voorbrug	106	CG	50
Sonesta St	Jagtershof	108	CD	57
Songeze Cr.	Eyethu	146	CP	53
Soni Rd	Athlone	102	CG	33
Sonke St	Kaya	146	CP	51
Sonneblom	Dunoon	42	BO	37
Sonneblom	Dunoon	42	BO	38
Sonneblom	Idasvallei	95	CA	78
Sonneblom Cr.	Bridgetown	103	CF	36
Sonneblom Rd	Bloemhof	61	BV	50
Sonneblom Rd	Stellenridge	62	BV	51
Sonneblom St	Parow Nth	60	BW	43
Sonneblom St	Uitsig	87	CB	44
Sonneblom St	Wellington	15	AT	92
Sonnedou	Stellenbosch	95	BY	75
Sonnedou Cl.	Plattekloof	60	BV	43
Sonnedou Rd	Pelikan Pk	142	CQ	36
Sonnemeisie St	Elim	90	CA	55
Sonnemeisie St	Elim	90	CB	55
Sonnendal Way	Marinda Hgts	89	BZ	52
Sonnet Cr.	Morgenster Hoogte	63	BU	55
Sonnet Quay	Marina Da Gama	159	CV	30
Sonneweelde	Goedemoed	46	BP	54
Sonny Leon Rd	Charlesville	104	CF	40
Sonny Rd	Vredelust	60	BW	46
Sonop St	Morgenster Hoogte	63	BU	55
Sonop St	Wellington	15	AW	93
Sonskyn St	Churchill	59	BX	42
Sonskyn St	Sunray	61	BX	49
Sonstraal Rd	Eversdal Hgts	46	BS	51
Sonstraal Rd	New Orleans	19	BB	94
Sonte Cl.	Vredekloof Hgts	47	BS	55
Sontie St	Elim	90	CB	55
Sonto St	Mxolisi Phetani	125	CL	50
Sonwabile Dr.	Crossroads	124	CK	44
Sonwabile Dr.	Crossroads	124	CK	45
Sonwabo St	Eyethu	146	CP	53
Sony St	Kaya	146	CP	51
Sonya St	Tafelsig (M.Plain)	145	CS	50
Sonyathi St	Bloekombos	49	BQ	63
Sonzicht Cl.	Brackenfell Sth	63	BX	57
Sophia St	Kalkfontein II	107	CD	53
Sophia St	Oranjezicht	82	CC	23
Sopraan St	Macassar	149	CS	65
Sopwith Rd	Kensington	84	BZ	34
Sorbonne St	Helderberg Pk	175	DA	75
Sorrel Way	Pelikan Pk	142	CQ	36
Sorrel Way	Pelikan Pk	142	CR	36
Sorrento Rd	St James	187	CZ	27
Soshanna Way	Kenridge	61	BU	49
South Access Rd	Montague Gdns Ind.	42	BR	36
South Arm Rd	Foreshore	82	BY	24
South Ave	Athlone	102	CF	34
South Ave	Kewtown	103	CF	35
South Ave	Somerset Rdg	170	CU	72
South Cl.	Montagu's Gift	141	CO	34
South East Temporal	Rocklands (M.Plain)	145	CS	47
South Link	Athlone	102	CF	34
South Rd	Plumstead	120	CM	30
South Rd	Table View	41	BP	33
South Rd	Table View	41	BP	34
South Rd	Table View	41	BQ	34
South Rd	Table View	42	BQ	35
South St	KWV	22	BG	88
South St	Wellington	10	AS	92
South Way	Pinelands	102	CD	33
South Wk	Pinelands	102	CD	33
Southam Cl.	Eersterivier	128	CN	61
Southdale Rd	Edgemead	58	BV	37
Southdene	Wesbank	107	CH	51
Southern Cross	Rocklands (M.Plain)	144	CS	46
Southern Cross Ave	Southfork	175	DB	75
Southern Cross Ave	Thembokwezi	125	CM	49
Southern Cross Ave	Thembokwezi	125	CK	50
Southern Cross Dr.	Bel Ombre	119	CM	23
Southern Cross Dr.	Silverhurst	119	CM	25
Southern Cross Dr.	Witteboomen	119	CM	23
Southern Cross St	Salberau	86	CB	41
Southern Hills Dr.	Lavender Hill	159	CT	30
Southern Right Cir.	Kommetjie	183	DA	13
Southey St	Flintdale Est.	140	CP	30
Southfield Rd	Plumstead	120	CN	29
Southfield Rd	Plumstead	120	CN	30
Southfork Cl.	Southfork	175	DB	75
Southgate Rd	Retreat	140	CR	30
Southgate St	Woodstock	82	CA	26
Soutpansberg Rd	Lavender Hill East	160	CU	32
Sovereign	Plumstead	140	CO	30
Spaanschemat River Rd	Barbarossa	119	CN	26
Spaanschemat River Rd	Fir Grove	139	CQ	24
Spaarman Ave	Alphen	119	CM	26
Span St	Lakeside	159	CV	27
Spandau Rd	Park Village	127	CK	58
Spaniel	Strandfontein	162	CT	40
Spanish Oak St	Oak Glen	62	BW	53
Spanner Cr.	Philippi East	125	CL	48
Sparaxis Ave	Welgedacht	60	BT	44
Sparden Rd	Northpine	63	BU	58
Sparks Mahamba St	Kuyasa	147	CS	55
Sparks Mahamba St	Kuyasa	147	CS	57
Sparman St	Park Estates	170	CX	72
Sparrman Ave	Monte Vista	59	BV	39
Sparrow	Acacia Pk	58	BX	36
Sparrow	Joostenberg	48	BO	62
Sparrow	Rocklands (M.Plain)	144	CS	45
Sparrow Cr.	Flamingo Vlei	41	BQ	33
Sparrow Mkhonto	Weltevreden Val. (M.Plain)	123	CN	42
Sparrow Rd	Langeberg Rdg	47	BR	56
Sparrow St	Bishop Lavis	105	CD	43
Sparrow St	Penlyn Est.	103	CH	36
Sparrow Wk	Sunbird Pk	107	CF	54
Sparrowhawk Cl.	D'urbanvale	29	BN	50
Sparrowhawk Cr.	D'urbanvale	29	BN	50
Sparrowhawk Rd	Pelikan Pk	142	CR	35
Sparta Way	Joe Slovo Pk	57	BU	34
Spatalla Cl.	Gordon Hgts	180	DD	79
Spatalla Cl.	Gordon Hgts	180	DE	79
Spearhead Quay	Marina Da Gama	159	CV	30
Speciosa	Anesta	113	CF	75
Spectra Rd	Retreat	140	CR	28
Spek Boom Ave	New Orleans	19	BA	91
Spekboom	Delft Sth	125	CJ	50
Spekboom Pl.	Leonsdale	86	CA	42
Spekboom St	Edenpark	62	BU	54
Speke St	Observatory	83	CC	29
Speldebos Cr.	Protea Village	64	BV	59
Speldekussing Cl.	Protea Village	64	BW	59
Speldekussing Cl.	Protea Village	64	BV	60
Spencer Rd	Claremont	101	CH	29
Spencer Rd	Woodstock	83	CB	28
Spencer St	Goodwood Est.	59	BX	39
Spencer St	Goodwood Est.	86	BY	39
Spencer St	Maitland	84	CA	31
Spes Bona Ave	Avondale	60	BW	44
Spes Bona Rd	Fisantekraal	31	BJ	56
Spes Bona Rd	Phesantekraal	30	BJ	51
Spes Bona Rd	Phesantekraal	30	BJ	53
Spes Bona Rd	Vrymansfontein	29	BJ	50
Spes Bona St	William Lloyd	23	BD	94
Spey Rd	Manenberg	123	CK	39
Speyer Dr.	Silversands	107	CH	54
Sphingo Rd	Philippi East	125	CM	47
Sphinx St	Blue Downs	108	CH	56
Spicatus Cl.	Gordon Hgts	179	DE	78
Spier Cl.	Mitchells Plain	144	CR	45
Spilbergen St	Bothasig	58	BT	38
Spilhaus Ave	Hohenort	119	CK	25
Spilhaus Ave	Hohenort	119	CL	25
Spilhaus St	Kaymor	62	BX	53
Spin Rd	Sack's Circle Ind.	89	CB	51
Spin St	Cape Town Cen.	82	CB	23
Spin St	Parow Ind.	87	CB	45
Spin St	Rosebank	101	CE	30
Spin St	Wellington	10	AS	92
Spine Rd	Bongani	145	CQ	50
Spine Rd	Driftsands	147	CO	55
Spine Rd	Graceland	146	CP	53
Spine Rd	Ilitha Pk	146	CQ	52
Spine Rd	Mfuleni	127	CM	56
Spine Rd	Mfuleni	127	CN	56
Spine Rd	Rocklands (M.Plain)	144	CS	46
Spine Rd	Strandfontein	161	CU	38
Spine Rd	Strandfontein	162	CT	42
Spine Rd	Strandfontein	162	CU	39
Spine Rd	Strandfontein	163	CT	44
Spine Rd	Tafelsig (M.Plain)	145	CR	48
Spine Rd	Tafelsig (M.Plain)	145	CR	49
Spinnaker Ave	Lakeside	159	CV	28
Spinnaker Cl.	Pelikan Pk	141	CR	33
Spinner Cl.	Hout Bay Harbour	136	CR	14
Spioenkop Rd	Heideveld	104	CG	40
Spitfire	Rocklands (M.Plain)	163	CT	45
Spitfire Cr.	Kraaifontein	47	BQ	58
Spitfire St	Factreton	84	BY	34
Spitfire St	The Hague	106	CF	50
Spitsberg Rd	Bishop Lavis	105	CE	43
Spitskop St	Greenfield	108	CH	56
Spitskop St	Heideveld	104	CF	40
Spitz Cl.	Strandfontein	162	CT	40
Spitz Way	Strandfontein	162	CT	40
Spitzkop St	Tafelsig (M.Plain)	145	CS	49
Spohr	Delft Sth	125	CK	48
Spolander St	Oak Glen	62	BW	52
Spoon St	Lakeside	159	CV	27
Spoonbill Cl.	Imhoff's Gift	184	DB	15
Spoonbill Cl.	Pelikan Pk	142	CR	35
Spoonbill Cr.	Pelikan Pk	142	CR	35
Spoonbill Cr.	Seawinds	159	CU	30
Spoonbill Cr.	Seawinds	160	CU	31
Spoonbill Way	Electric City	127	CN	58
Spooner Rd	Strandfontein	162	CT	40
Spoor La.	Maitland	83	CB	30
Spoor Way	Joostenberg	48	BP	59
Spoorbaan St	Woodstock	83	CA	29
Spoorweg Rd	Greenlands	88	CA	48
Sporrie St	Kleinvlei	127	CJ	58
Sporrie St	Vierlanden	30	BM	52
Sport Pienaar Rd	Newlands	101	CG	29
Sport Way	Durbanville	46	BQ	52
Sportica Cr.	Bellville	61	BV	49
Spray Rd	Bloubergrant	24	BN	30
Spreeu	Rocklands (M.Plain)	144	CS	44
Spreeu Cr.	Morningstar	46	BP	51
Spreeu St	Joostenberg	48	BP	59
Sprigg Rd	Rondebosch East	102	CH	32
Sprigg Rd	Table View	41	BQ	34
Spring Cl.	Hill View	127	CK	57
Spring Cl.	Montagu's Gift	141	CO	34
Spring Gdns	Pinelands	84	CC	33
Spring St	Tafelsig (M.Plain)	145	CS	48
Spring St	Woodstock	83	CB	27
Springbok Cl.	Pine Acres	175	DC	77
Springbok Cl.	Pinelands	102	CD	34
Springbok Cr.	Balvenie	86	CB	42
Springbok Rd	Langeberg Rdg	47	BR	56
Springbok Rd	Loevenstein	61	BW	47
Springbok Rd	Russel's Rest	128	CL	59
Springbok Rd	Sea Point	81	BZ	21
Springbok Rd	Uitzicht	46	BO	54
Springbok Rd	Wellington	15	AU	92
Springbok St	Kleinvlei	127	CJ	58
Springbok St	Klipkop	87	BZ	45
Springbok St	New Orleans	19	BA	92
Springbok St	New Orleans	19	BB	92
Springbok St	Scarborough	192	DJ	18
Springbok St	Silvertown	102	CF	34
Springbok St	Silvertown	103	CF	35
Springbok St	Soneike II	89	BZ	54
Springbok Way	Fish Hoek	186	DA	23
Springer Cl.	Marina Da Gama	159	CU	29
Springerskuil	Wesbank	107	CH	51
Springfield Cl.	Rondebosch	102	CF	31

Abbreviations used: Ave – Avenue, A.H. – Agricultural Holding, A.L. – Algemene Landgoed, Blvd – Boulevard, Cen. – Central, Cir. – Circle, Cl. – Close, Cr. – Crescent, Ct – Court, Dr. – Drive, Est. – Estate, Ext. – Extension, Hgts – Heights, Ind. – Industrial, Gdns – Gardens, Gr. – Grove, La. – Lane, (M.Plain) - Mitchells Plain, Nth – North, Pl. – Place, Pk – Park, Rd – Road, Rdg. – Ridge, S.H. – Small Holding, Sq. – Square, St – Street, Sth – South, Ter. – Terrace, Tn – Turn, Val. – Valley, Wk – Walk

STREET NAME	SUBURB NAME	PG	GRID	
Springfield Rd	Oakdale	61	BW	49
Springfield Rd	Oakdale	61	BW	50
Springfield Rd	Rondebosch	102	CF	31
Springfield St	Belhar	107	CD	51
Springfield St	Parklands	25	BM	33
Springfield St	Parklands	25	BL	33
Springfield St	Schaap Kraal	122	CL	36
Springfield St	Schaap Kraal	122	CM	37
Springfield St	Wesbank	107	CF	52
Springfield Ter.	District Six	82	CB	25
Springfontein Ave	Eversdal	62	BT	52
Springwood Cir.	Westlake	159	CU	27
Spruce Way	Weltevreden Val. (M.Plain)	144	CO	43
Spruit Cr.	Die Oude Spruit	63	BX	56
Spruit Rd	Dunoon	27	BN	40
Spruit St	Klipdam	90	CB	55
Spumanté	Durmonte	30	BN	53
Spumanté	Durmonte	30	BM	53
Spurwing Ave	Marina Da Gama	159	CU	30
Spurwing Ave	Villa Italia	57	BW	33
Spurwing Dr.	Electric City	127	CN	58
Spurwing Way	Steenberg	139	CS	24
Spurwing Way	Steenberg	158	CT	24
Spyker St	Somerset West	170	CV	74
Spykerman St	Silveroaks	90	CC	56
Squaw Rd	Steenberg	159	CT	30
Squier Rd	Durbanville	45	BQ	49
Squire Rd	Simon's Town	191	DE	24
Squires Cr.	Heathfield	140	CQ	28
Squires Rd	Heathfield	140	CP	28
Squirrel	Cloetesville	95	BY	75
Squirrel Ave	Westlake Est.	158	CU	25
Squirrel Cl.	Fir Grove	139	CQ	25
Squirrel Cr.	Eastridge (M.Plain)	145	CR	48
Squirrels Way	Rondebosch	101	CG	30
Squlac Cl.	Malibu Village	127	CJ	56
St Agatha Cr.	Lavender Hill	160	CT	31
St Agnes St	Lavender Hill	160	CT	31
St Aidan Rd	Lavender Hill	160	CT	31
St Aidans Rd	Lansdowne	121	CJ	33
St Alban	Lavender Hill	160	CT	31
St Alban Rd	Clarkes	86	CC	42
St Albert Rd	Lavender Hill	160	CT	32
St Albert Rd	Lavender Hill	160	CX	32
St Alexander Cir.	Lavender Hill	160	CT	31
St Alexander Rd	Lavender Hill	160	CT	31
St Alexander Rd	Lavender Hill	160	CX	32
St Alexis Rd	Lavender Hill	160	CT	32
St Alexis Rd	Lavender Hill	160	CX	32
St Alma Rd	Lansdowne	121	CJ	32
St Ambrose Cir.	Lavender Hill	160	CT	32
St Ambrose Rd	Lavender Hill	160	CT	32
St Ambrose Rd	Lavender Hill	160	CX	32
St Andrew Ave	Northern Paarl	18	AZ	88
St Andrew Rd	Lavender Hill	160	CT	31
St Andrews Ave	Rondebosch	101	CF	29
St Andrews Cl.	Connaught	87	CB	44
St Andrews Cl.	Connaught	87	CB	46
St Andrews Dr.	Greenways	174	DA	73
St Andrews Dr.	Greenways	174	DA	74
St Andrews Mews	Sunset Links	57	BT	31
St Andrews Rd	Claremont	101	CH	30
St Andrews Rd	Oakdale	61	BW	50
St Andrews Rd	Rondebosch	101	CF	29
St Andrews Rd	Sea Point	81	CA	19
St Anne St	Lavender Hill	160	CT	32
St Annes	Sunningdale	25	BN	31
St Anthony Rd	Heathfield	140	CQ	29
St Anthony Rd	Lavender Hill	160	CT	31
St Anthony Rd	Lavender Hill	160	CX	32
St Athans Rd	Athlone	102	CG	34
St Augustine Ave	Northern Paarl	18	AZ	88
St Augustine Rd	Lavender Hill	160	CT	31
St Augustine Rd	Lavender Hill	160	CX	32
St Barbara Rd	Lavender Hill	160	CT	31
St Barnabas Rd	Lavender Hill	160	CT	31
St Bartholomew Rd	Lavender Hill	160	CT	31
St Basil St	Lavender Hill	160	CT	32
St Beatrice St	Lavender Hill	160	CT	32
St Bede St	Lavender Hill	160	CT	32
St Bede's Rd	Three Anchor Bay	81	BZ	20
St Bedes Way	Clarkes	86	CC	42
St Bedes Way	Epping Ind.	86	CB	39
St Benedict St	Lavender Hill	160	CT	32
St Bernard	Wellington	15	AT	93
St Bernard Ave	Northern Paarl	18	AZ	88
St Bernard Cr.	Lavender Hill	160	CT	32
St Bernard Rd	Belgravia	102	CG	34
St Blaise Cr.	Lavender Hill	160	CT	32
St Blaise St	Lavender Hill	160	CT	32
St Blaize	Strandfontein	161	CT	38
St Blaize St	Ruyterwacht	86	CA	40
St Blaize Way	Skoongesig	45	BO	50
St Bonaventure St	Lavender Hill	160	CT	32
St Boniface Rd	Lavender Hill East	160	CT	32
St Brendan Rd	Lavender Hill	160	CT	32
St Bridget St	Lavender Hill	160	CT	32
St Bruno Rd	Lavender Hill	160	CT	32
St Catherine Rd	Lavender Hill East	160	CU	32
St Catherine Rd	Plumstead	120	CN	28
St Cecilia St	Lavender Hill	160	CT	31
St Charles Rd	Grassy Pk	141	CP	33
St Charles Rd	Lavender Hill East	160	CU	31
St Christopher Way	Amanda Glen	46	BS	52
St Clair Rd	Clarkes	86	CC	42
St Clair Rd	Plumstead	120	CN	28
St Clements Way	Lotus River	141	CQ	34
St Conute St	Lavender Hill	160	CT	32
St Crispin Rd	Wellington	10	AR	92
St Croix Dr.	Harbour Island	179	DD	75
St Croix St	Anchorage Pk	175	DC	78
St David St	Wellington	15	AT	92
St David's Rd	Claremont	101	CH	30
St Dennis Rd	Claremont	101	CH	30
St Dominique St	Adriaanse	87	CC	43
St Edward Rd	Lavender Hill East	160	CU	31
St Edward Rd	Lavender Hill East	160	CU	32
St Emillion Rd	Somerset West	151	CS	72
St Emillion Rd	Somerset West	170	CT	72
St Francis Ave	Northern Paarl	18	AZ	88
St Francis Pl.	Strandfontein	162	CT	39
St Francis Rd	Grassy Pk	141	CP	33
St Francis Rd	Heathfield	140	CP	28
St Francis Way	Skoongesig	45	BO	50
St Frusquin Rd	Belgravia	102	CG	34
St George Ave	Northern Paarl	18	AZ	88
St George St	Simon's Town	194	DJ	25
St George St	Somerset West	171	CU	75
St George St	Wellington	15	AU	92
St Georges Mall	Cape Town Cen.	82	CA	23
St George's Rd	Claremont	101	CH	30
St George's Rd	Green Point	81	BZ	21
St Georges St	Oakdale	61	BX	49
St Geran Cl.	Blouberg Sands	24	BL	30
St Gotha Cl.	Clarkes	86	CC	42
St Gotha Cl.	Clarkes	86	CB	39
St Gothas Rd	Belgravia	102	CG	34
St Heiler's Rd	Muizenberg	159	CX	29
St Helena Cl.	Bloubergstrand	24	BM	29
St Helena Cl.	Strandfontein	161	CT	38
St Helena St	Portlands (M.Plain)	144	CP	46
St Helena St	Strandfontein	161	CT	38
St Irene Rd	Lavender Hill East	160	CU	32
St Irene Rd	Lavender Hill East	160	CX	33
St James Cl.	Bonnie Brae	47	BP	57
St James Cl.	Bonnie Brae	47	BO	58
St James Cr.	Wellington	15	AU	92
St James Cr.	Wellington	15	AU	94
St James Park	Weltevreden Val. (M.Plain)	124	CN	43
St James Rd	Kingston	61	BX	48
St James Rd	Sea Point	81	BZ	20
St James Rd	St James	187	CZ	27
St James St	Vredehoek	82	CC	24
St James St	Vredehoek	100	CD	23
St Joan's Rd	Plumstead	120	CN	28
St John St	Anchorage Pk	175	DC	78
St John's Rd	Durbanville	45	BQ	49
St Johns Ave	Northern Paarl	18	AZ	88
St Johns Cr.	Wellington	15	AU	92
St Johns Rd	Cape Town Cen.	82	CB	23
St John's Rd	Durbanville	45	BP	49
St John's Rd	Kalk Bay	186	DA	26
St John's Rd	Lansdowne	121	CK	33
St John's Rd	Sea Point	81	CA	19
St John's St	Oakdale	61	BW	49
St Johns Ter.	Claremont	120	CJ	29
St Johns Ter.	Wynberg	120	CL	28
St John's Wood Cl.	Parklands	41	BO	32
St John's Wood Cr.	Parklands	41	BO	32
St Joseph Cr.	Wellington	15	AU	92
St Joseph Rd	Plumstead	120	CN	28
St Joseph's Rd	Lansdowne	121	CL	34
St Joseph's Rd	Lansdowne	122	CL	35
St Julian Rd	Belgravia	102	CG	34
St Kilda Rd	Crawford	102	CH	33
St Kilda Rd	Crawford	121	CJ	33
St Lawrence Cl.	Seawinds	159	CU	30
St Lawrence Cl.	Seawinds	159	CW	27
St Lawrence Cl.	Seawinds	160	CU	31
St Leger Rd	Claremont	101	CH	29
St Linus Cl.	Seawinds	159	CU	30
St Linus Cl.	Seawinds	159	CW	27
St Louis Cl.	Seawinds	159	CU	30
St Louis Cl.	Seawinds	159	CW	27
St Louis Way	Grassy Pk	141	CQ	31
St Lucia	Skoongesig	45	BO	50
St Lucia Cr.	Coniston Pk	159	CU	30
St Lucia Pl.	Strandfontein	162	CT	39
St Lucia Pl.	Strandfontein	162	CV	42
St Lucia St	Coniston Pk	159	CU	30
St Lucina Cl.	Seawinds	159	CU	30
St Lucina Cl.	Seawinds	159	CW	27
St Lucy Cl.	Seawinds	160	CU	31
St Lucy Cl.	Seawinds	160	CX	32
St Luke	Wellington	15	AT	93
St Luke Cl.	Seawinds	160	CU	31
St Luke Cl.	Seawinds	160	CX	32
St Luke's Rd	Claremont	101	CH	30
St Lukes Way	Eversdal	62	BT	51
St Malo Ave	Everglen	46	BS	51
St Malo Cl.	Brackenfell Sth	63	BX	57
St Margaret Cl.	Somerset West	171	CT	75
St Marks Rd	Claremont	101	CH	29
St Mark's Rd	Hout Bay	116	CL	14
St Mark's St	District Six	82	CB	24
St Mark's St	Eversdal	62	BT	51
St Martins La.	Harbour Island	175	DC	75
St Mary Rd	Plumstead	120	CN	28
St Matthews Way	Amanda Glen	46	BS	51
St Mauri Rd	Belgravia	102	CG	34
St Michaels Cr.	Bonnie Brae	47	BP	57
St Michael's Rd	Claremont	101	CH	30
St Michael's Rd	Grassy Pk	141	CQ	33
St Michael's Rd	Observatory	83	CC	29
St Michael's Rd	Tamboerskloof	81	CB	21
St Michael's St	Capricorn	159	CW	30
St Michel Ave	Everglen	45	BS	50
St Omer St	Paarlzicht	19	BC	92
St Pancras Rd	Belgravia	102	CG	34
St Patrick	Fresnaye	81	CB	19
St Patrick Ave	Lavender Hill	160	CT	31
St Patrick Ave	Lavender Hill East	160	CU	32
St Patrick Ave	Northern Paarl	18	AZ	89
St Patrick Ave	Seawinds	160	CU	31
St Patrick St	Wellington	15	AU	92
St Patricks Green	Summer Greens	58	BV	36
St Patrick's Rd	Claremont	101	CG	30
St Patrick's St	Capricorn	159	CW	30
St Paul Cl.	Bonnie Brae	47	BP	57
St Paul Cl.	Bonnie Brae	47	BO	58
St Paul St	Wellington	15	AU	92
St Paul's Ave	Cravenby	87	CA	43
St Pauls Cl.	Eversdal	62	BT	52
St Paul's Cr.	Rondebosch	101	CF	29
St Peter Ave	Seawinds	160	CU	31
St Peter St	Wellington	15	AU	92
St Peters Rd	Mowbray	101	CD	29
St Peters St	Uitzicht	31	BN	55
St Phillips St	District Six	82	CB	25
St Pierre Cr.	Tijgerhof	57	BW	33
St Quintons Rd	Oranjezicht	81	CC	22
St Ralph Rd	Seawinds	160	CU	31
St Ralph Rd	Seawinds	160	CX	32
St Raymond Rd	Seawinds	160	CU	31
St Regis Rd	Seawinds	160	CU	31
St Richard Rd	Seawinds	160	CU	31
St Robert La.	Seawinds	160	CU	31
St Robert La.	Seawinds	160	CX	32
St Roberts Rd	Seawinds	160	CU	31
St Sebastion St	Seawinds	160	CU	31
St Silas Rd	Belgravia	102	CG	34
St Simon St	Lavender Hill	160	CT	31
St Simon St	Wellington	15	AU	92
St Simon's Rd	Belgravia	102	CG	34
St Stainlas St	Seawinds	160	CU	31
St Stephen Ave	Seawinds	160	CU	31
St Stephens Rd	Pinelands	84	CC	32
St Stephen's Rd	Claremont	101	CH	30
St Swithin Rd	Lavender Hill East	160	CU	31
St Teresa St	Wellington	15	AU	92
St Theresa Cr.	Seawinds	160	CU	31
St Thomas Cl.	Anchorage Pk	175	DC	78
St Thomas Cl.	Anchorage Pk	175	DB	78
St Thomas Rd	Claremont	101	CH	30
St Thomas St	Anchorage Pk	175	DC	78
St Thomas St	Anchorage Pk	175	DB	78
St Thomas St	Lavender Hill	160	CT	31
St Thomas St	Wellington	15	AU	92
St Timothy St	Seawinds	160	CU	31
St Titus Cr.	Seawinds	159	CU	30
St Titus Cr.	Seawinds	160	CU	31
St Tropez St	Uitzicht	31	BN	56
St Urban	Seawinds	159	CU	30
St Ursula Cl.	Seawinds	159	CU	30
St Ursula Cl.	Seawinds	159	CW	27
St Valentine Cl.	Seawinds	160	CU	31
St Valentine Cl.	Seawinds	160	CX	32
St Victor Cl.	Seawinds	160	CU	31
St Victor Cl.	Seawinds	160	CX	32
St Vincent Dr.	Belhar	106	CD	50
St Vincent La.	Lavender Hill East	160	CU	31
St Vincent La.	Lavender Hill East	160	CX	32
St Wenceslas St	Seawinds	160	CU	31
St William Cr.	Seawinds	159	CU	30
St William Rd	Seawinds	160	CU	31
St Winifred St	Seawinds	160	CU	31
St.Albans Cl.	Bishopscourt	119	CJ	26
St.James St	Somerset West	170	CU	74
Staal St	Brackenfell Ind.	63	BT	58
Stable Cl.	Mitchells Plain	144	CS	44
Stable Cl.	Noordhoek Manor	157	CX	21
Stable Cr.	Mitchells Plain	144	CS	45
Stable Rd	Grassy Pk	141	CR	32
Stable Rd	Mitchells Plain	144	CS	45
Stables	Schaap Kraal	123	CM	40
Stacey St	Tafelsig (M.Plain)	145	CS	50
Stadens Ct	Edgemead	59	BT	39
Stadler Rd	Bloubergstrand	24	BM	28
Stadzicht St	Schotsche Kloof	81	CA	22
Staff Rd	Rondebosch East	102	CH	32
Stafford	Parklands	25	BM	33
Stafford St	Claremont	120	CJ	29
Stag Cr.	Eastridge (M.Plain)	145	CR	48
Staines Rd	Plumstead	120	CN	29
Stal St	Cape Town Cen.	82	CB	23
Stallion Way	Mitchells Plain	144	CR	44
Stamen St	Retreat	140	CS	28
Stamford Rd	Grassy Pk	141	CQ	32
Stamford Rd	Kenilworth	120	CK	28
Stamperhout	Delft Sth	125	CJ	49
Stanberry Rd	Rugby	84	BY	31
Standard La.	Wynberg	120	CL	28
Stanford Bridge	Weltevreden Val. (M.Plain)	124	CN	43
Stanford Mateyisa Cr.	Nonqubela	126	CN	52
Stanford Rd	Rondebosch	102	CG	31
Stanford Rd	Rondebosch	102	CH	31
Stanford Way	Edgemead	58	BV	38
Stanhope Rd	Claremont	120	CJ	29
Stanley Jonasi St	Manenberg	104	CH	40
Stanley Pl.	Mouille Point	81	BY	20
Stanley Rd	Bracken Hgts	62	BU	54
Stanley Rd	Claremont	101	CH	29
Stanley Rd	Highlands Est.	122	CM	38
Stanley Rd	Observatory	83	CB	29
Stanley Rd	Parklands	25	BM	33
Stanley Rd	Rondebosch	101	CF	28
Stanley Rd	Zoo Pk	47	BQ	57
Stanley St	Cape Town Cen.	82	BZ	23
Stanley St	Hoogstede	62	BV	54
Stanley St	Perm Gdns	128	CK	59
Stanlou Rd	Bellville	88	BY	48
Stapelia St	Welgedacht	60	BT	45
Stapelkop	Wesbank	107	CG	51
Star Cl.	Salberau	86	CB	41
Star Effort	Noordhoek Manor	157	CX	21
Starboard Cr	Strandfontein	162	CT	42
Starck Rd	Elsies River Ind.	86	BZ	41
Starck St	St Dumas	90	CC	55
Stardust Cr.	Weltevreden Val. (M.Plain)	144	CO	43
Starfish Cl.	Kraaifontein	47	BQ	58
Starfish Cr.	Milnerton	41	BS	33
Starfish La.	Big Bay	24	BL	28
Starfish Pl.	Woodlands (M.Plain)	144	CP	45
Starke Rd	Bergvliet	139	CQ	26
Starke Rd	Bergvliet	140	CQ	27
Starke Rd	Dreyersdal	140	CR	27
Starke Rd	Durbanville	46	BQ	51
Starking	Lindida	96	CA	79
Starking	Lindida	96	CB	80
Starlight Wk	Thembokwezi	125	CM	49
Starlight Wk	Thembokwezi	125	CK	50
Starling La.	Steenberg	139	CS	24
Starling Rd	Bishop Lavis	105	CD	44
Starling St	Penlyn Est.	103	CH	36
Starling St	Penlyn Est.	122	CJ	36
Starling St	Somerset Hgts	127	CJ	57
Stasie	Wellington	10	AR	91
Stasie Rd	Brackenfell	63	BV	55
Stasie Rd	Brackenfell	63	BW	56
Stasie Rd	Eersterivier	128	CL	60
Stasie Rd	Fisantekraal	31	BK	58
Stasie Rd	Protea Hoogte	63	BX	57
Stasie Rd	Stellenbosch	95	CC	75
Stasie St	Belmont Pk	48	BR	60
Stasie St	Belmont Pk	48	BS	60
Statice	Lentegeur (M.Plain)	145	CP	47
Statice Sq.	Kewtown	103	CE	35
Statice St	Kewtown	103	CE	35
Station Arcade	Parow	87	BZ	43
Station Rd	Athlone	102	CF	33
Station Rd	Blackheath Ind.	108	CF	57
Station Rd	Claremont	101	CH	28
Station Rd	Fish Hoek	186	DB	24
Station Rd	Heathfield	140	CQ	28
Station Rd	Kuilsrivier Ind.	89	CB	54
Station Rd	Lakeside	159	CV	28
Station Rd	Maitland	84	CA	31
Station Rd	Manenberg	123	CJ	40
Station Rd	Montague Gdns Ind.	58	BT	36
Station Rd	Montague Gdns Ind.	58	BU	36
Station Rd	Mowbray	101	CD	29
Station Rd	Observatory	83	CC	29
Station Rd	Retreat	140	CR	28
Station Rd	Retreat Ind. Area	140	CS	28
Station Rd	Rondebosch	101	CF	29
Station Rd	Simon's Town	191	DH	24
Station Rd	Summer Greens	58	BW	35
Station Rd	Townsend Est.	85	BZ	38
Station Rd	Wynberg	120	CL	29
Station St	Blackheath Ind.	108	CF	57
Station St	Croydon	149	CP	63
Station St	KWV	22	BG	88
Station St	Woodstock	82	CB	26
Steamboat Cl.	Strandfontein	162	CT	39
Steamboat Cl.	Strandfontein	162	CV	42
Steamboat Rd	Strandfontein	162	CT	39
Stearman	Rocklands (M.Plain)	163	CT	45
Steed Cl.	Grassy Pk	141	CQ	32
Steeleik Cl.	Eikenbosch	90	CC	57
Steelpoort Cr.	Delft	106	CG	49
Steen Ave	Somerset West	151	CS	72
Steen Rd	Sonstraal	46	BR	52
Steen St	Maitland	84	CA	32
Steenberg Blvd	Westlake Est.	158	CU	25
Steenberg Cl.	Frogmore Est.	159	CU	28
Steenberg Rd	Frogmore Est.	159	CU	28
Steenberg Rd	Tokai	139	CS	24
Steenberg Rd	Westlake	159	CU	27
Steenberg Rd	Westlake Est.	158	CU	26
Steenberg Rd	Westlake Est.	158	CU	24
Steenberg St	Tafelsig (M.Plain)	145	CS	48
Steenbok Cl.	Pinelands	102	CD	33
Steenbok Rd	Langeberg Rdg	47	BR	55
Steenbok Rd	Loevenstein	60	BW	46
Steenbok Rd	Lotus River	142	CP	35
Steenbok St	New Orleans	19	BB	92
Steenbok St	Ruwari	63	BV	58
Steenbok St	Soneike II	89	BZ	54
Steenbok St	Uitzicht	46	BO	54
Steenbok Way	Fish Hoek	186	DB	24

Index to Street Names

Steenboksberg — Teal Rd

STREET NAME	SUBURB NAME	PG	GRID	
Steenboksberg	Tafelsig (M.Plain)	145	CR	49
Steenboksberg	Tafelsig (M.Plain)	145	CP	50
Steenbras Rd	Eersterivier	128	CM	59
Steenbras Rd	Groenvallei	62	BX	53
Steenbras St	Brooklyn	83	BZ	30
Steenbras St	Parow	86	BY	42
Steenbras St	Tafelsig (M.Plain)	145	CR	49
Steengroef Rd	Pinelands	84	CC	32
Steenkamp St	Sarepta	89	CB	52
Steenkamp St	Sarepta	89	BY	54
Steenkamp St	William Lloyd	23	BD	93
Steenoven St	Bothasig	42	BS	37
Steenoven St	Bothasig	42	BS	38
Steensway Rd	Hout Bay	116	CM	14
Steenveld St	Bellair	62	BW	53
Stegman Rd	Claremont	101	CH	28
Stegman Rd	Claremont	101	CH	29
Stegman Way	Glencairn Hgts	191	DD	24
Stein St	Klein Nederburg	19	BC	94
Stein St	Wellington	15	AT	94
Steinbeck Cl.	Bishopscourt	119	CK	26
Steinberg St	Labiance	89	BZ	52
Stella Rd	Montague Gdns Ind.	42	BS	35
Stella Rd	Montagu's Gift	141	CO	34
Stella Rd	Plumstead	120	CN	30
Stella Rd	Plumstead	140	CO	30
Stella Rd	Somerset West	152	CS	75
Stella Rd	Thornton	85	CA	36
Stella Rd	Wetton	121	CL	34
Stella St	Chrismar	61	BW	50
Stella Way	Tafelsig (M.Plain)	145	CR	50
Stella Way	Tafelsig (M.Plain)	145	CS	50
Stellen Cl.	Marina Da Gama	159	CV	29
Stellenberg	Pinelands	84	CC	34
Stellenberg	Welgelegen	113	CD	76
Stellenberg Ave	Kenilworth	120	CK	29
Stellenberg La.	Die Bos	174	CY	74
Stellenberg Rd	Belhar	106	CD	50
Stellenberg Rd	Belhar	106	CH	48
Stellenberg Rd	Bellair	62	BV	53
Stellenberg Rd	Bellair	62	BW	53
Stellenberg Rd	Somerset West	151	CR	71
Stellenberg Rd	Vredenberg	62	BV	52
Stellenberg St	Parow Ind.	87	CB	45
Stellenberg St	Parow Ind.	87	CC	45
Stellenberg St	Salberau	86	CB	40
Stellenbosch Rd	Belhar	105	CD	45
Stellenbosch Rd	Belhar	105	CE	46
Stellenbosch Rd	Belhar	106	CE	49
Stellenbosch Rd	Wesbank	107	CE	52
Stellenbosch Rd	Wimbledon	108	CE	55
Stellenboschkloof Rd	Bloemendal	110	CD	66
Stellenboschkloof Rd	Uiterwyk	92	CC	63
Stellenboschkloof Rd	Vlottenburg	111	CD	67
Stellendal Rd	Somerset West	170	CU	74
Stellenhof Cl.	Edgemead	58	BU	38
Stellenhof St	Somerset West	171	CW	75
Stellenrijk St	Wellington	11	AQ	95
Stellenryk St	Stellenryk	62	BT	52
Stellentia Rd	Stellenbosch	94	CC	74
Stellentia Rd	Stellenbosch	112	CD	74
Stellita	Cloetesville	95	BY	75
Stemmet Rd	Penlyn Est.	103	CH	35
Stephan Way	Green Point	81	BY	21
Stephanie St	Casablanca	175	DB	76
Stephanie St	Wellington	10	AS	93
Stephen Rd	Montagu's Gift	142	CO	35
Stephen Rd	Tokai	139	CS	26
Stephen St	Gardens	81	CC	22
Stephenson St	Belhar	88	CC	49
Stepping Stones Rd	Eversdal	45	BS	50
Sterket	Pelikan Pk	142	CR	36
Sterkfontein St	Groenvallei	62	BX	53
Sterlig	Kirstenhof	158	CT	26
Sterlig Rd	Eversdal	61	BT	50
Sterling Cl.	Parklands	25	BN	34
Sterling Cr.	Parklands	25	BN	34
Sterling St	Vierlanden	30	BN	51
Sterlitzia	Lentegeur (M.Plain)	145	CP	47
Sterlitzia Rd	Stellenberg	62	BU	51
Sterlitzia Rd	Stellenberg	62	BX	52
Stern Cl.	Bakoven	98	CF	18
Sterretjie Cr.	Roosendaal	107	CF	51
Sterretjie Cr.	Roosendaal	107	CG	53
Sterretjie St	Groenvlei	18	BA	89
Stethoek	Vredehoek	82	CC	23
Stetson Rd	Leonsdale	86	CA	42
Steur Rd	Nooitgedacht	104	CE	42
Steve Biko Cr.	Weltevreden Val. (M.Plain)	123	CM	41
Steve Biko Rd	Harare	146	CR	52
Steve Biko Rd	Harare	146	CS	51
Steve Biko Rd	Mandela Pk	146	CQ	53
Steve Tshwete Rd	Umrhabulo Triangle	147	CQ	56
Steve Tshwete Rd	Umrhabulo Triangle	147	CR	56
Steve Tshwete St	Fisantekraal	31	BK	58
Steven	Peerless Pk Nth	48	BQ	59
Steven St	Bothasig	42	BS	38
Steven St	Bothasig	43	BS	39
Stevens Cl.	Grassy Pk	141	CQ	33
Stevens Rd	Grassy Pk	141	CQ	33
Steward Cl.	Bonnie Brae	47	BP	57
Steward Cl.	Bonnie Brae	47	BO	58
Steward St	De Oude Renbaan	22	BH	88
Stewart St	Sir Lowry's Pass	176	CZ	82
Stewart St	Soneike I	89	CA	54
Stewart St	Townsend Est.	58	BX	37
Stewart St	Townsend Est.	85	BY	37
Stewart St	Tygerdal	58	BX	37
Steyn Rd	Brooklyn	84	BY	31
Steyn St	Eastridge (M.Plain)	145	CQ	49
Steyn St	Rome	174	CY	73
Steynberg Rd	Parow Nth	60	BW	43
Steyning St	Woodstock	82	CB	26
Steynsrust Rd	Somerset West	150	CR	70
Steynsrust Rd	Somerset West	151	CR	71
Steytler St	Denneburg	23	BD	91
Steytler St	Peerless Pk East	47	BR	58
Steytler St	Peerless Pk East	48	BQ	60
Steytler St	Peerless Pk East	48	BR	59
Stibitz St	Westlake Est.	158	CU	25
Stiebeui St	Franschhoek Nth	75	BX	105
Stignant Cr.	Claremont	121	CJ	31
Stignant Rd	Claremont	121	CJ	31
Stillewater St	Tygerberg Ind. Pk	31	BL	57
Stillson Pl.	Eureka	87	CC	44
Stillson Pl.	Eureka	87	CB	46
Stilt Ave	Table View	41	BQ	33
Stilton Rd	Wynberg	120	CM	29
Stilwaney Cr.	Bellville Sth Ind.	88	CA	50
Stilwaney Cr.	Marlow	89	CA	51
Stimberg	Dunoon	42	BO	37
Stingel Rd	Retreat	140	CS	28
Stinkhout	Arbeidslus	96	CB	80
Stinkhout Ave	New Orleans	19	BB	91
Stinkhout Cl.	Onverwacht	175	DC	76
Stinkhout St	Die Oude Spruit	63	BX	56
Stinkhout St	Forest Village	127	CM	58
Stinkhout St	Rouxville	90	CA	56
Stinkwood Dr.	Noordhoek	156	CW	18
Stint Rd	Montagu's Gift	141	CO	33
Stirling	Rocklands (M.Plain)	144	CS	45
Stirling Cl.	Belhar	107	CD	52
Stirling Rd	Newlands	101	CH	27
Stirling Rd	Royal Cape	121	CM	31
Stirling Rd	West Beach	24	BN	30
Stirling St	District Six	82	CB	24
Stirling St	Lemoenkloof	18	BC	88
Stirling St East	Lemoenkloof	18	BB	88
Stirrup Cl.	Noordhoek Manor	157	CX	20
Stirrup Cr.	Kenilworth Pk	121	CK	31
Stirrup La.	Hout Bay	117	CM	16
Stirrup St	Mitchells Plain	144	CR	44
Stock Rd	Philippi	124	CL	45
Stock Rd	Philippi	124	CM	45
Stock St	Bonteheuwel	104	CE	40
Stockenstrom St	Belgravia	88	BY	50
Stockenstrom St	Belgravia	88	BY	49
Stockholm St	Uitzicht	47	BO	55
Stockley Rd	Lansdowne	121	CK	33
Stockton St	Somerset West	170	CW	72
Stofberg St	Paarlzicht	19	BC	91
Stoffel Smit	Stellenbosch	95	CB	75
Stoke St	Sunningdale	24	BM	30
Stoke St	Sunningdale	24	BL	29
Stoker St	Parow Ind.	87	CA	46
Stokery Rd	Wellington	10	AR	91
Stone	Idasvallei	96	CA	79
Stone Cl.	Dennedal	139	CS	26
Stone Cl.	Salberau	86	CA	41
Stone Gate	High Gate	107	CG	53
Stone Rd	Sea Point	81	BZ	20
Stone St	Parklands	25	BM	34
Stone Way	Northpine	63	BU	57
Stonebridge End	Parklands	25	BM	33
Stonebridge End	Parklands	25	BL	33
Stonebridge St	Parklands	25	BM	33
Stonebridge St	Parklands	25	BL	33
Stonehedge Rd	Hanover Pk	122	CK	36
Stonehill	Hout Bay	137	CP	17
Stonehurst Ave	Somerset West	169	CT	70
Stonehurst Ave	Somerset West	170	CT	71
Stonelands Rd	Hanover Pk	122	CK	36
Stork	Rocklands (M.Plain)	144	CS	44
Stork La.	Flamingo Vlei	41	BP	32
Stork St	Morgenster Hoogte	63	BT	57
Stork St	Ocean View	184	DC	15
Stork St	Weltevreden Val. (M.Plain)	124	CM	44
Stork Way	Sunnydale	185	DA	20
Storm Cl.	Eersterivier	128	CL	59
Stormberg	Wellington	15	AV	91
Stormberg Cr.	Bonnie Brae	47	BQ	57
Stormberg Cr.	Bonnie Brae	47	BP	58
Stormkaap Rd	Eersterivier	128	CM	60
Storms River Way	Manenberg	123	CJ	39
Storms River Wk	Manenberg	123	CJ	39
Stormsrivier St	Welgevonden	30	BN	53
Stormvlei	Wesbank	107	CH	51
Stormvoel Sq.	Seawinds	160	CU	31
Stow Rd	Eersterivier	128	CN	61
Stowe Cl.	Westlake Est.	158	CU	25
Stowe Cr.	Westlake Est.	158	CU	25
Stowe La.	Westlake Est.	158	CU	25
Stowe St	Woodstock	83	CB	27
Straalen Cl.	Barbarossa	120	CM	27
Strand	Die Boord	113	CD	75
Strand	Jamestown	112	CG	74
Strand Manor Cr.	Tarentaalplaas	175	CZ	75
Strand Mews St	Tarentaalplaas	175	CY	75
Strand Rd	Macassar Beach	148	CS	62
Strand Rd	Sanlamhof	88	BY	50
Strand Rd	Stikland Hospital	89	BY	51
Strand Ridge Cr.	Tarentaalplaas	175	CY	75
Strand St	Cape Town Cen.	82	CA	23
Strand St	Green Point	81	BZ	22
Strand St	Woodstock	83	CB	27
Strandblom St	Annandale	90	BZ	55
Strandfontein Rd	Lotus River	142	CP	36
Strandfontein Rd	Montagu's Gift	142	CO	35
Strandfontein Rd	Pelikan Pk	142	CR	36
Strandfontein Rd	Schaap Kraal	122	CM	35
Strandfontein Rd	Strandfontein	161	CU	38
Strandloper	Rocklands (M.Plain)	144	CS	44
Strandloper Cr.	Somerset West	170	CV	72
Strandloper Rd	Sunnydale	185	DA	19
Strandveld	Wesbank	107	CG	51
Strangman	Park Estates	174	CY	72
Strangman St	Somerset West	171	CT	78
Stranton Rd	Wynberg	120	CM	29
Strarrenberg Ave	Perm Gdns	128	CK	59
Strasbourg Cr.	Uitzicht	47	BO	55
Strat Caldecott Cr.	Woodlands (M.Plain)	124	CN	44
Stratford Ave	Eersterivier	128	CM	60
Stratford Ave	Eersterivier	128	CN	59
Stratford Path	Pinelands	84	CC	33
Stratford Way	Meadowridge	139	CO	26
Strathallan Rd	Rondebosch	102	CF	32
Strathcona Rd	Oranjezicht	99	CD	22
Strathearn Ave	Camps Bay	98	CE	18
Strathmore Cl.	Edgemead	59	BT	39
Strathmore La.	Camps Bay	98	CD	18
Strathmore Rd	Camps Bay	98	CD	18
Stratus	Rocklands (M.Plain)	145	CS	47
Strauss	Delft Sth	125	CJ	48
Strauss Ave	Retreat	140	CS	30
Strauss Cl.	Adriaanse	105	CD	43
Strauss St	Protea Hoogte	63	BX	56
Strawberry La.	Belle Constantia	139	CP	25
Strawberry La.	Blouberg Sands	24	BM	30
Strawberry La.	Dennemere	127	CJ	58
Strawberry La.	Malibu Village	127	CK	56
Streatham	Parklands	25	BM	33
Strelitzia	Belhar	87	CC	46
Strelitzia	Belhar	105	CD	46
Strelitzia Ave	Tygerdal	58	BX	38
Strelitzia Rd	Kommetjie	183	DC	11
Strelitzia St	Gordon Hgts	180	DD	79
Strelitzia St	Klein Nederburg	19	BB	92
Strelitzia St	Kleinvlei	127	CJ	58
Strelitzia St	Somerset West	151	CS	71
Stroebel St	Ravensmead	87	CA	45
Stromboli	Tafelsig (M.Plain)	145	CS	48
Struben Rd	Claremont	120	CJ	27
Struben St	Somerset West	171	CW	75
Strubens Rd	Observatory	83	CC	29
Strubens Rd	Observatory	101	CD	29
Stuart Cl.	Dennedal	139	CS	25
Stuart Cl.	Somerset West	171	CX	75
Stuart Rd	Rondebosch	102	CG	31
Stuart St	Somerset West	171	CU	75
Stuartfield Ave	Wynberg	120	CK	27
Stuckeris St	District Six	82	CB	25
Stucki St	Wellington	11	AS	95
Student Way	Strandfontein	162	CT	41
Students Way	Plumstead	120	CN	28
Studley St	Plumstead	140	CO	30
Study Cl.	Flamingo Vlei	41	BP	33
Study St	Flamingo Vlei	41	BQ	33
Study St	Table View	41	BP	33
Stuiwer St	Vierlanden	30	BN	51
Stuka	Rocklands (M.Plain)	163	CT	45
Stuka La.	The Hague	106	CF	50
Stuka St	Factreton	85	BZ	35
Stulo St	Crossroads	124	CK	44
Sturke Rd	Selborne	61	BV	47
Suddie Cl.	Steenberg	158	CT	23
Suffolk Ave	Weltevreden Val. (M.Plain)	144	CP	43
Suffolk Rd	Lakeside	159	CV	27
Suffolk St	Claremont	120	CJ	29
Suffolk St	Maitland	84	CA	31
Sugarbird Cr.	Seawinds	159	CU	30
Sugarbird La.	Steenberg	139	CS	24
Sugarloaf Cr.	Tafelsig (M.Plain)	145	CS	48
Sugarloaf Rd	Manenberg	104	CG	39
Sugarloaf Rd	Tafelsig (M.Plain)	145	CS	48
Sugarloaf Way	Somerset West	152	CS	78
Suid Agter Paarl	Paarl	20	BF	81
Suid Agter Paarl	Paarl	38	BJ	85
Suid St	Belrail	88	BY	49
Suiderkruis St	Forest Glade	127	CK	58
Suidooster	Stellenbosch	95	CB	78
Suidwal	Stellenbosch	95	CC	76
Suidwal	Stellenbosch	95	CC	77
Suikerbekkie St	Amstelhof	23	BD	93
Suikerbekkie St	Somerset West	152	CS	76
Suikerbekkie St West	Joostenberg	48	BO	60
Suikerbekkie St West	Joostenberg	48	BO	61
Suikerbos	Delft Sth	125	CK	49
Suikerbos	Green Oaks	95	BY	75
Suikerbos	Green Oaks	95	BY	77
Suikerbos	Lentegeur (M.Plain)	144	CO	45
Suikerbos Ave	New Orleans	19	BA	91
Suikerbos Cr.	Plattekloof	59	BU	42
Suikerbos La.	Somerset West	170	CW	74
Suikerbos La.	Westlake Est.	158	CT	25
Suikerbos Rd	Belhar	105	CD	46
Suikerbos Rd	Belhar	106	CD	47
Suikerbos Rd	Durbanville	45	BQ	50
Suikerbos Rd	Durbanville	45	BR	49
Suikerbos St	Bellair	62	BV	52
Suikerbos St	Bridgetown	103	CE	36
Suikerbos St	Protea Village	63	BV	58
Suikerbos St	Protea Village	64	BW	59
Suikerbossie	Dunoon	42	BO	37
Suikerbossie	Dunoon	42	BO	38
Suikerbossie Dr.	Forest Village	127	CM	58
Suikerbossie Dr.	Harbour Island	179	DF	75
Suikerkan Cr.	Eikenbosch	90	CC	57
Suikerkan Cr.	Protea Village	63	BW	58
Suker St	Bellville Sth Ext. 5	88	BZ	49
Sulani Dr.	Nonqubela	126	CN	52
Sulani Dr.	Nonqubela	146	CO	52
Sullivan Rd	Retreat	140	CS	30
Sullivan Rd	Retreat	159	CT	30
Sullivan St	Belhar	106	CD	49
Sullivan St	Belhar	106	CH	48
Sultan	Die Boord	112	CE	74
Sultan	Die Boord	113	CE	75
Sultana Cl.	Uitzicht	47	BO	55
Sultana Rd	Sonstraal	46	BQ	52
Sultana Rd	Table View	41	BO	33
Sultana St	Groenvlei	18	BA	89
Sultana St	Shirley Pk	89	BY	52
Sultana St	Somerset West	151	CR	71
Sultana St	Wellington	15	AT	94
Sumatra Ave	Bloubergstrand	24	BK	27
Sumatra Cl.	Portlands (M.Plain)	144	CP	46
Summer Cl.	Montagu's Gift	141	CO	34
Summer Cl.	Summerville	48	BS	59
Summer Clouds Rd	Eversdal	61	BT	50
Summer Cr.	Hill View	127	CK	57
Summer Cr.	Mandalay	125	CM	47
Summer Greens Dr.	Summer Greens	58	BV	36
Summer Pl.	Kirstenhof	158	CT	26
Summer Pl.	Mandalay	125	CM	47
Summerfield Cl.	Mitchells Plain	144	CR	45
Summerfield Cl.	Mitchells Plain	144	CS	43
Summerfield Cl.	Parklands	25	BN	34
Summerhaze	Eversdal Hgts	46	BS	51
Summerley Rd	Kenilworth	120	CK	29
Summerseat Cl.	Gardens	81	CC	21
Summerveld St	Somerset West	170	CW	72
Summerwood Way	Sonstraal Hgts	46	BQ	54
Summit Rd	Hanover Pk	122	CK	35
Summit St	Tafelsig (M.Plain)	145	CR	48
Summit Way	Nova Constantia	139	CP	24
Sun Cl.	Thembokwezi	125	CL	49
Sun King Cr.	Sonstraal Hgts	46	BR	54
Sun Rd	Bishop Lavis	105	CE	43
Sun Valley Ave	Hohenort	119	CL	25
Sunbird Cir.	Kommetjie	183	DB	13
Sunbird Cl.	Blouberg Rise	25	BN	31
Sunbird Cl.	D'urbanvale	45	BO	50
Sunbird Cl.	Kommetjie	183	DB	13
Sunbird Cl.	D'urbanvale	45	BO	50
Sunbird Ct	Bridgetown	103	CE	37
Sunbird Dr. East	Wimbledon	107	CF	54
Sunbird Dr. North	Sunbird Pk	107	CF	54
Sunbird Dr. South	Sunbird Pk	107	CG	54
Sunbird Link	Pelikan Pk	142	CR	35
Sunbird Way	Electric City	127	CN	58
Sunbury Rd	Elfindale	140	CQ	29
Sunbush Cl.	Hout Bay	137	CP	16
Sundale Dr.	Durbell	45	BS	50
Sunday Ct	Delft	106	CG	49
Sunday Peak Rd	Heideveld	104	CG	39
Sunderland	Rocklands (M.Plain)	163	CT	45
Sunderland St	Dunoon	42	BP	37
Sunderland St	Factreton	84	BY	34
Sunderland St	Factreton	85	BY	35
Sunderland St	Kensington	84	BY	33
Sundew	Protea Village	63	BW	58
Sundew	Stellenbosch	95	BY	75
Sundew Rd	Lotus River	141	CP	34
Sundew Rd	Lotus River	142	CP	35
Sundown Wk	Pinati	122	CJ	35
Sundu Rd	Thembokwezi	125	CM	48
Sunflower	Lentegeur (M.Plain)	145	CP	45
Sunflower Cl.	Bridgetown	103	CF	36
Sunflower Cr.	Eersterivier	127	CM	58
Sunflower Rd	Lavender Hill East	160	CU	31
Sunflower Rd	Lavender Hill East	160	CX	32
Suni Cr.	Goedemoed	46	BP	53
Suni St	Soneike II	89	BZ	54
Sunlands Ave	Lansdowne	121	CK	33
Sunmaid	Fairyland	19	AZ	93
Sunningdale	Stellenberg	62	BU	51
Sunningdale Dr.	Sunningdale	25	BL	31
Sunningdale Dr.	Sunningdale	25	BM	31
Sunningdale Rd	Kenilworth	120	CK	28
Sunningdale Way	Northpine	63	BU	58
Sunningdale Way	Northpine	63	BV	58
Sunninghill Rd	Wynberg	120	CL	29
Sunny	Northpine	63	BV	58
Sunny Way	Pinelands	84	CC	32
Sunny Way	Surrey	103	CG	37
Sunnybrae Rd	Rondebosch	101	CG	30
Sunnybrook Way	Elfindale	140	CQ	30
Sunnycove Steps	Fish Hoek	186	DC	25
Sunnydale Rd	Sunnydale	185	DA	19
Sunnyside Cr.	Woodstock	83	CA	29

Abbreviations used: Ave – Avenue, A.H. – Agricultural Holding, A.L.– Algemene Landgoed, Blvd – Boulevard, Cen. – Central, Cir. – Circle, Cl. – Close, Cr. – Crescent, Ct – Court, Dr. – Drive, Est. – Estate, Ext. – Extension, Hgts – Heights, Ind. – Industrial, Gdns – Gardens, Gr. – Grove, La. – Lane, (M.Plain) - Mitchells Plain, Nth – North, Pl. – Place, Pk – Park, Rd – Road, Rdg. – Ridge, S.H.– Small Holding, Sq. – Square, St – Street, Sth – South, Ter. – Terrace, Tn – Turn, Val. – Valley, Wk – Walk

STREET NAME	SUBURB NAME	PG	GRID	
Sunnyside Rd	Crawford	102	CH	33
Sunnyside Rd	Edgemead	58	BU	37
Sunray Rd	Fish Hoek	186	DB	24
Sunridge	Wesbank	107	CG	51
Sunrise	Pinelands	84	CB	33
Sunrise Cir.	Capricorn	159	CX	30
Sunrise Cir.	Ndabeni	84	CB	32
Sunrise Cl.	Barbarossa	140	CO	27
Sunrise Cl.	Edgemead	58	BU	38
Sunset Ave	Hout Bay	116	CM	13
Sunset Cl.	Fish Hoek	185	DA	22
Sunset Cl.	Hout Bay	116	CM	13
Sunset Cl.	Pinelands	84	CC	32
Sunset Cl.	Salberau	86	CB	41
Sunset Cl.	Salberau	86	CB	39
Sunset Cl.	Scottsdene	64	BV	60
Sunset Cl.	Sonstraal Hgts	46	BQ	53
Sunset Cr.	Macassar	149	CR	63
Sunset Cr.	Pinelands	84	CC	31
Sunset Cr.	Weltevreden Val. (M.Plain)	144	CQ	43
Sunset Dr.	Admirals Pk	175	DC	78
Sunset Dr.	Anchorage Pk	179	DD	77
Sunset Dr.	Somerset West	151	CQ	73
Sunset St	Philippi	124	CM	45
Suntsu Cr.	Umrhabulo Triangle	147	CQ	56
Sunwood Dr.	Tokai	139	CS	25
Superior Way	Portlands (M.Plain)	144	CQ	45
Supermarine St	Kensington	84	BZ	34
Supply Rd	Eersterivier	128	CN	61
Suraya St	Casablanca	175	DA	76
Surbiton Rd	Rosebank	101	CE	30
Surcingle Ave	Hout Bay	117	CN	16
Sureboy Dali St	Weltevreden Val. (M.Plain)	124	CM	43
Surf Rd	Strandfontein	162	CV	40
Surf St	Sea Point	80	CA	18
Surf Way	Kommetjie	183	DB	12
Suria Wk	Hanover Pk	122	CJ	37
Surin Cr.	Northpine	63	BT	58
Suring Cl.	Plattekloof	59	BV	42
Suring St	Plumstead	140	CO	28
Suring St	Wellington	15	AT	92
Surran Rd	Hanover Pk	122	CJ	36
Surran Rd	Hanover Pk	122	CK	36
Surran Rd	Newfields	122	CJ	36
Surrey Pl.	Green Point	81	BY	21
Surrey Rd	Mowbray	101	CD	30
Surrey St	Claremont	120	CJ	29
Surrey St	Townsend Est.	85	BZ	38
Surwood Wk	Hanover Pk	122	CK	35
Susan Ave	Bakoven	98	CF	18
Susan Cl.	Brentwood Pk	126	CJ	51
Susan Cl.	Kraaifontein	47	BQ	55
Susan St	Rosendal	61	BU	50
Susan St	Tafelsig (M.Plain)	145	CS	50
Susan Way	Brentwood Pk	126	CJ	51
Susan Way	Tokai	139	CS	26
Susanne Ave	Bel Ombre	119	CM	25
Sussex	Brackenfell Sth	90	BY	57
Sussex Rd	Blue Downs	108	CH	56
Sussex Rd	Observatory	101	CD	29
Sussex Rd	Tokai	139	CS	25
Sussex Rd	Weltevreden Val. (M.Plain)	144	CP	43
Sussex Rd	Wynberg	120	CL	29
Sussex Rd	Wynberg	120	CM	29
Sussex St	Claremont	120	CJ	29
Sussex St	Stellenryk	62	BU	52
Sussex St	Woodstock	82	CB	26
Suther Cl.	Hout Bay	116	CN	14
Sutherland St	Belhar	106	CD	49
Sutherland St	Belhar	106	CH	48
Sutherland St	Claremont	120	CJ	29
Sutherland St	Claremont	120	CK	30
Sutherland St	Ruyterwacht	86	CA	39
Sutton Rd	Fairways	141	CO	31
Suurberg Ct	Edgemead	59	BT	39
Suurberg St	Tafelsig (M.Plain)	145	CS	49
Suurbessie	Arbeidslus	96	CA	80
Suurbraak St	Eersterivier	128	CL	60
Suzanne Ave	Hout Bay	137	CQ	17
Suzanne Cr.	Brackenfell Sth	63	BX	57
Suzanne St	Denneburg	23	BD	91
Swaan Cr.	Jacarandas	90	CB	56
Swaan Rd	Somerset West	170	CV	72
Swakop Cr.	Park Village	127	CK	58
Swakop Ct	Delft	106	CG	49
Swakop Rd	Manenberg	123	CJ	39
Swalle St	Somerset West	171	CU	76
Swallow Cr.	Seawinds	159	CU	30
Swallow La.	Dreyersdal	139	CS	26
Swallow La.	Kommetjie	183	DB	13
Swallow Rd	Phumlani	142	CQ	36
Swallow Rd	Woodlands (M.Plain)	144	CP	44
Swallow St	D'urbanvale	29	BN	50
Swallow St	Flamingo Vlei	41	BQ	32
Swallow St	Joostenberg	48	BP	60
Swallow St	Maitland Gdn Village	83	CB	30
Swallow St	Ocean View	184	DC	15
Swallow Way	Scarborough	192	DJ	18
Swallow Way	Sunbird Pk	107	CF	54
Swan Cir.	Ocean View	184	DC	15
Swan Cl.	Plumstead	140	CP	29
Swan La.	Bergvliet	140	CQ	28
Swan Rd	Bishop Lavis	105	CD	43
Swan Rd	Bishop Lavis	105	CE	43
Swan St	Amanda Glen	46	BS	52
Swan St	Pelikan Pk	161	CV	38
Swanmore Rd	Rondebosch	102	CG	31
Swansea Rd	Newlands	101	CH	27
Swanson St	Woodstock	83	CB	28
Swart Rd	Athlone	102	CG	33
Swart St	Aurora	45	BQ	48
Swart St	Harbour Island	179	DE	77
Swart St	Kylemore	97	BZ	86
Swart St	Morgenster Hoogte	63	BT	56
Swartberg	Brackenfell	63	BW	55
Swartberg	Brackenfell	63	BV	58
Swartberg	Wellington	15	AV	91
Swartberg Ave	Bonnie Brae	47	BP	57
Swartberg Cr.	Welgevonden	46	BO	54
Swartberg Rd	Eversdal	62	BU	51
Swartberg St	Epping Ind.	86	CA	39
Swartberg St	Tafelsig (M.Plain)	145	CR	49
Swartbooi	Kayamandi	94	BZ	74
Swartdam Rd	Belthorn Est.	102	CH	34
Swarthout Cr.	Plattekloof	60	BV	43
Swarthout St	St Dumas	90	CC	56
Swartklip Rd	Eastridge (M.Plain)	145	CQ	49
Swartklip Rd	Lentegeur (M.Plain)	145	CO	48
Swartklip Rd	Mandalay	125	CM	48
Swartklip Rd	Strandfontein	165	CT	52
Swartklip Rd	Tafelsig (M.Plain)	146	CS	51
Swartkops St	Wesbank	107	CG	51
Swartland Cr.	Belhar	89	CC	52
Swartvlei St	Lemoenkloof	18	BC	89
Swartysterhout Rd	Bonteheuwel	103	CE	38
Swartz	Kayamandi	94	CA	74
Swawel	Onderpapegaaiberg	94	CC	72
Swawel Ave	Macassar	149	CR	65
Swawelstert Rd	Fairyland	19	AZ	94
Swaweltjie St	Amstelhof	23	BD	93
Swaweltjie St	Mikro Pk	90	CB	56
Sweet Home Way	Heathfield	140	CP	28
Sweet Pea	Dalvale	19	AY	91
Sweet Pea	Dalvale	19	AZ	94
Sweet Valley Rd	Bergvliet	140	CQ	28
Sweet William	Lentegeur (M.Plain)	145	CP	47
Sweet William	Lentegeur (M.Plain)	145	CP	50
Sweetwater Cl.	The Lakes	184	CZ	18
Sweetwell Ave	Voorbrug	106	CG	50
Swellendam St	Portlands (M.Plain)	145	CR	47
Swellengrebel	Die Boord	113	CE	75
Swellengrebel Ave	Bothasig	42	BS	38
Swellenhof Way	Marinda Hgts	89	BZ	52
Swellenhof Way	Marinda Hgts	89	BY	54
Swelleni St	Scottsdene	64	BT	60
Swemmer St	Beacon Valley (M.Plain)	145	CP	47
Swentu	Kayamandi	94	BZ	74
Swift	Seawinds	159	CU	30
Swift Cl.	Montagu's Gift	141	CO	32
Swift La.	Steenberg	158	CT	24
Swift St	Flamingo Vlei	41	BQ	33
Swift St	Salt River	83	CB	28
Swinford St	Connaught	87	CB	43
Swing Rd	Winslow	179	DD	77
Swiss Rd	Lansdowne	121	CK	34
Swisshoek St	Tygerberg Ind. Pk	31	BL	57
Swityi Cr.	Philippi East	125	CM	47
Sword Dancer Cl.	Silvermine Village	157	CX	19
Swordfish	Rocklands (M.Plain)	144	CS	45
Sybil La.	Camps Bay	98	CE	18
Sybil Rd	Ottery	121	CM	33
Sybrand Rd	Sybrand Pk	102	CE	32
Sycamore Cr.	Eastridge (M.Plain)	145	CR	47
Sycamore Cr.	Highbury	107	CE	53
Sycamore Cr.	Silverglade	185	DA	22
Sycamore St	Fairie Knowe	185	DA	19
Sycamore Way	Bridgetown	103	CE	36
Sydney Carter Cl.	Woodlands (M.Plain)	124	CN	44
Sydney Rd	Mowbray	101	CD	30
Sydney Rd	Wynberg	120	CM	29
Sydney St	District Six	82	CB	24
Sydney St	Green Point	81	BZ	21
Sydney St	Oakdale	61	BX	48
Sydney Taylor Cr.	Woodlands (M.Plain)	144	CO	45
Sydow St	Maitland	83	CB	30
Sydow St	Scottsdene	64	BU	60
Sydwell Mayona St	Kuyasa	147	CS	55
Sydwell Mayona St	Kuyasa	147	CS	57
Syfred Douglas	N1 City	59	BX	40
Syfret Rd	Rondebosch	102	CF	31
Sylvan Cl.	Oranjezicht	99	CD	22
Sylvan Rd	Wynberg	120	CM	28
Sylvaner Cl.	Zevenzicht	90	CC	58
Sylvaner Rd	Northpine	63	BU	58
Sylvaner Rd	Northpine	63	BV	58
Sylvaner St	Somerset West	151	CR	71
Sylvester Rd	Retreat	140	CR	30
Sylvester St	Wellington	10	AS	92
Sylvia Ave	Eersterivier	128	CM	61
Sylvia Rd	Claremont	120	CJ	27
Sylvia St	De Tuin	47	BS	55
Sylvia St	Kalkfontein II	107	CD	53
Symphony Ave	Dalvale	19	AY	92
Symphony Ave	Steenberg	159	CT	29
Symphony Ave	Steenberg	159	CT	30
Symphony Ave East	Dalvale	19	AY	93
Symphony Ave East	Dalvale	19	AZ	92
Symphony Ave West	Groenheuwel	19	AZ	92
Symphony Cl.	Sonstraal Hgts	46	BR	54
Symphony Way	Belhar	88	CC	49
Symphony Way	Belhar	106	CD	48
Symphony Way	Delft Sth	125	CK	48
Symphony Wk	Mitchells Plain Cen.	145	CQ	47
Synagogue St	Bellville Sth Ext. 5	88	BY	48
Synagogue St	Lemoenkloof	18	BC	89
Syringa Cl.	Bellair	62	BW	51
Syringa Cl.	Peers Hill	186	DA	23
Syringa Cr.	Belhar	106	CE	47
Syringa Cr.	Thornton	85	CA	37
Syringa Rd	Bergvliet	140	CR	28
Syringa Rd	Gordon Strand	179	DD	76
Syringa St	Bonteheuwel	103	CE	38
Syringa St	Forest Village	127	CM	58
Syringa St	Hanover Pk	122	CJ	37
Syringa St	Hillcrest Hgts	127	CL	57
Syringa St	Mikro Pk	90	CB	55
Syrus Gate	High Gate	107	CG	54
Sysen St	Blackheath Ind.	108	CF	56
Sysie St	Amstelhof	23	BD	93
Sysie St	Loucharmante	90	CC	56
T				
T.Jaxa St	Mfuleni	126	CK	54
T.Maxakatha St	Mfuleni	126	CK	53
T.Mfelane St	Mfuleni	126	CK	53
T.Mlanjeni St	Mfuleni	126	CK	53
T.Sebina St	Mandela Pk	147	CQ	55
T.Tokwana St	Mfuleni	126	CJ	53
T.Tokwana St	Mfuleni	126	CK	53
Taaibos	Arbeidslus	96	CA	80
Taaibos	Lentegeur (M.Plain)	144	CO	46
Taaibos	Leonsdale	86	CA	41
Taaibos Cl.	D'urbanvale	45	BO	49
Taaibos Cl.	Eastridge (M.Plain)	145	CR	47
Taaibos Cl.	Loevenstein	60	BW	45
Taaibos Cl.	Plattekloof	60	BU	43
Taaibos Cl.	Protea Hoogte	63	BW	57
Taaibos Rd	Bonteheuwel	103	CE	38
Taaibos Rd	Gordon Strand	179	DD	76
Taaibos St	Eversdal Hgts	46	BS	51
Taaibos St	Rouxville	90	CA	56
Tabak St	De Oude Renbaan	22	BH	88
Table Bay Blvd	Woodstock	83	CA	28
Tabora Way	Newlands	100	CH	26
Tabulele Ave	Victoria Mxenge	146	CO	52
Tacoma Rd	Belhar	106	CD	47
Tafa St	Victoria Mxenge	146	CO	52
Tafelberg	Brackenfell	63	BW	55
Tafelberg	Park Village	127	CK	58
Tafelberg Rd	Belhar	106	CE	50
Tafelberg Rd	Bishop Lavis	104	CD	41
Tafelberg Rd	Bishop Lavis	104	CE	42
Tafelberg Rd	Bonnie Brae	47	BP	57
Tafelberg Rd	Greenfield	108	CH	56
Tafelberg Rd	Lavender Hill East	160	CU	32
Tafelberg Rd	Oranjezicht	99	CE	22
Tafelberg St	Bothasig	58	BT	36
Tafelberg St	Bothasig	58	BU	36
Tafelberg St	Tafelsig (M.Plain)	145	CR	49
Tafelberg St	Tafelsig (M.Plain)	145	CS	50
Tafelberg St	Tafelsig (M.Plain)	146	CS	51
Tafelberg Way	Kenridge	45	BS	49
Tafelberg Way	Kenridge Hgts	45	BS	49
Tafelsig St	Panorama	59	BV	42
Tafeni St	Bloekombos	49	BR	63
Tagus Way	Manenberg	123	CK	39
Tahiti Cl.	Capri	185	DB	19
Tahiti St	Portlands (M.Plain)	144	CQ	46
Tahoe Cl.	Malibu Village	127	CK	56
Taillefer St	Courtrai	22	BG	88
Tailor Green	Summer Greens	58	BW	35
Take-a-Walk Cl.	Noordhoek	156	CX	18
Tala Cr.	Eyethu	146	CO	53
Talana	Lindida	96	CA	80
Talana Cl.	Claremont	120	CJ	27
Talana Cl.	Leonsdale	86	CA	42
Talana Cl.	Zevendal	90	CC	58
Talana Rd	Claremont	120	CJ	27
Talana Rd	Mabille Pk	89	CA	53
Talana Rd	Sack's Circle Ind.	89	CB	51
Talc St	Belthorn Est.	122	CJ	35
Taleni Sq.	Eyethu	146	CO	53
Talent St	Plumstead	140	CP	29
Talhana Hill	Somerset West	151	CQ	72
Taljaard St	Morgenster Hoogte	63	BT	56
Tallent St	Churchill	59	BX	42
Tallent St	Glenlily	86	BY	42
Tallis	Delft Sth	125	CK	48
Tally Ho Rd	Mitchells Plain	144	CS	45
Talma Rd	Muizenberg	187	CY	29
Talma St	Voorbrug	106	CG	50
Tamani Rd	Brown's Farm	123	CM	41
Tamarisk	Delft Sth	125	CJ	48
Tamarisk Cl.	Nova Constantia	139	CP	24
Tamarisk Cl.	Uitsig	87	CC	44
Tamarisk Cr.	Vredenberg	62	BV	52
Tamarisk Ct	Delft Sth	125	CJ	49
Tamarisk La.	Nova Constantia	139	CP	24
Tamarisk St	Brantwood	89	CB	53
Tamarisk St	Wellway Pk East	46	BO	52
Tamarix Rd	Thornton	85	CA	37
Tambo Rd	Mandela Pk	146	CR	54
Tambo Rd	Mandela Pk	147	CR	55
Tambo Rd	Masiphumelele	184	DA	18
Tambo St	Fisantekraal	31	BJ	58
Tambo St	Fisantekraal	32	BJ	59
Tambo St	Gugulethu	104	CF	40
Tamboekie	Amandelrug	90	CA	56
Tamboekie Cr.	Vredekloof	62	BT	54
Tamboekie Pl.	Leonsdale	86	CA	41
Tamboekie Pl.	Leonsdale	86	BZ	41
Tamboerskloof Rd	Tamboerskloof	81	CB	21
Tambotie	Delft Sth	125	CJ	50
Tambotie Ave	New Orleans	19	BB	91
Tambotie Cl.	Blommendal	61	BW	50
Tambotie Cl.	Plattekloof	60	BU	43
Tambotie Cr.	Tygerdal	58	BX	38
Tambotie Cr.	Wellway Pk East	46	BO	52
Tambotie Cr.	Wellway Pk East	46	BP	52
Tambotie Rd	Thornton	85	CA	36
Tambotie St	Eastridge (M.Plain)	145	CR	47
Tambotie St	Forest Hgts	127	CK	57
Tambotie St	Hillcrest Hgts	127	CL	57
Tambourine St	Cafda Village	141	CS	31
Tambourine St	Voorbrug	106	CD	48
Tambourine St	Voorbrug	106	CH	48
Tamo Rd	Retreat	140	CS	28
Tamsyn Cl.	De Tijger	60	BX	44
Tana Rd	Retreat	140	CS	28
Tana St	Mfuleni	126	CJ	53
Tana St	Portlands (M.Plain)	144	CQ	46
Tana Way	Delft	106	CF	49
Tanabaru St	Schotsche Kloof	81	CA	22
Tancred St	Athlone	102	CG	33
Tandanani Cr.	Mxolisi Phetani	125	CM	50
Tandazo Dr.	Victoria Mxenge	126	CN	51
Tandazo Dr.	Victoria Mxenge	146	CO	51
Tanel Rd	Pinati	122	CK	35
Tanga St	Eyethu	146	CP	53
Tangana Ave	Thembokwezi	125	CM	49
Tangana Ave	Thembokwezi	125	CK	50
Tanglewood Cr.	Milnerton	57	BU	31
Tanglewood Cr.	Sunset Links	57	BU	31
Tango Cr.	Retreat	140	CS	29
Tango Sq.	Mitchells Plain Cen.	145	CR	47
Tania Cl.	Lentegeur (M.Plain)	145	CO	48
Tania St	Casablanca	175	DA	76
Tania St	Kalkfontein II	107	CD	53
Tanja Rd	Hohenort	119	CL	25
Tanner Ave	Athlone	102	CG	33
Tanner Ave	Athlone	102	CG	34
Tanner Rd	Windsor Pk	47	BS	57
Tanner St	William Lloyd	23	BD	92
Tano St	Delft	106	CF	49
Tanqua St	Delft	106	CG	48
Tantallon Ct.	Dennemere	108	CH	57
Tantallon Ct.	Dennemere	108	CE	55
Tantalon Rd	Rondebosch	101	CF	29
Taoge Ct	Delft	106	CG	49
Tapiola Way	Edgemead	58	BU	37
Tara Cl.	Sonstraal Hgts	46	BQ	54
Tara Rd	Sonstraal Hgts	46	BQ	53
Taranto	Strandfontein	162	CT	41
Tarentaal	Onderpapegaaiberg	94	CC	72
Tarentaal	Rocklands (M.Plain)	144	CS	44
Tarentaal Cr.	Okavango Pk	63	BT	57
Tarentaal Rd	Bridgetown	103	CE	36
Tarentaal Rd	Bridgetown	103	CE	37
Tarentaal St	Amanda Glen	46	BS	52
Tarentaal St	Amstelhof	23	BD	94
Tarentaal St	Electric City	127	CN	58
Tarentaal St	Joostenberg	48	BP	61
Tarentaal St	Macassar	149	CS	65
Tarentaal St	Mikro Pk	90	CB	55
Tarentaal St	Wellington	15	AT	92
Tarka Rd	Eversdal Hgts	46	BR	51
Tarley Rd	Wynberg	120	CL	29
Taronga Rd	Crawford	102	CH	33
Taronga Rd	Crawford	121	CJ	33
Tarpon Cl.	Eersterivier	128	CN	60
Tarryn Cl.	Lemoenkloof	18	BC	87
Tasco Cr.	Jagtershof	108	CD	57
Tasman	Forest Glade	128	CL	59
Tasman Rd	Observatory	83	CB	29
Tasman St	Claremont	101	CH	30
Tassel Berry Cr.	Vredekloof Hgts	47	BS	55
Tatum Rd	Retreat	140	CS	29
Taulon	Groenvlei	18	BA	88
Taunton Rd	Wynberg	120	CM	29
Taurus	Everite	63	BU	57
Taurus	Mbekweni	15	AV	91
Taurus Cl.	Ocean View	189	DD	15
Taurus Rd	Joe Slovo Pk	57	BU	34
Taurus Rd	Phoenix	57	BU	33
Taurus Rd	Surrey	103	CG	38
Taurus Rd	Surrey	103	CH	38
Taurus Way	Ocean View	184	DC	15
Tay St	Woodstock	83	CB	27
Tayee St	Jamestown	113	CH	75
Taylor	Stellenbosch	95	CB	75
Taylor St	Beaconvale	87	CA	43
Taylor St	Oakdene	89	CC	53
Taylor St	Parowvallei	87	BZ	43
Teachers Way	Strandfontein	162	CT	41
Teak Pl.	Eastridge (M.Plain)	145	CR	47
Teak Rd	Bonteheuwel	103	CE	38
Teal Ave	Electric City	127	CN	58
Teal Cl.	Imhoff's Gift	184	DB	16
Teal Cl.	Silvermine Village	157	CX	19
Teal Rd	Montagu's Gift	141	CO	32

STREET NAME	SUBURB NAME	PG	GRID	
Tebe St	Victoria Mxenge	146	CO	51
Teck	Woodstock	82	CB	26
Tecno Cr.	Epping Ind.	85	CA	38
Tecno Cr.	Epping Ind.	85	CB	38
Tecoma Cr.	Plattekloof	60	BV	43
Tecoma Cr.	Thornton	85	CB	37
Tecoma Cr.	Wellington	10	AS	94
Tecoma Rd	Flintdale Est.	140	CP	30
Tecoma Rd	Flintdale Est.	141	CP	31
Tecoma Rd	Ridgeworth	61	BU	50
Tecoma St	Perm Gdns	127	CJ	58
Tecoma St	Perm Gdns	128	CJ	59
Tecoma Way	Pinelands	84	CC	34
Tecoma Way	Scarborough	192	DJ	18
Tedder Ave	Simon's Town	194	DJ	26
Teddington Rd	Oakdale	61	BX	48
Teddington Rd	Rondebosch	101	CF	29
Tedric St	Kaymor	89	BY	52
Tee Cl.	Lakeside	159	CV	27
Tee Cl.	Lakeside	159	CW	27
Tee St	Westlake	159	CU	27
Teebus Way	Delft	106	CG	49
Teerhout	Delft Sth	125	CJ	49
Teeruintjie Sq.	Roosendaal	107	CE	51
Tees Rd	Manenberg	123	CK	39
Tegno	Tegnopark	112	CF	73
Tekana Cr.	Nonqubela	126	CN	52
Tekstiel St	Parow Ind.	87	CB	45
Tekstiel St	Parow Ind.	87	CC	45
Tekwane Cl.	Crossroads	124	CK	44
Tele St	Mfuleni	126	CJ	53
Teleki Cr.	Groenvlei	18	BA	88
Telford Ave	Athlone	102	CG	33
Telford St	Parklands	25	BM	34
Telford Way	Edgemead	58	BU	38
Telford Way	Meadowridge	140	CP	27
Temba Cr.	Mfuleni	126	CL	54
Tembalethu St	Mfuleni	126	CL	54
Tembe St	Athlone	102	CF	33
Tembelihle	Mbekweni	15	AW	92
Tembu St	Kaya	146	CP	51
Temperance Rd	Retreat	140	CR	30
Tempest	Rocklands (M.Plain)	163	CT	45
Templar St	Camelot	107	CF	53
Temple St	Gatesville	103	CG	37
Templeman St	Durbanville	45	BQ	48
Templier St	Paarl	22	BE	88
Temporal	Rocklands (M.Plain)	145	CS	47
Tenby Rd	Wynberg	120	CM	29
Tenerife Cl.	Bloubergstrand	24	BN	29
Tennant	Stellenbosch	95	CA	75
Tennant Cr.	Belhar	107	CD	51
Tennant Rd	Windsor Pk	47	BS	57
Tennant Rd	Windsor Pk	47	BR	56
Tennant Rd	District Six	82	CB	24
Tennant St	Kenilworth	120	CK	28
Tennant St	Klippiesdal	19	BC	91
Tennent Rd	Athlone	102	CG	34
Tennessee Ave	Colorado (M.Plain)	144	CO	44
Tennessee Ave	Mitchells Plain	144	CR	44
Tennis Cr.	Beacon Valley (M.Plain)	145	CP	48
Tennyson Rd	Windsor Pk	47	BR	57
Tennyson Rd	Zoo Pk	47	BQ	57
Tennyson St	Mandalay	125	CM	48
Tennyson St	Salt River	83	CB	28
Tenor Cl.	Belhar	106	CD	49
Tenth	De Oude Renbaan	22	BH	88
Tenth Ave	Avon	86	CA	41
Tenth Ave	Beacon Valley (M.Plain)	145	CQ	47
Tenth Ave	Belmont Pk	48	BR	61
Tenth Ave	Belmont Pk	48	BR	59
Tenth Ave	Belmont Pk	48	BR	60
Tenth Ave	Boston	60	BX	46
Tenth Ave	Boston	61	BX	47
Tenth Ave	Cafda Village	140	CS	30
Tenth Ave	Da Gama Pk	190	DE	21
Tenth Ave	Eikendal	47	BS	58
Tenth Ave	Eikendal	48	BS	59
Tenth Ave	Fairways	141	CO	31
Tenth Ave	Fish Hoek	186	DB	23
Tenth Ave	Florida	87	CB	44
Tenth Ave	Hazendal	102	CE	33
Tenth Ave	Kayamandi	94	CA	74
Tenth Ave	Kensington	84	BY	34
Tenth Ave	Kensington	84	BZ	34
Tenth Ave	Leonsdale	86	CA	41
Tenth Ave	Retreat	140	CR	30
Tenth Ave	Schaap Kraal	142	CQ	36
Tenth Ave	Tafelsig (M.Plain)	146	CS	51
Tenth St	Bishop Lavis	104	CD	42
Tenth St	Elnor	86	CC	42
Tenth St	Kensington	84	BZ	33
Tenth St	Rusthof	174	DA	74
Tenth St	Rusthof	175	DA	75
Terblanche St	De Zoete Inval	22	BH	87
Terblanche St	Silveroaks	90	CC	55
Terblans Rd	Bonteheuwel	103	CE	38
Tercentenary Way	Glen Rdg	191	DD	24
Teremain Rd	Ottery	121	CN	33
Terence McCaw Cr.	Woodlands (M.Plain)	124	CN	45
Terez Cl.	Uitzicht	47	BO	55
Terhoven	Park Estates	174	CY	72
Terminus Rd	Nyanga	123	CJ	42
Terminus Steps	Bakoven	98	CF	17
Termo	Tegnopark	112	CF	73
Tern Cl.	Parklands	25	BN	32
Tern Cr.	Pelikan Pk	141	CR	33
Tern La.	Steenberg	139	CS	24
Tern Rd	Montagu's Gift	141	CO	33
Tern St	Pelikan Pk	161	CU	38
Tern St	Table View	41	BQ	32
Terra Rd	Wellington	12	AW	81
Terrace Hill	Silverhurst	119	CN	23
Terrace St	Wellington	10	AR	93
Terrapin La.	Table View	41	BQ	34
Tertia St	Voorbrug	106	CG	50
Tertius St	Amanda Glen	46	BS	52
Teslaarsdal	Wesbank	107	CG	51
Teslaarsdal	Wesbank	107	CG	53
Tessa Cr.	Lentegeur (M.Plain)	145	CO	48
Tester Rd	Vierlanden	30	BN	51
Tetra	Triangle Farm	89	BY	51
Tetyana Cr.	Nonqubela	126	CN	52
Teubes Rd	Kommetjie	183	DC	12
Teviot Plain	Voorbrug	106	CF	50
Texas Ave	Colorado (M.Plain)	144	CO	44
Texel Ct	Marina Da Gama	159	CV	30
Texel St	Ruyterwacht	86	CA	39
Textile St	Dal Josafat Ind.	22	BD	89
Thaba St	Fisantekraal	32	BJ	59
Thabo Mbeki Cr.	Mandela Pk	147	CR	55
Thakudi St	Wallacedene	48	BS	61
Thakudi St	Wallacedene	64	BT	62
Thame Cr.	Nonqubela	126	CN	52
Thames Ave	Bishop Lavis	104	CD	41
Thames Ave	Manenberg	123	CJ	39
Thames Cl.	Portlands (M.Plain)	144	CQ	46
Thames La.	Manenberg	123	CJ	39
Thames Wk	Manenberg	123	CJ	39
Thamsanga Rd	Nyanga	124	CK	43
Thamsanqa Rubusana	Weltevreden Val. (M.Plain)	123	CN	42
Thanda St	Umrhabulo Triangle	147	CQ	57
Thandabantu	Dunoon	42	BO	37
Thandanani	Mbekweni	15	AW	92
Thandanani	Mbekweni	15	AU	94
Thandanani St	Crossroads	124	CK	44
Thandeka	Dunoon	42	BO	37
Thandeka	Gugulethu	104	CH	40
Thandeka St	Ekuphumuleni	146	CQ	53
Thandi Modise Cr.	Mandela Pk	146	CQ	54
Thandisiwe	Mbekweni	15	AW	92
Tharina St	Somerset Pk	171	CW	75
Thatch Rd	Tokai	139	CS	25
Thatch St	Somerset West	151	CS	73
Thatcher St	Constantia Vale	119	CN	25
Thatchers Way	Durbanville	45	BQ	49
Thatchwood Cr.	Sonstraal Hgts	46	BQ	54
Thaxter Rd	Muizenberg Nth	159	CW	28
The Aloes Cl.	Peers Hill	186	DA	23
The Avenue	Salt River	83	CC	27
The Avenue	Silverhurst	119	CN	24
The Avenue	Stellenbosch	95	CC	77
The Bay Cl.	Somerset West	170	CW	72
The Bend	Bergvliet	140	CR	28
The Bend	Edgemead	58	BV	38
The Bend	Pinelands	102	CD	31
The Cedars Ave	Rocklands (M.Plain)	144	CS	44
The Cedars Ave	Rocklands (M.Plain)	144	CS	45
The Cheviots	Camps Bay	99	CD	19
The Close	Dreyersdal	140	CS	27
The Close	Fish Hoek	186	DA	24
The Cobbles	Rondebosch	101	CG	29
The Cobbles Rd	Table View	41	BO	34
The Crescent	Durbanville	45	BP	50
The Crescent	Durbanville	45	BP	47
The Crescent	Pinelands	84	CC	33
The Crossing	Pinelands	84	CC	32
The Dale	Fish Hoek	185	DA	22
The Dale	Silverglade	185	DA	22
The Dell	Dreyersdal	139	CS	26
The Dell	Pinelands	84	CC	33
The Downs Rd	Manenberg	123	CK	39
The Drive	Camps Bay	98	CE	18
The Fairway	Camps Bay	98	CE	18
The Fairway	Pinelands	102	CD	32
The Gables	Aurora	45	BQ	48
The Glade	Silverglade	185	DA	22
The Glen	Pinelands	84	CC	33
The Glen	Sea Point	81	CA	19
The Glen	Silverglade	185	DA	22
The Grange	Villa Italia	57	BW	33
The Grange Ave	Rondebosch	101	CF	28
The Grange Rd	Camps Bay	98	CD	18
The Hague Ave	The Hague	106	CF	50
The Hague Ave	The Hague	106	CE	49
The Hague St	Malibu Village	127	CJ	55
The Hamptons	Parklands	25	BN	34
The Hills	Durbanville Hills	45	BR	50
The Lane	Rondebosch	102	CG	31
The Link	Noordhoek Manor	157	CX	21
The Link	Park Village	127	CK	58
The Mead	Pinelands	84	CC	32
The Meadow	Edgemead	58	BV	38
The Meadows	Camps Bay	98	CD	18
The Meadway	Camps Bay	98	CE	18
The Mews	Glenhaven	89	CA	51
The Needle	Somerset West	151	CQ	71
The Needles Way	Hout Bay	118	CM	19
The Old Rd	Hout Bay	137	CP	17
The Orchards Cl.	Somerset West	171	CW	76
The Oval	Pinelands	84	CC	32
The Paddocks	Durbanville	45	BR	49
The Promenade	Hout Bay	137	CQ	16
The Reeds St	Welgedacht	60	BT	45
The Ridge	Clifton	98	CD	17
The Row	Muizenberg	159	CX	29
The Saddle	Barbarossa	120	CN	28
The Sanctuary	Kirstenhof	158	CT	26
The Stables	Strandfontein	162	CT	41
The Stables	Strandfontein	162	CV	42
The Steps	Newlands	101	CG	27
The Triangle	Pinelands	84	CC	32
The Tuscans	Villa Italia	57	BW	33
The Valley Wk	Silverhurst	119	CM	26
The Vines Cr.	Somerset West	171	CW	76
The Vineyard	Table View	41	BO	32
The Vinyard Cr.	Somerset West	171	CW	76
The Woods	Newlands	101	CG	27
Theal Rd	Tijgerhof	57	BX	33
Theal Rd	Wetton	121	CM	34
Theal St	Parow Nth	59	BW	42
Theatre Cr.	Weltevreden Val. (M.Plain)	144	CQ	43
Thebus Way	Eureka	87	CC	43
Thebus Way	Eureka	87	CB	46
Theescombe St	Wesbank	107	CH	51
Theewater Rd	Groenvallei	62	BX	53
Thekwane Rd	Philippi East	125	CL	47
Thelema Cl.	Zevendal	90	CC	58
Thelma Cl.	Bellville	62	BV	52
Thelma Rd	Claremont	120	CJ	28
Themba Ngesi St	Mandela Pk	147	CS	56
Themba Ngesi St	Mandela Pk	147	CS	58
Thembani Rd	Gugulethu	123	CJ	40
Thembisa	Gugulethu	104	CH	40
Thembrlihle St	Crossroads	124	CK	45
Theo St	Morgenster Hoogte	63	BT	56
Theomar Ct	Hohenort	119	CM	25
Theresa Ave	Oudekraal	98	CG	18
Therese St	Tafelsig (M.Plain)	145	CR	49
Thermo St	Triangle Farm	88	BZ	50
Theron Cr.	Strand	174	CZ	73
Theron St	Edgemead	58	BU	36
Theron St	Paarl	22	BE	88
Theronsberg St	Tafelsig (M.Plain)	145	CR	49
Thesen St	Dal Josafat Ind.	18	BC	89
Thetford Gr.	Parklands	25	BM	33
Thetford Rd	Parklands	25	BM	33
Thetha Cr.	Umrhabulo Triangle	147	CQ	57
Thetis Wk	Woodlands (M.Plain)	144	CO	44
Thetis Wk	Woodlands (M.Plain)	144	CR	43
Theunisen St	Somerset West	171	CT	77
Theys	William Lloyd	19	BC	94
Theys	William Lloyd	19	BA	94
Thibault	Mostertsdrift	96	CC	79
Thibault Ave	Somerset West	171	CT	75
Thibault Cr.	Richwood	42	BQ	38
Thibault Rd	Marina Da Gama	159	CV	29
Thibault Rd	Newlands	101	CH	27
Thibault St	Glen Ive	62	BU	52
Thibault St	Morgenster Hoogte	63	BU	55
Thibault St	Ruyterwacht	86	CA	39
Thibaza St	Umrhabulo Triangle	147	CP	58
Thicket Rd	Mowbray	101	CE	30
Thicket St	Newlands	101	CH	28
Thiele Rd	Ottery East	121	CM	33
Thierry	Karindal	96	CC	79
Third	De Oude Renbaan	22	BH	88
Third Ave	Belgravia	103	CG	35
Third Ave	Belmont Pk	48	BR	60
Third Ave	Bosonia	90	CB	55
Third Ave	Boston	61	BX	47
Third Ave	Boston	87	BY	46
Third Ave	Claremont	120	CJ	30
Third Ave	Cravenby	87	CA	43
Third Ave	Da Gama Pk	190	DE	21
Third Ave	Eikendal	48	BS	59
Third Ave	Elsies River Ind.	86	BZ	41
Third Ave	Fairways	121	CN	32
Third Ave	Fish Hoek	186	DB	24
Third Ave	Florida	87	CA	44
Third Ave	Glenlily	86	BY	42
Third Ave	Glenlily	87	BY	43
Third Ave	Grassy Pk	141	CQ	33
Third Ave	Hazendal	102	CE	33
Third Ave	Kenilworth	120	CK	30
Third Ave	Kensington	84	BZ	32
Third Ave	Lotus River	142	CP	35
Third Ave	Maitland	84	CA	33
Third Ave	Manenberg	123	CK	39
Third Ave	Mitchells Plain Cen.	145	CQ	47
Third Ave	Nyanga	123	CK	42
Third Ave	Paarl	22	BD	88
Third Ave	Retreat	140	CR	29
Third Ave	Rondebosch East	102	CG	32
Third Ave	Rondebosch East	102	CH	32
Third Ave	Schaap Kraal	142	CP	36
Third Ave	Vanguard	103	CG	38
Third Ave	Wellington	10	AS	93
Third Cr.	Fish Hoek	186	DB	24
Third Cr.	Vredelust	60	BX	46
Third Rd	Heathfield	140	CQ	29
Third Rd	Montague Gdns Ind.	58	BT	35
Third St	Bishop Lavis	104	CD	42
Third St	Firgrove	150	CR	67
Third St	Maitland	84	CA	33
Third St	Mxolisi Phetani	125	CL	49
Third St	Mxolisi Phetani	125	CL	50
Third St	Rusthof	174	DA	74
Third St	Welcome	103	CF	38
Third St	Wellington	10	AR	91
Thirlmere Rd	Plumstead	120	CN	29
Thirteenth	De Oude Renbaan	22	BH	88
Thirteenth Ave	Boston	60	BX	46
Thirteenth Ave	Boston	61	BX	47
Thirteenth Ave	Da Gama Pk	190	DE	21
Thirteenth Ave	Factreton	84	BY	34
Thirteenth Ave	Factreton	84	BZ	34
Thirteenth Ave	Fish Hoek	186	DB	23
Thirteenth Ave	Florida	87	CB	44
Thirteenth Ave	Kayamandi	94	CA	74
Thirteenth Ave	Schaap Kraal	142	CR	36
Thirteenth Ave	Valhalla	86	CA	40
Thirteenth St	Avon	86	CA	41
Thirteenth St	Bishop Lavis	105	CD	43
Thirteenth St	Kensington	84	BZ	33
Thirtieth Ave	Elnor	86	CB	42
Thirty-Fifth Ave	Adriaanse	87	CC	43
Thirty-Fifth Ave	Avonwood	87	CA	43
Thirty-Fifth Ave	Bishop Lavis	105	CD	44
Thirty-Fifth Ave	Elnor	86	CC	42
Thirty-First Ave	Elnor	86	CC	42
Thirty-Fourth Ave	Elnor	86	CC	42
Thirty-Fourth St	Balvenie	87	CC	43
Thirty-Ninth Ave	Eureka	87	CC	43
Thirty-Second Ave	Balvenie	86	CB	42
Thirty-Second St	Avonwood	86	CB	42
Thirty-Sixth Ave	Elnor	86	CC	42
Thirty-Third Ave	Elnor	86	CC	42
Thistle Ave	Somerset West	171	CV	75
Thistle St	Bishopscourt	119	CJ	25
Thistle St	Eersterivier	128	CL	58
Thobile Cr.	Kaya	146	CP	52
Thom St	Paarl	22	BD	88
Thom St	Paarl	22	BD	89
Thom St	Somerset West	171	CU	78
Thomas	Delft Sth	125	CJ	48
Thomas	Rusthof	174	DB	74
Thomas Bowler Ave	Edgemead	58	BU	38
Thomas Bowler Ave	Edgemead	59	BT	39
Thomas Cr.	Grassy Pk	141	CR	32
Thomas Cr.	Montagu's Gift	142	CO	35
Thomas Mchelm	Florida	87	CB	44
Thomas Nkobi	Weltevreden Val. (M.Plain)	123	CN	41
Thomas Rd	Balvenie	86	CB	42
Thomas Rd	Kenilworth	120	CK	29
Thomas Rd	Ndabeni	84	CB	32
Thomas St	Simon's Town	194	DJ	25
Thomas St	Valhalla Pk	104	CE	41
Thomas Tucker Ave	Blue Downs	127	CJ	56
Thompson Cl.	Ocean View	184	DC	16
Thompson St	Park Estates	170	CX	71
Thomson Rd	Claremont	101	CH	30
Thongothi St	Brown's Farm	123	CM	42
Thongothi St	Kuyasa	147	CR	56
Thor Cir.	Thornton	85	CB	35
Thor Cl.	Salberau	86	CB	40
Thor St	Valhalla	86	CA	40
Thorn St	Newlands	100	CH	26
Thornbury Rd	Plumstead	120	CN	29
Thorne Cl.	Barbarossa	120	CN	27
Thorne St	William Lloyd	19	BC	92
Thornhill Rd	Green Point	81	BZ	22
Thornhill Rd	Rondebosch	102	CE	31
Thornton Cl.	Dieprivier	140	CP	28
Thornton Rd	Athlone	102	CG	34
Thornton Rd	Belthorn Est.	121	CJ	34
Thornton Rd	Crawford	102	CH	34
Thornton Rd	Dieprivier	140	CP	28
Thornwick Rd	Plumstead	120	CM	28
Thorpe Cl.	Steenberg	157	CT	22
Three Anchor Bay Rd	Three Anchor Bay	81	BY	20
Three Firs Cr.	Tafelsig (M.Plain)	145	CS	47
Thrush La.	Bridgetown	103	CF	36
Thrush La.	Montagu's Gift	141	CO	32
Thrush St	Electric City	127	CN	58
Thukumbela St	Lwandle	175	CZ	77
Thuliswa	Dunoon	42	BO	37
Thuliswa	Dunoon	42	BO	38
Thunberg St	Monte Vista	59	BV	39
Thunderbolt	Rocklands (M.Plain)	144	CS	45
Thunzi St	Tarentaalplaas	170	CX	74
Thuthuzela St	Dunoon	42	BO	37
Thuyn St	Bothasig	42	BS	38
Thyme	Lentegeur (M.Plain)	144	CP	45
Thyme Cl.	Somerset West	171	CW	77
Thyme Cl.	Vredenberg	62	BV	53
Thys Witbooi Rd	Capricorn	160	CV	31
Tiara Way	Leonsdale	86	CA	42
Tiber Cl.	Portlands (M.Plain)	144	CQ	46
Tiber St	Manenberg	123	CK	39
Tickner St	Wellington	10	AR	92
Tico's Way	Silvermine Village	157	CX	19
Tide St	Woodstock	83	CA	27
Tiekiedraai Rd	Vierlanden	30	BN	51
Tienie Britz St	Beaconvale	87	BZ	45
Tienie Meyer Rd	Belrail	88	BY	48
Tienie Meyer Rd	Hardekraaltjie	87	BY	46
Tierberg Cl.	The Crest	46	BO	53
Tierberg Cr.	Welgevonden	30	BN	54
Tierberg Cr.	Welgevonden	30	BM	53

Abbreviations used: Ave – Avenue, A.H. – Agricultural Holding, A.L.– Algemene Landgoed, Blvd – Boulevard, Cen. – Central, Cir. – Circle, Cl. – Close, Cr. – Crescent, Ct – Court, Dr. – Drive, Est. – Estate, Ext. – Extension, Hgts – Heights, Ind. – Industrial, Gdns – Gardens, Gr. – Grove, La. – Lane, (M.Plain) - Mitchells Plain, Nth – North, Pl. – Place, Pk – Park, Rd – Road, Rdg. – Ridge, S.H.– Small Holding, Sq. – Square, St – Street, Sth – South, Ter. – Terrace, Tn – Turn, Val. – Valley, Wk – Walk

STREET NAME	SUBURB NAME	PG	GRID
Tierberg Rd	Avondale	60	BW 44
Tierberg Rd	Avondale	60	BX 44
Tierberg Rd	Avondale	87	BY 44
Tierberg St	Bothasig	42	BS 36
Tierboskat	Eastridge (M.Plain)	145	CR 48
Tierhout St	Blommendal	62	BW 51
Tierkloof St	Tafelsig (M.Plain)	145	CS 50
Tiffany Cl.	Rust-en-vrede	119	CN 26
Tiger Ave	Langeberg Rdg	47	BR 56
Tiger Moth	Rocklands (M.Plain)	163	CT 45
Tiger St	Mxolisi Phetani	125	CM 49
Tigerlily Cr.	Protea Village	64	BV 59
Tigris	Eden	113	CG 76
Tigris St	Eindhoven	125	CJ 50
Tijger Villas	Kenridge	61	BU 49
Tijgerhof St	Tijgerhof	57	BW 32
Tijuana St	Malibu Village	127	CK 55
Tiburg St	Uitzicht	31	BN 55
Tiller Arm Wk	Marina Da Gama	159	CV 30
Tillers Green	Summer Greens	58	BW 36
Timbavati St	Welgevonden	46	BO 54
Timber La.	Retreat	140	CS 28
Timber Way	Bergvliet	139	CQ 26
Timberlost Cl.	Somerset West	151	CQ 71
Timberlost La.	Hout Bay	118	CM 19
Timberon St	Paarl	22	BD 88
Timberton Cl.	Highbury	107	CE 54
Timmerman Cl.	Glen Rdg	191	DD 25
Timmerman St	Clamhall	60	BX 43
Timor Cl.	Portlands (M.Plain)	144	CQ 46
Timour Hall Rd	Plumstead	120	CN 28
Tindale Rd	Dieprivier	140	CP 28
Tindale Rd	Durbanville Hills	45	BR 50
Tindall	Idasvallei	96	CA 79
Tinka	Morgen Gronde	63	BX 55
Tinkers Cr.	Summer Greens	58	BV 36
Tinkers Pl.	Summer Greens	58	BV 36
Tinkers Rd	Summer Greens	58	BV 36
Tinktinkie	Onderpapegaaiberg	94	CC 72
Tinktinkie Rd	Die Wingerd	46	BP 53
Tinktinkie Rd	Die Wingerd	46	BS 54
Tinktinkie St	Mikro Pk	90	CB 55
Tinktinkie St	Somerset Hgts	127	CJ 57
Tinktinkie St	Somerset West	152	CS 76
Tinktinkie St	William Lloyd	23	BD 94
Tintagel Cl.	West Beach	24	BN 30
Tintagel Rd	West Beach	24	BN 30
Tintinkie St	Macassar	149	CS 65
Tinus de Jongh Cl.	Woodlands (M.Plain)	124	CN 44
Tiny Court Cl.	Fisantekraal	31	BK 58
Tiny Naude St	Springbok Pk	63	BV 55
Tiny Neethling St	Springbok Pk	63	BV 55
Tiobelle Cr.	Jamestown	113	CH 75
Tioga Cr.	Jamestown	113	CH 75
Tipston Cl.	Eersterivier	128	CN 61
Tiptol	Devon Pk	112	CD 72
Tipu	Greenlands	88	CA 49
Tipu	Hindle Pk	107	CH 54
Tipuane Pl.	Hazelwood Pk	185	CZ 20
Tipuane Pl.	Hazelwood Pk	185	DC 22
Tishbe Cl.	Bonnie Brook	47	BQ 57
Tissot Rd	Heathfield	140	CR 29
Titania Way	Meadowridge	140	CP 27
Titian St	De La Haye	89	BY 51
Titus	Tennantville	95	CA 75
Titus Ave	Rusthof	175	DA 75
Titus Cl.	Greenways	174	DA 74
Titus Rd	Mandalay	125	CM 48
Titus St	Mountain View	19	BB 92
Titus St	Scottsville	47	BS 57
Titus St	Scottsville	63	BT 57
Titus Way	The Vines	140	CO 27
Tivan Cr.	Vredekloof Hgts	47	BS 55
Tiverton Rd	Plumstead	120	CN 29
Tiverton Rd	Plumstead	120	CN 30
Tiverton St	Parklands	25	BM 34
Tivoli Pl.	Edgemead	58	BV 38
Tiwani St	Driftsands	125	CL 50
Tiwani St	Driftsands	126	CL 51
Tiwani St	Nonqubela	126	CN 53
Tobago Cl.	Portlands (M.Plain)	144	CP 46
Tobago Pl.	Macassar	149	CR 64
Tobago Way	Capri	185	DB 20
Tobago Way	Portlands (M.Plain)	144	CP 46
Tobiano Rd	Milnerton	41	BS 34
Tobin St	Scottsdene	64	BU 60
Tobruk	Strandfontein	162	CU 40
Tobruk Rd	Plumstead	120	CM 28
Toby Rd	Surrey	103	CH 37
Toefy	Cloetesville	95	BY 75
Toeskouer Rd	Belthorn Est.	102	CH 34
Toeskouer Rd	Belthorn Est.	121	CJ 34
Tokai Ct	Marina Da Gama	159	CV 29
Tokai Rd	Kirstenhof	140	CS 27
Tokai Rd	Northpine	63	BU 58
Tokai Rd	Steenberg	139	CS 24
Tokai Rd	Tokai	139	CS 25
Tokay St	Sonstraal	46	BR 52
Tokazi Rd	Ekuphumuleni	146	CQ 53
Tokia Rd	Helderberg Pk	175	DA 75
Tolbos	Delft Sth	125	CJ 49
Tolbos Cl.	Plattekloof	60	BU 43
Tolbos Cl.	Protea Village	64	BW 59
Tolbos Rd	Bonteheuwel	103	CE 38
Tolbos Rd	Bonteheuwel	103	CF 37
Tole St	Eyethu	146	CO 52
Toledo Rd	Montana/Durrheim	104	CG 42
Toleni Rd	Brown's Farm	124	CL 43
Toleni Rd	Kenilworth	120	CK 28
Tolerance Rd	Lansdowne	121	CL 34
Tolerance Rd	Retreat	140	CR 30
Toll Rd	Rondebosch	101	CF 29
Tolletjie Cr.	Roosendaal	107	CE 51
Tolo Cl.	Gugulethu	104	CF 40
Tolofiya	Philippi East	125	CM 47
Tolofiya St	Kuyasa	147	CR 56
Tolpen Rd	Pinati	122	CK 35
Tom St	Mabille Pk	89	CA 53
Tom St	Nyanga	123	CK 42
Tomahawk	Strandfontein	163	CT 45
Tomahawk St	Kensington	84	BZ 33
Tomson St	Goodwood Est.	85	BY 38
Tonbridge Rd	Heathfield	140	CR 29
Toner St	Avondale	60	BX 45
Toner St North	Avondale	60	BX 45
Toner St South	Avondale	87	BY 45
Tongaat	Papegaaiberg Ind. Pk	95	CA 75
Tontel Cr.	Roosendaal	107	CE 51
Tontel Cr.	Roosendaal	107	CG 53
Tontelhout	Delft Sth	125	CK 49
Tony Maloma St	Kuyasa	147	CS 55
Tony Maloma St	Kuyasa	147	CS 58
Tony Yengeni St	Crossroads	124	CK 44
Tooi Ave	Rusthof	174	DA 74
Tooting La.	Woodstock	83	CC 27
Top Rd	Fresnaye	81	CB 19
Topaas Cl.	Welgelegen	59	BT 41
Topaz	Fairdale	126	CJ 53
Topaz Cl.	Kommetjie	183	DB 13
Topaz Cl.	Pelikan Pk	161	CT 37
Topaz St	Sheridon Pk	159	CU 29
Topaz St	Somerset West	150	CR 70
Topaz Ter.	San Michel	157	CX 20
Topaz Way	San Michel	157	CX 20
Toplands	Voorbrug	106	CG 50
Topsham Rd	Ottery East	121	CN 34
Topsham Rd	Plumstead	120	CM 30
Torbay Rd	Grassy Pk	141	CQ 33
Torbay Rd	Green Point	81	BZ 21
Toring Rd	Retreat	141	CR 31
Torino Cr.	Brackenfell Sth	63	BW 57
Tornado Cir.	The Hague	106	CF 49
Torquay Ave	Claremont	120	CK 27
Torquay Cl.	Parklands	25	BN 33
Torrens Rd	Royal Cape	121	CM 32
Torrey Ave	Jamestown	113	CH 75
Torricelli St	Belhar	88	CC 50
Torrid Rd	Surrey	103	CG 38
Torrington Cr.	Parklands	25	BM 33
Torsig	Weltevreden Val. (M.Plain)	144	CP 43
Torsig	Weltevreden Val. (M.Plain)	144	CR 43
Tortel St	Wellington	15	AT 92
Tortelduif	Onderpapegaaiberg	94	CC 72
Tortelduif Cl.	Durbanville	46	BP 52
Tortelduif Cl.	Durbanville	46	BS 54
Tortelduif St	Jacarandas	90	CC 57
Tortelduif St	Macassar	149	CS 65
Tortuga Cl.	Barbarossa	119	CN 26
Tosca Cl.	Eastridge (M.Plain)	145	CQ 49
Tosca Cr.	Sonstraal Hgts	46	BR 54
Tosca Cr.	Uitzicht	47	BO 55
Toscana Cl.	Northpine	63	BU 58
Toscana Cl.	Northpine	63	BV 56
Toscana Way	Parklands	25	BM 33
Tosti	Delft Sth	125	CJ 49
Totem Rd	Lansdowne	121	CJ 32
Totius Rd	Townsend Est.	85	BY 37
Totius Rd	Welgemoed	60	BV 45
Totius St	Clamhall	60	BX 43
Totius St	Somerset West	170	CT 73
Totnes Rd	Plumstead	121	CN 31
Totness Ave	Bakoven	98	CF 18
Toto Biza St	Kuyasa	147	CS 55
Tottum Way	Proteaville	46	BO 51
Toucan Way	Blouberg Rise	25	BN 31
Toulon Ave	Plumstead	140	CP 29
Toulon St	Uitzicht	31	BN 56
Toulouse Cl.	Vredekloof	62	BT 53
Touraine Ave	Vredekloof	62	BU 53
Touraine St	Bel Ombre	119	CM 24
Tourmaline Rd	Fairdale	107	CH 54
Tourmaline Rd	Silversands	107	CH 54
Tousberg Rd	Manenberg	104	CG 39
Touws St	Mfuleni	126	CJ 53
Touws Way	Delft	106	CF 49
Tower Quay	Marina Da Gama	159	CW 30
Towerkop St	Manenberg	104	CG 39
Towerkop St	Tafelsig (M.Plain)	145	CS 50
Towers Rd	Muizenberg	159	CX 29
Townsend Ave	The Vines	140	CO 27
Townsend St	Acacia Pk	58	BX 36
Townsend St	Rome	174	CY 73
Townsend St	Townsend Est.	58	BX 37
Townsend St	Townsend Est.	85	BY 37
Townsend St	Townsend Est.	85	BZ 38
Townsend St	Tygerdal	58	BX 37
Tracer St	The Hague	106	CF 49
Tracey Ave	Weltevreden Val. (M.Plain)	124	CN 44
Track Cr.	Montague Gdns Ind.	58	BU 36
Tracy Cl.	Lentegeur (M.Plain)	145	CO 48
Tracy St	Casablanca	175	DB 76
Tracy St	Casablanca	175	DB 76
Trader St	Dennemere	108	CH 58
Tradouw	Wesbank	107	CG 51
Tradouw St	Belhar	89	CC 51
Tradouw St	Tafelsig (M.Plain)	145	CR 49
Tradouw Way	Delft	106	CG 49
Trafalgar Cr.	Malibu Village	127	CK 55
Trafalgar Cr.	Simon's Town	194	DJ 25
Trafalgar Dr.	Strandfontein	162	CT 40
Trafalgar Pl.	Simonskloof	194	DJ 25
Trafalgar Rd	Admirals Pk	175	DC 78
Trafalgar Sq.	Sea Point	81	CA 19
Trafalgar St	Cape Town Cen.	82	CA 23
Trafalgar St	Portlands (M.Plain)	145	CR 47
Trafalgar St	Russel's Rest	128	CL 60
Trafford Cl.	Edgemead	58	BV 38
Trafford Rd	Blackheath Ind.	108	CG 57
Traka St	Kaymor	89	BY 52
Traka Way	Delft	106	CF 48
Tralee Rd	Heathfield	140	CR 29
Traminer Ct	Northpine	63	BV 58
Traminer St	Somerset West	170	CT 72
Tramore Rd	Plumstead	140	CP 29
Tramore Rd	Plumstead	140	CP 30
Tramore Rd	Plumstead	141	CO 31
Trampoline St	Beacon Valley (M.Plain)	145	CQ 47
Tramway Rd	Sea Point	80	CA 18
Trans Karoo	Parow Ind.	87	CC 46
Trans Oranje	Parow Ind.	88	CB 47
Transport Cl.	Parow East	87	BY 45
Transvaal St	Paarden Eiland	83	BZ 29
Transvaal St	Paarden Eiland	83	CA 30
Transvalia	Uniepark	96	CB 79
Travers Rd	Newlands	101	CH 29
Traviata Ave	Scottsdene	64	BT 59
Treaty Rd	Woodstock	83	CB 27
Trebanio	Welgedacht	44	BS 46
Treble Cl.	Belhar	106	CD 49
Tredoux St	Beaconvale	87	CA 43
Tredoux St	Beaconvale	87	CA 44
Tredree Steps	Simon's Town	194	DJ 25
Tree Rd	Camps Bay	98	CE 18
Treehaven Rd	Claremont	121	CJ 31
Trek Rd	Gardens	99	CD 20
Trellis Rd	Tokai	139	CS 25
Tremaine Cl.	Mandalay	125	CN 48
Trematon Rd	Athlone	102	CF 32
Trenance Rd	Ottery	121	CM 33
Trengrove	Uniepark	96	CB 79
Trent Rd	Gardens	81	CB 21
Trent Rd	Plumstead	140	CP 29
Trent Rd	Vergesig	45	BQ 48
Trentham Rd	Plumstead	120	CN 30
Treurnich St	Paarl	22	BF 88
Trevor Rd	Lansdowne	121	CJ 32
Trevor Siljeur Rd	Capricorn	160	CU 31
Trevor Vilakazi	Weltevreden Val. (M.Plain)	123	CN 42
Trevor Vilakazi St	Mandela Pk	147	CQ 55
Trevor Way	Matroosfontein	86	CC 41
Trewwa Sq.	Roosendaal	107	CE 51
Triangle	Dal Josafat Ind.	18	BB 90
Trichardt St	Welgemoed	60	BU 45
Trichardt St	Welgemoed	60	BV 45
Trident	Rocklands (M.Plain)	144	CS 46
Trier Cl.	Vredekloof Hgts	47	BS 55
Trigg Rd	Capri Village	184	DB 17
Trill Rd	Observatory	83	CC 28
Trimaran Cl.	Sun Valley	185	DA 20
Trinidad Cl.	Capri	184	DB 18
Trinidad Cl.	Macassar	149	CR 63
Trinidad Cl.	Portlands (M.Plain)	144	CQ 46
Trinity La.	Rondebosch	102	CG 31
Triplets Way	Somerset West	153	CS 79
Trippens Cl.	Vierlanden	30	BN 52
Trippens Cl.	Vierlanden	30	BM 53
Tripper Way	Epping Ind.	86	CB 40
Tristan Cr.	Strandfontein	161	CT 38
Tristan St	Bergsig	46	BO 52
Tristania Ave	Ottery	121	CN 33
Triton Way	Phoenix	57	BV 33
Tritonia	Lentegeur (M.Plain)	145	CP 47
Tritonia Ave	Welgedacht	60	BU 45
Tritonia Dr.	Vredekloof Hgts	47	BS 55
Tritonia Rd	Table View	40	BO 30
Triumph St	Beacon Valley (M.Plain)	145	CQ 47
Trolley St	Tafelsig (M.Plain)	145	CS 47
Trolley St	Tafelsig (M.Plain)	145	CP 50
Trombone Cl.	Belhar	106	CD 49
Trompen Way	Edgemead	58	BU 38
Trompet St	Steenberg	159	CT 30
Troon Cr.	Sunningdale	25	BL 31
Troon Mews	Sunset Links	57	BT 31
Troop Rd	Wynberg	120	CM 30
Tropicana Rd	Weltevreden Val. (M.Plain)	144	CO 43
Trotter Rd	Strandfontein	143	CS 41
Troupant	Onderpapegaaiberg	94	CC 72
Trout Cl.	Pelikan Pk	142	CQ 35
Trout Way	Strandfontein	162	CT 39
Trovato Cl.	Mitchells Plain	144	CR 45
Trovato Cl.	Mitchells Plain	144	CR 43
Trovato Link	Wynberg	120	CL 27
Truman Rd	Claremont	101	CH 30
Trumpet Rd	Belhar	106	CD 49
Truro Cr.	Westlake Est.	158	CU 25
Truter St	Northern Paarl	18	AZ 89
Tryall Rd	Sunningdale	24	BL 30
Tryall Rd	Sunningdale	25	BL 31
Tsazo St	Mfuleni	126	CJ 53
Tsessebe Rd	Lotus River	142	CP 35
Tshaka Cr.	Nonqubela	146	CO 53
Tshitshi St	Brown's Farm	124	CL 44
Tshitshi St	Ilitha Pk	146	CQ 51
Tshitshi St	Ilitha Pk	146	CS 52
Tshona Cr.	Umrhabulo Triangle	147	CP 57
Tshona Cr.	Umrhabulo Triangle	147	CP 57
Tshonyane St	Bloekombos	48	BQ 62
Tshungulwana St	Nonqubela	126	CN 52
Tsietsi Mashinini	Weltevreden Val. (M.Plain)	123	CN 42
Tsitsikama St	Tafelsig (M.Plain)	145	CR 49
Tsitsikamma Way	Lavender Hill East	160	CU 32
Tsitsikamma Way	Lavender Hill East	160	CX 33
Tsolo St	Kaya	146	CP 51
Tsotsa Cr.	Nonqubela	126	CN 53
Tuba Cl.	Belhar	106	CD 49
Tuberose	Lentegeur (M.Plain)	144	CP 46
Tucana Cl.	Ocean View	189	DD 15
Tudor Ave	Tokai	139	CS 26
Tudor Cl.	Bergvliet	139	CQ 26
Tugela Ave	Thembokwezi	125	CM 49
Tugela Cir.	Plattekloof Glen	59	BW 40
Tugela Ct	Delft	106	CH 49
Tugela La.	Manenberg	123	CK 39
Tugela Rd	Bonnie Brook	47	BQ 57
Tugela Rd	Vygeboom	46	BR 51
Tugela St	Manenberg	123	CK 39
Tugela Way	Portlands (M.Plain)	144	CP 46
Tugwell Cr.	Edgemead	59	BU 39
Tuin	Dr Malan	95	CC 78
Tuin Sq.	Cape Town Cen.	82	CB 23
Tuin St	Franschhoek Sth	79	BZ 108
Tuin St	Gardens	81	CC 21
Tukela St	Mfuleni	126	CJ 53
Tula Cl.	Vredekloof Hgts	47	BS 55
Tulana	Sonstraal Hgts	46	BQ 54
Tulani St	Kaya	146	CP 51
Tulani St	Kaya	146	CQ 51
Tulbach Ave	Milnerton	57	BV 32
Tulbach Cr.	Belhar	89	CC 51
Tulbach Cr.	Belhar	107	CD 51
Tulbach Rd	Portlands (M.Plain)	144	CR 46
Tulbach St	Stellenryk	62	BU 52
Tulbagh	Paarlzicht	19	BC 91
Tulbagh Cl.	Brackenfell Sth	63	BX 56
Tulbagh Cr.	Churchill	60	BX 43
Tulbagh Rd	Kenridge	45	BS 49
Tulbagh Rd	Richwood	42	BQ 37
Tulbagh St	Bothasig	58	BT 38
Tulbagh St	Brooklyn	83	BY 30
Tulbagh St	Monte Vista	59	BV 39
Tulbagh St	Monte Vista	59	BW 39
Tulbagh St	Park Estates	174	CY 71
Tulbagh St	Wellington	11	AQ 95
Tulip	Bishop Lavis	104	CD 42
Tulip	D'urbanvale	29	BN 49
Tulip	D'urbanvale	45	BO 49
Tulip	Lentegeur (M.Plain)	144	CP 45
Tulip	Sarepta	89	CC 52
Tulip	Sarepta	89	BY 54
Tulip Cl.	Ottery East	121	CN 34
Tulip Cl.	Whispering Pines	175	DC 75
Tulip Rd	Grassy Pk	141	CQ 33
Tulip Rd	Parow Nth	60	BW 43
Tulip Rd	Retreat	140	CR 29
Tulip St	Amanda Glen	46	BS 52
Tulip St	Dunoon	26	BN 37
Tulip St	Protea Hoogte	63	BW 56
Tulip St	Protea Hoogte	63	BW 57
Tulip St	Weltevreden Val. (M.Plain)	124	CN 44
Tulip Tree Cl.	Hazelwood Pk	185	CZ 20
Tulip Tree Cl.	Hazelwood Pk	185	DC 22
Tullyallen Rd	Rondebosch	101	CG 30
Tulp Cl.	Perm Gdns	128	CJ 59
Tulp Cr.	Roosendaal	107	CE 51
Tulp St	Bellville Sth	88	CA 49
Tulp St	Wellington	15	AT 92
Tulsa Cl.	Malibu Village	127	CK 56
Tuna Rd	Nooitgedacht	104	CE 42
Tunce Cr.	Eyethu	146	CP 54
Tunce St	Kaya	146	CP 52
Tunica Rd	Graceland	146	CP 54
Tunnel St	Tafelsig (M.Plain)	145	CR 48
Tunny Cr.	Strandfontein	162	CT 39
Tunny St	Strandfontein	162	CT 39
Turban Cr.	Eersterivier	127	CM 58
Turf Club Dr.	Milnerton	41	BS 33
Turf Club Dr.	Milnerton	57	BT 34
Turf Hall Rd	Lansdowne	121	CJ 34
Turf Hall Rd	Lansdowne	121	CJ 33
Turf Hall Rd	Manenberg	123	CJ 35
Turf Hall Rd	Newfields	103	CH 37
Turf Hall Rd	Newfields	122	CJ 36
Turf Hall Rd	Primrose Pk	103	CH 37
Turf Hall Rd	Primrose Pk	103	CH 38
Turf Way	Strandfontein	162	CT 41
Turfburg Wk	Hanover Pk	122	CK 37
Turffontein Rd	Somerset West	170	CV 73
Turflyn Wk	Pinati	122	CJ 35
Turfontein La.	Milnerton Rdg	41	BR 34
Turinga St	Balvenie	86	CB 42

STREET NAME	SUBURB NAME	PG	GRID	
Turinga St	Balvenie	87	CB	43
Turk St	De Oude Renbaan	22	BH	88
Turkey Rd	Phumlani	142	CQ	35
Turkeyberry La.	Hout Bay	137	CQ	16
Turks Head Cl.	Marina Da Gama	159	CV	30
Turksvy Rd	Bonteheuwel	103	CE	38
Turkwel Ct	Delft	106	CG	49
Turnberry	Parklands	25	BM	33
Turnberry	Sunningdale	25	BM	31
Turnberry	Sunningdale	25	BL	33
Turnberry Cl.	D'urbanvale	45	BO	49
Turnberry Cl.	Greenways	174	DB	74
Turner Cr.	Durbanville	46	BQ	51
Turner Rd	De La Haye	61	BX	50
Turner Rd	Windsor Pk	47	BS	56
Turner St	Morgenster	63	BU	56
Turnstone Way	Pelikan Pk	142	CR	35
Turquoise Cl.	Rocklands (M.Plain)	145	CS	47
Turquoise Cl.	San Michel	157	CU	19
Turquoise Cr.	Pelikan Pk	161	CT	37
Turquoise Cr.	Sheridon Pk	159	CU	29
Turquoise Way	San Michel	157	CX	19
Turskvy	Lentegeur (M.Plain)	144	CO	45
Tuscany Cr.	Uitzicht	47	BO	55
Tussen Rd	Doornhoogte	103	CH	36
Tussendal Ave	Dreyersdal	140	CR	27
Tutu Ave	Umrhabulo Triangle	147	CP	57
Tutu Ave	Umrhabulo Triangle	147	CQ	56
Tutu Ave	Umrhabulo Triangle	147	CQ	58
Tuvana St	Scottsdene	64	BT	61
T'wagen Rd	Marina Da Gama	159	CV	30
Twecu Cr.	Nonqubela	146	CO	53
Tweed Rd	Rondebosch	101	CG	29
Twelfth	De Oude Renbaan	22	BH	88
Twelfth Ave	Avon	86	CA	41
Twelfth Ave	Belmont Pk	48	BR	60
Twelfth Ave	Boston	60	BX	46
Twelfth Ave	Boston	61	BX	47
Twelfth Ave	Cafda Village	140	CR	30
Twelfth Ave	Da Gama Pk	190	DE	21
Twelfth Ave	Eikendal	47	BS	58
Twelfth Ave	Fish Hoek	186	DB	23
Twelfth Ave	Florida	87	CB	44
Twelfth Ave	Hazendal	102	CE	33
Twelfth Ave	Kensington	84	BY	34
Twelfth Ave	Kensington	84	BZ	34
Twelfth Ave	Oakdale	61	BX	48
Twelfth Ave	Schaap Kraal	142	CQ	36
Twelfth Ave	Tafelsig (M.Plain)	146	CS	51
Twelfth Cl.	Kayamandi	94	CA	74
Twelfth St	Bishop Lavis	105	CD	43
Twelfth St	Elsies River Ind.	86	BZ	41
Twelfth St	Kensington	84	BZ	33
Twelfth St	Rusthof	175	DA	75
Twent Pl.	Westlake	159	CU	27
Twent Rd	Westlake	159	CU	27
Twentieth Ave	Fish Hoek	185	DA	21
Twentieth Ave	Norwood	86	CB	41
Twentieth St	Elsies River Ind.	86	CA	41
Twenty Steps	Bakoven	98	CF	17
Twenty-Eighth Ave	Avonwood	86	CB	42
Twenty-Eighth Ave	Norwood	86	CB	42
Twenty-Eighth St	Norwood	86	CB	42
Twenty-Fifth Ave	Norwood	86	CB	42
Twenty-First Ave	Avonwood	86	CA	42
Twenty-First Ave	Fish Hoek	185	DA	21
Twenty-First Ave	Norwood	86	CA	42
Twenty-First Cl.	Avonwood	86	CA	42
Twenty-First St	Avon	86	CA	41
Twenty-First St	Elsies River Ind.	86	CA	41
Twenty-Fourth Ave	Norwood	86	CB	42
Twenty-Ninth Ave	Elnor	86	CB	42
Twenty-Ninth St	Avonwood	86	CA	42
Twenty-Second Ave	Avonwood	86	CA	42
Twenty-Second Ave	Norwood	86	CB	42
Twenty-Seventh Ave	Norwood	86	CB	42
Twenty-Seventh St	Norwood	86	CB	41
Twenty-Sixth Ave	Clarkes	86	CB	42
Twenty-Sixth St	Leonsdale	86	CA	42
Twenty-Third Ave	Norwood	86	CB	42
Twenty-Third St	Elsies River Ind.	86	BZ	41
Twickenham Cr.	Beacon Valley (M.Plain)	145	CP	48
Twickenham Rd	Mowbray	101	CD	30
Twickenham Way	Edgemead	58	BV	38
Twilley St	Kenilworth Pk	120	CK	30
Twine Rd	Plumstead	120	CN	29
Twist St	Danena	61	BU	49
Twofold Rd	Sonstraal Hgts	46	BP	54
Twyford Rd	Rondebosch	102	CG	31
Tyatyeka St	Bloekombos	48	BR	62
Tyawe St	Nomzano	175	CY	76
Tyayo St	Umrhabulo Triangle	147	CQ	56
Tydemanhof	Lindida	96	CA	79
Tydemanhof	Lindida	96	CB	80
Tyeku St	Nonqubela	146	CO	53
Tyger Cr.	Klipkop	87	BZ	45
Tyger Falls Blvd.	Bellville	61	BU	48
Tygerberg	Brackenfell	63	BW	55
Tygerberg Rd	Richwood	42	BQ	38
Tygerberg Cl.	Strand	174	CY	74
Tygerberg Rd	Bonnie Brae	47	BQ	57
Tygerberg Rd	Durbanville Hills	45	BR	50
Tygerberg Rd	Durbanville Hills	45	BR	48
Tygerberg Rd	Richwood	43	BP	39
Tygerberg Rd	Roozeboom	43	BO	42
Tygerberg Rd	Springfield	44	BQ	44
Tygerberg St	Elsies River Ind.	86	BZ	41
Tygerberg St	Richmond Est.	59	BX	41
Tygerberg St	Richmond Est.	86	BY	41
Tygerbergvallei Rd	Bellville	61	BT	48
Tygerbergvallei Rd	De Bron	45	BS	48
Tygerpoort	Groenvallei	62	BX	53
Tygervallei St	Parow	86	BY	42
Tyhume St	Mfuleni	126	CJ	53
Tyilana St	Tarentaalplaas	175	CY	75
Tyinirhi Rd	Brown's Farm	124	CL	43
Tyne Ave	Riverton	86	BZ	40
Tyne Rd	Klein Begin	48	BS	60
Tyne Rd	Wynberg	120	CM	29
Tyne St	Belhar	107	CD	51
Tyne St	Belhar	107	CD	51
Tynemouth Rd	Plumstead	120	CN	30
Tynemouth Rd	Plumstead	121	CN	31
Tynemouth Rd	Plumstead	141	CO	31
Typhoon	Rocklands (M.Plain)	145	CS	47
Typhoon St	Factreton	85	BZ	35
Tyrian Cl.	West Beach	24	BN	30
Tyrone Cl.	Connaught	87	CB	43
Tyrone Rd	Wynberg	120	CL	29
Tyume St	Eyethu	146	CP	53
Tyune St	Delft	106	CH	49

U

STREET NAME	SUBURB NAME	PG	GRID	
Ubisi	Mbekweni	15	AW	91
Ubohlobo St	Crossroads	124	CK	44
Ubuntu Cr.	Mxolisi Phetani	125	CM	50
Ubuntu St	Crossroads	124	CK	44
Ubuntu St	Crossroads	124	CM	46
Ubuntu St	Guguletu	104	CH	41
Ubunye St	Crossroads	124	CK	44
Uduli	Mbekweni	15	AV	91
Ugaga St	Mfuleni	127	CM	55
Ugwidi St	Mfuleni	127	CM	55
Uiehout	Delft Sth	125	CK	48
Uil	Onderpapegaaiberg	94	CC	72
Uil Rd	Mikro Pk	90	CB	56
Uintjie Cr.	Roosendaal	106	CE	50
Uintjie St	Bonteheuwel	104	CD	40
Uintjie St	Vierlanden	30	BM	51
Uit Kerk St	Wellington	10	AR	93
Uit Kerk St	Wellington	10	AP	94
Uitenhage Way	Portlands (M.Plain)	144	CR	46
Uiterwyk Cl.	Mitchells Plain	144	CR	45
Uiterwyk Cl.	Mitchells Plain	144	CR	43
Uiterwyk Rd	Belhar	106	CD	49
Uiterwyk Rd	Belhar	106	CH	48
Uiterwyk St	Welgedacht	44	BS	45
Uitgift St	Somerset West	171	CT	78
Uithof St	Frogmore Est.	159	CU	27
Uitkamp	D'urbanvale	29	BN	50
Uitkamp Cl.	De Bron	45	BS	48
Uitkamp Cl.	De Bron	45	BP	47
Uitkyk Cr.	Voorbrug	106	CG	50
Uitkyk St	Franschhoek Sth	79	BY	107
Uitkyk St	Wellington	15	AW	93
Uitsig	Rozendal	96	CC	80
Uitsig	Stellenbosch	95	CC	75
Uitsig Ave	Uitsig	87	CC	44
Uitsig Ave	Uitsig	87	CC	45
Uitsig Cl.	Fir Grove	139	CQ	24
Uitsig Cl.	Mitchells Plain	144	CR	45
Uitsig Cl.	Mitchells Plain	144	CR	43
Uitsig Cl.	Zevendal	90	CC	58
Uitsig Rd	Durbanville	46	BQ	52
Uitsig Rd	Marina Da Gama	159	CV	29
Uitsig Rd	Silverhurst	119	CN	26
Uitsig Rd	Sunray	62	BX	49
Uitsig St	Panorama	59	BV	42
Uitspan Cl.	Whispering Pines	175	DC	75
Uitspan St	Scottsville	47	BS	56
Uitspan St	Scottsville	63	BT	57
Uitspanning St	Groenvlei	18	BA	89
Uitvlugt Rd	Pinelands	84	CC	32
Uitvlugt Rd	Pinelands	84	CC	33
Uitvlugt Rd	Ridgeworth	61	BV	49
Uitzicht Cr.	Richwood	42	BP	38
Uitzicht Heights	Uitzicht	46	BO	54
Uitzig Dr.	Somerset West	170	CT	73
Uitzight	Selborne	61	BV	47
Ukanyo St	Guguletu	104	CG	41
Ukelele Rd	Belhar	106	CD	49
Ukhetshe Cl.	Mfuleni	127	CM	55
Ukhosi St	Mfuleni	126	CM	54
Ukhozi St	Mfuleni	126	CM	54
Ukhuni Cl.	Tygerdal	58	BX	37
Ulex Rd	Gordon Strand	179	DD	76
Ulin Cr.	Macassar	149	CS	63
Ullswater	Pinelands	84	CB	34
Ullswater Rd	Coniston Pk	159	CU	29
Ullswater Rd	Ravensmead	87	CB	45
Ulm Cl.	Strandfontein	162	CT	41
Ulm Way	Strandfontein	162	CT	41
Ulster Rd	Royal Cape	121	CM	31
Ultra Ave	Scottsdene	64	BU	60
Ultra Ave	Scottsdene	64	BV	60
Ulundi St	Crossroads	124	CK	44
Ulunthu St	Guguletu	104	CH	40
Ulunthu St	Mfuleni	126	CK	53
Ulwadle St	Crossroads	124	CJ	44
Umbane	Mbekweni	15	AV	92
Umbashe St	Mfuleni	126	CJ	53
Umbashe St	Mfuleni	126	CK	52
Umbashe St	Mfuleni	126	CK	53
Umbeluzi St	Mfuleni	126	CJ	53
Umbethe	Mbekweni	15	AW	92
Umbilo Ct	Delft	106	CG	48
Umblo St	Mfuleni	126	CJ	53
Umcelu St	Mfuleni	127	CM	55
Umculo	Mbekweni	15	AW	92
Umdloti St	Mfuleni	126	CK	53
Umdudo	Mbekweni	15	AV	91
Umdudo	Mbekweni	15	AU	94
Umfolozi St	Delft	106	CH	50
Umfolozi St	Mfuleni	126	CJ	53
Umfuli Rd	Delft	106	CG	49
Umfuli St	Mfuleni	126	CJ	53
Umgeni Ave	Bonnie Brook	47	BQ	57
Umgeni St	Mfuleni	126	CJ	53
Umgeni Way	Delft	106	CG	49
Umgqungqo St	Crossroads	124	CK	44
Umgwali St	Mfuleni	126	CJ	53
Umhlatuzana St	Mfuleni	126	CK	53
Umhlontlo Dr.	Joe Slovo Pk	57	BU	34
Umkhomazi St	Mfuleni	126	CJ	53
Umkomaas Ave	Bonnie Brook	47	BQ	56
Umkomaas Ave	Bonnie Brook	47	BP	58
Umkonto	Mbekweni	15	AW	92
Umlazi St	Mfuleni	126	CK	53
Umlilo	Mbekweni	15	AV	92
Ummah Cl.	District Six	82	CB	25
Umnga	Langa	85	CC	36
Umnga Ave	Joe Slovo Pk	57	BU	34
Umngeni St	Kaya	146	CP	52
Umnquna Ct	Joe Slovo Pk	57	BU	34
Umnquna Ct	Joe Slovo Pk	57	BU	31
Umnyama	Mbekweni	15	AW	91
Umnyathi St	Mfuleni	126	CJ	53
Umsi	Philippi East	125	CL	47
Umsunduze St	Mfuleni	126	CK	53
Umswi St	Mfuleni	126	CM	54
Umswi St	Mfuleni	127	CM	55
Umtali St	Kenridge Hgts	45	BR	48
Umtata Dr.	Joe Slovo Pk	57	BV	34
Umtata Rd	Nyanga	124	CK	43
Umtata St	Mfuleni	126	CJ	53
Umthathi Ave	Joe Slovo Pk	57	BU	34
Umthi	Mbekweni	15	AV	92
Umthi Cl.	Tygerdal	58	BX	37
Umthuma Cr.	Joe Slovo Pk	57	BU	34
Umthuma Cr.	Joe Slovo Pk	57	BU	31
Umtwalume St	Mfuleni	126	CK	53
Umvoti St	Delft	106	CG	48
Umvoti St	Mfuleni	126	CK	53
Umyezo Dr.	Philippi East	125	CL	47
Umzinyathi St	Mfuleni	126	CJ	53
Umzumbe St	Mfuleni	126	CK	53
Unanyano	Mbekweni	15	AW	92
Uncle Andy's Dr.	Boschenmeer Est.	39	BJ	90
Undine Rd	Eversdal Hgts	61	BT	50
Ungqobe St	Mfuleni	126	CM	54
Ungqobe St	Mfuleni	127	CM	55
Unie	Uniepark	96	CB	79
Unie St	Bellville Sth	88	CA	49
Unie St	Klipkop	87	BZ	44
Union Ave	Newlands	100	CG	26
Union Ave	Newlands	101	CG	27
Union Ave	Pinelands	84	CB	33
Union Ave	Pinelands	84	CC	32
Union Ave	Pinelands	84	CC	33
Union Rd	Fairways	121	CN	32
Union Rd	Milnerton	57	BW	31
Union Rd	Milnerton	57	BW	32
Union St	Franschhoek Sth	79	BZ	107
Union St	Gardens	81	CC	22
Union St	Hout Bay	137	CP	16
Union St	Kenilworth Pk	120	CJ	30
Union St	Lochnerhof	170	CX	71
Union St	Lochnerhof	170	CX	72
Union St	Lochnerhof	174	CY	72
Union St	Northern Paarl	18	AZ	89
Union St	Simon's Town	194	DJ	24
Union Way	Matroosfontein	86	CC	41
Unity Dr.	Somerset West	170	CV	73
Unity Rd	Belgravia	103	CH	35
Unity Rd	Retreat	140	CR	30
Unity St	Kuyasa	147	CR	55
Unity St	Kuyasa	147	CS	58
University Dr.	Pinelands	85	CC	35
University St	Cape Town Cen.	81	CB	22
Uno Rd	Milnerton	57	BV	32
Unocofu St	Mfuleni	126	CM	54
Upington St	Portlands (M.Plain)	144	CS	46
Upington St	William Lloyd	23	BD	92
Uplands Ave	Milnerton	57	BV	32
Upper 5th Ave	Manenberg	123	CK	40
Upper Adelaide Rd	Woodstock	82	CC	26
Upper Albert Rd	Tamboerskloof	81	CB	21
Upper Alma Rd	Rosebank	101	CE	29
Upper Angelina Ave	Bishopscourt	101	CH	27
Upper Auret St	Paarl	22	BD	88
Upper Balfour St	Salt River	83	CC	27
Upper Bebington Ave	Bishopscourt	120	CK	27
Upper Berg Ave	Somerset West	171	CW	77
Upper Bloem St	Schotsche Kloof	81	CA	22
Upper Bosman	Paarl	22	BF	87
Upper Bowwood Rd	Claremont	120	CJ	27
Upper Cambridge St	Woodstock	82	CC	26
Upper Camp Rd	Ndabeni	83	CB	30
Upper Canterbury St	Gardens	82	CB	23
Upper Chamberlain St	Salt River	83	CC	27
Upper Clarens Rd	Fresnaye	81	CA	19
Upper Coventry Rd	Woodstock	82	CB	26
Upper Coventry Rd	Woodstock	82	CC	26
Upper Duke St	Woodstock	82	CB	26
Upper Duke St	Woodstock	82	CC	26
Upper Durban Rd	Mowbray	101	CD	29
Upper Grove Ave	Claremont	120	CJ	28
Upper Hillwood Rd	Bishopscourt	120	CJ	27
Upper Holly St	Newlands	100	CH	25
Upper Isabel Ave	Bishopscourt	120	CJ	27
Upper Kenridge Way	Kenridge Hgts	45	BR	49
Upper Keppel St	Woodstock	82	CC	26
Upper Kildare Cr.	Fish Hoek	186	DA	23
Upper Kinrae Cr.	Fish Hoek	186	DA	23
Upper Kloof Ave	Gardens	81	CC	21
Upper Lady Grey St	Paarl	18	BC	88
Upper Lang St	Groenvlei	18	BA	87
Upper Leeuwen St	Schotsche Kloof	81	CA	22
Upper Liesbeek Rd	Rosebank	101	CE	29
Upper Lincoln St	Loevenstein	61	BW	47
Upper Maynard St	Vredehoek	82	CC	23
Upper Melbourne Rd	Woodstock	82	CC	26
Upper Mill St	Lemoenkloof	18	BC	87
Upper Mill St	Vredehoek	82	CC	23
Upper Mountain Rd	Somerset West	152	CS	76
Upper Mountain Rd	Woodstock	82	CC	26
Upper Noreen Ave	Bishopscourt	119	CJ	26
Upper Orange St	Oranjezicht	81	CC	22
Upper Orange St	Oranjezicht	99	CD	22
Upper Orange St	Somerset West	170	CU	73
Upper Paradise Rd	Newlands	100	CH	26
Upper Paradise Rd	Newlands	100	CG	25
Upper Park La.	Strandfontein	162	CV	42
Upper Park La.	Strandfontein	162	CT	41
Upper Park St	Wellington	10	AS	92
Upper Pepper St	Schotsche Kloof	81	CA	22
Upper Plein	Lemoenkloof	18	BC	88
Upper Portswood Rd	Green Point	81	BZ	22
Upper Primrose Ave	Bishopscourt	119	CK	26
Upper Primrose Ave	Bishopscourt	120	CK	27
Upper Pypies Plain	Devil's Peak Est.	82	CC	24
Upper Quarterdeck Rd	St James	187	CZ	27
Upper Queens Rd	Woodstock	82	CC	26
Upper Rd	Newlands	101	CE	28
Upper Recreation Rd	Fish Hoek	186	DA	23
Upper Recreation Rd	Fish Hoek	186	DB	23
Upper Rhine Rd	Sea Point	81	BZ	20
Upper Roodebloem Rd	Woodstock	83	CC	27
Upper Rose St	Bishopscourt	119	CJ	25
Upper School St	Strandfontein	162	CT	41
Upper Shepards	Somerset West	171	CW	77
Upper Sidmouth Ave	Bishopscourt	120	CJ	27
Upper Silva St	Brooklyn	83	BZ	30
Upper Station Rd	Ndabeni	84	CB	31
Upper Thistle Ave	Newlands	100	CH	25
Upper Torquay Ave	Bishopscourt	120	CJ	27
Upper Tree Rd	Camps Bay	98	CE	18
Upper Tree Rd	Camps Bay	99	CE	19
Upper Union St	Gardens	81	CB	21
Upper Warwick St	Woodstock	82	CB	26
Upper Watt St	Harbour Island	179	DE	77
Upper Wheelan St	Newlands	101	CG	27
Upshire Cl.	Epping Forest	86	CC	41
Upton Park	Weltevreden Val. (M.Plain)	124	CN	43
Upton Rd	Eersterivier	128	CN	61
Upton Rd	Eersterivier	128	CJ	61
Ural Cr.	Tafelsig (M.Plain)	145	CS	48
Uranium St	Beroma	88	BZ	50
Uranium St	Triangle Farm	89	BZ	51
Uranuim	Vanguard	103	CF	37
Uranus	Rocklands (M.Plain)	144	CS	46
Uranus Cl.	Salberau	86	CB	41
Uranus Cl.	Salberau	86	CB	39
Urfield Rd	Lavender Hill	160	CT	31
Urha St	Mfuleni	126	CK	53
Urmarah Ave	Bel Ombre	119	CM	25
Urmarah Cl.	Bel Ombre	119	CM	25
Ursa Cl.	Ocean View	189	DD	16
Ursina Cl.	Hout Bay	136	CP	14
Ursinia Ave	Welgedacht	60	BT	45
Ursula Rd	Valhalla Pk	104	CE	41
Usasaza	Dunoon	26	BN	38
Usk Rd	Manenberg	123	CK	39
Usuthu Cr.	Delft	106	CG	48
Utah Cl.	Retreat	140	CS	28
Utah Pl.	Colorado (M.Plain)	124	CN	44
Utica Way	Strandfontein	162	CT	41
Utrecht St	Malibu Village	127	CJ	56
Utrecht St	Monte Vista	59	BV	39
Uvuko Cr.	Mxolisi Phetani	126	CM	51
UWC Access Rd	Belhar	88	CC	47
Uxam Wk	Philippi East	124	CL	46
Uxbridge Rd	Muizenberg Nth	159	CW	28
Uxolo St	Crossroads	124	CK	45
Uxomoyi St	Mfuleni	127	CM	55
Uys St	Denneburg	22	BD	90
Uys St	Denneburg	23	BD	91
Uzani	Mbekweni	15	AW	92

Abbreviations used: Ave – Avenue, A.H. – Agricultural Holding, A.L.– Algemene Landgoed, Blvd – Boulevard, Cen. – Central, Cir. – Circle, Cl. – Close, Cr. – Crescent, Ct – Court, Dr. – Drive, Est. – Estate, Ext. – Extension, Hgts – Heights, Ind. – Industrial, Gdns – Gardens, Gr. – Grove, La. – Lane, (M.Plain) - Mitchells Plain, Nth – North, Pl. – Place, Pk – Park, Rd – Road, Rdg. – Ridge, S.H.– Small Holding, Sq. – Square, St – Street, Sth – South, Ter. – Terrace, Tn – Turn, Val. – Valley, Wk – Walk

STREET NAME	SUBURB NAME	PG	GRID	
V				
Vaal Ct	Delft	106	CG	49
Vaal La.	Belthorn Est.	121	CJ	34
Vaal Rd	Bishop Lavis	104	CD	41
Vaal Rd	Milnerton	57	BV	32
Vaalblom	Arbeidslus	96	CB	80
Vaalboom Ave	New Orleans	19	BB	91
Vaalbos Rd	Bonteheuwel	104	CE	39
Vaalrivier Way	Portlands (M.Plain)	144	CP	46
Vakwana St	Nonqubela	146	CO	53
Vala St	Mxolisi Phetani	125	CM	50
Valangentabo St	Driftsands	126	CL	51
Valbonne Ave	Somerset West	150	CS	70
Valda St	Casablanca	175	DA	76
Valderrama Rd	Sunningdale	25	BN	32
Vale Rd	Rondebosch	101	CG	29
Valencia St	Blokombos	48	BR	62
Valencia St	Uitzicht	47	BO	55
Valencia Way	Mitchells Plain	144	CR	45
Valentino Dr.	Kirstenhof	159	CT	27
Valentino Dr.	Kirstenhof	159	CU	27
Valentyn	Cloetesville	95	BZ	75
Valentyn Rd	Tijgerhof	57	BW	32
Valentyn Rd	Tijgerhof	57	BW	33
Valerie Cl.	Tuscany Glen	127	CL	56
Valhalla	Sunningdale	25	BM	31
Valhalla Cr.	Tuscany Glen	127	CK	57
Valhalla Dr.	Bonteheuwel	104	CD	40
Valhalla Dr.	Charlesville	104	CF	41
Valhalla Dr.	Matroosfontein	86	CC	41
Valiant Rd	Tuscany Glen	127	CK	56
Valk La.	Mikro Pk	90	CB	56
Valk Way	Bridgetown	103	CE	36
Valkenier	Jagtershof	90	CC	57
Vallee Lustre	La Pastorale	113	CG	76
Vallei St	Wellington	15	AV	93
Valleizicht St	Brackenfell Sth	63	BX	58
Valley	Harbour Island	179	DE	77
Valley Cl.	Tafelsig (M.Plain)	145	CR	48
Valley Cr.	Weltevreden Val. (M.Plain)	144	CO	43
Valley Ct	Rocklands (M.Plain)	144	CS	45
Valley Oak St	Oak Glen	62	BW	53
Valley Oak St	Oak Glen	62	BX	52
Valley Rd	Austinville	108	CH	56
Valley Rd	Hout Bay	117	CM	17
Valley Rd	Hout Bay	117	CM	18
Valley Rd	Hout Bay	117	CN	15
Valley Rd	Hout Bay	117	CN	16
Valley Rd	Hout Bay	118	CM	19
Valley Rd	Hout Bay	137	CO	15
Valley Rd	Kenilworth	120	CJ	28
Valley Rd	Murdock Valley	195	DL	28
Valley Rd	Natte Valley	52	BP	78
Valley Rd	Natte Valley	53	BP	79
Valley Rd	Sweet Valley	139	CR	25
Valley St	Riverton	86	BZ	40
Valley St	Sunset Glen	108	CH	55
Valley View	Retreat	140	CS	29
Valley View Dr.	Hout Bay	116	CN	14
Valley Walk Cl.	Bel Ombre	119	CM	26
Valley Wk	Silverglade	185	DA	22
Valliant Blvd	Somerset West	169	CT	70
Valliant Blvd	Somerset West	170	CT	71
Vallie St	Cravenby	87	CB	43
Valmar Rd	Valmary Pk	45	BR	50
Valotta Ave	Brantwood	89	CA	53
Valour Cl.	Summer Greens	58	BW	35
Vals Ct	Delft	106	CG	49
Valsheide Cr.	Roosendaal	106	CE	50
Vampire St	Macassar	168	CT	64
Van Aarde St	Brandwag	90	BZ	55
Van Aarde St	Sir Lowry's Pass	176	CZ	82
Van Arckel St	Wynberg	120	CL	27
Van Arkel St	Bothasig	58	BT	36
Van Arkel St	Welgemoed	61	BU	47
Van Blerk St	Des Hampden	89	CB	53
Van Brakel	Park Estates	170	CX	72
Van Breda St	Barbarossa	120	CN	27
Van Breda St	Durbanville	45	BR	49
Van Breugel St	Bothasig	42	BS	37
Van Broekhuizen St	Groenvlei	18	BA	88
Van Broekhuizen St	Soneike I	89	CA	54
Van Bruggen Ave	Hohelzen	61	BW	47
Van Bruggen St	De Tijger	60	BW	43
Van Bruggen St	Soneike I	89	BZ	54
Van Coppenhagen	Rozendal	96	CB	79
Van Coppenhagen	Rozendal	96	CB	80
Van de Graaf	Welgemoed	60	BV	46
Van de Graaf Rd	Flamingo Vlei	41	BQ	33
Van de Leur Rd	Belhar	107	CD	51
Van de Leur St	Brooklyn	84	BZ	31
Van den Bos St	William Lloyd	23	BD	92
Van der Berg Cr.	Franschhoek Nth	75	BW	105
Van der Berg Cr.	Strand Halt	170	CW	73
Van der Bijl St	Belmont Pk	48	BR	60
Van der Bijl St	Sack's Circle Ind.	88	CB	50
Van der Byl	Stellenbosch	95	CB	76
Van der Byl Ave	Durbanville	46	BQ	51
Van der Byl St	Harbour Island	179	DE	77
Van der Byl St	Uit-kyk	171	CW	75
Van der Graaff Dr.	Table View	41	BP	34
Van der Heever Cr.	Scottsdene	64	BT	60
Van der Heever St	Goodwood Est.	58	BX	38
Van der Heever St	Soneike I	89	BZ	54
Van der Heiden St	Welgemoed	60	BU	46
Van der Horst Ave	Kommetjie	183	DB	11
Van der Lingen Sq.	Lemoenkloof	18	BC	88
Van der Lingen St	Paarl	18	BC	88
Van der Lingen St	Paarl	18	BC	89
Van der Merwe Cr.	Blomvlei	61	BV	47
Van der Merwe Rd	Somerset West	171	CU	77
Van der Merwe St	Huguenot	18	BC	90
Van der Merwe St	Peerless Pk East	47	BR	58
Van der Merwe St	Peerless Pk East	48	BR	59
Van der Merwe St	Strand	174	CZ	73
Van der Merwe St	Wellington	11	AR	95
Van der Poel Way	Bergvliet	139	CP	26
Van der Poels Doordrift St	Lemoenkloof	18	BC	87
Van der Poels St	Lemoenkloof	18	BC	88
Van der Poels St	Lemoenkloof	18	BC	87
Van der Poll Ave	Kommetjie	183	DC	12
Van der Poll Rd	Tokai	139	CS	25
Van der Ross Rd	Eikendal	63	BT	58
Van der Spuy	Beaconvale	87	CA	43
Van der Spuy	Lemoenkloof	18	BC	89
Van der Spuy St	Monte Vista	59	BV	39
Van der Spuy St	Van Ryneveld	174	CZ	72
Van der Stael Rd	Bothasig	42	BS	37
Van der Stael Rd	Bothasig	42	BS	37
Van der Stel	Mostertsdrift	95	CC	78
Van der Stel Ave	Kenridge	45	BS	49
Van Der Stel Ave	Brooklyn	84	BZ	31
Van der Stel Ave	Kenridge	61	BT	49
Van der Stel St	Beaconvale	87	CA	43
Van der Stel St	Bloomsburg	23	BD	91
Van der Stel St	De Kuilen	89	CB	54
Van der Stel St	Groenheuwel	19	BA	92
Van der Stel St	Kempenville	61	BX	49
Van der Stel St	Lochnerhof	170	CX	72
Van der Stel St	New Orleans	19	BB	92
Van der Stel St	Oakdale	61	BW	50
Van der Stel St	Sunkist	61	BX	49
Van der Stel St	Townsend Est.	85	BY	37
Van der Walt St	Welgemoed	60	BU	45
Van der Westhuizen Ave	Durbanville	46	BQ	51
Van Doesburg Ave	Bothasig	58	BT	38
Van Dyck St	De La Haye	88	BY	50
Van Dyk	Lindida	96	CA	80
Van Eck	Sack's Circle Ind.	88	CB	50
Van Eck St	Somerset Pk	171	CW	75
Van Eeden	Bracken Hgts	62	BU	54
Van Eyck Cr.	De La Haye	62	BX	51
Van Eyssen St	Churchill	61	BX	42
Van Eyssen St	Glenlily	86	BY	42
Van Goen St	Maitland Gdn Village	83	CB	30
Van Goens St	Bothasig	42	BS	38
Van Gogh Cr.	Malibu Village	127	CJ	56
Van Gogh Rd	Somerset West	151	CR	74
Van Gogh Rd	Somerset West	152	CR	75
Van Gogh St	De Duin	59	BW	41
Van Gogh St	Macassar	149	CS	66
Van Her Rd	Somerset West	151	CS	73
Van Holdt St	Newlands	101	CH	27
Van Hoogstraten Rd	Hout Bay	137	CP	16
Van Hoorn Rd	Table View	41	BP	33
Van Imhoff Way	Kommetjie	183	DC	11
Van Jaarsveld Rd	Welgemoed	60	BU	46
Van Kampz St	Camps Bay	98	CE	18
Van Kemp St	Ruyterwacht	86	CA	39
Van Louw St	Wellington	15	AV	93
Van Niekerk St	Kingston	61	BX	49
Van Niekerk St	Oakdale	61	BX	48
Van Niekerk St	Paarl	22	BE	88
Van Niekerk St	Park Estates	170	CX	72
Van Nierop Cr.	Sonnedal	59	BV	42
Van Oudtshoorn Rd	Hout Bay	137	CP	15
Van Passel St	Bothasig	58	BT	37
Van Passel St	Bothasig	58	BT	38
Van Reede	Dalsig	113	CD	75
Van Reede	Die Boord	112	CE	74
Van Reede	Die Boord	113	CD	75
Van Reenen Cl.	Newlands	100	CH	26
Van Reenen Cl.	Newlands	100	CG	25
Van Reenen Rd	Constantia Vale	119	CN	25
Van Reenen Rd	Table View	41	BP	33
Van Reenen St	Bloubergstrand	24	BM	28
Van Reenen St	Newlands	100	CG	26
Van Reenen St	Richmond	86	BY	41
Van Rensburg Rd	Goodwood Est.	58	BX	38
Van Rensburg Rd	Goodwood Est.	85	BY	38
Van Rheede	Greenways	174	DA	73
Van Rheede Rd	Table View	41	BP	34
Van Rhyn Cr.	Tafelsig (M.Plain)	145	CS	48
Van Riebeeck	Franschhoek Sth	79	BZ	108
Van Riebeeck	Stellenbosch	95	CC	77
Van Riebeeck Ave	Kenever	61	BT	49
Van Riebeeck Ave	Kenridge	45	BS	49
Van Riebeeck Rd	De Kuilen	89	CA	54
Van Riebeeck Rd	Eersterivier	128	CM	61
Van Riebeeck Rd	Eersterivier	128	CJ	59
Van Riebeeck Rd	Gaylee	108	CH	58
Van Riebeeck Rd	Kuilsrivier Ind.	108	CD	56
Van Riebeeck Rd	St Dumas	90	CC	55
Van Riebeeck St	Bothasig	58	BT	38
Van Riebeeck St	Brackenfell	63	BV	55
Van Riebeeck St	Brooklyn	83	BZ	30
Van Riebeeck St	Park Estates	174	CY	72
Van Riebeeck St	Peerless Pk East	48	BS	59
Van Riebeeck St	Richmond Est.	59	BX	41
Van Riebeeck St	Richmond Est.	86	BY	41
Van Riebeeckshof Rd	De Bron	61	BT	48
Van Riebeeckshof Rd	Door De Kraal	61	BT	47
Van Riebeeckshof Rd	Welgedacht	44	BS	45
Van Riebeeckshof Rd	Welgedacht	60	BT	46
Van Riet Ave	Welgemoed	60	BU	46
Van Rooyen Rd	Retreat	140	CR	29
Van Rooyen St	Groenvlei	18	BA	88
Van Rooyen St	Groenvlei	18	BC	87
Van Ryn Rd	Vlottenburg	111	CF	68
Van Ryn St	Barbarossa	120	CN	27
Van Ryneveld Ave	Devil's Peak Est.	82	CC	24
Van Ryneveldt St	Van Ryneveld	174	CZ	72
Van Sande St	Flintdale Est.	140	CP	30
Van Schalkwyk Rd	Rondebosch East	102	CH	32
Van Schoor	Belhar	106	CD	50
Van Spilbergen	Park Estates	170	CX	71
Van Ster Ave	Forest Hgts	127	CL	58
Van Taack	Brandwacht	113	CE	76
Van Tonder St	Ruwari	63	BW	58
Van Tromp St	Belgravia	88	BY	50
Van Tromp St	Park Estates	170	CX	71
Van Vrede St	Bothasig	58	BU	37
Van Vuuren St	Plumstead	140	CO	30
Van Wageringen St	Bothasig	42	BS	37
Van Wouw St	Labiance	89	BZ	52
Van Wyk Rd	Retreat	159	CT	29
Van Wyk St	Brandwag	90	BZ	55
Van Wyk St	Maitland	83	CA	30
Van Wyk St	Parowvallei	87	BZ	44
Van Wyksvlei Rd	Wellington	15	AU	93
Van Zyl Rd	Strand Halt	170	CW	74
Van Zyl St	Belrail	88	BY	50
Van Zyl St	De Zoete Inval	22	BH	88
Van Zyl St	Somerset West	171	CU	75
Van Zyl Way	Bergvliet	139	CP	26
Vancouver Cl.	Capri	184	DB	18
Vancouver Cl.	Portlands (M.Plain)	144	CQ	46
Vancouver Cr.	Capri	184	DB	18
Vanderer	Dennemere	127	CJ	57
Vanderer	Dennemere	127	CN	55
Vanessa Cr.	Lentegeur (M.Plain)	145	CO	48
Vangaurd Rd	Tuscany Glen	127	CK	57
Vanguard	Foreshore	82	CA	26
Vanguard Dr.	Acacia Pk	58	BW	36
Vanguard Dr.	Bonteheuwel	103	CD	38
Vanguard Dr.	Epping Ind.	85	CC	38
Vanguard Dr.	Hanover Pk	122	CJ	37
Vanguard Dr.	Schaap Kraal	122	CL	38
Vanguard Dr.	Schaap Kraal	123	CL	39
Vanguard Dr.	Schaap Kraal	123	CN	41
Vanguard Dr.	Schaap Kraal	123	CO	42
Vanguard Dr.	Schaap Kraal	144	CQ	43
Vanguard Dr.	Surrey	103	CH	37
Vanguard Dr.	Thornton	85	CA	38
Vanguard Dr.	Vanguard	103	CG	37
Vanguard Dr.	Wingfield	85	BY	37
Vanilla Ave	Silversands	107	CH	54
Vanqa St	Tarentaalplaas	175	CY	75
Vans Rd	Dreyersdal	140	CS	27
Vanyaza St	Guguletu	104	CG	41
Vaphi Cr.	Victoria Mxenge	146	CO	52
Varing	Delft Sth	125	CJ	49
Varing	Lentegeur (M.Plain)	144	CO	45
Varing Cl.	Belhar	106	CD	47
Varkens Vlei Rd	Schaap Kraal	123	CN	40
Varkens Vlei Rd	Schaap Kraal	142	CO	38
Varkens Vlei Rd	Schaap Kraal	143	CO	39
Varney's Rd	Green Point	81	BZ	21
Varsity St	Tamboerskloof	81	CB	21
Vasco Blvd	Vasco Est.	59	BX	39
Vasco Blvd	Vasco Est.	86	BY	39
Vasco da Gama Blvd.	Cape Town Cen.	82	CA	24
Vasco St	Brooklyn	83	BZ	30
Vasco St	Brooklyn	84	BZ	31
Vatala	Philippi East	125	CM	47
Vati St	Kaya	146	CP	52
Vatican St	Uitzicht	31	BN	55
Vatican St	Uitzicht	31	BN	56
Vaughn St	Blomtuin	62	BW	51
Vcqunta Way	Langa	103	CE	37
Veerheide Cl.	Perm Gdns	128	CJ	59
Veerheide Cl.	Perm Gdns	128	CJ	60
Veerheide Cr.	Roosendaal	106	CE	50
Veerpyl St	Beacon Valley (M.Plain)	145	CP	47
Vega Cl.	Ocean View	184	DC	15
Vega Rd	Retreat	140	CR	28
Vega St	Tuscany Glen	127	CK	57
Vega St East	Tuscany Glen	127	CK	57
Velani Cr.	Kaya	146	CO	51
Velapi Cr.	Nonqubela	126	CN	52
Veld Cl.	Rocklands (M.Plain)	144	CS	45
Veld Rd	Belgravia	103	CG	35
Velden Rd	Wynberg	120	CL	28
Veldvy Cr.	Roosendaal	107	CE	51
Veleli	Guguletu	104	CH	40
Velili St	Kaya	146	CP	51
Velisa Cr.	Umrhabulo Triangle	147	CQ	57
Velisa St	Umrhabulo Triangle	147	CQ	57
Velma Rd	Retreat	141	CR	31
Velocity St	Primrose Pk	122	CJ	37
Velocity St	Primrose Pk	122	CN	36
Velvet Cr.	Tuscany Glen	127	CK	56
Vena Cr.	Nonqubela	126	CN	53
Vendome	Groenvlei	18	BA	89
Venfolo St	Eyethu	146	CP	53
Venice	Marina Da Gama	159	CW	29
Venice Cl.	Eikenbosch	90	CC	57
Venice Cl.	Portlands (M.Plain)	144	CQ	46
Venning St	Somerset West	170	CU	74
Venster Ct	Edgemead	59	BT	39
Venster St	Manenberg	104	CG	39
Venter St	Durbanville	45	BP	49
Venter St	Mandalay	125	CL	48
Venter St	Morgenster Hoogte	63	BU	56
Ventnor Rd	Claremont	120	CJ	29
Ventnor Rd	Muizenberg	159	CW	30
Ventura	Rocklands (M.Plain)	144	CS	46
Ventura Cl.	Scottsdene	64	BV	59
Ventura Rd	Factreton	84	BY	34
Ventura Rd	Factreton	85	BY	35
Ventura Rd	Kensington	84	BY	33
Ventura St	Wingfield	85	BY	35
Ventura Ter.	Scottsdene	64	BV	59
Venus	Rocklands (M.Plain)	144	CS	45
Venus Ave	Bel Ombre	119	CM	25
Venus Ave	Phoenix	57	BU	33
Venus Cir.	Sunset Beach	41	BS	31
Venus Cl.	Bel Ombre	119	CM	25
Venus Cl.	Salberau	86	CB	41
Venus Cl.	Salberau	86	CB	39
Venus Cr.	Bishop Lavis	104	CE	42
Venus St	Kaya	146	CP	52
Venus St	Sarepta	89	CC	53
Venus St	Somerset Hgts	127	CK	57
Venus Way	Matroosfontein	86	CC	41
Venus Way	Ocean View	189	DD	15
Venus Way	Ottery	121	CL	33
Vera St	Scottsdene	64	BT	59
Verbena	Lentegeur (M.Plain)	145	CP	47
Verbena Cl.	Stellenberg	62	BU	51
Verbena Rd	Belhar	87	CC	46
Verbena Rd	Gordon Strand	179	DD	77
Verbena Rd	Sonstraal Hgts	46	BQ	53
Verbena St	Paarden Eiland	83	BZ	29
Verbena St	Peerless Pk East	63	BT	57
Verbena St	Sarepta	89	CC	52
Verbena St	Somerset West	170	CV	73
Verbena St	Wellington	15	AT	93
Verbena Way	Pinelands	102	CD	34
Vercueil St	Paarl	22	BE	88
Verdi	Delft Sth	125	CJ	48
Verdi Blvd	Sonstraal Hgts	46	BQ	54
Verdi Blvd	Sonstraal Hgts	46	BR	54
Verdi Cl.	Mandalay	125	CN	48
Verdi Rd	Strandfontein	162	CT	42
Verdi St	De Duin	59	BW	41
Verdi St	Protea Hoogte	63	BW	57
Verdi St	Steenberg	159	CT	29
Verdot Cl.	Table View	41	BO	33
Verdun	Franschhoek Sth	79	CB	108
Verdun St	Courtrai	22	BH	87
Verdun Way	Strandfontein	162	CT	40
Vereeniging Cir.	Ruyterwacht	86	CA	39
Verenigde St	Kalkfontein II	107	CD	53
Vergelegen Ave	Somerset West	171	CT	78
Vergelegen Cl.	Kleinbosch	59	BT	40
Vergelegen Cl.	Mitchells Plain	144	CR	45
Vergelegen La.	Belhar	106	CD	50
Vergelegen St	Bellair	62	BW	52
Vergelegen St	Bellair	62	BW	53
Vergelegen St	Kleinbosch	59	BT	40
Vergelegen Way	Mitchells Plain	144	CQ	45
Vergenoeg	Krigeville	113	CD	77
Vergenoeg St	Brackenfell Sth	63	BW	58
Vergenoeg St	Brackenfell Sth	63	BX	57
Vergenoegd	Voorbrug	106	CG	50
Vergenoegd Rd	Richwood	42	BQ	37
Vergenoegd St	Bellair	62	BW	52
Vergenoegd St	Somerset West	151	CR	71
Vergesig Rd	Eversdal Hgts	61	BT	50
Vergesig Rd	Skoongesig	29	BN	50
Vergezicht	Groenvlei	18	BA	88
Verheul Cl.	La Rochelle	62	BV	52
Veritas	Brackenfell	63	BW	56
Veritas	Brackenfell	63	BV	58
Veritas	D'urbanvale	45	BO	49
Verkouteren Cr.	Bloubergstrand	24	BL	27
Verlore St	Eersterivier	128	CN	59
Verlorenvlei Cr.	Delft	106	CH	50
Vermeer Rd	Somerset West	152	CR	75
Vermeer St	De La Haye	61	BX	50
Vermont Rd	Colorado (M.Plain)	124	CN	44
Vernon Rd	Northpine	63	BU	58
Vernon Rd	Northpine	63	BV	56
Vernon Rd	Plumstead	120	CM	28
Vernon Rd	Tuscany Glen	127	CL	57
Vernon Terrace Cr.	District Six	82	CB	24
Verona	Oak Glen	62	BW	53
Verona Villas	Skilpadvlei	45	BP	50
Veronica Cr.	Lentegeur (M.Plain)	145	CO	48
Veronica Rd	Lentegeur (M.Plain)	145	CO	48
Veronica St	Casablanca	175	DB	76
Veronica St	Kalkfontein II	107	CD	53
Verreweide	Universiteits-oord	95	CB	77
Verreweide St	Elim	90	CB	55
Versailles Cl.	La Rochelle	62	BV	51
Versailles St	Wellington	10	AR	92
Versailles St	Wellington	10	AS	91
Versseriver Rd	Bothasig	42	BS	38

Index to Street Names

Verster Ave — Welcome Zenzile St

STREET NAME	SUBURB NAME	PG	GRID	
Verster Ave	Somerset West	171	CT	78
Verster Rd	Belgravia	103	CG	35
Verster St	Eikendal	47	BS	58
Verster St	Lemoenkloof	18	BC	88
Versveld Ave	Hohenort	119	CL	25
Versveld Cr.	Tafelsig (M.Plain)	145	CS	48
Versveld Rd	Goodwood Est.	86	BY	39
Versveld Rd	Richmond Est.	86	BY	41
Versveld Rd	Vasco Est.	86	BY	40
Vertrou Rd	Belthorn Est.	102	CH	34
Verwey St	Morgenster Hoogte	63	BT	55
Verwood Rd	Muizenberg	159	CW	28
Verwood Rd	Muizenberg Nth	159	CW	28
Vesperdene Rd	Green Point	81	BZ	22
Vesta	Park Village	127	CK	58
Vesuvius Ave	Strandfontein	162	CT	42
Vesuvius Cr.	Tafelsig (M.Plain)	164	CT	48
Vet Ct	Delft	106	CG	49
Vetta Shell Way	Richwood	42	BP	38
Via Appia	Somerset West	171	CV	77
Via Appia	Somerset West	171	CW	76
Via Appia	Strandfontein	163	CT	43
Via Campari	Welgevonden	46	BO	54
Via Campari Ave	Richwood	42	BQ	38
Via Campari Ave	Richwood	42	BP	37
Via Firenza	Goedemoed	46	BP	54
Via Milano St	Sonstraal Hgts	46	BP	54
Via San Marco St	Sonstraal Hgts	46	BO	54
Via Toscana St	Goedemoed	46	BP	54
Via Veneto	Sonstraal Hgts	46	BP	54
Viben Ave	Brackenfell Ind.	63	BT	57
Viben Ave	Brackenfell Ind.	63	BT	58
Vibra St	Hanover Pk	122	CK	37
Vicci St	Malibu Village	127	CK	55
Vickers Rd	Kensington	84	BZ	33
Vickers St	The Hague	106	CF	49
Victor St	Hout Bay	136	CP	14
Victor St	Hout Bay	137	CP	15
Victoria	Paarl	18	BC	88
Victoria Ave	Hout Bay	136	CP	14
Victoria Ave	Hout Bay	137	CQ	15
Victoria Cl.	Blouberg Sands	24	BL	30
Victoria Cl.	Blouberg Sands	24	BL	29
Victoria Cl.	Portlands (M.Plain)	144	CQ	45
Victoria Cl.	Summer Greens	58	BW	35
Victoria Cl.	Tokai	139	CS	25
Victoria Cr.	Marlborough Pk	63	BT	55
Victoria Dr.	Summer Greens	58	BW	35
Victoria Hamlet	D'urbanvale	45	BO	49
Victoria Mxenge	Weltevreden Val. (M.Plain)	123	CN	42
Victoria Mxenge Cr.	Mandela Pk	146	CR	54
Victoria Rd	Bantry Bay	80	CB	18
Victoria Rd	Camps Bay	98	CE	18
Victoria Rd	Flintdale Est.	141	CP	31
Victoria Rd	Grassy Pk	141	CQ	32
Victoria Rd	Grassy Pk	141	CR	32
Victoria Rd	Hout Bay	116	CL	14
Victoria Rd	Hout Bay	117	CN	15
Victoria Rd	Hout Bay	117	CJ	15
Victoria Rd	Hout Bay	137	CO	15
Victoria Rd	Oakdale	61	BX	48
Victoria Rd	Oudekraal	98	CH	17
Victoria Rd	Pelikan Pk	141	CR	33
Victoria Rd	Plumstead	120	CN	29
Victoria Rd	Salt River	83	CC	28
Victoria Rd	Sea Point	80	CA	18
Victoria Rd	Tuscany Glen	127	CK	56
Victoria Rd	Tuscany Glen	127	CL	56
Victoria Rd	Woodstock	82	CB	26
Victoria Rd	Wynberg	120	CM	28
Victoria Rd	Wynberg	120	CL	30
Victoria St	Gardens	81	CB	22
Victoria St	Parow	86	BZ	42
Victoria St	Parow	87	BY	43
Victoria St	Retreat	140	CS	28
Victoria St	Richmond Est.	86	BY	41
Victoria St	Somerset West	170	CV	73
Victoria St	Somerset West	170	CW	72
Victoria St	Stellenbosch	95	CC	76
Victoria St	Stellenbosch	95	CC	77
Victoria St	Van Ryneveld	174	CZ	72
Victoria St	Windsor Pk	47	BR	58
Victoria St	Zoo Pk	47	BR	57
Victoria Way	Blouberg Sands	24	BL	30
Victoria Wk	Woodstock	82	CB	26
Victorskloof Rd	Hout Bay	117	CM	15
Victory Ave	Pinelands	84	CB	33
Victory Cl.	Scottsdene	64	BU	60
Victory Cl.	Victoria	194	DJ	24
Victory La.	Simon's Town	194	DJ	24
Victory Rd	Retreat	140	CR	30
Victory Rd	Woodlands (M.Plain)	144	CQ	44
Victory South	Scottsdene	64	BU	60
Victory St	Wynberg	120	CM	30
Victory Way	Victoria	194	DJ	24
Vidal Cr.	Strandfontein	162	CT	39
Vidor Rd	Tuscany Glen	127	CL	57
Vienna St	Portlands (M.Plain)	144	CQ	46
Vienna Way	Grassy Pk	141	CQ	31
Vierhout	Morgen Gronde	63	BX	55
Vierlanden Rd	Vierlanden	30	BN	51
View Mount Way	Somerset West	170	CT	73
Viewfield Rd	Somerset West	170	CT	73
Viking Rd	Tuscany Glen	127	CL	57
Viking Way	Epping Ind.	85	CB	36

STREET NAME	SUBURB NAME	PG	GRID	
Viking Way	Epping Ind.	85	CB	38
Viking Way	Epping Ind.	86	CB	40
Vilakazi Cr.	Masiphumelele	184	DA	18
Viljoen Cr.	Tafelsig (M.Plain)	145	CS	49
Viljoen Cr.	Wellington	15	AU	92
Viljoen Ct	Edgemead	58	BU	37
Viljoen St	Brandwag	90	BZ	55
Viljoen St	Denneburg	22	BD	90
Viljoens Wk	Parkwood	141	CO	32
Villa Caponero Rd	Plattekloof Village	59	BT	41
Villa Ciambri	Welgevonden	46	BO	54
Villa Cl.	Weltevreden Val. (M.Plain)	144	CP	43
Villa da Sol Cl.	Bonnie Brae	47	BQ	57
Villa Mont St	Somerset West	171	CV	76
Villa Palazzo	Vredekloof Hgts	47	BS	55
Villa Park	Weltevreden Val. (M.Plain)	124	CN	44
Village Cl.	Kenever	61	BT	49
Village Cl.	Sunset Beach	41	BR	31
Village Cl.	Vredekloof	62	BT	54
Village Cr.	Sunset Beach	41	BR	31
Village Green	Kirstenhof	159	CU	27
Village Green	Kirstenhof	159	CW	27
Village Green Cl.	Plumstead	140	CO	29
Village Green St	Greenways	174	DA	73
Village La.	Noordhoek	156	CW	18
Village Pl.	Parklands	41	BO	32
Village Wk	Parklands	41	BO	32
Villette St	Blomtuin	62	BV	51
Villiers St	Morgenster Hoogte	63	BT	56
Villion St	De Zoete Inval	39	BJ	88
Vimba St	Umrhabulo Triangle	147	CP	57
Vimy Ridge	Strandfontein	162	CT	40
Vin Doux St	Durmonte	30	BN	53
Vincent Ave	Rondebosch	102	CG	31
Vincent Cl.	Montagu's Gift	142	CO	35
Vincent Rd	Manenberg	103	CH	38
Vincent Rd	Tuscany Glen	127	CK	57
Vincent St	Maitland	83	CA	30
Vine Rd	Bergvliet	140	CQ	27
Vine Rd	Woodstock	83	CC	27
Vine Rd	Wynberg	120	CL	29
Vine St	Gardens	81	CB	22
Vineyard Ave	Austinville	108	CH	56
Vineyard Ave	Hout Bay	117	CN	18
Vineyard Cl.	Alphen	119	CM	26
Vineyard Cl.	Alphen	120	CM	27
Vineyard Cl.	Silverhurst	119	CN	23
Vineyard La.	Kenridge	45	BS	49
Vineyard Rd	Bergvliet	139	CR	26
Vineyard Rd	Claremont	101	CH	28
Vineyard Rd	Dreyersdal	140	CR	27
Vineyard Rd	Ridgeworth	61	BV	50
Vineyard Rd	Tuscany Glen	127	CK	56
Vineyard St	Kayamandi	94	CA	74
Vineyard Way	Hout Bay	137	CP	16
Vink Cl.	Loucharmante	90	CB	56
Vink Rd	Rocklands (M.Plain)	144	CS	44
Vink Rd	Sunnydale	185	DA	19
Vink St	Amstelhof	23	BD	93
Vink St	Bellville Sth	88	CA	49
Vink St	Flamingo Vlei	41	BP	32
Vink St	Morningstar	46	BP	51
Vink St	Wellington	15	AU	91
Vinkenberg	Morgen Gronde	63	BX	55
Viola	Lentegeur (M.Plain)	144	CP	46
Viola Cl.	Mandalay	125	CN	48
Viola Cr.	Welgedacht	60	BU	45
Viola Rd	Blouberg Rise	25	BN	31
Viola Rd	Clamhall	60	BX	43
Viola Rd	Table View	40	BO	30
Viola St	Retreat	159	CT	29
Viola St	Vredekloof Hgts	47	BS	55
Violet Cr.	Wimbledon	108	CH	55
Violet Rd	Belgravia	103	CG	35
Violet Rd	Claremont	120	CJ	27
Violet Rd	Tuscany Glen	127	CL	56
Violet St	Sarepta	89	CC	52
Violet St	Tarentaalplaas	175	DA	75
Violin Cr.	Belhar	106	CD	49
Viooltjie	Lentegeur (M.Plain)	145	CP	47
Viooltjie St	Blomtuin	61	BV	50
Viooltjie St	Plumstead	140	CO	28
Virgilia Cl.	Bay Pk	175	DC	76
Virginia Ave	Vredehoek	82	CC	23
Virginia Cr.	Weltevreden Val. (M.Plain)	144	CO	40
Virgo Cl.	Everite	63	BU	57
Virgo Rd	Surrey	103	CH	38
Virgo St	Morgenster Hoogte	63	BT	56
Virgo St	Ocean View	189	DD	15
Virgo St	Phoenix	57	BU	33
Virtue Cl.	Tuscany Glen	127	CK	57
Vis St	Macassar	149	CS	64
Visagie St	Bothasig	58	BU	37
Visagie St	Dolphin Beach	40	BP	30
Visagie St	Dolphin Beach	41	BP	31
Visagie St	Klipkop	87	BZ	44
Visagie St	Monte Vista	59	BV	39
Visagie St	Parowvallei	87	BZ	43
Visagie St	Parowvallei	87	BZ	44
Viscount	Rocklands (M.Plain)	145	CS	47
Viscount Cr.	Plattekloof Village	59	BT	42
Viscount St	The Hague	106	CF	49
Visier Jagters	Jagtershof	90	CC	57
Visser	Rusthof	174	DA	74
Visser	Stellenbosch	95	CC	76

STREET NAME	SUBURB NAME	PG	GRID	
Visser Ave	Wynberg	120	CK	27
Visser Cl.	Tuscany Glen	127	CL	56
Visser St	Morgenster Hoogte	63	BT	56
Visser St	Peerless Pk East	47	BS	58
Visser St	Peerless Pk East	48	BR	59
Vissershoek Cl.	Somerset West	150	CS	70
Vissershof Rd	Bothasig	59	BT	39
Vissershof Rd	Bothasig	59	BT	39
Vissershok Rd	Durbanville	45	BP	49
Vissershok Rd	Meerendal	29	BM	47
Vissershok Rd	Skilpadvlei	45	BO	49
Vissershok Rd	Vissershok	27	BK	41
Vissershok Rd	Vissershok	28	BK	43
Vissershok Rd	Vissershok	28	BL	45
Vista Cl.	Lekkerwater	184	DB	18
Vista Cl.	Tuscany Glen	127	CL	57
Vista Rd	Claremont	101	CH	29
Vista Rd	Tuscany Glen	127	CK	57
Vistula La.	Manenberg	123	CK	39
Vistula Rd	Manenberg	122	CK	38
Vistula Rd	Manenberg	123	CK	39
Vita Nova Ave	Tokai	139	CS	25
Viva St	Crossroads	124	CK	44
Vivaldi	Delft Sth	125	CJ	48
Vivaldi	Schuilplaats	113	CG	76
Vivaldi Cl.	Sonstraal Hgts	46	BQ	54
Vivaldi Cl.	Vygeboom	46	BQ	54
Vivaldi St	Morgenster Hoogte	63	BU	55
Vivian Mathe St	Kuyasa	147	CS	55
Vivian Mathe St	Kuyasa	147	CS	58
Vivian Matthee	Klein Nederburg	19	BB	93
Vixen Rd	Tuscany Glen	127	CK	56
Vlaeberg	Brackenfell	63	BW	55
Vlaeberg Cl.	Voorbrug	106	CF	50
Vlaeberg Cl.	Voorbrug	106	CH	48
Vlaeberg Cl.	Welgevonden	46	BO	54
Vlaeberg Rd	Welmoed Est.	109	CG	62
Vlaeberg Rd	Welmoed Est.	110	CH	63
Vlaeberg Rd	Welmoed Est.	129	CJ	63
Vlaeberg St	Tafelsig (M.Plain)	145	CS	47
Vlagskip St	Strandfontein	161	CT	38
Vlamboom Cl.	Hill View	127	CK	57
Vlamboom Cl.	Hill View	127	CN	55
Vlamboom Cr.	Blommendal	61	BW	50
Vlamboom Cr.	Plattekloof	60	BU	43
Vlamboom Cr.	Vredekloof	62	BT	53
Vlamboom Cr.	Vredekloof	62	BT	54
Vlamboom Rd	Bonteheuwel	103	CE	38
Vlamboom Rd	Bonteheuwel	104	CE	39
Vlamboom Sq.	Bonteheuwel	103	CE	38
Vlamboom Sq.	Bonteheuwel	103	CF	37
Vlamboom St	Forest Hgts	127	CK	57
Vlamboom St	Ottery	121	CN	33
Vlamdoring Cr.	Rouxville	90	BZ	56
Vlei Rd	Green Point	81	BY	21
Vlei Rd	Heathfield	140	CQ	29
Vlei Rd	Knole Pk	142	CO	36
Vlei Rd	Meerendal	29	BN	48
Vlei Rd	Muizenberg	159	CX	29
Vlei Rd	Muizenberg Nth	159	CV	28
Vlei Rd	Pelikan Pk	141	CR	34
Vlei Rd	Schaap Kraal	142	CQ	37
Vlei Rd	Scottsville	47	BS	56
Vlei Rd	Scottsville	63	BT	57
Vlei St	Durbanville	45	BP	49
Vlei St	Kempenville	61	BX	48
Vlei St	Kingston	61	BX	48
Vlei St	KWV	22	BH	88
Vlei St	Mabille Pk	89	CA	53
Vlei St	Parowvallei	87	BZ	44
Vleihall Rd	Hanover Pk	122	CK	36
Vleiland	Morgen Gronde	63	BX	56
Vleiroos	Lentegeur (M.Plain)	144	CO	45
Vleiroos Cl.	Plattekloof	60	BU	43
Vleiroos Sq.	Roosendaal	106	CE	50
Vleiroos St	Bellville	61	BU	48
Vleiroos St	Kenridge	61	BU	48
Vliegtuig St	Factreton	85	BY	35
Vlier	Bo Dalsig	113	CE	76
Vlier Cl.	Onverwacht	175	DC	76
Vlier Cl.	Onverwacht	175	DB	77
Vlier La.	Ottery	121	CN	33
Vlok St	Beaconvale	87	CA	44
Vlok St	Somerset West	170	CT	73
Vloot St	Bellville Sth	88	CA	49
Vlottenburg Rd	Vlottenburg	111	CE	68
Voel Ct	Delft	106	CG	49
Voël St	Belgravia	102	CG	34
Voël St	Belgravia	103	CG	35
Voëlberg Way	Eversdal	62	BU	51
Voëlvlei St	Groenvallei	62	BX	53
Voëlvlei St	Groenvallei	62	BX	52
Voëlvlei St	Tafelsig (M.Plain)	145	CS	49
Voetboog Rd	Schotsche Kloof	81	CA	22
Vogelgezang St	Belhar	107	CD	51
Vogelgezang St	District Six	82	CB	25
Vogevlei Main Rd	Wesbank	107	CG	52
Vogue	Tuscany Glen	127	CL	57
Voigt St	Dal Josafat Ind.	18	BC	89
Voilet	Lentegeur (M.Plain)	144	CP	45
Vokwana Way	Langa	103	CD	35
Volga Cl.	Portlands (M.Plain)	144	CQ	46
Volga St	Eindhoven	125	CJ	50
Volks St	Paarlzicht	19	BC	91
Volksang St	Cafda Village	140	CS	30

STREET NAME	SUBURB NAME	PG	GRID	
Volschenk St	Clamhall	60	BX	43
Volschenk St	De La Haye	62	BX	51
Volstedt Rd	The Palms	170	CX	73
Volstruis	Rocklands (M.Plain)	144	CS	44
Volstruis Rd	Bridgetown	103	CF	37
Volta Ct	Delft	106	CF	50
Volta Rd	Belhar	88	CC	50
Volta Rd	Retreat	140	CS	28
Volta St	Dal Josafat Ind.	19	AY	91
Volute Cir.	Sunset Beach	41	BS	31
Volvo St	Beacon Valley (M.Plain)	145	CQ	47
Von Braun St	Sarepta	89	CB	52
Von Willigh Cr.	Oakdene	89	CC	53
Vondel Rd	Edgemead	58	BV	38
Voogdy St	Soneike I	89	BZ	54
Voor St	Wellington	10	AS	92
Voor St	Wellington	10	AS	93
Voorbrug Ave	Somerset West	150	CS	70
Voorbrug Rd	Delft	106	CG	49
Voorbrug St	Voorbrug	106	CG	50
Voorbrug St	Voorbrug	106	CH	50
Voorhoede Cl.	Mitchells Plain	144	CQ	44
Voorjaar St	Surrey	103	CG	37
Voorschoten St	Dal Josafat Ind.	18	BA	90
Voorspoed Cl.	Voorbrug	106	CG	50
Voorspoed Rd	Surrey	103	CH	37
Voortrekker Rd	Bellville	87	BY	46
Voortrekker Rd	Belrail	88	BY	49
Voortrekker Rd	Durbanville	45	BP	50
Voortrekker Rd	Durbanville	45	BP	47
Voortrekker Rd	Maitland	84	CA	33
Voortrekker Rd	Maitland	85	BZ	36
Voortrekker Rd	Parow	86	BY	42
Voortrekker Rd	Parow East	87	BY	44
Voortrekker Rd	Ruyterwacht	86	CA	40
Voortrekker Rd	Somerset West	170	CW	74
Voortrekker Rd	Townsend Est.	85	BZ	38
Voortrekker Rd	Vasco Est.	86	BZ	40
Voortrekker Rd	Woodstock	83	CB	29
Vooruitsig Rd	Surrey	103	CH	37
Vorster Ave	Wetton	121	CL	34
Vorster St	Dal Josafat Ind.	19	AY	91
Vorster St	Peerless Pk East	48	BS	59
Vos St	Cape Town Cen.	82	CA	25
Voskuil	Morgen Gronde	63	BX	55
Vosmaar St	Dal Josafat Ind.	18	AZ	90
Vrede	Krigeville	113	CD	76
Vrede Rd	Frogmore Est.	159	CU	28
Vrede Rd	Tuscany Glen	127	CL	56
Vrede St	Beaconvale	86	BZ	42
Vrede St	Belrail	88	BY	48
Vrede St	Cape Town Cen.	82	CB	23
Vrede St	Durbanville	45	BQ	50
Vrede St	Voelvlei	89	CA	52
Vrede St	Wellington	15	AW	93
Vredehoek Ave	Vredehoek	82	CC	23
Vredekloof Rd	Vredekloof	62	BT	53
Vredekloof Rd	Vredekloof	62	BT	54
Vredelust	Cloetesville	95	BZ	75
Vredelust	Vredelust	60	BX	46
Vredelust St	Somerset West	151	CQ	71
Vredenberg Dr.	Eversdal	62	BU	51
Vredenburg	Devonvallei	112	CD	72
Vredenburg Ave	Rosebank	101	CE	30
Vredenburg Circus	Rosebank	101	CE	30
Vredenburg La.	Cape Town Cen.	81	CB	22
Vredenburg St	Bothasig	58	BT	38
Vredenburg St	Kleinbosch	59	BT	40
Vredenburg St	Mitchells Plain	144	CQ	43
Vredendal Rd	Athlone	102	CF	34
Vredendal St	Portlands (M.Plain)	144	CR	46
Vredenhof	Claremont	101	CG	29
Vredenhof Cr.	Edenpark	62	BU	54
Vredenhof Rd	Edgemead	58	BV	37
Vredenhof Rd	Guldenland	174	CY	74
Vredeveld	Morgen Gronde	90	BY	55
Vreem St	Bothasig	58	BU	37
Vriedenhof Rd	Wynberg	120	CM	28
Vriende St	Oranjezicht	82	CC	23
Vryburger Ave	Bothasig	58	BT	37
Vryburger Ave	Bothasig	58	BT	38
Vryburger Ave	Bothasig	58	BU	37
Vryburger St	Tygerdal	59	BX	39
Vrygrond Ave	Capricorn	159	CV	30
Vrygrond Ave	Capricorn	160	CV	31
Vrykyk St	Paarl	22	BF	89
Vrymansfontein St	De Bron	45	BS	48
Vrystaat Rd	Paarden Eiland	83	BY	30
Vuka Rd	Nyanga	124	CK	43
Vukani St	Mxolisi Phetani	125	CM	49
Vukani St	Mxolisi Phetani	125	CM	50
Vukayi St	Lwandle	175	CZ	77
Vukuthu St	Brown's Farm	124	CL	44
Vukuthu St	Ilitha Pk	146	CQ	52
Vula St	Eyethu	146	CO	52
Vulcan La.	Hout Bay Harbour	136	CR	13
Vulcan Rd	Tuscany Glen	127	CL	57
Vulindlela St	Lwandle	175	CZ	76
Vulindlela St	Lwandle	175	CZ	77
Vultee Cr.	Tuscany Glen	127	CK	57
Vulture Rd	Pelikan Pk	142	CQ	35
Vumazonke St	Nonqubela	126	CN	52
Vumbululu Cr.	Umrhabulo Triangle	147	CP	57
Vumile St	Eyethu	146	CP	53
Vumingoma	Mbekweni	15	AW	92

Abbreviations used: Ave – Avenue, A.H. – Agricultural Holding, A.L.– Algemene Landgoed, Blvd – Boulevard, Cen. – Central, Cir. – Circle, Cl. – Close, Cr. – Crescent, Ct – Court, Dr. – Drive, Est. – Estate, Ext. – Extension, Hgts – Heights, Ind. – Industrial, Gdns – Gardens, Gr. – Grove, La. – Lane, (M.Plain) - Mitchells Plain, Nth – North, Pl. – Place, Pk – Park, Rd – Road, Rdg. – Ridge, S.H.– Small Holding, Sq. – Square, St – Street, Sth – South, Ter. – Terrace, Tn – Turn, Val. – Valley, Wk – Walk

STREET NAME	SUBURB NAME	PG	GRID	
Vundisa Cr.	Bloekombos	48	BR	62
Vuurlelie Cr.	Roosendaal	106	CE	50
Vuurpyl Cr.	Thornton	85	CA	38
Vuurpyl Rd	Belhar	88	CC	47
Vuurpyl Rd	Bonteheuwel	103	CE	38
Vuurpyl St	Wellington	15	AT	92
Vuyani St	Kaya	146	CP	51
Vuyani St	Kaya	146	CP	52
Vuyisile Mini	Weltevreden Val. (M.Plain)	123	CN	42
Vuyisile Mini St	Mandela Pk	147	CQ	55
Vuyisile Mini St	Mandela Pk	147	CP	55
Vuyiswa Cl.	Bloekombos	48	BR	62
Vuyo Rd	Capricorn	160	CV	31
Vyeboom Rd	Bonteheuwel	103	CE	38
Vyeboom St	Forest Village	127	CM	57
Vygeboom Cl.	Vygeboom	45	BR	50
Vygeboom Cr.	Vygeboom	46	BR	51
Vygeboom Rd	Vygeboom	46	BR	51
Vygeboom Rd	Vygeboom	46	BR	51
Vygie	Acacia Pk	58	BX	36
Vygie	Weltevrede	68	BX	75
Vygie Ave	Blackheath Ind.	108	CF	56
Vygie Ave	Blackheath Ind.	108	CF	57
Vygie Ave	Kleinvlei	127	CJ	58
Vygie Cl.	Belhar	106	CD	47
Vygie Cl.	Ottery East	121	CN	34
Vygie Cr.	Roosendaal	106	CE	50
Vygie Ct	Kewtown	102	CF	34
Vygie Pl.	Pelikan Pk	142	CR	36
Vygie Rd	Bishop Lavis	104	CE	42
Vygie Rd	Gordon Strand	179	DD	77
Vygie Rd	Uitsig	87	CB	44
Vygie St	Bellair	62	BW	51
Vygie St	Blomtuin	62	BW	51
Vygie St	Durbanville	45	BQ	50
Vygie St	Durbanville	45	BP	47
Vygie St	Groenvlei	18	BA	89
Vygie St	Hanover Pk	122	CJ	36
Vygie St	Morgenster	63	BU	56
Vygie St	Parow Nth	59	BW	42
Vygie St	Scarborough	192	DJ	18
Vygie St	Wellington	15	AT	92
Vygiekraal Rd	Sand Ind.	122	CJ	38
W				
W Nzala St	Gugulethu	123	CK	40
W. Songqeqo St	Hout Bay	137	CO	16
W. Stemele St	Mfuleni	126	CK	53
W. Thafeni St	Mfuleni	126	CK	53
W. Thafeni St	Mfuleni	126	CL	53
W.D.Hambley Rd	Langeberg Rdg	47	BR	55
W.Fanti Pl.	Driftsands	147	CQ	55
Waaierpalm	Weltevrede	94	BY	74
Waaiertjie Cr.	Roosendaal	106	CF	50
Waaihoek Rd	Durbanville Hills	45	BR	49
Waaihoek Rd	Heideveld	104	CG	39
Waaihoek St	Tafelsig (M.Plain)	145	CR	49
Waarburgh Rd	Joostenberg	48	BP	61
Waarburgh Rd	Joostenberg	48	BP	62
Waarburgh Rd	Joostenberg	49	BO	65
Waarnemer Sq.	Factreton	85	BZ	35
Wabash Rd	Schaap Kraal	123	CK	39
Waboom	Delft Sth	125	CK	49
Waboom	Harbour Island	179	DF	75
Waboom	Lentegeur (M.Plain)	144	CO	45
Waboom	Weltevrede	94	BY	74
Waboom	Weltevrede	94	BZ	73
Waboom Ave	Amandelrug	90	CA	56
Waboom Ave	New Orleans	19	BA	91
Waboom Cr.	Plattekloof	59	BU	42
Waboom Rd	Durbanville Hills	45	BR	49
Waboom Rd	Proteavallei	60	BT	46
Waboom St	Edenpark	62	BU	54
Waboom St	Eersterivier	128	CN	59
Waboom St	Sunnydale	185	DA	19
Waboom St	Sunnydale	185	DB	22
Waboomberg Cl.	Tafelsig (M.Plain)	145	CR	49
Wade Rd	Claremont	120	CJ	29
Wade St	Rome	174	CY	73
Wader Cr.	Flamingo Vlei	41	BQ	33
Wadham La.	Woodstock	83	CC	27
Wagenaar St	Bothasig	58	BT	37
Wagenaar St	Monte Vista	59	BV	40
Wagenaar St	Monte Vista	59	BW	39
Waggie Rd	Blackheath Ind.	108	CG	55
Wag-'n-Bietjie Cl.	Rouxville	90	CA	56
Wagner	Delft Sth	125	CJ	48
Wagner Cl.	Mandalay	125	CM	48
Wagner Cr.	Belhar	106	CD	49
Wagner St	Protea Hoogte	63	BW	56
Wagner Way	Sonstraal Hgts	46	BR	54
Wagner Way	Steenberg	159	CT	29
Wagon Drift Rd	Groenvallei	62	BW	53
Wagtail Cl.	Dreyersdal	139	CS	26
Wagtail St	Joostenberg	48	BQ	60
Wagtail Way	Somerset West	171	CW	77
Wagtail Way	Sunbird Pk	107	CF	54
Wagter St	Wellington	15	AT	92
Wahid St	Penlyn Est.	103	CH	35
Wahlizwa St	Tarentaalplaas	175	CY	75
Waikiki	Kraaifontein	47	BQ	58
Wailea	Kraaifontein	47	BQ	58
Wairakei Cl.	Whispering Pines	175	DB	77
Wairoa Way	Skilpadvlei	45	BP	49
Wakefield Cl.	Connaught	87	CC	43

STREET NAME	SUBURB NAME	PG	GRID	
Wakefield Rd	Rondebosch	102	CG	31
Wakefield Rd	Wynberg	120	CL	28
Walaza Rd	Nyanga	124	CK	43
Walburgh St	Mountain View	19	BB	92
Waldemar St	Oakdene	89	CC	53
Walder	Paarl	22	BE	88
Waldheim Cl.	Weltevreden Val. (M.Plain)	144	CR	45
Waldheim Cl.	Weltevreden Val. (M.Plain)	144	CS	43
Waldorf Pl.	Silversands	107	CH	54
Waldrift Cl.	Edgemead	59	BU	39
Waldstadt Ave	Silversands	107	CH	54
Wale St	Cape Town Cen.	81	CA	22
Wale St	Cape Town Cen.	82	CA	23
Walker	Wallacedene	48	BS	61
Walker Cr.	Belhar	107	CD	51
Walker St	Aurora	45	BP	48
Wall St	Portlands (M.Plain)	145	CQ	47
Wallaby Wk	Zoo Pk	47	BQ	56
Wallace	Delft Sth	125	CJ	48
Wallace Paton Cr.	Woodlands (M.Plain)	144	CO	45
Wallace St	Townsend Est.	58	BX	37
Wallace St	Townsend Est.	85	BY	37
Wallace St	Townsend Est.	85	BZ	37
Wallace St	Tygerdal	58	BX	37
Wallasey	Sunningdale	25	BM	31
Wallendorf St	Fairfield	87	BY	44
Wallflower	Lentegeur (M.Plain)	145	CP	47
Wallflower St	Paarden Eiland	83	CA	29
Wallis Rd	Hazendal	102	CE	33
Walloon Rd	Barbarossa	140	CO	27
Walmer Cl.	West Beach	25	BN	31
Walmer Cr.	Wesbank	107	CH	51
Walmer Rd	District Six	82	CC	25
Walmer Rd	Parkwood	141	CO	32
Walmer Rd	Woodstock	82	CB	26
Walmer St	Eyethu	146	CP	53
Walmer Wk	Parkwood	141	CO	32
Walnut Ave	Amandelrug	90	CA	56
Walnut Cl.	Sonstraal Hgts	46	BP	54
Walnut Rd	Lansdowne	121	CK	33
Walnut St	Bellair	62	BW	52
Walnut Way	Mitchells Plain	144	CR	44
Walotta Cl.	Halalie	46	BO	52
Walrus	Rocklands (M.Plain)	163	CT	45
Walrus St	Kensington	84	BZ	34
Wals	Mitchells Plain Cen.	145	CQ	47
Wals Ave	Cafda Village	141	CS	31
Walsall Rd	Plumstead	120	CN	28
Walter Battiss Rd	Woodlands (M.Plain)	124	CN	44
Walter Levy St	Panorama	59	BW	41
Walter Rd	Three Anchor Bay	81	BZ	20
Walter Sisulu Rd	Ekuphumuleni	146	CQ	53
Walter Sisulu Rd	Mandela Pk	147	CR	55
Walter Sisulu Rd	Umrhabulo Triangle	147	CR	57
Walter St	Elim	89	CA	54
Walter St	Protea Hoogte	63	BW	57
Walters Cl.	Grassy Pk	141	CR	32
Walters Way	Bergvliet	139	CP	26
Waltham Cross St	Paarl	22	BF	88
Waltham Rd	Epping Forest	86	CC	41
Waltham Rd	Lansdowne	102	CH	32
Waltham Way	Meadowridge	140	CP	27
Waltham Way	Northpine	63	BU	58
Walton	Delft Sth	125	CJ	48
Walton Cr.	Sunningdale	25	BN	31
Walton Pl.	Klein Begin	48	BS	61
Walton Rd	Cafda Village	140	CR	30
Walton Way	Bridgetown	103	CF	36
Walvis Rd	Strandfontein	162	CT	39
Wamakers St	Belhar	107	CD	51
Wamkelekile	Mbekweni	15	AV	92
Wanda Cr.	Tafelsig (M.Plain)	145	CR	50
Wandel Cr.	Woodlands (M.Plain)	144	CP	45
Wandel St	Gardens	81	CB	22
Wandel St	Gardens	82	CB	23
Wanderers Cl.	Fir Grove	139	CQ	25
Wanderers Cl.	The Crest	30	BN	53
Wanderers Cl.	The Crest	30	BM	53
Wanderers Cr.	Beacon Valley (M.Plain)	145	CP	48
Wandsworth	Parklands	25	BM	33
Wankie Cl.	Portlands (M.Plain)	145	CR	47
Wapenlyn Cl.	Bothasig	42	BS	37
Wapenlyn Way	Bothasig	42	BS	37
Wapiti	Factreton	84	BY	34
Wapnick St	Peerless Pk East	48	BR	59
Wapnick St	Peerless Pk East	48	BR	60
Wapnick St	Peerless Pk East	48	BS	59
Waratah	Eersterivier	128	CN	60
Warbler Ave	Somerset Rdg	170	CT	72
Warbler Cl.	Marconi Beam	57	BU	34
Warbler Ct	Bridgetown	103	CE	37
Warbler Rd	Pelikan Pk	142	CQ	36
Warbler Way	Electric City	128	CN	59
Warblers Cl.	Bel Ombre	119	CM	26
Warblers Way	Bel Ombre	119	CM	25
Warbreck Rd	Lansdowne	121	CK	34
Ward La.	Grassy Pk	141	CQ	33
Warden Cr.	Penlyn Est.	122	CJ	35
Wargrave Rd	Kenilworth	120	CK	30
Warhawk	Rocklands (M.Plain)	163	CT	45
Warner	Simon's Town	191	DE	24
Warner Cr.	Riverton	86	BZ	40
Warren Cl.	Retreat	140	CS	29
Warren St	Fairfield	60	BX	44
Warren St	Tamboerskloof	81	CB	21

STREET NAME	SUBURB NAME	PG	GRID	
Warrenside	Retreat	140	CS	29
Warrenville Ter.	Cape Town Cen.	82	CB	23
Warries	Bloomsburg	23	BD	92
Warrington Rd	Claremont	121	CJ	31
Warsaw	Strandfontein	162	CT	41
Warthog St	Uitzicht	46	BO	54
Warwick Cir.	West Beach	24	BN	30
Warwick Cr.	Eersterivier	128	CN	61
Warwick Pl.	West Beach	24	BN	30
Warwick Rd	West Beach	24	BN	30
Warwick St	Claremont	101	CH	28
Warwick St	Vredehoek	82	CC	23
Warwick St	Woodstock	82	CB	26
Washington Cl.	Eikenbosch	90	CC	57
Washington Dr.	Colorado (M.Plain)	144	CO	44
Washington Dr.	Langa	103	CD	37
Washington Rd	Claremont	102	CH	31
Washington St	Boston	60	BW	46
Washington St	Boston	60	BX	46
Washington St	Langa	103	CD	35
Washington St	Langa	103	CD	37
Washington St	Malibu Village	127	CK	55
Washington Way	Portlands (M.Plain)	144	CR	46
Wasp Cl.	Strandfontein	163	CT	43
Wassenar Cl.	Westlake	159	CV	27
Wassenar Cl.	Westlake	159	CW	27
Water	Rozendal	96	CB	80
Water Oak St	Oak Glen	62	BW	53
Water St	Claremont	101	CH	29
Water St	Simon's Town	194	DJ	25
Water Way	Marina Da Gama	159	CV	29
Water Way	Winslow	179	DD	77
Waterberg	Brackenfell	63	BW	55
Waterberg Cr.	Bonnie Brae	47	BP	57
Waterberg Cr.	Bonnie Brae	47	BO	58
Waterberg Cr.	Tafelsig (M.Plain)	145	CS	48
Waterberg Rd	Heideveld	104	CF	40
Waterberry	Wesbank	107	CF	51
Waterberry Cr.	Greenlands	88	CA	48
Waterberry Cr.	Greenlands	88	CA	49
Waterbessie St	Amandelrug	90	CA	55
Waterblom	Lentegeur (M.Plain)	144	CO	45
Waterblommetjie St	Wellington	14	AT	90
Waterbok Cr.	Goedemoed	46	BP	53
Waterbok St	New Orleans	19	BA	92
Waterbok St	Soneike II	89	BZ	54
Waterbom St	Wesbank	107	CG	52
Waterboom	Weltevrede	94	BY	74
Waterboom Ave	Belhar	88	CC	47
Waterbossie Cl.	Protea Village	64	BW	59
Waterbuck Cl.	Eastridge (M.Plain)	145	CR	48
Waterbury Rd	Plumstead	120	CM	29
Watercress La.	Pelikan Pk	141	CR	34
Waterfall La.	Hout Bay	118	CM	19
Waterfall Rd	Simon's Town	191	DH	24
Waterford Ave	Lotus River	141	CP	34
Waterford Ave	Lotus River	142	CP	35
Waterford Cir.	Kirstenhof	159	CU	27
Waterford Cl.	Plumstead	140	CP	29
Waterford Rd	Blouberg Rise	25	BN	31
Waterford Rd	Connaught	87	CC	43
Waterford Rd	Connaught	87	CB	46
Waterford Rd	Elfindale	140	CP	29
Waterford Rd	Plumstead	140	CO	29
Waterford St	Somerset West	171	CU	78
Waterfront Rd	Bellville	61	BV	48
Waterheide Sq.	Roosendaal	106	CF	50
Waterhout	Delft Sth	125	CK	48
Waterhout St	Perm Gdns	128	CK	56
Watering St	Parow	86	BZ	42
Waterkant St	Cape Town Cen.	82	CA	23
Waterkant St	Green Point	81	BZ	22
Waterkant St	Lemoenkloof	18	BC	89
Waterkant St	Wellington	15	AU	92
Waterkloof Rd	De Bron	61	BT	48
Waterland	Morgen Gronde	63	BX	55
Waterland Rd	Blue Downs	108	CH	56
Waterlily	Lentegeur (M.Plain)	145	CP	47
Waterlily Cl.	The Lakes	184	CZ	18
Waterloo Ave	Weltevreden Val. (M.Plain)	123	CN	42
Waterloo Gr.	Wynberg	120	CL	28
Waterloo Rd	Lansdowne	121	CK	32
Waterloo Rd	Strandfontein	162	CT	41
Waterloo Rd	Wynberg	120	CL	28
Waterloo St	Malibu Village	127	CK	56
Waterman St	Forest Glade	127	CL	58
Watermeyer Rd	Blouberg Rise	25	BN	31
Waternooientjie St	Elim	90	CB	55
Watersmeet Rd	Somerset West	152	CS	76
Waterval St	Tafelsig (M.Plain)	145	CR	49
Waterville	Sunningdale	25	BM	31
Waterway	Kewtown	102	CE	34
Waterways Ave	Harbour Island	175	DC	75
Watford Ave	Athlone	102	CG	33
Watford Cl.	Wembley Pk	107	CE	53
Watford Cr.	Weltevreden Val. (M.Plain)	144	CP	43
Watford St	Wesbank	107	CG	52
Wathi St	Umrhabulo Triangle	147	CQ	58
Watshaya St	Nomzano	175	CY	76
Watson Cl.	Simon's Town	195	DK	27
Watson Rd	Muizenberg	159	CX	29
Watson St	Cape Town Cen.	81	CB	22
Watson Wk	Tokai	139	CS	25
Watsonia	Lentegeur (M.Plain)	145	CP	47
Watsonia Cl.	Ottery East	121	CN	34

STREET NAME	SUBURB NAME	PG	GRID	
Watsonia Cl.	Pinelands	102	CD	34
Watsonia Cl.	Plattekloof	60	BU	43
Watsonia Cl.	Wellington	15	AT	92
Watsonia Cr.	Big Bay	24	BK	28
Watsonia La.	Scarborough	192	DJ	18
Watsonia Rd	Belhar	88	CC	47
Watsonia Rd	Belhar	106	CD	47
Watsonia Rd	Bloubergrant	24	BN	29
Watsonia Rd	Bloubergrant	40	BO	30
Watsonia Rd	Durbanville	45	BQ	50
Watsonia Rd	Durbanville	45	BP	47
Watsonia Rd	Murdock Valley	195	DL	27
Watsonia Rd	Stellenberg	62	BU	52
Watsonia Rd	Thornton	85	CB	37
Watsonia St	Devil's Peak Est.	82	CC	24
Watsonia St	Gordon Hgts	180	DD	79
Watsonia St	Kleinvlei	127	CJ	58
Watsonia St	Tygerdal	58	BX	38
Watsonia Way	Lotus River	141	CP	33
Watt	Dal Josafat Ind.	19	AY	91
Watt	Dennemere	108	CH	58
Watt St	Harbour Island	179	DE	75
Watt St	Kaymor	62	BX	53
Wattle	Acacia Pk	58	BX	36
Wattle	Rosedale	128	CK	59
Wattle Cl.	Greenfield	108	CH	56
Wattle Gr.	Pinelands	84	CB	33
Wattle La.	Parkwood	141	CO	32
Wattle Rd	Chapman's Peak	156	CW	16
Wattle Rd	Grassy Pk	141	CQ	33
Wattle St	Loevenstein	60	BW	45
Wattle St	Sarepta	89	CC	52
Watussi Cl.	Strandfontein	163	CT	43
Watussi Cl.	Strandfontein	163	CU	43
Watussi Dr.	Strandfontein	163	CT	43
Wavell Ave	Simon's Town	194	DJ	26
Waveren	Lindida	96	CA	80
Waveren Ave	Somerset West	151	CQ	73
Waveren Sq.	Ruyterwacht	86	CA	39
Waveren St	Voorbrug	106	CD	49
Waveren St	Voorbrug	106	CH	48
Waverev Rd	Sonstraal	46	BR	52
Waverley Cl.	Barbarossa	140	CO	27
Waverley Rd	Observatory	101	CD	29
Wavern Cl.	Richwood	42	BQ	37
Waxberry St	Dunoon	26	BN	37
Waxbill La.	Steenberg	139	CS	24
Waxbury	Macassar	148	CR	62
Way Rd	Penhill	128	CK	60
Wayfarer Ave	Tijgerhof	57	BW	33
Wayside Rd	Bishop Lavis	104	CD	41
Wayside Rd	Rondebosch	101	CF	30
Weatherly St	Epping Ind.	86	CA	39
Weaver Bird Ave	Dennedal	139	CR	26
Weaver Cl.	Villa Italia	57	BW	33
Weaver Ct	Bridgetown	103	CE	35
Weaver St	Flamingo Vlei	41	BP	32
Weaver St	Sonstraal Hgts	46	BR	53
Weaver Way	Electric City	127	CM	58
Weavers End	Kommetjie	183	DB	13
Weavers Way	Somerset West	171	CU	75
Webb St	Greenways	174	DA	74
Weber	Dalvale	19	AY	91
Weber	Delft Sth	125	CJ	48
Weber	Idasvallei	96	CA	79
Weber Cl.	Belhar	106	CD	49
Weber Cr.	Penlyn Est.	122	CJ	35
Weber St	Brackenfell	63	BV	57
Weber St	Sarepta	89	CB	53
Webersvallei	Jamestown	112	CH	74
Webersvallei	Jamestown	113	CH	75
Webley Cl.	Jagtershof	108	CD	56
Webner St	Florida	87	CA	44
Webner St	Florida	87	CB	44
Webster Cl.	The Vines	140	CO	27
Wedge Rd	Fairways	121	CN	31
Wedge St	Lakeside	159	CV	27
Wedge St	Lakeside	159	CW	27
Wedgewood	Sonstraal Hgts	46	BQ	54
Wedgewood Cl.	Edgemead	58	BV	37
Wedgewood Cl.	Sonstraal Hgts	46	BR	54
Weenen Rd	Milnerton	57	BV	32
Weg St	Macassar	149	CS	64
Wege	Brandwacht	113	CE	76
Wegner Ave	Ottery East	121	CN	34
Weidenhof St	Stellenbosch	95	CC	75
Weijlandzicht	Durbanville	45	BO	49
Weimar Rd	Churchill	59	BX	42
Weimar St	Glenlily	86	BY	42
Weinsberg Rd	Silversands	107	CH	53
Weir Rd	Lansdowne	121	CK	34
Weir Rd	Milnerton	57	BW	31
Weiss St	Paarl	22	BD	89
Welbedacht	Voorbrug	106	CG	50
Welbedacht	Voorbrug	106	CH	48
Welbedacht Rd	Groenvallei	62	BW	53
Welbeloon Cl.	Welgelee	63	BT	55
Welbeloond Ave	Nova Constantia	139	CP	24
Welbeloond Cl.	Mitchells Plain	144	CR	45
Welbeloond Cl.	Mitchells Plain	144	CR	43
Welbevind Way	Hout Bay	117	CN	16
Welby Rd	Surrey	103	CH	37
Welcome La.	Kensington	84	BZ	33
Welcome Zenzile St	Kuyasa	147	CS	55
Welcome Zenzile St	Kuyasa	147	CS	58

Index to Street Names

Weldra Cr. — Ysterhout Cl.

STREET NAME	SUBURB NAME	PG	GRID
Weldra Cr.	Northpine	64	BT 59
Weldra Rd	Clarkes	86	CC 42
Wele Cl.	Kaya	146	CP 52
Welegemeend	Pinelands	84	CC 34
Welgedacht Dr.	Welgedacht	60	BT 45
Welgedacht Dr.	Welgedacht	60	BU 45
Welgegund	Welgelee	63	BT 55
Welgelee Rd	Fir Grove	139	CQ 25
Welgelee Rd	Welgelee	63	BT 55
Welgelegen Ave	High Constantia	139	CO 23
Welgelegen Ave	Strandfontein	162	CU 39
Welgelegen Ave	Voorbrug	106	CG 50
Welgelegen Rd	Mowbray	101	CD 29
Welgelegen Rd	Richwood	42	BQ 38
Welgelegen St	Bellville	61	BV 47
Welgelegen St	Lemoenkloof	18	BC 88
Welgelegen St	Lemoenkloof	18	BC 87
Welgelegen St	Table View	41	BO 32
Welgelegen St	Welgedacht	44	BS 46
Welgemeend St	Bellville	88	BY 47
Welgemeend St	Gardens	81	CC 22
Welgemeend St	Kleinbosch	59	BT 40
Welgemoed St	Bellville	61	BV 47
Welgemoed St	Welgemoed	61	BU 47
Welgevallen	Welgelegen	113	CD 76
Welgevonden Blvd	Stellenbosch	95	BY 75
Welgevonden Blvd	Weltevrede	67	BX 74
Welgevonden Blvd South	Stellenbosch	95	BY 75
Welgezicht Cr.	Uitzicht	47	BO 55
Welington Way	Parklands	25	BN 34
Welkom Rd	Plumstead	140	CO 29
Welkom St	Portlands (M.Plain)	144	CS 46
Welkom St	Portlands (M.Plain)	145	CS 47
Welkom St	Welgelee	63	BT 55
Well Rd	Hout Bay	117	CN 17
Wellesley St	Factreton	84	BY 34
Wellington	Portlands (M.Plain)	144	CR 46
Wellington Ave	Wynberg	120	CM 28
Wellington Rd	Durbanville	45	BP 50
Wellington Rd	Durbanville	46	BP 51
Wellington Rd	Wellway Pk East	46	BO 52
Wellington Rd	Wynberg	120	CM 29
Wellington St	Bloekombos	49	BR 63
Wellington St	Oakdale	61	BW 49
Wellington St	The Crest	30	BN 53
Wellington St	The Hague	106	CF 49
Wellington St	Vasco Est.	59	BX 39
Wellington St	Vasco Est.	86	BY 40
Wellington Wk	Wynberg	120	CM 28
Welmar Rd	Pinati	122	CJ 35
Welmoed Way	Somerset West	169	CT 70
Welmoed Way	Somerset West	170	CT 71
Weltevrede Cr.	Bonnie Brae	47	BP 57
Weltevrede Cr.	Welgelee	63	BT 55
Weltevrede Cr.	Welgelee	63	BV 56
Weltevrede St	Wellington	15	AU 92
Weltevreden Ave	Rondebosch	101	CF 30
Weltevreden Ave	Rondebosch	102	CG 31
Weltevreden Dr.	The Vines	140	CO 27
Weltevreden Parkway	Weltevreden Val. (M.Plain)	124	CN 43
Weltevreden Parkway	Weltevreden Val. (M.Plain)	144	CQ 43
Weltevreden Rd	Pinelands	84	CC 34
Weltevreden Rd	Rocklands (M.Plain)	144	CS 44
Weltevreden Rd	Schaap Kraal	123	CN 40
Weltevreden Rd	Schaap Kraal	143	CO 41
Weltevreden Rd	Strandfontein	163	CT 46
Weltevreden Rd	Weltevreden Val. (M.Plain)	144	CO 43
Weltevreden St	Gardens	81	CB 22
Weltevreden St	Paarl	22	BF 88
Weltevreden St	Stanlou	61	BX 48
Welton St	Lavender Hill	160	CT 31
Welvanpas St	Wellington	11	AR 95
Welvanpas St	Wellington	11	AS 95
Welway Rd	Altydgedacht	45	BR 48
Welwitschia	Delft Sth	125	CJ 50
Welwyn Ave	Pinelands	84	CB 34
Wembley Ave	Plumstead	140	CO 29
Wembley Cl.	Weltevreden Val. (M.Plain)	143	CO 42
Wembley Dr.	Schaap Kraal	143	CO 42
Wembley Dr.	Weltevreden Val. (M.Plain)	143	CO 42
Wembley Rd	Gardens	82	CC 23
Wembley Rd	Wembley Pk	107	CE 53
Wembley Way	Edgemead	58	BV 38
Wembley Way	Matroosfontein	86	CC 41
Wembley Way	Northpine	63	BU 58
Wembley Way	Northpine	63	BV 56
Wemmershoek St	Heemstede	62	BW 52
Wemmershoek St	Tafelsig (M.Plain)	145	CS 49
Wemmerspan Rd	Edgemead	58	BV 38
Wemyss St	Brooklyn	84	BY 31
Wena Cl.	Umrhabulo Triangle	147	CP 58
Wendtland St North	Fairfield	60	BX 44
Wendtlandt St	Fairfield	87	BY 44
Wendy Cr.	Tafelsig (M.Plain)	145	CR 50
Wendy Rd	Heathfield	140	CR 29
Wendy Way	Northgate	59	BW 42
Wenlock Rd	Newlands	101	CH 28
Wenlock St	Des Hampden	89	CA 53
Wenning Rd	Sonstraal	46	BR 52
Wenning St	De La Haye	89	BY 51
Wenning St	Parow Nth	60	BW 43
Wens Way	Belthorn Est.	102	CH 34
Wentworth	D'urbanvale	45	BO 49
Wentworth Blvd	Sunningdale	24	BM 30
Wentworth Blvd	Sunningdale	24	BL 29
Wentworth Mews	Sunset Links	57	BT 31
Wentworth St	Greenways	174	DA 73
Wentworth Wk	Southfork	175	DB 75
Wentzel	Rusthof	174	DA 74
Wentzel Rd	Steenberg	159	CU 29
Wepener Link	Belhar	107	CD 51
Wepener Link	Belhar	107	CG 53
Wepener St	Plumstead	140	CO 30
Werda Rd	Durbanville	46	BQ 53
Werda St	Sack's Circle Ind.	88	CA 49
Werde St	Flintdale Est.	141	CP 31
Werk St	Ndabeni	83	CB 30
Wesbank Main Rd	Wesbank	107	CF 52
Weskrom Rd	Claremont	102	CH 31
Wesley	Bergvliet	140	CQ 27
Wesley Mabuza St	Nyanga	123	CK 41
Wesley Rd	Scottsville	63	BT 56
Wesley Rd	Sunnydale	185	DA 19
Wesley St	Cape Town Cen.	82	CB 23
Wesley St	Claremont	120	CJ 29
Wesley St	Gardens	82	CB 23
Wesley St	Oakdene	89	CC 54
Wesley St	Observatory	83	CC 28
Wesley St	Park Estates	174	CY 72
Wesley Way	Sir Lowry's Pass	176	CZ 81
Wespoort Dr.	Eastridge (M.Plain)	145	CQ 47
Wespoort Dr.	Mitchells Plain	144	CR 44
Wespoort Dr.	Portlands (M.Plain)	144	CQ 46
Wessel	Hoogstede	62	BU 54
Wessel	Kuilsrivier Ind.	89	CC 54
Wessel Cir.	Montana/Durrheim	104	CF 41
Wessel Cr.	Retreat	140	CR 29
Wessel Lourens	Sonnekuil	89	CA 53
Wessel Lourens	Sonnekuil	89	BY 54
Wessel Lourens Cr.	Tygerdal	59	BX 39
Wessel Lourens Dr.	Vredekloof	62	BT 53
Wessel Lourens Dr.	Vredekloof	62	BT 54
Wessel St North	Avondale	60	BX 45
Wessel St South	Avondale	87	BY 45
Wessels	Green Point	81	BZ 22
Wessels Rd	Kenilworth	120	CK 29
Wessels Rd	Table View	24	BN 28
Wessex Rd	Paarden Eiland	83	CA 28
Wessex Rd	Paarden Eiland	83	CA 29
Wessox St	Marlow	89	CA 54
West	Cloetesville	95	BZ 75
West Cl.	Salberau	86	CB 41
West Coast Rd	Blouberg Sands	24	BJ 29
West Cr.	Winslow	175	DC 76
West Cr.	Winslow	179	DD 76
West Flower Cl.	Montagu's Gift	141	CO 33
West Flower Cl.	Pelikan Pk	141	CR 34
West Link	Athlone	102	CF 33
West Peak Cl.	Somerset West	152	CS 78
West Quay Rd	Foreshore	82	BZ 23
West Rd	Bishop Lavis	105	CD 44
West Rd	Grassy Pk	141	CQ 32
West Rd	Somerset West	170	CU 72
West St	Cape Town Cen.	82	BZ 23
West St	Cravenby	87	CA 43
West St	Northern Paarl	18	AZ 89
West St	Park Estates	174	CZ 72
West St	Parow East	87	BY 45
West St	Wellington	10	AS 92
Westbank Main Rd	Wesbank	107	CF 51
Westbank Main Rd	Wesbank	107	CG 51
Westbourn Gr.	Parklands	25	BN 34
Westbourn Gr.	Parklands	25	BL 33
Westbrooke Rd	Athlone	102	CG 34
Westbury Circus	Wynberg	120	CL 30
Westbury Cr.	Highbury	107	CE 53
Westbury Rd	Muizenberg	159	CX 30
Westbury Rd	Rondebosch	101	CF 30
Westchester Mews	Milnerton	57	BT 32
Westerdale Rd	Meerendal	29	BN 47
Westerdale Rd	Vissershok	28	BN 46
Westerford Rd	Rondebosch	101	CG 28
Westerford Way	Hout Bay	137	CO 15
Westering	Wesbank	107	CG 51
Westerkim Rd	Skoongesig	45	BO 50
Western Blvd	Green Point	81	BY 21
Western Blvd	Green Point	81	BZ 22
Westerwijk Ave	Plattekloof Glen	59	BW 39
Westerwyk Cl.	Strandfontein	163	CU 43
Westford Rd	Hout Bay	136	CQ 14
Westfort Rd	Woodstock	83	CC 27
Westgate St	Observatory	83	CC 28
Westhof	De Bron	45	BS 48
Westhof	De Bron	45	BP 47
Westhoven St	Dal Josafat Ind.	18	BA 89
Westleton Way	Edgemead	58	BV 36
Westlake Ave	Stonehurst	158	CV 26
Westlake Dr.	Pollsmoor	158	CT 26
Westlake Dr.	Westlake Est.	158	CU 25
Westleigh Ave	Parklands	25	BN 33
Westminister Cl.	Portlands (M.Plain)	144	CR 46
Westminister Rd	Woodstock	83	CB 28
Westminster Rd	Lansdowne	121	CK 34
Westminster Rd	Noordhoek Manor	157	CX 20
Westminster Rd	Noordhoek Manor	157	CV 20
Westmore Rd	Gardens	81	CC 21
Westoe Rd	Observatory	101	CD 29
Weston	Kalk Bay	186	DA 26
Westray Steps	St James	187	CZ 27
Westridge Cir.	Sweet Valley	139	CR 26
Westridge Cl.	Sweet Valley	139	CR 26
Westside Cr.	Weltevreden Val. (M.Plain)	144	CQ 43
Westwind Rd	Tijgerhof	57	BV 33
Wetton Rd	Kenilworth	120	CL 29
Wetton Rd	Kenilworth	120	CL 30
Wetton Rd	Wetton	121	CL 34
Wetton Rd	Wynberg	120	CL 29
Wetton Rd	Youngsfield	121	CL 31
Wetwyn Rd	Ottery	121	CL 33
Wexford Rd	Connaught	87	CC 43
Wexford Rd	Vredehoek	82	CC 24
Weybridge	Wesbank	107	CG 51
Weyburn Rd	Lotus River	141	CP 34
Weyers Ave	Durbanville	45	BQ 50
Weymouth Rd	Observatory	101	CD 29
Wharf St	Cape Town Cen.	82	CA 24
Wheatfield Rd	Belthorn Est.	121	CJ 34
Wheatstone St	Belhar	88	CC 50
Wheelan St	Newlands	101	CH 27
Wherry Rd	Muizenberg	159	CX 29
Whimbrell Way	Pelikan Pk	142	CQ 35
Whippet Cl.	Strandfontein	162	CT 40
Whippet Cl.	Strandfontein	162	CV 42
Whistletree Cr.	Sonstraal Hgts	46	BP 54
Whitburn Way	Edgemead	58	BU 38
Whitby Rd	Plumstead	120	CM 28
White Hart La.	Weltevreden Val. (M.Plain)	124	CN 44
White Oak St	Oak Glen	62	BW 53
White Rd	Retreat Ind. Area	140	CS 28
White Rd	Rondebosch	101	CG 29
White St	Nooitgedacht	105	CE 43
White St	Plumstead	140	CO 29
White Water Cl.	Bloubergstrand	24	BM 28
Whitehall Cl.	Portlands (M.Plain)	145	CR 47
Whiteheart St	Jamestown	113	CH 75
Whitehouse Way	Epping Forest	86	CB 41
Whitford St	Tamboerskloof	81	CB 22
Whiting Cr.	Eersterivier	128	CN 59
Whitley	Rocklands (M.Plain)	145	CS 47
Whitney Cr.	Eersterivier	128	CN 61
Whittle Cr.	Onverwacht	175	DC 76
Whittle Way	Seaforth Sound	194	DJ 26
Whittlers Way	Hout Bay	117	CN 17
Whluwolu St	Crossroads	124	CK 45
Whytes Way	Simon's Town	191	DE 24
Wicht Cr.	District Six	82	CB 24
Wicht St	Lavender Hill	141	CS 31
Wicht St	Richmond	86	BY 41
Wickboom La.	Simon's Town	194	DJ 25
Wicklow Rd	Plumstead	120	CN 28
Wicklow Rd	Royal Cape	121	CM 32
Wielblom Cl.	Protea Village	64	BW 59
Wielblom Cl.	Roosendaal	106	CF 50
Wielblom Cl.	Roosendaal	106	CH 48
Wien Rd	Silversands	107	CH 54
Wiener Rd	Newlands	101	CH 28
Wiener St	Vasco Est.	59	BX 40
Wiener St	Vasco Est.	86	BY 40
Wienheim Pl.	Silversands	107	CH 53
Wiersma Rd	Rondebosch	101	CF 29
Wiersma St	Mabille Pk	89	CA 53
Wigam Way	Parklands	25	BN 34
Wigtown Rd	Green Point	81	BZ 21
Wijnland Villas	Bellair	62	BV 52
Wilberforce	Park Estates	174	CY 71
Wilberforce St	Lochnerhof	170	CX 71
Wilberforce St	Park Estates	170	CX 71
Wild Olive Cr.	Protea Village	63	BW 58
Wild Olive Cr.	Whispering Pines	175	DB 77
Wild Olive La.	Big Bay	24	BK 28
Wild Olive La.	Big Bay	24	BL 29
Wild Rose Cr.	Sonstraal Hgts	46	BP 54
Wildebees	Uitzicht	46	BO 54
Wildebees Rd	Eastridge (M.Plain)	145	CR 48
Wildebees Rd	Lotus River	142	CQ 35
Wildebees St	Somerset Hgts	127	CJ 57
Wildeboom Rd	Gordon Strand	179	DD 77
Wildebosch	Lieberheim	113	CG 76
Wildegans Way	Tarentaalplaas	175	DA 76
Wildeklawer	Green Oaks	95	BY 75
Wildeklawer	Green Oaks	95	BY 77
Wildeklawer	Stellenbosch	95	BY 75
Wilderness Rd	Claremont	120	CJ 29
Wildevoëlvlei Rd	Heron Pk	184	DB 16
Wilfrank Cr.	De Tuin	47	BS 55
Wilfrank Cr.	De Tuin	47	BP 58
Wilfred Rd	Simon's Town	194	DJ 23
Wilgas Way	Somerset West	171	CT 76
Wilge	Bracken Hgts	62	BU 54
Wilge Ave	Rusdal	108	CF 57
Wilge Ct	Delft	106	CG 49
Wilge Rd	Bishop Lavis	104	CD 41
Wilge Rd	Claremont	121	CJ 31
Wilge St	Forest Village	127	CM 58
Wilgeboom	Northpine	64	BU 59
Wilgehof Cl.	Mitchells Plain	144	CQ 45
Wilgen Ct	Edgemead	59	BU 39
Wilger	Cloetesville	95	BZ 76
Wilger	Delft Sth	125	CJ 49
Wilger Cr.	Tygerdal	58	BX 37
Wilger Rd	Sonnedal	59	BV 42
Wilger Sq.	Bridgetown	103	CE 36
Wilger St	Amanda Glen	46	BS 52
Wilgerboom	Lentegeur (M.Plain)	144	CO 45
Wilgerivier Cl.	Portlands (M.Plain)	144	CQ 45
Wilgespruit Cr.	Langeberg Rdg	47	BR 55
Wilgespruit Cr.	Lemoenkloof	18	BB 89
Wilhelmina Rd	Somerset West	171	CT 76
Wilhelmina Schaefer St	Gustrow	175	DA 75
Wilhelmina St	Franschhoek Sth	79	BZ 107
Wilhelmina St	Rondebosch	101	CF 29
Wilhelmus Rd	Surrey	103	CH 37
Wilkinson St	Gardens	81	CB 22
Wilkinson St	Newlands	101	CG 28
Wilkshire St	Belgravia	103	CG 35
Will Nero Link	Connaught	87	CB 44
Will Nero Link	Connaught	87	CB 46
Willem Basson St	Wellington	10	AS 94
Willem St	Bothasig	42	BS 37
Willesden Rd	Camps Bay	98	CE 18
Willet Cr.	Pelikan Pk	141	CR 34
William Arendse Rd	Penlyn Est.	122	CJ 35
William Cl.	Gustrow	175	DB 75
William Cl.	Gustrow	175	DB 77
William Cr.	Belhar	88	CC 48
William Dabs St	Brackenfell	63	BV 55
William Frederick Rd	Bergvliet	139	CP 26
William Hartel	Bellville Sth Ind.	88	CA 50
William Link	Belhar	107	CD 51
William Link	Belhar	107	CG 53
William Mason Rd	Bishop Lavis	105	CD 43
William Mason St	Ysterplaat	84	BY 31
William Mkhaba St	Kuyasa	147	CS 56
William Penn St	Milnerton	41	BS 34
William Rd	Observatory	101	CD 29
William Rd	Penlyn Est.	103	CH 35
William Sergeant St	Sir Lowry's Pass	176	CZ 81
William St	Bloekombos	48	BR 62
William St	Maitland	84	CA 32
William St	Oakdene	89	CC 53
William St	Scottsdene	64	BT 61
William St	Woodstock	82	CB 26
William Stewart St	Gustrow	175	DA 75
William Taylor Way	Marlow	88	CA 50
Williams	Cloetesville	95	BY 75
Williams	Cloetesville	95	BZ 75
Williams Ave	Grassy Pk	141	CQ 34
Williams Ave	Wellington	15	AV 91
Williams St	Avondale	87	BY 44
Williams St	Fairfield	87	BY 44
Williams St	Northern Paarl	18	AZ 89
Williams St	Sir Lowry's Pass	176	CZ 82
Willie Cr.	Scottsdene	64	BT 60
Willie Faasen St	N1 City	59	BX 40
Willie Hofmeyer Ave	Sanlamhof	88	BY 50
Willie St	Wesbank	107	CE 52
Willie van Schoor Ave	Oakdale	61	BV 49
Willis St	Athlone	102	CG 34
Willis St	Lotus River	141	CQ 34
Williston Rd	Knole Pk	142	CO 36
Willoughby Dr.	Chapman's Peak	156	CW 17
Willoughby Dr.	Chapman's Peak	156	CX 17
Willow Ave	New Orleans	19	BB 91
Willow Cl.	Green Oaks	95	BY 75
Willow Rd	Belle Constantia	139	CP 25
Willow Rd	Blouberg Rise	25	BN 31
Willow Rd	Kaymor	62	BX 52
Willow Rd	Kaymor	62	BX 53
Willow Rd	Kaymor	89	BY 52
Willow Rd	Lotus River	141	CP 33
Willow Rd	Newlands	100	CH 26
Willow Rd	Observatory	83	CC 30
Willow Rd	Parkwood	141	CO 32
Willow Rd	Rosedale	128	CK 59
Willow Rd	Somerset West	170	CU 73
Willow Rd	Weltevreden Val. (M.Plain)	143	CO 42
Willow Rd	Wetton	121	CL 34
Willow Ridge	Milnerton	41	BS 33
Willow St	Chapman's Peak	156	CW 16
Willow St	Eastridge (M.Plain)	145	CR 48
Willow St	Hillcrest Hgts	127	CL 57
Willow St	Silveroaks	90	CC 55
Willow St	Sunnydale	185	CZ 19
Willow Way	Belhar	106	CD 47
Willow Way	Hout Bay	137	CO 15
Willow Way	Penhill	128	CK 61
Willow Way	Pinelands	84	CC 34
Willow Way	Sir Lowry's Pass	176	CZ 81
Willow Wk	Parkwood	141	CO 32
Willowbrook	Sonstraal Hgts	46	BQ 54
Willowbrooke La.	Alphen	119	CM 26
Willowmere Rd	Elfindale	140	CQ 29
Willowmore Cl.	Portlands (M.Plain)	144	CR 46
Willowspring	Voorbrug	106	CG 50
Willowspring	Voorbrug	106	CH 52
Wills Rd	Rosebank	101	CF 29
Wilmar St	Lavender Hill	160	CT 30
Wilmot Rd	Tijgerhof	57	BW 32
Wilshammer St	Cape Town Cen.	88	BY 48
Wilson Rd	Wynberg	120	CM 29
Wilton Dyeshana St	Gugulethu	123	CK 41
Wilton Dyeshana St	Gugulethu	123	CL 41
Wilton Mkwayi St	Mandela Pk	146	CR 54
Wiltshire Cr.	Kirstenhof	159	CU 27
Wiltshire Pl.	Kirstenhof	159	CU 27
Wiltshire Pl.	Kirstenhof	159	CW 27
Wimbledon Cr.	Weltevreden Val. (M.Plain)	143	CO 42
Wimbledon Rd	Blackheath Ind.	108	CE 56
Wimbledon Rd	Blackheath Ind.	108	CF 55
Wimbledon Rd	Blackheath Ind.	108	CG 55

Abbreviations used: Ave – Avenue, A.H. – Agricultural Holding, A.L.– Algemene Landgoed, Blvd – Boulevard, Cen. – Central, Cir. – Circle, Cl. – Close, Cr. – Crescent, Ct – Court, Dr. – Drive, Est. – Estate, Ext. – Extension, Hgts – Heights, Ind. – Industrial, Gdns – Gardens, Gr. – Grove, La. – Lane, (M.Plain) - Mitchells Plain, Nth – North, Pl. – Place, Pk – Park, Rd – Road, Rdg. – Ridge, S.H.– Small Holding, Sq. – Square, St – Street, Sth – South, Ter. – Terrace, Tn – Turn, Val. – Valley, Wk – Walk

STREET NAME	SUBURB NAME	PG	GRID	
Wimbledon St	Beacon Valley (M.Plain)	145	CP	48
Wimbledon Way	Edgemead	58	BV	38
Wimbledon Way	Parklands	25	BN	33
Wimbrel Ave	Table View	41	BQ	32
Wimple La.	Ottery East	121	CN	34
Wincester Ln.	Westlake Est.	158	CU	24
Winch Way	Blouberg Sands	24	BM	30
Winchester Ave	Bishopscourt	119	CJ	25
Winchester Ave	Noordhoek Manor	157	CX	21
Winchester Cl.	Dreyersdal	140	CS	27
Winchester Cr.	Jagtershof	108	CD	56
Winchester Rd	Blue Downs	127	CJ	56
Winchester Rd	Blue Downs	127	CN	55
Winchester Rd	Observatory	101	CD	29
Winchester Rd	West Beach	24	BN	30
Wincraig St	Brackenfell	63	BW	56
Windblom Rd	Bloubergstrand	24	BM	28
Windburg Ave	Devil's Peak Est.	82	CC	24
Windell Rd	Goodwood Est.	85	BY	38
Windell Rd	Plattekloof	60	BW	43
Windell St	Brackenfell Sth	63	BW	57
Windell St	Durbanville	46	BP	51
Windermere Rd	Muizenberg	159	CW	30
Windflower	Wesbank	107	CF	51
Windhoek	Arauna	63	BU	55
Windhover St	Kirstenhof	159	CT	27
Windjammer Rd	Anchorage Pk	175	DC	77
Windjammer Rd	Anchorage Pk	175	DB	78
Windjammer Rd	Anchorage Pk	179	DD	77
Windlass Way	Blouberg Sands	24	BM	29
Windmeul St	St Michaels	63	BU	56
Windmeul St	St Michaels	63	BV	56
Windmill	Wellington	12	AV	82
Windsor Cl.	Noordhoek Manor	157	CX	21
Windsor Cl.	Ottery East	121	CN	34
Windsor Cl.	Portlands (M.Plain)	145	CR	47
Windsor Cl.	West Beach	24	BN	29
Windsor Ct	Edgemead	59	BU	39
Windsor La.	Dennedal	139	CS	26
Windsor Park Ave	Elfindale	140	CQ	30
Windsor Pl.	Ruyterwacht	86	CA	40
Windsor Rd	Diep River	140	CO	28
Windsor Rd	Dreyersdal	140	CS	27
Windsor Rd	Kalk Bay	186	DA	26
Windsor Rd	Lansdowne	121	CJ	33
Windsor Rd	Oostersee	60	BX	45
Windsor Rd	Plumstead	120	CN	28
Windsor Rd	Somerset West	171	CT	76
Windsor Rd	West Beach	24	BN	30
Windsor St	Camelot	107	CF	53
Windsor Way	Northpine	64	BU	59
Winery	Altydgedacht	44	BS	46
Winery Rd	Somerset West	150	CO	69
Winery Rd	Somerset West	150	CP	68
Winery Rd	Somerset West	150	CR	68
Winery Way	Devonvallei	112	CD	73
Wingate Cr.	Sunningdale	25	BN	31
Wingate Sq.	Sunningdale	25	BN	31
Wingerd Dr.	Vredekloof	62	BT	53
Wingerd Dr.	Vredekloof	62	BU	53
Wingerd Rd	Nova Constantia	139	CQ	24
Wingerd Rd	Somerset West	170	CT	72
Wingerd Rd	Sonstraal	46	BR	52
Wingfield	Factreton	85	BZ	35
Wingfield Pl.	Monte Vista	59	BW	39
Wingfield Rd	Bothasig	42	BS	36
Wingfield St	Wellington	10	AR	92
Winkle Way	Clovelly	186	DA	24
Winkle Way	Sunset Beach	41	BS	31
Winnie Mandela Cr.	Mandela Pk	147	CQ	55
Winnipeg Rd	Coniston Pk	159	CU	30
Winnipeg St	Portlands (M.Plain)	144	CQ	45
Winslow Cr.	Eersterivier	128	CN	61
Winstonia Rd	Sea Point	81	BZ	20
Winstonia Rd	Sea Point	81	CA	20
Winter Cl.	Montagu's Gift	141	CO	34
Winter Cr.	Surrey	103	CG	37
Winter Pl.	Belhar	107	CD	51
Winterberg	Brackenfell	63	BW	55
Winterberg	Wellington	15	AV	91
Winterberg	Wellington	15	AU	94
Winterberg Rd	Heideveld	104	CG	39
Winterberg Rd	Lavender Hill East	160	CU	32
Winterberg Rd	Lavender Hill East	160	CX	33
Winterberg St	Bonnie Brae	47	BP	57
Winterberg St	Bonnie Brae	47	BO	58
Winterhoek Rd	Durbanville Hills	45	BR	49
Winterhoek St	Edgemead	58	BV	36
Winterhoek St	Tafelsig (M.Plain)	145	CS	49
Winterswynd Way	Bishopscourt	119	CJ	25
Winterton St	Edgemead	59	BT	39
Wintervogel Cl.	Mitchells Plain	144	CS	45
Wintervogel Cl.	Mitchells Plain	144	CS	43
Winton Cl.	Strandfontein	163	CT	43
Winton Cr.	Woodbridge Island	57	BW	31
Winton Rd	Blue Downs	127	CJ	56
Wireless Rd	Kommetjie	183	DB	13
Wisbeach Rd	Sea Point	81	BZ	20
Wistaria Ave	Pinelands	102	CD	34
Wistaria Cl.	Dolphin Beach	41	BP	31
Wisteria Cl.	Newlands	101	CG	28
Wisteria Cl.	Somerset West	171	CW	77
Wisteria Rd	Belhar	87	CC	46
Wisteria Rd	Claremont	120	CJ	29
Wisteria Rd	Claremont	120	CK	30
Wisteria Rd	Ridgeworth	61	BV	49
Wisteria St	Klein Nederburg	19	BC	92
Wisteria St	Klein Nederburg	19	AZ	94
Wit Els Ave	New Orleans	18	BA	90
Witberg	Brackenfell	63	BV	55
Witberg	Brackenfell	63	BV	58
Witberg Rd	Heideveld	104	CG	39
Witboom Rd	Kenridge	45	BS	49
Witels	Delft Sth	125	CJ	49
Witels Cl.	Plattekloof	60	BV	43
Witels St	Eersterivier	128	CN	59
Witels St	Morgenster Hoogte	63	BU	55
Withaak Cl.	Die Oude Spruit	63	BX	56
Withycombe Cl.	Barbarossa	119	CN	26
Witkaree St	Springbok Pk	62	BV	54
Witkaree St	Tygerdal	58	BX	37
Witneys La.	Newlands	101	CG	28
Witogie St	Amstelhof	23	BD	93
Witsenberg Rd	Lavender Hill East	160	CU	32
Witsuikerbos St	Bellville Ext. 53	60	BU	46
Witteberg	Wellington	15	AV	91
Wittebol St	Perm Gdns	128	CK	59
Wittebomen Cl.	Mitchells Plain	144	CS	45
Witteboom	Normandie	64	BW	59
Witteboomen Rd	Silverhurst	119	CN	24
Witzenberg	Belhar	106	CD	49
Witzenberg Dr.	Eversdal	61	BU	50
Witzenberg Dr.	Eversdal	62	BU	51
Witzenberg Rd	Durbanville Hills	45	BR	49
Witzenberg St	Tafelsig (M.Plain)	145	CR	49
Wodehouse Cr.	The Vines	140	CO	27
Wodin Rd	Newlands	101	CH	28
Woko Cr.	Victoria Mxenge	146	CO	51
Wolborough Rd	Kenilworth	120	CK	28
Wolf	Delft Sth	125	CK	48
Wolf Kibel Cr.	Woodlands (M.Plain)	124	CN	45
Wolf Power Cl.	Lekkerwater	184	CY	18
Wolfberg Rd	Heideveld	103	CF	38
Wolfberg St	Tafelsig (M.Plain)	145	CS	49
Wolfe St	Wynberg	120	CL	28
Wolga	Bishop Lavis	104	CD	41
Wolhuter Rd	Selborne	61	BV	47
Wolmarans St	Flintdale Est.	141	CO	31
Wolmunster St	Rosebank	101	CE	29
Wolraad Rd	Maitland	85	BZ	35
Wolseley Cl.	Richwood	42	BQ	38
Wolseley Cl.	Richwood	42	BQ	37
Wolseley St	Panorama	59	BV	41
Wolsey Rd	Lansdowne	102	CH	32
Woltemade	Die Boord	113	CE	75
Woltemade Rd	Stellenberg	62	BU	52
Woltemade St	Park Estates	170	CX	71
Woltemade St	Park Estates	170	CX	72
Woltenburg Cl.	Mitchells Plain	144	CR	45
Woltenburg Cl.	Mitchells Plain	144	CR	43
Wolvengat	Wesbank	107	CG	51
Wolwedans Cr.	Belhar	107	CD	51
Wolwefontein Ave	Northpine	64	BU	59
Wonderboom Ave	New Orleans	19	BA	91
Wonderboom St	Eversdal Hgts	46	BS	51
Wonker	Voorbrug	106	CG	50
Wonker	Voorbrug	106	CH	48
Wood Cl.	Capri Village	184	DB	18
Wood Cl.	San Michel	157	CX	19
Wood Dr.	Parklands	25	BM	33
Wood Dr.	Parklands	25	BN	33
Wood Dr.	Parklands	25	BN	34
Wood Dr.	Sunridge	41	BP	33
Wood Dr.	Table View	41	BO	34
Wood Rd	Capri Village	184	DB	18
Wood Rd	Hout Bay	137	CP	16
Wood Rd	Ottery	121	CM	32
Wood Rd	Rondebosch	102	CF	31
Wood Rd	Rondebosch	102	CG	31
Wood St	Eersterivier	128	CM	60
Wood Way	Simon's Town	190	DD	22
Wood Way	Simon's Town	191	DD	23
Woodbine Rd	Rondebosch	101	CF	28
Woodburn Cr.	Gardens	99	CD	21
Woodbury Ave	Ottery East	121	CN	34
Woodbury Cl.	Lansdowne	121	CK	32
Woodbury Cr.	Weltevreden Val. (M.Plain)	143	CQ	43
Woodbury La.	Epping Forest	86	CC	41
Woodbury Rd	Lansdowne	121	CJ	32
Woodbury Rd	Lansdowne	121	CK	32
Woodbush Way	Northpine	63	BU	58
Woodcutters Cl.	Hout Bay	117	CN	17
Woodcutters Way	Summer Greens	58	BV	36
Wooddale Rd	Ottery East	121	CN	34
Woodford Ave	Camps Bay	99	CE	19
Woodford Ave	Camps Bay	99	CE	18
Woodford Rd	Epping Forest	86	CC	42
Woodford Rd	Epping Forest	86	CB	39
Woodgate Rd	Plumstead	120	CN	30
Woodgate Rd	Plumstead	120	CO	30
Woodglen	Schuilplaats	113	CF	75
Woodhead Cl.	Camps Bay	99	CE	19
Woodhead Dr.	Edgemead	59	BT	39
Woodhead St	Tafelsig (M.Plain)	145	CS	48
Woodlands	Barbarossa	120	CN	28
Woodlands	Bergvliet	140	CR	27
Woodlands Cl.	Kraaifontein	47	BQ	58
Woodlands Cl.	Parklands	25	BM	32
Woodlands Cl.	Pinelands	84	CC	32
Woodlands Dr.	Richwood	42	BP	37
Woodlands Dr.	Sonstraal Hgts	46	BQ	54
Woodlands Rd	Ottery	121	CL	34
Woodlands Rd	Ottery	121	CM	34
Woodlands Rd	Ottery East	121	CN	34
Woodlands Rd	Rondebosch	101	CF	30
Woodlands Rd	Somerset West	170	CT	74
Woodlands Rd	Woodstock	82	CB	26
Woodlands Way	Edgemead	58	BU	38
Woodlands Way	Parklands	25	BM	32
Woodley Rd	Plumstead	120	CN	30
Woodley Rd	Plumstead	141	CO	31
Woodman	Idasvallei	96	CA	80
Woodpecker	Seawinds	160	CU	31
Woodpecker Cl.	Fish Hoek	186	DA	23
Woodpecker Cl.	Ottery	122	CL	35
Woodpecker Cl.	Ottery	122	CN	36
Woodpecker Rise	Somerset West	171	CW	77
Woodpecker Way	Sunbird Pk	107	CF	54
Woodrow Way	Pelikan Pk	141	CR	34
Woodroyd La.	Rondebosch	101	CF	28
Woodside Ct	Rondebosch	102	CF	32
Woodside Dr.	Pinelands	84	CC	33
Woodside Rd	Lansdowne	121	CK	34
Woodside Rd	Ottery	121	CM	33
Woodside Rd	Tamboerskloof	81	CB	21
Woodville Rd	Flintdale Est.	140	CP	29
Woodville Rd	Lotus River	141	CP	34
Woodward Cl.	Ocean View	184	DC	16
Woodward Cl.	Ocean View	184	DC	17
Woodwind Cir.	Retreat	159	CT	30
Woody St	Tafelsig (M.Plain)	145	CS	48
Woolf Way	Kenridge	61	BT	49
Woollens St	Dal Josafat Ind.	22	BD	89
Woolmore St	Hazendal	102	CE	33
Woolsack Dr.	Rondebosch	101	CE	29
Woolsack Dr.	Rosebank	101	CE	29
Worcester Cl.	Norwood	86	CA	41
Worcester Cl.	Richwood	42	BQ	38
Worcester Cl.	Richwood	42	BQ	37
Worcester Rd	Claremont	120	CJ	29
Worcester Rd	Sea Point	81	BZ	19
Worcester Rd	Woodstock	83	CC	25
Worcester St	Hout Bay	136	CP	14
Worcester St	Hout Bay	137	CP	15
Worcester St	Panorama	59	BV	41
Wormwood La.	Woodstock	83	CC	27
Wortelboom	Delft Sth	125	CK	49
Worthing Mews	Sunset Links	57	BT	32
Worthing Way	Parklands	25	BM	33
Woudenberg	Morgen Gronde	63	BX	55
Wrasse St	Soneike II	89	BZ	54
Wraysbury Cl.	Claremont	101	CH	29
Wren Cl.	Montagu's Gift	141	CO	33
Wren Sargent Cr.	Woodlands (M.Plain)	144	CO	45
Wren St	Brooklyn	84	BY	31
Wren Way	Meadowridge	140	CP	27
Wrensch Rd	Churchill	59	BX	42
Wrensch Rd	Glenlily	87	BY	43
Wrensch Rd	Observatory	83	CC	29
Wright Cl.	Woodlands (M.Plain)	144	CP	45
Wright St	Woodstock	82	CB	26
Wuppertal	Eersterivier	128	CL	60
Wuprertal Cl.	Mitchells Plain	144	CQ	44
Wurzburg Ave	Lansdowne	121	CJ	32
Wuthering Heights	Sonstraal Hgts	46	BR	54
Wycombe Ave	Rust-en-vrede	119	CN	26
Wydgelee Cr.	Wesbank	107	CG	51
Wye La.	Manenberg	123	CK	39
Wye Rd	Manenberg	123	CK	39
Wye Rd	Schaap Kraal	123	CK	39
Wyecroft Rd	Observatory	101	CD	29
Wyehill Cl.	Retreat	140	CS	29
Wyehill Way	Retreat	140	CS	29
Wygt St	Northern Paarl	18	AZ	89
Wyland Rd	Bothasig	58	BT	38
Wylant St	Welgemoed	61	BU	47
Wynand Rd	Muizenberg Nth	159	CW	28
Wynberg Pl.	Wynberg	120	CM	29
Wynberg St	Paarlzicht	19	BC	91
Wyndover Rd	Claremont	102	CH	31
Wyngaard Link	Ocean View	184	DC	16
Wyngaard Link	Ocean View	184	DC	17
Wynn Rd	Goodwood Est.	85	BY	38
Wynne St	Avondale	87	BY	44
Wynne St	Fairfield	87	BY	44
Wynsam Sq.	Flintdale Est.	141	CQ	31
Wynyard St	Oranjezicht	82	CC	23
Wynyard St	Table View	41	BP	32
Wyoming St	Stellenridge	62	BV	51
Wytham Ave	Kenilworth	120	CK	28
Wythenshawe Ave	Pinelands	84	CB	34
X				
X E Magqwashe St	Gugulethu	123	CK	41
Xaba Rd	Nyanga	124	CK	43
Xabiso Sq.	Eyethu	146	CP	53
Xafile Cr.	Victoria Mxenge	146	CO	52
Xaki St	Tarentaalplaas	170	CX	74
Xaki St	Tarentaalplaas	171	CX	75
Xam Cl.	Crossroads	124	CK	45
Xameni Cr.	Victoria Mxenge	146	CO	52
Xaso Cr.	Victoria Mxenge	126	CN	51
Xavier St	Hohelzen	61	BW	47
Xawuka Cr.	Nonqubela	126	CN	52
Xelela St	Umrhabulo Triangle	147	CQ	57
Xelo St	Nomzano	175	CZ	76
Xengxe	Nonqubela	146	CO	53
Xhala Cr.	Nonqubela	126	CN	52
Xhalanga	Dunoon	42	BO	37
Xhalanga	Dunoon	42	BO	38
Xhalanga	Philippi East	124	CM	46
Xhalanga Ave	Joe Slovo Pk	57	BV	34
Xhalanga Ave	Joe Slovo Pk	57	BU	31
Xhegwana Cl.	Nonqubela	126	CN	52
Xibi St	Nonqubela	146	CO	53
Xobo St	Driftsands	126	CL	51
Xola St	Mxolisi Phetani	125	CM	50
Xolani Rd	Ekuphumuleni	146	CQ	53
Xolani Sq.	Guguletu	104	CH	41
Xolile Donster St	Crossroads	124	CJ	44
Xuka Ct	Delft	106	CG	48
Xuka St	Mfuleni	126	CJ	53
Xwayi Cr.	Driftsands	126	CL	51
Xyris Way	Matroosfontein	86	CC	42
Y				
Yacht	Strandfontein	162	CT	41
Yacht Rd	Sanddrift	57	BW	34
Yakhani St	Mxolisi Phetani	125	CM	50
Yanta Ave	Nyanga	123	CK	42
Yardley Cl.	Epping Forest	86	CC	42
Yarmouth Rd	Muizenberg	159	CW	29
Yarmouth St	Somerset West	170	CW	72
Yarrow Rd	Milnerton	57	BV	32
Yarrowdale	Pinelands	84	CB	34
Yataghan La.	Crofters Valley	185	CY	19
Yawl Rd	Pelikan Pk	141	CR	34
Yazo St	Umrhabulo Triangle	147	CQ	56
Yeki St	Victoria Mxenge	146	CO	52
Yekiso Cl.	Langa	103	CE	37
Yellow Oak St	Oak Glen	62	BW	53
Yellow Oak St	Oak Glen	62	BX	52
Yellowood Cl.	Somerset West	171	CW	76
Yellowood Rd	Weltevreden Val. (M.Plain)	143	CO	42
Yellowstone Cr.	Coniston Pk	159	CU	30
Yellowwood Cl.	Parklands	25	BN	33
Yellowwood Cr.	Dieprivier	140	CO	28
Yellowwood Cr.	Tygerdal	58	BX	37
Yellowwood Dr.	Noordhoek	156	CW	18
Yellowwood Rd	Bonteheuwel	103	CE	38
Yellowwood Rd	Eersterivier	127	CM	58
Yellowwood Rd	Greenlands	88	CA	48
Yellowwood St	Eastridge (M.Plain)	145	CR	47
Yellowwood St	Tafelsig (M.Plain)	145	CS	47
Yellowwood St	Tafelsig (M.Plain)	164	CT	47
Yena St	Umrhabulo Triangle	147	CQ	56
Yengeni Cr.	Mxolisi Phetani	125	CM	50
Yeoman St	Mitchells Plain	144	CQ	45
Yeoville Rd	Vredehoek	82	CC	23
Yew St	Salt River	83	CB	27
Yeyi Cr.	Eyethu	146	CP	54
Yeza Rd	Nyanga	124	CK	43
Yinlan	Vredekloof Hgts	47	BS	55
Yisa St	Ilitha Pk	146	CQ	52
Ylang-Ylang St	Silversands	107	CH	54
Yoksal Rd	Lavender Hill	160	CT	31
Yolan Du Preez St	Fisantekraal	31	BK	58
Yomelela Ave	Dunoon	26	BN	38
York	Muizenberg	159	CX	29
York Cl.	Hout Bay Harbour	136	CR	13
York Cl.	Milnerton Rdg	41	BS	34
York Cl.	Milnerton Rdg	41	BS	33
York Cl.	Parklands	25	BM	33
York Cr.	Malibu Village	127	CK	56
York Cr.	Ottery	122	CM	35
York La.	Parklands	25	BM	33
York La.	Rosebank	101	CE	30
York Pl.	Klein Begin	48	BS	60
York Rd	Green Point	81	BZ	22
York Rd	Lansdowne	121	CK	34
York Rd	Ottery	122	CL	35
York Rd	Rosebank	101	CE	29
York Rd	Stellenryk	62	BT	52
York Rd	Wellington	10	AR	92
York Rd	Windsor Park Est.	47	BR	58
York Rd	Windsor Pk	47	BR	57
York Rd	Wynberg	120	CM	29
York St	Bloubergstrand	24	BM	28
York St	Claremont	120	CJ	30
York St	Cravenby	87	CB	43
York St	Klein Begin	48	BS	60
York St	Manenberg	123	CK	39
York St	Winslow	175	DC	77
York St	Woodstock	83	CB	27
York Way	Matroosfontein	86	CC	42
Yorkshire Cl.	Kirstenhof	159	CU	27
Yorkshire Cl.	Kirstenhof	159	CW	27
Yorkshire St	Lansdowne	121	CK	34
Yorkton Rd	Grassy Pk	141	CR	32
Yoto St	Lwandle	175	CZ	76
Young La.	Tokai	139	CS	26
Young La.	Wynberg	120	CL	28
Young St	Park Estates	174	CY	72
Ypres	Courtrai	22	BH	87
Ysberg St	St Michaels	63	BU	55
Yselstein St	Glencairn Hgts	191	DD	24
Ysterhout	Delft Sth	125	CJ	49
Ysterhout Ave	New Orleans	19	BB	91
Ysterhout Ave	New Orleans	19	AZ	94
Ysterhout Cl.	Plattekloof	60	BU	43

STREET NAME	SUBURB NAME	PG	GRID	
Ysterhout Cr.	Rouxville	90	CA	56
Ysterhout St	Stikland Hospital	62	BW	51
Ysterhout St	Vredekloof	62	BT	54
Ysterplaat St	Brooklyn	84	BZ	31
Yubel Rd	Retreat	140	CS	29
Yudelmans La.	Plumstead	120	CN	29
Yusuf Arafat Cr.	Mandela Pk	146	CR	54
Yusuf Dadoo St	Mandela Pk	146	CR	53
Yusuf Dr.	Schotsche Kloof	81	CA	22
Yusuf Gool Blvd.	Gatesville	103	CG	37
Yusuf Rd	Welcome	103	CF	38
Yuyu St	Nonqubela	126	CN	52
Yvette St	De Tijger	60	BW	44
Yvonne Rd	Plumstead	120	CN	30
Yvonne St	Beacon Valley (M.Plain)	145	CP	48
Yvonne St	Hohelzen	61	BW	47
Yvonne St	Scottsdene	64	BT	60
Z				
Z.K.Matthews Cr.	Driftsands	147	CQ	56
Z.Memani Rd	Nyanga	123	CJ	42
Zaanstrom Cl.	Dennemere	108	CH	57
Zabalazo	Mbekweni	15	AX	91
Zaida St	Casablanca	175	DA	75
Zak St	Schaap Kraal	123	CK	39
Zakhele St	Kaya	146	CQ	51
Zakhele St	Kaya	146	CQ	52
Zakheni St	Mxolisi Phetani	125	CM	49
Zakuza	Mbekweni	15	AV	91
Zaleni St	Kaya	146	CP	51
Zalkin St	Rugby	57	BX	32
Zalman St	Kenridge	61	BT	49
Zama Cl.	Gugulethu	104	CG	40
Zama St	Ilitha Pk	146	CR	52
Zamani	Mbekweni	15	AX	91
Zamani St	Mxolisi Phetani	125	CM	50
Zambesi Ave	Belthorn Est.	121	CJ	34
Zambesi Rd	Bonnie Brook	47	BQ	57
Zambezi Ct	Delft	106	CF	49
Zambezi St	Kenridge Hgts	45	BS	48
Zambezi St	Mfuleni	126	CK	54
Zambezi St	Mfuleni	126	CK	52
Zambezi Way	Portlands (M.Plain)	144	CQ	46
Zami Joseph St	Kuyasa	147	CS	55
Zanazo St	Bloekombos	48	BR	62
Zandberg St	Somerset West	151	CQ	71
Zanddrift Cl.	Brackenfell Sth	63	BX	56
Zandile St	Bloekombos	48	BR	62
Zandkloof Ave	Voorbrug	106	CG	50
Zandkloof Dr.	Langeberg Glen	47	BQ	56
Zandkloof Park	Goedemoed	46	BO	54
Zandkloof Rd	Goedemoed	46	BO	54
Zandkloof Rd	Sonstraal Hgts	46	BO	54
Zandvlei Cl.	Mitchells Plain	144	CQ	45
Zandvliet	Kirstenhof	158	CU	26
Zandvliet Cl.	Richwood	42	BQ	37
Zandvliet Rd	Macassar	149	CR	65
Zandvliet Rd	Macassar	149	CS	65
Zandvliet St	Somerset West	152	CS	75
Zandvoort Cl.	Northpine	63	BU	58
Zandvoort Rd	Edgemead	58	BV	38
Zandwijk Cl.	Sunnydale	185	DA	20
Zandzicht Cl.	Uitzicht	47	BO	55
Zantsi Cr.	Crossroads	124	CK	45
Zantsi St	Kaya	146	CP	52
Zaphola	Mbekweni	15	AX	91
Zaragoza St	Wesbank	107	CE	52
Zarobi Rd	Lotus River	141	CP	34
Zastron Rd	Milnerton	57	BV	32
Zazulwana Cr.	Brown's Farm	124	CL	43
Zeanette St	Casablanca	175	DB	76
Zebra Cr.	Eastridge (M.Plain)	145	CR	48
Zebra St	Goedemoed	46	BP	54
Zee Ct	Marina Da Gama	159	CV	29
Zeederberg St	Paarl	22	BE	88
Zeekoe Rd	Lotus River	141	CP	34
Zeekoe Rd	Lotus River	141	CQ	34
Zeekoevlei Rd	Pelikan Pk	142	CR	36
Zeekoevlei Rd	Pelikan Pk	142	CS	35
Zeekoevlei Rd	Zeekoevlei	161	CT	35
Zeeland Cr.	West Riding	41	BO	34
Zeeland St	Ruwari	63	BV	57
Zeepaard Way	Dennemere	108	CH	57
Zeepaard Way	Dennemere	108	CH	58
Zeerust Cl.	Portlands (M.Plain)	144	CR	46
Zeezicht Cl.	Richwood	42	BP	38
Zelani Mkhonza St	Kuyasa	147	CS	55
Zelani Mkhonza St	Kuyasa	147	CS	58
Zelda St	Elsies River Ind.	86	BZ	41
Zelda St	Hohelzen	61	BW	47
Zenith Cr.	Rocklands (M.Plain)	145	CS	47
Zenith Rd	Vanguard	103	CF	38
Zenith Way	Matroosfontein	86	CC	42
Zenzile St	Bloekombos	48	BR	62
Zephania Mothopeng	Weltevreden Val. (M.Plain)	123	CM	41
Zepplin St	The Hague	106	CF	49
Zero	Rocklands (M.Plain)	163	CT	45
Zethu St	Kaya	146	CP	52
Zetler	William Lloyd	23	BD	92
Zeus Cl.	Eureka	87	CC	44
Zeus Cl.	Woodlands (M.Plain)	144	CP	44
Zeus Dr.	Phoenix	57	BU	33
Zeus St	Park Village	127	CK	58
Zevendal Way	Zevendal	90	CC	58
Zevenzicht Dr.	Zevenzicht	90	CC	58
Zibeleni Pl.	Mfuleni	127	CL	55
Ziduli St	Victoria Mxenge	146	CO	52
Zifandel Cl.	Zevenzicht	90	CC	58
Zikhonkwane Rd	Philippi East	124	CM	46
Zimri St	Marlow	88	CA	50
Zinfandel St	Somerset West	151	CR	71
Zingela St	Umrhabulo Triangle	147	CQ	56
Zingisa St	Kaya	146	CP	52
Zingisa St	Kaya	146	CS	52
Zingizani	Mbekweni	15	AW	91
Zinnia	Lentegeur (M.Plain)	145	CP	47
Zinnia Cr.	Dalvale	19	AY	92
Zinnia Cr.	Dalvale	19	BA	94
Zinnia Rd	Ridgeworth	61	BV	50
Zinnia Rd	Silvertown	103	CF	35
Zinnia Rd	Tygerdal	58	BX	37
Zinnia Rd	Uitsig	87	CB	44
Zinnia St	Franschhoek Nth	75	BX	104
Zinnia St	Protea Hoogte	63	BX	57
Zinnia St	Sarepta	89	CC	52
Zinto St	Kaya	146	CP	51
Zinzani	Mbekweni	15	AX	92
Zion Rd	Claremont	120	CJ	27
Zion St	Paarl	22	BD	88
Zion St	Paarl	22	BE	88
Ziquamo Ave	Mfuleni	127	CL	55
Zircon Cir.	Sheridon Pk	159	CU	29
Zirconia Cr.	Highbury	108	CD	55
Zisa Cr.	Umrhabulo Triangle	147	CQ	56
Zither St	Steenberg	159	CT	30
Ziwane St	Lwandle	175	CZ	77
Zodiac Rd	Ocean View	183	DC	14
Zodiac St	Kaya	146	CQ	51
Zodiac St	Kaya	146	CQ	52
Zoete Inval Cl.	Mitchells Plain	144	CR	44
Zoetendal Cr.	Edgemead	59	BT	39
Zoetendal Pl.	Plattekloof Glen	59	BW	39
Zoetendal St	Somerset West	171	CV	75
Zola Cr.	Mfuleni	126	CL	54
Zola Mtsoni St	Kuyasa	147	CS	55
Zola Nqini St	Kuyasa	147	CS	56
Zomerlust Ave	Huis-in-bos	139	CP	24
Zomerlust Rd	Bergvliet	140	CR	27
Zongothi St	Brown's Farm	124	CM	43
Zonne Way	East Rock	62	BU	52
Zonnebloem La.	Belhar	106	CD	49
Zonnebloem St	Athlone	102	CF	32
Zonnebloem St	Table View	41	BO	33
Zonnekus Rd	Milnerton	57	BW	31
Zonnenburg St	Stellenryk	62	BT	52
Zonneweelde	Goedemoed	46	BP	54
Zonneweelde	Goedemoed	46	BS	54
Zono St	Bloekombos	48	BQ	62
Zorba Rd	Pinati	122	CK	35
Zorina Cl.	Bellville	61	BU	50
Zotshoba	Mbekweni	15	AW	91
Zoutendyk Steps	Fish Hoek	186	DC	24
Zoutman Cl.	Hout Bay	136	CQ	14
Zoutman Rd	Hout Bay	136	CQ	14
Zuba	Mbekweni	15	AW	91
Zuiderzee Cr.	Malibu Village	127	CJ	56
Zuidmeer St	Huguenot	18	BB	90
Zulu Dr.	Tarentaalplaas	175	CY	75
Zurich Cl.	Portlands (M.Plain)	144	CQ	46
Zurich St	Uitzicht	47	BO	56
Zuurberg Rd	Heideveld	104	CF	39
Zuzani Cr.	Nonqubela	126	CN	52
Zuzile St	Mandela Pk	146	CR	54
Zwaans Rd	Retreat	140	CR	28
Zwaanswyk	Karindal	96	CC	79
Zwaanswyk Rd	Steenberg	139	CS	23
Zwaanswyk Rd	Steenberg	139	CS	24
Zwaanswyk Rd	Steenberg	157	CT	22
Zwartkops Rd	Schaap Kraal	123	CK	39
Zwelethu	Mbekweni	15	AW	92
Zwelethu St	Wimbledon	107	CG	54
Zwelitsha	Mbekweni	15	AW	92
Zwelitsha	Mbekweni	15	AT	94
Zwelitsha Dr.	Nyanga	124	CJ	43
Zwelitsha Dr.	Nyanga	124	CK	43
Zwelonke Ave	Nyanga	123	CJ	41
Zwelonke Ave	Nyanga	123	CM	39
Zydenbos Ave	Somerset West	171	CW	75
Zyster St	Wellington	10	AS	93

SUBURB NAME	PG	GRID	
Aanhou Wen	96	CC	79
Acacia Park	58	BX	36
Admirals Park	179	DD	78
Adriaanse	87	CC	43
Airlie	139	CP	25
Airport Industria	105	CG	43
Alphen	119	CL	26
Altydgedacht	45	BR	47
Amanda Glen	62	BT	52
Amandelrug	90	CA	55
Amandelsig	90	CB	56
Amstelhof	23	BD	93
Anchorage Park	175	DC	77
Anesta	113	CF	75
Annandale	90	BZ	56
Arauna	63	BU	55
Arbeidslus	96	CA	80
Athlone	102	CF	33
Atlantic Beach Estate	205	BE	26
Atlantis Industria	200	AM	30
Atlantis Town Centre	199	AH	32
Aurora	45	BP	48
Austinville	108	CH	56
Avon	86	CA	41
Avondale (Atlantis)	201	AJ	31
Avondale (Bellville)	60	BX	45
Avonwood	86	CB	42
Bakoven	98	CF	18
Balvenie	86	CB	42
Bantry Bay	80	CB	18
Barbarossa	120	CN	27
Barnet Molokwana Corner	126	CN	53
Bay Park	175	DC	76
Bay View Village	191	DG	23
Beacon Valley (M.Plain)	145	CP	48
Beaconhill	199	AH	33
Beaconvale	87	BZ	43
Bel Ombre	119	CM	24
Belgravia (Bellville)	88	BY	50
Belgravia (Vygekraal)	103	CG	35
Belhar	106	CD	48
Bellair	62	BV	52
Bellavista	22	BD	90
Bellavista Ext.1	18	BC	90
Belle Constantia	139	CP	25
Bellville	61	BV	48
Bellville Central	88	BY	48
Bellville Ext. 22	62	BV	52
Bellville Ext. 36	61	BU	50
Bellville Ext. 38	62	BU	51
Bellville Ext. 41	61	BT	50
Bellville Ext. 43	61	BT	48
Bellville Ext. 53	60	BT	46
Bellville South	88	CA	49
Bellville South Industrial	89	CA	51
Bellville Sth Ext. 5	88	BZ	49
Belmont Park	48	BR	60
Belrail	88	BY	48
Belthorn Estate	121	CJ	34
Belvedere Noordhoek	157	CX	19
Belville Ext. 19	62	BV	51
Belville Sth Ext. 7	88	BZ	49
Bergsig	46	BO	52
Bergvliet	140	CQ	27
Beroma	88	BZ	50
Big Bay	24	BL	28
Bishop Lavis	104	CD	42
Bishopscourt	119	CJ	26
Blackheath Industria	108	CF	56
Bloekombos	48	BR	62
Bloemhof	61	BV	50
Blommendal	62	BW	51
Blomtuin	61	BW	50
Blomvlei	61	BV	47
Bloomsburg	23	BD	91
Blouberg Rise	25	BN	31
Blouberg Sands	24	BM	30
Bloubergrant	24	BN	30
Bloubergstrand	24	BJ	27
Bloubergstrand	24	BM	28
Blue Downs	127	CJ	56
Bo Dalsig	113	CE	76
Bongani	145	CP	50
Bonnie Brae	47	BP	57
Bonnie Brook	47	BQ	57
Bonteheuwel	104	CE	39
Bosonia	89	CB	54
Boston	61	BX	47
Bothasig	58	BT	37
Bracken Heights	62	BU	54
Brackenfell	63	BV	56
Brackenfell Industria	63	BT	57
Brackenfell South	63	BX	58
Brandwacht	113	CE	77
Brandwag	90	BZ	55
Brantwood	89	CA	53
Brentwood Park	126	CJ	51
Bridgetown	103	CF	36
Broadlands	175	CZ	77
Brooklyn	83	BZ	30
Browns Farm	123	CL	42
Cafda Village	141	CS	31
Camelot	107	CF	53
Camps Bay	98	CE	18
Cape Town Central	82	CA	23
Capri	185	DB	19
Capricorn	160	CV	31
Casablanca	175	DB	76
Century City	57	BW	34
Chantecler	62	BT	52
Chapman's Peak	156	CX	16
Charlesville	104	CF	40
Chrismar	61	BW	50
Churchill	59	BX	42
Clamhall	60	BX	43
Claremont	120	CJ	29
Clarkes	86	CC	42
Clifton	80	CC	18
Cloetesville	95	BZ	75
Clovelly	186	CZ	24
Clunie	139	CQ	23
Colorado (M.Plain)	144	CO	44
Coniston Park	159	CU	30
Connaught	87	CB	43
Constantia Vale	119	CN	25
Constantia Village	119	CN	25
Courtrai	22	BH	87
Cravenby	87	CB	43
Crawford	102	CH	33
Crossroads	124	CK	44
Croydon	149	CP	63
Da Gama Park	190	DE	21
Dal Josafat Industrial Township	18	BA	90
Dalsig	113	CE	76
Dalvale	19	AY	92
Danarand	89	CC	54
Danena	61	BU	49
De Bron	45	BS	48
De Bron	61	BT	48
De Duin	59	BW	41
De Kuilen	89	CB	54
De La Haye	89	BY	51
De Oude Renbaan	22	BH	88
De Tijger	60	BW	44
De Tuin	47	BS	55
De Villier's	88	BY	49
De Zoete Inval	22	BH	88
Delft	106	CG	49
Delft South	125	CJ	49
Delro	126	CL	54
Denneburg	23	BD	91
Dennedal	139	CR	25
Dennemere	108	CH	57
Des Hampden	89	CB	53
Devil's Peak Estate	82	CC	24
Devon Park (Eersterivier)	128	CL	60
Devon Park (Stellenbosch)	112	CD	72
Devonvallei	112	CD	72
Die Boord	113	CD	75
Die Bos	174	CY	74
Die Oude Spruit	63	BX	56
Die Rand	95	CA	76
Die Werf	113	CE	75
Die Wingerd (Durbanville)	46	BP	53
Die Wingerd (Stellenbosch)	113	CE	75
Dieprivier	140	CP	28
Diepwater (Wesbank)	107	CG	52
District Six (Zonnebloem)	82	CB	24
Dolphin Beach	40	BP	30
Door De Kraal	61	BT	47
Doornhoogte	103	CG	36
Dr Malan	95	CC	78
Dreyersdal	140	CR	27
Driftsands	147	CP	56
Dunoon	42	BO	37
D'urbanvale	29	BN	49
Durbanville	46	BQ	51
Durbanville Ext. 37	46	BP	53
Durbanville Hills	45	BR	49
Durbell	45	BS	50
Durmonte	30	BN	53
Duynefontein	204	AY	26
Eagles Nest	118	CN	22
East Rock	62	BU	52
Eastridge (M.Plain)	145	CR	48
Eden	113	CF	76
Edenpark	62	BU	54
Edgemead	58	BU	38
Edward	122	CN	35
Eersterivier	128	CM	60
Eikenbosch	90	CC	57
Eikendal	48	BS	59
Eindhoven	106	CH	50
Ekuphumuleni	146	CQ	53
Electric City	127	CN	58
Elfindale	140	CQ	30
Elim	90	CA	55
Elnor	86	CC	42
Elriche	18	BB	90
Elsies River Industrial	86	BZ	41
Epping Forest	86	CC	41
Epping Industrial	85	CB	38
Eskom	61	BV	50
Eureka	87	CC	44
Everglen	45	BS	50
Everite	63	BV	57
Eversdal	62	BT	51
Eversdal Ext. 21	62	BT	52
Eversdal Ext. 4	62	BU	51
Eversdal Heights	46	BS	51

SUBURB NAME	PG	GRID
Eversdal Heights	61	BT 50
Ex-skool	95	CA 75
Eyethu	146	CP 53
Factreton	85	BY 35
Fairdale	126	CJ 54
Fairfield	60	BX 44
Fairie Knowe	185	DA 19
Fairways (Cape Town)	121	CN 32
Fairways (Stellenbosch)	113	CE 75
Fairyland	19	AZ 93
Faure	148	CO 62
Ferndale	62	BV 54
Fir Grove	139	CQ 25
Firgrove	150	CR 67
Fisantekraal	31	BK 58
Fishhoek	186	DA 23
Flamingo Vlei	41	BQ 33
Flintdale Estate	141	CP 31
Florida	87	CA 44
Foreshore	82	BZ 25
Forest Glade (Constantia)	139	CS 24
Forest Glade (Eersterivier)	127	CL 58
Forest Heights	127	CL 58
Forest Village	127	CM 57
Franschhoek North	75	BW 105
Franschhoek South	79	BY 108
Fresnaye	81	CB 19
Frogmore Estate	159	CU 28
Gardens	81	CC 22
Gatesville	103	CH 36
Gaylands	139	CO 26
Gaylee	108	CG 57
Gersham	107	CD 53
Glen Alpine	118	CM 22
Glen Ive	62	BU 52
Glen Ridge	191	DD 25
Glencairn Heights	191	DD 24
Glenhaven	89	CA 51
Glenlily	86	BY 42
Goedemoed	46	BP 53
Good Hope	146	CR 51
Goodwood Estate	85	BY 38
Gordon Heights	180	DD 79
Gordon Strand	175	DC 76
Graceland	146	CQ 54
Grassy Park	141	CQ 32
Green Oaks	95	BY 75
Greenfield	108	CH 57
Greenlands	88	CA 48
Greenpoint	81	BY 22
Greenways	174	DA 73
Griffiths Mxenge	146	CQ 54
Groenheuwel	19	AZ 91
Groenvallei	62	BX 53
Groenvlei	18	BA 88
Grootbosch	138	CO 21
Guguletu	104	CH 41
Guldenland	174	CZ 74
Gustrow	175	DB 75
Haasendal	90	BZ 57
Haasendal	90	CA 57
Hagley	107	CF 52
Halalie	46	BO 52
Hanover Park	122	CK 36
Harare	146	CS 53
Harbour Heights	194	DJ 25
Harbour Island	179	DE 76
Harrington's Place	113	CE 75
Hazendal	102	CE 33
Heathfield	140	CQ 29
Heemstede	62	BW 53
Heideveld	104	CF 39
Helderberg Park	175	DA 75
Heron Park	184	DB 17
High Constantia	119	CN 23
High Gate	107	CG 53
Highbury	107	CE 54
Highlands Estate	122	CM 38
Hill View	127	CK 57
Hillcrest Heights	127	CL 56
Hillrise	61	BX 49
Hindle Park	107	CH 54
Hohelzen	61	BW 47
Hohenort	119	CL 25
Hoogstede	62	BV 54
Hope Of Constantia	139	CP 23
Hout Bay	137	CO 15
Hout Bay Harbour	136	CR 13
Huguenot	18	BC 90
Huis-in-bos	139	CO 24
Idasvallei	96	CA 79
Ilitha Park	146	CQ 52
Imhoff's Gift	184	DB 15
Jacarandas	90	CB 57
Jagtershof	108	CD 57
Jan Kriel	90	CA 55
Joe Slovo Park	57	BU 34
Joostenberg	48	BO 60
Kaapzicht	59	BW 40
Kalk Bay	186	DA 26
Kalkfontein I	107	CD 52
Kalkfontein II	107	CD 52
Karindal	96	CC 79
Kaya	146	CP 52
Kayamandi	94	CA 74
Kaymor	62	BX 53
Kempenville	88	BY 49
Kenever	61	BT 49
Kenilworth	120	CK 29
Kenilworth Park	121	CK 31
Kenridge	45	BS 49
Kenridge Ext. 3	61	BU 49
Kenridge Ext. 4	61	BU 48
Kenridge Heights	45	BS 49
Kensington	84	BZ 33
Kewtown	102	CE 34
Khayelitsha	166	CT 58
Killarney Gardens	42	BP 37
King Edward Rest	194	DJ 24
Kingston	61	BX 49
Kirstenhof	159	CT 27
Klein Begin	48	BS 60
Klein Constantia	138	CP 22
Klein Nederburg	19	BC 92
Klein Nederburg (Durbanville)	46	BP 53
Klein Parys	23	BE 91
Klein Zevenwacht	90	CB 58
Kleinbos	170	CX 74
Kleinbosch	59	BT 40
Kleingeluk	113	CE 75
Kleinvallei	94	CC 73
Kleinvlei	127	CJ 58
Klipdam	90	CB 55
Klipkop	87	BZ 45
Klippiesdal	19	BC 91
Knole Park	142	CO 36
Kommetjie	183	DA 14
Kraaifontein Ext. 17	47	BQ 57
Kraaifontein Industry	48	BQ 60
Krigeville	113	CD 76
Kromrivier	95	CB 76
Kuilsrivier Industria	108	CD 55
Kuyasa	147	CS 56
KWV	22	BG 88
La Rochelle	62	BV 51
Labiance	89	BZ 52
Lakeside	159	CV 27
Langa	103	CD 36
Langeberg Glen	47	BQ 56
Langeberg Ridge	47	BR 56
Langeberg Village	46	BP 53
Langgewacht	170	CW 72
Lansdowne	121	CK 33
Lavender Hill	160	CT 31
Lavender Hill East	160	CU 32
Lekkerwater	184	DA 18
Lemoenkloof	18	BB 88
Lentegeur (M.Plain)	144	CO 46
Leonsdale	86	CA 42
Lieberheim	113	CG 76
Lindida	96	CA 80
Lochnerhof	170	CX 71
Loevenstein	60	BW 46
Lotus River	141	CP 34
Loucharmante	90	CB 56
Loumar	89	BY 51
Lusthof	170	CX 72
Lwandle	175	CZ 76
Mabille Park	89	CA 53
Macassar	149	CS 64
Macassar Beach	168	CT 63
Maitland	84	CA 33
Maitland Garden Village	84	CC 31
Malibu Village	127	CK 56
Mandalay	125	CM 48
Mandela Park	147	CQ 55
Manenberg	123	CJ 39
Marconi Beam	57	BU 34
Marina Da Gama	159	CV 29
Marinda Heights	89	BZ 52
Marine Oil Refinery	191	DF 24
Marlborough Park	63	BT 55
Marlow	88	CA 50
Masiphumelele	184	DA 18
Matroosfontein	86	CC 41
Maycape	108	CE 55
Mbekweni	15	AW 91
Meadowridge	140	CP 27
Meadowsteads	156	CX 18
Melkbosstrand	204	BC 26
Metro Industrial Township	56	BX 30
Mikro Park	90	CB 56
Milnerton	41	BS 33
Milnerton Ext. 6	41	BS 34
Milnerton Ridge	41	BS 34
Mimosa	88	CA 50
Misty Cliffs	189	DH 17
Mitchells Plain	144	CR 45
Mitchells Plain Centre	145	CQ 47
Modderdam	105	CD 44
Montague Gardens Industrial	58	BT 35
Montagu's Gift	141	CO 34
Montana/Durrheim	104	CF 42
Monte Vista	59	BV 39
Morgen Gronde	63	BX 55
Morgenster	63	BU 56
Morgenster Hoogte	63	BT 56
Morningstar	46	BP 51
Mostertsdrift	95	CC 78
Mouille Point	81	BY 21
Mountain Veiw	19	BB 91
Mountainside Estate	179	DD 78
Mountainview	179	DD 78
Mowbray	102	CD 31
Muizenberg	159	CX 29
Muizenberg North	159	CV 28
Murdock Valley	195	DL 28
Mxolisi Phetani	125	CM 50
N1 City	59	BX 40
Ndabeni	84	CB 32
New Orleans	19	BB 91
Newfields	122	CJ 37
Nieuw Maastrecht	44	BR 43
Nomzano	175	CY 76
Nonqubela	126	CN 52
Nooitgedacht	104	CE 42
Noordhaven	157	CW 19
Noordhoek Manor Retirement Village	157	CX 20
Normandie	64	BW 59
Northern Paarl	18	AZ 89
Northgate	59	BW 42
Northpine	63	BU 58
Norwood	86	CB 41
Nova Constantia	139	CP 24
Nyanga	123	CJ 42
Oak Glen	62	BW 52
Oakdale	61	BV 49
Oakdale	61	BW 49
Oakdene	89	CC 53
Observatory	83	CC 29
Ocean View	184	DC 15
Ocean View	189	DD 16
Okavango Park	63	BT 57
Onderpapegaaiberg	94	CC 72
Onverwacht	174	CZ 74
Onverwacht	175	DC 76
Oostersee	60	BX 45
Oranjezicht	81	CC 22
Ottery	121	CM 33
Ottery	122	CM 35
Ottery East	121	CN 34
Oude Westhof	44	BS 44
Paarden Eiland	83	BZ 29
Paarl	22	BE 88
Paarlzicht	19	BC 91
Pagasvlei	139	CO 24
Panorama	59	BV 41
Papegaaiberg Industrial Park	95	CA 75
Park Estates	170	CX 72
Park Village	127	CK 58
Parklands	25	BM 33
Parkwood	141	CP 32
Parow	87	BY 43
Parow East	87	BY 45
Parow Industria	87	CB 46
Parow North	59	BW 42
Parowvallei	87	BZ 44
Peerless Park East	47	BS 58
Peerless Park East	48	BR 59
Peerless Park North	48	BQ 59
Peers Hill	185	DA 22
Peers Hill	186	DA 23
Pelikan Park	141	CS 33
Pelikan Park	142	CS 36
Pelikan Park	161	CU 37
Penhill	128	CK 60
Penlyn Estate	122	CJ 35
Perm Gardens	128	CK 59
Philippi	124	CL 44
Philippi East	124	CL 46
Phoenix	57	BU 33
Phumlani	142	CQ 36
Pinati	122	CK 35
Pine Acres	175	DC 77
Pine Haven	190	DG 22
Pinelands	84	CC 33
Plattekloof	60	BU 43
Plattekloof Glen	59	BW 40
Plumstead	120	CN 29
Pollsmoor	158	CT 25
Porter Estate	139	CR 23
Portlands (M.Plain)	144	CR 46
Primrose Park	122	CJ 38
Protea Hoogte	63	BW 57
Protea Park	201	AK 32
Protea Village	64	BV 59
Proteavallei Ext. 16	60	BT 46
Proteaville	46	BO 51
Rabiesdale	19	BC 92
Ravensmead	87	CA 45
Refinery	42	BR 38
Retreat	140	CS 29
Retreat Industrial Area	159	CT 28
Richmond	86	BY 41
Richmond Estate	86	BY 40
Richwood	42	BP 38
Ridgeworth	61	BV 50
Riverton	86	BZ 40
Robinvale	201	AJ 33
Rocklands (M.Plain)	144	CS 45
Rome	174	CY 73
Rondebosch	101	CF 30
Rondebosch East	102	CH 32
Rondevallei	107	CE 53
Rondevallei	107	CE 52
Roosendaal	107	CF 51
Rosebank	101	CE 29
Rosedale	128	CK 59
Rosendal (Bellville)	61	BU 50
Rouxville	90	CA 56
Royal Cape	121	CN 31
Rozendal (Stellenbosch)	96	CB 79
Rugby	57	BX 31
Rusdal	108	CE 57
Russel's Rest	128	CL 60
Rust-en-vrede	119	CN 26
Rusthof	174	DA 74
Ruwari	63	BV 57
Ruyteplaats Private Mountain Estate	117	CM 15
Ruyterwacht	86	CA 39
Sack's Circle Industrial	88	CB 50
Salberau	86	CB 41
Salt River	83	CC 28
San Michel	157	CX 20
Sand Industria	122	CK 38
Sanddrift	57	BV 34
Sanlamhof	88	BY 50
Sarepta	89	CC 53
Saxenburg Industrial Park	108	CE 57
Saxon Industrial	88	BZ 50
Saxonsea	199	AG 31
Scarborough	192	DJ 18
Schaap Kraal	143	CP 39
Schotsche Kloof	81	CA 22
Schuilplaats	113	CF 76
Scottsdene	64	BU 60
Scottsville	47	BS 57
Sea Point	81	CA 19
Seaforth Sound	194	DJ 26
Seawinds	160	CU 31
Selborne	61	BV 47
Sheridon Park	159	CU 29
Sherwood	199	AG 32
Shirley Park	89	BY 52
Sillery	139	CO 25
Silverglade	185	DA 22
Silverhurst	119	CN 25
Silvermine Village	185	CY 20
Silveroaks	90	CC 55
Silveroaks	90	CC 56
Silversands	107	CH 53
Silverstream	62	BU 52
Silvertown	103	CF 35
Silvertown	147	CP 55
Simon's Town	191	DG 23
Simonskloof	194	DJ 25
Simonswyk	95	CB 78
Skilpadvlei	45	BP 49
Skoongesig	45	BO 50
Somerset Heights	127	CJ 57
Somerset Park	171	CW 75
Somerset West	170	CT 74
Soneike I	89	CA 54
Soneike II	89	BZ 54
Sonnedal	59	BV 42
Sonnekuil	89	BZ 53
Sonstraal	46	BR 52
Southfork	175	DB 75
Springbok Park	62	BV 54
St Dumas	90	CC 56
St James	187	CZ 27
St Michaels	63	BU 55
Stanlou	61	BX 48
Steenberg	159	CT 29
Stellenberg	62	BU 51
Stellenbosch Central	95	CB 76
Stellenridge	62	BV 51
Stellenryk	62	BT 52
Stikland Hospital	62	BX 51
Stonehaven	185	DA 20
Strand	174	CY 73
Strand Halt	170	CW 74
Strandfontein	163	CT 43
Strandvale	170	CW 73
Streenberg	158	CT 23
Summer Greens	58	BV 36
Summerville	48	BS 60
Sun Valley	185	DA 20
Sunbird Park	107	CF 54
Sunkist	61	BX 49
Sunningdale	25	BM 31
Sunnydale	185	DA 19
Sunray	61	BX 49
Sunridge Ext. 5	41	BP 34
Sunset Beach	41	BS 32
Sunset Glen	127	CJ 55
Sunsetlinks	57	BU 31
Surrey	103	CH 38
Sweet Valley	139	CQ 25
Sybrand Park	102	CE 32
Table View	41	BP 32
Tafelsig (M.Plain)	145	CS 49
Tamboerskloof	81	CB 21
Tarentaalplaas	175	CY 75
Tegnopark	112	CF 73
Temperance Town	179	DD 78
Tennantville	95	CA 75
The Crest	46	BO 53
The Hague	106	CF 49
The Lakes	184	CZ 18

Cape Town Suburbs A-Z

Aalwyn St — Diaz

SUBURB NAME	PG	GRID
The Palms	170	CX 73
The Range	86	CC 41
The Vines	140	CO 27
Thembokwezi	125	CM 49
Thornton	85	CA 36
Three Anchor Bay	81	BZ 20
Tijgerhof	57	BW 32
Tokai	139	CS 25
Townsend Estate	85	BY 38
Triangle Farm	88	BZ 50
Tuscany Glen	127	CK 57
Tygerdal	58	BX 38
Uit-kyk	171	CW 75
Uitsig	87	CC 44
Uitzicht	47	BO 55
Umrhabulo Triangle	147	CQ 57
Uniepark	96	CB 79
Universiteits-oord	95	CB 77
Valhalla	86	CA 40
Valhalla Park	104	CE 41
Valmary Park	46	BR 51
Van Riebeeckstrand	204	AZ 26
Van Ryneveld	174	CZ 72
Vanguard	103	CF 38
Vasco Estate	86	BY 40
Vergesig	45	BQ 48
Victoria	194	DJ 24
Victoria Mxenge	126	CN 51
Vierlanden	30	BN 52
Villa Italia	57	BW 33
Voelvlei	89	CA 52
Voorbrug	107	CH 51
Vosfontein	62	BV 52
Vredehoek	82	CC 23
Vredekloof	62	BT 54
Vredekloof Heights	47	BS 55
Vredelust	60	BX 46
Vredenberg	62	BV 53
Vygeboom	46	BR 51
Vygekraal (Belgravia)	103	CG 35
Wallacedene	48	BS 61
Welcome	103	CF 38
Welcome Glen	190	DD 21
Welgedacht	60	BT 45
Welgelee	63	BT 55
Welgelegen (Durbanville)	59	BU 41
Welgelegen (Stellenbosch)	113	CD 76
Welgemoed	60	BU 46
Welgevonden	30	BN 54
Wellington	15	AT 92
Wellway Park	46	BO 52
Wellway Park East	46	BO 52
Weltevrede	94	BY 74
Weltevreden Valley (M.Plain)	144	CO 43
Wembley Park	107	CE 53
Wesbank (Diepwater)	107	CG 52
West Beach	24	BN 30
West Riding	41	BO 34
Westlake	159	CU 27
Westlake Estate	158	CU 25
Wetton	121	CL 34
Whispering Pines	175	DB 76
William Lloyd	23	BD 93
Wimbledon	108	CF 55
Windsor Estate	47	BQ 58
Windsor Park	47	BR 57
Wingfield	85	BY 36
Wingfield North Camp	58	BW 37
Winslow	179	DD 77
Winston Estate	170	CX 73
Witteboomen	119	CM 23
Woodbridge Island	57	BW 31
Woodlands	191	DE 23
Woodlands (M.Plain)	144	CO 44
Woodstock	83	CB 27
Wynberg	120	CL 28
Youngsfield	121	CL 31
Ysterplaat	84	BY 32
Zevendal	90	CC 58
Zevenwacht	90	CC 58
Zevenzicht	90	CC 58
Zonnebloem (District Six)	82	CB 24
Zoo Park	47	BR 57

Index to Street Names Other Towns

A

STREET NAME	TOWN NAME	PG	GRID
Aalwyn St	Langebaan	209	LF 11
Aalwynbos	Robertson	221	RO 11
Aandblom St	Ceres	207	CH 12
Aandblom St	Langebaan	209	LF 10
Aandblom St	Worcester	216	WR 15
Aan-De-Doorns Rd	Worcester	219	WV 16
Aan-De-Doorns Rd	Worcester	219	WW 17
Aan-De-Doorns Rd	Worcester	220	WW 18
Aanhuizen St	Swellendam	224	SX 10
Aas	Saldanha	210	SC 12
Abalone	Melkbos (Atlantic Beach Est.)	205	BE 26
Abattoir St	Malmesbury	212	MD 12
Abattoir St	Worcester	217	WR 18
Abdol	Saldanha	210	SC 10
Abelia Ave	Malmesbury	212	MD 12
Abeloni	Saldanha	210	SB 11
Aberdeen St	Hermanus	228	HG 13
Abraham Julies	Saldanha	210	SC 13
Abraham St	Worcester	219	WV 14
Acacia	Hermanus	228	HG 12
Acacia Cl.	Atlantis (Protea Pk)	201	AK 33
Acacia Cr.	Atlantis (Protea Pk)	201	AK 32
Acacia Cr.	Atlantis (Protea Pk)	201	AK 33
Acacia St	Caledon	225	CB 10
Acacia St	Grabouw	227	GV 12
Acasia Ave	Bredasdorp	197	BS 12
Adam St	Bredasdorp	197	BR 11
Adam St	Grabouw	227	GV 12
Adam St	Saldanha	211	SB 14
Adams St	Worcester	219	WV 15
Adderley St	Robertson	221	RR 11
Adderley St	Worcester	216	WS 14
Adderly Rd	Langebaan	208	LB 13
Addison St	Atlantis (Avondale)	201	AJ 31
Adenium St	Atlantis (Protea Pk)	201	AK 33
Adonis	Langebaan	208	LB 11
Adriatic Ave	Atlantis (Avondale)	201	AJ 31
Affodil St	Malmesbury	212	MD 12
Africa Ave	Worcester	219	WT 16
Africa Ave	Worcester	220	WT 20
Africa St	Montagu	222	MQ 12
Africa St	Robertson	221	RP 12
Agri Ave	Caledon	225	CC 12
Agterlang St	Bredasdorp	197	BR 12
Ainsdale Way	Melkbos (Atlantic Beach Est.)	204	BC 26
Aintree	Langebaan	208	LB 14
Akasia Ave	Malmesbury	212	MD 12
Akasia Ave	Swellendam	224	SZ 11
Akasia Way	Worcester	216	WQ 17
Akker Ave	Robertson	221	RR 12
Akker St	Caledon	225	CD 12
Akkerendam	Atlantis (Sherwood)	199	AG 33
Akkerhout	Malmesbury	212	MC 12
Alabama	Langebaan	209	LF 11
Alabama	Saldanha	210	SD 13
Alabama Rd	Saldanha	211	SB 14
Alabama St	Langebaan	209	LH 10
Alacrity St	Atlantis (Saxonsea)	199	AG 31
Albany St	Malmesbury	212	MC 12
Albatros Cr.	Langebaan	209	LG 12
Albatros St	Saldanha	211	SB 16
Albatros St	Worcester	218	WV 13
Albatros St	Worcester	219	WV 14
Albatross Pl.	Atlantis (Robinvale)	199	AH 32
Albert Cr.	Ceres	207	CG 12
Albert Cr.	Ceres	207	CH 12
Albert St	Robertson	221	RQ 11
Alberta Ave	Robertson	221	RP 11
Alberto St	Atlantis (Avondale)	201	AJ 31
Albertyn St	Caledon	225	CB 11
Albertyn St	Hermanus	228	HG 12
Albertyn St	Kleinmond	226	KP 12
Albertyn St	Worcester	219	WT 16
Albuca St	Langebaan	209	LJ 10
Aldegrande Way	Langebaan	209	LF 12
Alec Craven Cr.	Worcester	215	WS 12
Aletta Van As Cl.	Langebaan	208	LE 12
Alfa St	Malmesbury	212	MD 10
Alfa St	Malmesbury	212	ME 10
Algeria Ct	Atlantis (Sherwood)	199	AG 33
Alheit St	Ceres	207	CG 10
Alheit St	Kleinmond	226	KP 12
Alice St	Swellendam	224	SX 10
Alice St	Worcester	219	WT 14
Alicia	Saldanha	210	SC 12
Alisa Cir.	Melkbos (Atlantic Beach Est.)	204	BC 26
All Saints St	Bredasdorp	197	BT 12
All Saints St	Bredasdorp	197	BT 11
Allegheny La.	Atlantis (Sherwood)	199	AG 32
Allegheny La.	Atlantis (Sherwood)	199	AG 33
Allister St	Worcester	219	WU 17
Aloe Cr.	Atlantis (Protea Pk)	201	AK 33
Aloe Way	Worcester	215	WR 11
Alpha St	Worcester	220	WU 18
Alpina Ave	Robertson	221	RP 11
Alusia Cr.	Kleinmond	226	KO 12
Alvera St	Worcester	219	WV 16
Alwyn St	Swellendam	224	SZ 11
Amandel St	Worcester	219	WU 17
Amandelboom Ave	Kleinmond	226	KM 12
Amandelrug St	Malmesbury	212	MA 12
Amarrila St	Villiersdorp	223	VM 11
Amaryllis Cr.	Atlantis (Protea Pk)	201	AK 33
Amble Way	Melkbos (Melkbosstrand)	205	BD 25
Amersfoort St	Worcester	216	WQ 15
Amorgos St	Langebaan	208	LC 12
Amstelveen Rd	Atlantis (Avondale)	201	AJ 31
Amy Cl.	Atlantis (Avondale)	201	AK 31
Amy St	Saldanha	211	SB 15
Anchorage Rd	Langebaan	209	LG 11
Anderson St	Montagu	222	MP 12
Andre St	Saldanha	211	SA 17
Andrew Whyte St	Swellendam	224	SX 10
Andries St	Montagu	222	MQ 12
Andros St	Langebaan	208	LC 12
Anemoon St	Malmesbury	212	MD 12
Anemoon St	Swellendam	224	SZ 11
Anemoon St	Swellendam	224	TA 11
Angelier Ct	Atlantis (Protea Pk)	201	AK 32
Angelier St	Malmesbury	212	MD 12
Angelier St	Montagu	222	MO 13
Anglese Ct	Atlantis (Sherwood)	199	AG 33
Angus St	Malmesbury	212	MB 10
Anita St	Malmesbury	212	MC 11
Anker Cl.	Langebaan	209	LG 11
Ann Cr.	Worcester	215	WP 10
Anna Ave	Atlantis (Saxonsea)	199	AG 31
Anna Ave	Atlantis (Saxonsea)	199	AH 32
Antelope Ave	Atlantis (Avondale)	201	AJ 31
Anthony St	Robertson	221	RP 12
Antonia Seini St	Langebaan	209	LG 11
Antonio St	Saldanha	210	SC 12
Antrim St	Atlantis (Beaconhill)	199	AH 32
Anubis Cr.	Atlantis (Avondale)	201	AJ 31
Anys	Malmesbury	212	ME 12
Apple Cr.	Grabouw	227	GU 12
Arbor Dr.	Grabouw	227	GU 11
Arc St	Hermanus	229	HE 16
Arcadia St	Darling	213	DD 12
Arcadia St	Hermanus	228	HH 11
Arcadia St	Malmesbury	212	MB 11
Arcadia St	Malmesbury	212	MB 12
Ardennes Cr.	Atlantis (Beaconhill)	199	AH 32
Arend	Langebaan	209	LF 11
Arend St	Tulbagh	206	TX 12
Arende St	Saldanha	210	SC 10
Arendse St	Worcester	219	WT 17
Areos	Langebaan	208	LB 11
Aries St	Worcester	219	WU 15
Arion Dr.	Atlantis (Beaconhill)	199	AG 33
Arion Dr.	Atlantis (Saxonsea)	199	AH 32
Arion St	Ceres	207	CF 12
Aristea La.	Kleinmond	226	KL 11
Aristia Cl.	Atlantis (Protea Pk)	201	AK 33
Arkhani St	Worcester	219	WU 17
Armagh St	Hermanus	228	HH 12
Arnaud St	Malmesbury	212	MB 12
Arries St	Saldanha	210	SC 11
Artemis	Langebaan	208	LB 11
Arthur St	Worcester	219	WU 14
Arum La.	Worcester	215	WR 11
Arum Rd	Hermanus	228	HG 10
Arum St	Ceres	207	CH 12
Arundel Ct	Atlantis (Sherwood)	199	AH 33
Arundel St	Hermanus	228	HH 11
Arundo Sq.	Atlantis (Protea Pk)	201	AK 33
Ascot Cir.	Langebaan	208	LB 14
Ascot Pl.	Langebaan	208	LA 14
Ash Gr.	Worcester	215	WQ 11
Ash St	Robertson	221	RQ 12
Assegaai St	Tulbagh	206	TX 13
Aster Ave	Bredasdorp	197	BS 12
Aster Ave	Robertson	221	RP 11
Aster Cl.	Atlantis (Protea Pk)	201	AK 33
Aster Cr.	Atlantis (Protea Pk)	201	AK 33
Aster St	Malmesbury	212	MD 12
Aster St	Montagu	222	MP 13
Aster St	Worcester	216	WR 15
Asteria	Langebaan	208	LB 11
Atalantes St	Melkbos (Melkbosstrand)	204	BB 26
Athens Ave	Atlantis (Saxonsea)	199	AG 31
Athens Ave	Atlantis (Saxonsea)	199	AG 32
Athlone St	Ceres	207	CG 10
Athlone St	Swellendam	224	SX 11
Atlantic Ave	Melkbos (Duynefontein)	203	AX 26
Atlantic Ave	Melkbos (Duynefontein)	204	AY 26
Atlantic Beach Dr.	Melkbos (Atlantic Beach Est.)	205	BD 26
Atlantic Beach Dr.	Melkbos (Atlantic Beach Est.)	205	BE 26
Atlantic Links	Melkbos (Melkbosstrand)	204	BC 26
Atlantic Links	Melkbos (Melkbosstrand)	204	BC 27
Atlas St	Ceres	207	CF 12
Auction St	Malmesbury	212	MB 12
Auge St	Swellendam	224	SX 12
August	Robertson	221	RS 12
August Kotzenberg St	Atlantis (Atlantis Ind.)	200	AN 28
Avenhoorn St	Atlantis (Saxonsea)	199	AG 32
Aventine Ave	Atlantis (Beaconhill)	199	AH 32
Avocado Cr.	Grabouw	227	GU 11
Avocet	Langebaan	209	LF 11
Axel	Saldanha	210	SC 13
Azalea Cl.	Atlantis (Protea Pk)	201	AK 33
Azalea Cr.	Atlantis (Protea Pk)	201	AK 33
Azalia St	Malmesbury	212	MD 11

B

STREET NAME	TOWN NAME	PG	GRID
Baadjies St	Bredasdorp	197	BR 11
Baai	Saldanha	210	SC 11
Baartman Cr.	Worcester	220	WT 19
Babblers Pl.	Atlantis (Saxonsea)	199	AH 32
Babblers Pl.	Atlantis (Saxonsea)	199	AF 34
Badskop Cr.	Montagu	222	MO 12
Bahumi St	Worcester	217	WS 20
Bain St	Worcester	216	WS 14
Baker St	Swellendam	224	SX 11
Balfour St	Hermanus	228	HG 11
Balgowan St	Atlantis (Saxonsea)	199	AG 32
Balsamine Cl.	Atlantis (Protea Pk)	201	AK 33
Bam St	Villiersdorp	223	VM 12
Banie St	Montagu	222	MQ 12
Barber St	Saldanha	210	SC 12
Baring St	Worcester	216	WS 14
Barker St	Melkbos (Duynefontein)	204	AY 26
Barkley St	Worcester	215	WS 12
Barlawiet St	Malmesbury	212	MC 10
Barleria St	Atlantis (Protea Pk)	201	AK 32
Barlinka St	Ceres	207	CJ 12
Barlinka St	Worcester	219	WU 17
Barlinka Way	Montagu	222	MP 13
Barnacle Cir.	Melkbos (Atlantic Beach Est.)	204	BC 26
Barnard St	Villiersdorp	223	VL 12
Barocca St	Malmesbury	212	MA 11
Barocca St	Malmesbury	212	MA 12
Barry St	Montagu	222	MR 11
Barry St	Robertson	221	RQ 11
Barry St	Robertson	221	RQ 10
Basil February	Saldanha	210	SC 13
Basil February	Saldanha	210	SC 12
Basil Newmark St	Caledon	225	CB 10
Basson St	Langebaan	209	LJ 10
Bastaan St	Bredasdorp	197	BR 11
Batana Rd	Caledon	225	CD 13
Batavier Cl.	Langebaan	208	LE 12
Batavier Cr.	Langebaan	208	LE 11
Bath St	Montagu	222	MQ 11
Bath St	Montagu	222	MQ 12
Bato Way	Melkbos (Melkbosstrand)	204	BB 26
Bato Way	Melkbos (Melkbosstrand)	204	BC 26
Bauermeester	Langebaan	209	LH 10
Bauhinia Cl.	Atlantis (Protea Pk)	201	AK 32
Baxa St	Worcester	217	WS 21
Bay View Rd	Saldanha	211	SB 15
Beach Rd	Kleinmond	226	KN 12
Beach Rd	Kleinmond	226	KM 12
Beach Rd	Melkbos (Melkbosstrand)	204	BB 26
Beach Rd	Melkbos (Melkbosstrand)	204	BC 25
Beach Rd	Saldanha	211	SB 15
Beatrice St	Worcester	219	WU 14
Beaverhead La.	Atlantis (Sherwood)	199	AG 32
Beaverhead La.	Atlantis (Sherwood)	199	AH 32
Beck La.	Worcester	215	WS 13
Beekberg Cr.	Atlantis (Beaconhill)	199	AH 32
Beet St	Ceres	207	CH 11
Begonia Cir.	Atlantis (Protea Pk)	201	AK 32
Begonia St	Malmesbury	212	MD 12
Begonia St	Villiersdorp	223	VM 11
Behr Cir.	Saldanha	210	SC 10
Behr St	Bredasdorp	197	BR 12
Belderblom St	Swellendam	224	SX 12
Belelie St	Worcester	219	WU 15
Belgrove Cir.	Melkbos (Atlantic Beach Est.)	204	BC 26
Belinda St	Worcester	219	WV 16
Bell St	Bredasdorp	197	BR 12
Bell St	Montagu	222	MQ 11
Bellona St	Atlantis (Saxonsea)	199	AG 32
Bengal St	Atlantis (Avondale)	201	AJ 31
Benguella La.	Langebaan	209	LG 11
Benjamin Cl.	Langebaan	209	LG 10
Benjamin St	Worcester	219	WT 17
Benneth Cr.	Worcester	219	WV 17
Bentele St	Worcester	217	WS 20
Bento St	Atlantis (Avondale)	201	AJ 31
Berea St	Swellendam	224	SX 11
Berg St	Bredasdorp	197	BT 12
Berg St	Caledon	225	CB 10
Berg St	Hermanus	229	HF 14
Berg St	Montagu	222	MQ 11
Berg St	Montagu	222	MQ 10
Berg St	Saldanha	211	SC 14
Berg St	Swellendam	224	SW 13
Berg St	Villiersdorp	223	VL 11
Berg-en-Zee Dr.	Hermanus	229	HE 14
Bergman St	Ceres	207	CG 11
Bergplaats Ct	Atlantis (Sherwood)	199	AH 32
Bergroos St	Atlantis (Protea Pk)	201	AK 32
Bergroos St	Worcester	216	WR 15
Bergsig La.	Worcester	215	WR 11
Bergsig St	Ceres	207	CH 11
Bergsig St	Robertson	221	RO 12
Bergzicht St	Malmesbury	212	MB 11
Bergzicht St	Malmesbury	212	MB 12
Berlyn Sq.	Atlantis (Sherwood)	199	AG 32
Bernard Rudolf St	Worcester	217	WQ 18
Berta	Saldanha	210	SC 10
Berzelia St	Atlantis (Protea Pk)	201	AJ 32
Berzelia St	Atlantis (Protea Pk)	201	AK 32
Besembos	Malmesbury	212	ME 11
Besselaar Way	Worcester	216	WR 16
Bester St	Ceres	207	CJ 11

Abbreviations used: Ave – Avenue, A.H. – Agricultural Holding, A.L.– Algemene Landgoed, Blvd – Boulevard, Cen. – Central, Cir. – Circle, Cl. – Close, Cr. – Crescent, Ct – Court, Dr. – Drive, Est. – Estate, Ext. – Extension, Hgts – Heights, Ind. – Industrial, Gdns – Gardens, Gr. – Grove, La. – Lane, (M.Plain) - Mitchells Plain, Nth – North, Pl. – Place, Pk – Park, Rd – Road, Rdg. – Ridge, S.H.– Small Holding, Sq. – Square, St – Street, Sth – South, Ter. – Terrace, Tn – Turn, Val. – Valley, Wk – Walk

STREET NAME	TOWN NAME	PG	GRID
Betana St	Malmesbury	212	MC 10
Bethel St	Swellendam	224	SY 10
Bethel St	Worcester	219	WT 17
Beverley Ave	Atlantis (Beaconhill)	199	AH 32
Biccard St	Malmesbury	212	MB 12
Biesenbach St	Worcester	216	WP 16
Bifolia St	Langebaan	209	LJ 10
Bighorn Ct	Atlantis (Sherwood)	199	AH 32
Bignolia Cir.	Atlantis (Protea Pk)	201	AK 32
Biko	Robertson	221	RS 12
Biko St	Malmesbury	212	ME 12
Binga Sq.	Atlantis (Sherwood)	199	AH 32
Binne St	Ceres	207	CG 12
Bird La.	Hermanus	228	HG 12
Bird La.	Worcester	216	WS 15
Bird St	Malmesbury	212	MC 11
Birdie	Langebaan	209	LF 11
Birdland St	Langebaan	209	LG 12
Birkenhead Dr.	Melkbos (Atlantic Beach Est.)	205	BD 27
Birkenhead Dr.	Melkbos (Melkbosstrand)	204	BC 26
Bishop Ave	Atlantis	201	AK 34
Biskop St	Saldanha	210	SC 11
Bittern Cr.	Atlantis (Saxonsea)	199	AG 31
Blackdown Cr.	Atlantis (Beaconhill)	199	AH 32
Bleshoender St	Worcester	218	WV 13
Bloekom	Malmesbury	212	MD 11
Bloekom Ave	Bredasdorp	197	BR 12
Bloekom Ave	Robertson	221	RR 12
Bloekom St	Ceres	207	CH 13
Bloekombos	Robertson	221	RO 11
Bloem St	Malmesbury	212	MC 12
Bloem St	Montagu	222	MQ 11
Bloembosch Rd	Atlantis	201	AM 33
Bloemendal	Langebaan	209	LH 11
Blombos	Robertson	221	RO 11
Blouberg La.	Atlantis (Beaconhill)	199	AH 32
Bloubos	Robertson	221	RO 12
Bloubos	Robertson	221	RO 11
Bloukrans La.	Atlantis (Sherwood)	199	AH 32
Bloupunt La.	Montagu	222	MS 11
Blue Bell St	Worcester	219	WU 16
Bluegum Gr.	Worcester	215	WQ 11
Bob Loubser St	Kleinmond	226	KP 12
Bodla Ave	Worcester	220	WT 19
Boegoebos	Robertson	221	RO 11
Boekenhout Ave	Kleinmond	226	KM 12
Boesaks St	Montagu	222	MP 12
Bogey	Langebaan	209	LG 11
Bogey	Langebaan	209	LF 11
Bokmakierie St	Worcester	219	WV 14
Bokomo Rd	Malmesbury	212	MC 12
Bokwa Sq.	Atlantis (Saxonsea)	199	AG 32
Boland St	Villiersdorp	223	VL 12
Bon Aventura Ave	Atlantis (Avondale)	200	AJ 30
Bon Chretien St	Ceres	207	CH 13
Bonaero Ave	Bredasdorp	197	BS 11
Bond St	Bredasdorp	197	BU 12
Bonekruid	Malmesbury	212	MD 11
Bontebok Ave	Bredasdorp	197	BR 12
Bontebok St	Swellendam	224	SZ 11
Bos St	Grabouw	227	GV 13
Bos St	Grabouw	227	GV 12
Boschheuvel St	Worcester	216	WQ 16
Bosduif Ave	Melkbos (Van Riebeeckstrand)	204	AZ 26
Bosheuwel Ave	Robertson	221	RQ 12
Bosjemansrivier	Worcester	215	WQ 13
Bosman St	Worcester	215	WS 13
Bossanger St	Atlantis (Saxonsea)	199	AH 32
Bossanger St	Atlantis (Saxonsea)	199	AF 34
Bot River Rd	Kleinmond	226	KM 12
Botha Cr.	Worcester	215	WS 12
Bothma Cr.	Worcester	216	WQ 15
Botsane Ave	Worcester	220	WT 20
Botterblom St	Darling	213	DE 12
Bottlebrush St	Atlantis (Protea Pk)	201	AK 32
Boundary Rd	Saldanha	211	SC 14
Boundary Way	Worcester	215	WQ 11
Bowater Cl.	Melkbos (Melkbosstrand)	205	BD 25
Bowenia Ct	Atlantis (Sherwood)	199	AG 32
Bowline	Saldanha	210	SC 12
Bowsprit End	Melkbos (Atlantic Beach Est.)	205	BE 27
Boxhill Cl.	Atlantis (Beaconhill)	199	AH 32
Boyd St	Malmesbury	212	MB 12
Boyes St	Caledon	225	CC 11
Brahmaan St	Malmesbury	212	MB 10
Brakkefontein	Melkbos (Melkbosstrand)	202	AS 27
Brakkefontein	Melkbos (Melkbosstrand)	203	AT 27
Brand	Melkbos (Melkbosstrand)	204	BC 25
Brand St	Bredasdorp	197	BT 11
Brand St	Swellendam	224	SX 11
Brander St	Saldanha	211	SB 15
Brandvalley	Worcester	215	WQ 13
Brandwacht Way	Worcester	215	WQ 11
Breakers Ave	Melkbos (Melkbosstrand)	204	BC 26
Breakers Ave	Melkbos (Melkbosstrand)	204	BC 27
Breakwater Cove	Melkbos (Atlantic Beach Est.)	205	BE 26
Breakwater Cove	Melkbos (Atlantic Beach Est.)	205	BF 26
Brecon St	Atlantis (Beaconhill)	199	AH 32
Bree St	Bredasdorp	197	BU 12
Bree St	Langebaan	209	LH 10
Bree St	Malmesbury	212	MC 12
Bree St	Montagu	222	MQ 11
Breërivier Cr.	Worcester	219	WU 15
Brett St	Worcester	216	WQ 17
Breusing St	Worcester	216	WR 17
Brevity La.	Worcester	215	WQ 12
Brik Cl.	Langebaan	208	LE 11
Brink St	Montagu	222	MR 11
Brittlestar Dr.	Melkbos (Atlantic Beach Est.)	205	BD 27
Brittlestar Dr.	Melkbos (Atlantic Beach Est.)	205	BE 27
Bromvoël St	Worcester	218	WV 13
Brooks St	Worcester	219	WV 15
Brown St	Montagu	222	MQ 11
Brown St	Swellendam	224	SY 11
Brown St	Villiersdorp	223	VM 12
Brutus Ave	Atlantis (Saxonsea)	199	AG 32
Bruydegom Rd	Saldanha	211	SB 14
Buckingham Cr.	Ceres	207	CG 12
Buffelskraal	Worcester	215	WS 12
Buffelsnek Ct	Atlantis (Sherwood)	199	AG 32
Buirski St	Swellendam	224	SX 10
Buitekant St	Bredasdorp	197	BT 12
Buitekant St	Darling	213	DD 10
Buitekant St	Hermanus	228	HG 11
Buitekant St	Malmesbury	212	MC 11
Buitekant St	Montagu	222	MQ 12
Buitekant St	Swellendam	224	SX 11
Buitenkant St	Caledon	225	CC 10
Buitenkant St	Tulbagh	206	TW 11
Buitenkant St	Villiersdorp	223	VM 12
Buitenkant St	Villiersdorp	223	VM 11
Buitenkant St	Worcester	219	WU 15
Bunting Cr.	Atlantis (Robinvale)	201	AJ 32
Buren St	Robertson	221	RQ 12
Buren St	Worcester	216	WQ 15
Burg	Malmesbury	212	MB 11
Burger St	Montagu	222	MO 12
Burton Port St	Saldanha	211	SC 15
Burwana	Robertson	221	RS 12
Busa St	Worcester	217	WS 20
Butler St	Worcester	215	WS 13
Byvanger St	Worcester	218	WV 13

C

STREET NAME	TOWN NAME	PG	GRID
C.R.Louw St	Kleinmond	226	KP 12
Cabinet St	Montagu	222	MP 13
Caelian St	Atlantis (Beaconhill)	199	AH 33
Caledon La.	Worcester	215	WQ 11
Caledon St	Darling	213	DC 13
Caledon St	Grabouw	227	GT 11
Caledon St	Villiersdorp	223	VK 12
Calendula St	Worcester	219	WU 16
Callithea Rd	Langebaan	208	LC 11
Calton St	Atlantis (Beaconhill)	199	AH 33
Cambedo Ave	Kleinmond	226	KM 12
Canara Ct	Atlantis (Saxonsea)	199	AG 32
Canary	Langebaan	209	LG 12
Canary Cl.	Atlantis (Saxonsea)	199	AH 32
Canary Cl.	Atlantis (Saxonsea)	199	AF 34
Canterbury St	Hermanus	228	HH 11
Caperock Cl.	Melkbos (Melkbosstrand)	205	BD 25
Capitoline St	Atlantis (Beaconhill)	199	AH 33
Capricorn St	Saldanha	210	SC 11
Carinus St	Worcester	216	WP 16
Carl Cr.	Worcester	219	WV 17
Carmel Cir.	Atlantis (Beaconhill)	199	AH 33
Carmichael	Melkbos (Duynefontein)	204	AY 26
Carnation Ave	Bredasdorp	197	BS 12
Carnation St	Worcester	219	WU 16
Carnoustie Dr.	Melkbos (Melkbosstrand)	204	BC 26
Carnoustie Dr.	Melkbos (Melkbosstrand)	204	BC 27
Caroline St	Bredasdorp	197	BT 11
Carr St	Worcester	217	WS 18
Carr St	Worcester	220	WT 18
Carson St	Ceres	207	CG 10
Casos Rd	Langebaan	208	LC 11
Casos Rd	Langebaan	208	LD 12
Castalis St	Atlantis (Protea Pk)	201	AK 32
Castle St	Montagu	222	MO 12
Castlehill Cir.	Atlantis (Beaconhill)	199	AH 33
Cathcart St	Caledon	225	CC 11
Cathcart St	Worcester	215	WS 12
Caudata Cl.	Langebaan	209	LH 11
Cavallo Cr.	Malmesbury	212	MB 10
Cawdor St	Atlantis (Saxonsea)	199	AG 32
Cedar Gr.	Worcester	215	WQ 11
Ceder Ave	Robertson	221	RR 12
Celtis Ave	Grabouw	227	GU 11
Cemetery Rd	Caledon	225	CC 10
Cemetery Rd	Caledon	225	CB 10
Centaur St	Atlantis (Avondale)	200	AJ 30
Cereal St	Bredasdorp	197	BS 11
Ceres St	Atlantis (Avondale)	200	AJ 30
Cerf St	Worcester	219	WV 14
Cestrum Ave	Robertson	221	RP 11
Chakkie	Saldanha	210	SC 13
Chanda Cl.	Atlantis (Sherwood)	199	AG 32
Chapman	Saldanha	210	SD 13
Charel Uys Dr.	Atlantis	201	AK 31
Charel Uys Dr.	Atlantis (Atlantis Ind.)	200	AL 30
Charel Uys Dr.	Atlantis (Avondale)	201	AJ 31
Charel Uys Dr.	Atlantis (Avondale)	201	AJ 32
Charel Uys Dr.	Atlantis (Sherwood)	199	AF 32
Charel Uys Dr.	Atlantis (Sherwood)	199	AE 31
Charlene St	Worcester	219	WU 16
Charles Duminy Cl.	Atlantis (Atlantis Ind.)	201	AK 31
Charles Hoffe Ave	Melkbos (Duynefontein)	204	AY 25
Charles Hoffe Ave	Melkbos (Van Riebeeckstrand)	204	AZ 25
Charles Matthews St	Atlantis (Atlantis Ind.)	200	AL 30
Charles Matthews St	Atlantis (Atlantis Ind.)	201	AL 31
Charles Piers St	Atlantis (Atlantis Ind.)	200	AM 30
Charnwood Cl.	Atlantis (Sherwood)	199	AG 32
Charon St	Grabouw	227	GV 12
Charter St	Caledon	225	CD 12
Chasmanthe Cl.	Langebaan	209	LJ 11
Chat La.	Atlantis (Robinvale)	199	AH 32
Chavonnes St	Caledon	225	CD 11
Cheviot Dr.	Atlantis (Beaconhill)	199	AH 33
Chieftain St	Atlantis (Saxonsea)	199	AG 32
Chios Cl.	Langebaan	208	LD 11
Chris Hani St	Malmesbury	212	ME 12
Christopher Starke St	Atlantis (Atlantis Ind.)	200	AK 30
Christopher Starke St	Atlantis (Atlantis Ind.)	201	AK 31
Church St	Caledon	225	CC 12
Church St	Darling	213	DD 11
Church St	Hermanus	228	HG 12
Church St	Hermanus	228	HH 11
Church St	Malmesbury	212	MB 12
Church St	Montagu	222	MR 11
Church St	Saldanha	211	SC 14
Church St	Villiersdorp	223	VK 12
Church St	Worcester	216	WS 14
Cilicia Cr.	Atlantis (Avondale)	200	AJ 30
Cilliers St	Ceres	207	CG 12
Cilliers St	Worcester	215	WS 13
Cilliers St	Worcester	215	WS 12
Cinsaut St	Malmesbury	212	MA 12
Cinsaut St	Montagu	222	MP 13
Claassen St	Worcester	216	WS 17
Clairvaux St	Robertson	221	RQ 10
Claredon St	Bredasdorp	197	BV 12
Clarence St	Worcester	219	WU 14
Clarendon	Darling	213	DB 12
Clarendon Cl.	Atlantis (Sherwood)	199	AG 32
Clarke St	Saldanha	210	SC 11
Classic Cl.	Worcester	216	WP 15
Claude Samuel St	Worcester	219	WU 15
Clearwater Rd	Atlantis (Sherwood)	199	AG 32
Cleon Cl.	Langebaan	208	LD 11
Cleveland Cl.	Atlantis (Beaconhill)	199	AH 33
Cliff Rd	Hermanus	228	HH 11
Clipper St	Atlantis (Saxonsea)	199	AG 32
Clipston Cr.	Atlantis (Sherwood)	199	AG 32
Cloete St	Ceres	207	CG 11
Cloete St	Langebaan	209	LG 10
Clovelley St	Worcester	220	WT 18
Clubhouse Dr.	Langebaan	209	LF 13
Coetzee St	Robertson	221	RP 12
Coetzee St	Villiersdorp	223	VL 11
Cogmans Cl.	Montagu	222	MS 11
Coldrey St	Swellendam	224	SY 10
Cole	Darling	213	DC 12
Cole St	Worcester	215	WS 12
Colebrook St	Atlantis (Avondale)	200	AJ 30
Coledizea Ave	Worcester	220	WT 20
Coligny St	Malmesbury	212	MB 13
Coligny St	Robertson	221	RP 12
College Rd	Caledon	225	CC 11
College St	Hermanus	228	HG 13
Colombo St	Langebaan	209	LF 11
Coly La.	Atlantis (Robinvale)	201	AJ 32
Combrink St	Worcester	216	WS 16
Commaille Rd	Melkbos (Melkbosstrand)	204	BB 26
Commaille Rd	Melkbos (Melkbosstrand)	204	BC 25
Commisioner St	Swellendam	224	SY 10
Cona Ave	Worcester	220	WT 20
Concept Rd	Langebaan	209	LG 11
Concordia Cr.	Atlantis (Sherwood)	199	AG 32
Concordia St	Worcester	219	WU 17
Constant Dr.	Langebaan	209	LG 12
Constantia St	Robertson	221	RQ 10
Constitution St	Caledon	225	CB 12
Contour St	Hermanus	229	HE 16
Coral Cl.	Grabouw	227	GT 11
Coral Pl.	Atlantis (Avondale)	201	AJ 32
Cord Grass Way	Melkbos (Atlantic Beach Est.)	205	BD 27
Cormorant Cl.	Langebaan	209	LJ 11
Coronation Rd	Hermanus	228	HH 11
Coronation St	Swellendam	224	SZ 11
Cosmos Cl.	Atlantis (Protea Pk)	201	AK 32
Cosmos St	Atlantis (Protea Pk)	201	AK 31
Cotswold St	Atlantis (Robinvale)	199	AH 33
Cottage	Saldanha	210	SC 12
Cottager St	Atlantis (Avondale)	200	AJ 30
Courier St	Atlantis (Saxonsea)	199	AG 32
Courser Cir.	Atlantis (Robinvale)	199	AH 32
Courser La.	Atlantis (Robinvale)	201	AJ 32
Court La.	Bredasdorp	197	BV 12
Cowies St	Atlantis (Beaconhill)	199	AH 33
Cowrie La.	Melkbos (Atlantic Beach Est.)	205	BE 26
Cradock St	Worcester	215	WS 12
Crane St	Worcester	218	WV 13
Crassula St	Caledon	225	CB 12
Crescent Ave	Bredasdorp	197	BS 12
Croeser St	Malmesbury	212	MB 11
Cross St	Hermanus	229	HE 16
Cross St	Montagu	222	MO 12
Crotz St	Worcester	219	WV 14
Crow Ct	Atlantis (Robinvale)	199	AH 32
Cuckoo Ave	Atlantis (Robinvale)	199	AH 32
Culemborg St	Worcester	216	WQ 16
Cumberland Ct	Atlantis (Sherwood)	199	AG 32
Cupido St	Grabouw	227	GV 12
Cupido St	Montagu	222	MP 12
Curlew St	Atlantis (Robinvale)	199	AH 32
Curlew St	Atlantis (Robinvale)	201	AJ 33
Curry St	Worcester	219	WV 14
Cybelle St	Atlantis (Avondale)	200	AJ 30
Cypres St	Caledon	225	CB 10
Cyprug St	Swellendam	224	SX 11

D

STREET NAME	TOWN NAME	PG	GRID
D.F. Malherbe St	Kleinmond	226	KP 12
D.F. Strauss St	Kleinmond	226	KP 12
Da Gama	Saldanha	211	SC 14
Da Gama St	Langebaan	209	LG 10
Daffodil St	Robertson	221	RP 12
Daffodil St	Swellendam	224	SZ 11
Daffodil St	Worcester	219	WU 16
Dagbreek St	Malmesbury	212	MB 13
Dagbreek St	Robertson	221	RO 12
Dagbrekker St	Atlantis (Robinvale)	201	AJ 32
Dageraad St	Atlantis (Avondale)	200	AJ 30
Dageraad St	Langebaan	209	LH 11
Dageraad St	Saldanha	211	SC 14
Dahlia	Malmesbury	212	MC 12
Dahlia St	Atlantis (Protea Pk)	201	AK 31
Dahlia St	Montagu	222	MP 13
Dahlia St	Robertson	221	RP 13
Dahlia St	Saldanha	211	SC 14
Dahlia St	Swellendam	224	SZ 11
Dahlia St	Worcester	219	WU 16
Dam St	Bredasdorp	197	BV 11
Daniels Ave	Worcester	220	WT 20
Darling Cr.	Atlantis (Beaconhill)	199	AH 33
Darling Rd	Malmesbury	212	MD 12
Darling Rd	Malmesbury	212	ME 11
Darters Pl.	Atlantis (Robinvale)	199	AH 32
Dassen St	Langebaan	209	LG 11
Dassenberg Rd	Atlantis	200	AK 30
Dassenberg Rd	Atlantis	200	AL 28
Dassenberg Rd	Atlantis	200	AN 27
Dassenberg Rd	Atlantis	202	AO 26
Dassenberg Rd	Atlantis (Avondale)	198	AH 30
Dassenberg Rd	Atlantis (Avondale)	198	AF 30
Dassenberg Rd	Atlantis (Robinvale)	199	AD 31
Datura St	Atlantis (Protea Pk)	201	AK 32
David Cloete St	Atlantis (Atlantis Ind.)	201	AL 32
David Miller St	Atlantis (Atlantis Ind.)	200	AL 28
David St	Grabouw	227	GV 12
Davids St	Montagu	222	MQ 11
Davids St	Worcester	219	WU 14
Davids St	Worcester	219	WT 14
Dawn Rd	Langebaan	209	LG 12
Dawood St	Worcester	219	WU 14
Daybreak St	Langebaan	209	LG 11
Dayi St	Robertson	221	RS 12
De Doorns Cr.	Worcester	215	WQ 13
De Goede St	Hermanus	228	HG 11
De Jongh St	Worcester	216	WQ 17
De Kock St	Malmesbury	212	MC 10
De Kock St	Montagu	222	MR 11
De Kock St	Worcester	216	WS 15
De Korte St	Atlantis (Atlantis Ind.)	200	AL 30
De La Haye Cl.	Langebaan	209	LF 13
De La Haye Dr.	Langebaan	209	LF 13
De La Port St	Swellendam	224	SW 13
De Lat Bat Way	Worcester	216	WR 16
De Possel St	Caledon	225	CC 11
De Swantje Cl.	Langebaan	208	LE 12
De Villiers St	Bredasdorp	197	BT 12
De Villiers St	Bredasdorp	197	BT 11
De Villiers St	Caledon	225	CB 11
De Villiers St	Robertson	221	RP 11
De Villiers St	Villiersdorp	223	VK 11
De Villiers St	Worcester	215	WS 13
De Visch	Saldanha	211	SB 15
De Vos Malan St	Caledon	225	CC 10
De Vos St	Kleinmond	226	KP 12
De Vos St	Worcester	215	WS 13
De Vos St	Worcester	218	WT 13
De Waal St	Worcester	216	WS 14
De Wet St	Robertson	221	RP 12
De Wet St	Worcester	219	WT 15
De Wist St	Swellendam	224	SY 12
De Wit St	Robertson	221	RP 12
Deerlodge Rd	Atlantis (Sherwood)	199	AG 32
Dellville Ct	Atlantis (Sherwood)	199	AG 32
Delos St	Langebaan	208	LC 12
Delphi	Langebaan	208	LB 11
Delphinium St	Darling	213	DD 11
Delphinium St	Swellendam	224	TA 11
Delport St	Kleinmond	226	KO 12
Demas St	Worcester	219	WV 14
Demeter La.	Ceres	207	CH 10
Dempers St	Caledon	225	CB 11
Denise St	Worcester	219	WV 17
Denne Ave	Bredasdorp	197	BR 12
Denne Ave	Malmesbury	212	MD 12
Denne Ave	Robertson	221	RR 12
Denne Cr.	Ceres	207	CH 10
Denne La.	Worcester	216	WR 16
Denne St	Caledon	225	CE 13
Deon Britz St	Worcester	215	WS 12
Dewar	Atlantis (Sherwood)	199	AG 32
Diadem Cl.	Melkbos (Melkbosstrand)	204	BB 26
Diana St	Atlantis (Saxonsea)	199	AG 32
Dias Cr.	Ceres	207	CJ 11
Dias Cr.	Langebaan	209	LG 11
Diaz	Malmesbury	212	MA 11

STREET NAME	TOWN NAME	PG	GRID	
Diaz Rd	Saldanha	210	SC	10
Diaz St	Saldanha	211	SC	15
Dick de Klerk	Worcester	216	WP	15
Dickens St	Worcester	219	WU	14
Dido St	Atlantis (Saxonsea)	199	AG	32
Die Bad Rd	Melkbos (Duynefontein)	204	AY	25
Die Hoek	Langebaan	209	LG	12
Die Rand St	Swellendam	224	SX	10
Diedam St	Saldanha	210	SC	11
Diomede Cl.	Melkbos (Melkbosstrand)	204	BB	26
Dirk Brand St	Worcester	218	WT	13
Dirkie Uys St	Bredasdorp	197	BT	12
Dirkie Uys St	Grabouw	227	GT	11
Dirkie Uys St	Hermanus	228	HG	12
Dirkie Uys St	Malmesbury	212	MB	11
Dirkie Uys St	Robertson	221	RR	12
Disa	Langebaan	209	LG	10
Disa Ave	Bredasdorp	197	BT	12
Disa Ave	Robertson	221	RP	11
Disa Cl.	Atlantis (Protea Pk)	201	AJ	31
Disa St	Atlantis (Protea Pk)	201	AJ	32
Disa St	Atlantis (Protea Pk)	201	AK	31
Disa St	Caledon	225	CB	12
Disa St	Ceres	207	CH	12
Disa St	Grabouw	227	GU	12
Disa St	Hermanus	228	HG	12
Disa St	Malmesbury	212	MD	12
Disa St	Swellendam	224	SZ	11
Disa St	Tulbagh	206	TX	11
Disa St	Villiersdorp	223	VM	12
Disa St	Worcester	216	WR	15
Distillery Rd	Worcester	218	WT	12
Doddington St	Atlantis (Avondale)	200	AJ	30
Doleriet	Saldanha	210	SB	11
Dolfyn St	Saldanha	211	SC	14
Dollie	Saldanha	210	SC	13
Dolpen	Saldanha	210	SC	12
Dolphin St	Hermanus	228	HG	12
Dolphin View Cl.	Melkbos (Atlantic Beach Est.)	205	BF	26
Dommisse St	Worcester	216	WS	14
Don St	Saldanha	210	SC	11
Doncaster St	Saldanha	211	SB	15
Donkin	Darling	213	DC	12
Donkin Sq.	Caledon	225	CC	11
Donkin St	Caledon	225	CC	11
Donsie St	Saldanha	211	SA	17
Doornrivier	Worcester	215	WS	12
Dorah St	Atlantis (Saxonsea)	199	AG	32
Dordrecht Ave	Robertson	221	RQ	12
Doreen Cr.	Worcester	215	WP	10
Doringboom Ave	Kleinmond	226	KM	12
Doringbos	Robertson	221	RO	12
Dorp St	Malmesbury	212	MA	12
Dorpsig St	Bredasdorp	197	BU	12
Dove St	Saldanha	211	SA	17
Dr. Brewer St	Malmesbury	212	MC	11
Dr. Euvrard St	Malmesbury	212	MB	11
Dr. Euvrard St	Malmesbury	212	MB	12
Dresford St	Melkbos (Duynefontein)	204	AY	26
Driftwood Way	Melkbos (Atlantic Beach Est.)	205	BE	27
Dromedaris St	Melkbos (Melkbosstrand)	204	BC	26
Drommedaris	Saldanha	210	SD	13
Drommedaris Ave	Robertson	221	RR	13
Drommedaris Cr.	Worcester	216	WQ	16
Drommedaris St	Ceres	207	CJ	12
Drommedaris St	Melkbos (Van Riebeeckstrand)	204	AZ	26
Drostdy St	Swellendam	224	SY	12
Du Plessis St	Grabouw	227	GV	12
Du Preez St	Bredasdorp	197	BU	11
Du Preez St	Montagu	222	MP	12
Du Toit La.	Worcester	215	WS	13
Du Toit St	Ceres	207	CG	12
Du Toit St	Malmesbury	212	MC	12
Du Toit St	Montagu	222	MQ	12
Du Toit St	Swellendam	224	SX	10
Du Toit St	Villiersdorp	223	VL	12
Du Toits St	Bredasdorp	197	BU	11
Dudley Way	Worcester	219	WV	17
Duif La.	Atlantis (Robinvale)	199	AH	32
Duif St	Tulbagh	206	TX	12
Duiker Ave	Atlantis (Robinvale)	199	AH	32
Duiker Ave	Saldanha	211	SA	17
Duiker La.	Worcester	215	WQ	11
Duiker Rd	Melkbos (Van Riebeeckstrand)	204	AZ	26
Duiker St	Hermanus	228	HG	11
Duiker St	Hermanus	228	HG	12
Dukulu St	Worcester	217	WS	21
Duncan Rd	Worcester	220	WU	18
Duncan Way	Worcester	219	WV	17
Dune Ave	Bredasdorp	197	BR	12
Dunker St	Melkbos (Duynefontein)	204	AY	26
Durban St	Darling	213	DB	12
Durban St	Darling	213	DC	12
Durban St	Worcester	218	WU	13
Durban St	Worcester	219	WT	15
Durban St	Worcester	219	WW	16
Durban St	Worcester	220	WX	18
Duthie St	Malmesbury	212	MB	11
Duynbeeck	Langebaan	209	LH	10
Duynbeek St	Atlantis (Avondale)	200	AJ	30
Dwars St	Caledon	225	CD	12
Dwars St	Langebaan	209	LG	10
Dwesa La.	Atlantis (Sherwood)	199	AG	32
Dyasi Ave	Worcester	220	WT	21

E

STREET NAME	TOWN NAME	PG	GRID	
Eagle Rd	Melkbos (Van Riebeeckstrand)	204	AZ	26
Eagle St	Worcester	218	WV	13
Eagles Nest	Atlantis (Robinvale)	199	AH	32
East St	Hermanus	228	HH	11
East St	Tulbagh	206	TX	11
Ebbflow Cl.	Melkbos (Melkbosstrand)	205	BD	25
Eben Donges Ave	Robertson	221	RR	12
Ebenhaeser St	Grabouw	227	GT	11
Eddie Prins Dr.	Worcester	216	WQ	17
Edelweis St	Swellendam	224	SZ	11
Edgar Cr.	Melkbos (Duynefontein)	203	AX	26
Edgar Cr.	Melkbos (Duynefontein)	204	AY	26
Edinburgh Pl.	Atlantis (Saxonsea)	199	AH	32
Edward Cr.	Melkbos (Duynefontein)	204	AY	25
Edward Philcox St	Worcester	215	WQ	13
Edward Rd	Atlantis (Avondale)	200	AJ	30
Edward St	Worcester	219	WU	14
Eel Grass Way	Melkbos (Atlantic Beach Est.)	205	BD	26
Eerste Ave	Bredasdorp	197	BS	11
Egret Ave	Atlantis (Robinvale)	201	AJ	32
Egret St	Langebaan	209	LJ	10
Eich St	Worcester	215	WR	13
Eighteenth Ave	Melkbos (Melkbosstrand)	204	BB	26
Eighth Ave	Caledon	225	CD	13
Eighth Ave	Darling	213	DB	12
Eighth Ave	Kleinmond	226	KN	12
Eighth Ave	Melkbos (Melkbosstrand)	204	BC	25
Eighth Ave	Saldanha	211	SB	15
Eighth St	Hermanus	229	HF	17
Eighth St	Kleinmond	226	KN	12
Eike Ave	Bredasdorp	197	BU	12
Eike Ave	Grabouw	227	GU	12
Eike Ave	Malmesbury	212	MD	12
Eike La.	Tulbagh	206	TW	12
Eike La.	Worcester	216	WQ	16
Eike St	Ceres	207	CH	11
Eikenhof St	Worcester	219	WT	17
Eiland St	Ceres	207	CJ	12
Elara	Langebaan	208	LB	11
Elberta St	Ceres	207	CJ	12
Elberta St	Grabouw	227	GU	12
Elegangs Cl.	Langebaan	209	LH	12
Eleventh Ave	Darling	213	DB	12
Eleventh Ave	Kleinmond	226	KO	12
Eleventh Ave	Kleinmond	226	KM	12
Eleventh Ave	Melkbos (Melkbosstrand)	204	BC	26
Eleventh Ave	Saldanha	211	SB	15
Eleventh St	Kleinmond	226	KO	12
Elf St	Langebaan	209	LG	11
Elita St	Saldanha	210	SC	10
Elizabeth Cr.	Atlantis (Saxonsea)	199	AG	31
Elizabeth St	Worcester	219	WU	16
Elk La.	Atlantis (Sherwood)	199	AG	32
Ella St	Grabouw	227	GV	12
Ellefsen Cl.	Langebaan	209	LF	12
Elliot Way	Worcester	219	WV	17
Ellis St	Swellendam	224	SZ	12
Ellis St	Worcester	216	WP	15
Elm Ave	Robertson	221	RR	12
Elmboog La.	Worcester	219	WT	14
Eluxolweni	Robertson	221	RS	12
Empress Rd	Worcester	219	WU	14
Enchantress Cr.	Atlantis (Saxonsea)	199	AG	31
Enderstein St	Langebaan	209	LH	10
Engelbrecht St	Worcester	216	WS	14
Engels	Langebaan	209	LJ	11
Engin	Saldanha	210	SC	12
Epson St	Langebaan	208	LC	13
Erica Cl.	Hermanus	229	HE	14
Erica Cl.	Langebaan	209	LH	10
Erica Cr.	Atlantis (Protea Pk)	201	AJ	31
Erica Cr.	Atlantis (Protea Pk)	201	AJ	32
Erica Cr.	Kleinmond	226	KO	12
Erica Cr.	Villiersdorp	223	VN	11
Erica St	Grabouw	227	GU	12
Erica St	Robertson	221	RO	12
Erica St	Worcester	216	WR	15
Erika St	Bredasdorp	197	BV	12
Erika St	Swellendam	224	TA	11
Esperance	Worcester	215	WQ	13
Esperance St	Worcester	219	WU	17
Espiegle St	Atlantis (Saxonsea)	199	AG	32
Esseboom Ave	Kleinmond	226	KM	11
Essenhout Ave	Grabouw	227	GT	11
Essenhout Cr.	Tulbagh	206	TX	13
Essenhout St	Malmesbury	212	MD	11
Essop St	Worcester	219	WT	17
Esterhuysen St	Worcester	216	WQ	17
Ethel Way	Worcester	215	WQ	11
Europa St	Bredasdorp	197	BR	12
Eve Ave	Atlantis (Avondale)	200	AJ	30
Eve St	Saldanha	211	SB	14
Evita Bezuidenhout Blvd	Darling	213	DC	12
Excelsior Way	Worcester	219	WU	17
Eybers St	Worcester	217	WR	18
Eyland St	Atlantis (Saxonsea)	199	AG	32

F

STREET NAME	TOWN NAME	PG	GRID	
Fabriek Rd	Bredasdorp	197	BS	11
Fabriek St	Ceres	207	CH	12
Fabriek St	Ceres	207	CG	12
Fabriek St	Darling	213	DC	12
Fabriek St	Malmesbury	212	MD	11
Fabriek Way	Bredasdorp	197	BR	11
Fairbain St	Swellendam	224	SY	11
Fairbairn St	Worcester	216	WS	15
Fairbairn St	Worcester	219	WT	16
Fairfield St	Atlantis (Saxonsea)	199	AG	31
Fairview St	Worcester	219	WU	17
Fairway Dr.	Langebaan	209	LG	12
Fairway Heights Dr.	Worcester	216	WP	14
Fairways Ave	Hermanus	228	HF	13
Fakier	Worcester	219	WU	15
Falcons Pl.	Atlantis (Robinvale)	199	AH	32
Falken Cl.	Langebaan	209	LF	12
Fame St	Atlantis (Saxonsea)	199	AG	31
Fanie Dreyer Dr.	Melkbos (Melkbosstrand)	204	BC	26
Farleigh Ct	Atlantis (Sherwood)	199	AG	32
Faroek Way	Worcester	219	WV	17
Faure Cr.	Worcester	216	WP	17
Faure St	Ceres	207	CG	11
Faure St	Malmesbury	212	MB	12
Faure St	Swellendam	224	SX	12
Feik	Saldanha	210	SC	13
Felicia Cr.	Atlantis (Protea Pk)	201	AJ	31
Felicia Cr.	Langebaan	209	LH	12
Felicity St	Worcester	219	WU	16
Felix St	Montagu	222	MP	12
Fell St	Grabouw	227	GV	12
Fernande St	Atlantis (Saxonsea)	199	AG	31
Fernkloof Dr.	Hermanus	229	HE	15
Fernkloof Dr.	Hermanus	229	HE	14
Ferraria St	Langebaan	209	LJ	11
Ferry	Saldanha	210	SC	12
Ficus Ave	Robertson	221	RR	12
Ficus St	Malmesbury	212	MD	11
Field St	Worcester	216	WS	17
Fifteenth Ave	Darling	213	DB	12
Fifteenth Ave	Kleinmond	226	KM	11
Fifteenth Ave	Melkbos (Melkbosstrand)	204	BC	26
Fifth Ave	Caledon	225	CD	12
Fifth Ave	Darling	213	DC	12
Fifth Ave	Hermanus	229	HF	17
Fifth Ave	Kleinmond	226	KO	12
Fifth Ave	Kleinmond	226	KM	12
Fifth Ave	Melkbos (Melkbosstrand)	204	BC	25
Fifth Ave	Saldanha	211	SB	15
Fifth Ave	Tulbagh	206	TW	12
Fifth St	Hermanus	229	HE	17
Fifth St	Kleinmond	226	KN	12
Figilante St	Atlantis (Saxonsea)	199	AG	31
Fir Ave	Bredasdorp	197	BT	11
Fir Ave	Hermanus	229	HE	16
Fir Cl.	Hermanus	229	HE	16
First Ave	Caledon	225	CD	12
First Ave	Ceres	207	CG	11
First Ave	Darling	213	DC	12
First Ave	Hermanus	229	HE	17
First Ave	Kleinmond	226	KO	12
First Ave	Kleinmond	226	KM	12
First Ave	Melkbos (Melkbosstrand)	204	BC	25
First Ave	Robertson	221	RP	11
First Ave	Tulbagh	206	TX	12
First St	Hermanus	229	HE	17
First St	Kleinmond	226	KM	12
Fisant La.	Ceres	207	CG	10
Fisant St	Worcester	218	WV	13
Fisante St	Tulbagh	206	TW	13
Fisher St	Worcester	216	WS	16
Fisher St	Worcester	219	WT	16
Fiskaal St	Atlantis (Robinvale)	199	AH	33
Flameck St	Malmesbury	212	MC	10
Flamingo Park	Atlantis (Robinvale)	201	AJ	32
Flamingo Rd	Melkbos (Van Riebeeckstrand)	204	BA	26
Flamingo St	Langebaan	209	LH	10
Flamingo St	Saldanha	211	SB	16
Flamingo St	Worcester	215	WP	11
Flamink	Malmesbury	212	ME	10
Flat St	Hermanus	229	HF	15
Fletcher St	Bredasdorp	197	BT	11
Fleur St	Robertson	221	RO	12
Floksie St	Malmesbury	212	MD	12
Floors Brand	Langebaan	209	LG	11
Flora Ave	Hermanus	228	HG	11
Flora Cl.	Atlantis (Avondale)	200	AJ	30
Flower St	Hermanus	228	HG	12
Flower St	Langebaan	209	LG	12
Fluks St	Montagu	222	MQ	12
Fontein St	Grabouw	227	GT	12
Fonteinhout Ave	Kleinmond	226	KM	11
Ford St	Malmesbury	212	MB	11
Ford St	Worcester	216	WR	17
Forest Rd	Grabouw	227	GT	11
Forte	Saldanha	210	SC	12
Fortuin St	Bredasdorp	197	BR	11
Fortuin St	Ceres	207	CJ	11
Fortuin St	Grabouw	227	GV	12
Fortuin St	Worcester	219	WU	14
Fortune St	Atlantis (Avondale)	200	AJ	30
Fountain St	Darling	213	DD	11
Fourie St	Hermanus	228	HG	12
Fourteenth Ave	Darling	213	DB	12
Fourteenth Ave	Melkbos (Melkbosstrand)	204	BC	26
Fourteenth St	Kleinmond	226	KO	12
Fourth Ave	Caledon	225	CD	12
Fourth Ave	Ceres	207	CG	11
Fourth Ave	Darling	213	DC	12
Fourth Ave	Hermanus	229	HE	17
Fourth Ave	Hermanus	229	HF	17
Fourth Ave	Kleinmond	226	KO	12
Fourth Ave	Melkbos (Melkbosstrand)	204	BC	25
Fourth Ave	Saldanha	211	SB	15
Fourth Ave	Tulbagh	206	TW	12
Fourth La.	Ceres	207	CG	11
Fourth St	Hermanus	229	HE	17
Fourth St	Kleinmond	226	KM	12
Fourth St	Worcester	217	WR	19
Foxcroft Cr.	Melkbos (Duynefontein)	203	AX	26
Francis Auden St	Worcester	215	WQ	13
Francis St	Atlantis (Saxonsea)	199	AG	31
Franklin St	Worcester	216	WR	17
Fransman St	Worcester	219	WT	17
Fred Mann St	Worcester	217	WR	20
Fred Mann St	Worcester	217	WS	20
Freeman St	Robertson	221	RQ	10
Freemans La.	Bredasdorp	197	BT	12
Freesia Ave	Robertson	221	RP	10
Freesia Cl.	Atlantis (Protea Pk)	201	AJ	31
Freesia Cl.	Atlantis (Protea Pk)	201	AM	32
Freesia St	Caledon	225	CB	12
Freesia St	Ceres	207	CJ	12
Freesia St	Swellendam	224	TA	11
Freesia St	Tulbagh	206	TX	11
Freesia St	Worcester	219	WU	16
Fregat Cl.	Langebaan	208	LE	11
Freislich St	Worcester	215	WS	13
Fremont La.	Atlantis (Sherwood)	199	AG	32
Frere St	Worcester	215	WS	13
Fresia St	Malmesbury	212	MD	12
Frigate	Saldanha	210	SC	12
Frouenfeider St	Caledon	225	CC	12
Fuchsia St	Atlantis (Protea Pk)	201	AJ	32
Fuchsia St	Worcester	219	WU	16
Fulang Ave	Worcester	217	WS	21
Fulang Ave	Worcester	220	WT	20
Fullard St	Swellendam	224	SY	11
Fulmar Rd	Langebaan	209	LG	11
Fynbos St	Hermanus	229	HF	14

G

STREET NAME	TOWN NAME	PG	GRID	
G.J.H.Steenkamp St	Kleinmond	226	KP	12
Gaffley St	Grabouw	227	GV	12
Galico St	Langebaan	209	LH	10
Galjoen St	Saldanha	210	SC	11
Galjoot Cl.	Langebaan	208	LE	11
Galtonia St	Atlantis (Protea Pk)	201	AJ	32
Gannet Rd	Melkbos (Van Riebeeckstrand)	204	AZ	26
Garden St	Darling	213	DD	11
Gardenia	Grabouw	227	GU	12
Gardenia Ave	Ceres	207	CJ	12
Gardenia Ave	Malmesbury	212	MD	12
Gardenia St	Atlantis (Protea Pk)	201	AJ	32
Gardenia St	Atlantis (Protea Pk)	201	AK	32
Gardenia St	Worcester	219	WU	16
Gars St	Malmesbury	212	MB	13
Garthland St	Worcester	219	WU	17
Gasnat St	Worcester	219	WU	17
Gazania La.	Kleinmond	226	KL	11
Gazania St	Swellendam	224	TA	11
Gazania St	Atlantis (Protea Pk)	201	AJ	32
Gazonia St	Atlantis (Protea Pk)	201	AJ	32
Geel St	Bredasdorp	197	BR	11
Geelbek St	Saldanha	211	SC	14
Geelhout Ave	Kleinmond	226	KM	11
Geelhout Ave	Malmesbury	212	ME	11
Geelhout Ave	Robertson	221	RR	13
Geldenhuys St	Malmesbury	212	MC	12
Geldenhuys St	Worcester	216	WP	16
George St	Robertson	221	RO	12
George St	Worcester	219	WT	14
Geranium Cr.	Atlantis (Protea Pk)	201	AJ	32
Gerrit Maritz St	Kleinmond	226	KP	12
Gerrit Rd	Worcester	219	WU	17
Gertse St	Worcester	219	WV	15
Gerwyn Owen St	Atlantis (Atlantis Ind.)	200	AL	30
Ghika St	Atlantis (Saxonsea)	199	AG	31
Gholf Cr.	Ceres	207	CJ	11
Gideon Basson	Atlantis (Atlantis Ind.)	200	AN	29
Gie La.	Worcester	215	WS	13
Gill St	Grabouw	227	GV	12
Gladiola St	Malmesbury	212	ME	12
Gladiolus	Langebaan	209	LH	12
Gladiolus Cl.	Atlantis (Protea Pk)	201	AJ	32
Glaeser St	Worcester	216	WS	15
Glasogie St	Worcester	219	WV	14
Glen	Saldanha	211	SB	14
Glen Avon St	Worcester	220	WT	18
Glen Barry Rd	Swellendam	224	SW	12
Glen Mist	Saldanha	210	SC	13
Glencoe St	Worcester	219	WU	17
Glenn Cr.	Worcester	216	WR	14
Gloriosa Cl.	Atlantis (Protea Pk)	201	AJ	32
Godetia St	Malmesbury	212	MD	12
Goede Hoop Dr.	Langebaan	208	LE	12
Goede Hoop Dr.	Langebaan	209	LF	13
Goede Hoop St	Atlantis (Saxonsea)	199	AG	31
Goede Hoop St	Melkbos (Melkbosstrand)	204	BC	26
Goedehoop Ave	Robertson	221	RR	13
Goedehoop La.	Worcester	215	WP	12
Goetham St	Montagu	222	MP	12
Golf St	Bredasdorp	197	BT	11
Golf St	Bredasdorp	197	BS	12
Goliath Cr.	Ceres	207	CH	12

Abbreviations used: Ave – Avenue, A.H. – Agricultural Holding, A.L.– Algemene Landgoed, Blvd – Boulevard, Cen. – Central, Cir. – Circle, Cl. – Close, Cr. – Crescent, Ct – Court, Dr. – Drive, Est. – Estate, Ext. – Extension, Hgts – Heights, Ind. – Industrial, Gdns – Gardens, Gr. – Grove, La. – Lane, (M.Plain) - Mitchells Plain, Nth – North, Pl. – Place, Pk – Park, Rd – Road, Rdg. – Ridge, S.H.– Small Holding, Sq. – Square, St – Street, Sth – South, Ter. – Terrace, Tn – Turn, Val. – Valley, Wk – Walk

STREET NAME	TOWN NAME	PG	GRID	
Goniwe St	Malmesbury	212	ME	12
Good Hope St	Saldanha	210	SC	12
Good Shed St	Bredasdorp	197	BR	11
Gordon St	Worcester	219	WU	16
Gothenburg	Atlantis (Avondale)	201	AJ	31
Gouda St	Atlantis (Avondale)	198	AH	30
Goudveld Ct	Atlantis (Sherwood)	199	AG	32
Goukamma Ct	Atlantis (Sherwood)	199	AG	32
Gouna Cr.	Atlantis (Sherwood)	199	AG	32
Gousblom La.	Kleinmond	226	KL	11
Gousblom La.	Langebaan	209	LF	10
Gousblom St	Caledon	225	CB	12
Gousblom St	Malmesbury	212	MD	12
Governer St	Worcester	215	WS	13
Graaf St	Montagu	222	MQ	11
Graaff St	Villiersdorp	223	VL	11
Graan	Malmesbury	212	MB	13
Grampian Cr.	Atlantis (Beaconhill)	199	AH	33
Granaatbos	Robertson	221	RO	11
Grand Slam St	Langebaan	209	LG	12
Granny Smith Rd	Grabouw	227	GV	11
Greenwood La.	Worcester	216	WR	15
Grens Rd	Saldanha	211	SD	14
Grey St	Darling	213	DC	12
Grey St	Worcester	219	WT	15
Grey St	Worcester	219	WU	15
Groeneveld St	Worcester	216	WQ	15
Groenewald St	Swellendam	224	SX	12
Groenkop Cl.	Atlantis (Sherwood)	199	AG	32
Groenvlei St	Saldanha	210	SC	11
Groot Eiland	Worcester	215	WQ	13
Grosvenor Ave	Atlantis (Avondale)	199	AH	31
Grosvenor Ave	Atlantis (Avondale)	201	AJ	31
Grosvenor Ave	Atlantis (Saxonsea)	199	AG	31
Growers St	Ceres	207	CG	12
Grundel St	Atlantis (Avondale)	200	AJ	30
Guardian Cl.	Atlantis (Avondale)	200	AJ	30
Guernsey St	Malmesbury	212	MB	10
Gullcry Cl.	Melkbos (Melkbosstrand)	205	BD	25
Gullhaven	Atlantis (Robinvale)	201	AJ	32
Gum Grove St	Robertson	221	RQ	12
Gunter St	Villiersdorp	223	VL	12
Guthrie St	Hermanus	229	HF	16
H				
H. Hattingh St	Worcester	216	WQ	17
H.H. de Kock St	Kleinmond	226	KP	12
Haakdoring St	Tulbagh	206	TW	13
Haarlem St	Atlantis (Avondale)	201	AJ	31
Hackney St	Malmesbury	212	MB	10
Hager Ave	Robertson	221	RP	11
Haig Ave	Atlantis	201	AK	34
Halam St	Worcester	217	WS	21
Ham St	Villiersdorp	223	VM	10
Ham St	Villiersdorp	223	VM	11
Ham St	Villiersdorp	223	VL	11
Hamerkop Rd	Melkbos (Duynefontein)	204	AZ	26
Hamerkop St	Worcester	219	WV	14
Hamlet St	Montagu	222	MR	12
Hammer St	Worcester	219	WU	14
Hanekam St	Malmesbury	212	ME	12
Hani St	Robertson	221	RS	12
Hannah Cl.	Atlantis (Avondale)	201	AJ	31
Hans De Lange St	Worcester	217	WQ	18
Harbour lights La.	Melkbos (Atlantic Beach Est.)	205	BE	27
Harbour Rd	Hermanus	228	HH	13
Harbour Rd	Kleinmond	226	KO	12
Harde Peer Ave	Kleinmond	226	KM	11
Harder St	Saldanha	211	SC	14
Haring St	Saldanha	211	SD	14
Harlem St	Worcester	216	WQ	16
Harmony La.	Hermanus	228	HG	12
Harold Ashwell Blvd.	Melkbos (Melkbosstrand)	204	BB	26
Harpuisbos La.	Langebaan	209	LJ	11
Harpuisbos St	Langebaan	209	LH	11
Harriet St	Worcester	219	WV	16
Harris St	Worcester	216	WR	17
Harrow St	Atlantis (Beaconhill)	199	AH	33
Harry Alexander Cl.	Atlantis (Atlantis Ind.)	201	AL	32
Harry Alexander Cr.	Atlantis (Atlantis Ind.)	201	AL	31
Hartebees La.	Worcester	215	WQ	11
Hartwig Ave	Worcester	219	WT	16
Hartwig Ave	Worcester	219	WT	17
Hartzenberg St	Worcester	219	WU	15
Haw St	Caledon	225	CC	11
Hawer St	Malmesbury	212	MB	13
Heath Fields Rd	Atlantis (Protea Pk)	201	AJ	32
Heath St	Worcester	216	WR	15
Heatlie St	Worcester	220	WU	18
Heemraad St	Caledon	225	CD	13
Heemraad St	Malmesbury	212	MC	11
Heemraad St	Swellendam	224	SX	12
Heerengraaf Dr.	Langebaan	208	LE	12
Heerengraaf Dr.	Langebaan	209	LF	12
Heide Ave	Bredasdorp	197	BU	11
Heide Ave	Robertson	221	RP	12
Heide Ave	Swellendam	224	SZ	11
Heide St	Caledon	225	CB	12
Heide St	Ceres	207	CH	12
Heide St	Malmesbury	212	MD	12
Heldersig St	Ceres	207	CJ	11
Helen La.	Worcester	215	WP	11
Helen St	Atlantis (Saxonsea)	198	AG	30
Helena St	Worcester	219	WT	14
Helena St	Worcester	219	WU	14

STREET NAME	TOWN NAME	PG	GRID	
Heller Blvd	Worcester	215	WQ	11
Helm St	Worcester	219	WV	14
Hendrickse St	Worcester	219	WU	14
Hendrik Boom St	Worcester	216	WQ	16
Hendrik St	Grabouw	227	GV	12
Hendriks Cr.	Melkbos (Duynefontein)	203	AX	26
Hendry Coert St	Worcester	219	WT	15
Hendry Gird St	Worcester	215	WR	13
Hendry St	Ceres	207	CH	12
Hennie Ferus Cr.	Worcester	219	WT	15
Henry Cr.	Melkbos (Duynefontein)	203	AX	26
Henry Cl.	Grabouw	227	GU	11
Henry Hill St	Worcester	216	WQ	17
Hercules St	Atlantis (Avondale)	201	AJ	31
Herculus St	Ceres	207	CJ	12
Hereford St	Malmesbury	212	MB	10
Herlille St	Saldanha	210	SC	10
Hermanus Steyn St	Swellendam	224	SX	12
Hermes Ave	Atlantis (Saxonsea)	199	AF	31
Heron Cr.	Melkbos (Duynefontein)	204	AY	26
Heron Rd	Langebaan	209	LG	12
Herons Pl.	Atlantis (Robinvale)	201	AJ	32
Hertzog St	Grabouw	227	GT	11
Heuningberg St	Bredasdorp	197	BV	12
Heuningbos Cl.	Langebaan	209	LJ	12
Heuwel St	Robertson	221	RO	12
Heuwel Way	Worcester	216	WS	15
Heyn St	Worcester	216	WS	14
Heyns St	Swellendam	224	SX	12
Hibiscus Ave	Bredasdorp	197	BR	12
Hibiscus Ave	Robertson	221	RP	11
Hibiscus Cl.	Atlantis (Protea Pk)	201	AJ	32
Hibiscus Cl.	Atlantis (Protea Pk)	201	AM	32
Hibiscus St	Langebaan	209	LF	11
Hibuskus St	Malmesbury	212	MD	12
Hibuskus St	Malmesbury	212	ME	10
Hickory La.	Worcester	216	WP	15
High St	Darling	213	DD	10
High St	Hermanus	228	HG	13
High St	Malmesbury	212	MB	12
High St	Swellendam	224	TA	11
High St	Tulbagh	206	TX	11
High St	Worcester	216	WS	16
High St	Worcester	216	WS	15
High St	Worcester	219	WT	14
Highgate Cr.	Atlantis (Beaconhill)	199	AG	33
Hildebrand St	Darling	213	DD	11
Hill St	Darling	213	DD	11
Hill St	Hermanus	228	HF	13
Hill St	Malmesbury	212	MA	12
Hisop	Malmesbury	212	MD	11
Hitchcock St	Worcester	219	WT	17
Hlalele Ave	Worcester	220	WT	20
Hobby La.	Atlantis (Robinvale)	201	AJ	33
Hoek	Saldanha	210	SC	13
Hoeker Cl.	Langebaan	209	LF	11
Hof St	Malmesbury	212	MA	12
Hoffman St	Bredasdorp	197	BT	11
Hofmeyer St	Grabouw	227	GT	11
Hofmeyr St	Montagu	222	MR	11
Hokim St	Robertson	221	RP	11
Holiday Rd	Langebaan	209	LG	11
Holland St	Atlantis (Saxonsea)	198	AF	30
Hollenbach St	Worcester	219	WT	14
Holomisa St	Malmesbury	212	ME	12
Holster St	Swellendam	224	SZ	11
Holtzapfel St	Ceres	207	CH	12
Holzapfel Rd	Tulbagh	206	TX	13
Homeria Cl.	Atlantis (Protea Pk)	201	AJ	31
Homeria Cl.	Atlantis (Protea Pk)	201	AM	32
Honeysuckle Cl.	Langebaan	209	LG	12
Honeyvale Rd	Atlantis	201	AN	34
Hoog St	Bredasdorp	197	BV	12
Hoog St	Grabouw	227	GT	12
Hoog St	Montagu	222	MQ	12
Hoogergeest Cr.	Atlantis (Saxonsea)	199	AG	31
Hooggelegen La.	Worcester	215	WS	12
Hoop Cr.	Atlantis (Saxonsea)	198	AG	30
Hoop Cr.	Atlantis (Saxonsea)	199	AG	31
Hoop St	Bredasdorp	197	BT	12
Hoop St	Malmesbury	212	MB	13
Hoop St	Robertson	221	RR	11
Hoopoe Ave	Atlantis (Robinvale)	201	AJ	33
Hoopvol St	Caledon	225	CD	13
Hoopvol St	Malmesbury	212	MC	10
Hoosain Cr.	Worcester	219	WU	17
Hope St	Caledon	225	CB	11
Hope St	Hermanus	228	HG	13
Hopley Ave	Robertson	221	RP	11
Hopley St	Bredasdorp	197	BU	12
Hopley St	Swellendam	224	SZ	11
Horak St	Malmesbury	212	MB	12
Horizon Cl.	Langebaan	209	LG	12
Horn Cr.	Melkbos (Duynefontein)	203	AX	26
Hornbill Cir.	Atlantis (Robinvale)	199	AH	33
Hospitaal St	Malmesbury	212	MB	11
Hospital Rd	Hermanus	228	HH	11
Hospital St	Montagu	222	MR	12
Hospital St	Robertson	221	RP	12
Hostel St	Bredasdorp	197	BT	11
Hout St	Malmesbury	212	MA	12
Hout St	Swellendam	224	SX	11
Hoy St	Hermanus	228	HF	12
Hugenoot Way	Worcester	215	WP	11
Hugenot St	Villiersdorp	223	VL	12

STREET NAME	TOWN NAME	PG	GRID	
Hugenote St	Malmesbury	212	MB	11
Hugo Naude La.	Worcester	215	WS	13
Hugo Naude St	Kleinmond	226	KP	12
Hugo St	Bredasdorp	197	BU	11
Hugo St	Ceres	207	CG	11
Hugo St	Worcester	216	WR	17
Human Cr.	Melkbos (Duynefontein)	203	AX	26
Human Cr.	Melkbos (Duynefontein)	203	AX	27
Human St	Caledon	225	CB	11
Hydrangea Cr.	Atlantis (Protea Pk)	201	AJ	32
I				
I.J.Singleton St	Kleinmond	226	KP	12
Ibasa Cl.	Atlantis (Protea Pk)	201	AJ	32
Ibasa Cl.	Atlantis (Protea Pk)	201	AM	32
Ibis Cl.	Langebaan	209	LJ	10
Ibis St	Atlantis (Robinvale)	199	AH	33
Icarus	Langebaan	208	LB	11
Idlewinds St	Worcester	220	WU	18
Imbeza Rd	Atlantis (Sherwood)	199	AG	33
Imhoff St	Malmesbury	212	MA	11
Immelman St	Malmesbury	212	MB	12
Impala St	Hermanus	228	HG	11
Impala St	Hermanus	228	HG	12
Impala Way	Worcester	215	WR	11
Independant St	Bredasdorp	197	BU	12
Industria Rd	Hermanus	228	HG	11
Industria St	Robertson	221	RR	12
Industrial St	Grabouw	227	GV	11
Industrie Rd	Malmesbury	212	MC	12
Industrie St	Langebaan	209	LG	11
Industry St	Caledon	225	CC	11
Inia	Malmesbury	212	MC	10
Insiswa Rd	Atlantis (Sherwood)	199	AG	33
Inverness Dr.	Melkbos (Melkbosstrand)	204	BC	26
Inverness Dr.	Melkbos (Melkbosstrand)	204	BC	27
Iresine Cl.	Atlantis (Protea Pk)	201	AJ	32
Iresine Cl.	Atlantis (Protea Pk)	201	AM	32
Iris Cr.	Swellendam	224	TA	11
Iris St	Ceres	207	CJ	12
Iris St	Malmesbury	212	ME	12
Iris St	Robertson	221	RO	12
Iris Way	Worcester	215	WR	11
Isaacs River Rd	Kleinmond	226	KM	11
Ismael St	Montagu	222	MQ	12
Ismail Way	Worcester	219	WV	17
Ixia Cl.	Atlantis (Protea Pk)	201	AK	33
Ixia St	Caledon	225	CB	12
Ixia St	Darling	213	DD	12
J				
J.S. Marais St	Kleinmond	226	KP	12
Jacana Cir.	Atlantis (Robinvale)	201	AJ	33
Jacaranda Cl.	Atlantis (Protea Pk)	201	AJ	32
Jacaranda Cl.	Atlantis (Protea Pk)	201	AM	32
Jacaranda St	Caledon	225	CB	10
Jacaranda St	Tulbagh	206	TW	12
Jack Ave	Worcester	220	WT	20
Jacob St	Ceres	207	CH	12
Jacob St	Grabouw	227	GV	12
Jacob Verster St	Saldanha	210	SC	11
Jacobs St	Saldanha	210	SC	11
Jacobus Burger St	Worcester	216	WQ	17
Jacobus Cr.	Melkbos (Duynefontein)	203	AX	27
Jaffe St	Saldanha	211	SB	14
Jag Cl.	Langebaan	208	LE	11
Jakaranda Ave	Robertson	221	RR	12
Jakaranda La.	Bredasdorp	197	BS	12
Jakaranda La.	Worcester	216	WR	15
Jakaranda La.	Worcester	216	WR	16
Jakaranda St	Darling	213	DD	12
Jakaranda St	Malmesbury	212	ME	12
Jakaranda St	Malmesbury	212	MD	12
Jakaranda St	Swellendam	224	SY	11
Jakoba St	Langebaan	209	LH	10
Jan Fiskaal	Malmesbury	212	ME	10
Jansen Cr.	Robertson	221	RP	12
Janssens Cr.	Melkbos (Melkbosstrand)	204	BA	26
Janszen St	Worcester	216	WQ	16
Jantjies St	Bredasdorp	197	BR	11
Januarie St	Montagu	222	MP	12
Januarie St	Worcester	219	WU	14
Japhta Cr.	Grabouw	227	GV	13
Japonica St	Malmesbury	212	ME	12
Japonika St	Robertson	221	RP	13
Jarque Rd	Worcester	219	WU	17
Jasmyn St	Malmesbury	212	MD	12
Jasmyn St	Robertson	221	RP	13
Jason St	Worcester	219	WV	15
Jean Welz St	Worcester	215	WS	13
Jeffery St	Ceres	207	CG	11
Jeremy St	Bredasdorp	197	BT	13
Job St	Malmesbury	212	MB	12
Johan De Jong St	Robertson	221	RQ	13
Johan Heyns St	Atlantis (Atlantis Ind.)	201	AL	31
Johan St	Saldanha	211	SA	17
John Daneel St	Kleinmond	226	KO	12
John Dreyer St	Atlantis (Atlantis Ind.)	201	AL	32
John St Leger Cr.	Atlantis (Atlantis Ind.)	200	AL	29
John van Niekerk St	Atlantis (Atlantis Ind.)	200	AK	30
John van Niekerk St	Atlantis (Atlantis Ind.)	200	AM	30
Johnson St	Montagu	222	MQ	12
Johnson St	Robertson	221	RP	12
Jolette St	Worcester	219	WU	17
Jones St	Robertson	221	RO	12

STREET NAME	TOWN NAME	PG	GRID	
Jonkershoek Rd	Atlantis (Sherwood)	199	AG	33
Jordaan St	Malmesbury	212	MC	12
Jordaan St	Worcester	216	WR	14
Jose Burman	Hermanus	228	HF	13
Josephine	Ceres	207	CJ	12
Josias Blanckenberg St	Atlantis (Atlantis Ind.)	201	AK	31
Joubert St	Caledon	225	CC	11
Joubert St	Ceres	207	CG	12
Joubert St	Montagu	222	MQ	12
Joubert St	Worcester	217	WS	18
Juan Hampshire Pl.	Atlantis (Atlantis Ind.)	200	AL	30
Jubel St	Robertson	221	RO	12
Jupiter St	Ceres	207	CJ	12
Jutten	Saldanha	211	SC	15
Jutten St	Langebaan	209	LG	11
K				
Kabeljou St	Langebaan	209	LJ	10
Kalanchoe St	Atlantis (Protea Pk)	201	AJ	32
Kalkoen St	Worcester	218	WW	13
Kalkoen St	Worcester	219	WW	14
Kalkoentjie Ave	Kleinmond	226	KO	12
Kalkoentjie St	Darling	213	DD	11
Kameelboom St	Malmesbury	212	ME	11
Kamfer Ave	Malmesbury	212	ME	11
Kamp St	Saldanha	211	SB	15
Kamp St	Saldanha	211	SA	16
Kamp St	Swellendam	224	SX	12
Kanapa St	Tulbagh	206	TX	13
Kanarie	Malmesbury	212	ME	10
Kanarie St	Atlantis (Robinvale)	201	AJ	33
Kanarie St	Worcester	218	WV	13
Kanetvlei	Worcester	215	WQ	13
Kanon St	Bredasdorp	197	BU	11
Kanon St	Swellendam	224	SX	11
Kanonkop St	Atlantis (Beaconhill)	199	AG	33
Karatara Rd	Atlantis (Sherwood)	199	AG	33
Karb St	Swellendam	224	SY	10
Karee Ave	Grabouw	227	GT	11
Karee St	Tulbagh	206	TW	12
Kareeboom St	Malmesbury	212	MD	12
Karel Landman St	Worcester	216	WR	17
Kariem St	Worcester	219	WU	14
Karoo Way	Worcester	215	WQ	11
Karree	Malmesbury	212	MA	11
Karri Ct	Atlantis (Sherwood)	199	AG	33
Kasteel St	Caledon	225	CE	12
Kasuur St	Tulbagh	206	TX	12
Katberg Ct	Atlantis (Sherwood)	199	AG	33
Katlagter St	Worcester	218	WW	13
Katlagter St	Worcester	219	WV	14
Katonkel St	Saldanha	210	SB	12
Kea Cl.	Langebaan	208	LC	12
Keerom St	Bredasdorp	197	BT	13
Keerom St	Caledon	225	CC	10
Keerom St	Grabouw	227	GT	12
Keerom St	Malmesbury	212	MC	12
Keerom St	Montagu	222	MQ	10
Keerom St	Swellendam	224	SX	12
Keerom St	Worcester	215	WS	13
Keet St	Ceres	207	CG	11
Kehrweider St	Atlantis (Saxonsea)	199	AF	31
Kelkie St	Langebaan	209	LF	11
Kemp Cr.	Melkbos (Duynefontein)	203	AX	27
Kenilworth	Langebaan	208	LD	11
Kenneth Rd	Worcester	219	WU	17
Kent Cr.	Atlantis (Saxonsea)	199	AF	31
Kerk St	Bredasdorp	197	BT	12
Kerk St	Robertson	221	RR	11
Kerk St	Swellendam	224	SX	12
Kerkhof St	Worcester	219	WT	15
Kerkplein	Swellendam	224	SX	12
Keros St	Langebaan	208	LC	11
Kerria Ave	Atlantis (Protea Pk)	201	AK	31
Kerria Ave	Atlantis (Protea Pk)	201	AK	32
Kersbos	Malmesbury	212	ME	11
Keurboom Ave	Kleinmond	226	KM	11
Keurboom Cl.	Atlantis (Protea Pk)	201	AK	33
Keurboom St	Malmesbury	212	MD	12
Keurboom Way	Worcester	215	WR	11
Keyter St	Worcester	215	WR	13
Khedama St	Worcester	217	WS	21
Khomas Cl.	Atlantis (Beaconhill)	199	AH	33
Khutwana Ave	Worcester	217	WS	20
Kiepersol	Malmesbury	212	MC	12
Kiepersol St	Tulbagh	206	TW	13
Kies St	Worcester	219	WV	14
Kiewiet	Langebaan	209	LF	11
Kiewiet La.	Atlantis (Robinvale)	201	AJ	33
Kiewiet St	Ceres	207	CG	10
Kiewiet St	Hermanus	229	HF	15
Kiewiet St	Worcester	218	WV	14
Kiewietjie Rd	Melkbos (Duynefontein)	204	AY	26
Kimolos Cl.	Langebaan	208	LC	12
King St	Robertson	221	RQ	12
Kinga Cr.	Montagu	222	MR	12
Kingfischer	Atlantis (Protea Pk)	201	AJ	32
Kingfisher Cl.	Melkbos (Van Riebeeckstrand)	204	BA	26
Kingfisher St	Langebaan	208	LE	11
Kingfisher St	Worcester	218	WV	13
Kingston St	Atlantis (Avondale)	201	AJ	31
Kinross Dr.	Melkbos (Melkbosstrand)	204	BC	26
Kinross Dr.	Melkbos (Melkbosstrand)	204	BC	27
Kintyre Way	Melkbos (Atlantic Beach Est.)	204	BC	26
Kirkia St	Atlantis (Protea Pk)	201	AJ	32

Index to Street Names
Other Towns

Kirschbaum St — Plantasie St

STREET NAME	TOWN NAME	PG	GRID	
Kirschbaum St	Worcester	219	WT	14
Kiso Cl.	Atlantis (Sherwood)	199	AG	33
Klapper St	Tulbagh	206	TW	13
Klapper St	Tulbagh	206	TX	12
Klapperbos	Robertson	221	RO	12
Klassen St	Montagu	222	MP	12
Klawer	Malmesbury	212	MB	13
Klein Dassenberg Rd	Atlantis	201	AL	34
Kleinbegin	Malmesbury	212	MB	11
Kleinberg St	Worcester	219	WU	17
Kleinhans St	Saldanha	210	SC	11
Kleinplaat Rd	Atlantis (Sherwood)	199	AG	33
Kleintjies St	Worcester	219	WU	17
Kleintrou St	Caledon	225	CE	13
Klerck St	Worcester	216	WR	17
Klipdrift	Worcester	215	WS	12
Klipheuwel Cr.	Atlantis (Beaconhill)	199	AH	33
Klipheuwel St	Swellendam	224	SZ	11
Kloof St	Bredasdorp	197	BU	12
Kloof St	Caledon	225	CC	10
Kloof St	Malmesbury	212	MA	12
Kloof St	Montagu	222	MQ	10
Kloof St	Robertson	221	RO	12
Kloof St	Swellendam	224	SX	11
Klue St	Worcester	216	WR	14
Kluwer	Saldanha	210	SC	12
Knopbos	Malmesbury	212	ME	11
Knysna Rd	Atlantis (Sherwood)	199	AG	32
Koch St	Malmesbury	212	MC	12
Kochia St	Atlantis (Protea Pk)	201	AJ	32
Kohler St	Montagu	222	MQ	11
Kohler St	Montagu	222	MR	12
Kok	Saldanha	210	SC	12
Koker Ave	Malmesbury	212	ME	11
Kolgans St	Worcester	218	WW	13
Kolgans St	Worcester	219	WW	14
Kolgha Ct	Atlantis (Sherwood)	199	AG	33
Kolie Nelson St	Worcester	216	WP	15
Kollebe St	Swellendam	224	SY	10
Kolo St	Worcester	220	WT	20
Koltander	Malmesbury	212	MD	12
Kompanie Rd	Melkbos (Melkbosstrand)	204	BB	26
Kompanje Cl.	Langebaan	209	LG	11
Konstitusie St	Robertson	221	RR	10
Koorts St	Worcester	216	WP	16
Koos Henning St	Worcester	215	WS	12
Korhaan Rd	Melkbos (Van Riebeeckstrand)	204	AZ	26
Korhaan St	Worcester	218	WW	13
Koring St	Malmesbury	212	MB	13
Koringblom St	Malmesbury	212	MD	12
Koringland St	Swellendam	224	TA	10
Kort St	Bredasdorp	197	BR	11
Kort St	Caledon	225	CC	11
Kort St	Ceres	207	CH	11
Kort St	Hermanus	228	HG	11
Kort St	Kleinmond	226	KM	12
Kort St	Langebaan	209	LH	10
Kort St	Malmesbury	212	MB	11
Kort St	Montagu	222	MQ	10
Kort St	Robertson	221	RR	11
Kort St	Swellendam	224	SX	11
Kosmos St	Malmesbury	212	ME	12
Koster St	Swellendam	224	SX	11
Kotze St	Langebaan	209	LJ	10
Kotze St	Worcester	216	WP	15
Kraai St	Worcester	218	WV	13
Kraalbaai Cl.	Langebaan	208	LD	11
Kraanvoël Cl.	Atlantis (Robinvale)	201	AJ	33
Kransbos Rd	Atlantis (Beaconhill)	199	AG	33
Kreef Cr.	Saldanha	211	SC	15
Kreupelhout Ave	Bredasdorp	197	BT	13
Kriegler St	Tulbagh	206	TW	11
Krige St	Caledon	225	CB	11
Krige St	Ceres	207	CH	10
Krige St	Worcester	218	WT	13
Krom St	Montagu	222	MQ	11
Kromrivier Rd	Atlantis (Sherwood)	199	AG	33
Krone St	Worcester	216	WS	17
Kroon St	Worcester	219	WU	14
Kruger	Langebaan	209	LJ	10
Kruisement St	Malmesbury	212	MD	11
Kruisvlei St	Tulbagh	206	TW	11
Krynauw St	Worcester	216	WP	16
Kudu La.	Worcester	215	WQ	11
Kuhn St	Worcester	215	WS	13
Kuiken St	Worcester	218	WW	13
Kuiken St	Worcester	219	WW	14
Kuil St	Caledon	225	CC	11
Kuruman St	Atlantis (Beaconhill)	199	AH	33
Kwaaiwater Way	Hermanus	229	HF	16
Kwartel Cl.	Atlantis (Robinvale)	201	AJ	33
Kwartel St	Worcester	218	WV	13
Kwevoël St	Worcester	218	WW	13
Kwevoël St	Worcester	219	WW	14
Kwikkie St	Atlantis (Robinvale)	201	AJ	33
Kwikkie St	Worcester	218	WV	13
Kwikstertjie	Langebaan	209	LH	13
Kwinana Ave	Worcester	217	WS	20
Kythnos St	Langebaan	208	LC	12

L

STREET NAME	TOWN NAME	PG	GRID	
La Rozette St	Saldanha	211	SB	15
Laatoe St	Worcester	219	WV	15
Lafontein St	Worcester	219	WU	17
Lagan Rd	Atlantis (Sherwood)	199	AG	33
Lagoon St	Kleinmond	226	KM	12
Lagoon St	Langebaan	209	LH	10
Laguna Cr.	Saldanha	211	SB	14
Laing St	Caledon	225	CB	11
Lakeman Cl.	Atlantis (Avondale)	201	AJ	31
Lakey St	Bredasdorp	197	BR	11
Lakey St	Robertson	221	RP	12
Lambrecht St	Villiersdorp	223	VL	11
Lancaster St	Melkbos (Duynefontein)	203	AX	27
Lands End	Melkbos (Atlantic Beach Est.)	205	BE	27
Lang St	Bredasdorp	197	BR	12
Lang St	Bredasdorp	197	BS	12
Lang St	Bredasdorp	197	BU	11
Lang St	Robertson	221	RR	12
Langeberg St	Robertson	221	RO	12
Langefontein Way	Bredasdorp	197	BV	12
Langfontein St	Darling	213	DD	11
Lantana Cr.	Atlantis (Protea Pk)	201	AJ	32
Lantana St	Malmesbury	212	MD	12
Lark St	Worcester	218	WV	13
Larks Pl.	Atlantis (Robinvale)	201	AJ	32
Larkspur Cl.	Atlantis (Protea Pk)	201	AJ	32
Laserena St	Worcester	219	WU	17
Lavalle St	Worcester	219	WU	17
Lavender Way	Worcester	215	WR	11
Lavinia Cl.	Atlantis (Avondale)	201	AJ	31
Le Grange St	Worcester	219	WV	14
Le Roux St	Ceres	207	CJ	11
Le Roux St	Montagu	222	MQ	12
Le Roux St	Robertson	221	RP	11
Le Roux St	Robertson	221	RQ	11
Le Roux St	Villiersdorp	223	VL	12
Le Seuer St	Melkbos (Melkbosstrand)	204	BB	26
Le Seur St	Melkbos (Duynefontein)	203	AX	27
Le Sueur St	Worcester	219	WU	15
Leander Cl.	Atlantis (Avondale)	201	AJ	31
Lebanon La.	Atlantis (Sherwood)	199	AG	33
Leda Cl.	Melkbos (Melkbosstrand)	204	BB	26
Leemida St	Malmesbury	212	MB	10
Leentjies St	Langebaan	209	LG	10
Leentjiesklip Cr.	Langebaan	208	LD	11
Leerdam St	Robertson	221	RQ	12
Leerdam St	Worcester	216	WQ	16
Leeubekkie Ave	Robertson	221	RP	11
Leeubekkie St	Malmesbury	212	MD	12
Leeuwin Ave	Robertson	221	RQ	12
Leipoldt Ave	Worcester	216	WS	17
Leipoldt Ave	Worcester	219	WT	16
Lekays St	Montagu	222	MQ	12
Lelie	Langebaan	209	LF	10
Lelie	Malmesbury	212	ME	12
Lelie Cl.	Atlantis (Protea Pk)	201	AK	33
Lelie St	Caledon	225	CC	11
Lelie St	Swellendam	224	TA	11
Lelie Way	Bredasdorp	197	BR	11
Lemoenbos Cl.	Langebaan	209	LJ	11
Leonard St	Worcester	219	WU	17
Libertas St	Worcester	216	WQ	15
Lichtenstein St	Swellendam	224	SW	13
Liesbeeck La.	Worcester	215	WQ	11
Lighthouse Rd	Melkbos (Atlantic Beach Est.)	205	BE	26
Lighthouse Rd	Melkbos (Atlantic Beach Est.)	205	BF	26
Lily St	Worcester	219	WU	16
Limoneum	Langebaan	209	LH	11
Linaria Rd	Hermanus	228	HG	13
Linaria St	Atlantis (Protea Pk)	201	AJ	32
Lind St	Swellendam	224	SY	11
Linde Cr.	Melkbos (Duynefontein)	203	AX	27
Linde Cr.	Melkbos (Duynefontein)	203	AX	27
Linde La.	Worcester	216	WR	15
Linde St	Caledon	225	CB	10
Lindenberg St	Worcester	215	WS	13
Link	Langebaan	209	LG	12
Lipizzaner St	Malmesbury	212	MB	10
Lisboa St	Atlantis (Saxonsea)	199	AF	31
Litus St	Montagu	222	MP	12
Livanos Pl.	Atlantis (Saxonsea)	199	AF	31
Livingsea Cl.	Melkbos (Melkbosstrand)	204	BC	25
Lizo St	Worcester	217	WS	21
Lobelia St	Atlantis (Protea Pk)	201	AJ	32
Loch St	Hermanus	229	HF	15
Loch St	Worcester	215	WS	12
Loedolf St	Malmesbury	212	MA	12
Loerie La.	Atlantis (Robinvale)	201	AJ	32
Loerie St	Worcester	219	WV	14
Loff St	Worcester	219	WT	17
Lombard St	Worcester	220	WT	18
Londi St	Worcester	217	WS	21
London Rd	Hermanus	228	HH	11
Long St	Darling	213	DD	11
Long St	Hermanus	228	HG	13
Long St	Malmesbury	212	MB	11
Long St	Montagu	222	MR	12
Longtail St	Atlantis (Robinvale)	201	AJ	33
Lonsdale Ct	Atlantis (Sherwood)	199	AG	33
Lood	Saldanha	210	SC	13
Loop	Darling	213	DB	12
Loop St	Langebaan	208	LC	13
Loop St	Langebaan	208	LD	14
Loop St	Langebaan	208	LB	13
Loop St	Montagu	222	MQ	10
Loop St	Robertson	221	RQ	12
Loop St	Robertson	221	RP	11
Loop St	Tulbagh	206	TW	11
Lord Roberts	Hermanus	228	HG	13
Los St	Langebaan	208	LC	12
Losperds Cr.	Melkbos (Duynefontein)	203	AX	27
Lotus St	Ceres	207	CH	12
Loubser St	Malmesbury	212	MC	11
Louis Lange St	Worcester	217	WR	18
Louis Trichard St	Grabouw	227	GT	11
Louis Trichardt St	Worcester	216	WQ	17
Louise St	Worcester	219	WT	14
Lourens St	Bredasdorp	197	BU	12
Lourens St	Swellendam	224	SY	11
Louw St	Ceres	207	CH	12
Louw St	Malmesbury	212	MC	10
Louwtjie Rothman	Atlantis (Atlantis Ind.)	200	AM	30
Louwtjie Rothman	Atlantis (Atlantis Ind.)	201	AM	31
Louzaan St	Worcester	219	WU	17
Lovebird La.	Atlantis (Robinvale)	201	AJ	32
Loveday St	Hermanus	228	HG	11
Lower Beach Rd	Kleinmond	226	KO	11
Lowry Cole St	Malmesbury	212	MB	11
Lubitania Pl.	Atlantis (Saxonsea)	199	AF	31
Lublin Cl.	Atlantis (Sherwood)	199	AG	33
Luckhoff St	Kleinmond	226	KP	12
Lukasrand Rd	Atlantis (Beaconhill)	199	AH	34
Lupine	Malmesbury	212	ME	12
Lusernbos	Robertson	221	RO	11
Lusisi	Hermanus	228	HJ	10
Lusitania St	Saldanha	211	SB	15
Lusiteno	Malmesbury	212	MB	10
Luyt St	Hermanus	228	HF	13
Luyt St	Hermanus	228	HG	13
Luyt St	Worcester	215	WS	13
Lyell St	Ceres	207	CH	11
Lyell St	Ceres	207	CJ	12
Lyn	Saldanha	210	SC	13
Lyner St	Worcester	219	WT	16
Lyons St	Worcester	216	WS	14
Lyster Cir.	Atlantis (Robinvale)	201	AJ	32

M

STREET NAME	TOWN NAME	PG	GRID	
Maarman St	Bredasdorp	197	BR	11
Maasdam St	Saldanha	210	SC	11
Macdonald St	Ceres	207	CG	10
Mackay St	Caledon	225	CC	12
Mackeral St	Saldanha	211	SC	14
Madeliefie La.	Langebaan	209	LF	11
Madiba St	Worcester	217	WS	21
Magnet Cir.	Atlantis (Saxonsea)	199	AF	32
Magnet St	Atlantis (Saxonsea)	199	AF	31
Magnolia	Tulbagh	206	TX	11
Magnolia Ave	Malmesbury	212	ME	11
Magnolia La.	Hermanus	228	HG	12
Magnolia La.	Hermanus	228	HF	12
Magnolia Rd	Bredasdorp	197	BS	12
Magnolia St	Atlantis (Protea Pk)	201	AJ	32
Magnolia St	Atlantis (Robinvale)	201	AJ	32
Magnolia St	Montagu	222	MP	13
Magnolia St	Villiersdorp	223	VN	11
Magouka St	Worcester	219	WV	14
Magpie St	Worcester	218	WV	13
Mahem Cr.	Atlantis (Robinvale)	201	AJ	33
Main Rd	Grabouw	227	GR	12
Main Rd	Hermanus	228	HG	11
Main Rd	Hermanus	228	HG	13
Main Rd	Hermanus	229	HF	15
Main Rd	Kleinmond	226	KL	12
Main Rd	Kleinmond	226	KP	12
Main Rd	Kleinmond	226	KN	12
Main Rd	Saldanha	211	SB	14
Main Rd	Villiersdorp	223	VK	11
Main Rd	Villiersdorp	223	VL	12
Main St	Caledon	225	CD	13
Main St	Caledon	225	CD	12
Main St	Langebaan	209	LH	10
Main St	Langebaan	209	LG	10
Main St	Langebaan	209	LF	11
Maitland St	Darling	213	DC	11
Maitland St	Worcester	215	WS	12
Majuba Cl.	Atlantis (Beaconhill)	199	AH	33
Makade Ave	Worcester	217	WS	21
Makaolo Ave	Worcester	220	WT	20
Makou St	Tulbagh	206	TW	13
Makou St	Worcester	218	WW	13
Malan St	Malmesbury	212	MC	11
Malan St	Worcester	215	WS	13
Malan St	Worcester	218	WT	12
Malgas	Saldanha	210	SE	12
Malgas Cr.	Langebaan	209	LG	10
Malgas St	Atlantis (Robinvale)	201	AJ	33
Malgas St	Saldanha	211	SB	16
Malherbe St	Ceres	207	CG	12
Malherbe St	Robertson	221	RQ	10
Malherbe St	Villiersdorp	223	VL	12
Malmok St	Worcester	218	WW	13
Malva Cl.	Atlantis (Protea Pk)	201	AK	33
Malva St	Robertson	221	RO	12
Malvas Ave	Kleinmond	226	KO	12
Malvern Rd	Atlantis (Sherwood)	199	AG	33
Malvern St	Atlantis (Beaconhill)	199	AH	33
Mamali St	Worcester	217	WS	21
Mankopan St	Grabouw	227	GV	13
Mannikin St	Worcester	218	WW	13
Marais St	Worcester	219	WT	17
March	Langebaan	209	LG	13
March Cr.	Worcester	220	WT	19
Marcus St	Langebaan	209	LG	11
Marcus St	Saldanha	211	SC	15
Maree St	Villiersdorp	223	VL	12
Maria Cl.	Atlantis (Avondale)	201	AJ	31
Marigold St	Atlantis (Protea Pk)	201	AK	32
Marigold St	Atlantis (Protea Pk)	201	AJ	32
Marigold St	Worcester	219	WU	16
Marina St	Ceres	207	CJ	12
Marina St	Langebaan	209	LH	10
Marine Ave	Kleinmond	226	KO	11
Marine Dr.	Hermanus	228	HG	12
Marine Dr.	Hermanus	228	HG	13
Marinus St	Grabouw	227	GV	12
Maritz St	Ceres	207	CG	12
Maritz St	Worcester	217	WS	19
Marius Smit St	Worcester	218	WT	12
Marjolein St	Malmesbury	212	MD	11
Mark St	Atlantis Town Centre	199	AH	32
Mark St	Malmesbury	212	MB	12
Mark St	Robertson	221	RQ	10
Mark St	Worcester	216	WS	15
Market St	Montagu	222	MQ	12
Market St	Tulbagh	206	TW	11
Maroela Ave	Kleinmond	226	KO	12
Maroela St	Tulbagh	206	TX	11
Marone St	Worcester	219	WT	17
Marra St	Langebaan	209	LH	10
Mars St	Ceres	207	CJ	12
Mars St	Worcester	216	WQ	16
Marsvalla Cl.	Langebaan	209	LF	12
Marsvalla Way	Langebaan	209	LF	13
Marthina Cl.	Worcester	219	WT	15
Martilda Dr.	Langebaan	209	LF	12
Martin St	Worcester	219	WT	14
Mary Kirk St	Grabouw	227	GT	11
Maspaal	Saldanha	210	SC	12
Master's Way	Worcester	216	WP	14
Matheran St	Atlantis (Saxonsea)	199	AF	31
Matopo Cr.	Atlantis (Beaconhill)	199	AH	34
Matroos Ave	Worcester	220	WT	20
Matsila Ave	Worcester	217	WS	21
Matsila Ave	Worcester	220	WT	21
Matthee St	Bredasdorp	197	BU	12
Mauritius St	Atlantis (Saxonsea)	199	AF	31
Max Harris St	Grabouw	227	GT	12
May Ave	Worcester	217	WS	21
May Cr.	Melkbos (Duynefontein)	203	AX	26
May Cr.	Melkbos (Duynefontein)	203	AX	27
May St	Swellendam	224	SZ	12
Mayflower St	Saldanha	210	SC	12
Mayinjana Ave	Worcester	217	WS	20
Mayinyana Ave	Worcester	220	WT	20
Maynier St	Swellendam	224	SY	10
Mazula St	Worcester	217	WS	20
Mbotshelwa Ave	Worcester	220	WT	20
Mbutho St	Worcester	217	WS	21
McAlister St	Worcester	217	WR	18
McFarlane St	Hermanus	228	HF	13
Medland St	Ceres	207	CH	12
Meerhoff St	Worcester	216	WQ	16
Meermin Rd	Atlantis (Avondale)	199	AH	32
Meermin Rd	Atlantis (Avondale)	201	AJ	31
Meeu St	Langebaan	209	LJ	10
Meeu St	Tulbagh	206	TW	13
Meeu St	Worcester	218	WW	13
Mega St	Ceres	207	CG	11
Meiring St	Tulbagh	206	TX	10
Meiring St	Worcester	216	WS	16
Melba St	Atlantis (Robinvale)	201	AJ	33
Melck St	Langebaan	209	LJ	10
Melia St	Atlantis (Protea Pk)	201	AJ	32
Melianthus	Langebaan	209	LJ	12
Melk Rd	Ceres	207	CJ	12
Melkbos Cl.	Langebaan	209	LJ	11
Melkbos St	Malmesbury	212	MC	12
Melkbosstrand Rd	Melkbos (Melkbosstrand)	204	BC	28
Melkhout Ave	Kleinmond	226	KM	11
Melkhout Cr.	Bredasdorp	197	BT	13
Melkhout St	Tulbagh	206	TX	12
Melos Cl.	Langebaan	208	LD	11
Meltevreden St	Swellendam	224	SX	11
Mendip St	Atlantis (Beaconhill)	199	AH	34
Mentor Cr.	Atlantis (Avondale)	201	AJ	31
Mercer St	Worcester	216	WS	15
Merchant Wk	Melkbos (Duynefontein)	204	AY	26
Mercury St	Saldanha	210	SC	11
Merenstein	Langebaan	209	LG	10
Merenstein St	Langebaan	209	LG	10
Meresteyn Cl.	Atlantis (Avondale)	201	AJ	31
Meresteyn Cl.	Atlantis (Avondale)	201	AM	32
Merestyn Rd	Saldanha	211	SB	14
Mermaid Rd	Langebaan	209	LG	12
Mesabi St	Atlantis (Beaconhill)	199	AH	34
Metcale St	Caledon	225	CC	11
Meteren Cr.	Atlantis (Avondale)	201	AJ	31
Meul St	Malmesbury	212	MB	12
Meul St	Montagu	222	MQ	11
Meul St	Swellendam	224	SY	10
Mexican St	Atlantis (Saxonsea)	198	AE	30
Meyer Cr.	Robertson	221	RP	12
Meyer St	Bredasdorp	197	BR	11
Meyer St	Swellendam	224	SZ	11
Mgxaji St	Worcester	217	WS	21
Middel St	Bredasdorp	197	BR	11
Middel St	Montagu	222	MQ	11
Middel St	Montagu	222	MR	10

Abbreviations used: Ave – Avenue, A.H. – Agricultural Holding, A.L.– Algemene Landgoed, Blvd – Boulevard, Cen. – Central, Cir. – Circle, Cl. – Close, Cr. – Crescent, Ct – Court, Dr. – Drive, Est. – Estate, Ext. – Extension, Hgts – Heights, Ind. – Industrial, Gdns – Gardens, Gr. – Grove, La. – Lane, (M.Plain) - Mitchells Plain, Nth – North, Pl. – Place, Pk – Park, Rd – Road, Rdg. – Ridge, S.H.– Small Holding, Sq. – Square, St – Street, Sth – South, Ter. – Terrace, Tn – Turn, Val. – Valley, Wk – Walk

STREET NAME	TOWN NAME	PG	GRID
Middelburg St	Atlantis (Saxonsea)	199	AF 31
Middelburg St	Langebaan	209	LG 10
Middelburg St	Saldanha	211	SB 14
Middelpos	Saldanha	210	SB 11
Middenrak Cr.	Atlantis (Saxonsea)	199	AF 31
Middle River Rd	Kleinmond	226	KL 11
Milkwood	Hermanus	229	HF 16
Mill St	Caledon	225	CC 12
Millhurst St	Worcester	219	WU 17
Milner St	Hermanus	229	HF 15
Milner St	Worcester	215	WS 12
Mimosa Ave	Malmesbury	212	ME 11
Mimosa Ave	Malmesbury	212	MD 11
Mimosa Ave	Robertson	221	RP 11
Mimosa Cl.	Darling	213	DD 12
Mimosa Rd	Hermanus	228	HG 10
Mimosa St	Grabouw	227	GU 12
Mimosa Way	Worcester	216	WR 16
Minetoba Ave	Caledon	225	CD 13
Minetoka St	Langebaan	209	LF 11
Mitchell St	Bredasdorp	197	BS 12
Mitchell St	Hermanus	228	HF 13
Mitchell St	Hermanus	228	HG 13
Mizpah St	Saldanha	210	SC 11
Mkhiwane Ave	Worcester	220	WT 19
Mnga Ave	Worcester	220	WT 20
Mngcunube Ave	Worcester	220	WT 20
Mockingbird St	Worcester	218	WV 13
Moffat St	Hermanus	228	HF 13
Mogammad St	Worcester	219	WV 17
Mohammed	Montagu	222	MP 12
Moll St	Malmesbury	212	MB 13
Moller St	Swellendam	224	SX 13
Molteno St	Grabouw	227	GT 11
Monk St	Saldanha	210	SC 11
Montagu St	Atlantis (Saxonsea)	198	AE 30
Monte Vista St	Worcester	219	WU 17
Montezuma La.	Atlantis (Sherwood)	199	AG 33
Montreal Dr.	Atlantis (Beaconhill)	199	AG 33
Montreal Dr.	Atlantis (Sherwood)	199	AG 32
Mooising St	Bredasdorp	197	BV 12
Moolman St	Swellendam	224	SY 10
Moonstone St	Saldanha	210	SC 12
Moorfoot Cl.	Atlantis (Beaconhill)	199	AH 34
Mooring View Cl.	Melkbos (Atlantic Beach Est.)	205	BE 27
Moorrees St	Malmesbury	212	MB 11
Moorrees St	Malmesbury	212	MB 12
Moosa St	Worcester	219	WT 17
Mopani	Malmesbury	212	ME 11
Mopanie St	Tulbagh	206	TX 13
Moreson St	Bredasdorp	197	BV 11
Morgenson Cl.	Atlantis (Saxonsea)	199	AG 33
Morgenson Cl.	Atlantis (Saxonsea)	199	AF 34
Morne La.	Worcester	215	WP 10
Morris St	Ceres	207	CH 12
Morris St	Worcester	219	WU 14
Mortimer Cr.	Atlantis (Sherwood)	199	AF 33
Mosko St	Villiersdorp	223	VL 10
Mossel La.	Hermanus	228	HG 12
Mossel River Dr.	Hermanus	229	HF 16
Mossie	Langebaan	209	LH 13
Mossie	Malmesbury	212	ME 10
Mossie Cr.	Atlantis (Robinvale)	201	AJ 32
Mossie Cr.	Atlantis (Robinvale)	201	AJ 33
Mossie St	Worcester	218	WV 13
Mostert	Malmesbury	212	MD 11
Mostert Rd	Melkbos (Melkbosstrand)	204	BB 26
Mostert Rd	Melkbos (Melkbosstrand)	204	BC 26
Mosterthoek Ave	Ceres	207	CH 10
Mountain Dr.	Hermanus	228	HG 12
Mozambique St	Swellendam	224	SX 11
Mozart St	Atlantis (Avondale)	201	AJ 31
Mpinda St	Worcester	217	WS 20
Mpoza St	Worcester	220	WT 19
Mqwebedu Ave	Worcester	220	WT 20
Mt Pleasant St	Darling	213	DD 11
Mthathi Ave	Worcester	220	WT 19
Mtwazi St	Worcester	217	WS 20
Mtwazi St	Worcester	220	WT 20
Muelen Cl.	Langebaan	209	LF 12
Muhafu St	Robertson	221	RS 12
Muisvoël	Malmesbury	212	ME 10
Muisvoël St	Worcester	219	WV 14
Muller St	Montagu	222	MO 12
Muller St	Robertson	221	RO 12
Muller St	Swellendam	224	SY 11
Muller St	Villiersdorp	223	VL 12
Multana St	Worcester	219	WU 17
Munisipale St	Malmesbury	212	MC 12
Munnik St	Ceres	207	CG 11
Murchison St	Ceres	207	CH 11
Murray St	Saldanha	210	SC 11
Murray St	Swellendam	224	SY 10
Murray St	Swellendam	224	SY 11
Murray St	Worcester	216	WS 16
Museum St	Bredasdorp	197	BU 11
Museum St	Tulbagh	206	TW 11
Muskadel St	Montagu	222	MP 13
Muskadel St	Worcester	219	WU 17
Mussel Rd	Hermanus	228	HG 11
Musson St	Hermanus	228	HF 13
Musson St	Hermanus	228	HG 13
Myburgh St	Swellendam	224	SY 10
Myburgh St	Villiersdorp	223	VL 11
Myburgh St	Worcester	216	WP 16

STREET NAME	TOWN NAME	PG	GRID
Mydrecht	Langebaan	209	LH 10
Mykonos St	Langebaan	208	LC 12
Mylne St	Worcester	219	WT 15
Myna La.	Atlantis (Robinvale)	201	AJ 33
Myna St	Worcester	218	WV 13
Myrtle Ave	Malmesbury	212	ME 12
Myrtle St	Hermanus	228	HG 12
N			
Namen St	Atlantis (Saxonsea)	199	AF 32
Nantes St	Caledon	225	CD 12
Napier St	Worcester	216	WS 14
Napier St	Worcester	219	WT 14
Napoleon Ave	Melkbos (Duynefontein)	203	AX 26
Napoleon Ave	Melkbos (Duynefontein)	203	AX 27
Napoleon Ave	Melkbos (Duynefontein)	204	AY 27
Napoleon Cr.	Atlantis (Saxonsea)	199	AF 31
Narcissus Ave	Melkbos (Duynefontein)	203	AX 26
Nassau	Langebaan	209	LH 10
Nassau Cr.	Robertson	221	RQ 13
Nassau St	Worcester	216	WQ 15
Naude St	Ceres	207	CH 12
Nautilus Cir.	Melkbos (Atlantic Beach Est.)	205	BD 26
Nautilus St	Atlantis (Saxonsea)	198	AF 30
Nautilus St	Saldanha	211	SC 15
Naxos St	Langebaan	208	LC 12
Ndamoyi St	Worcester	220	WT 19
Ndyalvan Cr.	Worcester	217	WS 21
Ndzima St	Worcester	217	WS 20
Ndzishe Rd	Worcester	217	WS 21
Nederburg St	Worcester	216	WQ 16
Neethling	Robertson	221	RQ 12
Neethling St	Kleinmond	226	KP 12
Neethling St	Worcester	219	WT 17
Neil Hare Rd	Atlantis (Atlantis Ind.)	200	AL 29
Neil Hare Rd	Atlantis (Atlantis Ind.)	200	AL 30
Neil Hare Rd	Atlantis (Atlantis Ind.)	200	AN 28
Neil Hare Rd	Atlantis (Atlantis Ind.)	200	AN 29
Neil Hare Rd	Atlantis (Atlantis Ind.)	200	AN 30
Neil Hare Rd	Atlantis (Atlantis Ind.)	201	AL 31
Neil Hare Rd	Atlantis (Atlantis Ind.)	201	AM 31
Nel St	Montagu	222	MQ 12
Nel St	Worcester	215	WS 13
Nelly La.	Atlantis (Robinvale)	201	AJ 33
Nelson St	Swellendam	224	SX 11
Nemesia	Langebaan	209	LH 12
Nemesia Ave	Kleinmond	226	KO 12
Nemesia La.	Atlantis (Protea Pk)	201	AJ 32
Nemesia La.	Atlantis (Protea Pk)	201	AM 32
Nemesia St	Darling	213	DD 12
Nemesia St	Malmesbury	212	ME 12
Neptune St	Saldanha	211	SB 14
Nerie St	Langebaan	209	LG 12
Nerina Ave	Malmesbury	212	ME 11
Nerina La.	Kleinmond	226	KL 11
Nerina Pl.	Atlantis (Protea Pk)	201	AJ 32
Nerina Rd	Hermanus	228	HG 12
Nerina Rd	Robertson	221	RP 12
Nerina St	Atlantis (Protea Pk)	201	AJ 32
Nerina St	Caledon	225	CB 12
Nerina St	Darling	213	DD 12
Nerina St	Kleinmond	226	KO 12
Nerina St	Swellendam	224	SZ 11
Nerina St	Tulbagh	206	TX 11
Nerina St	Worcester	216	WR 15
Nerina St	Worcester	216	WR 16
Nerine St	Grabouw	227	GU 12
Net	Saldanha	210	SC 13
Neuman St	Bredasdorp	197	BT 11
New Cross St	Caledon	225	CC 12
New Row	Caledon	225	CC 11
New St	Caledon	225	CC 11
Newark St	Melkbos (Melkbosstrand)	205	BD 26
Newlands Rd	Atlantis (Sherwood)	199	AG 32
Newmarket St	Langebaan	208	LB 14
Newmarket St	Langebaan	208	LB 13
Ngethu Ave	Worcester	220	WT 20
Ngulube St	Worcester	220	WT 19
Nguni St	Malmesbury	212	MB 10
Nichol St	Hermanus	228	HF 13
Nick Prinsloo St	Worcester	216	WP 17
Nicobar St	Atlantis (Avondale)	201	AJ 32
Niesbos Cl.	Atlantis (Sherwood)	199	AG 32
Nightingale Rd	Atlantis (Avondale)	201	AJ 32
Nightingale St	Worcester	218	WV 13
Nimrod St	Atlantis (Saxonsea)	198	AF 30
Nineteenth Ave	Melkbos (Melkbosstrand)	204	BB 26
Ninth Ave	Caledon	225	CD 13
Ninth Ave	Darling	213	DB 12
Ninth Ave	Kleinmond	226	KN 12
Ninth Ave	Kleinmond	226	KM 12
Ninth Ave	Melkbos (Melkbosstrand)	204	BC 26
Ninth Ave	Saldanha	211	SB 15
Ninth St	Hermanus	229	HF 17
Ninth St	Kleinmond	226	KN 12
Nirvana St	Worcester	220	WU 18
Nivinia Ave	Kleinmond	226	KO 12
Njila Ave	Worcester	220	WT 20
Nkentsha St	Worcester	217	WS 21
Nkentsha St	Worcester	220	WT 21
Nkunzani St	Worcester	220	WT 20
Noble St	Worcester	219	WV 14
Nobuhle St	Malmesbury	212	ME 12
Nonkqubela St	Malmesbury	212	ME 12
Nooitgedacht Cr.	Worcester	215	WQ 13

STREET NAME	TOWN NAME	PG	GRID
Noord Dam St	Saldanha	210	SC 10
Noord St	Langebaan	209	LG 10
Noordzees St	Saldanha	210	SC 11
Norman Murray St	Atlantis (Atlantis Ind.)	200	AL 30
Northway	Hermanus	228	HF 12
Nottingham Rd	Atlantis (Sherwood)	199	AG 32
Nottinghill Cr.	Atlantis (Beaconhill)	199	AH 34
November St	Worcester	219	WT 17
Ntlakotlala	Robertson	221	RS 12
Nuwe Rust St	Caledon	225	CC 10
Nuwe St	Bredasdorp	197	BU 12
Nuxia St	Grabouw	227	GT 11
Nyibiba Ave	Worcester	220	WT 19
Nywerheid Cr.	Malmesbury	212	MD 11
O			
Oak St	Caledon	225	CB 10
Oak St	Swellendam	224	SZ 11
Oberon St	Saldanha	211	SC 14
Obiqua Cr.	Tulbagh	206	TW 12
Ocean Mist Cl.	Melkbos (Atlantic Beach Est.)	205	BE 26
Ocean Mist Cl.	Melkbos (Atlantic Beach Est.)	205	BF 26
October St	Bredasdorp	197	BR 12
October St	Robertson	221	RP 12
October St	Worcester	219	WT 16
Odendaal St	Swellendam	224	SY 11
Odysseus	Langebaan	208	LB 11
Oester St	Langebaan	209	LJ 10
Oester St	Saldanha	210	SC 10
Okkerneut St	Malmesbury	212	MD 11
Old Darling Rd	Darling	213	DD 12
Old Darling Rd	Darling	213	DC 11
Oldenburgh St	Atlantis (Avondale)	201	AJ 31
Oleander Ave	Malmesbury	212	MC 12
Olienhout La.	Caledon	225	CC 10
Olifant St	Tulbagh	206	TX 12
Olivier St	Worcester	216	WP 17
Olm La.	Worcester	216	WR 15
Olyf Dr.	Worcester	216	WQ 16
Omardien St	Worcester	219	WV 15
Omega St	Malmesbury	212	ME 11
Oog	Saldanha	210	SC 12
Oos St	Bredasdorp	197	BT 12
Oosterdam St	Saldanha	210	SC 11
Oosterland St	Atlantis (Avondale)	201	AJ 31
Oostewal Rd	Langebaan	209	LH 10
Oostewal Rd	Langebaan	209	LG 11
Oostewal Rd	Langebaan	209	LF 12
Oostewal St	Langebaan	209	LJ 10
Oostewal St	Langebaan	209	LH 10
Orange La.	Worcester	215	WQ 11
Orange St	Atlantis (Saxonsea)	199	AF 32
Oranje St	Ceres	207	CG 12
Orchard St	Grabouw	227	GU 12
Orchard St	Worcester	219	WU 17
Orchid St	Atlantis (Protea Pk)	201	AJ 32
Orion St	Saldanha	210	SC 11
Orlando Rd	Melkbos (Melkbosstrand)	204	BC 26
Orley St	Robertson	221	RP 12
Orothamnus St	Hermanus	228	HH 11
Orpheus	Langebaan	208	LB 11
Oslo	Saldanha	210	SC 11
Osprey Cl.	Langebaan	208	LE 11
Osprey St	Worcester	218	WW 13
Osprey St	Worcester	218	WV 13
Ottawa La.	Atlantis (Sherwood)	199	AG 32
Otto du Plessis Dr.	Melkbos (Koeberg Nuclear Power Station)	203	AW 26
Otto du Plessis Dr.	Melkbos (Koeberg Nuclear Power Station)	203	AW 27
Otto Du Plessis St	Worcester	216	WP 16
Ou Kaapse Rd	Grabouw	227	GU 12
Ou Meul St	Bredasdorp	197	BS 12
Ou Meul St	Bredasdorp	197	BS 13
Ou Meul St	Bredasdorp	197	BR 10
Ouderbrug Rd	Grabouw	227	GU 12
Outeniekwa St	Atlantis (Beaconhill)	199	AH 34
Overberg Cr.	Atlantis (Beaconhill)	199	AH 34
Owen St	Ceres	207	CG 11
Owen St	Ceres	207	CJ 11
Oyster La.	Melkbos (Atlantic Beach Est.)	205	BD 26
P			
P.G. Nelson St	Malmesbury	212	MB 11
Packham St	Worcester	216	WP 16
Paddy St	Robertson	221	RP 12
Padiachy St	Bredasdorp	197	BR 11
Padro St	Langebaan	209	LG 11
Palm Cr.	Tulbagh	206	TW 12
Palm La.	Worcester	216	WR 16
Palm St	Swellendam	224	SZ 11
Palmboom St	Malmesbury	212	MD 12
Palmer Ave	Atlantis (Avondale)	199	AH 31
Palmiet	Malmesbury	212	MA 11
Palmiet St	Kleinmond	226	KP 12
Palomino St	Malmesbury	212	MB 11
Panarama Cr.	Langebaan	209	LH 10
Panday St	Worcester	219	WT 17
Panorama Dr.	Saldanha	211	SB 14
Panorama Rd	Swellendam	224	SX 10
Papawer St	Robertson	221	RP 10
Pappagaai	Malmesbury	212	ME 10
Pappegaai St	Saldanha	211	SC 14
Paradise Way	Worcester	215	WQ 11
Paragon St	Atlantis (Avondale)	199	AH 31

STREET NAME	TOWN NAME	PG	GRID
Parakeet St	Worcester	218	WW 13
Parakeet St	Worcester	218	WV 13
Paraside	Langebaan	209	LF 12
Parel Ave	Robertson	221	RQ 12
Park	Langebaan	209	LJ 10
Park Cl.	Darling	213	DC 11
Park Dr.	Langebaan	209	LJ 11
Park La.	Worcester	216	WR 15
Park St	Bredasdorp	197	BS 12
Park St	Bredasdorp	197	BT 11
Park St	Ceres	207	CH 10
Park St	Montagu	222	MQ 12
Parker Cr.	Saldanha	211	SA 16
Parker St	Worcester	219	WT 15
Parks Ave	Robertson	221	RP 11
Paros Cl.	Langebaan	208	LC 12
Parring St	Montagu	222	MQ 12
Parrot St	Worcester	218	WV 13
Partridge Pl.	Melkbos (Duynefontein)	204	AZ 26
Passage	Villiersdorp	223	VL 12
Pastorie St	Darling	213	DD 11
Pastorie St	Malmesbury	212	MC 11
Paterson St	Hermanus	228	HG 12
Patricia Cr.	Grabouw	227	GV 13
Patrys	Langebaan	209	LF 12
Patrys Ave	Atlantis (Robinvale)	201	AJ 33
Patrys La.	Ceres	207	CG 10
Patrys St	Tulbagh	206	TW 13
Patrys St	Worcester	218	WV 13
Patterson St	Bredasdorp	197	BS 11
Paul Kruger St	Robertson	221	RQ 10
Paul Kruger St	Robertson	221	RQ 11
Paul Niemand St	Kleinmond	226	KP 12
Paul St	Worcester	219	WT 17
Peaceful St	Langebaan	209	LG 12
Peach Ave	Grabouw	227	GU 11
Pear Limpet La	Melkbos (Atlantic Beach Est.)	205	BD 26
Pearl Dr.	Langebaan	209	LF 13
Peckham St	Swellendam	224	SX 11
Pedro	Malmesbury	212	MA 12
Pegasus	Langebaan	208	LB 11
Pegel St	Worcester	216	WR 14
Pekeur St	Montagu	222	MQ 12
Pekeur St	Swellendam	224	SZ 12
Pelican Ave	Atlantis (Robinvale)	201	AJ 33
Pelican Parade	Melkbos (Van Riebeeckstrand)	204	AZ 26
Pelican St	Langebaan	208	LE 11
Pelican St	Saldanha	211	SB 16
Pelikaan St	Worcester	218	WV 13
Pella Rd	Atlantis (Avondale)	199	AE 32
Pella Rd	Atlantis (Avondale)	199	AF 34
Pells St	Worcester	216	WS 16
Penelope St	Atlantis (Avondale)	199	AH 31
Penguin Pl.	Langebaan	209	LJ 11
Penguin Pl.	Melkbos (Van Riebeeckstrand)	204	AZ 26
Penguin St	Worcester	218	WW 13
Peperboom Ave	Malmesbury	212	ME 11
Peperbos	Robertson	221	RO 12
Percheron St	Malmesbury	212	MB 10
Perel	Saldanha	210	SB 11
Periwinkel Way	Melkbos (Atlantic Beach Est.)	205	BD 26
Perkijt Dr.	Langebaan	209	LF 13
Perkins St	Worcester	217	WS 18
Perkins St	Worcester	220	WT 18
Perlemoen St	Saldanha	210	SC 10
Pescadora Cr.	Atlantis (Saxonsea)	199	AG 31
Petersen Cl.	Langebaan	209	LF 11
Petrel Cr.	Atlantis (Protea Pk)	201	AJ 33
Petrel St	Langebaan	209	LG 12
Petrel St	Worcester	219	WV 14
Petro St	Grabouw	227	GV 12
Petrus Cr.	Melkbos (Duynefontein)	204	AY 26
Petunia	Malmesbury	212	ME 12
Petunia La.	Atlantis (Protea Pk)	201	AJ 32
Petunia St	Darling	213	DD 11
Petunia St	Robertson	221	RP 13
Petunia St	Swellendam	224	TA 11
Phillip St	Ceres	207	CH 10
Phillips La.	Montagu	222	MO 12
Phlox Cr.	Atlantis (Protea Pk)	201	AJ 32
Phlox Pl.	Atlantis (Protea Pk)	201	AJ 32
Piek Cl.	Grabouw	227	GT 11
Piet Le Roux St	Kleinmond	226	KP 12
Piet Retief St	Malmesbury	212	MA 12
Piet Retief St	Montagu	222	MQ 12
Piet Retief St	Robertson	221	RQ 10
Piet Retief St	Robertson	221	RQ 11
Pieter Bergh St	Malmesbury	212	MC 12
Pieter van Eck St	Atlantis (Atlantis Ind.)	200	AK 30
Pieterse St	Worcester	219	WU 15
Pietersen St	Robertson	221	RP 12
Piet-my-Vrou Rd	Melkbos (Duynefontein)	204	AY 25
Pigeon St	Worcester	218	WV 13
Piketberg Rd	Malmesbury	212	MB 11
Pikkewyn	Langebaan	209	LF 11
Pikkewyn St	Atlantis (Robinvale)	201	AJ 33
Pikkewyn St	Saldanha	211	SA 15
Pinard St	Malmesbury	212	MC 12
Pine St	Ceres	207	CG 12
Pine St	Grabouw	227	GV 12
Pinotage St	Malmesbury	212	MA 12
Plaatjies St	Bredasdorp	197	BR 11
Planet	Saldanha	210	SC 12
Plantasie St	Bredasdorp	197	BU 12
Plantasie St	Ceres	207	CG 10

Index to Street Names
Other Towns
Plantation St — Victoria St

STREET NAME	TOWN NAME	PG	GRID
Plantation St	Caledon	225	CB 10
Plataan St	Malmesbury	212	ME 11
Plataan Way	Worcester	216	WR 15
Platbos Rd	Atlantis (Sherwood)	199	AG 32
Plein St	Bredasdorp	197	BT 12
Plein St	Caledon	225	CD 12
Plein St	Caledon	225	CC 11
Plein St	Hermanus	228	HG 12
Plein St	Malmesbury	212	MB 12
Plein St	Swellendam	224	SX 12
Plein St	Tulbagh	206	TW 11
Plettenberg St	Worcester	216	WQ 16
Plover Cl.	Langebaan	208	LD 11
Plover La.	Atlantis (Robinvale)	201	AJ 33
Plover St	Worcester	215	WP 11
Plum Ave	Grabouw	227	GU 12
Plum Ave	Grabouw	227	GU 11
Pluto St	Ceres	207	CJ 12
Pluto St	Saldanha	210	SC 11
Pokwas St	Montagu	222	MQ 12
Polack St	Robertson	221	RQ 12
Populier Ave	Malmesbury	212	ME 12
Populier La.	Worcester	216	WR 15
Porter St	Ceres	207	CG 12
Porter St	Ceres	207	CG 11
Porter St	Worcester	216	WS 14
Porter St	Worcester	219	WT 14
Posberg St	Langebaan	209	LH 10
Potgieter St	Ceres	207	CG 12
President St	Bredasdorp	197	BU 12
President St	Saldanha	211	SC 15
Prestwick Cl.	Melkbos (Melkbosstrand)	204	BC 26
Prestwick Cl.	Melkbos (Melkbosstrand)	204	BC 27
Pretorius St	Ceres	207	CH 12
Prince Albert St	Villiersdorp	223	VL 12
Prince Alfred Rd	Caledon	225	CB 10
Prince Rupert St	Atlantis (Saxonsea)	199	AF 32
Prins St	Bredasdorp	197	BR 11
Prins St	Grabouw	227	GT 12
Propeller	Saldanha	210	SC 12
Prospect St	Darling	213	DD 11
Prospect St	Malmesbury	212	MB 12
Protea Ave	Bredasdorp	197	BU 11
Protea Ave	Robertson	221	RP 12
Protea Ave	Swellendam	224	SZ 11
Protea Cir.	Malmesbury	212	ME 12
Protea Cr.	Atlantis (Protea Pk)	201	AJ 32
Protea Rd	Hermanus	228	HG 13
Protea Rd	Hermanus	229	HG 14
Protea Rd	Kleinmond	226	KO 12
Protea Rd	Montagu	222	MO 12
Protea St	Caledon	225	CB 12
Protea St	Ceres	207	CH 12
Protea St	Darling	213	DD 11
Protea St	Grabouw	227	GU 12
Protea St	Langebaan	209	LF 11
Protea St	Tulbagh	206	TX 11
Protea St	Villiersdorp	223	VM 12
Protea Way	Worcester	216	WR 16
Puffin Rd	Langebaan	209	LG 12
Q			
Qaba Cr.	Worcester	220	WT 19
Quaelberg St	Swellendam	224	SW 13
Quail Cr.	Atlantis (Robinvale)	201	AJ 33
Quaterdeck Rd	Langebaan	209	LG 12
Queen St	Worcester	219	WT 14
Queen Victoria St	Darling	213	DD 11
Queens St	Swellendam	224	TA 11
Quellerie Rd	Worcester	216	WQ 15
Quellerie St	Worcester	216	WQ 16
Quenet Cr.	Worcester	219	WT 15
Quint St	Worcester	219	WT 17
R			
Raats Ave	Villiersdorp	223	VK 12
Rabie Ave	Worcester	215	WS 13
Rabie St	Malmesbury	212	MA 12
Raed-Na-Gael	Hermanus	229	HE 14
Railway St	Malmesbury	212	MC 12
Rainbird St	Worcester	219	WV 14
Rainier St	Malmesbury	212	MA 12
Rainier St	Malmesbury	212	MB 12
Rainier St	Worcester	219	WU 14
Rand St	Bredasdorp	197	BR 11
Rand St	Bredasdorp	197	BR 11
Rand St	Ceres	207	CJ 12
Rattray St	Worcester	217	WS 18
Rattray St	Worcester	220	WT 18
Raven Ave	Saldanha	211	SA 17
Raven St	Caledon	225	CE 12
Raven St	Malmesbury	212	MC 11
Rawson St	Montagu	222	MQ 11
Raymond Cr.	Melkbos (Duynefontein)	204	AY 26
Raymond Pollet Dr.	Worcester	217	WS 19
Recreation St	Bredasdorp	197	BS 12
Redonda Ct	Atlantis (Sherwood)	199	AG 33
Reflector	Saldanha	210	SC 12
Reflector St	Atlantis (Saxonsea)	199	AF 32
Regatta View Cl.	Melkbos (Atlantic Beach Est.)	205	BE 26
Regatta View Cl.	Melkbos (Atlantic Beach Est.)	205	BF 26
Regent	Hermanus	228	HG 12
Reid St	Ceres	207	CG 11
Reiger St	Melkbos (Melkbosstrand)	204	BB 26
Reinecke St	Ceres	207	CG 11

STREET NAME	TOWN NAME	PG	GRID
Reisie St	Swellendam	224	SZ 11
Reisie St	Swellendam	224	SZ 12
Reitz St	Robertson	221	RR 11
Reitz St	Robertson	221	RQ 11
Reitz St	Swellendam	224	SX 11
Rekreasie St	Bredasdorp	197	BT 12
Rendezvous St	Worcester	219	WU 17
Rendlesham La.	Atlantis (Sherwood)	199	AG 33
Renonkal St	Montagu	222	MO 13
Renosterbos St	Malmesbury	212	MC 11
Renostervoël La.	Atlantis (Robinvale)	201	AJ 33
Republic St	Bredasdorp	197	BU 11
Repulse St	Saldanha	210	SC 11
Reservoir	Hermanus	229	HE 16
Reservoir	Hermanus	229	HF 16
Reservoir St	Malmesbury	212	MA 12
Restless Waver St	Saldanha	210	SC 11
Retief St	Ceres	207	CG 12
Retief St	Worcester	216	WP 16
Re-Union St	Bredasdorp	197	BU 12
Reyger La.	Worcester	215	WQ 11
Reygersdal Dr.	Atlantis	201	AM 34
Reygersdal Dr.	Atlantis (Avondale)	199	AH 31
Reygersdal Dr.	Atlantis (Protea Pk)	201	AJ 32
Rheebok St	Malmesbury	212	MC 11
Rhenius St	Swellendam	224	SX 12
Rhode Cr.	Ceres	207	CH 12
Rhode St	Worcester	219	WT 17
Rhodes St	Malmesbury	212	MB 13
Richter St	Robertson	221	RP 12
Ridge St	Grabouw	227	GV 12
Riebeeck St	Malmesbury	212	MB 12
Riebeeck St	Worcester	216	WS 15
Rietbaai Cl.	Langebaan	208	LD 11
Rietsanger La.	Atlantis (Robinvale)	201	AJ 33
Rietvalley St	Ceres	207	CG 13
Rijger Ave	Robertson	221	RR 13
Riley St	Worcester	216	WR 17
Ring St	Swellendam	224	SZ 11
Rio Rd	Melkbos (Melkbosstrand)	204	BC 26
River St	Bredasdorp	197	BS 11
River St	Bredasdorp	197	BR 12
River St	Robertson	221	RP 11
Riverside St	Bredasdorp	197	BR 11
Riverside St	Hermanus	229	HE 16
Riviera St	Worcester	219	WU 17
Rivierkant St	Ceres	207	CG 10
Robbejacht Cir.	Langebaan	208	LE 12
Robben Rd	Melkbos (Melkbosstrand)	204	BB 26
Robben St	Langebaan	209	LG 11
Robejaria	Saldanha	210	SE 13
Robert St	Atlantis (Saxonsea)	199	AF 32
Robertson Dr.	Worcester	220	WT 20
Robertson Rd	Worcester	216	WS 17
Robertson St	Robertson	221	RQ 11
Robey St	Worcester	219	WU 17
Robin St	Hermanus	228	HG 12
Robin St	Worcester	218	WV 13
Robinsons St	Worcester	215	WS 12
Rochester St	Hermanus	228	HH 11
Rocklands St	Hermanus	228	HH 12
Rockpool La.	Melkbos (Atlantic Beach Est.)	205	BE 27
Rodger St	Langebaan	209	LF 10
Rog St	Malmesbury	212	MB 11
Rokewood St	Grabouw	227	GU 12
Rolbos	Robertson	221	RO 11
Rolihlahla St	Malmesbury	212	ME 12
Roller La.	Atlantis (Robinvale)	201	AJ 33
Roller St	Worcester	218	WV 13
Roman Cl.	Hermanus	228	HH 10
Roman St	Saldanha	211	SC 14
Roman St	Worcester	219	WU 15
Rondeheuwel Cr.	Atlantis (Beaconhill)	199	AH 34
Rood St	Malmesbury	212	MB 12
Roede Vos Cr.	Langebaan	209	LH 11
Roodezand St	Robertson	221	RQ 12
Rooibekkie	Langebaan	209	LH 13
Rooibekkie St	Atlantis (Robinvale)	201	AJ 33
Rooibekkie St	Worcester	218	WV 13
Rooiberg Cl.	Atlantis (Beaconhill)	199	AH 34
Rooiborsie St	Atlantis (Robinvale)	201	AK 33
Rooibroodbos	Robertson	221	RO 11
Rooiels La.	Tulbagh	206	TW 12
Rooi-Els Way	Worcester	216	WR 17
Rooikrans Ave	Malmesbury	212	ME 11
Roos St	Ceres	207	CG 12
Roos St	Malmesbury	212	MD 12
Roos St	Robertson	221	RO 13
Roos St	Swellendam	224	SZ 11
Roosenberg	Langebaan	209	LH 10
Roosmaryn La.	Atlantis (Protea Pk)	201	AJ 32
Roosmaryn St	Malmesbury	212	MD 11
Rosa Ave	Robertson	221	RP 11
Rosane St	Worcester	219	WT 17
Rosita St	Robertson	221	RP 12
Rossouw St	Montagu	222	MR 12
Rossouw St	Tulbagh	206	TW 11
Rossouw St	Worcester	216	WQ 15
Rostic St	Langebaan	209	LG 12
Rothman St	Bredasdorp	197	BT 11
Rothman St	Malmesbury	212	MC 12
Rothman St	Swellendam	224	SZ 10
Rotspunt Cl.	Melkbos (Melkbosstrand)	205	BD 25
Rotterdam St	Atlantis (Avondale)	199	AH 31
Rotterdam St	Saldanha	210	SC 11

STREET NAME	TOWN NAME	PG	GRID
Roux Rd	Worcester	216	WR 15
Roux Rd	Worcester	216	WQ 16
Roux Rd	Worcester	216	WP 15
Roux Rd	Worcester	216	WQ 15
Roux St	Bredasdorp	197	BT 11
Roxana St	Worcester	219	WU 17
Royal George Rd	Atlantis (Saxonsea)	199	AG 31
Royal George Rd	Atlantis (Saxonsea)	199	AF 34
Royal Saxon	Atlantis (Saxonsea)	199	AF 32
Royal St	Hermanus	228	HG 13
Rozenburg St	Malmesbury	212	MB 12
Rozette St	Atlantis (Avondale)	199	AH 31
Ruby Lamp La.	Melkbos (Atlantic Beach Est.)	205	BD 26
Ruiterbos Ct	Atlantis (Sherwood)	199	AG 33
Ruskin St	Worcester	219	WU 14
Russel Cl.	Grabouw	227	GV 12
Russel St	Grabouw	227	GV 12
Russel St	Worcester	219	WT 15
Russel St	Worcester	219	WT 14
Ryke St	Grabouw	227	GT 11
S			
Saayman St	Robertson	221	RP 12
Sababt St	Bredasdorp	197	BR 11
Sacco St	Montagu	222	MP 12
Sacramento Cir.	Atlantis (Saxonsea)	199	AG 31
Saffraan St	Grabouw	227	GV 12
Safraan St	Tulbagh	206	TX 11
Sagita St	Saldanha	210	SC 11
Sainsbury St	Robertson	221	RP 11
Sake	Grabouw	227	GV 12
Salamander Rd	Saldanha	211	SC 15
Saldanha	Saldanha	210	SD 13
Saldanha Heights	Saldanha	211	SC 14
Salie	Malmesbury	212	ME 12
Salie St	Worcester	219	WU 15
Salmander St	Langebaan	209	LG 12
Sam St	Grabouw	227	GV 12
Samos Rd	Langebaan	208	LC 11
Sampson Rd	Atlantis (Robinvale)	199	AH 33
Sampson St	Worcester	219	WU 15
Samuel Cl.	Melkbos (Duynefontein)	204	AY 27
Samuel Cl. Nth	Melkbos (Duynefontein)	204	AY 27
Samuel Cl. Sth	Melkbos (Duynefontein)	204	AY 27
Samuel Cr.	Melkbos (Duynefontein)	204	AY 26
Samuel Cr.	Melkbos (Duynefontein)	204	AY 27
Samuel St	Robertson	221	RS 12
Samuel Walters St	Worcester	217	WS 18
Samuel Walters St	Worcester	217	WS 19
Samuel Walters St	Worcester	220	WT 18
Sand Fig Way	Melkbos (Atlantic Beach Est.)	205	BD 26
Sand Reef Cove	Melkbos (Atlantic Beach Est.)	205	BE 27
Sand Shrimp La.	Melkbos (Atlantic Beach Est.)	205	BD 27
Sanderling	Langebaan	209	LJ 11
Sandpiper Cl.	Langebaan	209	LJ 11
Sandpiper St	Worcester	219	WV 14
Sandvygie Cl.	Langebaan	209	LJ 11
Sangster St	Worcester	216	WR 14
Santa Rosa St	Ceres	207	CJ 12
Santorini St	Langebaan	208	LC 11
Sarah Cl.	Atlantis (Saxonsea)	199	AG 31
Sardina St	Saldanha	210	SC 12
Sarel Cilliers St	Malmesbury	212	MC 12
Sarel Cilliers St	Malmesbury	212	MB 12
Sauer St	Caledon	225	CD 12
Saul Damon St	Worcester	219	WV 15
Saunders St	Montagu	222	MQ 12
Saunders St	Worcester	219	WU 14
Savannah St	Saldanha	210	SC 11
Saxonwold Rd	Atlantis	201	AL 34
Scafie St	Robertson	221	RO 11
Sceptre St	Atlantis (Saxonsea)	199	AF 32
Sceptre St	Saldanha	211	SB 14
Schaapen Cr.	Langebaan	209	LG 11
Schapejacht Cir.	Langebaan	208	LE 12
Schapejacht Cl.	Langebaan	209	LF 12
Scholtz St	Swellendam	224	SX 12
Schonken St	Worcester	215	WS 13
Schonland St	Worcester	216	WR 17
Schoonberg Cr.	Atlantis (Saxonsea)	199	AH 31
Schooner Cl.	Melkbos (Atlantic Beach Est.)	205	BE 27
Schoonspruit	Malmesbury	212	MC 12
Schoonspruit Way	Malmesbury	212	MD 11
Schrader Cl.	Langebaan	209	LJ 11
Schrywershoek Cl.	Langebaan	208	LD 11
Schuster St	Saldanha	211	SC 14
Schuter St	Saldanha	211	SC 14
Schwartzwald Rd	Atlantis (Sherwood)	199	AG 33
Scotsville Rd	Langebaan	208	LD 14
Scout La.	Hermanus	228	HF 13
Sea Bamboo La.	Melkbos (Atlantic Beach Est.)	205	BE 26
Sea Bride St	Saldanha	211	SC 14
Sea Eagle St	Saldanha	211	SA 16
Sea Hare Cir.	Melkbos (Atlantic Beach Est.)	205	BD 26
Sea Haven	Langebaan	209	LH 10
Sea Pumpkin Way	Melkbos (Atlantic Beach Est.)	205	BD 26
Sea Wheat Way	Melkbos (Atlantic Beach Est.)	205	BE 26
Seagull St	Melkbos (Van Riebeeckstrand)	204	AZ 26
Sealord	Langebaan	209	LF 11
Sealy St	Bredasdorp	197	BT 11
Seaview Cr.	Melkbos (Melkbosstrand)	205	BD 25
Second Ave	Caledon	225	CD 12
Second Ave	Ceres	207	CG 11
Second Ave	Darling	213	DC 11
Second Ave	Hermanus	229	HF 17

STREET NAME	TOWN NAME	PG	GRID
Second Ave	Hermanus	229	HE 17
Second Ave	Kleinmond	226	KO 12
Second Ave	Kleinmond	226	KM 12
Second Ave	Melkbos (Melkbosstrand)	204	BC 25
Second Ave	Robertson	221	RP 11
Second Ave	Saldanha	211	SB 15
Second Ave	Tulbagh	206	TX 12
Second St	Hermanus	229	HE 17
Second St	Kleinmond	226	KM 12
Seder	Caledon	225	CE 13
Seder St	Malmesbury	212	MD 11
Sederberg Cl.	Atlantis (Beaconhill)	199	AH 34
Sederberg Cr.	Ceres	207	CF 11
Seeberg Cl.	Langebaan	208	LD 11
Seeberg St	Hermanus	228	HG 11
Seeduiker St	Langebaan	209	LG 11
Seemeeu	Langebaan	209	LF 11
Seesprei Cl.	Melkbos (Melkbosstrand)	205	BD 25
Seester St	Saldanha	211	SA 17
Seinheuwel Cr.	Atlantis (Beaconhill)	199	AG 34
Sending St	Bredasdorp	197	BS 11
Sennet St	Worcester	217	WS 18
September St	Swellendam	224	SZ 12
September St	Worcester	219	WT 16
Seringboom St	Malmesbury	212	MD 12
Seritos	Langebaan	208	LC 12
Serruria St	Villiersdorp	223	VM 11
Seventeenth Ave	Darling	213	DB 12
Seventeenth Ave	Melkbos (Melkbosstrand)	204	BB 26
Seventh Ave	Caledon	225	CD 12
Seventh Ave	Darling	213	DB 12
Seventh Ave	Kleinmond	226	KN 12
Seventh Ave	Melkbos (Melkbosstrand)	204	BC 25
Seventh Ave	Saldanha	211	SB 15
Seventh St	Hermanus	229	HF 17
Seventh St	Kleinmond	226	KN 12
Shand St	Swellendam	224	SX 12
Shasta Rd	Atlantis (Sherwood)	199	AF 33
Shavs Ave	Caledon	225	CD 12
Sheard St	Worcester	216	WS 17
Shelley St	Worcester	219	WU 14
Sherwood Rd	Atlantis (Sherwood)	199	AG 32
Short St	Worcester	215	WR 11
Shortle St	Worcester	219	WU 15
Shrike St	Worcester	219	WV 14
Side St	Hermanus	229	HE 16
Siebelaar St	Swellendam	224	SZ 11
Siebert St	Swellendam	224	SX 11
Silesia Rd	Atlantis (Sherwood)	199	AF 33
Silimela St	Robertson	221	RS 12
Silver Clipper St	Saldanha	210	SC 11
Silverman St	Saldanha	211	SC 14
Silwerblaar	Worcester	216	WQ 17
Silwerboom St	Malmesbury	212	MD 12
Simanga Ave	Worcester	217	WS 21
Simmentaler St	Malmesbury	212	MB 10
Simon	Montagu	222	MP 12
Simunye	Saldanha	210	SC 12
Sipres Ave	Grabouw	227	GU 12
Sipres La.	Worcester	216	WR 15
Siqwela Ave	Worcester	220	WT 19
Siring La.	Worcester	216	WR 17
Sivuyile St	Malmesbury	212	ME 12
Siwangaza Ave	Worcester	220	WT 20
Sixteenth Ave	Darling	213	DB 12
Sixteenth Ave	Melkbos (Melkbosstrand)	204	BB 26
Sixteenth Ave	Melkbos (Melkbosstrand)	204	BC 26
Sixth Ave	Caledon	225	CD 12
Sixth Ave	Darling	213	DC 12
Sixth Ave	Hermanus	229	HF 17
Sixth Ave	Kleinmond	226	KN 12
Sixth Ave	Melkbos (Melkbosstrand)	204	BC 25
Sixth Ave	Saldanha	211	SB 15
Sixth Ave	Tulbagh	206	TW 13
Sixth St	Hermanus	229	HE 17
Sixth St	Kleinmond	226	KN 12
Skafu Ave	Worcester	220	WT 20
Skemer St	Malmesbury	212	MC 11
Skipper Cl.	Langebaan	209	LG 11
Skipper St	Saldanha	210	SC 10
Skool St	Bredasdorp	197	BS 11
Skool St	Kleinmond	226	KO 12
Skool St	Langebaan	209	LF 11
Skool St	Malmesbury	212	MA 12
Skool St	Swellendam	224	SX 11
Skurweberg Ave	Ceres	207	CF 11
Slabbert St	Ceres	207	CG 11
Slabbert St	Worcester	216	WP 16
Slanghoek La.	Worcester	215	WQ 13
Sleigh St	Langebaan	209	LG 11
Sleigh St	Langebaan	209	LG 12
Sleigh St	Langebaan	209	LG 10
Smal	Caledon	225	CC 12
Smal St	Langebaan	209	LH 10
Smal St	Robertson	221	RQ 10
Smith St	Bredasdorp	197	BT 12
Smith St	Darling	213	DB 12
Smith St	Langebaan	209	LH 10
Smith St	Robertson	221	RQ 12
Smith St	Worcester	216	WS 17
Smuts Ave	Hermanus	228	HH 12
Smuts St	Malmesbury	212	MB 12
Sneli Ave	Worcester	220	WT 20
Snip St	Atlantis (Robinvale)	201	AJ 33
Snipe	Langebaan	209	LF 11

Abbreviations used: Ave – Avenue, A.H. – Agricultural Holding, A.L.– Algemene Landgoed, Blvd – Boulevard, Cen. – Central, Cir. – Circle, Cl. – Close, Cr. – Crescent, Ct – Court, Dr. – Drive, Est. – Estate, Ext. – Extension, Hgts – Heights, Ind. – Industrial, Gdns – Gardens, Gr. – Grove, La. – Lane, (M.Plain) - Mitchells Plain, Nth – North, Pl. – Place, Pk – Park, Rd – Road, Rdg. – Ridge, S.H.– Small Holding, Sq. – Square, St – Street, Sth – South, Ter. – Terrace, Tn – Turn, Val. – Valley, Wk – Walk

STREET NAME	TOWN NAME	PG	GRID	
Sobukhwe St	Malmesbury	212	ME	12
Sofietjie St	Swellendam	224	SZ	11
Söhnge La.	Worcester	219	WT	15
Söhnge La.	Worcester	219	WT	16
Söhnge La.	Worcester	219	WT	17
Solomon St	Robertson	221	RP	12
Solon St	Worcester	219	WU	15
Somerset Cr.	Darling	213	DC	11
Somerset St	Darling	213	DC	11
Somerset St	Swellendam	224	SY	11
Somerset St	Worcester	218	WT	13
Somerset St	Worcester	219	WT	14
Sonneblom St	Malmesbury	212	ME	12
Sonneblom St	Robertson	221	RP	13
Sonneblom St	Swellendam	224	TA	11
Sonop St	Bredasdorp	197	BV	12
Sonop St	Malmesbury	212	MC	11
Sonskyn St	Robertson	221	RP	11
Sophia Cl.	Atlantis (Saxonsea)	199	AG	31
Sophia Cl.	Atlantis (Saxonsea)	199	AF	34
Sound of Jura St	Saldanha	211	SB	14
Southern Right Cl.	Melkbos (Atlantic Beach Est.)	205	BE	26
Southern Right Cl.	Melkbos (Atlantic Beach Est.)	205	BF	26
Sparrebos Rd	Atlantis (Sherwood)	199	AF	32
Sperwer La.	Atlantis (Robinvale)	201	AJ	33
Spes Bona St	Worcester	220	WU	18
Spica St	Caledon	225	CD	13
Spierdijk	Langebaan	209	LH	11
Spin St	Langebaan	209	LG	11
Spinner	Saldanha	210	SC	13
Spires Ave	Malmesbury	212	ME	11
Sporrie Cl.	Langebaan	209	LJ	11
Sport Ave	Caledon	225	CC	12
Sport St	Ceres	207	CJ	12
Spreeu	Langebaan	209	LF	11
Spreeu St	Worcester	218	WV	13
Sprengel St	Worcester	216	WS	16
Springbok La.	Worcester	215	WQ	11
Springfield Ave	Hermanus	228	HH	11
Springveldt St	Worcester	219	WT	17
Springveldt St	Worcester	219	WU	17
Springwater Cl.	Melkbos (Melkbosstrand)	205	BD	25
Spruit St	Caledon	225	CC	10
St Andrew St	Ceres	207	CH	12
St Andrews Cl.	Worcester	216	WP	16
St Antonio St	Atlantis (Saxonsea)	199	AF	32
St Croix St	Langebaan	209	LG	10
St Francis	Malmesbury	212	MB	12
St Francis St	Ceres	207	CH	12
St George St	Ceres	207	CH	12
St Georges St	Caledon	225	CB	11
St James St	Ceres	207	CH	12
St Jean Bajou Dr.	Langebaan	209	LF	13
St John St	Ceres	207	CH	12
St John St	Malmesbury	212	MC	12
St Jose St	Atlantis (Saxonsea)	199	AF	32
St Jude St	Ceres	207	CH	12
St Lawrence St	Atlantis (Saxonsea)	199	AF	32
St Lawrence St	Atlantis (Saxonsea)	199	AF	34
St Luke St	Ceres	207	CG	12
St Mark St	Ceres	207	CH	12
St Mathews St	Ceres	207	CH	12
St Paul St	Ceres	207	CH	12
St Peter St	Ceres	207	CG	12
St Peters	Hermanus	228	HG	13
St Thomas St	Ceres	207	CH	12
St Thomas St	Malmesbury	212	MB	12
Staal St	Montagu	222	MP	12
Stabroek	Atlantis (Saxonsea)	199	AG	31
Staff St	Ceres	207	CH	10
Stals St	Worcester	216	WQ	17
Stanley St	Ceres	207	CJ	11
Star Fish Way	Melkbos (Atlantic Beach Est.)	205	BD	26
Starboard End	Melkbos (Atlantic Beach Est.)	205	BE	27
Starking St	Ceres	207	CJ	12
Starling Rd	Atlantis (Robinvale)	199	AH	33
Starling Rd	Atlantis (Robinvale)	201	AJ	33
Stasie St	Swellendam	224	SY	11
Statice	Langebaan	209	LF	11
Station St	Darling	213	DD	11
Steenbok St	Hermanus	228	HG	12
Steenbras Rd	Hermanus	228	HH	10
Steenbras St	Saldanha	211	SC	14
Steenkamp St	Villiersdorp	223	VL	11
Steenkool	Saldanha	210	SB	12
Steenkool	Saldanha	210	SB	11
Steenloper Cl.	Langebaan	209	LJ	10
Steenloper St	Atlantis (Robinvale)	201	AJ	33
Steil St	Bredasdorp	197	BT	12
Stein St	Worcester	215	WS	13
Steinthal Rd	Tulbagh	206	TW	12
Stemmet	Hermanus	228	HF	13
Sterling St	Caledon	225	CD	13
Sterling Way	Melkbos (Atlantic Beach Est.)	205	BD	26
Sterreschans St	Atlantis (Saxonsea)	199	AG	31
Stettyn St	Worcester	219	WU	17
Stil St	Hermanus	228	HJ	10
Stillwater Cove	Melkbos (Atlantic Beach Est.)	205	BD	27
Stockenstrom St	Worcester	216	WS	15
Stofberg St	Worcester	219	WU	15
Stoffel Erasmus Cr.	Atlantis (Atlantis Ind.)	200	AL	28
Stokvis St	Saldanha	211	SD	14
Strand	Langebaan	208	LC	14
Strand	Langebaan	208	LB	13
Strand Rd	Melkbos (Van Riebeeckstrand)	204	BA	26

STREET NAME	TOWN NAME	PG	GRID	
Strand St	Hermanus	228	HH	11
Strandloper La.	Atlantis (Robinvale)	201	AJ	33
Strandloper St	Saldanha	211	SB	16
Strathblane Way	Melkbos (Melkbosstrand)	205	BD	26
Strathtyrum End	Melkbos (Atlantic Beach Est.)	204	BC	26
Strawberry St	Grabouw	227	GU	11
Streicher St	Swellendam	224	SY	10
Strelitzia St	Atlantis (Protea Pk)	201	AJ	32
Strelizia Pl.	Atlantis (Protea Pk)	201	AJ	32
Strelizia Pl.	Atlantis (Protea Pk)	201	AM	32
Strydom St	Montagu	222	MP	12
Stuart	Montagu	222	MP	12
Stynder St	Worcester	219	WT	16
Suffren St	Langebaan	209	LG	10
Sugerbird La.	Atlantis (Robinvale)	201	AJ	33
Sugget St	Worcester	216	WS	17
Suid Dam St	Saldanha	210	SC	11
Suid St	Bredasdorp	197	BT	12
Suid St	Malmesbury	212	MA	12
Suikerbekkie	Malmesbury	212	ME	11
Suikerbekkie La.	Atlantis (Robinvale)	201	AJ	34
Suikerbekkie St	Worcester	219	WV	14
Suikerbos St	Malmesbury	212	ME	11
Suikerkan St	Langebaan	209	LF	10
Suikerkan St	Langebaan	209	LF	11
Sultana Cr.	Ceres	207	CJ	12
Sultana Cr.	Montagu	222	MP	13
Summer Cr.	Langebaan	209	LG	12
Summerveld	Langebaan	208	LA	13
Summerveld	Langebaan	208	LB	12
Summerveld	Langebaan	208	LB	13
Sun Rd	Atlantis (Avondale)	199	AH	31
Sunbeam St	Saldanha	210	SC	12
Sunbird Dr.	Langebaan	209	LH	12
Sunbird Dr.	Langebaan	209	LJ	11
Sunbird St	Worcester	219	WV	14
Suncrest	Ceres	207	CJ	12
Sunny Way	Worcester	215	WR	12
Sunnybrae Cr.	Hermanus	228	HH	11
Sunset	Langebaan	209	LJ	12
Sunset Clam	Melkbos (Atlantic Beach Est.)	205	BD	26
Suring	Malmesbury	212	ME	10
Sutherland St	Worcester	216	WS	16
Suurberg Cl.	Atlantis (Beaconhill)	199	AG	34
Swaeltjie	Langebaan	209	LF	11
Swallow St	Worcester	218	WV	13
Swan St	Worcester	219	WV	14
Swanepoel St	Montagu	222	MR	11
Swart St	Bredasdorp	197	BT	12
Swart St	Worcester	219	WU	15
Swartdam Rd	Hermanus	228	HH	10
Swartrivier Rd	Kleinmond	226	KM	11
Swawel	Malmesbury	212	ME	10
Swawel St	Atlantis (Robinvale)	201	AJ	33
Sweetpea Ave	Robertson	221	RP	11
Sweetpea St	Worcester	219	WU	16
Swellendam St	Robertson	221	RQ	11
Swellengrebel St	Swellendam	224	SX	13
Swift St	Atlantis (Robinvale)	199	AH	33
Swift St	Atlantis (Robinvale)	201	AJ	33
Sybille Cr.	Atlantis (Saxonsea)	199	AF	31
Sybille Rd	Melkbos (Melkbosstrand)	205	BD	26
Syros St	Langebaan	208	LC	12
Sysie St	Worcester	219	WV	14
T				
Taaibos	Malmesbury	212	MD	11
Taaibos	Robertson	221	RO	11
Taambay St	Worcester	219	WT	17
Tahoe Rd	Atlantis (Sherwood)	199	AF	32
Tahoe Rd	Atlantis (Sherwood)	199	AF	33
Talana St	Hermanus	228	HG	11
Tall Timber Ave	Ceres	207	CG	11
Talmakkies Cr.	Saldanha	210	SC	10
Tamarisk Ave	Malmesbury	212	ME	11
Tamboer Cl.	Langebaan	208	LE	12
Tanner St	Montagu	222	MQ	11
Tantallon Cl.	Atlantis (Saxonsea)	199	AG	31
Tantallon Cl.	Atlantis (Saxonsea)	199	AF	34
Tarentaal Rd	Melkbos (Van Riebeeckstrand)	204	AZ	26
Tarentaal St	Tulbagh	206	TW	13
Tarentaal St	Worcester	218	WV	13
Tasman Cir.	Atlantis (Beaconhill)	199	AG	34
Taunus Ave	Atlantis (Beaconhill)	199	AG	34
Taylor St	Worcester	215	WS	13
Teal	Langebaan	209	LF	12
Tecoma Pl.	Atlantis (Protea Pk)	201	AJ	32
Tegno St	Malmesbury	212	MD	11
Tekoma Ave	Malmesbury	212	ME	12
Tenos Rd	Langebaan	208	LD	11
Tenth Ave	Caledon	225	CD	13
Tenth Ave	Darling	213	DB	12
Tenth Ave	Kleinmond	226	KN	12
Tenth Ave	Kleinmond	226	KM	12
Tenth Ave	Melkbos (Melkbosstrand)	204	BC	26
Tenth Ave	Saldanha	211	SB	15
Tenth St	Hermanus	229	HF	17
Tenth St	Kleinmond	226	KN	12
Tern	Langebaan	209	LJ	11
Ternate Cl.	Atlantis (Saxonsea)	199	AG	31
Ternate Cl.	Atlantis (Saxonsea)	199	AF	34
Terpentyn St	Malmesbury	212	MC	12
Teuton Rd	Melkbos (Melkbosstrand)	205	BD	26
The Meadows	Worcester	215	WQ	11
Theoha Ave	Worcester	220	WT	20

STREET NAME	TOWN NAME	PG	GRID	
Thera Rd	Langebaan	208	LC	11
Theron La.	Worcester	215	WS	13
Theron La.	Worcester	218	WT	13
Theron St	Ceres	207	CG	10
Theron St	Hermanus	229	HE	16
Theron St	Tulbagh	206	TW	11
Theunissen St	Swellendam	224	SY	11
Third Ave	Caledon	225	CD	12
Third Ave	Ceres	207	CG	11
Third Ave	Darling	213	DC	12
Third Ave	Hermanus	229	HF	17
Third Ave	Hermanus	229	HE	17
Third Ave	Kleinmond	226	KO	12
Third Ave	Kleinmond	226	KM	12
Third Ave	Melkbos (Melkbosstrand)	204	BC	25
Third Ave	Robertson	221	RP	11
Third Ave	Saldanha	211	SB	15
Third Ave	Tulbagh	206	TX	12
Third St	Hermanus	229	HE	17
Third St	Kleinmond	226	KM	12
Thirteenth Ave	Darling	213	DB	12
Thirteenth Ave	Kleinmond	226	KO	11
Thirteenth Ave	Kleinmond	226	KO	11
Thirteenth Ave	Melkbos (Melkbosstrand)	204	BC	26
Thirteenth St	Kleinmond	226	KO	12
Thomas St	Bredasdorp	197	BR	11
Thomas St	Worcester	219	WU	15
Thomas Williams Cr.	Atlantis (Atlantis Ind.)	200	AK	30
Thome Cl.	Atlantis (Saxonsea)	199	AG	31
Thome Cl.	Atlantis (Saxonsea)	199	AF	34
Thompson St	Montagu	222	MR	12
Thunborg Cl.	Langebaan	209	LF	12
Tidehigh Cl.	Melkbos (Melkbosstrand)	205	BD	25
Tienvoet St	Robertson	221	RP	11
Tier St	Tulbagh	206	TX	12
Tilney St	Swellendam	224	SX	12
Tim St	Worcester	219	WU	15
Tindall St	Robertson	221	RP	11
Tinktinkie	Langebaan	209	LH	12
Tinktinkie	Malmesbury	212	ME	10
Tinktinkie St	Worcester	219	WV	14
Tino Cl.	Langebaan	208	LC	12
Titus St	Worcester	219	WU	15
T'kalft Cl.	Langebaan	208	LE	12
Tobias St	Worcester	219	WU	15
Tobie Cl.	Langebaan	209	LJ	11
Toens St	Worcester	217	WS	19
Tokai Ct	Atlantis (Sherwood)	199	AF	33
Toli St	Worcester	220	WT	19
Tom Brink Rd	Atlantis (Atlantis Ind.)	200	AM	27
Tom Henshilwood St	Atlantis (Atlantis Ind.)	201	AK	31
Tomlinson St	Swellendam	224	SX	13
Ton	Saldanha	210	SC	13
Tonyn St	Saldanha	211	SD	14
Toronto Rd	Atlantis (Sherwood)	199	AF	32
Torteldulf	Malmesbury	212	ME	10
Tortelduif Cr.	Atlantis (Robinvale)	199	AH	33
Tortelduif St	Worcester	218	WW	13
Tortilis Cl.	Langebaan	209	LH	11
Tortilis Cr.	Langebaan	209	LH	12
Tosca St	Malmesbury	212	MC	11
Tradewinds Cir.	Melkbos (Atlantic Beach Est.)	205	BE	26
Tradewinds Cir.	Melkbos (Atlantic Beach Est.)	205	BE	27
Trafalgar St	Atlantis (Saxonsea)	199	AF	32
Transvaal Way	Worcester	215	WR	11
Transvaal Way	Worcester	215	WR	12
Trappes St	Worcester	219	WT	14
Traub St	Worcester	216	WS	17
Trewwa	Langebaan	209	LE	11
Trichard St	Saldanha	211	SC	14
Trichardt St	Swellendam	224	SX	12
Trigardt St	Ceres	207	CH	11
Trinity St	Caledon	225	CB	11
Trireem	Saldanha	210	SC	12
Triton Way	Melkbos (Atlantic Beach Est.)	205	BD	26
Troon Rd	Langebaan	209	LG	12
Troon Rd	Langebaan	209	LG	11
Trui St	Swellendam	224	SZ	11
Truter St	Malmesbury	212	MC	11
Truter St	Montagu	222	MO	12
Truter St	Robertson	221	RQ	11
Truter St	Worcester	219	WU	14
Truter St	Worcester	219	WT	14
Tsequa Rd	Worcester	217	WS	20
Tshazimpunzi	Robertson	221	RS	12
Tshwete St	Malmesbury	212	ME	10
Tuin St	Malmesbury	212	MB	12
Tulbagh St	Darling	213	DD	11
Tulbagh St	Worcester	216	WS	14
Tulip La.	Atlantis (Protea Pk)	201	AJ	32
Tulip Pl.	Atlantis (Protea Pk)	201	AJ	32
Tulip St	Robertson	221	RP	13
Tulleken St	Worcester	216	WQ	16
Tulpe St	Malmesbury	212	MC	12
Tuscaloosa St	Saldanha	211	SB	14
Tusha Ave	Worcester	220	WT	20
Tweede Ave	Bredasdorp	197	BR	11
Tweefontein Cr.	Worcester	215	WS	12
Twelfth Ave	Darling	213	DB	12
Twelfth Ave	Melkbos (Melkbosstrand)	204	BC	26
Twelfth St	Kleinmond	226	KO	12
Twentieth Ave	Melkbos (Melkbosstrand)	204	BB	26
Twenty-First Ave	Melkbos (Melkbosstrand)	204	BB	26
Twenty-Second Ave	Melkbos (Melkbosstrand)	204	BB	26
Tyodi Ave	Worcester	220	WT	20

STREET NAME	TOWN NAME	PG	GRID	
U				
Udam	Saldanha	210	SC	10
Uil St	Worcester	219	WV	14
Uiltjie Ave	Melkbos (Duynefontein)	204	AY	26
Uitkyk St	Bredasdorp	197	BV	11
Uitnood St	Robertson	221	RQ	10
Uitsig La.	Worcester	215	WR	11
Uitsig St	Bredasdorp	197	BT	12
Uitsig St	Ceres	207	CG	12
Uitsig St	Langebaan	209	LH	10
Uitsig St	Malmesbury	212	MC	11
Uitsig St	Swellendam	224	SX	12
Uitvlugt St	Montagu	222	MO	11
Uitvlugt St	Montagu	222	MO	12
Umzumaai Ave	Ceres	207	CG	11
Umzumaai La.	Ceres	207	CF	10
Undulata Cl.	Langebaan	209	LH	12
Unie St	Bredasdorp	197	BU	11
Unie St	Montagu	222	MQ	12
Union Ave	Villiersdorp	223	VL	12
Unity	Saldanha	210	SC	12
Upington St	Caledon	225	CC	11
Upington St	Villiersdorp	223	VL	12
Upington St	Villiersdorp	223	VK	12
Upper Union Ave	Villiersdorp	223	VL	11
Urchin La.	Melkbos (Atlantic Beach Est.)	205	BD	26
Ursinia La.	Kleinmond	226	KL	11
Ursinia St	Langebaan	209	LH	11
Uys St	Ceres	207	CG	12
V				
Valentine St	Bredasdorp	197	BR	11
Valk	Langebaan	209	LF	11
Valk	Malmesbury	212	ME	10
Valk St	Atlantis (Robinvale)	199	AH	33
Valley Omar St	Worcester	219	WT	17
Valleyfield Rd	Atlantis (Saxonsea)	199	AG	31
Van Arckel St	Worcester	216	WQ	16
Van Blommenstein St	Swellendam	224	SW	12
Van Boven St	Langebaan	209	LF	10
Van Brakel St	Bredasdorp	197	BT	12
Van Breda Dr.	Langebaan	208	LE	12
Van Breda Dr.	Langebaan	208	LE	11
Van Coppenhagen	Villiersdorp	223	VL	11
Van De Graaf St	Worcester	216	WP	16
Van de Graaf St	Worcester	216	WQ	15
Van Der Byl St	Bredasdorp	197	BT	12
Van Der Merwe St	Ceres	207	CG	11
Van Der Merwe St	Montagu	222	MR	11
Van Der Merwe St	Worcester	216	WR	14
Van Der Stel St	Darling	213	DD	12
Van Der Stel St	Robertson	221	RQ	10
Van Der Stel St	Tulbagh	206	TX	11
Van Dyk St	Swellendam	224	SX	11
Van Eeden St	Swellendam	224	SX	10
Van Goens St	Worcester	216	WQ	16
Van Graan St	Robertson	221	RQ	12
Van Huyssteen Ave	Worcester	219	WT	16
Van Huyssteen Ave	Worcester	219	WT	17
Van Immhof St	Swellendam	224	SX	11
Van Oudshoorn Rd	Swellendam	224	SW	12
Van Oudtshoorn St	Robertson	221	RQ	12
Van Reenen St	Robertson	221	RQ	11
Van Rensburg Cr.	Worcester	218	WT	12
Van Rhyn St	Worcester	217	WS	21
Van Riebeeck Ave	Robertson	221	RR	13
Van Riebeeck St	Bredasdorp	197	BU	12
Van Riebeeck St	Caledon	225	CB	11
Van Riebeeck St	Ceres	207	CH	10
Van Riebeeck St	Darling	213	DD	11
Van Riebeeck St	Montagu	222	MR	12
Van Riebeeck St	Saldanha	211	SB	14
Van Riebeeck St	Villiersdorp	223	VL	12
Van Riebeeck St	Villiersdorp	223	VK	12
Van Ryneveld St	Swellendam	224	SW	12
Van Spillberg St	Saldanha	211	SB	14
Van Staden St	Swellendam	224	SY	10
Van Turha	Montagu	222	MP	12
Van Wyk St	Grabouw	227	GV	12
Van Wyk St	Montagu	222	MP	12
Van Zyl Ave	Worcester	219	WU	16
Van Zyl Ave	Worcester	219	WT	17
Van Zyl St	Bredasdorp	197	BT	13
Van Zyl St	Montagu	222	MR	12
Van Zyl St	Robertson	221	RQ	11
Van Zyl St	Robertson	221	RP	11
Van Zyl St	Robertson	221	RR	12
Van Zyl St	Swellendam	224	SX	13
Vanguard	Saldanha	210	SC	12
Varing St	Malmesbury	212	MD	12
Veendam	Saldanha	210	SC	11
Veldkornet St	Swellendam	224	SX	11
Venoutiekraal La.	Worcester	215	WS	12
Venster St	Caledon	225	CB	11
Venus St	Ceres	207	CJ	12
Verbena	Malmesbury	212	ME	12
Verbena St	Atlantis (Protea Pk)	201	AK	32
Verdmuller St	Malmesbury	212	MC	11
Veronia St	Grabouw	227	GU	12
Vicky St	Worcester	215	WQ	12
Victor	Atlantis (Saxonsea)	199	AG	31
Victoria	Caledon	225	CC	11
Victoria St	Malmesbury	212	MB	13
Victoria St	Robertson	221	RQ	10

STREET NAME	TOWN NAME	PG	GRID	
Victoria St	Robertson	221	RR	10
Victoria St	Villiersdorp	223	VL	12
Victory Way	Worcester	216	WP	15
Viljoen St	Bredasdorp	197	BV	12
Viljoen St	Bredasdorp	197	BU	11
Viljoen St	Worcester	219	WT	17
Village St	Montagu	222	MR	12
Villiera St	Worcester	219	WU	17
Vink	Malmesbury	212	ME	10
Vink	Langebaan	209	LH	13
Vink St	Ceres	207	CG	10
Vink St	Worcester	219	WV	14
Vinkel	Malmesbury	212	MD	11
Viola Ave	Malmesbury	212	MC	12
Viola Ave	Robertson	221	RP	11
Violet La.	Atlantis (Protea Pk)	201	AK	32
Violet St	Worcester	219	WU	16
Viool St	Saldanha	210	SC	12
Viooltjie Cl.	Langebaan	209	LJ	11
Visarend	Malmesbury	212	ME	10
Visser St	Swellendam	224	SX	12
Visvanger Rd	Melkbos (Van Riebeeckstrand)	204	BA	26
Vlei	Darling	213	DB	12
Vogelgezang St	Bredasdorp	197	BV	11
Vogelvlei Rd	Atlantis	201	AM	34
Voight St	Worcester	216	WR	17
Volendam St	Langebaan	209	LH	11
Volhou St	Bredasdorp	197	BR	11
Volmoed St	Worcester	219	WU	17
Volstruis St	Worcester	219	WV	14
Von Manber St	Swellendam	224	SX	11
Vondeling St	Langebaan	209	LG	11
Vondeling St	Saldanha	211	SC	10
Voorhoutjie Cl.	Langebaan	209	LF	12
Voorschoten	Saldanha	210	SD	13
Voortrek St	Swellendam	224	SY	10
Voortrekker Rd	Malmesbury	212	MC	12
Voortrekker Rd	Robertson	221	RR	10
Voortrekker Rd	Robertson	221	RR	12
Voortrekker Rd	Robertson	221	RS	13
Voortrekker St	Ceres	207	CH	10
Voortrekker St	Ceres	207	CG	12
Voortrekker St	Darling	213	DD	11
Voortrekker St	Darling	213	DD	12
Voortrekker St	Grabouw	227	GT	11
Voortrekker St	Villiersdorp	223	VL	12
Voortrekker Way	Malmesbury	212	MB	11
Vos St	Ceres	207	CH	12
Vos St	Ceres	207	CF	11
Vos St	Ceres	207	CG	11
Vos St	Malmesbury	212	MC	12
Vraagom St	Saldanha	210	SC	11
Vrede St	Malmesbury	212	MA	12
Vrede St	Malmesbury	212	MB	12
Vreesniet St	Worcester	219	WU	17
Vreugde La.	Worcester	215	WR	11
Vultures St	Worcester	218	WV	13
Vygie Ave	Bredasdorp	197	BR	11
Vygie St	Caledon	225	CB	12
Vygie St	Darling	213	DE	12
Vygie St	Darling	213	DD	12
Vygie St	Langebaan	209	LF	10
Vygie St	Robertson	221	RP	12
Vysie Ave	Swellendam	224	TA	11

W

STREET NAME	TOWN NAME	PG	GRID	
Waboom Ave	Malmesbury	212	ME	11
Waboom St	Hermanus	229	HE	14
Waboom Way	Worcester	216	WQ	17
Wafra Cl.	Melkbos (Melkbosstrand)	205	BD	26
Wagenboomrivier	Worcester	215	WQ	13
Wagener St	Malmesbury	212	MB	13
Waldeck Cr.	Melkbos (Duynefontein)	204	AY	26
Walker Bay Cr.	Hermanus	229	HE	14
Wallbrugh St	Bredasdorp	197	BR	11
Waltham St	Worcester	219	WU	17
Wandel St	Malmesbury	212	MC	12
Wandel St	Malmesbury	212	MC	11
Wanderers Rd	Langebaan	209	LG	12
Wanderlust St	Melkbos (Ogieskraal)	204	AZ	27
Wapen Cl.	Langebaan	208	LE	12
Waratah Ave	Melkbos (Melkbosstrand)	205	BD	26
Waratah Way	Melkbos (Melkbosplaas)	205	BD	27
Waratah Way	Melkbos (Melkbosplaas)	205	BD	28
Warath St	Saldanha	211	SA	14
Warren St	Robertson	221	RQ	11
Waterkant St	Bredasdorp	197	BU	12
Waterkant St	Robertson	221	RQ	12
Waterkant St	Tulbagh	206	TW	12
Waterloo Cr.	Atlantis (Avondale)	199	AG	31
Waterloo Rd	Melkbos (Melkbosstrand)	205	BD	26
Waterloos St	Worcester	219	WT	15
Watermeyer Cr.	Worcester	216	WS	15
Watsonia Ave	Malmesbury	212	ME	12
Watsonia La.	Kleinmond	226	KL	11
Watsonia St	Caledon	225	CB	12
Watsonia St	Darling	213	DD	11
Watsonia St	Grabouw	227	GU	12
Watsonia St	Robertson	221	RP	13
Watsonia St	Villiersdorp	223	VM	11
Wattel Way	Worcester	216	WQ	16
Waveren St	Robertson	221	RQ	12
Waveren St	Tulbagh	206	TW	11
Weaver La.	Atlantis (Robinvale)	199	AH	34
Weaver St	Worcester	218	WV	13
Wedgewood Rd	Worcester	216	WP	15
Welgelegen	Malmesbury	212	MB	11
Weltevreden St	Worcester	219	WU	17
Wentzel St	Worcester	219	WT	17
Werda St	Worcester	219	WU	17
Wes St	Bredasdorp	197	BU	11
Wesfleur Cir.	Atlantis Town Centre	199	AH	32
Wesley Rd	Robertson	221	RP	11
Wessel St	Saldanha	211	SC	14
Wessels St	Montagu	222	MO	12
West Coast Rd	Atlantis (Atlantis Ind.)	202	AQ	25
West Coast Rd	Melkbos (Duynefontein)	203	AV	27
West Coast Rd	Melkbos (Melkbosstrand)	202	AS	26
West St	Malmesbury	212	MC	12
West St	Tulbagh	206	TX	11
Westcliff Rd	Hermanus	228	HH	11
Westcliff Rd	Hermanus	228	HH	12
Westerdam St	Saldanha	210	SC	10
Westerwyk	Langebaan	209	LH	10
Westminster St	Worcester	219	WU	17
Wethmar St	Malmesbury	212	MC	10
Wethmar St	Malmesbury	212	MC	11
Whipping	Saldanha	210	SC	12
White Mussel La.	Melkbos (Atlantic Beach Est.)	205	BD	27
White St	Robertson	221	RQ	11
White St	Robertson	221	RQ	11
White St	Worcester	219	WT	17
Wichtman Rd	Langebaan	209	LH	10
Wielewaal Cr.	Atlantis (Robinvale)	199	AH	33
Wige Ave	Bredasdorp	197	BS	11
Wilger La.	Tulbagh	206	TW	11
Wilger St	Caledon	225	CE	13
Wilger St	Malmesbury	212	ME	11
Wilhelm Thys La.	Montagu	222	MP	12
Willem Eksteen Cl.	Langebaan	208	LE	12
Willem Lourens Cr.	Montagu	222	MR	12
Willem Nel St	Robertson	221	RQ	10
Willenberg	Worcester	219	WU	14
William Gourlay St	Atlantis (Atlantis Ind.)	200	AM	30
William Robertson St	Swellendam	224	SW	12
William St	Swellendam	224	SZ	12
Williams St	Worcester	219	WV	14
Willie Van Wyk	Worcester	216	WP	17
Willow Way	Worcester	216	WR	16
Wilson La.	Worcester	216	WS	15
Windhoek Rd	Saldanha	211	SC	14
Windsor Cr.	Atlantis (Saxonsea)	199	AG	31
Windsor Cr.	Hermanus	228	HH	11
Windward Tn	Melkbos (Atlantic Beach Est.)	205	BE	27
Winkfield	Saldanha	210	SC	12
Winterbach	Worcester	216	WR	17
Wistaria	Malmesbury	212	MC	12
Witels Way	Worcester	216	WR	16
Witzenberg	Ceres	207	CG	11
Witzenberg La.	Ceres	207	CG	11
Witzenberg St	Tulbagh	206	TW	12
Wodehouse St	Worcester	215	WS	12
Wolff St	Ceres	207	CH	12
Wolraad Dr.	Langebaan	208	LE	11
Wolraad Dr.	Langebaan	209	LF	11
Woodpecker Cr.	Atlantis (Robinvale)	199	AH	33
Woodpecker St	Worcester	218	WV	13
Worcester St	Grabouw	227	GT	11
Worcester St	Grabouw	227	GU	11
Wyland St	Worcester	216	WQ	16
Wylo Rd	Langebaan	209	LH	10
Wyngaard St	Grabouw	227	GV	12
Wynruit	Malmesbury	212	MD	11

Y

STREET NAME	TOWN NAME	PG	GRID	
Yellowwood Way	Grabouw	227	GU	11
Yonge St	Worcester	215	WS	13
Yssel St	Worcester	219	WU	15
Ysterhout	Malmesbury	212	ME	11
Ysterklip Cl.	Hermanus	229	HE	16
Yzerfontein Rd	Darling	213	DC	11

Z

STREET NAME	TOWN NAME	PG	GRID	
Zambesi La.	Worcester	215	WQ	11
Zambesi St	Caledon	225	CD	12
Zeeland Cir.	Atlantis (Saxonsea)	198	AG	30
Zeeland St	Langebaan	209	LG	12
Zeus	Langebaan	208	LB	11
Zinnia Ave	Malmesbury	212	ME	12
Zinnia Pl.	Atlantis (Protea Pk)	201	AK	32
Zola St	Malmesbury	212	ME	10
Zuijdpool Cl.	Langebaan	209	LF	12
Zulch St	Ceres	207	CG	12

Abbreviations used: Ave – Avenue, A.H. – Agricultural Holding, A.L.– Algemene Landgoed, Blvd – Boulevard, Cen. – Central, Cir. – Circle, Cl. – Close, Cr. – Crescent, Ct – Court, Dr. – Drive, Est. – Estate, Ext. – Extension, Hgts – Heights, Ind. – Industrial, Gdns – Gardens, Gr. – Grove, La. – Lane, (M.Plain) – Mitchells Plain, Nth – North, Pl. – Place, Pk – Park, Rd – Road, Rdg. – Ridge, S.H.– Small Holding, Sq. – Square, St – Street, Sth – South, Ter. – Terrace, Tn – Turn, Val. – Valley, Wk – Walk

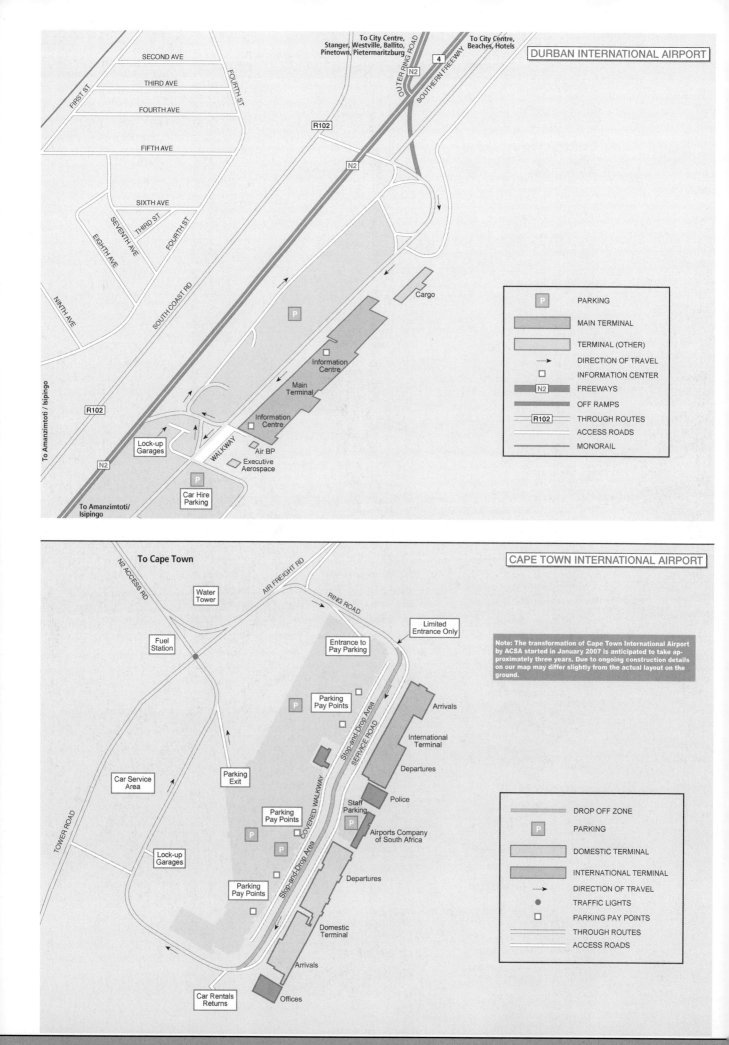

DURBAN INTERNATIONAL AIRPORT

SECOND AVE
THIRD AVE
FOURTH AVE
FIFTH AVE
SIXTH AVE
FIRST ST
FOURTH ST
THIRD ST
FOURTH ST
SEVENTH AVE
EIGHTH AVE
NINTH AVE
SOUTH COAST RD

To City Centre,
Stanger, Westville, Ballito,
Pinetown, Pietermaritzburg
To City Centre,
Beaches, Hotels
OUTER RING ROAD
SOUTHERN FREEWAY
N2
4

R102
N2

Cargo

P
Information Centre
Main Terminal
Information Centre
To Amanzimtoti / Isipingo
R102
N2
Lock-up Garages
WALKWAY
Air BP
Executive Aerospace
P
Car Hire Parking
To Amanzimtoti/ Isipingo

P — PARKING
— MAIN TERMINAL
— TERMINAL (OTHER)
→ — DIRECTION OF TRAVEL
□ — INFORMATION CENTER
N2 — FREEWAYS
— OFF RAMPS
R102 — THROUGH ROUTES
— ACCESS ROADS
— MONORAIL

CAPE TOWN INTERNATIONAL AIRPORT

To Cape Town
N2 ACCESS RD
AIR FREIGHT RD
RING ROAD
Water Tower
Fuel Station
Limited Entrance Only
Entrance to Pay Parking
P
Parking Pay Points
Stop-and-Drop Area
SERVICE ROAD
Arrivals
International Terminal
Departures
Car Service Area
Parking Exit
COVERED WALKWAY
Parking Pay Points
P
Staff Parking
Police
P
Airports Company of South Africa
TOWER ROAD
Lock-up Garages
P
Stop-and-Drop Area
Departures
Parking Pay Points
Domestic Terminal
Arrivals
Car Rentals Returns
Offices

Note: The transformation of Cape Town International Airport by ACSA started in January 2007 is anticipated to take approximately three years. Due to ongoing construction details on our map may differ slightly from the actual layout on the ground.

— DROP OFF ZONE
P — PARKING
— DOMESTIC TERMINAL
— INTERNATIONAL TERMINAL
→ — DIRECTION OF TRAVEL
● — TRAFFIC LIGHTS
□ — PARKING PAY POINTS
— THROUGH ROUTES
— ACCESS ROADS

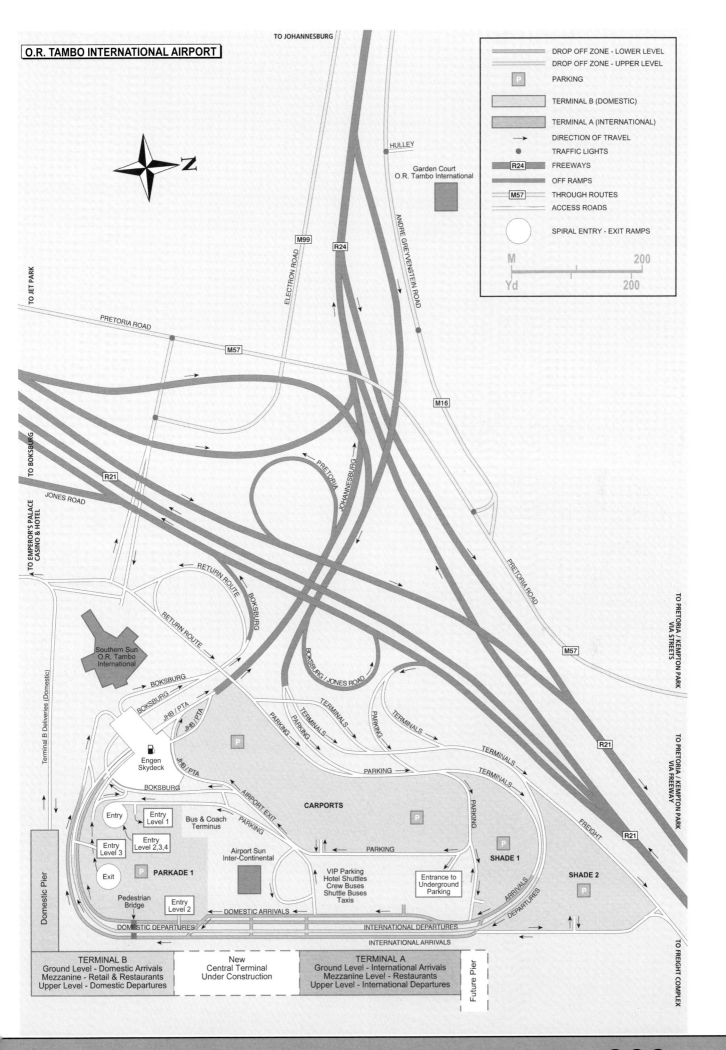

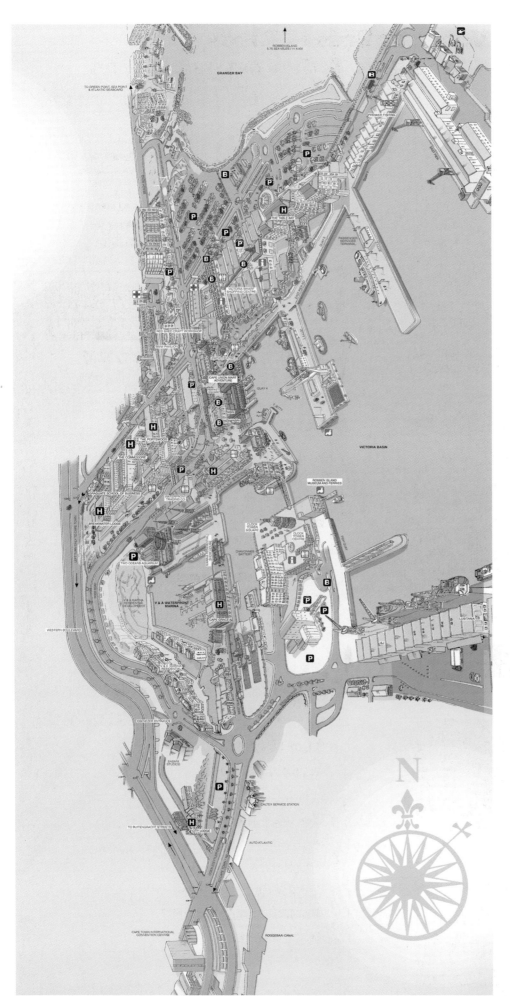

key:

- **i** INFORMATION
- **→** ENTRANCES
- **H** HOTELS
- SEALS
- **B** BUS STOPS
- ■ HELICOPTER CHARTERS
- **B** BANKS / ATM'S
- TOILETS

APPROXIMATE WALKING TIMES

Portswood Ridge/Commodore to Clock Tower
7 minutes

Commodore & Portswood Hotels to BMW Pavilion
5 minutes

Breakwater Lodge to Pierhead
9 minutes

Breakwater Lodge to Victoria Wharf
6 minutes

Cape Grace to Victoria Wharf
9 minutes

Cape Grace to Aquarium
5 minutes

Cape Grace to BMW Pavilion
15 minutes

City Lodge to Clock Tower
10 minutes

Table Bay Hotel to Clock Tower
15 minutes

Table Bay Hotel to Pierhead
12 minutes (via Victoria Wharf)

Victoria Wharf to Marina Residential
10 minutes (via Red Shed and past Aquarium)

Victoria Wharf to Aquarium
16 minutes

Victoria Wharf to Pierhead
10 minutes (past Quay 4)

Victoria Wharf to BMW Pavilion
6 minutes

Victoria Wharf to Nelson Mandela Gateway
16 minutes

Victoria Wharf to SA Maritime Museum
8 minutes

Red Shed to Craft Market
6 minutes

Visit our Sales Offices
For all your Wall map & Custom map needs

Johannesburg

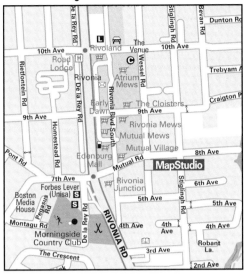

Cape Town

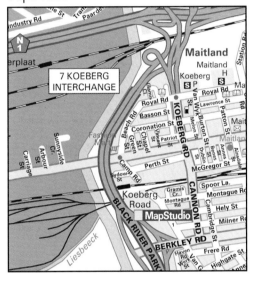

Durban

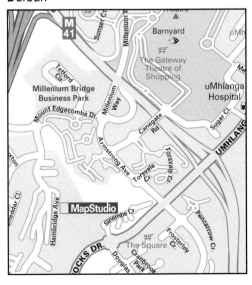

Johannesburg
7 Wessel Road, Rivonia,
P.O. Box 277,
Rivonia, 2128
Tel: +27 11 807-2292
Fax: +27 11 807-0409

Cape Town
Unit 7, M5 Freeway Park
(off Black River Parkway),
Maitland.
P.O. Box 1144,
Cape Town, 8000
Tel: +27 21 510-4311
Fax: +27 21 510-4766

Durban
Suite 3,
Sinembe Business Park,
8 Sinembe Crescent,
La Lucia Ridge
P.O. Box 1183,
uMhlanga Rocks, 4320
Tel: +27 31 566-2448
Fax: +27 31 566-1879

Find us:
See the maps to the left

0860 10 50 50

Wall Maps

Wall Maps for all your needs

Educational, regional, provincial, business, Southern Africa, Africa & the World

Whatever you need, we have the map for you

You can find:

- Capitals, towns, major & minor roads

- Sea routes

- Major airports

- Time zones

- Places of interest

- Provincial & country boundaries ......to name but a few

Custom Maps

Designed for your specific needs:

- Indicating your trading areas

- Personalised maps with logos

- Maps for diaries, calendars and brochures

- Enlargements

- Directional maps

- Trading maps with radii from centre point

- Separate country maps

Amendments ?

As part of our ongoing product improvement programme, we value your input.
This information together with your personal details (name and address) can be sent **Post Free** to the following address.

Freepost CB 11079
Attention: The Research Department
Map Studio
P.O. Box 1144
CAPE TOWN
8000

E-mail Address: research@mapstudio.co.za

Visit our Website:
www.mapstudio.co.za

0860 10 50 50

NOTES